How to Sell Your Ideas, Goods, and Services to the Government

Everything You Need
To Run A Business At Home

by

Matthew Lesko

Best Selling Author of *Information USA* and *Getting Yours*

Editor: Mary Ann Martello
Production: Beth Meserve
                Meserve Associates, Inc.
Cover Design: Lester Zaiontz
Cover Illustration: Mark Dagenais
Photographers: David W. Getty
                      Kim Travis
                      Steve Pope
                      Nicholas Carlson
                      Jerry Bielicki
                      Gerald McClard

FIRST EDITION

Library of Congress Cataloging-in-Publication Date

     Lesko, Matthew

     Everything You Need To Run A Business At Home

     ISBN 1-878346-36-9

The information in this book is continually updated on-line through the CompuServe Information Service. To subscribe call 1-800-524-3388 and ask for Representative 168.

Other books written by Matthew Lesko:

Getting Yours: The Complete Guide to Government Money

How to Get Free Tax Help

Information USA

The Computer Data and Database Source Book

The Maternity Sourcebook

Lesko's New Tech Sourcebook

The Investor's Information Sourcebook

The Federal Data Base Finder

The State Database Finder

The Great American Gripe Book II

Lesko's Info-Power II

What To Do When You Can't Afford Health Care

Government Giveaways for Entrepreneurs II

IRS Secrets, Shortcuts, and Savings

1001 Free Goodies and Cheapies

Free College Money, Termpapers & Sex(ed)

Free Stuff for Seniors

This book contains thousands of sources of money, help, and information designed to help anyone who wants to start a home-based business. You'll learn secrets like:

- How to tap into hundreds of billions of dollars of loans, grants, loan guarantees, and venture capital that you can use to start your business or even fix up your home to fit your business.

- How you can start your business with a lucrative government contract and even have the government do your marketing and paperwork for you.

- How you can take almost any job you're doing today for someone else and turn yourself into an independent freelancer working from home.

- How to get the best marketing advice, management expertise, tax help, and even legal help ALL FOR FREE.

- How to make money off your invention without hiring high priced attorneys and consultants.

- How to start an Import/Export business.

But more importantly, you'll <u>learn the philosophy and principles necessary to start any home-based business.</u> It doesn't matter what kind of business it might be — the spirit and philosophy of entrepreneurship remains the same. I'll show you step-by-step how I started my own home-based business in a one bedroom apartment with a phone, a desk, and business cards and turned it into one of the most successful information brokerage businesses in the country.

This Book is Out of Date

No matter how hard we try, we can't stop change. Phone numbers and even programs are bound to start changing as soon as we print the book. Please bear with us. In our information society, everything is out of date the day it is printed. Even the telephone book. Don't get frustrated if you call a number in this book and you happen to get some Chinese laundry. If doesn't mean all is lost. The office may just have moved or the number changed. Call the information operator for the location (if it is in Washington, call 202-555-1212) and ask for a new listing. The program name may have even changed. Be inventive if the directory assistance person doesn't show the listing that you're looking for. Most of these people can be incredibly helpful when they're asked for extra assistance.

Remember...It Takes Work

I hear so many authors say that all you have to do is buy their book and all your problems are solved. I feel that if you buy my book your problems have just begun. With this book you have thousands of sources and YOU have to do the work of following up on them. You just can't read this book and have your dreams fulfilled, you have to actually USE IT AND WORK AT IT. Your dreams won't come true by magic. You have to make telephone calls, lots of telephone calls, and then more follow-up calls. And follow up on any lead that is offered. Keep calling back for more help. And most importantly, keep a positive attitude and show lots of perseverance. But don't worry about all the work, that's actually the good part. Doing all the work is really a pleasure when you're doing it for yourself and you're learning. Work is only a bore when you're working for someone else or you don't like what you're doing. We all love to work, we just have to find what we love doing, and you can. Remember, it doesn't take a genius to run a business — look at all the idiots out there that are doing it. I flunked English in college and now have two New York Times Bestsellers. I even had two businesses that failed before I had a success. Why, back in the 1970s I had a computer software company that failed. I must have been the only one in the world with a computer business that failed back then. It could be that I failed because it wasn't the business that I truly wanted to be in. I've learned to trust my instincts since then and have found continuing success, and you can, too. It doesn't matter what your background is...you can do it.

Matthew Lesko

Table of Contents

Table of Contents

Introduction

The joys of being your own boss. The satisfaction of answering to no one but yourself. The convenience of not spending half your life in traffic. The pleasure of spending more quality time with your family. The benefit of growing your own life in the direction that you want to follow. These are some of the reasons why over 20,000,000 people now work from home and why the number continues to grow rapidly. More and more Americans are realizing that there is little security in working for a large corporation. And even more importantly, there is far less flexibility and growth potential at a big corporation than there would be if you took the plunge and started a business of your own.

Before the industrial revolution, most Americans worked from home. Back then you were either a farmer, who worked in the fields with your family, or you were some sort of craft person, working out of your home providing shoes, legal services, or other goods and services to the community. But shortly before the turn of the century, the industrialization of America was forcing people to leave their homes to work in factories, stores, and eventually office buildings. But now the tide is reversing. More and more people are leaving today's offices, factories, and stores and going back to work in their home. And those of us doing it find that our lives are so much more rewarding and fulfilling. Because most corporations have been unwilling to bend for employees who need to adjust their work schedules to accommodate two careers, children, and other responsibilities, workers have had to rethink the priorities in their lives. Is it worth it to slave away day after day for the giant conglomerate that refuses to give you the day off when your child is sick? After years of service, do you have any guarantee of job security in the future? Think again — a corporate conscience just doesn't exist these days, I'm sorry to report. That trend has driven more and more workers to decide to call their own shots.

Job Dissatisfaction and Bad Companies

As I've mentioned, there seem to be many reasons causing this shift back to working at home. I believe one of the most prevalent is job dissatisfaction. Most employees working for corporations today would rather be working for themselves, if they are truthful with themselves. We all know we're smarter than most of the people running things out there and we would love to have the opportunity of making all the decisions ourselves. We also hate the office politics that go on inside any organization. We see the people who get raises and promotions just because they suck up to the boss. And we all hate the endless meetings, water cooler dribble, and the useless gossip that seems to do nothing more than to provide insecure individuals an opportunity to feel important.

Companies themselves are also part of the problem. They are not taking care of people anymore. It used to be that if you worked for a large corporation, you had full health care, a pension plan, and probably a secure job for most of your working career. That's not the case anymore in our new economy. Companies don't want your loyalty anymore. They just want your work. And they are just as likely to fire you in good times as well as in bad times. Last year corporations made record breaking profits and at the same time had record breaking layoffs. Ten years ago such actions were unheard of in our country. But not anymore. It's also getting harder and harder to get a job with benefits like health care and a pension plan. It's also clear that unions aren't having much luck in insuring benefits for the average worker because they're in the process of shrinking. The trends are clear. Companies are looking out for themselves and forcing the individual worker to do the same. So, if you're doing a job you hate and they aren't treating you well, maybe it's time to take the hint and finally do something you really want to do in life.

Opportunities from the New American Corporation

Our country is in the midst of an economic transformation. And although it's hurting traditional employees, it is also making it easier for people to start a business in their own home. Why? Because businesses in this new economy are ideally suited for the home. In the industrial age it was downright impossible to start a business out of your home. Back then most new businesses required you to have a factory. Why do you think they called it the industrial age? These industrial opportunities required a lot of money and space for plant, equipment, and employees. But not so in the new economy. The growth of new businesses now are in the areas of information, services, and specialized products. And these kinds of businesses you can start with a phone, a desk, a business card, and a computer. Many of the hot businesses today, like Ben and Jerry's, Microsoft, and Mrs. Fields Cookies all started from humble home-based beginnings and grew into household names. So what pushed all of these budding entrepreneurs to find another way? I think that they've been fueled by the desire to work in a different way — for profit, for fun, to satisfy their individual interests, and to work around the other demands of life. It's worked successfully for thousands of people out there, now why shouldn't it work for all of us?

What's bad about big companies today is also good for home-based businesses. Companies are downsizing. They want to stay flexible and as a result, feel it's best to have as few full time employees as possible. They don't want the burden of paying for pension plans, health care, sick leave, discrimination suits, etc. And as a result they have created another buzz word called "outsourcing". They want to buy services on a contract basis instead of hiring full time employees. This is a natural market for home-based business. It is now easier to be a freelance editor working out of your home and getting work from publishers on a project by project basis. The market is also there for you to be a company's bookkeeper, personal manager, marketing specialist, or even a cleaning service and do it all out of your home because companies now don't want to make any commitments to a new full-time employee. H. Ross Perot was one of the first to take advantage of this trend. He started a home-based business that ran the computer operations of large corporations. He sold it to General Motors and is now a zillionnaire. And how many years has it been since he answered to anyone?

Business Opportunities From the New American Family

It's not only the change in corporate life that is creating new opportunities. The change in American families are creating even more opportunities for the home-based business. Over the past 15 years, families are working more and earning less. Wages for men have been decreasing over the past 15 years and the only way for a family to stay afloat is for the wife to enter the work force. And we know she has, because this is now a growth market for home-based businesses like daycare, shopping services, food delivery services, kids taxi services, clowns for parties, etc. Businesses that do the things that working moms don't have time to do are booming.

And what about seniors? They are now the fastest growing segment of the U.S. population. And they're not poor anymore. In the last 15 years the only age segment of men who experienced an increase in income has been men over 65. The growth in the seniors market is creating a need for home-based business opportunities that provide services like house maintenance, physical therapy, travel agents, investment advisors, and much, much more.

Better think again if you're under the impression that the corporation of past years will take care of you. It's now your job to take care of YOURSELF. Our changing world will keep handing out new opportunities every day. It's your job to go out there and take advantage of them.

Introduction

Success Stories

Nursing Her Baby and
Making $1,500 a Week Baking Cakes

Mother of five faces arrest for baking illegal cakes in her Westerville (dry) home.

Two years ago, Valerie Coolidge decided to make a little extra money while she was home taking care of her children. She had a great rum cake recipe, so she offered gourmet cakes for sale around the holidays. In one week alone, she had over $1,500 in cake orders. But she was nursing her baby and had not finished her Christmas shopping, so she finally had to cut off orders as the demand was incredible.

Valerie knew the market was there for her product, and went to the Ohio Department of Development to get the necessary permits for her new home-based business. The first

Valerie Coolidge
Owner of Gourmet Gifts in Westerville, OH

thing she learned was that she was breaking the law every time she made a rum cake even for her own family! The Department of Development explained that it is illegal to bake with alcohol in all but 11 states. She also learned that it is rarely enforced, but as she lives in a dry city, she decided to not push her luck. She revised her recipe to make it alcohol-free.

As a participant in the Women's Mentoring Program, Valerie is able to go over strategies and marketing ideas with her mentor, as well as learn about good and bad suppliers. Gourmet Gifts still operates out of Valerie's kitchen using her one oven, occasionally losing cakes to little fingers reaching up for a snack. Valerie even employs her older kids to help with cake cleanup and packaging.

Gourmet Gifts grew 2 1/2 times in the second year of operation, and over 500% in the third year. Valerie believes that to keep her priorities in line with God's will, she must put her family first and operate her business in an honest ethical manner. She believes these priorities have driven her newfound success.

Micro-Loan Gets Home Sewer, Single Mom of Four, Into Computerized Embroidery Business

Sandy Queen was trying to find a way that she could make money and take care of her four children after she and her husband divorced. She had sewn since she was a child, and tried to think of a way to put that talent to work for her.

Sandy lives in the country and had some buildings on her property which she now uses for a shop. With some help from a low interest Micro-Loan, Sandy was able to start a computerized embroidery shop. She designs logos, emblems, and initials on a computer monitor and then the machines sew them onto shirts, hats, sweat-shirts, and more. Schools, small businesses, and ball teams are some of her best customers.

Sandy Queen
Owner of SAQ Embroidery Specialist in Galloway, OH

After five years, Sandy is almost done repaying her loans. As part of an SBA women's mentoring program, Sandy can network, meet others, exchange ideas, and more.

Sandy says, "Working from home is great. It is becoming more popular, and home-based businesses are more accepted now." Tips that Sandy would offer are that word of mouth is a great advertisement and research is invaluable.

$20,000 Got This Man to Climb a Roof

Troy Schwan's main job was to wire houses for cable television, but on the side he owned a few houses, and was always looking to buy more.

When you buy a house, you want to know exactly what you are getting for your money, and that doesn't include any costly repairs that you didn't bargain for. That is when the idea for a home inspection business occurred to Schwan.

In researching home inspection companies, Troy decided to go with a particular franchise. He went to the bank initially for a loan, but they referred him to a Micro-

Troy Schwan
Owner of Schwan's Home Inspection Team in Fargo, ND

loan Program. The people there helped him put together a business plan and budget, and complete all the necessary forms. Troy had thoroughly checked the franchise company, talking to other owners and learning what the franchise had to offer before deciding to invest in this operation.

In North Dakota, home inspectors are still fairly rare, so part of the work Troy has had is to educate people as to why they need this service. Business is growing month by month, and Troy receives a great deal of support from the franchise main office, as well as their computer bulletin board service. The flexible schedule and being his own boss has made Schwan a very happy man.

At-Home Photographer
Adds More At-Home Businesses

Tired of searching for the scrap of paper with the plumber's number on it? What about the lady who hung your sister's wallpaper? Nancy Ersly has put together a directory to help answer all those kinds of questions.

When Nancy lost her job to yet another corporate reorganization, she decided to start a home-based commercial photography studio. She got a business card, her portfolio, a price list, and went knocking on doors. Nancy had several good clients, but was still looking for another business in addition to fill in some of the slow times.

When she was fixing up her older home, she kept cutting out contractor ads, and thought about putting them together in a directory. Format design, whether to charge advertisers or consumers, and distribution of the directory were all questions Nancy had to think through and answer for herself. She eventually came up with *The Resource Directory*, which is categorized alphabetically by type of business or service and is free to consumers.

Nancy Ersly
Owner of The Resource Directory in Sewickley, PA

Her first edition of the directory broke even, and her second book grew in size by 71% and even made some money. Nancy even got a copyright for the directory and is working on getting a trademark.

Part of what is nice about working from home for Nancy is the flexibility of time she now enjoys, but that is also the most challenging part of her business. She enjoys getting to see the fruits of her labor, and cannot imagine going back to a regular work environment. Nancy even has plans for several other ventures to help others who want to start a home-based business, as well as to adapt her own directory to other parts of the country.

Single Mom Figures Out Working at Home

Go for it. Those are words of advice from Donna Nissen, a person who put those words to use in her own life.

Donna was raising two young children when she found herself suddenly divorced. She had not gone to college earlier, so she decided that she should return to school to get training to help take care of her children the best way she could. Initially her area of focus was high tech communications, but a friend convinced her after graduation to switch to massage therapy, a field in which she had a deep interest.

Donna received her certification from the Pittsburgh School of Massage Therapy and went on to get a job giving massages in a hair salon. After some time, she decided to move her business into her home, which was quieter and more relaxing. All of her clients moved with her, and business remains good.

Donna's clients come from referrals by friends, family, and relatives. The local Small

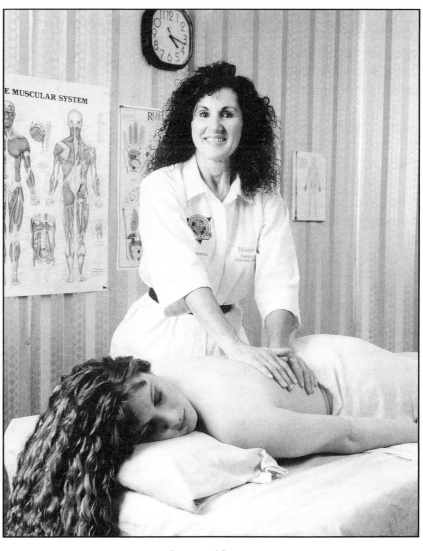

Donna Nissen
Owner of Nissen's Therapeutic Massage Center in Aliquippa, PA

Business Office was able to provide Donna with lots of good information on how to start a small business. Working from home allows Donna time to rest between clients, to do the usual household chores, and to keep her overhead to a minimum. Donna's business has tripled and she now plans to expand her office space and hire additional therapists. Donna truly believes in the positive benefits from massage therapy, and likes helping people feel healthier, happier, and more relaxed.

Retrained and Ready to Go

A back injury put an end to Larry Jaques' career as an auto mechanic. While out of work for over a year trying to recuperate, Larry's thoughts turned to what his next career move might be.

After advocating strongly with Workmen's Comp, Larry successfully completed a retraining program to become a computer electronics technician. He even graduated at the top of his class. Larry got a job working for a company, but when the company relocated forty miles away from his home, a two hour daily commute, he took a voluntary layoff.

Diversify! Computer Services was started four and a half years ago to assist new computer owners in learning more about the capabilities of their computers. Larry also works in database development, hardware and software sales, computer upgrades, and with the Internet and RIME network. Diversify! even had to diversity a little, as Larry is now working with more small businesses who are more likely to put money and time into training.

Larry Jaques
Owner of Diversity! Computer Services of Vista, CA

Working from home provides him a chance to set his own pace, eliminate commuting stress, focus on goals, and to generally feel better about his life. According to Larry, the one disadvantage is that the refrigerator is too close at hand! Having his own company has also given Larry a chance to use his creativity, as he designed a shade for a computer screen. He is getting a patent on the product and saved $650 by doing the patent search himself on the computer!

Making Santas At Home Gets Deborah on QVC

If you want to find a one of a kind Santa, then you have to head to the Upper Peninsula of Michigan or just tune into QVC.

Deborah Retaskie used to travel the local craft show circuit and would pick up different Santas for her sister who collects them. She knew there were Santa collectors out there, and thought she could make one of a kind old world Santas. She even came up with a certificate of authenticity and signs and dates all of her creations.

As her hobby-turned-business flourished, Deborah was able to quit her job as a home care provider for the elderly to

Deborah Retaskie
Owner of Superior Santas of Marquette, MI

devote all of her time to her company. Deborah uses recycled fabrics and furs for her St. Nicks, and even has one with a mink coat and hat! The Small Business Development Center helped her with financing, writing a business plan, and even provided her with trade show information.

Through the gift shows she attended, Deborah is now able to sell her products wholesale. In facts, she frequently sells out for the year very quickly. Her 9 and 14-year old kids even help out painting boots and dressing her Santas. When QVC toured the United States looking for some great products, they fell in love with Deborah's Santas and now offer them for sale on the show. Christmas happens year round at Deborah's house.

Mom From Michigan Makes $500
In Her First Day of Selling Driftwood

If you are looking for inspiration that happiness is just waiting for you, then spend some time talking with Peggy Iery. This woman loves what she is doing, and gets enjoyment from watching people look at and comment on her wonderful creations.

Peggy, like her sister Deborah Retaskie, was a home care provider for the elderly, but also had a hobby of making different items like pins, picture frames, or Santas out of driftwood. She took some of her handiwork to a local craft show. After making $500 in one morning, Peggy realized that a business was to be

Peggy Iery
Owner of Day Dreams and Driftwood of Marquette, MI

had using her talent. She went to her local Small Business Development Center (SBDC) which gave her pointers on how to become a legal business, and Day Dreams and Driftwood was born.

The SBDC also gave her moral support, networking assistance, and information about trade shows. Peggy even got a loan to finance the tools that she needed to make her job a little easier. The kids even help out. Peggy's 11-year old has his own line of driftwood products, and her 13-year old designed Peggy's first Santa. The Iery's get to live in a wonderful part of the country, with Lake Superior right out their back door. Peggy would have it no other way.

Love of Pets Turns Into a
Pet Sitting Business

One way K.P. Hill learned to meet her new neighbors was to first meet their pets.

The Hills, who had two dogs and cats, were building a house in a new neighborhood, and K.P. came up with the idea of a pet sitting business. Her first clients were people in her housing development. She started out part time eight years ago, and initially did not really need the income. Now her client base has grown to the point where she employs 2-5 independent contractors to help take care of people's pets in their homes.

K.P. is divorced now, and works at her business full-time. She says that there are tradeoffs in life, but she would not have it any other way and feels that all her needs are being met. Her advice to people starting out is to make sure that they know what their priorities are and to stick to them.

K.P. Hill of Indianapolis, IN
Owner of There's No Place Like Home

Government Grant Gets Mother of 7 Into Doll Business

It is not everyone who gets asked to hand their doll over for inspection, but Mrs. Sandy Belt has had the pleasure. She was one of the chosen few who got a chance to give their creations to President Clinton in honor of his support of small businesses.

Sandy has seven children, and had always sewn. She made the kids' clothes to save money. The Belts needed a second income, so Sandy began sewing a variety of things like dolls, quilts, and clothing. She did the local craft shows, but as she found out, many people didn't know how to move above these types of shows.

Sandy Belt
Owner of Town Folk in Marquette, MI

The Small Business Development Center was able to help her make Town Folk a successful company. They knew how marketable her products were, and provided her with information about large wholesale shows, and even gave her grant money so she could attend. Through these shows, McCalls saw her dolls and asked if she could design a specific product for them.

Sandy is now a freelance designer for several pattern companies and has sales reps who market her work. Her designs are frequently seen in craft magazines, as 95% of them use freelancers for their features.

Sandy's advice to would-be entrepreneurs is to never give up and to follow every lead. At the beginning, Sandy wrote many letters in an effort to get her goods into the marketplace, and received many rejections. Now she is in great demand, and will soon be featured in several books about America's craft artists.

The IRS Doesn't Scare Him

When most people hear the word audit, panic sets in. But for Tony Davis, that's when the fun begins.

After working for the IRS for seven years, Tony decided to work for a company representing people when they are faced with an audit. He then began his company, Preferred Tax Services, assisting people with their tax preparation as well as becoming an enrolled agent, which is someone sanctioned by the IRS to represent others in audit and collection proceedings.

Tony sees his job as educating his clients on how the IRS operates and what they will need to do. The government operates similarly to the military: you clock in and out, log on and off. Having his own business lets Tony have the flexibility to make his own schedule, set his own goals, and even check his own progress.

Although initially the business started mostly with tax preparation, it has evolved into more tax planning and audit preparation, with most of his customers coming from referrals. Tony's advice to others interested in home-based businesses is to look at your strengths and to build up your weaknesses.

Tony Davis of Carlsbad, CA
Owner of Preferred Tax Services

Thirty-three Years Strong

Having a home-based business is nothing new to Gwen Ogle. Her husband started as a sales rep working from home over thirty years ago, selling a variety of signs and displays for advertisement.

Initially, Gwen did the bookkeeping and keeping track of the orders, but then her husband developed Alzheimer's and was unable to keep up the sales end of the business. With encouragement from her husband, Gwen learned how to sell.

A home-based business allows Gwen to have more control over her day. She can even play golf if she wants to, as long as she completes her work for the week. Don't forget it takes tremendous self-discipline to work from home, but if you make a success of your business you can make as much money as you want.

Gwen has joined several organizations, such as the Chamber of Commerce, and networks with others whenever possible. Even though she is reaching retirement age, Gwen has no plans to retire and will work as long and as hard as she wants.

Gwen Ogle
Owner of Jere Ogle Sales in Coraopolis, PA

Near Death Experience Turns Into At-Home Seminar Company

Not everyone decides to take the time after almost dying to reflect upon their life, but Suzanne Green Metzger did.

Suzanne was a school teacher for fourteen years. When she was accidentally poisoned, she found herself on a gurney listening to doctors telling those around her that she would not live. When Suzanne did survive, she began to examine her life.

She quit her job and divorced her husband. After taking six months off, Suzanne needed to start working and began to do marketing for a company. Her next job was with a medical products company where she got to travel all around the country and made a great deal of money. But still she did not find happiness.

She began saving all the money she could and applied for every credit card, realizing that a bank would be reluctant to loan her money if she didn't have a job. Through her past jobs, Suzanne watched bright women not knowing how to get ahead in corporations. She developed seminars for these women with manuals and handouts to show how they could increase their effectiveness through communication.

Suzanne Green Metzger
Owner of Corporate Masters in Indianapolis, IN

Suzanne's company, Corporate Masters, now provides seminars to both men and women on a variety of topics dealing with professional and personal communication. Her local Small Business Development Center helped her to network and provided her with pointers on how her business could develop. Suzanne cannot imagine any other life, and has been nominated and received numerous awards for her work.

Freelance Artist Turns Into Inventor of Art Supplies

Laurel Ramsey is a freelance artist who often paints with water colors, and found she had to stop painting to get clean water to rinse her brushes. This was even more of a problem when she was far from a water source.

Laurel came up with the idea for the "Freshwater Rinse Well," which allows you to have a water supply wherever your work station happens to be. A 16 oz. bottle of water sits on top of a sink. You can open the valve to let in clean water, then hit another switch to let the dirty water fall to a chamber below.

Laurel drew out her idea on paper, and then built a prototype. She took this to the Small Business Administration who gave her step-by-step directions on how to prepare to sell the product, patent it, and go from the prototype to the actual product.

In her search for a manufacturer to make a mold, Laurel found a company who was willing to build and market her product for her. She signed a licensing agreement, and now her product is marketed in the United States and abroad.

Laurel Ramsey
Freelance Artist from Des Moines, IA

Take This Job and Love It

Fifteen years of interpreting government regulations and turning them into plain English for the readers of a large Washington, DC publisher left writer Kurt Samson dying for challenge and change. Spending over two hours a day getting back and forth to work only forced the issue.

Finally, he decided he'd had enough. Armed with several of Lesko's books, he decided to sell his expertise back to Uncle Sam.

Within days of giving notice to his employer, Kurt received a contract to interpret government regulations for the General Accounting Office. Because he already had a computer, fax, and copier at home, his overhead was next to nothing. And since he now has more time to spend with his family, he doesn't miss the drive one little bit.

Kurt Samson
Freelance Writer in Annapolis, MD

$10,000 Loan and Now
There Is Nothing Stopping Him

"There are a million businesses out there, a million jobs, and a million things to do." Those are words of wisdom from Ken McAlary.

Five years ago, Ken was laid off from his job as a lithographer, which was something he had done for over 35 years. He had six kids, a home, and $50 in his pocket, and decided it was time to start out on his own. McAlary now deals with over 2500 manufacturers, helping people and customers find the goods and services they need.

As his business grew, Ken realized that he needed to upgrade his computer system, so he took out a microloan for $10,000 to buy two computers — one for desktop publishing, and the other for his databases. Now there is no limit to what he can do. He provides mail order and printing services, and soon will be entering the liquidating and exporting market.

For Ken, having his own business provides the freedom for him to do what he wants when he wants, and there is no limit to the avenues his business can explore.

- Ken McAlary, owner of American Manufacturers Unlimited in Plainfield, NJ

Part-Time Hobby Turns Into
Full-Time Craft Business

Pat and Ed Endicott have always seemed able to keep themselves busy. They were both working full-time jobs, but managed to hold two boutiques in their home each year featuring over 800 different items which they made themselves. The items were made from calico quilted material and sewn into items such as coasters, hot pads, eyeglass cases, and clothes.

When Ed was laid off from a senior management position, they decided to move from Chicago to be near family and to put more emphasis on their craft business. They now have a full color catalog and their work is featured in many stores. Pat has taken many classes and workshops from the Small Business Administration which are held at the local university. She has learned a great deal from these classes and enjoys the networking and idea sharing. Pat is constantly surveying stores for new ideas, new products, goes to trade shows, and even puts together a newsletter four times a year.

Last April, Ed had a stroke, but they both have hopes for Ed's rehabilitation. Pat continues with the business, and she considers it her lifeline.

- Pat and Ed Endicott, owners of House of Threads and Wood, inc. in Rogers, AR

Husband's Layoff Gets Linda Into $90,000 Monogramming Business

It all started when her husband was laid off, and they needed some extra money. Linda Jones opened a business (initially with a friend) supplying the local schools with t-shirts, hats, and jackets featuring the school logo. A couple years later she bought her first monogramming machine so she could do the work herself. In 1990, Mrs. Jones' daughter began to need continuous IV treatment for her cystic fibrosis. What this meant for the business, was that it just moved into the house.

Linda said, "I was just used to being busy. I was PTA President, a volunteer at the schools. I was not one to sit around." With some help from the Small Business Development Center, Linda completed her business plan, did her resume, projected future income, and put together a portfolio to take to the bank. Her low interest loan allowed her to buy more machines, and even to build a 2,500 square foot building next to her house which is now the shop. In just three years, her income jumped from $16,000 to $90,000.

Small Town Monogramming now employs 13 people in a town with a total population of only 250 people. Some tips Linda would offer people is to emphasize quality, and that word of mouth is great free advertising.

- Linda Jones, owner of Small Town Monogramming in Fort Gay, WV

Cartoonist Loves Being a Freelancer

How many of us turn to the comics first when the paper arrives on Sunday morning? Jim Whiting has been helping us start our mornings off with a laugh for over 40 years.

Jim went to school on the GI Bill to get a good solid foundation in the art of cartooning. He sent cartoons to magazines for many years and at times it was either feast or famine. Jim eventually was lucky enough to have a comic feature syndicated by the L.A. Times Syndication service for many years.

Whiting says that working from home provides you with a great deal of freedom to set your own schedule. Vacations are even possible when you can arrange your deadlines accordingly. One problem many people face is insurance and retirement plans, and those concerns have to be considered when thinking about starting your own business.

For many years Jim has been part of a local Home-Based Business Association, which provides him a place to share ideas, network with others, and to keep up on the latest home office information.

Jim continues to draw cartoons for books, advertising copy, and other publications, and receives most of his referrals from past clients. Jim even keeps his name active on a listing for government contracts. Some words of advice from Jim for others who are considering home-based work is to keep trying, even in the face of rejection.

- Jim Whiting, Freelance Cartoonist from Solana Beach, CA

How to Start a Home-Based Business

Read this step-by-step procedure on how I started one of the most successful information brokerage businesses in the country, and how I did it all from a one-bedroom apartment. The basic philosophy and principles I discuss in the section apply to any home-based business. Read this section carefully. It will give you ideas for potential home-based businesses in the information industry. But more importantly, it will arm you with the courage and knowhow you need to take advantage of all the other chapters in this book that will point you to the money, help, and information you need to get your own home business started.

Matthew Lesko

How I Started With A Phone And A Desk And Turned It Into A Million Dollar Information Brokerage Business

All my life I wanted to start my own business. I didn't care what it was — I just wanted to learn how to feed myself and not work for someone else. I even considered selling hot dogs on the mall near the Washington Monument — I just wanted to be my own boss.

I started my first business when I got out of the Navy and hooked up with two other Vietnam Vets as partners. We scraped up a few thousand dollars in savings to start a little service business that provided information about the job market to military personnel who were overseas and due to return home soon. It was a bust and lasted only about six months. We lost all our money and didn't even get one single customer.

About a year later I tried again to start a business. It was a little software company I started with another person who was good at writing computer programs. We developed software to maintain mailing lists and called the system TOMALIS, which stood for Total Mailing List System. This was back in the days of mainframe computers, and the computer languages of the day went by names like Fortran and Cobol. That business also failed, but at least it took three years for this one to go under. This was back in the mid 1970s, and I felt that I must have been the only person in the world who had a computer business that went down the tubes during that "boom" time.

With another failed business under my belt, my hungry stomach was telling me that I had to go and get a real job to survive. I landed a job with a bunch of hot shots who were in the travel business but were also trying to get into the mergers and acquisitions business. I was hired to run the computers within the company, and it wasn't a bad job. No one else in the company

knew about computers and this made me look smart without really knowing much. But what really interested me were the hot shots running the company. In order to get close to them to see how they ran the business, I would volunteer to do anything. I'd hang around late at night when they were discussing big deals and volunteer to get coffee, donuts, do the xeroxing — anything to try to learn how to act like a big shot.

One day they came into my little office and asked me, not to get coffee, but to get information on how good or bad the rental car business was. It seems that they were considering making a bid to acquire Avis Rent-A-Car and needed some good market information to go along with the financial statements that they were poring over. I, of course, said YES, YES, YES. I was their "yes man", even though I knew nothing about the rental car business and had no idea where I was going to get this information.

I wanted to do this so badly I could almost taste it. This was one giant step up from coffee and xeroxing that lucky people are offered once in life, and I didn't want to blow it. I saw myself as a young turk on the way up the ladder of success. But I didn't have a clue where to go for the information I needed. I sat in my little office wondering if I could make the grade. I sat there staring at my desk hoping something would pop into my head and give me the magic answer. I stared at the telephone and then picked it up thinking, "Here I am in Washington, DC needing to know about the rental car business. Who can I call? Why not the government? I pass by all those big buildings every day on the way to work. Maybe someone there can help me."

Well it worked. By starting with the government information operator, I was able to work my way through a dozen more calls and referrals until I finally found an expert in the rental car business. It turned out to be a man who used to be the president of Hertz and was now in Washington and bored out of his mind with his government job. He actually invited me to lunch so he could tell me everything he knew. I was shocked! I couldn't believe that in 45 minutes on the telephone I could locate a real expert who was willing to tell me everything I needed to know about the rental car business. And he even wanted to take me to lunch!

Afterwards I was so excited about the information I had just received that I burst into a meeting my boss was having with his hot shot merger and acquisition buddies. He was eager to hear everything that I learned from my lunch right then and there. They were blown away, and so was I. We couldn't believe that a young turk like me who didn't know anyone could get such information that we had all assumed was privileged and confidential. This was a lot more satisfying than staying up until midnight attempting to debug some computer program. In those days there weren't any personal computers, and everyone worked on the same big computer. So if you needed a lot of computer time to debug a program you had to go down to the computer room at midnight when no one else

was using it. In the end, the big shots, the ones I was trying to be like, got a lot more excited about the information I got on the rental car business than with any program I ever wrote for them.

I was hooked. I was constantly getting information for these people on anything they would ask for. But it didn't last long — the company was going under, even though I had no idea it was even in trouble. I guess I still wasn't so close to the big shots after all. Again, it was time to find another job or start another business. I had a few thousand dollars in the bank, and a wife with a good job, so I figured that could support me for awhile in a new venture.

The new business would be exactly what I was doing for my hot shot bosses. I would try to be a consultant to people in the merger and acquisition business and get all the information that they needed to make their business a success, but were unable to find themselves.

This time, success finally happened. The business grew from just me, a telephone and a desk in my one bedroom apartment to over 30 employees and a million and a half dollars in sales in a little more than three years. Even after two failing businesses, I finally realized my first success, and I'll show how you can do it too.

Five Basic Steps For Starting
An Information Brokerage Company
With As Little Money As Possible

A recent listing of Inc. Magazines fastest growing businesses in the United States showed that over 33% of those businesses started with less than $10,000 in capital. That can happen because we're no longer in an industrial economy where it takes a lot of money to open up a business. Instead, we're living in a service and information economy where is takes very little money to start and grow a business. An information brokerage company fits this model to a tee. Here's my list of the steps you should take to get started:

Step #1

Get a *personal computer* that can handle at least word processing and has the capability of adding a modem in order to tap into commercial and public databases. Even if you don't plan to use this feature now, it might be helpful to have it in the future as your business grows.

Step #2

Establish a *telephone and a desk* that you can call an office. An answering machine or a voice mail message system is a minimum requirement for you to be in touch with other staff members.

Step #3

Print envelopes, *letterhead*, and business cards. Decide on a simple design printed on a medium grade paper. If you try to get too fancy on the cheap it looks bad. Stay simple and classic in all of your materials for your business.

Step #4

Believe the notion that we live in an information society, and if you are willing to make enough telephone calls you can gather information on almost anything.

Step #5

Find a *customer* and do whatever it takes to make them happy and keep coming back for your service or product.

Steps #1, #2 and #3 are pretty easy to accomplish. There are a lot of people who will take your money and provide you with those items. Steps #4 and #5 are a little more difficult to achieve but still possible now that you have this manual. The following chapters will not only show you how to tap into the world's largest source of free information, but will also show you how to find and keep customers while spending next to nothing of your own money.

What You DON'T Need To Start An Information Brokerage Business

Everybody is always telling entrepreneurs about all the essentials they need. Well, I think it's just as important to tell entrepreneurs what they don't need. After starting four businesses of my own and after having two failures, here is what I believe you should be extra careful to avoid.

1. Too Much Professional Advice

If you're starting a business with a limited supply of capital, too much professional advice is going to kill you. If you try to surround yourself with all the trappings of business success, you're soon going to go out of business.

Remember, you and your time are the most valuable resources in your business. Succeeding in business is a "beat the clock" game. If you're spending a lot of your time meeting with lawyers and accountants or choosing fancy "power" furniture, you'll have little time to concentrate on the *one* thing that is most important to your success...getting a client. This is the most critical success factor of any new business. Without a client, everything else is meaningless.

When I started my first business, I got the high priced accountants, the high priced lawyers, the power business cards, and power furniture, but I went out of business. And who won? It was the accountants, lawyers, and furniture salesmen. They were all smart enough to get paid and I was out on the street.

Your clients don't care what kind of accounting system you use or what legal structure you have formed. And having the right look, whether it be impressive business cards or furniture, may only affect your business 5% or 10%. This is a very insignificant percentage, especially if you have

no business. Furthermore, it's a waste of time if you're spending a half a day choosing furniture when you could be spending a half a day getting a client. Remember, 99% of your clients won't care what kind of furniture you have. The only person who cares about what kind of furniture you have is the furniture salesman.

2. Too Much Money

Anyone can start a business if given $1 million bucks. It doesn't take a lot of creativity to spend money to buy advertising in your local newspaper. But what are you going to do next year when your business doesn't have an extra $1 million around? Instead of learning how to buy space, you should first learn how to get your local paper to write a FREE story about your business! The price is right and it's more effective than advertising because you're also getting a big, respected institution, the newspaper, to endorse you. It will also earn you credibility in the local business community, and that can serve as a spark to get your new business off the ground.

Too much money for a novice entrepreneur can make you fat, lazy, and not very creative. The key to developing a strong business is learning how to get sales using the least amount of money, not the most amount of money.

3. Too Perfect A Product

A beginner entrepreneur can easily get hung up on trying to develop the perfect product. Most of us can never be perfect, but we can still be successful. Entrepreneurs can easily get trapped into believing that their product or service has to be just right before they offer it to the public.

Trying to be flawless can lead to failure, and being a perfectionist can cause you to go broke before you even get your product to market. Be careful that your perfectionist attitude isn't really a mask for your own insecurities. What your family and friends will think about your product doesn't matter, because the object of a product should be its sale to a potential customer. Customers come with all different kinds of needs that would be impossible to satisfy all the time, and very few customers are willing to pay for perfection. Go open up your own closets and look at all the mediocre stuff that you've purchased over the years.

Until you start asking people for money you really don't know what they will buy. Your product is probably going to change dozens of times before it reaches its final form. And this metamorphosis is due to customer feedback, your most important information source. Introduce your product as soon as possible so that you can stay in business long enough to find out how to improve that product. Then listen to your customer. He's the expert you need to listen to.

Few of us are smart enough to read minds but we're all smart enough to listen. If you offer a product to ten people and five of them say they would buy it if it were green, go right out and paint the thing green, so you can make a few sales.

If you spend too much time designing the ultimate product you'll probably be wrong anyway and have very few resources left to learn from your mistakes. Overdesigning a product isn't just a failure of the small entrepreneur. Do you remember Ford's Edsel or Coca Cola's New Coke? Now those were big failures.

4. A Board of Directors

Anytime you get three people in a room to talk about an idea there will always be at least one naysayer. Finding potential problems is always easy to do. If an idea was perfect, it wouldn't be an idea anymore; it would already be a product or service provided by someone else.

For ideas to work, it usually takes the passion and commitment of one person. This kind of spirit doesn't come from a board of directors that engages in group decision making. Although democratic, this process usually results in ideas where everyone owns a small piece of the end product and no one person is committed to the complete picture. The "vision" for a new product can often be lost in this way.

Board meetings can be a big waste of time for struggling entrepreneurs. Entrepreneurs have to live from moment to moment, often making quick, reflexive decisions so they can immediately move to the next decision. The temperament required for entrepreneuring is very different from the temperament needed to placate a diverse group such as a board of directors.

5. An MBA

I have a BS in Business and an MBA and I believe that it took me two failing businesses to "unlearn" all that I was taught in my six years of business school. I was brainwashed into believing such things as: "If you need money, you go to the bank." When I was starting my businesses I quickly learned that a bank is the **last** place an entrepreneur with no money should go. Business schools spend a lion's share of the time teaching you how to run big businesses like General Motors, and that kind of business plan has little relevance to the small, struggling entrepreneur.

The jargon you learn in business school certainly is helpful if you want to get a job in big business. But if you are a small entrepreneur, much of what they teach you will just interfere with your natural instincts. There is no magic to most operations associated with running a business. Accounting is keeping a checkbook.

Production is making sure that your product costs less than what you sell it for. But in the beginning, marketing can sometimes seem magical. Finding and keeping a customer is what any new business is all about, and that doesn't take an MBA to figure out. It just takes a lot of door pounding and return calling.

6. Government Forms

Don't tell the government this because I could get in trouble. I believe that entrepreneurs should even forget about government licenses and forms for starting a business.

After I had two businesses that failed, I got rid of the accountants, the lawyers, the power furniture, and power business cards, and I also didn't file any local, county, state, or federal forms. Don't get me wrong — I did file my tax return because I never mess around with the IRS and you shouldn't either. The government forms I'm talking about are the permits, licenses, and applications necessary to do business. My theory is that filing all these forms takes time and energy. Because your time is very important, you'd be better off to concentrate that time on what is the critical success factor of your business...getting customers.

If you don't file the necessary forms there isn't much that can happen to you. At the pace that the government works, it will take them three years to find you. And by then, you'll either be out of business, or you'll be successful enough to pay the $25 fine and file whatever forms are necessary.

What You DO Need To Start
An Information Brokerage Business

Just like in real estate where you are always told that there are three things that are key to making a fortune...location, location, and location. Well, the same goes for the information brokerage business where there are three things that are critical to its success...customers, customers, and more customers. Customers make it all happen. Your business is nothing without them. If you get a customer and have a strong desire to make that customer happy, you can figure out all the rest of it by yourself.

You Don't Have To Be A Know-It-All

As an information broker, you are basically getting information for free and selling it to customers for as much as you can get for it. You may not know everything you need to know about every little information source that is available to you, but in the beginning that won't matter. You will learn this as you get clients. What happens is that your clients will make you smart about your own business. When I started I barely knew two or three major sources in Washington, like the Department of Commerce and the Library of Congress. But after a year and a half of doing projects for clients, I learned 90% of everything I know today, and that's 15 years ago. You'll go up the learning curve fast when you're constantly trying to get new information for clients. That's why it's important to get clients as soon as possible. If you're trying to get information for pretend clients, you're not going to have the same motivation and you won't get the real feedback you need to be able to make the proper adjustments for the next client. Even consider working for free for a potential client. It's better than doing nothing. This way you are at least honing your skills at gathering information and getting better at it all the time.

So, there are basically only two things you should be spending your time on...looking for customers or satisfying those customers. In the information brokerage business, everything else is a detail that shouldn't be your first priority.

What Are You Going To Sell And To Whom?

The problem with the information brokerage business is that you are basically a generalist who knows how to find information on just about anything. It's a great skill to have but it can create some serious marketing problems. How do you go about selling everything to everyone? It's very difficult, believe me, I've tried it. In the beginning of my business, I was telling people that I could give them information to solve any kind of problem. It took me awhile to realize that people have specific kinds of problems and they can only use you if you identify these specific problems and tell them you can get them the answer that they're looking for.

Before I could get customers I had to show them how I could solve their specific problems like: financial information on their competitors, or information on the size of little known markets. They don't have "anykind" questions. No matter how good you are, you're not going to be successful if you go in to sell someone that you can answer "anykind" questions. The best you're going to get from the potential client is "Ok, Mr. Information Broker. When I have an 'anykind' question I'll give you a call." They'll never have one. So they'll never call.

Remember Rich People Have More Money

Besides finetuning your sales pitch you also have to consider finetuning your customer base. The big question is: Who are you going to sell to?

Some people are in business to make money. Some people are in business to save the world. And some are in business to do both things. If you're in business to save the world, you better get out. You'll be much happier becoming a non-profit organization or joining a religious order. Saving the world is too expensive to do as an entrepreneur.

That leaves us with the other two options to work with: making a buck and making a buck and saving the world. IF you're interested in making money and saving the world, you first have to make money in order to be around long enough to save the world. So we're down to just trying to make money (the good old fashioned American way). With this in mind, information brokers might be smart to remember what Willy Sutton said when asked why he robbed banks. He said; "Because that's where the money is". Information brokers have to live by the same slogan if they want to stay in business. It may be that poor people have a lot more information needs than rich people do, but poor people barely have enough money to pay for food and certainly aren't going to pay for information, no matter how useful the information might be. Rich people on the other hand, have money to spend on finding out how they can get richer, and they are willing and able to spend it.

Consumers Or Business?

Now that I've finished stating the obvious, let me talk about something that may not be as clear. Is the market for your information going to be aimed at consumers or businesses? Both groups have information needs and both have wealthy as well as poor constituents. I've sold information to both groups and have developed some rules of thumb for selling to each of these different groups.

Businesses, especially the big companies, are more accustomed to paying for information than consumers are. That's because they're all spending someone else's money. They're all trying to accomplish their goals as easily as possible. That means when they need information to make their decisions it's easier and quicker to buy it than to go out and find it themselves.

More and more businesses are realizing the value of having good information for good decision making. Whether big or small, a business can't succeed today unless it keeps up on the latest information. Business in the 90's is a fast changing environment, and unless companies are willing to keep up to date on what is going on in their markets, competition, technology, and regulations, they'll soon be out of business.

The information brokerage business is very similar to any other kind of service business, like the shoeshine business, for instance. Anyone can shine their own shoes, but people with a few extra bucks would rather pay someone $2 to do it for them. As an information broker, you have to find people who understand the value of having clean shoes and have a few extra bucks to have someone else clean them.

That's why I believe that selling to businesses or organizations is a better place to start when looking for customers. It's just an easier sell, with more available dollars to spend.

A Nitch Or Not

You also have to decide if you want to develop a "hook". That's a marketing term to make it easier for people to purchase your services. It's taking the situation we mentioned earlier about "any kind of a problem" and refining it even further. It makes it easier to attract the attention of customers if you can say you specialize in some interesting aspect of the information brokerage industry. I was fortunate enough to have started in Washington, DC and developed the hook of government information. The other businesses that were around when I started were either in New York City or California, and didn't have my advantage of being located so close to government sources. It gave me an instant edge over my competitors, even though I had no more experience gathering information than they did.

There are a number of ways of describing the niche that you want to develop for your business. You can define it by the customer group that you specialize in helping: small businesses, environment-related businesses, or non-profit organizations. Or you can define it by the area of information you want to deal with, such as: health information, company information, or international information. Another way you can describe your business is by the medium of the information you want to provide, such as: only database searches, only document retrieval, or only interviewing industry experts.

How To Find Customers

It's a game of beat the clock. You have to find enough customers to feed yourself before you run out of money. With all the time in the world anyone can eventually teach themselves, through trial and error, how to find enough customers to sustain a business. But no one gives you all the time in the world. Your time will be limited to the amount of money you have to keep living on while you search for customers. That's why success is a game of beat the clock.

In order to stay alive for the longest amount of time it's best to spend as little as possible on each attempt to get customers. This is why having a lot of money can be a big problem in starting an information brokerage business. Sure, you can spend tens of thousands of dollars by placing full page advertisements in the *Wall Street Journal* or some other national newspaper. But it's very unlikely that such advertisements will ever pay for themselves. People who place big advertisements like that normally do it because they are in it for the long haul. They're big established organizations who have already figured out what works and what doesn't work. They know if they don't get back the money

they spend on the ad this year they'll get it back next year, or the year after. You have to try to make sure you're going to be in business next year, and that's why you have to use your money wisely, and in smaller ways than a flashy *Wall Street Journal* ad.

Businesses that survive in the long run are those that learn how to run lean and mean. If you only know how to succeed with lots of money, you're eventually going to be out of business. Every business experiences business cycles, just like the economy does. There are good times and there are recessions. If you know only how to live in good times, what are you going to do in the recessions? What you'll do is go out of business. The businesses you see folding during the bad economic times are the ones who never learned how to operate their businesses lean and mean. They figured that the good times would last forever. So don't start that way. If you start with a lean and mean approach, you'll not only learn how to survive the bad times, but you'll also make a lot more money during the good times.

Five Ways To Get Customers
Without Breaking Your Bank

You have to be both creative and persistent. As soon as you start implementing one customer generating project, you should immediately be trying to think of more ways to get customers. The secret to successful marketing is to always plan for failure. You should be thinking about what you are going to do when your first plan fails, instead of wasting your time thinking about what to do when it succeeds. You may think that this is negative thinking, but I see it more as survival thinking. Anybody can handle success. That's easy. But can you handle defeat? That's the trick in business and in life, and you have to be prepared for it. Though no one goes into business hoping for a failure, it's a fact that failure is going to occur a heck of a lot more often than success. So that's what you should be training yourself for and trying to plan for.

Here are six things to think about as you plan for your next failure:

#1: Make 100 Phone Calls A Day

One of the hardest things to do in any business is to make cold calls. If you're not willing to do this, it's doubtful that you're serious about being in business. Everybody makes cold calls, and you should too. It's a great way to learn what you really know about your business, and to learn what you need to learn.

Making cold calls will help you determine what's both right and wrong with your business. By trying to sell something directly to a customer, you will immediately start learning what you have to change in your business to make a sale. If you call a hundred people and half of them say they would buy your product if it was orange, then it's obvious what to do. You go home and paint your product orange and call those customers again. This is the type of market research you'll get back by cold calling on customers. And this is much better than doing original market research before you start your business. I personally don't believe in market research before a business is started. It takes just as much energy to ask someone *to actually buy* something than it does to ask if they would consider buying something if it were made available to them. To me, market research seems like a trial run. Why not just run the real race?

Who Do You Call?

The most important thing is to keep calling. You'll never have the perfect list of potential customers to call. This is a sales and learning experience. After making 100 calls you'll wind up with a dozen other kinds of people to call, because you will learn from calling people. There will be people who you will call who will tell you about other opportunities, and that's how you're going to get the perfect customer list to call. The object is to just take the best available list you can think of and start calling.

If you are thinking local, you can call your local Chamber of Commerce and they can give you a list of the largest organizations in your community to contact. It's usually a free list or it costs very little. The Chamber may also have a library that will be stocked with all kinds of other local lists, like high tech firms or medical facilities in your area. Additional local lists can be identified from the section below entitled "Free Mailing Lists Of Customers".

If you're thinking national or international, you can get these lists too. To find appropriate professional associations, go to the library and find Gale's *Encyclopedia of Associations*. This book lists all trade associations and trade publications, and it's well indexed.

What follows are some helpful hints on what to say when you make these important first calls.

STEP #1
The most important thing to remember is to ask for their business. But before you do that, you will probably talk about a lot of other things first. Be personable, friendly, and receptive to their conversation.

STEP #2
Do you know who you are going to ask for? If you don't, that's OK. When someone answers the phone you can say something like this:

> *"Hi, I'm Matthew Lesko, with Information USA and I was told that you have someone in your organization who is in charge of buying information services. Can you help me figure out who that might be?"*

A starting paragraph like this is bound to lead to someone in the organization. But the most important part of calling and saying something like this is that you talk in an optimistic and energetic tone. If you call up and start talking in a negative tone like: *"You don't need any information today do you?"* People will want to please you and they can do that by saying you're right, they don't need anything, and hang up on you.

After making a few calls not knowing who to ask for, you'll start learning that there's probably only one person in an organization who buys your kind of information. It could be the Director of Marketing, the Sales Manager, the Corporate Librarian, or even President of the company if it's a small business.

STEP #3
What do you say when you get to the person who might be interested in the information you have to offer? You might want to start by saying something like this:

> *"Hi, I'm Matthew Lesko with Information USA, and I want to know who I might send some literature to about my information services. My service taps into all the latest information technology to make sure that your business knows the best places to make money."*

This should be enough to get you started. At this point a few things may happen. They'll tell you to go away. Then take their advice and go away, it's not worth any more effort. Or, they'll tell you the name and address of someone to send some information to. Or, they'll ask you more about your services. Or, they might not say anything. With this kind of opening, you should start saying things that may be of interest to them. Like, how you helped some other similar company in the neighborhood, or how you have a new source of information you would like to come in and tell them about. If it looks like there's an open door to learning more about your services, be sure that you step through it!

STEP #4
Send your material out to that company as soon as possible. If you don't have an official brochure, send a customized letter describing your services. In today's fast changing society, I feel it's almost better not to have a brochure. Using your personalized letterhead is a good way to keep your business flexible, because your ideas about your business are going to be changing all the time. It's very likely that as soon as you print 10,000 copies of some brochure you're going to want to change it. The longer you can put the production and expense of something like a brochure off, the better.

STEP #5
Wait a week or so after you send your literature and then call them back. You may want to say something like this:

"Mr. Schilling, you may not remember me. We spoke last week about how my information services may be able to help your company. I just called to make sure you received my literature and to see if you had any questions about how services like mine might help your business."

During this conversation you will also want to try and get an appointment to see someone at that company in person. Or tell them you can give them a price proposal for a specific project. You may want to say something like this:

"Mr. Schilling, I know it's a little complicated to understand how our services can solve a lot of your problems, and I think the best way to explain what we do is for me to give you a no obligation price quote. Let's pick an area that might be of interest to you, maybe information on a competitor, or a new customer and I'll be happy to tell you how much it will cost to get you this information. What do you say? Give me a topic. I'll give you a quote. And, you can use it today, tomorrow or never. No obligation, honest."

#2: Start A Free Newsletter

This idea worked wonders for me. Before I used the newsletter idea, I was placing one inch advertisements in the Wall Street Journal. It was the most that I could afford, and it wasn't getting me any interest or business. When you're offering a service that is pretty complicated to explain, it's difficult to say anything much in one inch of space. Almost every response was worthless. I would even get people who would write their name in crayon on napkins and send it in to me. It was pathetic.

Then I had a bright idea that I would put out a free newsletter on how to get free information.

I only knew a few sources at the time, because I wasn't really even in business yet. I had no customers. The newsletter was only four pages long. The first three pages talked about the information sources I knew something about. But page four described some of the kinds of services I could provide. When potential clients received my newsletter it seemed that they finally had something to relate to, because my phone hasn't stopped ringing since.

Potential clients could really relate to the newsletter for a number of reasons. It showed how smart I was by describing a half dozen information sources and anyone reading it would not know at least one of them. So they thought I was smart because I knew more than they did. (By the way, never worry about showing how dumb you are. The people who are smarter than you won't hire you anyway. But there are a whole lot of people dumber than you and these are the ones that you're after.) But I also think the newsletter did more than just that. It gave potential clients suggestions as to the type of information they could get. If they read my description of how you could get information about companies filed at the Securities and Exchange Commission, that might raise new questions, such as, "Hey, I wonder if you can get information about companies that file at the Federal Communications Commission?" and they would call me.

Never Worry About Giving Away Secrets

People have always asked me if I worried about giving away my secrets about finding information because then people wouldn't need me. That never bothered me. Look, I'm telling you how you can go into business and compete with me. There are no secrets in life, just lazy people. And the more money people get, the lazier they become. When people are buying a service, what they are really buying is trust. Think about it — would you go to a doctor or lawyer if you didn't trust them? The same is true for the information brokerage business. You first have to develop trust with a client no matter what your business is. If you belong to a fancy "union" like the doctors and lawyers do, trust almost automatically comes with the letters after the name. But the information brokerage business has no fancy union, so you have to develop another way to build trust with your clients. Giving free samples is a great way to do this, and it doesn't cost you anything because it's only words on paper. For the same amount of money it would cost to print up a brochure telling people how great you are, you can print a free newsletter that will actually give people something of value — information.

And as for somebody taking the information in your newsletter and finding out what they need themselves instead of hiring you, don't worry about it — that's going to happen anyway. You have no control over that. The people who want to do it themselves will find a way to do it themselves no matter what. It's the other people you want as clients, the people who don't want to do it themselves and have the money to pay someone else to do it for them.

I've been giving away free samples for close to 20 years and it has only helped, and never hurt my business. And it feels good too.

It doesn't have to be much of a newsletter, It could be only two sides of an 8 1/2 by 11 inch paper. It could be only one color if you want. The critical point is not color and size, it's just getting it done, and getting it out there in front of potential customers.

#3: Get Free Publicity

It doesn't get better than this. Why pay thousands of dollars for a one minute ad on television when you can get 7 minutes, 15 minutes, or even an hour for free? The way you do this is through publicity. You've seen it all the time as a consumer — people talking about their books on talk shows, or the local

entrepreneur talking about his business on the local TV News. You can do that too.

Publicity is the main reason my newsletter was so successful. When I first published the newsletter, I didn't send it directly to potential customers, but instead sent it to the press. And because I was interested in finding businesses as clients, I sent it to the business press announcing a *free newsletter on how to get free information*. When you offer the press something that is going to be helpful to their readers, they're bound to be interested in it and want to let others know about it.

Within weeks I was receiving up to 500 inquiries a month. And these were real inquiries on real business stationery — not notes on napkins written in crayon. At that point, I was hooked on the value of publicity. I was shocked that I could send something out to the media and they would tell their readers about it, and it didn't cost me anything.

You don't have to offer the media a free newsletter. You can just have a press release and offer important tips right on the press release. Maybe something like "Ten Information Secrets For Small Business".

You can send your press release to all kinds of media, not just the obvious ones. You can start with the business media like I did, or you can use the general media like newspapers, radio or TV, either locally or nationally. No matter who you decide to send your press release to, you have to remember to call these media sources after you send out your material. Try to talk them into using it. You'll probably even have to send the material all over again after you call. The media in this country gets inundated with press releases. And the only way to have any hope that they'll take a second look at your press release is by talking to them after they've seen it. A press release has got to be eye catching and upbeat too, in order to spark the media's interest.

Here are some sources that may be helpful in identifying media. You can contact these organizations directly or go to your local library and look at their publications for free.

1) Local and National TV and Radio Talk Shows
   "Talk Show Selects"
   Broadcast Interview Source
   2233 Wisconsin Avenue NW
   Washington, DC 20007-4112
   202-333-4904

2) National Radio, TV Newspapers and Magazines
   Gales Research
   Directory of Publications and
      Broadcast Media
   Gale Research, Inc.
   835 Penobscot Building
   Detroit, MI 48226-4094
   313-961-2242

3) Local United Way
   Most local United Way organizations maintain excellent listings of all local media and will give you a copy for free or for very little cost.

4) A Good Reference Library
   Most good reference librarians will be familiar with available directories listing media sources. Ask for their assistance while you're at the library doing research.

I've included a sample press release to show you that there is no magic in writing a good one. You should try as much as you can to be provocative in your writing, different, exciting, fun, rude, or anything else you can think of to get anyone's attention. There is a lot of noise out there in the media and you have to fight for just a little bit of coverage. But remember, the important point is just to get one out there. Don't agonize about what you're going to say in this first press release. Just give it your best shot. Learn from it. Then start all over and try it again.

Sorry. The following press release is just a sample. I'm no longer offering free subscriptions to my newsletter.

PRESS RELEASE

December 1, 1995
Contact: Matthew Lesko
301-924-0556

FREE NEWSLETTER ON HOW TO GET
...FREE INFORMATION

Research expert and information guru Matthew Lesko is giving away the store. That's right! He's sharing his most important information secrets that he's spent a lifetime uncovering in a free 4-page newsletter so that small business can learn the power of information. He's willing to show you:

- how to get information on your most ruthless competitor by tapping into revealing state records;
- how to get free market studies on hot new products by calling little known government offices;
- how to get access to free mailing lists of customers from government agencies when people have to provide their addresses;
- how to find free expertise on money making investment opportunities in foreign countries.

Lesko's giving away the names, addresses, and even the telephone numbers of all his contacts. What — is he crazy? No, he just believes that information is the key to success for any small business and he's willing to give out free samples to prove his point. Even if your business has all the money it needs, the key to any success is the right information. If you don't know how to spend your money wisely, you'll be out of business in no time. Don't blow the opportunity to make your small business a success — get Matthew Lesko's information secrets, and put them to work for you!

Why pay for market studies when you can get them for free? Why pay high priced private investigators to spy on your competitors when you can learn about them for free?

Matthew Lesko operates an information consulting business that has an impressive track record showing business clients around the country how they can use information to grow their business. If you would like a copy of his free newsletter, contact:

Matthew Lesko
Information USA, Inc
PO Box E
Kensington, DC 20895
301-924-0556

Matthew Lesko is available for interviews.

InformationUSA

INFORMATION USA INC.
P. O. BOX E
KENSINGTON, MD 20895-0418
301-924-0556   FAX 924-1329

#4: Free Speeches

Giving speeches to trade and professional associations is like making the perfect sales call to 100 different businesses all at one time. Dozens or hundreds of potential customers come to these gatherings to hear how you can help them. It doesn't get better than that, and the potential for important future contacts to be made at events like this can be awesome.

You'd have to make thousands of calls to make contacts like this. You can make it happen with just a few calls to the right organizations. You can be a speaker at trade and professional associations, local societies or business groups, at local junior colleges, or even at local libraries. It all depends on who you think the market is for your business.

If you think your clients would be marketing managers in large companies, contact the American Marketing Association in Chicago, Illinois. Through them you can get a listing of their upcoming conferences and the names and addresses of conference chairmen. They're always looking for speakers, especially free speakers. So if you call and say that you'd be happy to speak on the subject of "How To Get Free Marketing Information", you could have a good shot of being included on the next program. There are thousands of trade and professional associations you can speak to. To find which ones may be the best for you to contact, go to the library and find Gale's *Encyclopedia of Associations*. This book lists all associations and it's well indexed. There are also books listing upcoming meetings and conventions that may be interested in booking interesting speakers.

Local groups are also always looking for free speakers. Your local Chamber of Commerce can help you identify groups like a local marketing society, advertising club, auto salesmen group, or any group of 10 people meeting once a month

for a rubber chicken lunch or dinner. An awful lot of business is initiated at these kinds of gatherings.

You can also speak at the local public library. Most libraries offer their facilities to people who want to give free speeches to the community. So if this is your market, check it out, because a lot of these organizations will probably even do the advertising for a speech for you. Any advertising of your speech will promote you as an "expert" in your field, and bring about even more people as contacts that could help your business grow.

#5: Free Mailing Lists Of Customers

There is always some slick salesman out there who will be willing to sell you a mailing list of people they are convinced are your customers. My experience tells me that the best lists for information brokerage customers are those you collect yourself, or are members of specific small professional societies. Generic lists, like the names of directors of marketing for large corporations are not going to get you much response in a direct mailing. It would probably be better to call 100 or so organizations and get the specific name yourself of someone who buys information services.

Oftentimes, membership lists are much more profitable to mail information about your product or service to. These could be lists such as the local advertising executives club or the National Association of Bank Marketing Executives. Lists like these are not usually sold by mailing list salesmen, but are normally only available by going directly to the society themselves. You can locate relevant national societies by going to the library and looking at the book we mentioned earlier called Gale's *Encyclopedia of Associations*. To identify local professional groups, contact your local Chamber of Commerce or your local reference librarian.

Let's also talk about how to get free mailing lists. In marketing, the old adage "you get what you pay for" is not always true — it's more "you get what you work hard for". If you do a little work you can get some promising lists for free.

Start with your state office of economic development. You can find them by calling the operator located in your state capital. This is the office that is most interested in business development in your state. People in this office keep track of what kinds of business are located in the state, how big they are, etc. Many of these offices even maintain special lists like, companies who sell products overseas, or companies who are in the high tech business. It's worth a couple of calls to snoop around, because knowing this kind of information might come in handy in solving information requests for clients.

One of the best sources of business is your state office of corporations. From this office you can get lists of all the new businesses that started in your state. It seems that it's usually the new businesses that are trying to solve problems and need information to get ahead. The old businesses are usually cutting back and trying not to buy anything, while the new businesses are trying to grow. Many states are set up to provide lists of new businesses stating the name, address, and phone number along with the names of the owners. These can turn out to be great leads.

Also check your state licensing office. That's the office where all professionals have to register their activities, like doctors, lawyers, accountants, physical therapists, nursing home administrators, or travel agents. Remember, once the information touches the government in any way (such as through registration or licensing procedures), the information about that business becomes public, and that means that it's now your information, too.

How To Keep A Customer

The most expensive thing you'll ever do as an information broker is to try to get a new customer. Getting repeat customers is a lot cheaper than finding new ones. You've already sold them once, so they're convinced of the value and need of your service. With very little effort you can generate new business from old clients. Here's some ways to do this:

1) A Quick Call With Hot Info

Many times it only takes a simple call to an old client to remind them that they have an information problem you can cure very easily. You know the old saying, "out of sight, out of mind". Well, it works the same for customers too. But you should not call giving the impression that you only want to get more money from them, even though every one knows that's what you're doing. It's much better to call with some free hot news you thought they would be interested in, like an article in the newspaper that may influence their business. You wanted to make sure they didn't miss it, and you would be happy to fax it to them. Your clients are busy people and they will be more interested in giving you their time if they feel that you have their interest at heart, along with your own.

2) A Sample Of A Continuing Report

You can offer past clients continuation services. If they had an information problem once, you can make sure that they don't have it again by providing a monthly, automatic updating service. For example, if your client contracted you once to get information on their competitor, you can offer to update the information every month for a fee of $150. This way they will stay on top of the situation knowing what their competitors are doing, and won't have to call you in an emergency when their boss needs to know something about the current competition. You will have already provided that information to them.

3) A Freebie Document

Without calling or writing proposals for continuation services you can easily generate new business by just sending a freebie with a little sticky note saying:

"Thought you'd be interested in this. Give me a call if I can help."

You can look for articles that deal with the last project you worked on for them. Or, you can contact relevant government agencies and get copies of free reports to send to them. For example, if you had a client that once asked you for information on the Cable TV industry, you can call the U.S. Federal Communications Commission and get free copies of the latest reports showing trends in the industry. Almost any business owner is interested in this kind of information, especially if its current. It's the kind of thing that most business owners just don't have the time to do.

It's all about communication — the more you communicate with new and established clients, the more those clients will identify new ways to use your services.

What's Good and Bad About Using Computers In The Information Age

Food Processors, PCs, and Other Miracle Products

Before you purchase a database, first think about what you are actually buying. Is it the steak or the sizzle? Many of today's commercial database vendors are selling their services the way food processor sales reps sold their wares a few years back. Remember the sales pitch that this kitchen appliance could make the entire meal every day of the week? However, after buying this expensive gadget we found that puree of steak did not taste as good as a charcoaled piece of meat and that carrot mousse didn't suit our children's taste buds. Now we all have this expensive equipment cluttering up the kitchen counter that we use a few times a month to make coleslaw or milk shakes because the blender we bought 10 years ago is stashed away in the attic. Remember when simple was better?

This phenomenon has struck personal computers. A few years ago, buyers were sold on the belief that the world would pass them by if they did not have a PC. Furthermore, this sophisticated machine would solve all their problems and organize their lives like never before. We were told that daily tasks such as balancing the checkbook or keeping track of recipes would virtually disappear. However, PC owners discovered that because they never balanced their checkbook by hand, they were never going to do it by computer. It actually was more complicated and took longer to use the computer than the old fashioned way. And, keeping 50 or so recipes in a $1,000 machine that is located at the other end of the house proved to be inconvenient. Soon people realized that the "practical applications," like word processing and spread sheets, were not typical household

functions. As a result of this revelation, computer sales began to plummet.

Waiting For The Technology To Mature

One can safely predict that computers will eventually be easier, cheaper, and more practical to use as the sophistication of the technology improves. The same pattern occurred with the introduction of the automobile. It took decades to get it right, and even now, cars are being improved in subtle ways all the time.

When cars first rolled off the assembly line, the primary advantages they offered over the horse as a traditional means of transportation were technology and novelty. An automobile cost at least ten times more than a horse. These complex machines were difficult to start and required special fuel that was hard to come by. Special clothing, goggles, and other paraphernalia were necessary for protection against dust and the elements. And cars were very limited in where they could go due to the lack of good roadways. All of these problems could not compare with the simple act of jumping on a horse and going anywhere. It was obvious that the horse still was the fastest, most convenient, and most inexpensive mode of transportation. But even then people were willing to be oversold on the use of a new technology. In other words, they bought the sizzle instead of the steak. And those who waited until the cost was worth the benefit of the application found that as the technology improved, the new product was faster, cheaper, and easier to use than the original. With the increase in available software, or highways in the case of automobiles, there were many more uses and applications for the new product than the old one.

By waiting for the technology to evolve into a cost effective alternative for a specific application, consumers who held on to their horses before buying the first automobiles found that they got to their destinations a lot sooner for a lot less money than the new car buyer. And when these patient consumers purchased the later model of automobile, they found that their later model machine could do a great deal more than the ones that rolled off the first production line, with a lot less kinks to be worked out.

Pros And Cons Of Databases

Overselling Computerized Databases

A similar story continues to unfold with online databases. Slick sales reps tell us that we can solve all of our information problems with their databases. Again buyers, because of their infatuation with the technology, are dazzled with the notion of getting the answer to a million dollar question by simply dialing up an all knowing computer. In order to avoid spending money on novelty items, one has to see if the price of obtaining information via high tech means is worth the money compared to relying on traditional alternatives.

Helpful With Large Amounts of Info

Databases are especially good at handling large amounts of information, and there are literally hundreds of computerized systems that perform this function. These services index and abstract everything from all business-oriented periodicals to those that can provide such bibliographic help only in a certain subject area such as energy. If this is your field of interest, you should think about what you will be paying for. Most of these types of databases are aimed at the professional user and can be expensive. Studies show that the average professional user of databases spends about $100 per hour. What kind of information will you be able to access at that price?

A $100 Seminar On How To Shop At Macy's

Many of the professional databases are also very complicated to use. It is the only industry where commercial vendors charge their customers for taking a course on how to spend money on their products. Wouldn't it be something if Macy's Department Store charged you to take a class on how to shop at their store? This should be a clue that databases and their applications are not for everyone. Especially if you know that you'll be using a database very infrequently.

Much of the material that is online is also available in print form. So you may be paying $100 per hour for the convenience of not dropping by your local library to look up the indexes manually. At $100 an hour, you could buy an awful lot of library help.

Non Discriminating Computers

Also remember that these bibliographic databases sometime create more problems than they solve. Searching a large database on a subject can easily churn out 500 articles for you to review. The problem now comes in trying to identify the worthwhile articles, not to mention actually obtaining those which you select. The computer is attempting to cope with the information explosion by providing the capability to index any and all data that are generated. However, the computer does a very poor job at being selective. It cannot tell you whether an article is good or bad. This problem is only getting worse because anyone with a word processor can be a publisher within days and the commercial vendors are always eager to acquire new databases.

After you get bombarded with some 500 citations racing across the screen, you still may have to make a half dozen telephone calls to locate a real expert in the field who can suggest which are the best and most current articles to read. Or this expert may be able to give you the answer right over the telephone. Even better, he may be able to tell you what will be online next year because he is in the midst of writing or reviewing articles and manuscripts on that subject. **Remember, even though a report or survey is contained in a database, that does not guarantee it is the latest available information.** Many databases still rely on printed documentation, so many times there may be less expensive and easier ways to get your hands on more current information. In the chapter "Using Industry Sources And Overcoming The Negative Researching Syndrome", use the resources listed in the section "Government Experts".

Is Speed Worth The Price?

Getting information to you quickly is another function that databases and telecommunications do exceedingly well. Here again, you must decide whether the convenience is worthy of the expense. Having the Associated Press wire service available during the day at $10 to $20 per hour may not be cost effective for you and your business unless you are a million dollar business. Most of us barely get through the morning newspaper which costs a mere 50 cents and usually contains the highlights of what is reported on the wire service. And it's not yet feasible to scan your newspapers via computer either in bed or while commuting to work. No doubt getting the price of stocks as they are traded on the floor of the stock exchange at $75.00 per hour may be worth it if you are a big time investor and have to know what the stock market is doing minute-by-minute. But for most of our investment decisions, reading the stock quotes in our local morning paper is usually good enough. There are many professional applications in addition to big time investing in which speed would be worth a significant premium. It is wise to make sure that paying for this convenience is honestly necessary to you and your organization.

Help If You Are Reinventing The Wheel

Another aspect of telecommunications which appears to have much more usable potential is the ability of like minded people to communicate instantly. The pace at which civilization develops seems dependent upon the speed at which ideas are refined and shared with others. Thus, it seems reasonable to assume that some day soon one person on one side of the street will not waste his or her time wrestling with a problem which has already been solved by someone else on the opposite side of the street. Telecommunications can aid in the process of making information more available.

We once spoke to a veterinarian in Iowa who was faced with treating a three-legged dog and was uncertain how to proceed. As a member of a veterinarian bulletin board, he posed his question to this professional forum via computer. By the next morning, there were answers from doctors in Florida and Massachusetts who had treated similar cases. He did not have to wait for the next annual meeting of veterinarians or for a relevant article to be published in the Journal of Veterinarian Medicine. Overnight, he had his question answered and was free to tackle other unsolved problems because his time was now free to go on to other things.

Databases Are Here To Stay

By presenting all these negative aspects, we hope it is now more obvious that databases contribute only a few pieces to solving a big information puzzle. Many times the cost far exceeds the benefit. However, like the automobile, online databases are here to stay, and in time, they will become more reasonably priced and offer applications users never dreamed could exist.

The online database business, like other segments of the information industry, is a buyer's beware market. **Access to a $1,000 computerized information system that one** firm is selling may be available for free or a modest charge from some public or non-profit organization.

Some suggestions about purchasing databases are described next which are intended to help you save some money while utilizing this current technology.

Money Saving Online Tips

Use The Free Database First

This may sound obvious, but the real problem is that you may not be aware of **free online databases**. The free ones cannot afford to hire an expensive sales team to promote their systems. Here are some examples of how prices may vary widely for the same product:

- You can tap into weather information on over seven systems at prices ranging from $3 to $90 an hour, or you can access the National Weather Service's free database provided by the Federal government, which happens to be the basis for all the other sources of weather information.

- Online encyclopedias can cost up to $75 per hour if you are accessing systems like Dow Jones or BRS, or you can pay as little as $6 per hour on CompuServe or Delphi. Oftentimes, it is the exact same file.

- City or state demographics can cost over $100 an hour from such vendors as DIALOG, BRS or Chase Econometrics, or you can use the free database offered by Conway Data, Inc. in Atlanta, Georgia (404-446-6996).

- The latest economic statistics that are sold on such systems as DRI and Chase for as much as $160 an hour can also be accessed for free from an electronic bulletin board maintained by the U.S. Department of

Commerce. Chances are the data are probably available sooner from this free source.

Lesko's Info-Power, a monthly newsletter published by Information USA, Inc., frequently identifies unadvertised bulletin boards and databases that are free.

Consider Off-Line Alternatives

Typically what many commercial database vendors do is find data that are available in other formats, such as hard copy, off-line printout and computer tape. You can often save a lot of money by not accessing online systems but rather getting the information in less high tech ways. Here are some examples:

- Legi-Slate, Commerce Clearing House, and Congressional Quarterly will charge you up to $190 an hour to find out the current status of legislation, or you can telephone for free searches and even obtain computer printouts on all the bills you are monitoring by using a free database maintained by the U.S. Congress.

- Services such as Data Resources, I.P. Sharp, and Chase Econometrics will charge you $100 per hour to obtain demographic information on any country in the world, or you can call the International Demographic Center at the U.S. Bureau of the Census and request a free printout of the same information which may even be more current.

- Dialog charges $45 an hour for information on U.S. exports, and the Trade Information Branch at the U.S. Department of Commerce will give you much of the same information for free. Also, the data will be more current because this government office is where Dialog gets the information it sells.

- Control Data Corp. allows you to access a file called FARPS that will tell you where to get money in the government for your project, or you can contact the U.S. General Services Administration which maintains the file and this government agency will do free searches for you.

- An energy bibliographic database maintained by the U.S. Department of Energy in Tennessee is sold by DIALOG or it can be accessed directly from the government for free.

Use Database Wholesalers and Intermediaries

Many commercial vendors have initiation fees and monthly minimums which can increase your hourly cost considerably if you are not going to be a large user. One way to cut out these extra fees, at least until you see what your volume will be, is to use a database wholesaler or intermediary. For example, if you are a subscriber to MCI, you receive access to the Dow Jones service without paying an additional initiation charge. You may begin to see more of these opportunities as the telecommunications industry develops further.

If you are a first time database user and are interested in the non-consumer oriented electronic systems, it may be wise to have someone else do your searching. Even some so-called "user friendly" databases are not as easy to use as their vendors claim. Online charges at $100 an hour can translate into a hefty bill if you are just learning the system. Companies called information brokers will usually handle this for you. The best way to find available brokers is to contact your local reference librarian. They are in a good position to tell you what is available locally. If you have trouble with this approach, you may find help by calling: DIALOG Information Services, Customer Service, 1-800-334-2564.

This major commercial database vendor maintains a list, by city, of those organizations which will provide this service tailored to your

needs. Be sure to ask if a nearby public, academic, or specialized library might perform online retrieval services because chances are, this would be a cheaper alternative. For example, the Brooklyn Business Library will do database searches and charge only for direct out-of-pocket costs. An information broker is likely to cost you three to four times as much. The following reference book identifies over 8,400 databases available in a variety of electronic formats:

Gale's *Directory of Databases*
    1994, 2 volume set ($300)
    Gale Research Co.
    P.O. Box 33477
    Detroit, MI 48232-5477
    313-961-2242
    1-800-877-4253
    Contact: Sandy Gore, extension 1394

If you have a PC with a modem but have been reluctant to access the more complicated business databases, you can call Easynet. This firm will search some seven major vendors for you and send the results to you via your computer. Easynet covers most of the major business databases and claims that their average search cost is $17.00.

    EASYNET Telebase Systems, Inc.
    435 Devon Park Dr., Suite 600
    Wayne, PA 19087
    1-800-220-9553
    610-293-4700

Save With Evening Discounts

Most of the commercial database vendors offer discounts if you access their systems during the evening hours and other non-prime times. According to a survey of vendors, the average savings amounted to 50%, which means that if you encounter any volume at all, it would pay for you to hire someone to come into your office in the evening just to access certain databases. Here is a sample of such discounts offered by some of the major vendors:

ADP Network Services	50%
BRS	62% to 80.9%
CompuServe	52%
DataNet	84.4%
Dialog	53.3%
Dow Jones	22% to 78%
Delphi	45%
Mead Data Central	50%
NewsNet	25%
Source	62.7%

Save On Telecommunications Software

In this case, the cheapest may be the best. A paper presented at the 1985 National Online Conference concluded that there was little difference between using a free telecommunications product for the IBM-PC called PC-TALK and a $120 product called Instantcom. To obtain a copy of PC-TALK, contact your local IBM users group.

How To Use Your Computer...
To Sell Government Information

Besides tapping into government information with your computer you can also load large government files into your computer, then turn around and make money selling the information in smaller bits to interested companies. Here are some examples:

Selling Government Contract Information

There's a database with millions of records at the U.S. General Services Administration that shows who got government contracts from what government agency and for how much. There's a great business opportunity here in selling this information to the following groups:

A: Businesses and freelancers who are looking to get government contracts and would like to know who in the government might buy their product.

B: Small and minority businesses who are looking for subcontracting work. There are laws requiring companies who get large government contracts to subcontract to small and minority businesses.

C: Government contractors who are interested in keeping tabs on what contracts their competitors are winning.

For more information on the price and availability of these files contact: Federal Procurement Data System Division, Federal Procurement Data Center, General Services Administration, 4040 N. Fairfax Dr., Suite 900, Arlington, VA 22203, 202-401-1529.

Selling Government Grant Information

This is an interesting database that very few people know is available. It contains the name and address of everyone who got a government grant, direct payment, loan, or loan guarantee. For large programs like Social Security it only gives a total dollar amount for a small geographical area, like a congressional district. But for other programs it gives the names and addresses of people like those who got money for their business, money to be work on their video program, money to travel overseas, etc.

The market for this information may not be as obvious as the one for government contracts, but, believe me the market is there. Here are some examples to start with:

A: College and university researchers who want to know who is giving out research grants and who's getting them.

B: Insurance salesmen who are looking to sell business polices to companies who just got large government loans or grants.

C: Mailing list brokers who are looking for hot lists of people who get government money.

D: Banks and other financial services companies who are always looking for people who just got large amounts of money so that they can manage it for them (hold it in their bank or invest for them).

For more information on the price and availability of these files contact: Federal

Assistance Programs Retrieval System (FAPRS), Federal Domestic Assistance Catalog Staff (WKU), General Services Administration, Ground Floor, Reporters Building, 300 7th St., SW, Washington, DC 20407, 202-708-5126.

Selling Government Statistics

Everyone needs data at one time or another. That's one of the main reasons that the information brokerage business has become so big. And one way more and more clients are going to want their data is in a form that their particular computer system can read. As an information broker, you can take data from government computerized files, and slice it up and reformat it for your clients.

For example, you can go to major statistical agencies like the U.S. Bureau of Census, the U.S. Bureau of Labor Statistics, U.S. Department of Agriculture, and the U.S. Department of Commerce and copy all the data files that have information showing the makeup of the people that live in your city. Banks, restaurants, and other businesses need this information in order to make informed decisions about the growth of their business. You can add value to this information by providing it in a format that is compatible with their computer (Lotus, dBase, etc.), and you can constantly send them updates to keep this information current for them.

The contact persons for the major statistical agencies listed above are as follows:

1) Agriculture and Food Statistics
   National Agriculture Statistics Service
   Director, Estimates Division
   U.S. Department of Agriculture
   5175 S Building
   14th and Independence Ave., SW
   Washington, DC 20250
   202-720-3896

2) Economic and Demographic Statistics
   Bureau of the Census
   U.S. Department of Commerce

Data User Service Division
Customer Service
Washington, DC 20233
301-457-4100

3) Crime Statistics
   Uniform Crime Reporting Section
   Federal Bureau of Investigations (FBI)
   U.S. Department of Justice-GRB
   7th and D Streets, NW
   Washington, DC 20535
   202-324-5038

4) Economics-National, Regional and International
   Bureau of Economic Analysis
   U.S. Department of Commerce
   1441 L St., NW
   Washington, DC 20230
   202-606-9900

5) Education Statistics
   Office of Educational Research and Improvement
   555 New Jersey Ave., NW, Room 300
   Washington, DC 20208-5641
   1-800-424-1616

6) Health Statistics
   National Center for Health Statistics
   U.S. Department of Health and Human Resources
   6525 Belcrest Road
   Hyattsville, MD 20782
   301-436-8500

7) Employment, Prices, Living Conditions, Productivity, and Occupational Safety and Health
   Bureau of Labor Statistics
   U.S. Department of Labor
   2 Massachusetts Ave., NE
   Washington, DC 20212
   Information   202-606-7828
   Publications   202-606-7828, ext. 6

8) Import and Export Statistics
   World Trade Reference Room

U.S. Department of Commerce
Room 2233
Washington, DC 20230
202-482-2185

9) World Import and Export Statistics
World Trade Statistics
U.S. Department of Commerce
Room 2233
Washington, DC 20230
202-482-5242

There are literally thousands of places in the government you can get computerized data and resell it to customers. For example:

- You can get the names and addresses of all the people subscribing to a government publication on the environment and sell the information to non-profits who raise money to address environmental issues.

- You can get copies of all the Freedom of Information Act letters filed at a government agency like the Food and Drug Administration. Then scan these letters into your computer and sell this as a service to anyone who sends in a Freedom of Information Act request to get copies of everyone else's Freedom of Information Act requests.

- You can get the names of all the people who borrow money and use an asset as collateral and sell these names to mailing list companies, insurance companies, or bankers. This is the kind of information available from state offices.

Look closer at the section of this manual that describes government sources of information. From this you'll get all kinds of new ideas if you keep in mind that 99% of all government information is public. Just call offices you're interested in and see if they make their data available in computer readable formats. Then, you will only be limited by your imagination.

How To Write A Proposal

You may not even have to. Most information brokers work on projects ranging from $50 to $5,000. If it's a $50 project you're involved in, you certainly don't want to spend a whole lot of time writing proposals. You could spend the whole $50 just on proposal writing. But if the client wants a proposal, you should give it to him.

A small contract can be handled with just a few lines. You could say something like this:

Sample Small Project Proposal Letter

Mr. Jeff Bean
Carbon Steel Company
270 Price Street
Pittsburgh, Pa 18726

Dear Mr. Bean:

Thank you for calling us today to help you with your information requirements. As per our conversation, our task will be to identify any and all public documents filed to the State of Maryland Office of the Secretary of State under the name of Republic Steel, Inc. Our fee for this is $50.00, and is payable whether or not documents have been filed by this company.

We will report to you no later than Wednesday, April 29, 1995.

Again, thank you for your business.

Sincerely,

Matthew Lesko
President

On a short project, there is very little to lose if you have a miscommunication with the client. So if you can get away with a verbal agreement, all the better because it costs you nothing. You can play it safe by sending a note like the one above to serve as a backup agreement. But it's a different story for bigger projects. When there's some serious money involved, it's important to lay out everyone's expectations on paper before you begin the project. You should state what services you are going to perform and describe some of the limitations of the research process. Sometimes it's necessary to reassure new clients that you won't lie, cheat, or steal to get the information.

Below is a sample copy of a proposal letter for a more involved project.

Sample Large Project Proposal Letter

September 7, 1994

Mr. Steve Robbins
Graham Products Inc.
309 Palm Avenue
San Diego, CA 97213

Dear Mr. Robbins:

Thank you for thinking of us to assist you with your data needs. I feel that we can be of great assistance and I look forward to having an opportunity to show you how well our company can perform for you.

The objective of our research will be to seek the following information:
   The Market Structure and Pricing for Clean Room Swabs in the United States.

The types of information we will attempt to find will include but not be limited to the following:
   1)   The names and addresses of the major manufacturers;

   2)   An estimate on their size (market share and/or sales); and

   3)   Prices charged for typical quantities at the manufacturing and distributors level.

The research methodology for this project will include:

   1)   Interviews with executives from major manufacturers and distributors of clean room swabs;

   2)   Interviews with federal industry experts who monitor this market; and

   3)   Interviews with executives in trade associations and industry journals which cover this market.

Information USA, Inc. does not guarantee that all the information desired will be found, but we do guarantee that all the sources described above will be researched and that we will give our best effort to accomplish the stated objectives.

Because of the nature of the project we cannot guarantee that this information is available and exactly how long it will take to obtain it. Our expertise is in obtaining difficult information inexpensively. The initial cost of performing this research will be between 10 and 12 hours of research time at $100 per hour. At this juncture we will have either obtained all the information or will have enough to provide you with a good estimate of market share. Or, we will be able to tell you whether we can obtain the stated information objectives and how much more research it will take to accomplish this.

The final written report will highlight the results of our findings. You will receive copies of all reports, articles, and other public and private documents we collect during the course of our research. You will also receive the names, addresses, and telephone numbers of all sources which provide us with information so that Graham Products can collect this data for itself in the future. Where and when appropriate we will computerize our findings for you. This can be done by providing you with the information on diskette or through an intermediary such as NEWSNET or CompuServe. Also, because this research will only identify the majority of sources available and not explore the total universe of sources, our report will identify the likelihood of uncovering any additional information through more exhaustive investigation.

To insure Graham Products' confidentiality, all research will be conducted in the corporate name of Information USA.

Research can begin upon receipt of a $500 down payment. It is expected that the research will take approximately three weeks to complete. You will be billed the balance upon acceptance of the final report. The price includes all charges, including communications fees. However, the price does not cover the cost of purchasing any outside market studies. Such items will be billed separately, and Information USA will consult with you for authority and billing arrangements before any purchase is made. This price is guaranteed for four weeks from the date of this letter but is subject to change thereafter.

Thank you for allowing me this opportunity to present our services. Please feel free to call me should you have any questions concerning this proposal.

Sincerely,

Matthew Lesko
President

Beginning Your Research Project

Cultivating a successful list of clients — it's the single most important element of your business. It may take weeks and even months of phone calls and then follow up calls to finally convince a customer to take a chance on you and give you some work. Show these clients that you'll execute their research project thoroughly and in a timely manner. If you are able to accomplish this, you may make a repeat customer for yourself simply by completing this first assignment. Over time, this client will come to rely on you for accurate information sources, knowing that he can come to you time and time again to retrieve the information that he needs. Mark my words, that client will be more than willing, even eager to pay premium dollars for your expertise!

Months of setting up your office with the right equipment and talking to the right people to get the choice research assignments will be worthless if you don't have a clear understanding of how to actually find the information that has been requested of you. How do you begin to get on with this first very important assignment to gather information?

Let's begin with the basic request for information from the client. Has he been specific about the information that he wants you to find? Or has he instead given you a vague outline of what information he thinks he needs? The most important task that you can accomplish at the beginning of a project is to clarify with the client and yourself the exact information that you have been asked to search for. This clarification just might be the key to the success or failure of the project, and will probably determine whether this client will come to you in the future with other projects.

Oddly enough, one of the biggest obstacles you may encounter is coming across too much information for your client — an avalanche of information, so to speak. It's a vital part of your assignment to understand just how much information your client needs to proceed on to the next step of his project. Chances are, he will not be interested in seeing mounds of extraneous information that will only confuse him. Therefore, narrowing the goals of the project to fit the clients' needs will save you important time and will demonstrate to the client that you are indeed a quick study and get down to business quickly.

A Case Study

Let's suppose that a client contacts you to discuss the development of an outlet mall that he is contemplating, along with a group of investors. He has identified available real estate close to a high volume National Park, and has convinced a group of investors that this could be a potential goldmine for an outlet-type mall. The investors will not go ahead until they have some important questions answered regarding this project. The client comes to you for those answers because he knows that you won't present him with useless information that will only slow down the deal and complicate the situation. He knows that sometimes too much information can make a potential investor edgy and can point up other questions that the investors now want answered. You should begin to set up a plan to accomplish the goals set up in Plan One phase of a project.

Stage One: Questions To Be Answered

A. Could the proposed area sustain a mall, based on available demographic information?

1. Population statistics for a 100-mile radius
2. Tourist attendance statistics for the Park and general area over the last five years.

Research Sources:
- Local Chamber of Commerce
- State Office of Tourism
- State Tourism Office for National Park Visitors
- U.S. Department of Commerce for population and business pattern statistics
- State Labor Office for local labor statistics
- State Economic Development Office for appropriate projections

B. What methods would be most successful in attracting qualified merchants to the outlet mall?
1. Compile leasing requirements from a sampling of retail merchandisers
2. What are specific demographic requirements for their customer base?
3. What size of retail development are they most interested in participating in?

Resource Sources:
- Contact three major retail merchandisers already included in outlet malls, such as:
  Eddie Bauer
  The Gap
  Nike Athletic Shoe Manufacturers

C. General industry information regarding mall outlets
1. How do they draw merchandisers?
2. How do they allocate appropriate space to a retailer?
3. What major problems have they encountered?
4. How do they successfully manage their particular outlet?

Resource Sources:
- Talk with a store manager of an outlet mall.
- Check to see if there is an association for discount outlet owners in the area.
- Check to see if a trade publication exists for this particular industry.
- Attend a local Chamber of Commerce function where local merchandisers would be available to exchange information.

Much of the information for this report can be obtained easily over the telephone. Your local library is an excellent source for information on associations, trade publications, and regularly scheduled meetings held by leaders in that industry. The reference volume that accompanies this operations manual will give you helpful starting points within state and federal government offices, but you can always begin your search of federal offices by calling the Washington, DC information operator at 202-555-1212. Keep in mind too, that your local telephone directory lists most state offices, and by simply going through these pages you will no doubt find additional sources that you hadn't initially thought to contact. Online services are growing tremendously as an information source, often containing more up to date research than information found in publications.

This initial work will define the first stage of your research project. Some points you thought to be crucial to your research project may lose their importance in the face of more important information. For example, factors such as location might take on added significance as you learn more about local zoning restrictions. Often the information gathered from this phase will direct the work necessary to complete the second phase. This initial work may even define the project more clearly in the eyes of your client, and he'll be grateful to you for accomplishing this.

How To Write A Report

"If no one reads your report, your research is worthless." That's the one thing you should keep in mind when preparing a report for a client. Also, think about the newspaper *USA Today* and the local news on your television. These two organizations understand the communication of information better than anyone else in our society.

We live in a society with a lot of noise, a whole lot of noise. Everyone is competing for our attention. Think of it — we now have over 100 television channels and now they're talking about 300 channels being available soon. There are thousands of magazines published each year and they are adding more all the time. And, some 20,000 people subscribe to the INTERNET where they have some 8,000 special interest groups. And this keeps growing as we speak. Your report has to fight for your client's attention just like all these other media sources. But, you may say, "Yeah, my client paid big bucks for my report so she is definitely going to read it." **Wrong**. If it's boring, she's just going to skim it to see if there is anything really important or new in it, and then forget about it because it was boring. Or if she can't find the information in your report fast enough, she's going to get frustrated and probably never hire you again. So keep remembering that presentation is just as important as substance. The American people are the best entertained people in the world, and you have to be aware of that if you want to successfully communicate with them.

Answer the questions first. Your clients are busy people. They hired you to save them time, not to waste their time. It's not like in high school or college when you wrote about a lot of

extra things in your term papers just to fill up pages. Clients don't need filler — they need answers. So, if the client asked you to get the size of the market for BBQ utensils in Southern New Jersey and you couldn't get the exact figure, don't beat around the bush about how much of everything else you were able to find. Answer the question up front. Give an answer, even if it's only your best guess, and then explain how you arrived at the number. Then you can go into how much other information you found while conducting your research.

Document Interviews. This is a technique that many researchers fail to do. I believe that interviews should be treated the same as any other source of documented information. For example, if you found the size of the BBQ utensil market in an article in *Time* Magazine, you should also pass along a copy of this article to your clients. You should do the same for interviews — if you spoke to an expert who told you the size of the BBQ utensil market, you should also include the highlights of this interview on a separate sheet of paper. The paper could look something like this:

Sam Gibbons
Industry Analyst
U.S. Department of Commerce
Washington, DC
202-377-4995

- the largest sellers of BBQ utensils in the United States are Acme, Craft, and Iron Works

- the market has grown over 30% in the last two years and is expected to grow another 10% next year

- the size of the market in the United States must be over $200 million dollars and probably double that in the rest of the world

Report writing was one of the hardest parts of the business for me to learn. You have to know that I flunked English in college. So writing did not come naturally to me, even though I now have two New York Times Best Sellers and write a syndicated column for the New York Times. Any writing ability I have has come from writing reports for clients. So I feel that if I could do it and do it effectively, anyone can.

For:
XYZ Company
123 Main St.
Anywhere, USA
October 25, 1995

Report on Outlet Mall Venture

Prepared by:
Toni Murray
Information USA, Inc.
P.O. Box E
Kensington, MD 20895

As requested, I conducted interviews with three merchandisers, The Gap (415-737-4883), Nike (503-671-4299), and Eddie Bauer (206-861-4844) to ascertain their criteria and, understand their procedures for setting up outlet stores.

In surveying the three retail merchandisers, the consensus of opinion confirmed that the outlet mall concept was booming and that their outlet ventures were all doing extremely well. The criteria for choosing location for their stores was the same for each company:

1. That the mall should be located on a major highway with maximum accessibility.
2. That the area be tourist oriented and that there be year round traffic.

Nike revealed their outlet stores were doing better than their Nike Township stores. They also confided that they were considering producing products especially for their stores in outlet malls. The Gap is newer to the outlet concept of selling so the information that they can provide is not as extensive. They only have five stores, but are planning to open 20-25 outlet stores in the next five years. Eddie Bauer is well established in the outlet market presently, having 37 outlets. They look specifically for a mall that has other upscale stores.

In questioning the three retail merchandisers about criteria for considering a new location to open an outlet store, the subject of location within the mall was of major importance to all of the merchandisers. Visibility from the highway and visibility within the mall is extremely important to all merchandisers. Juggling positions of retailers will be an extremely important factor to be considered when choosing stores you wish to target to participation in this outlet mall. Strip malls are preferred over enclosed malls for two reasons. Strip malls are less expensive to maintain and they allow more visibility for merchandisers. The terms "center court", "end caps" and "anchor tenant" emerged repeatedly from these interviews. All of these terms relate to positioning within the mall. Anchor tenant is the store that appeals to all customers and will have the biggest draw. Center court is the space in the middle of the mall that has the most visibility. "End caps" are the spaces at the end of each side of the strip mall that are normally filled by a major retailer, with name recognition.

Eddie Bauer, whose parent company is Spiegel, mentioned that if Spiegel participated they would want a pod space (pod being a separate building adjacent to the mall). A synopsis of each interview with the merchandisers is included at the end of this report.

The Nike representative shared the name of the Silverthorne Outlet Mall in Colorado when I inquired about an outlet location in the Rocky Mountain Region of the United States. The manager of the Silverthorne Mall informed me that the mall was owned by a Virginia real estate corporation. I discovered that this company owns 79 outlet malls throughout the United States. Their Silverthorne Outlet Mall has 258,000 square feet and the anchor stores for this mall are Nike and Liz Claiborne, each with about 8,000 square feet. The "center court" position is held by Levi with 10,000 square feet.

In the course of my research, I learned of an industry publication that covers the outlet mall industry. The title of the publication is *Value Retail News* of Clearwater, Florida (813-536-4047). A complimentary copy of this newspaper has been ordered. It can be used as a valuable tool in keeping abreast of current market trends within this industry.

To summarize the findings of the interviews with the Gap, Nike, and Eddie Bauer:

1. For an outlet mall to be successful, a location on Highway 89 or 90 must be a priority.
2. This discount mall must be positioned so maximum visibility from the highway is achieved.
3. Planning of the mall structure should incorporate the factors of anchor stores and end caps. Also, enough land should be purchased to allow for building of pods should large merchandisers wish to join the mall;
4. Statistics need to be compiled and presented.
   - that travel east and west on Highway 90 and north and south on Highway 89 is sufficient to support an outlet mall.
   - population statistics of a 200 mile radius of Livingston must be presented to prove that there is year round population to draw on. These statistics should be supported with mention of the regional differences of Montana versus city drivers. (Montanans count miles, not hours, when driving, and expect to drive long distances to shop.) Figures on winter tourism in Yellowstone Park and at Bozeman's ski resort and Big Sky should be included with this information.
   - Weather statistics to dispel the myth of arctic winters making Montana roads impassable in the winter months should be included. The following reports will aid in this presentation.

Demographic Data
Montana State Travel Office (406-444-2654)

Yellowstone National Park Travel Data - This report details the number of vehicles and visitors that entered Yellowstone National park from the North entrance (Gardiner, MT) in 1994.

Visitors	455,410
Vehicles	366,122

Gross Lodging Tax Revenue - Reports are provided for the city of Gardiner, the city of Livingston, and for Park County. A tax of 4 percent of lodging price is collected by all motels, hotels, and bed and breakfasts.

	1st Quarter	2nd Quarter	3rd Quarter	4th Quarter
Gardiner	$3,254	$17,378	$48,051	$6,798
Park County	$24,193	$75,583	$184,443	$35,181
Livingston	$6,287	$13,106	$34,452	$7,954

Montana State Labor Office (406-444-2639)

Population for Park County	199214,786
Livingston	6,978
(part of Park County)	
Labor Force for Park County	19938,804
Employment for Park County	19938,361
Employment Gains for Park County	1990-19931,013

Institute for Tourism and Recreation Research (406-994-2090)
The University of Montana

The following information is taken from the institute report, *A Profile of Visitors to Montana: I-94*, published in 1992. The report is based on 1990 statistics.

The institute estimates that 140,000 non-resident groups enter Montana on Interstate 94. 7 percent (9,800) of that group exit Montana via Highway 89 North and enter Yellowstone Park.

The following information is taken from the institute report, *A profile of Visitors to Montana: Highway 89 South*, published in 1992. The report is based on 1990 statistics.

The institute estimates that 107,0000 non-resident groups enter Montana via Highway 89 South as they leave Yellowstone park.

Recommendations for continuing research:

1. Contact Mike Riley (406-994-2090) at the Montana State University Business school regarding a report he is currently writing for the Museum of the Rockies on tourism in the Bozeman area.

2. Contact and interview 30 possible merchandisers who might participate in the Mall.

3. Contact State Highway Department to obtain their statistics on east-east and north-south traffic out of Livingston.

4. Research actual site location information including:
   a) land available for sale along I-90 and Highway 89
   b) tax costs of land
   c) zoning restrictions
   d) city and state restrictions and regulations governing the land.

5. Plan a comprehensive public relations campaign addressing all positive and negative issues in order to win city approval of project.

6. Prepare presentation folders for all outlet merchandisers you plan to approach to participate.

Why Government Information Is Necessary For An Information Brokerage Business

Our changing economy has created both good and bad news for entrepreneurs. The bad news is that while our country may no longer produce the best cars in the world, the good news is our country has become the premier producer of information in the world. And now that the entire planet has been transformed into the information age using computers and databases that are available worldwide, this is even better news. Maybe it doesn't matter if we don't make the best cars anymore. Here's more good news for entrepreneurs — the largest source of information in the world happens to be the U.S. government. And because we live in a democracy, anyone can get all this information for free, or at very little cost. Because of this demand, as an entrepreneur in the information age there's a lot of money to be made providing information to people who need it and don't know how to get it. With the government as your source, you've got it made. You can get your product for free, and sell it to your customers for as much as the market will bear. It's kind of like running a gas station and having a free oil well in your backyard.

Government Is America's Biggest Industry

What people have failed to realize is that government in the United States now represents over 37% of the country's total Gross National Product. If you think the computer industry is big, think again. Look at the accompanying chart and you'll see that the percentage of GNP that accounts for the computer industry is peanuts compared to the government. Look at farming, health, and automobiles, and you'll see that government is bigger than any of them. If you ever go to Washington you'll see that there are no smokestacks in the city because our

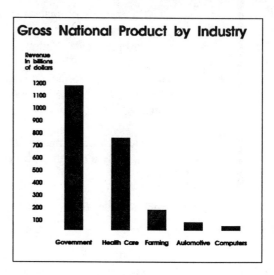

government doesn't make things — it's a government that produces paper, information, and expertise.

More Books Than All The Commercial Publishers

Did you know that all the major commercial publishers in the United States produce a total of about 50,000 books a year? This means that there are only about 50,000 new titles in all the libraries and bookstores around the country in a single given year. But did you also know that one little publisher in the government, called the National Technical Information Service (NTIS), publishes over 100,000 titles a year? Strangely enough, most people have never heard of the NTIS. Yet, it's the major source for reports published by federal agencies. I've seen government studies that show this agency is only publishing about 20% of what it actually could generate. So if NTIS was doing a perfect job they would have about 500,000 new titles a year. This is ten times the number of books published by all the commercial publishers in the country — and that's a lot of information.

And Better, Too

You must also remember that government publications are going to be better than the books you find in the bookstores or libraries. Ok, maybe they won't be as sexy looking but they sure will be more thorough. When you buy a book in the bookstore from an author like me, you get a book that the author spent maybe a year or two or sometimes as long as five years of his life working on. Five years is a long time for an author to work on a book. Authors have to eat every day, and there are very few of them able to spend five years on a book and still keep food on the table.

When you get a book from the government it is very likely that some government agency spent over 100 man years producing it. Much of government information and expertise is a result of large projects or contracts, and when the government studies something, they REALLY study it. That's what most of us say is wrong with the government...the fact that they spend *too* much time and money on everything. As an information broker this works to your advantage, because it will provide you with the most complete work available on any given subject.

Who Else But The Government Can Afford To Do It

Who else can afford to spend $3 billion dollars counting all the noses and toilets in the United States? That's what the U.S. government spent on the last census. They actually count people, toilets, and a whole lot of other things. Not even the biggest companies in the world such as General Motors or Proctor & Gamble and the like, can afford to spend that much money collecting information for just one study. But our government can and does, spending big money collecting information every day. And you can get it for free.

700,000 Free Experts

In addition to information in the form of reports, books and other publications, the government also has expertise. And it employs more experts than any other business in the world. Where else are you able to talk to experts on subjects like pasta, crayons, poplar trees, and even jelly beans, and all without it costing you a cent. I estimate that there are approximately 700,000 experts in the federal government that are each getting paid up to $80,000 a year just to study topics like these. And these experts are available to you for the price of a telephone call if you know where to look for them.

It may sound like an oxymoron to say "government expert", but after talking to thousands of them over the years, I truly believe that most government experts are more knowledgeable and more unbiased than those so called "private experts" who charge a lot of money to express their educated opinions. Let me give you some examples. Let's say your stock broker calls you up. You consider her to be an investment expert and she recommends putting all your money into biotechnology. Now think about it: Is that stock broker really an expert in biotechnology? No, she's an expert in calling people on the phone and getting them to invest their money in something. Most likely that stock broker just learned how to spell biotechnology that morning!

If you really want to learn about biotechnology you can call one of dozens of experts in the government who spend their careers doing nothing but studying biotechnology. So, when you call a government biotechnology expert, they could have been studying the industry for the last ten years of their life. These are not people, like investment advisors, who are trying to guess what everyone else in the market is doing. They are experts who live with the facts and figures in their head because that is their one area of study and expertise. Based on their study, they know today what trends and opportunities will show up in places like the Wall Street Journal in weeks, months, or even years. For another investment story see the chapter entitled "The Art Of Getting A Bureaucrat To Help You".

Using Free Government Experts As An Information Broker

It's important to realize the tremendous value of these government experts. As an information broker you can actually get better information from these experts than from the private professionals who charge high fees. It works for most any kind of specific expertise, be it marketing, legal, economic, and even medical.

Let's look at medical information as an example. Most of us believe that we have to go to local doctors to get the latest medical information, but that's not true at all. Doctors are probably the one group in America that is suffering the most from IES (Infomus Explosus Syndrome). IES means that the information in their discipline is growing so fast that there is no way they can possibly keep up on everything that is going on in their field and continue to take care of their patients. You've seen the headlines about health in the news — they're discovering new treatments, causes, and cures for diseases every day. Most doctors barely have enough time to read the *New England Journal Of Medicine* once a month, and this only provides them with a handful of articles.

Instead of relying on a busy doctor, who may not have the most up to date information and will also charge you a lot of money, you can call a government expert for free. The National Institute of Health spends billions of dollars every year studying every conceivable disease or ailment that you can think of. So instead of going to your local physician to determine the latest cure for anything from arthritis to hemorrhoids, you can call a government expert who is spending his career studying that disease. And these experts are also handing out lots of money to other experts around the world to study this disease. So why hope that your local doctor has had time to read the latest edition of the *New England Journal Of Medicine* when you can call a government expert who can tell you what will be in the *New England Journal of Medicine* next year, because they are conducting that research today.

This is also true of lawyers. Think about it. Where do the laws come from in our country? The government, right? So when you want to get the answer to a legal question, don't hire a lawyer when instead you can go to the government and get the answer for free. For example, maybe you're interested in buying a franchise and after talking to a franchise salesman you decide you better get some legal advice. If you call that friend of a friend who is an attorney for advice, they will go and read up on the franchise law for you. The attorney knows that the law changes every day and she better go find out what the latest revision is. Remember that this attorney is probably charging you somewhere between $100 and $200 an hour to get this information. Instead, you can make a call to the U.S. Federal Trade Commission and talk to a franchise attorney who helped write the law. In short, why pay someone $200 to learn the law for you when you can talk to someone who wrote the law, and it will cost you absolutely nothing?

Why Doesn't The Average Person Understand The Value Of Government Information?

I've been selling government information for close to 20 years now and I still can't come up with a simple answer to this question. I believe that it all comes from a combination of circumstances. First and foremost, most people hate their government. This is true because the only dealing most citizens have with government bureaucracy is with the Internal Revenue Service (IRS), the Division of Motor Vehicles, and what they read in the newspapers about the latest government screwup. Most of us are sick and disgusted with the waste and "shenanigans" that seem to characterize our government in daily headlines.

Let's look at these government agencies. Of course, everyone hates paying taxes. It's just unAmerican to feel otherwise. But the Division of Motor Vehicles is hated by most of us for a different reason. It's probably the only government agency that most of us come into contact with during our lives. At one time or another we all have to get our drivers license renewed. You've all been there. You stand in line for hours and finally come face-to-face with some bureaucrat who has been answering the same question a thousand times that day. She hates her job and treats you miserably. You treat her miserably back, and struggle through talking with her just to get the whole thing done. But you're not done. She tells you to stand in another line. And after waiting in this second line for what seems forever you're in front of another miserable person who also hates his boring job. And you wind up having one of the worst days of your life, and you rightly blame it all on the Division of Motor Vehicles in your state. With the only government experience taking place at the Division of Motor Vehicles, it's obvious that the government wouldn't be on

the top of anyone's list when they start thinking about where to get help and information.

The other major source of interaction most people have with the government is through the media. And with what we read about IRS scandals, Housing and Urban Development (HUD) scandals, hammers for $1,000 at the Defense Department, sex scandals on Capitol Hill, and more, we end up having little respect for government as a whole. These stories used to bother me a lot when I first started promoting government information, because they were so counter to the story I was trying to tell, but they don't bother me now. I've learned to better understand the role of the media in our society, which is to present the news. News is what's different in our society each day, and thank goodness the bad stuff is still what's different. When the good stuff becomes what's different, or news, then our society is really in trouble. The media's job is to find and expose what's wrong in our government and then we're all supposed to want to see it fixed. It's also very easy for the press to find someone in the government screwing up. We live in a democracy, and therefore, what work the government does is all public information open to public scrutiny. With over 15 million government workers on the payroll it's pretty easy to find someone screwing up. The media can't find someone in your house or small business screwing up because it's a private place of business, but once you get arrested or something like that, then your screwup becomes public information.

Day in and day out the average American is being bombarded with stories on how the government screwed up today. After hearing that over and over again, and not having any other personal experience except the bad one with the Division of Motor Vehicles, it's easy to see why a good upstanding American is going to go out of their way to avoid any contact with a lazy, shiftless bureaucrat.

Are The Rich Smart Or Welfare Queens?

There are some other myths about the government that keep us from using it like we should. I'm sure you've heard statements like this: "It's unAmerican to use the government. Our country is built on people who do everything for themselves. The only people who use the government are welfare queens or crooks who take congressmen and senators to lunch". I was brought up believing that this statement was practically a part of the Bill Of Rights. That belief changed when I got to Washington. Now I see that all the fat cats in our society have made it big because of help from the government. If your definition of a welfare queen is someone who takes money from the government and really doesn't need it, then some of our most famous current cultural heros can be called welfare queens.

People like H. Ross Perot — he made his fortune getting government contracts. He built his business into being worth zillions of dollars, and then he sold it to General Motors. And as soon as he left General Motors he started another business getting government contracts. General Motors even tried to sue him for leaving and starting up a competing business that went after government contracts.

Ross is not alone. Lee Iacocca turned Chrysler around because he went to Washington and got a $1.2 billion loan from the government. I laughed when he made a big deal about repaying the loan. I grew up thinking all loans had to be repaid. Donald Trump built his whole business on government money programs that helped him buy and fix up property. "Mr. Dealmaker" even brags in his first book about how his first million dollar deal involved government property

in Cincinnati. I was shocked to learn that even John Wayne got a government giveaway. That's right, John Wayne, who stood for everything America likes to believe about being a rugged "do-it-by-yourself" individualist. His private yacht was a converted U.S. Navy mine sweeper that was purchased at a government auction. But myths die hard even when the facts prove those myths wrong.

Uncle Sam Doesn't Advertise

So far I've only been talking about what goes on in the mind of the average American that stops them from using the government, but there are also a few things going on in the government that aren't helping things either. A big problem is that the government does not advertise the fact that most of this money and help is available to the average citizen. The reasons that they don't advertise can be put into two basic categories. For programs like grants, loans, and other money giveaways, it's difficult for a bureaucrat to ask Congress to kick in an extra million dollars to advertise the fact that they are trying to give away hundreds of millions of dollars. That seems to be a real tough sell for a bureaucrat. If they make such a request when fighting for their budget on Capitol Hill a Congressman would obviously say: "Why do you need the money in the first place? If you have to advertise that you want to give this money away, there can't be a need. So we're going to cut your budget!" No good bureaucrat ever wants a member of Congress to consider cutting their budget, because that could mean their job.

There's a different problem with the non-money stuff like all of the available government information and expertise. Most government information has not been created so that you can make a lot of money selling it. You're never going to see big signs in the government saying "FREE INFO: COME AND GET IT". The information that has been collected and created has all come about because of some law or policy. The fact that you can profit from it is just a byproduct of its original intent.

A good example is the U.S. Census. We've all heard of it, and we all know that it contains a lot of information about the kinds of people that live in the United States. But did you know that the real reason we do the Census is because our Constitution says that periodically we have to count the number of people living in this country so that we can figure out how many Congressmen and Senators we should have? So as a byproduct of the Constitution, we now have a $3 billion dollar market study that we can use to figure out the best place to open up a jewelry store, the best place to live, or where to look for rich people, among other things.

The same is true for other government information. The experts at the U.S. Department of Labor that forecast the supply and demand of various kinds of jobs in our country are doing this so that our government can better understand the effects of industry downsizing on government programs such as unemployment insurance. So if you're thinking about a new career, don't rely on reading an issue of *U.S. News and World Report* that talks about jobs in the year 2000. That article was written by some reporter who spent maybe a day, a week, or perhaps a month studying the subject. Instead, call the expert at the U.S. Department of Labor, who's been studying the topic for the last 15 years of his life.

The same is true for people like the aquaculture expert at the U.S. Department of Agriculture. An expert like this is on the payroll making $60,000 a year and studying the future of aquaculture because, some day, the availability of fish off our coasts might not be adequate to feed our population and we have to be ready with alternatives. But in the meantime, if you're interested in investing in an excelsior farm, this would be the office to contact. They have to know more about this subject than anyone else in the world because the future of America may depend on it.

The Art Of Getting A Bureaucrat To Help You

Our greatest asset as information seekers is that we live in a society inhabited by people who are dying to talk about what they do for a living. However, in this world of big bureaucracies and impersonal organizations, it is rare that any of us get a chance to share what we know with someone who is truly interested. Perhaps that explains why psychiatrists are in such great demand. They are great listeners, and not many average Americans are these days.

This phenomenon can actually work to your advantage — almost anyone can find an expert on any topic if you are willing to make an average of seven telephone calls to eventually locate that expert.

The Value Of Experts In
Today's Information Age

Using experts can be your answer to coping with the information explosion. Computers handle some problems of the information explosion because they are able to categorize and index vast amounts of data. However, many computerized databases fail to contain information that is generated by non-traditional sources, like documents that are buried in state and federal agencies.

Another problem is that many databases suffer from lack of timeliness because they offer indexes to articles and most publishers have long lead times for getting the material into print. And in our fast changing society, having the most current information is crucial, and these articles are often not as current or up to date as they should be.

Computers also contribute to a more serious problem. Because of their ability to store such large quantities of data, computers aggravate the information explosion by fueling the information overload. If you access one of the major databases on a subject such as Maine potatoes, most likely you will be confronted with a printout of 500 or more citations. Do you have the time to find and read all of them? How can you as a non-expert tell a good article from one that will just waste your valuable time retrieving and reading it?

The first step to cut through this volume of information is to find an expert specializing in Maine potatoes. Yes, such an individual exists! This person already will have read those 500 articles and will be able to identify the relevant ones that meet your information needs. This expert will also be able to tell you what will be in the literature next year on the subject of Maine potatoes, because he is probably in the midst of writing or reviewing forthcoming articles right now. And if you are in search of a fact or figure, this government bureaucrat might know the answer right off the top of his head. The best part of this research strategy is that all this valuable information can be accumulated for just the price of a telephone call.

Case Study: How To Find Mr. Potato

The techniques for locating an expert can best be illustrated by a classic story from the days when I was struggling to start my first information brokerage company in 1975.

At the time the business amounted to just a desk and telephone crowded into the bedroom of my apartment. As so often happens in a fledgling enterprise, my first client was a friend. His problem was this: "I've got to have the latest information on the basic supply and demand of Maine potatoes within 24 hours."

My client represented a syndicate of commodity investors which invests millions of dollars in Maine potatoes. When he called, these potatoes were selling at double their normal price and he wanted to know why. I knew absolutely nothing about potatoes, but thought I knew where to find out. The agreement with my client was that I would be paid only if I succeeded in getting the information (no doubt you've guessed I no longer work that way).

Luck With
The First Telephone Call

The first call I made was to the general information office of the U.S. Department of Agriculture. I asked to speak to an expert on potatoes. The operator referred me to Mr. Charlie Porter. I wondered if this Mr. Porter was a department functionary with responsibility for handling crank calls, but the operator assured me that he was an agriculture economist specializing in potatoes. I called Mr. Porter and explained how I was a struggling entrepreneur who knew nothing about potatoes and needed his help to answer a client's urgent request. Charlie graciously gave me much of the information I needed, adding that he would be happy to talk at greater length either over the phone or in person at his office. I decided to go see him and meet a real expert face to face.

Only Problem Was Getting Out Of
Charlie Porter's Office

For 2 1/2 hours the next morning, the Federal government's potato expert explained in minute detail the supply and demand of Maine potatoes. Charlie Porter showed me computer printouts that reflected how the price had doubled in recent weeks. For any subject that arose during our conversation, Charlie had immediate access to a reference source. Rows of books in his office covered every conceivable aspect of the potato market. A strip of ticker tape that tracked the daily price of potatoes from all over the country lay across his desk.

Here in Charlie's office was everything anyone might ever want to know about potatoes. The problem, it turned out, was not in getting enough information, but how to gracefully leave his office. Once Charlie started talking, it was hard for him to stop. It seemed that Charlie Porter had spent his lifetime studying the supply and demand of potatoes and finally someone with a genuine need sought his expertise on the subject closest to his heart.

One Potato....Two Potato....

When I finally had to tell Charlie that I really had to leave, he pointed across the hall in the direction of a potato statistician whose primary responsibility was to produce a monthly report showing potato production and consumption in the United States. From this statistician I was to learn about all the categories of potatoes that are tallied. It turns out the U.S. Department of Agriculture counts all the potato chips sold every month, even how many Pringle potato chips are consumed in comparison to say, Lay's Potato Chips. The statistician offered to place me on the mailing list to receive all this free monthly data.

The Art Of Getting An Expert To Talk

The information explosion requires greater reliance on experts in order to sift through this proliferation of enormous data. Cultivating an expert, however, demands an entirely different set of skills from using a library or a publication. You must know how to treat people so that they are ready, willing, and able to give you the information that you need. It is human nature for almost anyone to want to share their knowledge, but your approach will determine whether you ultimately get the expert to open up to your questions. So it is your job to create an environment that makes an individual want to share his expertise. Remember when dealing with both public and private sector experts, they will get the same paycheck whether they give you two weeks worth of free help or if they cut the conversation short after a minute or two. They will decide whether you'll get all of the information that you're asking for.

Expectations: The 7-Phone Call Rule

There is no magic to finding an expert. It is simply a numbers game which seems to take an average of seven telephone calls to find the answer you're looking for. Telephone enough people and keep asking each for a lead. The magic lies in how much information the expert will share once you find the right individual. This is why it is essential to remember "the 7-phone call rule", and never stop at the second or third lead that seems to be going nowhere.

If you make several calls and begin to get upset because you are being transferred from one person to another, you will be setting yourself up to fail once you locate the right expert. What is likely to happen is that when your "Charlie Porter" picks up his telephone he is going to hear you complaining about how sick and tired you are of getting the runaround from his organization and colleagues. If you don't sound like you are going to be the highlight of Charlie's day, he will instantly figure out how to get rid of you fast.

This explains why some people are able to get information and others fail. Seasoned researchers know it is going to take a number of telephone calls and they will not allow themselves to get impatient. After all, the runaround is an unavoidable part of the information gathering process. Consequently, the first words that come out of your mouth are extremely important because they set the stage for letting the expert want to help you.

Ten Basic Telephone Tips

Here are a few pointers to keep in mind when you are casting about for an expert. These guidelines amount to basic common sense but

are very easy to forget by the time you get to that sixth or seventh phone call.

1) Introduce Yourself Cheerfully
The way you open the conversation will set the tone for the entire interview. Your greeting and initial comment should be cordial and cheerful. They should give the feeling that this is not going to be just another telephone call, but a pleasant interlude in his or her day.

2) Be Open And Candid
You should be as candid as possible with your source since you are asking the same of him. If you are evasive or deceitful in explaining your needs or motives, your source will be reluctant to provide you with information. If there are certain facts you cannot reveal such as client confidentiality, explain just that. Most people will understand.

3) Be Optimistic
Throughout the entire conversation you should exude a sense of confidence. If you call and say "You probably aren't the right person" or "You don't have any information, do you?" it makes it easy for the person to say "You're right, I can't help you." A positive attitude will encourage your source to stretch his mind to see what information he might have that could possibly help you.

4) Be Humble And Courteous
You can be optimistic and still be humble. Remember the old adage that you can catch more flies with honey than you can with vinegar. People in general, and experts in particular, love to tell others what they know, as long as their position of authority is not questioned or threatened. In fact, if they are made to feel like an expert by the way you treat them, chances are that they will give you more information than they originally intended.

5) Be Concise
State your problem simply. A long-winded explanation may bore your contact and reduce your chances for getting a thorough response.

6) Don't Be A "Gimme"

A "gimme" is someone who says "give me this" or "give me that", and has little consideration for the other person's time or feelings. Remember to "ask" for information or a particular document that you're interested in.

7) Be Complimentary

This goes hand in hand with being humble. A well placed compliment about your source's expertise or insight about a particular topic will serve you well. In searching for information in large organizations, you are apt to talk to many colleagues of your source, so it wouldn't hurt to convey the respect that your "Charlie Porter" commands, for example, "Everyone I spoke to said you are the person I must talk with." It is reassuring for anyone to know that they have the respect of their peers.

8) Be Conversational

Avoid spending the entire time talking about the information you need. Briefly mention a few irrelevant topics such as the weather, the Washington Redskins, or the latest political campaign. The more social you are without being too chatty, the more likely that your source will open up to you.

9) Return The Favor

You might share with your source information or even gossip you have picked up elsewhere. However, be certain not to betray the trust of either your client or another source. If you do not have any relevant information to share at the moment, it would still be a good idea to call back when you are further along in your research when you might have information of value to offer.

10) Send Thank You Notes

A short note, typed or handwritten, will help ensure that your source will be just as cooperative in the future.

Case Study: Jelly Beans

In our information society, which produces thousands of databases and other resources every day, it seems that most decision makers rely primarily on traditional information sources. More often than not executives will spend lots of time and money trying to determine the size of a market or information about a competitor, and if the answer cannot be found through conventional sources, the corporate decision is made without the information. This does not have to be the case.

We believe that you can find solid information for almost any problem, no matter how sensitive the issue may be, if you use some unorthodox research techniques. To illustrate this point, here is a step-by-step account of how one of our researchers succeeded in gathering figures on the U.S. market for jelly beans when a Fortune 500 firm came up emptyhanded after exhausting all traditional sources. The prevailing view both inside and outside the industry was that this piece of the information puzzle could not be obtained.

It should be said at the outset that the estimates Information USA, Inc. finally obtained must not be regarded as 100% accurate, but they do represent the best available figures and, most likely, come within 10% to 15% of the actual number.

Opening Round

Faced with the problem of finding the U.S. market for jelly beans, we already knew that our client had contacted the major market research firms, did some literature searches, and came up with practically no useful information. As is evident from this case study, this information hunt occurred when Ronald Reagan was President and jelly beans happened to be the

candy of choice of several very high government officials.

1) The first call was to the U.S. Department of Commerce to locate the government's jelly bean expert. We were referred to Cornelius Kenny, the confectionery industry expert. Mr. Kenny was out that day and would call us back when he returned to the office.

2) A search of Gale's *Encyclopedia of Associations* identified four relevant trade associations. However, upon contacting them we were told that they provide information only to their members.

3) The White House seemed like a good bet because of Ronald Reagan's fondness for jelly beans and the resulting publicity. The Public Affairs office at 1600 Pennsylvania Avenue said that it never obtained statistical information on the industry but could tell us tales about a lifesize water buffalo and portraits of the President constructed of jelly beans. However, they suggested that we contact several lobbying organizations. Calls to these groups proved fruitless.

4) A call to the U.S. Bureau of the Census uncovered John Streeter, an analyst who monitors the panned candy industry. He told us:

* jelly beans have never been counted and there would be no way to get the answer;

* the non-chocolate panned candy category within the Bureau's Annual Confectionery Survey contains jelly beans;

* the seasonal category of the non-chocolate panned candies, according to his estimates,

contains 90% jelly beans because most jelly beans are sold during Easter and that jelly beans are about the only non-chocolate panned manufactured candy sold on a seasonal basis;

* $37,804,000 worth of non-chocolate panned candy was shipped by U.S. manufacturers in 1984, which represents about 48,354,000 pounds; the figures for total non-chocolate panned candy for 1984 totaled $251,525,000 and 237,308,000 pounds; and

* government regulations prohibited him from revealing the names of jelly bean manufacturers, but he did refer us to two trade associations he thought might help.

So this analyst at the Census Bureau, who tried to discourage us with warnings that no such figure for the jelly bean market exists, actually gave us quite a lot of concrete information as well as some valuable leads to pursue.

Armed and Dangerous
With A Little Information

At this point, we had a market estimate from one government expert based on a figure generated by the U.S. Bureau of the Census. It may have sounded like the answer we were after, but taking that figure to our client at this juncture would have been premature and possibly irresponsible. The main drawback was that the estimate reflected only one person's opinion, and although he was an expert, he was not a true industry observer as one would be if they were actually in the business of selling jelly beans. Our strategy now was to find people in the industry who could give us their interpretation of these figures.

The Census expert referred us to one of the trade associations we had already contacted. However, when we called back saying that Mr. Streeter at the Census Bureau suggested we call them, the association promptly responded with a

list of the 25 major jelly bean manufacturers. This is an example of how using the name of a government expert can get you in the door and get you the information you're looking for. When we phoned several manufacturers, they laughed when we told them of our effort to ascertain the market for jelly beans. Jelly beans had never been counted, they told us, and their advice was to give up.

At this point Mr. Kenny, the confectionery expert at the U.S. Department of Commerce called us back and he, too, said that the market had never been measured. However, he did hazard a guess that the jelly bean market could be roughly 50% of the total Census figure for Non-Chocolate Panned Candy.

A separate call to a private research group which does trend analysis by surveying grocery stores shared its estimate that 90% of all jelly beans are sold at Easter.

Easier To Be A Critic Than A Source

Our lack of success in dealing with a few manufacturers caused us to change tactics. Instead of asking them to estimate the size of the jelly bean market, we began asking them what they thought of the figures we received from the industry analysts at the Commerce Department, as well as the Census Bureau. We decided to try to find someone who actually filled out the Census survey and get a reaction to the Census figures. We spoke with the owner of Herbert Candies, a small candy company. He gave us his 1984 jelly bean production and cost statistics, told us he filled out the Census report, and readily explained what he thought the Census statistics meant in terms of jelly bean production and cost. Furthermore, using his calculator, he helped us arrive at national figures for 1984. He also told us which companies manufacture 80% of the jelly beans produced in the country.

Now, armed with actual figures for 1984 jelly bean production, average cost per pound, average number of jelly beans in a pound, and the percentage of jelly beans produced during Easter, we resumed calling manufacturers — this time to get their opinion of our figures. This was the real turning point in dealing with the manufacturers. Because everyone in the industry knew that there were no exact numbers on the size of the jelly bean market, as professionals they were afraid to give a figure because anyone could say it was wrong. However, because they were experts in the business, they were not afraid to criticize someone else's information. Reactions from insiders were just what we needed to help hone a good working number. The manufacturers were able to tell us why our figures were good or not and they gave us sound reasons why the numbers should be adjusted, such as "Based on our sales figures your numbers sound a little low," or "Not all manufacturers report to the Bureau of the Census, so that figure may be low."

To show how this tactic prompted many manufacturers to be candid about both the industry and their sales in particular, here are highlights of our conversations with nine companies. What is presented below may seem to be too detailed, but after reviewing them we hope that it proves our point about how open business executives can be about their company.

1) Owner, Herbert Candies (small manufacturer and retailer)
* 90% of jelly beans are sold at Easter
* 60% of Census seasonal category are jelly beans
* average cost of jelly beans is $1 per pound
* when President Reagan first got into office the jelly bean market shot up 150% but now it is back to normal
* Four companies have 80% of the market, with E.J. Brach the largest at 40%, Brock the second largest, followed by Herman Goelitz and Maillard
* Herbert Candies sold 30,000 pounds of jelly beans this past year and 90% at Easter; 10,000 were gourmet beans at $3.20 per pound and 20,000 were regular jelly beans at $2.80 per pound

2) Marketing Department, Nabisco Confectionery
* suggested we call SAMI, a private market research firm
* estimated 90% of jelly beans are sold at Easter
* confirmed that E.J. Brach has 40% of the market

3) Vice President of Marketing and Sales, Herman Goelitz (producer of "Bellies", Ronald Reagan's favorite)
* between 35% and 50% of his jelly beans are sold at Easter
* $1.00 per pound could be the average retail price
* a retailer can purchase jelly beans at $.60 per pound
* the retail price ranges between $1.25 and $5 per pound

4) General Manager, Burnell's Fine Candy (manufacturer of hanging bag jelly beans)
* 75% of jelly beans are sold at Easter
* $.60 to $.75 per pound is average manufacturer's price
* $1.59 is the average retail price
* 75% of Census seasonal category is probably jelly beans

5) Senior VP of Marketing and Sales, E.J. Brach (largest manufacturer)
* produces 24 million jelly beans annually at an average price of $.86 per pound
* there are approximately 100 beans per pound
* Brach's selling price is about industry average
* they have about 50% of the market
* 90% of the jelly beans sold at Easter sounds too high

6) Product Manager of Marketing Department, Brock Candy (second largest manufacturer)
* 85% to 95% of all jelly beans are sold at Easter

* average price paid by retailers is $.59 to $.99 per pound
* there are 130 to 140 jelly beans in a pound
* E.J. Brach has 40% to 50% of the jelly bean business — 32 to 45 million jelly beans sold in a year sounds correct given Brock's production figures; but probably it is closer to the high side
* Brock Candy is number 2 in the industry
* there are not many jelly bean manufacturers and basing total production on E.J. Brach's sales figures is a good way to arrive at an industry estimate

7) Traffic Manager, Powell Confectionery (medium size producer)
* 75% of jelly beans are sold at Easter judging from Powell's sales
* average retail price $.75 to $.80 per pound and the average manufacturer's price is $.65 to $.70 per pound
* 35 to 45 million jelly beans per year sounds reasonable
* it seems fair to double E.J. Brach production figures to get the total market because it has about 50% share of the market

8) President, Ferrara Panned Candy (largest panned candy producer)
* familiar with Census data and believes that jelly beans represent about 75% to 80% of the seasonal sales; 80% to 90% of all jelly beans are sold at Easter
* 32 to 45 million pounds per year seems a bit low
* E.J. Brach has 50% of the packaged jelly bean market but has less than half of the bulk jelly bean market

9) New Product Development Manager, Farley Candy
* familiar with Census data and believes that the numbers are understated because not all companies report their figures

* an industry estimate of 32 to 50 million pounds per year seems low

So much for all those who discouraged us from even tackling this issue of the market for jelly beans. All the data poured forth during these telephone conversations provided more information than our Fortune 500 client ever expected.

Deciding On An Estimate

As you can see from the interviews outlined above, traffic managers all the way up to company presidents were willing to give us their best estimate of the size of the market and even divulge their own company's sales figures.

After government experts, the figure seemed to cluster around the 45 to 50 million pound range. It may not be that obvious from just reading the highlights of our interviews, but that consensus became apparent after talking with about a dozen people associated with the industry.

Information Exchange
Is A People Business

It is just surprising what company executives and government experts are willing to tell you if they are approached in the right way. You can find the answer to any question (or at least a good estimate) as long as you expect to make many phone calls and you treat each person on the other end of the telephone in a friendly, appreciative way.

The biggest difference between those who succeed in their information quest and those who fail boils down to whether or not they believe the information exists. If you persist in thinking the information can be found, nine times out of ten you will get what you need.

Coping With Misinformation

One of the major problems encountered by researchers is determining the accuracy of the information that they have collected. If you are doing traditional market research and using primary sources, accuracy is not that complicated. Traditional market researchers are well aware of survey methods, sampling techniques, and computing errors using statistical standard deviation analysis. However, if you are a desk researcher, like Information USA, Inc. which relies on secondary sources and expert opinion, how do you compute the standard deviation for error? The answer is that you cannot use hard statistical techniques, but you can employ other soft forms of error checking.

Major Causes for Error and Prevention Tactics

Problem #1: Lost In The Jargon

It is not uncommon for researchers to be dealing frequently in areas of expertise where they do not have complete command of the industry jargon. In such situations it is easy to believe that you have found the exact information needed only to find out later that you missed the mark considerably. This is a common trap to fall into when fishing in unfamiliar waters. And if you have to do the job quickly, it is easy to believe that you know more than you really do or to avoid getting the complete explanation of specific jargon because you do not want to waste the time of the expert who is giving you the information. Here is an experience of a U.S. Department of Agriculture expert which illustrates this point.

This government expert received a call one day from an assistant at the White House. This hot shot, who acted pretty impressed with himself, said he was in a meeting with both the President and the head of the Meat Packers Association and needed to know right then the official number of cows in the United States. The livestock expert asked the presidential aide if that was exactly what he meant and then when he impatiently responded "Yes," the bureaucrat told him the figure. Within minutes the White House staffer called back and said the president of the Meat Packers Association laughed at him and claimed that there were twice as many cows. The assistant then realized he needed the number of all cows — including "male cows" — as well as all female ones.

The White House aide had a problem with semantics, probably a city slicker who never knew the difference between cows and cattle. This can happen to anyone, not only a cocky Presidential aide. For example, if you want to know the market for computers, a more specific question to ask is are you talking about free standing units or central processing units?

Solution #1: Act A Little Dumb

In order to prevent this type of embarrassment, you have to find an expert with whom you are comfortable. When I say comfortable, I mean someone you can go to and ask dumb questions. You will get the most help if you act very humble in your approach. If you request information with the arrogance of the White House staffer, you may be given only the facts you ask for and nothing more. However, if you call up an expert and say something like "Oh God, can you please help me? I don't really know much about this, but my boss needs to

know how many cows there are in the country."
With more than a hint of indecision in your
voice and honestly admitting you don't know
much about the field, the expert is more likely
to ask you some key questions that will ensure
that you get the right figures. He may even
enjoy giving you the information that you need,
and not just resent your phone call.

Problem #2: Believing The Written Word Or A Computer

This is a more serious problem than the
difficulties and confusion surrounding industry
jargon. Mastering the terminology just requires
a little homework. However, overcoming a deep
seated belief that information either from a
computer, in published sources, or from the
government is always accurate can be like
changing your religion. It took me years, as well
as dozens of professional embarrassments, to
overcome this problem.

Just because a figure appears in print does not
make it gospel. Remember the saying, "Figures
don't lie, but liars can figure." Keep this in mind
before betting the farm on anything you read in
print, even if it comes out of a computer. A
good illustration which follows pertains to
Census Bureau information.

A few years ago we were doing a market study
on stereo speakers and discovered that the
figures the U.S. Bureau of the Census had for
this market were off by over 50 percent. No one
in the industry complained to the government
because the industry was small and couldn't be
bothered. But most of the companies involved
knew that the figure was misleading and so had
no use for the Census report. Another case is a
Fortune 500 company which told us that for
over five years it filled out the U.S. Census form
under the wrong Standard Industrial Code (SIC).
An important caveat — this firm ranks as the
number two manufacturer in the industry.

You have to remember that number crunchers at
the Census Bureau and other such organizations
are not always interested in the meaning behind
the numbers. Much of their work is simply
taking a number from block A, adding it to the
number in block B, and placing the result in
block C. Verifying where the numbers come
from is not their job.

Published sources are an even bigger problem
than government data. Many believe that what
you read in a magazine or a newspaper or hear
on television or radio must be true. Nonsense!
Anyone and their brother can be interviewed by
a magazine or newspaper, and usually what they
say will get printed in a magazine or quoted on
the air as long as it is not too outrageous.
Sometimes you are more likely to get it into
print if what you're saying **is** outrageous. After
all, most news stories are just accounts of what
someone said as interpreted by a journalist.

The more general the media, the less accurate its
reporting may be about an industry. In other
words, an article in the ice cream industry trade
magazine is more likely to be accurate than a
similar story in the *New York Times*. The trade
journal will have reporters who cover that
particular industry and they will more than likely
be able to flush out bad data. The newspaper, on
the other hand, will do only one ice cream story
a year, and will print almost anything it hears.
So just because someone is quoted in an article
does not mean that the information is correct.

I have seen much of this firsthand when on
nationwide book promotion tours. In newspaper
interviews or on radio and television talk shows,
I can say almost anything and they will print or
broadcast it, as is. I will give countless facts and
figures based on my own biased research
(remember that I am trying to sell books), and
hardly ever will I be questioned or seriously
challenged about the authenticity of my research.
I don't know if it is laziness, apathy, or just
plain lack of time that allows so much
unchallenged information to be presented in the

media. I have even blatantly lied to a reporter who thought of himself as a clone of CBS' Mike Wallace of "60 Minutes." Before I started doing media interviews, I assumed that any good reporter worth his or her salt could find holes in what I presented and would expose me as some kind of fraud. I didn't know how they would do it, but I guess my own insecurity prompted me to prepare for the worst. The reality is that most reporters spend little or no time studying the topic before they interview you, and if you become annoyed or angry, especially with this Mike Wallace type described above, you can blow them away with an exaggerated fact or half-truth that he will never be able to verify.

Solution #2: Find Another Industry Expert

Whether a figure comes from the Census Bureau, a trade magazine or off a television program, your best bet for determining whether the number is accurate is to track down an industry expert and ask him to comment on the figure. What you are seeking is their biased opinion about the accuracy of the stated figure. If the expert believes the figure is correct but doesn't know why, find another expert.

Problem #3: Trusting An Expert

This may seem to contradict what I just said in the solution to problem #2, but stick with me and you'll see the difference.

There are many times when you cannot start with published or printed data and all you can do is pick the brains of experts within the industry. This means that you will be getting facts and figures based on the best available guess from experts. Many times this is the only way to get the information you need.

Getting this type of soft data can be full of danger. After having worked for hours trying to find a friendly soul to share with you his innermost thoughts about the facts and figures of an industry or company, you do not want to turn him off with an antagonistic remark about the accuracy of his data.

Solution #3: Ask Why?

The best way to judge whether a source is knowledgeable about the fact or figure they have given you is to ask them how they arrived at that number. Such a question will likely initiate one of the following responses:

"I don't know. It's the best I can think of."
- A response like this will be a clue that the expert may not know what he is talking about and you should continue your search for a more knowledgeable and willing expert.

"This is the figure I read from an industry association study."
- This should lead you to verify that such a study was conducted and to attempt to interview people involved with the report and its findings.

"The industry figure is XX because our sales are half that and we are number 2 in the industry."
- This is probably one of the best types of answers you can get. Any time an industry expert gives you a figure based on something he is positive about, you can almost take it to the bank. The best you can do after this is to find other industry analysts and ask them to comment on the figure you were given.

Misinformation can lead to a decision making disaster. Following the simple techniques described above can take you a long way down the road to making good decisions based on near perfect information.

Using Industry Sources And Overcoming The "Negative Researching Syndrome"

When you cannot find company information from traditional sources or government documents, it may be necessary to dig around the industry in order to uncover it. This is likely to be the only place you can turn to when you really want:

1) the scoop on a company's pricing policy;
2) facts on distribution channels for a given product;
3) details about a company's potential future strategy; or
4) estimates on the profitability of a privately held company.

The researchers at Information USA, Inc. are seeing many more research projects which fall into this category, and would like to share with you some of our recent experiences in solving this type of problem.

Two Pronged Approach

Unlike traditional research work, hunting for specific information within an industry involves two separate approaches. The first is identifying potential sources. The second and equally difficult job is developing a strategy for interviewing these sources.

Although most researchers probably would think that the biggest problem is figuring out what organizations and companies to contact, we find this not to be the case when dealing with industry sources. We believe that the toughest challenges our researchers face are improving their techniques and attitudes for obtaining information. Other types of research are not as "technique sensitive," because relying on industry sources means getting in close range to the target company. Although technique can be

the major trouble spot, let's tackle the problem of sources first.

Identifying Industry Sources

When I refer to industry sources, I am talking about those organizations and individuals whose business it is to know what is going on in the overall industry as well as activities among individual companies. These are the sources which can provide sensitive information that you cannot find elsewhere. Those who know their business and industry have to know about pricing, profitability, and even the strategy of those companies which comprise a particular industry. Most likely these individuals have never seen a given company's in-house strategic plan or a private company's profit and loss statement, but they are usually knowledgeable enough to give you estimates which can be as close as plus or minus 15% of the actual figures. They also will be familiar with an industry's "rule of thumb" in terms of operation, and can offer educated guesses on important figures, like sales based on the number of employees, or production based on the size of equipment, or strategy based on purchasing plans and sales literature. A researcher's job is to find industry people in a position to know and then to get them to share this knowledge.

Starting Points For Sources

Here are six major checkpoints for identifying industry sources:

I. Government Experts:

These sources can be the easiest to talk with and also can usually suggest leads to sources who in turn will identify others within the industry.

Normally these are analysts within the Federal government and sometimes within state government. Their job it is to monitor a specific industry either for the purpose of formulating government policy or preparing market analysis which is used by both the public and private sectors. These people are the most plugged into a given industry.

Examples of U.S. government industry experts whose focus is primarily on policy are Energy Department specialists who study potential applications for wind energy, or biotechnology experts at the Department of Agriculture who stay current on this research field as it pertains to the food industry. In contrast, those federal experts whose orientation is geared toward market analysis are found at the Department of Commerce who produce the annual *U.S. Industrial Outlook*, and the analysts at the U.S. International Trade Commission who investigate the impact of imports on American industry.

Finding policy oriented experts can be difficult because they are scattered throughout the vast federal bureaucracy. Try to determine which agency in the government probably follows a particular industry under which a given company falls. For food products, try the U.S. Department of Agriculture and the U.S. Food and Drug Administration; for products involving pesticides, check with the U.S. Environmental Protection Agency; for companies in new technologies, contact the Office of Technology Assessment on Capitol Hill. Other resources which will help you identify where these policy experts are hiding include:

1) *U.S. Government Manual* (Government Printing Office);

2) *Lesko's Info-Power II* by Matthew Lesko, (published by Information, USA, Inc.);

3) Local Federal Information Center (look in the U.S. government section of your local telephone book under General Services Administration); or

4) The Washington or district office of your U.S. Representative or Senator.

Below are the main telephone numbers for finding the two major offices which have 100 or more experts with market analysis orientation who cover most every industry. Simply call and ask to speak to the expert who studies golf balls or music instruments or whatever industry you are investigating:

- International Trade Administration (ITA), U.S. Department of Commerce, Washington, DC 20230, 202-482-1461: over 100 analysts who monitor all the major industries in the U.S. and the companies within these industries ranging from athletic products to truck trailers; and

- U.S. International Trade Commission (ITC), Office of Industries, 500 E St., SW, Room 504, Washington, DC 20436, 202-205-3296: experts who analyze the impact of world trade on U.S. industries ranging from audio components to x-ray apparatus.

There are no concrete rules for locating state industry experts. Every state government works differently, and the level of expertise varies tremendously. However, there is a trend at the state level to accumulate more data especially within those industries, for instance, high-tech companies, which the state sees as having potential for contributing to their economic development. The starting place for finding a specialist is the state's Department of Commerce and Economic Development. These offices are located in the state capital and are easy to track down by telephoning the state government operator.

II. Industry Observers:

Industry observers may be affiliated either with trade magazines or trade associations. They are in a position to oversee what is going on in the industry and they collect details about specific companies within that industry. Associations can identify the magazines and other publications that report on their industry and vice versa. If you have trouble getting started, contact either the federal analysts at the ITA and ITC described above or consult the *Encyclopedia of Associations* (Gale Research Company) at a local library.

You have to be careful who you talk to when contacting these various organizations. Usually when you call a trade association looking for information about the industry, they will connect you with the library; and when you contact a magazine, you are likely to be switched to the research department. These offices are good to touch base with, but they normally know about only the more obvious published material and are not very helpful in getting answers to more difficult questions.

After you have contacted the libraries or research departments of these organizations, be sure to call back with a different tactic in order to get through to the association executives and editors of trade magazines. These are the people who are immersed in the industry and pick up bits and pieces of information about companies which rarely show up in the published literature.

III.   The Distribution Chain:

People within the chain of distribution can be wholesalers, jobbers, distributors or anyone who acts as an intermediary between the manufacturer and the end user. Although not all products are sold through middlemen, many are, and if the company under investigation uses middlemen they can be an information bonanza. Most people in these kinds of businesses are down to earth types who generally like people and are approachable. What is also advantageous about dealing with distributors is that they normally handle the products of the company you are interested in as well as those of its competitors.

As a result they can be very helpful in comparing strategies and assessing market share.

Who do you talk to in these organizations? You try to talk to the buyers or sales reps. This normally does not leave many people in between. How do you find these organizations? Usually it is quite easy — most trade associations or magazines can provide you with lists. Or, it is also easy to call up your target company and pretend you want to purchase one of their products, at which point they will be more than happy to inundate you with the names and telephone numbers of suppliers.

IV.   Customers:

This may sound foolish to some, but for most industries customers are approachable and often prove to be valuable sources of company information. By talking to the buyers of a half dozen major retail chains, you can determine the market for goods ranging from tablecloths to toys. And the buyers at a dozen or so major food chain stores can give you a clear picture of almost any consumer food product. What is selling like hotcakes and what is gathering dust on the shelves can be invaluable marketing information.

How do you find a company's customers? If they fall into groups like supermarkets or department stores, their industry will be organized enough so you can contact the relevant trade association or trade magazines for a listing of members. Many times the target company's literature will proudly display major clients or customers. Most industries also produce a buyer's guide which will identify these sources. Again, the association or trade magazines should be aware of such publications.

V.   Competitors:

Contacting the competitors of a target company may be difficult if they are also your competitor. If the company is not in the same industry as your firm, or someone else is doing the research, competitors can often provide all the information sought. Obviously these are the people who really have to know about the target company. They are in the best position to know how well the company is doing compared to them and what their competitor is likely to do in the future.

VI.   Suppliers And Complimentary Product Manufacturers:

Don't overlook suppliers to the target company. These companies can be very helpful because the target company is just a customer to them and what they know about a company they are likely to assume that everyone knows. Many suppliers are directly dependent upon the success of their customer and make it their business to know how well they are doing and can offer predictions about future plans. Their livelihood depends upon knowing this information. Tire manufacturers have to know all about automobile companies and the manufacturers of equipment which make shoes have to know all about shoe companies. The same holds true for complimentary products like BBQ utensils and charcoal briquettes, or electric popcorn poppers and popcorn kernels.

The same technique described earlier for finding customers can also be used for locating suppliers and complimentary product manufacturers.

Preventing Early Pitfalls and Other Techniques

Developing a good technique is crucial when digging for information within an industry. Finding a source is simply a numbers game, and by following the outline presented above anyone doing the research will eventually run into a couple of people who will have most of the answers you need. However, creating the proper atmosphere for that source to want to share information with you is contingent on both

attitude and technique. Here are some of the major problems you are likely to encounter.

A bad start leads to depression. I've seen this happen to even the best of researchers. They will start out confident about a project investigating a company's pricing policy or profitability. After spending a half a day on the project and talking to a half dozen industry experts, they are ready to throw in the towel and give up. What normally happens is that the researcher has run into trouble getting through to anyone who knows much about the company or anyone they did talk to has been full of negative comments such as "There's no way to get that kind of information."

After initial feedback like this, it's natural for researchers to begin to believe what they are hearing and to forget about their past research triumphs. This faulty start can be even more devastating to a novice who has yet to complete a number of research projects. This problem intensifies as the researcher continues because all the negative feedback poisons their relaxed, friendly interviewing style and upbeat attitude. This pessimism creeps into their voice when talking to people within the industry. Soon they will start a conversation by saying things like "You don't have any information on company X, do you?"

Once this begins to happen the researcher should stop immediately and get some help. This "Negative Researching Syndrome" will begin to feed on itself and will only get worse and worse unless something drastic happens to change this course.

How do you cure "Negative Researching Syndrome"? Well it isn't easy, and unless the researcher is very experienced, it usually requires the help of a senior researcher. What we usually do when we sense a researcher falling into this trap is to tell him that it is a bad time of day to be making these kinds of calls, or to quit for the day. Another approach is to suggest the researcher pick up the next day but only after we have had a chance to get together to talk about the project. Before our session I try to make sure the researcher is given an easy short term project just to build up their confidence. Then we brainstorm about one or all of the following strategies:

1) Try a different segment of the industry. Instead of talking with distributors, switch to retailers; move from customers to government experts and so on. Try anything to find someone in the industry who may be more willing to talk.

2) Describe past success stories. We will remind the researcher of projects in the past where we started out thinking that we were never going to get anything and how it all eventually came together. I'll even describe some of my own personal experiences doing research where experts said it couldn't be done. And, of course, we'll remind them that this is really the reason we are getting paid. If it was easy, no one would need us.

3) Try a different "story line." This is explained next.

A Bad "Story Line" Can Kill A Project

A bad story line can also be the chief cause of "Negative Researching Syndrome." What do we mean by a story line? It is the explanation or reason the researcher gives for needing the information. If the researcher is uncomfortable with the story, a potential source will sense this unease and be reluctant to talk. In most research this is not a problem. In traditional projects, conventional reference sources are used for gathering information, and all you have to do is identify yourself and ask whether certain information is available. However, in dealing with industry sources the situation changes markedly; they are not comfortable just knowing the researcher's name and affiliation. Industry sources want to know what you are after and

why. And this is when the story line can make or break your chances for success.

Being comfortable with a "story line" can be a complicated process. The bottom line is that you are not after information that is proprietary. Consequently, it is essential for **you** to feel comfortable with what you are saying, because if you don't no one will open up to you and give you the real facts that you need to write a credible research report for your client.

If you are uneasy that your story line is too far fetched or something you don't know enough details about, you will fail to convince yourself or the people that you're speaking to, and as a result your efforts will backfire. Saying that you work for the FBI or write for the *Nuts and Bolts* Magazine are the kinds of stories that spell trouble. Furthermore, most researchers are basically too honest to stretch the truth that far and it begins to eat into their conscience. As they do get deeper into the research, the guilt that they feel will aggravate the troubling "Negative Researching Syndrome," and the researcher is bound to wind up empty handed, with little or no relevant information.

Here are a few sample explanations that may not be too improbable:

- Your company is doing a market study on all the companies within the industry. [Not just the target company.]

- You are trying to write an article about the industry and plan to submit it to a trade magazine.

- You are a student working on a paper. [Not a highly useful story but usually one that is easy to live with.]

- You have a client or your boss wants you to investigate the possibility of developing a competing brand and you are trying to get industry comments about such an idea.

[People will more likely give opinions than information on a company, but their opinions will often include company information.]

- You are working on a speech about the industry and trying to get some background material.

Also, if your story is too negative or "predatory," no one will **want** to give you the information. This, too, will show up when you are talking with industry experts and cause a researcher to come up empty handed. In other words, don't call up an industry source and say, "I am with company X, which is a major competitor of company Y. Can you tell me about the pricing strategy of company Y so that we can try to put them out of business?" Many researchers worry that this is really what they are doing through their research efforts, and this anxiety and belief will lead to "Negative Researching Syndrome", along with failure to gather any valuable information.

Choosing the right story line can determine the success or failure of your project. Be sure you can live with it and feel comfortable and honest, and that this explanation will make those in the industry comfortable enough to share information with you. If a researcher's story line does not meet these two criteria, be prepared for a long, hard, and more than likely, frustrating and unsuccessful hunting expedition.

Money for Your
Home-Based Business

Federal Money Programs For Your Business

The following is a description of the federal funds available to small businesses, entrepreneurs, inventors, and researchers. This information is derived from the *Catalog of Federal Domestic Assistance* which is published by the U.S. Government Printing Office in Washington, DC. The number next to the title description is the official reference for this federal program. Contact the office listed below the caption for further details. The following is a description of the terms used for the types of assistance available:

Loans: money lent by a federal agency for a specific period of time and with a reasonable expectation of repayment. Loans may or may not require payment of interest.

Loan Guarantees: programs in which federal agencies agree to pay back part or all of a loan to a private lender if the borrower defaults.

Grants: money given by federal agencies for a fixed period of time and which does not have to be repaid.

Direct Payments: funds provided by federal agencies to individuals, private firms, and institutions. The use of direct payments may be "specified" to perform a particular service or for "unrestricted" use.

Insurance: coverage under specific programs to assure reimbursement for losses sustained. Insurance may be provided by federal agencies or through insurance companies and may or may not require the payment of premiums.

* Money to Run An Agriculture Related Business, Recreation Related Business or Teenage Business

(10.406 Farm Operating Loans)
Director
Farm Credit Programs Loan Making Division
Consolidated Farm Service Agency
U.S. Department of Agriculture
Washington, DC 20250   (202) 720-1632

Objectives: To enable operators of not larger than family farms through the extension of credit and supervisory assistance, to make efficient use of their land, labor, and other resources.

Types of Assistance: Direct Loans; Guaranteed/Insured Loans.

Uses and Use Restrictions: Loan funds may be used to: (1) Purchase livestock, poultry, fur bearing and other farm animals, fish, and bees; (2) purchase farm, forestry, recreation, or nonfarm enterprise equipment; (3) provide operating expenses for farm, forestry, recreation, or nonfarm enterprise; (4) meet family subsistence needs and purchase essential home equipment; (5) make minor real estate improvements; (6) refinance secured and unsecured debts; (7) pay property taxes; (8) pay insurance premiums on real estate and personal property; (9) finance youth projects; (10) plant softwood timber on marginal land; (11) make annual operating (OL) loans to delinquent borrowers for production purposes, or subordinations to delinquent borrowers to enable them to obtain annual operating credit from another lending source; and (12) support other miscellaneous purposes.

Money Available Per Year: Direct Loans: $500,000,000; Guaranteed Loans: $1,735,000,000.

Range and Average of Financial Assistance: Insured loans up to $200,000; guaranteed loans up to $400,000; Insured average loan size: $41,000; Guaranteed average loan size $105,700 for fiscal year 1994. Average guaranteed loan was $101,000.

* Money to Farmers, Ranchers, and Aquaculture Businesses

(10.407 Farm Ownership Loans)
Administrator
Farmers Home Administration
U.S. Department of Agriculture
Washington, DC 20250   (202) 720-1632

Objectives: To assist eligible farmers, ranchers, and aquaculture operators, including farming cooperatives, corporations, partnerships, and joint operations, through the extension of credit and supervisory assistance to: Become owner-operators of not larger than family farms; make efficient use of the land, labor, and other resources; carry on sound and successful farming operations; and enable farm families to have a reasonable standard of living.

Types of Assistance: Direct Loans; Guaranteed/ Insured Loans.

Uses and Use Restrictions: Loan funds may be used to: (1) Enlarge, improve, and buy family farms; (2) refinance and restructure debts to reestablish the farming operation on a sound financial base; (3) provide necessary water and water facilities; (4) provide basic soil treatment and land conservation measures; (5) construct, repair, and improve essential buildings needed in the operation of a family farm; (6) construct or repair farm dwellings; (7) improve, establish, or buy a farm-forest enterprise; (8) provide facilities to produce fish under controlled conditions; (9) finance nonfarm enterprises; (10) develop energy conserving measures; and (11) acquire farmland by socially disadvantaged individuals who will be provided the technical assistance necessary in applying for an insured farm ownership loan.

Money Available Per Year: Direct Loans: $78,081,000; Guaranteed Loans: $540,674,000.

Range and Average of Financial Assistance: Maximum insured $200,000, maximum guaranteed $300,000. Average insured $78,375, Guaranteed, $162,570.

* Grants to Market Food Related Products Overseas

(10.600 Foreign Agricultural Market Development and Promotion)
Assistant Administrator
Commodity and Marketing Programs
Foreign Agricultural Service
U.S. Department of Agriculture
Washington, DC 20250   (202) 720-2705

Objectives: To create, expand, and maintain markets abroad for U.S. agricultural commodities.

Types of Assistance: Direct Payments for Specified Use (Cooperative Agreements).

Uses and Use Restrictions: Cooperative program: Funds may be used for trade servicing, consumer promotion, market research, and to provide technical assistance to actual or potential foreign purchasers. Types of activities and amounts of funds are annually negotiated between the Foreign Agricultural Service (FAS) and Cooperators and authorized in annual marketing plans. Programs are prioritized through a jointly conducted strategic planning process which identifies the major constraints to market expansion on a commodity by market basis. Unless specifically approved otherwise, Government funds may be used only in direct support of activities conducted outside the United States.

Money Available Per Year: Direct payments: $20,000,000 in 1995.

Range and Average of Financial Assistance: $9,000 to $8,000,000; $935,000.

* Grants to Sell Food Related Products Overseas

(10.601 Market Promotion Program)
Assistant Administrator
Commodity and Marketing Programs
Foreign Agricultural Service
U.S. Department of Agriculture
Washington DC 20250   (202) 720-2705

Objectives: To encourage the development, maintenance, and

expansion of commercial export markets for U.S. agricultural commodities through cost-share assistance to eligible trade organizations that implement a foreign market development program. Priority for assistance is provided for agricultural commodities or products in the case of an unfair trade practice. Funding of the program is accomplished through the issuance by the Commodity Credit Corporation (CCC) of a dollar check to reimburse participants for activities authorized by a specific project agreement.

Types of Assistance: Direct Payments for Specified Use (Cooperative Agreements).

Uses and Use Restrictions: Market Promotion Program (MPP) funds are provided through program agreements that provide for partial reimbursement of eligible promotional expenses in activity plans approved by the Foreign Agricultural Service (FAS). Unless specifically approved otherwise, government funds may be used only in direct support of activities conducted outside the United States. Three basic program types operate under the auspices of the program: MPP participants are eligible for a generic promotional program and/or a brand-identified promotional program (EIP). Funding of promotional activities include consumer advertising, point of sale demonstrations, public relations, press servicing activities, participation in trade fairs and exhibits, market research, and technical assistance. Export Incentive Program: The third program involves Commodity Credit Corporation (CCC) agreements with U.S. commercial entities which either own the brand(s) of the product(s) to be promoted or have sole agency agreements for such brands(s) in each country in which CCC resources will be expended. The Export Incentive Program operated under the MPP and Cooperative programs prior to 1993. Funds are usually limited to direct promotion expenses such as consumer advertising, point of sale demonstrations, public relations and press servicing activities, and participation in trade fairs and exhibits.

Money Available Per Year: Direct payments: $75,000,000.

Range and Average of Financial Assistance: $44,000 to $11,680,000; $2,023,753.

* Money to Local Communities Near National Forests To Help Businesses Grow or Expand

(10.670 National Forest-Dependent Rural Communities)
Deputy Chief
State and Private Forestry
Forest Service
U.S. Department of Agriculture
P.O. Box 96090
Washington, DC 20090-6090   (202) 205-1394

Objectives: Provide accelerated assistance to communities faced with acute economic problems associated with federal or private sector land management decisions and policies or that are located in or near a national forest and are economically dependent upon forest resources. Aid is extended to these communities to help them to diversify their economic base and to improve the economic, social, and environmental well-being of rural areas.

Types of Assistance: Project Grants; Direct Loans; Use of Property, Facilities, and Equipment; Training.

Uses and Use Restrictions: Economically disadvantaged rural

communities may request assistance in identifying opportunities that will promote economic improvement, diversification, and revitalization. Eligibility assistance is coordinated through a community action team and plan. Programs may include upgrade of existing industries, development of new economic activity in non-forest related industries, technical assistance, training and education directed towards meeting the community's planned goals. Assistance requested will be coordinated with other U.S. Department of Agriculture (USDA) agencies and targeted to provide immediate help to those rural communities in greatest need. Grants, loans and assistance are available to those communities meeting the eligibility requirements. Loans may be made available to economically disadvantaged communities for the purpose of securing technical assistance and service to aid in the development and implementation of community action plans.
Money Available Per Year: $4,900,000 in 1995.
Range and Average of Financial Assistance: $5,000 to $30,000.

* Loans to Non-Profits to Lend Money to New Businesses

(10.767 Intermediary Relending Program)
Rural Business and Cooperative Development Service
Room 6321, South Agriculture Building
Washington, DC 20250-0700   (202) 690-4100
Objectives: To finance business facilities and community development.
Types of Assistance: Direct Loans.
Uses and Use Restrictions: An entity that receives an Intermediary Relending Program (IRP) loan from the Rural Development Administration (RDA) is referred to as an intermediary. Intermediaries must relend all of the loan funds received from the IRP loan, for business facilities or community development in rural areas. An entity that receives a loan from an intermediary is referred to as an ultimate recipient. The maximum loan to any one intermediary is $2 million. The maximum term is 30 years and the interest rate is one percent per annum. Intermediaries may not use IRP funds to finance more than 75 percent of the cost of an ultimate recipient's project or for a loan of more than $150,000 to one ultimate recipient.
Money Available Per Year: Loans: $88,038,000.
Range and Average of Financial Assistance: $250,000 to $2,000,000; $773,810.

* Loans to Businesses in Small Towns

(10.768 Business and Industrial Loans)
Administrator
Rural Business and Cooperative Development Service
U.S. Department of Agriculture
Washington, DC 20250-0700   (202) 690-1553
Objectives: To assist public, private, or cooperative organizations (profit or non-profit), Indian tribes or individuals in rural areas to obtain quality loans for the purpose of improving, developing or financing business, industry, and employment and improving the economic and environmental climate in rural communities including pollution abatement and control.

Types of Assistance: Guaranteed/Insured Loans.
Uses and Use Restrictions: Financial assistance may be extended for: (a) Business and industrial acquisition, construction, conversion, enlargement, repair, modernization, development costs; (b) purchasing and development of land, easements, rights-of-way, buildings, facilities, leases or materials; (c) purchasing equipment, leasehold/improvements, machinery and supplies; and (d) pollution control and abatement. Maximum loan size is $10,000,000 and maximum time allowable for final maturity is limited to 30 years for land and buildings, the usable life of machinery and equipment purchased with loan funds, not to exceed 15 years, and 7 years for working capital. Interest rates on guaranteed loans are negotiated between the lender and the borrower. For loans of $2 million or less, the maximum percentage of guarantee is 90 percent. For loans over $2 million but not over $5 million, the maximum percentage of guarantee is 80 percent. For loans in excess of $5 million, the maximum percentage of guarantee is 70 percent. Losses on principal advanced, including protective advances, and accrued interest, may be guaranteed to the lender. Loans may not be made or guaranteed (a) to pay off a creditor in excess of the value of the collateral, (b) for distribution or payment to the owner, partners, shareholders, or beneficiaries of the applicant or members of their families when such persons shall retain any portion of their equity in the business, (c) for projects involving agricultural production, (d) for transfer of ownership of a business unless the loan will keep the business from closing, or prevent the loss of employment opportunities in the area, or provide expanded job opportunities, (e) for the guarantee of lease payments, (f) for financing community antenna television services or facilities, (g) for charitable and educational institutions, churches, fraternal organizations, hotels, motels, tourist homes, convention centers, tourist, recreation or amusement facilities, lending and investment institutions and insurance companies, (h) for any legitimate business activity where more than 10 percent of the annual gross income is derived from legalized gambling, (i) for guarantee of loans made by other federal agencies except those made by Banks for Co-ops, Federal Land Bank or Production Credit Associations, and (j) for any project which is likely to result in transfer of business or employment from one area to another or cause production which exceeds demand. Interested parties should contact the Rural Development Administration (RDA) or Farmers Home Administration (FmHA) State Office nearest them. The B&I program was formerly operated by FmHA. Until the newly created RDA field structure is in place, FmHA will continue to administer the program at the local level.
Money Available Per Year: Guaranteed Loans: $500,000,000.
Range and Average of Financial Assistance: $65,000 to $7,500,000; $1,030,928 (average size) for B&I guaranteed loans.

* Grants to Non-Profits to Lend Money to New Businesses

(10.769 Rural Development Grants)
Director
Community Facilities Loan Division
Rural Business and Cooperative Development Service
U.S. Department of Agriculture
Washington, DC 20250   (202) 720-1490
Objectives: To facilitate the development of small and emerging

private business, industry, and related employment for improving the economy in rural communities.

Types of Assistance: Project Grants.

Uses and Use Restrictions: Rural business enterprise grant (RBEG) funds may be used to establish revolving funds, provide operating capital and finance industrial sites in rural areas including the acquisition and development of land and construction, conversion, enlargement, repair or modernization of buildings, plants, machinery, equipment, access streets and roads, parking areas, transportation serving the site, utility extensions, necessary water supply and waste disposal facilities, pollution control and abatement incidental to site development, provide technical assistance, pay fees, and refinancing. Television demonstration grant (TDG) funds may be used for television programming to demonstrate the effectiveness of providing information on agriculture and other issues of importance to farmers and other rural residents.

Money Available Per Year: Grants: $45,500,000.

Range and Average of Financial Assistance: $7,000 to $1,000,000; $166,000.

* Loans to Companies That Provide Electricity to Small Towns

(10.850 Rural Electrification Loans and Loan Guarantees)
Administrator
Rural Electrification Administration
U.S. Department of Agriculture
Washington, DC 20250-1500   (202) 720-9540

Objectives: To assure that people in eligible rural areas have access to electric services comparable in reliability and quality to the rest of the Nation.

Types of Assistance: Direct Loans.

Uses and Use Restrictions: Long-term, direct loans to qualified organizations for the purpose of supplying central station electric services on a continuing basis in rural areas. The Rural Electrification Administration (REA) also makes direct loans primarily for generation and transmission projects.

Money Available Per Year: Direct Loans: $725,000,000; Guaranteed Loans: $275,000,000.

Range and Average of Financial Assistance: Direct Loans: $268,000 to $34,824,000; $3,223,057. Loan Guarantees: $630,000 to $157,871,600; $42,991,600.

* Loans to Companies That Provide Telephone Service to Small Towns

(10.851 Rural Telephone Loans and Loan Guarantees)
Administrator
Rural Utilities Services
U.S. Department of Agriculture
Washington, DC 20250   (202) 720-9540

Objectives: To assure that people in eligible rural areas have access to telephone service comparable in reliability and quality to the rest of the Nation.

Types of Assistance: Direct Loans.

Uses and Use Restrictions: Long-term direct loans to qualified organizations for the purpose of financing the improvement, expansion, construction, acquisition, and operation of telephone lines, facilities, or systems to furnish and improve telephone service in rural areas. "Rural area" is defined as any area of the United States, its territories, and possessions not included within the boundaries of any city, village, or borough having a population in excess of 1,500 inhabitants. Rural areas include both farm and non-farm populations.

Money Available Per Year: Direct Loans: $236,000,000; Guaranteed Loans: $120,000,000.

Range and Average of Financial Assistance: Direct Loans: $474,000 to $31,833,000; 7,137,900. Guaranteed Loans: $1,264,000 to $35,277,000; $7,137,900.

* Extra Loans to Companies That Provide Telephone Service to Small Towns

(10.852 Rural Telephone Bank Loans)
Administrator
Rural Utilities Services
U.S. Department of Agriculture
Washington, DC 20250   (202) 720-9540

Objectives: To provide supplemental financing to extend and improve telephone service in rural areas.

Types of Assistance: Direct Loans.

Uses and Use Restrictions: Long-term loans to qualified organizations for the purpose of supplying and improving telephone service in rural areas.

Money Available Per Year: Direct Loans: $175,000,000.

Range and Average of Financial Assistance: Direct Loans: $455,000 to $14,800,800; $4,605,200.

* Grants and Loans to Telephone Companies That Then Provide Financing to Small Businesses

(10.854 Rural Economic Development Loans and Grants)
Administrator
Rural Utilities Service
U.S. Department of Agriculture
Washington, DC 20250   (202) 720-9552

Objectives: To promote rural economic development and job creation projects, including funding for project feasibility studies, start-up costs, incubator projects, and other reasonable expenses for the purpose of fostering rural development.

Types of Assistance: Direct Loans; Project Grants.

Uses and Use Restrictions: Projects which promote rural economic development and job creation. Maximum amount of grant or loan is $400,000. Maximum term of loan is ten years at zero interest rate.

Money Available Per Year: Loans/Grants: $13,025,000 in 1995.

Range and Average of Financial Assistance: $10,000 to $400,000; $191,000.

* Free Plants to Nurseries

(10.905 Plant Materials for Conservation)
Deputy Chief For Technology
Soil Conservation Service
U.S. Department of Agriculture
P.O. Box 2890

Washington, DC 20013   (202) 720-3905

Objectives: To assemble, evaluate, select, release, and introduce into commerce, and promote the use of new and improved plant materials for soil, water, and related resource conservation and environmental improvement programs.

Types of Assistance: Provision of Specialized Services.

Uses and Use Restrictions: Plant materials are used in all phases of the soil and water conservation program. Plant materials are only produced for field testing to determine the plant's value for use on conservation cooperators properties in conjunction with Soil Conservation Districts, State Agricultural Experiment Stations, State Crop Improvement Associations, and other federal and state agencies, and to provide commercial producers with breeder and foundation quality seeds. Other plants or seed are not provided to landowners. Large-scale production is conducted.

Money Available Per Year: Salaries and expenses: $8,745,000.

Range and Average of Financial Assistance: Not applicable.

* Grants to Communities That Provide Money And Help To Small Business Incubators

(11.300 Economic Development-Grants for Public Works and Development Facilities)
David L. McIlwain, Director
Public Works Division
Economic Development Administration
Room H7326
Herbert C. Hoover Building
U.S. Department of Commerce
Washington, DC 20230   (202) 482-5265

Objectives: To promote long-term economic development and assist in the construction of public works and development facilities needed to initiate and encourage the creation or retention of permanent jobs in the private sector in areas experiencing severe economic distress.

Types of Assistance: Project Grants.

Uses and Use Restrictions: Grants for such public facilities as water and sewer systems, industrial access roads to industrial parks, port facilities, railroad sidings and spurs, tourism facilities, vocational schools, business incubator facilities, and infrastructure improvements for industrial parks. Qualified projects must fulfill a pressing need of the area and must: (1) tend to improve the opportunities for the successful establishment or expansion of industrial or commercial plants or facilities; (2) assist in the creation of additional long-term employment opportunities; or (3) benefit the long-term unemployed/ underemployed and members of low-income families. In addition, proposed projects must be consistent with the currently approved Overall Economic Development Program for the area, and for the Economic Development District, if any, in which it will be located, and must have adequate local share of funds with evidence of firm commitment and availability. Projects must be capable of being started and completed in a timely manner.

Money Available Per Year: Grants: $195,000,000.

Range and Average of Financial Assistance: No specific minimum or maximum project amount - $99,375 to $4,745,000; $969,922.

* Grants to Communities To Help Small Businesses Start or Expand

(11.302 Economic Development Support for Planning Organizations)
Luis F. Bueso
Director Planning Division
Economic Development Administration
Room H7319, Herbert C. Hoover Building
Washington, DC 20230   (202) 482-2873

Objectives: To assist in providing administrative aid to multi-county districts, redevelopment areas and Indian tribes to establish and maintain economic development planning and implementation capability and thereby promote effective utilization of resources in the creation of full-time permanent jobs for the unemployed and the underemployed in areas of high distress.

Types of Assistance: Project Grants.

Uses and Use Restrictions: Grants are used for staff salaries and other planning and administrative expenses of the funded economic development organization.

Money Available Per Year: Grants: $21,484,000.

Range and Average of Financial Assistance: $25,000 to $113,000; $60,000.

* Grants to Communities That Help Finance New or Old Businesses Due to New Military Base Closings

(11.307 Special Economic Development and Adjustment Assistance Program-Sudden and Severe Economic Dislocation (SSED) and Long-Term Economic Deterioration (LTED))
David F. Witschi, Director
Economic Adjustment Division
Economic Development Administration
Room H7327, Herbert C. Hoover Building
U.S. Department of Commerce
Washington DC 20230   (202) 482-2659

Objectives: To assist state and local areas develop and/or implement strategies designed to address adjustment problems resulting from sudden and severe economic dislocation such as plant closings, military base closures and defense contract cutbacks (SSED), or from long-term economic deterioration in the area's economy (LTED).

Types of Assistance: Project Grants.

Uses and Use Restrictions: Under the SSED Program, grants may be made to develop an adjustment strategy in response to sudden and severe economic dislocation (Adjustment Strategy Grant), or to implement such strategies (Adjustment Implementation Grants). Implementation grants may be made for the construction of public facilities, the provision of public services, business development, technical assistance, training, or any other activity that addresses the economic adjustment problem. Under the LTED Program, grants generally are made for the establishment or recapitalization of a Revolving Loan Fund (RLF).

Money Available Per Year: Grants: $165,000,000.

Range and Average of Financial Assistance: No specific minimum level; maximum levels new RLF, $500,000; RLF recaps $300,000; SSED Adjustment Implementation Grants, $1,000,000.

* Grants to Fishermen Hurt By Oil and Gas Drilling on the Outer Continental Shelf

(11.408 Fishermen's Contingency Fund)
Chief, Financial Services Division
National Marine Fisheries Service
1315 East West Highway
Silver Spring, MD 20910   (301) 713-2396

Objectives: To compensate U.S. commercial fishermen for damage/loss of fishing gear and 50 percent of resulting economic loss due to oil and gas related activities in any area of the Outer Continental Shelf.
Types of Assistance: Direct Payments with Unrestricted Use.
Uses and Use Restrictions: None.
Money Available Per Year: Direct payments: $625,000.
Range and Average of Financial Assistance: Range: $500 to $25,000; Average: $6,000.

* Grants To Fishermen Hurt By Foreign Fishing Vessels

(11.409 Fishing Vessel and Gear Damage Compensation Fund)
Chief, Financial Services Division
Attn: National Marine Fisheries Service
U.S. Department of Commerce
1315 East-West Highway
Silver Spring, MD 20910   (301) 713-2396

Objectives: To compensate U.S. fishermen for the loss, damage, or destruction of their vessels by foreign fishing vessels and their gear by any vessel.
Types of Assistance: Direct Payments with Unrestricted Use.
Money Available Per Year: Direct payments: $1,000,000.
Range and Average of Financial Assistance: $600 to $150,000; $7,350.

* Grants to Develop New Technologies For Your Business

(11.612 Advanced Technology Program)
Mr. George Uriano, Director
Advanced Technology Program
National Institute of Standards and Technology
Gaithersburg, MD 20899   (301) 975-5187
To receive application kits:
Ms. Gail Killen   (301) 975-2636

Objectives: To assist U.S. businesses in creating and applying pre-competitive generic technology and research results necessary to: (1) commercialize significant new discoveries and technologies rapidly, and (2) refine manufacturing technologies. The ultimate objective is to improve U.S. industry competitiveness.
Types of Assistance: Project Grants (Cooperative Agreements).
Uses and Use Restrictions: The assistance is to be used to aid U.S. joint research and development ventures, U.S. businesses and independent research organizations. Funding for joint

ventures is limited to a minority share and five years duration. All other awards must not exceed $2 million nor exceed three years. Single applicants must pay indirect costs. No awards can be used to fund existing or planned research programs that would otherwise be conducted in the same time period.
Money Available Per Year: Grants and Cooperative Agreements: $417,105,000 in 1995.
Range and Average of Financial Assistance: Range: $500,000 to $19,000,000; Average: $5,100,000.

* Grants to Organizations That Help Minorities Start Their Own Businesses

(11.800 Minority Business Development Centers)
Assistant Director
Office of Operations
Room 5063, Minority Business Development Agency
U.S. Department of Commerce
14th and Constitution Avenue, NW.
Washington, DC 20230   (202) 482-2366

Objectives: To provide business development services for a minimal fee to minority firms and individuals interested in entering, expanding, or improving their efforts in the marketplace. Minority business development center operators provide a wide range of services to clients, from initial consultations to the identification and resolution of specific business problems.
Types of Assistance: Project Grants.
Uses and Use Restrictions: The Minority Business Development Agency (MBDA) competitively selects and funds approximately 100 MBDCs to provide management and technical assistance to minority clients located in designated Metropolitan Statistical Areas (MSAs) throughout the country. Recipients of MBDC funds provide clients with advice and counseling in such areas as preparing financial packages, business counseling, business information and management, accounting guidance, marketing, business/industrial site analysis, production, engineering, construction assistance, procurement, and identification of potential business opportunities. The agency does not have the authority to make loans to minority businesses. Program funds are restricted to providing management and technical assistance.
Money Available Per Year: Grants: $23,924,000.
Range and Average of Financial Assistance: Awards have ranged from $165,000 to $1,074,526, with the average award being $218,000.

* Grants to Organizations That Help American Indians Start Their Own Businesses

(11.801 American Indian Program)
Assistant Director
Office of Operations, Room 5063
Minority Business Development Agency
U.S. Department of Commerce
14th and Constitution Avenue, NW
Washington, DC 20230   (202) 482-2366

Objectives: To provide business development service to

American Indians interested in entering, expanding, or improving their efforts in the marketplace. To help American Indian business development centers and American Indian business consultants to provide a wide range of services to American Indian clients, from initial consultation to the identification and resolution of specific business problems.

Types of Assistance: Project Grants.

Uses and Use Restrictions: The Minority Business Development Agency (MBDA) competitively selects and funds six Indian Business Development Centers (IBDC's) and one American Indian Business Consultant (AIBC) recipient to provide management and technical assistance to American Indians located throughout the country. Recipients of AIP funds provide clients with advice and counseling in such areas as preparing financial packages, business counseling, business information and management, accounting guidance, marketing, business/industrial site analysis, production, engineering, construction assistance, procurement and identification of potential business opportunities. MBDA does not have the authority to make loans to American Indian firms. Program funds are restricted to providing management and technical assistance.

Money Available Per Year: Grants: $1,906,500.

Range and Average of Financial Assistance: Awards range from $169,125 to $254,200, based on the availability of agency funds.

* Grants to Help Minority Businesses Enter New Markets

(11.802 Minority Business Resource Development)
Ms. Theresa Speake
Assistant Director for Program Development
Room 5096, Minority Business Development Agency
U.S. Department of Commerce
14th and Constitution Avenue, NW
Washington, DC 20230   (202) 482-5770

Objectives: The resource development activity provides for the indirect business assistance program conducted by MBDA. These programs encourage minority business development by identifying and developing private markets and capital sources; decreasing minority dependence on government programs; expanding business information and business services through trade associations; promoting and supporting the mobilization of resources of federal agencies and state and local governments at the local level; and assisting minorities in entering new and growing markets.

Types of Assistance: Project Grants (Cooperative Agreements).

Uses and Use Restrictions: Funds will be used in support of the MBDA policy statement on funding the Resource Development program. MBDA is charged under Executive Order 11625 with fostering new minority business enterprises and maintaining and strengthening existing firms to increase their opportunities to participate and receive the benefits of our economic system. MBDA will use a portion of its program funds to award contracts grants, and cooperative agreements public and private sector grantees which best demonstrate the ability to carry out MBDA's goals and objectives. Financial assistance under this program is to be targeted toward organizations which have the greatest potential developing access to capital market and other opportunities, and which can clearly demonstrate contributions

to be made to MBDA's goals and objectives. The performance of each individually funded grantee will be evaluated each year. The results of this evaluation will be critical in determining whether the organization will receive a new award.

Money Available Per Year: Grants: $2,202,000 in 1995.

Range and Average of Financial Assistance: Awards ranged from $2,500 to $235,000; $97,000.

* Grants to Organizations That Will Help You Sell To the Department of Defense

(12.002 Procurement Technical Assistance For Business Firms)
Defense Logistics Agency
Cameron Station
Office of Small and Disadvantaged Business
    Utilization (DLA-U), Room 4B130
Alexandria, VA 22304-6100   (202) 274-6471

Objectives: To assist eligible entities in the payment of the costs of establishing new Procurement Technical Assistance (PTA) Programs and maintaining existing PTA Programs.

Types of Assistance: Project Grants (Cooperative Agreements).

Uses and Use Restrictions: Recipients are to provide marketing and technical assistance to business firms in selling their goods and services to the Department of Defense (DoD), other federal agencies, and state and local governments. It also enhances the business climate and economies of the communities being served. Based on annual appropriations, the DoD cost-share will not exceed 50 percent of the net cost of a single PTA Program, excluding any federal funds and other income. The DoD share may be increased up to 75 percent for an existing program or new start that qualifies solely as servicing a distressed area. In no event shall the DoD share of the net program cost exceed $150,000, or $300,000 in the case of a statewide program or a program providing multi-area coverage (Indian Program). Further, a state and Defense Contract Management District (DCMD) dollar award limitation will be established each year dependent on the total dollar amount authorized for the program.

Money Available Per Year: Cooperative Agreements: $12,000,000 in 1995.

Range and Average of Financial Assistance: In 1992, $23,372 to $300,000; $146,733.

* Loans to Start A Business On An Indian Reservation

(15.124 Indian Loans - Economic Development)
Director
Office of Economic Development
Bureau of Indian Affairs
1849 and C Street, NW, Room 4060
Washington, DC 20240   (202) 208-5324
Contact: Jerry Folsom

Objectives: To provide assistance to Indians, Alaska Natives, tribes, and Indian organizations to obtain financing from private and governmental sources which serve other citizens. When otherwise unavailable, financial assistance through the Bureau is provided eligible applicants for any purpose that will promote the economic development of a Federal Indian Reservation.

Types of Assistance: Direct Loans; Guaranteed/ Insured Loans; Provision of Specialized Services.

Uses and Use Restrictions: Loans may be used for business, industry, agriculture, rehabilitation, housing, education, and for relending by tribes and Indian organizations to members of such organizations. Funds must be unavailable from other sources on reasonable terms and conditions. Funds may not be used for speculation. Except for educational purposes, Bureau financial assistance must be used on or near a federal Indian Reservation.

Money Available Per Year: Total Funds: $29,791,000.

Range and Average of Financial Assistance: $350 to over $1,000,000; Average: $100,000.

* Grants to Start Indian-Owned Businesses

(15.145 Indian Grants - Economic Development)
Jerry Folsom
Office of Economic Development
Bureau of Indian Affairs
1849 C Street, NW, Room 4060
Washington, DC 20240 (202) 208-5324

Objectives: To provide seed money to attract financing from other sources for developing Indian owned businesses; to improve Indian reservation economies by providing employment and goods and services where they are now deficient.

Types of Assistance: Project Grants; Direct Payments for Specified Use.

Uses and Use Restrictions: Grants must be used for development of profit oriented businesses which will have a positive economic impact on Indian reservations. Grants will provide no more than 25 percent of project costs. Grants are limited to $100,000 for individuals and $250,000 to Indian tribes.

Money Available Per Year: Grants: $3,900,000.

Range and Average of Financial Assistance: $810 to $250,000; Average: $39,400.

* Grants To Small Coal Mine Operators To Clean Up Their Mess

(15.250 Regulation of Surface Coal Mining and
Surface Effects of Underground Coal Mining)
Arthur Abbs, Chief
Division of Regulatory Programs
Office of Surface Mining Reclamation
  and Enforcement
U.S. Department of the Interior
1951 Constitution Ave., NW
Washington, DC 20240 (202) 208-2651

Objectives: To protect society and the environment from the adverse effects of surface coal mining operations consistent with assuring the coal supply essential to the Nation's energy requirements.

Types of Assistance: Project Grants; Direct Payments for Specified Use.

Uses and Use Restrictions: Grants for permanent program development are available to fund staff and related costs in connection with preparing state legislative proposals; preparing state regulations; preparing permanent program applications to the Office of Surface Mining Reclamation and Enforcement; and for other related purposes. Administration and enforcement grants are awarded to assist states that have received approval of permanent regulatory programs. Small Operator Assistance Program Operational grants are awarded to states and eligible individuals for contracting with qualified laboratories to provide hydrologic and geologic data on behalf of eligible small coal operators. Funded cooperative agreements provide for state regulation of coal mining activities on federal lands. Technical assistance is available on any aspect of regulating surface impacts of coal mining.

Money Available Per Year: $51,661,000. (Includes all cooperative agreements and State Grants except SOAP grants.) Small Operator Assistance: $1,760,000.

Range and Average of Financial Assistance: Administration and Enforcement $84,899 to $12,479,711. This represents an average of $2.1 million (est) in FY 1995.

* Grants to Environmental Engineering Companies to Help The Environment

(15.503 Small Reclamation Projects)
Dick L. Porter, Chief
Contracts and Repayment Division
Bureau of Reclamation
U.S. Department of the Interior
Washington, DC 20240 (202) 208-3014
or
Ron Willhite
Loan Program Coordinator
Resources Management
Bureau of Reclamation
U.S. Department of the Interior
Denver, CO 80225 (303) 236-8410

Objectives: To encourage state and local participation in the development of projects under federal reclamation laws, with emphasis on rehabilitation and betterment of existing projects for the purposes of significant conservation of water, energy, the environment, water quality control and to provide for federal assistance in the development of similar projects located in the 17 western most contiguous states and Hawaii.

Types of Assistance: Direct Loans; Project Grants.

Uses and Use Restrictions: Loans and grants for calendar year 1993 up to $33,300,000 for individual projects whose total cost cannot exceed $50,000,000. Projects can be single-purpose irrigation or drainage, or multipurpose, including municipal and industrial water supplies, flood control, fish and wildlife, recreation development, and hydroelectric power. Irrigation is a required purpose in all projects. Construction grants can be made for up to 50 percent of the costs allocated to flood control, fish and wildlife enhancement and recreation development, if such development is of general public benefit. In recent years the scope of the program has expanded to include Indian water development, groundwater recharge, wastewater reclamation and reuse, and wetlands development. All planning studies, the loan application report, water rights, and rights-of-way costs must be contributed by applicant. The loan costs allocated to irrigation and irrigation drainage are interest-free. The costs allocated to municipal and industrial water, hydroelectric power, the loan portion of costs allocated to flood control, fish and wildlife and recreation, and costs associated with serving excess land holdings are reimbursable with interest.

Money Available Per Year: Grants and loans: $3,000,000; Salaries and expenses: $600,000.

Range and Average of Financial Assistance: Loans: $2,000,000 to $33,300,000; Average: $20,000,000.

* Money To Help Start A Business in the Virgin Islands

(15.875 Economic and Political Development of the Territories and the Trust Territory of the Pacific Islands)
Assistant Secretary
Office of Territorial and International Affairs
U.S. Department of the Interior
Washington, DC 20240   (202) 208-4822

Objectives: To promote the economic, social, and political development of the territories, leading toward greater self-government for each of them.

Types of Assistance: Project Grants.

Uses and Use Restrictions: The base program provides federal funding for support of the operations of the American Samoa Government, including the Judiciary, the Northern Mariana Islands and the Trust Territory of the Pacific Islands, and the freely associated states of the Federated States of Micronesia and the Republic of the Marshall Islands. In addition, federal funding is provided for capital improvement programs and economic development in American Samoa, Guam, the Northern Mariana Islands, the Trust Territory of the Pacific Islands and the Virgin Islands.

Money Available Per Year: Grants: $74,110,000.

Range and Average of Financial Assistance: Not applicable.

* Money to Fishermen Who Have Their Boats Seized By A Foreign Government

(19.204 Fishermen's Guaranty Fund)
Mr. Stetson Tinkham
Office of Fisheries Affairs
Bureau of Oceans and International Environmental
  and Scientific Affairs
Room 5806, U.S. Department of State
Washington, DC 20520-7818   (202) 647-2009

Objectives: To provide for reimbursement of losses incurred as a result of the seizure of a U.S. commercial fishing vessel by a foreign country on the basis of rights or claims in territorial waters or on the high seas which are not recognized by the United States. Effective November 28, 1990, the United States acknowledges the authority of coastal states to manage highly migratory species, thus reducing the basis for valid claims under the Fishermen's Protective Act.

Types of Assistance: Insurance.

Money Available Per Year: Reimbursement of Losses: $186,000.

* Grants to Build An Airport

(20.106 Airport Improvement Program)
Federal Aviation Administration
Office of Airport Planning and Programming
Airports Financial Assistance Division
APP-500
800 Independence Avenue, SW
Washington, DC 20591   (202) 267-3831

Objectives: To assist sponsors, owners, or operators of public-use airports in the development of a nationwide system of airports adequate to meet the needs of civil aeronautics.

Types of Assistance: Project Grants; Advisory Services and Counseling.

Uses and Use Restrictions: Grants can be made for planning, construction, or rehabilitation at a public-use airport or portion thereof. Eligible work consists of: (1) airport master plans; (2) airport system plans; (3) airport noise compatibility plans; (4) land acquisition; (5) site preparation; (6) construction, alteration, and rehabilitation of runways, taxiways, aprons, and certain roads within airport boundaries; (7) construction and installation of airfield lighting, navigational aids, and certain offsite work; (8) safety equipment required for certification of airport facility; (9) security equipment required of the sponsor by the Secretary of Transportation by rule or regulation for the safety and security of persons and property on the airport; (10) snow-removal equipment; (11) terminal development; (12) aviation-related weather reporting equipment; (13) equipment to measure runway surface friction; (14) burn area training structures and land for that purpose, on or off airport; (15) agency-approved noise compatibility projects; (16) relocation of air traffic control towers and navigational aids (including radar) if they impede other projects funded under the Airport Improvement Program (AIP); (17) land, paving drainage, aircraft deicing equipment and structures for centralized deicing areas; and (18) projects to comply with the Americans with Disabilities Act of 1990, Clean Air Act, and Federal Water Pollution Control. Grants may not be made for the construction of hangars, most automobile parking facilities, buildings not related to the safety of persons on the airport, decorative landscaping or artwork, or routine maintenance and repair. Technical advisory services are also provided. Formula funds are available to primary commercial service airports (defined as a public airport which enplanes annually more than 10,000 passengers and receives scheduled passenger service of aircraft) and to cargo service airports (defined as an airport which is served by aircraft providing air transportation of only property (including mail) with annual landed weight in excess of 100,000,000 pounds). Discretionary funds may be used at any eligible facility.

Money Available Per Year: Grants: $1,500,000,000.

Range and Average of Financial Assistance: $12,600 to $34,354,194; Average: $1,172,000.

* Grants to Bus Companies

(20.509 Public Transportation for Nonurbanized Areas)
Federal Transit Administration
Office of Grants Management
Office of Capital and Formula Assistance
400 Seventh Street, SW

Washington, DC 20590 (202) 366-2053
Objectives: To improve, initiate, or continue public transportation service in nonurbanized areas by providing financial assistance for the acquisition, construction, and improvement of facilities and equipment and the payment of operating expenses by operating contract, lease, or otherwise. Also to provide technical assistance for rural transportation.
Types of Assistance: Formula Grants.
Uses and Use Restrictions: Section 18 funding may be used for eligible capital expenses, project administration, and operating expenses needed to provide efficient and coordinated public transportation service in nonurbanized areas. Funds may also be used for user side subsidies for nonurbanized public transportation and for rural segments of intercity bus service. Projects must provide for the maximum feasible coordination of public transportation sources assisted under this Section with other transportation services, and must provide for the maximum feasible participation of private operators. A set percentage of the state's annual apportionment, 10 percent in fiscal year 1993, and 15 percent in fiscal year 1994 and thereafter) must be spent to carry out a program for the development and support of intercity bus transportation, unless the governor certifies that such needs are adequately met. Rural Transit Assistance Program (RTAP) funds may be used for technical assistance, training, research, and related support services.
Money Available Per Year: Grants: $158,831,000. The RTAP was fully funded under the new transit planning and research program. The estimated obligations for FY 1994 and 1995 included $4.6 Million for RTAP.
Range and Average of Financial Assistance: Not applicable.

* Grants to Become A Women-Owned Transportation Related Company

(20.511 Human Resource Programs)
Director, Office of Civil Rights
Federal Transit Administration
U.S. Department of Transportation
400 Seventh Street, SW, Room 7412
Washington, DC 20590 (202) 366-4018
Objectives: To provide financial assistance for national and local programs that address human resource needs as they apply to public transportation activities particularly in furtherance of minority and female needs.
Types of Assistance: Project Grants (Cooperative Agreements); Dissemination of Technical Information.
Uses and Use Restrictions: Projects may include, but are not limited to, employment training programs, outreach programs to increase minority and female employment in public transportation activities, research on public transportation manpower and training needs, and training and assistance for minority-and women-owned business opportunities including assistance in seeking venture capital, obtaining surety bonding, obtaining management and technical services, and contracting with public agencies organized for such purposes.
Money Available Per Year: Grants, Cooperative Agreements: $1,189,000.
Range and Average of Financial Assistance: None established.

* Grants To U.S. Shipping Companies That Have To Pay Their Employees Higher Salaries Than Foreign Shipping Companies

(20.804 Operating Differential Subsidies)
Associate Administrator for Maritime Aids
Maritime Administration
U.S. Department of Transportation
400 Seventh Street, SW
Washington, DC 20590 (202) 366-0364
Objectives: To promote development and maintenance of the U.S. Merchant Marine by granting financial aid to equalize cost of operating a U.S. flag ship with cost of operating a competitive foreign flag ship.
Types of Assistance: Direct Payments for Specified Use.
Uses and Use Restrictions: Title VI of the Act provides for the payment of operating-differential subsidy on vessels to be used in a foreign service in the foreign commerce of the United States, which has been declared to be essential by the Secretary of Transportation under Section 211 of the Act. Operating subsidy is based on the difference between the fair and reasonable cost of certain items of operating expense and the estimated cost of the same items of expense if the vessels were operated under foreign registry.
Money Available Per Year: $214,356,000.
Range and Average of Financial Assistance: $8,000 to $14,200; $10,000.

* Money For Airlines to Fly To Small Towns And Make A Profit

(20.901 Payments for Essential Air Services)
Director, Office of Aviation Analysis, P-50
U.S. Department of Transportation
400 Seventh Street, SW
Washington, DC 20590 (202) 366-1030
Objectives: To assure that air transportation is provided to eligible communities by subsidizing air carriers when necessary to provide service.
Types of Assistance: Direct Payments for Specified Use.
Uses and Use Restrictions: When necessary, subsidy payments are made to air carriers providing air services at certain points. Subsidy is paid to cover the carrier's operating loss, plus a profit element.
Money Available Per Year: Direct payments to air carriers: $25,600,000.
Range and Average of Financial Assistance: For continental United States: $36,814 to $850,472 annually per point; $358,866 annually per point average.

* Grants To Women-Owned Businesses in Transportation

(20.902 Student Training and Education Program)
Office of Small and Disadvantaged Business
   Utilization, S-40
Office of the Secretary
400 Seventh Street, SW

Washington, DC 20590   (202) 366-1930

Objectives: To support Historically Black Colleges and Universities (HBCUs) in advancing the development of potential by providing quality education to minority students. This project will strengthen HBCU efforts to promote the full diversification of the work force by implementing programs and developing curriculums dedicated to providing a continuous pool of individuals to occupy professional and management positions in the Nation's work force, including minority, women-owned and disadvantaged business enterprises (DBEs). This project will provide opportunities for DBEs to enhance their knowledge and skills in the field of transportation and their involvement with the HBCUs and minority students.

Types of Assistance: Project Grants.

Uses and Use Restrictions: Financial assistance under this section may be used by educational institutions and non-profit organizations to design and carry out programs to encourage, promote and assist minority entrepreneurs and businesses in getting transportation-related contracts, subcontracts and projects. Funds may also be used to develop educational programs designed to enhance DBEs' knowledge of the transportation field, thereby increasing their capabilities to compete successfully for transportation-related contracts. In addition, this project will attract more of the Nation's young talent into transportation-related careers through their academic studies and through practical experience.

Money Available Per Year: Grants: $800,000.

Range and Average of Financial Assistance: $50,000 to $80,000 per HBCU.

* Grants to Women-Owned Businesses To Help Get Contracts From The Department of Transportation

(20.903 Support Mechanisms for Disadvantaged Businesses)
Office of Small and Disadvantaged Business
  Utilization, S-40
Office of the Secretary
400 Seventh Street, SW
Washington, DC 20590   (202) 366-1930

Objectives: To develop support mechanisms, including liaison and assistance programs, that will enable Disadvantaged Business Enterprises (DBEs) to take advantage of transportation-related contracts. Recipients will provide a communications link between the Department of Transportation; its grantees, recipients, contractors, subcontractors; and minority, women-owned and disadvantaged business enterprises in order to increase their participation in existing DOT programs and to provide more DBEs with DOT contracting opportunities.

Types of Assistance: Project Grants (Cooperative Agreements).

Uses and Use Restrictions: Financial assistance under this section may be given for projects which respond to needs as outlined in each respective program solicitation announcement (letter). Such assistance must provide a special level of effort or service in the delivery of management and technical assistance to minority, women-owned and disadvantaged business enterprises (DBEs) in order to overcome historic flaws in the free enterprise system and provide the opportunity for successful and full participation in that system. Types of management and technical assistance may include financial services, marketing assistance and referral services.

Money Available Per Year: Grants: $1,000,000 in 1995.

Range and Average of Financial Assistance: Average $95,000.

* Loans To Start A Credit Union

(44.002 Community Development Revolving Loan
Program for Credit Unions)
Mr. Ron Lewandowski
Community Development Revolving Loan Program
  for Credit Unions
National Credit Union Administration
1775 Duke St.
Alexandria, VA 22314   (202) 518-6490

Objectives: To support community based credit unions in their efforts to: (1) stimulate economic development activities (in the community they service), which result in increased income, ownership, and employment opportunities for low-income residents; and (2) to provide basic financial and related services to residents of their communities.

Types of Assistance: Direct Loans.

Uses and Use Restrictions: In order to meet the objectives of the Community Development Revolving Loan Program for Credit Unions, an applicant approved for participation must provide a variety of financial and related services designed to meet the particular needs of the low-income community served. Federal funds loaned under the Revolving Loan Program may be used for services that include activities aimed towards: (1) supporting and stimulating economic development and revitalization efforts within the low-income community, such as: (a) improving housing conditions and increasing home ownership through a variety of mechanisms including self-help and co-op housing development projects, assistance in securing and leveraging mortgages, site development and construction financing; and (b) increasing employment opportunities by aiding existing businesses and promoting the establishment of new businesses. Recipients are encouraged to use funds available through the Revolving Loan Program to serve as a catalyst to attract and stimulate the investment of capital from other private and public sources to promote economic development activities within the community; (2) providing member services such as financial counseling; and (3) increasing the membership and the capitalization base such as: (a) membership drives; (b) campaigns to encourage members to increase their share deposits through systematic savings, utilizing such methods as payroll deductions allotments; and (c) businesses and other organizations serving the community to maintain share deposits or contribute financially in other ways to projects supported by the credit union. Loans up to $300,000, will be made to credit unions. All loans must be repaid to the Community Development Revolving Loan Fund for Credit Unions within the shortest time compatible with sound business practice and with the objectives of the program, but in no case will the term exceed 5 years. Loans made under this program shall bear interest at a rate of 2 percent per annum. Semi-annual interest and principal payments are required by the Revolving Loan Program.

Money Available Per Year: Direct Loans: $1,800,000

Range and Average of Financial Assistance: $25,000 to $200,000; $135,000.

* Grants To Publish Books For A Limited Audience

(45.132 Promotion of the Humanities-Subventions)
Division of Research Programs
Subventions, Room 318
National Endowment for the Humanities
Washington, DC 20506   (202) 606-8207

Objectives: To ensure through grants to publishing entities the dissemination of works of scholarly distinction in the humanities.

Types of Assistance: Project Grants.

Uses and Use Restrictions: Awards are made to assist publication of materials of significance from all fields of the humanities. Grants are made in the fixed amount of $7,000; in a single application cycle a press may submit up to four applications and receive up to $28,000 (no more than four grants). Subventions take into account plant, paper, printing, binding, editorial, and overhead costs, but exclude royalties paid to authors.

Money Available Per Year: Grants: $5,720,000. (Note: In FY 1994 the budgets for the following programs were combined into one: 45.146, Editions; 45.147, Translations; and 45.132, Subventions. The program is called Scholarly Publications and is comprised of the three funding categories, Editions, Translations, and Subventions.

Range and Average of Financial Assistance: The fixed award amount is $7,000.

* Money If Your Business Was Hurt By A Natural Disaster or Drought

(59.002 Economic Injury Disaster Loans)
Office of Disaster Assistance
Small Business Administration
409 3rd Street, SW
Washington, DC 20416   (202) 205-6734

Objectives: To assist business concerns suffering economic injury as a result of certain Presidential, SBA, and/or Department of Agriculture declared disasters.

Types of Assistance: Direct Loans; Guaranteed/Insured Loans (including Immediate Participation Loans).

Uses and Use Restrictions: Up to 30 years for repayment. $500,000 limit on amount: economic injury governs. Funds can be provided to pay current liabilities which the small concern could have paid if the disaster had not occurred. Working capital for limited period can be provided to continue the business in operation until conditions return to normal. No funds available for realty, equipment repair or acquisition: the interest rate is not to exceed 4 percent.

Money Available Per Year: $76,563,000.

Range and Average of Financial Assistance: Direct loans: Up to $1,500,000; $50,725.

* Money For Small Businesses Owned by Low-Income People In Areas Of High Unemployment

(59.003 Loans for Small Businesses)
Director, Loan Policy and Procedures Branch
Small Business Administration
409 Third Street, SW
Washington, DC 20416   (202) 205-6570

Objectives: To provide direct loans to small businesses owned by low-income persons or located in any area having a high percentage of unemployment, or having a high percentage of low income individuals. (Guaranteed Loans, including Immediate Participation Loans are provided under program 59.012.)

Types of Assistance: Direct Loans; Advisory Services and Counseling.

Uses and Use Restrictions: To assist in establishing, preserving, and strengthening small businesses owned by low-income persons or located in areas of high unemployment. Excludes publishing media, radio and television, non-profit enterprises, speculators in property, lending or investment enterprises, gambling enterprises, and financing real property held for investment. Funds must not otherwise be available on reasonable terms.

Money Available Per Year: Loans: $8,502,000.

Range and Average of Financial Assistance: Direct Loans: Up to $150,000; Average: $67,694.

* Money For Businesses Hurt By Physical Disaster Or Drought

(59.008 Physical Disaster Loans)
Office of Disaster Assistance
Small Business Administration
409 3rd Street, SW
Washington, DC 20416   (202) 205-6734

Objectives: To provide loans to the victims of designated physical-type disasters for uninsured losses.

Types of Assistance: Direct Loans; Guaranteed/Insured Loans (including Immediate Participation Loans).

Uses and Use Restrictions: Loans made to homeowners, renters, and businesses to repair and/or replace damaged and/or destroyed real property and/or personal property to its pre-disaster conditions. Credit elsewhere test required for all applicants to determine interest rates. Loans to homeowners/tenants made up to 30 years. Limit of $100,000 for repair/ replacement of real property; $20,000 for repair/replacement of personal property, or a combined maximum of $120,000. The loan limit may be increased by 20 percent to provide protective measures from damages caused by physical disasters. The interest rate for homeowners/tenants who have credit available elsewhere is determined by a formula based on the cost of money to the U.S. Government, but not to exceed 8 percent. The interest rate for homeowners/tenants who do not have credit available elsewhere is 1/2 of the formula rate, but not to exceed 4 percent. Loans to business may not exceed $500,000. For businesses determined to be able to obtain credit elsewhere, the interest rate is based on a formula, but not to exceed 8 percent, with maturities not to exceed 3 years. For non-profit organizations determined to be able to obtain credit elsewhere, the interest rate is based on a formula, with maturities not to exceed 30 years. For businesses and non-profit organizations determined to be unable to obtain credit elsewhere, the interest rate may not exceed 4 percent, with maturities up to 30 years. Under certain circumstances, homeowners and businesses may be eligible for refinancing of existing liens. There are restrictions on the use of funds for voluntary relocation. In the case of a Major Source of

Employment, the $500,000 limitation on physical disaster loans may be waived. Provisions of Flood Disaster Protection Act of 1973 apply.
Money Available Per Year: Loans: $411,627,000.
Range and Average of Financial Assistance: Direct home loans up to $240,000 limit plus $200,000 additional in some special cases to refinance existing liens and $48,000 additional for protective measures. Direct business loans up to $1,500,000 with additional amounts are available for major source of employment. In fiscal year 1994, average loans were: $24,117 (Home); $66,079 (Business).

* Money To Start A Venture Capital Company

(59.011 Small Business Investment Companies)
Director, Office of Investments
Investment Division
Small Business Administration
409 Third Street, SW
Washington, DC 20416   (202) 205-6510
Objectives: To establish privately owned and managed investment companies, which are licensed and regulated by the U.S. Small Business Administration; to provide equity capital and long term loan funds to small businesses; and to provide advisory services to small businesses.
Types of Assistance: Direct Loans; Guaranteed/ Insured Loans; Advisory Services and Counseling.
Uses and Use Restrictions: The investment companies provide management and financial assistance on a continuing basis to eligible small business concerns. Financial assistance is provided by making long-term loans to these small concerns, and/or by the purchase of debt or equity type securities issued by these firms. Emphasis is on providing assistance to the pioneering, innovating-type concerns developing new products, processes, and markets. Specialized investment companies organized/ licensed under Section 301(d) of the authorizing statute (SSBICs) must restrict eligibility of small concerns financed by such investment companies to those owned and operated by individuals whose participation in the free enterprise system has been hampered by social or economic disadvantages. Debentures and/or participating securities are issued by the SBIC and guaranteed by SBA for a term not to exceed 10 years. Section 301(d) licensees (SSBICs) may also apply for the sale of a limited amount of their preferred stock to SBA. All investment companies generally may not self-deal, take control, finance "big business," or invest over 20 percent (30 percent for SSBICs) of private capital in any single small concern.
Money Available Per Year: Direct Loans: $15,000,000; Guarantees: $665,210,000.
Range and Average of Financial Assistance: Guarantee Loans: $50,000 to $90,000,000; Average: $1,480,000.

* Up to $750,000 to Start Your Own Business

(59.012 Small Business Loans)
Director, Loan Policy and Procedures Branch
Small Business Administration

409 Third Street, SW
Washington, DC 20416   (202) 205-6570
Objectives: To provide guaranteed loans to small businesses which are unable to obtain financing in the private credit marketplace, but can demonstrate an ability to repay loans granted. Guaranteed loans to low-income business owners or businesses located in areas of high unemployment, non-profit sheltered workshops and other similar organizations which produce goods or services; to small businesses being established, acquired or owned by handicapped individuals; and to enable small businesses to manufacture, design, market, install, or service specific energy measures.
Types of Assistance: Guaranteed/Insured Loans (including Immediate Participation Loans).
Money Available Per Year: Loans: $8,994,000,000.
Range and Average of Financial Assistance: Guarantee Loans: Up to $750,000; Average: $215,993.

* Loans To Local Organizations That Finance Small Businesses

(59.013 Local Development Company Loans)
Office of Rural Affairs and Economic Development
Small Business Administration
409 3rd Street, SW
Washington, DC 20416   (202) 205-6485
Objectives: To make federal loans to local development companies to provide long-term financing to small business concerns located in their areas. Local development companies are corporations chartered for the purpose of promoting economic growth within specific areas.
Types of Assistance: Guaranteed/Insured Loans.
Uses and Use Restrictions: Loans to local development companies are for the purchase of land, buildings, machinery, and equipment, or for constructing, expanding, or modernizing buildings. Loans are not available to local development companies to provide small businesses with working capital or for refinancing purposes. Loans may not exceed 25 years.
Money Available Per Year: Loans: $50,316,000
Range and Average of Financial Assistance: Guarantee Loans: Up to $1,000,000; $500,000.

* Help For Contractors and Others To Get Bonded To Obtain Contracts

(59.016 Bond Guarantees for Surety Companies)
Dorothy Kleeschulte, Assistant Administrator
Office of Surety Guarantees
Small Business Administration
409 3rd Street, SW
Washington, DC 20416   (202) 205-6540
Objectives: To guarantee surety bonds issued by commercial surety companies for small contractors unable to obtain a bond without a guarantee. Guarantees are for up to 90 percent of the total amount of bond.
Types of Assistance: Insurance (Guaranteed Surety Bonds)
Uses and Use Restrictions: Contracts of $1.250 million or less, where a surety bond is required but not available privately without an SBA guarantee. Guarantee is limited to bid, payment,

and performance bonds (and ancillary bonds incidental to the performance of a specific contract). Guarantee is provided directly to the surety, and only on a case-by-case basis, for a particular contract. Guarantee covers up to 90 percent of surety's losses on that contract.

Money Available Per Year: Bond-guarantees SBA shares to surety companies: $1,555,076,000

Range and Average of Financial Assistance: Size range of contracts awarded and bonded, $475 to $1,250,000; Average Contract: $144,479; Average Guarantee: $127,983.

* Low Interest Loans For Persons With Disabilities To Start A Business

(59.021 Handicapped Assistance Loans)
Director, Loan Policy and Procedures Branch
Small Business Administration
409 Third Street, SW
Washington, DC 20416   (202) 205-6570

Objectives: To provide direct loans for non-profit sheltered workshops and other similar organizations that produce goods and services; and to assist in the establishment, acquisition, or operation of a small business owned by handicapped individuals. (Guaranteed Loans, including Immediate Participation Loans, are provided under program 59.012.)

Types of Assistance: Direct Loans.

Uses and Use Restrictions: HAL-1 (non-profit organizations) loan proceeds may be used for working capital and construction of facilities if a construction grant is not available from other Government sources. No loan may be used for training, education, housing, or other supportive services for handicapped employees. HAL-2 (small business concerns): To be used for construction, expansion, or conversion of facilities; to purchase building, equipment, or materials; and for working capital. Excludes speculation, publishing media, radio and television, non-profit enterprises, speculators in property, lending or investment enterprises, and financing of real property held for sale or investment. For both HAL-1 and HAL-2, loans must be of such sound value or so secured as reasonably to assure repayment.

Money Available Per Year: Direct Loans: $9,553,000

Range and Average of Financial Assistance: $500 to $350,000; Average: $95,305.

* Loans to Veterans To Start A Business

(59.038 Veterans Loan Program)
Director, Loan Policy and Procedures Branch
Small Business Administration
409 Third Street, SW
Washington, DC 20416   (202) 205-6570

Objectives: To provide loans to small businesses owned by Vietnam-era and disabled veterans.

Types of Assistance: Direct Loans.

Uses and Use Restrictions: To construct, expand, or convert facilities; to purchase building equipment or materials; for working capital. Excludes gambling establishments, publishing media, radio and television, non-profit enterprises, speculators in property, lending or investment enterprises, and financing of real property held for investment; also excludes funds to

indiscriminately relocate the business. Funds must not otherwise be available on reasonable terms, nor used to pay off a loan to an unsecured creditor who is in a position to sustain loss. Guaranty loans under the regular Business Loan Program must be used if available before a direct loan can be considered.

Money Available Per Year: Loans: $12,000,000.

Range and Average of Financial Assistance: $1,000 to $150,000; Average: $75,845.

* Money To Local Organizations To Finance Small Businesses

(59.041 Certified Development Company Loans [504 Loans])
Office of Rural Affairs and Economic Development
Small Business Administration
409 3rd Street SW
Washington, DC 20416   (202) 205-6485

Objectives: To assist small business concerns by providing long-term fixed rate financing for fixed assets through the sale of debentures to private investors.

Types of Assistance: Guaranteed/Insured Loans.

Uses and Use Restrictions: Loans are to assist small businesses in the acquisition of land and buildings, construction, expansion, renovation and modernization, machinery, and equipment. Loans may have either a 10 or 20 year term.

Money Available Per Year: Guaranteed Loans: $2,078,571,000.

Range and Average of Financial Assistance: Up to $1,000,000; Average: $307,700.

* Loans To Minority Businesses That Want To Do Business With The Government

(59.042 Business Loans for 8(a) Program Participants)
Director, Loan Policy and Procedures Branch
Small Business Administration
409 Third Street, SW
Washington, DC 20416   (202) 205-6570

Objectives: To provide direct and guaranteed loans to small business contractors receiving assistance under the subsection 7(j) 10 and section 8(a) of the Small Business Act (15 U.S.C. 636 (a)), who are unable to obtain financing on reasonable terms in the private credit marketplace, but can demonstrate an ability to repay loans granted. Terms not to exceed 25 years.

Types of Assistance: Direct Loans; Guaranteed/ Insured Loans (including Immediate Participation Loans).

Uses and Use Restrictions: To construct, expand, or convert facilities, to acquire machinery, buildings, equipment, supplies, or materials. Loans for working capital are limited to manufacturers. Funds must not otherwise be available in the private credit marketplace on reasonable terms, nor must they be used to pay off a loan to an unsecured creditor who is in a position to sustain a loss.

Money Available Per Year: Direct Loans: $4,989,000.

Range and Average of Financial Assistance: Direct Loans: Up to $150,000; $750,000 with written authorization by the Associate Administrator for Minority Small Business and Capital Ownership Development. Average direct loan: $154,839. Guaranteed Loans range up to $750,000.

* Grants To Local Organizations That Help Women Start Their Own Businesses

(59.043 Women's Business Ownership Assistance)
Harriet Fredman
Office of Women's Business Ownership
Small Business Administration
409 3rd Street, SW
Washington, DC 20416   (202) 205-6673

Objectives: To promote the legitimate interest of small business concerns owned and controlled by women and to remove, in so far as possible, the discriminatory barriers that are encountered by women in accessing capital and other factors of production.

Types of Assistance: Project Grants (Cooperative Agreements or Contracts).

Uses and Use Restrictions: To establish demonstration projects for the benefit of small business concerns owned and controlled by women. The services and assistance provided by the demonstration projects are to include financial, management and marketing training and counseling to start-up or established on-going concerns.

Money Available Per Year: Cooperative Agreements: $4,000,000

Range and Average of Financial Assistance: $35,000 to $250,000; Average: $150,000.

* Grants To Local Organizations That Help Veterans Start Their Own Businesses

(59.044 Veterans Entrepreneurial Training and Counseling)
Reginald Teamer or William Truitt
Office of Veteran Affairs
Small Business Administration
6th Floor, 409 3rd Street, SW
Washington, DC 20416   (202) 205-6773

Objectives: To design, develop, administer, and evaluate an entrepreneurial and procurement training and counseling program for U.S. veterans.

Types of Assistance: Project Grants (Cooperative Agreements).

Uses and Use Restrictions: Funds shall be used to provide veterans and their dependents assistance to start and manage their businesses. The assistance may be in the form of intensive train-ing, counseling, and other specialized services.

Money Available Per Year: Grants: $445,000.

Range and Average of Financial Assistance: $28,000 to $100,000; Average: $75,600.

* Grants To Small Businesses That Want To Plant Trees on Government Land

(59.045 Natural Resource Development)
William F. Berry
Office of Procurement Assistance
Small Business Administration
409 3rd St., SW
Washington, DC 20416   (202) 205-6470

Objectives: To make grants to states to contract with small business concerns to plant trees on state or local government owned land.

Types of Assistance: Project Grants.

Uses and Use Restrictions: Assistance can be used for tree planting on state or local government owned land. Funds cannot be used to pay for land or land charges. This program requires performance to be contracted with small business.

Money Available Per Year: Grants: $18,000,000.

Range and Average of Financial Assistance: The amount of the allocation is based on population.

* Money To Local Organizations To Provide Micro-Loans

(59.046 Microloan Demonstration Program)
SBA Central Office
Office of Financial Assistance   (202) 205-6570
or write to:
Office of Financing
Loan Policy and Procedures Branch
Small Business Administration
409 Third Street SW, Eighth Floor
Washington, DC 20416

Objectives: To assist women, low-income, and minority entrepreneurs, business owners, and other individuals possessing the capability to operate successful business concerns and business concerns in areas suffering from lack of credit due to economic downturn through the establishment of the Microloan Demonstration Program. Under the program the Small Business Administration (SBA) will make loans to private, non-profit and quasi-governmental organizations (intermediaries) which will, in turn, make loans in amounts up to $25,000 to start up, newly established, or growing concerns for the provision of working capital or the acquisition of materials, supplies, or equipment.

Types of Assistance: Formula Grants; Project Grants; Direct Loans.

Uses and Use Restrictions: Loans to intermediaries with terms and restrictions as provided in Public Law 102-366 and subsequent regulations as published in the Federal Register.

Money Available Per Year: Loans: $65,016,000.

Range and Average of Financial Assistance: New program, information not yet available.

* Money For Disabled Veterans To Start New Businesses

(64.116 Vocational Rehabilitation for Disabled Veterans)
Central Office
U.S. Department of Veterans Affairs
Washington, DC 20420

Objectives: To provide all services and assistance necessary to enable service-disabled veterans and service persons hospitalized pending discharge to achieve maximum independence in daily living and, to the maximum extent feasible, to become employable and to obtain and maintain suitable employment.

Types of Assistance: Direct Payments with Unrestricted Use; Direct Payments for Specified Use; Direct Loans; Advisory

Services and Counseling.

Uses and Use Restrictions: The program provides for direct payment to service providers for the entire cost of tuition, books, fees, supplies, and other services. As part or all of a rehabilitation program, individuals may receive services and training designed to help them live with a reduced dependency on others in their homes and communities. Counseling services are provided to the individual during his or her participation in the program. In addition to disability compensation, the veteran receives a monthly subsistence allowance. Advances of up to $666 may be made to veterans to meet unexpected financial difficulties. These advances do not bear interest and are repaid out of future subsistence allowance payments. Although no set repayment period is established, the monthly rate of repayment may not generally be less than 10 percent. In general, a new advance may not be made until a previous advance has been fully repaid. Usually, the training phase of the rehabilitation program may not exceed 4 years nor may training be provided more than 12 years after the individual becomes eligible to apply for the program. Following training, or sometimes as the whole of a rehabilitation program, the veteran may also receive up to 18 months of counseling, job placement and post-placement services. The veteran may receive an employment adjustment allowance equal to 2 months of subsistence during this period of services, but only if employability was achieved as a result of services received in a program which included a training phase. Veterans who meet certain requirements may receive an initial supply of goods and commodities to start a small business.

Money Available Per Year: Direct payments: $279,840,000; Loan advances: $1,964,000.

Range and Average of Financial Assistance: Full cost of tuition, books, fees, supplies and rehabilitation services; Monthly full-time allowances range from $366 for a single veteran to $535 for a veteran with two dependents, plus $39 for each dependent in excess of two. Non-interest bearing loans of up to $732 and a work-study allowance not to exceed the higher of 25 times the federal or state minimum hourly wage times the number of weeks in the veteran's period of enrollment.

* Help For Retired Military To Start A Business

(64.123 Vocational Training for Certain Veterans Receiving VA Pension)
Central Office
U.S. Department of Veterans Affairs
Washington, DC 20420

Objectives: To assist new pension recipients to resume and maintain gainful employment by providing vocational training and other services.

Types of Assistance: Direct Payments for Specified Use; Advisory Services and Counseling.

Uses and Use Restrictions: The program provides for direct payment to service providers for the entire cost of tuition, books, fees, supplies, and other services. Counseling services are provided to the individual throughout participation in the program. The training phase of the program usually may not exceed 24 months and may not generally begin after January 1, 1996. Following training, or instead of training, the veteran may be provided up to 18 months of employment assistance. Veterans

who meet certain eligibility requirements may be provided an initial supply of goods and commodities to start a business. Earnings while in a vocational training program do count as income for pension, and may affect the amount received. However, a pensioner's eligibility for health care is protected for 3 years following loss of pension benefits because of income from work or training.

Money Available Per Year: $1,280,000.

Range and Average of Financial Assistance: Actual costs of books, supplies, tuition, and fees.

* Money To Invest In Companies Overseas

(70.002 Foreign Investment Guaranties)
Information Officer
Overseas Private Investment Corporation
1100 New York Ave., NW
Washington, DC 20527   (202) 336-8799

Objectives: To guarantee loans and other investments made by eligible U.S. investors in friendly developing countries and emerging economies throughout the world, thereby assisting development goals and improving U.S. global competitiveness, creating American jobs and increasing U.S. exports.

Types of Assistance: Guaranteed/Insured Loans; Direct Loans.

Uses and Use Restrictions: To guarantee loans for investments in developing countries, as an encouragement to private U.S. investment and to support, finance and insure projects that contribute to the economic and social development of the host country and have a positive impact on the U.S. economy. The Overseas Private Investment Corporation (OPIC) screens out projects that might have a negative effect on U.S. employment or the environment.

Money Available Per Year: Loan Guaranties: $500,000,000

Range and Average of Financial Assistance: $10,000,000 to $75,000,000; Average: $2,300,000.

* Insurance Against Your Business In Another Country Being Hurt By Foreign Politics

(70.003 Foreign Investment Insurance)
Information Officer
Overseas Private Investment Corporation
1100 New York Ave., NW
Washington, DC 20527   (202) 336-8799

Objectives: To insure investments of eligible U.S. investors in developing friendly countries and areas, against the risks of inconvertibility, expropriation, war, revolution and insurrection, certain types of civil strife, and business interruption. Special programs to insure contractors and exporters against arbitrary drawings of letters of credit posted as bid, performance or advance payment guaranties, energy exploration and development, leasing operations.

Types of Assistance: Insurance.

Uses and Use Restrictions: To encourage private U.S. investment in developing countries by protecting against certain political risks inherent in such investment. Investments, if not of a short-term nature, qualify for insurance if they contribute to the economic and social development of the host country and do not adversely affect U.S. employment. Special criteria may be applied to investments in natural resources extraction projects and large and sensitive projects. No insurance can be issued if investment has been made or committed prior to registration; applicant must obtain approval of foreign government for the investment, for insurance purposes.

Money Available Per Year: Insurance: $5,000,000; Contracts Issued: $3,600,000,000

Range and Average of Financial Assistance: $67,500 to $200,000,000; Average: $20,000,000.

* Free Patent Rights To Government Discoverers of Energy Saving Ideas

(81.003 Granting of Patent Licenses)
Robert J. Marchick
Office of the Assistant General Counsel
  for Patents
U.S. Department of Energy
Washington, DC 20585   (202) 586-2802

Objectives: To encourage widespread utilization of inventions covered by Department of Energy (DOE) owned patents.

Types of Assistance: Dissemination of Technical Information.

Uses and Use Restrictions: Nonexclusive, revocable licenses are granted by the Department of Energy (DOE) to responsible applicants with plans for development and/or marketing on approximately 2,000 DOE owned U.S. patents. Exclusive and partially exclusive licenses may also be granted. Similar licenses on approximately 1,000 DOE owned foreign patents may be accorded to U.S. citizens and corporations, and to others under terms and conditions which depend upon particular facts. Licenses for use or sale in the U.S. may normally be granted only to licensees that agree to manufacture in the U.S. Copies of U.S. patents may be obtained from the U.S. Patent and Trademark Office, Dept. of Commerce, Washington, DC 20231, at $1.50 per copy.

Money Available Per Year: (Salaries) Not identifiable.

Range and Average of Financial Assistance: Not applicable.

* Money To Work On An Energy-Related Invention

(81.036 Energy-Related Inventions)
George Lewett, Director
Office of Technology Evaluation and Assessment
National Institute of Standards and Technology
Gaithersburg, MD 20899   (301) 975-5500
or
Terry Levinson
Inventions and Innovation Division
Energy-Related Inventions Programs (CE-521)
U.S. Department of Energy
1000 Independence Avenue, SW
Washington, DC 20585   (202) 586-1479

Objectives: To encourage innovation in developing non-nuclear energy technology by providing assistance to individual and small business companies in the development of promising energy-related inventions.

Types of Assistance: Project Grants; Use of Property, Facilities, and Equipment; Advisory Services and Counseling; Dissemination of Technical Information.

Uses and Use Restrictions: The assistance provided includes evaluation of energy-related inventions, limited funding assistance, where appropriate, advice concerning engineering, marketing, business planning. Grantee may petition for waiver of government patent rights. No equity capital is provided. Thirty grants were made to inventors in fiscal year 1992. Funds are available in fiscal year 1995 for grants.

Money Available Per Year: Grants: $5,700,000.

Range and Average of Financial Assistance: Past awards average $83,000.

* Grants To Local Organizations That Help Women and Minorities Get Department of Energy Contracts

(81.082 Management and Technical Assistance for Minority Business Enterprises)
Sterling Nichols
Office of Minority Economic Impact
U.S. Department of Energy
Forrestal Building
Room 5B-110, MI-1
Washington, DC 20585   (202) 586-1594

Objectives: (1) To support increased participation of minority, and women-owned and operated business enterprises (MBE's); (2) to develop energy-related minority business assistance programs and public/private partnerships to provide technical assistance to MBE's; (3) to transfer applicable technology from national federal laboratories to MBE's; and (4) to increase the Department of Energy's (DOE) high technology research and development contracting activities.

Types of Assistance: Advisory Services and Counseling.

Uses and Use Restrictions: Services provided include: (1) Identification and compilation of DOE high technology procurement opportunities; (2) technical assistance to minority businesses and communities; (3) dissemination of DOE energy-technology opportunities to MBE's; (4) financial proposal and bid assistance to MBE's; and (5) match business opportunities in public and private organizations with minority business firms and educational institutions. The services provided by the Office of Minority Economic Impact (MI) are outside of the scope of similar services provided by DOE's Office of Small and Disadvantaged Business Utilization (OSDBU), as authorized by its charter, Public Law 95-507.

Money Available Per Year: Contracts and Grants: $382,000.

* Grants To Develop Energy Savings Products

(81.086 Conservation Research and Development)
Barbara Twigg
Office of Management and Resources
Conservation and Renewable Energy
Washington, DC 20585   (202) 586-8714

Objectives: To conduct a balanced long-term research effort in the areas of buildings, industry, transportation. Grants will be offered to develop and transfer to the non-federal sector various energy conservation technologies.

Types of Assistance: Project Grants.

Uses and Use Restrictions: Assistance may be used in the form of cost-shared contracts, cooperative agreements, or grants to non-profit institutions and organizations to develop and transfer energy conservation technologies to the scientific and industrial communities, state, and local governments.

Money Available Per Year: Grants: $3,700,000.

Range and Average of Financial Assistance: $50,000 to $500,000; Average: $200,000.

* Grants To Work On Solar Energy Products

(81.087 Renewable Energy Research and Development)
Barbara Twigg
Office of Management and Resources
U.S. Department of Energy
Washington, DC 20585   (202) 586-8714

Objectives: To conduct balanced research and development efforts in the following energy technologies; solar buildings, photovoltaics, solar thermal, biomass, alcohol fuels, urban waste, wind, and geothermal. Grants will be offered to develop and transfer to the nonfederal sector various renewable energy technologies.

Types of Assistance: Project Grants.

Uses and Use Restrictions: Assistance may be used to develop and transfer renewable energy technologies to the scientific and industrial communities, state, and local governments.

Money Available Per Year: Grants: $2,100,000.

Range and Average of Financial Assistance: From $10,000 to $100,000.

* Grants To Develop Uses of Fossil Fuels

(81.089 Fossil Energy Research and Development)
Mr. Dwight Mottet
Fossil Energy Program, FE-122
U.S. Department of Energy
Germantown, MD 20545   (301) 903-2787

Objectives: The mission of the Fossil Energy (FE) Research and Development program is to promote the development and use of environmentally and economically superior technologies for supply, conversion, delivery and utilization of fossil fuels. These activities will involve cooperation with industry, DOE Laboratories, universities, and states. Success in this mission will benefit the Nation through lower energy costs, reduced environmental impact, increased technology exports, and reduced dependence on insecure energy sources.

Types of Assistance: Project Grants; Project Grants (Cooperative Agreements).

Uses and Use Restrictions: Emphasis is on fundamental research and technology development.

Money Available Per Year: Grants and cooperative agreements: $86,064,000

Range and Average of Financial Assistance: $30,000 to $26,300,000; $2,967,000.

* Grants To Small Businesses To Develop Energy Information Databases

(81.091 Socioeconomic and Demographic Research, Data and Other Information)
Georgia R. Johnson
U.S. Department of Energy
Forrestal Building
Room 5B-110
Washington, DC 20585   (202) 586-1593

Objectives: (1) To provide financial support for developing and enhancing socioeconomic and demographic research, data, and other information which would help to determine minority energy consumption and usage patterns; (2) to evaluate the percentage of disposable income spent by minorities on energy compared to national usage patterns; (3) to develop policy analysis and economic indicators relating to the Department of Energy's (DOE) policies and programs and for use in the development of assessments for legislative and regulatory actions of DOE and other federal and state agencies; (4) to develop appropriate technical information to assist minority educational institutions and minority businesses; and (5) develop technical information on energy conservation and related efficiency options.

Types of Assistance: Project Grants.

Uses and Use Restrictions: Financial support, in whole or in part, may be provided for: (1) Salaries; (2) materials and supplies; (3) equipment; (4) travel; (5) publication costs; (6) services required for conducting research; (7) assessments; or (8) the development of other information. Restrictions on the use of funds is incumbent upon contract or grant provisions.

Money Available Per Year: Grants: $780,000.

Range and Average of Financial Assistance: Not applicable.

* Grants To Figure out How To Make Money Out of Department of Energy Information and Discoveries

(81.103 Technology Integration)
C. Sink
Office of Technology Development, EM-52
Environmental Restoration and Waste Management
Washington, DC 20545   (301) 903-7928

Objectives: To transfer technologies/information from the U.S. Department of Energy (DOE) to industry, universities, other federal agencies and vice versa, to develop public participation in the nation's environmental, technological needs, and to develop public/private partnership with companies of all sizes.

Types of Assistance: Project Grants (Cooperative Agreements).

Uses and Use Restrictions: Financial assistance is provided in support of the objectives stated above. Restrictions or the use of funds depend on the specific collaborative agreements. Applicants must meet the guidelines established by the Department of Energy.

Money Available Per Year: $13,100,000.

Range and Average of Financial Assistance: $550,000 to $5,500,000.

* Grants To Work With Local Schools To Train Your Workers

(84.228 Educational Partnerships)
Educational Networks Division
Room 502, 555 New Jersey Avenue, NW
Washington, DC 20208-5644   (202) 219-2116

Objectives: To encourage the creation of alliances between public elementary and secondary schools or institutions of higher education and the private sector in order to: (1) Apply the resources of the private and non-profit sectors of the community to the needs of elementary and secondary schools or institutions of higher education in that community to encourage excellence in education; (2) encourage businesses to work with educationally disadvantaged students and with gifted students; (3) apply the resources of communities for the improvement of elementary and secondary education or higher education; and (4) enrich the career awareness of secondary or postsecondary school students and provide exposures to the work of the private sector.

Types of Assistance: Project Grants; Project Grants (Contracts).

Uses and Use Restrictions: An eligible partnership may use funds received under this program for one or more of the following activities: (1) Model cooperative projects designed to apply the resources of the private and non-profit sectors of the community to improve the education of students in the public elementary and secondary schools of the local educational agency or institutions of higher education in that community; (2) projects designed to encourage business concerns and other participants in the eligible partnership to work with educationally disadvantaged students and with gifted students in the elementary and secondary schools of local educational agencies or institutions of higher education; (3) projects designed to encourage business concerns and other participants from the private sector to address the special educational needs of disadvantaged students or gifted and talented students, or both, in public elementary and secondary schools or institutions of higher education; (4) projects designed to enrich the career awareness of public secondary students or postsecondary students through exposure to officers and employees of business concerns and other agencies and organizations participating in the eligible partnership; (5) projects for statewide activities designed to carry out the purpose of this program including the development of model state statutes for the support of cooperative arrangements between the private and non-profit sectors and the local educational agencies or institutions of higher education within the state; (6) special training projects for staff designed to develop the skills necessary to facilitate cooperative arrangements between the private and non-profit sectors and the public elementary and secondary schools of local educational agencies or institutions of higher education; (7) academic internship programs for students or teachers, including if possible the opportunity to earn academic credit, involving activities designed to carry out the purpose of this program; and (8) projects encouraging tutorial and volunteer work in public elementary and secondary schools or institutions of higher education by personnel employed by business concerns and other participants in the eligible partnership.

Money Available Per Year: Grants: $4,135,564.

Range and Average of Financial Assistance: $220,588 to $400,000.

* Grants To Businesses That Employ People With Disabilities

(84.234 Projects with Industry)
Dr. Thomas E. Finch
Rehabilitation Services Administration
Office of Assistant Secretary for Special Education
  and Rehabilitation Services
U.S. Department of Education
Washington, DC 20202   (202) 205-9796

Objectives: To create and expand job and career opportunities for individuals with disabilities in the competitive labor market, to provide appropriate placement resources by engaging private industry in training and placement.

Types of Assistance: Project Grants; Project Grants (Cooperative Agreements).

Uses and Use Restrictions: Funds may be used to support projects to prepare persons with disabilities for gainful employment. Any industrial, business, or commercial enterprise; labor union employer; community rehabilitation program provider; trade association; Indian tribe or tribal organization; designated state unit; or other agency or organization with the capacity to create and expand job opportunities for individuals with disabilities.

Money Available Per Year: (Grants) $22,071,000.

Range and Average of Financial Assistance: Range for continuations $30,000 to $350,000; Average: $140,000. New awards $125,000 to $375,000; $175,000.

* Grants To Local Organizations To Improve The Literacy of Commercial Drivers of Local Businesses

(84.247 Commercial Drivers Education)
Paul Geib, Division of National Programs
Office of the Assistant Secretary for Vocational
  and Adult Education
U.S. Department of Education
400 Maryland Avenue, SW
Washington, DC 20202-7242   (202) 205-5864
or

Carroll F. Towey
Division of Adult Education and Literacy
Office of the Assistant Secretary for Vocational
  and Adult Education
400 Maryland Avenue, SW
Washington, DC 20202-7320   (202) 205-9791

Objectives: To establish and operate adult education programs that increase the literacy skills of eligible commercial drivers to successfully complete the knowledge test requirements under the Commercial Motor Vehicle Safety Act of 1986.

Types of Assistance: Project Grants.

Uses and Use Restrictions: Funds must be used for projects designed to increase the literacy skills of eligible commercial drivers to successfully complete the knowledge test requirements under the Commercial Motor Vehicle Safety Act of 1986.

Money Available Per Year: Grants: $340,000.

Range and Average of Financial Assistance: $10,000 to $250,000.

* Grants to Producers of Honey, Cotton, Rice, Soybeans, Canole, Flaxseed, Mustard Seed, Rapeseed, Safflower, Sunflower Seed, Feed Grains, Wheat, Rye, Peanuts, Tobacco, and Dairy Products.

(10.051 Commodity Loans and Purchases)
Cotton, Grain and Rice Price Support Division
Agricultural Stabilization and Conservation Service
U.S. Department of Agriculture
P.O. Box 2415
Washington, DC 20013   (202) 720-7641

Objectives: To improve and stabilize farm income, to assist in bringing about a better balance between supply and demand of the commodities, and to assist farmers in the orderly marketing of their crops.

Types of Assistance: Direct Payments with Unrestricted Use; Direct Loans.

Uses and Use Restrictions: Price support loans and purchases give farmers a ready means of promoting more orderly marketing. Price support loans to producers are "nonrecourse which means that producers have the option of forfeiting the collateral to CCC at loan maturity if market prices fall below the support level." If market prices are above the support level, producers can repay their loans and market their commodities. If the commodity is stored on the farm, the farmer is responsible for maintaining the quality and quantity of the commodity. Eligible commodities are feed grains, wheat, rice, rye, peanuts, tobacco, and dairy products (purchases only). Eligible commodities for which only loans are available also include honey, upland cotton, extra-long staple cotton, sugar, soybeans, canola, flaxseed, mustard seed, rapeseed, safflower, and sunflower seed. Beginning with the 1986 crop, the Secretary of Agriculture has the authority to permit commodity loan repayments at less than the original loan principal under the "marketing loan" provision. Loan deficiency payments will be offered for 1993-crop feed grains, wheat, rye, upland cotton, rice, soybeans, canola, flaxseed, mustard seed, rapeseed, safflower, sunflower seed, and honey if the loan repayment rates for these commodities are less than the established loan levels. To receive loan deficiency payments, producers must agree to forego obtaining a loan on the eligible quantity. For upland cotton, rice, soybeans, canola, flaxseed, mustard seed, rapeseed, safflower, sunflower seed, and honey; applications for payment must be filed before beneficial interest in the commodity is lost and the payment rate will equal the amount by which the loan rate exceeds the loan repayment rate in effect at the time the application is approved. Upland cotton, rice, soybeans, canola, flaxseed, mustard seed, rapeseed, safflower and sunflower seed loan deficiency payments and any gain realized from repaying a loan at a level lower than the original loan level (marketing loan) for these commodities are subject to a $75,000 per "person" payment limitation. For honey only, for the 1989 and 1990 crops, the value of loan forfeitures or deliveries were limited to $250,000 per "person". The Food, Agriculture, Conservation, and Trade Act of 1990 provides that for honey, each person's total market gains and loan deficiency payments shall be limited as follows: For the 1991 crop year, $200,000; for the 1992 crop year, $175,000; for the 1993 crop year, $150,000; for the 1994

crop year, $125,000; for the 1995 crop year, $100,000; for the 1996 crop year, $75,000; and for the 1997 and 1998 crop years, $50,000. The forfeiture limit for honey for each person for the 1991 through 1994 and subsequent years corresponds to the above amounts.

Money Available Per Year: Commodity purchases: $1,096,976,000; Loans: $8,336,213,000.

Range and Average of Financial Assistance: Direct payments (Purchases): Range not available. Loans: $50 to $76,000,000; Average: $24,288.

* Grants to Producers of Cotton

(10.052 Cotton Production Stabilization)
Deputy Administrator
Policy Analysis
Agricultural Stabilization and Conservation Service
P.O. Box 2415
U.S. Department of Agriculture
Washington, DC 20013   (202) 720-7583

Objectives: To assure adequate production for domestic and foreign demand for fiber, to protect income for farmers, to take into account federal costs, to enhance the competitiveness of U.S. cotton for domestic mill use and export, and to conserve our natural resources.

Types of Assistance: Direct Payments with Unrestricted Use.

Uses and Use Restrictions: To be eligible for 1994 crop program benefits, producers agreed to reduce their historical plantings--farm acreage base--of upland cotton by at least 11.0 percent and of extra long staple (ELS) cotton by at least 15.0 percent. The acreage removed from production must be maintained in approved conservation uses and, except in designated summer fallow and arid regions, one-half must be planted to a cover crop, not to exceed 5 percent of the base. In regions where cover crops must be planted, cost-share assistance is available to producers for establishing a multi-year perennial cover on up to 50 percent of the acreage removed from production and maintained in conservation uses (ACR). The cost-share assistance is equal to 25 percent of the cost for establishing the practice. Once cost-shares are received, the acreage devoted to the perennial cover must be maintained for 3 years after the calendar year in which the practice is established. Benefits include target price "deficiency" payments, which are made on planted acreage less 15 percent of the crop acreage base when the national average market price falls below the established target price. The 1994 target price for upland cotton is 72.9 cents per pound; the ELS cotton target price is 102.0 cents per pound, which is 120 percent of the ELS loan rate. An advance deficiency payment equal to 50 percent of the estimated rate will be made available to producers who request such payment and sign a program contract for the upland cotton program. Upland cotton producers repay loans at the lesser of the loan rate or either the adjusted world price in effect for the week in which the loan redemption occurs or a fixed loan repayment rate if established by the Secretary, but not less than 70 percent of the loan rate.

Money Available Per Year: Direct cash and certificate payments: $363,054,000.

Range and Average of Financial Assistance: Up to $250,000 per person. As of January 11, 1994, the average deficiency payment per producer for the 1992 upland cotton crop was $10,333 and an estimated $6,399 for the 1993 crop. (Cotton, feed grain, wheat and rice deficiency and diversion payments, in total, may not exceed $50,000 to any one person for the 1991 through 1997 crop years. The total of any (1) gains realized by repaying a loan at a level lower than the original loan level; (2) deficiency payments for wheat or feed grains attributable to a reduction in the statutory loan level; and (3) loan deficiency payments may not exceed $75,000 per person for each of the 1991 through 1997 crops. The total payment limitation, which includes inventory reduction payments and payments representing compensation for resource adjustment (other than diversion payments and cost-share assistance) or public access for recreation, combined with the above mentioned payments, is $250,000 per person for each of the 1991 through 1997 crops.)

* Grants To Dairy Farmers Whose Milk Is Contaminated Because of Pesticides

(10.053 Dairy Indemnity Program)
Emergency Operations and Livestock
  Program Division
Agricultural Stabilization and Conservation Service
U.S. Department of Agriculture
P.O. Box 2415
Washington, DC 20013   (202) 720-7673

Objectives: To protect dairy farmers and manufacturers of dairy products who through no fault of their own, are directed to remove their milk or dairy products from commercial markets because of contamination from pesticides which have been approved for use by the federal government. Dairy farmers can also be indemnified because of contamination with chemicals or toxic substances, nuclear radiation or fallout.

Types of Assistance: Direct Payments with Unrestricted Use.

Uses and Use Restrictions: Fair market value for the milk is paid to the dairy farmer who is unable to market because of any of the violating substances, and the fair market value of the dairy product is paid to the manufacturer who is unable to market because of pesticide residue. No payment may be made to any dairy farmer or any manufacturer whose milk or dairy product was removed from the market as a result of his negligence or his willful failure to follow procedures prescribed by the federal government.

Money Available Per Year: Direct payments: $200,000.

Range and Average of Financial Assistance: $88 to $95,000; $40,000.

* Grants to Producers of Corn, Sorghum, Barley, Oats, and Rye

(10.055 Feed Grain Production Stabilization)
Deputy Administrator
Policy Analysis
Agricultural Stabilization and Conservation Service
U.S. Department of Agriculture
P.O. Box 2415
Washington, DC 20013   (202) 720-4418

Objectives: To assure adequate production for domestic and foreign demand, to protect income for farmers, to take into account federal costs, to enhance the competitiveness of United States exports, to combat inflation, to conserve our natural resources, and to comply with statutory requirements.

Types of Assistance: Direct Payments with Unrestricted Use.

Uses and Use Restrictions: To be eligible for 1994 crop program benefits, program participants agree to reduce their historical plantings--crop acreage base--of corn, sorghum, and barley and oats by 0 percent. The acreage removed from feed grain production must be maintained in approved conservation uses. In regions where cover crops must be planted, cost-share assistance is available to producers for establishing a multi-year perennial cover on up to 50 percent of the acreage removed from production and maintained in conservation uses (ACR). The cost-share assistance is equal to 25 percent of the cost for establishing the practice. Once cost-shares are received, the acreage devoted to the perennial cover must be maintained for 3 years after the calendar year in which the practice is established. Benefits include target price protection with deficiency payments. Deficiency payments are made whenever market prices received by producers during the months of September 1994 through January 1995 for corn and sorghum and June 1994 through October 1994 for barley and oats average below the respective target prices. The 1993 target prices per bushel are as follows: Corn $2.75; sorghum $2.61; barley $2.36; and oats $1.45. In addition, to compensate for adjusted commodity price support rates, emergency compensation (also known as Findley) payments may be made, if the average market price falls below the basic price support rate, to provide the same total return to the producer as if price support rates had not been adjusted. The maximum combined payment rate per bushel (deficiency plus emergency compensation) is the difference between the target price and the national average price support rate. The price support rates per bushel are: $1.89 for corn, $1.80 for sorghum, $1.54 for barley, $0.97 for oats, and $1.61 for rye. Producers who request such payments will receive 50 percent of the estimated deficiency payment in cash after a program contract is signed and before compliance with program requirements is met. Program contracts are binding and liquidated damages will be assessed for failure to fulfill the terms of the contract.

Money Available Per Year: Direct cash and certificate payments: $2,017,300,000.

Range and Average of Financial Assistance: Up to $250,000 per person. As of January 11, 1994, the average deficiency payment per producer for the 1992 crop was $5,196 and an estimated $2,765 for the 1993 crop. (Cotton, feed grain, wheat and rice deficiency and diversion payments, in total, may not exceed $50,000 to any one person for the 1991 through 1997 crop years. The total of any (1) gains realized by repaying a loan at a level lower than the original loan level; (2) deficiency payments for wheat or feed grains attributable to a reduction in the statutory loan level; and (3) loan deficiency payments may not exceed $75,000 per person for each of the 1991 through 1997 crops. The total payment limitation, which includes inventory reduction payments and payments representing compensation for resource adjustment (other than diversion payments and cost-share assistance) or public access for recreation, combined with the above mentioned payments, is $250,000 per person for each of the 1991 through 1995 crops.)

* Grants To Producers of Wheat

(10.058 Wheat Production Stabilization)
Deputy Administrator
Policy Analysis
Agricultural Stabilization and Conservation Service
U.S. Department of Agriculture
P.O. Box 2415
Washington, DC 20013   (202) 720-4418

Types of Assistance: Direct Payments with Unrestricted Use.

Uses and Use Restrictions: To be eligible for 1994 crop program benefits, producers are not required to reduce their historical plantings -- crop acreage base -- of wheat. A 0 percent acreage reduction program is in effect. Benefits include target price "deficiency" payments which, under the standard program, are made if wheat prices during the months of June 1994 through October 1994 average below the target price of $4.00 per bushel. In addition, to compensate for adjusted commodity price support rates, emergency compensation (also known as "Findley") payments may be made, if the average market price falls below the basic price support rate, to provide the same total return to the producer as if price support rates had not been adjusted. The maximum payment rate per bushel is the difference between the target price and the national average price support rate of $2.72 per bushel. Producers who request such payments will receive 50 percent of the estimated deficiency payment in cash after a program contract is signed and before compliance with program requirements is met. Program contracts are binding and liquidated damages will be assessed for failure to fulfill the terms of the contract.

Money Available Per Year: Direct cash and certificate payments: $1,969,000,000.

Range and Average of Financial Assistance: Up to $250,000 per person. As of January 11, 1994, the average deficiency payment per producer for the 1992 crop was $2,776 and an estimated $3,629 for the 1993 crop. (Cotton, feed grain, wheat and rice deficiency and diversion payments, in total, may not exceed $50,000 to any one person for the 1991 through 1997 crop years. The total of any (1) gains realized by repaying a loan at a level lower than the original loan level; (2) deficiency payments for wheat or feed grains attributable to a reduction in the statutory loan level; and (3) loan deficiency payments may not exceed $75,000 per person for each of the 1991 through 1997 crops. The total payment limitation, which includes inventory reduction payments and payments representing compensation for resource adjustment (other than diversion payments and cost-share assistance) or public access for recreation, combined with the above mentioned payments, is $250,000 per person for each of the 1991 through 1997 crops.)

* Grants To Producers Of Wool and Mohair

(10.059 National Wool Act Payments)
Manager, Federal Crop Insurance Corporation
U.S. Department of Agriculture
2101 L Street NW, Suite 500
Washington, DC 20250
Mailing address:
Federal Crop Insurance Corporation
U.S. Department of Agriculture

Washington, DC 20250   (202) 254-8460

Objectives: To encourage continued domestic production of wool at prices fair to both producers and consumers in a manner which will assure a viable domestic wool industry in the future.

Types of Assistance: Direct Payments with Unrestricted Use.

Uses and Use Restrictions: Payments when required are made to growers to supplement farm income. No restrictions are placed on the use of these funds.

Money Available Per Year: Total indemnities: $979,412,000; Premium subsidy to farmers through direct writings and reinsured companies: $109,800,000.

Range and Average of Financial Assistance: Level of assistance varies according to policy, crop and indemnities paid.

* Grants To Producers of Rice

(10.065 Rice Production Stabilization)
Deputy Administrator
Policy Analysis
Agricultural Stabilization and
   Conservation Service
U.S. Department of Agriculture
P.O. Box 2415
Washington, DC 20013   (202) 720-7923

Objectives: To assure adequate production for domestic and foreign demand, to protect income for farmers, to take into account federal costs, to enhance the competitiveness of U.S. exports, and to conserve our natural resources.

Types of Assistance: Direct Payments with Unrestricted Use.

Uses and Use Restrictions: The 1994 crop rice program includes a 0 percent acreage reduction program. To be eligible for 1994 crop program benefits, producers must agree to limit 1994 rice acreage to no more than the farms rice base. The acreage removed from rice production must be maintained in approved conservation uses. In regions where cover crops must be planted, cost-share assistance is available to producers for establishing a perennial cover on up to 50 percent of the acreage removed from production and maintained in conservation uses (ACR). The cost-share rate is equal to 25 percent of the cost for establishing the practice. The acreage devoted to the perennial cover must be maintained for 3 years. Benefits include target price "deficiency payments" which are made if rice prices during the first five months of the marketing year (August-December) average below the target price. The target price for the 1994 crop is $10.71 per hundred weight. The maximum deficiency payment rate is the difference between the target price and the national average loan and purchase rate, which is $6.50 per hundred weight for the 1994 crop. Producers who request such payments will receive 50 percent of the estimated deficiency payments in cash after a program contract is signed and before compliance with program requirements is met. Producers may repay loans at a rate which is the lower of the loan rate or the higher of the world price of such rice, as determined by the Secretary, or the loan level times 70 percent. Producers who elect to forego obtaining a loan or purchase agreement on eligible production are eligible to receive loan-deficiency payments. The payment rate is the difference between the loan rate and world price of national-average-quality rice. The payment is available on loan eligible production for which the producer agrees to forego obtaining a loan or purchase agreement. Marketing certificates may be paid to producers if the world price is below the minimum loan repayment level as calculated for national-average-quality rice.

Money Available Per Year: Direct cash and certificate payments: $844,500,000.

Range and Average of Financial Assistance: Up to $250,000 per person. As of January 11, 1994, the average deficiency payment per producer for the 1992 crop was $20,116 and an estimated $10,750 for the 1993 crop. Cotton, feed grain, wheat and rice deficiency and diversion payments, in total, may not exceed $50,000 to any one person for the 1991 through 1997 crop years. The total of any (1) gains realized by repaying a loan at a level lower than the original loan level; (2) deficiency payments for wheat or feed grains attributable to a reduction in the statutory loan level; and (3) loan deficiency payments may not exceed $75,000 per person for each of the 1991 through 1997 crops. The total payment limitation, which includes inventory reduction payments and payments representing compensation for resource adjustment (other than diversion payments and cost-share assistance) or public access for recreation, combined with the above mentioned payments, is $250,000 per person for each of the 1991 through 1997 crops.

* Grants To Feed Livestock in An Emergency

(10.066 Emergency Livestock Assistance)
Emergency Operations and Livestock
 Programs Division
Agricultural Stabilization and
 Conservation Service
U.S. Department of Agriculture
P.O. Box 2415
Washington, DC 20013   (202) 720-5621

Objectives: To provide emergency feed assistance to eligible livestock owners, in a state, county, or area approved by the Executive Vice President, CCC, where because of disease, insect infestation, flood, drought, fire, hurricane, earthquake, hail storm, hot weather, cold weather, freeze, snow, ice, and winterkill, or other natural disaster, a livestock emergency has been determined to exist. These programs also provide feed assistance to eligible livestock owners for the preservation and maintenance of livestock in any county contiguous to a county where a livestock emergency has been determined to exist.

Types of Assistance: Direct Payments with Unrestricted Use.

Uses and Use Restrictions: Direct payments are for unrestricted use. Feed on which cost-sharing is received and CCC-owned feed grain purchased or donated: (a) Must be fed to the producer's livestock; (b) may not be resold; and (c) must be utilized during the established feeding period.

Money Available Per Year: Direct cash payments: $80,000,000.

Range and Average of Financial Assistance: $10 to $50,000; $3,411.

* Grants to Producers of Grain

(10.067 Grain Reserve Program)
Manager, Federal Crop Insurance Corporation
U.S. Department of Agriculture
2101 L Street NW, Suite 500

Washington, DC 20250
Mailing address:
 Federal Crop Insurance Corporation
 U.S. Department of Agriculture
 Washington, DC 20250   (202) 254-8460

Objectives: To insulate sufficient quantities of grain from the market to increase price to farmers. To improve and stabilize farm income and to assist farmers in the orderly marketing of their crops.

Types of Assistance: Direct Payments with Unrestricted Use.

Uses and Use Restrictions: For the 1990 crop wheat reserve and 1992 crop corn, grain sorghum, and barley authorized under the Food, Agriculture, Conservation, and Trade Act of 1990, the loan may be repaid at any time without penalty.

Money Available Per Year: Total indemnities: $979,412,000; Premium subsidy to farmers through direct writings and reinsured companies: $227,026,000.

Range and Average of Financial Assistance: Level of assistance varies according to policy, crop and indemnities paid.

* Loans To Family Farms That Can't Get Credit

(10.437 Interest Assistance Program)
FmHA County Supervisor in the county where the proposed farming operation will be located
or
FmHA
U.S. Department of Agriculture
Washington, DC 20250

Objectives: To aid not larger than family sized farms in obtaining credit when they are temporarily unable to project a positive cash flow without a reduction in the interest rate.

Types of Assistance: Guaranteed/Insured Loans.

Uses and Use Restrictions: Interest Assistance Program can be used on any of the three types of guaranteed loans. The three types and loan purposes are as follows: (1) Farm Ownership (FO) Loans - to buy, improve, or enlarge farms. Uses may include construction, improvement, or repair of farm homes and service buildings; improvement of on-farm water supplies; installation of pollution control or energy conservation measures; and establishing non-agricultural enterprises that help farmers supplement their farm income; (2) Operating Loans (OL) - to pay for items needed for farm operations, including livestock, farm and home equipment, feed, seed, fertilizer, fuel, chemicals, hail and other crop insurance, family living expenses, minor building improvements, water system development, hired labor, pollution abatement, and methods of operation to comply with the Occupational Safety and Health Act; and (3) Soil and Water (SW) - to develop, conserve, or make proper use of land and water resources, including development of wells and other sources of water, irrigation systems, drainage improvements, and improvements associated with forestry, fish farming, land protection, or pollution control. Loan limits are as follows: Real estate loans (FO and SW) - $300,000. For FO and SW loans, the County Supervisor can approve loans up to $260,000, the District Director up to $270,000, and the State Director or designee has the remaining authority to the maximum loan amount of $300,000. Operating (chattel) loans - $400,000. For OL loans, the County Supervisor can approve loans up to $350,000, the

District Director up to $360,000, and the State Director or designee has the full authority of $400,000.

Money Available Per Year: Subsidized Guaranteed Loans: $230,000,000.

Range and Average of Financial Assistance: $1 to $400,000.

* Premium Subsidies To Agriculture

(10.450 Crop Insurance)
Manager
Federal Crop Insurance Corporation
U.S. Department of Agriculture
2101 L Street NW, Suite 500
Washington, DC 20250
Mailing address:
Federal Crop Insurance Corporation
U.S. Department of Agriculture
Washington, DC 20250   (202) 254-8460

Objectives: To promote the national welfare by improving the economic stability of agriculture through a sound system of crop insurance and providing the means for the research and experience helpful in devising and establishing such insurance.

Types of Assistance: Insurance.

Uses and Use Restrictions: For the purpose of encouraging the broadest possible participation in the insurance program, thirty percent of each producer's premium as calculated by the corporation on any coverage under the corporation's and reinsured companies' policies of insurance of up to a maximum of 65 percent of the recorded or appraised yield, as adjusted, shall be paid by the corporation in accordance with Public Law 96-365. Insurance is available on crops in more than 3,000 agricultural counties in 50 states. Producers are not indemnified for losses resulting from negligence or failure to observe good farming practices. Insurance is offered on the following crops and/ or commodities: Almonds, apples, barley, dry beans, beans (canning and processing), citrus, citrus trees, corn for silage/grain, cotton, ELS cotton, cranberries, dry peas, figs, flax, forage production, forage seeding, fresh plums, grain sorghum, grapes, table grapes, hybrid corn seed, hybrid sorghum seed, macadamia nuts, macadamia trees, nursery stock, oats, onions, green peas, peppers, peaches, peanuts, pears, popcorn, potatoes, prunes, raisins, rice, rye, safflower, soybeans, special citrus (CA), stonefruit, sugar beets, sugarcane, sunflowers, sweet corn (canning and freezing), sweet corn (fresh market), tobacco, tomatoes (fresh market), tomatoes (canning and processing), walnuts, and wheat.

Money Available Per Year: Total Indemnities: $1,435,921,000. Premium Subsidy: $690,094,000.

Range and Average of Financial Assistance: Level of assistance varies according to policy, crop and indemnities paid.

State Money and Help For Your Business

Who Can Use State Money?

All states require that funds be used solely by state residents. But that shouldn't limit you to exploring possibilities only in the state in which you currently reside. If you reside in Maine, but Massachusetts agrees to give you $100,000 to start your own business, it would be worth your while to consider moving to Massachusetts. Shop around for the best deal.

Types Of State Money And Help Available

Each state has different kinds and amounts of money and assistance programs available, but these sources of financial and counseling help are constantly being changed. What may not be available this year may very well be available next. Therefore, in the course of your exploration, you might want to check in with the people who operate the business "hotlines" to discover if anything new has been added to the states' offerings.

Described below are the major kinds of programs which are offered by most of the states.

Information

Hotlines or One-Stop Shops are available in many states through a toll-free number that hooks you up with someone who will either tell you what you need to know or refer you to someone who can. These hotlines are invaluable — offering information on everything from business permit regulations to obscure financing programs. Most states also offer some kind of booklet that tells you to how to start-up a business in that state. Ask for it. It will probably be free.

Small Business Advocates operate in all fifty states and are part of a national organization (the National Association of State Small Business Advocates) devoted to helping small business people function efficiently with their state governments. They are a good source for help in cutting through bureaucratic red tape.

Funding Programs

Free Money can come in the form of grants, and works the same as free money from the federal government. You do not have to pay it back.

Loans from state governments work in the same way as those from the federal government — they are given directly to entrepreneurs. Loans are usually at interest rates below the rates charged at commercial institutions and are also set aside for those companies which have trouble getting a loan elsewhere. This makes them an ideal source for riskier kinds of ventures.

Loan Guarantees are similar to those offered by the federal government. For this program, the state government will go to the bank with you and co-sign your loan. This, too, is ideal for high risk ventures which normally would not get a loan.

Interest Subsidies On Loans is a unique concept not used by the federal government. In this case, the state will subsidize the interest rate the bank is charging you. For example, if the bank gives you a loan for $50,000 at 10 percent per year interest, your interest payments will be $5,000 per year. With an interest subsidy you might pay only $2,500 since the state will pay the other half. This is like getting the loan at 5 percent instead of 10 percent.

Industrial Revenue Bonds Or General Obligation Bonds are a type of financing that can be used to purchase only fixed assets, such as a factory or equipment. In the case of Industrial Revenue Bonds the state will raise money from the general public to buy your equipment. Because the state acts as the middleman, the people who lend you the money do not have to pay federal taxes on the interest they charge you. As a result, you get the money cheaper because they get a tax break. If the state issues General Obligation Bonds to buy your equipment, the arrangement will be similar to that for an Industrial Revenue Bond except that the state promises to repay the loan if you cannot.

Matching Grants supplement and abet federal grant programs. These kinds of grants could make an under-capitalized project go forward. Awards usually hinge on the usefulness of the project to its surrounding locality.

Loans To Agricultural Businesses are offered in states with large rural, farming populations. They are available solely to farmers and/or agribusiness entrepreneurs.

Loans To Exporters are available in some states as a kind of gap financing to cover the expenses involved in fulfilling a contract.

Energy Conservation Loans are made to small businesses to finance the installation of energy-saving equipment or devices.

Special Regional Loans are ear-marked for specific areas in a state that may have been hard hit economically or suffer from under-development. If you live in one of these regions, you may be eligible for special funds.

High Tech Loans help fledgling companies develop or introduce new products into the marketplace.

Loans To Inventors help the entrepreneur develop or market new products.

Local Government Loans are used for start-up and expansion of businesses within the designated locality.

Childcare Facilities Loans help businesses establish on-site daycare facilities.

Loans To Women And/Or Minorities are available in almost every state from funds specifically reserved for economically disadvantaged groups.

Many federally funded programs are administered by state governments. Among them are the following programs:

The SBA 7(A) Guaranteed and *Direct Loan* program can guarantee up to 90 percent of a loan made through a private lender (up to $750,000), or make direct loans of up to $150,000.

The SBA 504 establishes Certified Development Companies whose debentures are guaranteed by the SBA. Equity participation of the borrower must be at least 10 percent, private financing 60 percent and CDC participation at a maximum of 40 percent, up to $750,000.

Small Business Innovative Research Grants (SBIR) award between $20,000 to $50,000 to entrepreneurs to support six months of research on a technical innovation. They are then eligible for up to $500,000 to develop the innovation.

Small Business Investment Companies (SBIC) license, regulate and provide financial assistance in the form of equity financing, long-term loans, and management services.

Community Development Block Grants are available to cities and counties for the commercial rehabilitation of existing buildings or structures used for business, commercial, or industrial purposes. Grants of up to $500,000 can be made. Every $15,000 of grant funds invested must create at least one full-time job, and at least 51 percent of the jobs created must be for low and moderate income families.

Farmers Home Administration (FmHA) Emergency Disaster Loans are available in counties where natural disaster has substantially affected farming, ranching or aquaculture production.

FmHA Farm Loan Guarantees are made to family farmers and ranchers to enable them to obtain funds from private lenders. Funds must be used for farm ownership, improvements, and operating purposes.

FmHA Farm Operating Loans to meet operating expenses, finance recreational and nonagricultural enterprises, to add to family income, and to pay for mandated safety and pollution control changes are available at variable interest rates. Limits are $200,000 for an insured farm operating loan and $400,000 for a guaranteed loan.

FmHA Farm Ownership Loans can be used for a wide range of farm improvement projects. Limits are $200,000 for an insured loan and $300,000 for a guaranteed loan.

FmHA Soil And Water Loans must be used by individual farmers and ranchers to develop, conserve, and properly use their land and water resources and to help abate pollution. Interest rates are variable; each loan must be secured by real estate.

FmHA Youth Project Loans enable young people to borrow for income-producing projects sponsored by a school or 4H club.

Assistance Programs

Management Training is offered by many states in subjects ranging from bookkeeping to energy conservation.

Business Consulting is offered on almost any subject. Small Business Development Centers are the best source for this kind of assistance.

Market Studies to help you sell your goods or services within or outside the state are offered by many states. They all also have State Data Centers which not only collect demographic and other information about markets within the state, but also have access to federal data which can pinpoint national markets. Many states also provide the services of graduate business students at local universities to do the legwork and analysis for you.

Business Site Selection is done by specialists in every state who will identify the best place to locate a business.

Licensing, Regulation, And Permits information is available from most states through "one-stop shop" centers by calling a toll-free number. There you'll get help in finding your way through the confusion of registering a new business.

Employee Training Programs offer on-site training and continuing education opportunities.

Research And Development assistance for entrepreneurs is a form of assistance that is rapidly increasing as more and more states try to attract high technology-related companies. Many states are even setting up clearing-houses so that small businesses can have one place to turn to find expertise throughout a statewide university system.

Procurement Programs have been established in some states to help you sell products to state, federal, and local governments.

Export Assistance is offered to identify overseas markets. Some states even have overseas offices to drum up business prospects for you.

Assistance In Finding Funding is offered in every state, particularly through regional Small Business Development Centers. They will not only identify funding sources in the state and federal governments but will also lead you through the complicated application process.

Special Help For Minorities And Women is available in almost every state to help boost the participation of women and minorities in small business ventures. They offer special funding programs and, often, one-on-one counseling to assure a start-up success.

Venture Capital Networking is achieved through computer databases that hook up entrepreneurs and venture capitalists. This service is usually free of charge. In fact, the demand for small business investment opportunities is so great that some states require the investor to pay to be listed.

Inventors Associations have been established to encourage and assist inventors in developing and patenting their products.

Annual Governors' Conferences give small business people the chance to air their problems with representatives from state agencies and the legislature.

Small Business Development Centers (SBDCs), funded jointly by the federal and state governments, are usually associated with the state university system. SBDCs are a god-send to small business people. They will not only help you figure out if your business project is feasible, but also help you draw up a sensible business plan, apply for funding, and check in with you frequently once your business is up and running to make sure it stays that way.

Tourism programs are prominent in states whose revenues are heavily dependent on the tourist trade. They are specifically aimed at businesses in the tourist industries.

Small Business Institutes at local colleges use senior level business students as consultants to help develop business plans or plan expansions.

Technology Assistance Centers help high tech companies and entrepreneurs establish new businesses and plan business expansions.

On-Site Energy Audits are offered free of charge by many states to help control energy costs and improve energy efficiency for small businesses. Some states also conduct workshops to encourage energy conservation measures.

Minority Business Development Centers offer a wide range of services from initial counseling on how to start a business to more complex issues of planning and growth.

Business Information Centers (BICs) provide the latest in high-tech hardware, software, and telecommunications to help small businesses get started. BIC is a place where business owners and aspiring business owners can go to use hardware/software, hard copy books, and publications to plan their business, expand an existing business, or venture into new business areas. Also, on-site counseling is available.

U.S. Small Business Administration (SBA) Programs

The SBA offices listed under each state can provide you with detailed information on the following programs:

Small Business Innovative Research Grants (SBIR): Phase I awards between $20,000 to $50,000 to entrepreneurs to support six months of research on a technical innovation. Phase II grants are an additional $500,000 for development. Private sector investment funds must follow.

International Trade Loans: Guaranteed long-term loans through private lenders to develop or expand export markets, or to recover from the effects of import competition. Maximum guaranteed loan is $1,000,000 for fixed assets and an additional $250,000 for working capital and/or export revolving line of credit.

Contract Loan: Short-term loans are available to small businesses to finance the costs of labor and materials on contracts for which the proceeds are assignable. Program guarantees up to 90 percent of loans not in excess of $750,000. Qualifying small businesses must be in business for at least 12 calendar months prior to the date of the loan application.

General Contractor Loans: Small general construction contractors may obtain short-term loans or loan guarantees for residential or commercial construction or rehabilitation of property to be sold. The SBA will guarantee up to 90 percent of qualifying loans made by private lenders up to a maximum of $750,000. Direct loans can be up to $150,000.

7(a) Loan Guaranty Program: This program is used to fund the varied long-term needs of small businesses. It is designed to promote small business formation and growth by guaranteeing long-term loans to qualified firms. Can guarantee up to $750,000, generally between 70%-90% of the loan value, at an interest rate not to exceed 2.75 over the prime lending rate. Maturities are up to 10 years for working capital; up to 25 years for fixed assets.

7(a) Loan Guaranty Program
Low Documentation Loan Program (LowDoc): Purpose is to reduce the paperwork involved in loan requests of $100,000 or less. A one-page application is used and it relies on the strength of the individual applicant's character and credit history.

7(a) Loan Guaranty Program
GreenLine Program: Intended to finance short-term, working-capital needs of small businesses. Loan advances are usually made against a borrower's certified level of inventory and accounts payable.

7(a) Loan Guaranty Program
Vietnam-Era and Disabled Veteran Loan Program: Assists disabled veterans of any era who can't secure business financing from private sector or other guaranty loan sources. Veterans can apply for loans to establish a small business or expand an existing small business. The maximum is $150,000.

7(a) Loan Guaranty Program
Handicapped Assistance Loans: Assists individuals with disabilities and public/private nonprofit organizations for the employment of the handicapped. Financing is available for starting/acquiring or operating a small business. There are 2 programs of assistance: HAL-1 and HAL-2.

> ***HAL-1:*** Financial assistance is available to state and federal-chartered organizations that operate in the interest of disabled individuals. Applicants must provide evidence that the business is operated in the interest of handicapped individuals.

> ***HAL-2:*** Financial assistance is provided to handicapped persons who provide evidence that their business is a for-profit operation, qualifies as a small business, is 100% owned by 1 or more handicapped individuals, and the handicapped owner(s) must actively participate in managing the business.

7(a) Loan Guaranty Program
Women's Prequalification Loan Program: Provides women business owners a pre-authorized loan guaranty commitment. It provides a quick response to loan requests of $250,000 or less.

7(a) Loan Guaranty Program
Secondary Market: Lenders who hold business loans guaranteed by the SBA may improve profitability and liquidity by selling the guaranteed portions of those loans in the secondary market. Banks, savings and loan companies/ credit unions and pension funds, and insurance companies are frequent buyers.

8(a) Participant Loan Programs: Makes financial assistance available to 8(a) certified firms. Applicants must be participants in the 8(a) Program and eligible for contractual assistance. Loans can be made directly or through lending institutions under the agency's immediate participation or guaranty programs. Loans may be used for facilities/equipment or working capital.

7(m) MicroLoan Demonstration Program: Aimed at small businesses needing small-scale financing/technical assistance for start-up or expansion. Short-term loans of up to $25,000 are made to small businesses for the purchase of machinery and equipment, furniture and fixtures, inventory, supplies and working capital.

502 Local Development Company Program: Provides long-term, fixed asset financing through certified development companies. Proceeds are provided as follows: 50% by an unguaranteed bank loan, 40% by an SBA guaranteed debenture, 10% by the small business customer. The maximum SBA debenture is $1 million.

504 Certified Development Company Program: Provides long-term, fixed asset financing through certified development companies. Proceeds are provided as follows: 50% by an unguaranteed bank loan, 40% by an SBA guaranteed debenture, 10% by the small business customer. The maximum SBA debenture is $1 million.

Surety Bond Program
Prior Approval Program: Aimed at small construction/service contractors; surety/insurance companies; minority/women's groups; federal/state agencies; state insurance depts.; federal/state and other procurement officials.

Surety Bond Program
Preferred Surety Bond (PSB) Program: Aimed at small construction and service contractors; surety/insurance companies; minority and women's groups; federal/state agencies; state

insurance depts.; federal and state and other procurement officials. The decision to issue a surety bond guarantee is made by participating sureties. There are participating sureties authorized by SBA to issue/monitor and service bonds without prior SBA approval. SBA guarantees surety bonds for construction, service/supply contracts up to $1.25 million.

Export Working Capital Program (EWCP): Replaces the Export Revolving Line of Credit Program. EWCP will allow up to a 90% guarantee on private-sector loans of up to $750,000 for working capital. Loans can be for single or multiple export sales and can be extended for pre-shipment working capital and post-shipment exposure coverage.

Disaster Assistance Loan Program: A disaster-assistance loan program for nonagricultural victims. Eligibility is based on financial criteria. Interest rates fluctuate according to statutory formulas. There is a lower rate available to applicants without credit available elsewhere, not to exceed 4%, and a higher interest rate for those with credit available elsewhere, not to exceed 8%.

Disaster Assistance to Businesses
Loans for Physical Damage: Available to qualified businesses for uninsured losses up to $1.5 million for businesses of any size to repair/replace business property to pre-disaster conditions. Loans may be used to replace/repair equipment, fixtures, inventory, and leasehold improvements.

Disaster Assistance to Businesses
Economic Injury Disaster Loan (EIDL): For businesses that sustain economic injury as a result of a disaster. Working capital loans are made to help businesses pay ordinary/necessary expenses which would have been payable barring disaster. Maximum loan amounts is $1.5 million EIDL and physical damage loans combined unless the business meets the criteria for major source of employment.

Disaster Assistance to Businesses
Loan for Major Source of Employment (MSE):
For business, large and small, and nonprofit organizations. The $1.5 million limit may be waived for businesses that employ 250 or more in an affected area.

Disaster Assistance to Individual Homeowners and Renters:
Real Property: Loans available to qualified homeowner/renter applicants for uninsured losses up to $200,000 to repair/restore a primary residence to pre-disaster condition. Homeowners may apply for an additional 20% for disaster mitigation. This is a long-term program for individual disaster losses.

Disaster Assistance to Individuals Homeowners and Renters:
Personal Property: Loans available to qualified homeowner/renter applicants for uninsured losses up to $40,000 to repair/replace personal property such as clothing, furniture, cars, etc.

Government Contracting
Certificate of Competency: Helps small businesses to receive government contracts by providing an appeal process to low-bidder businesses denied government contracts by contracting officers for perceived lack of ability to satisfactorily perform.

Government Contracting
Prime Contract: Program increases small business opportunities in the federal acquisition process through initiation of small business set-asides, identification of new small business sources, counseling small businesses on how to do business with the federal government, and assessment of compliance with the Small Business Act through surveillance reviews.

Government Contracting
Breakout Program: Promotes/influences and enhances the break-out of historically sole-source items for full and open competition in order to effect significant savings to the federal government.

Government Contracting
Natural Resources Sales Assistance Program:
Timber Sales: Set-aside program maintains small businesses in the forest products industry by providing them with preferential bidding opportunities for purchasing timber offered by the federal government. Joint operation of the SBA and federal timber-selling agencies throughout the U.S.

National Small Business Tree Planting Program: Allocates grants to the states/trust territories for the purpose of contracting with small businesses to plant trees on land owned and controlled by state/local governments. Federal dollars are matched by community funds.

Government Contracting
Procurement Automated Source System (PASS): A computerized data base of small businesses nationwide which are interested in federal procurement opportunities. Information on each company includes a summary of capabilities, ownership and qualifications.

Small Business Technology Transfer Program (STTR) Pilot Program: This is similar in philosophy and objectives to the SBIR program. It has a requirement that the small firm competing for the Small Business Technology Transfer Program (STTR) Research and Development (R&D) project must collaborate with a nonprofit research institution. This is a joint venture project from the initial bid submission to project completion. Available to small high-tech R&D firms.

Alabama

* Southern Development Council
Everett Strong
401 Adams Ave. #680   205-264-5441
Montgomery, AL 36130   Fax: 205-264-6712

State of Alabama Economic Development Loan Fund: Favorable, long-term, fixed rates for land and building, construction, machinery and equipment, renovation/ expansion, and working capital, for manufacturing only. $400,000 maximum, $35,000 minimum for any single project. Provides 40 percent of financing needs, 60 percent to be provided through private lender or owner equity. Can be used with Industrial Revenue Bonds.

SBA 504: For any type of business. Provides loans using 50 percent conventional bank financing, 40 percent Small Business Administration (SBA) involvement through Certified Development Companies, and 10 percent owner equity injection. A fixed asset loan, usually below market. Maximum amount $750,000, minimum $50,000. Loan can be used for land, building, construction, renovation/ expansion, and machinery and equipment.

SBA 7(a) Loan Guarantee: Guarantees up to 90 percent of a loan made through a private lender, up to a maximum of $750,000. Can be used for working capital, inventory, machinery and equipment, and land and building. Can be used for debt refinancing if lender is changed to another bank. Available only to those unable to obtain a loan from conventional sources.

Alabama's Economic Development Float Loan Program: A short term (12 months) "gap financing" at below market rates. The Program allows the Alabama Dept. of Economic and Community Affairs (ADECA) to lend appropriated Community Development Block Grant (CDBG) program funds. The objective is to assist in the creation and retention of jobs for low/moderate income persons. Funds can be used for purchasing land/buildings and equipment; site improvements; construction and renovation of buildings or operating capital. Must present a letter of credit to ADECA for collateral. The maximum is $10,000,00 for any single project; minimum is $1,000,000 for any single project; and $2,500,000 minimum for total amount of project. Eligible business are warehousing/ distribution centers, or other projects deemed to have significant economic impact. A minimum of 1 new job must be created per $10,000 of funds in the project. At least 51% of the jobs created must go to people from low/moderate incomes.

* Alabama Development Office
Sherman Shores
401 Adams Ave. #600   205-242-0400
Montgomery, AL 36130   Fax: 205-264-6712

Appalachian Regional Commission Grant: 205-242-5446
Provides supplemental funding for economic development projects under its Jobs and Private Investment Program. Funds, which supplement federal or state-administered federal funds, can be used to reduce the local matching requirement to a minimum of 20 percent of total project cost. Eligible activities include access roads, water and sewer system installation, rail spurs, and dock facilities.

State Industrial Development Authority Bonds: 205-242-0434
Interest free loans are available to qualified applicants to finance a portion of the cost of construction of speculative buildings intended for industrial use. Qualified applicants must be city or county industrial development boards. No loan may be greater than 25 percent of the anticipated total cost of the building.

State Industrial Site Preparation Grants: 205-242-0475
Grants can be made to counties, municipalities, local industrial development boards, airport authorities, and economic development councils organized as public corporations to pay a portion of the costs of site improvements on land to which they hold the title in order to attract new industry or to assist an existing industry in expansion.

EDA Funds: 205-242-5488
The Economic Development Administration (EDA) of the United States Department of Commerce may provide funds for industrial development in the form of grants and loans for technical assistance, public works, and business loan guarantees.

Industrial Revenue Bonds: Long-term loans with interest rates below conventional rates for land and building acquisition, construction, and machinery and equipment for manufacturing facilities. $10 million maximum. Can finance 100 percent of project.

* State Treasurer
Linked Deposits Office
Lisa Cook
204 Alabama State House
Montgomery, AL 36130   205-242-7517

The Wallace Plan For Linked Deposits/Small Business
Loan: 205-242-7535
Lower (usually by 2 percent) than conventional rate loan. Can be used for land and buildings, equipment, repairs/ renovations, rent, utilities, insurance, taxes, legal or accounting fees, wages, inventory. Any small business in Alabama with less that 150 employees is eligible and has debts equal to or greater than 25 percent of assets. One job must be created for each $15,000 of loan amount. Loans above $250,000 must create one job for every $10,000 of loan. Deposits are placed for a two-year period.

The Wallace Plan For Linked Deposits/ Agricultural Loan:
      205-242-7535
Lower (usually by 2%) than conventional rate loan can be used for feed, seed, fertilizer, chemicals, veterinary or legal/accounting fees, energy costs, crop insurance, equipment purchases, harvesting expense, labor, land rent, livestock, and repair costs. Any person, corporation, or partnership engaged in the production of agricultural products that derives at least 70 percent of their income from farming is eligible. Loans are up to $100,000 for a maximum term of one year. May apply every four years. Must have debts equal to or greater than 25 percent of assets, and have interest cost as a substantial portion of expenses.

This is a two-part program: 1) Mortgage - low down payment financing program for first time buyers; 2) Savings Plan - competitive, premium returns for first time home buyers.

* Small Business Administration
2121 Eighth Ave. N, Suite 200   205-731-1344
Birmingham, AL 35202-2398   Fax: 205-731-1404
See the chapter introduction for a description of SBA programs.

Alaska

---

* Department of Commerce and Economic Development (DCED)
P.O. Box 110804
Juneau, AK 99811-0804   907-465-2017
or

Yarmon Investments
840 K St., #201
Anchorage, AK 99501   907-276-4466
The Polaris Fund, L.P.: Provides equity capital to young companies whose ideas and talents can lead to exceptional growth in sales and profits. They make their initial assessment based on a business plan which the Department of Commerce and Economic Development (DCED), or a Small Business Development Center can assist you with.

Division of Investments   907-465-2510 Juneau
          907-562-3779 Anchorage
Small Business and Economic Development Revolving Loan Fund: Financing is available to small businesses that are located within rural areas for industrial or commercial ventures to support the start-up and expansion of businesses that will create significant long-term employment and help diversify the economy. Interest rates are below the prevailing market rates. Loan amounts from $10,000 to $150,000.

Small Business Loan Assumption Program: Assists purchasers in the assumption of an existing small business loan. Factors considered are ability to provide sufficient collateral and have knowledge of Alaska economic conditions, business potential for growth, ability to repay the loan, and potential to create more jobs and provide additional services to the community.

Commercial Fishing Loan Program
Permit, Vessel and Gear Loans: Direct loans to individuals up to $100,000 at 10.5 percent interest for up to 15 years. Loans may be made to individuals who have been State residents for a continuous period of two years immediately preceding the date of application, do not have occupational opportunities available other than commercial fishing, or are economically dependent on commercial fishing for a livelihood, and for whom commercial fishing has been a traditional way of life in Alaska. Funds may be used to facilitate the repair, restoration or upgrade of exiting vessels and gear, for purchase of limited entry permits, gear and vessels.

Limited Entry Permits Loan Program: Loans up to $300,000 at 10.5 percent interest for up to 15 years are made to individual commercial fisherman who have been State residents for the two years immediately preceding the date of application and have held a limited entry permit, commercial fishing or crew member license for the year preceding the date of application. Applicants whose eligibility have been affected by the Exxon oil spill in 1989 should contact the division for further information.

SPAR Spill Prevention and Response   907-465-5250
Underground Storage Tank Assistance Fund: Assists owners of underground storage tanks to test, assess, clean up, and upgrade underground storage tanks. Grants and reimbursement programs are available. Reimbursement for tank testing is available for up to 50 percent of cost, not to exceed $300 per tank, maximum of $1,200 per facility. For site assessment, 50 percent of cost not to exceed $800 per tank, maximum of $2,300 per facility. For cleanup, grants of up to $1 million to cover 90 percent of cost, and no-interest loan for remaining 10 percent. For upgrade or closure, 60 percent of eligible costs up to a grant maximum of $60,000.

* Alaska Industrial Development and Export Authority (AIDEA)
480 West Tudor Rd.   907-561-8050
Anchorage, AK 99503-6690   Fax: 907-561-8998
Business Assistance Program: Provides up to 80% guarantee of the principal balance to the financial institution making the loan. Can make project financing/ refinancing, working capital loans available for projects that might not otherwise be financed. Guarantees up to $1 million are made on loans for real property/ equipment or working capital for projects that stabilize the economic base or create or maintain employment. A new program established by the Legislature targets entrepreneurs in rural areas and provides a streamlined approval process for guarantees on loans of $75,000 or less.

Development Finance Program: To be eligible for funding, a project must be essential for the economic well being of an area and must produce adequate revenues to repay the bonds sold to finance the project. The Alaska Industrial Development and Export Authority (AIDEA) works closely with local governments and approves projects compatible with the local economy and supported by the community. When projects require financing of more than $10 million in bonds, legislative approval is necessary.

Export Assistance Program: Designed to facilitate international trade. Program offers guarantees to financial institutions which provide exporters with pre-shipment/ post-shipment loans. Guarantees may total up to 90% of the transaction plus interest or $1 million, whichever is less.

Tax-Exempt Umbrella Bond (Loan Participation) Program: Working through financial institutions, the Alaska Industrial Development and Export Authority (AIDEA) participates up to 80% in permanent financing for public use projects such as ports/airports and docks. Borrowers apply at a qualified bank; the bank applies to AIDEA. Bank retains a minimum of 20% share in the principal amount. AIDEA participation limit is 80% or up to $10 million. Terms can be up to 15 or 25 years based on a 75% loan to value ratio. The project may not exceed 90% of the cost of the project or 75% of the appraised value of the project, whichever is less, unless the amount of the loan in excess of this limit is federally insured or guaranteed or is insured by a qualified mortgage insurance company.

Taxable Umbrella Bond (Loan Participation) Program: Working through financial institutions, the Alaska Industrial Development and Export Authority (AIDEA) participates up to 80% in permanent financing for business enterprises such as hotels/shopping centers, office buildings/ warehouses, and airplanes. The project may be newly constructed/newly acquired or refinanced. Borrowers apply at taxable bonds; the bank applies to AIDEA. The bank retains a minimum of 20% share in the principal amounts. AIDEA participation limit is 80% or up to $10 million. Terms can be up to 15 or 25 years based on a 75% loan to value ratio. The project may not exceed 90% of the cost of the project or 75% of the appraised value of the project, whichever is less, unless the amount of the loan in excess of this limit if federally insured or guaranteed or is insured by a qualified mortgage insurance company.

* Agricultural Stabilization and Conservation Service

State Executive Director
800 W. Evergreen
Suite 216
Palmer, AK 99645   907-745-7982

Agricultural Conservation Grant Program: This program was established to solve soil, water, and related resource problems in farming. Persons eligible are those that have produced agricultural products in commercial quantities. Up to 75 percent of costs of implementing conservation practices (windbreaks, grass waterways, minimum tillage, slope management, grass seeding, tree planting, woodlot improvement, etc.) are eligible. Maximum of $3,500 per applicant per year. Not a "start-up" type of grant.

* Farmers Home Administration

634 S. Bailey
Suite 103   907-745-2176
Palmer, AK 99645   Fax: 907-745-5398

Farm Ownership Loans and Operating Loans: For established farms, generally inside the "railbelt" region. Guaranteed loans up to $300,000 for ownership; $400,000 for operating loans. Insured loans up to $200,000 for ownership as well as operating loans. Must be able to demonstrate ability to farm and to repay the loan, but unable to obtain sufficient credit elsewhere.

Business and Industrial Loans: Assistance to individuals, corporations, public or private organizations in a rural area or city of less than 50,000 population, to obtain quality loans for economic development. Nearly any purpose except recreational or tourist type projects are eligible. Loan guarantees of up to 90 percent. Loans may be up to $10 million. Projects which create or save jobs have the highest priority.

* Alaska Department of Natural Resources

Division of Agriculture
P.O. Box 949
Palmer, AK 99645-0949   907-745-7200

Agricultural Revolving Loan Fund: Available to individual farmers, ranchers, homesteaders, partnerships or corporations who are Alaska residents and can demonstrate experience in the farming business. Provides direct short term loans (1-year) up to $200,000. Product processing and land clearing loans up to $250,000, farm development loans up to $1 million. Interest rates at 8 percent with varying pay back periods.

* Department of Community and Regional Affairs

Rural Development Fund
333 W. 4th Ave. #220
Anchorage, AK 99501-2341

Anchorage:	907-269-4500; Fax: 907-269-4520
Bethel:	907-543-3475
Dilingham:	907-842-5135
Fairbanks:	907-452-7126
Juneau:	907-465-4814
Kotzebue:	907-442-3696
Kodiak:	907-486-5736
Nome:	907-443-5457

Entrepreneur Rural Development Fund: Available to small enterprises at least six months old or where the owner has considerable experience in the same business. A maximum of $25,000 may be borrowed for construction, purchase of equipment, inventory, and working capital.

Lender Participation Rural Development Fund: Matches other lenders in the financing of large projects than that of the Entrepreneur fund. Up to $100,000 may be borrowed as long as the business is able to raise an equal amount from bank financing or other sources and can explain why more private funds are not available.

Child Care Programs Coordinator:
Child Care Grant Program: Grants, and technical assistance in grant expenditures and recordkeeping are available. Must have a current Alaska child care license, participate in the Day Care Assistance Program (municipalities which have licensed child care facilities) and provide child care under an attendance payment policy. Funds can be used for staff wages, staff training, food for the children, toys and equipment for the children, and parent involvement activities.

* Alaska Energy Authority

Loan Officer
P.O. Box 190869
701 East Tudor Rd.
Anchorage, AK 99519-0869   907-561-7877

Bulk Fuel Revolving Loan Fund: Assists communities in purchasing bulk fuel oil. A private individual who has a written endorsement from the government body of the community is eligible. Loan amount may not exceed 90 percent of the wholesale price of the fuel being purchased. Maximum loan amount is $50,000. Loan must be repaid within one year.

* Community Enterprise Development Corporation (CEDC)
1577 C St., Suite 304
Anchorage, AK 99501   907-274-5400
Fisheries Boat and Equipment Loan Program: Assists Western
Alaska coastal residents to enter or remain in the area's
commercial fishers. Boat and equipment loans of up to $25,000
at 12 percent interest. Applicants must reside in a western Alaska
village from Cape Seppings to Port Heiden, and provide 10
percent equity and all program processing costs. Priority is given
to those fishing under utilized fisheries and new entrants to
commercial fisheries.

Rural Development Loan Fund: Direct loans ranging from
$10,000 to $150,000 at 7 percent interest to rural individuals or
organizations. Funds may be used for a wide variety of purposes
including land, facility and equipment acquisition, construction
and expansion, business acquisition, purchase of supplies, and
working capital and start-up costs.

Direct Financing: Direct financing through equity investments
and loans are made to business enterprises. To improve the
economic well-being of communities, families and individuals in
rural Alaska by promoting efficient, productive and self-
sustaining business enterprises. Participation available to Native
profit organizations serving communities with low incomes. Also
provides information and technical assistance in business
development and management.

* Chief of Industry Services and Trade
National Oceanic and Atmospheric Administration
National Marine Fisheries Services
P.O. Box 21668
Juneau, AK 99802-1668   907-586-7224
*Fisheries Development Grants and Cooperative Agreements
Program:* Emphasis is on the development of the groundfish
resources off Alaska. Some work also underway on Alaska trade
issues, aquaculture, product development and product quality
assurance. A resource for serious fisheries development pilot
projects, large and small. Good resource for fisheries
development pilot project. Annual application period occurs in
winter. Each year the agency publishes priorities for types of
projects based on industry needs.

* Railbelt Community Development Corp.
619-Warehouse Ave., #256
Anchorage, AK 99501   907-277-5161
*Small Business Administration (SBA) Business Expansion Loan
Program -SBA 504 Program:* Loan is provided by the Railbelt
Community Development Corporation. Provides fixed-rate, long-
term financing to small business when expansion will create or
maintain job opportunities. Business must be an established,
healthy small business unable to obtain private funds for the
entire amount of a proposed expansion project. Fund up to 40
percent of a project's cost to a maximum of $750,000 at a fixed
rate below market interest rate, 50 percent conventional
financing, 10 percent owner equity. Funds may be used for land
or building purchase, new building construction and/or building
rehabilitation, machinery and equipment purchase, or leasehold
improvements.

* Alaska Commercial Fishing and Agriculture Bank (CFAB)
P.O. Box 92070
Anchorage, AK 99509   907-276-2007
Established by Alaska Statute, CFAB is a private lending
cooperative in which borrowers become members. Loans may be
made for harvesting, marketing, or processing of fish or
agriculture products. Interest rates are determined by the periodic
sale of Farm Credit bonds in the national market.

* Alaska State ASCS Office
State Executive Director
800 W. Evergreen, #216
Palmer, AK 99645   907-745-7982
Forestry Incentive Program: Cost sharing eligible to non-
industrial forest landowners with a minimum of 10 acres of
forest land. Up to 65 percent of costs of implementing forest
practices (tree planting, timber stand improvement, and site
preparation for natural regeneration). Maximum of $10,000 per
applicant per year.

* Small Business Administration (SBA)
222 West 8th Ave.
P.O. Box 67   907-271-4022
Anchorage, AK 99513-7559   Fax: 907-271-4545
See the chapter introduction for a description of SBA programs.

Arizona

* Arizona Office of Economic Development
Business Finance Unit
Department of Commerce
3800 N. Central, #1500
Phoenix, AZ 85012   602-280-1341
Community Development Block Grant: Regional grants are
awarded to communities for development projects such as water,
wastewater, community facilities, streets and curbs. Communities
then loan the money to business for the projects. State Set-Aside
Grants work the same way except they are for economic
development in rural communities.

Eximbank Guarantees and Insurance: Conventional bank loan to
finance production and shipment of goods for export guaranteed
up to 90 percent of the bank loan by the U.S. Export-Import
Bank. The Federal Credit Insurance Administration writes an
insurance policy guaranteeing repayment if oversees buyer does
not pay due to political risk.

Revolving Energy Loans: Companies with a minimum of two
years of business operations, engaged in the manufacture of
energy-conserving or energy-related products, or those installing
renewable energy or energy conserving products in their own
facilities. Funds may be used for fixed asset plant expansion for
manufacturers of energy-related products, energy-conserving
retrofits, or short term contract financing of production of
energy-related products. Loan amounts range from $50,000 to
$500,000. Interest rates are fixed.

Farmers Home Administration (FHA)
602-640-5086; 602-640-5088
Loan Guarantees: A commercial bank loan guaranteed up to 90 percent by the FHA. Minimum guarantee is $500,000.

Economic Development Administration 602-379-3750
Loan Guarantees: A commercial bank loan guaranteed up to 80 percent by the EDA.

* Small Business Administration (SBA)
2828 N. Central Ave., #800 602-640-2316
Phoenix, AZ 85004-1025 Fax: 602-640-2360
SBA 502: Fixed asset loan. Maximum loan amount is $750,000. SBA guarantees up to 85-90 percent of the loan. Less restrictive job creation requirements than the SBA 504 program.

See the chapter introduction for a description of SBA programs.

Arkansas

* Arkansas Development Finance Authority (ADFA)
100 Main St., Suite 200 501-682-5908
Little Rock, AR 72201-8023 Fax: 501-682-5859
Industrial Development Bond Guaranty Program: Offers taxable and tax exempt bond financing to both small and large businesses. Umbrella bonds, available to small businesses, spread the costs of the bond issue among all of the borrowers. ADFA also can provide interim financing for approved projects awaiting bond issuance. Available to manufacturing facilities.

Export Finance: Short-term loans to businesses based on export transactions. Financing is provided through the exporter's local bank which funds 10 percent of the loan value.

Tax Credit Program: Assists in the development of rental housing for owners of low income rental housing.

* Arkansas Industrial Development Commission
Community Development Division
One State Capitol Mall 501-682-1211
Little Rock, AR 72291 Fax: 501-682-7341
Industrial Revenue Bonds: Provides guarantees for local governments which issue bonds for local industrial development such as infrastructure development, new or expanding industries, downtown revitalization of public works. Maximum guarantee is $2 million with a term of 10 to 15 years.

Enterprise Zone Program 501-682-7310
Established to stimulate growth and create jobs in areas with high poverty, unemployment, or other economic distress. Provides tax incentives designed to encourage new business locations and expansions in designated geographic areas where there are serious economic problems. Eligible firms are manufacturing, warehouse operations employing 100 or more (no retail sales), and computer firms.

Community Assistance Division 501-682-5193
Community Development Block Grants (CDBG)
State Economic Infrastructure Fund: CDBG Funds have been granted to communities for improving the quality of life for lower to moderate income families. Grant funds are used by the community which make locating and expansion of businesses by providing utility extensions and capacity expansions, building rehabilitation, airport expansions, etc.

Economic Development Set-Aside: 501-682-1151
Portions of the CDBG fund have enabled communities to take advantage of specific economic development including industrial locations and expansion. Projects include water and sewer systems, fire protection, and flood control. The community loans the funds they receive to businesses for development and finance job-creating activities.

* Arkansas Science and Technology Authority
100 Main St.
Suite 450 (Technology Center)
Little Rock, AR 72201 501-324-9006
Promotes science and technology in both the public and private sectors and works to support scientific research and job creating technology development.

Applied Research Grant Programs: For companies in need of research and development and would welcome working with an Arkansas college or university to have this work completed on a cost-sharing basis.

Small Business Innovation Research Grants: Offers small business assistance in obtaining these grants for research and development. A federal program which insures that small businesses share in the expenditure of federal research dollars.

Seed Capital Investment Program: Program seeks to invest in innovative Arkansas companies that utilize new products or processes in their businesses. Does not fund entire projects, just the initial working capital portion of the financing package.

* Farmers Home Administration
700 West Capitol, Suite 5331
Little Rock, AR 72203 501-324-6281
Business and Industrial Loan Program: Works to improve economic conditions in rural areas. Guarantees up to 90 percent of a loan made by local lender. Loans can be made for capital improvements, machinery, real estate, and working capital. Limited to rural areas (towns of 50,000 population or less), no loans for actual agricultural production. General loan size from $500,000 to $10 million (less than $500,00 will refer to SBA).

* Small Business Administration (SBA)
2120 Riverfront Dr.
Suite 100 501-324-5278
Little Rock, AR 72202 Fax: 501-324-5199
See the chapter introduction for a description of SBA programs.

* Arkansas Capital Corporation
   800 Pyramid Place
   221 West Second St.
   Little Rock, AR 72201   501-374-9247
A private, non-profit corporation that provides fixed-rate financing for projects which do not meet the requirements for conventional bank loans. Most loans are in the $100,000 to $500,000 range and can be used for fixed assets or working capital. Projects must increase or maintain employment, and major portion of loan must be used for fixed assets.

* Certified Development Corporations (CDCs):
   Certified Development Corporations are non-profit organizations licensed by the Small Business Administration to administer small business loan programs for new or expanding businesses for the purpose of promoting economic growth in a particular area. Contact one in your area.

Batesville: White River Planning and Development District, Inc., Hwy. 25N, PO Box 2396, Batesville, AR 71901; 501-793-5233

Fort Smith: Western Arkansas Planning and Development District, Inc., PO Box 2067, Fort Smith, AR 72901; 501-785-2651

Harrison: Northwest Arkansas Certified Development Company, PO Box 190, Harrison, AR 72601; 501-741-5404

Hot Springs: West Central Arkansas Planning and Development District, Inc., PO Box 1067, Hot Springs, AR 71901; 501-624-1036

Jonesboro: East Arkansas Planning and Development District, 2905 King, Jonesboro, AR 72401; 501-932-3957

Little Rock: Arkansas Certified Development Corporation, 221 West 2nd, Suite 800, Little Rock, AR 72201; 501-374-8841

Lonoke: Central Arkansas Certified Development Corporation, PO Box 187, Lonoke, AR 72086; 501-676-2721

Magnolia: Southwest Arkansas Regional Development Company, PO Box 767, Magnolia, AR 71753; 501-234-7620

California

* California Department of Commerce
   801 K St., Suite 1700
   Sacramento, CA 95814
Office of Local Development   916-322-1394
Community Development Block Grant (CDBG) Program: Assists small business and developers in creating and/or retaining jobs in California. Conventional bank financing provides $2 for every $1 of CDBG. Fixed rate, no lower than 4 points below prime. Maximum loan amount $500,000. Maximum loan amount:

$500,000. Loan can be used for purchase of land and improvements, purchase of existing building(s) and improvements, building construction, machinery/equipment, working capital, inventory, off-site improvements.

SBA 502: Provides loans at market rate using 50 percent conventional bank financing, Small Business Administration (SBA) provides 40 percent, and 10-20 percent owner equity. Maximum loan 40 percent of project, not to exceed $750,000. Loan can be used for purchase of land and improvements, purchase of existing building(s) and improvements, building construction, machinery/equipment, renovation and restoration.

SBA 7(a): Provides capital to meet short-and-long term needs. Conventional bank financing provides the loan. The Small Business Administration (SBA) guarantees up to 90 percent of the loan amount to $155,000, 85 percent over $155,000. 10-33 percent equity required. Maximum loan guarantee $750,000. Loans can be used for land and improvements, purchase of existing building(s) and improvements, building construction, machinery/ equipment, working capital, inventory, business buy-outs.

Rural Economic Development Infrastructure Program: Assists financing rural public infrastructure projects which serve a specific business and result in the creation/ retention of permanent, private sector jobs.

Office of Business Development   916-324-8211
Enterprise Zones: Designed to encourage job-producing business development in designated sections of cities or counties. State tax credits as well as incentives offered by cities and counties are available to firms that hire new employees or make new investments in these areas.

Main Street Development   916-322-3520

* California Statewide Certified Development Corporation
   129 C St.
   Davis, CA 95616   916-756-9310
SBA 504: Provides loans using 50 percent conventional bank financing, the Small Business Administration (SBA) provides 40 percent, and 10-20 percent owner equity. A fixed asset loan, below market. Maximum loan amount is 40 percent of project, not to exceed $750,000. Loan can be used for purchase of land and improvements, purchase of existing building(s) and improvements, building construction, machinery/equipment, renovation and restoration.

* Small Business Administration (SBA)
   (Los Angeles)
   330 N. Brand
   Glendale, CA 91203   818-552-3210
or
   Small Business Administration (SBA)
   Mike Chung
   211 Main St.   415-744-6820
   San Francisco, CA 94105-1988   Fax: 415-744-6812

Local Offices

Fresno	209-487-5189
Los Angeles	213-894-2956
Sacramento	916-551-1426
San Diego	619-557-7252
San Francisco	415-744-6820
Santa Ana	714-836-2494
Ventura	805-642-1866

See the chapter introduction for a description of SBA programs.

* California World Trade Commission

Export Finance Office
107 S. Broadway
Suite 8039
Los Angeles, CA 90012   213-897-3997

Export Financing Program: Small Business firms experienced in exporting may apply for financial assistance in their exporting business. Guarantees for short term loans and insurance to support export of California goods and commerce fees.

* Certified Development Corporations

California Capital Small Business
  Development Corporation
926 J St., Suite 1500
Sacramento, CA 95814   916-442-1729

California Coastal Rural Development Corporation
Five East Gabilan St.
Suite 218
Salinas, CA 93902   408-424-1099

California Regional Urban Development Corporation
3932 Harrison St.
Oakland, CA 94611   415-652-5262

CAL Southern Small Business Development Corporation
600 B St.
Suite 2200
San Diego, CA 92189   619-232-7771

Hancock Urban Development Corporation
3600 Wilshire Boulevard
Suite 926
Los Angeles, CA 90010   213-382-4300

Pacific Coast Regional Urban Development Corporation
3810 Wilshire Boulevard
Suite 1901
Los Angeles, CA 90010   213-739-2999

SAFE BIDCO
145 Wikiup Dr.
Santa Rosa, CA 95403   707-577-8621

Valley Small Business Development Corporation
2344 Tulare St., Suite 302
Fresno, CA 93721   209-268-0166

Contact one of the above certified development corporations for application and inquiries on the following programs.

Underground Storage Tank Loan Program: Assists small businesses with underground storage tanks to upgrade, repair or remove underground storage tanks used to store petroleum. Low interest loans offered through Regional Development Corporations and Small Business Development Centers. Maximum loan $350,000.

Loan Guarantee Program: Permits Regional Development Corporations to use state funds to guarantee loans made by banks or financial institutions to small businesses. Funds can be used for working capital or short term credit needs. Maximum guarantee is 90 percent of the outstanding principal balance to a maximum of $350,000. Loans are guaranteed up to 90 percent of the outstanding principal balance.

Small Business Energy Conservation Program: Offers small businesses the opportunity to obtain low cost loan funds through the Regional Development Corporations to finance the installation of energy-saving equipment or devices. Interest rate will be 5 percent below the prime rate at the time of closing the loan. Loan amounts range from $15,000 to a maximum of $150,000. Term of loan not to exceed five years.

Hazardous Waste Reduction Loan Program: Low-cost loan funds are offered through the Regional Development Corporations for the acquisition and installation of hazardous waste reduction equipment or processes. Loan amounts range from $20,000 to a maximum of $150,000.

Colorado

* Office of Business Development

1625 Broadway, Suite 1710   303-892-3840
Denver, CO 80202   Fax: 303-892-3848
          1-800-592-5920 in Colorado

Colorado Long Term Lending Program: Most for-profit businesses are eligible. Priority is given to primary dollar-importing businesses. Long-term loans of between $100,000 to $500,000 per project for the financing of machinery, equipment, or real estate purchases. Recipients have the choice of a fixed or variable rate loan. Priority will be given to dollar-importing businesses.

Revolving Loan Fund for Energy: For energy efficiency improvements in small businesses. Assists in financing the acquisition and installation or upgrading of equipment, materials and energy using devices that will result in a savings in the business' utility costs. Loans range from $20,000 to $40,000 and will generally not exceed $60,000.

Rural Development Financing Program: The Office of Economic Development allocates and administers federal community development funds which are set aside for business finance projects. Loans, loan guarantees, equity investments or, under special circumstances, grants are provided for projects which create or retain jobs principally for low or moderate income persons. Financing will not exceed $250,000 per project. State participation up to 35 percent of a project, 10 percent owner equity, at least 55 percent other sources. Funds may be used for working capital, fixed assets, real estate, and construction. Not all metropolitan areas are eligible as they have their own Community Development Block Grant programs.

Economic Development Commission Funds: Allocates appropriated general fund revenues for economic development. Incentives such as infrastructure improvements, site development costs and loans to businesses are possible. Requires that at least one job be created for every $5,000 in state assistance, no more than 35 percent of the project be financed by the state, at least 10 percent in owner equity be provided. Terms are negotiated on a case-by-case basis.

* Colorado Housing and Finance Authority (CHFA)
   1981 Blake St.   303-297-7329
   Denver, CO 80202   1-800-877-2432 in Colorado
Quality Investment Capital Program: This loan program works in conjunction with the SBA 504 program (see Small Business Administration below). Provides fixed-rate financing for small business loans guaranteed by the SBA. The program stabilizes interest rates on the guaranteed portion of an SBA 7(a) loan. Maximum CHFA participation is $750,000 and a business may have no more than $750,000 outstanding on all SBA loans. Funds may be used for working capital, equipment purchase, business expansion, and real estate acquisition. See SBA 7(a) Loan Guarantee Program for terms.

Export Credit Insurance Program/Export Accounts Receivable Financing Program: Designed to help small exporters and those who have limited experience with exporting and extending credit to overseas customers. Provides credit insurance protection against commercial credit and political risks and can be used only to cover payments due for shipped exports. It covers 90 percent of commercial risk and 100 percent of political risk. Helps exporters finance their accounts receivable insured under this program by providing a financial bridge while those payments are outstanding. Financing is fully negotiable and depends on the individual needs and resources of the exporter as well as the contract that it covers. Financing will only cover the term of the export contract.

* Colorado Department of Local Affairs
   1313 Sherman St., Suite 521
   Denver, CO 80203   303-866-2156
Taxable Bond Financing for Fixed Assets: Industrial Development Revenue Bonds and Taxable Bonds are available for the purchase of land, building, equipment, and related soft costs for projects in the $500,000 to $20 million range. Interest rates are generally near the prime rate.

Enterprise Zones: These zones provide incentives for private enterprises to expand and for new businesses to locate in economically distressed areas of the state. A few of the tax incentives are a 3 percent investment tax credit for investments in equipment use exclusively in an enterprise zone, a job tax credit or refunds against state income taxes of $500 for each newly hired employee, hired in connection with a "new business" facility located in an enterprise zone for at least one year, an additional credit or refund of $500 per new business facility employee may be claimed by businesses which add value to agricultural commodities through manufacturing or processing, credit to rehabilitate vacant buildings.

* Colorado FmHA State Office
   655 Parfet St., Room E100
   Lakewood, CO 80215   303-236-2801
Business and Industrial Loan Program: Eligible projects must be located outside the boundary of a city of 50,000 or more. Development in adjacent urban areas is acceptable if the population density is less than 100 persons per square mile. Priority will be given to those projects located in open country, rural communities, and towns of 25,000 and smaller. Funds may be used for working capital or purchase of fixed assets. Guarantees of up to 90 percent for amounts up to $10 million. Alcohol fuel production facilities are eligible for up to $20 million. Loans are at market rates and may be fixed or variable.

Farm Operating Loans: Provides direct loans and loan guarantees to meet the operating expenses of family-size farms. Loans may be used for any purpose that facilitates successful operation of the farm. Loan guarantees up to 90 percent for amounts up to $400,000 at market rates that may be fixed or variable. Direct loans up to $200,000. Interest rates depend on the cost of money to the government at time of application. Applicants who have current FmHA farm ownership, soil and water, recreation, or operating loans are not eligible for this program.

Farm Ownership Loans: Direct and guaranteed loans to buy, improve, or enlarge family-size farms. Funds may be use to buy land, build or improve existing structures and facilities, and improve farm land and forests. Loan guarantees up to 90 percent for amounts up to $300,000 at market rates that may be fixed or variable. Direct loans up to $200,000. Interest rates depend on the cost of money to the government at time of application. Applicants who have current FmHA farm ownership, soil and water, recreation, or operating loans are not eligible for this program.

Limited Resource Farm Loans: Direct loans to low-income farmers and ranchers to buy, improve or enlarge family-size farms. Funds may be used to buy land, build or improve existing structures and facilities, and improve farm land and forests. Direct loans up to $200,000 at reduced interest rates that may be fixed or variable. Applicants who have current FmHA farm ownership, soil and water, recreation, or operating loans are not eligible for this program.

* Colorado Agricultural Development Authority
   (CADA)
   700 S. Kipling, #4000
   Lakewood, CO 80215   303-239-4114
Agricultural Processing Feasibility Grant Program: May be used only for the development of a report or study that analyzes the

feasibility of processing an agricultural commodity produced in Colorado. Maximum award is $15,000. Grants must be equally matched with a cash or in-kind contribution by applicant. Businesses need the approval of the local government where the proposed project is to be located.

Quality Agricultural Loan Program: The Colorado Agricultural Development Authority (CADA) works in conjunction with the Farmers Home Administration (FmHA) to provide fixed-rate financing on the guaranteed portion of a FmHa agricultural loan for farmers and ranchers. Funds can be used for working capital or purchase of fixed assets associated with the establishment or operation of the farm.

* Small Business Administration (SBA)
U.S. Customs House
999 18th St., #701   303-294-7186
Denver, CO 80202   Fax: 303-294-7153
See the chapter introduction for a description of SBA programs.

* Colorado Development Companies (CDC)
Four Colorado development companies lend to small and medium-sized businesses at fixed rates for terms of 10 to 20 years. Companies must create one job for every $15,000 they receive in financing. Contact your local CDC:

Colorado Springs: Pikes Peak Regional Development Corporation, 228 N. Cascade, #208, Colorado Springs, CO 80903, 719-471-2044. (El Paso County)

Denver: Community Economic Development of Colorado, 1111 Osage St., Suite 110, Denver, CO 80204, 303-893-8989. (statewide focus)

Denver: Denver Urban Economic Development of Colorado, 303 West Colfax Ave., Suite 1025, Denver, CO 80204, 303-296-5570. (City and County of Denver)

Pueblo: SCEDD Development Company, P.O. Box 1900, 212-West 13th, Pueblo, CO 81003, 719-545-8680. (19 counties)

SBA 504 Fixed Asset Loan Program: Provides long-term fixed rates for fixed asset purchases. At least one job must be created for every $15,000 in SBA assistance unless the project will produce a high community impact. Loans provided up to $750,000 or 40 percent of total project cost, whichever is less.

ACCESS Loan Program: ACCESS works in conjunction with the Small Business Administration's (SBA) 504 program. Together, they provide small businesses with long-term fixed rates on up to 95 percent of the financed portion of the fixed asset purchase (land and building, equipment, machinery). The ACCESS program cannot provide working capital. Loans are provided in amounts of $100,000 or more (no maximum). Industrial, manufacturing and wholesale distribution concerns located in enterprise zones are eligible for a lower rate. Through Access, businesses can borrow from local private lends which might not have been able to provide financing for total project needs.

* Colorado Department of Local Affairs
1313 Sherman St., #521
Denver, CO 80203   303-866-2205
Community Development Block Grant Funds: Available to cities and counties for the commercial rehabilitation of existing buildings or structures used for business, commercial, or industrial purposes. Funds are then loaned to businesses. Every $15,000 of funds invested must create at least one full-time job, and at least 51 percent of the jobs created must be for low- and moderate-income families. A number of rural areas have created local revolving loan funds which assist in financing new and expanded businesses in their communities.

* Colorado Venture Management
4845 Pearl East Circle, Suite 300
Boulder, CO 80301   303-440-4055
CBM Equity Fund: Provides equity financing for start-up businesses in the state through private venture capital partnerships. CVM will run the seed capital fund. Focus is on start-up and early stage investments in service and technology-based businesses. Investments will be considered in the range of $25,000 to $300,000.

Connecticut

---

* Connecticut Development Authority
Business Development Division
865 Brook St.
Rocky Hill, CT 06067   203-258-4200
Growth Fund: Direct state loans to small businesses in amounts up to $1 million for building, equipment, and working capital from $50,000 to $500,000. Available to those unable to obtain sufficient conventional financing on satisfactory terms or amounts, or for whom such assistance is important to locate or continue operations in Connecticut, and have sales less than $10,000,000. Eligible economic development projects are those that create or retain jobs, facilitate the export of goods and services or involve new products or services with potential for significant future contribution to the state's economy.

Business Assistance Fund: Direct state loans to businesses unable to obtain conventional financing on satisfactory terms or amounts, or for whom such state assistance is important to locate or continue operations in Connecticut. Loans available up to $250,000 to small contractors, private water companies, minority business enterprises holding a state contract, a business in an enterprise zone. Loans up to $500,000 for any business adversely affected by either a natural disaster or economic emergency as determined by the Commissioner of Economic Development.

Naugatuck Valley Fund: Available to companies engaged in manufacturing, processing or assembling of raw materials or finished products, or the significant servicing, overhaul or rebuilding of products, together with wholesale distribution of manufactured products who are unable to obtain sufficient private financing. Must create or retain one new job for every

$10,000 obtained from the Fund. State loans of up to $200,000 for companies in the Naugatuck Valley and certain other towns for real estate projects, machinery and equipment, and working capital.

Investment Financing: Provides direct state loans and investments in developing businesses that present the greatest potential future contribution to Connecticut's job growth and economic bases. Eligibility is the same as the Growth Fund with priority to firms that have high-tech jobs, high value added production techniques or services, strong export sales, high growth and high profitability potential and have achieved market penetration. Loans amounts range between $250,000 and $500,000.

Mortgage Insurance Fund: State guarantee of bank loan for land and building, machinery and equipment up to $15,000,000, and $5,000,000 for equipment. Economic development projects for manufacturing, research, office, warehouse hydroponic or aquaponic facility, energy conservation, pollution abatement.

CT Business Development Corp.:
SBA 504 Program: Sponsor for participation in the federal SBA 504 Program. Fixed rate loan up 40 percent of project cost to a maximum of $750,000. 50 percent conventional bank financing, minimum of 10 percent owner equity for the purchase of buildings and equipment.

Self-Sustaining Bond Program: Taxable and tax exempt bond financing for manufacturing, public water supply, solid waste disposal, local district heating and cooling, and state and local government projects. Amounts and terms subject to market conditions.

Manufacturing Assistance Act: 100 percent exemption from local property taxes for a period of four years on the purchase of new manufacturing equipment. Low interest loans and grants to manufacturers expanding productive capacity.

Urban Enterprise Zones Programs: Offers special investment incentives and financing programs to businesses located in any of 11 different zones.

Environmental Clean-up Fund: Loans up to $200,000 per year to business property owners unable to obtain clean-up financing from conventional sources.

Environmental Assistance Fund: Loans up to $250,000 or loan guarantees for projects focused on pollution prevention through manufacturing process changes.

* Department of Economic Development (DED)
    865 Brook St.
    Rocky Hill, CT 06067   203-258-4200
Manufacturing Assistance Fund: For business retention or expansion. $70 million in loans and loan guarantees; $20 million for defense diversification projects. Funding and tax credits for new machinery and equipment.

* Connecticut Innovation, Inc. (CII)
    40 Coldspring Rd.
    Rocky Hill, CT 06067   203-563-5851
Risk Capital: Provided for the development phase of a new product or process. Neither a loan nor a grant, this fund reimburses up to 60 percent of expenses on a regular basis, with other financing making up the balance. Payback is derived from a royalty based on sale of the product.

Innovation Development Loan Fund: Provides working capital for companies with new products and processes ready for manufacture, promotion, and sale.

The Technology Assistance Center
Yankee Ingenuity Initiative Grants: Designed to support cooperative ventures between businesses and public and private higher education institutions.

Small Business Innovation Research Grants (SBIR): Bridge grants for companies between Phase I and Phase II of federal SBIR grants, enabling companies to continue work while federal Phase II decisions are awaited.

Product Development Financing: Risk capital investments to fully develop innovative high technology ideas into products. Seek a return through royalties and generally accept the technology as a form of security.

Product Marketing Financing: Helps bring newly developed high technology products to market, or to expand markets. Funding is provided on a loan basis, usually with equity participation.

Connecticut Seed Venture Fund (CSV): Privately operated venture capital fund for corporate growth rather than product development.

Business and Academic Partnerships
Charles Goodyear Grants: Program is intended to encourage inventiveness through joint technology research between a college or university and a state firm. Projects are funded for up to two years and $200,000. Business partners must match the grant with cash or in-kind contributions to the school. Any public or private Connecticut college or university offering high technology courses may apply, in partnership with a state firm.

Elias Howe Grants: These grants are awarded for one year. Most grants are under $200,000, but there is no funding limit. Grants may be used to purchase equipment, service, and supplies that improve technology education and research.

Apollos Kinsley Grants: Program encourages cooperation between Connecticut public and private colleges and universities. Grants are given to partnerships of these institutions. Awards of up to $100,000 are given for one year.

* **Small Business Administration (SBA)**
  330 Main St.   203-240-4700
  Hartford, CT 06106   Fax: 203-240-4659
  See the chapter introduction for a description of SBA programs.

Delaware

* **Delaware Development Office**
  John S. Riley
  99 Kings Highway
  P.O. Box 1401
  Dover, DE 19903   302-739-4271

IRB Industrial Revenue Bonds: Eligible applicants are manufacturing facilities, first-time farmers, and 501(c)(3) organizations. State or local authority issues tax-exempt revenue bonds. Loan amounts range from $75,000 to $10,000. Usual terms of financing are 15 to 20 years on real estate and 5 to 10 years on equipment. Up to 30 years is allowed. Funds can be used for land/building acquisition, building construction and renovation, machinery and equipment. 501(c)(3) organizations may finance fixed assets and use bond proceeds for working capital.

The Small Business Revolving Loan and Credit Enhancement Fund: Available to small businesses with 100 or less employees. Normally 80% bank funds, 25% direct loan through the Delaware Development Office. Loan amounts can go up to $100,000. Funds can be used for financing working capital and fixed assets. "Blended rate" is equal to below conventional bank financing rates. Bank terms negotiates: 1 to 5 years for the Delaware Development Office portion.

SBA 504 U.S. Small Business Administration Section 504 Debentures: Available to small businesses with profits less than $2,000,000, and net worth less than $6,000,000. Normally 50% bank funds, 40% SBA-guaranteed bonds, and 10% equity. Funds can be used to finance land/building acquisitions, building construction and renovation, machinery and equipment. Amounts range from $120,000 to $2,500,000. "Blended rate" is equal to below conventional bank financing rates. Bank terms are negotiated.

SBA 7A U.S. Small Business Administration Guaranteed Loans: Business size varies with different industries. Funds can be used for working capital, land and building, machinery and equipment. SBA guarantees up to 90% of bank loan, with a maximum of $750,000. Interest rates and terms of financing are negotiated with the bank.

Delaware Technical Innovation Program (DTIP): Available to any applicant located in Delaware or relocating to Delaware, who has been granted a Phase I SBIR award and has submitted a Phase II SBIR application. Amounts are up to $50,000. Form of financing: Grant which bridges Phase I and Phase II of SBIR program.

* **Tax Incentives**
  Targeted Industry Tax Incentives
  Corporate Income Tax Credits: Available to manufacturers, wholesalers, laboratories or similar facilities used for scientific, agricultural, or industrial research, development or testing, computer processors, engineering firms, consumer credit reporting services, any combination of these services, and the administration and management support required for any of these activities who invest a minimum of $200,000 in a new or expanded facility and hires a minimum of five new employees. Program provides credits of $250 for each new employee and $250 for each $100,000 investment. Credits may not exceed 50% of the company's pre-credit tax liability in any one year.

* **Targeted Area Tax Credits**
  Corporate Income Tax Credits: Firms which qualify for targeted industry credits and locate in one of the targeted areas, qualify for corporate income tax credits of $500 for each new business and $500 for each new $100,000 investment. Targeted areas: real property that is owned by any level of government or any of their agencies; real property owned by a non-profit organization which is organized and operated solely for the purpose of fostering economic development; real property which has been approved as a Delaware Foreign Trade Zone, and 30 low-income Census Tracts throughout the state. Qualifying firms will not be subject to gross receipts taxes for the first 5 years and will then have these gross receipts taxes reduced on a declining scale for a period of 10 years.

  Retention and Expansion Tax Credits: Corporate income tax credits and gross receipts tax reductions are available to manufacturers and wholesalers planning new facilities or large expansions. Companies investing a minimum of $1 million or 15% or the unadjusted basis in the facility are eligible to receive 75% of Blue-Collar Tax Credits. Maximum annual credit cannot exceed $500,000.

  Investor Tax Credits: Personal income tax credits are available to individuals who invest in approved Delaware small businesses. Tax credits of 15%, applicable to no more than $100,000 or investment per investor in any one company, will be provided. Tax credits can be spread over five years.

* **Green Industries Tax Credits:**
  Waste Reductions: Manufacturers that reduce chemical waste by 20% or other wastes by 50%, are granted a $250 corporate income tax credit for each 10% reduction.

  Industry Credits: Eligible firms: manufacturers whose production inputs are comprised of at least 25% recycled materials; those firms that engage in the processing of materials removed from solid waste stream for resale as input to manufacturers; and firms who collect, distribute recycled materials, and/or materials removed from solid waste stream for recycling. Qualifying firms receive $250 corporate income tax credit. Also qualify for the 10 year gross receipts tax reductions.

Public Utility Tax Rebates for Industrial Users: Industrial firms meeting the criteria for targeted industries tax credits are eligible for a rebate of 50% of the Public Utilities Tax imposed on new or increased consumption of gas and electricity for five years. The public utilities tax rate is 4.25%.

* Property Tax Incentives:

New Construction- City of Wilmington: Grants property tax reductions for new construction in targeted areas within the city. The city allows a 100% credit on the increased assessments for a period of 5 or 7 years depending on the use of the facility and its location within the city.

Property Improvements - City of Wilmington: Offers a 100% reduction in property taxes for 5 or 7 years on increased assessments to qualified improvements to existing buildings.

New Construction and Renovations - New Castle County: Exempts some qualified commercial and industrial construction or renovations within the city from county property taxes at a rate of 100% for the first year, decreasing 10% a year until the full tax rate is attained. Applies only to new construction or renovations. Exemption is generally non-transferrable.

New Industrial, Manufacturing, Warehousing or Commercial Construction - City of Newark: Partially exempts all new industrial, manufacturing, and warehousing enterprises from real estate taxes levied on the increase in assessed valuation of the property attributable to new construction, for ten years. Exemptions begin at 100% for the first year and decrease 10% annually for ten years.

New Construction and Renovation - City of Dover: Grants tax waivers for eligible residential, commercial or office use projects within a defined target area. Must have a market value of materials and labor which exceeds $15,000. Tax waiver is for 10 years. Applies only to new construction and renovation. The city has placed a $1,000 cap on building permit fees for qualifying projects in the target area. Also offers a 100% waiver of impact fees for projects which maximize land use in the target area (e.g. with strong mixed use residential, commercial, and office combination).

Kent County Property Tax Abatements: Manufacturers, financial institutions, wholesalers, home offices, and operating units of insurance companies who invest at least $75,000 in a new or expanded facility and hire 4 new employees are eligible. Property taxes are reduced from 90% to 0% over the period of 10 years.

Delaware Access Program: Designed to give banks a flexible and non-bureaucratic tool to make business loans that are somewhat riskier than a conventional bank loan, in a manner consistent with safety and soundness. Designed to use a small amount of public resources to generate a large amount of private bank financing; providing access to bank financing for many businesses that might otherwise not be able to obtain such access. Eligible applicants are any commercial/industrial, agriculture business. The form of financing is 100% bank financing. The interest rates and the terms of financing are negotiated with the bank. the funds can be used to finance both working capital and fixed assets.

* Small Business Administration (SBA)
 1 Rodney Square, Suite 412
 920 N. King St. 302-573-6295
 Wilmington, DE 19801 Fax: 302-573-6060
See the chapter introduction for a description of SBA programs.

* Delaware Development Corporation
 99 Kings Highway
 P.O. Box 1401 302-739-4271
 Dover, DE 19903 Fax: 302-739-5749
SBA 504 Loans: Provides loans using 50 percent conventional bank financing, 40 percent Small Business Administration (SBA) involvement through Certified Development Companies, and 10 percent owner equity. A fixed-asset loan in amounts up to $750,000. Loan can be used for land and building, construction, machinery and equipment, and renovation/expansion. Interest rates are generally 1.1 percent above U.S. Treasury Bond rates.

* Wilmington Department of Commerce
 City County Building
 800 French St.
 Wilmington, DE 19801 302-571-4169
The Wilmington Department of Commerce offers Industrial Revenue Bond financing and other programs. Additionally, it's developing the key Brandywine and Christina Gateways in Center-City Wilmington and assisting in development of other parts of the city. Staff members are also available to reduce regulatory hold-ups. The Department of Commerce can also provide you with free publications.

* New Castle County Economic Development Corporation
 704 King St.
 1st Federal Plaza, Suite 536
 Wilmington, DE 19801 302-656-5050
The New Castle County Economic Development Corporation (NCCEDCO) offers SBA 504 and Industrial Revenue Bonds. Additionally, NCCEDCO offers small business counseling and is active in the development of the New Castle County Airport.

* Wilmington Economic Development Corp.
 605A Market St. Mall
 Wilmington, DE 19801 302-571-9088
The Wilmington Economic Development Corporation (WEDCO) provides financing through its direct lending program, the SBA 504 program, and other governmental mechanisms. WEDCO is also involved in the Brandywine Industrial Complex and offers management assistance to small businesses in the City of Wilmington.

* Sussex County Department of Economic Development
Sussex County Courthouse
P.O. Box 589   302-855-7770
Georgetown, DE 19947   Fax: 302-855-7773
The Sussex County Department of Economic Development issues
Industrial Revenue Bonds. In addition, it's developing the Sussex
County Industrial Airpark and assisting in development of other
parts of the County.

* Central Delaware Chamber of Commerce
9 Lockerman St.
Treadway Towers, Suite 2A   302-678-3028
P.O. Box 576   1-800-624-2522
Dover, DE 19903   Fax: 302-678-0189
This is the economic development agency in Kent County
providing assistance in site selection, demographics, and
statistical information as well as support to new and expanding
firms.

District Of Columbia

* Office of Business and Economic Development
Lloyd Levermore or Pamela Cook
Financial Services Division
717 14th St., NW, 10th Floor
Washington, DC 20005   202-535-1980
Revolving Loan Fund: Can be used for direct loans in
conjunction with private funds. Funds will be used primarily to
provide guarantees for bank loans.

Business Development Loan Program: Offers direct loans for gap
financing, construction, equipment purchases, inventory, and
working capital. Funds can also be used to provide financing for
development projects.

Commercial Development Assistance Program: Designed to
encourage investment in small neighborhood commercial businesses, CDAP offers direct loans in conjunction with private
funds. Typical fund uses are bridge financing, gap financing,
acquisition of equipment, fixtures and furniture, inventory, and
limited working capital.

Facade Loan Program: Designed to help revitalize neighborhood
commercial corridors, this loan program offers direct loans to
commercial property owners and business owners for the
renovation of their building facades. Loan amounts are up to
$25,000 at interest rates of 3%.

Met Grant Program: Designed to mitigate the disruptive costs
suffered by businesses as a result of the Metro System's
construction of the *Green Line,* this program can provide loans
of up to $30,000 and grants of up to $20,000 per year. Projects
must be CDBG-eligible and are only open to firms that had been
sited along the Green Line's construction route. Loans may be
funded at interest rates of 4% and must be repaid within five
years of the Green Line's completion. Highly flexible, the

program may underwrite equipment, inventory and even working
capital costs.

Development Zones Loan Program (DZLP): Seeking to
encourage the revitalization of the Alabama Avenue, DC Village,
and Anacostia Development Zones, this business development
program offers firms locating in these areas up to $200,000 or
90% of a project's cost. Low interest gap financing, typically set
between 3% to 6%, may be used to secure land, equipment,
inventory, leasehold improvements and working capital. Projects
meeting federal Community Development Block Grant (CDBG)
standards, and furthering a specific zone's development goals,
may access loans amortized over a term of up to twenty years,
depending on the particular use of funds.

* Economic Development Finance Corporation (EDFC)
1660 L St., NW
Suite 308
Washington, DC 20036   202-775-8815
The Economic Development Finance Corporation (EDFC) is a
quasi-public venture capital organization capitalized with public
and private funds that provides equity capital and loans to DC
businesses that meet EDFC's established investment criteria. The
EDFC can provide financial assistance in a number of creative
ways ranging from direct business loans to equity investments.

* Washington District Small Business Administration
1111 18th St., NW
6th Floor
P.O. Box 1993   202-606-4000
Washington, DC 20036   Fax: 202-634-1803
See the chapter introduction for a description of SBA programs.

Florida

* Bureau of Economic Assistance
Florida Department of Community Affairs
2740 Centerview Dr.
Rhyne Building
Tallahassee, FL 32399-2100   904-488-3581
Florida Enterprise Zone Program: Designed to benefit the most
distressed areas of Florida. Benefits for businesses that locate
within these zones or hire workers living within these zones
include property tax credits and community tax credits, sales tax
exemptions, corporate income tax credits, and credits against
sales and corporate taxes for job creation.

* Florida Department of Commerce
Bureau of Business Assistance
107 W. Gains St., Collins Building
Tallahassee, FL 32399-2000
Business Finance Section   904-487-0466
SBA 504 Loan Program: Provides loans using 50 percent
conventional bank financing, 40 percent SBA involvement

through Certified Development Companies, and 10 percent owner equity. A fixed asset loan in amounts up to $700,000. Funds can be used for land and building, construction, machinery and equipment, and renovation/ expansion.

SBA 7(a) Loan Guarantee Program: Guarantees up to 90 percent of a loan made through a private lender, up to $750,000. Can be used for start-up capital, working capital, inventory, machinery and equipment, and land and building. Available only to those unable to obtain a loan from conventional sources. Direct loans are made up to $150,000.

* Florida Department of Commerce
Bureau of Business Assistance
Business Finance Section
107 W. Gains St., Collins Building
Tallahassee, FL 32399-2000
Small Business Innovation Research
Grants (SBIR)   904-488-9357
The SBIR program stimulates innovate research among small technology-based business. They provide for financing of the very early research and development phase of innovation that meet the needs of the participating agencies. Assists in registering potential proposers with the agencies. Provides small businesses with information on proposal writing and with the names and addresses of the participating agencies to contact.
> *Phase I*: Awards between $20,000 to $50,000 to support six months of effort to demonstrate the scientific and technical merit and feasibility of the innovation.

> *Phase II*: Awards are an additional $500,000 for two years to further development the innovation through the prototype stage. Projects with potential will receive special consideration for a Phase II award.

> *Phase III*: Private sector investment is required to support a project to commercialization.

Economic Development Transportation Fund (EDTF): The EDTF fund is available to local governments in need of financial assistance for transportation projects which will facilitate economic development. The local governmental body must apply on behalf of a company that is considering an expansion or location of new facilities and that has an existing or anticipated transportation problem.

* Economic Development and Commercial Revitalization
Bureau of Community Assistance
2740 Centerview Dr., Rhyne Building
Tallahassee, FL 32399-2100   904-488-3581
Small City Community Development Block Grant (CDBG): Available to cities populations of 50,000 or less or counties with populations of less than 200,000. Designed to address and resolve specific community and economic development needs for low and moderate income families. The state sets aside CDBG funds to assist private entities for the purpose of creating or retaining jobs for low and moderate income persons.Funds can be used for the acquisition, construction, rehabilitation, or

installation of commercial or industrial buildings, structures and other real property and for public and private improvements.

* Small Business Administration (SBA)
501 E. Polk St., #104	813-228-2594
Tampa, FL 33602-3945	Fax: 813-228-2111

Small Business Administration (SBA)
7825 Baymeadows Way, Suite 100B   904-443-1900
Jacksonville, FL 32256   Fax: 904-443-1980

Small Business Administration (SBA)
Palm Beach Executive Plaza
5601 Corporate Way, Suite 402
West Palm Beach, FL 33407-2044   407-689-3922

Small Business Administration (SBA)
1320 S. Dixie Highway, Suite 501
Coral Gables, FL 33146-2911   305-536-5521
                                        Fax: 305-536-5058
See the chapter introduction for a description of SBA programs.

* Community and Business Loan Program
4440 NW 25th Place
Gainesville, FL 32606   904-338-3425
The Farmers Home Administration (FmHA), an agency of the U.S. Department of Agriculture, makes loans and grants in rural areas, including towns, for housing, farming, community facilities, and business and industry. A firm wishing to establish itself in a rural area, population of 50,000 or less, or an existing firm that needs to expand may be eligible for a loan guarantee through a commercial lender. Loans may be used for land, building, and equipment, working capital, and in certain cases for refinancing debt. Loans in amounts in excess of $500,000. The FmHA has established goals for business and industry loans to businesses operated by women and/or minorities, job producing enterprises in deeply distressed areas and modernizing and upgrading run-down business centers in rural areas.

* Certified Development Corporations (CDCs)
Certified Development Corporations are non-profit organizations licensed by the Small Business Administration to administer small business loan programs for new or expanding businesses for the purpose of promoting economic growth in a particular area. Contact one in your area:

Gainesville: North Central Florida Areawide Development Company, Inc., 235 S. Main St., Suite 205, Gainesville, FL 32601, 904-336-2199. Operating Area: Alachua, Bradford, Columbia, Dixie, Gilchrist, Hamilton, Lafayette, Madison, Suwannee, Taylor and Union Counties

Jacksonville: Jacksonville Local Development Company, Inc., 128 East Forsyth St., Florida Theatre Building, Suite 505, Jacksonville, FL 32202, 904-630-1914. Operating Area: Duval County

St. Petersburg: St. Petersburg Certified Development Corporation, P.O. Box 2842, St. Petersburg, FL 33701, 813-892-5108. Operating Area: City of St. Petersburg

Tallahassee: Florida First Capital Finance Corporation, Inc., Florida Department of Commerce, Collins Building, 107 West Gaines St., Tallahassee, FL 32399-2000, 904-487-0466. Operating Area: Statewide

Tampa: Tampa Bay Economic Development Corporation, Office of Urban Development, 306 East Jackson St., 7th Floor East, P. O. Box 3330, Tampa, FL 33601-3330, 813-242-5418. Operating Area: City of Tampa

Georgia

* Georgia Department of Community Affairs
    1200 Equitable Building
    100 Peachtree Street, NW
    Atlanta, GA 30303
    Steed Robinson   404-656-6200
    Brian Williamson   404-656-2900

Community Development Block Grant (CDBG): Regular Round Economic Development Program and CDBG Employment Incentive Program. The purpose of these two programs is to expand economic opportunities in cities and counties, principally for persons of low and moderate income. Only projects which cannot be funded through private lenders are eligible. Projects must create or retain jobs for low and moderate income persons. Loans are usually made at below-market rates with favorable terms. The maximum loan amount for the CDBG Regular Round is $500,000, for the EIP program, $300,000.

Revolving Loan Fund Programs   404-656-2900
Revolving loan funds are administered by Regional Development Centers to help business expand and create jobs. There are other similar programs in Georgia cities and counties (see Community Development Block Grants above).

Appalachian Region Business Development Revolving Loan Fund: Below market rate loans to businesses for projects that support downtown development, create and save jobs, and/or preserve and enhance historic downtown buildings. Must be located within one of the 35 "Appalachian Region" counties in North Georgia. One job is to be created or saved for every $20,000 loaned. 50 percent of total project cost must be provided by loan or equity injection. Maximum loan amount is $75,000.

Tax Exempt Industrial Bond Financing: Industrial Development Bonds are a type of long-term, low-interest rate financing available for manufacturing facilities. Private financial services firms issue the bonds.

Taxable Composite Bond Financing: Projects are pooled into a single bond issue of $15 million or more. Private financial services firms issue the bonds.

Job Tax Credit: As of March, 1994, there was no information provided. The Georgia legislature is considering legislation that will significantly expand the Job Tax Credit Program and will initiate other Georgia tax credits for businesses.

Industrial Revenue Bonds (IRB): Local Industrial Development Authorities issue IRB's to small and minority businesses.

Surety Bond Guarantee Program: Enables small contractors to obtain the surety bonds necessary to compete for government and non-government contracts. Permits a small business contractor to obtain a surety bond when the company might otherwise be too inexperienced to obtain a bond.

Business Infrastructure Finance (BIF) Program: This program is intended to facilitate and enhance job creation and/or retention for low and moderate income persons by providing a flexible and expedient financing mechanism to assist eligible industries with the financing of various privately owned infrastructure. Projects that create employment, greater job security, better working conditions, job training, enhancement of workplace skills and advancement opportunities receive the greatest consideration. BIF projects must always create or retain employment principally for low and moderate income persons. The Maximum BIF loan amount is $300,000. Loan amounts cannot exceed 90% of the specific project cost. Rates will generally not exceed a rate of prime plus 3%. Maximum term of the loan shall be five years.

Employment Incentive Program (EIP): This is a financing program capitalized with state CDBG funds that may be used by private business along with conventional private financing to carry out economic development projects which will result in employment of low and moderate income persons. Activities encompass two areas: 1) grant to local governments for the installation of public infrastructure which will support an eligible economic development project (public water and sewer systems, distribution and/or collection lines, wastewater treatment projects, rail spurs, and various other types of public facilities). 2) Grants to local governments who may then loan the EIP proceeds to a sub-recipient industry to finance various fixed assets which will be used in an eligible economic development project. EIP projects must always create or retain employment principally for low and moderate income persons. The maximum EIP grant or loan amount is $250,000. The term of an EIP loan generally ranges between 4 and 10 years depending upon the assets to be financed.

Appalachian Regional Commission Infrastructure Funds: Provides federally funded grants to cities and counties in the north Georgia area for infrastructure improvements that will result in the creation of permanent jobs. The purpose of the program is to assist with the economic development of Appalachian Region counties in Georgia. Grant amounts are available up to $200,000 for individual projects. No more than 80% of the funds may come from federal sources. Most activities providing water and sewer services are eligible as long as program objectives are met by the proposed project. Projects related to the supply, storage, treatment, and transmission of water are eligible, and projects related to the collection, storage, and treatment of sewage are eligible.

* Department of Housing and Urban Development
Richard Russell Building
75 Spring Street, SW
Atlanta, GA 30303   404-331-4001

U.S. Department of Housing and Urban Development (HUD)
Community Planning and Development
Section 108 Loan Guarantees: Section 108 provides communities
with an efficient source of financing for housing rehabilitation,
economic development, and large scale physical development
projects. Eligible applicants: Metropolitan cities and urban
counties, and nonentitlement communities that are assisted in the
submission of applications by states that administer the
Community Development Block Grant (CDBG) program.
Eligible activities include: acquisition of real property,
rehabilitation of publicly owned real property, housing
rehabilitation, economic development, related relocation,
clearance and site improvements, payment of interest on the
guaranteed loan and issuance costs of public offerings, and debt
service reserves. All projects and activities must principally
benefit low and moderate income persons, or aid in the
elimination or prevention of slums and blight, or meet other
community development needs. Maximum repayment period for
a loan guarantee is twenty (20) years.

Rural Development Administration (RDA)
Intermediary Relending Program: The purpose is to finance
business facilities and community development projects in rural
areas. This is achieved through loans made by the Rural
Development Administration (RDA) to intermediaries. The
intermediaries relend the funds to ultimate recipients for business
facilities or community development. Intermediaries may be
private non-profit corporations, public agencies, Indian groups,
or cooperatives. At least 51% of the owners or members of both
intermediaries and ultimate recipients must be U.S. citizens or
admitted for permanent residence. Must be unable to obtain the
proposed loan elsewhere at reasonable rates and terms. Loans
must be for the establishment of new businesses, the expansion
of existing businesses, creation of employment opportunities,
saving of existing jobs, or community development projects.
Repayment of loans are scheduled over a period of up to 30
years. The term of loans from intermediaries to ultimate
recipients is set by the intermediary.

Georgia Business and Industry Guaranteed Loan Program: The
purpose is to improve, develop, or finance business, industry and
employment in an effort to favorably impact the economic and
environmental climate of rural communities. Loans may be made
in areas outside the boundary of a city of 50,000 or more in
population and its immediate adjacent urbanized areas with a
population density of no more than 100 persons per square mile.
Can provide up to a 90% loan guarantee (normally does not
exceed 80%). The loans are limited to a maximum of $10
million. Loan funds may be used in developing or financing
business or industry, increasing employment and controlling or
abating pollution; real estate purposes, machinery and equipment,
and working capital. A minimum of 10% tangible balance sheet
equity is required. Balance sheet equity of at least 20-25% will
be required for new businesses, and businesses without full
personal or corporate guarantees.

Rural Business Enterprise Grants (RBEG): Used to support the
development of small emerging private business enterprises in
rural areas. Small and emerging private businesses would
generally be ones that will employ 50 or less new employees and
have less than $1,000,000 in projected gross revenues. These
grant funds may be used to finance and develop small and
emerging private business enterprises in rural areas including but
not limited to the following: acquisition and development of
land, easements, and rights of way; construction, conversion,
enlargement, repairs or modernization of buildings, plants,
machinery, equipment, access streets and woods, parking areas,
utilities, and pollution control and abatement facilities; start-up
operating costs and working capital; technical assistance for proposed grantee projects; refinancing of debts; financial assistance
to third parties through a loan; training in connection with technical assistance; production of television programs to provide
information on issues of importance to farmers and rural
residents.

Financing for Small Municipal and Rural Community Facility
Projects: Rural communities and small incorporated towns/cities
not larger than 20,000 based on the latest decennial population
census of the U.S. are eligible to apply. Applicants must be
unable to obtain the financing from other sources and/or their
own resources at rates and terms they can afford. Public bodies
and non-profit corporations can be eligible applicants. Funds can
be used for construction, land acquisition, legal fees, architect
fees, capitalized interest, equipment, initial operation and
maintenance costs, project contingencies, and any other cost that
is determined by the Rural Development Administration (RDA)
to be necessary for the completion of the project. Direct loans
may be obtained for 100% of eligible project costs subject to
adequate security, ability to repay, applicant's authority to
borrow, and availability of funds. Guaranteed loans - same as for
direct loans as determined by private lender and approved by
RDA.

Financing for Small Municipal and Rural Water and Wastewater
Systems: Guaranteed loans, direct loans, and grants are available.
Rural communities and small incorporate towns/cities not larger
than 10,000 based on the latest decennial population census of
the U.S. are eligible to apply. Applicants must be unable to
obtain the financing from other sources and/or their own
resources at rates and terms they can afford. Funds can be used
for construction, loan acquisition, legal fees, engineering fees,
capitalized interest, equipment, initial operation and maintenance
costs, project contingencies. Projects must be primarily for the
benefit of rural owners.

Guaranteed loans may be fixed or floating rate. May be obtained
for 100% of eligible project costs subject to adequate security,
ability to repay, applicant's authority to borrow, and availability
of funds. Repayment terms: up to 40 years based on applicant's
authority and life expectancy of the system.

Direct Loans have three categories: Market Rate (income of
$30,974); Intermediate Rate (income not more than $30,974 but
do not qualify for the poverty rate); Poverty Rate (income
$14,350 or 80% of market rate (80% of $30,794 = $24,779)).
Present Rates: Market Rate is 5.375 percent; Intermediate Rate
is 5.125 percent; Poverty Rate is 5 percent.

Grants cannot be received in conjunction with a guaranteed loan. They are used to supplement direct loans for the purpose of reducing user rate costs to a reasonable level when compared to comparable systems and similar size communities with similar economic and income conditions. The actual amount of grant funds awarded to the applicant will be determined based on the grant dollars required to reduce the user rates for users to a reasonable level up to the maximum amount of 55 percent or 75 percent.

* Community and Business Programs Division
  Farmers Home Administration
  Georgia State Office
  355 East Hancock Avenue
  Athens, GA 30610   706-546-2171
Special Grant Programs
Emergency Water Assistance Grants: Objective is to assist the residents of rural areas that have experienced a significant decline in quantity or quality of water to obtain adequate quantities of water that meet the standards set by the Safe Drinking Water Act. Grants may be made to public bodies and private non-profit corporations serving rural areas. Funds can be used for waterline extensions from existing systems; construction of new waterlines; repairs to an existing system; significant maintenance to an existing system; construction of new wells, reservoirs, transmission lines, treatment plants, and other sources of water; equipment replacement; and connection and/or tap fees. The maximum grant for alleviating a significant decline in quantity, or quality of water available from water supplies in rural areas is $500,000. The maximum grant available for repairs, partial replacement, or significant maintenance to remedy an acute shortage is $75,000.

Solid Waste Management Grant Program: Objectives are to reduce or eliminate pollution of water resources and improve planning and management of solid waste sites. Grants may be used to evaluate current landfill conditions to determine threats to water resources; provide technical assistance and/or training to enhance operator skills in the maintenance and operations of active landfills; provide technical assistance and/or training to help communities reduce the solid waste stream; and provide technical assistance and/or training for operators of landfills which are closed or will be closed in the near future.

Georgia's Freeport Law: A local option freeport amendment to the Georgia Constitution was submitted by the General Assembly and approved by Georgia's voters in November 1976. As a result, any local political subdivision now has wide flexibility in making a decision about this incentive. Under the law, all freeport decisions are in local hands — whether to have freeport at all, when to implement it, what kinds of inventory to exempt, the percentage of inventory exempted, and whether to have the law effective throughout the county or only for certain of its political subdivisions. Types of inventory exempted: Class 1: Manufacturer's raw materials and goods-in-process. Class 2: Finished goods held by the original manufacturer. Class 3: Finished goods held by the distributors, wholesalers, and manufacturers destined for out-of-state shipment.

Even after a local referendum has been passed, local officials retain their freedom to exercise further options: Defer full implementation of freeport of put freeport into effect on any scale, small or large, in increments of 20/40/60/80/100%. These levels are determined strictly by local officials.

Twenty Percent Investment Tax Credit: Also called the rehabilitation tax credit, it is an economic incentive that encourages the rehabilitation and reuse of historic buildings for business purposes. These will be found in cities of all sizes in all parts of the state. The majority will be found within downtown historic districts. The rehab tax credit provides a dollar for dollar reduction of Federal income taxes due for those taxpayers who can use the credit. The amount of the credit is equal to 20% of qualifying costs of rehabilitating the building. The building must be certified as historic. The work done on the building must also be certified. The total of qualifying rehab expenses must exceed the larger of $5,000 or the adjusted basis of the building. (Please note: This information provides only general guidance retarding the 20% investment tax credit. Professional tax advisors or legal counsel should be consulted for detailed information).

State Historic Preservation Tax Incentives: Designed to encourage rehabilitation of both residential and commercial historic buildings that might otherwise be neglected. The law provides an owner of historic property which has undergone substantial rehabilitation an eight-year freeze on property tax assessments. For the ninth year, the assessment increases by 50% of the difference between the recorded first year value and the current fair market value. In the tenth and following years the tax assessment will then be based on the current fair market value. The rehabilitation project must meet a rehabilitation test. If the property is: *Residential* (owner occupied — rehabilitation must increase the fair market value of the building by at least 50 percent. *Mixed-use* (primarily residential and partially income-producing property) — rehabilitation must increase the fair market value of the building by at least 75 percent. *Commercial and Professional Use* (income producing property) — rehabilitation must increase the fair market value of the building by at least 100 percent.

* Georgia Department of Administrative Services
  Small and Minority Business Coordinator
  200 Piedmont Avenue
  Suite 1620, West Floyd Building
  Atlanta, GA 30334   404-656-6315
Georgia Minority Subcontractors Tax Credit: In an effort to assist minority-owned businesses, the State of Georgia provides an income tax credit to any company which subcontracts with a minority owned firm to furnish goods, property, or services to the State of Georgia. This includes, but is not restricted to, the construction of any building or structure for the state. A minority owned business can be one of the following: a business which is owned by a member of a minority race, or a partnership of which a majority of interest is owned by one or more members of a minority race, or a public corporation of which a majority of the common stock is owned by one or more members of a minority race. The law allows a corporation, partnership, or individual, in computing Georgia taxable income, to subtract

from federal taxable income or federal adjusted gross income 10% of the amount of qualified payments to minority subcontractors.

City Business Improvement Districts: Permits the formation of special taxing district designed to promote the economic development of city commercial areas. Approved districts may provide supplemental services within the district's boundaries in order to improve and promote the district as a whole. Supplemental services include advertising, promotion, sanitation, security, and business recruitment and development.

Community Improvement Districts: Permits commercial areas to form special tax districts to pay for exceptional infrastructure needs. These "community improvement districts" (CID) do not replace standard city and county infrastructure improvement programs but supplement them by providing a means to pay for facilities which may be specially required in densely developed areas. Projects which can be funded include street and road construction and maintenance, sidewalks and streetlights, parking facilities, water systems, sewage systems, terminal and dock facilities, public transportation, and park facilities and recreational areas.

* **Office of Adult Literacy Programs**
  Mr. Robert Wofford
  1800 Century Place, NE
  Atlanta, GA 30345   404-679-1644

  Mr. Ted Banks
  Georgia Department of Revenue
  270 Washington Street, Suite 507
  Atlanta, GA 30334   404-656-4096
Georgia Department of Technical and Adult Education
Georgia Department of Revenue
Georgia Tax Credit for Adult Basic Skills Education: Designed to encourage businesses to provide or sponsor basic skills education programs for their employees. The program provides tax credits under Article 2 of Chapter 7 of Title 48 of the Official Code of Georgia Annotated, 48-7-41. The amount of tax credit shall be equal to one-third of the costs of education per full-time equivalent student, or $150 per full-time equivalent student, whichever is less, for each employee who has successfully completed an approved adult basic skills education program. The tax credit granted to any employer pursuant to the Code shall not exceed the amount of the taxpayer's income liability for the taxable year as computed without regard to this Code section.

* **Georgia Tech Research Institute**
  Economic Development Laboratory
  Atlanta, GA 30332   404-894-6121
Georgia Procurement Assistance Center: The major purpose is to promote economic and business development in Georgia and provide assistance and directions to firms in the procurement market. The Center helps firms solicit bids and locate procurement opportunities with the Department of Defense and area military facilities seeking certain goods and services. The

Center will offer assistance as long as the firm shows interest and effort. The Center also offers a computer matching service that matches opportunities listed in the *Commerce Business Daily* with client capabilities. Although all other services are free of charge, a yearly fee of $150 is charged to companies who want to participate in the computer matching service. Also includes federal, state, and local government contracts.

* **Georgia Department of Technical and Adult Education**
  Keith Johnson, Manager
  Training Information Services
  Suite 660, South Tower
  1 CNN Center
  Atlanta, GA 30303-2705   404-679-1700
Quick Start: The State of Georgia's internationally known training program for new and expanding business and industries. Quick Start directly provides a full range of high quality customized training services at no cost to client companies. These services cover not only job specific skills but also automation, productivity enhancement and human resource development training. Examples: Statistical Process Control, Programmable Logic Controller, and Team Skills training. Also provides comprehensive training for office operations such as corporate headquarters, billing and remittance centers, and telecommunications operations such as customer service centers.

* **Georgia Department of Labor**
  Andrea Harper
  Acting Assistant Commissioner
  Job Training Division
  Suite 650, Sussex Place
  148 International Boulevard
  Atlanta, GA 30303   404-656-7392
Job Training Partnership Act (JTPA): Offers employers the opportunity to hire people who have been trained in specific occupational areas such as secretarial, health care, welding, construction and other occupations in demand. The on-the-job training program assists employers who hire JTPA participants by reimbursing up to 50% of the employee's wages during the training period. This program is especially effective for new and expanding industries and can be linked with the Quick Start program.

* **Economic Development Administration (EDA)**
  401 West Peachtree Street, NW
  Suite 1820
  Atlanta, GA 30308-3510   404-730-3000
The Economic Development Administration (EDA) was established under the Public Works and Economic Development Act of 1965, to generate new jobs, to help protect existing jobs, and to stimulate commercial and industrial growth in economically distressed areas of the U.S.

Public Works Grants: Public and private non-profit organizations and Indian Tribes to help build or expand public facilities essential to industrial and commercial growth. Typical projects are industrial parks, access roads, water and sewer lines, port and airport termination developments.

Technical Assistance Grants: Communities and firms to find solutions to problems that stifle economic growth. Funds are used for studies to determine economic feasibility of resource development to establish jobs and provide on the scene assistance for innovative economic development techniques.

Planning Grants: States, cities, regional planning councils, and Indian Tribes to help pay for the expertise needed to plan, coordinate, and implement comprehensive economic development programs.

University Center Program Grants: Awarded to colleges/universities to utilize available resources to provide technical assistance to clients and address the economic development programs and opportunities of their service area.

Revolving Loan Fund (RLF) Grants: Awarded to help depressed areas overcome specific capital market gaps and to encourage greater private sector participation in economic development activities. RLF grantees make fixed asset and/or working capital loans to area businesses.

Economic Adjustment Program Grants: Assist state and local governments in solving recent and anticipated severe adjustment problems, resulting in abrupt and serious job losses and to help areas implement strategies to reverse and halt long term economic deterioration, i.e., natural disasters and military installation closures.

* Georgia Housing and Finance Authority
    Charlie Schroder or Jean Prasher
    60 Executive Parkway, NE
    Suite 250
    Atlanta, GA 30329   404-679-4840
or
    Georgia Department of Industry, Trade, and Tourism
    Kevin Langston
    285 Peachtree Center Avenue, NE
    Atlanta, GA 30303   404-656-3571
Georgia Housing and Finance Authority (GHFA):
Export Financing Assistance for Georgia Business: The Georgia Housing and Finance Authority and a number of "Satellite" organizations, in cooperation with the Georgia Department of Industry, Trade, and Tourism and the Export Import Bank of the U.S. (Eximbank), offers assistance to small and medium-sized Georgia businesses seeking to obtain financing for export sales. For businesses whose primary need is understanding and developing foreign markets, information and matchmaker services are provided by the Georgia Department of Industry, Trade, and Tourism (GDITT). These services include access to trade shows and incoming trade missions, placement in "Made in Georgia USA" product catalogues, and representation at Trade Days events sponsored by U.S. embassies abroad. GDITT also serves as a source of solicited and unsolicited leads for international sales, joint venture, licensing, and distribution opportunities.

* The Export-Import Bank of the U.S.
    811 Vermont Avenue, NW
    Washington, DC 20571-0999   202-566-4490
Export-Import Bank: An independent U.S. Government agency that helps finance the sale of U.S. goods and services to foreign buyers. It does this in two ways: 1) provides loans directly to foreign buyers; and 2) it encourages U.S. suppliers or their banks to extend credit terms to foreign buyers by providing credit risk protection, and in some cases, fixed-rate funding support. Also helps U.S. exporters obtain pre-export financing through its Working Capital Guarantee Program.

* The Community Investment Services Department
    Federal Home Loan Bank
    1475 Peachtree Street, NE
    Atlanta, GA 30309-3037   404-888-8436
Federal Home Loan Bank
Community investment Services: The fund provides long-term funds to its member institutions for lending in their communities. Funds may be used to assist first-time home buyers, for loans to small businesses, for the rehabilitation of historic districts, for community redevelopment programs, and for home mortgages for low- and moderate-income families. The maturities offered are up to 20 years at fixed rates.

* Georgia Housing and Finance Authority
    Charlie Schroder
    60 Executive Parkway South, NE
    Suite 250
    Atlanta, GA 30329   404-679-4840
Pre-Treatment/Wastewater Treatment Revolving Loan Fund: The Georgia Housing and Financing Authority (GHFA), in conjunction with the Economic Development Administration (EDA), offers low-cost financing to manufacturing and certain other businesses for the construction of wastewater treatment and pre-treatment facilities. Minimum private investment to program loan dollar ratio of 2:1 required. Eligible area includes 100 EDA-qualified Georgia counties. Loan amounts available range from $166,667 to $500,000. Maximum term of two years, with long-term take out available to qualified borrowers through GHFA.

REA Zero Interest Loan Program: 202-720-9552
Rural Electrification Administration: 202-720-0410
Blaine Stockton or Mark Wyatt
The program provides grants and zero-interest loans to Rural Electrification Administration (REA) borrowers for public-private projects for economic development and job creation. Eligible applicants include any REA borrower. REA borrowers may apply for funds during the first 14 days of any month. Funds available: $13.025 million is to be available in fiscal year 1994 in the loan program and over $19 million in the grant program.

* Georgia Environmental Facilities Authority
    Paul Burks, Executive Director
    2090 Equitable Building
    100 Peachtree Street
    Atlanta, GA 30303   404-656-0938

Assists local governments in constructing and rehabilitating solid waste and water and sewer facilities necessary for public purposes and for commercial, residential, and industrial development. Eligible applicants are cities, counties, solid waste and water and sewer authorities in the state of Georgia.

Water and Sewer Regular Loan Program: The interest rate charges is based on the rate paid by the state for the bond issue which supplied that year's loan funds. The maximum loan term is 20 years. Currently, the maximum amount of funds that can be loaned for any one project is $2 million.

Economic Development Set-Aside (EDSA) Program: The applicant must provide evidence in writing that a new employer would not be able to open his facility, or that an existing employer would not be able to expand or retain jobs without the improvements made possible by the loan. The maximum loan term is 20 years. The maximum funds available are $2 million.

Environmental Emergency Loan Program: The applicant must show that the project is needed to protect the community's health or safety from an immediate hazard. The interest rate for the emergency loan program is 2%. The maximum loan term is 10 years. The maximum loan amount is $75,000.

Regional Solid Waste Management Incentive Grant Program: Eligible applicants are local governments interested in forming regional coalitions to address their solid waste management needs on a regional basis. Eligible grant activities include, but are not limited to, developmental activities which may lead to the establishment of formal coalitions for regional integrated solid waste management, such as regional feasibility studies or efficiency assessments, regional recycling studies, engineering services, legal services, municipal solid waste characterization studies, public participation, regional solid waste management plan amendments required to form a regional coalition, and municipal solid waste landfill site screening studies. No more than 75% of the total activity cost can be paid for by the grant program. A local 25% cash match is required and must be available for expenditure at the time of the grant award.

1993 Recycling and Solid Waste Facilities Loan Program: Eligible applicants are Georgia local governments that wish to finance multi-jurisdictional recycling and solid waste management facilities. Eligible projects are composting and/or recycling proposals will receive high rating. Other eligible projects include materials recovery facilities and recovered materials processing facilities; municipal solid waste landfills and other such systems or facilities. The maximum loan term is 20 years. This loan program has a maximum of $1,000,000 per loan for recycling and solid waste management needs.

Georgia Department of Natural Resources
Verona Barnes   404-656-4708
State Revolving Loan Fund for Wastewater Treatment: Makes low interest loans to local governments for improving wastewater treatment facilities. Loans are currently made at four percent interest to local governments for projects that will eliminate violations of clean water regulations and provide for community growth. Loans are limited to $6 million, and are repaid over a 20

year period. A 4% closing fee is charged to fund the administrative costs of the program.

* Small Business Administration (SBA)
1720 Peachtree Rd NW
6th Floor
Atlanta, GA 30309   404-347-7416
See the chapter introduction for a description of SBA programs.

* Business Development Corporation of Georgia
4000 Cumberland Parkway
Suite 1200-A
Atlanta, GA 30339   404-434-0273
The Business Development Corporation (BDC) provides loans of $100,000 to $1,250,000 for up to 20 years to qualified businesses (no grants).

* Georgia Development Authority
Agricultural Loan Division
2082 E. Exchange Pl, #102
Tucker, GA 30084   404-493-5700
Agribusiness Start-up Assistance: This program allows local commercial banks to offer agribusiness enterprises tax-exempt interest rates. Businesses that deal directly with food or forestry are eligible. Borrowers must have no more than 100 employees and gross sales of existing business must be under $2 million during the preceding year. Loans may go up to $1 million.

* Georgia Department of Natural Resources
Historic Preservation Section
205 Butler Street, S.E., #1462
Atlanta, GA 30334   404-656-2840
Twenty Percent Investment Tax Credit: The ITC is an economic incentive that encourages the rehabilitation and re-use of historic buildings for business purposes. The rehab tax credit provides a dollar for dollar reduction of Federal income taxes for equity investors. Buildings must be certified historic through the Historic Preservation Section.

* Georgia Housing and Finance Authority
60 Executive Parkway South
Suite 250
Atlanta, GA 30329   404-679-0644
                        1-800-350-HOME Outside Metro Atlanta
Georgia Housing Trust Fund for the Homeless: Low-interest loans and grants for affordable housing activities. Primary criteria is impact on homelessness. Available to public-private partnerships.

Low Income Housing Tax Credits: Tax credit against annual tax liability for 10 years for development of rental housing. At least 20 percent of project's units must be occupied by tenants earning no more than 60 percent of an area's median income. Projects must have zoning in place, utilities to site, and site control.

Rental Rehabilitation Program: "Forgivable" loans to investors and property owners for 50 percent of eligible costs to rehabilitate substandard rental housing. Applicant must own property which must be located in a locally designated target area, and be substandard or failing HUD standards.

* Economic Development Administration
Atlanta Regional Office
401 W. Peachtree Street, NE, Suite 1820
Atlanta, GA 30308-3510   404-730-3000
Business Loan Guarantee Program: Guarantees up to 80 percent of the principal and interest of loans to be made to private borrowers for the purchase of fixed assets and/or working capital purposes for projects located in areas eligible for EDA assistance. Equity investment is 15 to 25 percent of total loan. Minimum loan amount is $600,000.

* Farmers Home Administration (FmHA)
Georgia State Office
355 East Hancock Avenue
Athens, GA 30610   706-546-2171
Business and Industrial Loan Program: Assistance is provided in the form of loan guarantees. FmHA contracts to reimburse the lender for a maximum of 90 percent of principal and interest. Loans are limited to areas outside the boundaries of cities of 50,000 or more. Basic uses for loans include developing or financing business or industry, increasing employment, and controlling or abating pollution. Funds can be used for land, buildings, machinery and equipment, working capital and pollution control facilities.

* Local or Certified Development Corporations
Certified Development Company of
  Northeast Georgia
305 Research Drive
Athens, GA 30610   706-548-3141

Atlanta Local Development Corporation
230 Peachtree Street, NW, Suite 1650
Atlanta, GA 30303   404-658-7000

The Business Growth Corporation of Georgia
4000 Cumberland Parkway, Suite 1200-A
Atlanta, GA 30339   404-434-0273

CSRA Local Development Corporation
2123 Wrightsboro Road
P.O. Box 2800
Augusta, GA 30904   706-737-1823

Fulton County Certified Development
  Corporation
141 Pryor St., Suite 5001
Atlanta, GA 30303   404-730-8073

Coastal Area District Development Authority
P.O. Box 1917

127 F Street
Brunswick, GA 31521   912-264-7315

Southwest Georgia Economic Development Corp.
30 East Broad Street
P.O. Box 346
Camilla, GA 31730   912-336-5617

Uptown, Inc.
P.O. Box 1237
Columbus, GA 31902   706-571-6057

North Georgia Certified Development
  Corporation
503 West Waugh Street
Dalton, GA 30720   706-272-2300

Middle Flint Area Development Corporation
228 W. Lamar St.
Americus, GA 31709   912-928-8729

Heart of Georgia Area Development
  Corporation
501 Oak Street
Eastman, GA 31023   912-374-4771

Georgia Mountains Regional Economic
  Development Corporation
1010 Ridge Road
Gainsville, GA 30501   706-536-3431

Troup County Local Development Corporation
P.O. Box 357
LaGrange, GA 30240   716-883-1655

Development Corporation of Middle Georgia
600 Grand Building
Mulberry Street
Macon, GA 31201   912-751-6160

Oconee Area Development Corporation
P.O. Box 707
Milledgeville, GA 31061   912-453-4328

Small Business Assistance Corporation
31 W. Congress St.
Savannah, GA 31402   912-232-4700

Southeast Georgia Development Corporation
3395 Harris Road
Waycross, GA 31501   912-285-6097

South Georgia Area Development Corporation
327 West Savannah Avenue
P.O. Box 1223
Valdosta, GA 31601   912-333-5281
Local or Certified Development Corporations: These corporations offer some local or SBA Section 502/503/7(a) loan funding for qualified small businesses in Georgia. Contact one of the above for further information:

* Venture Capital Network of Atlanta (VCN)
230 Peachtree Street, NW, Suite 1650
Atlanta, GA 30303   404-658-7000
The Venture Capital Network (VCN) of Atlanta matches entrepreneurs and individual investors through a confidential computerized database. Entrepreneurs most likely to benefit are those that require from $25,000 to $750,000 in equity financing. A fee is charged for registration.

* Georgia Capital Network
Georgia Tech Advanced Technology
   Development Center
430 10th Street NW
Suite N-116
Atlanta, GA 30318   404-894-5344
A confidential computerized matching service introducing entrepreneurs with new promising businesses that are too small for other equity sources to investors interested in early-state financing.

Hawaii

* Director of Finance
State of Hawaii
P.O. Box 150
Honolulu, HI 96810   808-586-1518
Local Bond Issues: The State of Hawaii has enacted legislation enabling the State to issue special purpose revenue bonds for manufacturing, processing or industrial enterprises, utilities serving the general public, and qualified health care facilities. The maximum interest rate for general obligation bonds is 8 percent. No limit is specified for revenue bonds.

* Hawaii Capital Loan Program
P.O. Box 2359
Honolulu, HI 96804   808-586-2576
Hawaii Capital Loan Program: Provides direct loans, or loans in participation with financial institutions, or the Small Business Administration to small businesses who are unable to obtain private financing. Funds can be used for plant construction, conversion or expansion, land acquisition for expansions, and purchase of equipment, machinery, supplies or materials, or for working capital. Maximum loan amount is $1 million. Current interest rate is 5 percent. Preference is given to businesses with job creating potential; use local resources or by-products; displace imports; create export opportunities, in the commercial or service sector; in research or development; in Pacific basin activities.

Hawaii Innovation Development Program: Loans are available to inventors to develop any early stage invention or new product which has not been exploited commercially. Loans are for the purpose of financing acquisitions of equipment, machinery, materials or supplies, or for working capital. Funds must be unavailable elsewhere.

* State Department of Agriculture
1428 South King Street
Honolulu, HI 96814   808-948-0145
Farmers unable to secure financing from conventional or other governmental sources may qualify for a Department of Agriculture loan.

* Small Business Administration (SBA)
Prince Kuhio Federal Building
Room 2213, Box 50207
300 Ala Moana Boulevard   808-541-2990
Honolulu, HI 96850-4981   Fax: 808-541-2976
See the chapter introduction for a description of SBA programs.

Idaho

* Idaho Department of Commerce
Economic Development Division
P.O. Box 83720
Boise, ID 83720   208-334-2470
Industrial Revenue Bonds (IRBs): Industrial Revenue Bonds allow Idaho businesses to borrow money at tax-exempt interest rates, up to $10 million, which are significantly lower than conventional rates. Fixed asset financing of land, buildings, machinery and equipment used in manufacturing, production, processing or assembly. A local public corporation issues bonds to finance the project. IRB's for small project's, $200,000 to $1 million, can be done similar to a commercial loan. Bonds over $1 million may find lower cost financing in the bond market (with letter of credit).

Community Development Block Grants: Available to cities and counties for the commercial rehabilitation of existing buildings or structures used for business, commercial or industrial purposes. Grants of up to $500,000 can be made. Every $10,000 of grant funds invested must create at least one full-time job and at least 51 percent of the jobs created must be for low and moderate-income families. Industrial site development such as site preparation, construction of water and sewer facilities, access roads, railroad spurs, etc.

* Small Business Administration (SBA)
1020 Main Street, Suite 290   208-334-1696
Boise, ID 83702-5745   Fax: 208-334-9353
See the chapter introduction for a description of SBA programs.

* Certified Development Corporations
Panhandle Area Council, Inc.
11100 Airport Drive
Hayden, ID 83835   208-772-0584

Clearwater Economic Development Assoc.
1626 B Sixth Avenue North
Lewiston, ID 83501   208-746-0015

Treasure Valley Certified Development
Corporation/Ida-Ore Planning and
Development Association
10624 W. Executive
Boise, ID 83704   208-322-7033

Region IV Development Corporation/
Region IV Development Association
P.O. Box 1844
Twin Falls, ID 83303   208-736-3064

Eastern Idaho Development Corporation
Southeast Idaho Council of Governments
ISU Business and Technology Center
1651 Alvin Ricken Drive
Pocatello, ID 83201   208-233-4032

East Central Idaho Development Company/
East Central Idaho Planning and Development
Association
P.O, Box 330
310 N. 2nd E
Rexburg, ID 83440   208-356-4524

Certified Development Corporations: Contact one of the following six Certified Development Corporations/ Economic Development Districts for information on the SBA 504 Program and Revolving Loan Fund.

SBA 504 Program: Provides loans using 50 percent conventional bank financing, 40 percent Small Business Administration (SBA) involvement through Certified Development Companies and 10 percent owner equity. A fixed asset loan in amounts up to $750,000. Loan can be used for land and building, construction, machinery and equipment and renovation/expansion.

Revolving Loan Fund: For business seeking to start up or expand. Loans must have job creation criteria. Some have fixed dollar requirements for each job created. Funding is not available in all counties. Interest rates are generally below prime interest rate. Used most often for loans under $100,000. Can be combined with SBA 7(a) Program.

* Farmers Home Administration (FmHA)
Community and Business Programs
3232 Elder
Boise, ID 83705   208-334-1836

FmHA Business and Industrial Loans: Assistance is provided in the form of loan guarantees. The Farmers Home Administration (FmHA) contracts to reimburse the lender for a maximum of 90 percent loan, but 60-70 percent is typical. Loans are limited to areas outside the boundaries of cities of 50,000 or less. Loans include development or improvement of land, buildings, machinery and equipment. May provide some working capital. Minimum guarantee is $500,000, maximum loan amount is $10 million. Interest rate may be fixed or variable. Hotels, restaurants and recreational business are not eligible. Public facility loans and grants also available for infrastructure development.

* Idaho Department of Water Resources
Energy Resources Division
1301 North Orchard
Boise, ID 83720   1-800-334-SAVE (7283) in ID
Energy Conservation Loans: Loans to businesses for energy conservation improvements to existing buildings, or new construction. Energy savings must have simple payback of less than 10 years. Interest rate of 6 percent term of 5 years. Maximum loan of $50,000.

* Economic Development Administration
304 N. 8th, #441
Boise, ID 83702   208-334-1521
or
Economic Development Districts
EDA Loans and Grants: Grants to communities for industrial site development and 80 percent loan guarantees for loans equal to or greater than $600,000 for individual enterprises. One job must be created for every $10,000. Available only to those unable to obtain a loan from conventional sources. Grants to communities for site preparation and construction of water and sewer facilities, access roads, railroad spurs, etc. Frequently combined with other funding sources such as the Community Development Block Grant. Matching funds of varying proportions are required.

* Association of Idaho Cities
3314 Grace
Boise, ID 83703   208-344-8594
or
Local City Council or Mayor
Revenue Allocation Financing: (Also known as increment financing) Tax exempt bonds for community development in designated areas. Amount of funding dependent upon increased property values within revenue allocation area. Only available within incorporated cities.

In addition to the government sponsored programs, there are many other financial loan and grant programs available through private institutions and private investors that you may wish to consider. You can obtain details on individual private assistance programs currently being offered by contacting the institutions directly.

Illinois

*** Illinois Department of Commerce and
Community Affairs**
James R. Thompson Center
100 W. Randolph St., Suite 3-400
Chicago, IL 60601   312-814-7179

In addition to programs listed below, *The Economic Development Resource Catalog* is available which provides financing programs that are available to Illinois communities and local governments.

Specific telephone numbers are located next to the program where applicable. If not noted, contact the above number.

Build Illinois Small Business Micro Loan Program: Provides direct financing at below-market interest rates in cooperation with private sector lenders. Money can be used for the same purposes as the SBD Loan Program above. Maximum amount to be loaned is $100,000.

Farmers Home Administration Business and Industrial Loan Program: Loan Guarantees in order to create or retain jobs in rural areas. Funds can be used for land and buildings, machinery and equipment, working capital. Guarantees from $500,000 to $10 million. Eligible business are those operating in areas where population density is less than 100 persons per square mile, and not in cities of 40,000 persons or more. Encourages loans which would not otherwise be made.

Equity Investment Fund: Provides financing to technology-based companies with significant potential for job creation. Funds can be used for real estate, machinery, equipment, working capital, organizational expenses, research and development costs. Can finance up to one-third of the total project cost with a maximum of $250,000.

Business Innovation Fund: Provides financing for technology-driven projects which might not attract traditional lenders or venture capitalists. Provides financial aid to start-up ventures which are in early to middle stage development and have a proprietary product or service. Aid up to $100,000 is offered for projects matched with private resources. Repayment is on a royalty basis when product is developed and sold in the marketplace.

Energy Conservation Interest Write-Down Grant Program: Provides direct grants to pre-pay loan interest for the purpose of reducing borrowing costs in cooperation with private sector lenders. Provides 100 percent of the total loan interest costs or a maximum of $10,000. Grant is based on the term of the loan, or the first five years of the loan, whichever is less. Purpose of the program is to help small businesses retrofit existing buildings and/or equipment with new energy efficient items. Money can be used for upgrading existing structures or equipment; insulation; meter improvement; efficient windows and lighting fixtures, HVAC systems, heat pumps, and use of hot water. The business must get an approved loan from an Illinois lending institution before applying for the grant.

Small Business Innovation and Research Grant Program (SBIR): SBIR federal grants finance research and development of small companies desiring to participate in government research. Money can be used for research and analytical efforts of the firm and costs for consultants and subcontractors. SBIR can help build scientific and technical leadership, attract other sources of funding, and augment research and development.

Illinois Fixed-Rate Financing Fund: Links federal, state, and private financing by using public finds in combination with the Small Business Administration SBA 7(a) Guaranteed Loan Program, bank funds, and equity.

Revolving Loan Program: Administered jointly by community action agencies and DCCA links private and public financing.

Money can be used for fixed assets, and working capital. Average loan is $50,000. A minimum of one job must be created for and filled for each $3,000-$5,000 of CSBG investment.

Cook County Economic Development Revolving Loan Fund: Provides financing to businesses located within Cook County, outside the City of Chicago and several other large cities. Funds can be used for real property acquisition; acquisition, construction, or rehabilitation of commercial or industrial buildings and other improvements; machinery and equipment acquisition and installation; and working capital. Loan amounts between $25,000 and $300,000 are available at an interest rate of one-half of the prime rate. Must create and retain jobs for low and moderate-income persons. At least one new job must be created for every $10,000 in funds, or one job must be retained for every $5,000.

Illinois Export Development Authority (IEDA): IEDA was created to provide export financing to small and medium-sized business. They have the authority to issue $1 million in bonds to fund export loans through commercial banks, including loans for pre-export activities. Financing is available in the form of short term loans which can be arranged through the IEDA and a local bank or other financial institution. Money can be used for pre-shipment financing -- working capital to produce goods or services, post-shipment financing -- to allow the exporter to sell the goods or services at competitive prices and terms. At least 25 percent of the final value of the goods or services must be produced in Illinois.

Export Import Bank Credit Insurance: Insurance program available through ExIm Bank for exports who grant short-term credit to foreign buyers. The insurance protects exporters who grant credit for up to 90 percent of commercial losses and 100 percent of political losses.

ExIm Working Capital Guarantee: Designated banks may apply for delegated authority under this program. This allows the banks to guarantee up to $300,000 without prior Eximbank approval. The guarantees cover working capital loans for export activity.

Technology Challenge Grant Program: Program is intended to find new ways to keep businesses competitive in the world marketplace. Grants may be used to respond to unique opportunities for which no other source of funding is available or as awards for exemplary and outstanding research. The Governor's Science Advisor and a private sector coalition of scientists will provide guidance on the types of projects to be financed.

Technology Investment Program: Provides a source of funding for new and existing firms which need to research and develop new products, processes or technologies to improve their productivity. Program will provide equity type investments, in qualified securities, or up to $500,000 or 50 percent of a project, whichever is less.

Marketing Staff
Build Illinois Small Business Development Loan Program: Provides direct financing for small businesses at below-market

interest rates in cooperation with private sector lenders for expansion and subsequent job creation or retention. Purpose of the program is to help small businesses create or retain jobs and assist in providing businesses with the opportunity to expand. Money can be used for acquisition of land and buildings, construction, renovation or leasehold improvements, purchase of machinery and equipment, and inventory and working capital. Loans do not exceed 25 percent of a project. Maximum amount for any one business project is $750,000. One job must be created or retained for every $3,000 loaned. 55 percent-80 percent conventional financing, 10-25 percent Small Business Development Loan Program, 10-20 percent owner equity.

Community Services Block Grant Business Loan Programs (CSBG): CSBG funding is to make affordable, long term, fixed-rate financing available to small businesses which are starting or expanding in Illinois and creating employment opportunity for low-income workers.

International Business Division   312-814-7164
International Finance Assistance Programs:
Office of Export Development Finance: Assists exporters to secure financing sources and to expedite such financing. Provides counseling on state and federal resources and helps match exports with financiers and credit insurance organizations. Also assists in assembly of loan packages and issues related to export financing.

Enterprise Zone Program   312-814-3130
Purpose of the program is to stimulate economic growth and neighborhood revitalization at the local level. Numerous state incentives are offered to encourage companies to locate or expand in enterprise zones. Local units of government typically offer additional incentives to further encourage economic growth and investment in the local enterprise zone.

* Illinois Development Finance Authority (IDFA)
     Marquite D. Russell
     Director of Marketing
     2 North LaSalle Street, Suite 980
     Chicago, IL 60602   312-793-5586
Industrial Revenue Bonds: Provide tax exempt low interest loans for manufacturers. Funds can be used for purchase of land, manufacturing machinery and equipment, facility construction, construction-related charges, and purchase of used buildings. Minimum loan amount $1.5 million, maximum is $10 million.

Illinois Venture Capital Fund: Provides seed capital for enterprises seeking to develop and test new products, processes, technologies and inventions.

Direct Loan Program: The Illinois Development Finance Authority (IDFA) provides supplemental financing for small and medium-sized businesses undertaking a fixed-asset project which will result in increase employment opportunities. Can finance up to 30 percent of a fixed asset project, not to exceed $250,000.

Employee Ownership Assistance Act: Designed to encourage employees of plants which are about to be closed to acquire the

facility and operate it as an employee-owned business. The program can provide small grants to fund feasibility studies and direct loans for up to 50 percent of the acquisition cost.

Title IX Revolving Loan Fund: Projects up to $100,000 to manufacturers in areas designated by the Federal Economic Development Administration. Fixed interest rate of 7.5%. Loan maturities up to 10 years.

Business Development Loan: Projects to $5,000 to $25,000 to small companies in Cook or Williamson counties for building renovation, and the purchase and installation of machinery and equipment. Borrowers required to inject 20% equity. Interest rate is fixed at 7.5%.

Programs For Business
     Direct Loan: Offers supplemental financing to small and mid-sized companies for expansion or modernization projects. Can be used to finance the acquisition of land, buildings, and machinery and equipment. Program contributes up to 30% of a project's fixed-asset costs, up to $250,000, in conjunction with conventional bank financing.

     Commercial Lease: IDFA purchases up to $200,000 of new equipment and leases that equipment to a business over a designated period of time. At the end of the lease, the lessee has the option of purchasing the equipment by remitting 10% of the original purchase price to IDFA.

     Rural Development Loan: IDFA finances businesses in rural communities with populations of less than 25,000. The loan contributes up to 75% of a project's fixed-asset costs, up to $150,000. Long-term financing is available at 6% fixed-rate of interest.

     Micro Loan Program: Provides small and emerging businesses with capital for start-up or expansion purposes. Loans up to $25,000 are available for the purchase of fixed assets, inventory, and working capital.

     Solid Waste Disposal Revenue Bonds: IDFA issues tax-exempt Solid Waste Disposal Revenue Bonds on behalf of privately owned solid waste disposal companies which provide services to the general public. Funds may be used for acquisition of fixed assets, including land, building, and equipment, as well as building construction or renovation.

     Multi-Family Housing Bonds: Tax-exempt bonds for housing developers that provide housing to low and moderate income residents. Funds can be used to purchase, build, or rehabilitate housing developments. Long term financing at rates below prime.

Programs For Units of Local Government
     Bonds: IDFA offers local governments cost-efficient and time efficient ways to finance vital improvement projects. Bonds carry a double tax-exemption, and low interest rates.

     Leases: IDFA's tax-exempt leases are for low cost projects ranging from $100,000 to $1 million. IDFA can help finance a variety of real estate and equipment purchases, such as equipment or water towers.

Tax/Revenue Anticipation Notes: To finance short-term working capital needs. Allows local governments to realize cash management savings.

Programs For Not-For-Profit Corporations

Bonds: Tax-exempt bonds on behalf of qualified not-for-profit corporations at interest rates significantly lower than conventional financing. Proceeds can be used to purchase, construct, renovate or equip a facility for use by the not-for-profit corporation in its operations.

Leases: Tax-exempt leasing is an effective alternative to bond financing for transactions which are smaller in project size or exclusively for equipment needs.

* Small Business Administration (SBA)

500 West Madison, Suite 1250   312-353-4528
Chicago, IL 60661-2511   Fax: 312-886-5108
See the chapter introduction for a description of SBA programs.

Tax Credits

Illinois Department of Revenue   217-782-3128
State Investment Credit: Investment tax credit against Illinois' Personal Property Replacement Income Tax for purchases of property, including buildings, used in manufacturing, mining, or retail businesses.

State Investment and Jobs Credits: Tax credits against Illinois' Personal Property Replacement Income Tax for purchases of property, including buildings, used in manufacturing, mining or retail businesses if the base employment of the firm has increased at least one percent over the preceding year. This tax credit benefits those employers who place new property in service and also increases their employment.

Training Expenses Credit: An income tax credit of 1.6 percent of qualified educational or vocational training costs accrued or paid for employee training in semi-technical, technical, semi-skilled or skilled fields.

Indiana

* Indiana Department of Commerce
Peter Rekis
One North Capitol, Suite 700   317-233-1094
Indianapolis, IN 46204-2288   Fax: 317-232-6786
Agricultural Development Corporation: Issues tax-exempt revenue bonds for financing agricultural enterprises. May finance farm land, equipment, buildings, improvements and additions, and breeding stock. For some projects being a first-time farmer is required.

Indiana Capital Assistance for Small Enterprises Program: Provides working capital in the form of grants and loans to small business owners.

Industrial Revenue Bonds: Issues tax-exempt bonds for financing industrial development projects. Bonds are payable from project revenues. Projects are generally manufacturing enterprises.

Investment Incentive Program: Provides loans for low-interest loans to expanding to relocating businesses. Grants or loans are made to eligible cities, towns, and counties which then make the loan to the firm to finance land, or buildings and equipment.

Strategic Development Fund: Program attempts to team up two or more Indiana businesses by offering grant or loan money in the form of matching dollars. Program is designed to foster creativity and cooperation between industrial sectors or regions of the state. Some project ideas include marketing programs, technology deployment, cooperative research, export development programs, apprentice programs.

Dinosaur Building Program Industrial Recovery Site: Designed to rejuvenate large, vacant buildings, usually 20 years or older with at least 300,0000 square feet. Two tax incentives are offer to businesses interested in locating its facility here. One is an inventory tax credit, the other an investment tax credit.

EnterpriseZones: Designed to help revitalize specific distressed areas and to create jobs for zone residents. There are currently fourteen enterprise zones. Through this program there are prime business sites available to meet a wide variety of facility requirements. Some of the tax and financial incentives offered to businesses locating in an enterprise zone are as follows:

Gross Income Tax Exemption: Businesses new to an enterprise zone are exempt from the gross income tax, and all enterprise zone income exceeding the income earned in the zone prior to its designation is exempt from the gross income tax.

Employment Expense Call: Income tax credit for the lesser of 10% of resident employee wages or $1,500 per employee.

Inventory Tax Credit: Property tax credit in the amount of depreciable personal tax liability on inventory in an enterprize zone.

Equity InvestmentCredit: Individual investors receive up to a 30 percent income tax credit for the purpose of equity in start-up or expanding enterprise zone firms.

There are also other tax incentives available for businesses not located in an Enterprise Zone such as *Inventory/ Interstate Inventory Tax Exemption,* and *Property Tax Abatement.*

International Trade Development Office:
Foreign Trade Zones (FTZ): An FTZ is a secured area legally outside of U.S. Customs territory. Foreign and domestic goods

may enter a zone to be stored, distributed, exhibited, combined with other foreign and domestic products, or used in other manufacturing operations. While the goods are in the FTZ, no U.S. duties are paid on them. FTZ's are located in Indianapolis, South Bend, and Burns International Harbor.

Export Finance Program: Provides short-terms loans for export orders up to a maximum of $500,000. This enables Indiana companies to offer more advantageous terms on letters of credit to foreign companies.

Trade Show Assistance Program: Provides financial assistance to companies planning to attend trade shows overseas. It is designed to help small and medium-sized companies realize their export potential through participation in international trade fair and exhibitions. Companies can be reimbursed for up to $5,000 of the cost directly attributable to the trade show.

International Business Education Program: Provides financial assistance to Indiana businesses seeking marketing analyses, technical information for competitive and marketing assistance or education programs on international issues. Funding is provided to Indiana firms to work with a state university on these programs.

The Capital Access Program: Designed to enable lenders to make business loans that carry a higher degree of risk than loans made under customary lending policies. Provides lenders with default protection that encourages them to extend financing they would not ordinarily offer. Financing is available to businesses that would otherwise be unable to obtain loans. The borrower makes a premium payment of between 1.5% and 3.5% of the loan amount, the lender matches that payment, and the Indiana Development Finance Authority (IDFA) matches the combined total of the borrower's and the lender's payments. For each loan, the total reserve contribution can range from a minimum of 6% of the loan to a maximum of 17.5%.

Industrial Development Project Loan Guaranty Program: The Indiana Development Finance Authority (IDFA) may guarantee a variety of financial instruments (loans, leases, bonds, letters of credit) made for the benefit of industrial development projects, mining operations, or agricultural operations that involve the processing of agricultural products. The most important requirement is that the financing encourages the creation or retention of employment in Indiana. Maximum amount for a guaranty is limited to $2,000,000. Most guaranties provided are for amounts less than $500,000. Maximum term: 20 years.

Underground Storage Tank Guaranty Program: The Indiana Development Finance Authority (IDFA) may guarantee a loan made to a petroleum marketer, petroleum retailer or political subdivision for the upgrade or replacement of underground storage tanks. Maximum amount is $200,000. Plans for the upgrade for tank replacement must be approved by the Indiana Department of Fire and Building Services.

Agricultural Loan and Rural Development Loan Guaranty Program: A loan made for the benefit of an agricultural enterprise or rural development project. Maximum amount is $300,000.

Bond Program: Types of projects for which the IDFA may issue bonds include the construction of new buildings, the acquisition or expansion of existing buildings, the acquisition of machinery, equipment or other fixtures, or the construction of pollution control facilities. A fee of $2,500 is charged by the IDFA, and requires the entity for which the bonds are issued to pay the Authority's issuer's counsel fees.

Export Finance Program: The Indiana Development Finance Authority and the International Trade Division (ITD) work in partnership with the Export-Import Bank of the United States (Eximbank) to provide export financing assistance to qualified exporters. The partnership assists Indiana exporters to obtain Eximbank guaranties and loans by packaging and submitting applications to Eximbank.

State Private Activity Bond Ceiling: The state ceiling (sometimes called "volume cap") is the maximum dollar amount of tax-exempt private activity bonds that may be issued within a year. All bond-issuing authorities must report to the IDFA when issuing tax-exempt private activity bonds. A fee of $500 per report is charged to cover administrative costs. At the end of each year, if the dollar amount of bonds issued is less than the state ceiling, the remaining volume may be carried forward for a period of 3 years by those entities planning to issue exempt facility bonds, qualified mortgage bonds, qualified student loan bonds or qualified redevelopment bonds.

* Indiana Statewide Certified Development Corporation
8440 Woodfield Crossing, Suite 315
Indianapolis, IN 46240   317-469-6166
Provides long-term fixed asset financing up to $500,000 in low-interest subordinated mortgages for small businesses.

* Corporation for Innovation Development
1 American Square, Suite 2150
Indianapolis, IN 46204   317-269-2350
Encourages the entrepreneurial spirit through increased access to venture capital. Activities include providing venture capital as well as equity and financing to established industries.

* Department of Economic Development
City of Fort Wayne
840 City-County Building
Fort Wayne, IN 46802   219-427-1127
Community Corporation - Ft. Wayne Community Development: Provides financial assistance at low interest rates. Designed to work in conjunction with private financing through seven programs.

* Small Business Administration (SBA)
Robert Gastineau, Deputy Director
Finance Division
429 N. Pennsylvania, #100   317-226-7272
Indianapolis, IN 46204-1873   Fax: 317-226-7259
See the chapter introduction for a description of SBA programs.

* **Metro Small Business Assistance Corporation**
  306 Civic Center Complex
  1 NW Martin Luther King Blvd.
  Evansville, IN 47708   812-426-5857
SBA Loan Guarantees and Direct Loans: Provides technical assistance to implement Small Business Administration (SBA) finance programs.

* **Indiana Small Business Development Corporation**
  Cynthia Burt, Comptroller
  One North Capital, Suite 1275   317-264-2820
  Indianapolis, IN 46204-2026   Fax: 317-264-2806
Enterprise Development Fund: Purpose of the Fund is to make loans to develop local investment pools for seed capital and local opportunity pools to help disadvantaged business and "non-traditional" entrepreneurs with financing.

Small Business Incubator Program: Provides grants available only in economically disadvantages areas, loans, or loan guarantees to community organizations for the purpose of establishing incubators. Funds can be used for the acquisition and renovation of existing facilities, acquisition of equipment, and operating expenses for the first 12 months. Both for-profit and not-for-profit corporations are eligible to participate in the program. Must match any funds provided, demonstrate a market-driven need for an incubator, and agree to provide assistance to incubator tenants. Loans or guarantees may not exceed the lessor of 50 percent of the total eligible project costs or $500,000. Grants may not exceed the lesser of 50 percent of the project costs or $250,000.

* **Metro Small Business Assistance Corporation**
  306 Civic Center Complex
  1 NW Martin Luther King Blvd.
  Evansville, IN 47708   812-426-5857
Working Capital Loan Pool: Provides short-term, working capital financing for small businesses in the city of Evansville and unincorporated areas of Vanderburg county.

* **Greater Bloomington Chamber of Commerce**
  116 West 6th Street
  Suite 100
  P.O. Box 1302
  Bloomington, IN 47402   812-336-6381
Venture Capital Club of South-Central Indiana: Provides a forum for new and existing businesses to present their case for funding before potential investors at monthly lunch meetings.

* **Mount Vernon Venture Capital Company**
  P.O. Box 40177
  Indianapolis, IN 46240   317-469-5888
The Mount Vernon Venture Capital Company makes equity-type investments -- normally loans with warrants. Investments are in the $100,000 to $400,000 range. This company mainly invests in enterprises that are past start-up.

* **Heritage Venture Partners II. Ltd.**
  135 N. Pennsylvania, #2380
  Indianapolis, IN 46204   317-635-5696
This company makes equity-type investments for a minimum of $400,000. In joint, ventures can make investments of up to $1 million.

* **CID Venture Partners**
  201 N. Illinois Street, #1950
  Indianapolis, IN 46204   317-237-2350
This company makes equity-oriented, direct investments in a wide range of industries and firms in various development stages.

Iowa

* **Department of Economic Development**
  200 East Grand Avenue
  Des Moines, IA 50309
Bureau of State Programs:
Division of Job Training   515-242-4819
Self Employment Loan Program (SELP): SELP offers low-interest loans up to $5,000 to low-income Iowans for self-employment ventures.

Small Business Loan Program: Provides limited financing to help new and expanding businesses through the sale of tax-exempt bonds and notes. Rates vary with the level of risk. Maximum loan amount is $10 million.

Bureau of Business Grants and Loans   515-242-4819
Division of Financial Assistance:
Community Economic Betterment Account (CEBA): Cities, counties or community colleges are eligible to apply on behalf of businesses that are expanding or are new business ventures in Iowa that increase the number of quality jobs in the state. Funds may be used to acquire and/or improve land and buildings, purchase machinery and equipment, working capital, and related projects costs. Loans are generally between $50,00 and $250,000.

Venture Capital Resources Fund: Provides an additional source in the way of equity financing of capital for small businesses that cannot get the full amount of financing needed from conventional sources for either a new or existing business. Loans range between $100,000 to $1 million.

Capital Access Program: Emphasis of this program is the revitalization of the livestock industry in Iowa. Assistance is provided in the form of loan guarantees and will vary from 4-1/2 percent to 10-1/2 percent depending on the characteristics of each loan.

Natural Rural Development Loan Program: Program is designed to assist in the revitalization and diversification of Iowa's rural economy. Available to any small business that locates or expands operations in a community with a population less than 20,000. Preference is given to light manufacturing, value added process projects, and/or projects that diversify the rural economy to emphasize development in areas other than agriculture. Loans are generally between $50,000 and $300,000. A Business Plan is necessary.

Community Development Block Grant:
Economic Development Set-Aside   515-242-4831
Any city under 50,000 population and all counties are eligible to apply on behalf of businesses that are expanding or are new business ventures in Iowa and who will increase the number of employment opportunities and increase the opportunity for low and moderate income individuals to find employment. Funds may be used to acquire and/or improve land and buildings, purchase machinery and equipment, working capital, and related project costs. Loans are generally between $25,000 and $200,000.

Community Development Block Grants:
Public Facilities Set-Aside   515-242-4825
Public Facilities Set-Aside funds assist with local infrastructure improvements such as sewer, water, street, and rail construction that support economic development. Priority given to projects creating the most jobs, those involving funds from local and private sources. Project must show benefit to low and moderate income persons usually in job creation. Cities under 50,000 population and all counties may apply. Project must support a specific identified development opportunity.

Bureau of Housing and Community Development
                                         515-242-4825
Division of Financial Assistance:
Community Development Block Grants: Available to cities and counties for the commercial rehabilitation of existing buildings or structures used for business, commercial, or industrial purposes principally for low and moderate income families.

Export Trade Assistance Program   515-242-4742
International Bureau:
Export Trade Assistance Program: Promotes the development of international trade activities and opportunities for exporters in the state through encouraging increased participation in overseas trade shows and trade missions. Eligibility includes being a resident or an entity with corporate offices in Iowa employing fewer than 500 individuals, exhibit products or services or samples of Iowa manufactured, processed or value-added products in conjunction with a foreign trade show or trade mission. Up to 75 percent of expenses directly attributed to cost of participating in a trade show or trade mission may be reimbursed, not to exceed $5,000 per event with a limit of three events in state's fiscal year.

* Iowa Product Development Corp. (IPDC)
    President
    200 East Grand Avenue
    Des Moines, IA 50309   515-242-4860
The Iowa Product Development Corporation (IPDC) was created to stimulate and encourage business development based on new products by the infusion of financial aid for invention and innovation where such aid is not reasonably available from commercial sources. Applicant may be either a new or existing business and must represent a venture that will maintain an Iowa presence, with the manufacturing of the product conducted in Iowa. Eligible projects should be advanced beyond the theoretic state and be readily capable of commercialization. A business plan will be necessary.

* Small Business Administration (SBA)
    210 Walnut, Room 749   515-284-4422
    Des Moines, IA 50309   Fax: 515-284-4572
See the chapter introduction for a description of SBA programs.

Kansas

* Kansas Dept. of Commerce and Housing
    700 SW Harrison Street, #1300
    Topeka, KS 66603-3712
Existing Industry Development Division   913-296-5298
Industrial Development Bonds (IDBs): Kansas cities and counties are authorized to issue IDBs for financing or construction of manufacturing facilities. They can be used to purchase or construct, or equip buildings, acquire sites, and enlarge or remodel buildings. The Existing Industry Division maintains records of bond activity within the state.

Venture Capital and Seed Capital: Privately run corporations were designed to create private risk capital for investment in smaller Kansas businesses. They seek projects that provide good, technically feasible ideas, the ability to generate a big profit, excellent management capability, and widespread market potential. Emphasis is placed on for development of a prototype product or process, a marketing study to determine the feasibility of a new product or process, or a business plan for the development and production of a new product or process.

Seed Capital - funds to a new business for such things as business and marketing planning, product development, and building prototypes.

Start-Up Capital - provided to a business which has generally been in business for less than one year and has some level of sales. Funds to be used for staffing and equipping the business.

Growth or Expansion Capital (Second Stage) - provided usually two to three years after start-up which allows the business to broaden its product line, expand geographically, and increase production.

Acquisition Capital (Third Stage) -- investments in a mature business which may be in a position to be acquired. Financing may be used to restructure the business to make it more attractive for acquisition.

Small Cities CDBG Program:
Community Development Division   913-296-3004
Small Cities Community Development Block Grant (CDBG):

Awarded to cities and counties with populations less than 50,000 for projects which stimulate or support local economic activity, principally for persons of low and moderate income. Funds may be used for public facilities, housing rehabilitation, and economic development projects.

Rental Rehabilitation Program: Designed to ensure an adequate supply of standard rental housing is available to lower-income tenants. Funds are offered through local government units, with an emphasis on rehabilitation of family housing.

Enterprise Zones   913-296-3485
Designed to "expand and renew the local economy and improve the social and economic welfare of residents in economically distress zone areas located within the cities of Kansas." Allows qualified business and industry located in an approved enterprises zone to take enhanced job expansion and investment income tax credits and sales tax exemptions on specific capital improvements.

Low Income Housing Tax Credits   913-296-2686
Designed to encourage investment in the supply of low and moderate income rental housing. Tax credits are available to qualified applicants for new construction, acquisition and rehabilitation.

Community Strategic Planning Assistance Act: The Act provides grant funding to non-metropolitan counties for the development and implementation of comprehensive countywide and multi-county economic development strategic plans. Planning grants are available up to $20,000. Action grants are not to exceed $40,000 and require a 100% local match. Action grants help sustain local commitment by providing funds.

* Business Tax Bureau
     Kansas Department of Revenue
     Docking State Office Building, 3rd Floor
     P.O. Box 12001
     Topeka, KS 66612-2001   913-296-2461
Job Expansion and Investment Credits: Designed to encourage businesses to expand employment and capital investment. It allows a qualifying business to receive $100 income tax credits for creating new jobs and investing capital in the state. Assists both new business and existing businesses to expand. A higher level of tax credits are available if located in an enterprise zone.

* Kansas Technology Enterprise Corporation (KTEC)
     112 West 6th Street
     Suite 400   913-296-5272
     Topeka, KS 66603   Fax: 913-296-1160
Through the following programs, the Kansas Technology Enterprise Corporation (KTEC) serves inventors, researchers, corporations, investors and entrepreneurs. In addition, they conduct an annual high tech expo.

Applied Research Matching Grants: The Kansas Technology Enterprise Corporation (KTEC) funds 40 percent of the cost of industry research and development (R&D) projects which lead to

job creation in Kansas. Industrially-focused Centers of Excellence are operated at several major universities.

Seed Capital Fund: Provides equity financing for high tech product development. Matching funds are provided for the Small Business Innovation Research Program.

KTEC Centers of Excellence: University based research centers providing product development, seminars, research, consulting, networking and training.

> *Advanced Manufacturing Institute (AMI):* Located on the campus of Kansas State University. Purpose is to improve manufacturing practiced by Kansas companies. These include automated and flexible manufacturing and assembly systems, process planning, processing of engineering materials, special developmental efforts, and technology transfer.

> *Center for Excellence in Computer-Aided Systems Engineering (CECASE):* Located on the campus of the University of Kansas. Mission is to assist companies with computer-aided analysis and design of advanced engineering systems. Also, is committed to the development of prototype software products.

> *Center for Technology Transfer (CTT):* Located in Pittsburgh State University. Provides assistance to industries through the development and transfer of technology. Focus is on the research, testing and development of plastic, wood and printing products and processes. Assists new and expanding industries to implement cutting edge technologies.

> *Higuchi Biosciences Center (HBC):* Located on the campus of the University of Kansas. Serves as a hub of pharmaceutical research and development. Mission is pre-clinical drug delivery, drug development, drug testing and research.

> *National Institute for Aviation Research (NIAR):* Located at the Wichita State University. Integrates higher education, government and business in cooperative efforts to advance the nation's aviation industry. Conducts research and technology transfer to meet industry challenges.

Innovative Technology Enterprise Corporation (ITEC): Assists innovators in the development and commercialization of marketable ideas in technology. Emphasis is placed on training, counseling, and advising of inventors and individuals with innovative ideas, making it easier to navigate the process of commercializing technologies.

Kansas Technology Resource Data Base (KTR): Catalogues research and technical information, refers clients to faculty researchers and laboratories for testing new products or processes, assists inventors in locating enterprises or entrepreneurs that may have applications for their innovations, provides management assistance and expertise to small enterprises of special importance to the economy, and encourages the use of state resources at educational institutions and Small Business Development Centers.

Mid-America Manufacturing Technology Center: A not-for-profit organization that primarily provides hands-on consulting to small and medium sized manufacturers to help them become more competitive. More than 65 engineers and technical specialists are employed throughout the region. Helps manufacturers implement improvement programs, troubleshoot technical equipment and production problems, and locate hard-to-find vendors. Other services include seminars, product testing, whole company assessments, industry networks, and demonstrations of equipment and software.

Grant Programs

Small Business Innovation Research (SBIR) Grants: Helps small businesses obtain Federal Small Business Innovation Research (SBIR) awards by providing grants to support proposal preparation. Offers a network for SBIR concept evaluation, identification of appropriate SBIR solicitation topics, federal agency contact, and technical assistance.

Training Equipment Grants: Provides matching monies to two-year academic institutions for the purpose of providing advanced equipment for workforce training. It's an opportunity to link the business, the educational facility, and the state closer together to provide the workforce with the training and skills for today's jobs.

Industrial Liaison: Targets the retention and expansion of current businesses. Assists firms in identifying and solving production or other technical problems, improving production processes, and capitalizing on advanced production techniques and technologies.

Seed Capital

Ad Astra Fund: Provides seed capital monies to start-up or early stage companies with an advanced technology base.

Ad Astra Fund II: In 1993 the legislature dedicated $1.5 million to seed capital for 1994. This is the first new seed capital money appropriated since 1988. Private investors are being contacted to invest in Ad Astra Fund II.

Special Projects Fund: Unexpected opportunities have provided for the Patent Depository Library, coder/ decoder sites in nine locations, and assisted in financing the proposal that won the Mid-America Manufacturing Technology Center grant for Kansas.

Projects Include:

Ad Astra Fund Management: Contract to assist the managers of the Ad Astra Fund in providing business services to the Ad Astra companies.

Public Information Director: Individuals attend community and civic organization meetings throughout the state giving presentations on the Kansas Technology Enterprise Corporation (KTEC).

Innovative Technology Enterprise Corporation: Ongoing funding of the Kansas Technology Enterprise Corporation' (KTEC) subsidiary which assists inventors.

Ad Astra Fund II Marketing Program: Assists in attracting outside investments in the new seed capital fund.

Total Quality Project Management: Ongoing project to develop Total Quality Management (TQM) at the state government level in Kansas.

* Kansas Development Finance Authority
Jayhawk Tower #1000
700 SW Jackson Street
Topeka, KS 66603-3758   913-296-6747
The Authority is authorized to issue bonds for the purpose of financing capital improvements facilities, industrial enterprises, agricultural business enterprises, educational facilities, health care facilities, and housing developments. Several small projects can be combined into one large bond issue.

* Kansas Association of Certified Development Companies
Box 46, Emporia State University
1200 Commercial Street
Emporia, KS 66801-5057   316-342-7041
SBA 504 Program: Provides loans using 50 percent conventional bank financing, 40 percent SBA involvement through Certified Development Companies, and 10 percent owner equity. A fixed asset loan in amounts up to $1 million. Loan can be used for land and building, construction, machinery and equipment, and renovation/ expansion.

* Small Business Administration (SBA)
Wichita District Office
100 E. English Street, #510   316-269-6273
Wichita, KS 67202   Fax: 316-269-6499

Small Business Administration (SBA)
Kansas City District Office
323 W. 8th, #501   816-374-5557
Kansas City, MO 64105   Fax: 816-374-6759
See the chapter introduction for a description of SBA programs.

* Farmers Home Administration
1200 SW Executive Drive
P.O. Box 4653
Topeka, KS 66604   913-271-2700
Business and Industrial Loan Program: This program provides loan guarantees to businesses and industries to benefit rural areas. Loans are made in any area outside the boundary of a city of 50,000 or more and its adjacent urbanized areas with population density of no more than 100 persons per square mile. Any legal entity, including individuals, public and private organizations, and federally recognized Indian tribes may borrow under its program. Priority is given to applications for projects in open country, rural communities and towns of 25,000 and smaller. Primary purpose is to create and maintain employment and improve the economic and environmental climate in rural communities. Guarantees of up to 90 percent of the principal and interest.

Kentucky

* Kentucky Development Finance Authority (KDFA)

Capital Plaza Tower
24th Floor   502-564-4554
Frankfort, KY 40601   Fax: 502-564-7697

Small Business Loans: The Kentucky Development Finance Authority (KDFA) is a state government agency and makes loans for fixed asset financing for business start-ups and expansions. Loans are available to small businesses with fewer than 100 employees for fixed asset project costs of less than $100,000. KDFA loans up to 45 percent of project costs. Loans supplement other financing. Loans can be used for most types of business activities except retail or commercial development projects. Interest rate is at or below market rate.

Tax-Exempt Industrial Revenue Bonds: Issued by state and local governments, Industrial Revenue Bonds (IRBs) offer low-cost financing for manufacturing projects costing less that $10 million.

Industrial Bonds in Distressed Counties: Private companies placing new manufacturing plants in certain economically distressed Kentucky counties can recoup the cost of the facilities through tax incentives. These state bond financed projects can include the land and buildings used for manufacturing, along with storage warehousing, and related office facilities.

* Commonwealth Small Business Development Corporation (CSBDC)

Capital Plaza Tower
24th Floor
Frankfort, KY 40601   502-564-4320

State Loans for Small Businesses: Long term fixed interest rate financing loans for up to 40 percent of the costs of expansions by qualifying Kentucky small businesses are available, 50 percent conventional financing, and 10 percent owner equity. Maximum loan per single small business project is $750,000 or $35,000 per job created. Fixed assets eligible for financing include land and/or building purchases, new building construction and/or building rehabilitation, and machinery and equipment purchases. Funds are disbursed at the completion of the project. Business must obtain interim financing and the CSBDC loan commitment will assist in securing the interim financing.

* Cabinet for Economic Development

Office of Business and Technology
Capital Plaza Tower
500 Mero Street
Frankfort, KY 40601   502-564-7670

State Bridge Grants for Innovative Research (SBIR): Kentucky businesses participating in Small Business Innovative Research contracts with federal agencies are eligible for state bridge grants. Grants bridge the period between the completion of a company's award for the first phase of a federal research project and the second phase award to help eliminate interruptions in the firm's development and growth in highly competitive technologies.

Kentucky Jobs Development Authority: Service or technology related companies such as data processing, research and development, and other non-manufacturing companies are eligible. Companies must provide a minimum of 75% of their services for persons located outside the state and must employ a minimum of 25 persons. The company receives a 100% credit against state income tax produced by the project, and a wage assessment equal to 5% of the gross payroll as inducements. These are limited to 50% of the approved costs or 10 years, whichever is first.

Kentucky Rural Economic Development Authority (KREDA) Incentives: Corporations, partnerships, sole partnerships, or business trusts that establish new manufacturing plants or expand existing manufacturing operations in qualifying Kentucky counties are eligible. Funds can be used for land, buildings, fixtures, and equipment for new and expanded manufacturing, together with storage, warehousing, and related office facilities. Costs can include all expenditures for land, site development, utility extensions, architectural and engineering services, construction or rehabilitation, and purchases and installation of equipment and fixtures. Companies can receive credits against Kentucky state income tax. Approved projects can be financed by conventional financing or by state bonds with either a lease or lease-purchase agreement.

Kentucky Industrial Development Authority: Any manufacturing company which is locating or expanding operations in Kentucky is eligible. Eligible projects are defined as land acquisition, building construction and fixtures used primarily for manufacturing purposes. Other associated costs may also be included. As an incentive, the company is allowed a 100% tax credit against Kentucky income tax which arises from the project.

Kentucky Industrial Revitalization Authority: Existing manufacturing companies which employ 25 persons and are faced with an imminent closure due to lack of productivity or profitability by outdated equipment are eligible. Building improvements, equipment purchases or other elements allowing the company to stay in business are eligible projects. The company receives a combination of a Kentucky income tax credit and the right to invoke an employee wage assessment equal to 6% of the gross payroll.

* Cabinet for Economic Development

Sara Bell, Director
Capital Plaza Tower, 24th Floor
500 Metro St.   502-564-4554
Frankfort, KY 40601   Fax: 502-564-7687

Enterprise Zone Program: Enterprise zones were initiated to bring new or renewed development to targeted areas, and to make businesses and industry in those areas more competitive. Special tax incentives and eased regulations are available to businesses located in special zones. There are ten enterprise zones.

* Kentucky Craft Marketing Program
Small Business Division
39 Market Plaza
Frankfort, KY 40601-1942   502-564-8076

Education, Arts, Humanities Program: Small businesses producing crafts items can obtain state guaranteed loans ranging from $2,000 to $20,000 from local banks. Loans can be used to finance inventory, and for the purchase, repair or renovation of equipment. To qualify, product must be juried and a thorough business plan must be submitted along with application.

* Small Business Administration (SBA)
Federal Building, Room 188
600 Dr. Martin Luther King, Jr. Place
Louisville, KY 40202   502-582-5971
                              Fax: 502-582-5009

See the chapter introduction for a description of SBA programs.

* Kentucky Department of Local Government
Division of Community Programs
1024 Capital Center Drive
Frankfort, KY 40601   502-564-2382

Community Development Block Grant Loan (CDBG): Available to cities and counties for the commercial rehabilitation of existing buildings or structures used for business, commercial, or industrial purposes. The cities and counties loan the grant funds to business to be used for fixed assets and for the creation or retention of jobs. At least 51 percent of the jobs created must be for low-and moderate-income families.

* Farmers Home Administration
771 Corporate Drive, Suite 200
Lexington, KY 40503   606-224-7300

FmHA Business and Industrial Guarantee Loan Program: Offers loan guarantees of up to 90 percent of principal and interest on conventional loans to businesses and industries in rural areas of Kentucky. The FmHA designates the eligible rural areas and are in areas with populations of less than 50,000. Priority is given where areas are in open country, rural communities, and cities of 25,000 or fewer. Funds can be used to purchase land, buildings, machinery, equipment, furniture, and fixtures; to finance construction, expansion, or modernization of buildings; and to provide start-up and working capital.

* Economic Development Administration (EDA)
771 Corporate Plaza, Suite 200
Lexington, KY 40503   606-233-2596

EDA Loan Guarantee: The EDA can guarantee up to 80 percent of a loan made by a private lender. Guaranteed loans can be used to finance both fixed assets and working capital for businesses in eligible counties. EDA loans are generally for larger firms and range from about $500,000 to $10,000,000. Priority is given to projects that are labor intensive, with assistance usually limited to no more than $20,000 per permanent job created or saved.

Bowling Green:
Barren River Area Development
District   502-781-2381
Catlettsburg:
FIVCO Area Development District   606-739-5191
Maysville:
Buffalo Trace Area Development
District   606-546-6874
Elizabethtown:
Lincoln Trail Area Development
District   502-769-2393
Florence:
Northern Kentucky Area
Development   606-283-1885
Hazard:
Kentucky River Area Development
District   606-436-3158
Hopkinsville:
Pennyrile Area Development
District   502-886-9484
Lexington:
Urban County Economic Development
Office   606-258-3131
London:
Cumberland Valley Area Development
District   606-864-7391
Louisville:
Louisville and Jefferson County Economic
Development Office   502-625-3051
Mayfield:
Purchase Area Development District   502-247-7171
Owensboro:
Green River Area Development
District   502-926-4433
Owingsville:
Gateway Area Development District   502-674-6355
Russell Springs:
Lake Cumberland Area Development
District   502-866-4200

Business Loans by Local Governments: Loans for local business start-ups and expansions are available through several Kentucky city and county governments and area development districts. Loans are generally restricted to $500,000 or less, or to a specified amount per job created or saved. Interest rates are typically at or below-market rates.

* Commonwealth Venture Capital Fund
Office of Financial Management and
    Economic Analysis
261 Capital Annex
Frankfort, KY 40601   502-564-2924

State Venture Capital Funds Loans and Investments: Small businesses showing a potential for long-term growth may obtain start-up and early stage financing assistance at competitive rates from a state venture capital fund. Loans, loan guarantees or equity investments of up to $500,000 can be obtained by a qualifying small business which must be Kentucky based and employ fewer than 100 people.

* Kentucky Highlands Investment Corporation (KHIC)
  P.O. Box 1738
  London, KY 40743   606-864-5175
A small business investment company licensed by the SBA, provide both short term and long term financing assistance to small businesses in Southeastern Kentucky. Venture capital loans and equity capital investments for higher-risk projects are available for start-ups, expansions, and relocations of manufacturing and services firms. Participation usually ranges from $50,000 to $750,000. Terms and interest rates are negotiated.

* The Cumberland Fund
  433 Chestnut Street
  Berea, KY 40403   606-986-2373
Private Loans: Appalachian Counties: Loans and financial planning assistance are available to qualifying new and expanding manufacturing businesses in the 49 Appalachian counties of Kentucky. Loans range from $10,000 to $150,000. Funds can be used for working capital or to finance fixed assets.

Louisiana

* Louisiana Dept. of Economic Development
  101 France Street, Suite 115
  P.O. Box 94185
  Baton Rouge, LA 70804-9185
Finance Division:
Industrial Development Bonds   504-342-3000
Can be used to finance industrial sites and buildings, equipment, storage facilities and pollution abatement and control projects. The facilities are then leased to the participating company at a rental sufficient to retire the bonds. When bonds are use for pollution abatement projects, they may be issued in unlimited amounts.

Enterprise Zones: Companies locating in specially-designated Enterprise Zones are eligible for a package of tax incentives in addition to those available elsewhere in the state. Incentives include a one-time tax credit of $2,500 for each new job created at start-up or added to the payroll during the five years of the program. There is also an exemption from most state and local sales taxes on building materials and operating equipment.

10-Year Industrial Tax Exemption: New manufacturing operations and expansions can receive an exemption from property taxes on industrial buildings, machinery and equipment for 10 years. Improvements to industrial land are also exempt.

Jobs Tax Credit: Companies may take a one-time tax credit ranging from $100 to $250 for each net new job created as the result of the start-up of new business or expansion of an existing one. Credits can be used to satisfy state corporate income tax obligations. Manufacturing companies can elect to take this credit in lieu of the industrial property tax exemption or the benefits of the Enterprise Zone program.

* Louisiana Economic Development Corp.
  Department of Economic Development
  P.O. Box 94185
  Baton Rouge, LA 70804-9185   504-342-3000
Small Business Innovative Research Matching Grant Program: Issues grants to Louisiana small businesses that have received Small Business Innovative Research (SBIR) Phase 1 grant funds. Any out-of-state firm which agrees to relocate headquarters and research and development operations to Louisiana and has received a Federal SBIR Phase 1 research award. Matches SBIR grant on a one-to-one basis not exceeding $50,000. Funds to be used for research and related costs not covered by the federal SBIR grant or contract. It acts as gap funding between Phase I and Phase II awards.

Venture Capital Incentive Program: This program stimulates availability of venture capital and encourages formation of seed and venture capital funds through three different programs.

The Louisiana Venture Capital Co-Investment Program works with venture capital funds to invest in Louisiana businesses. Matches up to 1/4 of a venture capital investment round with a qualified Venture Capital Fund.

The Louisiana Venture Capital Match Program matches $1 for every $2 of private investment in a Venture Capital Fund.

Small Business Equity Program: Participation loans and loan guarantees up to $2,000,000 per project. Guaranty funds can be used for purchase of fixed assets, equipment or machinery, line of credit for accounts receivable or inventory. Uses of funds from participation loans can be used to purchase fixed assets, equipment or machinery, working capital.

Small Business Linked Deposit: Eligible to small business with less than 150 employees to create new jobs or saving present jobs. Maximum per project is $200,000.

SBA 504: Loan guaranty available to small businesses. Conventional bank financing 50 percent, SBA participation 40 percent, owner equity 10 percent. Maximum loan $750,000.

* Small Business Administration
  1661 Canal Street, Suite 2000   504-589-6685
  New Orleans, LA 70112   Fax: 504-589-2339
See the chapter introduction for a description of SBA programs.

Maine

* Department of Economic and Community Development
  Shelley Toppan, Director
  219 Capital St.
  State House Station #130
  Augusta, ME 04333   207-624-6800
Community Development Block Grant Program (CDBG): Available to cities and counties for the commercial rehabilitation

of existing buildings or structures used for business, commercial, or industrial purposes, which are then loans to businesses. Grants of up to $500,000 can be made. Every $15,000 of grant funds invested must create at least one full-time job, and at least 51 percent of the jobs created must be for low- and moderate-income families. The following programs originate from the CDBG.

Development Fund: Flexible interest rate, repayment period, and qualifying requirements. It is limited to 40 percent of a project with a maximum of $100,000. Can finance working capital as well as fixed assets.

Interim Finance Program: Primarily a source of affordable working capital or construction financing based on need. A minimum of $500,000 must be requested.

Community Revitalization Grant Program: Funds are used for housing rehabilitation, downtown revitalization or public infrastructure. In some cases, portions of the grants can be loaned to private entities for commercial or industrial projects.

* **Finance Authority of Maine (FAME)**
  David Markovchick, Director
  83 Western Avenue
  P.O. Box 949   207-623-3263
  Augusta, ME 04332-0949   Fax: 207-623-0095

Commercial Loan Insurance Program: Designed to promote economic development by providing business borrowers access to capital that would otherwise be denied by lender due to unacceptable level of credit risk. Must be exhibit responsible ability to repay loan. Insures up to 90 percent of a commercial loan. Loan proceeds may be used for purchase of, and improvements to real estate, fishing vessels, and machinery and equipment.

Small Business and Veterans Loan Insurance Program: Helps small businesses that cannot obtain conventional financing. Will insure up to 90 percent of a loan to a maximum of $1,000,000. For eligible Maine veterans, the amount is increased to $1,100,000. Must employ 50 or fewer employees or gross sales less than $5 million.

SMART-E Bond Program: Tax-exempt, fixed-asset financing for manufacturing facilities. SMART-E will finance up to 90 percent of a loan by grouping it with other similar loans and selling tax-exempt bonds to finance them. Maximum loan is $7 million. Assets that can be financed with loan proceeds include land and depreciable assets.

Municipal Securities Approval Program: Issues Industrial Revenue Bonds. Proceeds may be used for land, land improvements, buildings, machinery and equipment, financing and interest charges, engineering, legal services, surveys, cost estimates and studies.

Maine Job Start Program: A revolving direct loan program designed to provide eligible small business people with necessary capital to start, expand, or strengthen a business operation.

Targeted to business that cannot obtain financing through conventional sources (even with loan insurance). Maximum available loan is $10,000. Interest rate is 2 percent below the prime interest rate. Applicant must have annual gross household income at or below 80 percent of the federal median income.

Potato Marketing Improvement Fund: Provides direct loans to potato growers and packers to construct modern storages, packing lines, and sprout inhibitor facilities. Long-term, fixed-rate loans at below market interest rates are available to help finance construction or improvements to storage and packing facilities. Participating loans can finance between 45 and 55 percent of the costs of eligible construction and improvements.

Linked Investment Program for Agriculture and Small Business: State funds are invested in financial institutions which then lend out funds at reduced interest rates to Maine farmers and small business people.

Occupational and Safety Loan Fund Program: Targeted direct loans to Maine businesses seeking to make workplace safety improvements. A business may borrow up to $50,000 for up to 10 years. Interest rate is 3 percent fixed. Funds can be used to purchase, improve, or erect equipment which reduces workplace hazards or promotes health and safety of employees.

Export Financing Services:

Working Capital Insurance provides additional security to bankers.

Export Credit Umbrella Insurance reduces international credit risks, allows an exporter to offer credit terms to foreign buyers in a competitive market, and offers the opportunity to obtain current cash flow against foreign receivables. Provided by the Export-Import bank of the United States (Eximbank).

Either FAME or Eximbank is responsible for up to 100 percent of a loan made by a financial institution to the exporter.

Underground Oil Storage Facility Program: A replacement program that provides 100 percent loan insurance to lenders, or direct loans to borrowers for the removal, replacement and disposal of underground marketing and distribution tanks for oil, petroleum products or petroleum by-products. Must be an owner of an underground oil storage facility and may be either an individual or business engaged in the marketing or distribution of oil, petroleum products or petroleum by-products to persons or entities other than the owner. Funds must be used for the removal, replacement and/or disposal of marketing or distribution tanks for oil, petroleum products or by-products.

Underground Oil Storage Tank Removal and Replacement Program: Provides 100% loan insurance to lenders, or direct loans to business borrowers, for the removal, replacement and disposal of underground tanks for oil, petroleum products or petroleum by-products. Loans must be used for the removal, replacement and/or disposal of storage tanks for oil, petroleum products or petroleum by-products, or for installation of air quality equipment required by state law.

Non-Traditional Lenders' Loan Insurance Program: Individuals, trusts and other organizations that are not ordinarily in the business of making loans may apply to FAME for insurance up to 80% of commercial loans. Maximum insurance exposure may not exceed $200,000 per borrower. If the lender has the right to take a future equity position in the business being financed, the insurance is limited to 50% of the loan.

Natural Resource Entrants Loan Insurance Program: Authorized to insure up to 90% of a loan to an eligible borrower mae by either a lender or the seller of the agricultural or fishing enterprise. Borrower must have a net worth of $100,000 or less. Insured loan amount may not exceed $225,000.

Agricultural Operating Loan Insurance Program: Designed to assist agricultural enterprises in obtaining seasonal lines of credit. Generally used to insure up to 75% of loans which are used to pay for the costs associated with raising crops. The term of the loan cannot exceed 15 months and FAME's insurance amount not to exceed $250,000.

Economic Recovery Loan Program: Direct lending program designed to assist small businesses in their effort to remain viable during difficult economic times. The program is available to assist both existing firms and new business ventures. Borrower requests should be the minimum amount necessary to complete the project under consideration, not to exceed $200,000. Interest rates will not exceed Wall Street Prime plus 4%.

Overboard Discharge Replacement Program: Provides 100% loan insurance to lenders on loans made for the removal, rehabilitation or replacement of certain wastewater disposal systems which result in discharges into fresh or salt water. Maximum insured loan under this program is $1,000,000. Interest rates and loan terms are negotiated between the borrower and lender. Loan term may not exceed 10 years.

Waste Reduction and Recycling Loan Program: The Authority will sometimes request that businesses intending to finance projects designed to reduce and recycle waste submit proposals for loans of up to $50,000. Interest rates on loans are fixed at 8% or 4%, with the lower rate available to projects receiving 50% or more of the financing from sources other than the Authority.

Revenue Obligation Securities Program: The Finance Authority of Maine (FAME) is authorized to issue tax-exempt Industrial Revenue Bonds to finance any project authorized under the U.S. Internal Revenue Code, Section 103, including manufacturing facilities, solid waste projects and loans for non-profit corporations. Proceeds may be used for land, buildings, machinery and equipment, financing and interest charges, engineering, legal services, surveys, cost estimates and studies. Offers low financing rates.

Investment Banking Services: For borrowers seeking larger amounts of capital for major commercial projects. The Finance Authority of Maine (FAME) can help ensure that Maine businesses have available to them the best possible financial programs and services.

Adaptive Equipment Loan Program: Provides low interest loans to assist disabled persons in becoming more productive member of the community. Businesses may also borrow to make their facilities more accessible to physically challenged individuals. May also be used to enable a business to make physical and structural changes necessary to allow a business to hire disabled workers.

* Small Business Administration (SBA)
Federal Building
40 Western Avenue, Room 512   207-622-8378
Augusta, ME 04330   Fax: 207-622-8277
See the chapter introduction for a description of SBA programs.

* Farmers Home Administration (FmHA)
444 Stillwater Ave., Suite 2
P.O. Box 405
Bangor, ME 04402-0405   207-990-9160
FmHA Business and Industry Program: Assistance is provided in the form of loan guarantees. The Farmers Home Administration (FmHA) contracts to reimburse the lender for a maximum of 80 percent of on loans up to $10,000,000. Loans are limited to areas outside the boundaries of cities of 50,000 or more. Priority is given to communities with less than $25,000, as well as to job creation and retention. Basic uses for loans include developing or financing business or industry, and increasing employment. Maximum term for fixed-asset or working capital loans is 30 years, for machinery and equipment 15 years, for working capital 7 years. Interest rate may be fixed or variable.

* Economic Development Administration
Department of Commerce
40 Western Avenue
Augusta, ME 04330   207-622-8271
EDA Loans and Grants: Low-interest loans or grants to communities may be used to develop land or to make improvements to public facilities in order to promote development and business expansions.

* Certified Development Companies
Androscoggin Valley Council of Governments
70 Court Street
Auburn, ME 04210   207-783-9186

Coastal Enterprises, Inc.
P.O. Box 268
Wiscasset, ME 04578   207-882-7552

Eastern Maine Development Corporation
1 Cumberland Place, #300
Bangor, ME 04401   207-942-6389

Northern Kennebec Regional Planning Commission
7 Benton Avenue
Winslow, ME 04902   207-873-0711

Northern Maine Regional Planning Commission
P.O. Box 779
Caribou, ME 04736   207-498-8736

Lewiston/Auburn Economic Growth Council
P.O. Box 1188
Lewiston, ME 04243   207-784-0161

Certified Development Companies (CDC): CDCs are SBA certified and intended to assist communities, both urban and rural, by stimulating the growth and expansion of small businesses primarily through financial assistance. Financial assistance may be provided through the Development Company loan programs.

Certified Development Corporations also package applications for other programs. Each administering organization sets its own policies regarding the targeting of particular industries.

Regional Revolving Loan Funds: Capitalized with either public or private grants. These pools of money are loaned to expanding companies in order to fill financing gaps that will allow viable projects to proceed.

SBA 504 Program: Provides loans using 50 percent conventional bank financing, 40 percent Small Business Administration (SBA) involvement through Certified Development Companies, and 10 percent owner equity. Maximum loan amount is $750,000. Loan can be used for fixed assets (land and building, construction, machinery and equipment, and renovation/expansion).

Child Care Loans: Coastal Enterprises, Inc. is able to make loans to child care providers to expand or improve a child care business and to prospective child care providers to start-up a business.

Maryland

* Maryland Industrial Development Financing
   Authority (MIDFA)
   217 East Redwood Street, Suite 2244
   Baltimore, MD 21202   410-333-6932

Export Financing Program: For industrial/ commercial businesses engaged in the export of Maryland products or services, this program insures up to 90 percent of a conventional loan of from $10,000 to $5 million. Proceeds may be used to finance pre-and/or post-shipment working capital needs and standby letters of credit required by the foreign buyer.

Supplementary Export Financing Assistance: The Maryland International Division and the Maryland Industrial Development Financing Authority (MIDFA) can arrange specialized financing for exports through the Export-Import Bank of the United States. MIDFA can package and coordinate applications. In addition,

MIDFA serves as administrator for the Foreign Credit Association, which provides insurance against commercial and political risks associated with foreign receivables. Can be used in conjunction if the Export Financing Program.

Conventional Program: For industrial/ commercial businesses except certain retail establishments. Insures up to 80 percent or $1 million, whichever is lower, of a conventional loan. Proceeds may be used to finance fixed assets such as land, building, machinery and equipment, working capital, government contracts, revolving credit lines. Projects normally range from $35,000 to $5 million. Interest rates of loan are determined by the lender.

Enterprise Zone Program: For industrial/ commercial business except certain retail establishes located in State Enterprise Zones. Insures up to 90 percent or $500,000, whichever is lower, of a conventional loan. Proceeds may be used to finance fixed assets such as land, building, machinery and equipment, working capital, and government contracts. Projects normally range from $35,000 to $500,000. Interest rates of loan are determined by the lender. Advantages of locating in an enterprise zone include property-tax reduction and income tax credits to eligible firms.

Tax Exempt Program: Issues tax-exempt revenue bonds for manufacturers which may be totally or partially insured. Projects normally range from $200,000 to $10 million. Proceeds may be used for fixed assets such as land, new buildings, new machinery and equipment, existing buildings and use equipment. Interest rates are tax-exempt, floating, or fixed-rate as determined by bond purchaser or market conditions.

Taxable Bond Program: For industrial/ commercial businesses with certain exceptions. Insurance level varies with each project but is limited to $5 million. Can be used to finance fixed assets such as land, building-new or existing, permanent financing may be coupled with construction loan, new machinery and equipment.

Seafood and Aquaculture Loan Fund: Available to individuals or businesses involved in seafood processing or aquaculture. Can be used for construction, acquisition, renovations, and excavation of real property and acquisition of equipment and fixtures. Fixed interest rate at 2% below prime. Normal project ranges from $20,000 to $800,000.

Maryland Small Business Development Financing Authority (MSBDFA)   410-333-6975
Surety Bond Guarantee Assistance Program: Assists small contractors in obtaining bid, performance and payment bonds for government and public utility contracts. For small businesses employing fewer than 50 full-time employees or those with annual gross sales less than $10 million. Program guarantees up to 90% of the face value of issued bonds. Proceeds guarantee reimbursement of bid, payment, or performance bonds up to $1 million. Guarantee may not exceed term of the contract. Must have been denied bonding by a surety within 90 days of submitting an application, subcontract no more than 75 percent of the dollar value of the contract, and show that the contract will have substantial economic impact.

Long-Term Guaranty Program: Available to businesses owned 70% or more by socially and economically disadvantaged persons. Loan guarantee may not exceed the lesser of 80% of the loan or $600,000. Funds can be used for business working capital, acquisition of machinery or equipment, and real property improvements. Variable interest rate, no more than 2% over prime. MSBDFA can guarantee up to 80% of a loan made by a lending institution to a qualified applicant, and may provide an interest subsidy of up to 4%.

Contract Financing Program: Helps businesses owned 70% or more by socially and economically disadvantaged persons. Direct loans up to $500,000. Loan guarantees up to 90% not to exceed a maximum participation of $500,000. Funds can be used as working capital required to begin, continue and complete government or public utility contracts; acquisition of machinery or equipment to perform contracts.

Equity Participation Investment Program
Technology Component and Business Acquisition Component: Helps technology based business and business acquisitions which will be owned 70% or more by disabled, socially or economically disadvantaged persons. Technology based businesses - equity investment or loans up to $500,000; Business acquisitions - equity investments or loans up to 25% of initial investment or $500,000, whichever is less. Funds can be used for purchase of machinery and equipment, leasehold improvements, furniture and fixtures, inventory, working capital, real estate acquisitions, construction or major renovation, sign package and supplies, and purchase of stock aid the corporation.

Franchise Component: Available to franchises that are or will be owned 70% or more by disabled, socially or economically disadvantaged persons. Normal project range is $50,000 to $1.5 million. Equity investments or loans up to 45% or initial investment of $100,000, whichever is less. Funds can be used for purchase of machinery and equipment, leasehold improvements, furniture and fixtures, inventory, working capital, purchase of franchise, real estate acquisition, construction or renovation, franchise fees.

International Financing
Trade Financing Program: Available to industrial/ commercial businesses which are engaged in the export and import of goods through Maryland ports and airports as well as service providers to the overseas market. Normal range of project is $10,000 to $5 million. Insured up to lower of 90% of obligation or $1 million for export financing and 80% for all others. The actual amount of insurance varies with each transaction. Can be used to finance pre and/or post shipment working capital needs, standby letters of credit required by the foreign buyer, import letters of credit, and revolving credit lines. Loans can be conventional, floating or fixed rate as determined by lender.

Maryland Energy Financing Administration   410-333-4782
Maryland Energy Financing Program: Sale of revenue bonds are used to help businesses seeking to conserve energy, co-generate energy, and produce fuels and other energy sources. Projects range from $200,000 to $80 million. Proceeds may be used for land acquisition, building acquisition, construction or

rehabilitation, machinery and equipment, and hydroelectric facilities.

* Development Credit Fund, Inc.
2530 N. Charles Street, Suite 200
Baltimore, MD 21218   410-467-7500
Development Credit Fund Program: Loan guarantees for businesses owned by socially and economically disadvantaged persons. Must show experience in the trade. Projects range from $5,000 to $575,000. Proceeds may be used for working capital, acquisition of machinery and equipment acquisition, and business acquisitions, business real estate. Interest rates are variable, none more than 2 percent over prime rate.

* Community Financing Group
Department of Economic and Employment
   Development
Redwood Tower, 217 East Redwood
Baltimore, MD 21202   410-333-4304
Community Development Block Grant: Available to cities and counties for the commercial rehabilitation of existing buildings or structures used for business, commercial, or industrial purposes. Grants of up to $500,000 can be made. Every $15,000 of grant funds invested must create at least one full-time job, and at least 51 percent of the jobs created must be for low- and moderate-income families.

Maryland Industrial Land Act (MILA): Available to political jurisdictions attempting to develop or redevelop industrial space. Amount of loan varies with each type of loan; up to 1005 for a shell building. Industrial park loans cannot exceed $1.5 million or 50% of the project cost. Funds can be used for acquisition of industrial land, industrial park development, shell building construction, rehabilitation of existing buildings for business incubators, and utility lines and access roads. Terms of loans vary with each type of loan. Normally, up to 20 years.

Maryland Industrial and Commercial Redevelopment Fund (MICRF): Available to political jurisdictions attempting to develop or redevelop commercial or industrial enterprises. Normal project range is $300,000 to $10 million. Funds can be used for fixed assets (land, building, machinery and equipment), infrastructure (roads, sewer lines, utilities, telecommunications), technical assistance studies and some other soft costs. Terms of loans vary; may be up to 25 years.

* Maryland Business Assistance Center
217 East Redwood Street, 10th Floor
Baltimore, MD 21202   410-333-6975
Maryland Industrial and Commercial Redevelopment Fund:
Loan/Grant Program: The fund makes loans or grants to political subdivisions to cover part of the project costs of an industrial or commercial redevelopment project. Subdivisions then use proceeds to guarantee loans to redevelopers.

Foreign Trade Zones: Manufacturers, exporters, importers and distributors can realize significant operating and financial advantages. Reduced customs duties and improved cash flow are just two of the many benefits.

Enterprise Incentive Deposit Fund: Interest rate subsidies can be provided for real estate and equipment financing. Businesses in certain rural high unemployment areas of the state may be eligible for the 3% subsidy.

Employee Training Programs: Provides business with the skilled manpower it needs to operate profitably. Offers performance based, short-term training which is conducted during the start-up phase of operations. These programs will assist in recruiting personnel and will screen applicants for whatever skills and aptitudes the company specifies.

SBA Pollution Control Loan Guarantee Program: Will guarantee 85% of the payments due for installation of pollution control facilities or equipment by eligible small businesses.

Industrial Development Revenue Bonds: Manufacturers and 501(c)(3) organizations may finance the acquisition of land, buildings, machinery and equipment with tax-exempt industrial development revenue bonds. The terms, amount and uses of industrial development bonds financing are limited by federal law.

Maryland Department of Economic and Employment Development   410-333-6975
Maryland Industrial Land Act: Authorizes loans to counties and municipalities for options and acquisition of industrial land, development of industrial parks, construction of buildings, and purchase of options, access ways, utilities, and rail rights of way needed to serve industrial sites. Loan amounts range from $750,00 to $1.5 million.

* **Department of Economic and Employment**
   Development
   217 East Redwood Street
   Baltimore, MD 21202   410-333-6975
Day Care Facilities Financing Programs (DCFP):
Day Care Facilities Loan Guarantee
Program   410-333-4308
Loan guarantees insure up to 80 percent of loans. The project must create or expand day care facilities in the state and the applicant must demonstrate an inability to obtain adequate financing through normal lending channels. Must demonstrate the ability to manage the facility, or contract for management services. Funds can be used for construction, renovation, purchase of land and building, equipment, supplies and working capital. Funds can also assist in the financing of the purchase of an existing center, provided the center will be expanded to accommodate additional clients.

Facilities for Elderly and Handicapped Adults: Guarantees of loans are made to individuals or businesses to finance the expansion or development of day care facilities for the elderly and for medically handicapped adults. Applicants who own or are acquiring a building for elderly or medically handicapped adult day care or wish to have an adult day care facility in the

home may be eligible to apply to the *Maryland House Rehabilitation Program* to finance any required alterations or modifications to the structure. The two programs are working together.

Loan guarantees are also available for Child Care.

Child Care Facilities Direct Loan Fund: Fund is designed to finance up to 50 percent of the "hard" costs for the expansion or development of a child care facility where care is provided for seven or more children. For those seeking to expand or develop day care facilities in the state, have demonstrated the ability to manage the facility, or contract for management services, and are unable to obtain necessary financing through normal lending channels. Funds may be used for construction, renovation, or acquisition of real property. $15,000 is the minimum that may be borrowed directly from the DCFP for a child care facility in the home.

* **Small Business Administration**
   Prince Georges County/Montgomery County
   10 North Calvert   410-962-4392
   Baltimore, MD 21202   Fax: 410-962-1805

   Washington District Small Business Administration
   1111 18th Street, NW, 6th Floor
   P.O. Box 1993   202-634-1500
   Washington, DC 20036   Fax: 202-634-1803
See the chapter introduction for a description of SBA programs.

Massachusetts

* **Massachusetts Community Development**
   Finance Corporation
   10 P.O. Square, Suite 1090
   Boston, MA 02109   617-482-9141
Venture Capital Program: Provides debt and equity financing to small, viable businesses for working capital. Preferred investment range is $75,000 to $300,000. Program provides up to one-third of the total financing required.

Real Estate Program: Flexible, short-term financing for residential, commercial or industrial real-estate projects. May provide 20 percent or up to $250,000 for projects that will construct affordable housing or develop commercial property.

Urban Initiative Fund: Will consider financing and technical assistance to businesses that are at least 51% minority owned; are located in an urban, low income minority community; have less than $500,000 in annual nest sales. The Urban Initiative Fund (UIF) also provides loans to non-profit, community-based organizations that are governed by a Board of Directors composed of at least 51% minority group members; are located in an urban, low income, minority community. UIF seeks innovative ways to strengthen the economic and social infrastructure of low income minority communities by building the capacity of small minority owned businesses and minority controlled community organizations. Financing is available for working capital, equipment purchases, leasehold improvements, new product development and startups. Loans range from $5,000 to $200,000 though the preferred investment range is under $100,000.

* Massachusetts Economic Stabilization Trust Fund
    100 Cambridge Street, #1302
    Boston, MA 02202   617-727-8158
Industrial Services Program: Provides funding for companies in mature industries which face permanent layoffs or plant closings. Funds are in the form of conventional loans at favorable rates of interest with flexible terms.

* Massachusetts Business Development
    Corporation
    One Liberty Square, 2nd Floor
    Boston, MA 02109   617-350-8877
Business Loans: Provides loans to firms which are unable to obtain financing through conventional sources. Loans may be used for purchase or construction of fixed business assets (land, plant, equipment) and for working capital. Can provide up to 100 percent of financing.

* Massachusetts Capital Resource Company
    420 Boylston Street
    Boston, MA 02116   617-536-3900
Provides unsecured loans in the form of debt and equity financing to small and medium-sized firms that are unable to obtain financing through conventional sources. Maximum loan amount is $5 million.

* Massachusetts Industrial Finance Agency
    Beth L. Brown, Marketing Coordinator
    75 Federal Street   617-451-2477
    Boston, MA 02110   Fax: 617-451-3429
Taxable Industrial Development Bond: Bonds are available for a wide range of industrial and commercial capital expansions, including manufacturing, warehouse and distribution, and research and development projects. Proceeds can be used for the acquisition, construction, or renovation of buildings and land, or for the purchase of equipment.

Tax-Exempt Industrial Development Bond Program: Bonds can be used by manufacturers planning to construct new facilities, expand or renovate existing facilities, or purchase new equipment.

Guaranteed Loan Program: Pools either tax-exempt or taxable IDBs into one large bond issue to enable smaller companies access to the public credit market.

Mortgage Insurance Program: Insures portions of loans from 10% to 40% with a ceiling of $500,000 for real estate and $250,000 for equipment.

Seafood Loan Fund: Provides low-rate, fixed-rate financing for companies engaged in the seafood processing industry. Direct loans of up to $200,000 are available.

Childcare Facilities Loan Fund: Provides direct loans of up to $250,000 to companies, developers, and non-profit organizations to be used for acquisition, renovation, construction, and permanent installed equipment for on-site day care facilities.

Economic Development Fund: Targeted to small businesses including industrial, commercial, not-for-profit, and service firms. Funds may be used for acquisition, renovation or construction of facilities and the purchase of machinery and equipment. Loans are either fixed or variable rates on case-by-case basis. Direct loans range from $50,000 to $300,000. Loans will generally have a maturity of up to five years.

Economic Stimulus Fund: Targeted to industrial enterprises such as manufacturers. Funds may be used for acquisition, renovation or construction of facilities and the purchase of machinery and equipment. Loans will be either fixed or variable. Generally have a maturity of up to five years. Direct loan amounts range from $50,000 to $500,000. There is a $1,000 non-refundable, non-creditable application fee. 1% of the total principal amount of the loan is due to the Massachusetts Industrial Finance Agency (MIFA) at closing.

Massachusetts Export Finance Guarantee Program: Available to any size or type business interested in exporting which is unable to obtain financing without this guarantee, including companies interested in exporting services to other countries. No less than 51% of all content (materials, labor) must come from Massachusetts. Loans may be used to purchase materials, services and labor for the production of goods or services for current or future export sales. Also used for foreign business development (marketing activities, trade fair participation, or promotional activities). There is no minimum on the loan amount that can be guaranteed under the Partnership. The program will not be cost effective for amounts less that $50,000. The maximum guarantee size is 70% of a loan amount of $500,000, whichever is less.

Massachusetts Export Partnership Application: Can help you access the pre-export working capital that your company needs. Sponsored in conjunction with Eximbank and the Massachusetts Office of International Trade and Investment (OITI), this program encourages lenders who otherwise might be reluctant to loan working capital to exporters to take advantage of Eximbank's 100% guarantee.

Application for Export Import Bank of the United States (Eximbank) Umbrella Policy: Available to any size, type of business interested in exporting. Companies must have an average export sales of below $2 million during the past two years. Eximbank insurance covers up to 95% of the exporter's short-term credit sales. With the insurance, exporters can increase their competitiveness in the foreign markets by offering more flexible payment terms to their overseas customers.

Applications for Non-Profit Institutions for Tax-Exempt or Taxable Bond Financing: Available to Massachusetts 501 (c)(3) not-for-profit borrowers (educational institutions, cultural institutions, long term care facilities, medical diagnostic imaging facilities, and research and development facilities). Bond proceeds may be used to acquire, renovate or construct buildings, and to purchase equipment and land. May also be used to refinance existing asset-based debt.

Application for IDB-Eligible Borrowers for Tax-Exempt Lease/Purchase Financing: Tax-exempt IDBs are available for manufacturers undertaking the fixed asset expansion projects. Can also be used for environmental projects, including recycling plants and sewage, sold waste and hazardous waste facilities. Tax-exempt lease proceeds may be used to finance the purchase and installation of equipment on a capital lease basis.

Application for Tax-Exempt or Taxable Bond Financing for Environmental Projects: Available for qualified solid waste, hazardous waste, waste water treatment, and energy generation projects. Proceeds may be used to acquire, renovate or construct buildings, and to purchase land and equipment. There is no minimum or maximum bond amount. The bond financing may not be cost-effective for amounts less than $1.5 million.

Working Capital Financing: Fidelity Funding, Inc. (FF) provides working capital financing for small and medium-sized companies. Will fund against commercial and government receivables.

* Massachusetts Government Land Bank
    One Court Street, Suite 200
    Boston, MA 02108   617-727-8257
Mortgage Financing: Below-market rates for mortgages in the $200,000 to $2 million range for industrial projects that increase jobs in areas of high unemployment and projects that provide lower-income housing.

* Executive Office of Communities and Development
    CDAG Program Director
    Division of Communities Development
    100 Cambridge Street
    Boston, MA 02202   617-727-7180
Community Development Action Grant: Grants are made to cities and towns for public actions in support of private investments. Projects should create or retain long-term employment and/or housing opportunities and revitalize distressed areas.

Economic Development Set Aside Program   617-727-7180
Loans at low interest rates and favorable terms for businesses locating, expanding, or starting-up in communities that are eligible for HUD Small Cities Community Development Block Grants.

* Farmers Home Administration
    451 West Street
    Amherst, MA 01002   413-253-4300
Business and Industry Loans: Loan guarantees for funds for business and industrial acquisition, construction, repair,

modernization, purchase of land, machinery and equipment, furniture and fixtures, start up and working capital, processing and marketing facilities, and pollution control. Minimum loan size is $500,00. Maximum loan size is $10 million.

Farm Loan Guarantees: Made to family farmers and ranchers to enable them to obtain funds from private lenders. Funds must be used for farm ownership, improvements, and operating purposes.

Farm Operating Loans: Loans to help meet operating expenses, finance recreational and nonagricultural enterprises to add to family income, and pay for mandated safety and pollution control changes. Available at variable interest rates. Limits are $200,000 for an insured farm operating loan and $400,000 for a guaranteed loan.

Farm Ownership Loans: Can be used to for a wide range of farm improvement projects. Limits are $200,000 for an insured loan and $300,000 for a guaranteed loan.

Soil and Water Loans: Must be used by individual farmers and ranchers to develop, conserve, and properly use their land and water resources and to help abate pollution. Interest rates are variable; each loan must be secured by real estate.

Youth Project Loans: Enable young people to borrow for income producing projects sponsored by a school or 4H club.

* Economic Development Administration
    545 Boylston Street
    Suite 601
    Boston, MA 02116   617-727-7001
Business Development Loans: Provides direct loans to be used for the acquisition of fixed assets, land preparation, building rehabilitation, and working capital for industrial or commercial enterprises. Loans are available for up to 65 percent of project cost.

* Small Business Administration (SBA)
    Boston District Office
    10 Causeway Street
    2nd Floor, Room 265   617-565-5590
    Boston, MA 02222-1093   Fax: 617-565-5598
See the chapter introduction for a description of SBA programs.

* Office of Community Planning and
Development Division
    Department of Housing and Urban Development
    10 Causeway Street, 3rd Floor
    Boston, MA 02222   617-565-5345
Community Development Block Grant: Available to cities and counties for the commercial rehabilitation of existing buildings or structures used for business, commercial, or industrial purposes. Grants of up to $500,000 can be made. Every $15,000 of grant funds invested must create at least one full-time job, and at least 51 percent of the jobs created must be for low- and moderate-income families.

Urban Development Action Grant: Awarded to communities which then lend the proceeds at flexible rates to eligible businesses. Projects whose total costs are less than $100,000 are not eligible. UDAG funds should leverage at least three to four times their amount in private sector investment.

* Executive Office of Communities and Development
　　100 Cambridge Street, 14th Floor
　　Boston, MA 02202　　　　　　617-727-8690
Community Development Block Grant -- Small Cities: Available to cities and counties for the commercial rehabilitation of existing buildings or structures used for business, commercial, or industrial purposes. Grants of up to $500,000 can be made. Every $15,000 of grant funds invested must create at least one full-time job, and at least 51 percent of the jobs created must be for low- and moderate-income families.

* Massachusetts Technology Development Corporation
　　148 State Street, 9th Floor
　　Boston, MA 02109　　　　　　617-723-4920
Makes both debt and equity investments to provide working capital to new and expanding high technology companies which have the capacity to generate significant employment growth in the state.

* The Thrift Fund
　　50 Congress Street, Suite 515
　　Boston, MA 02109　　　　　　617-227-0404
A loan pool established to fund job-intensive projects in areas of higher-than-average unemployment, supporting mature industries, and assisting small businesses.

Michigan

* Michigan Strategic Fund
　　P.O. Box 30234
　　525 W. Ottawa
　　3rd Floor Law Bldg.
　　Lansing, MI 48933
State Research Fund　　　　　　517-335-2139
Grants of $20,000 to $50,000 for prototype development and to support successful Phase I federal Small Business Innovation Research projects while awaiting Phase II funding. A minimum 25 percent cash match is required of applicants.

BIDCO Program　　　　　　517-373-7551
Provides different types of financing including subordinate loans with equity features, royalty financing for product development, straight equity investments and guaranteed loans under the SBA 7(a) program.

Tax-Exempt Bonds　　　　　　517-373-6213
Tax-exempt bonds are issued for up to $10 million per company to finance up to 100 percent of the cost of acquiring and/or rehabilitating fixed assets.

Capital Access Program　　　　　　517-373-7551
Allows banks to make business loans that are riskier than conventional bank loans by providing a type of portfolio insurance to guarantee loan payments.

Seed Capital Funds　　　　　　517-373-7551
Enterprise Development Fund: Invests in industrial technology, biomedical and biotechnology, computer, consumer and communications businesses.

Onset Seed Fund: Specializes in industrial technology, with a special emphasis on creating companies which will provide products to the major automotive companies, as well as to suppliers for use in their manufacturing processes.

Diamond Venture Associates: Focuses on manufacturing or product-oriented businesses and service-oriented businesses. Feasibility prototypes, marketing strategies and test marketing are some of the projects that can be funded.

Demery Seed Capital Fund: Specializes in product-oriented businesses and service organizations with a more intensive focus on food processing industries.

Alternative Investments Division:
Michigan Venture Capital Fund Program　　　517-373-4330
Invests in high growth, high margin companies with a potential return on investment of 35 percent or more.

* MERRA
　　1050 Sixth Street, Second Floor
　　Detroit, MI 48226　　　　　　313-964-5030
Small Business Innovation Research Grants: Award between $20,000 to $50,000 to entrepreneurs to support six months of research on a technical innovation. Second phase grants are an additional $500,000 for development. Private sector investment funds must follow.

* Michigan Certified Development Corporation
　　525 W. Ottawa
　　Lansing, MI 48909　　　　　　517-373-6378
SBA 504: Provides loans using 50 percent conventional bank financing, 40 percent SBA involvement through Certified Development Companies and 10 percent owner equity. A fixed asset loan in amounts up to $500,000. Loan can be used for land and building, construction, machinery and equipment and renovation/expansion.

* Michigan Department of Commerce
　　525 W. Ottawa
　　Lansing, MI 48909　　　　　　517-373-9017
Community Development Block Grants: Available to cities and counties for the commercial rehabilitation of existing buildings or structures used for businesses, commercial or industrial purposes. Grants of up to $500,000 can be made. Every $15,000 of grant funds invested must create at least one full-time job and at least 51 percent of the jobs created must be for low and moderate income families.

State Money - Minnesota

* Small Business Administration
515 MacNamara Bldg.
477 Michigan Avenue   313-226-6075
Detroit, MI 48226   Fax: 313-226-4769
See the chapter introduction for a description of SBA programs.

Minnesota

---

* Minnesota Department of Trade and
Economic Development
Paul Moe, Director
500 Metro Square
121 7th Place East
St. Paul, MN 55101-2146   Fax: 612-296-3287

Economic Development Program: 612-296-5005
Contact Economic Development Director, Local Unit of Government. Local communities may use grant funds to make a loan to a specific businesses for expansion or start up purposes. A community may receive only one grant per year, with a maximum award of $500,000.

Minnesota Public Facilities Authority   612-296-4704
Provides loans and grants to qualified governmental units for the acquisition and betterment of public land, buildings, facilities and improvements of a capital nature.

Capital Access Program   612-297-1391
To encourage loans to businesses, particularly small and medium sized businesses, from private lending institutions to foster economic development. The lender obtains additional financial protection through a special fund created by the lender, borrower and the State. The lender and borrower contribute between 3% and 7% of the loan to the fund. Loans made for industrial, commercial, or agricultural purposes, refinancing of enrolled loans is permissible. All loan terms are negotiated between borrower and lender.

Tourism Loan Program   612-296-6858
Low-interest revolving loan fund for resorts, campgrounds and other tourism related businesses.

Small Business Development Loan Program: Creates jobs and provides loans for business expansion. Makes small business loans through the issuance of industrial development bonds backed by a state funded reserve of 25 percent. Available to manufacturing and industrial businesses located or intending to locate in Minnesota, those with 500 employees or fewer. Funds can be used for acquisition of land, building, machinery and equipment, building construction and renovations development costs, legal and financial fees. Minimum available $250,000 up to a maximum of $4 million. Market rate of interest for similar securities at the time bonds are sold. Rates are fixed for the term of the loan.

Infrastructure Financing for Communities
The Small Cities Development Program: Awards grants to local governments for public infrastructure (water, waste

water, storm sewer and flood control projects) and for housing and commercial district rehabilitation projects. Housing and commercial grants are loaned to individuals to correct serious structural deficiencies and code violations in their homes and businesses.

The Public Facilities Authority: Provides low-interest loans and other financial assistance to local governments and sanitary districts for new or expanded wastewater treatment facilities that meet the requirements of the Clean Water Act.

Financial Resources for Businesses
The Minnesota Job Skills Partnership Board: Awards grants for cooperative education and training projects between business and educational institutions.

The Economic Recovery Grant Program: Awards grants to local governments who, in turn, either make loans for business development projects or finance public improvements that support business development projects.

The Urban Challenge Grant Program: Provides matching grants to non-profit organizations, who make low-interest loans to businesses located in distressed areas.

Technical Assistance for Businesses
The Site Location Program: Assists businesses that are interested in expanding or relocating to Minnesota. Help identify potential sites and act as liaisons between businesses and local and state government. Provide data on business location factors (labor supply and cost, tax comparisons, and other operating cost comparisons).

The Small Business Assistance Office: Provides information and assistance on all aspects of start up, operation and/or expansion of businesses. Small business may obtain counseling for the purposes of business financing, management assistance, training, publications and other technical needs.

The Minnesota Job Skill Partnership Board: Awards grants for cooperative education and training projects between Minnesota businesses and educational institutions.

The Environmental Ombudsman: Provides information and educational materials to help small businesses maneuver through the environmental permitting and regulation process effectively and efficiently. Also acts as a facilitator between the private sector and environmental agencies.

Growing Minnesota Industries
The Wood Industry Development Program: Works to enhance the state's growing forest products industry. Advises existing businesses and assists new and expanding businesses regarding suppliers, financing, marketing and other business concerns.

The Health Care Industry Development Program: Works to stimulate growth in medical products and health care industry. Seeks to create new jobs and investment by assisting new and existing business in relocation or expansion within Minnesota.

The Printing and Publishing Industry Development Program: Works to enhance growth in the state's printing and publishing industry. The specialist advises existing businesses, seeks to create new jobs and investment by assisting new and existing businesses in relocation or expansion within Minnesota. He enhances relationships among companies, service providers, trade associations, economic development groups and government agencies.

Technical Assistance for Communities

Technical Assistance: Representative who can assist community leaders in establishing long-term business development and job creation activities.

The Star Program: Provides a framework for local units of government. With the professional assistance program staff, participating cities complete a process of organization, information gathering, planning and marketing. The communities are well prepared to work with business prospects and have a plan for job creation and retention.

The Minnesota Main Street Program: Helps participants create and implement a comprehensive approach to economic development for central business districts.

The Business Retention and Expansion Program: Helps communities retain and create jobs at existing local firms through a survey of major employers.

The Picture-It-Painted Program: Assists community groups with restoration and revitalization projects. Applicants receive paint and other coatings to complete projects that will benefit the community.

The Tools Program: Computer database designed to facilitate research on economic development by businesses and communities. Easy access to data on various industries, allowing users to quickly identify industry trends in such areas as sales and employment.

* Minnesota Technology, Inc.
111 Third Avenue South, Suite 400
Minneapolis, MN 55401   612-338-7722
Promotes jobs and economic growth through technology assistance services, and technology information. An early stage seed capital fund is expected to be available in 1992.

* Indian Affairs Council
1819 Bemidji Avenue
Bemidji, MN 56601   218-755-3825
Provides resources for management and technical assistance for businesses owned by Minnesota-based Indians. A special revolving loan fund disburses funds on a case-by-case basis.

* Small Business Administration (SBA)
610-C Butler Square Building
100 North Sixth Street

Minneapolis, MN 55403   612-370-2303
See the chapter introduction for a description of SBA programs.

* Dept. of Housing and Urban Development
220 Second Street South
Minneapolis, MN 55401   612-370-3000
Urban Development Action Grant: Awarded to communities which then lend the proceeds at flexible rates to eligible businesses. Projects whose total costs are less than $100,000 are not eligible. UDAG funds should leverage at least three to four times their amount in private sector investment.

* Agri-Bank
375 Jackson Street
St. Paul, MN 55101   612-282-8800
Federal Land Bank Association: Provides long-term credit for land and other purchases to farmers and farm-related businesses.

Production Credit Association: Provides short- and intermediate-term credit to cover seasonal operating expenses, land improvements, and purchases of farm equipment, livestock, storage facilities and buildings.

Bank for Cooperatives: Credit services for agricultural and rural utility cooperatives.

* Farmer's Home Administration
375 North Jackson, Suite 410
St. Paul, MN 55101   612-290-3866
Business and Industrial Loans: Assistance is provided in the form of a loan guarantee of up to 90 percent of the principal and interest. Funds can be used for financing construction, conversion, acquisition, equipment and machinery, supplies of materials, and working capital.

* Initiative Funds
Northwest Minnesota Initiative Fund
4 West Office Building, #310
P.O. Box 975
Bemidji, MN 56601   218-759-2057

Midwest Minnesota Community Development
  Corp. (MMCDC)
803 Roosevelt Avenue
P.O. Box 623
Detroit Lakes, MN 56501   218-847-3191

Northeast Minnesota Initiative Fund
204 Ordean Building
424 West Superior Street
Duluth, MN 55802   218-726-4740

West Central Minnesota Initiative Fund
Norwest Bank
220 West Washington, Suite 205
Fergus Falls, MN 56537   218-739-2239

Southwest Minnesota Initiative Fund
163 Ninth Avenue
Granite Falls, MN 56241   612-564-3060

Central Minnesota Initiative Fund
58 1/2 East Broadway
P.O. Box 59
Little Falls, MN 56345   612-632-9255

Southeast Minnesota Initiative Fund
540 West Hill Circle
P.O. Box 570
Owatonna, MN 55060   507-455-3215

Initiative Funds: Private, non-profit organizations supplemented with funds from various public and private sources. Funds are distributed in grants and loans. The six initiative funds listed above are separate entities, and each has its own programs, funding levels, and guidelines. Call your regional Initiative Fund.

The Midwest Minnesota Community Development Corporation (MMCDC) receives grants and loans from public and private sources and re-lends these funds to businesses in the form of secured loans. The interest rate charged is normally at or near bank loan rates. The Revolving Loan Fund serves a five county area of Minnesota (Hubbard, Mahnomen, Beltrami, Clearwater, and Lake of the Woods). The Non-Profit National Corporations Loan Program serves rural communities with a population of 20,000 or less.

Mississippi

* **Mississippi Department of Economic and Community Development**
  P.O. Box 849
  1200 Walter Sillers Building   601-359-3449
  Jackson, MS 39205   Fax: 601-359-2832

Mississippi Business Investment Act: This program matches $1 of State money for each $2 of private funds generated for a project. Each project must create at least 10 new jobs within two years and create at least one new full-time job per $15,000 loaned. Applicants must be sponsored by their locality -- city, town, or county.

Industrial Revenue Bonds: Designed for companies interested in financing land, building, machinery and equipment, the bonds are issued by political subdivisions and backed by corporate guaranty.

Loan Guaranty Program: Guarantees private loans made to small businesses for development and expansion of commercial and industrial enterprises. Maximum loan is $200,000, and maximum guaranty is 74 percent of the loan, not to exceed $150,000.

SBA 504: Provides loans using 50 percent conventional bank financing, 40 percent Small Business Administration (SBA) involvement through Certified Development Companies, and 10 percent owner equity. A fixed-asset loan in amounts up to $750,000. Loans can be used for land and building, construction, machinery and equipment, and renovation/expansion.

Small Enterprise Development Finance Act: Provides loans for small projects that will increase employment and investment in small communities Loans are through the Mississippi Small Enterprise Development Corp.

Farm Reform Act (MFRA):
Emerging Crop Loan Programs: Aids farmers with the production of emerging crops. Provides for the payment of interest on the farmer's original bank loan through MFRA funds until the initial crop is harvested. Offers long-term repayment of the interest loan to the State.

Tax Credits:

Job Tax Credit: Five-year tax credit to the company's state income tax for credit each new job created by a new or expanding business.

Research and Development Jobs Tax Credit: Provides an additional five-year tax credit of $500 per year for each new R&D job created by new or expanding businesses.

Headquarters Jobs Tax Credit: Provides an additional five-year tax credit of $500 per year for each new job created by the transfer of a national or regional headquarters to Mississippi, provided that at least 35 jobs are created.

Child Care Tax Credit: Tax credit of 25 percent of the unreimbursed expenses of a child's care to new or existing businesses that provide or contract for child care for employees during the employees' work hours.

CDBG Program: Available to cities and counties for the commercial rehabilitation of existing buildings or structures used for business, commercial, or industrial purposes. Grants of up to $500,000 can be made. Every $15,000 of grant funds invested must create at least one full-time job, and at least 51 percent of the jobs created must be for low- and moderate-income families.

EDA Grant Program: Funds to be used by communities for site preparation and construction of water and sewer facilities, access roads, and rail spurs for new or relocating businesses. Communities are required to provide 20-50 percent matching funds.

EDA Guaranty Loan: Proceeds of the loan can be used to acquire land, buildings, and equipment. Guarantee is for 80-90 percent of a conventional loan. Loan guaranties are restricted to a maximum of $10,000 per job to be created.

* **Small Business Administration (SBA)**
  101 W. Capital
  Suite 400
  First Jackson Century   601-965-4378
  Jackson, MS 39201   Fax: 601-965-4294

See the chapter introduction for a description of SBA programs.

Missouri

* Missouri Dept. of Economic Development
P.O. Box 118
Jefferson City, MO 65102   314-751-0717
Missouri Economic Development Infrastructure Board Loan Guarantee: Works in the same way as an SBA 7(a) loan. Guarantees up to 85 percent of a maximum loan of $400,000. (see below)

Action Fund (MoDag) Program: Direct loans of up to $400,000 to be used as gap financing to supplement Community Development Block Grants.

Mo Bucks: Offers expanding companies low-interest, short-term loans based on creation of new jobs. Companies can get up to $25,000 for each new job created. Funds can be used for any costs involved in the expansion.

Tax Exempt Revenue Bonds: Can finance 100 percent of a project costing not more than $10 million in capital expenditures. Funds to be used for fixed assets only such as real property improvements, machinery, and equipment for manufacturing purposes.

Community Development Block Grant: Funds up to $500,000 are available to cities and counties. Every $10,000-$25,000 of funds invested must create at least one full time job,, and at least 51 percent of the jobs created must be for low-and-moderate income families.

* Small Business Administration (SBA)
911 Walnut Street, 13th Floor   816-426-3608
Kansas City, MO 64016   Fax: 816-426-5559
See the chapter introduction for a description of SBA programs.

Montana

* Board of Investments
Office of Development Finance
Capitol Station
Helena, MT 59620   406-444-0001
Coal Tax Loan Programs: Trust funds are established each year with proceeds from state coal taxes. Loans are made to Montana businesses that will create long-term benefits to the state's economy. Long-term, fixed-rate direct loans are available through approved financial institutions. The maximum loan can not exceed 10 percent of the prior year's deposits into the funds.

Federally Guaranteed Loan Programs: Financial institutions that have secured a federal guarantee on a fixed-rate loan to a business that is eligible for Board investment may sell the federally guaranteed portion of the loan to the Board at a pre-established rate. This program provides fixed-rate financing at lower-than-average interest rates. Proceeds may be used for the purchase of land, buildings, equipment, machinery, building expansion or repair, inventory, or funds for working capital.

Economic Development Linked Deposit Program: State funds are placed in long-term deposit with approved financial institutions to back-up loans to specific borrowers. The proceeds from this fixed-rate loan can be used for working capital, interim construction, inventory, site development, and acquisition of machinery, equipment and buildings, among other uses.

Business Loan Participation Program: May be used to finance commercial, multi-family or Small Business Administration (SBA) 504 loans, it allows approved Montana financial institutions the opportunity to "sell" up to 80 percent of an eligible business loan to the Board of Investments. The Board then owns a participation interest in both the financing and the security for an approved commercial loan that is serviced by the originating financial institution. Funds are targeted to long-term fixed-rate loans that have the potential to positively benefit economic development within the state.

SBA 504 Loan Participation Program: Essentially the same as the Business Loan Participation Program but in this case the Board funds a portion of a project financed under the SBA 504 Program.

Stand Alone Industrial Development Bond Program: Borrowers able to assume responsibility for funding their own projects can have the Board of Investments issue industrial development bonds. Projects must be in the public interest.

* Montana Capital Companies
Billings: Renaissance Capital Ltd. Partnership, 115 N. Broadway, Billings, MT 59101, 406-248-6771.

Billings: Treasure State Capital Ltd. Partnership, 512 N. 29th, Billings, MT 59101, 406-245-6102.

Billings: KBK Venture Capital Co. of Montana, 722 Third Avenue North, Billings, MT 59101, 406-256-2355.

Black Eagle: The Glacier Springs Company, P.O. Box 399, Black Eagle, MT 59414, 406-727-7500.

Butte: Southwest Montana Development Corp., 305 West Mercury, Butte, MT 59701, 406-723-4349.

Great Falls: Great Falls Capital Corporation, 9 Third Street North, Suite 305, Great Falls, MT 59401, 406-761-7978.

Missoula: First Montana Capital Corporation, 310 West Spruce Street, Missoula, MT 59802, 406-721-4466.

Venture, Equity or Risk Capital: The Montana legislature adopted an act to encourage the private sector in Montana to create organized pools of equity or venture capital that could be invested in Montana businesses. Through these companies, Montana Capital Companies invest funds in small businesses engaged in one of the following:

Manufacturing

Agricultural, fishery, or forestry production and processing

Mineral production and processing, except for conventional oil and gas exploration.

Nonfossil forms of energy generation

Transportation

Research and development of products or processes associated with any of the activities listed above

Wholesale or retail distribution activities for which products produced in Montana comprise 50% or more of gross sale receipts

Any activity conducted in the state for which 50% or more of the gross receipts are derived from the sale of products or services outside Montana

Tourism

* Local Government Assistance Division

Department of Commerce
1424 9th Avenue
Helena, MT 59620   406-444-3757

Community Development Block Grant Program: Available to cities and counties, and towns for the commercial rehabilitation of existing buildings or structures used for business, commercial, or industrial purposes. Grants of up to $500,000 can be made. Every $15,000 of grant funds invested must create at least one full-time job, and at least 51 percent of the jobs created must be for low- and moderate-income families.

County Land Planning Grant Program: County governments receive a percentage of the coal severance tax collected by the state, which may then be distributed by the counties to local planning boards. Funds are used for local land use planning, including downtown redevelopment, economic development, and capital improvements planning.

Local Impact Assistance Program: Funding is derived from the Montana coal severance tax. Loans and grants are awarded to local governments which have been required to expand the provision of public services as the result of large-scale development of coal mines and coal-using energy complexes.

* Department of Agriculture

Agriculture/Livestock Bldg.
Capitol Station
Helena, MT 59620-0201   406-444-2402

Junior Agriculture Loan Program: Direct, lower-interest rate financing to active members of rural youth organizations for junior livestock and other agricultural business loans. May also make direct loans to youths unable to participate as members of such organizations. Projects can involve crop and livestock production, custom farming, marketing and distribution processing. Loans shall not exceed $7,000.

Rural Assistance Loan Program: Provides loans to farmers and ranchers with modes financial investments in agriculture. Available to those who are unable to qualify for financing from

commercial lenders. Maximum loan amount is $25,000, not to exceed 80 percent of the loan value. Funds can be used to finance agricultural property such as livestock and farm machinery, improvements such as barns and irrigation systems, annual operating expenses, and agricultural land.

Montana Growth Through Agriculture Act (MGTA): Intent of MGTA is to create jobs and expand small agricultural business opportunities. The program receives a level of coal severance tax revenues for the purpose of funding seed capital loans, market enhancement and research grants, agricultural business incubators and foreign trade office activities.

Seed Capital Loans: Funds are specifically intended for the commercialization and marketing of new and innovative agricultural products or processes. Maximum loan amount in any one round of financing is $50,000.

Market Development Grant Program: Program is intended to benefit Montana's agricultural community by upgrading existing agricultural research capabilities, providing financial support to individual research projects, supporting organization improvements and marketing, facilitating the process of transferring research from the laboratory to the commercial marketplace. The project must demonstrate potential for commercial application by other prospective producers or processors, and the primary beneficiary of market development grants results must be the general public.

* Department of Natural Resources and Conservation

Water Development Bureau
1520 East 6th Avenue
Helena, MT 59620-2301   406-444-6668

Water Development Loan and Grant Programs: The state's coal severance tax provides grants, and two bonding authorities fund loans. Loans and grants available for such diverse water development projects as dam and reservoir construction, streambank stabilization and erosion control, development of water conservation measures, and water and sewer projects.

Reclamation and Development Grant Program: Funds projects that protect and restore the environment from damages resulting from mineral development and projects that meet other crucial state needs. Other projects may qualify if they enhance Montana's economy or develop, promote, protect, or otherwise further Montana's total environment and public interest.

* Small Business Administration (SBA)

301 S. Park, Room 528   406-449-5381
Helena, MT 59626   Fax: 406-449-5474

See the chapter introduction for a description of SBA programs.

* Montana Science and Technology Alliance

46 North Last Chance Gulch, Suite 2B
Helena, MT 59620   406-449-2778

The purpose of the Alliance is to provide a source of financing for technology-based, entrepreneurial development to revitalize

Montana industries and encourage new ones. They operate two financing programs:

Seed Capital Financing Program: Give priority to companies which incorporate advanced or innovative technologies, include plans for full commercialization and address one or more the Alliance's target technologies. Available to companies which cannot be financed through conventional financing do to the need for working capital and the lack of collaterizable assets but which hold realistic promise for rapid and significant growth. Maximum loan amount is $350,000 for a single round of financing and up to a total of $750,000 over multiple financing rounds. Program loans require a 100 percent co-investment from private sources.

Research and Development Financing Program:
Centers for Excellence Program: Assists in the accelerated development of technology in the state by providing a source of funds to research organizations for projects which have outstanding technological and commercial potential for development in the state.

Nebraska

* Nebraska Investment Finance Authority
1033 O Street, Suite 218
Lincoln, NE 68508   402-434-3900
Provides lower-cost financing for manufacturing facilities, certain farm property, healthcare, and residential development. Funds can be used for land, buildings or equipment. All types of manufacturing and industrial projects including assembling, processing, warehousing, distributing, and transporting are eligible for funding. Minimum loan is $700,000.

Industrial Development Revenue Bonds (IDRB): Lower-cost financing through tax-exempt bonds for manufacturing projects only. Proceeds can be used to buy land, plants, equipment and on-site utilities. Maximum loan is $10,000,000.

* Department of Economic Development
P.O. Box 94666
301 Centennial Mall South   402-471-3119
Lincoln, NE 68509   1-800-426-6505 in Nebraska
Community and Rural Development Division:
Community Improvement Financing: Encourages private investment in economically depressed areas for public improvements. Loans are available for land purchase, clearance, and sale, construction of streets, sidewalks, utilities, and parks.

Existing Business Assistance Division   402-471-4167
Economic Development Finance Program/ Community Development Block Grants: Direct loans or loan guarantees for fixed assets, real estate and working capital, grants for job training, and deferred loans to help meet equity requirements of commercial lender are available to businesses for job-creation

business development in towns under 2,500 population. Maximum loan is up to 50 percent of the project costs. The remaining portion to come from conventional financing. At least one job must be created for every $20,000, and a majority of the jobs created/retained must be for made available to low-and moderate-income people.

* Small Business Administration
11145 Mill Valley Road   402-221-4691
Omaha, NE   Fax: 402-221-3680
Small Business Assistance   402-471-3782
Small Business Innovation Research Program (SBIR): Provides small business concerns with an opportunity to propose innovation ideas that meet specific research and development needs of one or more of the eleven participating federal agencies and has the potential for future commercialization. Phase I awards are between $20,000 to $50,000 to entrepreneurs to support six months of research on a technical innovation. Phase II grants are an additional $500,000 to pursue further development. Phase III is for the commercialization of the results of Phase II and requires the use of private sector investment funds. Businesses can be added to a list of firms that are sent copies of the SBIR Pre-Solicitation Announcement.

See the chapter introduction for a description of SBA programs.

* Nebraska Economic Development Corporation (NEDC)
2631 O Street
Lincoln, NE 68510   402-475-2795
SBA 504: Provides loans using 50 percent conventional bank financing, 40 percent SBA involvement, and 10 percent owner equity. Loan-term fixed-asset financing in amounts up to $750,000. Loan can be used for land and building, construction, machinery and equipment, and renovation/expansion.

* Farmers Home Administration
Federal Building, Room 308
100 Centennial Mall North
Lincoln, NE 68508   402-437-5556
Business and Industrial Loan Program: The programs are to create and maintain employment, and improve the economic and environmental climate in rural areas with a population of 25,000 or less. Loan guarantees are available for business and industrial acquisitions, construction conversion, enlargement, repair and modernization, purchase of land, machinery and equipment, processing and marketing facilities, start-up and working capital, and pollution control. Guarantees up to 90 percent of project up to a maximum of $10 to $20 million dollars.

* Nebraska Research and Development Authority
NBC Center, Suite 660   402-475-5109
Lincoln, NE 68508   Fax: 402-475-5170
The Authority supports business development and technology transfer. Invests in "seed" capital in new businesses that export a substantial amount of their product or service outside of Nebraska. They take an equity position in the business created.

* Northeast Nebraska Venture Capital Network
405 Madison Avenue
Norfolk, NE 68702   402-371-4862
Encourages the development and expansion of home-grown enterprises. Private investors may provide seed capital for inventors, early stage financing for start-up firms, or expansion capital for established firms. Companies receiving funds must locate in a 20-county area in northeast Nebraska. Loan structure or equity position will vary with investors.

Nevada

* Nevada Commission of Economic Development
Capital Complex   702-687-4325
Carson City, NV 89710   Fax: 702-687-4450
Regional Development Grants: Provides matching grants to regional development organizations to encourage cooperative economic diversification.

* Nevada Department of Commerce
1665 Hot Springs Rd
Carson City, NV 89710   702-687-4250
Industrial Development Revenue Bonds (IDRBs): Tax-exempt industrial revenue bonds are available to manufacturing facilities for a maximum of 40 years and can provide up to 100 percent financing for land, building, improvements, and capital equipment for businesses incurring between $ 1-10 million in development costs.

* Department Commission of Economic Development
Capital Complex   702-687-4325
Carson City, NV 89710   Fax: 702-687-4450
Enterprise Zones: Offers incentives to businesses to encourage development in designated zones. Las Vegas and North Las Vegas are currently Enterprise zones.

Small Business Revitalization Program: Office specializes in creating loan packages for businesses and reviews and assesses expansion projects. The staff can also recommend the most efficient financing for a specific project and acts as an advocate for small businesses with commercial lenders. The program uses loans available from the public sector, such as the Small Business Administration 504 loan guarantees and the Nevada Revolving Loan Fund in order to encourage private sector investment in small business expansion projects.

Nevada Revolving Loan Fund Program: Funded through the Small Cities Community Development Block Grant, this program provides loans for small business expansion if low- and moderate-income jobs are created. Financing must not be available from conventional lenders. Loans of up to $100,000 are available for "gap financing". Rates are variable.

SBA 7(a) Loan Guarantee Program: Guarantees up to 90 percent of a loan, up to $750,000, made through conventional bank financing. Funds can be used for working capital, fixed asset acquisition, and leasehold improvements.

* Nevada State Development Corporation
350 S. Center Street, Suite 310
Reno, NV 89501   702-323-3625
SBA 504: Provides loans using 50 percent conventional bank financing, 40 percent SBA involvement through Certified Development Companies, and 10 percent owner equity. A fixed-asset loan in amounts up to $750,000. Loan can be used for land and building, construction, machinery and equipment, and renovation/expansion.

* Farmers Home Administration
Nevada State Development Corp.
350 South Center Street, Suite 310
Reno, NV 89501   702-323-3625
Business and Industry Loan Guarantee Program: This program provides loan guarantees to improve, develop, or finance business, industry and employment in rural areas.

Working Capital Guarantee Program: This program assists small and medium size exports obtain financing needed to produce goods and services for sales abroad by guaranteeing private lend loans.

* Small Business Administration (SBA)
District Office
301 East Stewart St., Room 301   702-388-6611
Las Vegas, NV 89125   Fax: 702-388-6469
See the chapter introduction for a description of SBA programs.

New Hampshire

* Industrial Development Authority
Frank J. Lass
4 Park Street, Room 302   603-271-2391
Concord, NH 03301-6313   Fax: 603-271-2396
Industrial Development Revenue Bond Financing: Tax exempt revenue bond financing is available through the Business Finance Authority (BFA). Advantages include 1005 financing. Lower interest costs to the company and no dilution of equity. Eligible applicants are manufacturing facilities, facilities for the disposal of waste material; small-scale power facilities for producing electric energy; water-powered electric generating facilities; water facilities for the collecting, purifying, storing or distributing of water for use by the general public. Bond proceeds may be used to finance the cost of land, buildings and equipment, as well as bond counsel fees and the development and financing costs of the project.

Guaranteed Loans
The Guarantee of Loans to Small Business Program: This program works in conjunction with the U.S. Small Business

Administration (SBA). For businesses seeking guarantees on loan amounts that exceed the SBA's capacity. The Business Finance Authority (BFA) guarantees amount shall not exceed 90% of the original principal amount of the loan. The BFA guarantee amount and the SBA guarantee amount shall not exceed $1,500,000. The loan amount used to finance working capital shall not exceed $500,000. There is a non-refundable application fee of $250.

Machinery and Equipment: Guarantees up to 35 percent of the cost of new industrial machinery and equipment. The maximum guarantee for any single project is $600,000.

The Capital Access Program (CAP): For small businesses experiencing difficulty obtaining lines of credit and funds for start-up or expansion. Encourages banks to make loans to businesses with more than conventional risk by creating an account designed to protect the lender. The account reduces lender risk by decreasing the bank's exposure on the loan. CAP is available to businesses with annual revenues of less than $5,000,000. Total loan amount may not exceed $500,000.

The Guarantee Asset Program (GAP): Designed to provide assistance to capital intensive businesses experiencing difficulty obtaining normal bank financing. BFA will guarantee up to 90% of a loan made by a bank to a qualifying business. The borrower must have at least 25 full time employees. No more than 40% of the gross proceeds of the loan may used to finance working capital. The maturity of a loan shall not exceed 5 years. The terms of the loan will be determined by the participating financial institution.

The Temporary Loans to Business Program: The BFA will warehouse taxable and tax-exempt bond issues and package them into a composite bond. By placing bonds through the BFA, businesses can minimize their financing costs. The total principal amount of the loan shall not exceed $2,000,000. Interested businesses should arrange to meet with the Senior Credit Officer of the BFA to discuss application procedures.

Secondary Market for Loans by Local Development Organizations Program: Local Development Organizations (LDO) can sell their existing loans to the BFA and use the proceeds for loans for business development. Any LDO dedicated to the promotion and development of business is eligible for this program. The applying LDO must have a detailed plan describing how the proceeds of the sale will be used to promote business and maintain and/or create employment opportunities. A non-refundable application fee of $250 will be charged for each loan submitted for consideration.

Aid to Local Development Organizations Program: To help LDOs create and maintain employment opportunities, the BFA may lend money to LDOs for the purpose of developing and expanding business opportunities in their market area. By providing LDOs with additional resources

for financing, the BFA can effectively foster economic growth through existing organizations dedicated to the development of business. Any local development organization dedicated to the promotion and development of business is eligible for this program. The terms of the loan to the business will determined by the participating LDO.

* Small Business Administration (SBA)
District Office
143 N. Main, Suite 202   603-225-1400
Concord, NH 03302-1257   Fax: 603-225-1409
See the chapter introduction for a description of SBA programs.

* Development Corporations
Concord Community Development Corp.
(Merrimack County)
45 Airport Road
P.O. Box 664
Concord, NH 03301

Granite State Economic Development Corporation
(Belknap, Chesire, Hillsborough, Strafford, Sullivan, Rockingham Counties)
P.O. Box 1491
Portsmouth, NH 03802   603-436-0009

* Farmers Home Administration (FmHA)
3rd Floor, City Center
89 Main Street
Montpelier, VT 05602   802-828-4472
FMHA Business and Industrial Development Loan Program: Guarantees loans to all types of businesses and industries to benefit rural areas. Available for projects in all municipalities in New Hampshire except Manchester and Nashua and communities immediately contiguous to these two cities. Loans can be used for business; construction, conversion, enlargement, repair and modernization; purchase and development of land and facilities, easements, leases, machinery and equipment, supplies or materials; certain housing development sites; processing and marketing facilities; working capital; pollution control.

* New Hampshire Office of State Planning
2-1/2 Beacon Street
Concord, NH 03301   603-271-2155
Community Development Block Grants (CDBG): Grants are awarded to municipalities who in turn loan the funds to help municipalities meet housing and community development needs by alleviating some form of physical or economical distress.

* Economic Development Administration
Federal Building
55 Pleasant Street
Concord, NH 03301   603-225-1624
Loan Guarantee Program: Available to business unable to obtain conventional financing. Guarantees up to 80 percent of project. Funds can be used for land and machinery, new construction or

rehabilitation of commercial or industrial buildings, and working capital. For each $20,000 of loan guarantee, a job must be created or saved.

* New Hampshire Port Authority
     555 Market Street, Box 506
     Portsmouth, NH 03801   603-436-8500
Foreign Enterprise Zone: Foreign traders can store, mix, blend, repack and assemble various commodities with an exemption from normal custom duties and federal excise taxes. Four areas in New Hampshire have been designated as Foreign Trade Zone 81. They are the Port Authority Terminal, Portsmouth; Portsmouth Industrial Park; Crosby Road Industrial Park, Dover; Manchester Airport (formerly Grenier Air Base, Manchester).

* Industrial Development Manager
     Public Service of New Hampshire (PSNH)
     1000 Elm Street
     Manchester, NH 03105   603-669-4000
Development Incentive Rate Contract: PSNH offers an incentive rate to its new or expanding commercial and industrial customers that will provide benefits to all PSNH customers. PSNH negotiates special rate contracts with existing or new customers having incremental load requirements of more than 300 kilowatts.

* NETAAC (New England Trade Adjustment
     Assistance Center)
     120 Boylston Street
     Boston, MA 02116   617-542-2395
Direct Loan Guarantees: Available to manufacturing firms for the purchase of equipment or plant expansions. Maximum available is $1 million.

Trade Adjustment Assistance: Manufacturing company must have experienced a decline in production or sales and an actual or threatened decrease in employment, attributable to increased imports of competitive products.

New Jersey

* New Jersey Economic Development Authority
     Capital Place One
     200 S. Warren Street, CN 990
     Trenton, NJ 08625   609-292-1800
Direct Loans: The New Jersey Economic Development Authority provides up to $500,000 in direct loans for qualified businesses unable to obtain conventional loans. Loans of up to $250,000 are available for working capital. Aimed at businesses in manufacturing, processing, or distributing that will either create jobs or are located in economically distressed areas. The interest rate is on par with the current federal discount rate.

Urban Centers Small Loan Program: Loans up to $30,000 to encourage merchants to remain in downtown urban areas. These

loans have set interest rates of 1 percent below the federal discount rate.

Revolving Line of Credit: A one year revolving line of credit of up to $100,000 for companies interested in exporting.

Fixed Asset Loans/Local Development Financing Fund: Loans are made for commercial and industrial projects in designated communities, for fixed assets only. Loans are for up to 25 years and range from $25,000 to $2 millions. Funds must be matched 1:1 from the public and private sector.

Loan Guarantees: Aids businesses needing additional security to receive a conventional loan or bond financing. The Authority can guarantee a portion of a loan for fixed assets or for working capital needs up to $1 million. These guarantees are aimed at businesses involved in manufacturing, processing, or distribution that will create a significant number of jobs or are located in economically distressed areas. The guarantees cover up to 90 percent of the loan, for a maximum of 10 years.

Industrial Revenue Bonds: Tax-exempt bonds for manufacturing needs, first-time farmers and certain non-profit organizations. The tax relief enjoyed by purchasers enables applicants to borrow money at more favorable interest rates. The Authority can also issue taxable bonds, as well as composite bonds when financing for smaller individual projects is grouped into a larger issue.

Real Estate Development Program: Develops business parks and other commercial facilities, acquiring and improving vacant or existing sites, and subdividing the sites for sale to businesses. Newly constructed facilities may qualify for a 15 year property tax abatement.

Economic Growth Bonds: Provide long-term loans at attractive, market interest rates for real estate acquisition/equipment, machinery, building/ construction/ renovations. Minimum loan size is approximately $750,000. Maximum tax-exempt bond amount for manufacturers is $10 million.

Bond Financing: Available to manufacturing facilities, governmentally owned public airports/docks/wharves/mass commuting facilities, water/sewer facilities/ sewage disposal facilities, solid waste disposal facilities, electric/gas furnishings facilities/hazardous waste facilities. Maximum tax-exempt bond amount for manufacturers is $10 million. Proceeds may be used for construction, purchase or renovations, equipment and machinery.

Statewide Loan Pool for Business: Businesses must either create or retain jobs; be located in a financially targeted municipality; or represent a targeted industry such as manufacturing, industrial, agricultural, etc. Assistance will not exceed $35,000 per job created or maintained.

Loan Guarantees: Preference is given to businesses that will create or maintain tax ratable, are located in an economically distressed area, or represent an important economic sector of the state and will contribute to New Jersey's growth/diversity. Guarantees of conventional loans of up to $1 million for working capital and guarantees of conventional loans/bond issues for fixed assets of up to $1.5 million are available.

New Jersey Worldwide: Available to businesses that want to enter the export market/expand export sales but unable to obtain funds elsewhere. At least 50% of the costs of the goods/services being financed must be added in New Jersey. Up to $1 million one-year revolving line of credit will be provided to finance confirmed foreign orders. The bank will provide 75% of the funds at its normal lending rate and EDA will provide the remaining 25% at its lending rate, but no lower than 5%.

Export Working Capital Loans: Any business exporting/planning to export goods/ services it has produced and unable to get financing on its own. A one-year revolving line of credit for up to $250,000 can be established annually. Funds can be used to purchase materials and production costs for confirmed orders. Interest is set at the federal discount rate but no lower than 5%.

Grow New Jersey Fund: Any for-profit business may be eligible for consideration. Borrower must create/retain a minimum of one job per $35,000 of assistance. May borrow up to $1 million to be used for fixed asset needs, such as real estate/machinery/ equipment/working capital. EDA provides 10% of the total loan amount for loans up to $155,000 and 15% for loans in excess of $155,000. No minimum is needed for working capital financing.

Financing for Small Businesses, Minority-Owned and Women-Owned Enterprises: Most of the funds are targeted to enterprises located in Atlantic City or providing goods/ services to customers in Atlantic City. Loans of up to $1 million are made for up to 15 years for real estate; 10 years for fixed assets; and up to 5 years for working capital. Interest rate is set at 200 basis points above 2/3 of the prevailing Moody's "A" rated Utility Index, but no lower than 5%.

New Jersey Contractors Assistance Program: Small contracting businesses/women businesses primarily in the Atlantic City area, are eligible. Help small contractors get performance bonds and bid successfully on major construction projects.

Recycling Loans: Available to businesses which collect/separate, process/convert post-consumer waste into new/marketable products. Loans may range from $50,000 - $500,000 or higher, depending on available funds. Financing is made for up to 10 years at 3% below the prime rate. Proceeds may be used for buildings/land/equipment and machinery/trucks and other vehicles/ professional engineering and architectural services.

Underground Storage Tank Improvement Loan Program: Available to small businesses with 100 employees or less that own their own underground storage tanks and demonstrate an economic hardship. Loans range from $5,000 to $100,000 are made to upgrade existing tanks or install new ones. Financing may be from 5-10 years at an interest rate from 2 1/2% to 6%.

* **New Jersey Urban Development Corp.**
    Capital Place One
    200 S. Warren Street, CN 990
    Trenton, NJ 08625　　　　　　　609-633-1100

Provides financial and other assistance for development projects in qualified communities. Working as a complement to other urban development programs, the UDC tries to give impetus to joint government/ private sector development programs. The UDC can buy, sell, and lease property, make loans, construct projects, enter into joint ventures, and buy and sell stock in subsidiaries it creates.

* **Office of Urban Enterprise Zones**
    New Jersey Department of Commerce and
    Economic Development
    20 W. State St., CN 829
    Trenton, NJ 08625-0829　　　　　609-292-1912
Urban Enterprize Zones Program: Provides incentives for urban development projects through tax credits and tax exemptions. In certain areas, businesses receive a 50 percent reduction in the 6 percent state sales tax on goods sold. The tax collected in those locations goes into a special State Treasury account, to be released later for use in development projects in amounts equal to the proportion of taxes paid by each participating city.

* **Small Business Administration (SBA)**
    60 Park Place, 4th Floor　　　　　201-645-2434
    Newark, NJ 07102　　　　　　Fax: 201-645-6265
See the chapter introduction for a description of SBA programs.

* **New Jersey Commission on Science and Technology**
    20 West State Street, CN 832
    Trenton, NJ 08625-0832　　　　　609-984-1671
Small Business Innovative Research Grants (SBIR): Award between $20,000 to $50,000 to entrepreneurs to support six months of research on a technical innovation. Second phase grants are an additional $500,000 for development. Private sector investment funds must follow.

* **Local Municipality**
    Small Cities Block Grant Program: Funding is available to businesses located in small cities and non-urban counties designated by the federal Department of Housing and Urban Development. Funds are awarded competitively for use on fixed assets only. 51 percent of jobs created by the project must go to low- and moderate-income workers, and the business must be unable to obtain financing from other sources.

* **New Jersey Commission on Science and Technology**
    20 West State Street, CN 832
    Trenton, NJ 08625-0832　　　　　609-984-1671
Helps small, technology-based companies in their formative years. Services include bridge grants for while they are waiting for the next installment of their SBIR funds; the Washington Technical Liaison, who helps companies obtain the SBIR grants; and Innovation Partnership Grants, which provide funds to assist academic researchers involved in projects of use to industry. The

state's major scientific research centers at Princeton University, the New Jersey Institute of Technology, Rutgers State University, the University of Medicine and Dentistry of New Jersey, and the Stevens Institute of Technology are linked to the program. The New Jersey Entrepreneur's Forum, supported by the Commission, gives new companies the benefit of advice and assistance from experienced business people.

* Casino Reinvestment Development Authority (CRDA)
1301 Atlantic Ave, 2nd Floor
Atlantic City, NJ 08401   609-347-0500
Funnels a portion of casino revenues into state development projects, by mandatory investment in CRDA taxable or tax-free bonds (1.25 percent of casino gross receipts). CRDA pays interest at 2/3rds of market rate, freeing funds for development use. The CRDA then makes loans to designated municipalities at below-market rate financing.

New Mexico

* Dept. of Economic Development and Tourism
Joseph Montoya Building
1100 St. Francis Drive
P.O. Box 20003
Santa Fe, NM 87503   505-827-0300
Revolving Loan Fund: Assists communities with loan funds that are then disbursed to local businesses to encourage development in designated areas. Funds may be used for acquisition of real property, construction, rehabilitation or installation of public facilities, improve community's infrastructure, and other activities that encourage economic development. Maximum loan amount is $250,000 per project.

Economic Development Department:
Community Development Block Grant (CDBG) Set-A-Side Loan Program: Grants are awarded to communities in non-metropolitan areas for community development projects in a defined geographic area to create new jobs for low-to-moderate-income persons. In turn, the communities provide low interest gap financing for business start up and expansion.

* State Investment Council
Ark Plaza, Suite 203
2025 South Pacheco Street
Santa Fe, NM 87505   505-827-4788
Severance Tax Permanent Fund:
Oil and Gas Loan Participations: New Mexico will purchase financial instruments such as certificates of deposit (using funds from its Severance Tax Permanent Fund) from private banks to support oil and gas production loans to qualified gas and oil producers. The aim is to encourage new oil and gas development in the state.

Real Property-Related Business Loans: Available to start or expand operations. Loan amounts from $500,000 to $2,000,000.

Venture Capital Investment Program: New Mexico has three venture capital programs, including one that targets high technology projects. Outside experts assess the feasibility of proposals before loans are granted. Recipients need not repay the state for unsuccessful projects, but if the project does succeed, the state receives royalty fees.

* Regulation and Licensing Department
Securities Division
725 St. Michaels Drive
Santa Fe, NM 87501   505-827-7140
"27 K" Exemption Program: A regulatory relief program for small businesses trying to raise capital. The exemption allows a corporation or limited partnership to make an offering of $1.5 million to an unlimited number of purchasers under certain circumstances (mostly related to requirements of doing business within the State of New Mexico), thus allowing them to sell shares of stock without adhering to a minimum price per share.

* State Board of Finance, DFM
131 S. Capitol Street
Batan Memorial Bldg., Room 203
Santa Fe, NM 87503   505-827-4980
Industrial Revenue Bonds: Bonds may be issued by counties or municipalities for use by manufacturing businesses only for capital development. Interest received by bondholders is exempt from federal and state taxes. 95 percent of proceeds must be used for hard costs (expenses subject to the allowance of depreciation).

* New Mexico Taxation and Revenue Dept.
Revenue Division
Returns Processing Bureau
P.O. Box 630
Santa Fe, NM 87504   505-827-0700
Investment Tax Credit: Available to manufacturing operations. For each $100,000 of equipment purchased (used directly and exclusively in a manufacturing process and subject to depreciation) by a company that simultaneously hires one employee, that company may receive credit against its gross receipts taxes or withholding tax due. A business must apply for the credit.

* Small Business Administration (SBA)
625 Silver SW, Suite 320   505-766-1870
Albuquerque, NM 87102   Fax: 505-766-1057
See the chapter introduction for a description of SBA programs.

* New Mexico Industry Development Corp.
1009 Bradbury Drive, SE
Albuquerque, NM 87106   505-246-6000
New Mexico Industry Development Corporation Revolving Loan: Using grants from the U.S. Economic Development Administration (EDA) and the Community Development Block Grant Program (CDBG), New Mexico makes these loans

available to small businesses in counties declared to be in a state of long-term economic deterioration. Funds are for fixed assets (land, buildings, machinery, equipment) with priority given to those who also have other sources of financing. Fixed-asset loans are for up to 15 years, and working capital loans are for up to 7 years. Rates under market level are possible.

* FmHA Business and Industrial Loan Program
Farmers Home Administration
Room 3414, Federal Building
517 Gold Ave. S.W.
Albuquerque, NM 87102   505-766-2463
To foster economic development in rural areas, this program offers guarantees to private lenders for projects by healthy, reliable companies that will benefit the community. Loans are for a wide range of rural and industrial purposes, including pollution control and transportation services. Projects should create jobs in areas with populations under 25,000.

* New Mexico Housing Authority
Joseph Montoya Building
1100 St. Francis Drive
Santa Fe, NM 87503   505-827-0258
Internal Revenue Service Low Income Housing Tax Credit Program: Private investors receive tax credits for use over a 10 year period. Housing units developed must meet low-income qualifications. Investors may receive credit if their project consists of new construction (9 percent), rehabilitation (9 percent), acquisition (4 percent), and uses federal subsidies. Portions of properties must be set aside for low-income residents.

Housing And Urban Development Rental Rehabilitation Program: Serves the twin purposes of offering grants to developers to rehabilitate existing housing and subsidies to tenants who live in them. This is a 50/50 matching program, where the Housing Authority provides 50 percent of the costs, as a grant, and the investor provides 50 percent from other funds. Allowable funds range from $5000 to rehabilitate an efficiency apartment, to $8500 for a single-family home with 3 or 4 bedrooms. Other restrictions apply.

New York

* New York State Urban Development Corp.
1515 Broadway
New York, NY 10036
Small and Medium-Sized Business Assistance Program   212-930-0356
Industrial Loans: A public finance and development authority that aims to create and retain jobs in economically distressed areas. It can provide low-interest financing for retooling and modernization to industrial businesses. Maximum loan is 50 percent of total project costs, or $15,000 per job created to a maximum of $750,000. Minimum loan amount is $75,000. Funds may be used for acquisition of land and/or buildings,

construction renovation and leasehold improvements, machinery and equipment, working capital.

Targeted Investment Program   212-930-0320
Provides low-cost financing to construct or renovate industrial, commercial, or mixed-use facilities and create substantial private sector jobs in economically distressed areas marked by high unemployment and physical blight. Funds may be used for construction, renovation and leasehold improvements, machinery and equipment. Financing usually does not exceed 33% of total project cost of $15,000 per job created and/ or retained. Maximum loan amount is $1,000,000.

Regional Economic Development Partnership Program (REDPP)   212-930-0297
Low-cost financing is available which will directly and quickly create and/or retain permanent jobs in New York State. Projects must not be financially feasible without Regional Economic Development Partnership Program (REDPP) participation. Program available to projects that involve either distressed areas, minority-and women-owned businesses, productivity improvement, dislocated workers, public assistance recipients or long-term unemployed persons.

Loans are limited to the lesser of $400,000 or 1/3 of project cost. Interest subsidies limited to lesser of $250,000 or 1/3 project cost feasibility studies capped at $40,000.

Business Development Loans: Available to industrial, manufacturing, commercial, research and development, tourism, agricultural and service companies for working capital, equipment and machinery, land acquisition, and acquisition, renovation or construction of facilities.

Tourism Destination Loans: Available for projects that involve the development of a recreational, educational, cultural or historical facility and will attract visitors from outside its region.

Business Development Grants: Available for feasibility studies to examine local takeover efforts, and to reduce financing costs through interest subsidies.

ERA Industrial Park Assistance Program: Loans or interest subsidy grants are available for the development of urban industrial park, industrial parks, and business incubators owned by municipalities, industrial development agencies or local development corporations. ERA assistance is available to eligible firms for specific projects that create or preserve substantial jobs, expand or retain businesses in the State or relocate to the State, and enhance physically substandard and insanitary areas. Loan proceeds can be used for acquisition or improvements of land and/or buildings, construction, renovation, and leasehold improvements, purchase machinery and equipment, and limited working capital uses. Eligible applicants include for-profit firms involved in manufacturing, warehousing, distribution and related industrial operations.

JOB Retention Working Capital Loan Fund: Provides working capital loans or working capital loans or loan guarantees to assist companies at imminent risk of reducing employment that have difficulty in securing conventional working capital financing. Projects must help to preserve a significant number of jobs that would otherwise be threatened. Minimum amount of loan is $500,000. May not exceed 80% or the total credit facility.

* Regional Economic Development Partnership Program (REDPP)

Business Infrastructure Assistance

Program: 212-930-0295

This program provides loans and grant combinations for infrastructure projects which foster business development. Eligible applicants are municipalities, a local development corporation, or an industrial development agency. Infrastructure activities eligible for business assistance include the construction of basic systems and/or facilities on public or privately-owned property including drainage and sewer systems, access roads and sidewalks, docks and wharves, water supply systems, and site clearance, preparation, improvement and demolition. Projects are funded up to $500,000 and may be no more that 49% of the total business infrastructure project cost.

Economic Development Assistance Grants

Program: 212-930-0297

Provided for programs related to the economic development of a region within the State. Grants may be used to benefit eligible local governments and non-for-profit organizations, including local development corporations and industrial development agencies. Among the specific program components: ICSS-Industrial and Commercial Site Surveys; BIDs-Business Improvement Districts; SBSC-Small Business Service Centers.

Child Care Assistance Program: The Regional Economic Development Partnership Program (REDPP) Child Care Assistance Program provides loans, grants and loan/grant combinations for child care projects that will establish or expand a not-for-profit child care facility. Loans may be made up to $250,000 of 60% or the total project costs, whichever is less. Funds may be used towards acquisition, design, construction, improvement or renovation of an eligible child care facility, purchase of machinery and equipment, and working capital. Grants may be made up to $100,000 or 40% of the total project, whichever is less. Grants can be used for feasibility studies directly related to the development of an eligible child care facility, acquisition, design, construction, improvement or renovation of an eligible child care facility, or purchase of permanently installed machinery and equipment. Maximum amount of assistance available in a loan/grant combination is $250,000 or 85% or the total project cost, whichever is less.

Tourism Destination Projects Program: A tourism destination is defined as a recreational, educational, cultural, or historical location/facility which is likely to attract a number of visitors from outside the economic development region in which the project is located. Loans may be used to purchase equipment and machinery, land acquisition, acquisition, renovation of construction of facilities, working capital, and/or soft costs. To be eligible an applicant must be a municipality, a local development corporation, or an industrial development agency that seeks to develop infrastructure that is directly related to an

eligible business development. Eligible assistance includes the construction of basic systems and/or facilities on public/privately owned property including; drainage and sewer systems; access roads and sidewalks; docks and wharves; water supply systems; and site clearance, preparation, improvement and demolition.

NYS Industrial Effectiveness Program

(IEP): 518-474-1131

Eligible applicants are industrial firms or groups of firms experiencing competitive problems and evidencing a management/ labor commitment to promote long-term stability. Grants are provided to manufacturing firms to undertake productivity and other operational improvements in cooperation with employees to remain competitive, profitable, and viable.

Strategic Industries Group Services Program

(SIGS): 518-474-1131

Matching funds are provided to stimulate industrial modernization activity among smaller manufacturing firms. Provides an incentive to industrial groups, trade associations, labor organizations, educational institutions, technology organizations, economic development organizations, consultant organizations, and other regional and local manufacturing related organizations to develop group projects and networks to solve competitive problems.

Direct Loans - NY Job Development Authority

(JDA): 212-818-1700

Low interest loans for permanent financing of facilities, machinery and equipment. Businesses may be owned by individuals, partnerships, for-profit corporations and not-for-profit corporations. Project must be able to retain or create employment. Loans may not exceed 40% or total project costs (60% for projects in distressed areas and for companies in need of special assistance). Funds can be used for acquisition, construction costs, purchase of machinery or equipment, architectural, engineering, legal, accounting and other related professional fees and costs of interim financing.

Loan Guarantees - NY Job Development Authority

(JDA): 212-818-1700

Businesses include manufacturers, wholesalers, distributors, research and development center, warehouse, offices, agri-business. Loan guarantees cover up to 80% of the project cost. Funds can be used for acquisition, construction costs, purchase of machinery and equipment, architectural, engineering, legal, accounting and other related professional fees and cost of interim financing. Projects must retain or create employment.

Rural Development Loan Fund (RDLF): 212-818-1700

RDLF loans are targeted to firms in municipalities with populations of 25,000 or less. Provides up to 20% of projects cost on loans ranging from $20,000 to $50,000. Eligible applicants are small businesses in economically distressed rural communities in order to increase private sector employment.

Long-Term Economic Development Fund: 212-818-1700

Low interest loans to help stimulate growth of business and job creation in areas of the state suffering long-term economic deterioration and decline, or sudden and severe job losses. Loan amounts up to $150,000. Priority will be given to projects that contribute to the revitalization of distressed locations.

Micro Loan Program - NY Job Development Authority (JDA): 212-818-1700
Targeted at small businesses to expand or create a product line or service. Lends up to 40% (some instances, 60%) of the eligible project costs. Program does not entertain requests for realty loans of less than $40,000 and machinery and equipment loans of less than $25,000.

New York Business Development Corporation: Responds to the needs of small business and the banking community through creative financing programs, providing medium and long-term loans. Loan proceeds may be used for working capital, real estate construction, acquisition, renovations, or machinery and equipment purchases. Loans range from $50,000 to $1 million.

Industrial Access Program: 518-457-8331
Provides funding for highway and bridge improvements. Must result in jobs being created or retained. Maximum of $1 million, are a 60% grant 40% interest free loan over five years. Can only be obtained after attempts to obtain other financing has failed.

Transportation Systems Management (TSM) Program: 518-473-2005
Assistance to develop and implement methods to address local transportation needs. Assistance to employers, companies, and regional organizations to establish local transportation programs especially for commuters.

DED Tourism Programs: 518-474-4116
Offers grants to Tourism Marketing Programs for county and regional tourism promotion agencies, and to encourage or promote tourism or tourism-related activities which feature the Erie Canal; offers Customer Relations Training to businesses that include regular public contact.

Infrastructure Investment Program: 212-930-0297
Applicant must be a local government; an industrial development agency; an urban renewal agency; or a local development corporation. Grant may be used to finance expenses, including soft costs (i.e. legal expenses, appraisal costs, engineering fees, etc.) in connection with site clearance, site preparation, or building demolition. Projects may be funded up to $400,000 or 80% of the total project cost, whichever is less.

Economic Development Assistance Grants Program: Provides assistance to not-for-profit organizations, including local development corporation and industrial agencies. Specific program components:
ICSS - Industrial and Commercial Site Surveys: Grants to local development corporations and industrial development agencies for the preparation of commercial or industrial site surveys to develop a database on the availability of such sites.

BIDs - Business Improvement Districts: Grants available to encourage merchant associations and others with the creation of business improvement districts in highly distressed areas.

SBSC - Small Business Service Centers: Grants available for the establishment of small business service centers to assist commercial/service area or industrial business with marketing assistance, business planning, tax and regulatory information.

TAPs - Training Assessment Programs: Grants available to conduct assessments or provide technical assistance to non-retail business in implementing quality management training programs.

Grants may also be used to establish or update strategic plans; provide benefits to a region; implement a firm or industry training program; or implement a training assessment program.

Entrepreneurial Assistance Program (EAP): 212-827-6170
Grants are provided to minority or women-owned business enterprise or dislocated workers. Purpose is to increase the business formation rates for minorities, women and dislocated workers; strengthen managerial and financial skills of new and existing minority, women and dislocated workers owned businesses; and assist in the growth and expansion of businesses owned by minorities or women.

Bonding Assistance Program (BAX): 212-818-1700
Provides surety bonding guarantees, loans and technical assistance to minority, women and small business contractors in meeting the payment/performance bonding requirements necessary to obtain construction contracts awarded by any public agency, authority or municipality.

NYS Minority and Women Owned Business Enterprise Program: 518-474-6346
Fosters the development and growth of minority and women-owned business enterprises.

Tax Incentives
Investment Tax Credit: 518-438-8581
Encourages new capital investment in productive capacity and replacement of outdated facilities. The credit rate for corporations is 5% of the first $350 million of investments, plus 4% for investments over that amount. The credit rate for personal income tax is 4%.

Research and Development Property Tax Investment Tax Credit: 518-457-2751
Provides an incentive for the purchase or improvement of research and development facilities. The tax credit rate is 9% for corporations and 7% for personal income tax. Property must have a useful life of at least 4 years and must be used for the purpose of research and development in the experimental or laboratory sense.

Corporate Franchise Tax Allocation Percentages: 518-438-8581
Business corporations are subject to tax only on the portion of their activities which are deemed to be attributable to activities in the state. Formulas have been devised for the purpose of determining that portion of a corporation's

business income and capital, investment income and capital, and subsidiary capital which is taxable in New York.

Sales Tax Exemptions: 518-438-8581
Promotes industry and prevention of multiple layers of sales taxation. In order to qualify for sales tax exemptions, businesses must register as vendors with the Dept. of Taxation and finance and file the appropriate exemption certificates with suppliers.

Retail Enterprise Credit: 518-438-8581
Provides an incentive for the rehabilitation of buildings of a retail facility. The credit is available to offset the personal income tax and the franchise tax on general business corporations.

International Banking Facility
Deduction: 518-457-2751
Promotes NY State as a location for international banking. Available to financing institutions which establish international banking facilities (IBFs) within NY to accept deposits from, and make loans to, foreign customers may take as a deduction the adjusted eligible net income of the IBF.

Expansion, Retention and Attraction Assistance
Program 212-930-0355
Provides low-cost loans to industrial firms involved in manufacturing, warehousing, distribution, or research and development and operating or proposing to move to New York State. Funds can be used for acquisition of land and/or buildings, construction, renovation, and leasehold improvements, machinery and equipment, and working capital. Maximum loan is 33 percent of total project cost, or $15,000 per job created and/ or retained. Minimum loan amount is $100,000.

Commercial Revitalization Program: 212-930-0320
Commercial revitalization for neighborhoods or major cities, or for the main streets of small cities and communities. Flexible, low-cost financing to owners of commercial properties in distressed commercial districts, to improve their appearance. Loans are available for exterior property improvements, and technical assistance (TA) grants for design and architectural supervision. Funds may be used for selected masonry repair, cleaning and repainting, new awnings and signs, street facade lighting, and miscellaneous building features. Maximum funding is $225,000 per project.

* Small and Medium-Sized Business Assistance (SAMBA)

Day Care Projects: 212-930-0355
Loans are available to assist day care centers that are located at the site of the sponsoring company or at a proximate site if sponsored by a consortium of eligible firms. Must be demonstrated that the day care project is necessary to improve or maintain productivity of the sponsoring company or companies. Maximum loan amount is $250,000 or 60% of the total project cost, whichever is less. Loans may be used for acquisition of real property, new construction or renovation, and acquisition of permanently installed equipment.

Regional Revolving Loan Trust Fund: 212-930-0297
Provides working capital loans and loan guarantees to small (100 or fewer full-time employees) businesses. Provides working capital loans up to $75,000 or 50% of the total project cost, whichever is less, and working capital loan guarantees up to 80% of the loan but not to exceed $80,000. Eligible corporations must be non-profit or public benefit corporations that serve a region of at least two entire counties. Projects must create or retain jobs, are located in distressed areas, are owned by minorities or women entrepreneurs, or which employ minorities, women or displaced workers, and leverage other public and/or private dollars.

* Minority and Women Business Development and Lending (MWBDL)

Franchise Loan Program: 212-930-0290
Encourages the establishment of minority and women-owned franchises in New York State. Offers loans to minorities and women seeking to acquire a new franchise. Loans shall not be less than $50,000 and generally shall not exceed $500,000. Generally, loan will not exceed 60% of the total project cost.

Governments Contractor Loan and Government-Sponsored
Residential Construction Loan Programs: 212-930-0290
Provides eligible enterprises with the funds necessary to help such enterprises perform on contracts with a governmental entity or authority. Loan amount shall not exceed 50% of the annual value of the contract(s) and the amount shall not be less than $20,000 and shall not exceed $500,000, and to enterprises perform on contracts in connection with government-sponsored residential construction or renovation.

Small, Minority and Women Owned Business Enterprises,
Transportation Capital Assistance and Guaranteed Loan
Program: 212-930-0290
Is designed to provide financial assistance to small businesses and minority and women-owned business enterprises engaged in government sponsored, transportation-related construction projects. Financial assistance will be provided in the form of working capital loans or loan guarantees. Loans and loan guarantees may be used to enable small businesses and to secure service, commodity or construction contracts on transportation projects. Interest rates and terms are determined at time of approval. Minimum loan amount is $20,000 and the maximum loan amount is $500,000.

Minority and Women Small Business Incubator Program:
Eligible entities must be organized as either a not-for-profit corporation or a business corporation. Loans shall not exceed the lesser of 75% of the total project cost or $650,000. Loans can be used to finance renovation and improvements to existing facilities, acquisition of machinery, equipment, and furnishings and construction of a new facility if necessary. A one-time operating grant, in the amount not to exceed $40,000, may be used to cover operating costs for the first 18 months of operation of the incubator.

Community-Based Revolving Loan Trust Funds: Decentralizes decision-making to not-for-profit community-based organizations throughout the State, creating a locally-administered loan program for working capital loans and fixed-asset or real estate financing to minority and women owned business enterprises (MEBEs). Loans for working capital are $35,000; and for fixed-asset or real estate financing are $50,000.

Loan Guarantee Program With Affiliated Lenders: Provides guarantees of loans underwritten by affiliated lenders to NY State certified MWBE contractors with current or pending government construction or supply contracts. Amount of the loan guarantee may equal 80% of the maximum loan amount permissible under the MWBDL program or $500,000, whichever is less. Loan guarantees are also available for projects which are eligible for franchise loans and business development loans.

Linked Deposit Program: The Community Development Credit Unions (CDCUs) will make loans to Minority and Women-Owned Business Enterprises. Loans are for a maximum of $20,000 per loan, and a term not to exceed five years.

Technical Assistance Program: Provides a variety of technical assistance programs for Minority and Women-Owned Business Enterprises.

> *The Small Contractor Technical Assistance Program:* Assists construction and supply contracting firms who require assistance in the development/ formulation of detailed financial, marketing, cost estimation, bonding, contract preparation, etc., to submit a bid proposal and compete in the marketplace.

> *The Regional Technical Assistance Program:* Provides project development assistance to MWBEs that need such assistance to enable them to complete their business and financing proposals to any state economic development program.

> *The Economic Development Zones Technical Assistance Program:* Provides assistance to minority, women and MWBEs, seeking to expand and/or acquire a franchise or other business enterprise.

> *The General Technical Assistance Program:* Provides business development assistance to minorities, women, and MWBEs, as required, through providers designated by UDC or selected jointly by UDC and the recipient.

* Urban and Community Development Program (UCDP)

Economic Development Study Grant Program: 518-473-6930
Available to local development corporations, business improvement districts, industrial development agencies and not-for-profit economic development and community development organizations. Enables communities to evaluate alternative development scenarios or aspects of development strategies. Grants range from $5,000 to $50,000. A cash match of at least 15% of the total project cost is required.

Targeted Area Development Assistance
Program: 212-930-0320
Provides loans and grants as well as study grants involving the

acquisition, construction, renovation or improvement of commercial, industrial, and mixed-use development projects in highly distressed communities. Loan amounts are between $250,000 and $1,000,000. Grants may not exceed $100,000.

Urban and Community Development Outreach
Programs: 212-930-0320
Designed to educate and inform potential applicants regarding the availability, objectives and requirements of public sector economic development programs. The UDC will award individual grants ranging in the amounts from $5,000 to not more than $60,000 to eligible not-for-profit organizations for the provision of outreach services.

Urban Project Planning Program: Provides grants for planning studies of major mixed-use urban projects which are likely to result in significant economic development in cities, municipalities and metropolitan areas within the state. May address issues such as zoning, development costs, design, and financial feasibility for projects covering sites encompassing a minimum of one city block or five acres. Grants range from $50,000 to $200,000 up to a maximum of 50% of the total project cost. Recipients must match grant dollar-for-dollar. Cities and municipalities are eligible.

Professional Services Assistance Program: 212-930-0320
Technical assistance to local development corporations, not-for-profit corporations, district management associations of business improvement districts, and municipalities. Services include real estate market/financial analysis/appraisal; architectural, construction cost estimating, structural, mechanical, civil, traffic, environmental and other engineering cervices; zoning, urban planning/land use analysis; and other real estate-related services in connection with development, renovation, and improvement of a development site.

* New York State Department of Economic Development
One Commerce Plaza
Albany, NY 12245
Industrial Effectiveness Program 518-474-1131
Technical and financial assistance for manufacturing firms to preserve and create permanent private sector jobs. Encourages firms to undertake productivity and other operational improvements to remain competitive, profitable, and viable, and by aiding local buyouts.

> *Grants:* Available to share the cost of a consultant to conduct productivity assessment of an industrial firm or group of firms; feasibility study for corporate restructuring or turnaround; feasibility study for local buyout.

> *Loans:* Working capital loans to improve productivity and for corporate restructuring or turnaround plans.

> Loans to support a local buyout.

Secondary Materials Program: Designed to encourage and foster the implementation of waste reduction techniques by industrial or commercial firms and the expansion of markets for secondary materials (materials destined for the wastestream that can be recovered for recycling).

Grants: Made to companies, with less than 500 employees or less than $10 million in gross annual sales, to evaluate specific technologies or processes. Grants can fund 80 percent of total cost to a maximum of $100,000.

Financial Assistance: Loans up to $250,000, principal reductions up to $125,000, loan guarantees, or interest subsidies up to 75 percent of the prime rate. interest subsidies up to 75 percent of the prime rate. Available to businesses for construction, alternation, repair or improvement of buildings or equipment to utilize secondary materials.

Agricultural Wastewater Loan Program   518-486-6291
Financial assistance to food processing and farm production enterprises for the construction of wastewater treatment facilities that will enable the firm to meed current environmental standards and reduce energy consumption. Financial assistance available are direct, low interest loans up to $250,000, principal reductions up to 50 percent of eligible loan, not to exceed $125,000, loan guarantees, and interest subsidies up to 75 percent of the prime rate. Made to applicants with less than 500 workers or less than $10 million in gross annual sales.

Economic Development Zones   518-473-6930
Offers incentives, and financial and other targeted assistance programs to businesses expanding or relocating to one of the 19 enterprise zones. Businesses may receive an investment tax credit, real property tax exemption, tax credit related to wages, reduction on utility bills, among other incentives.

Urban Development Corporation (UDC) Expansion, Retention and Attraction Program: Provides loans to industrial firms to create or preserve jobs through in-state expansion or relocation to the state.

Excelsior Linked Deposit Program: Allows eligible businesses to obtain loans from commercial banks at interest rates 2 to 3 percentage points lower than the prevailing bank rates. State funds will be deposited with the banks to encourage them to grant the loans to their customers at reduced rates. Small manufacturing and service businesses will be eligible. Projects must help improve the company's competitive position and profitability, and help create or retain jobs in New York State.

* New York Job Development Authority (JDA)
   Noel Blackwell
   605 Third Avenue
   New York, NY 10158   212-818-1700
Direct Loan Program: Assist with financing needs of companies expanding or building new facilities or starting a new business. Provides low interest loans for construction, acquisition or rehabilitation of plant facilities, and for machinery and equipment. Loans may not exceed 40 percent of total project cost. Most kinds of businesses are eligible except for retail establishments, hotels, or apartment buildings.

Loan Guarantee Program: This program provides guarantees of up to 80 percent of project cost for loans made by banking organizations. May be used for machinery and equipment and/or construction, acquisition, or rehabilitation of plant facilities for new or expanding companies. Most kinds of businesses are eligible except for retail establishments, hotels, or apartment buildings.

Bonding Assistance Program: Provides a limited guarantee on construction contracts of not more than $1,000,000 to small and/or minority-and women-owned contractors and subcontractors seeking to obtain construction contracts awarded by any governmental agency or authority.

Rural Development Loan Fund: The program is aimed at providing low-cost financing to small businesses in distressed rural areas and communities with less than 25,000 population. Loans range from $20,000 to $50,000 and are up to 20 percent of a project's total cost. Funds can be used for projects involving plant expansion, construction, acquisition or rehabilitation, purchase of machinery and equipment, and working capital.

Rural Areas Development Fund: Provides low-cost financing to businesses, individuals, and local public entities for economic and community development projects that provide jobs to displaced farm families, farm families needing additional income to supplement their farming operations, long-term unemployed, or persons on public assistance in rural areas.

Loans to businesses may be made to develop new businesses or expanding existing ones in manufacturing, service industries, and agribusiness. Proceeds may be used for infrastructure projects related to economic development, industrial parks and business incubators, child care centers, pollution control facilities and transportation facilities. Loans are available for real estate. machinery and equipment and working capital. Maximum loan is 90 percent of total project cost or $90,000, whichever is less.

XPORT Program: This is a joint program between the Job Development Authority and the Port Authority of New York and New Jersey. Offers payment in advance on accounts receivable from overseas customers through a revolving fund of $1.7 million. Has loaned $5.7 million in export financing to small businesses.

* New York State Science and Technology Foundation
   John Ciannamea, Manager
   99 Washington Ave., Suite 1730   518-474-4349
   Albany, NY 12210   Fax: 518-473-6876
Corporation for Innovation Development
Venture Capital Program   518-473-9741
Provides debt and equity capital to technology-based start-ups and young, growing business ventures in New York. Applicants must have innovative, technology-based products or services with significant potential for job creation. Investments normally range from $50,000 to $150,000 and is to be used primarily for working capital. Must be matched by loans or investments from other sources.

Small Business Innovation Research Promotion Program (SBIR) 518-473-9746
Assists small research firms gain a larger share of research funds available under the federal Small Business Innovation Research (SBIR) program.

> *Small Business Innovation Research Grants:* A federal program that awards between $20,000 to $50,000 to entrepreneurs to support six months of research on a technical innovation. Phase II grants are an additional $500,000 for development. Private sector investment funds must follow.

> *Small Business Innovation Research (SBIR) Matching Grants:* Designed to increase participation in the Federal SBIR Program by small, technology-based New York businesses. Matching contracts up to $50,000 awarded to successful Federal SBIR Phase I award winners. Awards are made at conclusion of Phase I research and upon application for Federal Phase II funds, bridging a "gap" for small firms. Technical assistance is also provided.

Technology and Disabilities Program:
John Ciannamea 518-473-9741
Funds development of marketable products originally researched and developed at an academic institution or non-profit organization to service the needs of disabled clientele. Awards of up to $30,000 are made on a competitive bases twice annually to further product development or refinement which address physical, sensory, mental and other health-related disabilities.

University-Industry Programs
Dr. Theresa A. Walker, Mgr; 518-473-9744
Centers for Advanced Technology Program:
Formed by partnerships among universities, private industry, and State governments to facilitate the development and transfer of technology from research universities into the private sector. Are designated in technology areas that have a direct impact on the State's economy. Each Center for Advanced Technology is eligible to receive up to $1 million in State support annually contingent upon a positive evaluation which includes peer review by experts from industry and academe.

Cornell Theory Center: National high-performance computing communications center designated and funded by the National Science Foundation. Vital resource for industrial, academic and government researchers who need the power of the most advanced computers to store large computational problems. The Center has also established a computing resource for biomedical research program and conducts special outreach programs for minorities and small businesses.

Northeast Parallel Architectures Center (NPAC): Seeks to put high-performance computing to work in industry. Parallel computing represents the future of high performance computing that is needed to solve the largest, most complex computational problems. The program is intended to enhance the competitive position of targeted industries; spur the formation of high tech start-up companies, and to apply the benefits of parallel computing to large, complex industrial problems.

New York State Education and Research Network (NYSERNet): A high-performance telecommunications network connecting universities, industry and government laboratories, schools, libraries and government agencies to computational resources. The Network's growing membership base includes research universities, industrial corporations, colleges, schools, hospitals and government offices.

National Center for Earthquake Engineering Research (NCEER): Conducts cooperative research to reduce the devastating impact of earthquakes on people, the communities in which they live, and the networks of lifeline systems that serve them. NCEER receives annual federal funding from the Nations Science Foundation and State matching support from the foundation. The center gathers data on earthquakes in the United States and around the world, sponsors conferences and seminars to increase public awareness of the natural disasters and keeps the world's engineering and construction communities up to date on the latest technologies.

State/Industry/University Cooperative Research Centers (SIUCRC): Designed to coordinate federal, state and industrial support for centers that undertake research and other activities that can contribute to local economic development and the competitiveness of U.S. industry. In addition to federal funding of as much as $2 million per center over eight years, each receives matching funding from the state and industrial sponsors.

Integrated Electronics Engineering Center at the State University of New York at Binghamton: Undertakes research to advance engineering and scientific knowledge regarding the technology of electronic imaging, which includes the capture, recording, storage, and reproduction of electronic images.

Center for Electronic Imaging Systems at the University of Rochester: Undertakes research to advance engineering and scientific knowledge regarding the technology of electronic imaging, which includes the capture, recording, storage, and reproduction of electronic images.

Achievement Awards Program: Encourages outstanding students to pursue higher education and careers in technical subject areas. The first, second and third place winners of the N.Y. Math League and the N.Y. Science Congress competitions receive scholarships of $1,200, $800, and $500 respectively, to be applied toward tuition at an accredited college or university in New York State.

* Industrial Technology Programs
Industrial Technology Councils Program (ITC): 518-474-6346
Serves as the State's main network for developing the high technology business and research base on a region by region basis. It is a conduit through which needed services are deployed to technology and manufacturing firms in each region. The Industrial Technology Council (ITC) also helps regional companies to apply and compete for federal research grants annually awarded through the SBIR program.

Industrial Technology Extension Services
(ITES):   518-474-4349
Consists of a network of technology specialists located throughout the State, who provide hands-on assistance to manufacturing firms. Technical personnel serve as field "agents", working one-on-one with small and medium sized manufacturing companies to bring the benefits of modern technology to the factory floor. Agents help companies to research, evaluate and implement technology and/or management-related productivity improvements. They also help companies obtain State Industrial Effectiveness Program grants, promote technology transfer with research laboratories and universities and act as the outreach arm of the federally funded Northeast Manufacturing Technology Center.

Northeast Manufacturing Technology Center
(NEMTC):   518-473-9746
This is a federally sponsored manufacturing technology center which works in conjunction with Industrial Technology Extension Services (ITES) agents to implement technology in the manufacturing work place. It is dedicated to modernizing industry.

New York Photonics Development Corporation (PDC): This is an independent, not-for-profit organization dedicated to cooperative research and development and commercialization of photonics technologies with the U.S. Air Force and other industrial partners. It works closely with the ITCs to provide effective technology transfer assistance to companies.

* Cooperative Finance and Development Programs
Corporation for Innovation Development Program
(CID):   518-473-9741
Supports the formation and growth of new technology companies by providing State investments and leveraged venture capital financing. Eligible firms can receive equity and/or debt financing of $250,000 or more for product marketing and development. Matching funding at a rate of 3 to 1 is required. Companies supported with CID investments comprise a diverse group of technologies, ranging from the manufacturers of three-dimensional computer displays to the exploration of novel treatments for life-threatening diseases.

Technology and Disabilities Program:
                                                    518-473-9741
Supports the development of highly promising, creative products and processes that are helping New York citizens with disabilities lead more enjoyable lives. Companies may apply for financing to further develop products which meet these criteria. Investment financing of up to $100,000 per project is available to companies, which may collaborate with a not-for-profit laboratory on innovative technologies with a high potential for commercialization.

Venture Line: 518-486-5438
Through a computerized database, VentureLine provides a convenient and confidential means of matching the financial needs of entrepreneurs and other businesses to the capital resources of investors and venture capital firms. Each week, the VentureLine database is reviewed to spot potential matches between applicant businesses and investors. Investors have the opportunity to confidentially review business applications before engaging in negotiations. Both businesses and entrepreneurs can explore financing opportunities, collaborative ventures, and licensing arrangements.

* Special Projects and Initiatives
The Science and Technology Foundation supports various Legislative initiative and other special projects targeted at the growth of New York State's technology infrastructure. These activities are:

Long Island Research Institute: A not-for-profit consortium of Brookhaven National Laboratory, Cold Spring Harbor Laboratory, the Center for Medical Biotechnology at SUNY Stony Brook, and North Shore University Hospital working cooperatively to promote technology transfer and the commercialization of technologies from the four institutions.

Long Island High Technology Incubator: This modern facility provides young, growing technology firms with state-of-the-art equipment and laboratory space for development in a highly supportive environment.

Marist College Small Business Network: Supports the development of a computer network to assist small businesses throughout New York, enabling member firms to retrieve database information, marketplace information, and to communicate with other members. An Electronic Incubator has been established to assist defense related firms, diversify and develop new products and markets.

New York Tech-Scan: A corporate recruitment and economic development tool that serves as an electronic catalogue and source book on New York State's high technology resources. Designed to provide easy access to wide range of information on the State's scientific and technological assets, its standing nationally and internationally, and its comparative advantage in key high-tech industries and critical technologies.

On-Campus Networks Initiative: A project to conduct a needs assessment of establishing an on-campus computer networks system among New York's colleges and universities.

Center for Integrated Manufacturing Studies: Designed to help small to medium-sized manufacturing firms adopt new technologies to become more competitive.

Syracuse Metropolitan Development Authority/ Syracuse University Research Park: Includes requisite infrastructural planning for future development of a research park on a 90 acre parcel within close proximity to several major educational and medical institutions in the Syracuse area, including Syracuse University, Crouse Irving Memorial Hospital and Hutchings Psychiatric Center.

* **New York State Department of Agriculture**
    and Markets
    Division of Agricultural Protection and
      Development Service
    One Winners Circle
    Capital Plaza
    Albany, NY 12235   518-457-7076

Agricultural Research and Development Grants: Grants are offered annually to farmers, agri-businesses, institutions and individuals with original ideas in production, processing and marketing of farm products. Maximum amount of loan is $50,000. Proceeds are focused on creation of jobs in the food and agriculture industry, new capital investment and expansion in the food and agriculture industry, market development and expansion, among others. (At present, no funds are available.)

* **New York State Energy Research**
    Development Authority
    William Reinhart
    Two Rockefeller Plaza
    Albany, NY 12223   518-465-6251

Economic Development Through Greater Energy-Efficiency (EDGE) Program: Provides technical and financial assistance to firms interested in reducing their energy use and related costs. Technical and financial support available for detailed engineering feasibility studies of innovative and energy-efficient process modifications. Financial assistance available for the demonstration of innovation energy-efficient process technology. Eligibility requirements include firms not using current, available technology; there are energy conservation measures that can be implemented; limited capital prevents a firm's expansion or modernization. Funding for Engineering Studies is up to $25,000 but not to exceed 50 percent and up to $500,000 for demonstrations but not to exceed 50 percent.

* **New York State Environment Facilities**
    Corporation (EFC)
    50 Wolf Road
    Albany, NY 12205   518-457-4114

Industrial Pollution Control Financing Program: The Environment Facilities Corporation (EFC) issues special obligation revenue bonds with provide low-cost loans to companies assisting industry in meeting its environmental responsibilities without incurring high financing costs. Eligible facilities include sewage treatment, solid waste disposal, resource recovery, water management, water supply, hazardous waste disposal. Bond interest is generally exempt from State and Federal income taxes. Several company projects at more than one location can be financed under one bond issue.

* **New York Business Development Corporation (NYBDC)**
    P.O. Box 738
    Albany, NY 12201   518-463-2268

Corporation Loan Program: Provides long-term loans available to small businesses in industrial, commercial and service-oriented businesses, that might otherwise have problems obtaining financing. The loans are a complement to or in participation with conventional lenders. The New York Business Development Corporation (NYBDC) share of the loan ranges from $50,000 to $1,000,000. Funds may be used for working capital, machinery and equipment, real estate construction, acquisition and renovations.

* **Small Business Administration (SBA)**
    Regional Office
    26 Federal Plaza
    Room 3100   212-264-2454
    New York, NY 10278   Fax: 212-264-4963

See the chapter introduction for a description of SBA programs.

* **Housing and Urban Development (HUD)**
    Regional Office
    26 Federal Plaza
    New York, NY 10278-0068   212-264-8068

Community Development Block Grants: Available to cities and counties for the commercial rehabilitation of existing buildings or structures used for business, commercial or industrial purposes. Grants of up to $500,000 can be made. Every $15,000 of grant funds invested must create at least one full-time job, and at least 51 percent of the jobs created must be for low- and moderate-income families.

North Carolina

* **North Carolina Department of Commerce**
    Commerce Finance Center
    430 North Salisbury Street
    Raleigh, NC 27611   919-733-4151

Small Business Development Division:

Long-term, Fixed Rate Financing Program: Allows North Carolina banks to win long-term fixed rate certificates of deposit from the State Treasurer and then re-lend the same money on a long-term, fixed rate basis to small businesses.

Industrial Revenue Bonds: Tax-exempt long-term, low interest financing available to manufacturing companies that will have a measurable economic impact on the community. Industrial firms may finance projects related to product manufacturing, distribution centers, or research and development facilities necessary to the manufacturing process. Generally, capital projects with investments under $10 million can be financed in full.

Industrial Development Bonds: For manufacturing companies that cannot qualify for financing that is exempt from federal taxes, North Carolina bond authorities can issue Industrial Development Bonds with interest income exempt from state income tax.

TIPP: Tarheel IRB Pool Program: Pooled industrial revenue bonds designed to allow small firms access to the IRB program. This enables borrowers in the $500,000 to $3,000,000 to use the bond vehicle cost effectively. Companies need a letter of credit from their bank. These bonds can have variable or fixed rates.

Job Creation Tax Credit: Companies creating full-time jobs in a designated economically-distressed counties may be eligible for a tax credit of $2,800 per job created and can be applied against state corporate or individual income taxes. The amount can offset up to 50 percent of a firm's state income tax. Companies can agree to hire a minimum of 20 new employees over two years, allowing them to still receive credits even if the county loses its distressed classification.

Industrial Building Renovation Fund: In certain economically distressed counties, companies may be eligible for funds to repair or renovate existing buildings for use as manufacturing and industrial operations. A firm can receive $1,200 per job created, up to a maximum of $250,000, for repair, renovation, or equipping a structure for industrial use. Funds used to benefit a private business, such as air-conditioning or equipment, are repayable at 2 percent interest. No repayment of funds is required where funds are used to provide a utility service to the building. The improvement is then loaned by the local government.

Manufacturer's Incentive Tax Formula: Can cut taxable income for businesses by up to 25 percent. This is an allocation formula that gives tax breaks to corporations that are located within North Carolina, even if they conduct a large volume of sales outside the state.

* State Tax Incentives and Advantages

Corporate Income Tax: North Carolina uses the latest federal tax code and your business benefits from accelerated depreciation and other tax saving mechanisms on its state tax return as follows:

Savings for Multi-State Companies: Double-weighted sales factor apportionment formula for multi-state corporations gives your business significant savings if you do business in more than one state.

Jobs Creation Tax Credit: State offers an income tax credit of $2,800 for every new manufacturing job created above a threshold of nine. Companies can lock in their eligibility for an additional two years with a letter of commitment for 20 new jobs in the 24-month period.

Sales and Use Taxes: Preferential rates provided by the State, that vary from the standard 4% rate and 2% total local option sales tax.

General Property Tax: Real property is assessed at full market value every 8 years. Personal property (autos, office equipment, industrial machinery) is assessed annually at approximately current market value less depreciation. Beneficial to businesses that otherwise might be subject to annual real property assessments. Also beneficial to areas where the original cost of equipment is used for tax purposes.

* State Financial Incentives and Advantages

North Carolina Industrial Development Fund (NCIDF): Loans and grants of up to $250,000 ($2,400 per job created) are available to companies that repair, renovate or equip existing buildings for industrial use in less developed counties. Loans and quick loan turn-arounds and repayment exemption where funds are used to provide public utility service to building.

Taxable Industrial Development Bond (TIDB): For manufacturers who do not qualify for tax exempt bonds. It provides increased savings of 35-75 basis points.

Community Development Block Grant (CDBG): Companies needing up to $1 million in loans or infrastructure improvements. Requirement is that at least 60% of the jobs created by filled by people whose income is in the low to moderate income category at the time of employment. These are also available to wholesale, retail and service companies.

Basic Buildings Program: Help develop small rural communities throughout the state. The state often constructs speculative industrial buildings, ready to be upfitted to specific industries. Using these buildings can cut the average start up time for a company from 29 to 13 weeks.

Business Energy Improvements Program: Low interest loans (approximately 65% of prime) are available for retrofitting existing buildings.

North Carolina Shared/Group FSC Program: Using the state's Group Foreign Sales Corporation, companies can obtain state and federal tax exemptions on a portion of their export profits. Exemption can range from 15-30% for federal and state tax purposes. Available to all North Carolina companies with export profits.

North Carolina Ports Tax Credit: Available to exporters who use the North Carolina ports at Morehead City and Wilmington and who are subject to the payment of North Carolina income taxes. They can apply and qualify for a tax credit. Tax credit can be earned on cargo wharfage and handling fees exceeding the average for the last 3 years inclusive of the current tax year. The maximum cumulative credit that may be taken may not exceed $1 million.

* Employment Security Commission (ESC)

Job Screening: The state Employment Security Commission (ESC) screens and recommends job applicants for any company locating in the state. All you have to do is provide the ESC with a list of job openings and requirements for each position.

* Other State Organizations Financial Incentives and Advantages:

Department of Community Colleges

Industrial Training Program: This program provides the following services at no cost to your company: selection/training of instructors; payment of instructor wages for the duration of the training program; lease/operation of a temporary training facility; training aids/materials; reimbursement of instructor travel expenses; and standard equipment required for training.

Department of Transportation (DOT)

Access Road Fund: Tax money is allocated to DOT to construct necessary site access roads for new plants that create a specific number of jobs.

Department of Environment, Health and Natural Resources

Environmental and Energy Saving Programs: The Office of Waste Reduction provides grants and technical assistance to help companies reduce and control industrial waste. (The Pollution Prevention Pays Program provides free on site technical assistance in process evaluation to reduce waste streams).

North Carolina First Flight, Inc.: Helps and encourages small businesses and provides one-time grants of up to $200,000 for the establishments of small business incubator facilities that provide low-rent space, shared support services and basic equipment. First Flight Fund #1 (FFF #1) provides seed equity investment capital for entrepreneurs engaged in developing and commercializing technological innovations. Provides initial investments of up to $50,000 and up to $100,000 in second and later-round investments.

North Carolina Biotechnology Center: Biotechnological companies locating in NC are eligible for four grant programs from the North Carolina Biotechnology Center. Grants support basic research, information sharing, education enhancement, job training instructional development. The state also has two loan programs that encourage technology transfer, research and development efforts.

Academic Research Initiation Grant: Seed funding for novel biotechnology-related research projects.

Institutional Development Grant: Broad institutional benefits such as establishment of core service facilities, purchase of multi-user equipment or recruitment of exceptional ability.

Event Support Grant: To promote information sharing related to scientific, educational or business aspects of biotechnology.

Education Enhancement Grant: Assists development of programs, activities, resources and personnel necessary for biotechnology education and job training in non-profit institutions, schools, community colleges, colleges, or universities.

Economic Development Finance Program (EDFP): Companies wishing to promote the initiation and expansion of commercial biotechnological applications can receive up to $250,000 of EDFP support for an 18-month period.

Small Business Innovative Research (SBIR) Matching Fund: Companies receiving SBIR funds are also eligible for up to $50,000 for activities that refine Phase I research and initiate work on Phase II project objectives.

North Carolina MCNC: (Access to the Center for Microelectronics). With a no-fee membership in the North Carolina Industry Participant Group, small businesses can gain access to the Center's resources at no charge. Also available are consulting and technology transfer assistance for a very nominal fee.

Center for Communications: Businesses can quickly access information they need to enhance their competitiveness in the market place and benefit from accelerated technology transfer. CONCERT network links more than 6,000 computer to Internet's worldwide resources, including national laboratories, advanced computer facilities and databases.

Industrial Extension Service (IES), School of Engineering, North Carolina State University: Assist industries with: in-plant presentation workshops; short courses and seminars; technical and supervisory workshops; video-based engineering education courses; Resource/Referral Center for industry, government and other educational institutions; and access to faculty and staff laboratory resources for applied research projects.

Industry Electrotechnology Laboratory (IEL): Offer a comprehensive lighting demonstration, a motors testing facility, a staff of professional problem-solvers, offices and a resource center featuring a library of the latest technical bulletins.

* Local Financial Incentives and Advantages

Community Incentives: Local governments negotiate individually with businesses to meet the individual needs of an organization. Using public and private resources, these initiatives and incentives are put together by various localities to attract industries that provide jobs to the area.

Government Funded Water and Sewer Improvements: To ensure a quality infrastructure, local governments will invest money in utilities up to the amount that will be recovered in taxes over an 8 to 10 year period.

City/County Industrial Parks: Local governments are authorized to invest up to .05% of their assessed property taxes in economic development projects. Some local governments have acquired industrial sites, developed properties and directly negotiated their sale or lease to companies interested in locating in the area by using this power.

Road Improvements: Allows local elected official to use tax dollars for road improvements to meet the needs of local businesses.

Rail Sidings: Businesses requiring high volume or critical rail service benefit from location in some communities that will share or reduce the cost of rail sidings.

Incentives for Industry by Private Entities: These groups of business people, such as committees of 100, use private resources to provide land, buildings and grants to industries willing to relocate to their area.

Turnkey Project Management: Businesses locating to the state benefit from development companies able to provide economical and efficient management of a new plant opening, from site selection to beneficial occupancy.

Professional Development/Relocation Services: Relocating companies benefit from the free services of a professional developer in addition to the assistance provided by the professional state coordinator. Assistance covers almost every aspect of relocation, including property control, design and construction, employee recruitment screening, training and establishment of good employee relations programs.

Job Training Partnership Act (JTPA) Funds: Over $93 million in JTPA funds are available to provide businesses with trained and skilled workers.

Small Business Administration (SBA) Subordinated Mortgages: Ten and twenty year loans are available with down payments as low as 10%. The SBA portion offers a loan for up to 40% of the project costs, with maximum participation of $750,000. Loan involves 50% participation by a local lender on a first mortgage.

Finance Center   919-733-5297
Farmers Home Administration Loan Guarantees: Guarantees private lenders up to 90 percent of the principal and interest on a loan. Borrowers must have up to 25 percent equity in the project to qualify. Maturities can be up to 30 years for real estate, 15 years for machinery, and 7 years for working capital. This is a program for communities with populations under 50,000.

Pollution Control Tax Breaks: Facilities for pollution control, recycling and recovery qualify for rapid depreciation on state income tax returns. North Carolina counties offer additional tax advantages for costs of this type of equipment.

* North Carolina Technological Development Authority
2 Davis Drive
Durham, NC 27709   919-990-8558
Seed and Incubator Capital: Through the Innovation Research Fund, up to $50,000 in seed money is available for development of new products or services. The Authority funds incubator facilities through its Incubator Facilities Program. It also conducts workshops across the state for those small business interested in the Innovation Research Fund and the Small Business Innovation Research program.

* Small Business Administration (SBA)
District Office
200 N. College St.
Suite A-2015   704-344-6563
Charlotte, NC 28202-2173   Fax: 704-344-6769
See the chapter introduction for a description of SBA programs.

* North Carolina Department of Economic
   and Community Development
Division of Community Assistance
1307 Glenwood Ave.
Suite 250
Raleigh, NC 27605   919-733-2850
Community Development Block Grants: Available to cities and counties, who in turn, loan the money to businesses for the commercial rehabilitation of existing buildings or structures used for business, commercial, or industrial purposes. Funds can be used for fixed assets and to partially finance working capital. Every $15,000 of funds invested must create at least one full-time job, and at least 51 percent of the jobs created must be for low- and moderate-income families.

* North Carolina Enterprise Corporation
P.O. Box 20429
Raleigh, NC 27619   919-781-2691
A private, for-profit corporation with a board of directors representing private and public interests that is financed by both sectors. The corporation provides equity-type financing to small and medium-sized business, principally for manufacturing. Provides long-term capital for long-term investment. It is aimed at expanding the rural economic base in the state.

* North Carolina Biotechnology Center
15 Alexander Drive
P.O. Box 13547
Research Triangle Park, NC 27709-3547
       919-541-9366
Supports biotechnology research as a means of improving the state's economy. The center does not actually perform research itself, but supports, coordinates, and educates in the field of biotechnology. Grants are available for academic research, large-scale projects at universities and non-profit institutions, economic development, and for groups wishing to organize conferences and workshops. These grants total several million dollars per year.

* Institute of Private Enterprise
University of North Carolina
The Kenan Center
CB 3440
Chapel Hill, NC 27599-3440   919-962-8201
Investment Contacts Network: A computerized matching service organized by the University of North Carolina's Institute of Private Enterprise. It matches investors with promising entrepreneurs. Entrepreneurs pay $100 for a six month listing, and investors pay $200 per year.

North Dakota

* Bank of North Dakota (BND)

For Student Loans Only:
Bank of North Dakota (BND)
700 East Main Avenue, Box 5509
Bismarck, ND 58502-5509   701-224-5685

All Other Loans:
Bank of North Dakota
1833 E. Bismarck Expressway
Bismarck, ND 58504   701-224-5674

Micro Business Loans: Available to all small business activities including home-based businesses, retail, services, and manufacturing.

TRIP Loans (Tourism and Recreation Investment Program): Available to all tourism related businesses and activities including recreation, historical sites, festival and cultural events, unique lodging and food services, and guide services.

Both types of loans will require a local financing institution to act as lead lender for the loan. The Bank of North Dakota will take up to 50 percent of the total loan, to a maximum of $10,000. Funds may be used to establish or purchase a new or existing business, finance the acquisition of real property, remodel or expand an existing business, purchase equipment, working capital, purchase inventory.

PACE (Partnership in Assisting Community Expansion): Available to manufacturing, processing, value-added processing and targeted service industries such as data processing, data communications and telecommunications. Funds can be used for working capital, equipment and real property. The Bank of North Dakota (BND) will fund up to $300,000 for interest rate buydown to a maximum of 5 percent below prime. BND will fund 70 percent to 85 percent of interest buydown. Community must fund remainder.

Small Business Loan Program: Loans of up to $250,000 to any business, through a local lender, for working capital, equipment and real property. Terms are 3-5 years for working capital, 5-7 years for equipment, and 12-15 years for real estate. Equity requirement is 25 percent for new businesses. Local lender is required for 30-40 percent of loan.

Business Development Loans: Available to any business. Local lender is required for up to 30 to 40 percent of total loan. The Bank of North Dakota (BND) share is up to $500,000 per project. Fund can be used for working capital, equipment and real property.

Match Program: Available to manufacturing and processing companies with a credit rate of "A" or better. The Bank of North Dakota's share will be limited to $25 million. Funds can be used for real estate and for purchase and lease of machinery and equipment.

Export-Import Bank Working Capital Guarantee   701-224-5674
Provides repayment guarantees of up to 90 percent to eligible lenders on secured loans.

Export-Import Bank Medium and Long Term Loans   701-224-5674
Covers up to 85 percent of the export value. Support export sales facing foreign competition backed with subsidized official financing.

Export Credit Insurance   701-224-5674
Offers insurance policies protecting U.S. exporters against the risk of nonpayment by a foreign debtor.

* Office of Urban Development

122 South 5th Street
Room 233
Grand Forks, ND 58201-1518   701-746-2545

Grand Forks Growth Fund: The fund is intended to provide gap and incentive financing for new or expanding businesses which have capacity to create new primary sector jobs and contribute to the local tax base. Funds can be used to provide temporary or permanent financing for capital costs (land, buildings, and infrastructure), equipment, working capital, seed capital, or other miscellaneous feasibility costs. A minimum 10 percent equity contribution is required. For requests in excess of $25,000, the applicant must obtain some levels of bank participation.

* Office of Intergovernmental Assistance

600 E. Boulevard Avenue
Bismarck, ND 58505   701-224-2094

Community Development Revolving Loan Fund: Borrow to be user or develop through loan to eligible local government. Loans amounts up to $300,000 per project for primary sector, $50,000 per project for retail sector. Funds can be used for fixed assets related to business and infrastructure. A dollar for dollar non-public match, and 10 percent minimum equity requirement. Job creation criteria for low to moderate income people.

Community Development Block Grants: Available to cities and counties for the commercial rehabilitation of existing buildings or structures used for business, commercial, or industrial purposes. Grants of up to $300,000 can be made. Every $15,000 of grant funds invested must create at least one full-time job, and at least 51 percent of the jobs created must be for low- and moderate-income families.

* Governor's Office

600 E. Boulevard Avenue
Bismarck, ND 58505   701-224-2200

Industrial Revenue Bonds: For developers, commercial or industrial users - sold through political subdivision. Up to 100 percent of cost of project for fixed assets and equipment. Market interest rates for 7-20 years. No equity requirements. For funding under $1 million on a first-come, first-served basis.

* Agricultural Products Utilization Commission

600 East Boulevard, 6th Floor
Bismarck, ND 58505-0020   701-224-4760

The Commission provides funding and assistance to private industry in the establishment of agricultural processing plants for the manufacturing and marketing of agricultural derived fuels, chemicals and other processed products.

* North Dakota Tax Commissioner

600 E. Boulevard Avenue
Bismarck, ND 58505-0599   701-224-2770

Special Tax Incentives for Businesses: Incentives include:

Five year property and corporation income tax exemptions for new business projects

Wage and salary income tax credits

Income tax credit for research expenditures and for investment in a North Dakota venture capital corporation

Deductions for selling or renting a business to a beginning business person or farmland to a beginning farmer

* Fargo-Cass County Economic Development Corporation

417 Main Avenue
Suite 401
Fargo, ND 58103   701-237-6132

SBA 504: Provides loans using 50 percent conventional bank financing, 40 percent Small Business Administration (SBA) involvement through Certified Development Companies, and 10 percent owner equity. A fixed asset loan in amounts up to $750,000. Loan can be used for land and building, construction, machinery and equipment, and renovation/expansion.

* Small Business Administration (SBA)

657 2nd Avenue N.
Room 218   701-239-5131
Fargo, ND 58108-3086   Fax: 701-239-5645

See the chapter introduction for a description of SBA programs.

* Center for Innovation and Business Development

Box 8103, University Station
University of North Dakota
Grand Forks, ND 58202   701-777-3132

Small Business Innovation Research Grant: Awards between $20,000 to $50,000 to entrepreneurs to support six months of research on a technical innovation. Phase II grants are an additional $500,000 for development. Private sector investment funds must follow.

First Seed Capital Group: Brings together investors and businesses. Focuses on business start-ups and equity capital investment for businesses with needs of less than $150,000.

* State Director

Farmers Home Administration
Third and Rosser Avenues
P.O. Box 1737
Bismarck, ND 58502-1737   701-250-4781

Business and Industrial Loan Programs: Provides loan guarantees to lenders. Proceeds can be used for working capital, equipment, and real property. Interest rates are negotiated between lender and borrower. Maximum terms: 7 years for working capital, 10 years for equipment, and 25 years for real property. Requires 10 percent equity for existing businesses and 20 percent-25 percent for new businesses. Additional funding allowed from any source. Only rural areas and areas with populations under 25,000 are eligible.

* Economic Development Administration (EDA)

P.O. Box 1911
Bismarck, ND 58502   701-250-4321

EDA Loan Guarantee: Guarantees up to 80 percent of the principal and interest on loans to businesses in designated areas of high unemployment or low income. Funding limits are determined by project need. Uses are for working capital, equipment, and real property. The guarantee is made to private lending institutions in designated EDA eligible areas. Projects must be of direct benefit to local residents and demonstrate long-term employment opportunities in the area.

* Capital Dimensions Inc.

400 East Broadway, Suite 420
Bismarck, ND 58501   701-222-0995

Myron G. Nelson Venture Capital Fund, Inc.: Established by legislation, this corporation provides a source of investment capital for the establishment, expansion, and rehabilitation of North Dakota businesses.

Roughrider Equity Corporation: A statewide development corporation designed to promote the development and expansion of new and existing primary sector businesses through the investment of equity funds.

Ohio

---

* Ohio Department of Development

P.O. Box 1001
Columbus, OH 43266-0101   1-800-848-1300

*Economic Development Financing
Division*   614-466-5420

Direct Loans: Loans are available for land and building acquisition, expansion or renovation, and equipment purchase. Industrial projects are preferred. The state can fund up to 30 percent of the total fixed cost of a project, up to $1 million. Interest is at a 5 percent fixed rate for 10-15 years. Equity must be at least 10 percent from the borrower and 25 percent conventional financing. Must create one job for every $10,000 received.

Industrial Revenue Bonds: For fixed assets and equipment for manufacturing projects. Provides up to 100 percent of eligible fixed assets at 75 percent of prime, at a floating or fixed rate for up to 20 years.

Ohio Enterprise Bond Fund: For building and land acquisition, construction, expansion or renovation, and equipment purchase for commercial or industrial projects between $1 million and $15 million. Long-term, fixed-rate for up to 25 years at treasury bond rates, plus 1-1/2 percent for up to 90 percent of project amount.

Pooled Bond Program   614-644-5645
Available to manufacturing projects between $400,000 and $10 million in size. Funds can be used for building acquisition, construction, expansion, or renovation and new equipment purchase. Can finance up to 100 percent of eligible fixed assets at 3-4 percent below current market rates, for up to 30 years. Borrower must submit letter of credit from lender and project must create or retain jobs. Projects are pooled in one issue for companies too small for traditional Industrial Revenue Bonds.

Office of Local Government Services   614-466-2285
Revolving Loan Funds: Targeted at projects that will create or retain jobs for low-to-moderate income households, and help develop, rehabilitate or revitalize a participating "small city" community. Must be used for fixed assets related to commercial, industrial, or infrastructure use. Loans available for users or developers, at 5-9 percent with flexible terms.

Community Development Block Grants: Available to cities and counties for the commercial rehabilitation of existing buildings or structures used for business, commercial, or industrial purposes. Grants of up to $350,000 can be awarded to cities or counties, who in turn, loan the money to user or developer. Projects must create or retain at least 5 jobs. At least 51% of the jobs created must be for low- and moderate-income families.

Office of Industrial Development   614-466-4551
Enterprise Zone Program: Offers up to 100 percent abatement of real estate or personal property taxes for up to 10 years. Business must retain or create jobs and establish, expand, renovate, or occupy a facility in an Enterprise Zone.

International Trade Division   614-466-5017
Export Credit Insurance: One year policy is backed by the Export-Import Bank of the United States for export sales made under short-term credit plans. Insurance covers 100 percent for political risks and 90 percent for commercial risks, for exporters with under $2 million sales who have not used Foreign Credit Insurance Agency policies in the past 2 years.

Ohio Thomas Edison Program
                    614-466-3887; 1-800-848-1300
Edison Technology Incubators: Low-cost space for technology-based businesses that reduces operating costs during start-up phase. Access to business, technical, and professional services. Rents and fees are at below market rates. Some incubators provide access to separate seed capital funds.

Edison Seed Development Fund: Links business and university research facilities and provides matching funds for development of product ideas to help turn new ideas into marketable products. Matching funds up to $50,000 for early stage research, and up to $250,000 in matching funds for advanced state research.

Small Business Innovation Research Program
                    614-466-5967; 1-800-848-1300
Small Business Innovative Research Grants (SBIR): Phase I Awards between $20,000 to $50,00 to entrepreneurs to support six months of research on a technical innovation. Phase II grants are an additional $500,000 for development. Private sector funds must follow.

SBIR Bridge Grants: Helps companies maintain continuity on SBIR Phase I projects during the federal funding gap between Phases I and II. Awards up to the amount of Phase I SBIR award, not to exceed $50,000.

Ohio Coal Development Program   614-466-3465
Financial assistance for clean coal research and development projects. Up to $75,000 or two-thirds of total project cost for research. Pilot and demonstration scale project up to $5 million or one-half of total project cost for a pilot project, one-third total project cost for a demonstration product. Funds can be issued in the form of a grant, loan, or loan guarantee.

Ohio Statewide Development Corporation   614-466-5043
SBA 504: Provides loans using 50 percent conventional bank financing, 40 percent SBA involvement through Certified Development Companies, and 10 percent owner equity. A fixed-asset loan in amounts up to $750,000. Loan can be used for land and building, construction, machinery and equipment, and renovation/expansion. Must create one Ohio job for every $35,000 received.

Minority Development Financing Commission
                    614-644-7708; 1-800-848-1300
Ohio Mini-Loan Program: Fixed asset and equipment loans for small business with less than 25 employees for projects of $100,000 or less. Targeted 50 percent allocation to businesses owned by minorities and women. Available for start-up or existing business expansion. Up to 45 percent guarantee of an eligible bank loan.

* Public Affairs Office
    Treasurer of the State
    Ohio State House, First Floor   614-466-8855
    Columbus, OH 43215   1-800-228-1102 in Ohio
Small Business Linked Deposit Program: Funds are available for fixed assets, working capital, and refinancing for small businesses, creating or retaining jobs. Rates are 3 percent below current lending rate fixed for two years.

Agricultural Linked Deposit Program: Provides funds for Ohio full-time farmers to help meet planning deadlines. Provides up to $100,000 per farm at reduced rate, approximately 4% below borrower's current rate.

Both categories must have bank loans from eligible state depositories.

* Small Business Administration (SBA)
2 Nationwide Plaza, Suite 1400   614-469-6860
Columbus, OH 43215-2592   Fax: 614-469-2391
See the chapter introduction for a description of SBA programs.

Oklahoma

* Oklahoma Development Finance Authority
301 NW 63rd
Suite 225
Oklahoma City, OK 73116-7904   405-848-9687
Loans: Provides funding in loan packages for manufacturing and industrial parks. It may loan up to 33 1/3 percent of a project's cost of land, buildings, and stationary manufacturing equipment with a first mortgage on the assets up to a maximum loan of $1 million. It may also loan up to 66 percent of a project's cost for land, buildings, and stationary manufacturing equipment secured with a first mortgage on the assets. Maximum loan is $2 million.

* Oklahoma Industrial Finance Authority
301 NW 63rd, Suite 225
Oklahoma City, OK 73116-7904   405-842-1145
Loans: Available to manufacturers plus recreational, agriculture processing, livestock processing and conditioning, and mine resource processors. The Authority can loan up to 66-2/3 percent of the cost of land, buildings and fixed equipment on a secured first mortgage and 33-1/3 percent on a second mortgage. Maximum loan amount is $1.25 million per project on a first mortgage, $750,000 on a second mortgage.

* Office of the State Treasurer
State Capitol Building, Room 217
Oklahoma City, OK 73105   405-521-3191
Oklahoma Small Business Linked Deposit Program: Loans are available of up to $1 million for small businesses and $5 million for industrial parks. Loan must create new jobs or preserve existing ones. Terms not to exceed two years, but may be renewed up to 2 additional years.

Agricultural Linked Deposit Program: Available for farmers who meet certain criteria. The linked deposit commitment cannot exceed 2 years, but may be renewed. The interest rates are fixed and are calculated based on the current T-note auction rate minus 3 percent.

* Small Business Administration (SBA)
District Office
200 NW 5th St.   405-231-4301
Oklahoma City, OK 73102   Fax: 405-231-4876
See the chapter introduction for a description of SBA programs.

* HUD Regional Office
Murrah Federal Building
200 NW Fifth St.
Oklahoma City, OK 73102-3202   405-231-4181
Urban Development Action Grants (UDAG): Awarded to communities which then lend the proceeds at flexible rates to eligible businesses. Projects whose total costs are less than $100,000 are not eligible. Urban Development Action Grant funds should leverage at least three to four times their amount in private sector investment.

* Oklahoma Department of Commerce
P.O. Box 26980
Oklahoma City, OK 73126-0980   1-800-879-6552
Community Affairs and Development
Division   405-841-9326
Community Development Block Grants - Economic Development Financing: Grants are awarded to cities and counties, who in turn provide gap financing to start-up and expanding businesses, for the commercial rehabilitation of existing buildings or structures used for business, commercial, or industrial purposes. Financing of up to $500,000 can be made per project. Purpose of the program is to create new jobs for low and moderate income persons in non-metropolitan areas of the state.

Small Business Demonstration Energy Conservation Grant Program: Provides grants to small businesses to provide practical demonstrations of energy conservation measures which have potential for widespread use.

Research and Planning Division   405-841-5156
Enterprise Zone Program: There are 27 cities, 9 counties and 35 Labor Surplus Areas that are designated enterprise zones. Incentives for qualified businesses locating in an enterprise zone includes double investment/new jobs tax credits, general obligation bond financing.

Capital Resources Division   405-841-5150
Export Finance Program: Helps to increase export opportunities and enhance the internal competitiveness of business by providing both export insurance coverage and access to working capital (based on insured accounts receivable).

* Farmers Home Administration
USDA Agriculture Building
Stillwater, OK 74074   405-624-4294
Business and Industrial Loan Program: Encourages the retention of jobs in rural areas. The Farmers Home Administration (FmHA) will guarantee up to 90 percent of a loan from a commercial institution.

* Venture Capital Exchange
Enterprise Development Center
University of Tulsa
600 South College Ave.   918-631-2684
Tulsa, OK 74104   ext. 3152 or 2684
A not-for-profit corporation geared toward linking entrepreneurs

and investors, Venture Capital Exchange (VCE) helps fill the gaps in equity financing options available in the $20,000--$500,000 range. It operates a database available only to designated investors and entrepreneurs. Matches are made anonymously, until an investor finds a business he is interested in. Then the two parties are introduced and VCE ends its role. The service costs $100 for both investors and entrepreneurs. Following are some of the Venture Capital Companies in Oklahoma:

Oklahoma City: Energy Seed Fund, Oklahoma Department of Commerce, Capital Resources Division, P.O. Box 26980, Oklahoma City, OK 73126-0980, 405-843-9770, ext. 161.

Oklahoma City: McGowan Investment Company, P.O. Box 270008, 4341 Will Rogers Parkway, Oklahoma City, OK 73137, 405-946-9706.

Oklahoma City: OKC Innovation Center, 101 Park Ave., Suite 500, Oklahoma City, OK 73102, 405-235-3127.

Tulsa: ML Oklahoma Venture Partners, L.P., 6100 S. Yale Avenue, Suite 2019, Tulsa, OK 74136, 918-491-6700.

Tulsa: Davis Venture Partners, L.P., One Williams Center, Suite 2000, Tulsa, OK 74172, 918-584-7272.

Tulsa: TSF Capital Corporation, 2407 East Skelly Dr., Suite 102, Tulsa, OK 74105, 918-747-2600.

Tulsa: Tulsa Innovation Center, 1216 Lansing, Tulsa, OK 74106.

* **Venture Capital Clubs**
   The three Venture Capital Clubs in Oklahoma offer forums where entrepreneurs can publicly present their ventures to potential investors:

Bartlesville: Venture Capital Club, Tri-County Business Assistance Center, 6105 S. Nowata Road, Bartlesville, OK 74006-6010, 918-333-3422.

Oklahoma City: The Oklahoma Venture Forum, P.O. Box 2176, Oklahoma City, OK 73101-2176, 405-636-9736.

Tulsa: Oklahoma Private Enterprise Forum, Metropolitan Tulsa Chamber of Commerce, 616 South Boston, Tulsa, OK 74119, 918-585-1201, ext. 242.

Oregon

---

* **Oregon Economic Development Department**
   775 Summer Street NE
   Salem, OR 97310
Business Finance Section   503-373-1240
Oregon Business Development Fund Loans (OBDF): Structures and issues loans to small businesses. Manufacturing, processing,

and tourism related projects are eligible. Emphasis on rural areas, enterprise zones, and businesses with 50 employees or less. Offers long-term fixed-rate financing land, buildings, machinery and equipment, permanent working capital. Preference given to projects which will create a minimum of one job every $15,000 of OBDF investment. 17 percent of OBDF money is set aside for OBDF loans of $50,000 or less. 15 percent of available money is set aside for emerging small business in economically depressed areas. Maximum loan is 40 percent of eligible project costs and may not exceed $250,000 per project. 10 percent owner equity required in most cases.

Industrial Development Revenue Bonds (IDRBs): Industrial revenue bonds are issued by the Economic Development Commission to qualified manufacturing, processing and tourism related facilities. Only manufacturing projects are exempt from federal taxes. Major program goal is job creation. Eligible companies may borrow from $500,000 to $10,000,000.

Composite Revenue Bond Program: Allows the state to combine several Industrial Development Revenue Bond projects into one bond issue. The composite" issue will be large enough to achieve an average issuance cost lower than individual borrowers within the issue could obtain alone. Each individual loan is secured by a letter of credit from borrower's bank. Tax exempt rates are typically 75-80 percent of conventional rates. Funds can be used to finance fixed assets.

Local Revolving Loan Funds: There are many revolving loan funds for small business financing administered by Oregon's local government, and development groups. These funds frequently come from sources such as Dept. of Housing and Urban Development (HUD) through the State of Oregon, and the Federal Economic Development Administration (EDA).

Community Development Section   503-378-3732
Community Development Block Grant Program (CDBG): Through grants to eligible cities and counties, individual businessesmay apply for direct loans for expansion or relocation. Grants are to be used for businesses which will create or retain permanent jobs, the majority of which will be made available to low and moderate income people. Money can be used for either a loan from the city or county to a business or to pay for construction of public infrastructure required to serve a business project. Must create or retain at least one job per $12,000 of CDBG funds. For public infrastructure projects, one job must be created or retain for every $20,000 of CDBG funds. Loans are for a maximum of $500,000 per project.

Special Public Works Fund (SPWF): Provides Lottery funds for construction of public infrastructure necessary to support business development projects that result in creation or retention of permanent jobs. Eligible to Oregon cities, counties, port districts, water districts, metropolitan service districts, and federally recognized Indian tribes. Funding is provided by loans or combination of loans and grants. Maximum award per project is $1 million, and at lease one permanent, full-time job must be created or retained for every $20,000 of SPWF assistance. Technical assistance grants up to $10,000 available for municipalities with populations of less than 5,000.

Business Development Division   503-373-1225
Enterprise Zone Program: There are 30 enterprise zones established to stimulate business investment. Firms locating or expanding on an enterprise zone is eligible for property tax relief. In addition, state and local government land within an enterprise zone not already designated for some public use is available for sale or lease at fair market value. Individual enterprise zones may offer other incentives.

* Oregon Economic Development Department

Ports Division/International Trade Division
1 World Trade Center
121 SW Salmon Street, Suite 300
Portland, OR 97204   503-229-5625
Oregon Port Revolving Loan Fund: Long-term loans to the 23 legally formed Port Districts are offered through this fund at lower than market interest rates. Individual loans may be made to a maximum of $500,000 per project. Money may be used for port development projects (infrastructure) or assist private business development projects. A wide variety of projects qualify such as water-oriented facilities, industrial parks, airports, and eligible commercial or industrial developments. Revolving fund loans may also be used for matching funds for grants from federal, state and local agencies.

In addition, port districts are authorized to issue *Tax Exempt Industrial Development Bonds* either for their own operations or for companies locating or expanding within the port districts.

* Portland Development Commission

1120 SW Fifth, Suite 1100
Portland, OR 97204   503-796-5300
The City of Portland has authority to issue *Industrial Development Revenue Bonds.* The city also administers several *Revolving Loan Funds* targeted to serve business within specific areas of the City.

* Oregon Department of Energy

625 Marion Street NE   503-373-1033
Salem, OR 97310   1-800-221-8035 in Oregon
Small-Scale Energy Loan Program (SELP): Finances energy conservation and renewable energy projects in Oregon. Projects may be sponsored by individuals, businesses, non-profit organizations, and municipal corporations. Eligible projects are those which conserve conventional energy such as electricity and natural gas; or produce renewable energy from geothermal or solar sources, or from water, wind, biomass, and some waste materials. Can be used for equipment costs, construction, certain design and consultant fees, some reserves, construction interest, and most loan closing costs. Interest rates are fixed and typically lower than market. Can finance eligible equipment costs, construction, certain design and consultant fees, some reserves, construction interest, and most closing costs.

Business Energy Tax Credit: Designed to encourage businesses to invest in energy conservation, use renewable energy resources and recycle. Examples of qualifying projects are weatherization,

energy-efficient lighting, and equipment to process and haul recyclable materials. Maximum allowable credit is 35 percent of the certified cost.

* Oregon State Treasury

159 State Capitol
Salem, OR 97310   503-378-4111
Commercial Mortgage Program: Provides financing for large real estate development projects. Allows financial institutions to sell real estate mortgages to state of Oregon which enables lenders to provide financing for large projects that they might not otherwise be able to finance. Usually the program consists of ten-year, fixed-rate loan with a 25 year amortization for Oregon properties with multi-purpose use. Maximum loan to value is 75 percent.

* Small Business Administration (SBA)

222 SW Columbia, Suite 500   503-326-2682
Portland, OR 97201-6605   Fax: 503-326-2808
See the chapter introduction for a description of SBA programs.

* Oregon Department of Agriculture

635 Capitol Street, NE
Salem, OR 97310   503-378-3775
Agricultural Opportunity Fund: Provides grants to private, non-profit organizations and to public agencies for agricultural promotion and marketing projects. Encourages expansion of existing agribusiness and to locate in Oregon.

* Oregon Resource and Technology Development Corporation (ORTDC)

1934 NE Broadway
Portland OR 97232   503-282-4462
Provides early-state capital to move products into commercial markets or to prove technical feasibility. Eligible to basic sector business and applied research and development projects likely to be successful commercially. Provides management assistance and technical referral services and sponsors a computer-based network to bring entrepreneurs and potential investors together.

Seed Capital Fund: Early found financing for new product development. Investment list is $500,000.

Applied Research: For research leading to commercially viable applications. Limit is $100,000 with a one-to-one match requirement.

* Department of Environmental Quality

Management Services Division
811 SW Sixth Avenue   503-229-6022
Portland, OR 97204-1390   1-800-452-4011 in Oregon
Pollution Control Tax Credit: Tax credits are provided to encourage the use of pollution control facilities that prevent, control or reduce air, water, noise, hazardous waste, or solid waste pollution, or recycle or dispose of used oil. An income tax

or excise tax credit of 50 percent of the cost of the facility that is allocable to pollution control is available.

Pennsylvania

* Government Response Team
Robert A. McNary
Commonwealth of Pennsylvania
Department of Commerce   717-787-8199
439 Forum Building   717-787-6500
Harrisburg, PA 17120   Fax: 717-234-4560

Machinery and Equipment Loan Fund (MELF): Available to manufacturing, industrial, agricultural processors, and mining operations. Uses of funds are for machinery and equipment, acquisition and upgrading, and related engineering and installation costs. Loans up to $500,000, or 50 percent of the total eligible projects costs, whichever is less. One job must be created or retained for each $25,00 of loan funds. Interest rate between 3-6 percent depending upon local unemployment rate.

Environmental Technology Loan Fund (ETLF): Financing available to recyclers of municipal waste and manufacturers using recycled municipal waste materials. Funds can be used for acquisition or upgrade of machinery and equipment. Loans amounts up to $100,000, or 50 percent of the total eligible projects costs, whichever is less. Interest rate is 3%.

Business Infrastructure Development Program (BID): Funds for specific infrastructure projects such as access roads, water and sewer treatment and distribution, energy facilities, parking lots, storm sewer distribution, bridges, rail facilities, port facilities, and land acquisition and clearance. Available to manufacturing, industrial, research and development, agricultural processors, or firms establishing a national or regional headquarters. Both grants and loans are awarded to local sponsors. Loans to private businesses at 3 to 6 percent interest rate depending upon the unemployment rate. For every $1 of state BID assistance at least $2 in private sector matching funds are required. One job for every $15,000 must be created.

Site Development Program (SDP): Grants are available for construction and rehabilitation projects, such as water and sewer facilities, access roads, and channel realignment. Usually the limit for each grant is $50,000, or 50 percent of the total cost. Projects in certain economically distressed areas may receive up to $100,000 in grant money. Funds are available to manufacturing, industrial, and travel-related firms.

Pennsylvania Economic Development Financing Authority (PEDFA):
Tax-Exempt Pooled Bond Program: Variable interest rate loans tied to market for tax-exempt bonds available to manufacturing, energy, solid waste disposal and transportation facilities. Funds can be used for land and building acquisition, building renovation and new construction, machinery and equipment acquisition and installation and tax-exempt bond refunding. Minimum loan amount $400,000 to a maximum of $10 million. 100 percent of the project can be financed.

Taxable Bond Program: Variable interest rate loans available to all types of businesses needing access to low-cost capital. These funds may be used to purchase land and buildings, building renovation and new construction, machinery and equipment acquisition and installation, and working capital. Loans in an amount no less than $400,000. 100 percent of the of the project cost can be financed.

Pennsylvania Industrial Development Authority (PIDA): Available to manufacturing, industrial, research and development, agricultural processors, or firms establishing a national or regional headquarters. Use of funds are for land and building acquisition, building construction and renovation, industrial park development, and multi-tenant spec building construction and renovation. Loans up to $2 million. No more than 30-60 percent of total eligible project costs depending upon firms size and area unemployment rate. Interest rates vary between 3-6 percent depending upon local unemployment rate. One job must be created for every $15,000 of loan funds. Interest rate is 5 percent.

Pennsylvania Capital Loan Fund (PCLF): Available to manufacturing, industrial, export services, advanced-technology firms, small business with fewer than 100 employees. Provides low-interest loans to firms for capital development projects that create new jobs. Funds can be used for land and building, building construction and renovation, machinery and equipment acquisition and installation, and working capital. Loans amounts up to $200,000, or 50 percent of the total eligible projects costs, whichever is less.

Two other Pennsylvania Capital Loan Fund programs are as follows:

> *PCLF - PennAg:* Available to agricultural processors with fewer than 100 employees. Uses of funds are the same as *Pennsylvania Capital Loan Fund* above with exception of working capital. Loan amounts are the same as *PCLF*.

> *PCLF - Apparel:* Available to apparel manufacturers for machinery and equipment acquisition and installation. Loans up to $200,000, or 50 percent of the total eligible project costs, whichever is less. Interest rate is 3 percent. One job must be created for every $15,000 of funds.

Pennsylvania Economic Development Partnership Fund (EDP Fund): Available to manufacturing, industrial, research and development, or firms establishing national and regional headquarters in distressed communities. Funds use are land and building acquisition, building construction and renovation, site preparation, and infrastructure. Loan and grant amounts vary depending upon the financial needs and type of project. For every $15,000 of funds, one job must be created. Interest rates range between 3-9 percent depending upon local unemployment rate.

Industrial Communities Action Program (ICAP): Aimed at the reuse of blighted industrial buildings for trade services, manufacturing, industrial, or research/development firms. Loans up to $1 million or 25% of the total project costs, whichever is less. The interest rate is 3%. Loan terms to private developers are negotiated by applicant and approved by the Dept. of Commerce on a case-by-case basis. Land or buildings must be provided as collateral, and the developer must provide 5% equity. Portion of repayments must be retained by applicant; and $50,000 cost per job to be created within 5 years. Loan funds can be used for land and building acquisition, construction/ renovation, demolition, clearance, environmental remediation, water/ sewer systems, access roads, site preparation, and utilities.

Industrial Communities Site Program (ICSP): Aimed at the reuse of blighted industrial sites to provide opportunities for manufacturing, industrial, or research and development firms. Grants up to $1.5 million. Grants will be disbursed upon execution of a contract. The funds can be used for land/building acquisition, demolition, infrastructure construction or rehabilitation, environmental clean-up and site preparation.

Pennsylvania Infrastructure Investment Authority (Pennvest): Aimed at communities needing clean drinking water distribution and treatment facilities and/or safe sewage/storm water conveyance and treatment facilities. Loans up to $11 million per project for one municipality; up to $20 million for more than one municipality; up to $350,000 for design and engineering; up to 100% of the total project costs. The interest rate is 1 to 5 percent, depending upon the resulting user rates in the community; terms depending upon the useful life of the asset being financed. Funds can be used for the design, engineering and construction of publicly/privately owned drinking water distribution and treatment facilities and/or sewage and storm water conveyance and treatment systems.

Recycling Incentive Development Account (RIDA): Aimed at recyclers of municipal waste and manufacturers using recycled municipal waste materials. Loans up to $300,000 or 50% of the total eligible project costs. Interest rate is 3 percent; the term is up to 7 years. A private-sector match is required; 10 percent equity required; may subordinate lien position; disbursement at closing; and $30,000 cost per job to be retained or created. Loan funds can be used for acquisition or upgrade of machinery and equipment.

Sunny Day Fund: Aimed at manufacturing, industrial, research/development companies that create employment opportunities. Loans up to 50 percent of the total eligible project costs; total project costs must be at least $10 million. Interest rate is 3-6 percent, depending upon local unemployment rate. At least 100 new jobs must be created; $15,000 cost per job to be created. Funds can be used for land /building acquisition, building construction/ renovation, and machinery and equipment.

* Pennsylvania Treasury Department
　Linked Deposit Program
　129 Finance Building
　Harrisburg, PA 17120　　　　　717-787-2520
Linked Deposit Program: Established to create and retain jobs through the financing of economic development projects, the Pennsylvania Treasury Department offers up to $200 million in support. Deposits of state funds are made in commercial banks

and Savings and Loans (S & L), which then make funds available as loans to new or expanding small businesses. Funds available to firms engaged in expanding or establishing a business within the state, employing fewer than 150 people. At least one full-time job, or equivalent, should be created or saved for every $15,000 to $25,000 loaned.

* Nursing Home Loan Agency
　Room 460, Forum Building
　Harrisburg, PA 17120　　　　　717-783-8523
Provides financing for the state's nursing homes, offering low-interest loans to those unable to find financing elsewhere. The loans enable these institutions to comply with required safety and fire codes. Financing is also available to convert unneeded hospital beds into nursing home beds.

* Revenue Bond and Mortgage Program
　Room 466, Forum Building
　Harrisburg, PA 17120　　　　　717-783-1108
Funds for this program are borrowed through a local Industrial Development Authority, with financing secured from private sector sources. Lenders do not pay taxes on interest earned from the loan and borrowers obtain interest rates lower than conventional ones. Funds may be used for purchase of land, buildings, machinery, or equipment.

* Office of Technology Development
　Forum Building, #352
　Harrisburg, PA 17120　　　　　717-787-4147
Technology Business Incubator Loan Program: Grants and loans are available to construct, acquire, renovate, equip and furnish buildings for use as small technology business incubator facilities. Funds are available for up to 50 percent of total project cost, or $650,000, whichever is less. Grants may be made for technology business incubators located in designated economically distressed communities. Must be occupied by for-profit firms engaged primarily in product and process development, product commercialization or manufacturing.

Incubators provide for space and business development services needed in the start-up phase. A list of current technology incubator facilities is available.

Research Grants Division:
Research Seed Grants: Provides grants of up to $35,000 to businesses that are developing or commercializing a new technology. Preference is given to firms with fewer than 50 employees.

* Ben Franklin Technology Centers
　Executive Director
　North East Tier BFTC
　125 Goodman Drive
　Lehigh University
　Bethlehem, PA 18015　　　　　215-758-5200

Executive Director
BFTC of Southeastern Pennsylvania
University City Science Center
3624 Market Street
Philadelphia, PA 19104   215-382-0380

President
BFTC of Western Pennsylvania
4516 Henry Street, Suite 103
Pittsburgh, PA 15213   412-681-1520

President
BFTC of Central/Northern Pennsylvania
105 Barbara II Building
University Park, PA 16802   814-863-4558

Ben Franklin Partnership Program: Funds research and development projects that will benefit the state's economy through commercialization of high tech advances. The four Ben Franklin Technology Centers, listed above, provide assistance in evaluating your ideas, developing business plans and introducing you to funding sources as well as provide information on the programs listed below.

Challenge Grant Program for Technological Innovation: Support may be in the form of grant awards, equity positions or investments with royalty payback provisions. Requires matching funds. Eligible activities include joint research and development between private companies and university, research and development by small companies, entrepreneurial development, including support for incubators, education and training.

Seed Venture Capital Funds: Provide equity financing to new businesses during their early stages of growth, including eligible firms located in small business incubators. Types of business eligible to receive investments include manufacturing firms, firms involved in international export-related mercantile ventures, and advanced technology and computer-related ventures. A firm must have 50 or fewer employees.

Environmental Technology Fund: Available to companies developing recycling processes or markets for recycled materials. Uses are research and development, and technology transfer. Grants available up to $100,000.

* **Small Business Administration (SBA)**
100 Chestnut Street, Suite 309   717-782-3840
Harrisburg, PA 17101   Fax: 717-782-4839
See the chapter introduction for a description of SBA programs.

* **Lackawanna County Industrial Development Authority**
200 Adams Ave.
Scranton, PA 18502   717-961-6829
or
Economic Development Council of
  Northeastern Pennsylvania
1151 Oak St.
Pittston, PA 18640-3795   717-655-5581
Lackawanna County Industrial Development Authority (LCIDA)

Low-Interest Loan Program: Provides short term loans to small businesses throughout Lackawanna County who are unable to obtain adequate financing through conventional sources. Jobs must be created/retained as a direct result of the proposal project. Applicants must show that the project is financially feasible. Determination of feasibility will be based upon the project's ability to provide sufficient cash flow to support loan repayment.

Interest rate is 4 1/2% per annum. Maximum loan participation is 50% of total project costs or $20,000 (i.e., $40,000 project @ 50% = $20,000 maximum loan). Most loans are expected to be in the range of $10,000 - $20,000. The loan term is 2 years maximum for working capital, and 3 years maximum for other. The loan process period is approximately 60-90 days.

* **Division of Loans and Technical Assistance**
Office of Program Management
490 Forum Bldg.
Harrisburg, PA 17120   717-783-5046
Storage Tank Loan Fund (STLF): This fund is designed to financially assist small storage tank facility owners/ operators identified by the Department of Environmental Resources (DER) as potentially liable for the release or danger of a release of regulated substances from a storage tank. Assistance consists of low-interest loans to help finance the cost of corrective actions ordered by DER. By assisting small storage tank owners with the repair/ replacement of storage tanks, the loan proceeds help alleviate problems which may otherwise cause job loss or business shutdown.

Rhode Island

* **Rhode Island Department of Economic Development (RIDED)**
7 Jackson Walkway
Providence, RI 02903   401-277-2601
Small Business Loan Fund: Provides fixed rate loans at lower rates to manufacturing, processing, and selected services. Funds can be used for fixed assets (acquisition and improvement of land, buildings and equipment including new construction), job creation criteria. Loans range from $25,000 to $150,000 for fixed assets and up to $30,000 for working capital. Program funds should average 25 percent of total project cost. Terms are for up to 15 years for land and buildings, machinery and equipment 10 years, and loans for working capital are for a maximum of 5 years.

Tax-Exempt Industrial Revenue Bonds: Tax-exempt Industrial Revenue Bonds, issued through the Rhode Island Industrial Facilities Corporation (RIIFC), may be used to finance fixed assets (land, building, new machinery and equipment and certain other "soft" costs) for a manufacturing project. Financing may cover the entire project up to $10 million.

Taxable Industrial Revenue Bonds: Taxable bonds are also issued through the Rhode Island Industrial Facilities Corporation

(RIIFC) for manufacturing and certain selected commercial facilities, including travel-tourist facilities. Financing may cover the entire project. Interest rates are usually floating. Terms of the loan and interest rates are established by the lender. Funds may be used for fixed assets (land, building, machinery and equipment, and related "soft" costs).

Rhode Island Industrial-RecreationalBuilding Authority (IRBA) Insured Bond and Mortgage: Debt insurance on tax-free bonds, taxable bonds and conventional mortgages. Insurance premiums are based on average annual outstanding principal balance for manufacturing, processing, office, wholesale, retail, and travel-tourist facilities. Funds can be used for new building acquisition, or additions/rehabilitation of existing buildings, new or used machinery and equipment. Limits on loans are 90 percent for real estate, 80 percent for machinery and equipment, 40 percent for second mortgages, and 75 percent for travel-tourist projects. IRBA can insure a minimum of $100,000 per project cost and maximum of $5 million.

Rhode Island Partnership for Science and Technology State Support SBIR: Program provides four categories of support to qualified SBIR applicants. The partnership pays for consulting that is provided by the Rhode Island Small Business Development Center in order to help applicants develop quality proposals. A Rhode Island company that submits a valid Phase I SBIR proposal to the federal government will receive a $1,000 grant to help defray the cost of preparing an application. A matching grant of 50 percent (up to a maximum of $2,500) is available to a Phase I recipient that uses a consultant who is a faculty member from any Rhode Island university or college. A Rhode Island Phase I SBIR grant recipient who submits a Phase II proposal is eligible to receive a matching state grant of 50 percent of the Phase I award up to a maximum of $25,000.

Applied Research Grants: Through the Rhode Island Partnership for Science and Technology, research grants are offered to business that can do research work with Rhode Island university, colleges or hospitals. For major, innovative projects with a minimum research budget of $200,000. Projects should offer the potential for commercialization with high profit. The Partnership will fund up to 60 percent of the research project.

Small Business Tax Incentives: Provides tax incentives for investments in qualified small companies less than four years old with annual gross revenue less than $2.5 million. Incentives are available to entrepreneurs or venture capital partnerships which meet the requirements of the program.

Two other certified development companies serve specific areas:
Newport	401-277-2601
Bristol County	401-245-0750

* Small Business Administration (SBA)
380 Westminster Street   401-528-4561
Providence, RI 02903   Fax: 401-528-4539
See the chapter introduction for a description of SBA programs.

Business Development Company
Financing   401-351-3036
The Business Development Company (BDC) offers direct revolving and terms loans and SBA guarantee and term loans to healthy Rhode Island Businesses. Loans up to 90 percent of project cost to a maximum of $600,000. Minimum is $100,000. Funds can be used for any business purpose.

Governor's Office of Energy Assistance   401-277-3370
RISE Energy ConservationProgram: Commercial and industrial firms can apply for an energy audit at subsidized cost. Based on the results of the study, the company may be eligible for a bank loan of $5,000 to $25,000 at rates up to 5 percent below market rate. Firms with $50,000 or more annual energy cost should contact the Governor's office, Smaller firms should contact RISE as above.

* Rhode Island Division of Taxation
Department of Administration
1 Capital Hill
Providence, RI 02908   401-277-3050
Child Daycare Tax Credits: Credits are available against the business corporation tax and other business taxes at 30 percent of amount of day care purchase and of the cost to establish and/or operate a licensed day care facility. Maximum annual credit is $30,000. Certain restrictions apply.

* RI Department of Environmental Management (RIDEM)
83 Park Street
Providence, RI 02903   401-277-3434
Hazardous Waste Reduction, Recycling and Treatment Program: Grants are available to companies in four categories for development of hazardous waste reduction, recycling or treatment facilities. The categories are: feasibility study - 90 percent up to $140,000; project design - 70 percent to 90 percent up to $75,000; construction - 50 percent to 90 percent up to $250,000; evaluation - 90 percent to 100 percent up to $50,000.

Technical Assistance:
Cities and Towns: The following communities have revolving loan funds or other economic incentives for businesses. They also provide site location and technical services to resident companies or other companies looking to expand/start a business.

Bristol	401-253-7010
Central Falls	401-728-3270
Cranston	401-461-1000
Cumberland	401-728-2400
East Providence	401-434-3311
Newport	401-846-9600
North Providence	401-232-0900
Pawtuckett	401-725-5200
Providence	401-351-4300
Warwick	401-738-2000
West Warwick	401-822-9215
Westerly	401-596-7355
Woonsocket	401-762-6400

South Carolina

* South Carolina State Development Board
P.O. Box 927
Columbia, SC 29202   803-737-0400

Industrial Revenue Bonds (IRB): Cities and counties are all authorized to issue taxable or nontaxable IRBs. Bonds are issued for terms of 40 years maximum, but terms of 10-25 years are common. Interest rates are generally lower than conventional rates, since they are negotiated between the purchaser and the company using the facility. They are usually secured by the real estate or tangible property of the project.

Loan Program: For business and industry construction. Grantee must employ 51 percent low- and moderate-income personnel. Interest rates are negotiable, and payback is required within 12 months.

* South Carolina Jobs
Economic Development Authority
1201 Main Street
Suite 1750   803-737-0079
Columbia, SC 29201   Fax: 803-737-0016

Tax-Exempt Industrial Revenue Bond Program (IRB): This program is designed to provide accessibility to the public finance market for small manufacturing and non-profit firms. This market allows for variable and/or fixed rate funds at low rates. Individual company funding requirements (for land and depreciable assets) should range between $500,000 and $10 million. The program offers the small borrowers reduced up front closing costs making IRBs more economical than ever. IRBs may be done on a pooled or stand-alone basis as individual applications warrant.

Community Development Block Grant: Available to cities and counties for the commercial rehabilitation of existing buildings or structures used for business, commercial, or industrial purposes. Grants of up to $500,000 can be made. Every $15,000 of grant funds invested must create at least one full-time job, and at least 51 percent of the jobs created must be for low- and moderate-income families.

Carolina Capital Investment Corporation:
Venture Capital Funding Program: Loans or equity funds are available directly to businesses for product and process innovations which will create employment and aid economic development. Eligibility is limited to private, for-profit businesses with a net worth of under $1 million--mostly in the manufacturing, industrial, or service sectors. Loans may be for capital expenditures and the purchase of new equipment, as well as for working capital needs. The maximum allowable funding is $75,000, which can be in the form of straight debt financing, straight equity financing, or a combination of the two.

Infrastructure Bond Bank Program: Long-term, low cost water and sewer financing. Eligibility is currently limited to counties, municipalities, special purpose or special service districts, and commissions of Public Works of the State. Eligible projects include any water supply, sewer system, sewage or wastewater treatment facility. Priority will also be give to projects with local funding commitment for complementary infrastructure needs such as transportation. Municipal bond financing allows the borrower a considerable degree of flexibility. Repayment schedules can be tailored to meet specific needs of the borrowers.

Export Working Capital Guarantee Program (EWCG): This program provides short-term, Pre-Export Working Capital financing. Available only to South Carolina businesses involved in international trade through exportation of goods and services from South Carolina. Program is limited to private for profit businesses. The EWCG program guarantee shall be limited to 85% of the borrowed amount, not to exceed $170,000. The remaining 15% of the credit risk must be covered through commercial banks or financial institutions. The term of the EWCG program may vary but in no case will exceed 180 days. Interest rates on the loan will be negotiated between the commercial bank and the exporter.

The Commercial Loan Program for Rural Communities: Low-cost financing for Small Business start-up and expansion. Eligibility is restricted to those businesses which are located in towns affiliated with the South Carolina Downtown Development Association, Inc. (SCDDA). Borrowers must enter into a contract which requires the creation of at least one permanent, full-time job for each $10,000 increment of loan proceeds. At least 51% of the jobs to be created must be available to persons who qualify as low-moderate income individuals. Proceeds may be used for the acquisition or renovation of fixed assets or for general working capital purposes. Loan amount is limited to 85 percent of a project's cost, not to exceed $500,000. The remaining 15 percent of project costs must come from commercial banks, savings and loan debt financing or additional equity, etc. Term of a loan may vary but not exceed ten years.

Palmetto Basic Building Fund (PBBF): Low-interest, mortgage loans for basic building projects of non-profit local development corporations. Fund is a revolving loan fund which has been established by providing non-profit local development corporations with intermediate term financing for basic building projects. The fund will promote industrial diversification and aid in the tax base in the respective county. Basic building must be multi-use industrial facilities that can be completed quickly to the individual design and engineering specifications of the majority of industrial projects. Loans range from $250,000 to $400,000 for buildings of 20,000 to 30,000 square feet in size. Loans can be up to 100 percent of the project's cost excluding the value of the land. Loans are two-year term loans with principal and accrued interest payable at maturity or upon the sale of properties. Interest rates on these loans are fixed at four percentage points below the current money center bank prime rate, but no less than 4 percent.

Scana Development Revolving Loan Fund: Short-term financing for manufacturing, industrial and service businesses. A revolving loan which has been established for the express purpose of encouraging, assisting, promoting, and cooperating in the economic development of the State of South Carolina. Loans to restaurants, cyclical and speculative businesses are precluded. Will create new economic opportunities, urge and advocate economic diversifications, and identify and attract additional capital from the private and public sectors. Eligibility is restricted to those firms that are served by South Carolina Electric and Gas Company. Proceeds may be used for the acquisition or renovation of fixed assets, debt refinancing or for general working capital purposes. Loan amount shall not exceed $50,000. The term of the loan may vary, but shall not exceed 60 months. The interest rate is established at the time of commitment, but shall not exceed 5 percent.

The Microenterprise Loan Program for Small Industry: Low-cost financing for small business expansion. Utilized Community Development Block Grant (CDBG) funds for the purpose of funding economic development loans to small manufacturing, retail and service businesses. Eligibility is restricted to those businesses which have been operable for two years, and employ fewer than 5 employees, one or more of whom owns the business. Borrowers must enter into a contract which requires the creation of at least one permanent, full-time job for each $10,000 increment of loan proceeds. At least 51 percent of the jobs to be created must be available to persons who are low-moderate income individuals. Proceeds may be used for acquisition or renovation of fixed assets or for general working capital purposes. The loan amount is limited to 85 percent of the project's cost, not to exceed $25,000.

Rural Development Administration Intermediary Relending Program: This program provides gap financing for business. It is intended to supplement existing financing available to small business to assist in overcoming financial obstacles that otherwise might prevent realization of a project. Private for profit enterprises located in the rural areas and cities of South Carolina with population of 25,000 or less are eligible to apply. Eligibility whether start-ups or expansions of existing operations, is generally confined to manufacturing, industrial or service business. Permanent full-time employment must be created or retained. Loan proceeds may be used for capital expenditures such as the acquisition, construction or renovation of buildings and land, and the purchase of new or used equipment. Working capital and debt refinancing will qualify under the program. Loans may be for up to $150,000, but may not exceed more than 75% of a project's cost. Loan term cannot exceed seven years.

* Business Development Corporation
    Suite 225, Enoree Building
    Koger Center
    111 Executive Center Drive
    Columbia, SC 29210   803-798-4064
Business Development Board (BDB): A source of funds for business development and expansion. The Business Development Board (BDB) operates as a widely-held stock company made up of bank and savings and loan members. The BDB provides loans for companies which cannot obtain them elsewhere. Terms may range to 10 years or longer, and interest rates are usually comparable to the market rate. The BDB also makes loans under Small Business Administration (SBA) guarantees. Funds are available for any sound business purpose, excluding debt financing or speculative purposes.

* Small Business Administration (SBA)
    Strom Thurman Federal Bldg.
    1835 Assembly Street
    Room 358   803-765-5376
    Columbia, SC 29201   Fax: 803-765-5962
See the chapter introduction for a description of SBA programs.

South Dakota

* Governor's Office of Economic Development
    711 East Wells Avenue   605-773-5032
    Pierre, SD 57501-3369   1-800-872-6190
Community Development Block Grant: An anti-poverty block grant program whose funds are channeled towards those services and activities that will have an impact on the causes of poverty. About 90 percent of the funding goes to Community Action Agencies which can use the funds in various ways, such as revolving loan funds. Some of the types of activities funds are used for are to assist low-income people to secure and retain employment, obtain and maintain housing, obtain emergency assistance to meet immediate needs such as health services, nutritious food, housing, or employment assistance.

Revolving Economic Development and Initiative Fund (REDI): Funded by a one year, 1 percent sales tax, the REDI funds are used for a low-interest revolving loan fund for economic development and job creation. Loans are available to any for-profit business or non-profit business cooperative, whether business start-ups, business expansions, or business relocation. Funds can be used for purchase of land and site improvements; construction, acquisition, or renovation of buildings; fees, services and other costs associated with construction; machinery and equipment, trade receivables; inventory; and other working capital needs. The fund may provide up to 45 percent of the total project cost and requires applicants to have matching funds available beforehand, including a 10 percent equity contribution. Interest rates begin at 3 percent, but will later be determined semi-annually. Terms are amortized up to 20 years.

Economic Development Finance Authority:
Industrial Revenue Bonds (IRB): Industrial Revenue Bonds may be issued by any municipality, county, or sanitary district and may be used to finance industrial, commercial, manufacturing, agricultural, natural resources, educational, and other facilities. IRBs are limited obligation bonds of the issuing municipality, and once issued, they are to be repaid exclusively from the revenue produced by the project being financed.

SBA 504: Provides loans using 50 percent conventional bank financing, 40 percent Small Business Administration (SBA) involvement through Certified Development Companies, and 10 percent owner equity. A fixed-asset loan (land, building, and equipment with a useful life of 10 years or more) in amounts up to $750,000. Administered through the South Dakota Development Corporation, eligible businesses may borrow up to $500,000 with a minimum of $50,000. One job is to be created for each $35,000 of loan amount.

Community Development Block Grants Special Projects Account: Allows the state to provide grants to local government, who in turn, loan funds to businesses which will locate in the community to create jobs which benefit low and moderate income persons.

Fastrack Loan Guarantee Program: Enables students who have an idea for a new business to obtain back financing guaranteed through the Fastrack Foundation. High school students in grades 9-12 are eligible to participate. A business plan should be prepared which should include market, competition, promotion ideas, costs and financing needs.

Agricultural Processing and Export Loan Program (APEX): Eligible to businesses that will use and add value to one or more of South Dakota's agricultural products; locate in a community with a population of less than 2,000; employ low income persons, farm families or displaced farm families. Funds may be used for purchase of land and associated site improvements; construction, acquisition or renovation of building; fees, services and other costs associated with construction; trade receivables; inventory; other working capital needs; refinancing of existing debt; and crop and livestock production. The loan can provide up to 70 percent of the total project cost. Maximum loan amount is $150,000. Interest rates are between five and seven percent.

* Department of Agriculture
    Office of Rural Development
    Anderson Bldg.
    445 East Capitol
    Pierre, SD 57501   605-773-3375

Agricultural Loan Participation Program: A vehicle for supplementing existing credit, this program is administered through local lenders, with the state Department of Agriculture providing up to 80 percent of the funding. Interest can be up to 10 percent, with a maximum loan length of 10 years. Applicants must have lived in South Dakota for the past two years, be at least 21 years old, and have derived at least 60 percent of their income in the past tax year from farming. Projects funded are those which show they will add value to, or create innovative uses for South Dakota agricultural products, especially those of which there is a surplus. Can also be used in developing viable new agricultural products and subsequent markets or enhancing the economic viability of the applicant or the rural community.

* Farmers Home Administration
    200 4th Street, SW
    Huron, SD 57350   605-352-1100

Guaranteed Business and Industrial Loans: Loans aimed at creating and maintaining employment and improving the economies of rural areas. Local lenders initiate and service the loans, while the Farmers Home Administration (FmHA) guarantees up to 90 percent of the loan. Potential borrowers who

want loans of $500,000 or less should apply to the Small Business Administration. Guarantees are limited to $10 million. Interest rates are determined between the borrower and the lender and can be fixed or variable. Eligible projects and costs are business and industrial acquisitions, construction, conversion, enlargement, repair or modernization; purchase of land, machinery and equipment, furniture and fixtures, and certain housing development sites; processing and marketing facilities, start-up and working capital; pollution control; feasibility studies.

Rural Rental Housing Loans: Loans are available to create, improve, or purchase modest but adequate housing units for people with low to moderate incomes and for those age 62 or older. Loans may be made for housing in open country and in communities with populations of up to $20,000. The borrowers must be unable to finance the housing with personal resources, and be unable to obtain credit from other sources. Funds can be used to build, purchase or repair apartment-style housing, buy and improve land on which the buildings are to be located, provide streets, water and waste disposal systems, supply appropriate recreation and service facilities, install laundry facilities and equipment, landscaping.

* Bureau of Indian Affairs
    Area Credit Office
    Federal Building
    115 4th Avenue, SE
    Aberdeen, SD 57401   605-226-7343

Economic Development Grant Program: Provides seed money to Indian entrepreneurs to establish and increase profit-making business ventures and employment on or near federal Indian reservations. Grants are awarded for up to 25 percent of the total project and may not exceed $100,000 for individuals. Applicants must be able to raise matching funds of at least 75 percent of the total project costs.

Indian Loan Guaranty Fund: Guarantees loans made by private lenders to individual Indians for up to 90 percent of the unpaid principal. Funds must be used for projects that will benefit the reservation economy, with a $350,000 limit on loans to individuals. A 20 percent equity contribution is required. Thirty years is the maximum maturity term for these loans. Interest rates may not exceed 2 3/4 percent of the New York prime.

Revolving Loan Fund: Makes direct loans to individual Indians for economic enterprises which will contribute to the economy of an Indian reservation. Applicants must be unable to obtain financing from other sources, and must use the Indian loan guaranty program before applying to the Revolving Loan Fund. Loans to individuals are limited to $500,000 with a 20 percent equity contribution required from the borrower. The duration of the loans is flexible (maximum of 30 years), and interest rates are determined by the Secretary of the Treasury.

* State Investment Council
    4009 West 49th, Suite 300
    Sioux Falls, SD 57106-3784   605-335-5023

The State Investment Council deals solely with venture capital funds that invest in equity or equity-participating instruments of businesses. The fund can invest only in businesses which have headquarters and the majority of their employees located within the state. The Investment Council's participation in a venture capital fund may not be greater than one-third of the total equity funds invested in the fund.

* Small Business Administration (SBA)
101 S. Main Street
Suite 101   605-330-4231
Sioux Falls, SD 57102-0572   Fax: 605-330-4215
See the chapter introduction for a description of SBA programs.

Tennessee

* Department of Economic and Community Development
Rachel Jackson State Office Building
320 Sixth Avenue North
Nashville, TN 37243-0405   615-741-6671
                                    1-800-342-1340 in Tennessee

Energy Division, 8th Floor:
Small Business Energy Loan Program: Small businesses with under 500 employees, local governments or not-for-profit companies in good financial shape can qualify for loans at 5 percent annual interest with varying repayment periods. Maximum amount is $100,000 for installing energy efficiency measures in an existing structure at least one year old. Energy improvements include: insulation, storm doors and windows, specially coated glass, energy control devices, furnace systems, solar heating, and energy efficient lighting.

Program Management Section   615-741-6201
Tennessee Industrial Infrastructure Program: Available to manufacturing and other types of economic activities which export more than half of their product or services outside of Tennessee, businesses where more than half of their product or services enters into the production of exported products, and uses which primarily result in import substitution or the replacement of imported products or services with those produced in Tennessee. This program provides grants and loans to local governments and businesses for job creation activities, including infrastructure improvements. Activities include those involved in water and wastewater systems, transportation, site improvements, and electrical and natural gas systems, among others.

Tennessee Small Cities Community Development Block Grants (CDBG) Industrial Grant/Loan Program: The state allocates a significant amount of its available Community Development Block Grant (CDBG) money for this program. Funds are awarded for grants and loans to assist industries in locating or expanding in Tennessee and providing jobs. Jobs must be for low and moderate income persons. Grants are made for public infrastructure, and loans are made for industrial buildings and equipment. Maximum loan generally is $500,000. Up to

$750,000 to businesses locating or expanding in a community designated as a distressed area.

Venture Capital: Works with private investors to inject seed capital into promising or expanding firms. Up to $500,000 is available for working capital or fixed assets in manufacturing, warehousing, distribution, and other non-retail firms. The Corporation is limited to 50 percent of the total investment in a project.

Bond Reservation Section   615-741-2373
Industrial Development Bonds: These are mostly taxable bonds issued by local governments on behalf of businesses. Often used to finance manufacturing, multi-family housing, and single-family housing, these bonds may provide 100 percent financing, with interest rates lower than for conventional bonds.

* Small Business Administration (SBA)
50 Vantage Way
Suite 201   615-736-5881
Nashville, TN 37228-1500   Fax: 615-736-7232
See the chapter introduction for a description of SBA programs.

* Tennessee Valley Authority (TVA)
400 W. Summit Hill Drive
O.C.H. 1E
Knoxville, TN 37902   615-632-3148
Special Opportunities Counties Program: There are approximately 24 Tennessee counties eligible for this program, the objective of which is to assist the Valley's poorest counties to create new private sector job opportunities and enable them to utilize local resources for economic development. The Tennessee Valley Authority (TVA) contributes no more than 50 percent of the project costs, and is based on a ration of $3,000 to $5,000 per job created. Investments may range from $2,000 for low-skilled jobs to $6,000 for high-skilled high-wage positions. TVA funds may go in combination with other federal or private funds to municipalities, industrial development authorities, or other non-profit organizations devoted to economic development. These entities may in turn lend the funds at TVA long-term borrowing rates.

* Farmers Home Administration (FmHA)
Department of Agriculture
3322 W. End Ave., Suite 300
Nashville, TN 37203   615-736-7341
FmHA Business and Industrial Loans: For rural areas outside cities of 50,000 or more with priority to areas of 25,000 or less population. This aid is in the form of loan guarantees in which the Farmers Home Administration (FmHA) guarantees private lenders up to 90 percent reimbursement of losses. Applicants deal directly with private lenders. Maximum loan is $10 million, with an alcohol fuel loan limit of $20 million. (For loans under $500,000, borrowers are advised to contact the Small Business Administration.) Terms are 30 years for land, building and fixtures, 15 years for machinery or equipment, and 7 years for working capital. Interest rates may be fixed or varied.

* Tennessee Technology Foundation (TTF)
P.O. Box 23184
Knoxville, TN 37933-1184   615-694-6772

A private, non-profit corporation created to stimulate growth in technology-based businesses in Tennessee, the Tennessee Technology Foundation (TTF) targets the "Technology Corridor" in the eastern part of the state where the Oak Ridge National Laboratory, the Tennessee Valley Authority, and the University of Tennessee are located. It provides services such as linking state, federal, and private sector resources, siting new facilities, identifying sources of capital and manpower for new or existing businesses, and helping with business plans for new companies. It also maintains a computerized inventory of real estate including both raw and improved land. The Foundation works to assist high technology businesses in technical areas and to help with the commercialization of research and development products.

Texas

---

* Texas Department of Commerce
P.O. Box 12728
Austin, TX 78711

Texas Capital Fund
Community Development Block Grant   512-320-9649

Awards are made to a city or county that in turn provides a loan to a specific business for "gap financing". Project must be located in a rural area generally with a population of 50,000 or less. Funds can be used for land, building, machinery and equipment, working capital, and infrastructure to businesses creating jobs of which 51% benefit low and moderate income persons. Minimum loan is $50,000, and maximum loan up to $500,000. Up to $2.5 million for infrastructure projects.

Industrial Revenue Bonds/Tax-Exempt Bond Program: May be issued by political subdivisions, the state Department of Commerce or conservation districts through the formation of industrial development corporations. Eligible projects are mostly manufacturing, but also include student loans. Proceeds may be used for land and depreciable property with limitations. Up to $10 million in tax exempt bonds may be issued. Also, in most cases, a letter of credit is needed for each project.

Taxable Bond Program: Taxable bonds may be issued for manufacturing, industrial, or commercial projects. There is no limit to the maximum size. Applicants must provide either a buyer for the bond or a letter of credit indicating the credit enhancement needed to rate the bonds.

Texas Enterprise Zone Program   512-320-9579

Provides incentives and regulatory relief to stimulate job creation and investment in economically distressed areas. Types of incentives include tax abatement to encourage business retention, expansion and start-ups, sales tax rebates available for businesses in the zone which are designated Enterprise Zone Projects.

Texas Rural Economic Development Fund   512-320-9649

Eligible to a manufacturing or industrial enterprise located in a rural city with a population of 50,000 or less or a county with a population of 200,000 or less and predominantly rural in character. Preference is given to food and fiber processing industries. Up to 85 percent of loan made by a commercial lender is guaranteed to the State. Funds can be used for land, buildings, equipment, facilities, working capital. Minimum loan is $50,000. Maximum loan is $350,000. Must create at least one job for every $35,000 of guarantee.

Texas Exporters Loan Guarantee Program   512-320-9662

A manufactured product with at least 25 percent Texas source components, labor or intellectual property is eligible as well as the export preparation of agricultural product or livestock. Up to 85% of loan made by commercial lender is guaranteed by the State. Funds can be used for raw materials, inventory, other manufacturing costs, marketing and equipment. Minimum loan is $10,000. Maximum loan is $350,000. Term of loan is 1 year or less.

Eximbank Working Capital Guarantee   512-320-9662

Export working capital loans are made through a commercial lender. Exporters may apply for preliminary commitments and then "shop" for a lender. Up to 90% of loan is guaranteed. Funds can be used for inventory and working capital. Minimum loan is $10,000 with no maximum. Loans are usually up to 12 months.

Texas Export Credit Umbrella Insurance
Program   512-320-9662

An insurance policy is underwritten by the Eximbank and is designed to stimulate the expansion of Texas exports to foreign countries by insuring a company's eligible export credit sales against loss due to political and commercial reasons.

Contract Loan Program: Guarantees available to contractors and subcontractors engaged in the construction, manufacturing and service industries. Business must provide a specific product or service under an assignable contract. Finance estimated cost of labor and material needed to perform on a specific contract.

Loans to Small General Contractors: Loan guarantees available to construction contractors and homebuilders. Funds can be used for construction, rehabilitation for property for resale. Maximum loan guarantee is $750,000.

Handicapped Assistance Loan: Available to companies 100 percent owned by one or more handicapped individuals who are actively involved in the management of the company. Funds can be used for working capital, fixed assets, improvements, some debt refinancing. Direct loans up to $150,000 and $750,000 on guarantee.

* Farmers Home Administration
District Office
101 S. Main, Suite 102
Temple, TX 76501   817-774-1307

Business and Industry Loan Program: Loan guarantees available for projects located in cities with a population of less than

50,000. Funds can be used for working capital, acquisition of fixed assets (can include land and building), improvements, and in some cases debt refinancing. Recommend projects over $50,000. Maximum loan is $10 million. Up to $20 million for alcohol fuel production facilities.

* Agriculture Finance Office
   Department of Agriculture
   P.O. Box 12847
   Austin, TX 78711
Linked Deposit Program   512-463-7686
Available for non-traditional alternative crops, processing facilities for agricultural products, and direct marketing initiatives. Funds can be used to purchase or lease land, buildings, equipment, seed, fertilizer, etc. Maximum loan is $100,000 for production, $250,000 for processing and marketing.

Rural Microenterprise Loan Program   512-463-7686
Loans or loan guarantees available to family owned and operated enterprises in rural Texas. Funds can be used for fixed assets and working capital. Maximum loan or guarantee is $15,000 for start-ups and $30,000 for existing businesses.

Texas Agricultural Finance Authority (TAFA)   512-463-7686
Loans, loan guarantees or revenue bonds available to small and medium size enterprises that contribute to the diversification of Texas agriculture. Funds can be used for fixed assets and working capital.

* Tyler Seed/Venture Growth Fund
   P.O. Box 2004
   Tyler, TX 75710   903-593-2004
Seed Capital Funds: Tyler and Smith counties have established seed capital funds which in invest in local companies. The funds are typically used to leverage other sources of funding.

* Small Business Administration (SBA)
   8625 King George Drive   214-767-7633
   Dallas, TX 75235-3391   Fax: 214-767-7870
See the chapter introduction for a description of SBA programs.

Utah

* Small Business Administration (SBA)
   Salt Lake District Office
   125 South State Street   801-524-5800
   Salt Lake City, UT 84138-1195   Fax: 801-524-4160
See the chapter introduction for a description of SBA programs.

* Deseret Certified Development Company
   Statewide
   7050 Union Park Center, Suite 570
   Midvale, UT 84047   801-566-1163

* Utah Technology Finance Corporation
   419 Wakara Way
   Salt Lake City, UT 84108   801-364-4346
Assists the incubation and growth of new and emerging high technology businesses, especially small businesses. Provides funds for research contracts, program grants, equity investments, convertible loans, and venture financing.

Vermont

* Vermont Industrial Development Authority
   56 East State Street   802-223-7226
   Montpelier, VT 05602   Fax: 802-223-7266
Industrial Loan Programs: Makes direct loans to eligible companies in amounts up to 40 percent of the cost of acquiring land, buildings, machinery, or equipment to be used in an industrial facility. Participation may not exceed $300,000 for real estate and $200,000 for machinery and equipment projects.

Industrial Revenue Bonds: Issues tax-exempt and taxable industrial revenue bonds to provide qualified borrowers with low interest funds for acquisition of land, machinery, buildings, or equipment for use in manufacturing facilities.

SBA 504: Provides loans using 50 percent conventional bank financing, 40 percent Small Business Administration (SBA) involvement through Certified Development Companies, and 10 percent owner equity. A fixed-asset loan in amounts up to $750,000. Loan can be used for land and building, construction, machinery and equipment, and renovation/expansion.

Agricultural Finance Program: The Authority makes low interest loans to family farmers and agricultural facility operators for real estate and machinery and equipment acquisition. Maximum loan amount is $50,000.

Debt Stabilization Program: The Authority re-lends funds borrowed from a Vermont bank consortium to refinance, at lower interest rates, operating debts of family farmers. The maximum loan amount is $150,000.

Vermont Job Start: Can lend up to $15,000 at 8 1/2% interest rate for low income person/businesses to expand or to start up a business.

* Agency of Development and Community Affairs
   109 State Street
   Pavilion Office Building
   Montpelier, VT 05602   802-828-2501
Economic Development Department:
Job Development Zones   802-828-3221
Job Development Zones are areas created for incentives such as tax credits, for communities to get new and existing business to locate in the area.

*Department of Housing and Community
Affairs*   802-828-3217
Vermont Community Development Program: Provides grant
funds to communities to improve housing, create and retain
employment opportunities, and improve public facilities in
support of housing and economic development activities to
benefit persons of lower income. These funds are then loans to
businesses for economic development.

Public Facilities Division   802-244-8744
Administers constructions grants and loans for engineering
planning for municipal pollution control and water supply
projects. Administers construction grand awards for pollution
control projects, construction loans for municipal water supply
and pollution control facilities through state and federal
programs.

* Vermont Housing Finance Agency
   230 St. Paul Street   1-800-864-0538
   Burlington, VT 05401   1-800-222-VHFA in VT
Multi-Family Development: Issues tax-exempt bonds and loans
the proceeds to developers of affordable housing. Issues low
income housing tax credits to developers of low income rental
housing.

* Northern Community Investment Corporation
   P.O. Box 904
   20 Main St.
   St. Johnsbury, VT 05819   802-748-5101
A private, non-profit, community-based corporation that assists
development in Vermont and northern New Hampshire. The
Northern Community Investment Corporation (NCIC) provides
capital and professional assistance to both small and large
businesses and community development projects. Some of its
services include: personalized technical assistance, direct
financing of $500,000 or more, attracting outside capital to
supplement its own resources in order to expand its investments,
developing industrial space for new or expanding businesses, and
investment in residential and commercial development.

* Small Business Administration (SBA)
   Room 205, 87 State Street   802-828-4422
   Montpelier, VT 05602   Fax: 802-828-4485
See the chapter introduction for a description of SBA programs.

Virginia

* Virginia Small Business Financing Authority (VSBFA)
   1021 E. Carey St.
   P.O. Box 798
   Richmond VA 23206-0798   804-371-8254
Loan Guaranty Program: Assists small businesses in obtaining
short-term capital to improve and expand their operations.
Provides a maximum guaranty to private lenders of 50 percent

of a bank loan, or $250,000 whichever is less. This is a program
that can be used by businesses which have already taken
advantage of the Small Business Administration (SBA) guaranty
program for fixed assets and are now in need of short-term
capital to finance current operations.

Industrial Development Bonds (IDBs): The Virginia Small
Business Financing Authority (VSBFA) issues tax-exempt
Industrial Development Bonds (IDBs) to provide a low-interest
source of capital to creditworthy small manufacturing firms for
their land, building and capital equipment needs. Minimum
project size is $250,000 and the total effective annual financing
costs average 80-90 percent of the Prime interest rate. They are
primarily interested in assisting businesses which are providers
of goods or services and which are owned or directly managed
by the applicant. Number of jobs created, fiscal impact of the
project on the locality, and opinion of the local governing body
regarding the project are all considered. An outside investor's
interest in a project should not exceed 49 percent.

Umbrella IDB Program: Tax exempt revenue bonds are issued
to small businesses for use in manufacturing projects. Funds can
be used for land, buildings and new capital equipment. Through
an Umbrella Program, the Authority provides small businesses
access to the public capital market's rates and terms for tax
exempt bonds, by pooling projects together in a single
"umbrella" bond. Applicants must present a letter of credit from
a financial institution guaranteeing the amount of the bond.

Taxable Bond Program: Provides long-term financing at
reasonable interest rates for land, building, and capital equipment
for small businesses. Requirements are similar to those for the
Umbrella IDB program. Applicants need a letter of credit from
a bank or other lending institution as a guaranty for the
financing. Then a triple A-rated bank provides a master letter of
credit and the Small Business Finance Authority issues the
commercial paper in the national market to fund the project. This
allows small businesses access to the low, short-term rates
available in the commercial paper market to finance long-term
projects.

Export Financing Assistance Program: The Virginia Small
Business Financing Authority (VSBFA) works in partnership
with the Export-Import Bank of the United States. (Eximbank)
through its City/State Program to provide easier access to
Eximbank financing programs and export credit insurance. A full
array of finance programs including working capital financing
for the exporter and financing for the foreign buyer, assists
businesses in gaining access to Eximbank guarantees and loans
by packaging and submitting applications according to Eximbank
guidelines. Also assists exporter in obtaining export credit
insurance.

Child Day Care Financing Program: Provides small direct loans
to child day centers for quality enhancement projects or to meet
or maintain child care standards. Examples: infant care
equipment or equipment needed to care for children with special
needs, playground improvements, and upgrades or minor
renovations to kitchens, bathrooms, and plumbing and electrical
systems.

*** Virginia Department of Housing
and Community Development**
205 N. Fourth Street
Richmond, VA 23219-1747   804-786-4474
Revolving Loan Funds: Administers two revolving loan funds which provide below market rate loans to manufacturing and related industries in eligible communities to finance land, buildings and equipment. One or two dollars of private investment is required for each dollar from the funds, and the maximum loan amount is limited by the number of permanent jobs created or maintained as a result of the financing.

Community Development Block Grants   804-786-4474
Available to cities and counties for projects which create or maintain jobs or which address the problems of community decline. The funds received by the city/county are, in turn, loaned to businesses. Eligible projects include the commercial rehabilitation of existing buildings or structures used for business, commercial, or industrial purposes, site development, access roads, railroad spans, water and sewer facilities. Every $15,000 of grant funds invested must create at least one full-time job, and at least 51 percent of the jobs created must be for low- and moderate-income families.

* Virginia Coalfield Economic Development Authority
P.O. Box 1060
Lebanon, VA 24266   703-889-0381
Provides financial assistance to new or expanding industries in far south-western Virginia through a revolving loan program. Businesses which will bring new income to the area may use the loans for real estate purchases, construction or expansion of buildings, and purchase of machinery and equipment. Job creation and average minimum hourly wage requirement apply.

Venture Capital Networks: There are various private venture capital firms and clubs in the state. The Department of Economic Development will refer inquirers to private investment firms for up to date information.

* Small Business Administration (SBA)
Richmond District Office
400 N. 8th Street, Room 3015   804-771-2400
Richmond, VA 23240   Fax: 804-771-8018

Small Business Administration (SBA)
District of Columbia Office
(Loudoun, Arlington, Fairfax Counties,
Alexandria and Fairfax City)
1111 18th Street, NW
P.O. Box 19993   202-634-1500
Washington, DC 20036   Fax: 202-634-1803
See the chapter introduction for a description of SBA programs.

* Farmer's Home Administration (FmHA)
400 North Eighth Street
Room 8213   804-771-2451
Richmond, VA 23240   804-771-2453 (program info)

Farm Loan Program: Provides loans and loan guarantees to farm families, rural communities, and rural non-farm citizens. Loans are available to finance homes, community facilities such as water or sewer systems, and non-farm businesses.

Business and Industrial Loan Program: Encourages the creation and retention of jobs in rural areas. FmHA will guarantee loans by commercial institutions up to 90 percent.

Federal Land Bank: A nationwide cooperative credit system making long-term loans available to eligible farmers and other rural residents. These loans are for agriculture-related purposes only, including: farm real estate, livestock, farm operating expenses, housing related to farm operations, and to refinance debts or remove a lien from farm land. Loans are also available for farm-related sites, capital structures, equipment, and working capital. Federal Land Bank offices are located in counties throughout the state.

* VEDCORP, Inc.
951 East Byrd Street, Suite 940   804-648-4802
Richmond, VA 23219   Fax: 804-648-4809
VEDCORP is a private, for-profit entity that makes investments in small businesses located in targeted areas of Virginia to encourages economic development and employment growth in these areas. Provides capital to businesses and entrepreneurs in support of their long term growth objectives. Investments range from $100,000 to $700,000 for five to eight years, repayments scheduled to match the cash flow expectations of the business, and an appropriate interest rate combined with an equity participation in the business.

Washington

*** Department of Community, Trade and
Economic Development**
P.O. Box 48300   206-586-8974
Olympia, WA 98504-8300   1-800-562-5677 in WA
Community Development Finance Program: Helps businesses obtain long-term start-up or expansion loans at reasonable interest rates and low down payments. Funds are available for real estate, new construction, renovation, major leasehold improvements, machinery and equipment, and working capital.

Development Loan Fund: Offers loans to businesses in economically distressed areas where jobs will be increased, especially for low- and moderate-income residents. The Fund provides the difference between the total amount of the project cost and the private financing available. Loans are usually at interest rates below market levels.

Coastal Loan Fund: Provides below-market rate loans to businesses in the five coastal counties of Clallam, Jefferson, Grays Harbor, Pacific and Wahkiakum for projects that will create permanent job opportunities for dislocated workers, the unemployed and lower-income persons.

Loans will purchase consulting assistance including accounting, engineering, architecture, design, market studies, feasibility analyses, tourism studies, land use planning, revitalization planning and strategic planning for community development.

* Department of Trade and Economic Development
2001 Sixth Avenue
Suite 2600   206-464-7350
Seattle, WA 98121   1-800-237-1233

Industrial Revenue Bonds: For acquisition, construction or improvement of manufacturing facilities. Bonds are tax-exempt, with interest paid to the buyer not subject to federal income tax. The result is lower interest rates. Bonds may be issued by cities, counties, or port districts on behalf of a private business project proposal.

Umbrella Bond Program: For small businesses with borrowing needs too small for Industrial Revenue Bonds. This program pools several requests for industrial financing into one umbrella bond issue.

Loan Packaging Assistance for Certified Minority and Women Owned Businesses and Minority and Women Owned Start-Up Businesses: Through the Community Development Finance (CDF) Program, you can schedule and appointment with the finance specialist assigned to your area. The finance specialist will work with you to identify public and private financing opportunities and will assist you in preparing application materials.

Community Development Block Grant Float Loans: Available to cities and counties. Eligible cities and counties may apply for a grant under this program to extend a short-term loan to a private business entity. Project must be proven necessary and appropriate to create or retain jobs; and must agree to create jobs. The interest rate will be negotiated based on the contribution the project will make to job creation or retention. The rate will be in the 5-7% range.

* Washington State Business Assistance Center
Dept. of Trade and Economic Development
919 Lakeridge Way SW, Suite A
Olympia, WA 98502   206-464-5832

Washington Economic Development Finance Authority: Provides financing for small export transactions, gives farmers who participate in federal, long-term land conservation programs an option to obtain lump-sum funds for machinery purchases, modernization, debt reduction or new business investment.

* Washington State Energy Office
809 Legion Way SE
P.O. Box 43165
Olympia, WA 98504-3165   206-956-2000

Industrial Program: Low-interest loans provided to fund energy efficiency measures. Provides technical assistance in the form of industrial energy efficiency studies for small-and medium-size manufacturing facilities.

* Export Assistance Center of Washington (EACW)
2001 Sixth Avenue, Suite 2100
Seattle, WA 98121   206-464-7123

Export Financing: Assists with the placement of a federal guarantee against commercial and political risks. The Export Assistance Center of Washington (EACW) is a designated City/State Cooperative entity for the Export-Import Bank of the U.S. (Exim), a federal agency in this field. The Foreign Credit Insurance Agency offers insurance against foreign receivables may be assigned to a commercial lender so that the exporter can receive payment prior to collection on the foreign invoice. EACW also can help businesses secure private sector financing, including equity capital, and works with several federal and state agencies that offer various financing and other assistance.

* Department of Revenue
Audit Section
1101 S. Eastside Street
Olympia, WA 98504-7470   206-753-3171

Distressed Area Tax Deferral Program: Sales or use tax deferral may be available for buildings, equipment, or machinery used in manufacturing, research, or development in distressed areas. Another provision is that one new job must be created for every $300,000 of investment. Repayment begin three years after completion of the project, with total repayment to be complete over the following five years.

* Small Business Administration
Seattle Regional Office
915 2nd Avenue, Room 1792   206-553-1420
Seattle, WA 98174-1088   Fax: 206-553-8635

See the chapter introduction for a description of SBA programs.

* Department of Agriculture
Farmers Home Administration
P.O. Box 2427
Wenatchee, WA 98807   509-662-4358

Business and Industry Loan Guarantee Program: The FmHa grants loan guarantees for up to 90 percent of a lender's losses on loans used for business or industry development. Individuals, as well as public and private organizations and Indian tribal groups in rural areas with under 50,000 population, are eligible. Priority is given to towns under 25,000 population. Funds can be used for buy-outs, construction, conversion, modernization and repair of buildings, purchase of land, equipment, furniture and fixtures, processing and marketing facilities, and pollution control, feasibility studies.

* Economic Development Administration
Jackson Federal Building
915 Second Avenue, Room 1856
Seattle, WA 98174   206-553-4740

Revolving Loan Funds: Grants are made to designated redevelopment areas, economic development districts, states, political subdivisions and Indian tribes to establish or expand revolving loan funds in depressed areas. These funds are loaned to businesses for fixed assets or working capital.

* Washington State Business Assistance Center
Dept. of Trade and Economic Development
919 Lakeridge Way SW, Suite A
Olympia, WA 98502   206-753-5632
Child Care Facility Fund: Makes direct loans at a fixed interest rate, guaranteed loans up to 80 percent of the loan, and matching grants on a dollar-for dollar basis with cash, goods, or services. Maximum loan amount is $25,000 to employers starting or expanding child care services. Funds can be used to make capital improvements in an existing licensed child care facility, start a licensed child care facility, including family child care homes, purchase equipment, and operations costs during the first three months of a new program.

West Virginia

* Governor's Office of Community and
Industrial Development
Community Development Division
Room B 553
State Capitol Complex, Bldg. 6
Charleston, WV 25305   304-558-4010
Grants In Aid Programs: Provides money for infrastructure construction or improvement to provide planned, orderly development of communities and to lay the basis for economic growth. Funds go for such projects as public utilities, access roads, public buildings, streets, and sidewalks.

Community Development Block Grant Program: Available to cities and counties, who in turn, loan the money to businesses for the commercial rehabilitation of existing buildings or structures used for business, commercial, or industrial purposes. Every $15,000 of funds invested must create at least one full-time job, and at least 51 percent of the jobs created must be for low and moderate-income families.

Appalachian Regional Commission: This Federal Commission provides discretionary funds to governor's for regional improvement in the areas of water quality, waste disposal, planning, access roads, and highways. The Department of Community Development has preliminary review jurisdiction over proposals.

* West Virginia Economic Development
Authority (WVEDA)
Building 6, Room 525
State Capitol Complex
Charleston, WV 25305   304-558-3650
Direct Loans: The WVEDA is a public corporation charged with promoting economic development through financial assistance to state industries for expansion or construction purposes. The Authority works in conjunction with other state industrial development agencies and lending institutions. It offers below market rates. Funds can be used for acquisition, construction and/or renovation of land, buildings, and equipment. Loans are mostly for manufacturing businesses. Can provide up to 45

percent of the total project cost, with a $500,000 limit per project.

State Industrial Development Pool Funds: A $50 million investment fund set up by the State Board of Investments, this money is available through the WVEDA to larger industrial development projects. Loan terms are similar to the revolving fund, but letters of credit are required. Rates are based on U.S. Treasury bill rates.

SBA 504: Provides long-term fixed-rate loans for small and medium-sized firms. SBA participation is 40 percent through the West Virginia Certified Development Corporation, 50 percent conventional bank financing, and 10 percent owner equity. A fixed-asset loan in amounts up to $750,000. Loan can be used for land and building, construction, machinery and equipment, and renovation/expansion.

Farmer's Home Administration Business and Industry Guaranteed Loan Program: This program covers up to 90 percent of the principal of a loan in order to protect investors.

* West Virginia State Tax Department
State Capitol
Room 417 West, Building 1
1800 Washington Street E
Charleston, WV 23505   304-348-2500
Small Business Tax Credit: To qualify, businesses must have an annual payroll of at most $1,700,000 and annual sales not exceeding $5,500,0000, and the median salary of the company's employees must be at least $12,000 per year. Must create at least 10 new jobs. Firm is then allowed 30 percent of its qualified investment as credit.

Warehouse "Freeport" Tax Exemption: Allows goods in transit to an out-of-state destination to be exempt from local ad valorem property tax when "warehoused" in West Virginia. Exemption is applicable for "property in the form of inventory in the flow of interstate commerce or while in transit is consigned to a warehouse, public or private, within the state for final destination outside the state".

Investment Tax Credits: Credit against *Business Franchise Taxes* for industrial expansion or revitalization is available to manufacturers and persons providing manufacturing services. Also available for utilities paying the Business and Occupational Tax and natural resource producers who pay Severance Taxes.

Credit against franchise taxes for investment in a qualified research and development project is available to producers of natural resources, manufacturers, generators of electric power and persons providing manufacturing services.

* Small Business Development Center
1115 Virginia Street E
Charleston, WV 25301   304-558-2960
See the chapter introduction for a description of SBA programs.

Wisconsin

* Wisconsin Housing and Economic Development Authority

P.O. Box 1728   608-266-0976
Madison, WI 53701-1728   Fax: 608-267-1099

Business Development Bonds: These are essentially industrial revenue bonds issued by the Wisconsin Housing and Economic Development Authority (WHEDA) on behalf of small businesses. Eligible projects qualify for low-cost, fixed-rate financing. Businesses need to supply lenders with a letter of credit from WHEDA to guarantee these bonds. Available to manufacturers and first-time farmers with gross sales of $35 million or less. Project funded must create or retain employment. Proceeds can be used for land, building, or equipment purchase or improvement. Other restrictions apply. Business Development Bonds generally range from $500,000 to $1 million with $10 million maximum.

Venture Capital Fund: Available to business that have fewer than 25 employees and gross sales of less than 2.5 million. Financing type is an equity investment. Investments are made to very early stage business ventures with potential for significant growth.

Wisconsin Community Capital   608-256-3441
Business must be located in a distressed community and must expect to create or retain 10 to 15 jobs for unemployed or underemployed residents within 2 years. Loans range between $30,000 to $200,000. Funds can be used for land, buildings, equipment, inventory, working capital.

* Department of Development

Roger M. Nacker
123 W. Washington Ave.
P.O. Box 7970   608-266-1386
Madison, WI 53707   Fax: 608-267-0436

Industrial Revenue Bonds: Available to manufacturing businesses for land, buildings, equipment, new or expanded facilities/equipment. Maximum loan amount is $10,000,000.

Wisconsin Development Fund:
Todd Boehm   608-266-0241
Technology Development Program: To be eligible for this program, the business must be a Wisconsin-based business applying in conjunction with a school in the University of Wisconsin System or another post-baccalaureate institution in Wisconsin. Preference is given to proposals with strong market potential, contributing to state economy and to research aims of education institution, and be completed within 2 years. The program provides loans or repayable grants up to 25 percent of total research costs, to fund product or process development research. Amounts range from $50,000 to $200,000.

Major Economic Development Projects:
Phillip Albert   608-266-7099
Projects are evaluated on the potential contribution to job creation or retention, new capital investment, infrastructure needs and local unemployment among others. Businesses may apply directly, or local government may apply on their behalf. Grants or loans up to 75 percent of the cost of the project.

Small Cities Community Development Block Grant Program:
Jim Frymark   608-266-2742
This program is federally funded. The Department administers the Small Cities portion of the Program. It is available to cities with populations under 50,000 (populations over 50,000 apply directly to the federal government) for economic development projects. The program focuses on job creation and retention with a requirement that a portion of the jobs be made available to persons of low- and moderate-income. Applicant must be a local government acting on behalf of a business. The assistance to the business is in the form of a loan with terms that vary based on the firm's need.

Employee Ownership Assistance:
Todd Kearney   608-266-6675
This program makes loans to employee groups to study the feasibility of converting an operating or recently-closed business to employee ownership. Loans are awarded on a competitive basis to those groups with greatest management ability and promise for success and where economic impact and affected employment is largest. The program requires a 25 percent match by borrowing group, unless hardship can be shown.

Small Business Innovation Research (SBIR) Program
Todd Boehm   608-266-0241
A federal Research and Development Program available to small businesses for projects at the earliest stage of research that have commercial potential. Phase I awards up to $50,000 over six months to evaluate the scientific and technical merit and feasibility of an idea. Phase II awards are up to $500,000 over two years to pursue the technological development of the innovation. Phase III is for commercialization with private or non-SBIR government funding. Each federal agency issues a solicitation bulletin, generally once a year, describing the areas of research it will fund.

SBIR Bridge Gap Financing   608-267-9383
Business that submit a Phase II proposal will be guaranteed up to $40,000 in state funding to "bridge the gap" in federal funding between the end of Phase I and the start of Phase II.

Bureau of International Development   608-266-1480
Export Development Loan Program   608-266-1480
Offers loans of up to $30,000 for small Wisconsin businesses wishing to enter exporting or to expand into new markets. Business must match a minimum of 60 percent of the loan funds.

Development Zone Program   608-267-2045
Businesses who expand, start or relocate in one of the 8 development zones in the state, and meet certain requirements may be eligible for tax benefits. Tax credits include a refundable jobs credit for hiring members of certain targeted groups, refundable sales tax credit for the amount of sales tax paid on building materials and equipment used in a trade or business, plus a non-refundable 2.5 percent location credit, non-refundable

2.5 percent investment credit, and a non-refundable 5 percent additional research credit.

Recycling Loan Program
Todd Kearney   608-266-6675
This program is designed to encourage new or expanding businesses to make products from recycled materials. Funds will be awarded to those recycling activities that best contribute to the state's goals.

Recycling Rebate Program
Todd Kearney   608-267-6675
This program is designed to offset the increased costs of making products from recycled materials. It also encourages the start-up and expansion of recycling firms, and the promotion of new markets for waste products. Firms may apply for a one-time rebate on qualified equipment, or up to five annual rebates, to offset the cost of a recycling process.

Minority Business Development Fund:
Robert Wynn   608-266-8380
This program provides financial support for early business planning, or to stimulate expansion or acquisition of an existing business. To qualify, a firm must be certified as a minority-owned business. Each project must retain or increase employment.

Minority Business Early Planning Grant Program:
Robert Wynn   608-266-8380
This program provides grants to minority entrepreneurs for business planning assistance and for feasibility studies.

Business Development Initiative for Persons With Disabilities:
Dale Versteen   414-227-4061
This program provides technical assistance for the start-up and expansion of small businesses interested in hiring persons with disabilities. Equity financing is also offered to firms owned by persons with disabilities for start-up and expansion, and to organizations providing service to disabled persons.

Minority Business Recycling Early Planning Grant Program:
Robert Wynn   608-266-8380
This program provides grants to minority entrepreneurs for business planning assistance and for feasibility studies to assist the start-up of recycling enterprises.

Public Facilities for Economic Development Program:
Paul Van Rooy   608-266-3278
This program provides grants or low-interest loans to communities to lend to a business for infrastructure improvements. Each project must result in direct job creation.

Major Economic Development Project Program:
Paul Smestad   608-266-3278
This program supports business-development projects that will have a substantial local, regional, or state-wide impact.

Customized Labor Training Fund:
This fund stimulates employment and business expansion by helping companies train or retrain workers in specialized skills.

Tax Incremental Financing (TIF):
Paul Van Rooy   608-266-3278
This is a funding mechanism for financing local economic development projects, created to help cities attract industrial and commercial growth in underdeveloped and blighted areas and to areas in need of rehabilitation.

Wisconsin Transportation Facilities Economic Assistance and Development Program:
Ken Leonard   608-267-7754
Enables the Department of Transportation secretary to approve transportation facilities improvements (rail, road, harbor, and airport) when transportation improvements is a part of an economic development project.

Area Development Manager Program:

Region 1:	Mary Ambros	715-836-2630
Region 2:	Mary Jo Carson	715-346-2043
Region 3:	Dennis Russell	414-498-6302
Region 4:	Ryron Rasmussen	608-266-0148
Region 5:	Dan Madden	608-267-2250
Region 6:	Larry Baker	414-238-2227
Region 7:	Vic Grassman	608-266-0563

Assists business expansions, promotes business retention, and helps local development organizations in their respective territories. Local economic development practitioners can turn to area development managers for assistance with long-term marketing and planning strategies.

Small Business Ombudsman Office:
Sara Burr   608-266-5489
Gives information on government regulations and financing alternatives to small businesses, particularly new entrepreneurs.

Women's Business Services Program:
Mary Strickland   608-266-0593
Helps women entrepreneurs start or expand their businesses, and improve their business operations. It identifies accessible sources of financing for these firms, and assists in business planning, financial projections, and cash-flow-statement preparation.

Permit Information Center: 608-266-9869
The center manages regulatory and permit clearance for economic development projects. It informs companies of all sizes about permit processes and deadlines, speeds up the issuance of permits, and resolves delays and communication problems.

Entrepreneurial Network Coordinator: 608-267-9384
Develops resources, programs, and policies to strengthen entrepreneurial network. Activities include business development and training workshops, and conferences.

Manufacturing Assessment Center:
Karl Arps   608-266-0165
The center helps small and medium manufacturers improve quality and productivity through professional assessment of operations, systems and layouts.

Recycling Specialist:
Bill Lehman   608-266-7068
Assists in identifying financing alternatives for business expansions in recycling.

Main Street Program: 608-267-3855
This program helps communities revitalize their downtowns. It offers a comprehensive range of professional services that follow a four-point approach: organization, promotion, design, and economic restructuring. Services include training for community based program managers; workshops; on-site visits, and ongoing technical support.

Community Preparedness Program:
Bill Zillmer   608-267-5100
The program assists community leaders in organizing and planning economic development strategies. The staff also provide technical assistance in developing/identifying resources for community economic development projects.

Business and Management Assistance Program:
Michael Malcheski   608-267-2252
The program provides management assistance, financial analysis, marketing/development advice to small companies and entrepreneurs.

American Indian Economic Development Liaison:
                                          608-267-0762
Provides advice, training, technical assistance, economic development information to the tribes, tribal communities, and American Indian entrepreneurs, and serves as state economic development liaison.

Physician Loan Assistance Program: 608-267-3837
The program provides repayment of medical school loans up to $50,000 to physicians who are willing to practice in medical-shortage areas. It helps communities that have shortages of primary care physicians and have had difficulty recruiting these physicians to their area.

Wisconsin Development Fund (WDF)
Economic Development Component:
James Frymark   608-266-2742
The program helps businesses create/retain jobs. An eligible local governmental unit must apply on behalf of the company for a loan based on the company's need.

WDF-Customized Labor Training Fund:
Todd Kearney   608-266-6675
This fund can provide grants to start-up, expanding and retooling companies for up to 50 percent of the cost of customized training or retraining of workers. Goals are to stimulate business expansion/creation, and to help modernize industrial base through introduction of new products and services.

WDF-Technology Development Fund:
Todd Boehm   608-266-9383
This program encourages research and development. It provides financial support to consortia of businesses and higher-education institutions, and promotes business retooling and diversification.

Applied Research in Technology Program:
Todd Boehm   608-266-0241
The program supports university research that has potential to benefit Wisconsin businesses.

Technology Based Incubator Program: 608-266-3278
The program offers financial assistance for feasibility studies to determine the need for a technology based incubator, and the initial operation and development of a proposed incubator.

Employee Ownership Assistance Loan Program:
Todd Kearney   608-266-6675
The Loan Program can help a group of employees seeking to purchase a business. The business under consideration must have closed or suffered substantial layoffs within one year prior to the group's application.

Community-Based Economic Development
Program: 608-266-3278
Designed to promote business activities within the state's economically-distressed areas. It awards grants to small businesses and to community-based organizations. Applicants can receive grants of up to 50 percent of the cost to study, create, or operate business incubators.

Community Development Planning Program: 608-266-3278
The program provides grants to communities in 18 northern counties to help strengthen and diversify their local economies. Grant awards are made for economic development projects and in implementing economic development projects that are part of an existing economic development plan.

Rural Economic Development Program: 608-266-3278
Grants and loans are available for planning and managerial assistance for rural businesses with fewer than 25 employees located in rural areas. Counties with less than 150 people per square mile or municipal units with a population of less than 4,000 are eligible.

Hazardous Pollution Audit Grant Program: 608-266-6675
The program helps businesses and communities determine both the amount of hazardous wastes they produce and the cost of preventing pollution. Maximum grant is $2,500, or 50% of the cost of a hazardous-pollution audit, whichever is less.

Tourism Development

Tourism Communication Program: 608-266-8773
Responsible for public information, publication production, media assistance, statewide events publicity, and special projects promotions producing the materials and publicity to ensure that Wisconsin tourism is visible to public.

Joint Effort Marketing (JEM) Program: 608-266-3750
Department may fund up to 75% of advertising expenses of qualifying projects that help promote the state in coordination with the tourism marketing plan.

JEM Newspaper Program: 608-266-8045
Businesses can take advantage of special low rates and get greater impact by purchasing advertising space in newspapers under the Wisconsin tourism logo.

Information Services Program: This program operates 7 highway information centers, 2 urban information centers, and a computerized response and inventory system.

Tourism Development Consultant Program:
608-267-0752
This program provides information on funding sources and feasibility assessment to individual businesses and developers. Development consultants advise and help promote the industry in their respective territories.

Heritage Tourism Program: 608-266-7299
The program is intended to help local communities identify tourist attractions and cultural and historic resources; profile the demographics of the tourist who come to their area; identify sources of competition; and develop a marketing plan.

* Export-Import Bank of the United States
811 Vermont Avenue, NW
Washington, DC 20571   202-566-8990
Working Capital Guarantee: Loan guarantees to assist small to medium-sized companies having the potential to export but inability to access working capital lines of credit from their banks to finance operations. Funds can be used for inventory, working capital, materials, labor, marketing activities. Other export credit programs available include medium and long term credit, and various types of export/import insurance.

* Small Business Administration (SBA)
310 W. Wisconsin Ave., #400   414-297-3941
Milwaukee, WI 53203   Fax: 414-297-4267

Small Business Administration
212 East Washington Avenue   608-264-5261
Madison, WI 53703   Fax: 608-264-5541
See the chapter introduction for a description of SBA programs.

* Wisconsin Business Development Finance
Corporation
P.O. Box 2717
Madison, WI 53701   608-258-8830
Wisconsin Business Development (WBD): Offers long-term financing at below conventional rates. Fund can be used for land, building, equipment, and certain soft costs such as architect, accounting, legal fees are also eligible. Wisconsin Business Development (WBD) participation may not exceed 40 percent or a maximum of $750,000 of the project cost.

* Farmers Home Administration (FmHA)
4949 Kirschling Court
Stevens Point, WI 54481   715-345-7600
Business and Industrial Loans: This program provides loan guarantees up to 90 percent of project cost. Businesses must be located in an area outside the boundary of a city of 50,000 or more. Priority will be given to projects in rural communities and communities of 25,000 or less. Funds can be used for land, buildings, equipment, inventory, and working capital. Special loans are also available for alcohol fuel projects.

* Northwest Planning Commission
302 Walnut Street
Spooner, WI 54801   715-635-2197
Program services businesses primarily in timer, and wood, manufacturing and tourism industries in Northwestern Wisconsin. Must create 1 job for every $5,000 loans to business. A subordinated loan covering 10 to 20 percent of project. Funds can be used for land, buildings, and equipment.

* Impact Seven
320 Industrial Avenue
Turtle Lake, WI 54889-9109   715-986-4171
Rural Development Loan Fund: Loans available with a preference to Northwest Wisconsin. Loans generally range between $40,000 to $150,000. One job must be created for each $20,000 of loan funds. Funds can be used for land, buildings, equipment, and inventory.

Venture Capital: Financing type is equity investment. Prefer businesses in Northwest Wisconsin but will consider anywhere in the state, any industry. Job creation is a criterion. Available from start-up to mature business buyout or expansion. No restrictions on use of funds.

* First Commercial Financial Corporation
330 South Executive Drive, #204
Brookfield, WI 53005   414-786-0699
Venture Capital: Financing type is equity investment. Most investments are for second state or later, and start-up funds are also available. Prefer biotech, high-tech, medical, communications, computers, electronics and other manufacturing. Will consider service or distribution businesses and businesses in other industry areas. Prefer investments in the midwest.

* Venture Investor of Wisconsin, Inc.
University Research Park
565 Science Drive, Suite A
Madison, WI 53711   414-272-4400
Venture Capital: Financing type is equity investment. Works with Wisconsin companies or those willing to be to start and develop their business. Preference is given to those having products or services with national market potential. Deals with early state companies as well as special situations such as new product launches or significantly changed corporate strategies.

Wyoming

* Division of Economic and Community Development
Department of Commerce
Barrett Bldg., 4th Floor N   307-777-7284
Cheyenne, WY 82002   Fax: 307-777-5840
1-800-262-3425 out of state
Planning and Marketing Grants: Local governments may apply for grants under this program on behalf of for-profit businesses.

Funds may be used to defray cost of feasibility studies, business plan preparation, marketing studies and test marketing. The for-profit business may be either a start-up or existing business planning to expand. Up to $25,000 available per applicant.

Main Street Program: Main Street communities have received funds from the Petroleum Violations Fund (PVF). PVF funds must be matched dollar for dollar with private funds and may be used for energy conservation related renovation projects in downtown areas.

Industrial Revenue Bonds: Private lenders purchase these bonds which provide low-interest loans for large business expansion. Maximum loan is $10 million, minimum loan is $500,000. Interest rates may be fixed or variable. A broker should be consulted for details. Division of Economic and Community Development can refer you to one.

Both of the following programs can be used for direct loans and loan guarantees, or in conjunction with other public or private financing sources.

Federally Funded Business Loan Program (Economic Development Block Grant): Offers low-interest loans to businesses creating jobs for low-to moderate income citizens. Funds can be to buy or lease land, buildings, machinery and equipment, construction and renovation. The state grants money to participating cities, towns and counties, which then loan it to your business at below-market rates. Up to $250,000 is available, but should not exceed 25 percent of total project cost. One position must be created for each $10,000 of loan funds. 51 percent of jobs created must be filled by low-to-middle income citizens.

State Funded Business Loan Program: Offers loans and loan guarantees at flexible rates and terms. A business must use Wyoming resources and employees and contribute to the state's basic economy. Service companies are generally not eligible. Applicants need equity equal to at least 20 percent of the total project cost and loans are usually limited to $750,000, or 60 percent of the total cost. 10 year maximum.

* **Office of the State Treasurer**
   State Capitol
   Cheyenne, WY 82002   307-777-7408
Small Business Assistance Act: Provides fixed-asset financing and 5-year interest rate subsidies of loans to be used for creating jobs. Wyoming residents who own and operate medium-sized industrial or manufacturing firms are eligible. Funds may be used to acquire land and buildings, purchase machinery and equipment, and build or renovate facilities.

State Linked Deposit Program: Offers a 5-year, fixed-rate interest subsidy at below market rate on loans used for creation and retention of jobs. Businesses may use funds for construction of plants, expansions of existing structures, equipment,

machinery, land, livestock, and capital. The maximum amount of the loan is $750,000. This must certify creation of jobs. Loans cannot give the business an unfair advantage over its competitors. Farm and ranch operations are not considered to be in competition with each other.

* **Wyoming Industrial Development Corporation**
   P.O. Box 3599
   Casper, WY 82602   307-234-5351
The corporation provides non-bank lending through various Small Business Administration programs and other public finance sources for companies with moderately strong credit risks. Funds may be used for acquiring fixed assets, renovation and construction of facilities, financing costs, or working capital. These loans range from $25,000 to $3 million, but most do not exceed $750,000. Some size restrictions and employment requirements apply. Depending on which program is used, the Small Business Administration will guarantee between 40 percent-90 percent of a loan. Terms run from between 7 to 10 years, with maturity in 25 years.

SBA 504 Program: Provides loans using 50 percent conventional bank financing, 40 percent SBA involvement through Certified Development Companies, and 10 percent owner equity. A fixed-asset loan in amounts up to $750,000. Loan can be used for land and building, construction, machinery and equipment, and renovation/expansion.

SBA 7(a) Guaranteed and Direct Loan: Guarantees up to 90 percent of a loan made through a private lender, up to 750,000. Can be used for working capital, inventory, machinery and equipment, and land and building. Available only to those unable to obtain a loan from conventional sources. Direct loans are made up to $150,000.

* **Western Research Institute**
   Box 3395
   Laramie, WY 82071   307-721-2327
Science, Technology and Energy Authority Program (STEA): Designed to assist business involved with advanced technology move from research and development to the marketplace. STEA leverages state funds with private and federal dollars to provide financing.

* **Farmers Home Administration**
   P.O. Box 820
   Casper, WY 82602   307-261-5144
Provides loan guarantees to help local industry in rural communities of less than 50,000. Program allows financial institutions to make loans beyond their capital limitations.

* **Small Business Administration**
   100 E. B Street, Room 4001   307-261-5761
   Casper, WY 82602-2839   Fax: 307-261-5499
See the chapter introduction for a description of SBA programs.

Venture Capital:
Finding A Rich Angel

With federal and state money getting harder to come by, and banks experiencing serious problems, anyone interested in starting his own business or expanding a current one may do well to look into venture capital. Venture capitalists are willing to invest in a new or growing venture for a percentage of the equity. Below is a listing of some of the associations, government agencies and businesses that have information available on venture capital.

In addition, there are Venture Capital Clubs throughout the country where entrepreneurs have a chance to present their ideas to potential investors and learn about the process for finding funds.

Associations

The National Venture Capital Association (NVCA)
1655 North Fort Meyer Drive
Suite 700
Arlington, VA 22209
703-351-5269
Fax: 703-351-5268

The association works to improve the government's knowledge and understanding of the venture capital process. Staff members can answer questions about federal legislation and regulations, and provide statistical information on venture capital. NVCA members include venture capital organizations, financiers and individuals investing in new companies.

The association publishes a membership directory that includes a listing of the members with addresses, phone numbers, tax numbers and contacts. There are now about 200 members. The directory is available for $10.

The Western Association of Venture Capitalists
3000 San Hill Road
Bldg. 1, Suite 190
Menlo Park, CA 94025
415-854-1322

Publishes a directory of its 110 members. The cost is $50.

National Association of Investment Companies
1111 14th Street NW, Suite 700
Washington, DC 20005
202-289-4336
Fax: 202-289-4329

It is composed of specialized Small Business Investment Companies (SSBICs). The SSBIC Directory lists about 120 companies across the country including names, addresses and telephone numbers. It also describes each company's investment preferences and policies. The 23-page publication costs $25.98.

It also publishes *Perspective*, a monthly newsletter geared toward specialized small business investment companies. This newsletter includes articles about legislation and regulations affecting SSBICs. (Note: This association was formerly called the American Association of Minority Enterprise Small Business Investment Companies (AAMESBIC)).

National Association of Small Business Investment Companies (NASBIS)
1199 North Fairfax Street, Room 200
Alexandria, VA 22314
703-683-1601
Fax: 703-683-1605

This association serves as an information clearinghouse on venture capital. Staff can direct you to venture capital sources, experts and literature.

The 1994-1995 membership directory, *Venture Capital: Where to Find It*, has 120 pages listing about 300 small business investment companies and specialized small business investment companies. It gives names, addresses, phone numbers, investment policies, industry preferences, and preferred dollar limits on loans and investments. The directory is available for $10. To order, send a check or money order to NASBIS Directory, P.O. Box 2039, Merrifield, VA 22116.

Technology Capital Network
201 Vassar Street
Cambridge, MA 02139
617-253-7163

This non-profit corporation tries to match entrepreneurs in need of capital with venture capital sources. Investors and entrepreneurs register for up to 12 months for $300.

Venture Capital Clubs

There are more than 150 Venture Capital Clubs worldwide where inventors can present their ideas to potential investors. At a typical monthly meeting, a couple of entrepreneurs may give short presentations of their ideas. It is a great way for entrepreneurs and potential investors to talk informally.

The International Venture Capital Institute (IVCI)
P.O. Box 1333
Stamford, CT 06904
203-323-3143

The IVCI publishes an annual directory of domestic and international venture groups (venture capital clubs). The cost of the *1995 IVCI Directory of Domestic and International Venture Groups*, which includes contact information for all of the clubs, is $19.95.

Association of Venture Capital Clubs
265 East 100 South, Suite 300
P.O. Box 3358
Salt Lake City, UT 84111
801-364-1100

The association was formed to facilitate and encourage creation and participation in growth-oriented businesses. The association publishes a directory of its members and will put you in touch with the club nearest you. If you are interested in starting a club, the association publishes a 15-chapter manual which sells for $50. Send to the attention of Lisa Rene Jones.

Below is a partial listing of clubs in the United States.

Alabama
(AL, LA, MO, TX)
Birmingham Venture Club, Chamber of Commerce, P.O. Box 10127, Birmingham, AL 35202; 205-323-5461, Fax: 205-250-7669. Attn: Patricia Fox.

Mobile Venture Club, c/o Mobile Area Chamber of Commerce, 451 Government Street, Mobile, AL 36652; 205-433-6951, Fax: 205-431-8608. Attn: Walter Underwood.

Alaska
Alaska Pacific Venture Club, 405 W. 27th Ave., Anchorage, AK 99503; 907-563-3993, Fax: 907-279-9319.

Arizona
Arizona Ventures, 2419 N. Black Canyon Hwy., Suite 4, Phoenix, AZ 85009; 602-254-8560, Fax: 602-254-9650. Attn: Merritt Chamberlain.

Arkansas
Venture Resources Inc., 100 South Main Street, Suite 416, Little Rock, AR 72201; 501-375-2004, Fax: 501-375-8317.

California
(CA, OR, WA)
Orange Coast Venture Group, c/o American Accounting, 23011 Moulton Parkway, F2 Laguna Hills, CA 92654; 714-855-0652, Fax: 714-859-1707. Attn: Renee Wagoner.

(CA, OR, WA)
Orange County Venture Group, P.O. Box 2011, Laguna Hills, CA 92654; 714-855-0652, Fax: 714-380-1128. Attn: Gregory Beck.

(CA, OR, WA)
Community Entrepreneurs Organization, P.O. Box 2781, San Rafael, CA 94912; 415-435-4461. Attn: Dr. Robert Crandall.

San Diego Venture Group, 750 B Street, Suite 2400, San Diego, CA 92101; 619-595-0284, Fax: 619-231-8055.

Colorado
Rockies Venture Club, Inc., 4950 East Evans, Suite 115, Denver, CO 80222; 303-831-4174. Attn: Maita Lester.

Connecticut
(CT, MA, MI, NJ, NY, IN, OH, PA, DC)
Connecticut Venture Capital Fund, 200 Fisher Drive, Avon, CT, 06001; 203-677-0183, Fax: 203-676-0405. Attn: Sam McKay.

District of Columbia
Baltimore-Washington Venture Group, Michael Dingman Center for Entrepreneurship, College Park, MD 20742-7215; 301-405-2144, Fax: 301-314-9152. Attn: Mark Feuerberg.

Florida
Gold Coast Venture Capital Club, 5820 North Federal, Suite A-2, Boca Raton, FL 33478; 407-997-6594, Fax: 407-997-6347. Attn: Mike Donnelly.

Florida
(FL, GA, TN, KY)
Gold Coast Venture Capital Club, 11401-A W. Palmetto Park Rd., Suite 202, Boca Raton, FL 33428; 407-488-4505, Fax: 407-487-4483.

Gold Coast Venture Capital Club, 5820 North Federal, Suite A-2, Boca Raton, FL 33478; 407-997-6594, Fax: 407-997-6347. Attn: Mike Donnelly.

(FL, GA, TN, KY)
Florida Venture Group, 2838 Kansas Street, Oviedo, FL 32765; 407-365-5374, Fax: 407-365-5374. Attn: Maryjim King.

Hawaii
Hawaii Venture Capital Association, University of Hawaii, OTTED, 2800 Woodlawn Drive, Suite 280, Honolulu, HI 96822; 808-526-1277, Fax: 808-524-2775.

Idaho
Rocky Mountain Venture Group, 2300 N. Yellowstone, Suite E, Idaho Falls, ID 83402; 208-526-9557, Fax: 208-526-0953. Attn: Dennis Cheney.

Treasure Valley Venture Capital Forum, Idaho Small Business Development Center, Boise State University College of Business, 1910 University Drive, Boise, ID 83725; 208-385-1640.

Iowa
Iowa City Development, ICAD Group, P.O. Box 2567, Iowa City, IA 52244; 319-354-3939, Fax: 319-338-9958. Attn: Marty Kelley.

Illinois
Madison Dearborn Partners, 70 West Madison, Suite 1330, Chicago, IL 60602; 312-732-5400, Fax: 312-732-4098.

Indiana
Venture Club of Indiana, P.O. Box 40872, Indianapolis, IN 46240-0872; 317-253-1244, Fax: 317-253-1244.

Kentucky
Kentucky Investment Capital Network, Capital Plaza Tower, 23rd Floor, Frankfort, KY 40601; 502-564-7140, Fax: 502-564-3256.

Mountain Ventures Inc., P.O. Box 1738, London, KY 40743; 606-864-5175, Fax: 606-864-5194.

Louisiana
(AL, LA, MO, TX)
Louisiana Seed Capital Corporation, 339 Florida St., Suite 525, Baton Rouge, LA 70801; 504-383-1508, Fax: 504-383-1513. Attn: Kevin Couhig.

(AL, LA, MO, TX)
Greater New Orleans Venture Capital Club, 301 Camp Street, New Orleans, LA 70130; 1-800-949-7890, Fax: 504-527-6950. Attn: Judy Houston.

Maryland
Mid Atlantic Venture Association (MAVA), 9690 Deereco Rd., Suite 800, Timonium, MD 21093; 410-560-2000, Fax: 410-560-1910. Attn: Maryanne Gray.

Massachusetts
Venture Capital Fund of New England, 160 Federal St., 23rd Floor, Boston, MA 02110; 617-439-4646, Fax: 617-439-4652.

Michigan
(CT, MA, MI, NJ, NY, IN, OH, PA, DC)
Southeastern Venture Capital, The Meyering Corporation, 206 30 Harper Ave., Suite 103, Harper Woods, MI 48225; 313-886-2331. Attn: Carl Meyering.

(CT, MA, MI, NJ, NY, IN, OH, PA, DC)
New Enterprise Forum, Chamber of Commerce, 211 E. Herron, Suite 1, Ann Arbor, MI 48104; 313-665-4433. Attn: Barb Sprague.

Minnesota
The Entrepreneurs Network, 1433 Utica Avenue S., Suite 70-3, Minneapolis, MN 55416; 612-542-0682.

St. Paul Venture Capital, 8500 Normandale Lake Blvd., Suite 1940, Bloomington, MN 55437; 612-830-7475, Fax: 612-830-7475.

Mississippi
Magnolia Venture Capital Corporation, P.O. Box 2749, Jackson, MS 39207; 601-352-5201, Fax: 601-355-1804.

Missouri
Venture Group Inc., 233 West 47th Street, Kansas City, MO 64112; 816-531-5585, Fax: 816-531-8818.

Missouri Innovation Center, 5650 A South Sinclair Road, Columbia, MO 65203; 314-446-3100, Fax: 314-446-3106.

Montana
(CO, MT, UT, NM, ID, AZ)
Montana Private Capital Network, 7783 Valley View Road, Poulson, MT 59860; 406-883-5470, Fax: 406-883-5470. Attn: Jon Marchi, President.

Nebraska
(IL, IA, NE, MN, WI, SD, ND, KS)
Grand Island Industrial Foundation, 309 West 2nd St., P.O. Box 1486, Grand Island, NE 68802-1486; 308-382-9210, Fax: 308-382-1154. Attn: Andrew G. Baird, II CED.

New Jersey
(CT, MA, MI, NJ, NY, IN, OH, PA, DC)
Venture Association of New Jersey, Inc., 177 Madison Ave., CN 1982, Morristown, NJ 07960; 201-267-4200, Fax: 201-984-9634. Attn: Amy or Jay Trien.

New York
(CT, MA, MI, NJ, NY, IN, OH, PA, DC)
Long Island Venture Group, CW Post Campus, Long Island University, College of Management, Deans Office, Worth Hall, Room 309, North Blvd., Brookville, NY 11548; 516-299-3017, Fax: 516-299-2786. Attn: Carol Caracappa.

(CT, MA, MI, NJ, NY, IN, OH, PA, DC)
New York Venture Group, 605 Madison Avenue, Suite 300, New York, NY 10022-1901; 212-832-7300, Fax: 212-832-7338. Attn: Burt Alimansky.

(CT, MA, MI, NJ, NY, IN, OH, PA, DC)
Westchester Venture Capital Network, c/o Chamber of Commerce, 222 Mamaroneck Avenue, White Plains, NY 10605; 914-948-2110, 914-948-0122.

Rochester Venture Capital Group, 100 Corporate Woods, Suite 300, Rochester, NY 14623.

Ohio
(CT, MA, MI, NJ, NY, IN, OH, PA, DC)
Greater Columbus Chamber of Commerce, Columbus Investment Interest Group, 37 N. High St., Columbus, OH 43215; 614-225-6087, Fax: 614-469-8250. Attn: Diane Essex.

(CT, MA, MI, NJ, NY, IN, OH, PA, DC)
Ohio Venture Association, Inc., 1127 Euclid Avenue, Suite 343, Cleveland, OH 44115; 216-566-8884, Fax: 216-696-2582. Attn: Joan McCarthy.

Oklahoma
Oklahoma Venture Forum, 101 North Broadway, P.O. Box 26788, Oklahoma City, OK 73126-0788; 405-636-9736 or 405-270-1050, Fax: 405-270-1090. Attn: Steve Thomas.

Oregon
Northwest Capital Network, P.O. Box 6650, Portland, OR 97228-6650; 503-282-6273, Fax: 503-282-2976. Attn: Dawn Lewis.

Oregon Enterprise Forum, 2611 Southwest Third Avenue, Suite 200, Portland, OR 97201; 503-222-2270 ext. 219, Fax: 503-241-0827. Attn: Carl Flipper.

Portland Venture Group, P.O. Box 2341, Lake Oswego, OR 97035; 503-697-5907, Fax: 503-697-5907. Attn: Glen Smith.

Pennsylvania
(CT, MA, MI, NJ, NY, IN, OH, PA, DC)
Delaware Valley Venture Group, 1234 Market St., Suite 1800, Philadelphia, PA 19107; 215-972-3960, Fax: 215-972-3900. Attn: Carolyn Keim.

Enterprise Venture Capital Corporation of Pennsylvania, 111 Market Street, Johnstown, PA, 15901; 814-535-7597, Fax: 814-535-8677.

South Dakota
Dakota Ventures Inc., P.O. Box 8194, Rapid City, SD 57709; 605-348-8441, Fax: 605-348-8452. Attn. Don Frankenfeld.

Tennessee
(FL, GA, TN, KY)
Mid-South Venture Group, 5180 Park Ave., Suite 310, Memphis, TN 38119; 901-761-3084, Fax: 901-685-5282. Attn: William Richey.

Tennessee Venture Capital Network (TCVN), 7 Cope Administration Building, Middle Tennessee State University, Murfreesboro, TN 37132; 615-898-2100, 800-344-TCVN. Attn: Richard Prince.

Texas
(AL, LA, MO, TX)
Houston Venture Capital Association, 1221 McKinney, Suite 2400, Houston, TX 77010; 713-750-1500, Fax: 713-750-1501. Attn: Lynn Gentry.

Texas Venture Capital Network, 8920 Business Park Dr., Suite 275, Austin, TX 78759; 512-794-9398, Fax: 512-794-0448.

Capital Southwest Venture Corporation, 12900 Preston Rd., Suite 700, Dallas, TX 75230; 214-233-8242, Fax: 214-233-7362.

Utah
(CO, MT, UT, NM, ID, AZ)
Mountain West Venture Group, c/o Bonneville Research, 48 Market St., #200, Salt Lake City, UT 84101; 801-364-5300. Attn: Robert Springmeyer.

Utah Ventures, 419 Wakara Way, Suite 206, Salt Lake City, UT 84108; 801-583-5922, Fax: 801-583-4105.

Vermont
Vermont Venture Network, P.O. Box 5839, Burlington, VT 05402; 802-658-7830, Fax: 802-658-0978.

Virginia
Richmond Venture Capital Club, 9101 Midlothian, Suite 900, Richmond, VA 23235; 804-560-7000. Attn: Sally Cook.

Washington
(CA, OR, WA)
Northwest Venture Group, P.O. Box 21693, Seattle, WA 98111; 206-746-1973.

West Virginia

Enterprise Venture Capital Company, P.O. Box 460, Summerville, WV 26651; 304-872-3000, Fax: 304-872-3040. Attn: William Bright.

Wisconsin

Wisconsin Venture Network, 823 N. Second St., Suite 605, Milwaukee, WI 53203; 414-278-7070.

International Clubs

Puerto Rico Venture Capital Club, P.O. Box 2284, Hato Rey, Puerto Rico, 00919; 1-809-787-9040. Attn: Danol Morales.

Johannesburg Venture Capital Club, 162 Anderson Street, P.O. Box 261425, EXCOM 2023 RSA, Johannesburg, South Africa, 2001. Attn: Graham Rosenthal.

Cape Town Venture Capital Association, c/o Arthur Anderson and Company, 12th Floor, Shell House, Capetown, South Africa, 8001. Attn: Colin Hultzer.

Canada Clubs

Edmonton Chamber of Commerce, 600 10123 99th St., Edmonton, Alberta Canada, T5J 3G9; 403-464-3560. Attn: Ace Cetinski.

Venture Capital/Entrepreneurship Club of Montreal, Inc., 1670 Sherbrooke St., East Montreal (Quebec) Canada, H2L 1M5; 514-526-9490. Attn: Claude Belanger.

Other groups with information on venture capital include:

The CPA Firm Coopers and Lybrand
1251 Avenue of the Americas
New York, NY 10020
212-536-2000
Fax: 212-536-1858

The firm publishes several publications on venture capital including *Three Keys to Obtaining Venture Capital*, *The Economic Impact of Venture Capital*, *Venture Capital: The Price of Growth*, and *Charting a Course for Corporate Venture Capital*. There is no charge for these publications.

Venture Economics, Inc.
22 Pittsburgh Street
Boston, MA 02210

617-345-2504
Attn: Kelly McGow

Publications are available from:
Securities Data Publishing
40 West 57th Street
11th Floor
New York, NY 10019
212-333-9274
Attn: David Fabel

Venture Capital Journal, a monthly periodical that cites new issues and trends in venture capital investments. Subscription rate is $845.

Pratt's Guide to Venture Capital Sources, an annual directory that lists 800 venture capital firms in the U.S. and Canada. It also includes articles recommending ways to raise venture capital. $249 + $5 shipping.

Venture Capital Journal Yearbook, an annual publication that summarizes investment activities of the previous year. It includes statistics and data about capital commitments and investment activities in specific industries. $195.

Additional Reading Material

A Venture Capital Primer for Small Business, a U.S. Small Business Administration publication that identifies what venture capital resources are available and explains how to develop a proposal for obtaining these funds ($2). SBA Publications, P.O. Box 30, Denver, CO 80201-0030. Item number FM5.

The Ernst & Young Guide to Financing for Growth. This is part of their entrepreneur series and includes bibliographical references and index. ($14.95) John Wiley & Son, 1 Wiley Dr., Somerset, NJ 08875, 800-225-5945. 1994.

Uncle Sam's Venture Capital

What Do Federal Express, Apple Computer, Staples and A Porno Shop on 42nd Street All Have In Common?...They All Used Government Venture Money To Get Started

A few years ago I read that the government provided money to a porno shop in New York City through a program call Small Business Investment Companies (SBIC). Since 1960 these organizations provided venture capital to over 75,000 businesses, so it's easy to see that one of these 75,000 business one could include a porno shop. Porno is a legitimate businesses in many areas of the country.

SBICs are licensed by the U.S. Small Business Administration but are privately owned and operate on a for profit basis. Their license allows then to pool their money with borrowed money from the government in order to provide financing to small businesses in the form of equity securities or long-term debt. These government subsidized investment companies have helped Compaq, Apple, Federal Express and Staples reach the big time. They have also helped small companies achieve success. They've financed Spencer and Vickie Jacobs' hot tub business in Columbus, Ohio, as well as taxi drivers in New York City who needed money to pay for the medallions which allows them to operate their own cab.

Uncle Sam's Venture Capital Boom

In 1994 new regulations were imposed that make it easier to become an SBIC. The budget for this program was also greatly expanded and as a result there will now be over $6 billion worth of financing available to entrepreneurs over the next few years. Now, that's not small.

With these new regulations and budget in place the government expects that were will soon be 200 additional SBICs waiting to serve American entrepreneurs.

Who Gets The Money?

Basically you have to be a small business to apply for this money, and their definition is companies that have less than $18 million in net worth and less than $6 million in profits. Wow, that's some small business. They seem particularly interested in businesses that offer a new product or service that has a strong growth potential. There is special consideration given to minorities and Vietnam Veterans.

But you do have to be armed with a business plan which should include the following:
1) Identify Your Company
2) Identify Your Product Or Service
3) Describe Your Product Facilities And Property
4) Detail Your Marketing Plan
5) Describe Your Competition
6) Describe Your Management Team
7) Provide A Financial Statement

Where to Apply

You can apply to more than one SBIC. Each acts as an independent company and they can provide money to both local or out-of-state businesses. At the end of this section is a listing of SBA licensed Small Business Investment Companies. However, this list is growing every day so it is wise to contact the following office to obtain a current list: Associate Administrator for Investment, U.S. Small Business Administration, Washington, DC 20416, 202-205-6510.

States Have Venture Money Too

It's not enough to only look at federal venture capital programs, because state governments also have venture capital programs and more and more states continue to start new ones. Some states, like Maryland, see the value in the new rule changes for becoming an SBIC and are beginning to apply to become a licensed participant of the Small Business Administration's program. Here is what is available from state governments at the time this book went to press. Be sure to check with your state to see what's new:.

1) Arkansas - Seed Capital Investment Program
2) Connecticut - Risk Capital
   - Product Design Financing
   - Seed Venture Fund
3) Illinois - Technology Investment Program
   - Illinois Venture Capital Fund
4) Iowa - Venture Capital Resources Fund
5) Kansas - Venture Capital and Seed Capital
   - Seed Capital Fund
   - Ad Astra Fund
   - Ad Astra Fund II
6) Louisiana - Venture Capital Incentive Program
7) Massachusetts - Venture Capital Program
8) Michigan - Enterprise Development Fund
   - Onset Seed Fund
   - Diamond Venture Associates
   - Semery Seed Capital Fund
   - Michigan Venture Capital Fund
9) Montana - Venture, Equity & Risk Capital
10) New Mexico - Venture Capital Investment Program
11) New York - Corporation for Innovation Development
12) North Carolina - North Carolina First Flight Inc.
13) North Carolina - Seed and Incubator Capital
14) Pennsylvania - Seed Venture Capital
15) South Carolina - Venture Capital Funding Program
16) Tennessee - Venture Capital

Contact your state office of economic development in your state capital for further information on venture capital available in your state (see the chapter entitled "State Money and Help For Your Business")

Alabama

Alabama Capital Corporation, David C. DeLaney, President, 16 Midtown Park East, Mobile, AL 36606; 205-476-0700, Fax: 205-476-0026.

Alabama Small Business Investment Company, Harold Gilchrist, Manager, 1732 5th Avenue North, Birmingham, AL 35203; 205-324-5231, Fax: 205-324-5234.

FJC Growth Capital Corporation, William B. Noojin, Manager, 200 West Court Square, Suite 750, Huntsville, AL 35801; 205-922-2918, Fax: 205-922-2909.

First SBIC of Alabama, David C. DeLaney, President, 16 Midtown Park East, Mobile, AL 36606; 205-476-0700, Fax: 205-476-0026.

Hickory Venture Capital Corporation, J. Thomas Noojin, President, 200 W. Court Square, Suite 100, Huntsville, AL 35801; 205-539-5130, Fax: 205-539-5130.

Arizona

First Commerce and Loan LP, Ross M. Horowitz, GP and Manager, 5620 N. Kolb, #260, Tucson, AZ 85715; 602-298-2500, Fax: 602-745-6112.

First Interstate Equity Corp., Edmund G. Zito, President, 100 West Washington Street, Phoenix, AZ 85003; 602-528-6647, Fax: 602-440-1320.

Sundance Venture Partners, L.P., (Main Office: Cupertino, CA), Gregory S. Anderson, Vice-President, 2828 N. Central Ave., Suite 1275, Phoenix, AZ 85004; 602-279-1101, Fax: 408-257-8111.

Arkansas

Capital Management Services, Inc., David L. Hale, President, 1910 North Grant Street, Suite 200, Little Rock, AR 72207; 501-664-8613, Fax: 501-664-6302.

Small Business Inv. Capital, Inc., Charles E. Toland, President, 10003 New Benton Hwy., P.O. Box 3627, Little Rock, AR 72203; 501-455-6599, Fax: 501-455-6556.

Southern Ventures, Inc., Jeffrey A. Doose, President, 605 Main Street, Suite 202, Arkadelphia, AR 71923; 501-246-9627, Fax: 501-246-2182.

California

ABC Capital Corp., Anne B. Cheng, President, 27 N. Mentor Ave., Pasadena, CA 91106; 818-355-3577, Fax: 818-355-5577.

AMF Financial, Inc., Ron Arehart, President, 4330 LaJolla Village Drive, Suite 110, San Diego, CA 92122; 619-546-0167, Fax: 619-455-0868.

Allied Business Investors, Inc., Jack Hong, President, 428 South Atlantic Blvd., Suite 201, Monterey Park, CA 91754; 818-289-0186, Fax: 818-289-2369.

Ally Finance Corp., Percy P. Lin, President, 9100 Wilshire Blvd., Suite 408, Beverly Hills, CA 90212; 310-550-8100, Fax: 310-550-6136.

Asian American Capital Corporation, David Der, President, 1251 West Tennyson Road, Suite #4, Hayward, CA 94544; 510-887-6888, Fax: 510-782-6432.

Astar Capital Corp., George Hsu, President, 429 S. Euclid Avenue, Suite B, Anaheim, CA 92802; 714-490-1149, Fax: 714-597-5950.

BNP Venture Capital Corporation, Edgerton Scott II, President, 3000 Sand Hill Road, Building 1, Suite 125, Menlo Park, CA 94025; 415-854-1084, Fax: 415-854-1084.

BT Capital Corp., (Main Office: New York, NY), 300 South Grand Avenue, Los Angeles, CA 90071.

BankAmerica Ventures, Inc., Patrick Topolski, President, 555 California Street, 12th Floor, c/o Dept. 3908, San Francisco, CA 94104; 415-953-3001, Fax: 415-622-4714.

Bentley Capital, John Hung, President, 592 Vallejo St., Suite #2, San Francisco, CA 94133; 415-362-2868, Fax: 415-398-8209.

Best Finance Corporation, Vincent Lee, General Manager, 4929 W. Wilshire Blvd., Suite 407, Los Angeles, CA 90010; 213-731-2268, Fax: 213-937-6393.

Calsafe Capital Corp., Ming-Min Su, President, Director, 245 East Main Street, Suite 107, Alhambra, CA 91801; 818-289-3400, Fax: 818-300-8025.

Charterway Investment Corporation, Tien Chen, President, 222 South Hill Street, Suite 800, Los Angeles, CA 90012; 213-687-8539, Fax: 213-626-8238.

Citicorp Venture Capital, Ltd., (Main Office: New York, NY), 2 Embarcadero Place, 2200 Geny Road, Suite 203, Palo Alto, CA 94303; 415-424-8000.

DSC Ventures II, LP, Daniel D. Tompkins, Jr. Manager, 20111 Stevens Creek Blvd., Suite 130, Cupertino, CA 95014; 408-252-3800, Fax: 408-252-0757.

Developers Equity Capital Corporation, Larry Sade, Chairman of the Board, 1880 Century Park East, Suite 211, Los Angeles, CA 90067; 213-277-0330, Fax: 310-277-4271.

Draper Associates, a California LP, Bill Edwards, President, c/o Timothy C. Draper, 400 Seaport Court, Suite 250, Redwood City, CA 94063; 415-599-9000, Fax: 415-599-9726.

Far East Capital Corp., Tom Wang, Pres., 123 S. Figueroa St., Los Angeles, CA 90012; 213-253-0599, Fax: 213-253-0566.

First American Capital Funding, Inc., Chuoc Vota, President, 10840 Warner Avenue, Suite 202, Fountain Valley, CA 92708; 714-965-7190, Fax: 714-965-7193.

First SBIC of California, Greg Forrest, President, 650 Town Center Drive, Seventeenth Floor, Costa Mesa, CA 92626; 714-556-1964, Fax: 714-546-8021.

First SBIC of California, (Main Office: Costa Mesa, CA), 5 Palo Alto Square, Suite 938, Palo Alto, CA 94306; 415-424-8011, Fax: 415-424-6830.

First SBIC of California, (Main Office: Costa Mesa, CA), 155 North Lake Ave., Suite 1010, Pasadena, CA 91109; 818-304-3451, Fax: 818-440-9931.

Fulcrum Venture Capital Corporation, Brian Argrett, President, 3683 Crenshaw Blvd., 4th Floor, Los Angeles, CA 90016; 213-299-8016, Fax: 213-299-8059.

G C & H Partners, James C. Gaither, General Partner, One Maritime Plaza, 20th Floor, San Francisco, CA 94110; 415-981-5252, Fax: 415-951-3699.

Hall, Morris & Drufva II, L.P., Ronald J. Hall, Managing Director, 25401 Cabbot Road, Suite 116, Laguna Hills, CA 92653; 714-707-5096, Fax: 714-707-5121.

Imperial Ventures, Inc., H. Wayne Snavely, President, 9920 South La Cienega Blvd., (P.O. Box 92991; L.A. 90009), Inglewood, CA 90301; 310-417-5928, Fax: 213-417-5874.

Jupiter Partners, John M. Bryan, President, 600 Montgomery St., 35th Floor, San Francisco, CA 94111; 415-421-9990, Fax: 415-421-0471.

LaiLai Capital Corp., Danny Ku, Pres. & General Mgr., 223 E. Garvey Avenue, Suite 228, Monterey Park, CA 91754; 818-288-0704, Fax: 818-288-4101.

Magna Pacific Investments, David Wong, President, 700 North Central Ave., Suite 245, Glendale, CA 91203; 818-547-0809, Fax: 818-547-9303.

Marwit Capital Corp., Martin W. Witte, President, 180 Newport Center Dr., Suite 200, Newport Beach, CA 92660; 714-640-6234, Fax: 714-759-1363.

Merrill Pickard Anderson & Eyre, Steven L. Merrill, President, 2480 Sand Hill Road, Suite 200, Menlo Park, CA 94025; 415-854-8600, Fax: 415-854-0345.

Myriad Capital, Inc., Chuang-I Lin, President, 328 S. Atlantic Blvd., Suite 200A, Monterey Park, CA 91754; 818-570-4548, Fax: 818-570-9570.

New West Partners II, Timothy P. Haidinger, Manager, 4350 Executive Drive, Suite 206, San Diego, CA 92121; 619-457-0723, Fax: 619-457-0829.

Northwest Venture Partners, (Main Office: Minneapolis, MN), 3000 Sand Hill Road, Building 3, Suite 245, Menlo Park, CA 94025.

Norwest Equity Partners IV, (Main Office: Minneapolis, MN), 3000 Sand Hill Road, Building 3, Suite 245, Menlo Park, CA 94025; 503-223-6622.

Norwest Growth Fund, Inc., (Main Office: Minneapolis, MN), 3000 Sand Hill Road, Building 3, Suite 245, Menlo Park, CA 94025.

Opportunity Capital Corporation, J. Peter Thompson, President, One Fremont Place, 39650 Liberty Street, Suite 425, Fremont, CA 94538; 510-651-4412, Fax: 510-651-0128.

Opportunity Capital Partners II, L.P., J. Peter Thompson, Gen Partner, 39650 Liberty Street, Suite 425, Fremont, CA 94538; 510-651-4412, Fax: 510-651-0128.

Positive Enterprises, Inc., Kwok Szeto, President, 1489 Webster Street, Suite 228, San Francisco, CA 94115; 415-885-6600, Fax: 415-928-6363.

Ritter Partners, William C. Edwards, President, 150 Isabella Avenue, Atherton, CA 94025; 415-854-1555, Fax: 415-854-5015.

San Joaquin Business Investment Group Inc., Joe Williams, President, 1900 Mariposa Mall, Suite 100, Fresno, CA 93721; 209-233-3580, Fax: 209-233-3709.

South Bay Capital Corporation, Charles C. Chiang, President, 18039 Crenshaw Blvd., Suite 203, Torrance, CA 90504; 213-515-1712, Fax: 213-324-9273.

Sundance Venture Partners, L.P., Larry J. Wells, General Manager, 10600 N. DeAnza Blvd., Suite 215, Cupertino, CA 95014; 408-257-8100, Fax: 408-257-8111.

Union Venture Corp., Kathleen Burns, Vice President, 445 South Figueroa Street, Los Angeles, CA 90071; 213-236-5658, Fax: 213-688-0101.

VK Capital Company, Franklin Van Kasper, Gen Partner, 50 California Street, Suite 2350, San Francisco, CA 94111; 415-391-5600, Fax: 415-397-2744.

Western General Capital Corporation, Alan Thian, President, 13701 Riverside Drive, Suite 610, Sherman Oaks, CA 91423; 818-986-5038, Fax: 818-905-9220.

Colorado
UBD Capital, Inc., Dennis D. Erickson, President, 1700 Broadway, Denver, CO 80274; 303-861-8811.

Connecticut
AB SBIC, Inc., Adam J. Bozzuto, President, 275 School House Road, Cheshire, CT 06410; 203-272-0203, Fax: 203-272-9978.

All State Venture Capital Corporation, Ceasar N. Anquillare, President, The Bishop House, 32 Elm Street, P.O. Box 1629, New Haven, CT 06506; 203-787-5029, Fax: 203-785-0018.

Capital Resource Co. of Connecticut, Morris Morgenstein, Gen Partner, 2558 Albany Avenue, West Hartford, CT 06117; 203-236-4336, Fax: 203-232-8161.

Financial Opportunities, Inc., Ms. Robin Munson, Manager, One Vision Drive, Enfield, CT 06082; 203-741-4444, Fax: 203-741-9716.

First New England Capital, LP, Richard C. Klaffky, President, 100 Pearl Street, Hartford, CT 06103; 203-293-3333, Fax: 203-549-2528.

Marcon Capital Corp., Martin A. Cohen, President, 49 Riverside Ave., Westport, CT 06880; 203-226-6893, Fax: 203-454-9658.

RFE Capital Partners, L.P., Robert M. Williams, Managing Partner, 36 Grove St., New Canaan, CT 06840; 203-966-2800, Fax: 203-966-3109.

SBIC of Connecticut Inc. (The), Kenneth F. Zarrilli, President, 965 White Plains Road, Trumbull, CT 06611; 203-261-0011, Fax: 203-452-9699.

TSG Ventures, Inc., Duane Hill, President, 1055 Washington Blvd., 10th Floor, Stamford, CT 06901; 203-363-5344, Fax: 203-363-5340.

Florida
Allied Financial Services Corp., (Main Office: Washington, DC), Executive Office Ctr., Suite 305, 2770 N. Indian River Blvd., Vero Beach, FL 32960; 407-778-5556, Fax: 202-569-9303.

Allied Investment Corp., (Main Office: Washington, DC), Executive Office Ctr., Suite 305, 2770 N. Indian River Blvd., Vero Beach, FL 32960; 407-778-5556, Fax: 202-659-2053.

BAC Investment Corp., Gregory Hobbs, Manager, 6600 NW 27th Ave., Miami, FL 33247; 305-693-5919, Fax: 305-693-7450.

Florida Capital Ventures, Ltd., Warren E. Miller, President, 880 Riverside Plaza, 100 W. Kennedy Blvd., Tampa, FL 33602; 813-229-2294, Fax: 813-229-2028.

J & D Capital Corp., Jack Carmel, President, 12747 Biscayne Blvd., North Miami, FL 33181; 305-893-0303, Fax: 305-891-2338.

Market Capital Corp., Donald Kolvenbach, President, 1102 North 28th Street, P.O. Box 31667, Tampa, FL 33631; 813-247-1357, Fax: 813-248-5531.

Pro-Med Investment Corporation, (Main Office: Dallas, TX), AmeriFirst Bank Building, 2nd Floor S, 18301 Biscayne

Boulevard, N. Miami Beach, FL 33160; 305-933-5858, Fax: 305-931-3054.

Quantum Capital Partners, Ltd., Michael E. Chaney, President, 4400 NE 25th Ave., Ft. Lauderdale, FL 33308; 305-776-1133, Fax: 305-776-1133.

Western Financial Capital Corp., (Main Office: Dallas, TX), AmeriFirst Bank Building, 2nd Floor S, 18301 Biscayne Blvd., N. Miami Beach, FL 33160; 305-933-5858, Fax: 305-931-3054.

Georgia
First Growth Capital, Inc., Vijay K. Patel, President/Manager, 4630 Chambers Road, Macon, GA 31206; 912-781-7131, Fax: 912-781-0066.

Investor's Equity, Inc., I. Walter Fisher, Pres., 945 E. Paces Ferry Rd., Suite 1735, Atlanta, GA 30326; 404-266-8300.

North Riverside Capital Corp., Tom Barry, President, 50 Technology Park/Atlanta, Norcross, GA 30092; 404-446-5556, Fax: 404-446-8627.

Renaissance Capital Corporation, Anita P. Stephens, President, 34 Peachtree Street, NW, Suite 2610, Atlanta, GA 30303; 404-658-9061, Fax: 404-658-9064.

Hawaii
Bancorp Hawaii SBIC, Robert Paris, President, 111 South King Street, Suite 1060, Honolulu, HI 96813; 808-521-6411, Fax: 808-521-4504.

Pacific Venture Capital, Ltd., Dexter J. Taniguchi, President, 222 South Vineyard Street, PH.1, Honolulu, HI 96813; 808-521-6502, Fax: 808-521-6541.

Illinois
Amoco Venture Capital Company, Wallace Lennox, President, 200 E. Randolph Drive, Mail Code 3905A, Chicago, IL 60601; 312-856-6523, Fax: 312-856-3060.

Business Ventures, Incorporated, Milton Lefton, President, 20 N. Wacker Dr., Suite 1741, Chicago, IL 60606; 312-346-1580, Fax: 312-346-6693.

Chicago Community Ventures, Inc., Phyllis George, President, 25 East Washington Blvd., Suite 2015, Chicago, IL 60603; 312-726-6084, Fax: 312-726-0167.

Combined Fund, Inc. (The), E. Patric Jones, President, 915 East Hyde Park Blvd., Chicago, IL 60615; 312-363-0300, Fax: 312-363-6816.

Continental Illinois Venture Corp., John Willis, President, 209 South LaSalle Street, (Mail: 231 S. LaSalle St.), Chicago, IL 60693; 312-828-8023, Fax: 312-987-0887.

First Capital Corp. of Chicago, John A. Canning, Jr., President, Three First National Plaza, Suite 1330, Chicago, IL 60670; 312-732-5400, Fax: 312-732-4098.

Heller Equity Capital Corporation, John M. Goense, President, 500 West Monroe Street, Chicago, IL 60661; 312-441-7200, Fax: 312-441-7378.

Neighborhood Fund, Inc. (The), James Fletcher, President, 1950 East 71st Street, Chicago, IL 60649; 312-753-5670, Fax: 312-493-6609.

Peterson Finance and Investment Company, James S. Rhee, President, 3300 West Peterson Ave., Suite A, Chicago, IL 60659; 312-539-0502, Fax: 312-583-6714.

Tower Ventures, Inc., Robert T. Smith, President, 3333 Beverly Road, Location A-C 254A, Hoffman Estates, IL 60179; 312-875-0571, Fax: 312-906-0164.

Walnut Capital Corp., Burton W. Kanter, Chairman of the Board, Two North LaSalle Street, Suite 2410, Chicago, IL 60602; 312-346-2033, Fax: 312-346-2231.

Indiana
1st Source Capital Corporation, Eugene L. Cavanaugh, Jr., VP, 100 North Michigan Street, (P.O. Box 1602; South Bend 46634), South Bend, IN 466011 219-235-2180, Fax: 219-235-2719.

Cambridge Ventures, LP, Ms. Jean Wojtowicz, President, 8440 Woodfield Crossing, #315, Indianapolis, IN 46240; 317-469-9704, Fax: 317-469-3926.

Circle Ventures, Inc., Carrie Walkup, Manager, 26 N. Arsenal Avenue, Indianapolis, IN 46201; 317-636-7242, Fax: 317-637-7581.

Iowa
MorAmerica Capital Corporation, David R. Schroder, VP, 101 2nd St., SE, Suite 800, Cedar Rapids, IA 52401; 319-363-8249, Fax: 319-363-9683.

Kansas
Kansas Venture Capital, Inc., Rex E. Wiggins, President, 6700 Antioch Plaza, Suite 460, Overland Park, KS 66204; 913-262-7117, Fax: 913-262-3509.

Kansas Venture Capital, Inc., (Main Office: Overland Park, KS), Thomas C. Blackburn, VP, One Main Place, Suite 806, Wichita, KS 67202; 316-262-1221, Fax: 316-262-0780.

Kentucky
Equal Opportunity Finance, Inc., Franin Justice, Jr., President, 420 S. Hurstbourne Pkwy., Suite 201, Louisville, KY 40222; 502-423-1943, Fax: 502-423-1645.

Mountain Ventures, Inc., Jerry A. Rickett, President, London Bank and Trust Building, 400 S. Main St., Fourth Floor, London, KY 40741; 606-864-5175, Fax: 606-864-5194.

Louisiana
Premier Venture Capital Corporation, G. Lee Criffin, President, 451 Florida Street, Baton Rouge, LA 70821; 504-389-4421, Fax: 504-389-4299.

Maine

Maine Capital Corp., David M. Coit, President, Seventy Center Street, Portland, ME 04101; 207-772-1001.

Maryland

American Security Capital Corp., Inc., Jim Henry, Investment Officer, 100 S. Charles Street, 5th Floor, Baltimore, MD 21203; 410-547-4205, Fax: 410-547-4990.

Greater Washington Investment, Inc., Haywood Miller, Manager, 5454 Wisconsin Avenue, Chevy Chase, MD 20815; 301-656-0626, Fax: 301-656-4053.

Security Financial and Investment Corp., Joseph Sirh, President, 7720 Wisconsin Avenue, Suite 207, Bethesda, MD 20814; 301-951-4288.

Syncom Capital Corp., Terry L. Jones, President, 8401 Colesville Road, #300, Silver Spring, MD 20910; 301-608-3207.

Massachusetts

Advent Atlantic Capital Co. LP, David D. Croll, Managing Partner, 75 State Street, Suite 2500, Boston, MA 02109; 617-345-7200, Fax: 617-345-7201.

Advent Industrial Capital Company LP, David D. Croll, Managing Partner, 75 State Street, Suite 2500, Boston, MA 02109; 617-345-7200, Fax: 617-375-7201.

Advent V. Capital Company LP, David D. Croll, Managing Partner, 75 State Street, Suite 2500, Boston, MA 02109; 617-345-7200, Fax: 617-345-7201.

Argonauts MESBIC Corporation, Kevin Chen, General Manager, 929 Worcester Road, Framingham, MA 01701; 508-820-3430, Fax: 508-872-3741.

BancBoston Ventures, Inc., Frederick M. Fritz, President, 100 Federal Street, P.O. Box 2016, Stop 01-31-08, Boston, MA 02110; 617-434-2442, Fax: 617-434-1383.

Business Achievement Corporation, Michael L. Katzeff, President, 1172 Beacon St., Suite 202, Newton, MA 02161; 617-965-0550, Fax: 617-345-7201.

Chestnut Capital Int'l II LP, David D. Croll, Managing Partner, 75 State St., Suite 2500, Boston, MA 02109; 617-345-7200, Fax: 617-345-7201.

Chestnut Street Partners, Inc., David D. Croll, President, 75 State Street, Suite 2500, Boston, MA 02109; 617-345-7220, Fax: 617-345-7201.

Commonwealth Enterprise Fund Inc, Gabrielle Greene, Manager, 10 Post Office Square, Suite 1090, Boston, MA 02109; 617-482-1881, Fax: 617-482-7129.

First Capital Corp. of Chicago, (Main Office: Chicago, IL), One Financial Center, 27th Floor, Boston, MA 02111; 617-457-2500, Fax: 617-457-2506.

LRF Capital, Limited Partnership, Joseph J. Freeman, Manager, 189 Wells Avenue, Suite 4, Newton, MA 02159; 617-964-0049, Fax: 617-965-4100.

Mezzanine Capital Corporation, David D. Croll, President, 75 State St., Suite 2500, Boston, MA 02109; 617-345-7200, Fax: 617-345-7201.

Northeast SBI Corp., Joseph Mindick, Treasurer, 16 Cumberland St., Boston, MA 02115; 617-267-3983, Fax: 617-267-3983.

Pioneer Ventures Limited Partnership, Frank M. Polestra, Managing Partner, 60 State Street, Boston, MA 02109; 617-742-7825, Fax: 617-742-7315.

Southern Berkshire Invst Corp., Henry Thornton, President, P.O. Box 669, Sheffield, MA 01257; 413-229-3106, Fax: 413-229-8857.

Transportation Capital Corp., (Main Office: New York, NY), 45 Newbury Street, Suite 207, Boston, MA 02116; 617-536-0344, Fax: 212-949-9836.

UST Capital Corp., Arthur F.F. Snyder, President, 40 Court Street, Boston, MA 02108; 617-726-7000, Fax: 617-726-7016.

Michigan

Dearborn Capital Corp., Gary L. Ferguson, President, c/o Ford Motor Credit Corp., The American Road, Dearborn, MI 48121; 313-337-8577, Fax: 313-390-4051.

Metro-Detroit Investment Co., William J. Fowler, President, 30777 Northwestern Highway, Suite 300, Farmington Hill, MI 48018; 313-851-6300, Fax: 313-851-9551.

Motor Enterprises, Inc., James Kobus, Manager, General Motors Building, Room 15-134, 3044 W. Grand Blvd., Detroit, MI 48202; 313-556-4273, Fax: 313-974-4499.

Mutual Investment Co., Inc., Timothy J. Taylor, Treasurer, 21415 Civic Center Drive, Mark Plaza Building, Suite 217, Southfield, MI 48076; 313-357-2020.

White Pines Capital Corp., Mr. Ian Bund, President & Mgr, 2929 Plymouth Road, Suite 210, Ann Arbor, MI 48105; 313-747-9401, Fax: 313-747-9704.

Minnesota

Capital Dimensions Ventures Fund, Inc., Dean R. Pickerell, President, Two Appletree Square, Suite 335, Minneapolis, MN 55425; 612-854-3007, Fax: 612-854-6657.

FBS SBIC, Limited Partnership, John M. Murphy, Jr., Managing Agent, 601 Second Avenue South, Minneapolis, MN 55402; 612-973-0988, Fax: 612-973-0203.

Milestone Growth Fund, Inc., Esperanza Guerrero, President, 2021 E. Hennepin Ave., Suite 155, Minneapolis, MN 55413; 612-378-9363, Fax: 612-378-9361.

Northland Capital Venture Partnership, George G. Barnum, Jr., President, 613 Missabe Building, Duluth, MN 55802; 218-722-0545, Fax: 218-722-7241.

Northwest Venture Partners, Robert F. Zicarelli, Manager, 2800 Piper Jaffray Tower, 222 South Ninth Street, Minneapolis, MN 55402; 612-667-1650, Fax: 612-667-1660.

Norwest Equity Partners IV, Robert Zicarelli, General Partner, 2800 Piper Jaffray Tower, 222 South Ninth Street, Minneapolis, MN 55402; 612-667-1650, Fax: 612-667-1660.

Norwest Growth Fund, Inc., Daniel J. Haggerty, President, 2800 Piper Jaffray Tower 222 South Ninth Street Minneapolis, MN 55402; 612-667-1650, Fax: 612-667-1660.

Mississippi
Sun-Delta Capital Access Center, Inc., Howard Boutte, Jr., VP, 819 Main Street, Greenville, MS 38701; 601-335-5291, Fax: 601-335-5293.

Missouri
Bankers Capital Corp., Raymond E. Glasnapp, President, 3100 Gillham Road, Kansas City, MO 64109; 816-531-1600, Fax: 816-531-1334.

CFB Venture Fund I, Inc., James F. O'Donnell, Chairman, 11 South Meramec, Suite 800, St. Louis, MO 63105; 314-854-7427, Fax: 314-234-2333.

CFB Venture Fund II, Inc., Bart S. Bergman, President, 1000 Walnut Street, 18th Floor, Kansas City, MO 64106; 816-234-2357, Fax: 816-234-2333.

MBI Venture Capital Investors, Inc., Anthony Sommers, President, 850 Main Street, Kansas City, MO 64105; 816-471-1700, Fax: 816-889-1798.

Midland Capital Corp., Neil E. Sprague, Manager, 1010 Walnut Street, Kansas City, MO 64106; 816-471-8000, Fax: 816-421-5351.

MorAmerica Capital Corporation, (Main Office: Cedar Rapids, IA), 911 Main St., Suite 2724A, Commerce Tower Bldg., Kansas City, MO 64105; 816-842-0114, Fax: 816-471-7339.

United Missouri Capital Corporation, Noel Shull, Manager, 1010 Grand Avenue, (P.O. Box 419226; K.C., MO 64141), Kansas City, MO 64106; 816-556-7333, Fax: 816-556-7143.

Nebraska
United Financial Resources Corp., Joan Boulay, Manager, 7401 "F" Street, (P.O. Box 1131; Omaha, NE 68101), Omaha, NE 68127; 402-339-7300, Fax: 402-734-0650.

New Jersey
Bishop Capital. L.P., Charles J. Irish, General Partner, 500 Morris Avenue, Springfield, NJ 07081; 201-376-0495, Fax: 201-376-6527.

CIT Group/Venture Capital, Inc., Colby W. Collier, Manager, 650 CIT Drive, Livingston, NJ 07932; 201-740-5429, Fax: 201-740-5555.

Capital Circulation Corporation, Judy Kao, Manager, 2035 Lemoine Avenue, Second Floor, Fort Lee, NJ 07024; 201-947-8637, Fax: 201-585-8288.

ESLO Capital Corp., Leo Katz, President, 212 Wright Street, Newark, NJ 07114; 201-242-4488, Fax: 201-242-4488.

First Princeton Capital Corporation, Michael Lytell, President, One Garret Mountain Plaza, 9th Floor, West Paterson, NJ 07424; 201-278-8111, Fax: 201-278-4290.

Fortis Capital Corporation, Martin Orland, President, 333 Thornall Street, 2nd Floor, Edison, NJ 08837; 908-603-8500, Fax: 908-603-8250.

Rutgers Minority Investment Co., Oscar Figueroa, President, 92 New Street, Newark, NJ 07102; 201-648-5287, Fax: 201-648-1110.

Tappan Zee Capital Corporation, Jack Birnberg, President, 201 Lower Notch Road, Little Falls, NJ 07424; 201-256-8280, Fax: 201-256-2841.

Transpac Capital Corporation, Tsuey Tang Wang, President, 1037 Route 46 East, Clifton, NJ 07013; 201-470-8855, Fax: 201-470-8827.

Zaitech Capital Corporation, Mr. Fu-Tong Hsu, President, 1037 Route 46 East, Unit C-201, Clifton, NJ 07013; 201-365-0047, Fax: 201-365-0977.

New Mexico
Albuquerque SBIC, Albert T. Ussery, President, 501 Tijeras Avenue, N.W., P.O. Box 487, Albuquerque, NM 87103; 505-247-0145, Fax: 505-843-6912.

New York
767 Limited Partnership, H. Wertheim and H. Mallement, 767 Third Avenue, c/o Harvey Wertheim, New York, NY 10017; 212-838-7776, Fax: 212-593-0734.

ASEA-Harvest Partners II, Harvey Wertheim, General Partner, 767 Third Avenue, New York, NY 10017; 212-838-7776, Fax: 212-593-0734.

American Asian Capital Corporation, Howard H. Lin, President, 130 Water Street, Suite 6-L, New York, NY 10005; 212-422-6880.

American Commercial Capital Corporation, Gerald J. Grossman, President, 600 Third Avenue, Suite 3810, New York, NY 10016; 212-986-3305, Fax: 212-983-4585.

Argentum Capital Partners, LP, Daniel Raynor, Chairman, 405 Lexington Avenue, New York, NY 10174; 212-949-8272, Fax: 212-949-8294.

Atlanta Investment Company, Inc., L. Mark Newman, Chairman of the Board, 650 5th Avenue, 15th Floor, New York, NY 10019; 212-956-9100, Fax: 212-956-9103.

BT Capital Corp., Noel E. Urben, Pres., 280 Park Ave.-32 West, New York, NY 10017; 212-454-1903, Fax: 212-454-2421.

Barclays Capital Investors Corp., Graham McGahen, President, 222 Broadway, 7th Floor, New York, NY 10038; 212-412-3937, Fax: 212-412-6780.

CB Investors, Inc., Edward L. Kock III, Pres., 270 Park Ave., New York, NY 10017; 212-286-3222, Fax: 212-983-0626.

CIBC Wood Gundy Ventures, Inc., Gordon Muessel, V.P., 425 Lexington Ave., 9th Floor, New York, NY 10017; 212-856-3713, Fax: 212-697-1554.

CMNY Capital II, L.P., Robert G. Davidoff, G.P., 135 E. 57th St., 26th Floor, New York, NY 10022; 212-909-8432, Fax: 212-980-2630.

CMNY Capital, L.P., Robert Davidoff, G.P., 135 E. 57th St., 26th Floor, New York, NY 10022; 212-909-8432, Fax: 212-980-2630.

Capital Investors & Management Corp., Rose Chao, Manager, 210 Canal Street, Suite 607, New York, NY 10013; 212-964-2480, Fax: 212-349-9160.

Chase Manhattan Capital Corp., Gustav H. Koven, President, 1 Chase Plaza, 7th Floor, New York, NY 10081; 212-552-6275, Fax: 212-552-2807.

Chemical Venture Capital Assoc., Jeffrey C. Walker, Managing Gen., 275 Park Avenue, 5th Floor, New York, NY 10017; 212-270-3220, Fax: 212-270-2327.

Citicorp Investments Inc., Barbara Wolfson, Unit Leader, 450 W. 33rd Street, New York, NY 10001; 212-736-8170, Fax: 212-594-2133.

Citicorp Venture Capital, Ltd, William Comfort, Chairman of the Board, 399 Park Avenue, 6th Floor, New York, NY 10043; 212-559-1127, Fax: 212-527-2496.

East Coast Venture Capital, Inc., Zindel Zelmanovitch, President, 313 West 53rd Street, Third Floor, New York, NY 10019; 212-245-6460, Fax: 212-265-2962.

Edwards Capital Company, Edward H. Teitlebaum, President, Two Park Avenue, 20th Floor, New York, NY 10016; 212-686-5449, Fax: 212-213-6234.

Elk Associates Funding Corp., Gary C. Granoff, President, 600 Third Avenue, 38th Floor, New York, NY 10016; 212-972-8550, Fax: 212-983-0571.

Empire State Capital Corporation, Dr. Joseph Wu, President, 170 Broadway, Suite 1200, New York, NY 10038; 212-513-1799, Fax: 212-513-1892.

Esquire Capital Corp., Wen-Chan Chin, President, 140 Veterans Memorial Highway, Commack, NY 11725; 516-462-6946, Fax: 516-462-6945.

Exim Capital Corp., Victor K. Chun, President, 241 5th Avenue, 3rd Floor, New York, NY 10016; 212-683-3375, Fax: 212-689-4118.

Fair Capital Corp., Rose Chao, Manager, 210 Canal Street, Suite 607, New York, NY 10013; 212-964-2480, Fax: 212-349-9160.

Fifty-Third Street Ventures, LP, Patricia Cloherty & Dan Tessler, 155 Main Street, Cold Spring, NY 10516; 914-265-4244, Fax: 914-265-4158.

First Pacific Capital Corp., Michael Cipriani, Manager, 273 Wyckoff Avenue, Brooklyn, NY 11237; 718-381-5095, Fax: 718-381-5192.

First Wall Street SBIC, LP, Alan Farkas, G.P., 26 Broadway, Suite 1320, New York, NY 10004; 212-742-3770, Fax: 212-742-3776.

Flushing Capital Corporation, Frank J. Mitchell, President, 137-80 Northern Boulevard, Flushing, NY 11354; 718-742-3770, Fax: 718-742-3776.

Freshstart Venture Capital Corporation, Zindel Zelmanovich, President, 313 West 53rd Street, 3rd Floor, New York, NY 10019; 212-265-2249, Fax: 212-265-2962.

Fundex Capital Corp., Howard Sommer, President, 525 Northern Blvd., Great Neck, NY 11021; 516-466-8551, Fax: 516-466-0180.

Genesee Funding, Inc., Stuart Marsh, President & CEO, 100 Corporate Woods, Rochester, NY 14623; 716-272-2332, Fax: 713-272-2396.

Hanam Capital Corp., Robert Schairer, President, 208 West 30th Street, Suite 1205, New York, NY 10001; 212-564-5225, Fax: 212-564-5307.

Hop Chung Capital Investors, Inc, Yon Hon Lee, President, 123 Walker Street, New York, NY 10013; 212-219-1777, Fax: 212-941-8159.

IBJS Capital Corp., Corbin R. Miller, President, One State Street, 8th Floor, New York, NY 10004; 212-858-2000, Fax: 212-858-2768.

Ibero American Investors Corp., Emilio Serrano, President, 104 Scio Street, Rochester, NY 14604; 716-262-3440, Fax: 716-262-3441.

InterEquity Capital Corporation, Irwin Schlass, President, 220 Fifth Avenue, 10th Floor, New York, NY 10001; 212-779-2022, Fax: 212-779-2103.

International Paper Cap. Formation, Inc., (Main Office: Memphis, TN), Frank Polney, Manager, Two Manhattanville

Road, Purchase, NY 10577; 914-397-1578, Fax: 914-397-1909.

J.P. Morgan Investment Corp., C. Seth Cunningham, Managing Director, 60 Wall Street, New York, NY 10260; 212-483-2323.

Kwiat Capital Corp., Sheldon F. Kwiat, President, 579 Fifth Avenue, New York, NY 10017; 212-223-1111, Fax: 212-223-2796.

M & T Capital Corp., T. William Alexander, President, One M & T Plaza, Buffalo, NY 14240; 716-842-5881, Fax: 716-842-5376.

Manhattan Central Capital Corp., David Choi, President, 1255 Broadway, Room 405, New York, NY 10001; 212-684-6411, Fax: 212-684-6474.

Medallion Funding Corporation, Alvin Murstein, President, 205 E. 42nd Street, Suite 2020, New York, NY 10017; 212-682-3300, Fax: 212-983-0351.

Minority Equity Cap. Co, Inc., Alvin N. Puryear, Chairman, 51 Madison Avenue, Suite 2212, New York, NY 10010; 212-779-4360, Fax: 212-725-2040.

NYBDC Capital Corp., Robert W. Lazar, President, 41 State Street, P.O. Box 738, Albany, NY 12201; 518-463-2268, Fax: 518-463-0240.

NatWest USA Capital Corporation, Orville G. Aarons, General Mgr, 175 Water Street, New York, NY 10038; 212-602-1200, Fax: 212-602-2149.

Norwood Venture Corp., Mark R. Littell, President, 1430 Broadway, Suite 1607, New York, NY 10018; 212-869-5075, Fax: 212-869-5331.

Pan Pac Capital Corp., Dr. In Ping Jack Lee, President, 121 East Industry Court, Deer Park, NY 11729; 516-586-7653, Fax: 516-586-7505.

Paribas Principal Incorporated, Steven Alexander, President, 787 Seventh Avenue, 33rd Floor, New York, NY 10019; 212-841-2000, Fax: 212-841-2146.

Pierre Funding Corp., Elias Debbas, President, 805 Third Avenue, 6th Floor, New York, NY 10022; 212-888-1515, Fax: 212-688-4252.

Pyramid Ventures, Inc., Annmarie O'Shea, Asst. VP, 280 Park Avenue--29 West, New York, NY 10017; 212-454-1702, Fax: 212-850-2629.

R & R Financial Corp., Imre Rosenthal, President, 1370 Broadway, New York, NY 10036; 212-356-1400, Fax: 212-356-0900.

Rand SBIC, Inc., Donald Ross, President, 1300 Rand Building, Buffalo, NY 14203; 716-853-0802, Fax: 716-854-8480.

Situation Ventures Corp. Sam Hollander, Pres., 56-20 59th St., Maspeth, NY 11378; 718-894-2000, Fax: 718-326-4642.

Square Deal Venture Capital Corp., Gloria Feibusch, Manager, 766 N. Main Street, New Square, NY 10977; 914-354-7917.

Sterling Commercial Capital,Inc., Harvey L. Granat, President, 175 Great Neck Road, Suite 404, Great Neck, NY 11021; 516-482-7374, Fax: 516-487-0781.

TLC Funding Corp., Philip G. Kass, President, 660 White Plains Road, Tarrytown, NY 10591; 914-332-5200, Fax: 914-332-5660.

Tappan Zee Capital Corporation, (Main Office: Little Falls, NJ), 120 N. Main St., New City, NY 10956; 914-634-8890.

Transportation Capital Corp., Paul Borden, President, 315 Park Avenue South 10th Floor, New York, NY 10010; 212-598-3225, Fax: 212-598-3102.

Triad Capital Corp. of New York, Lorenzo J. Barrera, President, 960 Southern Blvd., Bronx, NY 10459; 212-589-6541, Fax: 212-589-5101.

Trusty Capital Inc., Yungduk Hahn, President, 350 Fifth Avenue, Suite 2026, New York, NY 10118; 212-736-7653, Fax: 212-629-3019.

United Capital Investment Corp., Paul Lee, President, 60 East 42nd Street, Suite 1515, New York, NY 10165; 212-682-7210, Fax: 212-573-6352.

Vega Capital Corp., Victor Harz, President, 720 White Plains Rd., Scarsdale, NY 10583; 914-472-8550, Fax: 914-472-8553.

Venture Opportunities Corp., A. Fred March, President, 110 East 59th Street, 29th Floor, New York, NY 10022; 212-832-3737, Fax: 212-223-4912.

Winfield Capital Corp., Stanley M. Pechman, President, 237 Mamaroneck Avenue, White Plains, NY 10605; 914-949-2600, Fax: 914-949-7195.

Zenia Capital Corp., Zenia Yuan, President, 135-14 Northern Blvd., 2nd Floor, Flushing, NY 11354; 718-461-1778, Fax: 718-461-1835.

North Carolina

First Union Capital Partners Inc, Kevin J. Roche, Senior VP, One First Union Center, 18th Floor, 301 South College Street, Charlotte, NC 28288; 704-374-6487, Fax: 704-374-6711.

Heritage Capital Corp., Richard N. Brigden, VP, 2000 Two First Union Center, Charlotte, NC 28282; 704-372-5404, Fax: 704-372-6409.

NationsBanc SBIC Corporation, George W. Campbell, Jr., Pres., 901 W. Trade St., Suite 1020, Charlotte, NC 28202; 704-386-7720, Fax: 704-386-6662.

Springdale Venture Partners, LP, S. Epes Robinson, Gen Partner, 212 S. Tryon Street, Suite 960, Charlotte, NC 28281; 704-344-8290, Fax: 704-386-6695.

Ohio

A.T. Capital Corp., Donald C. Molten, Manager, 127 Public Square, 4th Floor, Cleveland, OH 44114; 216-737-4090, Fax: 216-737-3177.

Banc One Capital Partners Corp., (Main Office: Dallas, TX). 10 W. Broad St., Suite 200. Columbus, OH 43215; 614-221-0722.

Cactus Capital Company, Edward C. Liu, President, 870 High Street, Suite 216, Worthington, OH 43085; 614-436-4060, Fax: 614-436-4060.

Center City MESBIC, Steven Budd, President, 8 North Main Street, Dayton, OH 45402; 513-226-0457, Fax: 513-222-7035.

Clarion Capital Corp., Morton A. Cohen, President, Ohio Savings Plaza, Suite 1520, 1801 E. 9th Street, Cleveland, OH 44114; 216-687-1096, Fax: 216-694-3545.

National City Capital Corp, William H. Schecter, President, 1965 East Sixth St, Suite 400, Cleveland, OH 44114; 216-575-2491, Fax: 216-575-3355.

Rubber City Capital Corporation, Jesse T. Williams, Manager, 1144 East Market Street, Akron, OH 44316; 216-796-9167, Fax: 216-796-1876.

Society Venture Capital Corp., Carl G. Nelson, Chief Inv. Offcr, 127 Public Square, 4th Floor, Cleveland, OH 44114; 216-689-5776, Fax: 216-689-3204.

Oregon

Northern Pacific Capital Corp., Joseph P. Tennant, President, 937 S.W. 14th St., Suite 200, P.O. Box 1658, Portland, OR 97207; 503-241-1255, Fax: 503-299-6653.

U.S. Bancorp Capital Corp., Gary Patterson, President, 111 S.W. Fifth Avenue, Suite 1090, Portland, OR 97204; 503-275-5860, Fax: 503-275-7565.

Pennsylvania

CIP Capital, Inc., Winston Churchill, Jr., Manager, 300 Chester Field Parkway, Malvern, PA 19355; 215-251-5075, Fax: 215-651-5930.

Enterprise Venture Cap Corp. of Pennsylvania, Don Cowie, C.E.O., 111 Market Street, Johnstown, PA 15901; 814-535-7597, Fax: 814-535-8677.

Erie SBIC, George R. Heaton, President, 32 West 8th Street, Suite 615, Erie, PA 16501; 814-453-7964, Fax: 814-454-2640.

Fidelcor Capital Corporation, Elizabeth T. Crawford, Pres., Fidelity Building, 11th Floor, 123 South Broad Street, Philadelphia, PA 19109; 215-985-3722, Fax: 215-985-7282.

First SBIC of California, (Main Office: Costa Mesa, CA), Daniel A. Dye, Contact, P.O. Box 512, Washington, PA 15301; 412-223-0707, Fax: 714-546-8021.

Greater Phila. Venture Capital Corp., Inc., Fred S. Choate, Mgr., 351 E Conestoga Rd., Wayne, PA 19087; 215-254-8900.

Meridian Capital Corp., Joseph E. Laky, President, Horsham Business Center, Suite 200, 455 Business Center Drive, Horsham, PA 19044; 215-957-7520, Fax: 215-957-7521.

Meridian Venture Partners, Raymond R. Rafferty, Gen Part, The Fidelity Court Building, 259 Radnor-Chester Road, Radnor, PA 19087; 215-293-0210, Fax: 215-254-2996.

PNC Capital Corp., Gary J. Zentner, President, Pittsburgh National Building, Fifth Avenue and Wood Street, Pittsburgh, PA 15222; 412-762-2248, Fax: 412-762-6233.

Salween Financial Services, Inc., Dr. Daljeet Singh, President, 228 North Pottstown Pike, Exton, PA 19341; 215-524-1880, Fax: 215-524-9988.

Puerto Rico

North American Inv. Corporation, Rita V. de Fajardo, President, Mercantile Plaza Bldg., Suite 813, PO Box 1831, Hato Rey, PR 00919; 809-754-6178, Fax: 809-754-6181.

Rhode Island

Domestic Capital Corp., Nathaniel B. Baker, President, 815 Reservoir Avenue, Cranston, RI 02910; 401-946-3310, Fax: 401-943-6708.

Fairway Capital Corp., Paul V. Anjoorian, President, 285 Governor Street, Providence, RI 02906; 401-454-7500, Fax: 401-455-3636.

Fleet Venture Resources, Inc., Robert M. Van Degna, President, 111 Westminster Street, 4th Floor, Providence, RI 02903; 401-278-6770, Fax: 401-751-1274.

Moneta Capital Corp., Arnold Kilberg, Pres., 285 Governor St., Providence, RI 02906; 401-454-7500, Fax: 401-455-3636.

NYSTRS/NV Capital, Limited Partnership, Robert M. Van Degna, Managing Ptr., 111 Westminster Street, Providence, RI 02903; 401-276-5597, Fax: 401-751-1274.

Richmond Square Capital Corp., Harold I. Schein, President, 1 Richmond Square, Providence, RI 02906; 401-521-3000, Fax: 401-751-3940.

Wallace Capital Corp., Lloyd W. Granoff, President, 170 Westminster Street, Suite 300, Providence, RI 02903; 401-273-9191, Fax: 401-273-9648.

South Carolina

Charleston Capital Corporation, Henry Yaschik, President, 111 Church Street, P.O. Box 328, Charleston, SC 29402; 803-723-6464, Fax: 803-723-1047.

Floco Investment Co., Inc. (The), William H. Johnson, Sr., Pres., Highway 52 North, (P.O. Box 919; Lake City SC 29560), Scranton, SC 29561; 803-389-2731, Fax: 803-389-4199.

Lowcountry Investment Corp, Joseph T. Newton, Jr. President, 4444 Daley Street, P.O. Box 10447, Charleston, SC 29411; 803-554-9880, Fax: 803-745-2730.

Tennessee

Chickasaw Capital Corporation, Tom Moore, President, 67 Madison Avenue, Memphis, TN 38147; 901-383-6404, Fax: 901-383-6191.

International Paper Cap. Formation, Inc., Bob J. Higgins, VP and Control, International Place II, 6400 Poplar Avenue, Memphis, TN 38197; 901-763-6282, Fax: 901-763-7278.

Sirrom Capital, LP, George M. Miller, II, Manager, 511 Union Street, Suite 2310, Nashville, TN 37219; 615-256-0701, Fax: 615-254-0947.

Tennessee Venture Capital Corp., Wendell P. Knox, President, 201 Fourth Ave. North, Suite 850, P.O. Box 190034, Nashville, TN 37219; 615-244-6935, Fax: 615-254-1195.

Valley Capital Corp., Lamar J. Partridge, President, Suite 212, Krystal Building, 100 W. Martin Luther King Blvd., Chattanooga, TN 37402; 615-265-1557, Fax: 615-265-0619.

West Tennessee Venture Capital Corporation, Frank Banks, President, 5 North Third Street, Memphis, TN 38103; 901-522-9237, Fax: 901-527-6091.

Texas

AMT Capital, Ltd., Tom H. Delimitros, CGP, 8204 Elmbrook Dr., Suite 101, Dallas, TX 75247; 214-905-9760, Fax: 214-905-9761.

Alliance Business Investment Co., (Main Office: Tulsa, OK), 911 Louisiana, One Shell Plaza, Suite 3990, Houston, TX 77002; 713-224-8224, Fax: 713-659-8070.

Alliance Enterprise Corporation, Donald R. Lawhorne, President, North Central Plaza 1, Suite 710, 12655 North Central Expressway, Dallas, TX 75243; 214-991-1597, Fax: 214-991-1647.

Banc One Capital Partners Corp., Suzanne B. Kriscunas, President, 300 Crescent Court, Suite 1600, Dallas, TX 75201; 214-979-4360, Fax: 214-979-4355.

Capital Southwest Venture Corp., William R. Thomas, President, 12900 Preston Road, Suite 700, Dallas, TX 75230; 214-233-8242, Fax: 214-233-7362.

Catalyst Fund, Ltd., (The), Richard L. Herrman, Manager, Three Riverway, Suite 770, Houston, TX 77056; 713-623-8133, Fax: 713-623-0476.

Central Texas SBI Corporation, David G. Horner, President, 1401 Elm Street, Suite 4764, Dallas, TX 75202; 214-508-5050, Fax: 214-558-5060.

Charter Venture Group, Inc., Winston C. Davis, President, 2600 Citadel Plaza Dr, Suite 600, P.O. Box 4525, Houston, TX 77008; 713-622-7500, Fax: 713-552-8446.

Chen's Financial Group, Inc., Samuel S. C. Chen, President, 10101 Southwest Freeway, Suite 370, Houston, TX 77074; 713-772-8868, Fax: 713-772-2168.

Citicorp Venture Capital, Ltd., (Main Office: New York, NY), 717 North Harwood, Suite 2920-LB87, Dallas, TX 75201; 214-880-9670, Fax: 214-953-1495.

DC Bancorp Venture Capital Co., David G. Franklin, President, 901 Main Street, 66th Floor, Dallas, TX 23510; 214-508-0900, Fax: 214-508-0985.

FCA Investment Company, Robert S. Baker, Chairman, San Felipe Plaza, Suite 850, 5847 San Felipe, Houston, TX 77057; 713-781-2857, Fax: 713-781-7195.

First City, Texas Venture, Inc., Mr. J.R. Brlansky, Manager, 1001 Main Street, 15th Floor, P.O. Box 4517, Houston, TX 77002; 713-658-5421, Fax: 713-658-6548.

HCT Capital Corp., Vichy Woodward Young, Jr., Pres., 4916 Camp Bowie Blvd., Suite 200, Ft. Worth, TX 76107; 817-763-8706, Fax: 817-377-8049.

Houston Partners, SBIP, Harvard Hill, President, CGP, Capital Center Penthouse, 401 Louisiana, 8th Floor, Houston, TX 77002; 713-222-8600, Fax: 713-222-8932.

Jiffy Lube Capital Corporation, Mark Youngs, Manager, 700 Milam Street, P.O. Box 2967, Houston, TX 77252; 713-546-8910, Fax: 713-546-4154.

MESBIC Financial Corp. of Houston, Arturo Moreno, President, 401 Studewood, Suite 200, Houston, TX 77007; 713-869-8595, Fax: 713-546-2229.

MESBIC Ventures, Inc., Donald R. Lawhorne, President, 12655 N. Central Expressway, Suite 710, Dallas, TX 75243; 214-991-1597, Fax: 214-991-1647.

Mapleleaf Capital Ltd., Patrick A. Rivelli, Manager, Three Forest Plaza, Suite 1300, 12221 Merit Drive, Dallas, TX 75251; 214-239-5650, Fax: 214-701-0024.

Minority Enterprise Funding, Inc., Frederick C. Chang, President, 17300 El Camino Real, Suite 107-B, Houston, TX 77058; 713-488-4919, Fax: 713-488-3786.

NationsBanc Capital Corporation, David Franklin, President, 901 Main Street, 66th Floor, Dallas, TX 75202; 214-508-0900, Fax: 214-508-0985.

North Texas MESBIC, Inc., Allan Lee, President, 12770 Coit Road, Suite 525, (Box 832673; Richardson, TX 75083), Dallas, TX 75251; 214-991-8060.

Power Ventures, Inc., Donald R. Lawhorne, President, North Central Plaza 1, Suite 710, 12655 North Central Expressway, Dallas, TX 75243; 214-991-1597, Fax: 214-991-1647.

Pro-Med Investment Corporation, Mrs. Marion Rosemore, President, 17290 Preston Road, Suite 300, Dallas, TX 75252; 214-380-0044, Fax: 214-380-1371.

SBI Capital Corp., William E. Wright, President, 6305 Beverly Hill Lane, (P.O. Box 570368; Houston, TX 77257), Houston, TX 77057; 713-675-1188, Fax: 713-975-1302.

UNCO Ventures, Inc., John Gatti, President, 520 Post Oak Blvd., Suite 130, Houston, TX 77027; 713-622-9595, Fax: 713-622-9007.

United Oriental Capital Corp., Jai Min Tai, President, 908 Town and Country Blvd., Suite 310, Houston, TX 77024; 713-461-3909, Fax: 713-465-7559.

Ventex Partners, Ltd., Richard S. Smith, President, 1000 Louisiana, Suite 1110, Houston, TX 77002; 713-659-7860, Fax: 713-659-7855.

Victoria Capital Corp., Kenneth L. Vickers, President, One O'Connor Plaza, Victoria, TX 77902; 512-573-5151, Fax: 512-574-5236.

Victoria Capital Corp., (Main Office: Victoria, TX), 750 E. Mulberry, Suite 305, P.O. Box 15616, San Antonio, TX 78212; 512-736-4233.

Western Financial Capital Corp., Andrew S. Rosemore, President, 17290 Preston Road, Suite 300, Dallas, TX 75252; 214-380-0044, Fax: 214-380-1371.

Vermont

Green Mountain Capital, L.P., Michael Sweetman, General Mgr., P.O. Box 659, Stowe, VT 05672; 802-253-8142, Fax: 802-253-9857.

Queneska Capital Corporation, Albert W. Coffrin, III, Pres., 123 Church St., Burlington, VT 05401; 802-865-1806, Fax: 802-865-1891.

Virginia

Continental SBIC, Arthur Walters, President, 4141 N. Henderson Rd., Suite 8, Arlington, VA 22203; 703-527-5200, Fax: 703-527-3700.

East West United Investment Company, Dung Bui, President, 815 W. Broad Street, Falls Church, VA 22046; 703-536-0268, Fax: 703-536-8123.

Hampton Road SBIC, John A. Hornback, Jr., Pres., 420 Bank Street, P.O. Box 327, Norfolk, VA 23510; 804-622-2312, Fax: 804-622-5563.

Rural America Fund, Inc., Fred Russell, Chief Exec Offcr, 2201 Cooperative Way, Herndon, VA 22071; 703-709-6750, Fax: 703-709-6779.

Walnut Capital Corp., (Main Office: Chicago, IL), 8000 Tower Crescent Dr., Suite 1070, Vienna, VA 22182; 703-448-3771, Fax: 703-448-7751.

Wisconsin

Banc One Venture Corp., H. Wayne Foreman, President, 111 East Wisconsin Ave., Milwaukee, WI 53202; 414-765-2274, Fax: 414-765-2235.

Bando-McGlocklin SBIC, George Schonath, Chief Executive, 13555 Bishops Court, Suite 205, Brookfield, WI 53005; 414-784-9010, Fax: 414-784-3426.

Capital Investments, Inc., James R. Sanler, President, Commerce Building, Suite 540, 744 North Fourth Street, Milwaukee, WI 53203; 414-273-6560, Fax: 414-273-0530.

Future Value Ventures, Inc., William P. Beckett, President, 250 East Wisconsin Avenue, Suite 1875, Milwaukee, WI 53202; 414-278-0377, Fax: 414-278-7321.

M & I Ventures Corp., John T. Byrnes, President, 770 North Water Street, Milwaukee, WI 53202; 414-765-7910, Fax: 414-765-7850.

MorAmerica Capital Corporation, (Main Office: Cedar Rapids, IA), 600 East Mason Street, Milwaukee, WI 53202; 414-276-3839, Fax: 414-276-1885.

Polaris Capital Corp., Richard Laabs, President, One Park Plaza, 11270 W. Park Place, Suite 320, Milwaukee, WI 53224; 414-359-3040, Fax: 414-359-3059.

Microenterprise:
When You Need Just A Little Money
To Start A Big New Business

A recent survey showed that approximately 33% of the top 500 fastest growing small businesses in the U.S. started with less than $10,000. It doesn't take much money to start a business in today's information age and service economy. We're no longer in the manufacturing age, when you needed a lot of money to start a business because you needed to buy a plant and equipment. Today, many businesses are started with just a phone, a desk, and business cards. Traditional government money programs required entrepreneurs to ask for at least $50,000 to $100,000. Now the government has set up Microenterprise Programs where you can ask for just a little amount of money to make that big change in your life.

A Growing Unknown Resource

These programs are continually growing. They seem so successful that policy makers are finding new ways to make them grow. But this growth and success seems to be causing as many problems as the opportunities they are creating. On one hand the SBA programs recently increased the number of banks that participate in its microloan program from 100 to 200 and also added a subcategory of lenders to include for-profit and non-profit organizations. Grants under this program will increase from $45 million in 1995 to $98 million in 1997 and direct loans will increase from $120 million to $250 million during the same period. But, on the other hand I read that programs like the one at the U.S. Department of Housing and Urban Development fell short of quota by $1.5 billion because not enough people applied. This means that the poor bureaucrat could not give out all their money because not enough people applied. I even got a personal call from a local organization who had $50,000 of this money for

someone to open up a bakery, and no one applied for it.

66% Chance of Being a Microloan Winner

Each year thousands of people will be getting microloans to start or expand their businesses. Although data is not available for every program, one of the major microloan lenders estimates that 66% of the people who apply get their money. Here are a few examples of recent recipients:

- $5,000 to Street Smart, Inc., a street-hockey equipment distributor in Southeastern Pennsylvania

- $25,000 to Med-Ex Medical Express, a courier service that specializes in the health care field

- $15,000 to Jeannette Saunders and Pamela Marshall of Sacramento, CA to start P&J Word Processing Service

* Money To Start A Business In A Small Town

U.S. Department of Agriculture
Business and Industry Division
Room 6321 South
14th and Independence Ave., SW
Washington, DC 20250
202-720-7818

The Intermediary Relending Program (IRP) is a rural development program administered by the Farmers Home Administration (FmHA). The purpose is to provide loans for the establishment of new businesses, expansion of existing businesses, creation of employment opportunities, and community development projects in rural areas. Loans are made to intermediaries who relend funds to recipients for business facilities or community development. You can borrow up to $150,000 with a maximum term of 30 years and an interest rate one percent per annum. For information, copies of regulations, and forms, contact the office listed above.

Active/Approved IRP Loans

Alabama
Alabama-Tombigee Regional Commission, 12 Water St., Suite 200, Courthouse Annex, Camden, AL 36726; 205-682-4234.

Southeast Alabama Regional Planning and Development Commission, P.O. Box 1406, Dothan, AL 36302; 205-794-4093.

Alaska
Tanana Chiefs Conference, Inc., 122 First Ave., Fairbanks, AK 99701; 907-452-8251.

Arizona
Business Development Finance Corporation, 345 E. Toole Ave., Suite 300, Tucson, AZ 85701; 602-623-3377.

Arkansas
Arkansas Land and Farm Development Corporation, Rt. 2, Box 291, Brinkley, AR 72012; 501-734-1140.

Arkansas Enterprise Group, 708 Clinton St., Suite 111, Arkadelphia, AR 71732; 501-246-3945.

Southwest Arkansas Planning and Development District, Inc., P.O. Box 767, Magnolia, AR 71753; 501-234-4030.

California
California Statewide Certified Development Corporation, 129 C St., Davis, CA 95616; 916-756-9310.

California Coastal Rural Development Corporation, 5 E. Gabilan St., Suite 218, P.O. Box 2103, Salinas, CA 93902-2103; 408-424-1099.

Del Norte Economic Development Corporation, P.O. Box 728, Crescent City, CA 95531; 707-464-2169.

Arcata Economic Development Corporation, 630 Ninth St., P.O. Box 4168, Arcata, CA 95521; 707-822-4616.

Valley Rural Development Corporation, 955 N St., Fresno, CA 93721; 209-268-0166.

Crown Economic Development Corporation of Kings County, 1222 W. Lacy Blvd., Suite 101, Hanford, CA 93230-5901; 209-582-4326.

Colorado
Colorado Housing and Finance Authority, 1981 Blake St., Denver, CO 80202-1272; 303-297-2432.

Connecticut
none

Delaware
none

Florida
none

Georgia
Georgia Housing and Finance Authority, 60 Executive Parkway South, Suite 250, Atlanta, GA 30329; 404-679-4840.

Georgia Mountains Regional Economic Development Corporation, 1010 Ridge Rd., Gainsville, GA 30501; 404-536-3431.

South Georgia Area Resource Development Agency, Inc., 327 W. Savannah Ave., Valdosta, GA 31601; 912-333-5277.

Coastal Area District Development Authority, 1313 Newcastle St., Brunswick, GA 31250; 912-261-2500.

CSRA Rural Lending Authority, Inc., 2123 Wrightsboro Rd., Augusta, GA 30904-0800; 404-737-1823.

Middle Flint Area Development Corp., 203 E. College St., Ellaville, GA 31806; 912-937-2563.

Development Corporation of Middle Georgia, 600 Grand Building, 651 Mulberry St., Macon, GA 31201; 912-751-6160.

Hawaii
none

Idaho
Panhandler Area Council, Inc., 11100 Airport Dr., Hayden, ID 83835; 208-772-0584.

Ida-Ore Planning and Development Association, 10624 W. Executive, Boise, ID 83704; 208-322-7033.

East-Central Idaho Planning and Development Association, Inc., 310 N. 2nd East, Rexburg, ID 83440; 208-356-4524.

Illinois
Illinois Development Finance Authority, 2 N. La Salle, Suite 980, Chicago, IL 60602; 312-793-5586.

City of Flora, 122 N. Main St., Flora, IL 62839; 618-662-7111.

South Central Illinois Regional Planning and Development Commission, 120 Delmar Ave., Suite A, Salem, IL 62881; 618-548-4234.

Indiana
none

Iowa
Albia Industrial Development Corporation, 6 S. Main, Albia, IA 52531; 515-932-7053.

Dubuque County Courthouse, 720 Central Ave., Dubuque, IA 52001; 319-589-4441.

Upper Explorerland Regional Planning Commission, 134 W. Green St., P.O. Box 219, Postville, IA 52162; 319-864-7551.

Wright County Economic Development Commission, P.O. Box 214, Clarion, IA 50525; 515-532-6422.

Nishnabotna Valley Rural Electric Cooperative, 1317 Chatburn Ave., Harlan, IA 51537; 712-755-2166.

Sheldon Community Development Corporation, P.O. Box 276, Sheldon, IA 51201; 712-324-2813.

Kansas
Mid America, Inc., 1501 S. Joplin, Pittsburg, KS 66763; 314-231-8267.

South Central Kansas Economic Development District, Inc., River Park Place, Suite 580, 727 N. Waco, Wichita, KS 67203; 316-262-5246.

Pioneer Country Development, Inc., 317 N. Pomeroy Ave., Box 248, Hill City, KS 67642-0248; 913-674-3488.

Great Plains Development, Inc., 100 Military Plaza, 1 Dodge City, KS 67801; 316-227-6406.

Kentucky
Harlan Revitalization Association, P.O. Box 1709, Harlan, KY 40831; 606-573-7698.

Appalachian Investment Corporation, 431 Chestnut St., Suite 7, Berea, KY 40403; 606-986-2375.

Kentucky Highlands Investment Corporation, 400 S. Main St., London, KY 47476; 606-864-5175.

Purchase Area Development District, P.O. Box 588, Mayfield, KY 42066; 502-247-7171.

Louisiana
Kisatchie-Delta Regional Planning and Development District, Inc., 5212 Rue Verdun St., Alexandria, LA 71303; 318-487-5454.

North Delta Regional Planning and Development District, Inc., 2115 Justice St., Monroe, LA 71201; 318-387-2572.

Evangeline Economic and Planning District, P.O. Box 90070, 5 St. John St., Lafayette, LA 70509; 318-233-3215.

Maine
North Kennebec Regional Planning Commission, 7 Benton Ave., Winslow, ME 04901; 207-873-0711.

Oxford Hills Area Development Corporation, 174 Main St., Norway, ME 04268; 207-743-2425.

Coastal Enterprise, Inc., P.O. Box 268, Wiscasset, ME 04578; 207-882-7552.

Eastern Maine Development Corporation, 1 Cumberland Place, Bangor, ME 04401-8520; 207-942-6389.

Androscoggin Valley Council of Governments, 125 Manley Rd., Auburn, ME 04210; 207-783-9186.

Finance Authority of Maine, 83 Western Ave., Augusta, ME 04330; 207-623-3262.

Auburn Business Development Corporation, P.O. Box 642, Auburn, ME 04212; 207-784-0161.

Maryland
Garrett County Development Corporation, 313 E. Alder St., Old Courthouse, Room 307, Oakland, MD 21550; 301-334-1920.

Cumberland-Allegany County Industrial Foundation, Inc., One Commerce Dr., Cumberland, MD 21502; 301-777-5968.

Massachusetts
Southeastern Economic Development Corporation, 88 Broadway, Taunton, MA 02780; 508-822-1020.

Franklin County Community Development Corporation, 324 Wells St., Greenfield, MA 01301; 413-774-7404.

Michigan
Rural Michigan Intermediary Relending Program, 1235 Woodmere, Traverse City, MI 49684; 616-941-5858.

Northern Economic Initiatives Corporation, 1009 W. Ridge St., Marquette, MI 49855; 906-228-5571.

Minnesota
City of McIntosh, 115 Broadway NW, McIntosh, MN 56556; 218-563-3043.

Detroit Lakes Development Corporation, 1025 Roosevelt Ave., Detroit Lakes, MN 56501; 218-847-5658.

Caledonia Economic Development Authority, P.O. Box 232, Caledonia, MN 55921; 507-724-3632.

Minnesota's Community Development Corporation, P.O. Box 623, Detroit Lakes, MN 56502; 218-847-3191.

City of Crookston, P.O. Box 492, Crookston, MN 56716; 218-281-7979.

City of Lakefield, 301 Main St., Lakefield, MN 56150; 507-662-5457.

Prairieland Economic Development Corp. 2524 Broadway Ave., P.O. Box 265, Slayton, MN 56172; 507-836-6656.

Northwest Minnesota Initiative Fund, 722 Paul Bunyan Dr. NW, Bemidji, MN 56601; 218-759-2057.

City of Fergus Falls, P.O. Box 868, Fergus Falls, MN 56538-0868; 218-739-2251.

Midwest Minnesota Community Development Corporation, 803 Roosevelt Ave., P.O. Box 623, Detroit Lakes, MN 56502-0623; 218-847-3191.

City of Fosston, 220 E. First St., Fosston, MN 56542; 218-435-1959.

The Development Corporation of Austin, 1900 8th Ave. NW, Austin, MN 55912; 507-433-0345.

Northland Foundation (formerly Northeastern Minnesota Initiative Fund), 600 Providence Building, 332 W. Superior St., Duluth, MN 55802; 218-723-4040.

West Central Minnesota Initiative Fund, Norwest Bank Building, Suite 205, 220 W. Washington Ave., Fergus Falls, MN 56537; 218-739-2239.

Southeastern Minnesota Initiative Fund, P.O. Box 570, Owatonna, MN 55060; 507-455-3215.

City of Blooming Prairie, P.O. Box 68, Blooming Prairie, MN 55917; 507-583-7573.

Central Minnesota Initiative Fund, P.O. Box 59, Little Falls, MN 56345; 612-632-9255.

Red Lake Falls Development Corporation, 201 Second St., Red Lake Falls, MN 56750; 218-253-2484.

Mississippi
Southwest Mississippi Planning and Development District, Inc., 110 S. Wall St., Natchez, MS 39120; 601-446-6044.

Northeast Mississippi Planning and Development District, P.O. Box 600, Booneville, MS 38829; 601-728-6248.

Three Rivers Planning and Development District, 75 S. Main, P.O. Drawer B, Pontotoc, MS 38863; 601-489-2415.

South Delta Planning and Development District, Inc., P.O. Box 1776, Greenville, MS 38702; 601-378-3831.

Missouri
Rural Missouri, Inc., 1014 Northeast Dr., Jefferson City, MO 65109; 314-634-0136.

Green Hills Rural Development, Inc., 900 Main St., Trenton, MO 64683; 816-359-5086.

Montana
Bear Paw Development Corporation of Northern Montana, P.O. Box 1549, Harve, MT 59501; 406-265-9226.

Nebraska
South East Nebraska Development District, 2632 O St., Lincoln, NE 68510-1398; 402-475-2560.

Nebraska Economic Development Corporation, 139 S. 52nd St., Lincoln, NE 68510; 402-483-0382.

Nevada
Rural Nevada Development Corporation, 457 5th St., Ely, NV 89301; 702-289-8519.

New Hampshire
Belknap County Economic Development Council, 64 Count St., Laconia, NH 03246; 603-524-3057.

New Mexico
New Mexico Community Development Loan Fund, P.O. Box 4979, Albuquerque, NM 87196; 505-243-3196.

New Jersey
South Jersey Economic Development District, Inc., 800 E. Commerce St., Bridgeton, NJ 08302; 609-455-6593.

New York
Adirondack Economic Development Corporation, P.O. Box 747, Saranac Lake, NY 12983.

Southern Tier Enterprise Development Organization, Inc., 465 Broad St., Salamanca, NY 14779; 716-945-5301.

Lake Champlain/Lake George Region Revolving Loan Corporation, Amherst St., Lake George, NY 12845; 518-668-5773.

New York Job Development Authority, 605 3rd Ave., 26th Floor, New York, NY 10158; 518-474-7580.

North Country Alliance Local Development Corporation, 317 Washington St., Watertown, NY 13601; 315-785-2593.

Regional Economic Development and Energy Corporation of the Southern Tier Central Region, New York, 145 Village Square, Painted Post, NY 14807; 604-962-3021.

COMCO Development Corporation, 572 S. Salina St., Syracuse, NY 13202; 315-470-1888.

North Carolina
NC Rural Fund for Development, 728 Clermont Rd., New Bern, NC 28560; 991-638-3041.

Self-Help Ventures Fund, 413 E. Chapel Hill St., Durham, NC 27701; 919-683-3016.

Advancement, Inc., 711 N. Cedar St., Lumberton, NC 28358; 919-738-4851.

Dunn Area Committee of 100, Inc., 600 S. Magnolia Ave., Dunn, NC 28334; 919-892-2884.

Neuse River Development Authority, Inc., 223 Middle St., New Bern, NC 28563; 919-638-6724.

North Dakota
Lewis and Clark Regional Development Council, 400 E. Broadway Ave., Suite 418, Bismarck, ND 58501; 701-255-4591.

Lake Agassiz Regional Council, 417 Main Ave., Fargo, ND 58018; 701-239-5373.

Roosevelt-Custer Regional Council for Development, Pulver Hall, Dickinson, ND 58601; 701-277-1241.

Ohio
Enterprise Development Corporation, 900 E. State St., Athens, OH 45701; 614-592-1188.

Ashtabula County 503 Corporation, 36 W. Walnut St., Jefferson, OH 44047; 216-576-3759.

South Central Development Agency, 129 E. Main St., Hillsboro, OH 45133; 513-393-9599.

Oklahoma
Ozarks Corporation for Innovation Development, P.O. Box 1335, Durant, OK 74702; 405-924-5094.

Central Oklahoma Economic Development District, 400 N. Bell St., P.O. Box 3398, Shawnee, OK 74802-3398; 405-273-3213.

Logan County Economic Development Council, Inc., 212 W. Oklahoma St., Guthrie, OK 73044; 405-282-0060.

Miami Area Economic Development Service, 2 N. Main, Miami, OK 74350; 918-542-8405.

Rural Enterprises, Inc., 422 Cessna, P.O. Box 1335, Durant, OK 74702; 405-924-5094.

Oregon
Oregon Cascades West Council of Governments, 408 SW Monroe St., Corvallis, OR 97333; 503-757-6851.

Southern Oregon Economic Development District, 132 W. Main St., Suite 101, Medford, OR 97501-2746; 503-779-2608.

Mid-Willamette Valley Council of Governments, 105 High St. SE, Salem, OR 97301; 503-588-6177.

Pennsylvania
North Central Pennsylvania Regional Planning and Development Commission, P.O. Box 488, Ridgway, PA 15853; 814-772-6901.

Northern Tier Regional Planning and Development Comm., 507 Main St., Towanda, PA 18848; 717-265-9103.

Northwest Pennsylvania Regional Planning and Development Commission, Biery Building, Suite 406, Franklin, PA 16323; 814-437-3024.

Southern Alleghenies Planning and Development Commission, 541 58th St., Altoona, PA 16602; 814-946-1641.

Economic Development Council of Northeastern Pennsylvania, 1151 Oak St., Pittston, PA 18640-3795; 717-655-5581.

Jefferson Co. Development Council, Inc., R.D. 5, Box 47, Brookville, PA 15825; 814-849-3047.

Puerto Rico
Advancer Local Development Corp., Inc., Del Parque 403, 9th Floor, Santurce, PR 00912; 809-721-6797.

Rhode Island
none

South Carolina
Catawba Regional Development Corp., P.O. Box 450, Rock Hill, SC 29731.

Lake City Development Corporation, Inc., 159 S. Ron McNair Blvd., Lake City, SC 29560; 803-394-3771.

Lower Savannah Regional Development Corporation, P.O. Box 850, Aiken, SC 29802; 803-649-7981.

Carolina Capital Investment Corporation, 1201 Main St., Suite 1750, Columbia, SC 29201; 803-737-0079.

Santee-Lynches Regional Development Corporation, P.O. Box 1837, Sumter, SC 29151; 803-775-7381.

South Dakota
Northeast Council of Governments, P.O. Box 1985, Aberdeen, SD 57402-1985; 605-622-2595.

South Dakota Economic Development Finance Authority, 711 Wells Ave., Pierre, SD 57501; 605-773-5032.

First District Development Company, 124 First Ave. NW, Watertown, SD 57201; 605-886-7224.

Tennessee
First Tennessee Economic Development Corporation, 207 N. Boone St., Suite 800, Johnson City, TN 37604; 615-928-0224.

Cumberland Area Investment Corporation, 125 Burgess Falls Rd., Cookville, TN 38501; 615-432-4050.

South Central Tennessee Dev. District, 815 S. Main St., Columbia, TN 38402-1346; 615-381-2040.

Southeast Local Development Corporation, 216 W. 8th St., Suite 300, Chattanooga, TN 37402; 615-266-5781.

Southwest Tennessee Development District, 416 E. Lafayette, Jackson, TN 38301; 901-422-4041.

Areawide Development Corporation, P.O. Box 19806, Knoxville, TN 37939-2806; 615-524-8553.

Mid-Cumberland Area Development Corp., Stahlman Building, 211 Union St., Box 233, Nashville, TN 37201; 615-862-8828.

Texas
Brownwood Industrial Foundation, Inc., 521 E. Baker, Brownwood, TX 76801; 915-646-9535.

Utah
Utah Technology Finance Corporation, 185 S. State, Suite 208, Salt Lake City, UT 84111; 801-364-4346.

Deseret Certified Development Co., 4885 S. 900 East, Salt Lake City, UT 84117; 801-266-0443.

Vermont
Franklin County Industrial Development Corporation, 2 Federal St., St. Albans, VT 05478; 802-542-2191.

Vermont 503 Corporation, 58 E. State St., Montpelier, VT 05602; 802-223-7226.

Rutland Industrial Development Corporation, P.O. Box 39, 5 Court St., Rutland, VT 05702; 802-773-9147.

Northern Community Investment Corporation, P.O. Box 904, St. Johnsbury, VT 05819; 802-748-5102.

Virginia
Lake Country Development Corporation, P.O. Box 150, South Hill, VA 23970; 804-447-7101.

Virgin Islands
none

Washington
Tri-County Economic Development District, 347 W. Second, Suite A, Colville, WA 99114; 509-684-4571.

Evergreen Community Development Assoc., 2015 Smith Tower, Seattle, WA 98104; 206-622-3731.

West Virginia
Mid-Ohio Valley Regional Planning and Development Council, 1200 Grand Central Ave., Vienna, WV 26105; 304-295-9312.

West Virginia Economic Development Authority, Room M-146, State Capital, Charleston, WV 25305; 304-348-3650.

Wisconsin
Adams-Columbia Electric Cooperative, P.O. Box 70, Friendship, WI 53934-0079; 608-339-3346.

Impact Acceptance Corporation, Rt. 2, Box 8, Turtle Lake, WI 54889; 715-986-4171.

Northwest Wisconsin Business Development Corporation, 302 Walnut St., Spooner, WI 54801; 715-635-2197.

Wyoming
Division of Economic and Community Development, Barrett Building, 4N, Cheyenne, WY 82002; 307-777-7185.

Multi-State Intermediaries
Community Transportation Association of America, 725 15th St. NW, Suite 900, Washington, DC 20005; 202-628-1480.

Community Resource Group, Inc., 2705 Chapman Ave., Springdale, AR 72764; 501-756-2900.

Rural Community Assistance Corporation, 2125 19th St., Suite 203, Sacramento, CA 95818; 916-447-2854.

Housing Assistance Council, Inc., 1025 Vermont Ave. NW, Washington, DC 20005; 202-842-8600.

* Rural Business Grants

U.S. Department of Agriculture
Community Facilities Loan Division
14th and Independence Ave., SW
Washington, DC 20250
202-720-1490

The Rural Business Enterprise Grant Program (RBEG) is administered by the Rural Development Administration, and provides grant funds to a local or regional intermediary which, in turn, lends funds in a flexible manner to local businesses. Funds are designed to facilitate the development of small and emerging private business, industry, and related employment. Money can used for the acquisition and development of land, and the construction of buildings, plants, equipment, access streets and roads, parking areas, utility and service extensions, refinancing, fees, technical assistance, startup operating cost and working capital. Grant applications are available from Farmers Home Administration field offices, and you can contact the office listed above for more information.

Farmers Home Administration State Offices

Alabama
Horace Horn, Sterling Center, Suite 601, 4121 Carmichael Rd., Montgomery, AL 36106-3683; 205-279-3400.

Alaska
Ernest Brannon, 634 S. Bailey, Suite 103, Palmer, AK 99645; 907-745-2176.

Arizona
Alan Stephens, 3003 N. Central Ave., Suite 900, Phoenix, AZ 85012; 602-280-8700.

Arkansas
Michael L. Dunaway (Acting), 700 W. Capitol, P.O. Box 2778, Little Rock, AR 72203; 501-324-6281.

California
Michael Reyna, 194 W. Main St., Suite F, Woodland, CA 95695-2915; 916-668-2000.

Colorado
Ruth Rodriguez, 655 Parfet St., Room E-100, Lakewood, CO 80215; 303-236-2801.

Delaware-Maryland
John Walls, 4611 So. Dupont Hwy., Camden, DE 19934-9998; 302-697-4300.

Florida
Jan Shadburn, 4440 NW 25th Pl., P.O. Box 147010, Gainesville, FL 32614-7010; 904-338-3400.

Georgia
Laura Jean Meadows, Stephens Federal Building, 355 E. Hancock Ave., Athens, GA 30610; 706-546-2173.

Hawaii
Francis Blanco, Federal Building, Room 311, 154 Waianuenue Ave., Hilo, HI 96720; 808-933-3000.

Idaho
Loren Nelson, 3232 Elder St., Boise, ID 83705; 208-334-1301.

Illinois
Wallace Furrow, Illini Plaza, Suite 103, Champaign, IL 61820; 217-398-5235.

Indiana
John Thompson, 5975 Lakeside Blvd., Indianapolis, IN 46278; 317-290-3100.

Iowa
Ellen Huntoon, Federal Building, Room 873, 210 Walnut St., Des Moines, IA 50309; 515-284-4663.

Kansas
Bill Kirk, 1201 SW Summit Exec. Center, P.O. Box 4653, Topeka, KS 66604; 913-271-2700.

Kentucky
Tom Fern, 771 Corporate Plaza, Suite 200, Lexington, KY 40503; 606-224-7300.

Louisiana
Austin Cormier, 3727 Government St., Alexandria, LA 71302; 318-473-7920.

Maine
Seth Bradstreet, 444 Stillwater Ave., Suite 2, P.O. Box 405, Bangor, ME 04402-0405; 207-990-9106.

Massachusetts /Rhode Island/ Connecticut
William Bradley, 451 West St., Amherst, MA 01002; 413-253-4300.

Michigan
Donald Hare, 3001 Coolidge Rd., Suite 200, East Lansing, MI 48823; 517-337-6635.

Minnesota
Janice Daley, 410 Farm Credit Service Bldg., 375 Jackson St., St. Paul, MN 55101; 612-290-3842.

Mississippi
George E. Irvin, Federal Building, Room 831, 100 W. Capitol St., Jackson, MS 39269; 601-965-4316.

Missouri
William Shay (Acting), 601 Business Loop, 70 West, Parkade Center, Suite 235, Columbia, MO 65203; 314-876-0976.

Montana
Anthony Preite, 900 Technology Blvd., Suite B, P.O. Box 850, Bozeman, MT 59771; 406-585-2580.

Nebraska
Stanley Foster, Federal Bldg, Room 308, 100 Centennial Mall N, Lincoln, NE 68508; 402-437-5551.

New Jersey
Ernest Grunow, Tarnsfield Plaza, Suite 22, 1016 Woodland Rd., Mt. Holly, NJ 08060; 609-265-3600.

New Mexico
Steven Anaya, Federal Building, Room 3414, 517 Gold Ave. SW, Albuquerque, NM 87102; 506-766-2462.

New York
James Bay, The Galleries of Syracuse, 441 S. Salina St., Syracuse, NY 13202; 316-477-6400.

North Carolina
James Kearney, 4405 Bland Rd., Suite 260, Raleigh, NC 27609; 919-790-2731.

North Dakota
Charles Mertens, Federal Building, Room 208, 3rd and Rosser, P.O. Box 1737, Bismarck, ND 58502; 701-250-4781.

Ohio
Linda Page, Federal Building, Room 507, 200 N. High St., Columbus, OH 43215; 614-469-5606.

Oklahoma
Charles Rainbolt, USDA Agricultural Center, Stillwater, OK 74074; 405-624-4250.

Oregon
Scott Duff, Federal Building, Room 1590, 1220 SW 3rd Ave., Portland, OR 97204; 503-326-2731.

Pennsylvania
Cheryl Cook, 1 Credit Union Place, Suite 330, Harrisburg, PA 17110-2996; 717-782-4476.

Puerto Rico
Iliana Echegoyen, New San Juan Office Bldg., Room 501, 159 Carlos E. Chardon St., Hato Rey, PR 00918-5481; 809-766-5095.

South Carolina
Bernie Wright, Strom Thurmond Federal Bldg., 1835 Assembly St., Room 1007, Columbia, SC 29201; 803-765-5163.

South Dakota
Dallas Tonsager, Federal Building, Room 308, 200 4th St. SW, Huron, SD 57350; 605-352-1100.

Tennessee
David Seivers, 3322 West End Ave., Suite 300, Nashville, TN 37203-1071; 615-783-1308.

Texas
George Ellis, M.J. Pena, Federal Building, Suite 102, 101 S. Main, Temple, TX 76501; 817-774-1301.

Nevada
Sarah Mersereau, 1390 S. Curry St., Carson City, NV 89703-5405; 702-887-1222.

Utah
James Harvey, Federal Building, Room 5438, 125 S. State St., Salt Lake City, UT 84138; 801-524-4063.

Vermont/New Hampshire/ Virgin Islands
Roberta Harold, City Center, 3rd Floor, 89 Main St., Montpelier, VT 05602; 802-828-6001.

Virginia
Lloyd A. Jones, Culpeper Building, Suite 238, 1606 Santa Rosa Rd., Richmond, VA 23229; 804-287-1550.

Washington
George Aldaya, Federal Building, Room 319, 301 Yakima St., P.O. Box 2427, Wenatchee, WA 98807; 509-664-0240.

West Virginia
Robert Lewis, 75 High St., P.O. Box 678, Morgantown, WV 26505; 304-291-4791.

Wisconsin
Bryce Luchterhand, 4949 Kirschling Court, Stevens Point, WI 54481; 715-345-7625.

Wyoming
Derrel L. Carruth, Federal Building, Room 1005, P.O. Box 820, Casper, WY 82602; 307-261-5271.

* New Programs To Help The Poor
U.S. Department of Health and Human Services
Office of Community Services

370 L'Enfant Promenade, SW, Fifth Floor
Washington, DC 20447
202-401-9341

The Demonstration Partnership Program provides funds to stimulate eligible entities (mainly Community Action Agencies) to develop new approaches to provide for greater self-sufficiency of the poor. Many of the programs funded include micro-enterprise/ self-employment projects. The target populations have included homeless men, female heads of households, young minority males, families, and low-income women. Programs offer a range of services including technical assistance, small low-interest loans, business training, and more. For information on how you can start a program or for a listing of existing ones in your area, contact the office listed above.

Some of the awardees include:
North Coast Opportunities, Inc., Ukiah, CA

Central Vermont Community Action Council, Inc., Barre, VT

Southeast Iowa Community Action, Burlington, IA

Mayor's Office of Community Services, Philadelphia, PA

Elmore/Autauga Community Action Corp., Elmore, AL

* Help Those Help Themselves
U.S. Department of Health and Human Services
Office of Community Services
370 L'Enfant Promenade, SW
Fifth Floor
Washington, DC 20447
202-401-9346

The Discretionary Grants Program's goal is strengthen the American family, which includes improving access of youth living in low-income families to needed support services, including employment training and other transition to work services, and improving the integration, coordination, and continuity of other health and human services funded services. The program areas focus on employment opportunities and self-sufficiency among low-income individuals; however, they are not micro-enterprise oriented programs. This program supports projects which provide employment and ownership opportunities for low-income people through business, physical or commercial development and which generally improve the quality of the economic and social environment of low-income residents in economically-depressed areas. The emphases of projects must be on self-help and mobilization of the community-at-large. For application information contact the office listed above.

There are several set-aside programs available including:
Historically Black Colleges and Universities
Pre-Development Funds (assess feasibility of potential projects)
Youth Opportunities Unlimited
Community Food and Nutrition Program
Rural Housing
Community Facilities Development
National Youth Sports Program
Migrants and Seasonal Farmworkers

List of FY 93 Grant Awards Issued by ACF Office of Community Services

Urban and Rural Community Economic Development
Abyssinian Development Corp., 131 W. 138th St., New York, NY 10030; Amount: $500,000.

Allegheny West Civic Council, Inc., 845 N. Lincoln Ave., Pittsburgh, PA 15233; Amount: $340,000.

Arkansas Enterprise Group, 605 Main St., Suite 203, Arkadelphia, AR 71923; Amount: $371,050.

Asian Neighborhood Design, Inc., 80 Fresno St., San Francisco, CA 94133; Amount: $375,000.

Beech Corporation, 1615 N. Carlisle St., Philadelphia, PA 19121; Amount: $277,520.

Bethel New Life, Inc., 367 N. Karlov, Chicago, IL 60624; Amount: $468,336.

Chinese Economic Development Council, Inc., 65 Harrison Ave., Boston, MA 02111; Amount: $293,000.

Coalition For a Better Acre, 450 Merrimack St., Lowell, MA 01852; Amount: $310,000.

Coastal Enterprises, Inc., P.O. Box 268, Wiscasset, ME 04578; Amount: $275,000.

Collinwood Community Services Center, 813 E. 152nd St., Cleveland, OH 44110; Amount: $500,000.

Cypress Hills Local Development Corporation, 3152 Fulton St., Cypress Hills, NY 11208; Amount: $299,925.

Delta Foundation, Inc., 819 Main St., Greenville, MS 38701; Amount: $460,000.

Dorchester Bay Economic Development Corporation, 594 Columbia Rd., Suite 302, Dorchester, MA 02125; Amount: $500,000.

Eastside Community Investments, Inc., 26 N. Arsenal, Indianapolis, IN 46201; Amount: $500,000.

Hough Area Partners in Progress, Inc., 8610 Hough Ave., Cleveland, OH 44106; Amount: $84,000.

Impact Seven, Inc., 100 Digital Dr., Clear Lake, WI 54005; Amount: $495,000.

Knoxville Area Urban League, P.O. Box 1911, 2416 Magnolia Ave., Knoxville, TN 37901; Amount: $261,644.

Korean Community Center of East Bay (KCCEB), 3538 Telegraph Ave., Oakland, CA 94609; Amount: $150,000.

Latino Resource Organization, Inc., 2714 W. Pico Blvd., Suite 220, Santa Monica, CA 90405; Amount: $500,000.

Meri Weather, Inc., 178 State St., Meriden, CT 06450; Amount: $380,000.

Mid Bronx Desperadoes Community Housing Corporation, 1762 Boston Rd., Bronx, NY 10460; Amount: $500,000.

Mid Bronx Senior Citizens Council, Inc., 900 Grand Concourse, Bronx, NY 10451; Amount: $125,000.

Midwest Minnesota Community Development Corporation, 803 Roosevelt Ave., Detroit Lakes, MN 56501; Amount: $250,000.

Mountain Association for Community Economic Development, 433 Chestnut St., Berea, KY 40403; Amount: $500,000.

Neighborhood Development Corporation of Jamaica Plain, 31 Germania St., Jamaica Plain, MA 02130; Amount: $498,625.

New Community Corporation, 233 W. Market St., Newark, NJ 07103; Amount: $500,000.

Northeast Louisiana University, 700 University Ave., Monroe, LA 71209; Amount: $87,820.

Private Industry Council of Dade Co., Inc., 7900 NE 2nd Ave., Suite 603, Miami, FL 33138; Amount: $500,000.

Rural Enterprises, Inc., 422 Cessna, Durant, OK 74701; Amount: $500,000.

San Jose Development Corp., 111 N. Market St., Suite 150, San Jose, CA 95113; Amount: $488,834.

Science Park Development Corporation, 5 Science Park,New Haven, CT 06511; Amount: $500,000.

Southeast Development, Inc., 10 S. Wolfe St., Baltimore, MD 21231; Amount: $500,000.

Southwestern Community Services, Inc., 69Z Island St., Keene, NH 03430; Amount: $170,436.

St. Paul's Community Svcs., Inc., 451 Van Houten St., Paterson, NJ 07501; Amount: $250,000.

Vermont Slauson Economic Development Corporation, 5918 S. Vermont Ave., Los Angeles, CA 90044; Amount: $450,000.

Vine City Housing Ministry, 228 Maple Place, NW, Atlanta, GA 30314.

Walnut Hills Redevelopment Foundation, Inc., 2601 Melrose Ave., Suite 100, Cincinnati, OH 45206; Amount: $500,000.

West Central Missouri Community Action Agency, 106 W. 4th St., Appleton, MD 64724; Amount: $335,390.

White Mountain Apache Tribe, P.O. Box 700, Whiteriver, AZ 85941; Amount: $164,037.

Women Entrepreneurs of Baltimore, Inc., 28 E. Ostend St., Baltimore, MD 21230; Amount: $491,878.

Disadvantaged Youth Set-Aside
Eastside Community Investments, Inc., 26 N. Arsenal Ave., Indianapolis, IN 46201; Amount: $625,000.

Human Development Corporation of Metropolitan St. Louis, 929 N. Spring Ave., St. Louis, MD 63108; Amount: $729,488.

Tampa-Hillsborough Community Development Corporation, Inc., 1207 East M.L. King, Jr. Blvd., Tampa, FL 33603; Amount: $750,000.

Urban and Rural Community Economic Development/Set Aside
D.C. Private Industry Council, Inc., 1129 20th St. NW, Suite 200, Washington, DC 20036; Amount: $500,000.

Greater Atlanta Small Business Project, 10 Park Place South, Suite 305, Atlanta, GA 30303; Amount: $479,660.

Kentucky Highlands Investment Corp., P.O. Box 1738, London, KY 40741; Amount: $468,500.

Opa-Locka Community Development Corporation, 490 Opa-Locka Blvd., Suite 20, Opa-Locka, FL 33054; Amount: $492,254.

Urban and Rural Community Economic Development/ Developmental Set-Aside
Brownsville Area Revitalization Corporation, 322 Front St., Brownsville, PA 15417; Amount: $237,000.

Esperanza Housing and Community Development Corporation, 990 Highland Dr., #106, Solana Beach, CA 92075; Amount: $250,000.

Evergreen Community Development Corporation, P.O. Box 451, Lincoln City, OR 97367; Amount: $247,837.

Fathers, Inc.,1234 Columbus Ave., Roxbury Crossing, MA 02120; Amount: $188,159.

Great River Foundation, Inc., 118 N. Pearl, Suite 131, Natchez, MS 39120; Amount: $250,000.

Northeast Milwaukee Industrial Development Corporation, Inc., 531 E. Burleigh, Milwaukee, WI 53212; Amount: $250,000.

Washington County Council on Economic Development, 703 Courthouse Sq., Washington, PA 15301; Amount: $178,959.

Rural Housing Repairs and Rehabilitation
Community Action Human Resources Agency, P.O. Box 160, Coolidge, AZ 85228; Amount: $250,000.

Community Housing Improvement Systems and Planning Association, Inc., 600 E. Market St., Salinas, CA 93905; Amount: $250,000.

Community Services Programs of West Alabama, Inc., 601 17th St., Tuscaloosa, AL 35401; Amount: $93,206.

Corporation for Ohio Appalachian Development (C.O.A.D.), 1 Pinchot Place, P.O. Box 787, Athens, OH 45701; Amount: $250,000.

Foundation for Rural Housing, Inc., 4506 Regent St., Madison, WI 53705; Amount: $237,125.

Kentucky Mountain Housing Development Corporation, Inc., P.O. Box 729, Manchester, KY 40962; Amount: $250,000.

Louisa County Housing Foundation, Louisa County Courthouse, Louisa, VA 23093; Amount: $31,000.

Oregon Housing and Community Services Department, 1600 State St., Salem, OR 97310; Amount: $250,000.

Panhandle Area Council, 11100 Airport Dr., Hayden, ID 83835; Amount: $250,000.

Proyecto Azteca, P.O. Box 1014, San Juan, TX 78589; Amount: $250,000.

Renewal Unlimited, Inc., 135 Linn St., P.O. Box 77, Baraboo, WI 53913; Amount: $65,850.

Steuben Churchpeople Against Poverty, Inc., 108 Liberty St., Bath, NY 14810; Amount: $152,819.

United Methodist Relief Center, 690 Coleman Blvd., Mt. Pleasant, SC 29464; Amount: $150,000.

* Welfare Moms Can Start Their Own Business

U.S. Dept. of Health and Human Services
Office of Community Services
370 L'Enfant Promenade, SW, Fifth Floor
Washington, DC 20447
202-401-5282

If you're getting help from Aid to Families With Dependent Children (AFDC), you may be able to get free training on how to become an entrepreneur along with money to become your own boss. The program is called Job Opportunities for Low-Income Individuals (JOLI) program, which seeks to enhance the capacity and self-sufficiency of participating individuals. JOLI aims to help Aid to Families with Dependent Children (AFDC) recipients and others whose income falls below the federal poverty guidelines become self-sufficient by starting their own micro-enterprises or through employment in newly created permanent jobs. The program is designed to demonstrate and evaluate ways of creating new employment and business opportunities for certain low-income individuals through the provision of technical and financial assistance to private employers in the community, self-employment/micro-enterprise programs, and/or new business development programs. JOLI awards grants to non-profit organizations to develop these projects. Contact the office listed above for information of programs in your area or application information.

Job Opportunities for Low-Income Individuals

FY 93 Grantees

Ms. Julia Vindasius, Vice President, Arkansas Enterprise Group, 400 Main, Suite 118, Pine Bluff, AR 71606; 501-535-6233. Project Director: Ms. Julia Vindasius.

Mr. Noble L. Sissle, Executive Director, Tampa Hillsborough Community Development Corporation, Inc., 1207 East M.L. King Jr. Bldg., Tampa, FL 33603; 813-248-4232. Project Director: Noble L. Sissle.

Ms. Connie E. Evans, Executive Director, Women's Self-Employment Project, 166 W. Washington St., Suite 730, Chicago, IL 60602; 312-606-8255. Project Director: Lynette Boone.

Mr. John T. Patterson, Pres., South Bronx Overall Economic Development Corp., 370 E. 149th St., Bronx, NY 10455; 718-292-3113. Project Director: Valarie White or Nancy Lasher.

Ms. Peggy Powell, Executive Director, Home Care Associates Training Institute, Inc., 349 E. 149th St., Bronx, NY 10451; 718-993-7104. Project Director: Janet Saglio or Steve Dawson.

Rev. Steve L. Carlton, Chairman, Community Socio-Economical Center for Hope, 412 E. Fourth St., Lexington, NC 27292; 919-765-2366. Project Staff: Rev. Steve Carlton, Irene Perry, Bessie Singletary, Paul Fletcher, Garcia Howard.

Ms. Jean Ann Harris, Executive Director, Dilliard Building, Inc., 504 W. Elm St., Goldsboro, NC 27530; 919-734-8118. Project Director: Jean Ann Harris.

Mr. Donald Stricker, President, WSOS Community Action Comm., Inc., 109 S. Front St., P.O. Box 590, Fremont, OH 43420; 419-334-8911. Project Director: Ms. Billie Derivan.

Mr. Robert Jeffrey, Executive Dir., Black Dollar Days Task Force, 116-21st Ave., Seattle, WA 98122; 206-323-0534. Project Director: Zachary Bruce, Program Asst: Coletta Locke.

Mr. William Bay, President, Impact Seven, Inc., 100 Digital Dr., Clear Lake, WI 54005; 715-263-2532. Project Director: Dileep Rao.

FY 92 Grantees

John D. Arnold, Ph.D., Chief Executive Officer, PPEP Housing Development Corp., Inc., 802 E. 46th St., Tucson, AZ 85741; 602-622-3553. Contact Person: Frank Ballesteros.

Kerry N. Doi, Executive Director, Pacific Asian Consortium in Employment, 2525 W. 8th St., Suite 304, Los Angeles, CA 90057; 213-389-2373. Contact Person: Yusa Chang.

Dorothy Trujillo, Executive Director, Mi Casa Resource Center for Women, 571 Galapago St., Denver, CO 80204; 303-573-1302. Contact Person: Elsa Holguin, Project Director.

Jim Deffenbaugh, Executive Director, Panhandle Area Council, Inc., 11100 Airport Dr., Hayden, ID 83835; 208-772-0584. Contact Person: Jim Deffenbaugh.

Connie Evans, Executive Director, Women's Self-Employment Project, 166 W. Washington St., Suite 730, Chicago, IL 60602; 312-606-8255. Contact Person: Lynette Boone, Project Director.

Ms. Halcyon Blake, Chair, Board of Directors, Coastal Enterprises, Inc., P.O. Box 268, Water St., Wiscasset, ME 04578; 207-882-7552. Contact Person: Ron Phillips, President; Kathleen Kearny, Project Director.

Terry Polchies, Executive Director, Central Maine Indian Community Development Corporation, 132-144 N. Main St., P.O. Box 3040, Brewer, ME 04412-3040; 207-989-5971. Contact Person: Claire Bolduc or West Francis, Deputy Director.

Jill Goodman, Executive Director, The Human Development Corporation of Metropolitan St. Louis, 929 N. Spring Ave., St. Louis, MO 63108; 314-652-5100. Contact Person: Janice Washington.

Martin Eakes, Executive Director, Center for Community Self-Help, 413 E. Chapel Hill St., Durham, NC 27701; 919-683-3016. Contact Person: Katherine McKee, Project Director or Bryan Hassel.

Steven J. Budd, President, City-Wide Development Corporation, 1400 Miami Valley Tower, 40 W. Fourth St., Dayton, OH 45402-1883; 513-226-0457. Contact Person: Steven J. Budd.

FY 91 Grantees
Mr. George Yokoyama, Executive Director, Hawaii County Economic Opportunity Council, 34 Rainbow Dr., Hilo, HI 96720; 808-961-2681. Contact Person: Mr. George Yokoyama.

Mr. Dennis J. West, President, Eastside Community Investments, Inc., 3228 E. Tenth St., Indianapolis, IN 46201; 301-633-7303. Contact Person: Ms. Linda Gilkerson, Project Director.

Mr. John F. Else, President, Institute for Social and Economic Development, 1901 Broadway St., #313, Iowa City, IA 52240; 319-338-2331. Contact Person: Ms. Margaret Showers, Project Director.

Mr. Halcyon Blake, Chair, Board of Directors, Coastal Enterprises, Inc., P.O. Box 268, Wiscasset, ME 04578; 207-882-7552. Contact Person: Mr. Ron Phillips, President; Ms. Kathleen Kearny, Project Director.

Mr. John Zeller, Executive Director, Montgomery County Private Industry Council, 8500 Colesville Rd., Silver Spring, MD 20910; 301-495-0440. Contact Person: Dr. Janice S. Lohmann, Project Director (301-495-0451).

Ms. Michelle Richards, Executive Director, Ann Arbor Community Development Corporation, 2008 Hogback Rd., #2A Taylor, Ann Arbor, MI 48105; 313-677-1400 (CDC), 313-677-1444 (WISE Program). Contact Person: Ms. Lendell McEwen.

Mr. Adolphus Mooney, Chairman, Community Development Corporation of Kansas City, 2420 E. Linwood Blvd., #400, Kansas City, MO 64109; 816-924-5800. Contact Person: Ms. Carole Herron, Ms. Michelle Rousseau, Project Director (816-921-8111).

Mr. Jeffery K. Rupp, Executive Director, Human Resources Development Council, 321 E. Main St., Suite 300, Bozeman, MT 59715; 406-587-4486. Contact Person: Ms. Lynn Robson, Project Director.

Mr. Richard Recny, Chairman, Local Development Corporation of East New York, 116 Williams Ave., Brooklyn, NY 11207; 718-385-6700. Contact Person: Mr. Jeffery Stern, Executive Director; Ms. Sherry Roberts, Project Director.

Ms. Sara L. Lewis, Executive Director, Free the Children, Inc., 1200 Peabody St., Memphis, TN 38103; 901-276-0969. Contact Person: Mr. Malcolm Wallace, Project Director (901-276-0843).

FY 90 Grantees
Fairbanks Native Association, Inc., 310 First Ave., Fairbanks, AK 99701; 907-452-1648. Contact Person: Mr. Samuel S. Demientieff, Executive Director; Mr. Robert Keller, Project Director; Ms. Nellie Hamsley, Employment Coordinator.

East Central Arkansas Economic Development Corporation, 125 N. Grant, P.O. Box 709, Forrest City, AR 72335; 501-633-7686. Contact Person: Mr. Tommy Davis, Executive Director; Mr. Leroy Lacey, Project Director.

Women's Economic Growth, 1275 S. Main St., P.O. Box 605, Etna, CA 96027; 916-467-3100. Contact Person: Ms. Mimi VanSickle, Executive Director.

Greater Atlanta Small Business Project, 10 Park Place South, Suite 305, Atlanta, GA 30303; 404-659-5955. Contact Person: Mr. Maurice S. Coakley, Director; Mr. David Weber.

Institute for Social and Economic Development, 1901 Broadway, Suite 313, Iowa City, IA 52240; 319-338-2331. Contact Person: Dr. John F. Else, President; Ms. Margaret Showers, Project Director.

Grand Rapids Opportunities for Women, 144 E. Fulton, Grand Rapids, MI 49503; 616-774-3900. Contact Person: Ms. Bonnie K. Miller, President; Ms. Leanne Moss, Project Officer.

Omaha Small Business Network, 2505 N. 24th St., Douglas County, Omaha, NE 68110; 402-346-9262. Contact Person: John Cochran, Chairman; Ms. Leslie Redden, Project Director.

Greyston Family Inn of Yonkers, 144 Woodworth Ave., Yonkers, NY 10701; 914-376-3900. Contact Person: Ms. Sandra J. Holmes, Executive Director.

Private Industry Council of Snohomish Co., 917-134th St. SW, A-10, Everett, WA 98204; 206-743-9669. Contact Person: Ms. Emily Duncan, Executive Director; David Prince, Project Director.

CAP Services, Inc., 5499 Highway 10 East, Stevens Point, WI 54481; 715-345-5200. Contact: Mr. Karl S. Pnazek, CEO.

* Up To $5,000 For Refugees

U.S. Dept. of Health and Human Services
Office of Refugee Resettlement
370 L'Enfant Promenade, SW, Sixth Floor
Washington, DC 20447
202-401-4560

Refugees can receive technical assistance, training, or loans of up to $5,000 through a program called the Micro-Enterprise Development Project. The program allows states and public or private, non-profit organizations and institutions to apply to receive grants to develop and administer micro-enterprise programs consisting of small-scale financing ($5,000) available through microloans to refugees and technical assistance and support to these refugee entrepreneurs. For information on organizations which were awarded grants, contact the office listed above.

Awardees Include:
Church Ave. Merchants Block Association; Brooklyn, NY
Coastal Enterprises, Inc.; Wiscasset, ME
Center for Southeast Asian Refugee Resettlement;
  San Francisco, CA
Economic and Employment Development Center;
  Los Angeles, CA
Institute for Social and Economic Development; Iowa City, IA
International Refugee Center of Oregon; Portland, OR
Jewish Vocational Service; Boston, MA
Women's Self-Employment Project; Chicago, IL
Ethiopian Community Development Council; Arlington, VA
Interim Community Development Association; Seattle, WA
Kahlihi Palama Immigrant Services; Honolulu, HI
Lutheran Children and Family Services of Eastern Pennsylvania;
  Philadelphia, PA
Merced County Department of Economic and Strategic
  Development; Merced, CA
Institute for Cooperative Development; Manchester, NH
Institute for Social and Economic Development; Iowa City, IA

* Grants To Towns That Will Lend You Business Money
American Communities
Information Center
Office of Community Planning and
  Development
P.O. Box 7189
Gaithersburg, MD 20898-7189
800-998-9999

Cities can get grants that can be used to lend you money to start a small business. The Entitlement Grants is the largest component of the Community Development Block Grant Program and provides annual grants to entitled cities (population 50,000) and counties (population 200,000) to develop viable urban communities by providing decent housing and suitable living environment, and by expanding economic opportunities, principally for low- and moderate-income persons. The program provides funds to carry out a wide range of community development activities directed toward neighborhood revitalization, economic development, improved community facilities and services, and most recently micro-enterprise. Funds can be used to establish credit (direct loans and loan guarantees, revolving loan funds, and more) for the stabilization and expansion of micro-enterprises; provide technical assistance, advice, and business support services to owners of micro-enterprises; and provide general support to owners of micro-enterprises and organizations developing micro-enterprises. In 1994 there were 802 metropolitan cities and 135 urban counties which were awarded $3,003,7000. To learn if your community received funds and the person to contact in your area for more information, contact the office listed above. You may also contact the HUD office nearest you (listed below).

HUD Offices

New England Area
Boston Regional Office, Mary Lou Crane, Secretary's Representative, HUD-Boston Office, Thomas P. O'Neill, Jr. Federal Building, 10 Causeway St., Room 375, Boston, MA 02222; 617-565-5234.

Bangor Regional Office, Richard Young, Acting State Coordinator, HUD-Bangor Office, Casco Northern Bank Building, 23 Main St., Bangor, ME 04401-6394; 207-945-0467.

Burlington Regional Office, William Peters, Acting State Coordinator, HUD-Burlington Office, Room 244, Federal Building, 11 Elmwood Ave., P.O. Box 879, Burlington, VT 05402-0879; 802-951-6290.

Hartford Regional Office, Robert S. Donovan, Acting State Coordinator, HUD-Hartford Office, 330 Main St., Hartford, CT 06106-1860; 203-240-4523.

Manchester Regional Office, David B. Harrity, Acting State Coordinator, HUD-Manchester Office, Norris Cotton Federal Building, 275 Chestnut St., Manchester, NH 03103-2487; 603-666-7681.

Providence Regional Office, Michael Dziok, Acting State Coordinator, HUD-Providence Office, 330 John O. Pastore Federal Building and U.S. Post Office, Kennedy Plaza, Providence, RI 02903-1785; 401-528-5351.

Microenterprise

New York/New Jersey Area

New York Regional Office, Jose Cintron, Secretary's Representative, HUD-New York Office, 26 Federal Plaza, New York, NY 10278; 212-264-6500.

Albany Regional Office, John Petricco, Acting State Coordinator, HUD-Albany Office, 52 Corporate Circle, Albany, NY 12203-5121; 518-464-4200.

Buffalo Regional Office, Joseph Lynch, Acting State Coordinator, HUD-Buffalo Office, 5th Floor, Lafayette Court, 465 Main St., Buffalo, NY 14203-1780; 716-846-5755.

Camden Regional Office, Elmer Roy, Acting State Coordinator, HUD-Camden Office, 2nd Floor, Hudson Building, 800 Hudson Square, Camden, NJ 08102-1156; 609-757-5081.

Newark Regional Office, Diane Johnson, Acting State Coordinator, HUD-Newark Office, 13th Floor, One Newark Center, Newark, NJ 07102-5260; 201-622-7900.

Midatlantic Area

Philadelphia Regional Office, Karen Miller, Secretary's Representative, HUD-Philadelphia Office, Liberty Square Building, 105 S. 7th St., Philadelphia, PA 19106; 215-597-2560.

Baltimore Regional Office, Maxine Saunders, Acting State Coordinator, HUD-Baltimore Office, 5th Floor, City Crescent Building, 10 S. Howard St., Baltimore, MD 21201-2505; 410-962-2520.

Charleston Regional Office, Fred Roncaglione, Acting State Coordinator, HUD-Charleston Office, Suite 708, 405 Capitol St., Charleston, WV 25301-1795; 304-347-7000.

Pittsburgh Regional Office, Choice Edwards, Acting State Coordinator, HUD-Pittsburgh Office, 412 Old Post Office Courthouse, 7th Ave. and Grant St., Pittsburgh, PA 15219; 412-644-6428.

Richmond Regional Office, Mary Ann Wilson, Acting State Coordinator, HUD-Richmond Office, The 3600 Centre, 3600 W. Broad St., P.O. Box 90331, Richmond, VA 23230-0331; 804-278-4507.

Washington Regional Office, Jessica Franklin, State Coordinator, HUD-Washington, DC Office, Suite 300, Union Center Plaza, Phase II, 820 First St. NE, Washington, DC 20002-4205; 202-275-9200.

Wilmington Regional Office, David Sharbaugh, Acting State Coordinator, HUD-Wilmington Office, 824 Market St., Suite 850, Wilmington, DE 19801-3016; 302-573-6300.

Southeast Area

Atlanta Regional Office, Davey Gibson, Secretary's Representative, HUD-Atlanta Office, Richard Russell Federal Building, 75 Spring St. SW, Atlanta, GA 30303; 404-331-5136.

Birmingham Regional Office, Heagar Hill, Acting State Coordinator, HUD-Birmingham Office, Suite 300, Beacon Ridge Tower, 600 Beacon Parkway West, Birmingham, AL 35209-3144; 205-290-7617.

Caribbean Regional Office, Rosa Villalonga, Acting State Coordinator, HUD-Caribbean Office, New Jan Juan Office Building, 159 Carlos E. Chardon Ave., San Juan, PR 00918-1804; 809-766-6121.

Columbia Regional Office, Ted B. Freeman, Acting State Coordinator, HUD-Columbia Office, Strom Thurmond Federal Building, 1835 Assembly St., Columbia, SC 29201-2480; 803-765-5592.

Coral Gables Regional Office, Orlando L. Lorie, Acting Area Coordinator, HUD-Coral Gables Office, Gables One Tower, 1320 S. Dixie Highway, Coral Gables, FL 33146-2911; 305-662-4500.

Greensboro Regional Office, Larry J. Parker, Acting State Coordinator, HUD-Greensboro Office, Koger Building, 2306 W. Meadowview Rd., Greensboro, NC 27407-2707; 919-547-4001.

Jackson Regional Office, Sandra Freeman, Acting State Coordinator, HUD-Jackson Office, Dr. A.H. McCoy Federal Building, 100 W. Capitol St., Room 910, Jackson, MS 39269-1096; 601-965-5308.

Jacksonville Regional Office, James T. Chaplin, Acting Area, Coordinator, HUD-Jacksonville Office, Suite 2200, Southern Bell Tower, 301 W. Bay St., Jacksonville, FL 32202-5121; 904-232-2626.

Knoxville Regional Office, Mark Brezina, Acting Area Coordinator, HUD-Knoxville Office, Third Floor, John J. Duncan Federal Bldg., 710 Locust St., SW, Knoxville, TN 37902-2526; 615-545-4384.

Louisville Regional Office, Verna V. Van Ness, Acting State Coordinator, HUD-Louisville Office, 601 W. Broadway, P.O. Box 1044, Louisville, KY 40201-1044; 502-582-5251.

Memphis Regional Office, Bob Atkins, Acting State Coordinator, HUD-Memphis Office, One Memphis Place, 200 Jefferson Ave., Suite 1200, Memphis, TN 38103-2335; 901-544-3367.

Miami/South Dade Regional Office, Otis Pitts, Jr., Acting State Coordinator, HUD-Miami/South Dade Office, 10710 SW 211 St., Miami, FL 33189; 305-238-2851.

Nashville Regional Office, John H. Fisher, Acting State Coordinator, HUD-Nashville Office, 251 Cumberland Bend Dr., Suite 200, Nashville, TN 37228-1803; 615-736-5213.

Orlando Regional Office, M. Jeanette Porter, Acting Area Coordinator, HUD-Orlando Office, Langley Building, 3751 Maguire Blvd., Suite 270, Orlando, FL 32803-3032; 407-648-6441.

Tampa Regional Office, George A. Milburn, Jr., Acting Area Coordinator, HUD-Tampa Office, Timberlake Federal Building Annex, 501 E. Polk St., Suite 700, Tampa, FL 33602-3945; 813-228-2501.

Midwest Area
Chicago Regional Office, Edwin Eisendrath, Secretary's Representative, HUD-Chicago Office, Ralph Metcalfe Federal Building, 77 W. Jackson Blvd., Chicago, IL 60604; 312-353-5680.

Cincinnati Regional Office, William Harris, Acting Area Coordinator, HUD-Cincinnati Office, Room 9002, Federal Office Building, 550 Main St., Cincinnati, OH 45202-3253; 513-684-2884.

Cleveland Regional Office, Philip Giaconia, Acting Area Coordinator, HUD-Cleveland Office, Fifth Floor, Renaissance Building, 1350 Euclid Ave., Cleveland, OH 44115-1815; 216-522-4065.

Columbus Regional Office, Robert W. Dolin, Acting State Coordinator, HUD-Columbus Office, 200 N. High St., Columbus, OH 43215-2499; 614-469-5737.

Detroit Regional Office, Harry I. Sharrott, Acting State Coordinator, HUD-Detroit Office, Patrick V. McNamara Federal Building, 477 Michigan Ave., Detroit, MI 48226-2592; 313-226-7900.

Flint Regional Office, Gary T. LeVine, Acting Area Coordinator, HUD-Flint Office, Suite 200, 605 N. Saginaw St., Flint, MI 48502-1953; 313-766-5112.

Grand Rapids Regional Office, Ronald Weston, Acting Area Coordinator, HUD-Grand Rapids Office, 2922 Fuller Ave., NE, Grand Rapids, MI 49505-3499; 616-456-2100.

Indianapolis Regional Office, J. Nicholas Shelley, Acting State Coordinator, HUD-Indianapolis Office, 151 N. Delaware St., Indianapolis, IN 46204-2526; 317-226-6303.

Milwaukee Regional Office, Delbert F. Reynolds, Acting State Coordinator, HUD-Milwaukee Office, Henry S. Reuss Federal Plaza, 310 W. Wisconsin Ave., Suite 1380, Milwaukee, WI 53203-2289; 414-297-3214.

Minneapolis-St. Paul Regional Office, Thomas Feeney, Acting State Coordinator, HUD-Minneapolis-St. Paul Office, 220 Second St., South, Minneapolis, MN 55401-2195; 612-370-3000.

Springfield Regional Office, William Fattic, Acting Area Coordinator, HUD-Springfield Office, Suite 206, 509 W. Capitol St., Springfield, IL 62704-1906; 217-492-4085.

Southwest Area
Fort Worth Regional Office, Stephen Weatherford, Secretary's Representative, HUD-Fort Worth Office, 1600 Throckmorton, P.O. Box 2905, Fort Worth, TX 76113; 817-885-5401.

Albuquerque Regional Office, Michael R. Griego, Acting State Coordinator, HUD-Albuquerque Office, 625 Truman St. NW, Albuquerque, NM 87110-6443; 505-262-6463.

Dallas Regional Office, Acting Area Coordinator, HUD-Room 860, 525 Griffin St., Dallas, TX 75202-5007; 214-767-8359.

Houston Regional Office, George Rodriguez, Area Coordinator, HUD-Houston Office, Suite 200, Norfolk Tower, 2211 Norfolk, Houston, TX 77098-4096; 713-653-3274.

Little Rock Regional Office, John T. Suskie, Acting State Coordinator, HUD-Little Rock Office, Suite 900, TCBY Tower, 425 W. Capitol Ave., Little Rock, AR 72201-3488; 501-324-5931.

Lubbock Regional Office, Henry E. Whitney, Acting Area Coordinator, HUD-Lubbock Office, Federal Office Building, 1205 Texas Ave., Lubbock, TX 79401-4093; 806-743-7265.

New Orleans Regional Office, Robert Vasquez, Acting State Coordinator, HUD-New Orleans Office, Fisk Federal Building, 1661 Canal St., New Orleans, LA 70112-1887; 504-589-7200.

Oklahoma Regional Office, Edwin I. Gardner, Acting State Coordinator, HUD-Oklahoma City Office, Murrah Federal Bldg., 200 NW 5th St., Oklahoma, OK 73102-3202; 405-231-4181.

San Antonio Regional Office, A. Cynthia Leon, Acting Area Coordinator, HUD-San Antonio Office, Washington Square Building, 800 Dolorosa St., San Antonio, TX 78207-4563; 512-229-6800.

Shreveport Regional Office, Ben Wiley, Acting Area Coordinator, HUD-Shreveport Office, Suite 1510, 401 Edwards St., Shreveport, LA 71101-3107; 318-266-5385.

Tulsa Regional Office, James Colgan, Acting Area Coordinator, HUD-Tulsa Office, Suite 110, Boston Place, 1516 S. Boston Ave., Tulsa, OK 74119-4032; 918-581-7435.

Great Plains Area
Kansas City Regional Office, Joseph O'Hern, Secretary's Rep., HUD-Kansas City Office, Room 200, Gateway Tower II, 400 State Ave., Kansas City, KS 66101; 913-551-5462.

Des Moines Regional Office, William McNarney, Acting State Coordinator, HUD-Des Moines Office, Room 239, Federal Building, 210 Walnut St., Des Moines, IA 50309-2155; 515-284-4512.

Omaha Regional Office, Roger M. Massey, Acting State Coordinator, HUD-Omaha Office, Executive Tower Centre, 10909 Mill Valley Rd., Omaha, NE 68154-3955; 402-492-3101.

St. Louis Regional Office, Kenneth G. Lange, Acting Area Coordinator, HUD-St. Louis Office, Robert A. Young Federal Bldg., Third Floor, 1222 Spruce St., St. Louis, MO 63103-2836; 314-539-6560.

Rocky Mountain Area

Denver Regional Office, Anthony Hernandez, Secretary's Representative, HUD-Denver Office, 633 17th St., Denver, CO 80202; 303-672-5440.

Casper Regional Office, William Garrett, Acting State Coordinator, HUD-Casper Office, 4225 Federal Office Building, 100 E.B. St., P.O. Box 120, Casper, WY 82602-1918; 307-261-5252.

Fargo Regional Office, Keith Elliott, Acting State Coordinator, HUD-Fargo Office, Federal Building, 657 2nd Ave. North, P.O. Box 2483, Fargo, ND 58108-2483; 701-239-5136.

Helena Regional Office, Gerard Boone, Acting State Coordinator, HUD-Helena Office, Room 340, Federal Office Bldg., Drawer 10095, 301 South Park, Helena, MT 59626-0095; 406-449-5205.

Salt Lake City Regional Office, Richard Bell, Acting State Coordinator, HUD-Salt Lake City Office, 257 Tower, Suite 550, 257 E. 200 South, Salt Lake City, UT 84111-2048; 801-524-5379.

Sioux Falls Regional Office, Don Olson, Acting State Coordinator, HUD-Sioux Falls Office, Suite I-201, 2400 W. 49th St., Sioux Falls, SD 57105-6558; 605-330-4223.

Pacific/Hawaii Area

San Francisco Regional Office, Arthur Agnos, Secretary's Representative, HUD-San Francisco Office, Philip Burton Federal Building and U.S. Courthouse, 450 Golden Gate Ave., P.O. Box 36003, San Francisco, CA 94102; 415-556-4752.

Fresno Regional Office, Willie Mae Haskin, Acting Area Coordinator, HUD-Fresno Office, Suite 138, 1630 E. Shaw Ave., Fresno, CA 93710-8193; 209-487-5033.

Honolulu Regional Office, Gordon Y. Furutani, Acting State Coordinator, HUD-Honolulu Office, Suite 500, Seven Waterfront Plaza, 500 Ala Moana Blvd., Honolulu, HI 96813-4918; 808-541-1323.

Los Angeles Regional Office, Charles Ming, Acting Area Coordinator, HUD-Los Angeles Office, 1615 W. Olympic Blvd., Los Angeles, CA 90015-3801; 213-251-7122.

Las Vegas Regional Office, Benjamin Davis, Acting State Coordinator, HUD-Las Vegas Office, 1500 E. Tropicana Ave., Suite 205, Las Vegas, NV 89119-6516; 702-388-6500.

Phoenix Regional Office, Dwight A. Peterson, Acting State Coordinator, HUD-Phoenix Office, Two Arizona Center, Suite 1600, 400 N. 5th St., Phoenix, AZ 85004-2361; 602-379-4434.

Reno Regional Office, Andrew D. Whitten, Jr., Acting Area Coordinator, HUD-Reno Office, 1575 DeLucchi Lane, Suite 114, P.O. Box 30050, Reno, NV 89502-6581; 702-784-5356.

Sacramento Regional Office, Paul Pradia, Acting Area Coordinator, HUD-Sacramento Office, Suite 200, 777 12th St., Sacramento, CA 95814-1977; 916-551-1351.

San Diego Regional Office, Charles J. Wilson, Acting Area Coordinator, HUD-San Diego Office, Suite 300, Mission City Corporate Center, 2365 Northside Dr., San Diego, CA 92108-2712; 619-557-5310.

Santa Ana Regional Office, Samuel Sandoval, Acting Area Coordinator, HUD-Santa Ana Office, 3 Hutton Centre, Suite 500, Santa Ana, CA 92707-5764; 714-957-7333.

Tucson Regional Office, Sharon Atwell, Acting Area Coordinator, HUD-Tucson Office, Suite 700, Security Pacific Bank Plaza, 33 N. Stone Ave., Tucson, AZ 85701-1467; 602-670-6237.

Northwest/Alaska Area

Seattle Regional Office, Bob Santos, Secretary's Representative, HUD-Seattle Office, Seattle Federal Office Building, 909 First Ave., Suite 200, Seattle, WA 98104; 206-220-5101.

Anchorage Regional Office, Arlene Patton, Acting State Coordinator, HUD-Anchorage Office, Suite 401, University Plaza Building, 949 E. 36th Ave., Anchorage, AK 99508-4135; 917-271-4170.

Boise Regional Office, Gary Gillespie, Acting State Coordinator, HUD-Boise Office, Suite 220, Park IV, 800 Park Blvd., Boise, ID 83712-7743; 208-334-1990.

Portland Regional Office, Richard C. Brinck, Acting State Coordinator, HUD-Portland Office, 520 SW 6th Ave., Portland, OR 97204-1596; 503-326-2561.

Spokane Regional Office, Gary Rogers, Acting Area Coordinator, HUD-Spokane Office, 8th Floor East, Farm Credit Bank Building, W. 601 First Ave., Spokane, WA 99204-0317; 509-353-2510.

* Your State Can Get You Money

American Communities
Information Center
Office of Community Planning and
  Development
P.O. Box 7189
Gaithersburg, MD 20898-7189
800-998-9999

The State and Small Cities Program is the second largest component of the Community Development Block Grant (CDBG) program and aids communities that do not qualify for assistance under the CDBG Entitlement program. The grants assist communities in carrying out a wide range of community development activities directed toward neighborhood revitalization, economic development, and the provision of improved community facilities and services. Funds can also by used to provide assistance to public and private organizations, agencies, and other entities (including non-profits and for-profits) to facilitate economic development in supporting micro-enterprise. Funds can be used to establish credit (direct loans and loan guarantees, revolving loan funds, and more) for the stabilization and expansion of micro-enterprises; provide technical assistance, advice, and business support services to owners of micro-enterprises; and provide general support to owners of micro-enterprises and organizations developing micro-enterprises. In 1994, these funds totaled $1,287,300. If you are an interested citizen, you should contact your local officials for more information. If your local government or state officials cannot answer your questions, you may wish to contact the HUD Field Office that serves your area (look for the office closest to you from the list in the item above). Be aware that the state administers the program and determines which local projects receive funding.

* Public Housing Entrepreneurs

U.S. Department of Housing and Urban
    Development
Deputy Director of Resident Initiatives
451 Seventh St., SW, Room 4112
Washington, DC 20410
202-619-8201

Call yourself a handyman and get money to fix up your neighborhood. Money is set aside to give to public housing residents to modernize existing public housing projects. The money can also be used to provide residents with on-the-job training in construction and contractor related trades. It's called the Comprehensive Grant Program, and is available to Public Housing Agencies and Indian Housing Authorities of 250 housing units or more, which includes 897 public housing agencies nationwide. Contact your local Public Housing Authority for more information or you may contact the office listed above.

* Microloans

U.S. Small Business Administration (SBA)
409 Third St., SW, Suite 8300
Washington, DC 20416
202-205-6490

The U.S. Small Business Administration's Microloan Program was developed for those times when just a small loan can make the difference. Under this program, loans range from less than $100 to a maximum of $25,000. SBA has made these funds available to non-profit organizations for the purpose of lending to small business and they can also provide intense management and technical assistance. A microloan must be repaid on the shortest term possible — no longer than six years — depending on the earnings of the business. The interest rates on these loans will be competitive and based on the cost of money to the inter-mediary lender. This program is available in 44 states. To learn which non-profit organizations in your area offer this program call the Small Business Answer Desk at 800-8-ASK-SBA.

Approved Microloan Participants

Lenders
Alabama
Elmore Community Action Committee, Inc., 1011 W. Tallassee, P.O. Drawer H, Wetumpka, AL 36092. Contact: Marion D. Dunlap, 205-567-4361. Service Area: Autauga, Elmore and Montgomery counties.

Alaska
Community Enterprise Development Corporation of Alaska, 1577 C St. Plaza, Suite 304, Anchorage, AK 99501. Contact: Perry R. Eaton, 907-274-5400. Service Area: Statewide.

Arizona
Chicanos Por La Causa, Inc., 1112 E. Buckeye Rd., Phoenix, AZ 85034. Contact: Pete Garcia, 602-257-0700. Service Area: Urban areas of Maricopa and Pima counties, Graham and Gila counties (including Point of Pines Reservation and the Southwestern area of Fort Apache Reservation), Coconino and Mohave counties (including the Kaibab, Havasupai, and Hualapai Reservations and the Western portions of the Navajo and Hopi Reservations), Yavapai and La Paz counties

PPEP Housing Development Corp/, Micro Industry Credit Rural Organization, 802 E. 46th St., Tucson, AZ 85713. Contact: John D. Arnold, 602-622-3553. Service Area: Cochise, Santa Cruz, rural Maricopa, rural Pinal and rural Yuma counties.

Arkansas

Arkansas Enterprise Group, 605 Main St., Suite 203, Arkadelphia, AR 71923. Contact: Brian Kelley, 501-246-9739. Service Area: Southern portion of the state including Arkansas, Ashley, Bradley, Calhoun, Chicot, Clark, Cleveland, Columbia, Dallas, Desha, Drew, Garland, Grant, Hempstead, Hot Spring, Howard, Jefferson Lafayette, Lincoln, Little River, Miller, Monroe, Montgomery, Nevasa, Ouachita, Phillips, Pike, Polk, Pulaski, Saline, Sevier, and Union counties.

Delta Community Development Corp., 675 Eaton Rd., P.O. Box 852, Forrest City, AR 72335. Contact: Michael Jackson, 501-633-9113. Service Area: Cross, Crittenden, Monroe, Lee, and St. Francis counties.

White River Planning and Development District, Inc., 1652 White Dr., P.O. Box 2396, Batesville, AR 72503. Contact: Van C. Thomas, 501-793-5233. Service Area: Cleburne, Fulton, Independence, Izard, Jackson, Sharp, Stone, Van Buren, White, and Woodruff counties.

California

Arcata Economic Development Corporation, 100 Ericson Ct., Suite 100, Arcata, CA 95521. Contact: Kathleen E. Moxon, 707-822-4616. Service Area: Del Norte, Humboldt, Mendocino, Siskiyou, and Trinity counties.

Center for Southeast Asian Refugee Resettlement, 875 O'Farrell St., San Francisco, CA 94109. Contact: Vu-Duc Vuong, 415-885-2743. Service Area: Alameda, Contra Costa, Marin, Merced, Sacramento, San Francisco, San Joaquin, San Mateo, Santa Clara, and Stanislaus counties.

Coalition for Women's Economic Development, 315 W. Ninth St., Suite 705, Los Angeles, CA 90015. Contact: Mari Riddle, 213-489-4995. Service Area: Los Angeles county.

Valley Rural Development Corporation, 3417 W. Shaw, Suite 100, Fresno, CA 93711. Contact: Michael E. Foley, 209-271-9030. Service Area: Fresno, Kings, Kern, Stanislaus, Madera, Mariposa, Merced, Tuolumne, and Tulare counties.

Colorado

Greater Denver Local Development Corp., 1981 Blake St., Suite 406, P.O. Box 2135, Denver, CO 80206. Contact: Cecilia H. Prinster, 303-296-9535. Service Area: City of Denver, and Adams, Arapahoe, Boulder, Denver, and Jefferson counties.

Region 10 LEAP, Inc., P.O. Box 849, Montrose, CO 81402. Contact: Stan Broome, 303-249-2436. Service Area: West Central area including Delta, Gunnison, Hinsdale, Montrose, Ouray, and San Miguel counties.

Connecticut

New Haven Community Investment Corp., 809 Chapel St., 2nd Floor, New Haven, CT 06510. Contact: Salvatore J. Brancati, Jr., 203-776-6172. Service Area: Statewide.

Delaware

Wilmington Economic Development Corp., 605-A Market St. Mall, Wilmington, DE 19801. Contact: Edwin H. Nutter, Jr., 302-571-9088. Service Area: New Castle County, in the cities of Wilmington, Newark, New Castle, Middletown, Odessa, and Townsend.

District of Columbia

ARCH Development Corporation, 1227 Good Hope Rd. SE, Washington, DC 20020. Contact: Duane Gautier, 202-889-5023. Service Area: Portions of the District of Columbia commonly referred to as Adams Morgan, Mount Pleasant and Anacostia, Congress Heights, Columbia Heights, and 14th St. Corridor.

H Street Development Corporation, 611 H St., NE, Washington, DC 20002. Contact: William J. Barrow, 202-544-8353. Service Area: Portions of the District of Columbia including specific areas of the Northeast, Southeast and Northwest quadrants.

Florida

Community Equity Investments Inc., 302 N. Barcelona St., Pensacola, FL 32501. Contact: Daniel R. Horvath, 904-444-2234. Service Area: Western Panhandle including Bay, Calhoun, Escambia, Gadsden, Gulf, Jackson, Holmes, Liberty, Leon, Franklin, Wakulla, Walton, Washington, Okaloosa, and Santa Rosa counties.

United Gainesville Community Development Corporation, Inc., 214 W. University Ave., Suite D, P.O. Box 2518, Gainesville, FL 32602. Contact: Vian M. Cockerham, 904-376-8891. Service Area: North Central section including Alachua, Bradford, Columbia, Dixie, Gichrist, Hamilton, Jefferson, LaFayette, Levy, Madison, Marion, Putman, Suwanee, Taylor, and Union counties.

Georgia

Fulton County Development Corp., dba Greater Atlanta Small Business Project, 10 Park Place South, Suite 305, Atlanta, GA 30303. Contact: Maurice S. Coakley, 404-659-5955. Service Area: Fulton, Dekalb, Cobb, Gwinnett, Fayette, Clayton, Henry, Douglas, and Rockdale counties.

Small Business Assistance Corporation, 31 W. Congress St., Suite 100, Savannah, GA 31401. Contact: Tony O'Reily, 912-232-4700. Service Area: Chatham, Effingham, Bryan, Bulloch, and Liberty counties.

Hawaii

The Immigrant Center, 720 N. King St., Honolulu, HI 96817. Contact: Patrician Brandt, 808-845-3918. Service Area: Island of O'ahu within the city and county of Honolulu.

Idaho

Panhandle Area Council, 11100 Airport Dr., Hayden, ID 83835-9743. Contact: Jim Deffenbaugh, 208-772-0584. Service Area: Northern Panhandle including Benewah, Bonner, Boundary, Kotenai, and Shoshone counties.

Illinois

Greater Sterling Development Corporation, 1741 Industrial Dr., Sterling, IL 61081. Contact: Reid Nolte, 815-625-5255. Service Area: City of Sterling and Whiteside and Lee counties.

Illinois Development Finance Authority, 5310 Sears Tower, 233 S. Wacker, Chicago, IL 60606. Contact: Philip S. Howe, 312-793-5586. Service Area: Statewide with the exceptions of Peoria, Tazwell, Woodford, Whiteside, and Lee counties, the city of Sterling, and those portions of Chicago currently served by WSEP.

The Economic Council for the Peoria Area, 124 SW Adams St., Suite 300, Peoria, IL 61602. Contact: Michael Kuhns, 309-676-7500. Service Area: Peoria, Tazwell, and Woodford counties.

The Neighborhood Institute and Women's Self Employment Project, 166 W. Washington St., Suite 730, Chicago, IL 60602. Contact: Connie Evans, President, 312-606-8255. Service Area: Portions of the City of Chicago.

Indiana
Eastside Community Investments Inc., 26 N. Arsenal Ave., Indianapolis, IN 46201. Contact: Dennis J. West, 317-637-7300. Service Area: City of Indianapolis.

Metro Small Business Assistance Corp., 1 NW Martin Luther King Jr. Blvd., Evansville, IN 47708-1869. Contact: Debra A. Lutz, 812-426-5857. Service Area: Vanderburgh, Posey, Gibson, and Warrick counties.

Iowa
Siouxland Economic Development Corporation, 400 Orpheum Electric Building, P.O. Box 447, Sioux City, IA 51102. Contact: Kenneth A. Beekley, 712-279-6286. Service Area: Cherokee, Ida, Monoma, Plymouth, Sioux, and Woodbury counties.

Kansas
South Central Kansas Economic Development District, Inc., 151 N. Volutsia, Wichita, KS 67214. Contact: Jack E. Alumbaugh, 316-683-4422. Service Area: Butler, Chautauqua, Cowley, Elk, Greenwood, Harper, Harvey, Kingman, Marion, McPherson, Reno, Rice, Sedgwick and Sumner counties.

Center for Business Innovations, Inc., 4747 Troost Ave., Kansas City, MO 64110. Contact: Robert J. Sherwood, 816-561-8567. Service Area: Wyandotte, Johnson, Kansas City, and Leavenworth.

Kentucky
Kentucky Highlands Investment Corporation, 362 Old Whitley Rd., London, KY 40741. Contact: Jerry A. Rickett, 606-864-5175. Service Area: Bell Clay, Clinton, Harlan, Jackson, Knox, Laurel, McCreary, Pulaski, Rockcastle, Wayne, and Whitley counties.

Purchase Area Development District, 1002 Medical Dr., P.O. Box 588, Mayfield, KY 42066. Contact: Henry A. Hodges, 502-247-7171. Service Area: Western Kentucky including Ballard, Calloway, Carlisle, Futon, Graves, Hickman, McCracken, and Marshall counties.

Louisiana
Greater Jennings Chamber of Commerce, 414 Cary Ave., P.O. Box 1209, Jennings, LA 70546. Contact: Jerry Arceneaux, 318-824-0933. Service Area: Jeff Davis Parish.

Maine
Coastal Enterprises, Inc., P.O. Box 268, Water St., Wiscasset, ME 04578. Contact: Ronald L. Phillips, 207-882-7552. Service Area: Statewide excluding Aroostook, Piscataquis, Washington, Oxford, Penobscot, and Hancock counties.

Northern Maine Regional Planning Commission, 2 S. Main St., P.O. Box 779, Caribou, ME 04736. Contact: Robert P. Clark, 207-498-8736. Service Area: Aroostook, Piscataquis, Washington, Penobscot, and Hancock counties.

Community Concepts, Inc., 35 Market Sq., P.O. Box 278, South Parris, ME 04281. Contact: Charleen M. Chase, 207-743-7716. Service Area: Oxford County.

Maryland
Council for Equal Business Opportunity, Inc., The Park Plaza, 800 N. Charles St., Suite 300, Baltimore, MD 21201. Contact: Michael Gaines, 410-576-2326. Service Area: City of Baltimore and Ann Arundel, Baltimore, Carroll, Harford, and Howard counties.

Massachusetts
Economic Development Industrial Corporation of Lynn, 37 Central Sq., 3rd Floor, Lynn, MA 01901. Contact: Peter M. DeVeau, 617-592-2361. Service Area: City of Lynn.

Jobs for Fall River, Inc., One Government Center, Fall River, MA 02722. Contact: Paul L. Vigeant, 508-324-2620. Service Area: City of Fall River.

Springfield Business Development Fund, 26 Court St., Room 222, Springfield, MA 01103. Contact: James Asselin, 413-787-6050. Service Area: City of Springfield.

Western Massachusetts Enterprise Fund, 324 Wells St., Greenfield, MA 01301. Contact: Christopher Sikes, 413-774-7204. Service Area: Berkshire, Franklin counties, the towns of Chester and Chicopes within Hampden County, the towns of Athol, Petersham, Phillipston and Royalston within Worcester County and the following towns within Hampshire County: Amherst, Chesterfield, Cummington, Easthampton, Goshen, Hadley, Huntington, Middlefield, Northampton, Plainfield, Westhampton, Williamsburg, and Worthington.

Michigan
Ann Arbor Community Development Corp., 2008 Hogback Rd., Suite 2A, Ann Arbor, MI 48105. Contact: Michelle Richards Vasquez, 313-677-1400. Service Area: Washtenaw County.

Detroit Economic Growth Corporation, 150 W. Jefferson, Suite 1500, Detroit, MI 48226. Contact: Robert W. Spencer, 313-963-2940. Service Area: City of Detroit.

Flint Community Development Corp., 877 E. Fifth Ave., Building C-1, Flint, MI 48503. Contact: Bobby J. Wells, 313-239-5847. Service Area: Genessee County.

Northern Economic Initiatives Corp., 1009 W. Ridge St., Marquette, MI 49855. Contact: Richard Anderson, 906-228-5571. Service Area: Upper Peninsula including Alger, Baraga, Chippewa, Delta, Dickinson, Gogebic, Houghton, Iron, Keewenaw, Luce, Macinac, Marquette, Menonimee, Ontonagon, and Schoolcraft counties.

Minnesota
Northeast Entrepreneur Fund, Inc., Olcott Plaza, Suite 140, 820 Ninth St., North, Virginia, MN 55792. Contact: Mary Mathews, 218-749-4191. Service Area: Koochiching, Itasca, St. Louis, Aitkin, Carlton, Cook and Lake counties.

Women Venture, 2324 University Ave., St. Paul, MN 55114. Contact: Kay Gudmestad, 612-646-3808. Service Area: Cities of Minneapolis and St. Paul and Andra, Carver, Chicago, Dakota, Hennepin, Isanti, Ramsey, Scott, Washington, and Wright counties.

Minneapolis Consortium of Community Developers, 1808 Riverside Ave., Minneapolis, MN 55454-1035. Contact: Karen Reid, 612-338-8729. Service Area: Portions of the city of Minneapolis.

Northwest Minnesota Initiative Fund, 722 Paul Bunyan Dr., NW, Bemidji, MN 56601. 218-759-2057. Service Area: Beltrami, Clearwater, Hubbard, Kittsson, Lake of the Woods, Mahnomen, Marshall, Norman, Pennington, Polk, Red Lake, and Rousseau counties.

Mississippi
Delta Foundation, 819 Main St., Greenville, MS 38701. Contact: Harry J. Bowie, 601-335-5291. Service Area: Statewide excluding Issaquena, Sharkey, Humphreys, Madison, Leake, Kemper, Copiah, Hinds, Rankin, Newton, Smith, Jasper, Clarke, Jones, Wayne, and Greene counties.

Friends of Children of Mississippi, Inc., 4880 McWillie Circle, Jackson, MS 39206. Contact: Marvin Hogan, 601-362-1541. Service Area: Issaquena, Sharkey, Humphreys, Madison, Leake, Kemper, Copiah, Hinds, Rankin, Newton, Smith, Jasper, Clarke, Jones, Wayne, and Greene counties.

Missouri
Center for Business Innovations, Inc., 4747 Troost Ave., Kansas City, MO 64110. Contact: Robert J. Sherwood, 816-561-8567. Service Area: Statewide.

Montana
Capital Opportunities/District IX Human Resource Development Council, Inc., 321 E. Main St., Suite 300, Bozeman, MT 59715. Contact: Jeffery Rupp, 406-587-4486. Service Area: Gallatin, Park and Meagher counties.

Women's Opportunity and Resource Development, Inc., 127 N. Higgins Ave., Missoula, MT 59802. Contact: Kelly Rosenleaf, 406-543-3550. Service Area: Lake, Mineral, Missoula, Ravalli, and Sanders counties.

Nebraska
Rural Enterprise Assistance Project, P.O. Box 406, Walthill,

NE 68067. Contact: Don Ralston, 402-846-5428. Service Area: Boone, Brown, Burt, Cass, Cherry, Colfax, Custer, Dixon, Gage, Greeley, Jefferson, Johnson, Keya Paha, Knox, Lancaster, McPherson, Nance, Nemaha, Pierce, Rock, Saline, Saunders, Seward, Thurston, and Wayne counties.

West Central Nebraska Development District, Inc., 710 N. Spruce St., P.O. Box 599, Ogailala, NE 69153. Contact: Ronald J. Radil, 308-284-6077. Service Area: Arthur, Chase, Dawson, Dundy, Frontier, Furnas, Gosper, Grant, Hayes, Hitchcock, Hooker, Keith, Lincoln, Logan, Perkins, Red Willow and Thomas counties.

Nevada
Nevada Women's Fund, 210 S. Sierra St., Suite 100, Reno, NV 89501. Contact: Fritsi H. Ericson, 702-786-2335. Service Area: Statewide.

New Hampshire
Institute for Cooperative Community Development, Inc., 2500 N. River Rd., Manchester, NH 03106. Contact: Don Mason, 603-644-3103. Service Area: Statewide excluding Grafton, Carol and Coos counties.

Northern Community Investment Corp., c/o 20 Main St., St. Johnsbury, VT 05819. Contact: Carl J. Garbelotti, 802-748-5101. Service Area: Grafton, Carol and Coos counties.

New Jersey
Trenton Business Assistance Corp., Division of Economic Development, 319 E. State St., Trenton, NJ 08608-1866. Contact: James Harveson, 609-989-3509. Service Area: Portions of the city of Trenton.

Greater Newark Business Development Consortium, One Newark Center, 22nd Floor, Newark, NJ 07102-5265. Contact: Henry Hayman, 201-242-6237. Service Area: Bergen, Essex, Hudson, Middlesex, Monmouth, Morris, Passaic, and Somerset counties with the exception of the city of Jersey City.

Union County Economic Dev. Corp., Liberty Hall Corporate Center, 1085 Morris Ave., Suite 531, Union, NJ 07083. Contact: Maureen Tinen, 908-527-1166. Service Area: Union County.

Jersey City Economic Development Corp., 601 Pavonia Ave., Jersey City, NJ 07306. Contact: Thomas D. Ahearn, 201-420-7755. Service Area: City of Jersey City.

New Mexico
Women's Economic Self Sufficiency Team, 414 Silver South West, Albuquerque, NM 87102-3239. Contact: Agnes Noonan, 505-848-4760. Service Area: Statewide.

New York
Adirondack Economic Development Corporation, Trudeau Rd., P.O. Box 747, Saranac Lake, NY 12983. Contact: Ernest Hohmeyer. 518-891-5523. Service Area: Clinton, Essex, Franklin, Fulton, Hamilton, Herkimer, Jefferson, Lewis, Oneida, Oswego, St. Lawrence, Saratoga, Warren, and Washington counties.

Hudson Development Corp., 444 Warren St., Hudson, Ny 12534. Contact: Lynda S. Davidson, 518-828-3373. Service Area: Columbia county.

Manhattan Borough Development Corp., 15 Park Row, Suite 510, New York, NY 10038. Contact: Patricia Swann, 212-791-3660. Service Area: The borough of Manhattan.

Rural Opportunities, Inc., 339 East Ave., Rochester, NY 14604. Contact: W. Lee Beaulac, 716-546-7180. Service Area: Allegheny, Cattarauqua, Cayuga, Chatauqua, Erie, Genessee, Livingston, Niagara, Ontario, Orleans, Senece, Steuben, Wayne, Wyoming, and Yates counties.

North Carolina
Self-Help Ventures Fund, 413 E. Chapel Hill St., Durham, NC 27701. Contact: Robert Schall, 919-956-8526. Service Area: Statewide.

North Dakota
Lake Agassiz Regional Council, 417 Main Ave., Fargo, ND 58103. Contact: Irvin D. Rustad, 701-239-5373. Service Area: Statewide.

Ohio
Enterprise Development Corporation (formerly the Athens Small Business Center, Inc.), 900 E. State St., Athens, OH 45701. Contact: Karen A. Patton, 614-592-1188. Service Area: Adams, Ashland, Athens, Belmont, Brown, Carrol, Columbiana, Coshocton, Gallia, Guernsey, Harrison, Highland, Holmes, Jackson, Jefferson, Knox, Lawrence, Meigs, Monroe, Morgan, Muskinghum, Nocking, Noble, Perry, Pike, Ross, Scioto, Tuscarawas, Vinton and Washington counties.

Columbus Countywide Development Corp., 941 Chatham Lane, Suite 207, Columbus, OH 43221. Contact: Mark Barbash, 614-645-6171. Service Area: Franklin County and the City of Columbus.

Hamilton County Development Co., Inc., 1776 Mentor Ave., Cincinnati, OH 45212. Contact: David K. Main, 513-632-8292. Service Area: City of Cincinnati and Adams, Brown, Bugler, Clermont, Clinton, Highland, and Warren counties.

Women's Entrepreneurial Growth Organization of NE Ohio, 58 W. Center St., Suite 228, Akron, OH 44308. Contact: Susan Hale, 216-535-4523. Service Area: Ashtabula, Cuyahoga, Geauga, Lake, Lorain, Mahoning, medina, Portage, Stark, Summit, Trumbull, Wayne.

Oklahoma
Rural Enterprises, Inc., 422 Cessna St., Durant, OK 74701. Contact: Sherry Harlin, 405-924-5094. Service Area: Statewide.

Tulsa Economic Development Corp., 130 N. Greenwood Ave., Suite C, Tulsa, OK 74120. Contact: Frank F. McCrady III, 918-585-8332. Service Area: Adair, Canadian, Cherokee, Cleveland, Craig, Creek, Delaware, Haskell, Hayes, Hughes, Kay, Latimer, Leflore, Lincoln, Logan, McIntosh, Muskogee, Noble, Nowata, Okfuskee, Oklahoma, Okmulgee, Osage, Ottawa, Pawnee, Payne, Pittsburg, Pottawatomie, Rogers,

Seminole, Sequoyah, Wagoner, Washington, and Wayne counties including the city of Tulsa.

Oregon
Cascades West Financial Services, Inc., 408 SW Monroe St., Corvallis, OR 97333. Contact: Deborah L. Wright, 503-757-6854. Service Area: Benton, Clackamas, Hood River, Jefferson, Lane, Lincoln, Linn, Marion, Multnomah, Polk, Tillamook, Wasco, Washington, Yamhill.

Pennsylvania
The Ben Franklin Technology Center of Southeastern Pennsylvania, 3624 Market St., Philadelphia, PA 19104-2615. Contact: Phillip A. Singerman, 215-382-0380. Service Area: Bucks, Chester, Delaware, Montgomery, and Philadelphia counties.

The Washington County Council on Economic Development, 703 Courthouse Sq., Washington, PA 15301. Contact: Malcolm L. Morgan, 412-228-6816. Service Area: Southwestern area of Pennsylvania including Greene, Fayette, and Washington counties.

York County Industrial Development Corp., One Market Way East, York, PA 17401. Contact: David B. Carver, 717-846-8879. Service Area: York County.

Puerto Rico
Corporation for the Economic Development of the City of San Juan, Avenue Munos Rivera, #1127, Rio Piedras, PR 00926. Contact: Jesus M. Rivera Viera, 809-756-5080. Service Area: Territory wide.

South Carolina
Charleston Citywide Local Development Corporation, 496 King St., Charleston, SC 29403. Contact: Sharon Brennan, 803-724-3796. Service Area: City of Charleston.

Santee Lynches Regional Development Corp., 115 N. Harvin St., 4th Floor, Sumter, SC 29151-1837. Contact: James T. Darby, Jr., 803-775-7381. Service Area: Clarendon, Kershaw, Lee and Sumter counties.

South Dakota
Northeast South Dakota Energy Conservation Corporation, 414 Third Ave., East, Sisseton, SD 57262. Contact: Arnold Petersen, 605-698-7654. Service Area: Beadle, Brown, Buffalo, Campbell, Clark, Codington, Day, Edmunds, Faulk, Grant, Hand, Hyde, Jerauld, Kingsbury, McPherson, Marshall, Miner, Potter, Roberts, Sanborn, Spink, and Walworth counties.

Tennessee
South Central Tennessee Development District, 815 S. Main St., P.O. Box 1346, Columbia, TN 38402. Contact: Joe Max Williams, 615-318-2040. Service Area: Bedford, Coffee, Franklin, Giles, Hickman, Lawrence, Lewis, Lincoln, Marshall, Maury, Moore, Perry, and Wayne counties.

Texas
Business Resource Center Incubator, 4601 N. 19th St., Waco, TX 76708. Contact: Curtis Cleveland, 817-754-8898. Service

Area: Bell, Bosque, Coryell, Falls, Hill, and McLennan counties.

San Antonio Local Development Corp., 100 Military Plaza, 4th Floor City Hall, San Antonio, TX 78205. Contact: Robert Nance, 210-299-8080. Service Area: Atascosa, Bandera, Bexar, Comal, Frio, Gillespie, Guadalupe, Karnes, Kendall, Kerr, Medina, and Wilson counties.

Southern Dallas Development Corporation, 1402 Corinth, Suite 1150, Dallas, TX 75215. Contact: Jim Reid, 214-428-7332. Service Area: Portions of the city of Dallas.

Utah
Utah Technology Finance Corporation, 177 E. 100 South, Salt Lake City, UT 84111. Contact: Todd Clark, 801-364-4346. Service Area: Carbon, Emery, Grand, Iron, Juab, Milard, Salt Lake County, San Juan, Sanpete, Sevier, Tooele, Washington, and parts of Utah and Weber counties.

Vermont
Economic Development Council of Northern Vermont, Inc., 155 Lake St., St. Albans, VT 05478. Contact: Connie Stanley-Little, 802-524-4546. Service Area: Chittenden, Franklin, Grand Isle, Lamoille, and Washington counties.

Northern Community Investments Corporation, 20 Main St., St. Johnsbury, VT 05819. Contact: Carl J. Garbelotti, 802-748-5101. Service Area: Caledonia, Essex, and Orleans counties.

Virginia
Ethiopian Community Development Council, Inc., 1038 S. Highland St., Arlington, VA 22204. Contact: Tsehaye Teferra, 703-685-0510. Service Area: Prince William, Arlington and Fairfax counties and the cities of Alexandria and Falls Church.

Business Development Centre, Inc., 147 Mill Ridge Rd., Lynchburg, VA 24502. Contact: Karen Mauch, 804-582-6100. Service Area: Amherst, Appomattox, Bedford, Campell counties, cities of Lynchburg and Bedford, and the Town of Amherst.

People, Incorporated of Southwest Virginia, 988 W. Main St., Abingdon, VA 24210. Contact: Robert G. Goldsmith, 703-628-9188. Service Area: Buchanan, Dickenson, Lee, Russell, Scott, Washington, Wise counties and the cities of Bristol and Norton.

Washington
Snohomish County Private Industry Council, 917 134th St., SW, Suite A-10, Everett, WA 98204. Contact: Emily Duncan, 206-743-9669. Service Area: Adams, Chelan, Douglas, Grant, King, Kittitas, Klickitat, Okanogan, Pierce, Skagit, Snohomish, Whatcom, and Yakima counties.

Tri-Cities Enterprise Association, 2000 Logston Blvd., Richland, WA 99352. Contact: Dallas E. Breamer, 509-375-3268. Service Area: Benton and Franklin counties.

West Virginia
Ohio Valley Industrial and Business Development Corporation,

12th and Chapline Sts., Wheeling, WV 26003. Contact: Terry Burkhart, 304-232-7722. Service Area: Marshall, Ohio, Wetzel, Brooke, Hancock, and Tyler counties.

Wisconsin
Advocap, Inc., 19 W. First St., P.O. Box 1108, Fond du Lac, WI 54936. Contact: Richard Schlimm, 414-922-7760. Service Area: Fond du Lac and Winnebago counties.

Impact Seven, Inc., 100 Digital Dr., Clear Lake, WI 54005. Contact: William Bay, 715-263-2532. Service Area: Statewide with the exceptions of Fond du Lac, Kenosha, Milwaukee, Oasukee, Racine, Walworth, Waukesha, Washington, and Winnebago counties and inner city Milwaukee.

Northwest Side Community Development Corp., 5174 N. Hopkins Ave., Milwaukee, WI 53209. Contact: Howard Snyder, 414-462-5509. Service Area: Inner city Milwaukee.

Women's Business Initiative Corporation, 3112 W. Highland Blvd., Milwaukee, WI 53208. Contact: Becky Pileggi, 414-933-3231. Service Area: Kenosha, Milwaukee, Oazukee, Racine, Walworth, Washington, and Waukesha counties.

Technical Assistance Grant Recipients
Alaska
Southeast Alaska Small Business Development Center, 400 Willoughby Ave., Suite 211, Juneau, AK 99801-1724. Contact: Charles M. Northrip, 907-463-3789. Service Area: Through SBDC system, the Alaska Panhandle.

California
Women's Initiative for Self Employment, 450 Mission St., Suite 402, San Francisco, CA 94105. Contact: Etienne LeGrand, 415-247-9473. Service Area: specified sectors of the San Francisco Bay Area.

Connecticut
American Woman's Economic Development Corporation, Plaza West Office Centers, 200 W. Main St., Suite 140, Stamford, CT 06902. Contact: Fran Polak, 203-326-7914. Service Area: SW corner of state including Ansonia, Beacon Falls, Bethel, Bridgeport, Bridgewater, Brookfield, Danbury, Darien, Derby, Easton, Fairfield, Greenwich, Milford, Monroe, New Canaan, New Fairfield, New Milford, Newtown, Norwalk, Oxford, Redding, Ridgefield, Seymour, Shelton, Sherman, Stamford, Stratford, Trumbull, Weston, Westport, and Wilton counties.

District of Columbia
American Women's Economic Development Corporation, Washington DC Regional Training Center, 1250 24th St. NW, Suite 120, Washington, DC 20037. Contact: Susan P. Bari, 202-857-0091. Service Area: District of Columbia.

Florida
Lee County Employment and Economic Development Corporation, 2121 W. First St., Rear, P.O. Box 2285, Fort Myers, FL 33902-2285. Contact: Roy H. Kennix, 813-337-2300. Service Area: Community Redevelopment Areas of Lee

County including Charleston Park, Dunbar, Harlem Heights, North Fort Myers, and State Road 80.

Illinois
Women's Business Development Center, 8 S. Michigan Ave., Suite 400, Chicago, IL 60603. Contact: Linda Darragh, 312-853-3477. Service Area: Boone, Cook, DeKalb, DuPage, Kane, Kankakee, Kendall, Lake, McHenry, Will, and Winnebago counties.

Indiana
Hoosier Valley Economic Development Corp., 1613 E. Eighth St., P.O. Box 843, Jeffersonville, IN 47131-0843. Contact: Jerry L. Stephenson, 812-288-6451. Service Area: Clark, Crawford, Floyd, Harrison, Orange, Scott, and Washington counties.

Iowa
Institute for Social and Economic Development, 1901 Broadway, Suite 313, Iowa City, IA 52240. Contact: John F. Else, 319-338-2331. Service Area: Statewide.

Kansas
Great Plains Development, Inc., 100 Military Plaza, Suite 128, P.O. Box 1116, Dodge City, KS 67801. Contact: Carlyle Kienne, 316-227-6406. Service Area: State of Kansas.

Kentucky
Community Ventures Corporation, 200 W. Vine St., Fifth Floor, Lexington, KY 40507. Contact: Kevin R. Smith, 606-281-5475. Service Area: Anderson, Bourbon, Clark, Fayette, Harrison, Jessamine, Nicholas, Scott, and Woodford counties.

Massachusetts
Jewish Vocational Service, Inc., 105 Chauncy St., 6th Floor, Boston, MA 02111. Contact: Barbara S. Rosenbaum, 617-451-8147. Service Area: Greater Boston with particular emphasis on the Mattapan (Boston), North Dorchester (Boston), and Central Square (Cambridge) neighborhoods.

Michigan
Cornerstone Alliance, 185 E. Main, Benton Harbor, Berrien County, MI 49022-4440. Contact: D. Jeffrey Noel, 616-925-6100. Service Area: City of Benton Harbor and Berrien county.

Minnesota
Neighborhood Development Center, Inc., 663 University Ave., St. Paul, MN 55104. Contact: Mihailo Temali, 612-290-8150. Service Area: Districts 3, 5, 6, 8, 9, and 16 of the city of St. Paul.

Missouri
Community Development Corporation of Kansas City, 2420 E. Linwood Blvd., Suite 400, Kansas City, MO 64109. Contact: Donald Maxwell, 816-924-5800. Service Area: Cass, Clay, Platte, Ray and Jackson counties.

Montana
Montana Department of Commerce, SBDC Division, 1424 9th Ave., P.O. Box 200501, Helena, MT 59620-0501. Contact:

Gene Marcille, 406-444-4780. Service Area: Through the SBDC network, Cascade, Chouteau, Fergus, Glacier, Golden Valley, Judity Basin, Musselshell, Petroleum Pondera, Teton, Toole and Wheatland counties, and the Blackfeet, Flathead, and Fort Peck Reservations, and the Crow, Fort Belknap, Northern Cheyenne, and Rocky Boys Reservations and their Trust Lands.

Nebraska
Omaha Small Business Network, Inc., 2505 N. 24th St., Omaha, NE 68110. Contact: John R. Cochran, 402-346-8262. Service Area: Areas within the city of Omaha known as the North Omaha and South Omaha target areas.

New Jersey
New Jersey Small Business Development Center, 180 University Ave., Newark, NJ 07102-1895. Contact: Andrew B. Rudczynski, 201-648-5950. Service Area: Through the SBDC network, statewide.

New Mexico
New Mexico Community Development Loan Fund, P.O. Box 705, Albuquerque, NM 87103-0705. Contact: Vangie Gabaldon, 505-243-3196. Service Area: Statewide.

New York
Brooklyn Economic Development Corporation, 30 Flatbush Ave., Suite 420, Brooklyn, NY 11217-1197. Contact: John Bartolomeo, 718-522-4600. Service Area: The five boroughs of New York City.

North Carolina
North Carolina Economic Development Center, Inc., 4 N. Blount St., 2nd Floor, Raleigh, NC 27601. Contact: Billy Ray Hall, 919-715-2725. Service Area: Statewide.

Ohio
Women Entrepreneurs, Incorporated, 36 E. Fourth St., Suite 925, Cincinnati, OH 45202. Contact: Peg Moertil, 513-684-0700. Service Area: Brown, Butler, Clermont, Hamilton, and Warren counties.

Pennsylvania
Philadelphia Commercial Development Corporation, 1315 Walnut St., Suite 600, Philadelphia, PA 19107. 215-790-2200. Service Area: Bucks, Montgomery, Philadelphia, Chester, and Delaware counties.

Texas
Corpus Christi Chamber of Commerce/SBDC, 1201 N. Shoreline, P.O. Box 640, Corpus Christi, TX 78403. Contact: Robert R. Carey, 512-882-6161. Service Area: Nueces and San Patricio counties.

Vermont
Champlain Valley Office of Economic Opportunity, Inc., 191 North St., Burlington, VT 05401. Contact: Robert Kiss. 802-862-2771. Service Area: State of Vermont.

Virginia
The Commonwealth of Virginia Department of Economic

Development, 1021 E. Cary St., Richmond, VA 23219. Contact: David V. O'Donnell, 804-371-8253. Service Area: Through the SBDC network, the state of Virginia.

* State Microloan Programs

Contact the State Office of Economic Development listed in your state capital

or

See the chapter, *State Money and Help For Your Business*, page 33

In addition to the federal programs, many state governments are also putting their money into microloan opportunities. Here are a few microloan programs that are currently available at the state level:

Iowa - Self employment Loan Program ($5,000 for low-income)

Maine - Job Start Program ($10,000)

New York - Micro Loan Program - NY Job Development

North Dakota - Micro Business Loans

Ohio - Ohio Mini-Loan Program

South Carolina - Micro Enterprise Loan Program

Texas - Rural Microenterprise Loan Program

New programs are being added all the time, so be sure to contact your state capital for the most current information.

How to Become a Freelancer Working Out of Your Home

How To Become a Freelancer
With The Government

While you're between jobs or just thinking about quitting the one you have and want something to tide you over until you get your next one, you should seriously think about freelancing for the Federal government.

The Interior Department hires ecologists and geologists. The Justice Department hires business consultants. The Department of Energy hires conservation consultants. Here's a sample listing of the kinds of projects freelance consultants do for the Federal government:

Types of Government Freelancing

Landscaping	Business Consulting	Administrative Support
Carpentry Work	Photography	Services
Painting and Paper Hanging	Insurance Agents	Education and Training
Security Guards	Computer programming	Medical Services
Computer Services	Research	Social Services
Data Processing	Drafting	Special Study and Analysis
Detective Services	Interior Decorating	Wildlife Management
Electrical Work	Library Services	Salvage Services
Plumbing	Word Processing	Travel Agent
Accounting Services	Translation Services	Personnel Testing Services
Chaplain Services (Priest)	Courier and Messenger	Photography
Management Consulting	Cleaning Services	Animal Care
Engineering Services	Food Service	Mathematics and Computer
Information Retrieval	Auditing Services	Science
Services	Advertising Services	Environmental Research
Real Estate Agents	Nursing Services	Historians
Secretarial Services	Housekeeping Services	Recreation Research
Court Reporting		Economic Studies
Legal Services		More, More, More...

Practically every major agency hires freelance consultants to work on both small and large projects--which might be exactly what you need until you land a full-time job down the road.

The feds hire all kinds of professionals to perform consulting work, from accountants and business specialists, to computer experts, social scientists, and security and surveillance consultants. The offices listed below, called Offices of Small and Disadvantaged Business

Utilization, specialize in helping individuals and small businesses get involved in contracting with their agency.

Subcontracting

Not only do the feds themselves hire consultants, so do the large prime contractors who sell their products and services to them. By law, any large company that receives contracts worth $500,000 or more from the Federal government must make an effort to subcontract some of that contract to small businesses. So if a company, for example, gets a large computer consulting contract with the Defense Department, they'll have to make an effort to hire some freelance computer consultants of their own to work on the contract. And that could be you.

How to Find Subcontracting Work

All of the federal procurement offices or Offices of Small and Disadvantaged Business Utilization (SBDU) (see list below) can provide you with information regarding subcontracting. Many of the departments' prime contracts require that the prime contractor maximize small business subcontracting opportunities. The SBDU offices can show you the way.

Each of the large federal agencies listed below, except the Department of Education, maintain directories of large contractors who are looking to do work with the feds in your area of expertise. And since the companies listed in these directories, for the most part, have just landed big government contracts, they might very well be looking to take on more full-time employees to help fulfill those contracts. A great lead on new job openings that probably won't be listed in the Sunday newspaper!

Offices of Small and Disadvantaged Business Utilization

Note: Offices designated as Offices of Small and Disadvantaged Business Utilization (OSDBUs) provide procurement assistance to small, minority, 8(a) and women-owned businesses. Their primary function is to ensure that small and disadvantaged businesses receive their fair share of U.S. Government contracts. "OSDBUs" are the contacts for their respective agencies and are excellent sources of information.

Agency for International Development
320 21st St., NW, Room 1200A SA-14, Washington, DC 20523-1414; 703-875-1551, Fax: 703-875-1862. Attn: Mr. Ivan R. Ashley, Director, OSDBU.

Corporation for National Service
1100 Vermont Avenue, NW, Room 2101, Washington, DC 20525; 202-606-5166, ext. 363, Fax: 202-606-5127. Attn: Ms.

Donna Darlington, Director, Procurement and Grants Management Division.

Department of Agriculture
14th and Independence Ave., SW, Room 1323, South Bldg., Washington, DC 20250; 202-720-7117, Fax: 202-720-3001. Attn: Ms. Sharron Harris, Director, OSDBU.

Department of Commerce
14th and Constitution Ave, NW, Room H-6411, Washington, DC 20230; 202-482-1472, Fax: 202-482-0501. Attn: Mr. James P. Maruca, Director, OSDBU.

Department of Defense
Office of the Director for Small Business Programs, 3061 Defense Pentagon, Room 2A340, Washington, DC 20301-3061; 703-614-1151, 703-697-1688, 703-697-9383, Fax: 703-693-7014. Attn: (Vacant), Director, OSDBU.

Department of the Air Force
Office of the Secretary of the Air Force, The Pentagon - Room 5E271, Washington, DC 20330-1060; 703-697-1950, Fax: 703-614-9266. Attn: Mr. Anthony J. DeLuca, Director, OSDBU (SAF/SB).

Department of the Army
Office of the Secretary of the Army, 106 Army Pentagon, Washington, DC 20310-0106; 703-697-7753, Fax: 703-693-3898. Attn: Mr. Daniel R. Gill, Director, OSDBU.

Department of the Navy
Office of the Secretary of the Navy, 2211 Jefferson Davis Hwy., Arlington, VA 22244-5102; 703-602-2700, Fax: 703-602-2477. Attn: Mr. Don L. Hathaway, Director, OSDBU.

Defense Logistics Agency Headquarters
AQAU Cameron Station, Room 6-170, Alexandria, VA 22304-6130; 703-274-6471, Fax: 703-274-0565. Attn: Mr. Lloyd C. Alderman, Director, OSDBU.

Department of Education
400 Maryland Avenue, SW, Room 3120-ROB-3, Washington, DC 20202-0521; 202-708-9820, Fax: 202-401-6477. Attn: Mr. Daniel L. Levin, Director, OSDBU.

Department of Energy
1707 H Street, NW, Room 904, Washington, DC 20585; 202-254-5583, Fax: 202-254-3989. Attn: Mr. Leonel V. Miranda, Director, OSDBU (BU-1).

Department of Health and Human Services
200 Independence Ave., SW, Room 517D, Humphrey Bldg., Washington, DC 20201; 202-690-7300, Fax: 202-690-8772. Attn: Mr. Verl Zanders, Director, OSDBU.

Department of Housing and Urban Development
451 7th Street, SW, Room 3130, Washington, DC 20410; 202-708-1428, Fax: 202-708-7642. Attn: Director, OSDBU.

Department of the Interior
1849 C Street, NW, Room 2725, Washington, DC 20240; 202-

208-3493, Fax: 202-208-5048. Attn: Mr. Kenneth Kelly, Director, OSDBU.

Bureau of Indian Affairs, Division of Contracting and Grants Administration, 1951 Constitution Ave., NW, MS 334-SIB, Washington, DC 20245; 202-208-2825.

Department of Justice
12th and Pennsylvania Avenue, NW, Room 3235, Ariel Rios Bldg., Washington, DC 20530; 202-616-0521, Fax: 202-616-1717. Attn: Mr. Joseph K. Bryan, Director, OSDBU.

Department of Labor
200 Constitution Ave., NW, Room C-2318, Washington, DC 20210; 202-219-9148, Fax: 202-219-9167. Attn: Ms. June Robinson, Director, OSDBU.

Department of State
SDBU, Room 633, SA 6, Washington, DC 20522-0602; 703-875-6824, Fax: 703-875-6825. Attn: Ms. Durie White, Director, OSDBU.

Department of Transportation
400 7th Street, SW, Room 9414, Washington, DC 20590; 202-366-1930, Fax: 202-366-7228. Attn: Ms. Luz Hopewell, Director, OSDBU.

Department of the Treasury
1500 Pennsylvania Avenue, NW, Room 6100 - Annex, Washington, DC 20220; 202-622-0530, Fax: 202-622-2273. Attn: Ms. Debra Sonderman, Assistant Director, OSDBU.

Department of Veterans Affairs
810 Vermont Avenue, NW (005SB), Washington, DC 20420; 202-376-6996, Fax: 202-233-4952. Attn: Mr. Scott F. Denniston, Director, OSDBU (005SB).

Environmental Protection Agency
401 M Street, SW, Mail Code 123OC, Washington, DC 20460; 703-305-7777, Fax: 703-305-6462. Attn: Mr. Leon H. Hampton, Jr., Director, OSDBU.

Export-Import Bank of the U.S.
811 Vermont Avenue, NW, Room 1017, Washington, DC 20571; 202-566-8111, Fax: 202-566-7524. Attn: Mr. Daniel A. Garcia, Administrative Officer.

Farm Credit Administration
1501 Farm Credit Drive, McLean, VA 22102-5090; 703-883-4149, Fax: 703-734-5784. Attn: Mr. Darrell Cooper, Chief of Contracting and Procurement.

Federal Communications Commission
1919 M St., NW, Room 404, Washington, DC 20554; 202-634-6624. Attn: Ms. Sonna Stampone, Chief, Acquisitions Branch.

Federal Deposit Insurance Corporation (FDIC)
Minority and Women Outreach Program (MWOP), 550 17th St., NW, PA 2041, Washington, DC 20429; 202-942-3126, 202-942-3128, Fax: 202-942-3113. Attn: Mr. Paul Barnes, Deputy Director.

Federal Emergency Management Agency
500 C Street, SW, Room 407, Washington, DC 20472; 202-646-3743, Fax: 202-646-3695. Attn: Ms. Christine Makris, Chief, Policy and Evaluation Branch.

Federal Housing Finance Board (FHFB)
1777 F Street, NW, 3rd Floor, Washington, DC 20006; 202-408-2582, Fax: 202-408-2580. Attn: Mr. Ernest Roane, Contracting Officer.

Federal Mediation and Conciliation Service
2100 K Street, NW, Room 100, Washington, DC 20427; 202-653-5310, Fax: 202-653-2002. Attn: Mr. Dan Funkhouser, Director of Administrative Services.

Federal Trade Commission
6th and Pennsylvania Avenue, NW, Room 706, Washington, DC 20580; 202-326-2258/2257, Fax: 202-382-2050. Attn: Ms. Jean Sefchick, Chief of Procurement.

Fannie Mae
3900 Wisconsin Avenue, NW, Washington, DC 20016-2899; 202-752-3775, Fax: 202-752-3804. Attn: Ms. Kathy Dress, Director, Minority and Women-Owned Businesses Office of Diversity. Ms. Claudia White, Director, Minority and Women-Owned Businesses Office of Diversity.

Freddie Mac
7900 W. Park Drive, MILSTOP 915, McLean, VA 22102; 703-905-5329. Attn: Mr. Jay Inouye, Administrator, Minority Business Development.

General Services Administration
18th and F Streets, NW, Room 6029, Washington, DC 20405; 202-501-1021, Fax: 202-208-5938. Attn: Ms. Joan Parrott-Fonseca, Director, OSDBU (AU).

International Trade Commission
500 E Street, SW, Room 214, Washington, DC 20436; 202-205-2732. Attn: Ms. Lois Waterhouse, Contract Specialist.

Interstate Commerce Commission
12th and Constitution Avenue, NW, Room 1311, Washington, DC 20423; 202-927-5577, Fax: 202-927-5976. Attn: Mr. Virgil Schultz, Chief, Procurement Contracting Branch.

Library of Congress
Office of Contracts and Logistics, 1701 Brightseat Road, Landover, MD 20785; 202-707-0412, Fax: 202-707-8611. Attn: Mr. Napoleon Jasper, Procurement Policy Administrator.

National Aeronautics and Space Administration
NASA Headquarters, Mail Code K, Room 9K70, 300 E Street, SW, Washington, DC 20546; 202-358-2088, Fax: 202-358-3261. Attn: Mr. Ralph C. Thomas, III, Associate Administrator, OSDBU.

National Archives and Records Administration
8601 Adelphi Road, Room 4400, College Park, MD 20740-6001; 301-713-6755. Attn: Ms. Joyce Murray, Contract Specialist.

National Credit Union Administration
Office of Administration, 1775 Duke Street, Alexandria, VA 22314-3428; 703-518-6410, Fax: 703-518-6439. Attn: Mr. Ed Brosnan, Contract Specialist.

National Labor Relations Board
1099 14th Street, NW, Suite 6100, Washington, DC 20570; 202-273-4210, Fax: 202-273-4266. Attn: Ms. Paula Roy, Chief of Contracting and Procurement Section.

National Science Foundation
4201 Wilson Blvd., Room 590, Arlington, VA 22230; 703-306-1390. Attn: Dr. Donald Senich, Director, OSDBU.

Nuclear Regulatory Commission
Office of Small Business and Civil Rights, Washington, DC 20555; 301-415-7387, 301-415-7486. Attn: Mr. Vandy Miller, Director, Office of Small Business and Civil Rights.

Executive Office of the President
Office of Administration/General Services, New Executive Office Building, 725 17th Street, NW, Room 5001, Washington, DC 20503; 202-395-3314, Fax: 202-395-3982. Attn: Ms. Thelma Toler, Contract Administrator.

Office of Personnel Management
Procurement Division, Quality Assurance Branch, 1900 E Street, NW, Room 1452 - SB427, Washington, DC 20415; 202-606-2180. Attn: Ms. Faye Turner, Small Business Technical Advisor.

Office of the Comptroller of the Currency (OCC)
Acquisitions and Procurement Branch, 250 E Street, SW, Mail Stop 4-13, Washington, DC 20219; 202-874-5040, Fax: 202-874-5625. Attn: Ms. Mary Ellen Dorsey, Contract Specialist.

Office of the Thrift Supervision
Department of the Treasury, 1700 G Street, NW, 3rd Floor, Washington, DC 20552; 202-906-6346/7864. Attn: Mr. Columbus D. Jude, Sr., Advocate, Outreach Program for Small Businesses, Minority-Owned and Women-Owned Businesses.

Pennsylvania Avenue Development Corporation
1331 Pennsylvania Avenue, NW, Suite 1220 North, Washington, DC 20004-1703; 202-724-0761, ext. 44, Fax: 202-724-0246. Attn: Ms. Susan Zusy, Affirmative Action Project Manager.

Railroad Retirement Board
1310 G Street, NW, Suite 500, Washington, DC 20005; 202-272-7742, Fax: 202-272-7728. Attn: Ms. Marian Gibson, Director, OSDBU.

Resolution Trust Corporation (RTC)
801 17th Street, NW, Room 1201, Washington, DC 20434; 202-416-6925, Fax: 202-416-2466. Attn: Ms. Johnnie B. Booker, Vice President, Division of Minority and Women's Programs.

Small Business Administration
Director, Office of Procurement and Grants Management, 409

Third Street, SW, 5th Floor, Washington, DC 20416; 202-205-6622 (Speak with Director, Deputy Director or Contract Specialist).

Smithsonian Institution
Small and Disadvantaged Business Utilization Program, 915 L'Enfant Plaza, SW, Washington, DC 20560; 202-287-3508, Fax: 202-287-3490. Attn: Mr. Mauricio P. Vera, Small and Disadvantaged Business Utilization Program Manager.

Tennessee Valley Authority
1101 Market Street, EB2B, Chattanooga, TN 37402-2801; 615-751-6269, Fax: 615-751-6890. Attn: Mr. George Provost, Manager, OSDBU.

U.S. Postal Service
475 L'Enfant Plaza, SW, Room 3821, Washington, DC 20260-5616; 202-268-6578, Fax: 202-268-6573. Attn: Mr. Richard J. Hernandez, Manager, Vendor Programs.

United States Information Agency
400 6th St., SW, Room 1725, Washington, DC 20547; 202-205-5404, Fax: 202-401-2410. Attn: Ms. Georgia Hubert, Director, OSDBU.

More Help Selling Your Services

Need some help marketing your product or service to the government? The Procurement Assistance Offices are aware of the federal procurement process, and can help you draw up a sensible business plan. They can match the product or service you are selling with the appropriate agency, and then help you market your wares effectively. Several programs have online bid matching services. They can obtain specifications, get your name on solicitation mailing lists, and more. These offices are partially funded by the Department of Defense to assist businesses with Defense Procurement. To find out where these centers are located, see the following state by state listing, or contact:

Small and Disadvantaged Business
 Utilization Office
Cameron Station
Room 4B110
Defense Logistics Agency
Alexandria, VA 22304
703-274-6471

Department of Defense Procurement Technical Assistance Cooperative Agreement Program Recipient List

Alabama
Joseph L. Richardson, University of Alabama at Birmingham, Executive VP, 1717 11th Ave., S, Suite 419, Birmingham, AL 35294-4410; 205-934-7260, Fax: 205-934-7645.

Alaska
Ron Hadden, University of Alaska Anchorage, Small Business Development Ctr., 430 W. 7th Ave., Suite 100, Anchorage, AK 99501; 907-274-7232, Fax: 907-274-9524.

Arizona
Anson J. Arviso, The National Center for AIED, National Center Headquarters, 953 E. Juanita Ave., Mesa, AZ 85204; 602-831-7524, Fax: 602-491-1332.

Paul R. Roddy, Aptan, Inc., 360 N. Hayden Rd., Scottsdale, AZ 85257; 602-945-5452, Fax: 602-970-6355.

Arkansas
Toni Tosch, Board of Trustees, University of Arkansas, College of Business Administration, 120 Ozark Hall, Fayetteville, AR 72701; 501-337-5355, Fax: 501-337-5045.

California
Jane E. McGinnis, Merced County DE/SD, 1632 "N" St., Merced, CA 95340; 209-385-7312, Fax: 209-383-4959.

William Hobdy, Business Innovation Center, San Diego Incubator Corp., 3350 Market St., San Diego, CA 92102; 619-685-2949, Fax: 619-531-8829.

Thad C. Aaron, De Anza College, Business Division, C/O Amd Captan M/S 31, Sunnyvale, CA 94088-3453; 408-739-6283, Fax: 408-245-7618.

Colorado
Debra L. Larsen, Colorado Office of Business Development, Governor's Office, 1625 Broadway, Suite 1710, Denver, CO 80202; 303-620-8082, Fax: 303-892-3848.

Connecticut
Ronald Kipnis, Seatech, 1084 Shennecossett Rd., Groton, CT 06340; 203-449-8777, Fax: 203-449-9463.

Delaware
Onike Sawyer, Delaware State University, School of Business & Economics, 1200 N. Dupont Hwy., Dover, DE 19901; 302-739-5146, Fax: 302-739-3517.

Florida
Laura Subel, University of West Florida, Florida PTA Program, 11000 University Parkway, Pensacola, FL 32514; 904-444-2066, Fax: 904-444-2070.

Georgia
Robert A. (Duke) Walsh, Columbus College, Division of Continuing Education, One Arsenal Place, 901 Front Ave., Suite 106, Columbus, GA 31901-2727; 706-649-1092, Fax: 706-649-1094.

Charles P. Catlett, Jr., Georgia Technical Research Corp., Economic Development Institute, 400 Tenth St., CRB Room 246, Atlanta, GA 30332-0420; 404-894-6121, Fax: 404-853-9172.

Hawaii
Larry G. Nelson, State of Hawaii, Department of Business Economic Development & Tourism, 737 Bishop St., Suite 1900, Honolulu, HI 96813; 808-586-2598, Fax: 808-587-2777.

Idaho
Larry Demirelli, Idaho Department of Commerce, State of Idaho, 700 West State Street, Boise, ID 83720; 208-334-2470, Fax: 208-334-2631.

Illinois
Lorenzo Padron, Latin American Chamber of Commerce, The Chicago Pac, 2539 N. Kedzie Ave., Suite 11, Chicago, IL 60647; 312-252-5211, Fax: 312-252-7065.

Kim M. Meier, Black Hawk College District 503, 6600 34th Ave., Moline, IL 61265; 309-755-2200, Fax: 309-755-9847.

Lois Vanmeter, State of Illinois, Department of Commerce & Community Affairs, 620 E. Adams St., Third Floor, Springfield, IL 62701; 217-785-6310, Fax: 217-785-6328.

Indiana
Linnea Hokanson, Partners in Contracting Corporation, PTA Center, 200 Russell St., Suite 200E, Hammond, IN 46320; 219-932-7811, Fax: 219-932-5912.

David Schaaf, Indiana Small Business Corp., Government Marketing Assistance Group, One North Capitol Ave., Suite 1240, Indianapolis, IN 46204-2026; 317-264-5600, Fax: 317-264-2806.

Iowa
Bruce Coney, State of Iowa, Iowa Department of Economic Development, 200 East Grand Ave., Des Moines, IA 50309; 515-242-4888, Fax: 515-242-4893.

Kentucky
James A. Kurz, Kentucky Cabinet For Economic Development, Department of Community Development, 500 Mero St., 22nd Floor Cap Plaza Tower, Frankfort, KY 40601; 800-838-3266, Fax: 502-564-3256.

Louisiana
Phyllis McLaren, Jefferson Parish Economic Development Commission, The Bid Center, 1221 Elmwood Park, Suite 405, Harahan, LA 70123; 504-736-6550, Fax: 504-736-6554.

Stephen Killingsworth, Louisiana Productivity Center, University of Southwest Louisiana, P.O. Box 44172, 241 E.

Lewis St., Lafayette, LA 70504-4712; 318-782-6057, Fax: 318-262-5472.

Sherrie B. Mullins, Northwest Louisiana Government Procurement Center, Greater Shreveport Economic Development, 400 Edwards St., P.O. Box 20074, Shreveport, LA 71120-0074; 318-677-2530, Fax: 318-677-2534.

Maine
Eastern Maine Development District, Market Development Center, One Cumberland Pl, Suite 300, Bangor, ME 04401; 800-955-6549, Fax: 207-942-3548.

Maryland
Moses A. Cain, Morgan State University, School of Business & Management, Coldspring Lane & Hillen Rd., Baltimore, MD 21239-4098; 410-319-3861, Fax: 410-319-3532.

Paul W. Riley, Tri County Council For Western Maryland, 111 S. George St., Cumberland, MD 21502; 301-777-2158, Fax: 301-777-2495.

Massachusetts
Peter F. Hrul, Commonwealth of Massachusetts, Massachusetts Office of Business Development, 1 Ashburton Place, 21st Floor, Boston, MA 02108; 508-657-8600, Fax: 508-657-0158.

Michigan
Chapin W. Cook/Cindy Erickkson, Genesee County Metropolitan Planning Commission, PTA Center, 1101 Beach St., Room 223, Flint, MI 48502; 810-257-3010, Fax: 810-257-3185.

Pennie Southwell, Jackson Alliance For Business Development, PTA Center, 133 W. Michigan Ave., Jackson, MI 49201; 517-788-4455, Fax: 517-788-4337.

Judi Zima, Schoolcraft College, 18600 Haggerty, Livonia, MI 48152-2696; 313-462-4438, Fax: 313-462-4439.

Thomas Young, Thumb Area Consortium/Growth Alliance, Local Procurement Office, 3270 Wilson St., Marlette, MI 48453; 517-635-3561, Fax: 517-635-2230.

Denise Hoffmeyer, Northeast Michigan Consortium, 320 State St., P.O. Box 711, Onaway, MI 49765; 517-733-8548, Fax: 517-733-8069.

Delena Spates-Allen, Saginaw Future, Inc., Procurement Technical Assistance Center, 301 E. Genesee Ave., 3rd Floor, Saginaw, MI 48607; 517-754-8222, Fax: 517-754-1715.

Paula Boase, Downriver Community Conference, Economic Development, 15100 Northline, Southgate, MI 48195; 313-281-0700, Fax: 313-281-3418.

Janet E. Masi, Warren, Center Line, Sterling Heights Chamber of Commerce, 30500 Van Dyke Ave., Suite 118, Warren, MI 48093; 810-751-3939, Fax: 810-751-3995.

John Calabrese, West Central Michigan Employment & Training Consortium, PTA Center, 110 Elm St., Big Rapids, MI 49307; 616-796-4891, Fax: 616-796-8316.

Sandra Ledbetter, CEO Council, Inc., Government Contracting Office, 100 W. Michigan, Suite 294, Kalamazoo, MI 49007; 616-342-0000, Fax: 616-343-1151.

James F. Haslinger, Northwestern Michigan Council of Governments, PTA Center, P.O. Box 506, Traverse City, MI 49685; 616-929-5036, Fax: 616-929-5012.

Minnesota
Michael Melin, Minnesota Project Innovation, Inc., Government Marketing Assist, Mill Place, Suite 100, 111 Third Ave., S, Minneapolis, MN 55401-2551; 612-341-0641, Fax: 612-338-3483.

Mississippi
Charles W. "Skip" Ryland, Mississippi Contract Procurement Center, Inc., 3015 12th St., P.O. Box 610, Gulfport, MS 39502; 601-864-2961, Fax: 601-864-2969.

Missouri
Morris Hudson, Curators of University of Missouri, University Extension, 310 Jesse Hall, Columbia, MO 65211; 314-882-0344, Fax: 314-884-4297.

Guy Thomas, Missouri Southern State College, 3950 E. Newman Rd., Joplin, MO 64801-1595; 417-625-9313, Fax: 417-625-9782.

Montana
James F. Ouldhouse, Montana Tradeport Authority, 2722 Third Ave., North, Suite 300, Billings, MT 59101-2043; 406-256-6871, Fax: 406-256-6877.

Gregory L. Depuydt, Procurement Technical Institute, 305 W. Mercury, Suite 208, Butte, MT 59701-1659; 406-723-4061, Fax: 406-723-5345.

Karl J. Dehn, High Plains Development Authority, Inc., 2800 Terminal Dr., Suite 209, P.O. Box 2568, Great Falls, MT 59404; 406-454-1934, Fax: 406-454-2995.

Nebraska
Tawni Avery, Nebraska Department of Economic Development, Existing Business Assistance Division, 301 Centennial Mall, South, P.O. Box 94666, Lincoln, NE 68509-4666; 308-535-8213, Fax: 308-535-8175.

Nevada
Ray Horner, State of Nevada, Commission on Economic Development, Capitol Complex, Carson City, NV 89710; 702-687-4325, Fax: 702-687-4450.

New Hampshire
State of New Hampshire, Office of Business & Industrial Development, P.O. Box 1856, 172 Pembroke Rd., Concord, NH 03302-1856; 603-271-2591, Fax: 603-271-2629.

New Jersey
James F. O'Grady, County of Union New Jersey, Union County PTA Center, 1085 Morris Ave., Suite 531, Lib Hall, Union, NJ 07083; 908-527-1166, Fax: 908-527-1207.

John B. McKenna, Foundation At New Jersey Institute of Technology (NJIT), PTA Center, University Heights, Newark, NJ 07102; 201-596-3105, Fax: 201-596-5806.

New Mexico
Rita Cordova, State of New Mexico General Services Department, Procure Assistance Program, 1100 St. Francis Dr., Room 2006, Santa Fe, NM 87503; 505-827-0425, Fax: 505-827-0499.

New York
Carin Webb, Research Foundation State University of New York, Office of Research & Sponsored Program, P.O. Box 6000, Binghamton, NY 13902-6000; 607-777-2718, Fax: 607-777-2022.

Patricia Finn, South Bronx Overall Economic Development Corporation, Procurement, 370 E. 149th St., Bronx, NY 10455; 718-292-3113, Fax: 718-292-3115.

Thomas M. Livak, Cattaraugus County, Department of Economic Development, Plan & Tour, 303 Court St., Little Valley, NY 14755; 716-938-9111, Fax: 716-938-9438.

Solomon Soskin, Long Island Development Corporation, PTA Program, 255 Glen Cove Rd., Carle Place, NY 11514; 516-741-5690, Fax: 516-741-5851.

Gordon Richards, New York City Department of Business Services, Procurement Outreach Program, 110 William St., New York, NY 10038; 212-513-6472, Fax: 212-618-8987.

Roberta J. Rodriquez, Rockland Economic Development Corporation, Procurement, One Blue Hill Plaza, Suite 812, Pearl River, NY 10965; 914-735-7040, Fax: 914-735-5736.

North Carolina
Susan Dutton Kinney, University of North Carolina at Chapel Hill, Small Business & Tech Development Center, Room 300, Bynum Hall, Chapel Hill, NC 27599-4100; 919-571-4154, Fax: 919-571-4161.

North Dakota
Eric Nelson, University of North Dakota, North Dakota Small Business Development Center, Department of Grants & Contracts, P.O. Box 8164, Grand Forks, ND 58202-8164; 701-237-9678, Fax: 701-235-6706.

Ohio
Nancy Rogers, University of Cincinnati, Cece Small Business Development Center, 1111 Edison Dr., Cincinnati, OH 45216-2262; 513-948-2083, Fax: 513-948-2007.

Marc Graves, Greater Cleveland Growth Association, Cleveland Area Development Corporation, 200 Tower City Center, 50 Public Square, Cleveland, OH 44113; 216-621-3300, Fax: 216-621-6013.

Burt Schildhouse, Greater Columbus Chamber of Commerce, COGNAP, 37 N. High St., Columbus, OH 43215; 614-225-6952, Fax: 614-469-8250.

Ronda Gooden, Terra Community College, NCOPTA, 1220 Cedar St., Fremont, OH 43420; 419-332-1002, Fax: 419-334-2300.

Virginia K. Mullenax, Community Improvement Corporation of Lake County Ohio, NE Ohio Government Contract Assistance Center, 7750 Clocktower Dr., Kirtland, OH 44094-5198; 216-951-8488, Fax: 216-951-7336.

Kay A. Richmond, Lawrence Economic Development Corporation, Procure Outreach Center, 101 Sand & Solida Rd., P.O. Box 488, South Point, OH 45680; 614-894-3838, Fax: 614-894-3836.

William Horton, Central State University, Ohio Procurement & Technical Assistance Center, Wilberforce, OH 45384; 513-376-6514, Fax: 513-376-6598.

Stephen J. Danyi, Mahoning Valley Economic Development Corporation, Mahoning Valley Technical Procurement Center, 4319 Belmont Ave., Youngstown, OH 44505-1005; 216-759-3668, Fax: 216-759-3686.

Oklahoma
Denise Agee-Kennemer, Oklahoma Dept. of Vocational & Technical Education, Oklahoma Bid Assistance Network, 1500 W. Seventh Ave., Stillwater, OK 74074-4364; 405-743-5574, Fax: 405-743-6821.

Roy Robert Gann, Jr., Tribal Government Institute, 111 N. Peters, Suite 400, Norman, OK 73069; 405-329-5542, Fax: 405-329-5543.

Oregon
Jan Hurt, Organization for Economic Initiatives, Government Contract Acquisition Program, 99 W. 10th Ave., Suite 337-B, Eugene, OR 97401; 503-344-3537, Fax: 503-687-4899.

Pennsylvania
Daniel R. Shade, Southern Alleghenies Planning & Development Commission, PTA State of Pennsylvania, 541 58th St., Altoona, PA 16602; 814-949-6528, Fax: 814-949-6505.

Joseph E. Hopkins, Mon-Valley Renaissance, CA University of Pennsylvania, 250 University Ave., California, PA 15419; 412-938-5881, Fax: 412-938-4575.

Richard A. Mihalic, NW Pennsylvania Regional Planning & Development Commission, Specialized SVCS PTA, 614 Eleventh St., Franklin, PA 16323; 814-437-3024, Fax: 814-432-3002.

Chuck Burtyk, PIC of Westmoreland/Fayette, Procurement Assistance Center, 531 S. Main St., Greensburg, PA 15601; 412-836-2600, Fax: 412-836-8058.

Ronald F. Moreau, Indiana University of Pennsylvania, College of Business, Robertshaw Building, Room 10, 650 S. 13th St., Indiana, PA 15705-1087; 412-357-7824, Fax: 412-357-3082.

Robert J. Murphy, Johnstown Area Regional Industries, Defense PAC, 111 Market St., Johnstown, PA 15901; 814-535-8675, Fax: 814-535-8677.

A. Lawrence Barletta, Seda Council of Governments, R.D. 1 Box 372, Lewisburg, PA 17837; 717-524-4491, Fax: 717-524-9190.

Charles L. Rech, Trustees Univ. of Pennsylvania, SE-PA PTAP, 3733 Spruce St., Vance Hall, 4th Floor, Philadelphia, PA 19104-6374; 215-898-1219, Fax: 215-573-2135.

Gilbert M. Lutz, Southwest Pennsylvania Regional Development Council, Inc., Southwest Pennsylvania Local Development District, The Waterfront, 200 First Ave., Pittsburgh, PA 15222-1573; 412-391-5590, Fax: 412-391-9160.

Karen Ostroskie, Economic Development Council of Northeast Pennsylvania, Local Development District, 1151 Oak St., Pittston, PA 18640; 717-655-5581, Fax: 717-654-5137.

Robert W. Imhof, North Central Pennsylvania Regional Planning & Development Commission, North Central Business Development, P.O. Box 488, 651 Montmorenci Ave., Ridgway, PA 15853; 814-773-3162, Fax: 814-772-7045.

Peggy Cranmer, Northern Tier Regional Planning & Development Commission, Economic/Community Development, 507 Main St., Towanda, PA 18848-1697; 717-265-9103, Fax: 717-265-7585.

Susan Hart, West Chester University, Center For Study Connect & DBASES, 128 Elsie O. Bull Center, West Chester, PA 19383; 610-436-3337, Fax: 610-436-3110.

Puerto Rico
Pedro J. Acevedo, Commonwealth of Puerto Rico, Economic Development Administration, 355 Roosevelt Ave., Hato Rey, PR 00918; 809-753-6861, Fax: 809-751-6239.

Rhode Island
Daniel E. Lilly, Jr., Rhode Island Port Authority & Economic Development Corp., Financial Services, 7 Jackson Walkway, Providence, RI 02903; 401-277-2601, Fax: 401-277-2102.

South Carolina
Judy Radin-Sidlow, University of South Carolina, Frank L. Roddey SBDC of South Carolina, College of Business Administration, Columbia, SC 29208; 803-777-4907, Fax: 803-777-4403.

South Dakota
Kareen Dougherty, University South Dakota, South Dakota PTA Center, 414 E. Clark Patterson 112, Vermillion, SD 57069-2390; 605-330-6191, Fax: 605-330-6231.

Tennessee
Nell Tays-Hirsch, Center for Industrial Services, University of Tennessee, 226 Capitol Blvd., Suite 606, Nashville, TN 37219-1804; 615-532-8657, Fax: 615-532-4937.

Texas
Doug Nelson, Panhandle Regional Planning Commission, Economic Development Unit, P.O. Box 9257, Amarillo, TX 79105-9257; 806-372-3381, Fax: 806-373-3268.

Rogerio Flores, University of Texas at Arlington, Automation & Robotics Research Institute, Office of President, Box 19125, Arlington, TX 76019; 817-794-5978, Fax: 817-794-5952.

Michele Y. Reed, University of Texas at Brownsville, Office of President, 80 Fort Brown, Brownsville, TX 78520; 210-544-8812, Fax: 210-548-6522.

Corpus Christi Chamber of Commerce, Small Business Development Center, Chamber of Commerce Found, 1201 N. Shoreline, P.O. Box 640, Corpus Christi, TX 78403; 512-882-6161, Fax: 512-888-5627.

Ted Cadou, University of Houston, TIPS, 1100 Louisiana, Suite 500, Houston, TX 77002; 713-752-8477, Fax: 713-756-1515.

Otilo Castellano, Texas Technical University, College of Business Administration, 2579 South, Loop 289, Lubbock, TX 79423; 806-745-1637, Fax: 806-745-6207.

Glenn E. Harris, Angelina College, Procurement Assistance Center, P.O. Box 1768, Lufkin, TX 75902; 409-639-3678, Fax: 409-639-3863.

Dr. Charles Welch, Northeast Texas Community College, East Texas PTA Program, P.O. Box 1307, Mt. Pleasant, TX 75455; 903-572-1911, Fax: 903-572-0598.

Rosalie O. Manzano, San Antonio Procurement Outreach Program, Economic Development Department, P.O. Box 839966, San Antonio, TX 78283; 210-554-7133, Fax: 210-554-7160.

El Paso Community College, P.O. Box 20500, El Paso, TX 79998; 915-534-3405, Fax: 915-534-3420.

Utah
Johnny C. Bryan, Utah Department of Community & Economic Development, Utah Procurement Outreach Program, 324 South State St., Suite 504, Salt Lake City, UT 84111; 801-538-8791, Fax: 801-538-8825.

Vermont
Amy Erwin, George Mason University, Entrepreneurship Center, 4400 University Dr., Fairfax, VA 22030; 703-993-8300, Fax: 703-330-5891.

Robert E. McGhee, Crater Planning District Commission, The Procurement Assistance Center, 1964 Wakefield St., P.O. Box 1808, Petersburg, VA 23805; 804-861-1667, Fax: 804-732-8972.

Maxine B. Rogers, Southwestern Virginia Community College, Economic Development Division, P.O. Box SVCC, Richlands, VA 24641; 703-964-7334, Fax: 703-964-9307.

Washington

Morris A. Winter, Economic Development Council, Kitsap County, 4841 Auto Center Way, Suite 204, Bremerton, WA 98312; 206-643-0102, Fax: 206-643-6673.

Teena M. Kennedy, Economic Development Council, Snohomish County, 917 134th St., SW, Suite 103, Everett, WA 98204; 206-743-4567, Fax: 206-745-5563.

Cindy Blackwell, Spokane Area Economic Development Council, 221 N. Wall, Suite 310, P.O. Box 203, Spokane, WA 99210-0203; 509-624-9285, Fax: 509-624-3759.

West Virginia

Michael W. Walker, Regional Contracting Assistance Center,

1116 Smith St., Suite 202, Charleston, WV 25301; 304-344-2546, Fax: 304-344-2574.

Belinda Sheridan, Mid-Ohio Valley Regional Council, PTA Center, P.O. Box 247, Parkersburg, WV 26102; 304-295-8714, Fax: 304-295-7681.

Wisconsin

Ralph Steckman, Madison Area Technical College, Small Business PAC, 211 North Carroll St., Madison, WI 53703; 608-258-2330, Fax: 608-258-2329.

Mary Frey, Wisconsin Procurement Institute, 840 Lake Ave., Racine, WI 53403; 414-632-6321, Fax: 414-632-7157.

How Freelance Writers and Editors Can Get Government Contracts

Writers don't have to be starving artists — the Federal government hires freelancers to do all kinds of work, such as script writing, technical writing, editing, translations, and much more. Consider this:

* If you're a consumer writer, the Food and Drug Administration might be interested in using your skills to write an article on food safety for $1,200.

* If you're an editor, the U.S. Department of Agriculture might want to use you at a rate of $1,225 per week.

* Technical writers can land $25,000 contracts that NASA awards each year.

While many agencies have in-house writers on staff, sometimes the work load is just too much and they'll look outside for freelancers to do the projects. Not all hire freelance writers, so we've done the leg work for you and found out which agencies do. Don't forget to also check the general section on freelancing, as well as checking out state contracts.

To be considered for any kind of contract work with the government, you'll need to submit a standard capabilities statement with each agency with which you would like to work. This statement should be submitted on a standard form 129 (*SF-129*), which is available free from any of the contracting offices listed below.

Once they've received your *SF-129*, an agency will put you on the bidders mailing list so that when writing opportunities come up, you'll be notified. You'll then be asked to submit a closed bid for the project, with the lowest bid getting the work. Keep in mind, though, that on larger contracts of $25,000 and up, the government usually pays only on completion of the project, which could be six months or a year, depending on the size. So if you're going to bid, be sure you can survive that long before you get paid.

Here are some success stories of individuals and small businesses that have received writing contracts worth more than $25,000:

International Computer and Telecommunications of Lanham, MD, received *$1.99 million* to provide NASA headquarters with technical writing support services.

Gottlieb Associates of Washington, DC, received *$55,310* to edit a science magazine for the National Science Foundation.

Stone and Webster Engineering Corp. of Engelwood, CO, received *$192,839* to revise and update a book for the Department of Energy.

Graph Tech, Inc., of Arlington, VA, received *$57,418* to provide editorial services to the Federal Emergency Management Administration.

Bruce Valley of Alexandria, VA, received *$38,289* to write speeches for the Chairman of the Federal Deposit Insurance Corp.

The Blue Pencil Group, Inc., of Reston, VA, received *$27,900* to edit a scientific journal for the National Science Foundation.

Not all freelance writers get work through this kind of formal, bidded contract. Most writing and editing jobs are smaller, valued under $25,000, and are given out on a less formal basis — the procurement office might contact only three writers they know of and ask for bids, with the lowest getting the job.

Even smaller jobs in the range of, say, $2,500 or under are often awarded to writers that the Small Purchases Agent for an agency might have on his/her rolodex, especially those writers who can do work on an as-needed, last minute basis. So make sure that the Small Purchases Agent in each agency knows your name and has your resume on file — it's usually the people who are freshest in the agent's mind that gets these small, though often lucrative assignments.

Here are some examples of these smaller contracts:

Briere Associates of Arlington VA received *$2,000* to edit an investigation report for the International Trade Commission.

Richard Bellman received *$511* to write a paper on fair housing for the Department of Housing and Urban Development.

Peter Petrakis of Annapolis, MD, received *$2,500* to write a scientific report for the Public Health Service.

Paragon Solutions received *$23,011* to develop a users manual for the Department of Housing and Urban Development.

Rowena Itchon of Washington, DC, received *$2,000* for editing services from the Securities and Exchange Commission.

Barbara Snyder of Falls Church, VA, received *$625* to write a paper on drug abuse for the Department of Health and Human Services.

Don Hill of Virginia received *$2,500* to produce a series of training conference reports for the Office of Personnel Management.

In fact, when first starting out in government contracting, it's a good idea to complete a few of these smaller contracts before you try to land

any of the larger ones valued over $25,000. Showing a government agency that you have successfully completed smaller contracting work for them will make them more likely to award you larger jobs when you submit bids on them. Just as it is in the private sector, if all other things are equal, contracts often go to those companies with whose work the agency is most familiar.

Writers Contacts

Agriculture Department
Sedelta Verble
Office of Communications
Room 412A, Administration Building
U.S. Department of Agriculture
14th and Independence Aves., SW
Washington, DC 20250
202-720-2798

The U.S. Department of Agriculture's (USDA) Office of Public Affairs hires the services of writers, script writers, and editors to work on small projects such as videos from time to time. If you're interested in being considered for this work, you'll need to send in a *SF-129* capabilities statement for you or your company. Once on file, the USDA will contact you if they think you're right for the job.

Drug Enforcement Administration
Office of Procurement
Attn: Burdette Burton
Drug Enforcement Administration
Washington, DC 20537
202-307-7777

At times, the Drug Enforcement Administration (DEA) requires the services of technical writers and script writers to work on projects that can't be completed by in-house capabilities. These contracts are usually valued under $25,000. If you're interested in being considered for this work, you'll need to submit an *SF-129* that outlines your capabilities and experience. When writing projects come up, you'll then be notified and requested to submit bids on the contract.

Energy Department
Headquarters
Office of Procurement Operations
U.S. Department of Energy
1615 M St., NW
Washington, DC 20036
202-634-4552

In limited cases, the U.S. Department of Energy (DoE) seeks the services of freelance editors and technical writers. To be considered for this work and be placed on the bidders list, you'll need to submit an *SF-129* to this office.

Environmental Protection Agency
U.S. Environmental Protection Agency
Mail Code 1704
401 M St., SW
Washington, DC 20460
202-260-4359

This office at the Environmental Protection Agency (EPA) puts out the *EPA Journal*, a magazine specializing in environmental and regulatory issues. Occasionally, the *Journal* uses the services of freelancers to write articles of varying length for a negotiated fee. If you're interested in being considered for this work, you'll need to submit a capabilities statement and some relevant clips of your work.

Federal Emergency Management Administration
Federal Emergency Management Administration
Acquisitions Branch
500 C St., SW
Washington, DC 20472
202-646-4257

The Federal Emergency Management Administration (FEMA) puts out many educational and training materials relating to disaster management, and at times they hire freelance writers and editors to work on these materials. To be considered for this work and be placed on the bidders list, you'll need to submit an *SF-129* outlining your capabilities. These contracts are valued over $2,500.

Fish and Wildlife Service
Anne Tracy
Office of Public Affairs
Fish and Wildlife Service
1849 C St., NW
Room 3240
Washington, DC 20240
202-208-6286

The Public Affairs Office at the Fish and Wildlife Service (FWS) at times needs to hire freelance writers and editors to work on projects concerning issues such as wildlife and wetlands preservation. To be considered for this work, you'll need to submit a resume, a capabilities statement that outlines your experience, and some clips. If they're interested in using you, you'll be contacted when a relevant project arises.

Stephanie Smith
U.S. Fish and Wildlife Service
Office of Training and Education
Mail Stop 304
4401 N. Fairfax Dr.
Arlington, VA 22203
703-358-1781

This office at the Fish and Wildlife Service (FWS) produces environmental education and training materials that at times require the services of freelance editors and writers. To be considered for this work, you'll need to submit a resume, a capabilities statement that outlines your experience, and some clips. If they're interested in using you, you'll be contacted when a relevant project arises.

Food and Drug Administration
Judith Willis
FDA Consumer
5600 Fishers Lane
Rockville, MD 20857
301-443-3220

The Food and Drug Administration (FDA) puts out a magazine called the *FDA Consumer*, which specializes in food and drug issues. This magazine often uses freelance writers to research and write articles which the FDA is interested in having done. The articles usually run between 2,000 and 2,500 words, and the writers receive between $850 and $1,200 per article, depending on experience and the subject. If you're interested in being considered for this work, you'll need to submit your resume, along with relevant clips, to this office. If they're interested in using your services, you'll be notified when an appropriate project arises.

Forest Service
U.S. Forest Service
U.S. Department of Agriculture
P.O. Box 96090
Room 707 RP-E
Washington, DC 20090-6090
703-235-8165

On occasion, the Forest Service hires freelance editors, proofreaders, and technical writers to do contract work. This work often specializes in the earth sciences and may involve technical engineering reports. If you'd like to be notified when these contract opportunities arise, you'll need to submit an *SF-129* that outlines your capabilities and experience.

General Services Administration
Faith Payne
General Services Administration
XSP, Room 6022
18th and F Sts., SW
Washington, DC 20405
202-501-1021

The General Services Administration (GSA) often uses the services of freelance editors and writers to work on the publications they produce, such as government booklets, training catalogs, and so on. To be considered for this work, submit a resume, cover letter, and clips outlining your capabilities. If they're interested, you'll be notified when projects arise.

Health and Human Services
General Acquisitions
Public Health Service
U.S. Department of Health and Human Services
Parklawn Ave., Room 5-101
Rockville, MD 20857
301-443-6550

The U.S. Department of Health and Human Services (HHS) hires freelance editors and writers to work on health-related reports and publications. To be considered for this work, you'll need to submit an *SF-129* that outlines your capabilities and experience to this office. Once on file, this office will notify you when any projects come up that they think match your talents.

Housing and Urban Development
> Office of Procurement and Contracts
> U.S. Department of Housing and Urban Development
> 407 7th St., SW
> Room 5272
> Washington, DC 20410
> 202-708-1772

The U.S. Department of Housing and Urban Development (HUD) hires writers and editors to work on such projects as research papers departmental publications. To be considered for this work, you'll need to submit an *SF-129* to this office so that you can be placed on the bidders mailing list, which will notify you when writing contracts arise. Also, you should keep in contact with HUD's small purchase office, which also awards like contracts.

Interior Department
> Dinah Anderson
> Office of Administrative Services
> Branch of Acquisition Services
> 1849 C St., NW
> Mail Stop 2626
> Washington, DC 20240
> 202-208-3523

The Office of Administrative Services (OAS) division of the Interior Department contracts for the services of editors to support the production of departmental reports and publications. Interior also contracts for the service of translators (R608) and technical writers (T013). Commodity codes appear in parentheses. To be placed on the bidders list and receive notification when editing contract opportunities arise, you'll need to submit a capabilities statement in the form of a *SF-129*.

International Trade Commission
> U.S. International Trade Commission
> Procurement Division
> 500 E St., SW, Room 214
> Washington, DC 20436
> 202-252-2732

Occasionally the International Trade Commission (ITC) uses the services of freelance writers and editors to work on investigation reports that they issue. If you're interested in being considered for these small projects, you'll need to submit an *SF-129* to this office. If they're interested in using your services, they'll contact you when any projects arise.

Justice Department
> Office of Justice Programs
> 633 Indiana Ave., NW
> Room 542
> Washington, DC 20531
> 202-307-0608

At times, the Office of Justice Programs (OJP) requires freelance editors and writers for project support. If you're interested in being considered for this work, you'll first need to submit a capabilities statement to this office. If they're interested in possibly using you, they may set up an interview to further discuss your capabilities. After that, if they want to use you, you'll be notified when any relevant work comes up that they think best matches your abilities.

Labor Department
> Brenda Butler
> Office of Procurement Services
> U.S. Department of Labor
> 200 Constitution Ave., NW, Room S-5220
> Washington, DC 20210
> 202-219-6445

The U.S. Department of Labor hires freelancers to work on different projects, such as script writers as part of video projects. If you're interested in being considered for this work, you'll first need to submit an *SF-129* capabilities statement to this office. If they're interested in possibly using you, they may set up an interview to further discuss your capabilities. After that, if they want to use you, you'll be notified when any relevant work comes up that they think best matches your abilities.

National Aeronautics and Space Administration
> NASA Headquarters
> Washington, DC 20546
> 202-358-2090

NASA headquarters in Washington, DC, contracts for the services of both writers and editors. What follows are the different kinds of related services along with their respective Commodity Code numbers you'll need to know when applying to be placed on the bidders list to receive notice of up-coming contracting opportunities: translators (73890007); film script writers (78190003); and technical writing and editing (89990001).

> *Langley Research Center*
> NASA
> Hampton, VA 23681
> 804-864-1000

> *Ames Research Center*
> NASA
> Moffett Field, CA 94035
> 415-604-5000

> *Lewis Research Center*
> NASA
> Cleveland, OH 44135
> 216-433-4000

> *George C. Marshall Space Flight Center*
> Procurement Office/AP16
> Marshal Space Flight Center, AL 35812
> 205-544-2121

This Center contracts for script writing (89998221), technical writing (89998224), and creative writing (89998383).

> *Goddard Space Flight Center*
> NASA
> Greenbelt Rd.
> Greenbelt, MD 20771
> 301-286-6574

The above four NASA centers regularly contract for the services of technical writers. To be considered for this work, you'll need to first submit a *SF-129*, which is available from any of these offices. The Commodity Code for technical writing is 89990001.

National Park Service
Dyra Monroe
National Park Service
Contract Operations Branch
P.O. Box 37127
Washington, DC 20013-7127
202-523-0092

The National Park Service hires freelance writers and editors for contract work when projects arise. If you're interested in being placed on their bidders list so that you can receive notice when new contracts need filling, you'll need to submit an *SF-129* capabilities statement with this office.

National Science Foundation
National Science Foundation
Legislative and Public Affairs Office
4201 Wilson Blvd.
Arlington, VA 22230
703-306-1070

The National Science Foundation (NSF) hires freelance writing and editing services to work on various journals that they produce. To be put on the bidders list and receive notice of upcoming contract opportunities, you should submit an *SF-129* to this office.

National Technical Information Service
Anita Tolliver
National Technical Information Service
U.S. Department of Commerce
5285 Port Royal Rd., Room 203
Springfield, VA 22161
703-487-4720

National Technical Information Service (NTIS), the largest publisher and distributor of government technical information, occasionally hires freelancer editors and writers to work on their publications. To be considered for this contract work, you'll need to submit an *SF-129* summarizing your capabilities and experience. When relevant contracts arise, you'll be notified to submit bids on the projects.

Office of Personnel Management
U.S. Office of Personnel Management
1900 E St., NW, SB 427
Washington, DC 20415
202-606-2240

From time to time, the Office of Personnel Management (OPM) awards small writing contracts in the $2,500 range to freelancers to work on such projects as putting together conference reports and executive summaries. If you're interested in this work, you'll need to send in a capabilities statement, such as a resume, for you or your company. This statement should also include your hourly rate for proofreading and editing. If they're interested in using your services, you'll be contacted when any appropriate projects come up.

Postal Service
Headquarters Purchasing
Barbara Sauls
Services Purchasing
U.S. Postal Service

475 L'Enfant Plaza West, SW
Washington, DC 20260-6237
202-268-4100

For writing contracts worth $25,000 and over, you'll need to be placed on the Postal Service's list of suppliers. This office can send you the appropriate applications. When writing contracts arise, you'll be notified to submit competitive bids. The Postal Service awards contracts for both technical writing and technical manual production services, which includes editorial services such as proofreading, copy mark-up, and text writing. The Commodity Codes for these services are T013A and T013B. The code for Speech Writing is R416A, and for Language Translation it's R416.

Securities and Exchange Commission
U.S. Securities and Exchange Commission
450 5th St., NW
Washington, DC 20549

The Securities and Exchange Commission (SEC) occasionally hires freelance writers to write speeches. The standard rate for speech writing is about $2,000 per project. If you think you have the background to do this kind of work, submit a capabilities statement to the SEC. If they're interested in using your services, they'll contact you when an appropriate project comes up.

Smithsonian Institution
Office of Contracting and Property Management
Smithsonian Institution
955 L'Enfant Plaza, SW
Suite P114
Washington, DC 20024
202-287-3331

The Smithsonian often hires freelancers to work on their publications. Keep in mind, though, that this work does not include work on the *Smithsonian Magazine*, which is a completely separate entity. This part of the Smithsonian provides administrative publication support, along with the many different books that they publish. To be considered for this work, you'll need to submit an *SF-129* outlining your capabilities and experience, and if they're interested in using you, you'll be notified when opportunities arise.

Transportation Department
Office of the Secretary
U.S. Department of Transportation
(DOT)/OST
M-64, Room 9413
400 7th St., SW
Washington, DC 20590
202-366-4953

On occasion, the Department of Transportation (DoT) contracts for the services of writers and editors. To be notified when these opportunities arise, you'll need to submit an *SF-129* to this office.

Treasury Department
Wesley Hawley
Procurement Services Division
Treasury Department
1500 Pennsylvania Ave., NW, Room 1438

Washington, DC 20220
202-622-1300
To be considered for any writing and editing contracts that might arise, you'll need to submit a capabilities statement to this office or an *SF-129*.

Office of Procurement
SBA-PCR
Ollie Snyder
1301 Constitution Ave., NW
ICC Building, Room 3379
Washington, DC 20229
202-927-7131
On occasion, FMS requires the services of freelance editors and writers, and to get on the bidders' list, you need to submit an *SF-129* that outlines your capabilities.

Michelle James
Internal Revenue Service
Room 700 Constellation Centre
6009 Oxon Hill Rd.
Oxon Hill, MD 20749
202-283-1350

U.S. Secret Service
Procurement Division
1310 L St., NW, Room 730
Washington, DC 20223
202-435-6940

Columbus Jude
Advocate Outreach Program
Office of Thrift Supervision
1700 G St., NW
Washington, DC 20552
202-906-6346
The above departments within the U.S. Department of the Treasury contract for the service of writers and editors. To bid on writing contracts valued over $25,000, you'll need to complete and submit an *SF-129* application to be put on their solicitation mailing lists. These agencies also make smaller purchases of these services, and with your *SF-129* on file, they will contact you when any appropriate work comes up. Once on the mailing lists, you'll receive notice whenever these agencies are looking for bids on writing contracts.

U.S. Geological Survey
U.S. Geological Survey
12201 Sunrise Valley Dr.
MS-508 National Center
Reston, VA 22092
703-648-5768
The U.S. Geological Survey (USGS) hires freelance writers and editors to work on educational pamphlets and projects concerning the earth sciences. If you're interested in being considered for this work, you'll need to submit a capabilities statement to this office, along with relevant clips. If they're interested in using your services, they'll contact you when relevant projects arise.

How Artists, Designers, and Photographers Can Get Freelance Government Contracts

The federal government spends millions of dollars each year for the services of artists, graphic designers, illustrators, painters, calligraphers, photographers, computer graphics specialists, and any other art-related specialty. Because the government is involved, many artists might shy away from finding out how they can get in on these opportunities. But the following listing is put together to help you get in contact — with just one phone call — with the people who hire artists like yourself. Don't forget to check the general section on freelancing, as well as checking out state contracts.

It's difficult to get a clear estimate of the amount of government contracts that go to artists. If you count prime as well as subcontracts the figure could be as high as $20 to $30 million dollars. Here are what some of the major agencies spend each year:

Spending By Major Agencies On Artists

Department of Agriculture	$186,000
National Science Foundation	$187,500
Department of Labor	$400,000
Postal Service	$378,000
U.S. Geological Survey	$100,000
Food & Drug Administration	$200,000
Federal Emergency Management Agency	$ 25,000
U.S. Customs Service	$ 40,000
National Park Service	$1,900,000

Here are some examples of artists who have landed art contracts with the government:

Artists Who Received Government Contracts

Jacob Lawrence received **$95,000** to create a ceramic tile wall mosaic to be placed in the Joseph P. Addabbo Federal Building in Queens, NY. GSA.

Linda Sherman Design, Inc., of Gaithersburg, MD, received **$432,000** to provide graphic art and editorial support services to NASA.

Manuel Neri received **$100,000** to create a marble sculpture entitled "Ventana al Pacifico" that was placed outside the Gus J. Solomon Courthouse in Portland, Oregon. GSA.

Gerald Farrar & Associates, Inc., of Tulsa, OK, received **$3,540** to provide graphic art services to the Department of Energy.

Lehman-Scaffa Photo & Art of Silver Spring, MD, received **$12,000** to provide graphic arts services to the National Science Foundation, including viewgraphs, slides, charts, maps, mechanical and conceptual drawings, page layouts, publication covers, signs, typesetting, posters, prints and negatives and exhibit materials.

Hugh Moore & Associates of Alexandria, VA, received **$35,000** from the National Science Foundation to provide graphic art support services, including designing educational pieces for a national science program.

Inkwell, Inc., of Washington, DC, received **$10,000** from the USDA to provide graphic art support services.

Douglass Harding Group of Washington, DC, received **$32,000** from the USDA to provide graphic art support services.

Thomas Baldwin, Inc., of Alexandria, VA, received **$138,000** from the Forest Service to design the interior of the Service's National Visitors Center.

Standsbury Ronsaville Wood Inc., of Annapolis, MD, landed a contract from the National Park Service worth **$16,000** to provide graphic design services, including illustrations, layout, exhibit production, publication design, and more.

Nelson/Hendrickson of Purcellville, VA, landed a contract from the National Park Service worth **$72,948** to provide production-ready wayside exhibit plan packages.

Maria Alquilar received **$19,000** to create a high fired clay sculpture for the General Services Administration that was placed in the Main Border Station in San Luis, AZ.

Caleb Bach received **$18,000** to produce two paintings entitled "The Effects of Good and Bad Government" that were placed in the Seattle Courthouse.

Robert Brooks received **$4,000** to create a photographic mural that was placed in the U.S. Border Station in Fort Kent, ME. GSA.

Houston Conwill received **$49,000** to create a bronze sculpture on a granite platform that was placed in the Joseph P. Addabbo Federal Building in Queens, NY.

The painter, **Blue Sky**, received **$12,600** to create an oil painting entitled "Moonlight on the Great Pee Dee" which was placed in the J.M. McMillan Federal Building in Florence, SC. GSA.

Frank Smith received **$20,000** to create a ceramic tile wall mural for the Joseph P. Addabbo Federal Building in Queens, NY. GSA.

Another Color, Inc., received **$422,000** to provide graphic art and editorial support services to NASA.

Creative Service, Inc., received **$200,000** to provide graphic art and editorial support services to NASA.

Artists Who Received Money from the National Park Service 1991:

Lloyd Townsend	$ 6,663
Hugh Brown	$ 14,721
Robert Hynes	$ 4,020
Louis Glanzman	$ 9,362
Glenn Moy	$ 9,511
Charles Hazard	$ 3,528
Steven Patricia	$ 7,020
Robert Hynes	$ 8,786
Chris White Design	$ 50,974
Dorothy Novick	$ 4,056
G.S. Images	$236,294
General Graphics	$268,363
G.S. Images	$ 86,643
Specialty Graphics	$103,932
General Graphics	$ 17,246
Scribing Graphics	$100,167

We've put together an agency-by-agency listing of the people who will look at your work, get it reviewed, and put your name on their vendors list so you can get in on these contracting opportunities. In many cases we've also included the kinds of projects these agencies most often hire freelancers to work on from brochures and book design to exhibits and promotional posters.

When To Apply

Keep in mind that because new contracts are awarded at the beginning of the fiscal year in October, you should make sure that an agency you're interested in working for has seen your portfolio by late spring or early summer--this will give them enough time to consider you for the current fiscal year. Otherwise you may have to wait an entire year before you get any work, especially the larger contracts.

Find Out Past Winning Contracts

Because many art contracts are awarded on a competitive bid basis, you should be aware of successful bids in the past before you submit a bid of your own. Through a Freedom of Information Act Request from the agency in question, you can get copies of winning bids on art contracts from previous years. Remember, the competition on these contracts is very high, but most artists don't know how to use the Freedom of Information Act to give them the edge.

Small Contracts

For smaller contracts valued under $25,000, many agencies award Blanket Purchase Agreements (BPAs) to artists they want to use. Getting a BPA means that the agency agrees to offer you work up to a certain value over the period of the fiscal year, often up to $25,000. For larger jobs, the agency may send out project announcements to three artists on their bidder's list and ask for bid proposals. Each agency conducts the bidding procedure slightly differently.

For even small jobs, such as those for $2,500 or less, an agency may simply pull the name of an artist out of their rolodex and call them for a quote on a job. If they think the price is in line with what they want to spend, they'll simply award the job to that one artist. Many jobs are awarded on this basis.

Who To Contact For Contracts

Agriculture Department
James Schleyer
Design Division
Room 516A, U.S. Dept. of Agriculture
Washington, DC 20250
202-720-4337

Each year the U.S. Department of Agriculture (USDA) contracts out about 40% to 60% of its design work to free-lance artists. Contracts are awarded to freelancers through the procurement office, which maintains a list of approved artists that receive notification of requests for bids when a contract needs fulfilling. To get on this contracting list, artists must have their portfolios reviewed and approved. To set up an appointment to have your portfolio reviewed, contact James Schleyer, chief of the Design Division.

Commerce Department
Office of Administrative Operations
Visual and Electronic Communications Division
Design and Graphics
Room 2864
U.S. Department of Commerce
Washington, DC 20230
202-482-3061

The U.S. Department of Commerce contracts out about 20% of their graphics and design work to freelancers. This work often includes publication design, poster design, exhibits, presentation charts, framing and mounting, and much more. If you're interested in being considered for some of this work, contact the Graphics Branch and arrange for a portfolio review. If they can use the kind of work you do, they may decide to sign you to a Blanket Purchase Agreement where you'll receive up to a certain dollar amount of work throughout the year. This division awards about 40 BPAs each year.

Customs Service
U.S. Customs Service
1301 Constitution Ave., NW,
Graphics Department
Washington, DC 20229
202-927-0314

The Customs Service hires artists on a freelance basis to work on some of their projects that involve graphics, such as 30 x 40 presentation boards, color graphics, exhibits, and the like. To be considered for this work, you'll need to get your portfolio reviewed before June/July when the new contracts are awarded for the new fiscal year. If they're interested in using you, they may sign you to a blanket purchase agreement where you'll be awarded projects up to a certain total dollar amount over the year. The U.S. Customs Service spends between $30,000 and $40,000 per year on freelance graphic art.

Drug Enforcement Agency
        Chief, Contracting and Procurement Unit
        Drug Enforcement Agency
        1405 I St., NW
        Washington, DC 20537
        202-633-2894
From time to time the Drug Enforcement Agency (DEA) contracts for graphics support for their different programs, such as education and interdiction. If you're interested in doing freelance graphics work for the DEA, you'll need to submit an *SF-129* to this office. Once you're on file, if they're interested in using your talents, they'll contact you when an appropriate project comes up and ask you to submit a bid.

Energy Department
        William Talbot
        U.S. Department of Energy
        1000 Independence Ave., SW
        Washington, DC 20585
        202-586-2732
This office produces the technical graphics support for the Department of Energy (DoE), and they hire the services of design firms that can produce technical computer graphics. If your computer graphics company is interested in competing on DoE contracts, you'll need to submit a *Solicitation Mailing List Application (SF-129)*, which is available by contacting this office. This form asks you to provide basic background on your company, including size, computer capabilities, and experience. Once selected, graphics companies are kept on list, and when a job comes up, DoE will contact three or four firms and ask them to submit bids on the contract.

        Bob Stiefel
        Printing Operations
        U.S. Department of Energy
        1000 Independence Ave., SW, GE-116
        Washington, DC 20585
        202-586-6035
This graphics section of the Department of Energy (DoE) does exhibit design and construction and print media production. Once a year in March and April, Mr. Halvorson reviews the design contractors he's used over the previous year and decides if he wants to re-use them. If not, he interviews new design artists interested in doing print media work with DoE. This interview process includes a portfolio review. If selected as a contractor, designers are held under Blanket Purchasing Agreements and are called in on an irregular basis for bid sessions during which they bid against each other on the available projects. Contact Mr. Halvorson if you're interested in having your portfolio reviewed during March and April.

Environmental Protection Agency
        James Ingram
        Visual Information Specialist
        Editorial Services Division
        U.S. Environmental Protection Agency

        401 M St. SW, MS 1704
        Washington, DC 20460
        202-260-4359
The Environmental Protection Agency (EPA) hires the services of graphic artists to do all kinds of projects, including presentation exhibits, view graphs, slide shows, publication designs, cover illustrations, photography, and much more. To be considered for this work, you'll need to arrange with Mr. Ingram for an interview where you have your portfolio reviewed. EPA hires freelance artists three different ways. For small jobs with a quick turn-around, artists are used on a on-call basis, where EPA will call you up with a job they think you can do and ask for a price. If they like the price, you get the job. They also hold a certain number of artists under Blanket Purchasing Agreements, where you get work during the year adding up to a certain total amount of the agreement. For large projects, EPA will choose three artists on their vendors list and send out requests for proposals. The lowest bid gets the job.

Federal Emergency Management Agency (FEMA)
        Susan Rappa
        Graphics Department, Room 315
        Federal Emergency Management Agency
        500 C St., SW
        Washington, DC 20472
        202-646-3475
Federal Emergency Management Agency (FEMA) puts about ten graphic artists and designers under contract per year. If you're interested in showing your work to FEMA, contact Bill Sachs and arrange to go in for a portfolio review. If they're interested in using your services, you may be recommended for a Blanket Purchase Agreement where you'll be asked to submit bids on projects as they come up, with the lowest bid getting the job. FEMA spends about $25,000 per year on freelance art services.

Fish & Wildlife Service
        Tom Nebel
        U.S. Dept. of the Interior
        Fish & Wildlife Service
        1849 C St, NW, Room 3544
        Washington, DC 20240
        202-208-4111
The Fish & Wildlife Service (FWS) contracts out all kinds of graphic design services, from illustration and photography to calligraphy and book design. To be considered for these contracting opportunities you'll need to contact this office and set up a portfolio review. If you live in an area of the country other than the Washington, DC, area, you should contact the Fish & Wildlife Service field office nearest you. If they like your work and want to use you, FWS will notify you when projects matching your capabilities arise, and you'll be asked to make bids on them. On smaller projects, they may simply call you up and ask for a price and whether you can get the project done in the needed time.

Food & Drug Administration
        Jesse Nichols
        Office of Communications
        Food & Drug Administration
        5600 Fishers Ln., HFI-40
        Room 15A-19

Rockville, MD 20857
301-443-3210

The Food and Drug Administration (FDA) contracts graphic artists and designers to work on editorial illustrations, exhibit design, posters, photographic projects, and much more. If you're interested in being considered for this work, contact this office and arrange for a portfolio review. If they'd like to use your talents, they may decide to sign you to a Blanket Purchase Agreement where you'll receive up to a certain dollar amount of work throughout the year by bidding on individual projects as they arise. This office at FDA signs about 10 artists each year under freelance contract.

General Services Administration

Tim Hinton or Arlethia McGhee
Office of Graphic Design
U.S. General Services Administration
18th & F Sts., NW
Washington, DC 20405
202-501-0742

The General Services Administration (GSA) hires artists to do all kinds of work for them on a freelance basis, including publications, exhibits, slide shows, and audio-visual productions. To be considered for work with GSA, an artist needs to contact GSA and set up an appointment to have his or her portfolio reviewed. Once reviewed, artists are classified according to their strengths and the type of publications that are appropriate for their kind of work. The artists are then ranked according to the quality and style of their work. When a job needs to be contracted, GSA will contact three or four artists from their lists and ask them to submit bids. Bids are chosen based on both quality and price. Contact Tim Hinton or Arlethia McGee to set up a portfolio review.

Art-in-Architecture Program (PGA)
General Services Administration
18th & F Sts., NW
Washington, DC 20405
202-501-4228

By law, the federal government must spend 0.5% of the cost of constructing or purchasing new buildings or completing major repairs and alterations of existing buildings on artwork. Artwork can include sculptures, murals, photographs, paintings, ceramic tile displays, and can range from a couple of thousand dollars in cost to $100,000 or more, depending on the size of the project. To have your work considered for any upcoming projects, you'll need to receive a program application from this office, then submit it along with 35mm slides of work created within the last three years. You'll also need to include a current resume. Working with national, state, and local art agencies, GSA then nominates and selects artists to work on these projects.

Immigration & Naturalization Service

Glenn Brown
Printing Officer
Immigration & Naturalization Service
425 I St, NW, Room 2115
Washington, DC 20536
202-514-3210

Each year, the Immigration and Naturalization Service (INS) retains three graphic artists or companies on a bidders list who are contacted whenever a project comes up that the INS cannot do themselves in-house. Each are asked to submit a price on the job and the lowest gets it. Each August, Mr. Rutter reviews the portfolios of any new artists interested in being placed on the bidders list. The three artists chosen are the ones who can provide the necessary quality of work for the lowest amount of money. The kind of work that INS contracts out often includes one-, two-, and multi-color bar and pie charts for presentations, along with calligraphy for handlettered certificates. Contact Mr. Rutter in July or August to arrange for a portfolio review.

Internal Revenue Service

Buddy Kirk
Internal Revenue Service
111 Constitution Ave, NW, Room 1137
PC:M:PS:G
Washington, DC 20224
202-622-7330

The Internal Revenue Service (IRS) hires freelance artists to do exhibits, posters, computer graphics, illustrations, charts, brochures, flip charters, flyers, and much more. To be put on the vendors list and qualify to submit bids on projects, you'll need to have your portfolio reviewed by the IRS design group. If they are interested in your work and feel that they can use your special skills, you'll be placed on the list of vendors and receive notice when any relevant projects that require your skills arise. This IRS design group spends about $650,000 annually on contracts with artists.

Labor Department

Lionel White
Division of Audio-Visual Communication
U.S. Dept. of Labor
200 Constitution Ave., SW, Room 6311
Washington, DC 20210
202-219-7820

The Labor Department hires outside art contractors to do all kinds of projects, including cover-to-cover publications, name cards, graphic panels for exhibits, newsletters, editorial illustrations, book cover designs, stationery, and much more. If you're interested in being considered for these design contracting opportunities, contact this office and request that your name be placed on the mailing list of contract proposals that are mailed out each Spring. Upon receiving the proposals, you'll fill it out and return it, being sure to include background on your expertise, examples of technical experience, and price scale. A panel of experts will review the submitted portfolios and price proposals and choose the top applicants to work under Blanket Purchase Orders valued up to $25,000 annually. The Labor Department spends between $350,000 to $500,000 each year on freelance graphic art.

National Archives

Serene Werblood
National Archives and Records Administration
NEPP
Washington, DC 20408
202-501-6056

The graphics division of the publications office hires freelance graphics artists to work on such projects as lobby posters, books, marketing brochures, direct mail, and exhibit catalogs. Every year, this office keeps two or three freelance designers under contract with Blanket Purchasing Agreements, and for larger jobs, they send out requests for bids to artists on their vendor list. To be considered for contracting work with the publication division of the Archives, you'll need to contact this office and arrange to have your portfolio reviewed. If they like your work and think they can use you, you'll be put on their list of bidders. New contracts begin in October, so they like to have their prospective freelancers chosen by July/August.

National Institutes of Health

Ron Winterowd
National Institutes of Health
Medical Arts and Photography Branch
900 Rockville Pike
Mail Stop 1016
Bldg. 10, Room B-2L316
Bethesda, MD 20892
301-496-2868

The National Institutes of Health (NIH) contracts out about 50-70% of their art and photographic work, which includes publication design, illustration, exhibit fabrication, photography, video production, charts/ graphs, poster sessions, composites, and much more. To be considered for this contract work you'll need to contact this office and arrange for an interview and portfolio review. If they want to try you out, they use Open Market Requisition contracts, and if they'd like to keep you on for a longer time, they may decide to sign you to a Blanket Purchase Agreement where you'll receive contract work valued up to a certain dollar amount over the course of a year.

National Institute of Standards & Technology

Bill Welsh
Repro-Graphics
National Institute of Standards and Technology
Gaithersburg, MD 20899-0001
301-975-2631

The National Institute of Standards and Technology (NIST) graphics department does some work with freelance artists. If you're interested in finding out more, you'll need to contact this office and have your portfolio reviewed by the department. If they're interested in using you, they will use the standard contracting procedures: a bidder's list, blanket purchasing agreements, and so on.

National Oceanic & Atmospheric Administration

Diane Boxley
National Oceanic & Atmospheric Administration
Room 725, (083312)
6010 Executive Blvd.
Rockville, MD 20852
301-413-0907

The National Oceanic and Atmospheric Administration (NOAA) hires freelance artists to do work on exhibits, publications, silk screening, wall plaques, photography, and much more. To be considered for the work, you'll need to arrange to have your portfolio reviewed by Mr. Butts. If they are interested in using your talents, they may decide to sign you to a Blanket Purchase Agreement, where they'll provide you with on-going contract work up to a certain dollar value, or they may simply contact

you with a project in mind, ask for a price, and if they like it, you get it. For more information on the portfolio review process contact Mr. Butts at the office above.

National Park Service

Harper's Ferry Center
Contracting Branch
Administrative Annex
Taylor Street
P.O. Box 50
Harper's Ferry, WV 25425
304-535-6236

The National Park Service (NPS) contracts the services of all kinds of artists, illustrators, and photographers. To qualify for these contracting opportunities, you'll need to have your portfolio reviewed by the NPS. The review can be arranged through this office--either in person or sending copies of your work by mail. Once your portfolio is approved, you'll be placed on the bidders' list and receive notifications of projects in your area of specialty.

National Science Foundation

Division of Grants and Agreements
National Science Foundation
4201 Wilson Blvd.
Arlington, VA 22230
703-306-1210

Graphic artists and illustrators interested in doing contract work with the National Science Foundation (NSF) should send them samples of their work along with a statement summarizing their capabilities and areas of specialty. Upon receiving this information, the Division of Grants & Contracts will circulate your resume and samples among the different NSF program offices, which in turn will decide if they are interested in using your services. This is the procedure used on contracts less than $20,000 in value. Over that amount, NSF places a notice in the *Commerce Business Daily* for open bidding.

U.S. Postal Service

Terry McCaffery
Stamp Marketing Division
Office of Philatelic and Retail Services
U.S. Postal Service
475 L'Enfant Plaza
Room 4461-E
Washington, DC 20260
202-268-6576

This office oversees both the production and promotion of U.S. postal stamps, and they hire freelance artists to help support many of their projects, including posters, brochures, and stamps. If you're interested in doing this kind of work, you'll need to contact this office and arrange to have your portfolio reviewed, either in person, or by submitting tear sheets of your work. For graphic art on their promotional materials, they work three different ways. For projects under $2,000, they will simply contact the artist on file they think is best for the job or who can do it the fastest. For projects up to $5,000, they will normally use a Basic Pricing Agreement that is arranged with the artist for an entire year. For projects over $5,000, they will often ask for competitive bids from their list of vendors.

How to Become a Freelancer

Most of the stamps are done by freelance illustrators, 300 of whom they have on file. Contracts usually are for $3,000 per stamp or $10,000 for a block of four. In 1992, they contracted 26 artists to do 126 stamp designs. If you're interested in being considered for stamp illustration, you'll need to contact the above office and arrange to have your work reviewed. Depending on the project, contracts are awarded in a similar fashion to those for the Postal Services promotional materials described above.

> *Thad Dilley*
> Communications Department, Room 2P530
> U.S. Postal Service
> 475 L'Enfant Plaza
> Washington, DC 20260
> 202-268-2194

This department of the U.S. Postal Services contracts the services of graphic designers, illustrators, calligraphers, and photographers to work on their publication materials. To be put on their bidders list, you first need to send them a description of your graphics capabilities and specialties, and then make an appointment to go in for a portfolio review. If after reviewing your work, they are interested in using your talents, you'll be put on a bidders list and then notified when projects arise that you are qualified to complete.

Public Health Service

> *Paris Pacchione*
> Room 36-36
> U.S. Department of Health and Human Services
> Public Health Service
> 5600 Fishers Lane
> Rockville, MD 20857
> 301-443-1090

This technical services branch of the Public Health Service (PHS) works to meet the art requirements for the Indian Health Service, the Office of the Surgeon General, the Assistant Secretary of Health, and the Agency for Health Care Policy Review, among others. To help keep up with their heavy work load, they contract out a large amount of art projects, including silk screen posters, banners, brochures, plaques, exhibit designs, 3-D displays, and much, much more. If you're interested in doing work for them on a freelance basis, contact Harris Pacchione to arrange for a portfolio review. If they like your work and want to use your talents, you'll be put on a bidders list and perhaps offered a Blanket Purchasing Agreement and asked to bid on jobs as they come up during the year. Currently PHS maintains about 30 BPAs with freelance artists. For major jobs, they'll send out proposal requests to three vendors on their list and ask for proposals.

Alcohol, Drug Abuse, and Mental Health Administration

> *Gene Souder*
> Alcohol, Drug Abuse and Mental Health Administration
> Graphics Branch, Room 789
> 5600 Fishers Lane
> Rockville, MD 20857
> 301-443-4183

The Alcohol, Drug Abuse and Mental Health Administration (ADAMHA) hires freelance artists and design firms to work on

such projects as view graphs, exhibits, publications, logos, and much more. Each June 1st they award the new graphic design contracts for the new fiscal year, so if you're interested in being considered for this work, you'll need to contact this office and arrange for a portfolio review. Each year, about 15 firms and individuals are awarded Blanket Purchase Agreements where they are given up to a certain dollar amount of work throughout the year.

Work is also contracted by:
> Health Resources and Services Administration
> Ray Targrowski
> 301-443-1014

U.S. Geological Survey

> *Joy Durant*
> National Mapping Division
> U.S. Geological Survey
> 12201 Sunrise Valley Dr.
> MS-508 National Center
> Reston, VA 22092
> 703-648-6880

The National Mapping Division of the U.S. Geological Survey (USGS) contracts the work of freelance graphic designers to create pamphlets and educational pieces dealing with the earth sciences. Companies and individuals interested in being considered for contracting work should submit background information on their capabilities, along with samples of their work. If the USGS is interested in using your services, you'll be placed on a bidders list and notified when an appropriate contracting opportunity arises. For contracts valued under $2,500 the USGS will simply contact the artist they think is best suited for the job and who can do it in the needed time. The USGS awards about $100,000 in contracts annually for graphic art.

Small Business Administration

> Publications and Graphic Design Services
> Office of Public Communications
> U.S. Small Business Administration
> 409 Third St., SW
> Washington, DC 20416
> 202-205-6740

The Small Business Administration (SBA) contracts out about 70% of the graphics and art design work that they need. These projects include publication design, banners, name tags, over-sized presentation boards, pamphlets and brochures, and much more. If you're interested in being considered for contract work with SBA, contact Mr. Wheat and arrange for a portfolio review. If they'd like to use your services, they'll have your name put on a bidders list in SBA's Office of Procurement & Grants Management. When a project arises, Procurement will notify at least three artists on the bidders list and ask them to submit bids on the project.

Smithsonian Institute

> *Ann Garvey*
> Smithsonian Institute Press
> 470 L'Enfant Plaza
> Suite 7100
> Washington, DC 20560
> 202-287-3738, ext. 352

This office provides the graphic art and design support for much of the Smithsonian Institute, including all of the publications produced by the Smithsonian Institute Press (this does not include the *Smithsonian Magazine*, which is an entirely separate entity). Although much of the work is done in-house, they do occasionally hire the services of freelancers to work on projects that they don't have the time or expertise to complete themselves. This work may involve graphic design, mechanicals, and every so often, illustration work. To be considered for this work, you'll need to contact Mr. Carter and arrange for a portfolio review. If they are interested in your work, you'll be contacted to submit bids on projects as they come up, with the lowest bid taking the job.

State Department

Rose Grover
Graphics Division
U.S. Department of State
21st & C Sts., SW,
Room 1655
Washington, DC 20520
202-647-1082

When the different bureaus within the State Department need outside graphics support, they contact artists on a vendors list that they maintain. The kind of projects that get farmed out to freelancers are usually last minute projects that the Graphics Division doesn't have the time or capability to do, such as charts for congressional briefings. To be put on the vendors listing, an artist first needs to be cleared by Rose Grover, the head of the Graphics Division. This process may include a portfolio review. Once on the bidders list, artists can receive direct calls from the individual bureaus for bids on projects.

Treasury Department

Stu Gates
Printing and Graphics
U.S. Department of the Treasury
1500 Pennsylvania Ave., NW
Annex, Room B-39
Washington, DC 20220
202-622-2160

To handle some of their large and mid-level graphic design work, the Treasury contracts the services of outside design vendors. This work is awarded on a competitive basis through Blanket Purchase Agreements where the graphics/design firm or individual given contract work up to a certain pre-determined dollar value throughout the year on an as-needed basis. Contact this Division for more information on getting your portfolio reviewed and being considered for the bidders list.

U.S. Information Agency

Howard Cincotta
Visual Services
U.S. Information Agency
301 4th St., SW
Washington, DC 20547
202-619-4269

The U.S. Information Agency's (USIA) Visual Services does some work with freelance artists. If you're interested in finding out more, you'll need to contact this office and have your portfolio reviewed by the department.

How to Get Video Production and Voiceover Contracts From The Federal Government

Freelance video production is one of the fastest growing fields in federal contracting. In 1993, the Federal government spent almost **$21 million** dollars on the services of freelance video production people. That represents almost *one-quarter* of what the entire Federal government spent in the area of audio-visuals for 1993! Video tape production increased by 48% from 1989 to 1993. The growth of the video industry during these years translated directly into increased government business.

These projects often include video taping press conferences and meetings, making documentaries and training videos, and much more.

To get in line for this big government money spent on video production, you first need to know who does the hiring and who they're looking to hire. That's what the people in the following list can tell you. These Federal A-V contacts keep track of what their individual agency is doing and planning to do with video projects. They can help you get a better picture of whether you've got the expertise to do the kind of jobs that they need doing.

Video Production Contacts

Agriculture Department
Larry Quinn, Office of Communications, Video Teleconference and Radio Center, Room 1614 South Building, U.S. Department of Agriculture, Washington, DC 20250-1300; 202-720-6072.

Commerce Department
Robert B. Amdur, Director of Communications Services, Office of Public Affairs, U.S. Department of Commerce, Washington, DC 20230; 202-219-3605.

Defense Department
Paul Lewis, Defense Audiovisual Policy, OASD (PA) American Forces, Information Service, Defense Audiovisual Policy Office,

Suite 326, 601 N. Fairfax St., Alexandria, VA 22314-2007; 703-274-4872.

Education Department
Greg Grason, U.S. Department of Education, Room 2222, FOB #10, 600 Independence Ave., SW, Washington, DC 20202; 202-401-2559.

Energy Department
F. Chester Gray, Public Information Office, PA-5, U.S. Department of Energy, 1000 Independence Ave., SW, Washington, DC 20585; 202-586-4670.

Health & Human Services
Milo Mouch, U.S. Department of Health & Human Services, 200 Independence Ave., SW, Washington, DC 20201; 202-690-6076.

Housing & Urban Development
John Jones, HUD Training Academy, U.S. Department of Housing & Urban Development, 451 7th St., SW, Room 2180, Washington, DC 20410; 202-708-2009.

Interior Department
Stephen Brooks, Office of the Secretary, U.S. Department of the Interior, 1849 C St., NW, Washington, DC 20240; 202-208-6416.

Justice Department
Joe Kierlabor, U.S. Department of Justice, 1309 of Main Justice, 10th St. & Constitution Ave., NW, Washington, DC 20530; 202-616-3883.

Labor Department
Tom Accardy, Division of AV Communication Services, U.S. Department of Labor, Room N-6311, 200 Constitution Ave., NW, Washington, DC 20210; 202-219-7820.

State Department
Jane Dorset, S/S/EX Room 7512, U.S. Department of State, 2201 C St., NW, Washington, DC 20520; 202-647-9537.

Transportation Department
William Mosley, Public Affairs, Office of the Secretary, U.S. Department of Transportation, 400 7th St., SW, Suite 10413, Washington, DC 20590; 202-366-5582.

Treasury Department
Robert Harper, Office of Real and Personal Property, U.S. Department of the Treasury, 1500 Pennsylvania Ave., NW, Room 6140, Washington, DC 20220; 202-622-0500.

Veterans Affairs
Kevin Walls, Media Services 032B3, Department of Veterans Affairs, 810 Vermont Ave., NW, Washington, DC 20420; 202-273-7508.

Independent Federal Agencies

Corporation for National Service
Mike Berning, Office of Public Affairs, Corporation for National Service, 1200 New York Ave., NW, Washington, DC 20525; 202-606-5000.

Agency for International Development
Donna Wolf, USAID/LPA, Room 488D, Agency for International Development, Washington, DC 20523; 202-647-3499.

Environmental Protection Agency
Ed McRay, Office of the Comptroller (PM-225), Budget Division, U.S. Environmental Protection Agency, 401 M St., SW, Washington, DC 20460; 202-260-2070.

Equal Employment Opportunity Commission
Susan Taylor, Library Management Branch, Equal Employment Opportunity Commission, 1801 L St., NW, Washington, DC 20507; 202-663-4630.

Federal Emergency Management Agency
Bruce Marshall, Support Systems Branch, Federal Emergency Management Agency, 16825 South Seton Ave., Emmitsburg, MD 21727; 301-447-1260.

General Services Administration
J. Peter Glaws, Office of AV Services, General Services Administration, 18th & F Sts., NW, Room B33, Washington, DC 20405; 202-208-1421.

National Credit Union Administration
James L. Baylen, Administrative Office, National Credit Union Administration, 1775 Duke St., Alexandria, VA 22314; 703-518-6410.

National Aeronautics & Space Administration
Joseph Benton, Office of Public Affairs, National Aeronautics & Space Administration, 300 E St., SW, Code PS, Washington, DC 20546; 202-358-1743.

National Endowment for the Humanities
Barry Maynes, National Endowment for the Humanities, 1100 Pennsylvania Ave., NW, Room 201, Washington, DC 20506; 202-606-8233.

National Science Foundation
Susan Bartlett, Office of Legislative & Public Affairs, National Science Foundation, 4201 Wilson Blvd., Arlington, VA 22230; 703-306-1070.

Overseas Private Investment Corporation
Peter Ballinger, Overseas Private Investment Corporation, 1100 New York Ave., NW, Washington, DC 20527; 202-336-8400.

Pension Benefit Guaranty Corporation
Richard Petta, Communications & Public Affairs, Pension Benefit Guaranty Corporation, 1200 K St., NW, Washington, DC 20005-4026; 202-326-4040.

Selective Service System
Larry Waltman, Public Affairs Office, National Headquarters Selective Service System, 1515 Wilson Blvd., Arlington, VA 22209; 703-235-2053.

Small Business Administration
D.J. Caulfield, Publications & Graphic Design Services, Office of Public Communications, U.S. Small Business Administration, 409 Third St., SW, Washington, DC 20416; 202-205-6740.

Tennessee Valley Authority
Alan Carmichael, Communications, Tennessee Valley Authority, 400 W. Summit Hill Dr., Knoxville, TN 37902; 615-632-8018.

U.S. Information Agency
Martha Methee, Television and Film Service, U.S. Information Agency, Patrick Henry Building, Room 5122, 601 D St., NW, Washington, DC 20547; 202-501-7758.

How to Get a $150/Hour Business Consultant for Free

How to Get a $150/Hour
Business Consultant For Free

Small Business Development Centers (SBDCs) are probably the best deal the government has to offer to entrepreneurs and inventors. Where else in the world are you able to have access to a $150 an hour consultant for free? There are over 700 of these offices all over the country and they offer free (or very low cost) consulting services on any aspect of business including:

- how to write a business plan
- how to get financing
- how to protect your invention
- how to sell your idea
- how to license your product
- how to comply with the laws
- how to write a contract
- how to sell overseas
- how to get government contracts
- how to help you buy the right equipment

You don't even have to know how to spell ENTREPRENEUR to contact these offices. They cater to both the dreamer, who doesn't even know where to start, as well as to the experienced small business that is trying to grow to the next stage of development.

Why spend money on a consultant, a lawyer, an accountant, or one of those invention companies when you can get it all for free, and probably better, at your local SBDC?

Recently, I spoke with some entrepreneurs who used a California SBDC and each of them had nothing but praise for the services. A young man who dropped out of college to start an executive cleaning business said he received over $8,000 worth of free legal help from the center and said it was instrumental in getting his business off the ground. A woman who worked in a bank started her gourmet cookie business by using the SBDC

to help her get the money and technical assistance needed to get her venture going. And a man who was a gymnast raved about how the SBDC helped him get his personal trainer business off the ground.

Can something that is free be so good? Of course it can. Because most of the people who work there are not volunteers, they are paid for by tax dollars. So it's really not free to us as a country, but it is free to you as an entrepreneur. And if you don't believe me that the SBDCs are so good, would you take the word of Professor James J. Chrisman from the University of Calgary in Calgary, Alberta, Canada? He was commissioned to do an independent study of SBDCs and found that 82% of the people who used their services found them beneficial. And the businesses who used SBDCs had average growth rates up to 400% greater than all the other businesses in their area. Not bad. Compare this to the Fortune 500 companies who use the most expensive consulting firms in the country and only experience growth rates of 5% or less. So, who says you get what you pay for?

Small Business Development Centers

Alabama

Lead Center:
Office of State Director
Alabama Small Business Development Consortium
University of Alabama at Birmingham
1717 11th Ave. South, Suite 419
Birmingham, AL 35294-7645
205-934-7260
Fax: 205-934-7645

Small Business Development Centers

Auburn: Auburn University, Small Business Development Ctr., College of Business, Auburn, AL 36849, 205-844-4220.

Birmingham: University of Alabama at Birmingham, Small Business Development Center, 1601 11th Ave. S., Birmingham, AL 35294-2060, 205-934-6760.

Birmingham: Alabama Small Business Procurement System, University of Alabama at Birmingham, Small Business Development Center, 1717 11th Ave. South, Suite 419, Birmingham, AL 35294-4410, 205-934-7260.

Florence: University of North Alabama, Small Business Development Center, P.O. Box 5248, Keller Hall, School of Business, Florence, AL 35632-0001, 205-760-4629.

Huntsville: North East Alabama Regional Small Business Development Center, Alabama A&M University and University of Alabama in Huntsville, 225 Church St., NW, Huntsville, AL 35804-0343, 205-535-2061.

Jacksonville: Jacksonville State University, SBDC, 114 Merrill Hall, Jacksonville, AL 36265, 205-782-5271.

Livingston: Livingston University, Small Business Development Center, 212 Wallace Hall, Livingston, AL 35470, 205-652-9661, ext. 439.

Mobile: University of South Alabama, SBDC, 8 College of Business, Mobile, AL 36688, 334-460-6004.

Montgomery: Alabama State University, SBDC, 915 S. Jackson St., Montgomery, AL 36195, 334-269-1102.

Troy: Troy State University, Small Business Development Ctr., 102 Bibb Graves, Troy, AL 36082-0001, 334-670-3771.

Tuscaloosa: Alabama International Trade Center, University of Alabama, 250 Bidgood Hall, Tuscaloosa, AL 35487-0396, 205-348-7621.

Tuscaloosa: University of Alabama, SBDC, 250 Bidgood Hall, Tuscaloosa, AL 35487-0397, 205-348-7011.

Alaska

Lead Center:
Jan Fredericks
University of Alaska
Small Business Development Center
430 West 7th Avenue, Suite 110
Anchorage, AK 99501
907-274-7232
Fax: 907-274-9524
Outside Anchorage: 800-478-7232

Anchorage: University of Alaska-Anchorage SBDC, 430 West 7th Ave., Suite 110, Anchorage, AK 99501, 907-274-7232; Fax: 907-274-9524; outside Anchorage: 800-478-7232.

Fairbanks: University of Alaska-Fairbanks, SBDC, 510 Fifth Ave., Suite 101, Fairbanks, AK 99701, 907-456-1701; Fax: 907-456-1942; outside Fairbanks: 800-478-1701.

Juneau: Southeast Alaska Small Business Development Center, 400 Willow St., Juneau, AK 99801, 907-463-3789; Fax: 907-463-3929.

Wasilla: Matanuska-Susitna Borough, Small Business Development Center, 1801 Parks Highway, #C-18, Wasilla, AK 99654, 907-373-7232; Fax: 907-373-2560.

Arizona

Lead Center:
Arizona Small Business Development Center
9215 N. Black Canyon Highway
Phoenix, AZ 85021
602-943-9818
Fax: 602-943-3716

Flagstaff: Coconino County Community College, SBDC, 3000 N. 4th St., Suite 25, Flagstaff, AZ 86004, 602-526-5072; Fax: 602-526-8693; 1-800-350-7122.

Holbrook: Northland Pioneer College, Small Business Development Center, P.O. Box 610, Holbrook, AZ 86025, 602-537-2976; Fax: 602-524-2227.

Kingman: Mojave Community College, Small Business Development Center, 1971 Jagerson Ave., Kingman, AZ 86401, 602-757-0894; Fax: 602-787-0836.

Phoenix: Rio Salado Community College, Small Business Development Center, 301 West Roosevelt, Suite B, Phoenix, AZ 85003, 602-238-9603; Fax: 602-340-1627.

Phoenix: Gateway Community College, SBDC, 108 N. 40th St., Phoenix, AZ 85034, 602-392-5223; Fax: 602-392-5329.

Prescott: Yavapal College, Small Business Development Center, 1100 E. Sheldon St., Prescott, AZ 86301, 602-778-3088; Fax: 602-778-3109.

Sierra Vista: Cochise College, Small Business Development Center, 901 N. Colombo, Room 411, Sierra Vista, AZ 85635, 602-459-9778; Fax: 602-459-9737; 1-800-966-7943, ext. 778.

Thatcher: Eastern Arizona College, Small Business Development Center, 622 College Ave., Thatcher, AZ 85552-0769, 602-428-8590; Fax: 602-428-8462.

Tucson: Pima Community College, Small Business Development Center, 4903 E. Broadway, Suite 101, Tucson, AZ 85709, 602-748-4906; Fax: 602-748-4585.

Yuma: Arizona Western College, Small Business Development Center, 281 W. 24th St., #152 Century Plaza, Yuma, AZ 85364, 602-341-1650; Fax: 602-726-2636.

Arkansas

Lead Center:
Arkansas Small Business Development Center
University of Arkansas at Little Rock
Little Rock Technology Center Building
100 S. Main, Suite 401
Little Rock, AR 72201
501-324-9043
Fax: 501-324-9049

Arkadelphia: Henderson State University, Small Business Development Center, P.O. Box 7624, Arkadelphia, AR 71923, 501-246-5511, ext. 327.

Fayetteville: University of Arkansas at Fayetteville, Small Business Development Center, College of Business - BA 117, Fayetteville, AR 72701, 501-575-5148.

Jonesboro: Arkansas State University, Small Business Development Center, P.O. Drawer 2650, Jonesboro, AR 72467, 501-972-3517.

California

Lead Center:
California Small Business Development Center
California Department of Commerce
Office of Small Business
801 K Street, Suite 1700
Sacramento, CA 95814
916-324-5068
Fax: 916-322-5084

Aptos: Central Coast Small Business Assistance Center, 6500 Soquel Dr., Aptos, CA 95003, 408-479-6136; Fax: 408-479-5743.

Auburn: Sierra College, SBDC, 560 Wall St., Suite J, Auburn, CA 95603, 916-885-5488; Fax: 916-823-4704.

Bakersfield: Weill Institute, SBDC, 1330 22nd St., Bakersfield, CA 93301, 805-322-5881; Fax: 805-322-5663.

Chico: Butte College, Tri-County Small Business Development Center, 260 Cohasset Ave., Chico, CA 95926, 916-895-9017; Fax: 916-895-9099.

Chula Vista: Southwestern College, SBDC and International Trade Center, 900 Otay Lakes Rd., Bldg. 1600, Chula Vista, CA 91910, 619-482-6393; Fax: 619-482-6402.

Clearlake: Satellite Operation, Small Business Development Center, Hilltop Professional Ctr., Suite 205, Box 4550, Clearlake, CA 95422, 707-996-3440; Fax: 707-995-3605.

Crescent City: North Coast Small Business Development Center, 779 9th St., Crescent City, CA 95531, 707-464-2168; Fax: 707-465-6008.

Eureka: North Coast Satellite Center, 408 7th St., Suite "E", Eureka, CA 95501, 707-445-9720; Fax: 707-445-9652.

Fresno: Central California Small Business Development Center, 1999 Tuolumine St., Suite 650, Fresno, CA 93721, 209-237-0660; Fax: 209-237-1417.

Gilroy: Gavilan College, SBDC, 7436 Monterey St., Gilroy, CA 95020, 408-847-0373; Fax: 408-847-0393.

Irvine: Accelerate Technology Small Business Development Center, Graduate School of Management, Room 230, University of California, Irvine, CA 92717-3125, 714-856-8366; Fax: 714-725-2978.

La Jolla: Greater San Diego Chamber of Commerce, Small Business Development Center, 4275 Executive Square, Suite 920, La Jolla, CA 92037, 619-453-9388; Fax: 619-450-1997.

Los Angeles: Export Small Business Development Center of Southern California, 110 E. 9th, Suite 669, Los Angeles, CA 90079, 213-892-1111; Fax: 213-892-8232.

Merced: Satellite Operation, Small Business Development Center, 1632 N. St., Merced, CA 95340, 209-385-7312; Fax: 209-383-4959.

Modesto: Valley Sierra Small Business Development Center, 1012 11th St., Suite 300, Modesto, CA 95354, 209-521-6177; Fax: 209-521-9373.

Napa: Napa Valley College, Small Business Development Center, 1556 First St., Suite 103, Napa, CA 94559, 707-253-3210; Fax: 707-253-3068.

Oakland: East Bay Small Business Development Center, 2201 Broadway, Suite 701, Oakland, CA 94612, 510-893-4114; Fax: 510-893-5532.

Oxnard: Satellite Operation, SBDC, 300 Esplanade Dr., Suite 1010, Oxnard, CA 93030, 805-981-4633; Fax: 805-988-1862.

Pomona: Eastern Los Angeles County Small Business Development Center, 363 S. Park Ave., Pomona, CA 91766, 909-629-2297; Fax: 909-629-8310.

Riverside: Inland Empire Small Business Development Center, 2002 Iowa Ave., Suite 110, Riverside, CA 92507, 714-781-2345; Fax: 714-781-2345.

Sacramento: Greater Sacramento Small Business Development Center, 1787 Tribute Rd., Suite A, Sacramento, CA 95815, 916-263-6580; Fax: 916-263-6571.

San Jose: Silicon Valley - San Mateo County, Small Business Development Center, 111 N. Market St., #150, San Jose, CA 95113, 408-298-7694; Fax: 408-971-0680.

San Mateo: San Mateo County Satellite Center, Bayshore Corporate Center, 1730 S. Amphlett Blvd., Suite 208, San Mateo, CA 94402, 415-358-0271; Fax: 415-358-9450.

Santa Ana: Rancho Santiago Small Business Development Center, 901 East Santa Ana Boulevard, Suite 108, Santa Ana, CA 92701, 714-647-1172; Fax: 714-835-9008.

Santa Rosa: Redwood Empire, Small Business Development Center, 520 Mendocino Ave., Suite 210, Santa Rosa, CA 95401, 707-524-1770; Fax: 707-524-1772.

Stockton: San Joaquin Delta College, SBDC, 814 N. Hunter, Stockton, CA 95202, 209-474-5089; Fax: 209-263-6571.

Suisun: Solano County Small Business Development Center, 320 Campus Lane, Suisun, CA 94585, 707-864-3382; Fax: 707-864-3386.

Torrance: Southwest Los Angeles County Small Business Development Center, 21221 Western Ave., Suite 110, Torrance, CA 90501, 310-782-3861; Fax: 310-782-8607.

Van Nuys: Northern Los Angeles Small Business Development Center, 14540 Victory Boulevard, Suite #206, Van Nuys, CA 91411, 818-373-7092; Fax: 818-373-7740.

Visalia: Satellite Operation, Central California Small Business Development Center, 430 W. Caldwell, Suite D, Visalia, CA 93277, 209-625-3051/3052; Fax: 209-625-3053.

Colorado

Lead Center:
Colorado Small Business Development Center
Office of Economic Development
1625 Broadway, Suite 1710
Denver, CO 80202
303-892-3809; 303-892-3840
Fax: 303-892-3848

Alamosa: Adams State College, SBDC, Alamosa, CO 81102, 719-589-7372; Fax: 719-589-7522.

Aurora: Community College of Aurora, Small Business Development Center, 16000 E. Centretech Parkway, #A201, Aurora, CO 80011-9036, 719-341-4849.

Canon City: Canon City (Satellite) Small Business Development Center, 402 Valley Rd., Canon City, CO 81212, 719-442-1475.

Colorado Springs: Pikes Peak Community College/Colorado Springs Chamber of Commerce, Small Business Development Center, P.O. Drawer B, Colorado Springs, CO 80901-3002, 719-471-4836.

Craig: Colorado Northwestern Community College, Small Business Development Center, 50 Spruce Dr., Craig, CO 81625, 303-824-7078; Fax: 303-824-3527.

Delta: Delta Montrose Vocational School, SBDC, 1765 US Hwy 50, Delta, CO 81416, 303-874-8772; Fax: 303-874-8796.

Denver: Community College of Denver/ Denver Chamber of Commerce, Small Business Development Center, 1445 Market St., Denver, CO 80202, 303-620-8076; Fax: 303-534-3200.

Durango: Fort Lewis College, Small Business Development Center, Miller Student Center, Room 108, Durango, CO 81301, 303-247-9634; Fax: 303-247-7620.

Fort Collins: Fort Collins (Satellite), P.O. Box 2397, Fort Collins, CO 80522, 303-226-0881.

Fort Morgan: Morgan Community College, Small Business Development Center, 300 Main St., Fort Morgan, CO 80701, 303-867-4424; Fax: 303-867-7580.

Grand Junction: Mesa State College, SBDC, 304 W. Main St., Grand Junction, CO 81505-1606, 303-243-5242.

Greeley: Aims Community College/Greeley and Weld Chamber of Commerce, SBDC, 1407 8th Ave., Greeley, CO 80631, 303-352-3661; Fax: 303-352-3572.

Lakewood: Red Rocks Community College, Small Business Development Center, 13300 W. 6th Ave., Lakewood, CO 80401-5398, 303-987-0710; Fax: 303-969-8039.

Lamar: Lamar Community College, SBDC, 2400 S. Main, Lamar, CO 81052, 719-336-8141; Fax: 719-336-2448.

Littleton: Arapaho Community College/South Metro Chamber of Commerce, SBDC, 7901 S. Park Plaza, Suite 110, Littleton, CO 80120, 303-795-5855; Fax: 303-795-7520.

Pueblo: Pueblo Community College, Small Business Development Center, 900 West Orman Ave., Pueblo, CO 81004, 719-549-3224; Fax: 719-546-2413.

Stratton: Stratton (Satellite) Small Business Development Center, P.O. Box 28, Stratton, CO 80836, 719-348-5596; Fax: 719-348-5887.

Trinidad: Trinidad State Junior College, Small Business Development Center, 600 Prospect St., Davis Building, Trinidad, CO 81082, 719-846-5645.

Westminister: Front Range Community College, Small Business Development Center, 3645 West 112th Avenue, Westminister, CO 80030, 303-460-1032; Fax: 303-466-1623.

Connecticut

Lead Center:
Connecticut Small Business Development Center
University of Connecticut
School of Business Administration
Box U-41, Room 422, 368 Fairfield Rd.
Storrs, CT 06268
203-486-4135
Fax: 203-486-1576

Bridgeport: Business Regional B.C., Small Business Development Center, 10 Middle St., 14th Floor, Bridgeport, CT 06604-4229, 203-335-3800; Fax: 203-366-9105.

Bridgeport: University of Bridgeport, Small Business Development Center, 141 Linden Avenue, Bridgeport, CT 06601, 203-576-4538.

Danielson: Quinebaug Valley Community College, SBDC, 742 Upper Maple Street, Danielson, CT 06239-1440, 203-774-1133; Fax: 203-774-7768.

Hartford: University of Connecticut/MBA, Small Business Development Center, 1800 Asylum Ave., West Hartford, CT 06117, 203-241-4986; Fax: 203-241-4907.

Groton: University of Connecticut, Small Business Development Center, Administration Building, Room 313, 1084 Shennecossett Rd., Groton, CT 06340-6097, 203-449-1188; Fax: 203-445-3415.

Middletown: Middlesex County Chamber of Commerce, Small Business Development Center, 393 Main St., Middletown, CT 06457, 203-344-2158; Fax: 203-346-1043.

New Haven: Greater New Haven Chamber of Commerce, Small Business Development Center, 195 Church St., New Haven, CT 06506, 203-773-0782; Fax: 203-787-6730.

Stamford: Southwestern Area Commerce and Industry Association (SACIA), Small Business Development Center, One Landmark Square, Stamford, CT 06901, 203-359-3220; Fax: 203-967-8294.

Waterbury: Greater Waterbury Chamber of Commerce, Small Business Development Center, 83 Bank St., Waterbury, CT 06702, 203-757-0701; Fax: 203-756-3507.

Willmantic: Eastern Connecticut State University, Small Business Development Center, 83 Windham St., Willmantic, CT 06226-2295, 203-456-5349; Fax: 203-456-5670.

Delaware

Lead Center:
Delaware Small Business Development Center
University of Delaware
Purnell Hall, Suite 005
Newark, DE 19716
302-831-1555
Fax: 302-831-1423

City of Wilmington: Wilmington Economic Development Corporation, 605A Market Street Mall, Wilmington, DE 19801; 302-571-9088.

New Castle County: New Castle County Economic Development Corporation, First Federal Plaza, Suite 536, Wilmington, DE 19801; 302-656-5050

Sussex County: Sussex County Department of Economic Development, PO Box 589, 11 S. Race St., Georgetown, DE 19947; 302-855-7770; Fax: 302-855-7773

District of Columbia

Lead Center:
District of Columbia Small Business Development Center
Howard University
6th and Fairmont St., NW, Room 128
Washington, DC 20059
202-806-1550
Fax: 202-806-1777

Arlington: Marymount University, Small Business Development Center, Office of Continuing Education, 2807 N. Glebe Rd., Arlington, VA 22207-4299, 703-522-5600.

College Park: University of Maryland (UMCP), SBDC, College of Business and Management, Tydings Hall, College Park, MD 20742, 301-405-2144.

Landover: National Business League of Southern Maryland, Inc., Small Business Development Center, 1400 McCormick Dr., Landover, MD 20785, 301-883-6491.

Washington: Galludet University, Small Business Development Center, Management Institute, 800 Florida Ave., NE, Washington, DC 20002-3625, 202-651-5312.

Washington: George Washington University, Small Business Development Center, National Law Center, 720 20th St., NW, Suite SL-101B, Washington, DC 20052, 202-994-7463.

Florida

These centers provide assistance with Department of Defense procurement who continuously search for suppliers for its vast array of needs and offer many business opportunities for competent suppliers.

Lead Center:
Florida Small Business Development Center Network
University of West Florida
Downtown Center
19 W. Garden St., Suite 366
Pensacola, FL 32561
904-444-2060
Fax: 904-474-2092

AltaMonte Springs: Seminole Community College, Small Business Development Center, Seminole Chamber of Commerce, P.O. Box 150784, AltaMonte Springs, FL 32715-0784, 407-834-4404.

Boca Raton: Florida Atlantic University, Small Business Development Center, Building T-9, P.O. Box 3091, Boca Raton, FL 33431, 407-362-5620.

Cocoa: Brevard Community College, SBDC, 1519 Clearlake Rd., Cocoa, FL 32922, 407-951-1060, ext. 2045.

Dania: Small Business Development Center, 46 SW 1st Ave., Dania, FL 33304, 305-987-0100.

Deland: Stetson University, Small Business Development Center, School of Business Administration, P.O. Box 8417, Deland, FL 32720, 904-822-7326.

Fort Lauderdale: Small Business Development Center, Florida Atlantic University, Commercial Campus, 1515 West Commercial Blvd., Room 11, Fort Lauderdale, FL 33309, 305-771-6520.

Fort Pierce: Indian River Community College, Small Business Development Center, 3209 Virginia Ave., Room 114, Fort Pierce, FL 34981-5599, 407-468-4756.

Fort Myers: University of South Florida, Small Business Development Center, Sabal Hall, Rooms 219 and 220, 8111 College Parkway, Fort Myers, FL 33919, 813-489-4140.

Fort Walton Beach: University of West Florida, Fort Walton Beach Center, Small Business Development Center, 414 Mary Esther Cutoff, Fort Walton Beach, FL 32548, 904-244-1036.

Gainesville: Small Business Development Center, 214 W. University Ave., P.O. Box 2518, Gainesville, FL 32601, 904-377-5621.

Gainesville: FSBDC Product Innovation Program, Florida Product Innovation Center, 2622 NW 43rd St., Suite B-3, Gainesville, FL 32606, 904-334-1680.

Jacksonville: University of North Florida, Small Business Development Center, College of Business, 4567 St. John's Bluff Rd., S., Jacksonville, FL 32216, 904-646-2476.

Lynn Haven: Gulf Coast Community College, SBDC, 2500 Minnesota Ave., Lynn Haven, FL 32444, 904-271-1108.

Miami: Florida International University, SBDC, Trailer MO1, Tamiami Campus, Miami, FL 33199, 305-348-2272.

Ocala: Small Business Development Center, 110 East Silver Springs Blvd., P.O. Box 1210, Ocala, FL 32670, 904-629-8051.

Orlando: University of Central Florida, Small Business Development Center, P.O. Box 161530, Orlando, FL 32816, 407-823-5554.

Pensacola: University of West Florida, Small Business Development Center, Building 8, 11000 University Parkway, Pensacola, FL 32514, 904-474-2908.

St. Petersburg: University of South Florida, St. Petersburg Campus, Small Business Development Center, 830 First St. S., Room 113, St. Petersburg, FL 33701, 813-893-9529.

Sarasota: Small Business Development Center, 5700 N. Tamiami Trail, Sarasota, FL 33580, 813-359-4292.

Tallahassee: Florida A & M University, Small Business Development Center, 1157 Tennessee St., Tallahassee, FL 32308, 904-599-3407.

Tampa: University of South Florida, Small Business Development Center, College of Business Administration, 4202 Minnesota Ave., BSN 3403, Tampa, FL 32444, 813-974-4274.

West Palm Beach: Small Business Development Center, Prospect Place, Suite 123, 3111 S. Dixie Highway, West Palm Beach, FL 33405, 407-837-5311.

Georgia

Lead Center:
Georgia Small Business Development Center
University of Georgia, Chicopee Complex
1180 East Broad Street
Athens, GA 30602
706-542-5780
Fax: 706-542-6776

Albany: Small Business Development Center, Southwest Georgia District, Business and Technology Center, 230 S. Jackson Street, 3rd Floor, Suite 333, Albany, GA 31701, 912-430-4303; Fax: 912-430-3933.

Athens: Small Business Development Center, University of Georgia, Chicopee Complex, 1180 East Broad Street, Athens, GA 30602, 706-542-7436; Fax: 706-542-6776.

Atlanta: Morris Brown College, Small Business Development Center, 634 Martin Luther King Jr. Dr., NW, Atlanta, GA 30314, 404-220-0201; Fax: 404-220-0236.

Atlanta: Georgia State University, Small Business Development Center, Box 874, University Plaza, Atlanta, GA 30303-3083, 706-651-3550; Fax: 706-651-1035.

Augusta: Small Business Development Center, 1061 Katherine Street, Augusta, GA 30910, 706-737-1790; Fax: 706-731-7937.

Brunswick: Small Business Development Center, 1107 Fountain Lake Drive, Brunswick, GA 31525, 912-264-7343; Fax: 912-262-3095.

Columbus: Small Business Development Center, 928 45th St. North Bldg., Room 523, Columbus, GA 31902, 706-649-7433; Fax: 706-649-1928.

Decatur: DeKalb Chamber of Commerce, Small Business Development Center, 750 Commerce Drive, Decatur, GA 30030, 404-378-8000; Fax: 404-378-3397.

Gainesville: Small Business Development Center, 456 Jesse Jewel Parkway, Suite 302, Gainesville, GA 30501, 706-531-5881; Fax: 706-531-5684.

Lawrenceville: Gwinnett Technical Institute, Small Business Development Center, 1250 Atkinson Road, Lawrenceville, GA 30246, 404-339-2287; Fax: 404-339-2329.

Macon: Small Business Development Center, P.O. Box 13212, Macon, GA 91208-3212, 912-751-6592.

Marietta: Kennesaw State College, SBDC, P.O. Box 444, Marietta, GA 30061, 404-423-6450; Fax: 404-423-6564.

Morrow: Clayton State College, Small Business Development Center, P.O. Box 285, Morrow, GA 30260, 404-961-3440; Fax: 404-961-3428.

Rome: Floyd College, SBDC, P.O. Box 1664, Rome, GA 30162, 706-295-6326; Fax: 706-295-5732.

Savannah: Small Business Development Center, 450 Mall Blvd., Suite H, Savannah, GA 31405, 912-356-2755; Fax: 912-353-3033.

Statesboro: Small Business Development Center, Landrum Center, Box 6156, Statesboro, GA 30460, 912-681-5194; Fax: 912-681-0648.

Valdosta: Small Business Development Center, Valdosta Area Office, Baytree West Professional Offices, Suite 9, Baytree Rd., Valdosta, GA 31602, 912-245-3738; Fax: 912-245-3741.

Warner Robins: Middle Georgia Technical Institute, Small Business Development Center, 151 Asigian Blvd., Warner Robins, GA 31088, 912-953-9356; Fax: 912-953-9376.

Hawaii

Lead Center:
Hawaii Small Business Development Center
University of Hawaii at Hilo
200 W. Kawili St.
Hilo, HI 96720-4091
808-933-3515
Fax: 808-933-3683

Hilo: Small Business Development Center - Big Island, University of Hawaii at Hilo, 523 W. Lanikaula Street, Hilo, HI 96720-4091, 808-933-3515.

Lihue: Small Business Development Center - Kauai, Kauai Community College, 3-1901 Kaumualii Highway, Lihue, HI 96766-9591, 808-246-1748.

Kihei: Small Business Development Center - Maui, Maui Research and Technology Center, 590 Lipoa Parkway, Kihei, HI 96753, 808-875-2402.

Honolulu: Small Business Development Center - Oahu, Business Action Center, 1130 N. Merchant St., Suite 1030, Honolulu, HI 96817, 808-522-8131.

Idaho

Lead Center:
Idaho Small Business Development Center
Boise State University
College of Business
1910 University Drive
Boise, ID 83706-9987
208-385-1640
Fax: 208-385-3877

Idaho Falls: Idaho State University, Small Business Development Center, 2300 North Yellowstone, Idaho Falls, ID 83401, 208-523-1087; Fax: 208-523-1049.

Lewiston: Lewis-Clark State College, Small Business Development Center, 500 8th Avenue, Lewiston, ID 83501, 208-799-2465; Fax: 208-799-2831.

McCall: Boise Satellite Office, SBDC, Boise State Univ., College of Business, 415 Railroad, McCall, ID 83638, 208-634-2883.

Nampa: Boise Satellite Office, SBDC, Boise State Univ., College of Business, Canyon County Center, 2407 Caldwell Blvd., Nampa, ID 83651, 208-467-5707, ext. 4728.

Pocatello: Idaho State University, Small Business Development Center, 1651 Alvin Ricken Drive, Pocatello, ID 83201, 208-232-4921; Fax: 208-233-0268; 1-800-232-4921.

Post Falls: North Idaho College, Small Business Development Center, 525 W. Clearwater Loop, Post Falls, ID 83854, 208-769-3296.

Twin Falls: College of Southern Idaho, Small Business Development Center, Region IV, 315 Falls Ave., Twin Falls, ID 83303, 208-733-9554, ext. 2477; Fax: 208-734-6592.

Illinois

Lead Center:
Illinois Small Business Development Center Network
Dept. of Commerce and Community Affairs
620 East Adams Street, 6th Floor
Springfield, IL 62701
217-524-5856
Fax: 217-785-6328

Aurora: Waubonsee Community College/ Aurora Campus, Small Business Development Center, 5 East Galena Blvd., Aurora, IL 60506, 708-892-3334, Ext. 139; Fax: 708-892-3374.

Small Business Development Centers

Carbondale: Southern Illinois University/Carbondale, Small Business Development Center, Carbondale, IL 62901, 618-536-2424; Fax: 618-453-5040.

Centralia: Kaskaskia College (Satellite), Small Business Development Center, Shattuc Road, Centralia, IL 62801, 618-532-2049; Fax: 618-532-4983.

Chicago: Back of the Yards Neighborhood Council (Sub-Center), Small Business Development Center, 1751 West 47th Street, Chicago, IL 60609, 312-523-4419; Fax: 312254-3525.

Chicago: Greater North Pulaski Economic Development Corp., SBDC, 4054 West North Avenue, Chicago, IL 60639, 312-384-2262, Fax: 312-384-3850.

Chicago: Women's Business Development Center, Small Business Development Center, 8 South Michigan, Suite 400, Chicago, IL 60603, 312-853-3477; Fax: 312-853-0145.

Chicago: Olive-Harvey College, Small Business Development Center, 10001 South Woodlawn Drive, Chicago, IL 60628, 312-468-8700; Fax: 312-468-8086.

Chicago: Industrial Council of NW Chicago, Small Business Development Center, 2023 West Carroll, Chicago, IL 60612, 312-421-3941; Fax: 312-421-1871.

Chicago: Latin American Chamber of Commerce, Small Business Development Center, 539 North Kedzie, Suite 11, Chicago, IL 60647, 312-252-5211; Fax: 312-252-7065.

Chicago: Eighteenth Street Development Corp., Small Business Development Center, 1839 South Carpenter, Chicago, IL 60608, 312-733-2287; Fax: 312-733-7512.

Chicago: Loop Small Business Development Center, DCCA, State of Illinois Ctr., 100 West Randolph, Suite 3-400, Chicago, IL 60601, 312-814-6111; Fax: 312-814-2807.

Crystal Lake: McHenry County College, Small Business Development Center, 8900 U.S. Highway 14, Crystal Lake, IL 60012-2761, 815-455-6098; Fax: 815-455-3999.

Danville: Danville Area Community College, SBDC, 28 West North Street, Danville, IL 61832, 217-442-7232; Fax: 217-442-6228.

DeKalb: Northern Illinois University, SBDC, Department of Management, 305 East Locust, DeKalb, IL 60115, 815-753-1403; Fax: 815-753-2305.

Dixon: Sauk Valley College, SBDC, 173 Illinois Route #2, Dixon, IL 61021-9110, 815-288-5605; Fax: 815-288-5958.

Edwardsville: Southern Illinois University/ Edwardsville, SBDC, Campus Box 1107, Edwardsville, IL 62026, 618-692-2929; Fax: 618-692-2647.

Elgin: Elgin Community College, SBDC, 1700 Spartan Drive, Elgin, IL 60115, 708-697-1000, ext. 7923; Fax: 708-888-7995.

Evanston: Evanston Business and Technology Center, Small Business Development Center, 1840 Oak Ave., Evanston, IL 60201, 708-866-1841; Fax: 708-866-1808.

Freeport: Highland Community College (Satellite), Small Business Development Center, 2998 West Pearl City, Freeport, IL 61032-9341, 815-232-1362; Fax: 815-235-6130.

Glen Ellyn: College of DuPage, Small Business Development Center, 22nd and Lambert Road, Glen Ellyn, IL 60137, 708-858-2800, ext. 2771.

Grayslake: College of Lake County, SBDC, 19351 West Washington Street, Grayslake, IL 60030, 708-223-3633, 708-223-3612; Fax: 708-223-9371.

Harrisburg: Southeastern Illinois College (Satellite), 325 Poplar, Suite A, Harrisburg, IL 62946, 618-252-5001; Fax: 618-252-0210.

Ina: Rend Lake College, SBDC, Route #1, Ina, IL 62846, 618-437-5321, ext. 335.

Joliet: Joliet Junior College, SBDC, Renaissance Center, Room 319, 214 North Ottawa Street, Joliet, IL 60431, 815-727-6544, Ext. 1313; Fax: 815-722-1895.

Kankakee: Kankakee Community College, SBDC, Box 888, River Road, Kankakee, IL 60901, 815-933-0376; Fax: 815-933-0380.

Macomb: Western Illinois University, SBDC, 216 Seal Hall, Macomb, IL 61455, 309-298-2211; Fax: 309-298-2520.

Mattoon: Lake Land College, SBDC, South Route #45, Mattoon, IL 61938-9366, 217-235-3131; Fax: 217-258-6459.

East Moline: Black Hawk College, SBDC, 301 42nd Ave, East Moline, IL 61244, 309-752-9759, 309-752-0262; Fax: 309-755-9847.

Monmouth: Maple City Business and Technology (Satellite), SBDC, 620 South Main Street, Monmouth, IL 61462, 309-734-4664; Fax: 309-734-8579.

Oglesby: Illinois Valley Community College, SBDC, Building 11, Route 1, Oglesby, IL 61348, 815-223-1740; Fax: 815-224-3033.

Olney: Illinois Eastern Community College, SBDC, 233 East Chestnut, Olney, IL 62450, 618-395-3011; Fax: 618-395-1922.

Palos Hills: Moraine Valley College, SBDC, 10900 South 88th Avenue, Palos Hills, IL 60465, 708-974-5468; Fax: 708-974-0078.

Peoria: Bradley University, SBDC, 141 North Jobst Hall, 1st Floor, Peoria, IL 61625, 309-677-2992; Fax: 309-677-3386.

Rockford: Rock Valley College, SBDC, 1220 Rock Street, Rockford, IL 61102, 815-968-4087; Fax: 815-968-4157.

Springfield: Lincoln Land Community College, SBDC, 200 West Washington, Springfield, IL 62701, 217-524-3060; Fax: 217-782-1106.

East St. Louis: East St. Louis, DCCA, State Office Building, 10 Collinsville, East St. Louis, IL 62201, 618-583-2272; Fax: 618-588-2274.

Ullin: Shawnee College (Satellite), SBDC, Shawnee College Road, Ullin, IL 62992, 618-634-9618; Fax: 618-634-9028.

University Park: Governor's State University, SBDC, University Park, IL 60466, 708-534-4929; Fax: 708-534-8457.

Indiana

Lead Center:
Indiana Small Business Development Center
Economic Development Council
One North Capitol, Suite 420
Indianapolis, IN 46204
317-264-6871
Fax: 317-264-3102

Bloomington: Greater Bloomington Chamber of Commerce, Small Business Development Center, 116 W. 6th Street, Bloomington, IN 47404, 812-339-8937.

Columbus: Columbus Enterprise Development Center, Inc., SBDC, 4920 North Warren Drive, Columbus, IN 47203, 812-372-6480; Fax: 812-372-0228.

Evansville: Evansville Chamber of Commerce, Small Business Development Center, 100 NW Second Street, Suite 200, Evansville, IN 47708, 812-425-7232.

Fort Wayne: Northeast Indiana Business Assistance Corporation, Small Business Development Center, 1830 West Third Street, Fort Wayne, IN 46803, 219-426-0040.

Jeffersonville: Hoosier Valley Economic Opportunity Corporation, Small Business Development Center, 1613 E. 8th Street, Jeffersonville, IN 47130, 812-288-6451.

Indianapolis: Indiana University, Small Business Development Center, 342 Senate Ave., Indianapolis, IN 46204, 317-261-3030.

Kokomo: Kokomo-Howard County Chamber of Commerce, Small Business Development Center, P.O. Box 731, Kokomo, IN 46903, 317-457-5301.

Lafayette: Greater Lafayette Progress, Inc., Small Business Development Center, 122 N. Third, Lafayette, IN 47901, 317-742-2394.

Madison: Madison Area Chamber of Commerce, Small Business Development Center, 301 East Main Street, Madison, IN 47250, 812-265-3127.

Muncie: Muncie-Delaware County Chamber, Small Business Development Center, 401 South High Street, Muncie, IN 47308, 317-284-8144; Fax: 317-741-5489.

Portage: Northwest Indiana Forum, Inc., Small Business Development Center, 6100 Southport Rd., Portage, IN 46410, 219-762-1696.

Richmond: Richmond Area Chamber of Commerce, Small Business Development Center, 33 South 7th Street, Richmond, IN 47374, 317-962-2887.

South Bend: South Bend Chamber of Commerce, Small Business Development Center, 300 North Michigan Street, South Bend, IN 46601, 219-282-4350.

Terre Haute: Indiana State University, Small Business Development Center, School of Business, Terre Haute, IN 47809, 812-237-7676.

Iowa

Lead Center:
Iowa Small Business Development Center
Iowa State University
College of Business Administration
Chamblynn Building
137 Lynn Avenue
Ames, IA 50010
515-292-6351
Fax: 515-292-0020

Ames: Iowa State University, ISU Small Business Development Center, 137 Lynn Avenue, Ames, IA 50014, 515-292-6351; Fax: 515-292-0020.

Ames: ISU Small Business Development Center, ISU Ames Branch, 111 Lynn Avenue, Ames, IA 50014, 515-292-6355; Fax: 515-292-0020.

Audubon: ISU Small Business Development Center, ISU Audubon Branch, Circle West Incubator, P.O. Box 204, Audubon, IA 50025, 712-563-2623; Fax: 712-563-2301.

Cedar Falls: University of Northern Iowa, Small Business Development Center, Suite 5, Business Building, Cedar Falls, IA 50614-0120, 319-273-2696; Fax: 319-273-6830.

Council Bluffs: Iowa Western Community College, Small Business Development Center, 2700 College Road, Box 4C, Council Bluffs, IA 51502, 712-325-3260; Fax: 712-325-3424.

Creston: Southwestern Community College, Small Business Development Center, 1501 West Townline, Creston, IA 50801, 515-782-4161; Fax: 515-782-4164.

Davenport: Eastern Iowa Community College District, Small Business Development Center, 304 West Second Street, Davenport, IA 52801, 319-322-4499; Fax: 319-322-8241.

Small Business Development Centers

Des Moines: Drake University, Small Business Development Center, Drake Business Center, Des Moines, IA 50311-4505, 515-271-2655; Fax: 515-271-4540.

Dubuque: Dubuque Area Chamber of Commerce, Northeast Iowa Small Business Development Center, 770 Town Clock Plaza, Dubuque, IA 52001, 319-588-3350; Fax: 319-557-1591.

Iowa City: University of Iowa, Oakdale Campus, Small Business Development Center, 108 Pappajohn Business Adm. Bldg., Suite 5160, Iowa City, IA 52242, 319-335-3742; Fax: 319-335-1956.

Marion: Kirkwood Community College, Small Business Development Center, 2901 Tenth Avenue, Marion, IA 52302, 319-377-8256; Fax: 319-377-5667.

Mason City: North Iowa Area Community College, Small Business Development Center, 500 College Drive, Mason City, IA 50401, 515-421-4342; Fax: 515-424-2011.

Ottumwa: Indian Hills Community College, Small Business Development Center, 525 Grandview Avenue, Ottumwa, IA 52501, 515-683-5127; Fax: 515-683-5263.

Sioux City: Western Iowa Tech Community College, Small Business Development Center, 4647 Stone Ave., Bldg. B, Sioux City, IA 51102, 712-274-6418; Fax: 712-274-6429.

Spencer: Iowa Lakes Community College, Small Business Development Center, Gateway North Shopping Center, Highway 71 North, Spencer, IA 51301, 712-262-4213; Fax: 712-262-4047.

West Burlington: Southeastern Community College, Small Business Development Center, Drawer F, West Burlington, IA 52655, 319-752-2731, ext. 103; Fax: 319-752-4957.

Kansas

Lead Center:
Kansas Small Business Development Center
Wichita State University
1845 Fairmount
Wichita, KS 67260-0148
316-689-3193
Fax: 316-689-3647

Atchison: Benedictine College, Small Business Development Center, 1020 N 2nd St, Atchison, KS 66002, 913-367-5340, ext. 2425; Fax: 913-367-6102.

Augusta: Butler County Community College, Small Business Development Center, 600 Walnut, Augusta, KS 67010, 316-775-1124; Fax: 316-775-1370.

Chanute: Neosho County Community College, Small Business Development Center, 1000 S Allen, Chanute, KS 66720, 316-431-2820, ext 219; Fax: 316-431-0082.

Coffeyville: Coffeyville Community College, Small Business Development Center, 11th and Willow Sts., Coffeyville, KS 67337-5064, 316-252-7007; Fax: 316-252-7098.

Colby: Colby Community College, SBDC, 1255 South Range, Colby, KS 67701, 913-462-3984, ext. 239; Fax: 913-462-8315.

Concordia: Cloud County Community College, SBDC, 2221 Campus Drive, P.O. Box 1002, Concordia, KS 66901, 913-243-1435; Fax: 913-243-1459.

Dodge City: Dodge City Community College, Small Business Development Center, 2501 North 14th Avenue, Dodge City, KS 67801, 316-227-9247, ext. 247; Fax: 316-227-9200.

Emporia: Emporia State University, Small Business Development Center, 207 Cremer Hall, Emporia, KS 66801, 316-342-7162; Fax: 316-341-5418.

Fort Scott: Fort Scott Community College, Small Business Development Center, 32108 S Horton, Fort Scott, KS 66701, 316-223-2700; Fax: 316-223-6530.

Garden City: Garden City Community College, Small Business Development Center, 801 Campus Drive, Garden City, KS 67846, 316-276-9632; Fax: 316-276-9630.

Hays: Fort Hays State University, Small Business Development Center, 1301 Pine, Hays, KS 67601, 913-628-5340; Fax: 913-628-1471.

Hutchinson: Hutchinson Community College, Small Business Development Center, 815 N. Walnut, #225, Hutchinson, KS 67501, 316-665-4950; Fax: 316-665-8354.

Independence: Independence Community College, SBDC, College Ave. and Brookside, Box 708, Independence, KS 67301, 316-331-4100; Fax: 316-331-5344.

Iola: Allen County Community College, T.B.D., Small Business Development Center, 1801 N. Cottonwood, Iola, KS 66749, 316-365-5116; Fax: 316-365-3284.

Lawrence: University of Kansas, SBDC, 734 Vermont, Suite 104, Lawrence, KS 66044, 913-843-8844; Fax: 913-865-4400.

Liberal: Seward County Community College, Small Business Development Center, 1801 North Kansas, Liberal, KS 67905, 316-629-2650, ext. 148; Fax: 316-624-0637.

Manhattan: Kansas State University, SBDC, 2323 Anderson Ave., Suite 100, Manhattan, KS 66502-2947, 913-532-5529; Fax: 913-532-5827.

Ottawa: Ottawa University, Small Business Development Center, College Avenue, Box 70, Ottawa, KS 66067, 913-242-5200, ext. 5457; Fax: 913-242-7429.

Overland Park: Johnson County Community College, SBDC, CEC Bldg., Room 223, Overland Park, KS 66210-1299, 913-469-3878; Fax: 913-469-4415.

Parsons: Labette Community College, SBDC, 200 S. 14th, Parsons, KS 67357, 316-421-6700; Fax: 316-421-0921.

Pittsburgh: Pittsburgh State University, SBDC, Shirk Hall, Pittsburgh, KS 66762, 316-235-4920; Fax: 316-232-6440.

Pratt: Pratt Community College, Small Business Development Center, Hwy. 61, Pratt, KS 67124, 316-672-5641; Fax: 316-672-5288.

Salina: KSU-Salina College of Technology, Small Business Development Center, 2409 Scanlan Avenue, Salina, KS 67401, 913-826-2622,; Fax: 913-826-2936.

Topeka: Washburn University, Small Business Development Center, 101 Henderson Learning Center, Topeka, KS 66621, 913-231-1010, ext. 1305; Fax: 913-231-1063.

Wichita: Wichita State University, Small Business Development Center, Brennan Hall, 1845 Fairmount, Wichita, KS 67208, 316-689-3193; Fax: 316-689-3647.

Kentucky

Lead Center:
Kentucky Small Business Development Center
University of Kentucky
Center for Business Development
College of Business and Economics
205 Business and Economics Building
Lexington, KY 40506-0034
606-257-7668
Fax: 606-258-1907

Ashland: Ashland Small Business Development Center, Boyd-Greenup County Chamber of Commerce Building, P.O. Box 830, 207 15th Street, Ashland, KY 41105-0830, 606-329-8011; Fax: 606-325-4607.

Bowling Green: Western Kentucky University, Bowling Green Small Business Development Center, 245 Grise Hall, Bowling Green, KY 42101, 502-745-2901; Fax: 502-745-2902.

Cumberland: Southeast Community College, Small Business Development Center, Room 113, Chrisman Hall, Cumberland, KY 40823, 606-589-4514; Fax: 606-589-4941.

Elizabethtown: Elizabethtown Small Business Development Center, 238 West Dixie Avenue, Elizabethtown, KY 42701, 502-765-6737; Fax: 502-765-6737.

Highland Heights: Northern Kentucky University, North Kentucky Small Business Development Center, BEP Center, Room 463, Highland Heights, KY 41099-0506, 606-572-6524; Fax: 606-572-5566.

Hopkinsville: Hopkinsville Small Business Development Center, 300 Hammond Drive, Hopkinsville, KY 42240, 502-886-8666; Fax: 502-886-3211.

Lexington: University of Kentucky, Small Business Development Center, College of Business and Economics, 205 Business and Economics Building, Lexington, KY 40506-0034, 606-257-7666; Fax: 606-258-1907.

Louisville: Bellarmine College, Small Business Development Center, School of Business, 2001 Newburg Road, Louisville, KY 40205-0671, 502-452-8282; Fax: 502-452-8288.

Louisville: University of Louisville, SBDC, Center for Entrepreneurship and Technology, Room 122, Burhans Hall, Louisville, KY 40292, 502-588-7854; Fax: 502-588-8573.

Morehead: Morehead State University, Small Business Development Center, 207 Downing Hall, Morehead, KY 40351, 606-783-2895; Fax: 606-783-2678.

Murray: Murray State University, West Kentucky SBDC, College of Business and Public Affairs, Murray, KY 42071, 502-762-2856; Fax: 502-762-3049.

Owensboro: Owensboro Small Business Development Center, 3860 U.S. Highway 60 West, Owensboro, KY 42301, 502-926-8085; Fax: 502-684-0714.

Pikeville: Pikeville Small Business Development Center, 222 Hatcher Court, Pikeville, KY 41501, 606-432-5848.

Somerset: Eastern Kentucky University, Small Business Development Center, 107 West Mt. Vernon Street, Somerset, KY 42501, 606-678-5520; Fax: 606-678-8349.

Louisiana

Lead Center:
Louisiana Small Business Development Center
Northeast Louisiana University, Adm. 2-57
Monroe, LA 71209
318-342-5506
Fax: 318-342-5510

Alexandria: Small Business Development Center, 5212 Rue Verdun, Alexandria, LA 71306, 318-484-2123.

Baton Rouge: Capital Small Business Development Center, 9613 Interline Avenue, Baton Rouge, LA 70809, 504-922-0998.

Hammond: Southeastern Louisiana University, Small Business Development Center, Box 522, SLU Station, Hammond, LA 70402, 504-549-3831; Fax: 504-549-2127.

Lafayette: University of Southwestern Louisiana, Arcadiana Small Business Development Center, Box 43732, Lafayette, LA 70504, 318-262-5344; Fax: 318-262-5296.

Lake Charles: McNeese State University, Small Business Development Center, College of Business Administration, Lake Charles, LA 70609, 318-475-5529; Fax: 318-475-5529.

Monroe: Northeast Louisiana University, College of Business Administration, Monroe, LA 71209, 318-342-1224; Fax: 318-352-5506.

Monroe: Northeast Louisiana University, Small Business Development Center, Louisiana Electronic Assistance Program, College of Business Administration, Monroe, LA 71209, 318-342-1215; Fax: 318-342-1209.

Monroe: Northeast Louisiana University, Small Business Development Center, Adm. 2-57, Monroe, LA 71209, 318-342-5506; Fax: 318-342-5510.

Natchitoches: Northwestern State University, Small Business Development Center, College of Business Administration, Natchitoches, LA 71497, 318-357-5611; Fax: 318-357-6810.

New Orleans: University of New Orleans, Small Business Development Center, Louisiana International Trade, 2 Canal St., New Orleans, LA 70148, 504-568-8222.

New Orleans: Loyola University, SBDC, Box 134, New Orleans, LA 70118, 504-865-3474; Fax: 504-865-3347.

New Orleans: Southern University, Small Business Development Center, College of Business Administration, New Orleans, LA 70126, 504-286-5308; Fax: 504-286-5306 (call first).

New Orleans: University of New Orleans, Small Business Development Center, Lakefront Campus, College of Business Administration, New Orleans, LA 70148, 504-539-9292.

Ruston: Louisiana Tech University, Small Business Development Center, Box 10318, Tech Station, Ruston, LA 71271-0046, 318-257-3537; Fax: 318-257-3356.

Shreveport: Louisiana State University at Shreveport, Small Business Development Center, College of Business Administration, 1 University Place, Shreveport, LA 71115, 318-797-5144; Fax: 318-797-5156.

Thibodaux: Nicholls State University, Small Business Development Center, P.O. Box 2015, Thibodaux, LA 70310, 504-448-4242; Fax: 504-448-4922.

Maine

Lead Center:
Maine Small Business Development Center
University of Southern Maine
96 Falmouth Street
Portland, ME 04103-9989
207-780-4420
Fax: 207-780-4810

Auburn: Androscoggin Valley Council of Governments, Small Business Development Center, 125 Manley Rd., Auburn, ME 04210, 207-783-9186; Fax: 207-783-5211.

Bangor: Eastern Maine Development Corporation, Small Business Development Center, P.O. Box 2579, Bangor, ME 04401, 207-942-6389; Fax: 207-942-3548.

Caribou: Northern Maine Regional Planning Commission, SBDC, P.O. Box 779, 2 Main Street, Caribou, ME 04736, 207-498-8736; Fax: 207-493-3108.

Sanford: Southern Maine Regional Planning Commission, Small Business Development Center, Box Q, 255 Main Street, Sanford, ME 04073, 207-324-0316; Fax: 207-324-2958.

Wiscasset: Coastal Enterprises, Inc., Small Business Development Center, Walter Street, Box 268, Wiscasset, ME 04578, 207-882-7552; Fax: 207-882-7308.

Maryland

Lead Center:
Small Business Development Center
1420 N. Charles St.
Baltimore, MD 21201
410-837-4141
Fax: 410-837-4151

Annapolis: Anne Arundel Office of Economic Development, Small Business Development Center, 2660 Riva Rd., Annapolis, MD 21401, 410-224-4205; Fax: 410-222-7415.

Baltimore: Business Resource Center, SBDC, 3 W. Baltimore St., Baltimore, MD 21202, 410-605-0990; Fax: 410-605-0995.

Bel Air: Harford County Economic Development Office, SBDC, 220 S. Main St., Bel Air, MD 21014, 410-893-3837; Fax: 410-879-8043.

College Park: Manufacturing and Technology, Small Business Development Center, Dingman Center for Entrepreneurship, College of Business and Management, University of Maryland, College Park, MD 20742, 301-405-2144; Fax: 301-314-9152.

Columbia: Howard County Economic Development Office, Small Business Development Center, 6751 Gateway Drive, Columbia, MD 21043, 410-290-0066; Fax: 410-313-2662.

Cumberland: Western Region Small Business Development Center, 3 Commerce Drive, Cumberland, MD 21502, 301-724-6716; Fax: 301-777-7504.

Elkton: Cecil Community College, Eastern Region SBDC, 135 E. Main St., Elkton, MD 21921.

Glen Burnie: Arundel Center N, Small Business Development Center, 101 Crain Highway NW, Room 110B, Glen Burnie, MD 21601, 410-766-1910; Fax: 410-766-1911.

Landover: Suburban Washington Small Business Development Center, 1400 McCormick Dr., Suite 282, Landover, MD 20785, 301-883-6491; Fax: 301-883-6479.

Salisbury: Eastern Shore Small Business Development Center SubCenter, Salisbury State University, Perdue School of Business, 1101 Canden Ave., Salisbury, MD 21801, 410-546-4325; Fax: 410-548-5389.

Towson: Baltimore County Chamber of Commerce, Small Business Development Center, 102 W. Pennsylvania Ave., Towson, MD 21204, 410-832-5866; Fax: 410-821-9901.

Waldorf: Charles Community College, Southern Region Small Business Development Center, 235 Smallwood Village Center, Waldorf, MD 20601, 301-932-4155; Fax: 301-645-9082.

Westminster: Carroll County Economic Development, Small Business Development Center, 125 North Court Street, Room 103, Westminster, MD 21157, 410-857-8166; Fax: 410-848-0003.

Massachusetts

Lead Center:
Massachusetts Small Business Development Center
University of Massachusetts
205 School of Management
Amherst, MA 01003
413-545-6301
Fax: 413-545-1273

Boston: University of Massachusetts at Amherst, Minority Business Assistance Center, 250 Stuart Street, 5th Floor, Boston, MA 02116, 617-287-7750; Fax: 617-426-7854.

Chestnut Hill: Boston College, Metropolitan Regional Small Business Development Center, 96 College Road - Rahner House, Chestnut Hill, MA 02167, 617-552-4091; Fax: 617-552-2730.

Chestnut Hill: Boston College, Capital Formation Service/East, Small Business Development Center, 96 College Road - Rahner House, Chestnut Hill, MA 02167, 617-552-4091; Fax: 617-552-2730.

Fall River: University of Massachusetts at Dartmouth, Southeastern Massachusetts Regional Small Business Development Center, 200 Pocasset Street, P.O. Box 2785, Fall River, MA 02722, 508-673-9783; Fax: 508-674-1929.

Salem: Salem State College, North Shore Regional Small Business Development Center, 197 Essex Street, Salem, MA 01970, 508-741-6343; Fax: 508-741-6345.

Springfield: University of Massachusetts, Western Massachusetts Regional Small Business Development Center, 101 State Street, Suite #424, Springfield, MA 01103, 413-737-6712; Fax: 413-737-2312.

Worcester: Clark University, Central Massachusetts Regional Small Business Development Center, 950 Main Street, Worcester, MA 01610, 508-793-7615; Fax: 508-793-8890.

Michigan

Lead Center:
Michigan Small Business Development Center
2727 Second Avenue
Detroit, MI 48201
313-964-1798
Fax: 313-577-4222

Allendale: Ottawa County Economic Development Office, Inc., SBDC, 6676 Lake Michigan Drive, Allendale, MI 49401, 616-892-4120; Fax: 616-895-6670.

Ann Arbor: Merra Specialty Business Development Center, SBDC, 2200 Commonwealth, Suite 230, Ann Arbor, MI 48105, 313-930-0034; Fax: 313-663-6622.

Bad Axe: Huron County Economic Development Corporation (Satellite), SBDC, Huron County building, Room 303, Bad Axe, MI 48413, 517-269-6431; Fax: 517-269-7221.

Battle Creek: Kellogg Community College, Small Business Development Center, 450 North Avenue, Battle Creek, MI 49017-3397, 616-965-3023; 1-800-955-4KCC; Fax: 616-965-4133.

Benton Harbor: Lake Michigan College, Small Business Development Center, Corporate and Community Services, 2755 E. Napier, Benton Harbor, MI 49022-1899, 616-927-3571, ext. 247; Fax: 616-927-4491.

Big Rapids: Ferris State University, Small Business Development Center, Alumni 226, 901 S. State Street, Big Rapids, MI 49307, 616-592-3553; Fax: 616-592-3539.

Cadillac: Wexfor-Missaukee Business Development Center (Satellite), 117 W. Cass Street, Suite 1, Cadillac, MI 49601-0026, 616-775-9776; Fax: 616-775-1440.

Caro: Tuscola County Economic Development Corporation, Small Business Development Center, 1184 Cleaver Road, Suite 800, Caro, MI 48723, 517-673-2849; Fax: 517-673-2517.

Detroit: NILAC-Marygrove College, Small Business Development Center, 8425 West McNichols, Detroit, MI 48221, 313-945-2159; Fax: 313-864-6670.

Detroit: Wayne State University, Small Business Development Center, School of Business Administration, 2727 Second Avenue, Detroit, MI 48201, 313-577-4850; Fax: 313-577-8933.

Detroit: Comerica Small Business Development Center, 8300 Van Dyke, Detroit, MI 48213, 313-571-1040.

East Lansing: Michigan State University, International Business Development Center, 6 Kellogg Center, East Lansing, MI 48824-1022, 517-353-4336; Fax: 517-336-1009; 1-800-852-5727.

Escanaba: 1st Step, Inc., Small Business Development Center, 2415 14th Avenue, South, Escanaba, MI 49829, 906-786-9234; Fax: 906-786-4442.

Flint: Genesee Economic Area Revitalization, Inc. (Satellite), Small Business Development Center, 412 S. Saginaw Street, Flint, MI 48502, 313-238-7803; Fax: 313-238-7866.

Grand Rapids: Grand Rapids Community College, SBDC, Applied Technology Center, 151 Fountain N.E., Grand Rapids, MI 49503, 616-771-3600; Fax: 616-771-3605.

Hart: Oceana Economic Development Corporation (Satellite), Small Business Development Center, P.O. Box 168, Hart, MI 49420-0168, 616-873-7141; Fax: 616-873-3710.

Houghton: Michigan Technological University, Small Business Development Center, Bureau of Industrial Development, 1400 Townsend Drive, Houghton, MI 49931, 906-487-2470; Fax: 906-487-2858.

Howell: Livingston County Business Development Center, 404 E. Grand River, Howell, MI 48843, 517-546-4020; Fax: 517-546-4115.

Kalamazoo: Kalamazoo College, SBDC, Stryker Center for Management Studies, 1327 Academy Street, Kalamazoo, MI 49007, 616-383-8602; Fax: 616-383-5663.

Lansing: Lansing Community College, Small Business Development Center, P.O. Box 40010, Lansing, MI 48901, 517-483-1921; Fax: 517-483-9616.

Lapeer: Lapeer Development Corporation (Satellite), 449 McCormick Drive, Lapeer, MI 48446, 313-667-0080; Fax: 313-667-3541.

Marlette: Thumb Area Community Growth Alliance, Small Business Development Center, 3270 Wilson Street, Marlette, MI 48453, 517-635-3561; Fax: 517-635-2230.

Marquette: Northern Economic Initiative Corporation, Small Business Development Center, 1009 West Ridge Street, Marquette, MI 49855, 906-228-5571; Fax: 906-228-5572.

Mt. Clemens: Macomb County Business Assistance Network, 115 South Groesbeck Highway, Mt. Clemens, MI 48043, 313-469-5118; Fax: 313-469-6787,

Mt. Pleasant: Central Michigan University, Small Business Development Ctr., 256 Applied Business Studies Complex, Mt. Pleasant, MI 48859, 517-774-3270; Fax: 517-774-2372.

Muskegon: Muskegon Economic Growth Alliance, Small Business Development Center, 349 West Webster Avenue, Suite 104, P.O. Box 1087, Muskegon, MI 49443-1087, 616-722-3751; Fax: 616-728-7251.

Peck: Sanilac County Economic Growth (Satellite), 175 East Aitken Road, Peck, MI 48466, 313-648-4311; Fax: 313-648-4617.

Port Huron: St. Claire County Community College, SBDC, 323 Erie Street, P.O. Box 5015, Port Huron, MI 48061-5015, 313-984-3881, ext. 457; Fax: 313-984-2852.

Saginaw: Saginaw Future, Inc., Small Business Development Center, 301 East Genesee, Fourth Floor, Saginaw, MI 48607, 517-754-8222; Fax: 517-754-1715.

Scottville: West Shore Community College (Satellite), Business and Industrial Development, 3000 North Stiles Road, Scottville, MI 49454-0277, 616-845-6211; Fax: 616-845-0207.

Sidney: Montcalm Community College (Satellite), 2800 College Drive SW, Sidney, MI 48885, 517-328-2111; Fax: 517-328-2950.

Sterling Heights: Sterling Heights Area Chamber of Commerce (Satellite), 12900 Paul, Suite 110, Sterling Heights, MI 48313, 313-731-5400.

Traverse City: Northwestern Michigan College, Center for Business and Industry, 1701 East Front Street, Traverse City, MI 49684, 616-922-1105.

Traverse City: Travers Bay Economic Development Corporation, Traverse City Small Business Development Center, 202 East Grandview Parkway, P.O. Box 387, Traverse City, MI 49685-0387, 616-946-1596; Fax: 616-946-2565.

Traverse City: Greater Northwest Regional CDC, 2200 Dendrinos Drive, Traverse City, MI 49685-0506, 616-929-5000.

Traverse City: Traverse City Area Chamber of Commerce BDC, 202 E. Grandview Parkway, P.O. Box 387, Traverse City, MI 49685-0387, 616-947-5075.

Troy: Walsh/O.C.C. Business Enterprise Development Center, 340 E. Big Beaver, Suite 100, Troy, MI 48083, 313-689-4094; Fax: 313-689-4398.

University Center: Saginaw Valley State University (Satellite), Business and Industrial Development Institute, 2250 Pierce Road, University Center, MI 48710, 517-790-4000; Fax: 517-790-1314.

Minnesota

Lead Center:
Minnesota Small Business Development Center
Department of Trade and Economic Development
550 Metro Square, 121 7th Place E.
St. Paul, MN 55101
612-297-5773
Fax: 612-296-1290

Bemidji: Customized Training Center, SBDC, Bemidji Technical College, 905 Grant Avenue, SE, Bemidji, MN 56601, 218-755-4286; Fax: 218-755-4289.

Bloomington: Normandale Community College, Small Business Development Center, 9700 France Avenue South, Bloomington, MN 55431, 612-832-6560.

Brainerd: Brainerd Technical College, Small Business Development Center, 300 Quince Street, Brainerd, MN 56401, 218-828-5302; Fax: 218-828-5340.

Duluth: University of Minnesota at Duluth, Small Business Development Center, 10 University Drive, 150 SBE, Duluth, MN 55812, 218-726-8758.

Grand Rapids: Itasca Development Corporation, Grand Rapids Small Business Development Center, 19 NE Third Street, Grand Rapids, MN 55744, 218-327-2241; Fax: 218-327-2242.

Hibbing: Hibbing Community College, Small Business Development Center, 1515 East 25th Street, Hibbing, MN 55746, 218-262-6703.

International Falls: SBDC, Rainy River Community College, 1501 Hwy 71, International Falls, MN 56649, 218-285-2255; Fax: 218-285-2239.

Mankato: Mankato State University, Small Business Development Center, P.O. Box 3367, 410 Jackson St., Mankato, MN 56001, 507-387-5643.

Marshall: Southwest State University, Small Business Development Center, ST #105, Marshall, MN 56258, 507-537-7386; Fax: 507-537-6094.

Minneapolis: Minnesota Project Innovation, Small Business Development Center, Suite 410, 111 Third Avenue South, Minneapolis, MN 55401, 612-338-3280; Fax: 612-338-3483.

Minneapolis: SBDC, University of St. Thomas, 1000 LaSalle Ave., Suite MPL100, Minneapolis, MN 55403, 612-962-4500; Fax: 612-962-4410.

Moorhead: Moorhead State University, Small Business Development Center, 1104 7th Ave.S, MSU Box 303, Moorhead, MN 56560, 218-223-2280.

Owatonna: SBDC, Owatonna Incubator, Inc., P.O. Box 505, 560 Dunnell Dr., Suite #203, Owatonna, MN 55060, 507-451-0517; Fax: 507-455-2788.

Pine City: Pine Technical College, Small Business Development Center, 1100 4th St., Pine City, MN 55063, 612-629-7340.

Plymouth: SBDC, Hennepin Technical College, 1820 N. Xenium Lane, Plymouth, MN 55441, 612-550-7218; Fax: 612-550-7272.

Red Wing: Red Wing Technical Institute, Small Business Development Center, 2000 Pottery Place Dr., Suite 339, Red Wing, MN 55066, 612-388-4079.

Rochester: Rochester Community College, Small Business Development Center, 851 30th Avenue, SE, Rochester, MN 55904, 507-285-7536.

Rosemount: Dakota County Technical Institute, Small Business Development Center, 1300 145th Street East, Rosemount, MN 55068, 612-423-8262.

Rushford: SBDC, SE Minnesota Development Corp., P.O. Box 684, 111 W. Jessie St., Rushford, MN 55971, 507-864-7557; Fax: 507-864-2091.

St. Cloud: St. Cloud State University, Small Business Development Center, Business Resource Center, 4191 2nd St. S, St. Cloud, MN 56301, 612-255-4842.

Virginia: Minnesota Technology Inc., Small Business Development Center, Olcott Plaza, 820 N.9th St., Virginia, MN 55792, 218-741-4251.

Wadena: Wadena Technical College, Small Business Development Center, 222 Second Street, SE, Wadena, MN 56482, 218-631-1502; Fax: 218-631-2396.

White Bear Lake: North/East Metro Technical College, Small Business Development Center, 3500 Century Ave. N, Suite 200D, White Bear Lake, MN 55110, 612-779-5764.

Mississippi

Lead Center:
Mississippi Small Business Development Center
University of Mississippi
Old Chemistry Building, Suite 216
University, MS 38677
601-232-5001
Fax: 601-232-5650

Booneville: Northeast Mississippi Community College, Small Business Development Center, Cunningham Blvd., Holliday Hall, 2nd Floor, Booneville, MS 38829, 601-728-7751, ext. 317; Fax: 601-728-1165.

Cleveland: Delta State University, Small Business Development Ctr., P.O. Box 3235 DSU, Cleveland, MS 38733, 601-846-4236; Fax: 601-846-4235.

Decatur: East Central Comm. College SBDC, Broad St., P.O. Box 129, Decatur, MS 39327, 601-635-2111; Fax: 601-635-2150.

Ellisville: Jones Jr College SBDC, 900 Court St., Ellisville, MS 39437, 601-477-4165; Fax: 601-477-4166.

Gautier: Mississippi Gulf Coast Community College Small Business Development Center, Jackson County Campus, P.O. Box 100, Gautier, MS 39553, 601-497-9595; Fax: 601-497-9604.

Greenville: Delta Community College, Small Business Development Center, P.O. Box 5607, Greenville, MS 38704-5607, 601-378-8183; Fax: 601-378-5349.

Gulfport: MS Contract Procurement Center, SBDC, 3015 12th St., P.O. Box 610, Gulfport, MS 39502-0610, 601-864-2961; Fax: 601-864-2969.

Hattiesburg: Pearl River Community College, Small Business Development Center, 5448 U.S. Highway 49 South, Hattiesburg, MS 39401, 601-544-0030; Fax: 601-544-0032.

Itta Bena: Mississippi Valley State University SBDC, MS Valley State University, Itta Bena, MS 38941, 601-254-3601; Fax: 601-254-6704.

Jackson: Jackson State University, SBDC, Suite A1, Jackson Enterprise Center, 931 Highway 80 West, Jackson, MS 39204, 601-968-2795; Fax: 601-968-2796.

Long Beach: University of Southern Mississippi, Small Business Development Center, 136 Beach Park Place, Long Beach, MS 39560, 601-865-4578; Fax: 601-865-4581.

Lorman: Alcorn State University SBDC, P.O. Box 90, Lorman, MS 39095-9402, 601-877-6684; Fax: 601-877-6256.

Meridian: Meridian Community College, Small Business Development Center, 910 Highway 19 North, Meridian, MS 39307, 601-482-7445; Fax: 601-482-5803.

Mississippi State: Mississippi State University, Small Business Development Center, P.O. Drawer 5288, Mississippi State, MS 39762, 601-325-8684; Fax: 601-325-4016.

Natchez: Copiah-Lincoln Community College, SBDC, 823 Hwy. 61 North, Natchez, MS 39120, 601-445-5254.

Raymond: Hinds Community College, SBDC, International Trade Center, P.O. Box 1170, Raymond, MS 39154, 601-857-3536; Fax: 601-857-3535.

Ridgeland: Holmes Comm. College SBDC, 412 West Ridgeland Ave., Ridgeland, MS 39159, 601-853-0827; Fax: 601-853-0844.

Southaven: Northwest MS Comm. College SBDC, Desoto Center, 8700 Northwest Dr., Southaven, MS 38671, 601-342-1570; Fax: 601-342-5686.

Summit: Southwest MS Comm. College SBDC, College Dr., Summit, MS 39666, 601-276-3890; Fax: 601-276-3867.

Tupelo: Itawamba Community College, Small Business Development Ctr., 653 Eason Blvd., Tupelo, MS 38801, 601-680-8515; Fax: 601-680-8547.

University: University of Mississippi, Small Business Development Center, Old Chemistry Building, Suite 216, University, MS 38677, 601-234-2021; Fax: 601-232-5650.

Missouri

Lead Center:
Missouri Small Business Development Center
University of Missouri
Suite 300, University Place
Columbia, MO 65211
314-882-0344
Fax: 314-884-4297

Camdenton: Camden County Extension Center, Small Business Development Center, 113 Kansas, P.O. Box 1405, Camdenton, MO 65020, 314-346-2644; Fax: 314-346-2694.

Cape Girardeau: Southwest Missouri State University, Small Business Development Center, 222 N. Pacific, Cape Girardeau, MO 63701, 314-290-5965; Fax: 314-290-5651.

Chillicothe: Livingston County Extension Center, Small Business Development Center, 3rd Floor Library, 450 Locust, Chillicothe, MO 64601, 816-646-0811.

Chillicothe: Small Business Development Center, Chillicothe City Hall, 715 Washington St., Chillicothe, MO 64601-2229, 816-646-6920; Fax: 816-646-6811.

Clayton: St. Louis County Extension Center, Small Business Development Center, 121 S Meramac, Suite 501, Clayton, MO 63105, 314-889-2911; Fax: 314-854-6147.

Columbia: Boone County Extension Center, Small Business Development Center, 1012 N. Hwy UU, Columbia, MO 65205, 314-445-9792; Fax: 314-445-9807.

Columbia: State Marketing Specialist, Small Business Development Center, 300 University Place, Columbia, MO 65211, 314-882-2595; Fax: 314-884-4297.

Columbia: University Extension, SBDC, 821 Clark Hall, Columbia, MO 65211, 314-882-4142; Fax: 314-882-2595.

Columbia: University of Missouri at Columbia, Small Business Development Center, 1800 University Place, Columbia, MO 65211, 314-882-7096; Fax: 314-882-6156.

Forsyth: Taney County Extension Center, SBDC, P.O. Box 218, Forsyth, MO 65653, 417-546-2371; Fax: 417-546-2981.

Hannibal: Hannibal Satellite Center, Small Business Development Center, Hannibal, MO 63401, 816-385-6550; Fax: 816-385-6568.

Hillsboro: Jefferson County Extension Center, Small Business Development Center, Courthouse, #203, 725 Maple St., Hillsboro, MO 63050, 314-789-5391; Fax: 314-789-5059.

Independence: Jackson County Extension Center, Small Business Development Center, 1507 S. Noland Rd., Independence, MO 64055-1307, 816-252-5051; Fax: 816-252-5575.

Jackson: Cape Girardeau County Extension Center, Small Business Development Center, P.O. Box 408, 815 Highway 25S, Jackson, MO 63755, 314-243-3581; Fax: 314-243-1606.

Jefferson City: Cole County Extension Center, Small Business Development Center, 2436 Tanner Bridge Rd., Jefferson City, MO 65101, 314-634-2824; Fax: 314-634-5463.

Joplin: Missouri Southern State College, Small Business Development Center, 107 Mathews Hall, Joplin, MO 64801-1595, 417-625-9313; Fax: 417-625-9782.

Kansas City: Rockhurst College, Small Business Development Center, 1100 Rockhurst Road, Kansas City, MO 64110-2599, 816-926-4572; Fax: 816-926-4646.

Kansas City: Western Region, University of Missouri-Kansas City, Small Business Development Center, 5110 Cherry St., Kansas City, MO 64110, 816-235-2891; Fax: 816-235-2947.

Kansas City: Jackson County Extension Center, Small Business Development Center, 1901 NE 48th, Kansas City, MO 65118, 816-792-7760; Fax: 816-792-7779.

Kirksville: Northeast Missouri State University, Small Business Development Center, 207 E. Patterson, Kirksville, MO 63501, 816-785-4307; Fax: 816-785-4357.

Macon: Thomas Hill Enterprise Center, SBDC, P.O. Box 246, Macon, MO 63552, 816-385-6550; Fax: 816-385-6568.

Maryville: Northwest Missouri State University, Small Business Development Center, 423 N. Market St., Maryville, MO 64468, 816-646-6920; Fax: 816-646-6811.

Mexico: Audrain County Extension Center, Small Business Development Center, 101 N. Jefferson, 4th Floor Courthouse, Mexico, MO 65265, 314-581-3231; Fax: 314-581-3232.

Moberly: Randolph County Extension Center, Small Business Development Center, 417 E. Urbandale, Moberly, MO 65270, 816-263-3534; Fax: 816-263-1874.

Park Hills: Small Business Development Center, Mineral Area College, P.O. Box 1000, Park Hills, MO 63601-1000, 314-431-4593, ext. 283; Fax: 314-431-2144.

Poplar Bluff: Three Rivers Community College, SBDC, Business Incubator Building, 3019 Fair Street, Poplar Bluff, MO 63901, 314-686-3499; Fax: 314-686-5467.

Potosi: Washington County Extension Center, Small Business Development Center, 102 N. Missouri, Potosi, MO 63664, 314-438-2671; Fax: 314-438-2079.

Rolla: MO Enterprise Business Assistance Center, Small Business Development Center, 800 W. 14th St., Suite 111, Rolla, MO 65401, 314-364-8570; Fax: 314-364-6323.

Rolla: Phelps County Extension Center, SBDC, Courthouse, 200 N. Main, P.O. Box 725, Rolla, MO 65401, 314-364-3147; Fax: 314-364-0436.

Rolla: Center for Technology Transfer and Economic Development, University of Missouri at Rolla, Room 104, Nagogami Terrace, Rolla, MO 65401-0249, 314-341-4559; Fax: 314-341-6495.

Sedalia: Pettis County Extension Center, Small Business Development Center, 1012 A Thompson Blvd., Sedalia, MO 65301, 816-827-0591; Fax: 816-826-8599.

Springfield: Green County Extension Center, SBDC, 833 Boonville Ave., Springfield, MO 65802, 417-862-9284; Fax: 417-868-4175.

Springfield: Southwest Missouri State University, Small Business Development Center, Center for Business Research, 901 S. National, Springfield, MO 65804-0089, 417-836-5685; Fax: 417-836-7666.

St. Joseph: Buchanan County Extension Center, SBDC, 4125 Mitchell Ave., Box 7077, St. Joseph, MO 64507, 816-279-1691; Fax: 816-279-3982.

St. Louis: St. Louis County Extension Center, 207 Marillac, UMSI, 8001 Nttl. Bridge Rd, St. Louis, MO 63042, 314-731-3533; Fax: 314-731-0523.

St. Louis: St. Louis University, Small Business Development Center, 3750 Lindell Boulevard, St. Louis, MO 63108, 314-534-7232; Fax: 314-534-7023.

St. Peters: St. Charles County Extension Center, SBDC, 260 Brown Rd., St. Peters, MO 63376, 314-970-3000.

Union: Franklin County Extension Center, SBDC, 414 E. Main, P.O. Box 71, Union, MO 63084, 314-583-5141; Fax: 314-583-3500.

Warrensburg: Central Missouri State University, Center for Technology, Grinstead #75, Warrensburg, MO 64093-5037, 816-543-4402; Fax: 816-747-1653.

Warrensburg: Central Missouri State, Small Business Development Center, Grinstead #609, Warrensburg, MO 64093-5037, 816-543-4402; Fax: 816-543-8159.

West Plains: Howell County Extension Center, SBDC, 217 S. Aid Ave., West Plains, MO 65775, 417-256-2391; Fax: 417-256-8569.

Montana

Lead Center:
Montana Small Business Development Center
Department of Commerce
1424 Ninth Avenue
Helena, MT 59620
406-444-4780
Fax: 406-444-1872

Small Business Development Centers

Billings: Billings Area Business Incubator, Small Business Development Center, 2722 3rd Ave., #300 W., Billings, MT 59101, 406-256-6875; Fax: 406-256-6877.

Bozeman: Bozeman Human Resources Development Council, Small Business Development Center, 215 Mendenhall, Bozeman, MT 59715, 406-587-3113; Fax: 406-587-9565.

Butte: Butte REDI, Small Business Development Center, 305 W. Mercury Street, Suite 211, Butte, MT 59701, 406-782-7333; Fax: 406-782-9675.

Haver: Haver Small Business Development Center, Bear Paw Development Corporation, P.O. Box 1549, Haver, MT 59501, 406-265-9226; Fax: 406-265-5602.

Kalispell: Flathead Valley Community College, Small Business Development Center, 777 Grandview Drive, Kalispell, MT 59901, 406-756-3833; Fax: 406-786-3815.

Missoula: Missoula Incubator, Small Business Development Center, 127 N. Higgins, 3rd Floor, Missoula, MT 59802, 406-278-9234; Fax: 406-721-4584.

Sidney: Sidney Small Business Development Center, 123 W. Main, Sidney, MT 59270, 406-482-5024; Fax: 406-482-5306.

Nebraska

Lead Center:
Nebraska Small Business Development Center
Omaha Business and Tech. Ctr.
2505 N. 24th St., Suite 101
Omaha, NE 68110
402-595-3511

Chadron: Chadron State College, SBDC, Administration Building, Chadron, NE 69337, 308-432-6282.

Kearney: University of Nebraska at Kearney, Small Business Development Center, Welch Hall, 19th and College Drive, Kearney, NE 68849, 308-234-8344.

Lincoln: University of Nebraska at Lincoln, Small Business Development Center, Cornhusker Bank Bldg., 11th and Cornhusker Hwy., Suite 302, Lincoln, NE 68521, 402-472-3358.

North Platte: Mid-Plains Community College, Small Business Development Center, 416 North Jeffers, Room 26, North Platte, NE 69101, 308-534-5115.

Omaha: University of Nebraska at Omaha, Small Business Development Center, Peter Keiwit Conference Center, 1313 Farnam, Suite 132, Omaha, NE 68182, 402-595-2381.

Peru: Peru State College, Small Business Development Center, T.J. Majors Building, Room 248, Peru, NE 68421, 402-872-2274.

Scottsbluff: Small Business Development Center, Nebraska Public Power Building, 1721 Broadway, Room 400, Scottsbluff, NE 69361, 308-635-7513.

Wayne: Wayne State College, Small Business Development Center, Connell Hall, Wayne, NE 68787, 402-375-7575.

Nevada

Lead Center:
Nevada Small Business Development Center
University of Nevada at Reno
College of Business Administration, Room 411
Reno, NV 89577-0100
702-784-1717
Fax: 702-784-4305

Elko: Northern Nevada Community College, Small Business Development Center, 901 Elm Street, Elko, NV 89801, 702-738-8493.

Las Vegas: University of Nevada at Las Vegas, Small Business Development Center, College of Business and Economics, 4505 Maryland Parkway, Las Vegas, NV 89154, 702-739-0852.

New Hampshire

The following offices offer free consulting and information referral services. Nominal fees are charged for most training programs.

Lead Center:
New Hampshire Small Business Development Center
University of New Hampshire
108 McConnell Hall
Durham, NH 03824
603-862-2200
Fax: 603-862-4876

Durham: Office of Economic Initiatives, Heidelberg Harris Building, Technology Drive, Durham, NH 03824, 603-862-0710.

Durham: Small Business Development Center, Heidelberg Harris Building, 125 Technology Drive, Durham, NH 03824, 603-862-0700; Fax: 603-862-0701.

Keene: Keene State College, Small Business Development Center, Blake House, Keene, NH 03431, 603-358-2602; Fax: 603-358-3612.

Littleton: Small Business Development Center, P.O. Box 786, Littleton, NH 03561, 603-444-1053.

Manchester: Small Business Development Center, 1000 Elm Street, 8th Floor, Manchester, NH 03101, 603-624-2000; Fax: 603-627-4410.

Plymouth: Plymouth State College, Small Business Development Center, Hyde Hall, Plymouth, NH 03264, 603-535-2523; Fax: 603-535-2611.

Nashua: Center for Economic Development, Small Business Development Center, 188 Main Street, Nashua, NH 03062, 603-886-1233; Fax: 603-886-1164.

New Jersey

Lead Center:
New Jersey Small Business Development Center
Rutgers Graduate School of Management
University Heights
180 University Avenue
Newark, NJ 07102
201-648-5950
Fax: 201-648-1110

Atlantic City: Small Business Development Center, Greater Atlantic City Chamber of Commerce, 1301 Atlantic Avenue, Atlantic City, NJ 08401, 609-345-5600; Fax: 609-345-4524.

Camden: Rutgers - The State University Of New Jersey at Camden, Small Business Development Center, Business and Science Building, 2nd Floor, Camden, NJ 08102, 609-225-6221; Fax: 609-225-6231.

Jersey City: Hudson County Community College, 900 Bergen Ave., Jersey City, NJ 07093.

Lincroft: Brookdale Community College, Small Business Development Center, Newman Springs Road, Lincroft, NJ 07738, 908-842-8685; Fax: 908-842-0203.

New Brunswick: County of Middlesex, Dept. of Industrial and Economic Development, 150 Neilson St., New Brunswick, NJ 08901, 908-745-5836.

Newark: Rutgers - The State University of New Jersey at Camden, Small Business Development Center, University Heights, 180 University Ave., 3rd Floor, Newark, NJ 07102, 201-648-5950; Fax: 201-648-1110.

Paramus: Bergen Community College, Small Business Development Center, 400 Paramus Rd., 3rd Fl., Room A328, Paramus, NJ 07652, 201-447-7841.

Trenton: Mercer County Community College, Small Business Development Center, P.O. Box B, Trenton, NJ 08690, 609-586-4800; Fax: 609-890-6338.

Trenton: Mercer County Community College, Small Business Development Center, James Kerney Campus, N. Broad and Academy Sts., Trenton, NJ 08608, 609-586-4800, ext. 688.

Union: Kean College of New Jersey, Small Business Development Center, East Campus, Room 242, Union, NJ 07083, 908-527-2946; Fax: 908-527-2960.

Washington: Warren County Community College, Small Business Development Center, Route 57 West, Box 55A, Washington, NJ 07882-9605, 201-689-9620.

West New York: Hudson County Community College, 6501 Polk St., 3rd Fl., West New York, NJ 07306.

New Mexico

Lead Center:
New Mexico Small Business Development Center
Santa Fe Community College
P.O. Box 4187
Santa Fe, NM 87502-4187
505-438-1362
Fax: 505-438-1237

Alamogordo: New Mexico State University at Alamogordo, Small Business Development Center, 1000 Madison, Alamogordo, NM 87310, 505-434-5272.

Albuquerque: Albuquerque Technical Vocational Institute, Small Business Development Center, 525 Buena Vista SE, Albuquerque, NM 87106, 505-224-4246.

Carlsbad: New Mexico State University at Carlsbad, Small Business Development Center, 301 South Canal, P.O. Box 1090, Carlsbad, NM 88220, 505-887-6562.

Clovis: Clovis Community College, SBDC, 417 Schepps Blvd., Clovis, NM 88101, 505-769-4136.

Espanola: Northern New Mexico Community College, Small Business Development Center, 1002 N. Onate Street, Espanola, NM 87532, 505-753-7141.

Farmington: San Juan College, Small Business Development Center, 203 West Main, Farmington, NM 87401, 505-326-4321.

Gallup: University of New Mexico at Gallup, Small Business Development Center, P.O. Box 1395, Gallup, NM 87305, 505-722-2220.

Grants: New Mexico State University at Grants, Small Business Development Center, 709 E. Roosevelt Ave., Grants, NM 87020, 505-287-8821.

Hobbs: New Mexico Junior College, Small Business Development Center, 5317 Lovington Highway, Hobbs, NM 88240, 505-392-4510.

Las Cruces: Dona Ana Branch Community College, Small Business Development Center, Box 30001, Department 3DA, Las Cruces, NM 88003-0001, 505-527-7566.

Las Vegas: Luna Vocational Technical Institute, Small Business Development Center, Luna Camp, P.O. Drawer K. Las Vegas, NM 88701, 505-454-2595.

Los Alamos: University of New Mexico at Los Alamos, SBDC, P.O. Box 715, Los Alamos, NM 87544, 505-662-0001.

Los Lunas: University of New Mexico at Valencia, Small Business Development Center, 280 La Entrada, Los Lunas, NM 87031, 505-865-9596, ext. 317.

Roswell: Eastern New Mexico University at Roswell, SBDC, P.O. Box 6000, Roswell, NM 88201-6000, 505-624-7133.

Santa Fe: Santa Fe Community College, Small Business Development Center, South Richards Avenue, P.O. Box 4187, Santa Fe, NM 87502-4187, 505-438-1343.

Silver City: Western New Mexico University, Southwest Small Business Development Center, Glazer Hall, Continuing Education Department, P.O. Box 2672, Silver City, NM 88062, 505-538-6320.

Tucumcari: Tucumcari Area Vocational School, Small Business Development Center, 824 W. Hines, P.O. Box 1143, Tucumcari, NM 88401, 505-461-4413.

New York

Lead Center:
New York Small Business Development Ctr.
State University of New York
State University Plaza, S-523
Albany, NY 12246
518-443-5398; 1-800-732-7232
Fax: 518-465-4992

Albany: State University of New York at Albany (SUNY), Small Business Development Center, Draper Hall, 107, 135 Western Ave., Albany, NY 12222, 518-442-5577; Fax: 518-442-5582.

Albany: The National SBDC Research Network, State University of New York, State University Plaza, 85277, Albany, NY 12246, 518-443-5265; Fax: 518-443-5275.

Binghamton: SUNY at Binghamton, Small Business Development Center, P.O. Box 6000, Vestal Parkway East, Binghamton, NY 13902-6000, 607-777-4024; Fax: 607-777-4029.

Brockport: Small Business Development Center, 74 North Main Street, Brockport, NY 14420, 716-637-6660; Fax: 716-637-2102.

Bronx: Bronx Community College, SBDC, McCracken Hall, Room 14, West 181st St. and University Ave., Bronx, NY 10453, 718-220-6464; Fax: 718-563-3572.

Brooklyn: Kingsborough Community College, 2001 Oriental Blvd., Bldg. Tr Room 4204, Manhattan Beach, Brooklyn, NY 11235, 718-368-4619; Fax: 718-368-4629.

Brooklyn: Downtown Outreach Center, SBDC, 111 Livingston St., Room 208, Brooklyn, NY 11201, 718-596-7081; Fax: 718-596-6989.

Buffalo: State University College at Buffalo, Small Business Development Center, 1300 Elmwood Avenue, BA 117, Buffalo, NY 14222, 716-878-4030; Fax: 716-878-4067.

Cobleskill: Cobleskill Outreach Center, SBDC, SUNY Cobleskill, Warner Hall, Room 218, Cobleskill, NY 12043, 518-234-5528; Fax: 518-234-5292.

Corning: Corning Community College, Small Business Development Center, 24 Denison Parkway West, Corning, NY 14830, 607-962-9461; Fax: 607-936-6642.

Dobbs Ferry: Mercy College, Small Business Development Center, Westchester Outreach Center, Mercy College, 555 Broadway, Dobbs Ferry, NY 10522, 914-674-7845, ext. 485; Fax: 914-693-4996.

Farmingdale: SUNY College of Technology at Farmingdale, Small Business Development Center, Campus Commons, Farmingdale, NY 11735, 516-420-2765; Fax: 516-293-5343.

Fishkill: Marist College, Small Business Development Center, Fishkill Extension Center, 2600 Route 9, Unit 90, Fishkill, NY 12524-2001, 914-897-2607/2608/2609; Fax: 914-897-4653.

Geneseo: SUNY Geneseo, Small Business Development Center, 1 College Circle, Geneseo, NY 14454-1485, 716-245-5429; Fax: 716-245-5430.

Geneva: Geneva Outreach Center, Small Business Development Center at Geneva, 122 N. Genesee St., Geneva, NY 14456, 315-781-1253.

Hempstead: EOC Hempstead Outreach Center, SBDC, 269 Fulton Ave., Hempstead, NY 11550, 516-564-8672/1895; Fax: 516-481-4938.

Jamaica: York College, Small Business Development Center, Science Building, Room 107, The City University of New York, Jamaica, NY 11451, 718-262-2880; Fax: 718-262-2881.

Jamestown: Jamestown Community College, Small Business Development Center, P.O. Box 20, Jamestown, NY 14702-0020, 716-665-5754, 1-800-522-7232; Fax: 716-665-6733.

Kingston: Kingston SBDC, 649 Ulster Ave., Kingston, NY 12401, 914-339-1322; Fax: 914-339-1631.

New York: Harlem Outreach Center, SBDC, 163 W. 125th St., Room 1307, New York, NY 10027, 212-865-4299/4399; Fax: 212-865-0622.

New York: East Harlem Outreach Center, SBDC, 145 E 116th St., 3rd Floor, New York, NY 10029, 212-534-2729/4526; Fax: 212-410-1359.

New York: Midtown Outreach Center, SBDC, Baruch College, 360 Park Ave. South, Room 1101, New York, NY 10010, 212-802-6620; Fax: 212-802-6613.

New York: Pace University, SBDC, Pace Plaza, New York, NY 10038, 212-346-1899; Fax: 212-346-1613.

Oswego: SUNY at Oswego, SBDC, Operation Oswego County, 44 W. Bridge St., Oswego, NY 13126, 315-343-1545; Fax: 315-343-1546.

Plattsburgh: Clinton Community College, SBDC, Lake Shore Rd., Suite 9 South, 136 Clinton Point Dr., Plattsburgh, NY 12901, 518-562-4260; Fax: 518-563-9759.

Riverhead: Riverhead Outreach Center, Small Business Development Center, Suffolk County Community College, Riverhead, NY 11901, 516-369-1409/1507; Fax: 516-369-3255.

Rochester: Small Business Development Center-SUNY Brockport, Temple Bldg., 14 Franklin St., Suite 200 Rochester, NY 14604, 716-232-7310.

Sanborn: Niagara County Community College at Sanborn, Small Business Development Center, 3111 Saunders Settlement Road, Sanborn, NY 14132, 716-693-1910; Fax: 716-731-3595.

Southampton: Southampton Outreach Center, SBDC, Long Island University at Southampton, Abney Peak, Montauk Highway, Southampton, NY 11968, 516-287-0059/0071; Fax: 516-287-8287.

Staten Island: The College of Staten Island, SBDC, Sunnyside Campus, Room B140, 715 Ocean Terrace, Staten Island, NY 10301, 718-390-7645; Fax: 718-876-9378.

Stony Brook: SUNY at Stony Brook, Small Business Development Center, Harriman Hall, Room 109, Stony Brook, NY 11794, 516-632-9070; Fax: 516-632-7176.

Suffern: Rockland Community College at Suffern, Small Business Development Center, 145 College Road, Suffern, NY 10901, 914-356-0370; Fax: 914-356-0381.

Syracuse: Onondaga Community College at Syracuse, Small Business Development Center, Excell Bldg., Room 108, Route 173, Syracuse, NY 13215, 315-492-3029; Fax: 315-492-3704.

Troy: Manufacturing Technology Center, SBDC, New York Manufacturing Partnership, 385 Jordan Rd., Troy, NY 12180-8347, 518-286-1014. Fax: 518-286-1006.

Utica: SUNY College of Technology at Utica/Rome, Small Business Development Center, P.O. Box 3050, Utica, NY 13504-3050, 315-792-7546; Fax: 315-792-7554.

Watertown: Jefferson Community College, Small Business Development Center, Watertown, NY 13601, 315-782-9262; Fax: 315-782-0901.

White Plains: The Small Business Resource Center, Small Business Development Center, 222 Bloomingdale Road, 3rd Floor, White Plains, NY 10605-1500, 914-644-4116; Fax: 914-644-2184.

North Carolina

Lead Center:
North Carolina Small Business Development Center
University of North Carolina
4509 Creedmoor Road, Suite 201
Raleigh, NC 27612
919-571-4154
Fax: 919-571-4161

Asheville: Asheville Office, Small Business Development Center, 34 Wall St., Suite 707, Public Services Bldg., Asheville, NC 28805, 704-251-6025.

Boone: Appalachian State University, SBDC, Northwestern Region, Walker College of Business, Boone, NC, 28608, 704-262-2492; Fax: 704-262-2027.

Chapel Hill: Small Business Development Center, Central Carolina Region, 608 Airport Road, Suite B, Chapel Hill, NC 27514, 919-962-0389; Fax: 919-962-0389.

Charlotte: Small Business Development Center, Southern Piedmont Region, The Ben Craig Center, 8701 Mallard Creek Road, Charlotte, NC 28262, 704-548-1090; Fax: 704-548-9050.

Cullowhee: Small Business Development Center, Center for Improving Mountain Living, Western Carolina University, Cullowhee, NC 28723, 704-227-7494; Fax: 704-227-7422.

Elizabeth City: Elizabeth City State University, Small Business Development Center, Northeastern Region, P.O. Box 874, Elizabeth City, NC 27909, 919-335-3247; Fax: 919-335-3648.

Fayetteville: Fayetteville State University, Small Business Development Center, Cape Fear Region, Continuing Education Center, P.O. Box 1334, Fayetteville, NC 28302, 919-486-1727; Fax: 919-486-1949.

Greensboro: North Carolina A&T University/CH Moore Agricultural Research Center, Small Business Development Center, Box D-22, Greensboro, NC 27411, 910-334-7005; Fax: 910-334-7073.

Greenville: East Carolina University, Small Business Development Center, Eastern Region, 300 E. 1st St., Willis Bldg., Greenville, NC, 27858-4353, 919-757-6157; Fax: 919-757-6992.

Hickory: Catawba Valley Region, Small Business Development Center, 514 Hwy 321, Suite A, Hickory, NC 28601, 704-345-1110; Fax: 704-326-9117.

Small Business Development Centers

Pembroke: Pembroke State University, Office of Economic Development and SBTDC, Pembroke, NC 28372, 910-521-6603; Fax: 910-521-6550.

Raleigh: MCI Small Business Resource Center, 800 1/2 S. Salisbury St., Raleigh, NC 27601, 919-715-0520; Fax: 919-715-0518.

Rocky Mount: NC Wesleyan College, Small Business Development Center, 3400 N. Wesleyan Blvd., Rocky Mount, NC 27804, 919-985-5130; Fax: 919-977-3701.

Wilmington: University of North Carolina at Wilmington, SBDC, Southeastern Region, Room 131, Cameron Hall, 601 South College Road, Wilmington, NC 28403, 919-395-3744; Fax: 919-395-3815; Fax: 910-350-3990.

Winston-Salem: Winston-Salem University, SBDC, Northern Piedmont Region, P.O. Box 13025, Winston-Salem, NC 27110, 919-750-2030; Fax: 919-750-2031.

North Dakota

Lead Center:
North Dakota Small Business Development Center
University of North Dakota
118 Gamble Hall, Box 7308
Grand Forks, ND 58202
701-777-3700
Fax: 701-777-3225

Bismarck: Small Business Development Center, Bismarck Regional Center, 400 East Broadway, Suite 416, Bismarck, ND 58501, 701-223-8583; Fax: 701-255-7228.

Devils Lake: Devils Lake Outreach Center, Small Business Development Center, 417 5th Street, Devils Lake, ND 58301, 800-445-7232.

Dickinson: Small Business Development Center, Dickinson Regional Center, 314 3rd Avenue West, Drawer L, Dickinson, ND 58602, 701-227-2096; Fax: 701-225-5116.

Fargo: Small Business Development Center, Fargo Regional Center, 417 Main Avenue, Fargo, ND 58103, 701-237-0986; Fax: 701-235-6706.

Grafton: Grafton Outreach Center, Red River Regional Planning Council, Small Business Development Center, P.O. Box 633, Grafton, ND 58237, 800-445-7232.

Grand Forks: Small Business Development Center, Grand Forks Regional Center, The Hemp Center, 1407 24th Avenue S., Suite 201, Grand Forks, ND 58201, 701-772-8502; Fax: 701-775-2772.

Jamestown: Jamestown Outreach Center, Small Business Development Center, 210 10th St. SE, Box 1530, Jamestown, ND 58402, 701-252-9243; Fax: 701-251-2488/252-4837.

Minot: Minot Outreach Center, SBDC, 4215 E. Burdick Expy. Minot, ND 58701, 701-839-6641; Fax: 701-838-8955.

Minot: Small Business Development Center, Minot Regional Center, 1020 20th Avenue Southwest, P.O. Box 940, Minot, ND 58702, 701-852-8861; Fax: 701-838-2488.

Williston: Williston Outreach Ctr., Tri-County Economic Development Assn., SBDC, Box 2047, Williston, ND 58801, 800-445-7232.

Ohio

Lead Center:
Ohio Small Business Development Center
Department of Development
State Office Tower
P.O. Box 1001
Columbus, OH 43226-0101
614-466-2480
Fax: 614-466-0829

Akron: Small Business Development Center, Akron Regional Development Board, One Cascade Plaza, 8th Floor, Akron, OH 44308, 216-379-3170; Fax: 216-379-3164.

Athens: Ohio University, Small Business Development Center, Innovation Center, 20 E. Circle Dr., Athens, OH 45701, 614-593-1797; Fax: 614-593-1795.

Athens: Athens Small Business Center, Inc., 900 East State Street, Athens OH 45701, 614-592-1188.

Bowling Green: Wood County Small Business Development Center, WSOS Community Action Commission, Inc., P.O. Box 539, 121 E. Wooster St., Bowling Green, OH 43402, 419-352-3817; Fax: 419-353-3291.

Canton: Small Business Development Center, Greater Stark Development Board, 6000 Frank Ave. NW, Canton, OH 44704, 216-379-3170; Fax: 216-379-3164.

Celina: Wright State University, Lake Campus, Small Business Development Center, 7600 State Route 703, Celina, OH 45882, 419-586-0355; Fax: 419-586-0358.

Cincinnati: Cincinnati Small Business Development Center, IAMS Research Park, MC189, 1111 Edison Avenue, Cincinnati, OH 45216-2265, 513-948-2082; Fax: 513-948-2007.

Cincinnati: Clemont County Chamber of Commerce, Small Business Development Center, 4440 Glen Este-Withamsville Road, Cincinnati, OH, 513-753-7141; Fax: 513-753-7146.

Cincinnati: Cincinnati Minority Business Assistance Corporation, University of Cincinnati, Small Business Development Center, 2900 Reading Rd., Box 210167, Cincinnati, OH 45237-2810, 513-556-1922; Fax: 513-556-0097.

Cleveland: Northern Ohio Mfg. SBDC, Prospect Pk. Bldg., 4600 Prospect Ave., Cleveland, OH 44103-4314, 216-432-5364; Fax: 216-361-2900.

Cleveland: Women's Business Development Center of Cleveland, 601 Lakeside Ave., Cleveland, OH 44114, 216-654-4162; Fax: 216-664-3002.

Cleveland: Greater Cleveland Growth Association, SBDC, 200 Tower City Center, 50 Public Square, Cleveland, OH 44113-2291, 216-621-3300; Fax: 216-621-4617.

Columbus: Columbus Small Business Development Center, Columbus Area Chamber of Commerce, 37 North High Street, Columbus, OH 43215, 614-225-6082; Fax: 614-469-8250.

Columbus: Ohio Dept. of Development, Ohio Women's Business Resource Network, Small Business Development Center, 77 S. High St., 28th Floor, Columbus, OH 43266-0101, 800-849-1300, ext. 6-2682; Fax: 614-466-0829.

Coshocton: Coshocton Area Chamber of Commerce, Small Business Development Center, 124 Chestnut Street, Coshocton, OH 43812, 614-622-5411; Fax: 614-622-9902.

Dayton: Dayton Area Chamber of Commerce, Small Business Development Center, Chamber Plaza, 5th and Main Streets, Dayton, OH 45402-2400, 513-226-8239; Fax: 513-226-8254.

Dayton: Dayton Satellite, Center for Small Business Assistance, College of Business, 310 Rike Hall, Dayton, OH 45433, 513-873-3503; Fax: 523-873-3545.

Dayton: Microenterprise Development Program, Small Business Development Center, 1152 W. Third St., Dayton, OH 45407, 513-222-0065; Fax: 513-222-8658.

Dayton: City of Dayton MCBAP, SBDC, 1116 W. Stewart St., Dayton, OH 45408, 513-223-2164; Fax: 513-223-8495.

Dayton: Central State University, Miami Valley OPTA Outreach Center, Small Business Development Center, 100 Jenkins Hall, Dayton, OH 45384, 513-376-6514; Fax: 513-376-6598.

Defiance: Northwest Small Business Development Center, 1935 E. Second St., Suite D, Defiance, OH 43512, 419-784-3777; Fax: 419-782-4649.

Fremont: North Central Small Business Development Center, Fremont Office, Terra Technical College, 1220 Cedar Street, Fremont, OH 43420, 419-332-1002; Fax: 419-334-2300.

Hillsboro: Enterprise Center Small Business Development Center, 129 E. Main St., Hillsboro, OH 45132, 513-393-9599; Fax: 513-393-8159.

Jefferson: Ashtabula County Economic Development Council, Inc., Small Business Development Center, 36 West Walnut Street, Jefferson, OH 44047, 216-576-9134; Fax: 216-576-5003.

Kent: Kent Regional Business Alliance Small Business Development Center, Kent State Univ. Partnership, College of Business Admin., Room 302, Kent, OH 44242, 216-672-2750; Fax: 216-672-2448.

Kettering: EMTEC/Small Business Development Center, Southern Area Mfg. Small Business Development Center, 2171 Research Park, Kettering, OH 45420, 513-259-1361; Fax: 513-259-1303.

Lima: Lima Technical College, Small Business Development Center, 545 West Market Street, Suite 305, Lima, OH 45801, 419-229-5320; Fax: 419-229-5424.

Lorain: Lorain County Chamber of Commerce, Small Business Development Center, 6100 S. Broadway, Lorain, OH 44053, 216-246-2833; Fax: 216-246-4050.

Mansfield: Mid-Ohio Small Business Development Center, 246 E. 4th St., P.O. Box 44901, Mansfield, OH 44902, 800-366-7232; Fax: 419-522-6811.

Marietta: Marietta College, Small Business Development Center, 213 4th St., Marietta, OH 45750, 614-376-4832; Fax: 614-376-4801.

Marion: Marion Small Business Development Center, Marion Area Chamber of Commerce, 206 S. Prospect Street, Marion, OH 43302, 614-382-0181.

Mentor: Lakeland Community College, Lake County Economic Development Center, Small Business Development Center, Mentor, OH 44080, 216-951-1290; Fax: 216-951-7336.

New Philadelphia: Tuscarawas Chamber of Commerce, Small Business Development Center, 330 University Drive, NE, New Philadelphia, OH 44663, 216-339-3391; Fax: 216-339-2637.

Oxford: Miami University Small Business Development Center, Dept. of Decision Sciences, 336 Upham Hall, Oxford, OH 44045, 513-529-4841; Fax: 513-529-1469.

Piqua: Upper Valley Joint Vocational School, Small Business Development Center, 8811 Career Drive, North County Road 25A, Piqua, OH 45356, 513-778-8419; Fax: 513-778-9237.

Portsmouth: Portsmouth Area Chamber of Commerce, Small Business Development Center, 1206 Weller St., P.O. Box 1757, Portsmouth, OH 45662, 614-354-2833; Fax: 614-353-2695.

Shaker Heights: Western Reserve Minority Chamber of Commerce, Small Business Development Center, 20475 Farnsleigh, Shaker Heights, OH 44122, 216-283-4700; Fax: 216-283-5006.

Southpoint: Lawrence County Chamber of Commerce, Small Business Development Center, U.S. Route 52 and Solida Road, P.O. Box 488, Southpoint, OH 45680, 614-894-3838; Fax: 614-894-3836.

Springfield: Springfield Small Business Development Center, INC., 300 E. Auburn Ave., Springfield, OH 45505, 513-322-7821; Fax: 513-322-7874.

St. Clairsville: Department of Development of the CIC of Belmont County, Small Business Development Center, St. Clairsville Office, 100 East Main Street, St. Clairsville, OH 43950, 614-695-9678; Fax: 614-695-1536.

Steubenville: Greater Steubenville Chamber of Commerce, Small Business Development Center, 630 Market Street, P.O. Box 278, Steubenville, OH 43952, 614-282-6226; Fax: 614-282-6285.

Toledo: Toledo MCBAP, Economic Opportunity Planning Association, Small Business Development Center, 505 Hamilton St., Toledo, OH 43602, 419-242-7304; Fax: 419-242-8263.

Toledo: Northwest Ohio Women's Business Entrepreneurial Network, Small Business Development Center, Toledo Regional Growth Partnership, 300 Madison Ave., Toledo, OH 43604, 419-252-2700; Fax: 419-252-2724.

Youngstown: Youngstown State University, Cushwa Center for Industrial Development, Small Business Development Center, 410 Wick Ave., Youngstown, OH 44555, 216-742-3495; Fax: 216-742-3784.

Zanesville: Zanesville Area Chamber of Commerce, Small Business Development Center, 217 North Fifth Street, Zanesville, OH 43701, 614-452-4868; Fax: 614-454-2963.

Oklahoma

Lead Center:
Oklahoma Small Business Development Center Network
Southeastern Oklahoma State University
517 University
Durant, OK 74701
405-924-0277
1-800-522-6154
Fax: 405-924-7471

Ada: East Central State University, Small Business Development Center, 1036 East 10th, Ada, OK 74820, 405-436-3190; Fax: 405-436-3190.

Alva: Northwestern State University, Small Business Development Center, 709 Oklahoma Blvd., Alva, OK 73717, 405-327-0560; Fax: 405-327-8608.

Durant: Southeastern State University, Small Business Development Center, 517 University, Durant, OK 74701, 405-924-0277; Fax: 405-920-7471.

Enid: Phillips University, Enid Satellite Center, 100 South University Avenue, Enid, OK 73701, 405-242-7989; Fax: 405-237-1607.

Langston: Langston University, Minority Assistance Center, Hwy. 33 East, Langston, OK 73050, 405-466-3256; Fax: 405-466-3381.

Lawton: Lawton Satellite Center, Small Business Development Center, American National Bank Building, 601 SW "D", Suite 209, Lawton, OK 73501, 405-248-4946.

Miami: Miami Satellite, 215 I St. NE, Miami, OK 74354, 918-540-0575; Fax: 918-540-0575.

Midwest City: Rose State College, Procurement Specialty Center, 6420 Southeast 15th Street, Midwest City, OK 73110, 405-733-7348; Fax: 405-733-7495.

Oklahoma City: University of Central Oklahoma, SBDC, 621 N. Robinson, Suite 372, Oklahoma City, OK 73102, 405-232-1968; Fax: 405-232-1967.

Poteau: Carl Albert Junior College, Poteau Satellite Center, Small Business Development Center, 1507 South McKenna, Poteau, OK 74953, 918-647-4019; Fax: 918-647-1218.

Tahlequah: Northeastern State University, Small Business Development Center, Tahlequah, OK 74464, 918-458-0802; Fax: 918-458-2105.

Tulsa: Tulsa Satellite Center, State Office Building, 440 South Houston, Suite 507, Tulsa, OK 74107, 918-581-2502; Fax: 918-581-2745.

Weatherford: Southwestern State University, Small Business Development Center, 100 Campus Drive, Weatherford, OK 73096, 405-774-1040; Fax: 405-774-7091.

Oregon

Lead Center:
Oregon Small Business Development Center
44 W. Broadway, Suite 501
Eugene, OR 97401-3021
503-726-2250
Fax: 503-345-6006

Albany: Linn-Benton Community College, Small Business Development Center, 6500 S.W. Pacific Boulevard, Albany, OR 97321, 503-967-6112; Fax: 503-967-6550.

Ashland: Southern Oregon State College, Small Business Development Center, Regional Service Institute, Ashland, OR 97520, 503-482-5838, Fax: 503-482-5838.

Bend: Central Oregon Community College, Small Business Development Center, 2600 N.W. College Way, Bend, OR 97701, 503-383-7290; Fax: 503-383-7503.

Coos Bay: Southwestern Oregon Community College, Small Business Development Center, 340 Central, Coos Bay, OR 97420, 503-269-0123; Fax: 503-269-0323.

Eugene: Lane Community College, Small Business Development Center, 1059 Willamette Street, Eugene, OR 97401, 503-726-2255; Fax: 503-686-0096.

Grants Pass: Rogue Community College, Small Business Development Center, 214 SW 4th St., Grants Pass, OR 97526, 503-471-3515.

Gresham: Mount Hood Community College, Small Business Development Center, 323 NE Roberts Street, Gresham, OR 97030, 503-667-7658, Fax: 503-666-1140.

Klamath Falls: Oregon Institute of Technology, Small Business Development Center, 3201 Campus Drive, South 314, Klamath Falls, OR 97601, 503-885-1760; Fax: 503-885-1855.

Lincoln City: Oregon Coast Community College Service District, Small Business Development Center, 4157 NW Highway 101, Suite 123, Lincoln City, OR 97367, 503-994-4166; Fax: 503-996-4958.

Medford: Small Business Development Center, 229 N. Bartlett, Medford, OR 97501, 503-772-3478; Fax: 503-776-2224.

Milwaukie: Clackamas Community College, Small Business Development Center, 7616 S.E. Harmony Road, Milwaukie, OR 97222, 503-656-4447; Fax: 503-652-0389.

Ontario: Treasure Valley Community College, Small Business Development Center, 88 S.W. Third Avenue, Ontario, OR 97914, 503-889-2617, Fax: 503-889-8331.

Pendleton: Blue Mountain Community College, Small Business Development Center, 37 S.E. Dorion, Pendleton, OR 97801, 503-276-6233.

Portland: Portland Community College, Small Business Development Center, 123 N.W. 2nd Avenue, Suite 321, Portland, OR 97209, 503-273-2828; Fax: 503-294-0725.

Portland: Small Business International Trade Program, 121 S.W. Salmon Street, Suite 210, Portland, OR 97204, 503-274-7482, Fax: 503-228-6350.

Rosenburg: Umpqua Community College, Small Business Development Center, 744 S.E. Rose, Rosenburg, OR 97470, 503-672-2535; Fax: 503-672-3679.

Salem: Chemeketa Community College, Small Business Development Center, 365 Ferry Street S.E., Salem, OR 97301, 503-399-5181; Fax: 503-581-6017.

Seaside: Clatsop Community College, Small Business Development Center, 1761 N. Holladay, Seaside, OR 97138, 503-738-3347.

The Dalles: Columbia Gorge Community College, Small Business Development Center, 400 E. Scenic Dr., Suite 257, The Dalles, OR 97058, 503-298-3118, Fax: 503-298-3119.

Tillamook: Tillamook Bay Community College Service District, Small Business Development Center, 401 B Main St., Tillamook, OR 97141, 503-842-2551; Fax: 503-842-2555.

Pennsylvania

Lead Center:
Pennsylvania Small Business Development Center
University of Pennsylvania
The Wharton School, 444 Vance Hall
Philadelphia, PA 19104-6374
215-898-1219
Fax: 215-573-2135

Aliquippa: Beaver Valley Technology Center, Small Business Development Center, 300 Main Ave., W. Aliquippa Business and Technology Ctr., Aliquippa, PA 15001, 412-378-7422.

Bethlehem: Lehigh University, Small Business Development Center, Rauch Business Center #37, Bethlehem, PA 18015, 215-758-3980; Fax: 215-758-5205.

California: California University, SBDC, Mon Valley Renaissance Center, Box 62, California, PA 15419, 412-938-5938.

Clarion: Clarion University of Pennsylvania, Small Business Development Center, Dana Still Building, Clarion, PA 16214, 814-226-2060; Fax: 814-226-2636.

Erie: Gannon University, SBDC, Carlisle Building, 3rd Floor, Erie, PA 16541, 814-871-7714; Fax: 814-871-7383.

Exton: West Chester University, Small Business Development Center, Suite 201, 930 East Lancaster Ave., Exton, PA 19341, 215-363-5175.

Harrisburg: Kutztown University, Small Business Development Center, University Center, 2986 N. 2nd St., Harrisburg, PA 17110, 717-233-3120.

Huntingdon: Juniata College, Business Outreach Center, Small Business Development Center, 1700 Moore St., Huntingdon, PA 16652, 814-643-4310, ext. 633.

Indiana: Indiana University of PA, Small Business Development Center, 202 McElhaney Hall, Indiana, PA 15705, 412-357-2179.

Latrobe: St. Vincent College, Small Business Development Center, Alfred Hall, 4th Floor, Latrobe, PA 15650, 412-537-4572; Fax: 412-537-0919.

Lewisburg: Bucknell University, Small Business Development Center, Dana Engineering Building, Lewisburg, PA 17837, 717-524-1249; Fax: 717-524-1768.

Loretto: St. Francis College, Small Business Development Center, Business Resource Center, Loretto, PA 15940, 814-472-3200; Fax: 814-472-3202.

Small Business Development Centers

Mansfield: Mansfield Univ., Northern Tier Small Business Assistance Center, Rural Services Institute, Mansfield, PA 16933, 717-662-4972.

Philadelphia: Drexel University, Small Business Development Center, Department of Management, College of Business, Academic Building, Philadelphia, PA 19104, 215-895-2122.

Philadelphia: Temple University, Small Business Development Center, Room 6, Speakman Hall, 006-00, Philadelphia, PA 19122, 215-204-7282.

Philadelphia: LaSalle University, Small Business Development Center, 20th St. and Olney Ave., Philadelphia, PA 19141, 215-951-1416.

Philadelphia: University of Pennsylvania, Small Business Development Center, The Wharton School, 409 Vance Hall, Philadelphia, PA 19104-6357, 215-898-4861; Fax: 215-898-1299.

Pittsburgh: Duquesne University, Small Business Development Center, Rockwell Hall-Room 10 Concourse, 600 Forbes Avenue, Pittsburgh, PA 15282, 412-434-6233; Fax: 412-434-5072.

Pittsburgh: University Small Business Development Center, Room 343 Mervis Hall, Pittsburgh, PA 15260, 412-648-1544; Fax: 412-648-1693.

Scranton: University of Scranton, Small Business Development Center, St. Thomas Hall, Room 588, Scranton, PA 18510, 717-941-7588; Fax: 717-941-4053.

Villanova: Villanova University, Small Business Development Center, Management Dept., Ithan and Lancaster Aves., Villanova, PA 19085, 215-645-4382.

Washington: Washington and Jefferson College, Small Business Development Center, Center for Economic Development, Department of Economics and Business, Washington, PA 15301, 412-222-4400.

Wilkes-Barre: Wilkes College, Small Business Development Center, Hollenback Hall, 192 South Franklin Street, Wilkes-Barre, PA 18766, 717-824-4651, ext. 4340.

Rhode Island

Lead Center:
Rhode Island Small Business Development Center
Bryant College
1150 Douglas Pike
Smithfield, RI 02917
401-232-6111
Fax: 401-232-6416

Newport: Salve Regina University, SBDC, Miley Hall, Room 006, Newport, RI 02840, 401-849-6900; Fax: 401-847-0372.

North Kingstown: Rhode Island Small Business Development Center, Quonset P/D Industrial Park, 35 Belver Ave., Room 217, North Kingstown, RI 02852, 401-294-1228/1227; Fax: 401-294-6897.

Providence: Rhode Island SBDC, CCRI-Providence Campus, One Hilton St., Providence, RI 02905, 401-455-6088; Fax: 401-455-6047.

Providence: Bryant College, Small Business Development Center, 7 Jackson Walkway, Providence, RI 02903, 401-831-1330; Fax: 401-454-2819.

Providence: Rhode Island Small Business Development Center, Providence Campus, One Hilton Street, Providence, RI 02905, 401-455-6042; Fax: 401-455-6047.

South Carolina

Lead Center:
South Carolina Small Business Development Center
University of South Carolina
College of Business Administration
Columbia, SC 29208
803-777-4907
Fax: 803-777-4403

Alkan: University of South Carolina, Alkan Office, Small Business Development Center, 171 University Pkwy., Suite 100, School of Business, Alkan, SC 29801, 803-641-3646.

Beaufort: University of South Carolina at Beaufort, Small Business Development Center, 801 Carterat Street, Beaufort, SC 29902, 803-521-4143; Fax: 803-521-4198.

Charleston: Charleston Small Business Development Center, 901 E. Bay St., Suite 539, P.O. Box 20339, Charleston, SC 29413-0339, 803-727-2020; Fax: 803-727-2013.

Clemson: Clemson University, Small Business Development Center, 425 Sirrine Hall, Clemson, SC 29634-1392, 803-656-3227; Fax: 803-656-4869.

Columbia: University of South Carolina, USC Regional Small Business Development Center, College of Business Administration, Columbia, SC 29208, 803-777-5118; Fax: 803-777-4403.

Conway: Coastal Carolina, Small Business Development Center, School of Business Administration, Conway, SC 29526, 803-349-2170; Fax: 803-349-2445.

Florence: Florence Darlington Technical College, Small Business Development Center, P.O. Box 100548, Florence, SC 29501-0548, 803-661-8256; Fax: 803-661-8041.

Greenville: Greenville Chamber of Commerce, Small Business Development Center, 24 Cleveland St., Greenville, SC 29606, 803-239-3753; Fax: 803-282-8549.

Greenwood: Upper Savannah Council of Governments, Small Business Development Center, SBDC Exchange Building, 222 Phoenix Street, P.O. Box 1366, Greenwood, SC 29648, 803-227-6110; Fax: 803-229-1869.

Hilton Head: University of South Carolina at Hilton Head, Small Business Development Center, Suite 300, Kiawah Bldg., 10 Office Park Road, Hilton Head, SC 29928, 803-785-3995; Fax: 803-777-0333.

Orangeburg: South Carolina State College, Small Business Development Center, School of Business, 300 College Ave., Orangeburg, SC 29117, 803-536-8445; Fax: 803-536-8066.

Rock Hill: Winthrop University, Small Business Development Center, 119 Thurmond Building, Rock Hill SC 29733, 803-323-2283, Fax: 803-323-3960.

Spartanburg: Spartanburg Chamber of Commerce, SBDC, P.O. Box 1636, 105 N. Pine St., Spartanburg, SC 29304, 803-594-5080; Fax: 803-594-5055.

South Dakota

Lead Center:
South Dakota Small Business Development Ctr
University of South Dakota
414 East Clark
Vermillion, SD 57069-2390
605-677-5549
Fax: 605-677-5272

Aberdeen: Small Business Development Center, 226 Citizens Building, Aberdeen, SD 57401, 605-662-2252.

Pierre: Small Business Development Center, 105 South Euclid, Suite C, Pierre, SD 57501, 605-773-5941.

Rapid City: Small Business Development Center, 444 Mount Rushmore Road, Rapid City, SD 57709, 605-394-5311.

Sioux Falls: Small Business Development Center, 200 North Phillips, L103, Sioux Falls, SD 57102, 605-330-5756.

Tennessee

Lead Center:
Tennessee Small Business Development Center
Memphis State University
South Campus (Getwell Road), Building #1
Memphis, TN 38152
901-678-2500
Fax: 901-678-4072

Chattanooga: Chattanooga State Technical Community College, Small Business Development Center, 4501 Amnicola Highway, Chattanooga, TN 37406-1097, 615-697-4410; Fax: 615-698-5653.

Chattanooga: Southeast Tennessee Development District, Small Business Development Center, 25 Cherokee Blvd., Chattanooga, TN 37405, 615-266-5781; Fax: 615-267-7705.

Clarksville: Austin Peay State University, Small Business Development Center, College of Business, Clarksville, TN 37044-0001, 615-648-7764; Fax: 615-648-7475.

Cleveland: Cleveland State Community College, SBDC, Business and Technology, P.O. Box 3570, Cleveland, TN 37320-3570, 615-478-6247; Fax: 615-478-6251.

Columbia: Small Business Development Center, Memorial Building, Room 205, 308 West 7th Street, Columbia, TN 38401, 615-388-5674.

Cookeville: Tennessee Technological University, Small Business Development Center, College of Business Administration, P.O. Box 5023, Cookeville, TN 38505-0001, 615-372-3648; Fax: 615-372-6112.

Dyersburg: Dyersburg Community College, Small Business Development Center, P.O. Box 648, Dyersburg, TN 38024, 901-286-3200; Fax: 901-286-3201.

Hartsville: Four Lakes Regional Industrial Development Authority, Small Business Development Center, P.O. Box 63, Hartsville, TN 37074-0063, 615-374-9521; Fax: 615-374-4608.

Jackson: Jackson State Community College, Small Business Development Center, 2046 North Parkway Street, Jackson, TN 38310-3797, 901-424-5389; Fax: 901-425-2647.

Johnson City: East Tennessee State University, SBDC, College of Business, P.O. Box 70, 698A, Johnson City, TN 37614-0698, 615-929-5630; Fax: 615-929-5274.

Knoxville: Pellissippi State Technical Community College, SBDC, P.O. Box 22990, Knoxville, TN 37933-0990, 615-694-6660; Fax: 615-694-6583.

Knoxville: International Trade Center, 301 E. Church Avenue, Knoxville, TN 37915, 615-637-4283.

Memphis: Memphis State University, Small Business Development Center, 320 South Dudley Street, Memphis, TN 38104-3206, 901-527-1041; Fax: 901-527-1047.

Memphis: Memphis State University, Small Business Development Center, International Trade Center, Memphis, TN 38152, 901-678-4174; Fax: 901-678-4072.

Morristown: Walters State Community College, Small Business Development Center, Business/Industrial Services, 500 S. Davy Crockett Parkway, Morristown, TN 37813-688, 615-587-9722; Fax: 615-586-1918.

Murfreesboro: Middle Tennessee State University, Small Business Development Center, School of Business, P.O. Box 487, Murfreesboro, TN 37132, 615-898-2745; Fax: 615-898-5538.

Small Business Development Centers

Nashville: Tennessee State University, Small Business Development Center, School of Business, 330 10th Avenue North, Nashville, TN 37203-3401, 615-251-1178; Fax: 615-251-1178 (call first).

Texas

Lead Centers:
North Texas Small Business Development Center
Dallas County Community College
1402 Corinth Street
Dallas, TX 75215
214-565-5835
Fax: 214-565-5857

Houston Small Business Development Center
University of Houston
1100 Louisiana, Suite 500
Houston, TX 77002
713-752-8444
Fax: 713-752-8484

Northwest Texas Small Business Development Center
Center for Innovation
2579 South Loop 289, Suite 114
Lubbock, TX 79423
806-745-3973
Fax: 806-745-6207

South Texas Border Small Business Development Center
University of Texas at San Antonio
801 S. Bowie
San Antonio, TX 78205
210-558-2450

Abilene: Abilene Christian University, Caruth Small Business Development Center, College of Business Administration, ACU Station, Box 8307, Abilene, TX 79699, 915-674-2776; Fax: 915-674-2507.

Alvin: Alvin Community College, Small Business Development Center, 3110 Mustang Road, Alvin, TX 77511-4898, 713-338-4686; Fax: 713-388-4903.

Amarillo: West Texas State University, Panhandle Small Business Development Center, T. Boone Pickens School of Business, 1800 South Washington, Suite 110, Amarillo, TX 79102, 806-372-5151.

Athens: Trinity Valley Small Business Development Center, 500 South Prairieville, Athens, TX 75751, 903-675-7403; Fax: 903-675-6316.

Austin: Austin Small Business Development Center, 221 South IH 35, Suite 103, Austin, TX 78741, 512-326-2256; Fax: 512-447-9825.

Baytown: Lee College, SBDC, P.O. Box 818, Baytown, TX 77522-4703, 713-425-6309; Fax: 713-425-6307.

Beaumont: John Gray Institute/Lamar University, Small Business Development Center, 855 Florida Ave., Beaumont, TX 77705, 409-880-2367; Fax: 409-880-2201; 1-800-722-3443.

Bonham: Bonham Small Business Development Center (Satellite), Sam Raybourn Center, Bonham, TX 75418, 903-583-4811.

Brenham: Blinn College, Small Business Development Center, 902 College Ave., Brenham, TX 77833, 409-830-4137; Fax: 409-830-4116.

Bryan: Bryan/College Station Chamber of Commerce, Small Business Development Ctr., P.O. Box 3695, Bryan, TX 77806, 409-260-5222.

Corpus Christi: Corpus Christi Chamber of Commerce, Small Business Development Center, 1201 North Shoreline, Corpus Christi, TX 78403, 512-882-6161; Fax: 512-888-5627.

Corsicana: Navarro Small Business Development Center, 120 North 12th Street, Corsicana, TX 75110, 903-874-0658; Fax: 903-874-4187.

Dallas: International Business Center, 2050 Stemmons Freeway, World Trade Center, Suite #150, P.O. Box 58299, Dallas, TX 75258, 214-653-1777; Fax: 214-748-5774.

Denison: Grayson Small Business Development Center, 6101 Grayson Drive, Denison, TX 75020, 903-786-3551; Fax: 903-463-5284.

Denton: Denton Small Business Development Center (Satellite), P.O. Drawer P, Denton, TX 76202, 817-382-7151; Fax: 817-382-0040.

DeSoto: Best Southwest Small Business Development Center, 1001 N. Beckley, Suite 606D, DeSoto, TX 75115, 214-228-3783.

Edinburg: University of Texas/Pan American, Small Business Development Center, 1201 West University Drive, Edinburg, TX 78539-2999, 512-381-3361; Fax: 512-381-2322.

El Paso: El Paso Community College, Small Business Development Center, 103 Montana Avenue, Room 202, El Paso, TX 79902-3929, 915-534-3410; Fax: 915-534-3420.

Fort Worth: Tarrant Small Business Development Center, 1500 Houston Street, Room 163, 7917 Highway 80 West, Fort Worth, TX 76102, 817-244-7158; Fax: 817-877-9295.

Gainesville: Cooke Small Business Development Center, 1525 West California, Gainesville, TX 76240, 817-665-4785; Fax: 817-668-6049.

Galveston: Galveston College, Small Business Development Center, 4015 Avenue Q, Galveston, TX 77550, 409-740-7380; Fax: 409-740-7381.

Hillsboro: Hillsboro Small Business Development Center (Satellite), SOS Building, P.O. Box 619, Hillsboro, TX 76645, 817-582-2555, ext. 282.

Houston: North Harris Community College District, SBDC, 250 N. Sam Houston Parkway, Houston, TX 77060, 713-591-9320; Fax: 713-591-3513; 1-800-443-SBDC.

Huntsville: Sam Houston State University, SBDC, College of Business Administration, P.O. Box 2058, Huntsville, TX 77341, 409-294-3737; Fax: 409-294-3612.

Kingsville: Kingsville Chamber of Commerce, Small Business Development Center, 635 East King, Kingsville, TX 78363, 512-595-5088; Fax: 512-592-0866.

Lake Jackson: Brazosport College, SBDC, 500 College Drive, Lake Jackson, TX 77566, 409-266-3380.

Laredo: Laredo Development Foundation, SBDC, 616 Leal Street, Laredo, TX 78041, 512-722-0563.

Longview: Kilgore College, Small Business Development Center, 300 South High, Longview, TX 75601, 903-757-5857; Fax: 903-753-7920.

Lubbock: Texas Tech University, SBDC, Center for Innovation, 2579 South Loop 289, Suite 114, Lubbock, TX 79423, 806-745-1637; Fax: 806-745-6207.

Lufkin: Angelina Community College, SBDC, P.O. Box 1768, Lufkin, TX 75902, 409-639-1887; Fax: 409-639-4299.

Mt. Pleasant: Northeast Texarkana Small Business Development Center, P.O. Box 1307, Mt. Pleasant, TX 75455, 214-572-1911; Fax: 903-572-6712.

Odessa: University of Texas/Permian Basin, Small Business Development Center, 4901 East University, Odessa, TX 79762, 915-563-0400; Fax: 915-561-5534.

Paris: Paris Small Business Development Center, 2400 Clarksville Street, Paris, TX 75460, 214-784-1802; Fax: 903-784-1801.

Plano: Collin County Small Business Development Center, Plano Market Square, 1717 East Spring Creek Parkway, #109, Plano, TX 75074, 214-881-0506; Fax: 214-423-3956.

San Angelo: Angelo State University, Small Business Development Center, 2610 West Avenue N, Campus Box 10910, San Angelo, TX 76909, 915-942-2119; Fax: 915-942-2038.

San Antonio: UTSA, International Small Business Development Center, 801 S. Bowie, San Antonio, TX 78205, 512-227-2997; Fax: 512-222-9834.

Stafford: Houston Community College System, Small Business Development Center, 13600 Murphy Road, Stafford, TX 77477, 713-499-4870; Fax: 713-499-8194.

Stephenville: Tarleton State University, Small Business Development Center, Box T-158, Stephenville, TX 76402, 817-968-9330; Fax: 817-968-9329.

Texas City: College of the Mainland, Small Business Development Center, 8419 Emmett F. Lowry Expressway, Texas City, TX 77591, 409-938-7578; Fax: 409-935-5816.

Tyler: Tyler Small Business Development Center, 1530 South SW Loop 323, Suite 100, Tyler, TX 75701, 903-510-2975; Fax: 903-510-2978.

Victoria: University of Houston-Victoria, Small Business Development Center, 700 Main Center, Suite 102, Victoria, TX 77901, 512-575-8944; Fax: 512-575-8852.

Waco: McLennan Small Business Development Center, 4601 North 19th Street, Waco, TX 76708, 817-750-3600; Fax: 817-756-0776.

Wharton: Wharton County Junior College, Small Business Development Center, Administration Building, Room 102, 911 Boling Highway, Wharton, TX 77488-0080, 409-532-0604; Fax: 409-532-2201.

Wichita Fall: Midwestern State University, Small Business Development Center, Division of Business, 3400 Taft Blvd., Wichita Falls, TX 76308, 817-696-6738; Fax: 817-689-4374.

Utah

Lead Center:
Utah Small Business Development Center
University of Utah
102 West 500 South, Suite 315
Salt Lake City, UT 84101
801-581-7905
Fax: 801-581-7814

Cedar City: Southern Utah University, Small Business Development Center, 351 West Center, Cedar City, UT 84720, 801-586-5400; Fax: 801-586-5493.

Ephraim: Snow College, Small Business Development Center, 345 West 100 North, Ephraim, UT 84627, 801-283-4021; 801-283-6890; Fax: 801-283-6913.

Logan: Utah State University, Small Business Development Center, East Campus Building, Logan, UT 84322-8330, 801-797-2277; Fax: 801-797-3317.

Ogden: Weber State University, Small Business Development Center, College of Business and Economics, Ogden, UT 84408-3806, 801-626-7232; Fax: 801-626-7423.

Price: College of Eastern Utah, Small Business Development Center, 451 East 400 North, Price, UT 84501, 801-637-1995; Fax: 801-637-4102.

Orem/Provo: Utah State College, Small Business Development Center, School of Management, 800 W. 200 S, Orem, UT 84058, 801-222-8230; Fax: 801-225-1128.

Roosevelt: Uintah Basin Applied Technology Center, SBDC, 1100 East Lagoon, P.O. Box 124-5, Roosevelt, UT 84066, 801-722-4523; Fax: 801-722-5804.

St. George: Dixie College, Small Business Development Center, 225 South 700 East, St. George, UT 84770, 801-673-4811 ext 353; Fax: 801-673-8552.

Vermont

Lead Center:
Vermont Small Business Development Center
Vermont Tech. College
P.O. Box 422
Randolph, VT 05060-0422
802-464-7232
Fax: 802-728-3026

Burlington: Northwestern Vermont Small Business Development Center, 60 Main St, Suite 101, P.O. Box 786-GBIC, Burlington, VT 05402-0786, 802-658-9228; Fax: 802-860-1899.

Rutland: Southwestern Vermont Small Business Development Center, 256 N. Main St., REDC, Rutland, VT 05701-2413, 802-773-9147; Fax: 802-773-2772.

Springfield: Southeastern Vermont Small Business Development Center, Clinton Square-SRDC, P.O. Box 58, Springfield, VT 05156-0058, 802-885-2071; Fax: 802-885-3027.

St. Johnsbury: Northeastern Vermont Small Business Development Center, 44 Main St.,-NVDA, P.O. Box 640, St. Johnsbury, VT 05819-0640, 802-748-5181; Fax: 802-748-1223.

White River Jct: Central Vermont Small Business Development Center, P.O. Box 246, White River Jct., VT 05001, 802-295-3710; Fax: 802-295-3779.

Virginia

Lead Center:
Virginia Small Business Development Center
P.O. Box 798
Richmond, VA 23206-0798
804-371-8253
Fax: 804-225-3384

Abingdon: VA Highland Community College, Small Business Development Center, P.O. Box 828, Abingdon, VA 24212, 703-964-7345; Fax: 703-964-9307.

Arlington: George Mason University/ Arlington Campus, Small Business Development Center, 3401 N. Fairfax Dr., Arlington, VA 22201, 703-993-8129; Fax: 703-993-8130.

Big Stone Gap: Mt. Empire Community College, Southwest Small Business Development Center, Drawer 700, Route 23, Big Stone Gap, VA 24219, 703-523-6529; Fax: 703-523-4130.

Blacksburg: Western Virginia Small Business Development Center Consortium, VPI and SU, Economic Development Assistance Center, 404 Clay Street, Blacksburg, VA 24061-0539, 703-231-5278; Fax: 703-231-8850.

Blacksburg: New River Valley SBDC, 234 Donaldson Brown Center, Virginia Tech., Blacksburg, VA 24061-0539, 703-231-5278/231-4004; Fax: 703-231-8850.

Charlottesville: Central Virginia Small Business Development Center, 918 Emmet St. N, Suite 200, Charlottesville, VA 22903, 804-295-8198, Fax: 804-295-7066.

Fairfax: Northern Virginia Small Business Development Center, 4260 Chainbridge Road, Suite A-1, Fairfax, VA 22030, 703-993-2131; Fax: 703-993-2126.

Farmville: Longwood College, 515 Main St., Small Business Development Center, Farmville, VA 24592, 804-395-2086, Fax: 804-395-2359.

Fredericksburg: Rappahannock Region SBDC, 1301 College Ave., Seacobeck Hall, Fredericksburg, VA 22401, 703-899-4076.

Harrisonburg: James Madison University, Small Business Development Center, College of Business Building, Room 523, Harrisonburg, VA 22807, 703-568-3227; Fax: 703-568-3399.

Lynchburg: Lynchburg Regional Small Business Development Center, 147 Mill Ridge Road, Lynchburg, VA 24502, 804-582-6170; Fax: 804-582-6106.

Manassas: Small Business Development Center, Dr. William E.S. Flory, 10311 Sudley Manor Drive, Manassas, VA 22110, 703-335-2500; Fax: 703-335-1700.

Middletown: Lord Fairfax Community College, SBDC, P.O. Box 47, Middletown, VA 22645, 703-869-6649; Fax: 703-869-7881.

Norfolk: Hampton Roads Inc., Small Business Development Center, P.O. Box 327, 420 Bank Street, Norfolk, VA 23501, 804-622-6414; Fax: 804-622-5563.

Richlands: Southwest Virginia Community College, Small Business Development Center, P.O. Box SVCC, Richlands, VA 24641, 703-964-7345; Fax: 703-964-9307.

Richmond: Capital Area Small Business Development Center, 403 East Grace Street, Richmond, VA 23219, 804-648-7838; Fax: 804-648-7849.

Roanoke: The Blue Ridge Small Business Development Center, 310 First Street, S.W. Mezzanine, Roanoke, VA 24011, 703-983-0717; Fax: 703-983-0723.

South Boston: South Boston Small Business Development Center, P.O. Box 1116, 515 Broad St., South Boston, VA 24596, 804-575-0044, Fax: 804-572-4087.

Sterling: Loudoun County Small Business Development Center, 21515 Ridgetop Circle, Suite 220, Sterling, VA 22170, 703-430-7222; Fax: 703-430-9562.

Warsaw: Warsaw SBDC, P.O. Box 490, 106 W. Richmond Rd., Warsaw, VA 22572, 804-333-0286, 804-333-0183, 800-524-8915; Fax: 804-333-0187.

Wytheville: Wytheville Community College, Small Business Development Center, 1000 E. Main Street, Wytheville, VA 24382, 703-228-5541, ext 314; Fax: 703-228-2541.

Washington

Lead Center:
Washington Small Business Development Center
Washington State University
245 Todd Hall
Pullman, WA 99164-4727
509-335-1576
Fax: 509-335-0949

Aberdeen: Grays Harbor College, Small Business Development Center, 1602 Edward P. Smith Drive, Aberdeen, WA 98520, 206-532-9020.

Bellevue: Bellevue Community College, Small Business Development Center, 3000 Landerholm Circle, Bellevue, WA 98009, 206-641-2265; Fax: 206-453-3032.

Bellingham: Western Washington University, Small Business Development Center, College of Business and Economics, 415 Park Hall, Bellingham, WA 98225, 206-676-3899; Fax: 509-647-4844.

Centralia: Centralia Community College, Small Business Development Center, 600 West Locust Street, Centralia, WA 98531, 206-736-9391; Fax: 206-753-3404.

Everett: Edmonds Community College, Small Business Development Center, 917 134th Street, S.W., Everett, WA 98204, 206-745-0430; Fax: 206-745-5563.

Moses Lake: Big Bend Community College, Small Business Development Center, 7662 Chanute St., Bldg. 1500, Moses Lake, WA 98837-3299, 509-762-6239; Fax: 509-762-6329.

Mt. Vernon: Skagit Valley College, Small Business Development Center, 2405 College Way, Mt. Vernon, WA 98273, 206-428-1282; Fax: 206-428-1186.

Olympia: South Puget Sound Community College, Small Business Development Center, 2011 Mottman Road SW, Olympia, WA 98501, 206-754-7711; Fax: 206-586-6054.

Omak: Wenatchee Valley College, Small Business Development Center, P.O. Box 1042, Omak, WA 98841, 509-826-5107; Fax: 509-826-4604.

Pasco: Columbia Basin College, Small Business Development Center, 2600 North 20th, Pasco, WA 99301, 509-547-0511; Fax: 509-546-0401.

Seattle: South Seattle Community College, Small Business Development Center, 6000 16th Avenue, SW, Seattle, WA 98106, 206-764-5339; Fax: 206-764-5393.

Seattle: Washington State University at Seattle, Small Business Development Center, 2001 Sixth Avenue, Suite 2608, Seattle, WA 98121-2518, 206-464-5450.

Seattle: North Seattle Community College, Small Business Development Center, International Trade Institute, 9600 College Way North, Seattle, WA 98103, 206-527-3732; Fax: 206-527-3734.

Spokane: Community College of Spokane, Small Business Development Center, West 601 First, Spokane, WA 99204, 509-459-3741; Fax: 509-459-3433.

Tacoma: Washington State University at Tacoma, Small Business Development Center, 950 Pacific Avenue, Suite 300, Box 1933, Tacoma, WA 98401-1933, 206-272-7232; Fax: 206-597-7305.

Tacoma: Pierce College, Small Business Development Center, 9401 Farwest Drive, SW, Tacoma, WA 98498, 206-964-6776; Fax: 206-964-6746.

Vancouver: Columbia River Economic Development Council, SBDC, 100 E. Columbia Way, Vancouver, WA 98660-3156, 206-693-2555; Fax: 206-694-9927.

Wenatchee: Wenatchee Valley College, Small Business Development Center, 1300 Fifth Street, Wenatchee, WA 98801, 509-662-1651; Fax: 206-764-5393.

Yakima: Yakima Valley Community College, Small Business Development Center, P.O. Box 1647, Yakima, WA 98907, 509-575-2284; Fax: 509-575-2461.

West Virginia

Lead Center:
West Virginia Small Business Development Center
West Virginia Development Office
950 Kanawha Blvd.
Charleston, WV 25301
304-558-2960
Fax: 304-558-0127

Athens: Concord College, Small Business Development Center, Box D-125, Athens, WV 24712, 304-384-5103.

Fairmont: Fairmont State College, Small Business Development Center, Fairmont, WV 26554, 304-367-4125.

Huntington: Marshall University, Small Business Development Center, 1050 Fourth Avenue, Huntington, WV 25755, 304-696-6789.

Montgomery: West Virginia Institute of Technology, Small Business Development Center, Room 102, Engineering Building, Montgomery, WV 25136, 304-442-5501.

Morgantown: West Virginia University, Small Business Development Center, P.O. Box 6025, Morgantown, WV 26506, 304-293-5839.

Parkersburg: West Virginia University at Parkersburg, Small Business Development Center, Route 5, Box 167-A, Parkersburg, WV 26101, 304-424-8277.

Shepherdstown: Shepherd College, Small Business Development Center, 120 North Princess Street, Shepherdstown, WV 25443, 304-876-5261.

Wheeling: West Virginia Northern Community College, Small Business Development Center, College Square, Wheeling, WV 26003, 304-233-5900; ext. 206.

Wisconsin

Lead Center:
Wisconsin Small Business Development Center
University of Wisconsin
432 N. Lake Street, Room 423
Madison, WI 53706
608-263-7794
Fax: 608-262-3878

Eau Claire: University of Wisconsin at Eau Claire, Small Business Development Center, Schneider Hall, #113, Eau Claire, WI 54701, 715-836-5637.

Green Bay: University of Wisconsin at Green Bay, Small Business Development Center, 460 Wood Hall, Green Bay, WI 54302, 414-465-2089.

La Crosse: University of Wisconsin at LaCrosse, Small Business Development Center, School of Business, 323 N. Hall, La Crosse, WI 54601, 608-785-8782.

Madison: University of Wisconsin at Madison, Small Business Development Center, 3260 Grainger Hall, Madison, WI 53715, 608-263-2221.

Milwaukee: University of Wisconsin at Milwaukee, Small Business Development Center, 929 North Sixth Street, Milwaukee, WI 53203, 414-227-3240.

Oshkosh: University of Wisconsin at Oshkosh, Small Business Development Center, 157 Clow Faculty, Oshkosh, WI 54901, 414-424-1453.

Stevens Point: University of Wisconsin at Stevens Point, Small Business Development Center, Main Building, Stevens Point, WI 54481, 715-346-2004.

Superior: University of Wisconsin at Superior, Small Business Development Center, 29 Sundquist Hall, Superior, WI 54880, 715-394-8351.

Whitewater: University of Wisconsin at Whitewater, Small Business Development Center, 2000 Carlson Bldg., Whitewater, WI 53190, 414-472-3217.

Wyoming

Lead Center:
Wyoming Small Business Development Center
111 West 2nd Street, Suite 416
Casper, WY 82601
800-348-5207
307-234-6683
Fax: 307-577-7014

Cheyenne: Laramie County Community College, Small Business Development Center, 1400 East College Drive, Cheyenne, WY 82007, 307-632-6141, 800-348-5208; Fax: 307-632-6061.

Laramie: University of Wyoming, Small Business Development Center, P.O. Box 3620, University Station, Laramie, WY 82071, 307-766-3050, 800-348-5194; Fax: 307-766-3406.

Powell: Northwest Community College, Small Business Development Center, John DeWitt Student Center, Powell, WY 82435, 307-754-6067, 800-348-5203; Fax: 307-754-6069.

Rock Springs: Wyoming Small Business Development Center, P.O. Box 1168, Rock Springs, WY 82902, 307-352-6894, 800-348-5205; Fax: 307-352-6876.

Help For
Home-Based Inventors

Patents, Trademarks, and Copyrights

Most inventors realize that it's vitally important to protect their idea by copyrighting it and obtaining the necessary patents and copyrights, but did you know that it's also important to look around for loans and other grants to support your business while working on your invention? If you want an idea to become an actual product, you have to invest an awful lot of your time into its research, and not just on a part time basis. Loans and grants programs for inventors help you do just that — for example, Hawaii offers low cost loans to inventors, as do other states around the country. First, let's talk about getting the necessary information concerning trademark and patent procedures.

Patent and Trademark Office

United States patent and trademark laws are administered by the Patent and Trademark Office (PTO). States also have trade secret statutes, which generally state that if you guard your trade secret with a reasonable amount of care, you will protect your rights associated with that secret. The PTO examines patent and trademark applications, grants protection for qualified inventions, and registers trademarks. It also collects, assembles, and disseminates the technological information patent grants. The PTO maintains a collection of more than 5 million United States patents issued to date, several million foreign patents, and 1.2 million trademarks, together with supporting documentation. Here's how to find out what you need to do to patent your idea.

What a Great Idea

To help you get started with patenting your invention, the Patent and Trademark Offices will send you a free booklet upon request called

Summary of How the Patent Process Works. There are three legal elements involved in the process of invention: the conception of the idea, diligence in working it out, and reducing it to practice — i.e., getting a finished product that actually works. If you have a great idea you think might work, but you need time to develop it further before it is ready to be patented, what should you do?

Protect Your Idea for $6

You can file a Disclosure Statement with the Patent and Trademark Office, and they will keep it in confidence as evidence of the date of conception of the invention or idea.

Disclosure Statement
Commissioner of Patents and Trademarks
Patent and Trademark Office
Washington, DC 20231
Recorded Message   703-557-3158
Disclosure Office   703-308-HELP
Legal Counsel   703-308-HELP

Send an 8 1/2 x 13" drawing, a copy, signed disclosure, SASE, and a check or money order for $6 to file. Upon request, the above office will also send you a free brochure on Disclosure Statements.

This is the best way to keep the idea you are working on completely secret and yet document the date you conceived the idea. You can file the Disclosure Statement at any time after the idea is conceived, but the value of it will depend on how much information you put into it — so put as much detail into this statement as you can.

Another way to document the date of conception is to have someone vouch for you and your idea.

Explain your idea to another person who is able to understand it and have them acknowledge what you have said to them in a signed, dated, notarized affidavit. Keep the voucher statement in a safe place in case you should ever need to produce it as proof of conception.

Either of the above two methods produces documentation that can be used as evidence if someone else later claims to have thought of your idea first and patents it before you do. The drawback to the voucher method is that it does not preserve absolute secrecy as does filing a disclosure statement. The person you told may tell someone else, and then you might have a problem.

Telling the World

Another way to document the date of conception is to publish it in a journal. Suppose that while in your basement to see why your old furnace is not working, you trip over your stationary exercise bicycle, which you never use, and hit your head. You also hit upon a way to heat your home by hooking up the furnace to one of the bike wheels and pedalling for 15 minutes. You're not sure if this method will work with any other furnace except your own, but it might. If you publish this or any other idea in a journal, it is protected for a year.

Publication acts as collateral evidence of the date of conception. If you are the first to conceive of an idea, and no one else has previously filed a Disclosure Statement on it or taken a Voucher Affidavit or published it, then for a year no one can patent your idea. Note that during the year you have to patent your invention you may not know whether someone else has documented an earlier conception date. The other catch to this method is that you have only a year to act. The heat is on because after a year **you** are barred from patenting your own invention! This is because the government wants you to use a reasonable amount of diligence in putting the idea to work sooner rather than later.

The Purpose of Documenting The Date of Conception

If someone else should try to patent your idea, filing a Disclosure Statement shows that you thought of it first, although filing this statement does not legally protect your invention. Documentation of the conception date gives you time to patent your invention, and is invaluable if you need to prove when you thought of your idea if a dispute should arise. (Note that filing a Disclosure Statement gives you limited defensive legal protection only if you follow it up with a patent in two years. Unlike a patent, it cannot be used offensively, to stop someone else from patenting the same idea.) When you go to file for a patent, if you and a competitor get into a dispute as to who was the first to invent it, the Patent and Trademark Office (PTO) will hold an Interference Proceeding. If you thought of the idea first, your Disclosure Statement or Voucher Affidavit will go a long way towards establishing that you were the first inventor and should therefore receive the patent for it.

Research Resources That Can Help You Turn Your Idea Into Reality

While diligently working out the details of your invention you can use the extensive resources of over 150,000 scientific and technical journals, articles, and books at the Scientific Document Library at the PTO in Crystal City, VA.

Facilitating public access to the more than 25 million cross-referenced United States patents is the job of PTO's Office of Technology Assessment and Forecast (OTAF), 703-308-0322. It has a master database which covers all United States patents, and searches are available for a fee which is based on the size of the project. The minimum search fee is $150, but no fee is charged if the information you need is already contained in a report they have on hand. This office can run a search for you based on classification, sub-class, country, or company name, but not by work or topic. An OTAF search will not result in an in-depth patent search. (More on that, and how to find classifications in the *Conducting Your Own Patent Search* section below.) OTAF extracts information from its database and makes it available in a variety of formats, including publications, custom patent reports, and statistical reports. The purpose of most of the reports generated by an OTAF search is to reveal patent trends.

Copies of the specifications and drawings of all patents are available from PTO. Design patents and trademark copies are $1.50 each. Plant patents not in color are $10 each, while plant patents in color are $20 each. To make a request, you must have the patent number. For copies, contact:

Commissioner of Patent and Trademarks
U.S. Department of Commerce
U.S. Patent and Trademark Office (PTO)
P.O. Box 9
Washington, DC 20231
Public Information Line
703-308-HELP

Patenting Your Invention

To patent your invention, start by ordering the Patent Booklet called *General Information Concerning Patents*, and Application Form.

Superintendent of Documents
U.S. Government Printing Office
Washington, DC 20402
202-512-1800

The cost is $2 and may be charged to Mastercard, VISA or Choice Card. The booklet must be ordered by its stock number 003-004-00641-2.

The application will ask you for a written description, oath, and drawing where possible. The cost to file for a patent to individuals or small businesses of under 15 employees (defined by SBA standards) is $315. It generally takes 18 months to two years for the PTO to grant a patent, and rights start the date the patent is granted. If you use your invention prior to being granted a patent, you can put "patent pending" on your product. This warns competitors that you have taken the necessary steps, but otherwise affords you no legal protection. Before embarking on the patenting process, you should conduct a patent search to make sure no one else has preceded you.

Conducting Your Own Patent Search

Before investing too much time and money on patenting your idea, you will want to see if anyone has already patented it. The PTO will only conduct searches on a specific inventors' name that you request. The fee is $10 and covers a 10-year time span. You can request this service by calling 703-308-0595. If you wish to hire a professional to do your patent search, consult the local yellow pages or obtain a copy of *Patent Attorneys and Agents Registered to Practice Before the U.S. Patent and Trademark Office*. View this publication at the PTO Search Room, or obtain it from the U.S. Government Printing Office. Even if your search is not as in-depth as that of a patent attorney or a patent agent, you may still find the information that you need. You may conduct your patent search at the Patent and Trademark Office Search Room located at:

Patent and Trademark Office (PTO)
Washington, DC 20231
703-308-0595

You can also conduct your patent search at any one of the 72 Patent Depository Libraries (PDLs) throughout the country. For information about the Patent Depository Library Program and the location of a library near you, call the toll-free number listed below.

Office of Patent Depository Library
   Programs

U.S. Patent and Trademark Office
2021 Jefferson Davis Hwy., Suite 2004
Arlington, VA 22202
1-800-435-7735
703-308-3924

The mailing address is:
Office of Patent Depository Libraries Office
U.S. Patent and Trademark Office
Suite 2004
Washington, DC 20231

This office distributes the information to the 72 PDLs. The information is kept on CD-Rom discs, which are constantly updated, and you or the library personnel can use them to do a patent search. CD-Rom discs have been combined to incorporate CASSIS (Classification and Search Support Information System). CD-Rom discs do not give you online access to the PTO database. Online access will be available through APS (Automated Patent Systems) within two years. APS is presently available only to patent examiners, public users of the PTO Search Room and to 14 of the 72 Patent Depository Libraries on a pilot program basis. Each PDL with the online APS has its own rules regarding its use. To use the online APS at the PTO Search Room, you must first sign up and take a class at the Search Room. Online access costs $40 per connect hour, and the charge for paper used for printouts is additional.

If you do not live near a PDL, the three CD-Rom discs are available through subscription. You may purchase the Classification disc, which dates back to 1790, for $210; the Bibliography disc, which dates back to 1969, for $210; and the ASIST disc, which contains a roster of patent attorneys, assignees, and other information for $151. You can also conduct your patent search and get a copy of it through commercial database services such as:

Mead Data Central, NEXIS Express, LEXPAT; 1-800-543-6862, 1-800-543-6862, Fax: 513-865-7418. Searches are done free of charge on patent topics. The charge for information found is $30 for a list of abstracts, plus print charges. Copies of patents (which you may decide to order after viewing the listing, or order directly if you already know which patent you want) cost $20. Copies include full text and detailed description of drawings, but no actual drawing because it is pulled from the electronic database.

If complete secrecy or doing your own search is your object, you may also subscribe to LEXPAT through the full library service. The cost is $28 per hour access charge, plus 65 cents per minute connect time. To subscribe call 1-800-843-6476.

Derwent, 1420 Spring Hill Rd., Suite 525, McLean, VA 22102; 1-800-451-3451, 703-790-0400, Fax: 703-790-1426. Patent searches are $360 per hour, plus 80 cents per record and $40 per hour for technical time. Copies of patents are $13-$16 for the first 25 pages and 67 cents for each additional page thereafter.

Rapid Patent, 1921 Jefferson Davis Highway, Suite 1821D, Arlington, VA 22202; 1-800-457-0850, 703-920-5050, Fax: 703-413-0127. Minimum costs for patent searches are: $240 for Mechanical, $290 for Electrical or Chemical. They are done manually. Delivery time is 4 weeks. Copies of patents cost $3.25 for each 25 pages.

CompuServe, 1-800-848-8199. There is a $39.95 one-time fee. Search time is $12.50 per hour or 21 cents per minute. Searches are available for abstracts ($4), full listing ($4), or classification ($4).

If you are going to do your own patent search at your local Patent Depository Library, begin with the *Manual and Index to U.S. Patent Classifications* to identify the subject area where the patent is placed. Then use the CD-Rom discs to locate the patent. CD-Rom discs enable you to do a complete search of all registered patents but do not enable you to view the full patent, with all its specific details. Lastly, view the patent, which will be kept on microfilm, cartridge, or paper. What information there is to view varies by library, depending on what they have been able to purchase. If the library you are using does not have the patent you want, you may be able to obtain it through inter-library loan.

Copies of patents can be ordered from the PTO at 703-308-9726, or more quickly, but for a price, from commercial services such as Derwent or Rapid Patent. Depending on what each individual PDL has available, copies of patents can be obtained for no fee.

To obtain a certified copy of a patent, call 703-308-9726 (Patent Search Library at the PTO). The fee is $5 and you must have the patent number. For a certified copy of an abstract of titles, the fee is $15. For a certified copy of patent assignments, with a record of ownership from the beginning until present, call 703-308-9726. The cost is $15, and to request specific assignments you must have the reel and frame number.

Trademarks

Registering a trademark for your product or service is the way to protect the recognition quality of the name you are building. The PTO keeps records on more than 1.2 million trademarks and records. Over 500,000 active trademarks are kept on the floor of the library, while "dead" trademarks are kept on microfilm. Books contain every registered trademark ever issued, starting in 1870. You can visit the Patent and Trademark Office to research a trademark. You can then conduct your search manually for no charge or use their Trademark Search System (T-Search) for $40 per hour, plus ten cents per page and $25 per hour for office staff assistance time.

Trademark Search Library
2900 Crystal Dr.
Second Floor, Room 2B30
Arlington, VA 22202
703-308-9800/9805

If you can't do it yourself, you can hire someone to do the search for you. For an agent to do this, consult the local yellow pages under "Trademark Agents/Consultants" or "Trademark Attorneys". You can also locate an agent by calling your local bar association for a list of recommendations.

To conduct your own search at a Patent Depository Library use the CD-Rom disc on trademarks. It is not presently available for purchase. The CD-Rom disc contains trademarks but not images. Images can be found in the *Official Gazette*, which contains most current and pending trademarks. Subscriptions to the *Gazette* for trademarks cost $312 per year. The *Gazette* for patents costs $583 per year. Both are issued every two weeks and can be ordered from the U.S. Government Printing Office. You can also purchase an image file which contains pending and registered trademarks and corresponding serial or registration numbers through Thomson and Thomson by calling 1-800-692-8833. The information contained in it dates back to April 1, 1987 and is updated by approximately 500 images weekly. However, the PDL you use is likely to have an image of the trademark on microfilm or cartridge, and also have copies of the *Official Gazette*. If not, and you have the registration number, you may obtain a copy of the trademark you want for $1.50 from the PTO. Contact:

The Patent and Trademark Office
U.S. Department of Commerce
P.O. Box 9
Washington, DC 20231
Public Information Line
703-557-4636

There are also several commercial services you can use to conduct trademark searches.

CompuServe, 1-800-848-8199. Fees are: $39.95 one time charge, plus $12.80 per hour or 21 cents per minute online time, plus $4 per search and $4 for full entry call-up.

Trademark Scan produced by Thomson and Thomson. It can be purchased by calling 1-800-692-8833 (ask for online services), or accessed directly via Dialog. Trademark Scan is updated three times per week, and includes state and federal trademarks, foreign and domestic. To access Trademark Scan you must already have Dialog. The cost is $130 per hour. Call 703-524-8004 or 1-800-334-2564. The fax number for Trademark Producer Scan is 617-786-8273. Users who already own the database should use this number.

Derwent, 1-800-451-3451, is a commercial service that will conduct the search for you. They will access the Trademark Scan database via Dialog. Cost is $60 per mark plus $1 per record. If required, 24-hour turnaround time is available.

Visual image of trademarks are not available on any of the electronic services above.

Online services and database discs for both patents and trademarks are constantly being expanded. For information on an extensive range of existing and projected products, call the PTO Office of Electronic Information at 703-308-0322 and ask for the U.S. Department of Commerce, PTO Office of Information Systems' *Electronic Products Brochure*. For example, there is a Weekly Text File, containing text data of pending and registered trademarks. Information can be called up by using almost any term. It can be purchased from IMSMARQ, 215-834-5089, the Trademark Register through Bell Atlantic Gateway, 1-800-638-6363, and Thomson & Thomson, 1-800-692-8833.

How to Register a Trademark

Get a copy of the booklet, *Basic Facts about Trademarks* from the U.S. Government Printing Office. It is free upon request from the Trademark Search Library by calling 703-308-9800/9805. The mark you intend to use needs to be in use before you apply. The fee to register your trademark is $175. The time to process your registration can take up to 14 months.

The Right Way to Get a Copyright

Copyrights are filed on intellectual property. A copyright protects your right to control the sale, use of distribution, and royalties from a creation in thought, music, films, art, or books. For more information, contact:

> Library of Congress
> Copyright Office
> Washington, DC 20559
> 202-479-0700
> Public Information Office
> 202-707-3000

If you know which copyright application you require, you can call the Forms Hotline, open 7 days per week, 24 hours per day at 202-707-9100. The fee is $20 for each registration.

The Library of Congress provides information on copyright registration procedures and copyright card catalogs which cover 28 million works that have been registered since 1870. The Copyright Office will research the copyright you need and send you this information by mail. Requests must be made in writing and you must specify exactly what information you require. Contact the Copyright Office, Reference and Bibliography, Library of Congress, 101 Independence Ave., SE, Washington, DC 20559; 202-707-6850, Public Information 707-3000. The fee for the search is $30 per hour. You can get a certificate stating the search was conducted by qualified researchers. There is no fee if you conduct the search yourself, and staff at the Library of Congress will show you how to do it. You may then, if you wish, request a certificate. The Copyright Office will conduct its own search, but your work will probably reduce the time of the search and save you money.

Subscriptions to the following parts of the Library of Congress *Catalogue of Copyright*

Entries are available from the Superintendent of Documents, U.S. Government Printing Office, Washington, DC 20402-9325. Each lists material registered since the last issue was published. Order by stock number using Mastercard, VISA, check, or money order. To order, call the Government Printing Office Order Desk at 202-512-1800. Fax for delays in receiving orders: 202-512-2250. For help or complaints call the Superintendent of Documents Office at 202-512-1803 (publications), or 202-512-1806 (subscriptions).

Part 1: Nondramatic Literary Works - this quarterly costs $16 per year. Stock number 730-001-0000-2.

Part 2: Serials and Periodicals - this semiannual costs $5 per year. Stock number 730-002-0000-9.

Part 3: Performing Arts - this quarterly costs $16 per year. Stock number 730-003-0000-5.

Part 4: Motion Pictures and Filmstrips - this semiannual costs $5 per year. Stock number 730-004-0000-1.

Part 5: Visual Arts - this semiannual does not include maps and costs $5 per year. Stock number 730-005-00000-8.

Part 6: Maps - this semiannual costs $4 per year. Stock number 730-006-0000-4.

Part 7: Sound Recordings - this semiannual costs $7.50 per year. Stock number 730-007-0000-1.

Part 8: Renewal - this semiannual costs $5 per year. Stock number 730-008-0000-7.

Invention Scams: How They Work

Fake product development companies prey on amateur inventors who may not be as savvy about protecting their idea or invention as experienced inventors might be. Most of the bogus/fake companies use escalating fees.

The following is a description of how most of them operate:

-   The inventor is invited to call or write for free information.

-   The inventor is then offered a free evaluation of his idea.

-   Next comes the sales call. The inventor is told he has a very good potential idea and that the company is willing to share the cost of marketing, etc. Actual fact, there is no sharing with these companies. Most times the inventor has to come up with the money (usually several hundred dollars or more) for a patent search and a market analysis. Neither of these are worth anything.

-   Then the inventor receives a professional/impressive looking portfolio which contains no real information at all. All the paper crammed into this portfolio looks topnotch, but it's all computer generated garbage.

-   Upon receiving this portfolio, the inventor is lured into signing a contract that commits him to giving the company thousands of dollars to promote/license the product. The company sends some promotional letters to fulfill their obligation, but large manufacturers simply toss them into the trash.

After all this, the inventor has spent thousands of dollars, wasted a lot of time, and gotten nowhere with his product.

How To Avoid Losing a Fortune

According to the experts, the inventor should:

-   Beware of the come-ons offered by these unethical companies. Avoid using the invention brokers who advertise on TV late in the evening; in public magazines; those who offer 800 numbers; and those on public transit display signs.

-   When upfront money is required, look out. There are very few legitimate consultants who insist on a retainer or hourly fee.

-   Don't allow the enthusiasm of your idea to take over your inherent common sense. Talk to your patent attorney and see if he knows anything about this company. Plus, check with inventors associations in the state, and see what they have to say about this particular company.

-   Demand to know what percentage of ideas the company accepts. Legitimate brokers might accept 2 ideas out of every 100. The fake companies tend to accept about 99 out of 100.

-   Find out their actual success rate. Any corporation/ company that will not give you their success rate (not licensing agreements) is a company to stay away from.

-   Get an objective evaluation of your invention from reputable professionals. This will save you plenty of money on a bad idea.

A number of highly recommended programs are listed in the next section.

Free Help For Inventors

If you have a great idea and want to turn it into reality, don't rush out and spend what could be thousands of dollars for a private invention company and a patent attorney. You can get a lot of this help for free or at a fraction of the cost. There is a lot of help out there; university-sponsored programs, not-for-profit groups, state affiliated programs, profit-making companies, etc. Depending on the assistance and the organization, some services are free, others have reasonable fees.

Many of the inventors organizations hold regular meetings where speakers share their expertise on topics such as licensing, financing and marketing. These groups are a good place for inventors to meet other inventors, patent attorneys, manufacturers, and others with whom they can talk and from whom they can get help.

If the listings in the state-by-state section of this chapter do not prove to be useful, you can contact one of the following organizations for help.

1. Innovation Assessment Center
    2001 6th Ave.
    Suite 2608
    Seattle, WA 98121
    206-464-5450
    This service will evaluate your idea for a cost of $295. They also provide counseling services and can assist you with your patent search. They are part of the local Small Business Development Center.

2. Wisconsin Innovation Service Center
    402 McCutchan Hall
    University of Wisconsin - Whitewater
    Whitewater, WI 53190
    414-472-1365

The only service that is guaranteed is the evaluation. However, efforts are made to match inventors with exceptional high evaluation scores with manufacturers seeking new product ideas. (Do not offer direct invention development or marketing services). WISC charges a $165 flat fee for an evaluation. The goal is to keep research as affordable as possible to the average independent inventor. Most evaluations are completed within 60 - 90 days. Those inventions from specialized fields may require more time. WISC also provides preliminary patent searches via on-line databases to client.

3. Inventure Program
    Benjamin C. Swartz
    Inventure Program
    Drake Business Center
    2507 University
    Des Moines, IA 50311-4505
    515-271-2655
    INVENTURE is a program of the Drake University Business Development and Research Institute designed to encourage the development of valid ideas through the various steps to becoming marketable items. INVENTURE has no paid staff. The entire panel is made up of volunteers. The administration of the program is handled by existing staff from the Small Business Development Center and the College of Business and Public Administration. They will review items from **any person** regardless of their place of residence. They will review a product idea and check it for market feasibility. INVENTURE may link individuals with business and/or financial partners.

INVENTURE screens every product submitted, but will not consider toy/game or food items. Products are evaluated on 33 different criteria, (factors related to legality, safety, business risk, and demand analysis, to market acceptance/competition). It normally takes up to 6 weeks to receive results of the evaluation. Evaluators are experienced in manufacturing, marketing, accounting, production, finance and investments.

INVENTURE acts in a responsible manner to maintain confidence of an idea, but cannot guarantee confidentiality.

For assistance with business plans, financial projections, and marketing help, you're encouraged to contact your Small Business Development Center (SBDC).

To submit an idea to INVENTURE, follow the following directions:

1. Fill out a disclosure document.
2. Return to the INVENTURE office with a check for $100 made payable to Drake University (INVENTURE).
3. If an idea does not pass the initial screening, your check will be returned.

4. The Wal-Mart Innovation Network (WIN)
Center for Business Research and
 Development
College of Business Administration
Southwest Missouri State University
901 S. National Avenue
Springfield, MO 65804
417-836-5667/5680
The WIN program is essentially an innovation evaluation service designed to provide inventors with an honest and objective third-party analysis of the risks and potential of their ideas and inventions. If the invention or new product idea passes the tough screening process, the Center will automatically send your idea to Wal-Mart for an Assessment of

Marketability. Their expertise allows to provide qualified inventors with a second analysis of the marketability of their invention/new product idea. A WIN endorsement will increase the chances that others will be willing to listen. If the invention/product idea receives a "Fully recommended" market assessment, WIN will not take the development or commercialization of your invention or idea. But, if the invention has a reasonable chance of success, WIN will supply information about the Innovation Network (IN) resources in a particular state, (Do not assume their services are free). The only advance payment charged by WIN is the $150 evaluation fee. A "fully recommended" WIN Assessment of Marketability does not obligate Wal-Mart in any way. The WIN program is limited to consumer related ideas and inventions. The only promise is an honest and objective preliminary evaluation.

5. U.S. Department of Energy
U.S. Dept. of Energy, CE-521
Mail Stop SE-052
1000 Independence Ave., SW
Washington, DC 20585
202-586-1478
Fax: 202-586-1605
Innovative Concepts Program: InnCon operates in cycles of roughly 1-2 years. For each cycle, the InnCon Program chooses an energy-related topic and invites innovators to submit proposals for funding of projects that relate to that topic. As many as 15 innovators are awarded seed money to explore feasibility of their concepts. The program also seeks funding from other federal organizations; this increases the potential to yield commercial products.

The Innovative Concepts Program funds novel ideas for energy efficiency that are significant from existing technologies. Anyone who has an innovative concept that addresses the current InnCon topic is invited to apply. The InnCon Program has a mailing list of potential contributors, who are notified of opportunities to apply for. To add your name, contact: Raymond L. Watts, K6-54, Pacific Northwest Laboratory, Box 999, Richland, WA 99352; 202-586-1605, Fax: 509-376-8054

Energy-Related Inventions Program (ERIP):

The National Institute of Standards and Technology (NIST) works with the U.S. Department of Energy (DOE) to conduct ERIP. Anyone can submit an invention at any stage of development for a free evaluation from NIST. Average grant/contract award has been about $83,000, with the maximum award being just under $100,000. Any invention that could save/produce energy from nonnuclear sources can qualify. An invention is classified energy-related if it results in reducing consumption, increasing industry productivity, or helping in energy production. To submit an energy-related invention, write to: Office of Technology Evaluation and Assessment, National Institute of Standards and Technology, Gaithersburg, MD 20899. Ask for Evaluation Request (form 1019). Complete the form with a detailed written description with illustrations/drawings, if possible. One should point out how the invention will benefit the nation in terms of energy use. There is no fee/obligation, financial or otherwise, on submitting an invention. The types of support an inventor will get from ERIP is a NIST evaluation attesting that the concept is technically sound; an opportunity to attend the Commercialization Planning Workshops; an assessment of the market potential for the technology; consideration of his/her proposal for grant funding. (ERIP grants are one-time only awards).

6. U.S. Environmental Protection Agency
    Center for Environmental Research
    Information
    Cincinnati, OH 45260

Directory Description: Environmental Protection Agency, Office of Research and Development, 401 M Street, SW, Washington, DC 20460; 202-260-7676, Fax: 202-260-9761

The Office of Research and Development conducts an Agency wide integrated program of research and development relevant to pollution sources and control, transport and fate processes, health/ecological effects, measurement/monitoring, and risk assessment. The office provides technical reviews, expert consultations, technical assistance, and advice to environmental decision makers in federal, state, local, and foreign governments.

Center for Environmental Research Information

26 W. ML King Drive, Cincinnati, OH 45268, Calvin O. Lawrence, Director; 513-569-7391, Fax: 513-569-7566

A focal point for the exchange of scientific/technical information both within the federal government and to the public.

The Technology Transfer Branch

Works with laboratories, program offices, regions, academia, private sector to produce technology transfer products (i.e. reports, summaries, journal articles, design manuals, handbooks, seminars, workshops, and training courses) that aid states, local governments and the regulated community in complying with Environmental Protection Agency (EPA) regulations. Topics include groundwater remediation, pollution prevention, solid, hazardous wastes, sludge, small community water treatment, municipal wastewater treatment, air pollution.

The Research Communication Branch

Is responsible for working with laboratories, program offices, regions to produce information products that summarize research, technical, regulatory enforcement information that will assist non-technical audiences in under-standing environmental issues.

The Document Management Branch
Is responsible for the production and distribution of scientific and technical reports, responding to requests for publications, and quality control of information products through the application of standardized procedures for the production of documents.

Office of Exploratory Research
Robert Menzer, Acting Director, 401 M Street, SW, Washington, DC 20460; 202-260-5750, Fax: 202-260-0450
The Office of Exploratory Research (OER) plans, administers, manages, and evaluates the Environmental Protection Agency's (EPA) extramural grant research. It supports research in developing a better understanding of the environment and its problems. Main goals are: to support the academic community in environmental research; maintain scientific/technical personnel in environmental science/technology; to support research for the identification/solution of emerging environmental problems.

Goals are accomplished through four core programs:

1. The Research Grants Program:
Supports research initiated by individual investigators in areas of interest to the agency.

2. The Environmental Research Centers Program:
Has two components: The Academic Research Center Program (ARC) and the Hazardous Substance Research Centers Program (HSRC).

3. The Small Business Innovation Research (SBIR) Program:
Program supports small businesses for the development of ideas relevant to EPA's mission. Focuses on projects in pollution control development. Also receives 1.5% of the Agency's resources devoted to extramural Superfund research.

4. The Visiting Scientists Program:
Components are an Environmental Science and Engineering Fellows Program and a Resident Research Associateship Program. The Fellows Program supports ten mid-career post-doctoral scientists and engineers at EPA headquarters & regional offices. The Research Associateship Program attracts national and international scientists and engineers at EPA research laboratories for up to 3 years to collaborate with Agency researchers on important environmental issues.

Other programs available are:
A Minority Fellowship Program
A Minority Summer Intern Program
The Agency's Senior Environmental
  Employment Program (SEE)
The Federal Workforce Training Program
An Experimental Program to Stimulate
  Competitive Research (EPSCoR).

State Sources for Inventors

Below is a listing of a variety of inventors groups, listed state by state. Some organizations listed under the state where they are located are regional or national in scope. In states where there is no specific program for inventors, the Small Business Development Centers (under the U.S. Small Business Administration) can often be of help. They are usually found at the colleges and universities. The Small Business Development Center office is located at 409 Third St., SW, Suite 4600, Washington, DC 20416; 202-205-6766.

Alabama

Office for the Advancement of Developing Industries
University of Alabama - Birmingham
1075 13th South
Birmingham, AL 35205
205-934-2190
Inventors can receive help on the commercialization and patent processes and critical reviews of inventions in this office. Assessments can be made on an invention's potential marketability and assistance is available for patent searches. There is a charge for services.

Small Business Development Center
University of Alabama at Birmingham
Medical Towers Building
1717 11th Ave. South, Suite 419
Birmingham, AL 35294
205-934-7260
Fax: 205-934-7645
The center offers counseling for a wide range of business issues and problems.

U.S. Small Business Administration
Business Development
2121 8th Avenue, N, Suite 200
Birmingham, AL 35203-2398
205-731-1338
Fax: 205-731-1404
This office offers counseling for a wide range of business issues and problems.

Alabama Technology Assistance Program
University of Alabama at Birmingham
1717 11th Avenue S, Suite 419
Birmingham, AL 35294
205-934-7260

This program provides general assistance/funding information. Inventors meet other inventors and investors.

Alaska

UAA Small Business Development Center of Alaska
430 W. 7th Ave., Suite 110
Anchorage, AK 99501
907-274-7232
Fax: 907-274-9524
The SBDC provides general assistance, including free counseling to inventors on commercialization and patent processes, and arranging meetings between inventors, investors, manufacturers, and others who can be of help.

Arizona

Arizona SBDC Network
108 N. 40th Street, Suite 148
Phoenix, AZ 85034
602-392-5224
Fax: 602-392-5300
The center offers counseling for a wide range of business issues and problems.

Gateway Community College
Small Business Development Center
Kathy Evans, Director
108 N. 40th Street
Phoenix, AZ 85034
602-392-5233
The center provides inventor assistance and funding information to inventors.

Arkansas

Arkansas Inventors Congress
P.O. Box 411
Dardanell, AR 72834
501-229-4515
Contact Person: Garland Bull
The Arkansas Inventors Congress counsels inventors on commercialization and patent processes, and provides communications among inventors, manufacturers and financial people. It will provide assessments of the market potential on inventions. U.S. Patent and Trademark Office forms and publications are available. Dues are required.

Small Business Development Center
University of Arkansas at Little Rock
100 S. Main, Suite 401
Little Rock, AR 72201
501-324-9043
Fax: 501-324-9049
The center offers counseling for a wide range of business issues and problems.

California

Inventors of California
P.O. Box 6158
Rheem Valley, CA 94570
510-376-7541

This group holds regular meetings with speakers, promotes communications between inventors and manufacturers, and for a fee, provides critical reviews of inventions. Dues are required.

Inventors Workshop International
Inventor Center, Suite 304
3201 Corte Malpaso
Camarillo, CA 93012
805-484-9786

This foundation has chapters nationwide. They hold meetings, conduct seminars, and counsel inventors on important issues, including product development and market research. The foundation publishes journals and a guidebook. There are dues and subscription fees.

Invent Magazine
8 West Janss Rd.
A Thousand Oaks, CA 91360-3325

This is a nationally distributed magazine for inventors. It is not affiliated with any single inventors group. It is published quarterly, and there is a subscription fee.

Small Business Development Center
801 K Street, 17th Floor, Suite 1700
Sacramento, CA 95814
916-324-9234
916-322-3524

The center offers counseling for a wide range of business issues and problems.

Colorado

Affiliated Inventors Foundation, Inc.
2132 E. Bijou Street
Colorado Spring, CO 80909
719-635-1234

This foundation counsels inventors on commercialization and patent processes, and provides detailed information on the steps needed to reach commercialization. Preliminary appraisals, evaluations and other services are available for a fee.

Small Business Development Center
Office of Business Development
1625 Broadway, Suite 1710
Denver, CO 80202
303-892-3809
Fax: 303-892-3848

The center offers counseling for a wide range of business issues and problems.

Connecticut

Small Business Development Center
University of Connecticut
Box U-41, Room 422
368 Fairfield Road
Storrs, CT 06269-2041

203-486-4135
Fax: 203-486-1576

The center offers counseling for a wide range of business issues and problems.

Delaware

Small Business Development Center
University of Delaware
Purnell Hall
Newark, DE 19716
302-831-1555
Fax: 302-451-6750

The office offers free management counseling and seminars on various topics, and can counsel inventors on areas such as the commercialization and patenting processes. Services are by appointment only.

Delaware Technical Innovation Program (DTIP)
Delaware Development Office
99 Kings Highway
P.O. Box 1401
Dover, DE 19903
302-739-4271

Assistance is available to any applicant located in Delaware or relocating to Delaware, who has been granted a phase I SBIR award and has submitted a Phase II SBIR application. Amounts are up to $50,000. Form of financing: Grant - bridges Phase I and Phase II of SBIR program.

Agribusiness Diversification Development Program: The program was developed jointly with the Department of Agriculture for assisting innovative agricultural enterprises such as, but not limited to, aquaculture. Funding for the program is limited, and no funding will be available after June 30, 1994. For further information, contact the Delaware Development Office.

District of Columbia

U.S. Department of Commerce
U.S. Patent and Trademark Office
Washington, DC
703-305-8292

Also see Maryland for National Institute of Standards and Technology.

District of Columbia Small Business Development Center
Howard University
6th and Fairmount Street NW, Room 128
Washington, DC 20059
202-806-1550
Fax: 202-797-6393

The center offers counseling for a wide range of business issues and problems.

U.S. Small Business Administration
2328 19th St., NW
Washington, DC 20009
202-205-6977
Fax: 202-205-7064

This office provides general assistance and information on funding.

Florida

Florida Product Innovation Center
2622 NW 43rd Street, Suite B3
Gainesville, FL 32606
904-334-1600

Developed by the Florida Small Business Development Center, the Innovation Center offers individual guidance and group training in: determining technical feasibility of an idea; facilitating technology transfer from the laboratories to product development; patent, copyright, trademark and licensing procedures, etc. Individual consultation and assistance are free. Technical evaluations conducted by qualified engineers are $100.

Tampa Bay Inventors Council
Mr. Purdy, President
P.O. Box 2254
Largo, FL 34649
813-391-0315

This group counsels inventors on commercialization and patent processes, and provides critical reviews of inventions. It offers referrals and communications for inventors with manufacturers, venture capitalists, patent attorneys, etc. The annual dues are $30. Inventions range from electronics to women's hair products.

Small Business Development Center
University of West Florida
414 Marv Esther Cutoff
Fort Walton Beach, FL 32548
904-244-1036

The center offers counseling for a wide range of business issues and problems.

Florida SBDC Network
19 W. Garden St.
Pensacola, FL 32501
904-444-2060
Fax: 904-444-2070

The network provides general assistance; conducts market/ technical assessments; offers legal advice on patents and licensing; provides funding information; and assists in building a prototype. Inventor get to showcase their inventions and meet with other inventors and investors.

University of Central Florida
Small Business Development Center
P.O. Box 25000
CBA Suite 309
Orlando, FL 32816
407-823-5554
Fax: 407-823-5741

The center provides general assistance, funding information and conducts market assessments. Inventors meet other inventors.

Georgia

Inventors Association of Georgia
525 Page Ave. NE
Atlanta, GA 30307
404-427-8024

This association holds regular meetings where members are encouraged to report on progress on inventions. Counseling is available. A newsletter is published. The annual dues are $50 for corporate members, $25 for individuals.

Small Business Development Center
University of Georgia
Chicopee Complex
1180 East Broad Street
Athens, GA 30602
404-542-5760

The center offers counseling for a wide range of business issues and problems.

Hawaii

Inventors Council of Hawaii
P.O. Box 27844
Honolulu, HI 96827
808-595-4296

The council holds monthly meetings with topical speakers and some workshops. It serves as a Patent Information Center for the state, and publishes a monthly newsletter. Annual dues are $25.

Small Business Development Center
University of Hawaii at Hilo
523 W. Lanikaula Street
Hilo, HI 96720-4091
808-933-3515
Fax: 808-933-3683

The center offers counseling for a wide range of business issues and problems.

Idaho

Idaho Research Foundation, Inc.
University of Idaho
121 Sweet Ave.
Moscow, ID 83843-2309
208-883-8366

This foundation counsels inventors on commercialization and patent processes, and provides critical reviews on inventions. Computerized data searching and marketing service is available. It takes a percentage of intellectual property royalties.

Small Business Development Center
Boise State University
1910 University Drive
Boise, ID 83725
208-385-1640

The center offers counseling for a wide range of business issues and problems.

Idaho Small Business Development Center
P.O. Box 1238
Twin Falls, ID 83303
208-733-9554
Fax: 208-733-9316

The center conducts market assessments and provides funding information.

Idaho Small Business Development Center
Lewis-Clark State College
500 8th Ave.

Lewiston, ID 83501
208-799-2463
Fax: 208-799-2831
The center provides general assistance and funding information. They also conduct market assessments.

Idaho State University
Small Business Development Center
2300 N. Yellowstone
Idaho Falls, ID 83401
208-523-1087
Fax: 208-523-1049
The center provides general assistance and funding information, and conducts technical assessments. Inventors meet with other inventors and investors.

Illinois

Argonne National Laboratory
Energy Systems Division
9700 S. Cass Ave.
Argonne, IL 60439
708-252-8259
This organization published *Catalog of Organizations That Assist Inventors: Activities and Services, Edition II*, January 1990. It summarizes activities and services of 145 national, state and local programs and organizations in the U.S. and Canada that assist independent inventors or inventors associated with small businesses. It is available for $26.

Inventor's Council
53 W. Jackson, Suite 1643
Chicago, IL 60604
312-939-3329
This group provides a liaison between inventors and industries. It holds meetings and workshops on commercialization, evaluation, marketing, financing, etc., for U.S. and Canadian inventors. Dues are required.

Small Business Development Center
Department of Commerce and Community Affairs
620 East Adams St., 6th Floor
Springfield, IL 62701
217-524-5856; 217-785-6328
The center offers counseling for a wide range of business issues and problems, including commercialization and patent processes.

Small Business Development Center
Evanston Business and Technology Center
1840 Oak Avenue
Evanston, IL 60201
708-866-1817
Fax: 708-866-1808
The center provides general assistance and funding information.

Western Illinois University
Technical Center and Small Business Development Center
Seal Hall 214
Ma Comb, IL 61455
309-298-2211
Fax: 309-298-2520

The center provides general assistance; conducts market/technical assessments; provides investment and funding information; and aids in building a prototype. Inventors meet with other inventors and investors, and get the chance to showcase their inventions.

Indiana

The Inventors and Entrepreneurs Society of Indiana, Inc.
c/o Purdue University Calumet
Hammond, IN 46323
219-989-2354
Residents of Illinois, Michigan, and Kentucky are also served by this society. It holds monthly meetings, counsels inventors, offers educational information, and will assess market potential of specific inventions on request. It also publishes a newsletter. Annual dues are $30.

Small Business Development Center
Economic Development Council
One North Capitol, Suite 200
Indianapolis, IN 46204
317-634-1690
Fax: 317-264-6855
The center offers counseling for a wide range of business issues and problems.

Iowa

Drake Business Center
Drake University
2401 University Ave.
Des Moines, IA 50311-4505
515-271-2655
This center evaluates innovations for marketability, counsels inventors on commercialization, and helps match inventors with business persons. The fee for invention assessment is $100.

Small Business Development Center
Administrative Office, Iowa State University
Chamberlynn Building
137 Lynn Avenue
Ames, IA 50010
515-292-6351
Fax: 515-292-0020
The center offers counseling for a wide range of business issues and problems.

Iowa Small Business Development Center
Clark Marshall, Director
Gateway N
Spencer, IA 51301
712-262-4213
Fax: 712-262-4047
The center provides general assistance and funding information. inventors meet with other inventors and investors.

Kansas

Kansas Association of Inventors, Inc.
2015 Lakin
Great Bend, KS 67530
316-792-1375
This association primarily serves Kansas residents, but has

members from other states and from Canada. It holds monthly chapter meetings, assesses market potential of inventions, and provides for communications between inventors and manufacturers, investors, etc. There is a quarterly newsletter. Annual dues are $35.

Small Business Development Center
Wichita State University
Campus Box 148
Wichita, KS 67208
316-689-3193
Fax: 316-689-3647

The center offers counseling for a wide range of business issues and problems.

Kentucky

Center for Entrepreneur and Technology
University of Louisville
Burhans Hall, Room 121, Shelby Campus
Louisville, KY 40292
502-852-7854

This center counsels inventors on commercialization and patent processes and provides critical reviews of inventions. It provides assistance in technically refining inventions. There are no fees.

Bluegrass Inventors Guild
917 Watterson Trail
Louisville, KY 40299
502-244-5626

This group has informal monthly meetings, speakers, networking and counseling. Dues are $30/year.

Office of Business and Technology
500 Mero Street
Cabinet of Economic Development
Capital Plaza Tower
Frankfort, KY 40601
1-800-626-2930; 1-800-633-2007 (in KY)

This office provides self-help assistance in the form of related articles, marketing ideas, and technical information. If you have a patent, they will try to match you with an investor through their Investment Capitol Network data base.

Small Business Development Center
Kentucky Small Business Development Center
Center for Business Development
College of Business and Economics Building
205 Business and Economics Building
University of Kentucky
Lexington, KY 40506-0034
606-257-7668
Fax: 606-258-1907

The center offers counseling for a wide range of business issues and problems.

Kentucky Office of Business and Technology
Cabinet for Economic Development
Capital Plaza Tower
Frankfort, KY 40601
502-564-7670

Business and Technology Branch (BTB): Coordinates the activities and interrelationships of state/national/regional programs designed to help businesses become more competitive through the comprehensive application of technology in both day-to-day work and long-range plans. They are currently providing funding fronts to various technology-related agencies and organizations across the state, including regional technology transfer/assistance centers, and technology applications centers at state universities. They encourage the Commonwealth's innovative individuals and companies to participate in available research and development assistance programs such as the Small Business Innovation Research (SBIR) program.

Small Business Innovation Research (SBIR) Program: Designed to develop/expand technology-based firms by providing "idea" money, a valuable resource for firms that want to develop new technologies. The firm must be a small, for profit, American firm with fewer than 500 employees. **SBIR Bridge Grant:** was designed to assist Kentucky firms in continuing product development research projects begun under Federal Phase I SBIR awards.

Kentucky Transportation Center
Transportation Research Building
Lexington, KY 40506-0043
606-257-4513

The center works closely with various federal, state and local agencies, as well as the private sector to conduct research supported by a wide variety of sources. They also coordinate an experimental educational program through the Advanced Institute for Transportation Systems Science.

Louisiana

Small Business Development Center
Northeast Louisiana University
College of Business Administration
700 University Avenue
Monroe, LA 71209
318-342-5506
Fax: 318-342-5510

The center offers counseling for a wide range of business issues and problems.

Louisiana Department of Economic Development
P.O. Box 94185
Baton Rouge, LA 70804-9185
504-342-5371

The department provides general assistance.

Maine

Center for Innovation and Entrepreneurship
University of Maine
Maine Tech Center, 16 Godfrey Drive
Orono, ME 04473
207-581-1465

This center counsels inventors on the commercialization process, provides referrals for critical reviews of inventions and for financial and patent assistance, and conducts inventors' forums. It publishes a newsletter and bulletins. The communicative services are usually free; there are fees for educational services and materials.

Small Business Development Center
University of Maine at Machias
Math and Science Building
Machias, ME 04654
207-255-3313

The center offers counseling for a wide range of business issues and problems.

Department of Industrial Cooperation
5711 Boardman Hall, Room 117
Orono, ME 04469-5711
207-581-1488
Fax: 207-581-2202

Maine Inventors Network (MIN): A collaboration between the University of Maine and the University of Southern Maine. The network provides comprehensive services to guide new products from invention to marketplace, from concept to commercialization. The goal is to encourage and stimulate new business start-ups and add-on products for existing Maine manufacturers. MIN provides invention screening/evaluations. This process encourages the inventor to focus resources on sound ideas and avoid the costs of developing less feasible inventions. MIN will assist in identifying the technical needs of the inventor. They educate inventors about the various types of protection available such as patents, copyrights, and trademarks, and will then refer the inventor to proper legal counsel for a full assessment of their needs. MIN can channel the inventor or entrepreneur to the proper resources at the University of Southern Maine's Small Business Development Center and Small Business Development Center (SBDC) sub-centers for help in identifying the marketing needs of their invention. Advice on current or planned business ventures is also available. MIN and SBDC can refer the inventor to a variety of financing sources. MIN maintains up-to-date information on the needs and abilities of companies and manufacturers of Maine. MIN is a public service offered to the residents of Maine.

Inventrepreneurs Forum of Maine, Inc.: (Co-sponsored by the University of Maine, Department of Industrial Cooperation and the Maine Small Business Development Center. For more information contact: Don Forester at 797-3985 or Jake Ward 581-1488).

On March 15, 1984, the Inventrepreneurs Forum of Maine, Inc (IFM), was formed and became a non-profit incorporation in the state of Maine. It was organized to stimulate inventiveness and entrepreneurship, and to help innovators and entrepreneurs develop and promote their ideas. It allows inventors and entrepreneurs to join together, share ideas and hopefully improve the chance for success. It gives encouragement, professional expertise, evaluation assistance, confidentiality, and moral support of the University of Maine's Network, and the University of Southern Maine's Small Business Development Center. The Inventrepreneurs Forum of Maine, Inc, can help inventors find the answers to important questions/solutions to almost any problem. The Inventrepreneurs Forum of Maine, Inc, meets on the first Tuesday of each month from 6:30-9:00 PM at the University of Southern Maine, Campus Center, Rooms A, B and C on Bedford Street in Portland.

Maryland

Office of Energy-Related Inventions
National Institute of Standards and Technology
Gaithersburg, MD 20899
301-975-5500

The office evaluates all promising non-nuclear energy-related inventions, particularly those submitted by independent inventors and small companies for the purpose of obtaining direct grants for their development from the U.S. Department of Energy. Although individual grant or contract awards have exceeded $100,000, the average award is $70,000.

Small Business Development Center
Department of Economic and Employment Development
217 E. Redwood Street, 10th Floor
Baltimore, MD 21202
301-333-6995
Fax: 301-333-6608

The center offers counseling for a wide range of business issues and problems.

Massachusetts

Small Business Development Center
University of Lowell
450 Aiken Street
Lowell, MA 01854
508-458-7261

The center offers counseling for a wide range of business issues and problems.

Small Business Development Center
205 School of Management
University of Massachusetts
Amherst, MA 01003
413-545-6301

The center provides general assistance and funding information.

Small Business Association of New England
69 Hickory Drive
Waltham, MA 02254
617-890-9070
Fax: 617-890-4567

The association provides general assistance and funding information.

Michigan

Inventors Council of Michigan
Metropolitan Center for High Technology
2727 Second Ave.
Detroit, MI 48201
313-963-0616

The Council holds regular meetings with topical speakers, counsels inventors on the commercialization and patent processes through the statewide Small Business Development Centers, and provides communications among inventors, manufacturers, patent attorneys, and venture capitalists. There are annual dues.

Small Business Development Center
2727 Second Avenue
Detroit, MI 48201

313-577-4848
Fax: 313-577-4222
The center offers counseling for a wide range of business issues and problems.

Minnesota

Minnesota Project Innovation, Inc.
111 3rd Ave. S., Suite 410
Minneapolis, MN 55401-2554
612-338-3280
This project is affiliated with the Minnesota Dept. of Energy and Economic Development, U.S. Small Business Administration, and private companies. It provides referrals to inventors for sources of technical assistance in refining inventions.

Minnesota Inventors Congress (MIC)
1030 East Bridge Street
P.O. Box 71
Redwood Falls, MN 56283
507-637-2344
The Minnesota Inventors Congress (MIC) is a nonprofit organization established in 1958 to promote creativity, innovation, entrepreneurship by assisting the inventor and entrepreneur with education, promotion and referral. It's a professional organization composed of private individuals and corporations, who are creating and developing useful technologies. MIC is for inventors at every development stage — the novice and experienced; male or female; young and old; and supporters of invention and innovation. Workshops are also available. These are for individuals with ideas or inventions not yet successfully on the market; for companies, entrepreneurs looking for such inventions or new products.

"World's Oldest Annual Invention Convention", promotes the spirit of invention, innovation. Each year a 3 day convention presents more than 200 inventions and attracts some 10,000 visitors from around the world. The MIC provides a meeting place for:

1) Inventors to showcase their new products, connecting with manufacturers/investors, product test market, educational seminars, publicity, inventors network, and $1,500 in cash awards.
2) Manufacturers, marketers, investors and licenses seeking new products.
3) Inventors, viewers and exhibitors, seeking free counsel and literature on the invention development process.
4) Public to view the latest inventions, by adults and students, purchase MarketPlace products and meet global inventors.

The Inventors Resource Center
P.O. Box 71
Redwood Falls, MN 56283
1-800-468-3681 (in MN)
507-637-2344
The Minnesota Inventors Congress established this center as a focal point for a statewide invention support system. It offers walk-in services, referrals, literature, and a toll-free hotline in the state, 1-800-INVENT 1.

Small Business Development Center
Department of Trade and Economic Development
900 American Center Building
150 East Kellogg Blvd.
St. Paul, MN 55101
612-297-5570
Fax: 612-296-1290
The center offers counseling for a wide range of business issues and problems.

Mississippi

Confederacy of Mississippi Inventors
4759 Nailor Rd.
Vicksburg, MS 39180
601-636-6561
This group holds quarterly meetings, counsels inventors on patent processes, sponsors invention fairs at schools, and publishes a quarterly newsletter. Annual dues are $12.

Small Business Development Center
Old Chemistry Building, Suite 216
University, MS 38677
601-232-5001
Fax: 601-232-5650
The center offers counseling for a wide range of business issues and problems.

Mississippi State University
Small Business Development Center
P.O. Box 5288
Mississippi State, MS 39762
601-325-8684
Fax: 602-325-8686
The center provides general assistance; conducts market assessments; and provides funding information.

Small Business Development Center
Meridian Community College
Meridian, MS 39307
601-482-7445
Fax: 601-482-5803
The center provides general assistance and funding information; conducts market/technical assessments; and offers legal advice on patents and licensing. Inventors meet with other inventors and investors.

Missouri

Missouri Innovation Center
T-16 Research Park
Columbia, MO 65211
314-882-2822
This group provides communications among inventors, manufacturers, patent attorneys and venture capitalists, and provides general consultations. It is sponsored by the state, city of Columbia, and the University of Missouri. There are fees for some services.

Inventors Association of St. Louis
P.O. Box 16544
St. Louis, MO 63105
314-432-1291

Help for Home-Based Inventors

The group holds monthly meetings, provides communications among inventors, manufacturers, patent attorneys, and venture capitalists. It publishes a newsletter. There are annual dues.

Missouri Small Business Development Center (State Office)
University of Missouri
300 University Place
Columbia, MO 56211
314-882-0344
Fax: 314-884-4297

The center offers counseling for a wide range of business issues and problems.

Montana

Montana Science and Technology Alliance
46 North Last Chance Gulch, Suite 2B
Helena, MT 59620
406-449-2778

The Alliance provides funds to early stage, technology based companies seeking to commercialize products or processes in Montana.

Montana Inventors Association
RR #1, Box 31
Highwood, MT 59450
406-733-5031
Contact: Fred Davison

Small Business Development Center
Montana Department of Commerce
1424 Ninth Avenue
Helena, MT 59620
406-444-4780

The center offers counseling for a wide range of business issues and problems.

Nebraska

Nebraska Technical Assistance Center
University of Nebraska - Lincoln
P.O. Box 880535
W 191 Nebraska Hall
Lincoln, NE 68588-0535
402-472-5600; 1-800-332-0265 (in NE)

Found within the College of Engineering and Technology, the center offers counseling services to inventors on patents and trademarks. The free assistance is for preliminary information. For more technical help, the office will refer inventors elsewhere.

Small Business Development Center
University of Nebraska at Omaha
60th and Dodge Street
CBA, Room 407
Omaha, NE 68182
402-554-2521
Fax: 402-554-3747

The center offers counseling for a wide range of business issues and problems.

Association of SBDCs
1313 Farnam Street, Suite 132

Omaha, NE 68182-0472
402-595-2387
Fax: 402-595-2388

Organization's name and address may be given to individual inventors for referrals.

Nevada

Nevada Inventors Association
P.O. Box 9905
Reno, NV 89507
Contact: Don Costar

This association holds monthly meetings, workshops and publishes a monthly newsletter. It networks with other inventor associations to keep abreast of their activities. Annual dues are $25.

NITEC
Nevada Small Business Development Center 1032
University of Nevada Reno
Reno, NV 89557-0100
702-784-1717
Fax: 702-784-4337

The center provides general assistance and funding information. inventors meet with other inventors and get to showcase their inventions.

Nevada Small Business Development Center
University of Nevada Las Vegas
4505 Maryland Parkway
Las Vegas, NV 89154-6011
702-895-0652

The center provides general assistance and funding information. Inventors meet with other inventors.

New Hampshire

Service Corps of Retired Executives (SCORE)
Stewart Nelson Building
143 Main Street
Concord, NH 03302
603-226-7763
603-666-7561

SCORE offices offer counseling on a variety of questions and can help inventors with marketing, commercialization and related issues.

Small Business Development Center
University of New Hampshire
108 McConnell Hall
Durham, NH 03824
603-862-2200
Fax: 603-862-4468

The center offers counseling for a wide range of business issues and problems.

Small Business Development Center
1001 Elm Street
Manchester, NH 03261
603-624-2000

The Small Business Development Center provides general assistance and funding information, and offers legal advice on patents and licensing. Inventors meet with other inventors.

New Jersey

Corporation for the Application of Rutgers Research
Rutgers, The State University of New Jersey
P.O. Box 1179
Piscataway, NJ 08854
908-932-4445, ext. 4648

The Corporation counsels inventors on commercialization and patent processes, provides critical reviews of inventors, and assesses marketability. Equity for services.

National Society of Inventors
539 Laurel Place
South Orange, NJ 07079
201-596-3322

This society counsels inventors on the commercialization and patenting processes; provides critical reviews of inventions and provides communications among inventors, manufacturers, developers and venture capitalists. It holds monthly meetings and publishes a newsletter. There are annual dues.

Small Business Development Center
Rutgers University
180 University Avenue
3rd Floor - Ackerson Hall
Newark, NJ 07102
201-648-5950
Fax: 201-648-1110

The Small Business Development Center offers counseling for a wide range of business issues and problems.

New Mexico

Thunderbird Technical Group
(Also known as the Albuquerque Invention Club)
P.O. Box 30062
Albuquerque, NM 87190
505-266-3541

The contact is Dr. Albert Goodman, president of the club. The club meets on a monthly basis for speakers and presentations by different inventors. Members include patent attorneys, investors, and manufacturers. Annual dues are $10.

Small Business Development Center
Santa Fe Community College
P.O. Box 4187
Santa Fe, NM 87502-4187
505-438-1362
Fax: 505-438-1237

The center offers counseling for a wide range of business issues and problems.

New York

Center for Technology Transfer
State University of New York College of Oswego
209 Park Hall
Oswego, NY 13126-3599
315-341-2128

The center counsels inventors on the commercialization and patent processes, provides critical reviews of inventions, and provides prototype fabrication and development. There are fees or royalties from sales, as well as laboratory and materials costs.

Inventors Society of Western N.Y.
P.O. Box 23654
Rochester, NY 14692
716-454-6899

This non-profit organization provides inventors with information and guidance so the inventor can decide what is the best course of action. There are some fees for services, $65/year.

Small Business Development Center
State University of New York
SUNY Central Plaza S-523
Albany, NY 12246
518-443-5398
Fax: 518-465-4992

The center offers counseling for a wide range of business issues and problems.

New York State Energy Authority
Two Rockefeller Plaza
Albany, NY 12223
518-465-6251
Fax: 518-473-4549

The office provides general assistance, investment and funding information; conducts market and technical assessments; and assists in building a prototype.

New York State
Energy Research and Development Authority
Two Rockefeller Plaza
Albany, NY 12223
518-465-6251

The office provides general assistance and investment and funding information. It assists in building a prototype.

SUNY Institute of Technology
Small Business Development Center
P.O. Box 3050
Utica, NY 13504
315-792-7546
Fax: 315-792-7554

The center provides general assistance and funding information; conducts market/technical assessments; offers legal advice on patents and licensing, and assists in building a prototype. Inventors meet with other inventors.

Corporation For Innovation Development Program (CID)
John Ciannamea, Manager
Innovation Finance Program
New York State Science and Technology Foundation
99 Washington Avenue, Suite 1730
Albany, NY 12210
518-473-9741

The program provides debt and equity financing and management assistance for technology-based start-up companies with a working prototype or product ready for market. Makes equity and/or debt investments of $250,000 or more. Matching funds are required. Eligibility: Must have an innovative product/service ready for introduction to a large or rapid-growth market. Types of ventures that qualify are start-up companies. Some priority is given to firms in the electronics/information and medical/biological areas.

Energy Product Center
Peter Douglas
New York State Energy Research and
    Development Authority
2 Rockefeller Plaza
Albany, NY 12223
518-465-6251/6214

Supports ventures that promote the efficient use of energy while at the same time creating jobs and economic benefits in the State. Eligibility: Applicant need not be a NY State resident or doing business in NY at the time of application, but the product or service for which assistance is sought must be developed, produced or manufactured in NYS. Any individual or private enterprise with an innovation, energy related product/system appropriate for development in NYS may apply.

Solid Waste Management Technical Assistance Program
Thomas Lynch
New York State Department of
    Environmental Conservation
50 Wolf Road
Albany, NY 12233-4015
518-485-5856

Technical assistance is provided to enhance local planning and implementation of environmentally sound solid waste management programs. Assistance is provided to local governments, the private sector and individuals regarding such subjects as source separation, waste reduction/ recycling, composting, waste-to-energy and landfilling. Eligibility: For information, contact local regional office.

North Carolina

Innovation Research Fund
North Carolina Technology Development Authority
P.O. Box 13169
2 Davis Drive
Research Triangle Park, NC 27709-3169
919-990-8558

This fund provides financial assistance to enable inventors to commercialize inventions or develop improvements. The authority receives a return on its investments through royalties from sales of the sponsored product.

Small Business Development Center
University of North Carolina
4509 Creedmoor Road, Suite 201
Raleigh, NC 27612
919-571-4154
Fax: 919-571-4161

The center offers counseling for a wide range of business issues and problems.

North Dakota

Center for Innovation and Business Development
University of North Dakota
University Station, Box 8103
Grand Forks, ND 58202
701-777-3132

This center conducts seminars and workshops with speakers; counsels on the commercialization and patenting process;

provides communications among inventors, manufacturers, and patent attorneys. There are fees for services.

Small Business Development Center
118 Gamble Hall
University of North Dakota
University Station, Box 7308
Grand Forks, ND 58202-7308
701-777-3700
Fax: 701-777-3650

The center offers counseling for a wide range of business issues and problems.

Ohio

Ohio Inventors Association
9855 Sand Ridge Rd.
Millfield, OH 45761
614-797-4434

This association is affiliated with the Inventors Connection of Greater Cleveland, Inventors Club of Greater Cincinnati, Inventors Network of Columbus, Inventors Council of Dayton, etc. The Ohio Association helps local clubs and works to solve problems common to all inventors. Ron Docie, the contact person, is knowledgeable about a wide range of inventors' issues and keeps abreast of inventors' organizations.

Numbers for other organizations:
Inventors Connection of Greater Cleveland
                                            216-226-9681
Inventors Council of Dayton   513-294-7447
Inventors Club of Cincinnati   513-298-8423
Columbus Inventors Council   614-292-1993
Inventors Network of Columbus   614-291-7900

These associations all meet on a regular basis, provide communications among inventors, manufacturers, patent attorneys, etc., and often publish newsletters. There are annual dues.

Docie Marketing
9855 Sand Ridge Rd.
Millfield, OH 45761
614-797-4434

This profit-making company counsels inventors on the commercialization process, provides critical review of inventions and arranges meetings between inventors and manufacturers.

Small Business Development Center
Department of Development
30 East Broad Street, 23rd Floor
P.O. Box 1001
Columbus, OH 43226
614-466-2711
Fax: 614-466-0829

The center offers counseling for a wide range of business issues and problems.

NORSAC
SBIR Assistance Center
58 W. Center Street
Akron, OH 44308
216-375-2173

Fax: 216-762-3657
The center provides general assistance and funding information, and conducts market assessments.

Oklahoma

Invention Development Center
8230 SW 8th Street
Oklahoma City, OK 73128
405-376-2362

The center holds regular meetings, often with speakers, publishes a newsletter, and offers counseling and technical assistance to inventors. Annual dues are $25.

Oklahoma Inventors Congress
P.O. Box 18797
Oklahoma City, OK 73154-0797
405-848-1991

The Congress holds regular meetings with topical speakers, counsels inventors on the patent process, and publishes a monthly newsletter. It is affiliated with the Office of the Governor, Department of Commerce, National Congress of Inventors Organizations. Annual dues are $10.

Small Business Development Center
Southeastern Oklahoma State University
Station A, Box 2584
Durant, OK 74701
405-924-0277
Fax: 405-924-7071

The center offers counseling for a wide range of business issues and problems.

Inventors Assistance Program
Oklahoma Department of Commerce
P.O. Box 26980
6601 Broadway Extension
Oklahoma City, OK 73126-0980
405-841-5143

The program objective is to increase the number of new products manufactured in Oklahoma by assisting inventors, innovators, and entrepreneurs through the commercialization process. Can best be described as having two components: a referral/consulting service and a new product commercialization service. The referral and consulting service is offered at no charge. The new product commercialization service is currently free of charge, but this policy may change at any time. There are many facets to the commercialization process. The goal of the staff is to determine technical feasibility, patentability, and commercial feasibility. The analysis takes into consideration the type of new product, its present stage of development, and the skills and experience of the innovator. The staff will assist the innovator in deciding whether to manufacture or license the product. Business and marketing plan assistance can be provided. Licensee location and help with the negotiation process is also available, and if the product is licensed, the staff works with the licensee to develop a thorough marketing strategy.

Oregon

Small Business Development Centers (SBDCs) at three state colleges and the community colleges can counsel inventors and direct them where to go for patent process, etc. SBDCs at state colleges are: Southern Oregon State, 503-482-5838; Oregon Institute of Technology, 503-885-1760; and Eastern Oregon State, 1-800-452-8639.

Lane Community College
Oregon Small Business Development
   Center/Downtown Center
99 W. 10th Avenue, Suite 216
Eugene, OR 97401
503-726-2250
Fax: 503-345-6006

The center provides general assistance and funding information.

Small Business Development Center
123 NW 2nd St., Suite 321
Portland, OR 97209
503-273-2828
Fax: 503-294-0723

The center provides general assistance and funding information.

Oregon State Library
Patent and Trademark Depository
State Library Building
Salem, OR 97310
503-378-4239
Fax: 503-588-7119

Organizations name and address may be given to individual inventors for referrals.

Pennsylvania

American Society of Inventors
P.O. Box 58426
Philadelphia, PA 19102-8426
215-546-6601

Members are counseled on the commercialization and patent processes; critical reviews of inventions, and assessments of market potential are provided. The Society also offers technical assistance and referrals. There are dues.

Technology Commercialization
Lehigh University
Rauch Business Center #37
621 Taylor Street
Bethlehem, PA 18015
215-758-3446

The main focus is directed towards commercialization of university research although commercialization assistance is given to some private inventors each year. This group provides critical reviews of inventions and provides communication among inventors, manufacturers, patent attorneys, and venture capitalists. There are fees for services.

Small Business Development Center
Bucknell University
Dana Engineering Building, 1st Floor
Lewisburg, PA 17837
717-524-1249

The center offers counseling for a wide range of business issues and problems.

Small Business Development Center
La Salle University
1900 W. Olney Avenue
Philadelphia, PA 19141
215-951-1416
Fax: 215-951-1597
The center provides general assistance and funding information, and conducts market assessments. Inventors meet with investors.

Pennsylvania Small Business Development Center
423 Vance Hall
3733 Spruce Street
Philadelphia, PA 19104-6374
215-898-1219
Fax: 215-573-2135
The center provides general assistance and funding information. It also conducts market and technical assessments.

Rhode Island

Service Corps of Retired Executives (SCORE)
c/o U.S. Small Business Administration
380 Westinghouse, Room #511
Providence, RI 02903
401-528-4571
Volunteers in the SCORE office are experts in many areas of business management and can offer advice to inventors in areas including marketing and the commercialization process.

Small Business Development Center
7 Jackson Walkway
Providence, RI 02903
401-831-1330
The center offers counseling for a wide range of business issues and problems.

Small Business Development Center
Bryant College
1150 Douglas Pike
Smithfield, RI 20917
401-232-6111
Fax: 401-232-6416
The center provides general assistance and conducts market and technical assessments.

South Carolina

Center for Applied Technology (CAT)
Emerging Technology Center
Clemson University
511 Westinghouse Rd.
Pendleton, SC 29670
CAT Center   803-646-4000
Emerging Technology Center   803-646-4020
The center helps inventors on the commercialization and patent processes, assesses market potential of specific inventions and assists inventors in technically refining inventions. It works with the Small Business Development Center, South Carolina Research Authority, Battelle Institute and other organizations. Some services are free, others have nominal fees.

Small Business Development Center
South Carolina State College
School of Business Administration
Orangeburg, SC 29117
803-536-8445
The center offers counseling for a wide range of business issues and problems.

South Carolina Small Business Development Center
University of South Carolina
College of Business Administration
Columbia, SC 29208
803-777-4907
Fax: 803-777-4403
The center provides general assistance and funding information.

South Dakota

Dakota State University
SBIR PTAC Assistance Center
East Hall, Room 3
Madison, SD 57042
605-256-5555
This office can provide guidance to inventors on a wide range of issues: commercialization, patent process, marketability, etc. It has grant money available.

Small Business Development Center
University of South Dakota
School of Business
414 East Clark
Vermillion, SD 57069
605-677-5272
Fax: 605-677-5427
The center offers counseling for a wide range of business issues and problems.

Tennessee

Tennessee Inventors Association
P.O. Box 11225
Knoxville, TN 37939-1225
615-483-0151
Monthly meetings are held where a wide range of topical subjects are discussed: patenting, venture capital, marketing, etc. Workshops and invention exhibitions are held periodically. Annual dues are $30.

Venture Exchange Forum
P.O. Box 23184
Knoxville, TN 37933-1184
615-694-6772
The Forum holds monthly meetings, and arranges meetings between inventors and manufacturers. Annual dues are $25.

Small Business Development Center
Jackson State Community College
2046 North Parkway Street
Jackson, TN 38104
901-424-5389
The center offers counseling for a wide range of business issues and problems.

Texas

Technology and Economic Development
301 Terrow, Suite 119
College Station, TX 77843-8000
409-845-0538
The organization conducts workshops, provides counseling on commercialization and patent processes, offers critical reviews of inventions on a selected basis, assesses invention's marketability, and assists with patent searches. State appropriations, federal grants and subscriptions to newsletter are available.

Texas Inventors Association
4000 Rock Creek Drive, #100
Dallas, TX 75204
The association holds meetings, and provides counseling for inventors on commercialization and patent processes. There are annual dues.

North Texas-Dallas Small Business Development Center
Dallas Community College District
1402 Corinth Street
Dallas, TX 75215
214-565-5831
Fax: 214-565-5815
The center offers counseling for a wide range of business issues and problems.

Texas Tech University
Small Business Development Center
2579 S. Loop 289
Lubbock, TX 77002
806-745-1637
Fax: 806-745-6207
The center provides general assistance and funding information.

University of Houston
Small Business Development Center
Texas Product Development Center
1100 Louisiana, Suite 500
Houston, TX 77002
713-752-8440
Fax: 713-756-1515
The center provides general assistance and funding information; conducts market and technical assessments; and assists in building a prototype. Inventors meet with investors.

U.S. Department of Energy
Dallas Support Office
1420 W. Mockingbird Lane, Suite 400
Dallas, TX 75247
214-767-7245
Fax: 214-767-7231
The office provides general assistance and funding information

Utah

Utah Small Business Development Center
University of Utah
College of Business
Salt Lake City, UT 84101
801-581-7905

The center offers workshops, seminars and conferences, counsels inventors on the commercialization and patent processes, and supplies publications about patenting, licensing and financing. There are nominal fees for workshops, etc.

Utah Small Business Development Center
102 W. 500 S, Suite 315
Salt Lake City, UT 84101
801-581-7905
Fax: 801-581-7814
The center provides general assistance and funding information, and conducts market and technical assessments. Inventors meet with inventors and investors.

Science, Technology and Innovation State Office
P.O. Box 11
West Jordan, UT 84084
801-569-2973
The office provides general assistance and funding information, conducts market and technical assessments, and assists in building a prototype. Inventors meet with inventors and investors, and showcase their inventions.

Vermont

Economic and Development Office
State of Vermont
109 State Street
Montpelier, VT 05609
800-622-4553; 802-828-3221
Staff member Curt Carter can counsel inventors on the commercialization and marketing processes as well as other areas, and refer them to other places as needed. There are no fees.

Small Business Development Center
University of Vermont
Extension Service, Morrill Hall
Burlington, VT 05405
802-656-4479
Fax: 802-656-8642
The center offers counseling for a wide range of business issues and problems.

Virginia

Technology Commercialization
Virginia's Center for Innovative Technology
2214 Rock Hill Rd., #600
Herndon, VA 22070
703-689-3043
The center provides seed money to colleges and universities to set up entrepreneurship or innovation centers. Such centers are at the College of William and Mary, George Mason University, James Madison University, Longwood College, Old Dominion University, University of Virginia, and Virginia Commonwealth. Inventors are counseled on the commercialization and patent processes at these centers and can have their inventions assessed for market potential.

Small Business Development Center
Department of Economic Development
1021 East Cary Street, 11th Floor

Richmond, VA 23219
804-371-8258
Fax: 804-371-8137
The center offers counseling for a wide range of business issues and problems.

Small Business Development Center
918 Emmet Street North, Suite 200
Charlottesville, VA 22903-4878
804-295-8198
Fax: 804-979-3749
The center provides general assistance, and conducts market and technical assessments.

U.S. Department of Commerce
Patent and Trademark Office
Box 2863
Arlington, VA 22202
703-308-0658
Fax: 703-308-3718
The office provides general assistance, and offers legal advice on patents and licensing. Inventors meet with inventors.

Washington

Innovation Assessment Center
2001 6th Ave., Suite 2608
Seattle, WA 98121
206-464-5450
Part of the Small Business Development Center, this center performs commercial evaluations of inventions, counseling and provides assistance with patentability searches. There are fees for services.

Small Business Development Center
Washington State University
245 Todd Hall
Pullman, WA 99164
509-335-5260
Fax: 509-335-0949
The center offers counseling for a wide range of business issues and problems.

Small Business Development Center
Western Washington University
415 Parks Hall
Bellingham, WA 98227-9073
206-676-3899
Fax: 206-676-4844
The center provides general assistance, and investment and funding information.

West Virginia

Small Business Development Center
West Virginia Institute of Technology
Montgomery, WV 25136
304-442-5501
The center offers counseling for a wide range of business issues and problems.

West Virginia Small Business Development Office
West Virginia Development Office

115 Virginia Street, E
Charleston, WV 25301-2406
304-558-2960
Fax: 304-558-0127
The center provides information on investment and funding.

Wisconsin

Center for Innovation and Development
University of Wisconsin - Stout
103 First Ave, W
Menomonie, WI 54751
715-232-5026
The center counsels inventors on the commercialization and patent processes; provides critical reviews of inventions; assists inventors on technically refining inventions; and provides prototype development. There are fees for services.

Wisconsin Innovation Service Center
402 McCutchan Hall
UW-Whitewater
Whitewater, WI 53190
414-472-1365
Provides early stage market research for inventors. There are fees for services.

Small Business Development Center
University of Wisconsin
432 North Lake Street, Room 423
Madison, WI 53706
608-263-7794
Fax: 608-262-3878
The center offers counseling for a wide range of business issues and problems.

Wisconsin Department of Development
P.O. Box 7970
Madison, WI 53707
608-267-9383
Fax: 608-267-2829
The office provides information on investment and funding.

Wyoming

Small Business Development Center
Casper College
350 West A, Suite 200
Casper, WY 82601
307-235-4827
Barbara Stuckert, who works in the office, is able to help inventors on a wide range of issues including patenting, commercialization and intellectual property rights. There are no fees for services.

Canada

Innovative Center
156 Columbia Street W.
Waterloo, Ontario NN 26363
519-885-5870
Provides inventors with market research, idea testing, and helps guide inventors up to the patent stage.

How to Sell Your Ideas, Goods, and Services to the Government

How to Sell Your Ideas, Goods, and Services To The Government

If you produce a product or service, you've probably always wondered how you could offer what you produce to the biggest client in the world — the federal government. Have you thought of the government as being a "closed shop" and too difficult to penetrate? Well, I'm happy to say that you're entirely wrong on that score. The federal government spends over $180 billion each year on products ranging from toilet paper to paper clips and writes millions of dollars in contracts for services like advertising, consulting, and printing. Most Americans believe that a majority of those federal purchasing contracts have been eliminated over the last few years, but that's simply not true — they've just been replaced with new contracts that are looking for the same kinds of goods and services. Last year the government took action (either initiating or modifying) on over 350,000 different contracts. They buy these goods and services from someone, so why shouldn't that someone be you? To be successful doing business with the government, you need to learn to speak "governmenteze" to get your company into the purchasing loop, and I can show you how to accomplish that in just a few easy steps.

Step 1

Each department within the federal government has a procurement office that buys whatever the department needs. Most of these offices have put together their own *Doing Business With the Department of* _____ publication, which usually explains procurement policies, procedures, and programs. This booklet also contains a list of procurement offices, contact people, subcontracting opportunities, and a solicitation mailing list. Within each department is also an Office of Small and Disadvantaged Business Utilization, whose sole purpose is to push the interests of the small business, and to make sure these companies get their fair share of the government contracts. Another resource is your local Small Business Administration Office which should have a listing of U.S. Government Procurement Offices in your state.

Step 2

Once you have familiarized yourself with the process, you need to find out who is buying what from whom and how much, as well as who wants what when. There are three ways to get this important information.

A. Daily Procurement News
Each weekday, the *Commerce Business Daily* (CBD) gives a complete listing of products and services (that cost over $25,000) wanted by the U.S. government — products and services that your business may be selling. Each listing includes the following: the product or service, along with a short description; name and address of the agency; deadline for proposals or bids; phone number to request specifications; and the solicitation number of the product or service needed. Many business concerns, including small businesses, incorporate CBD review into their government marketing activities. To obtain a $208/year subscription, contact: Superintendent of Documents, U.S. Government Printing Office, Washington, DC 20402; 202-512-1800.

B. Federal Data Systems Division (FDSD)
This Center distributes consolidated information about federal purchases, including research and development. FDSD can tell you how much the federal government spent last quarter on products and services, which agencies made

those purchases, and who the contractors were that did business with the government. FDSD summarizes this information through two types of reports: The FDSD standard report and the FDSD special report. The standard report is a free, quarterly compilation containing statistical procurement information in "snapshot" form for over 60 federal agencies, as well as several charts, graphs, and tables which compare procurement activities by state, major product and service codes, method of procurement, and contractors. The report also includes quarterly and year-to-year breakdowns of amounts and percentages spent on small, women-owned, and minority businesses. Special reports are prepared upon request for a fee, based on computer and labor costs. They are tailored to the specific categories, which can be cross-tabulated in numerous ways. A special report can help you analyze government procurement and data trends, identify competitors, and locate federal markets for individual products or services. Your Congressman may have access to the Federal Procurement Database from his/her office in Washington, which you may be able to use for free. For more information, contact: Federal Data Systems Division, General Services Administration, 7th and D St., SW, Room 5652, Washington, DC 20407; 202-401-1529.

C. Other Contracts

For contracts under $25,000, you need to be placed on a department's list for solicitation bids on those contracts. The mailing list forms are available through the Procurement Office, the Office of Small and Disadvantaged Business Utilization, or your local Small Business Association office. Last year 18.7 billion dollars was spent on these "small" purchases, so these contracts are not to be overlooked.

Step 3: Subcontracting Opportunities

All of the federal procurement offices or Offices of Small and Disadvantaged Business Utilization (SDBU) can provide you with information regarding subcontracting. Many of the departments' prime contracts require that the prime contractor maximize small business subcontracting opportunities. Many prime contractors produce special publications which can be helpful to those interested in subcontracting. The SDBU Office can provide you with more information on the subcontracting process, along with a directory of prime contractors. Another good source for subcontract assistance is your local Small Business Administration (SBA) office, 1-800-827-5722. SBA develops subcontracting opportunities for small business by maintaining close contact with large business prime contractors and referring qualified small firms to them. The SBA has developed agreements and close working relationships with hundreds of prime contractors who cooperate by offering small firms the opportunity to compete for their subcontracts. In addition, to complete SBA's compliance respon-sibilities, commercial market representatives monitor prime contractors in order to assess their compliance with laws governing subcontracting opportunities for small businesses.

Step 4: Small Business Administration's 8(a) Program

Are you a socially or economically disadvantaged person who has a business? This group includes, but is not limited to, Black Americans, Hispanic Americans, Native Americans, Asian Pacific Americans, and Subcontinent Asian Americans. Socially and economically disadvantaged individuals represent a significant percentage of U.S. citizens, yet account for a disproportionately small percentage of total U.S. business revenues. The 8(a) program assists firms to participate in the business sector and to become independently competitive in the marketplace. SBA may provide participating firms with procurement, marketing, financial, management, or other technical assistance. A Business Opportunity Specialist will be assigned to each firm that participates, and is responsible for providing the firm with access to assistance that can help the firm fulfill its business goals. SBA undertakes an extensive effort to provide government contracting opportunities to participating businesses. SBA has the Procurement Automated Source System (PASS) which places your company's capabilities online so that they may be available to government agencies and major corporations when they request potential bidders for contracts and subcontracts. To apply for the 8(a) program, you must attend an interview session with an official in the SBA field office in your area. For more information, contact your local Small Business Administration Office, or you can call 1-800-827-5722 for the SBA office nearest you.

Step 5: Bond

A Surety bond is often a prerequisite for government and private sector contracts. This is particularly true when the contract involves construction. In order for the company to qualify for an SBA Guarantee Bond, they must make the bonding company aware of their capabilities based on past contract performance and meeting of financial obligations. SBA can assist firms in obtaining surety bonding for contracts that do not exceed $1,250,000. SBA is authorized, when appropriate circumstances occur, to guarantee as much as 90 percent of losses suffered by a surety resulting from a breach of terms of a bond.

Step 6: Publications

The Government Printing Office has several publications for sale which explain the world of government contracts. For ordering information, contact: Superintendent of Documents, Government Printing Office, Washington, DC 20402; 202-512-1800.

* *U.S. Government Purchasing and Sales Directory* ($23): The Directory is an alphabetical listing of the products and services bought by the military departments, and a separate listing of the civilian agencies. The Directory also includes an explanation of the ways in which the SBA can help a business obtain government prime contracts and subcontracts, data on government sales of surplus property, and comprehensive descriptions of the scope of the government market for research and development.

* *Guide to the Preparation of Offers for Selling to the Military* ($4.75)

* *Small Business Specialists* ($3.75)

* *Small Business Subcontracting Directory* ($7.00): designed to aid small businesses interested in subcontracting opportunities within the Department of Defense (DOD). The guide is arranged alphabetically by state and includes the name and address of each current DOD prime contractor as well as the product or service being provided to DOD.

* *Women Business Owners; Selling to the Federal Government* ($3.75)

* *Selling to the Military*, ($8.00)

Step 7: What is GSA?

General Services Administration (GSA) is the Government's business agent. On an annual budget of less than half a billion dollars, it directs and coordinates nearly $8 billion a year worth of purchases, sales, and services. Its source of supply is private enterprise, and its clients are all branches of the federal government. GSA plans and manages leasing, purchase, or construction of office buildings, laboratories, and warehouses; buys and delivers nearly $4 billion worth of goods and services; negotiates the prices and terms for an additional $2.3 billion worth of direct business between federal groups and private industry; sets and interprets the rules for federal travel and negotiates reduced fares and lodging rates for federal travelers; and manages a 92,000 vehicle fleet with a cumulative yearly mileage of over 1 billion. For a copy of *Doing Business With GSA, GSA's Annual Report*, or other information regarding GSA, contact: Office of Publication, General Services Administration, 18th and F Streets, NW, Washington, DC 20405; 202-501-1235. For information on GSA's architect and engineer services, such as who is eligible for GSA professional services contracts, how to find out about potential GSA projects, what types of contracts are available, and where and how to apply, contact: Office of Design and Construction, GSA, 18th and F Streets, NW, Washington, DC 20405; 202-501-1888. Information on specifications and standards of the federal government is contained in a booklet, *Guide to Specifications and Standards*, which is available free from Specifications Sections, General Services Administration, 470 E L'Enfant Plaza, SW, Suite 8100, Washington, DC 20407; 202-755-0325.

Step 8: Bid and Contract Protests

The General Accounting Office (GAO) resolves disputes between agencies and bidders for government contracts, including grantee award actions. The free publication, *Bid Protests at GAO; A Descriptive Guide*, contains information on GAO's procedures for determining legal questions arising from the awarding of government contracts. Contact Information Handling and Support Facilities, General Accounting Office, Gaithersburg, MD 20877; 202-275-6241. For Contract Appeals, the GSA Board of Contract Appeals works to resolve disputes arising out of contracts with GSA, the Departments of Treasury, Education, Commerce, and other independent government agencies. The Board also hears and decides bid protests arising out of government-wide automated data processing (ADP) procurements. A contractor may elect to use either the GSA Board or the General Accounting Office for resolution of an ADP bid protest. Contractors may elect to have their appeals processed under the Board's accelerated procedures if the claim is $50,000 or less, or under the small claims procedure if the claim is $10,000 or less. Contractors may also request that a hearing be held at a location convenient to them. With the exception of small claims decisions, contractors can appeal adverse Board decisions to the U.S. Court of Appeals for the Federal Circuit. For more information, contact: Board of Contract Appeals, General Services Administration, 18th and F Streets, NW, Washington, DC 20405; 202-501-0720. There are other Contract Appeals Boards for other departments. One of the last paragraphs in your government contract should specify which Board you are to go to if a problem arises.

Free Local Help:
The Best Place To Start To Sell To The Government

Within each state there are offices that can help you get started in the federal procurement process. As was stated previously, your local Small Business Administration (SBA) office is a good resource. In addition to their other services, the SBA can provide you with a list of Federal Procurement Offices based in your state, so you can visit them in person. Another place to turn is your local Small Business Development Center (look under Economic Development in your phone book). These offices are funded jointly by federal and state governments, and are usually associated with the state university system. They are aware of the federal procurement process, and can help you draw up a sensible business plan.

Some states have established programs to assist businesses in the federal procurement process for all departments in the government. These programs are designed to help businesses learn about the bidding process, the resources available, and provide information on how the procurement system operates. They can match the product or service you are selling with the appropriate agency, and then help you market your product. Several programs have online bid matching services, whereby if a solicitation appears in the *Commerce Business Daily* that matches what your company markets, then the program will contact you to start the bid process. They can then request the appropriate documents, and assist you in achieving your goal. These Procurement Assistance Offices (PAOs) are partially funded by the Department of Defense to assist businesses with Defense Procurement. For a current listing of PAOs contact:

Defense Logistics Agency
Office of Small and Disadvantaged
  Utilization
Bldg. 4, Cameron Station
Room 4B110
Alexandria, VA 22304-6100
703-274-6471

Let Your Congressman Help You

Are you trying to market a new product to a department of the federal government? Need to know where to try to sell your wares? Is there some problem with your bid? Your Congressman can be of assistance. Because they want business in their state to boom, they will make an effort to assist companies in obtaining federal contracts. Frequently they will write a letter to accompany your bid, or if you are trying to market a new product, they will write a letter to the procurement office requesting that they review your product. Your Congressman can also be your personal troubleshooter. If there is some problem with your bid, your Congressman can assist you in determining and resolving the problem, and can provide you with information on the status of your bid. Look in the blue pages of your phone book for your Senators' or Representatives' phone numbers, or call them in Washington at 202-224-3121.

Small Business Set-Asides

The Small Business Administration (SBA) encourages government purchasing agencies to set aside suitable government purchases for exclusive small business competition. A purchase which is restricted to small business bidders is identified by a set aside clause in the invitation for bids or request for proposals. There is no overall listing of procurements which are, or have been, set aside for small business. A small business learns which purchases are reserved for small business by getting listed on bidders' lists. It also can help keep itself informed of set aside opportunities by referring to the *Commerce Business Daily*. Your local SBA office can provide you with more information on set asides, as can the Procurement Assistance Offices listed at the end of this section. You can locate your nearest SBA office by calling 1-800-827-5722.

Veterans Assistance

Each Small Business Administration District Office has a Veterans Affairs Officer which can assist veteran-owned businesses in obtaining government contracts. Although there is no such thing as veterans set aside contracts, the Veterans Administration does make an effort to fill its contracts using veteran-owned businesses. Contact your local SBA office for more information.

Woman-Owned Business Assistance

There are over 3.7 million women-owned businesses in the United States, and the number is growing each year. Current government policy requires federal contracting officers to increase their purchases from women-owned businesses. Although the women-owned firms will receive more opportunities to bid, they still must be the lowest responsive and responsible bidder to win the contract. To assist these businesses, each SBA district office has a Women's Business Representative, who can provide you with information regarding government programs. Most of the offices hold a *Selling to the Federal Government* seminar, which is designed to educate the business owner on the ins and outs of government procurement. There is also a helpful publication, *Women Business Owners: Selling to the Federal Government*, which provides information on procurement opportunities available. Contact your local SBA

office or your Procurement Assistance Office (listed below) for more information.

Minority and Labor Surplus Area Assistance

Are you a socially or economically disadvantaged person who has a business? This group includes, but is not limited to, Black Americans, Hispanic Americans, Native Americans, Asian Pacific Americans, and Subcontinent Asian Americans. Socially and economically disadvantaged individuals represent a significant percentage of U.S. citizens yet account for a disproportionately small percentage of total U.S. business revenues. The 8(a) program assists firms to participate in the business sector and to become independently competitive in the marketplace. SBA may provide participating firms with procurement, marketing, financial, management, or other technical assistance. A Business Opportunity Specialist will be assigned to each firm that participates, and is responsible for providing the firm with access to assistance that can help the firm fulfill its business goals.

SBA undertakes an extensive effort to provide government contracting opportunities to participating businesses. SBA has the Procurement Automated Source System (PASS) which places your company's capabilities online so that they may be available to government agencies and major corporations when they request potential bidders for contracts and subcontracts. To apply for the 8(a) program, you must attend an interview session with an official in the SBA field office in your area. Some areas of the country have been determined to be labor surplus areas, which means there is a high rate of unemployment. Your local SBA office can tell you if you live in such an area, as some contracts are set asides for labor surplus areas. For more information, contact your local Small Business Administration office (call 1-800-827-5722 for the SBA office nearest you), or call the Procurement Assistance Office in your state (listed below.)

Federal Procurement
Assistance Offices

Alabama

University of Alabama at Birmingham, Alabama Small Business Development Consortium, 1717 11th Ave. S., Suite 419, Birmingham, AL 35294; 205-934-7260, Fax: 205-934-7645.

Alaska

University of Alaska/Anchorage, Small Business Development Center, 430 W. Seventh Ave., Suite 110, Anchorage, AK 99501; 907-274-7232, Fax: 907-274-9524.

Arizona

APTAN, Inc., 360 N. Hayden Rd., Scottsdale, AZ 85257; 602-945-5452, Fax: 602-970-6355.

National Center for American Indians Enterprise Development, National Center Headquarters, 953 E. Juanita Ave., Mesa, AZ 85204; 602-831-7524, Fax: 602-491-1332.

Arkansas

Board of Trustees, University of Arkansas, College of Business Administration/ESC, 120 Ozark Hall, Fayetteville, AR 72701; 501-337-5358, Fax: 501-337-5045.

California

c/o AMD, Procurement Assistance Center, m/s 31, 901 Thompson Place, P.O. Box 3453, Sunnyvale, CA 94088-3453; 408-739-6283.

Business Innovation Center, San Diego Incubator Corp., 3350 Market St., San Diego, CA 92102; 619-685-2949, Fax: 619-531-8829.

Merced County Office of Economic and Strategic Development, Contract Procurement Center, Karen Prentiss, 1632 N St., Merced, CA 95340; 209-385-7312, Fax: 209-383-4959.

Colorado

Office of Business Development, Governor's Office, 1625 Broadway, Suite 1710, Denver, CO 80202; 303-620-8082, Fax: 303-892-3848.

Connecticut

SEATECH, 1084 Shennecossett Rd., Gorton, CT 06340; 203-449-8777, Fax: 203-449-9463.

Delaware

Delaware State College, Dept. of Economics and Business, Dr. Winston Awadzi, 1200 N. Dupont Hwy., Dover, DE 19901; 302-739-5146, Fax: 302-739-3517.

Florida

University of West Florida, Florida Procurement Technical Assistance Program, 11000 University Parkway, Pensacola, FL 32514; 904-444-2066, Fax: 904-444-2070.

Georgia

Columbus College, Division of Continuing Education, 1 Arsenal Pl., 901 Front Ave., Columbus, GA 31901; 706-649-1092, Fax: 706-649-1094.

Georgia Tech Research Corporation, Economic Development Institute, 400 10th St., Atlanta, GA 30332-0420; 404-894-6121, Fax: 404-853-9172.

Hawaii

State of Hawaii, Department of Business, Economic Development and Tourism, Mr. Larry Nelson, P.O. Box 2359, Honolulu, HI 96813; 808-586-2598, Fax: 808-587-2777.

Idaho

State of Idaho, Mr. Larry Demirelli, Department of Commerce, 700 W. State St., Boise, ID 83720; 208-334-2470, Fax: 208-334-2631.

Illinois

Black Hawk College District 503, 6600 34th Ave., Moline, IL 61268; 309-755-2200, Fax: 309-755-9847.

Latin American Chamber of Commerce, The Chicago PAC, 2539 N. Kedzie Ave., Suite 11, Chicago, IL 60647; 312-252-5211, Fax: 312-252-7065.

State of Illinois, Department of Commerce and Community Affairs, 620 East Adams, 6th Floor, Springfield, IL 62701; 217-785-6310, Fax: 217-785-6328.

Indiana

Indiana Institute for New Business Ventures, Government Marketing Assistance Group, One North Capitol, Suite 1240, Indianapolis, IN 46204-2026; 317-264-5600, Fax: 317-264-2806.

Partners in Contracting Corp., PTA CTR, 200 Russell St., Suite 200E, Hammond, IN 46320; 219-932-7811, Fax: 219-932-5612.

Iowa

State of Iowa, Iowa Department of Economic Development, 200 E. Grand Ave., Des Moines, IA 50309; 515-242-4888, Fax: 515-242-4893.

Kentucky

Kentucky Cabinet for Economic Development, Department of Community Development, 500 Mero St., Capital Plaza Tower, 22nd Floor, Frankfort, KY 40601; 1-800-838-3266, Fax: 502-564-3250.

Louisiana

Jefferson Parish Economic Development Commission, The Bid Center, Ms. Phyllis McLaren, 1221 Elmwood Park Blvd., Suite 405, Harahan, LA 70123; 504-736-6550, Fax: 504-763-6554.

Louisiana Productivity Center/USL, Procurement Technical Assistance Network, P.O. Box 44172, 241 E. Lewis St., Lafayette, LA 70504-4172; 318-231-6767, Fax: 318-262-5472.

Northwest Louisiana Government Procurement Center, Greater Shreveport Economic Development, P.O. Box 20074, 400 Edwards St., Shreveport, LA 71120-0074; 318-677-2530, Fax: 318-677-2534.

Maine

Eastern Maine Development Corporation, Market Development Center, One Cumberland Place, Suite 300, Bangor, ME 04401; 207-942-6389, 1-800-339-6389 (ME), 1-800-955-6549, Fax: 207-942-3548.

Maryland

Morgan State University, School of Business and Mgmt., Dr. Otis Thomas, Cold Spring Lane and Hillen Road, Baltimore, MD 21239; 410-319-3861, Fax: 410-319-3532.

Tri-County Council for Western Maryland Inc., 111 S. George St., Cumberland, MD 21502; 301-777-2158, Fax: 301-777-2495.

Massachusetts

Commonwealth of Massachusetts, MA Office of Business Development, 1 Ashburton Place, 21st Floor, Boston, MA 02108; 508-657-8600, Fax: 508-657-0185.

Michigan

Genesee County Metropolitan Planning Commission, Procurement Technical Assistance Program, 1101 Beach St., Flint, MI 48502; 810-257-3010, Fax: 810-257-3185.

Jackson Alliance for Business Development, PTA Center, 133 W. Michigan Ave., Jackson, MI 49201; 517-788-4455, Fax: 517-788-4337.

Kalamazoo County CGA, Inc., Government Contracting Office, Ms. Sandra Ledbetter, 100 W. Michigan, Suite 294, Kalamazoo, MI 49007; 616-342-0000, Fax: 616-343-1151.

Downriver Community Conference, Economic Development Department, 15100 Northline, Southgate, MI 48195; 313-281-0700, Fax: 313-281-3418.

Northeast Michigan Consortium, 320 State St., P.O. Box 711, Onaway, MI 49765; 517-733-8548, Fax: 517-733-8069.

Northwest Michigan Council of Governments, Procurement Technical Assistance Center, Mr. James F. Haslinger, P.O. Box 506, Traverse City, MI 49685-0506; 616-929-5036, Fax: 616-929-5012.

Saginaw Future, Inc., Contract Procurement Office, 301 E. Genessee, 3rd Floor, Saginaw, MI 48607; 517-754-8222, Fax: 517-754-1715.

Schoolcraft College, Ms. Judi Zima, 18600 Haggerty Rd., Livonia, MI 48152-2696; 313-462-4438, Fax: 313-462-4439.

Thumb Area Consortium/Growth Alliance, Local Procurement Office, 3270 Wilson St., Marlette, MI 48453; 517-635-3561, Fax: 517-635-2230.

Warren, Center Line, Sterling Heights Chamber of Commerce, Ms. Janet E. Masi, 30500 Van Dyke Ave., Suite 118, Warren, MI 48093-2178; 810-751-3939, Fax: 810-751-3995.

West Central Michigan Employment and Training Consortium, Procurement Tech. Assistance, Mr. John Calabrese, 110 Elm St., Big Rapids, MI 49307; 616-796-4891, Fax: 616-796-8316.

Minnesota

Minnesota Project Innovation, Govt. Marketing Assistance, Mill Place, 111 3rd Ave., S, Suite 100, Minneapolis, MN 55401-2554; 612-341-0641, Fax: 612-338-3483.

Mississippi

Mississippi Contract Procurement Center, 3015 12th St., Gulfport, MS 39502; 601-864-2961, Fax: 601-864-2969.

Missouri

Curators of the University of Missouri, University Extension, 310 Jesse Hall, Columbia, MO 65211; 314-882-0344, Fax: 314-884-4297.

Missouri Southern State College, 3950 E. Newman Rd., Joplin, MO 64801-1595; 417-625-9313, Fax: 417-625-9782.

Montana

Montana Tradeport Authority, James F. Ouldhouse, 2722 3rd Ave., N., Suite 300 West, Billings, MT 59101; 406-256-6871, Fax: 406-256-6877.

High Plains Development Authority Inc., 2800 Terminal Dr., Suite 209, P.O. Box 2568, Great Falls, MT 59404; 406-454-1934, Fax: 406-454-2995.

Procurement Technical Institute, Greg Depuydt, 305 W. Mercury, Butte, MT 59701; 406-723-4061, Fax: 406-723-5345.

Nebraska

Nebraska Department of Economic Development, Existing Business Assistance Division, 301 Centennial Mall So., P.O. Box 94666, Lincoln, NE 68509-4666; 308-535-8213, Fax: 308-535-8175.

Nevada

State of Nevada, Commission on Economic Development, Mr. Ray Horner, Capitol Complex, Carson City, NV 89710; 702-687-4325, Fax: 702-687-4450.

New Hampshire
Office of Business and Industrial Development, P.O. Box 1856, 172 Pembroke Rd., Concord, NH 03302-1856; 603-271-2591, Fax: 603-271-2629.

New Jersey
New Jersey Institute of Technology, Procurement Technical Assistance Center, Mr. John McKenna, 240 Martin Luther King Blvd., Newark, NJ 07102; 201-596-3105, Fax: 201-596-5806.

Union County PTA Center, 1085 Morris Ave., Suite 531, Liberty Hall, Union, NJ 07083; 908-527-1166, Fax: 908-527-1207.

New Mexico
State of New Mexico, Procurement Assistance Program, 1100 St. Francis Dr., Room 2006, Santa Fe, NM 87503; 505-827-0425, Fax: 505-827-0499.

New York
Cattaraugus County, Department of Economic Development and Tourism, 303 Court St., Little Valley, NY 14755; 716-938-9111, Fax: 716-938-9438.

Long Island Development Corporation, Procurement Technical Assistance Program, 255 Glen Cove Rd., Carle Place, NY 11514; 516-741-5690, Fax: 516-741-5851.

New York City Department of Business Services, Procurement Outreach Program, 110 William St., New York, NY 10038; 212-513-6472, Fax: 212-618-8987.

Rockland Economic Development Corporation, Procurement Division, 1 Blue Hill Plaza, Suite 812, Pearl River, NY 10965; 914-735-7040, Fax: 914-735-5736.

South Bronx Overall Economic Development Corporation, 370 East 149th St., Bronx, NY 10455; 718-292-3113, Fax: 718-292-3115.

State University of New York, Office of Research and Sponsored Prog., P.O. Box 6000, Binghamton, NY 13902; 607-777-2718, Fax: 607-777-2022.

North Carolina
University of North Carolina at Chapel Hill, Small Business and Technology Development Center, Bynum Hall, Chapel Hill, NC 27599; 919-571-4154, Fax: 919-571-4161.

North Dakota
University of North Dakota, North Dakota Small Business Development Center, Department of Grants and Contracts, P.O. Box 8164, Grand Forks, ND 58202; 701-237-9678, Fax: 701-235-6706.

Ohio
Central State University, Ohio Procurement and Technical Assistance Ctr., Wilberforce, OH 45384; 513-376-6514.

Columbus Area Chamber of Commerce, Central Ohio Government Marketing Assistance Program, 37 N. High St., Columbus, OH 43215; 614-225-6952, Fax: 614-469-8250.

Community Improvement Corporation of Lake County, Northeast Ohio Government Contract Assistance Center, 7750 Clocktower Dr., Mentor, OH 44060; 216-951-8488, Fax: 216-951-7336.

Greater Cleveland Government Business Program, 200 Tower City Center, 50 Public Square, Cleveland, OH 44113; 216-621-3300, Fax: 216-621-6013.

Lawrence Economic Development Corporation, Outreach Center, 101 Sand and Solida Rd., P.O. Box 488, South Point, OH 45680; 614-894-3838, Fax: 614-894-3836.

Mahoning Valley Economic Development Corp., Mahoning Valley Technical Procurement Center, Stephen J. Danyi, 4319 Belmont Ave., Youngstown, OH 44505; 216-759-3668, Fax: 216-759-3680.

Terra Technical College, North Central Ohio Procurement Technical Assistance Program, 1220 Cedar St., Fremont, OH 43420; 419-332-1002.

University of Cincinnati, CECE-Extension Unit Small Business Ctr., Ms. Nancy Rogers, 1111 Edison Dr., IAMS Bldg., Cincinnati, OH 45216; 513-948-2083, Fax: 513-948-2007.

Oklahoma
Oklahoma Department of Vocational-Technical Education, Business Assistance and Development Division, 1500 W. Seventh Ave., Stillwater, OK 74074-4364; 405-743-5574, Fax: 405-743-6821.

Tribal Government Institute, 111 N. Peters, Suite 400, Norman, OK 73069; 405-329-5542, Fax: 405-329-5543.

Oregon
Organization for Economic Initiatives, Government Contract Acquisition Program, 99 W. 10th Ave., Eugene, OR 97401; 503-344-3537, Fax: 503-687-4899.

Pennsylvania
Chester County Department of Commerce, Office of Economic Development, 117 W. Gay St., West Chester, PA 19380; 610-436-3337, Fax: 610-436-3110.

Economic Development Council of Northeastern Pennsylvania, Local Development District, 1151 Oak St., Pittston, PA 18640; 717-655-5581, Fax: 717-654-5137.

Government Contracting Assistance, Slippery Rock University, Economic and Community Development Center, Slippery Rock, PA 16057-1326; 412-738-2346.

Indiana University of Pennsylvania, Dr. Robert Camp, Robertshaw Center, 650 S. 13th St., Suite 303, Indiana, PA 15705; 412-357-7824, Fax: 412-357-3082.

Johnstown Area Regional Industries, Defense Procurement Assistance Center, 111 Market St., Johnstown, PA 15901; 814-535-8675, Fax: 814-535-8677.

Kutztown University, Small Business Development Center, University Center, 2986 N. 2nd St., Harrisburg, PA 17110; 717-233-3120.

Lehigh University, Rach Business Center #37, 412 S. New St., Bethlehem, PA 18015; 215-758-3980.

Mon Valley Renaissance, California University of Pennsylvania, 250 University Ave., California, PA 15419; 412-938-5881, Fax: 412-938-4575.

Montgomery County Department of Commerce and Economic Development, #3 Stony Creek Office Center, West Marshall Street, Norristown, PA 19404; 215-278-5950.

North Central Pennsylvania Regional Planning and Development Commission, 651 Montmorenci Ave., Ridgway, PA 15853; 814-772-3162, Fax: 814-772-7045.

Northern Tier Regional Planning and Development Commission, 507 Main St., Towanda, PA 18848; 717-265-9103, Fax: 717-265-7585.

Northwest Pennsylvania Regional Planning and Development Commission, 614 Eleventh St., Franklin, PA 16323; 814-437-3024, Fax: 814-432-3002.

Private Industry Council of Westmoreland/ Fayette, Inc., Procurement Assistance Center, 531 S. Main St., Greensburg, PA 15601; 412-836-2600, Fax: 412-836-8058.

SEDA - Council of Governments, RD 1, Timberhaven, Lewisburg, PA 17837; 717-524-4491, Fax: 717-524-9190.

South Western Pennsylvania Regional Development Council, The Waterfront, 200 First Ave., Pittsburgh, PA 15222-1573; 412-391-5590, Fax: 412-391-9160.

Southern Alleghenies Planning and Development Commission, 541 58th St., Altoona, PA 16602; 814-949-6528, Fax: 814-949-6505.

Temple University, Room 6, Speakman Hall, Philadelphia, PA 19122; 215-787-5893.

Trustees University of Pennsylvania, SE-PA PTAP, 3733 Spruce St., Vance Hall, Philadelphia, PA 19104-6374; 215-898-1219, Fax: 215-573-2135.

Puerto Rico

Commonwealth of Puerto Rico (FOMENTO), Economic Development Administration, Mr. Pedro J. Acevedo, 355 Roosevelt Ave., Hato Rey, PR 00918; 809-752-6861, Fax: 809-751-6239.

Rhode Island

Rhode Island Department of Economic Development, Business Development Office, 7 Jackson Walkway, Providence, RI 02903; 401-277-2601, Fax: 401-277-2102.

South Carolina

University of South Carolina, College of Business Administration, Small Business Development Center, Columbia, SC 29208; 803-777-4907, Fax: 803-777-4403.

South Dakota

South Dakota Procurement Technical Assistance Center, School of Business, 414 E. Clark, Vermillion, SD 57069; 605-330-6191, Fax: 605-330-6231.

Tennessee

University of Tennessee, Center for Industrial Services, Mr. T.C. Parsons, 226 Capitol Boulevard Bldg., Suite 606, Nashville, TN 37219-1804; 615-532-8657, Fax: 615-532-4937.

Texas

Angelina College, Defense PTA Center, P.O. Box 1768, Lufkin, TX 75902; 409-639-3678, Fax: 409-639-3863.

El Paso Community College, P.O. Box 20500, El Paso, TX 79998; 915-534-3405, Fax: 915-534-3420.

Northeast Texas Community College, East Texas Procurement Technical Assistance Program, P.O. Box 1307, Mt. Pleasant, TX 75455; 903-572-1911, Fax: 903-572-0598.

Panhandle Regional Planning Commission, Economic Development Unit, P.O. Box 9257, Amarillo, TX 79105-9257; 806-372-3381, Fax: 806-373-3268.

San Antonio Procurement Outreach Center, Department of Economic and Employment Development, Ms. Rosalie O. Manzano, P.O. Box 839966, San Antonio, TX 78283; 210-554-7133, Fax: 210-554-7160.

Small Business Development Center, Chamber of Commerce, 101 N. Shoreline, Corpus Christi, TX 78401; 512-882-6161, Fax: 512-888-5627.

Texas Technical University, College of Business Administration, 2579 S. Loop 289, Lubbock, TX 79423; 806-745-1637, Fax: 806-745-6207.

University of Houston/TIPS, Texas Information Procurement Service, 1100 Louisiana, Houston, TX 77204; 713-752-8477, Fax: 713-756-1515.

University of Texas at Arlington, Automaton and Robotics Research Institute, P.O. Box 19125, Arlington, TX 76019; 817-794-5978, Fax: 817-794-5952.

University of Texas at Brownsville, Office of President, 80 Fort Brown, Brownsville, TX 78520; 210-544-8812, Fax: 210-548-5627.

Utah

Utah Department of Community and Economic Development, Utah Procurement Outreach Program, 324 S. State St., Suite 504, Salt Lake City, UT 84111; 801-538-8791, Fax: 801-538-8825.

Vermont

State of Vermont, Agency of Development and Community Affairs, 109 State St., Montpelier, VT 05609; 802-828-3221, Fax: 802-828-3258.

Virginia

Crater Planning District Commission, The Procurement Assistance Center, 1964 Wakefield St., P.O. Box 1808, Petersburg, VA 23805; 804-861-1667, Fax: 804-732-8972.

George Mason University, Entrepreneurship Center, 4400 University Dr., Fairfax, VA 22030; 703-993-8300, Fax: 703-330-5891.

Southwest Virginia Community College, Procurement Technical Center, Ms. Maxine B. Rogers, P.O. Box SVCC, Richlands, VA 24641; 703-964-7334, Fax: 703-964-9307.

Washington

Economic Development Council of Snohomish County, 917 134th St. SW, Everett, WA 98204; 206-743-4567, Fax: 206-745-5563.

Spokane Area Economic Development Council, P.O. Box 203, 221 N. Wall, Suite 310, Spokane, WA 99210-0203; 509-624-9285, Fax: 509-624-3759.

Economic Development Council of Kitsap County, 4841 Auto Center Way, Suite 204, Bremerton, WA 98312; 206-643-0102, Fax: 206-643-6673.

West Virginia

Mid-Ohio Valley Regional Council, Procurement Technical Assistance Center, P.O. Box 247, Parkersburg, WV 26105; 304-295-8714, Fax: 304-295-7681.

Regional Contracting Assistance Center, Inc., Mr. Mick Walker, 1116 Smith St., Suite 202, Charleston, WV 25301; 304-344-2546, Fax: 304-344-2574.

Wisconsin

Procurement Institute, Inc., 840 Lake Ave., Racine, WI 53403; 414-632-6321, Fax: 414-632-7157.

Madison Area Technical College, Small Business Assistance Center, 211 N. Carroll St., Madison, WI 53703; 608-258-2330, Fax: 608-258-2329.

Government Buys Bright Ideas From Inventors: Small Business Innovative Research Programs (SBIR)

The Small Business Innovative Research Program (SBIR) stimulates technological innovation, encourages small science and technology-based firms to participate in government-funded research, and provides incentives for converting research results into commercial applications. The program is designed to stimulate technological innovation in this country by providing qualified U.S. small business concerns with competitive opportunities to propose innovative concepts to meet the research and development needs of the federal government. Eleven federal agencies with research and development budgets greater than $100 million are required by law to participate: The Departments of Defense, Health and Human Services, Energy, Agriculture, Commerce, Transportation, and Education; the National Aeronautics and Space Administration; the National Science Foundation; the Nuclear Regulatory Commission; and the Environmental Protection Agency.

Businesses of 500 or fewer employees that are organized for profit are eligible to compete for SBIR funding. Non-profit organizations and foreign-owned firms are not eligible to receive awards, and the research must be carried out in the U.S. All areas of research and development solicit for proposals, and the 1995 budget for SBIR is $900 million. There are three phases of the program: Phase I determines whether the research idea, often on high-risk advanced concepts, is technically feasible, whether the firm can do high quality research, and whether sufficient progress has been made to justify a larger Phase II effort. This phase is usually funded for 6 months with awards up to $50,000. Phase II is the principal research effort, and is usually limited to a maximum of $500,000 for up to two years. The third phase, which is to pursue potential commercial applications of the research funded under the first two phases, is supported solely by non-federal funding, usually from third party, venture capital, or large industrial firms. SBIR is one of the most competitive research and development programs in government. About one proposal out of ten received is funded in Phase I. Generally, about half of these receive support in Phase II. Solicitations for proposals are released once a year (in a few cases twice a year). To assist the small business community in its SBIR efforts, the U.S. Small Business Administration publishes the Pre-Solicitation Announcement (PSA) in December, March, June, and September of each year. Every issue of the PSA contains pertinent information on the SBIR Program along with details on SBIR solicitations that are about to be released. This publication eliminates the need for small business concerns to track the activities of all of the federal agencies participating in the SBIR Program. In recognition of the difficulties encountered by many small firms in their efforts to locate sources of funding essential to finalization of their innovative products, SBA has developed the Commercialization Matching System. This system contains information on all SBIR awardees, as well as financing sources that have indicated an interest in investing in SBIR innovations. Firms interested in obtaining more information on the SBIR Program or receiving the PSA, should contact the Office of Technology, Small Business Administration, 409 3rd St., SW, MC/6470, Washington, DC 20416, 202-205-6450.

SBIR representatives listed below can answer questions and send you materials about their agency's SBIR plans and funding:

Department of Agriculture

Dr. Charles F. Cleland, Director, SBIR Program, U.S. Department of Agriculture, Small Business Association, 409 Third St., SW, 8th Floor, Washington, DC 20416; 202-205-7777.

Department of Defense

Mr. Robert Wrenn, SBIR Program Manager, OSD/SADBU, U.S. Department of Defense, The Pentagon, Room 2A340, Washington, DC 20301-3061; 703-697-1481.

Department of Education

Mr. John Christensen, SBIR Program Coordinator, U.S. Department of Education, 555 New Jersey Ave., NW, Room 602D, Washington, DC 20208; 202-219-2050.

Department of Energy

Dr. Samuel J. Barish, SBIR Program Manager, ER-16, U.S. Department of Energy, Washington, DC 20585; 301-903-3054.

Department of Health and Human Services

Mr. Veri Zanders, SBIR Program Manager, Office of the Secretary, U.S. Department of Health and Human Services, Washington, DC 20201; 202-690-7300.

Department of Transportation

Dr. George Kobatch, DOT SBIR Program Director, DTS-22, Research and Special Program Administration, Volpe National Transportation Systems Center, U.S. Department of Transportation, 55 Broadway, Kendall Square, Cambridge, MA 02142-1093; 617-494-2051.

Environmental Protection Agency

Mr. Donald F. Carey, SBIR Program Manager, Research Grants Staff (8701), Office of Research and Development, U.S. Environmental Protection Agency, 401 M St., SW, Washington, DC 20460; 202-260-7899.

National Aeronautics and Space Administration

Mr. Harry Johnson, Manager, SBIR Office, Code CR, National Aeronautics and Space Administration Headquarters, 300 E St., SW, Washington, DC 20546-0001; 202-358-0691.

National Science Foundation

Mr. Roland Tibbetts, Mr. Ritchie Coryell, Mr. Daryl G. Gorman, Mr. Charles Hauer, Dr. Sara Nerlove, SBIR Program Managers, National Science Foundation, 4201 Wilson Boulevard, Room 590, Arlington, VA 22230; 703-306-1391.

Nuclear Regulatory Commission

Ms. Marianne M. Riggs, SBIR Program Representative, Financial Management, Procurement, and Administrative Staff, Nuclear Regulatory Commission, Washington, DC 20555; 301-415-5822.

State Procurement Assistance

Have you ever wondered where the government buys all of the products that it works with each day? Well, they buy from small businesses just like yours that produce products such as:

- work clothing
- office supplies
- cleaning equipment
- miscellaneous vehicles
- medical supplies and equipment

Imagine what your bottom line could look like each year if you won just ONE lucrative government contract that would provide your business with a secure income! It might even buy you the freedom to pursue other clients that you wouldn't have the time or money to go after otherwise.

The following offices are starting places for finding out who in the state government will purchase your products or services.

State Procurement Offices

Alabama
Finance Department, Purchasing Division, 11 S. Union, Room 200, Montgomery, AL 36130; 205-242-7250.

Alaska
State of Alaska, Department of Administration, Division of General Services and Supply, P.O. Box 110210, Juneau, AK 99811-0210; 907-465-2253.

Arizona
State Purchasing, Executive Tower, Suite 101, 1700 W. Washington, Phoenix, AZ 85007; 602-542-5511.

Arkansas
Office of State Purchasing, P.O. Box 2940, Little Rock, AR 72203; 501-324-9312.

California
Office of Procurement, Department of General Services, 1823 14th St., Sacramento, CA 95814; 916-445-6942.

Colorado
Division of Purchasing, 225 E. 16th Ave., Suite 900, Denver, CO 80203; 303 866-6100.

Connecticut
State of Connecticut, Department of Administrative Services, Bureau of Purchases, 460 Silver St., Middletown, CT 06457; 203-638-3280.

Delaware
Purchasing Division, Purchasing Bldg., P.O. Box 299, Delaware City, DE 19706; 302-834-4550.

District of Columbia
Department of Administrative Services, 441 4th St. NW, Room 710, Washington, DC 20001; 202-727-0171.

Florida
General Service Department, Division of Purchasing, Knight Bldg., 2737 Centerview Dr., 2nd Floor, Tallahassee, FL 32399-0950; 904-488-8440.

Georgia
Administrative Services Department, 200 Piedmont Ave., Room 1308 SE, Atlanta, GA 30334; 404-656-3240.

Hawaii
Purchasing Branch, Purchasing and Supply Division, Department of Accounting and General Services, Room 416, 1151 Punch Bowl, Honolulu, HI 96813; 808- 586-0575.

Idaho
Division of Purchasing, Administration Department, 5569 Kendall, State House Mall, Boise, ID 83720; 208-327-7465.

Illinois
Department of Central Management Services, Procurement Services, 801 Stratton Bldg., Springfield, IL 62706; 217-782-2301.

Indiana
Department of Administration, Procurement Division, 402 W. Washington St., Room W-468, Indianapolis, IN 46204; 317-232-3032.

Iowa

State of Iowa, Department of General Services, Purchasing Division, Hoover State Office Building, Des Moines, IA 50319; 515-281-3089.

Kansas

Division of Purchasing, Room 102 North, Landon State Office Building, 900 SW Jackson St., Topeka, KS 66612; 913-296-2376.

Kentucky

Purchases, Department of Finance, Room 367, Capital Annex, Frankfort, KY 40601; 502-564-4510.

Louisiana

State Purchasing Office, Division of Administration, P.O. Box 94095, Baton Rouge, LA 70804-9095; 504-342-8010.

Maine

Bureau of Purchases, State House Station #9, Augusta, ME 04333; 207-287-3521.

Maryland

Purchasing Bureau, 301 W. Preston St., Mezzanine, Room M8, Baltimore, MD 21201; 410-225-4620.

Massachusetts

Purchasing Agent Division, One Ashburton Place, Room 1017, Boston, MA 02108; 617-727-7500.

Michigan

Office of Purchasing, Mason Bldg., P.O. Box 30026, Lansing, MI 48909, or 530 W. Ellegan, 48933; 517-373-0330.

Minnesota

State of Minnesota, 112 Administration Bldg., 50 Sherburne Ave., St. Paul, MN 55155; 612-296-6152.

Mississippi

Office of Purchasing and Travel, 1504 Sillers Bldg., 550 High St., Suite 1504, Jackson, MS 39201; 601-359-3409.

Missouri

State of Missouri, Division of Purchasing, P.O. Box 809, Jefferson City, MO 65102; 314-751-3273.

Montana

Department of Administration, Procurement Printing Division, 165 Mitchell Bldg., Helena, MT 59620-0135; 406-444-2575.

Nebraska

State Purchasing, Material Division, 301 Centennial Mall S., P.O. Box 94847, Lincoln, NE 68509; 402-471-2401.

Nevada

Nevada State Purchasing Division, 209 E. Musser St., Room 304, Blasdel Bldg., Carson City, NV 89710; 702-687-4070.

New Hampshire

Plant and Property Management, 25 Capitol St., State House Annex, Room 102, Concord, NH 03301; 603-271-2201.

New Jersey

Division of Purchase and Property, CN-039, Trenton, NJ 08625; 609-292-4886.

New Mexico

State Purchasing Division, 1100 St. Frances Dr., Joseph Montoya Bldg., Room 2016, Santa Fe, NM 87503; 505-827-0472.

New York

Division of Purchasing, Corning Tower, Empire State Plaza, 38th Floor, Albany, NY 12242; 518-474-3695.

North Carolina

Department of Administration, Division of Purchase and Contract, 116 W. Jones St., Raleigh, NC 27603-8002; 919-733-3581.

North Dakota

Central Services Division of State Purchasing, Purchasing, 600 E Blvd., I Wing, Bismarck, ND 58505-0420; 701-224-2683.

Ohio

State Purchasing, 4200 Surface Rd., Columbus, OH 43228-1395; 614-466-5090.

Oklahoma

Office of Public Affairs, Central Purchasing Division, Room B4, State Capital Bldg., Oklahoma City, OK 73105; 405-521-2110.

Oregon

General Services, Purchasing, 1225 Ferry St., Salem, OR 97310; 503-378-4643.

Pennsylvania

Procurement Department Secretary, N. Office Bldg., Room 414, Commonwealth and North St., Harrisburg, PA 17125; 717-787-5295.

Rhode Island

Department of Administration, Purchases Office, One Capital Hill, Providence, RI 02908-5855; 401-277-2317.

South Carolina

Materials Management Office, General Service Budget and Control Board, 1201 Main St., Suite 600, Columbia, SC 29201; 803-737-0600.

South Dakota

Division of Purchasing, 118 W. Capitol Ave., Pierre, SD 57501; 605-773-3405.

Tennessee

Purchasing Division, C2-211, Central Services Bldg., Nashville, TN 37219; 615-741-1035.

Texas

State Purchasing and General Services Commission, P.O. Box 13047, Austin, TX 78711; 512-463-3445.

Utah

Purchasing Division, Department of Administrative Services, State Office Bldg., Room 3150, Salt Lake City, UT 84114; 801-538-3026.

Vermont

Purchasing Division, 128 State St., Drawer 33, Montpelier, VT 05633-7501; 802-828-2211.

Virginia

Department of General Services, Purchasing Division, P.O. Box 1199, Richmond, VA 23209; 804-786-3172.

Washington

Office of State Procurement, 216 GA Building, P.O. Box 41017, Olympia, WA 98504-1017; 206-753-6461.

West Virginia

Department of Administration, Purchasing Section, Room E102, Building One, 1900 Kanawha Blvd. E, Charleston, WV 25305-0110; 304-558-2306.

Wisconsin

Division of State Agency Services, Bureau of Procurement, 101 E. Wilson, 6th Floor, P.O. Box 7867, Madison, WI 53707-7867; 608-266-2605.

Wyoming

Department of Administration, Procurement Services, 2001 Capitol Ave., Cheyenne, WY 82002; 307-777-7253.

Starting an Importing and Exporting Business

Starting an Importing and Exporting Business

If you've found that the domestic market for your product or service is dwindling, it's time to consider broadening your sales base by selling overseas. Hey, it's not as complicated as you might think. There is a lot of information available to us in this country about other countries that isn't even available in that particular country. In other words, we have access to things like marketing trend reports on countries like Turkey that business people in Turkey can't even get hold of! Important expertise and assistance for new and more experienced exporters continue to increase at both the federal and state level.

That widget that you invented in your garage so many years ago is now found in every hardware store in this country — why shouldn't it be in every French hardware store? Or the line of stationery that sold so well for you in this country could definitely be a hit in British stores that specialize in selling fine writing papers. So how do you go about finding what countries are open to certain imports and what their specific requirements are? If you're smart, you go to the best source around — the government — and make it work for you.

Polypropylene In Countries That Don't Even Count People

A few years ago a Fortune 500 company asked us to identify the consumption of polypropylene resin for 15 lesser developed countries. It was a project they had been working on without success for close to a year. After telexing all over the world and contacting every domestic expert imaginable, we too came up empty handed. The basic problem was that we were dealing with countries that didn't even count people, let alone polypropylene resin.

Our savior was a woman at the U.S. Commerce Department named Maureen Ruffin, who was in charge of the World Trade Reference Room. Ms. Ruffin and her colleagues collect the official import/export statistical documents for every country in the world as soon as they are released by the originating countries. Although the data are much more current and more detailed than those published by such international organizations as the United Nations, the publications available at this federal reference room are printed in the language of origin. Because none of the 15 subject countries manufacture polypropylene resin, Ms. Ruffin showed us how to get the figures by identifying those countries which produce polypropylene and counting up how much each of them exported to the countries in question. To help us even further, she also provided us with free in-house translators to help us understand the foreign documents.

Exporter's Hotline

The Trade Promotion Coordinating Committee has established this comprehensive "one-stop shop" for information on U.S. Government programs and activities that support exporting efforts. This hotline is staffed by trade specialists who can provide information on seminars and conferences, overseas buyers and representatives, overseas events, export financing, technical assistance, and export counseling. They also have access to the National Trade Data Bank.

Trade Information Center
U.S. Department of Commerce
Washington, DC 20230
800-USA-TRADE
202-482-0543
Fax: 202-482-4473
TDD: 800-833-8723

Country Experts

If you are looking for information on a market, company or most any other aspect of commercial life in a particular country, your best point of departure is to contact the appropriate country desk officer at the U.S. Department of Commerce. These experts often have the information you need right at their fingertips or they can refer you to other country specialists that can help you.

U.S. and Foreign Commercial Services
(FCS)
International Trade Administration
U.S. Department of Commerce
Room 2810
Washington, DC 20230   202-482-6220

All the Department of Commerce/US & FCS field offices around the country are listed later in this chapter. (You will also find a separate roster of international trade offices maintained by the states.)

ITA Country Desk Officers

A

ASEAN	Karen Goddin	202-482-3877	2032
Afghanistan	Tim Gilman	202-482-2954	2308
Albania	EEBIC	202-482-2645	7412
Algeria	Claude Clement	202-482-5545	2033
Angola	Finn Holm-Olsen	202-482-4228	3317
Anguilla	Michelle Brooks	202-482-2527	2039
Antigua/			
Barbuda	Michelle Brooks	202-482-2527	2039
Argentina	Randy Mye	202-482-1548	3021
Aruba	Michelle Brooks	202-482-2527	2039
Australia	Gary Bouck	202-482-4958	2036
Austria	Philip Combs	202-482-2920	3039
Armenia	BISNIS	202-482-4655	7413
Azerbaijan	Mark Siegelman	202-482-5680	7413

B

Bahamas	Mark Siegelman	202-482-5680	2039
Bahrain	Claude Clement		
	/Chris Carone	202-482-1860	2029B
Balkan States	EEBIC	202-482-2645	7412
Bangladesh	John Simmons	202-482-2954	2308
Barbados	Michelle Brooks	202-482-2527	2039
Belgium	Simon Bensimon	202-482-5401	3039
Belize	Michelle Brooks	202-482-2527	2039
Benin	Debra Henke	202-482-5149	3317

Bhutan	Tim Gilman	202-482-2954	2308
Bolivia	Rebecca Hunt	202-482-2521	2037
Botswana	Finn Holm-Olsen	202-482-4228	3317
Brazil	Horace Jennings	202-482-3871	3019
Brunei	Raphael Cung	202-482-4958	2036
Bulgaria	EEBIC	202-482-2645	7412
Burkina Faso	Philip Michelini	202-482-4388	3317
Burma	Gary Bouck	202-482-4958	2306
Burundi	Philip Michelini	202-482-4388	3317
Belarus	BISNIS	202-482-4655	7413

C

Cambodia	Gary Bouck	202-482-4958	2036
Cameroon	Debra Henke	202-482-5149	3317
Canada	Kathy Klein	202-482-3103	3033
Cape Verde	Philip Michelini	202-482-4388	3317
Caymans	Mark Siegelman	202-482-5680	2039
Central Africa			
Republic	Philip Michelini	202-482-4388	3317
Chad	Philip Michelini	202-482-4388	3317
Chile	Roger Turner	202-482-1495	3021
Columbia	Paul Moore	202-482-1659	2037
Comoros	Chandra Watkins	202-482-4564	3317
Congo	Debra Henke	202-482-5419	3317
Costa Rica	Mark Siegelman	202-482-5680	2039
Cuba	Mark Siegelman	202-482-5680	2039
Cyprus	Ann Corro	202-482-3945	3042
Czech Republic	EEBIC	202-482-2645	7412
Cote d'Ivoire	Philip Michelini	202-482-4388	3317

D

D'Jibouti	Chandra Watkins	202-482-4564	3317
Denmark	James Devlin	202-482-3254	3037
Dominica	Michelle Brooks	202-482-2527	2039
Dominican			
Republic	Mark Siegelman	202-482-5680	2039

E

E. Caribbean	Michelle Brooks	202-482-2527	3021
Ecuador	Paul Moore	202-482-1659	2037
Egypt	Thomas Sams		
	/Corey Wright	202-482-1860	2029B
El Salvador	Helen Lee	202-482-2528	2039
Equatorial			
Guinea	Philip Michelini	202-482-4388	3317
Ethiopia	Chandra Watkins	202-482-4564	3317
European			
Community	Charles Ludolph	202-482-5276	3036

F

Finland	James Devlin	202-482-3254	3037
France	Elena Mikalis	202-482-6008	3042

G

Gabon	Debra Henke	202-482-5149	3321
Gambia	Philip Michelini	202-482-4388	3317
Germany	Brenda Fisher	202-482-2435	3409
Germany	John Larsen	202-482-2434	3409
Ghana	Debra Henke	202-482-5149	3321
Greece	Ann Corro	202-482-3945	3042
Grenada	Michelle Brooks	202-482-2527	2039

Country	Contact	Phone	Code
Guatemala	Helen Lee	202-482-2528	2039
Guinea	Philip Michelini	202-482-4388	3317
Guinea-Bissau	Philip Michelini	202-482-4388	3317
Guyana	Michelle Brooks	202-482-2527	2039
H			
Haiti	Mark Siegelman	202-482-5680	2039
	Helen Lee	202-482-2528	2039
Hong Kong	Sheila Baker	202-482-3932	2317
Hungary	EEBIC	202-482-2645	7412
I			
Iceland	James Devlin	202-482-3254	3037
India	John Simmons		
	/John Crown		
	/Tim Gilman	202-482-2954	2308
Indonesia	Karen Goddin	202-482-3877	2036
Iran	Paul Thanos	202-482-1860	2029B
Iraq	Thomas Sams	202-482-1860	2029B
Ireland	Boyce Fitzpatrick	202-482-2177	3045
Israel	Paul Thanos	202-482-1860	2029B
Italy	Boyce Fitzpatrick	202-482-2177	3045
J			
Jamaica	Mark Siegelman	202-482-5680	2039
Japan	Ed Leslie		
	/Cynthia Cambell		
	/Eric Kennedy	202-482-2425	2320
Jordan	Paul Thanos	202-482-1860	2029B
K			
Kenya	Chandra Watkins	202-482-4564	3317
Korea	Jeffrey Donius		
	/Dan Duvall		
	/William Golike	202-482-4390	2327
Kuwait	Corey Wright		
	/Thomas Sams	202-482-5506	2033
Kazakhstan	BISNIS	202-482-4655	7413
Krygyz Republic	BISNIS	202-482-4655	7413
L			
Laos	Hong-Phong B. Pho	202-482-4958	2036
Lebanon	Corey Wright		
	/Thomas Sams	202-482-1860	2029B
Lesotho	Finn Holm-Olsen	202-482-4228	3317
Liberia	Philip Michelini	202-482-4388	3317
Libya	Claude Clement	202-482-5545	2033
Luxembourg	Simon Bensimon	202-482-5401	3039
Lativa	EEBIC	202-482-2645	7412
Lithuania	EEBIC	202-482-2645	7412
M			
Macau	Sheila Baker	202-482-3932	2317
Madagascar	Chandra Watkins	202-482-4564	3317
Malawi	Finn Holm-Olsen	202-482-4228	3317
Malaysia	Raphael Cung	202-482-4958	2036
Maldives	John Simmons	202-482-2954	2308
Mali	Philip Michelini	202-482-4388	3317
Malta	Robert McLaughlin	202-482-3748	3045
Mauritana	Philip Michelini	202-482-4388	3317
Mauritius	Chandra Watkins	202-482-4564	3321
Mexico	Shawn Ricks	202-482-0300	3022
Mongolia	Sheila Baker	202-482-3932	2317
Montserrat	Michelle Brooks	202-482-2527	2039
Morocco	Claude Clement	202-482-5545	2033
Mozambique	Finn Holm-Olsen	202-482-4228	3317
Moldova	BISNIS	202-482-4655	7413
N			
Namibia	Finn Holm-Olsen	202-482-4228	3317
Nepal	Tim Gilman	202-482-2954	2308
Netherlands	Simon Bensimon	202-482-5401	3039
Netherlands Antilles	Michelle Brooks	202-482-2527	2039
New Zealand	Gary Bouck	202-482-4958	2036
Nicaragua	Mark Siegelman	202-482-5680	2039
Niger	Philip Michelini	202-482-4388	3317
Nigeria	Debra Henke	202-482-5149	3317
Norway	James Devlin	202-482-4414	3037
O			
Oman	Paul Thanos	202-482-1860	2029B
P			
Pacific Islands	Gary Bouck	202-482-4958	2036
Pakistan	Tim Gilman	202-482-2954	2308
Panama	Helen Lee	202-482-2527	3021
Paraguay	Randy Mye	202-482-1548	2039
People/China	Cheryl McQueen		
	/Laura McCall	202-482-3583	2317
Peru	Rebecca Hunt	202-482-2521	2037
Philippines	Ed Oliver	202-482-3875	2036
Poland	EEBIC	202-482-2645	7412
Portugal	Mary Beth Double	202-482-4508	3045
Q			
Qatar	Paul Thanos	202-482-1860	2029B
R			
Romania	EEBIC	202-482-2645	7412
Russia	BISNIS	202-482-4655	7413
Rwanda	Philip Michelini	202-482-4388	3317
S			
Sao Tome & Principe	Debra Henke	202-482-4228	3317
Saudi Arabia	Chris Cerone		
	/Claude Clement	202-482-5545	2033
Senegal	Philip Michelini	202-482-4388	3317
Seychelles	Chandra Watkins	202-482-4564	3317
Sierra Leone	Philip Michelini	202-482-4388	3317
Singapore	Raphael Cung	202-482-4988	2036
Somalia	Chandra Watkins	202-482-4564	3317
South Africa	Emily Solomon	202-482-5148	3317
Spain	Mary Beth Double	202-482-4508	3045
Sri Lanka	John Simmons	202-482-2954	2308
St. Bartholomy	Michelle Brooks	202-482-2527	2039
St. Kitts-Nevis	Michelle Brooks	202-482-2527	2039
St. Lucia	Michelle Brooks	202-482-2527	2039

St. Martin	Michelle Brooks	202-482-2527	2039
St. Vincent			
Grenadines	Michelle Brooks	202-482-2527	3021
Sudan	Chandra Watkins	202-482-4564	3317
Suriname	Michelle Brooks	202-482-2527	3021
Swaziland	Finn Holm-Olsen	202-482-5148	3317
Sweden	James Devlin	202-482-4414	3037
Switzerland	Philip Combs	202-482-2920	3039
Syria	Corey Wright		
	/Thomas Sams	202-482-2515	2039
Slovak			
Republic	EEBIC	202-482-2645	7413
T			
Taiwan	Robert Chu		
	/Dan Duvall		
	/Paul Carroll	202-482-4390	2327
Tanzania	Vacant	202-482-4228	3317
Thailand	Jean Kelly	202-482-3875	2032
Togo	Debra Henke	202-482-5149	3317
Trinidad/			
Tobago	Michelle Brooks	202-482-2527	2039
Tunisia	Corey Wright		
	/Thomas Sams	202-482-1860	2029B
Turkey	Ann Corro	202-482-3945	3042
Turks & Caicos			
Islands	Mark Siegelman	202-482-5680	2039
U			
Uganda	Chandra Watkins	202-482-4564	3317
United Arab			
Emirates	Claude Clement	202-482-5545	2033
United			
Kingdom	Robert McLaughlin	202-482-3748	3045
Uruguay	Roger Turner	202-482-1495	3021
V			
Venezuela	Laura Zieger		
	Hatfield	202-482-4303	2037
Vietnam	Hong-Phong		
	B. Pho	202-482-4958	2036
Virgin Islands			
(UK)	Michelle Brooks	202-482-2527	2039
Y			
Yemen, Rep of	Paul Thanos	202-482-1860	2029B
Z			
Zaire	Philip Michelini	202-482-4388	3317
Zambia	Finn Holm-Olsen	202-482-4228	3317
Zimbabwe	Finn Holm-Olsen	202-482-4228	3317

State Department Country Experts

If you need information that is primarily political, economic or cultural in nature, direct your questions first to the State Department Country Desk Officers. An operator at the number listed below can direct you to the appropriate desk officer.

U.S. Department of State
2201 C Street NW
Washington, DC 20520
202-647-6575

Foreign Specialists
At Other Government Agencies

The following is a listing by subject area of other departments within the federal government which maintain country experts who are available to help the public:

1) **Mineral Resources:**
Bureau of Mines, U.S. Department of Interior, Division of International Minerals, 810 7th St. NW, Washington, DC 20241-0002, 202-501-9666.

2) **Foreign Agriculture:**
Foreign Agriculture Service, Agriculture and Trade Analysis Division, U.S. Department of Agriculture, Room 732, 1301 New York Ave., NW, Washington, DC 20005, 202-219-0700.

Food Safety and Inspection Service, International Programs, U.S. Dept. of Agriculture, Room 341-E, 14th and Independence Ave., SW, Washington, DC 20250-3700, 202-720-3473.

Animal and Plant Health Inspection Service, Import-Export, U.S. Department of Agriculture, 6505 Bellcrest Rd., Hyattsville, MD 20782, 301-436-8590.

Food Transportation, International Transportation Branch, U.S. Department of Agriculture, Room 1217 South Building, Washington, DC 20250, 202-690-1320.

3) **Energy Resources:**
Office of Export Assistance, U.S. Department of Energy, 1000 Independence Ave., SW, Washington, DC 20585, 202-586-7997.

Office of Fossil Energy, U.S. Dept. of Energy, 1000 Independence Ave., SW, Washington, DC 20585, 202-586-7297.

4) Economic Assistance to Foreign Countries:
Business Office, U.S. Agency for International Development, 320 21st St. NW, Washington, DC 20523, 703-875-1551.

5) Information Programs and Cultural Exchange:
U.S. Information Agency, 301 4th St. SW, Washington, DC 20547, 202-619-4700.

6) Seafood Certificates:
Inspection Certificates for Seafood Exports, National Oceanic and Atmospheric Administration, 1315 East-West Highway, Room 12554, Silver Spring, MD 20910, 301-713-2355.

7) Metric:
Office of Metric Programs, National Institute of Standards and Technology, Building 411, Room A146, Gaithersburg, MD 20899, 301-975-3690.

8) Telecommunications Information:
Bureau of International Communications and Information Policy, U.S. Department of State, Washington, DC 20520, 202-647-5231.

9) Fisheries:
Office of Trade and Industry Services, Fisheries Promotion and Trade Matters, National Marine Fisheries Service, 1315 East-West Highway, Silver Spring, MD 20910, 301-713-2379.

Fax Directory Of
Overseas Commercial Counselors

You can just say, "FAX IT", if you are looking for a market study, a client or any other piece of information in a given country and want the information as quickly as possible. Listed below are the fax numbers of the commercial officers who work at U.S. Embassies around the world. These officers are available to assist U.S. businesses succeed in selling their products overseas.

Algeria:
Algiers	011-213-2-69-18-63

Argentina:
Buenos Aires	011-54-1777-0673

Australia:
Sydney	011-61-2-221-0576
Brisbane	011-61-7-832-6247
Melbourne	011-61-3-510-4660
Perth	011-61-9-231-9444

Austria:
Vienna	011-43-1310-6917

Barbados:
Bridgetown	1-809-431-0179

Belgium:
Brussels (Emb)	011-32-2-512-6653
Brussels (EC)	011-32-2-513-1228
Antwerp	011-32-03-542-6567

Brazil:
Brasilia	011-55-61-225-9136
Belo Horizonte	011-55-31-335-3054
Rio de Janeiro	011-55-21-240-9738
Sao Paulo	011-55-11-853-2744

Cameroon:
Yaounde	011-237-23-07-53

Canada:
Ottawa	1-613-233-8511
Calgary	1-403-264-6630
Halifax	1-902-423-6861
Montreal	1-514-398-0711
Toronto	1-416-595-5466
Vancouver	1-604-687-6095

China:
Beijing	011-86-1-532-3297
Guangzhou	011-86-20-666-6409
Shanghai	011-86-21-433-1576
Shenyang	011-86-24-282-0074

Columbia:
Bogata	011-57-1-285-7945

Costa Rica:
San Jose	011-506-231-4783

Cote D'Ivoire:
Abidjan	011-225-22-32-59
African Dev Bk	011-225-22-2437

Czech Republic:
Prague	011-42-2-2421-4465

Denmark:
Copenhagen	011-45-31-42-01-75

Dominican Republic:
Santo Domingo	1-809-688-4838

Ecuador:
Quito	011-593-2-504-550
Guayaquil	011-593-4-324-558

Egypt:
Cairo	011-20-2-355-8368

Finland:
Helsinki	011-358-0-635-332

France:
Paris(EMB)	011-33-1-4266-4827
Paris (ORCD)	011-33-1-4524-7410
Bordeaux	011-33-56-51-60-42
Lyon	011-33-1-4266-4827

Marseille	011-33-91-550-947	Guadalajara	011-52-36-26-6549
Nice	011-33-16-9387-0738	Monterrey	011-52-83-45-7748
Strasbourg	011-33-88-24-0695	**Morocco:**	
Germany:		Casablanca	011-212-22-02-59
Bonn	011-49-228-334-649	Rabat	011-212-7-656-51
Berlin	011-49-30-238-6290	**Netherlands:**	
Dusseldorf	011-49-211-594-897	The Hague	011-31-70-363-29-85
Frankfurt	011-49-69-748-204	Amsterdam	011-31-20-5755-350
Hamburg	011-49-40-410-6598	**Nigeria:**	
Munich	011-49-89-285-261	Lagos	011-234-1-261-9856
Stuttgart	011-49-711-236-4350	**Norway:**	
Greece:		Oslo	011-47-2243-07-77
Athens	011-30-1-721-8660	**Pakistan:**	
Guatemala:		Karachi	011-92-21-568-3089
Guatemala	011-502-2-317-373	**Panama:**	
Honduras:		Panama	011-507-27-1713
Teguicigalpa	011-504-38-2888	**Peru:**	
Hong Kong:		Lima	011-51-14-33-4887
Hong Kong	011-852-845-9800	**Philippines:**	
Hungary:		Manila	011-63-2-818-2684
Budapest	011-36-1-142-2529	Asian Dev Bank	011-63-2-632-4003
India:		**Poland:**	
New Delhi	011-91-11-687-2391	Warsaw	011-48-22-21-63-27
Bombay	011-91-22-262-3850	**Portugal:**	
Calcutta	011-91-33-242-2335	Lisbon	011-351-1-726-9109
Madras	011-91-44-825-0240	Oporto	011-351-2-600-2737
Indonesia:		**Romania:**	
Jakarta	011-62-21-385-1632	Bucharest	011-40-1610-5316
Medan	011-62-61-518-711	**Russia:**	
Surabaya	011-62-31-574-492	Moscow	011-7-095-230-2101
Iraq:		**Saudi Arabia:**	
Baghdad	011-964-1-718-9297	Riyadh	011-966-1-488-3237
Ireland:		Dhahran	011-966-3-891-8332
Dublin	011-353-1-682-840	Jeddah	011-966-2-665-8106
Israel:		**Singapore:**	
Tel Aviv	011-972-3-663-449	Singapore	011-65-338-4550
Italy:		**South Africa:**	
Rome	011-39-6-4674-2113	Johannesburg	011-27-11-331-6178
Florence	011-39-55-283-780	Cape Town	011-27-21-254-151
Milan	011-39-2-481-4161	**Spain:**	
Naples	011-39-81-761-1869	Madrid	011-34-1-575-8655
Jamaica:		Barcelona	011-34-3-205-7705
Kingston	1-809-926-6743	**Sweden:**	
Japan:		Stockholm	011-46-8-661-1964
Tokyo	011-81-3-589-4235	**Switzerland:**	
Tokyo (TradeCtr)	011-81-3-987-2447	Bern	011-41-31-357-7336
Fukuoka	011-81-9-271-3922	Geneva(GATT)	011-41-22-749-4885
Osaka-Kobe	011-81-6-361-5978	Zurich	011-41-1-382-2655
Sapporo	011-81-11-643-0911	**Taiwan:**	
Kenya:		Taipei	011-886-2-757-7162
Nairobi	011-254-2-216-648	Kaohsiung	011-886-7-223-8237
Korea:		**Thailand:**	
Seoul	011-82-2-738-8845	Bangkok	011-66-2-255-2915
Kuwait:		**Trinidad & Tobago:**	
Kuwait	011-965-244-2855	Port-of-Spain	1-809-628-5462
Malaysia:		**Turkey:**	
Kuala Lumpur	011-60-3-242-1866	Ankara	011-90-312-467-1366
Mexico:		Istanbul	011-90-212-252-2417
Mexico City	011-52-5-207-8938	**United Arab Emirates:**	
Mexico City		Adu Dhabi	011-971-2-331-374
(Trade Center)	011-52-5-566-1115	Dubai	011-971-4-313-131

United Kingdom:
London   011-44-71-491-4022
U.S.S.R.:
Moscow   011-7-095-230-2101
Venezuela:
Caracas   011-58-2-285-0336
Yugoslavia:
Belgrade   011-38-11-645-096
Zagreb   011-38-41-440-235

Money For Selling Overseas

1) State Government Money Programs:

Some state government economic development programs offer special help for those who need financial assistance in selling overseas. See the section presented later in this chapter entitled *State Government Assistance To Exporters*.

2) Export-Import Bank Financing:

The Export-Import Bank facilitates and aids in the financing of exports of United States goods and services. Its programs include short-term, medium-term, and long-term credits, small business support, financial guarantees, and insurance. In addition, it sponsors conferences on small business exporting, maintains credit information on thousands of foreign firms, supports feasibility studies of overseas programs, and offers export and small business finance counseling. To receive *Marketing News* Fact Sheets, or the *Eximbank Export Credit Insurance* booklet, or the Eximbank's *Program Selection Guide,* contact: Export-Import Bank, 811 Vermont Ave. NW, Washington, DC 20571, 202-565-3901, 1-800-565-EXIM.

3) Small Business Administration (SBA) Export Loans:

This agency makes loans and loan guarantees to small business concerns as well as to small business investment companies, including those which sell overseas. It also offers technical assistance, counseling, training, management assistance, and information resources, including some excellent publications to small and minority businesses in export operations. Contact your local or regional SBA office listed in the blue pages of your telephone book under Small Business Administration, or Small Business Administration, Office of International Trade, 409 3rd St., SW, Washington, DC 20416, 202-205-6720.

4) Overseas Private Investment Corporation (OPIC):

This agency provides marketing, insurance, and financial assistance to American companies investing in 118 countries and 16 geographic regions. Its programs include direct loans, loan guarantees, and political risk insurance. The Overseas Private Investment Corporation (OPIC) also sponsors seminars for investment executives as well as conducts investment missions to developing countries. The Investor Services Division offers a computer service to assist investors in identifying investment opportunities worldwide. A modest fee is charged for this service and it is also available through the Lexis/Nexis computer network. Specific Info-Kits are available identifying basic economic, business, and political information for each of the countries covered. In addition, it operates:

Program Information Hotline
Overseas Private Investment Corporation
1100 New York Ave., NW
Washington, DC 20527
202-336-8799 (Hotline)
202-336-8400 (General Information)
202-457-7128 (Investor Services Division)
202-336-8636 (Public Affairs)
202-336-8680 (Press Information)
202-408-5155 (Fax)

5) Agency For International Development (AID):

The Agency for International Development (AID) offers a variety of loan and financing guarantee programs for projects in developing countries that have a substantial developmental impact or for the exportation of manufactured goods to AID-assisted developing countries. Some investment opportunities are region specific, which include the Association of Southeast Asian National, the Philippines, and Africa. For more information contact the Office of Investment, Agency for International Development, 515 22nd St. NW, Room 301, Washington, DC 20523-0231, 202-663-2280.

6) Grants to Train Local Personnel

The Trade and Development Agency has the authority to offer grants in support of short-listed companies on a transaction specific basis. These are usually in the form of grants to cover the cost of training local personnel by the company on the installation, operation, and maintenance of equipment specific to bid the proposal. Contact: Carol Stillwell, 703-875-4357; Fax: 703-875-4009.

7) Consortia of American Businesses in Eastern Europe (CABEE):

The Consortia of American Businesses in Eastern Europe (CABEE) provides grant funds to trade organizations to defray the costs of opening, staffing, and operating U.S. consortia offices in Eastern Europe. The CABEE grant program initially began operations in Poland, the Czech Republic, Slovikia, and Hungary, targeting five industry sectors: agribusiness/ agriculture, construction/housing, energy, environment, and telecommunications. Contact: CABEE, Department of Commerce, 14th and Constitution Avenue, Washington, DC 20230, 202-482-5004.

8) Consortia of American Businesses in the Newly Independent States (CABNIS):

This program was modeled after CABEE and stimulates U.S. business in the Newly Independent States (NIS) and assist the region in its move toward privatization. The Consortia of American Businesses in the Newly Independent States (CABNIS) is providing grant funds to nonprofit organizations to defray the costs of opening, staffing, and operating U.S. consortia offices in the NIS. Contact: CABNIS, Department of Commerce, 14th and Constitution Avenue, Washington, DC 20230, 202-482-5004.

Marketing Data, Custom Studies, And Company Information

Further information on any of the following services and products can be obtained by contacting a U.S. Department of Commerce/US & FCS field office listed later in this chapter, or by contacting the US & FCS at: United States and Foreign Commercial Services, U.S. Department of Commerce, Room 3810, HCH Building, 14th and Constitution Ave., NW, Washington, DC 20230, 202-482-4767 or call 1-800-USA-TRADE.

1) International Industry Experts:

A separate Office of Trade Development at the Commerce Department handles special marketing and company problems for specific industries. Experts are available in the following international market sectors:

Aerospace:	202-482-2835
Automotive and Consumer Goods:	202-482-0823
Basic Industries:	202-482-5023
Capital Goods and International Construction:	202-482-5023
Science and Electronics:	202-482-3548
Telecommunications:	202-482-4466
Service:	202-482-5261
Textiles and Apparel:	202-482-3737

You can also talk to industry desk officers at the Department of Commerce. They can provide information on the competitive strengths of U.S. industries in foreign markets from abrasives to yogurt. They are listed in the "Experts" section at the end of this book and have "COMMERCE" after their name. You can call the Department of Commerce at 202-482-2000 (main office) or 1-800-872-8723 (trade information) to locate specific industry analysts.

2) Trade Lists:

Directories of overseas customers for U.S. exports in selected industries and countries: They contain the names and product lines of foreign distributors, agents, manufacturers, wholesalers, retailers, and other purchasers. They also provide the name and title of key officials as well as telex and cable numbers, and company size data. Prices range up to $40 for a list of a category.

3) Country Trade Statistics:

The Export and Import Trade Database maintains worldwide export and import statistics tracked by mode of transportation and port of entry or exit. Customized tabulation and reports can be prepared to user specifications. Prices begin at $25 and vary depending on job size. Contact: Trade Data Services Branch at 301-457-2311.

4) Demographic and Social Information:

The Center for International Research compiles and maintains up to date global demographic and social information for all countries in its International Data Base (IDB). Printed tables are available on selected subjects for selected countries can be purchased for a minimum of $75. Contact: Systems Analysis and Programming Staff, 301-457-1403.

5) Customized Export Mailing Lists:

Selected lists of foreign companies in particular industries, countries, and types of business can be requested by a client. Gummed labels are also available. Prices start at $35.

6) World Traders Data Reports:

Background reports are available on individual firms containing information about each firm's business activities, its standing in the local business community, its creditworthiness, and overall reliability and suitability as a trade contact for exporters. The price is $100 per report.

7) Agent Distributor Service (ADS):

This is a customized search for interested and qualified foreign representatives on behalf of an American client. U.S. commercial officers overseas conduct the search and prepare a report identifying up to six foreign prospects which have personally examined the U.S. firm's product literature and have expressed interest in representing the firm. A fee of $250 per country is charged.

8) New Product Information Service:

This service is designed to help American companies publicize the availability of new U.S. products in foreign markets and simultaneously test market interest in these products. Product information which meets the criteria is distributed worldwide through Commercial News USA and Voice of America broadcasts. A fee is charged for participation.

9) Customized Market Studies:

At a cost of $800 to $13,500 per country per product, these studies are called "Comparison Shopping Service". They are conducted by the U.S. Embassy foreign commercial attaches and can target information on quite specific marketing questions such as:

- Does the product have sales potential in the country?
- Who is the supplier for a comparable product locally?
- What is the going price for a comparable product in this country?
- What is the usual sales channel for getting this type of product into the market?
- What are the competitive factors that most influence purchases of these products in the market (i.e., price, credit, quality, delivery, service, promotion, brand)?
- What is the best way to get sales exposure in the market for this type of product?
- Are there any significant impediments to selling this type of product?
- Who might be interested and qualified to represent or purchase this company's products?
- If a licensing or joint venture strategy seems desirable for this market, who might be an interested and qualified partner for the U.S. company?

10) Special Opportunities in the Caribbean Basin and Latin America:

Under the Caribbean Economic Recovery Act of 1983, the government has established special incentives for American firms wishing to do business with Latin American and Caribbean Basin companies. Seminars, workshops, business development missions, business counseling, as well as marketing and competitive information are available.

Latin America/Caribbean Business
Development Center
U.S. Department of Commerce
Washington, DC 20230
202-482-0841
Fax: 202-482-2218

11) New Markets In Eastern European Countries

The Eastern Europe Business Information Center is stocked with a wide range of publications on doing business in Eastern Europe. These include lists of potential partners, investment regulations, priority industry sectors, and notices of upcoming seminars, conferences, and trade promotion events. The center also serves as a referral point for programs of voluntary assistance to the region.

Eastern Europe Business Information Center
U.S. Department of Commerce
Washington, DC 20230
202-482-2645
Fax: 202-482-4473

12) Exporting to Japan: Japan Export Information Center (JEIC)

The Japan Export Information Center (JEIC) provides business counseling services and accurate information on exporting to Japan. The JEIC is the point of contact for information on business in Japan, market entry alternatives, market information and research, product standards and testing, tariffs, and non-tariff barriers. The center maintains a commercial library and participates in seminars on various aspects of Japanese business. Contact: Japan Export Information Center, (202) 482-2425; Fax: (202) 482-0469.

13) Office of Export Trading Company Affairs

The Office of Export Trading Company offers various information as well as promoting the use of export trading companies and export management companies; offers information and counseling to businesses and trading associations regarding the export industry; and administers the Export Trade Certificate of Review program which provides exporters with an antitrust "insurance policy" intended to foster joint export activities where economies of scale and risk diversification are achieved. Contact: Office of Export Trading Company Affairs, 202-482-5131; Fax: 202-482-1790.

14) U.S.-Asia Environmental Partnership

The U.S.-Asia Environmental Partnership (US-AEP) is a comprehensive service to help U.S. environmental exporters enter markets in the Asia/Pacific region. It is a coalition of public, private and non-governmental organizations which promotes environmental protection and sustainable development in 34 nations in the Asia/Pacific area. Contact: 1-800-USA-TRADE or 202-482-0543; Fax: 202-482-4473.

15) Business Information Service for the Newly Independent States (BISNIS)

The Business Information Service for the Newly Independent States (BISNIS) provides "one stop shopping" for U.S. firms interested in doing business in the Newly Independent States (NIS) of the former Soviet Union. Information is available on commercial opportunities in the NIS, sources of financing, up to date lists of trade contacts as well as on U.S. Government programs supporting trade and investment in the region. BISNIS publishes a monthly bulletin with information on upcoming trade promotion events, practical advice on doing business with NIS and other topics. Contact: BISNIS, 202-482-4655; Fax: 202-482-2293.

16) **Technical Assistance with Transportation Concerns**

The Department of Transportation provides technical assistance to developing countries on a wide range of problems in the areas of transportation policy, highways, aviation, rail and ports. It also supports AID in the foreign aid development program. Contact: Bernestine Allen, International Transportation and Trade, 202-366-4398; Fax: 202-366-7417; Herbert Baschner, Federal Aviation Administration, 202-267-3173; Fax: 202-267-5306; John Cutrell, Federal Highway Administration, 202-366-0111; Fax: 202-366-9626; Ted Krohn, Federal Railroad Administration, 202-366-0555; Fax: 202-366-7688; James Treichel, Maritime Administration, 202-366-5773; Fax: 202-366-3746.

17) **"Doing Business"**

The "Doing Business" television program is a half-hour long monthly televised business program sent by satellite to more than 100 countries highlighting innovation and excellence in U.S. business. The program consists of segments on new products, services, and processes of interest to overseas buyers and promising research. Contact: Paul Vamvas, Worldnet Television, 202-501-8450; Fax: 202-501-6689.

18) **Japan's Official Development Assistance Program:**

This program is the central source for information about how to access procurement through Japan's foreign aid program. Contact: Robert Lurensky, Office of Energy, Environment and Infrastructure, 202-482-4002, Fax: 202-482-0136; Elizabeth Johns, Office of Japan Trade Policy, 202-482-1820; Fax: 202-482-0469.

19) **Environmental Technology Network for Asia (ETNA):**

The Environmental Technology Network for Asia (ETNA) matches environmental trade leads sent from U.S.-Asia Environmental Partnership (USAEP) Technology Representatives located in 9 Asian countries with appropriate U.S.

environmental firms and trade associations that are registered with ETNA's environmental trade opportunities database. U.S. environmental firms receive the trade leads by Broadcast Fax system within 48 hours of leads being identified and entered electronically from Asia. Contact: 202-663-2674; Fax: 202-663-2760.

20) **Automated Trade Locator Assistance System:**

The SBAtlas is a market research tool which provides free of charge two types of reports: product-specific and country-specific. The product report ranks the top 35 import and export market for a particular good or service. The country report identifies the top 20 products most frequently traded in a target market. Contact: SBAtlas is available through SBA district offices, Service Corps of Retired Executives (SCORE) office, and Small Business Development Centers, to get the address and phone number to the nearest office call 1-800-U-ASK-SBA.

21) **Export Contact List Service (ECLS):**

This database retrieval service provides U.S. exporters with names, addresses, products, sizes and other relevant information on foreign firms interested in importing U.S. goods and services. Similar information is also available on U.S. exporters to foreign firms seeking suppliers from the U.S. Names are collected and maintained by Commerce district offices and commercial officers at foreign posts. Contact your nearest district Commerce office located in this book or call 1-800-USA-TRADE.

Trade Fairs And Missions

Trade fairs, exhibitions, trade missions, overseas trade seminars, and other promotional events and services are sponsored by the Export Promotion Services Group, U.S. and Foreign Commercial Services, U.S. Department of Commerce, 14th and E Streets, NW, Room 2810, Washington, DC 20230, 202-482-6220. This office or one of its field offices which are listed later in this chapter can provide additional details on these activities.

1) Industry-Organized, Government-Approved Trade Missions:

Such missions are organized by trade associations, local Chambers of Commerce, state trade development agencies, and similar trade-oriented groups that enjoy U.S. Department of Commerce support.

2) Catalog Exhibitions:

Such exhibitions feature displays of U.S. product catalogs, sales brochures, and other graphic sales materials at American embassies and consulates or in conjunction with trade shows. A Department of Commerce specialist assists in the exhibition. Call 202-482-3973; Fax: 202-482-2716.

3) Video Catalog:

This catalog is designed to showcase American products via video tape presentation. This permits actual product demonstrations giving the foreign buyer an opportunity to view applications of American products. Federal specialists participate in these sessions. Call 202-482-3973; Fax: 202-482-0115.

4) U.S. Specialized Trade Missions:

These missions are distinct from those mentioned above since the U.S. Department of Commerce plans the visits and accompanies the delegation. They are designed to sell American goods and services as well as establish agents or representation abroad. The Department of Commerce provides marketing information, advanced planning, publicity, and trip organization. Call 1-800-USA-TRADE.

5) U.S. Seminar Missions:

The objective here is to promote exports and help foreign representation for American exporters. However, unlike trade missions, these are designed to facilitate the sales of state-of-the-art products and technology. This type of mission is a one to two day "seminar" during which team members discuss technology subjects followed by private, sales-oriented appointments. Call 1-800-USA-TRADE.

6) Matchmaker Trade Delegations:

These Department of Commerce-recruited and planned missions are designed to introduce new-to-export or new-to-market businesses to prospective agents and distributors overseas. Trade Specialists from Commerce evaluate the potential firm's products, find and screen contacts, and handle logistics. This is followed by an intensive trip filled with meetings and prospective clients and in-depth briefings on the economic and business climate of the countries visited. Call Office of Export Promotion Services, 202-482-3119; Fax: 202-482-0178.

7) Investment Missions:

These events are held in developing countries offering excellent investment opportunities for U.S. firms. Missions introduce U.S. business executives to key business leaders, potential joint venture partners, and senior foreign government officials in the host country. Call Investment Missions, 202-336-8799; Fax: 202-408-5155.

8) Foreign Buyer Program:

This program supports major domestic trade shows featuring products and services of U.S. industries with high export potential. Government officials recruit on a worldwide basis qualified buyers to attend the shows. Call Export Promotion Services, 202-482-0481; Fax: 202-482-0115.

9) Trade Fairs, Solo Exhibitions, and Trade Center Shows:

The Department of Commerce organizes a wide variety of special exhibitions. These events range from solo exhibitions representing U.S. firms exclusively at trade centers overseas to U.S. pavilions in the largest international exhibitions. Call 1-800-USA-TRADE.

10) **Agent/Distributor Service (ADS):**
Looking for overseas representatives to expand your business and boost your export sales? Commerce will locate, screen, and assess agents, distributors, representatives, and other foreign partners for your business. Call 1-800-USA-TRADE.

11) **Trade Opportunities Program (TOP):**
The Trade Opportunities Program (TOP) provides companies with current sales leads from international firms seeking to buy or represent their products or services. TOP leads are printed daily in leading commercial newspapers and are also distributed electronically via the U.S. Department of Commerce Economic Bulletin Board. Call 202-482-1986; Fax: 202-482-2164.

12) **Travel and Tourism:**
The U.S. Travel and Tourism Administration (USTTA) promotes export earnings through trade in tourism. USTTA stimulates demand for travel to the U.S.; encourages and facilitates promotion in international travel markets by U.S. travel industry concerns; works to increase the number of new-to-market travel businesses participating in the export market; forms cooperative marketing opportunities for private industry and regional, state, and local government; provides timely data; and helps to remove government-imposed travel barriers. Call 202-482-4904, 202-482-4752; Fax: 202-482-2887.

13) **Gold Key Service:**
This customized service is aimed at U.S. firms which are planning to visit a country. Offered by many overseas posts, it combines several services such as market orientation briefings, market research, introductions to potential partners, and interpreters for meetings, assistance in developing a sound market strategy, and an effective followup plan. Call 1-800-USA-TRADE.

Special Programs for Agricultural Products

The following programs are specifically aimed at those who wish to sell agricultural products overseas. Agricultural exporters should also be sure not to limit themselves only to programs under this heading. Programs listed under other headings can also be used for agricultural products.

1) **Office Space for Agricultural Exporters:**
The Foreign Agriculture Service (FAS) maintains overseas agricultural trade offices to help exporters of U.S. farm and forest products in key overseas markets. The facilities vary depending on local conditions, but may include a trade library, conference rooms, office space, and kitchens for preparing product samples. Contact: Foreign Agriculture Service, U.S. Department of Agriculture, 14th and Independence Ave. SW, Washington, DC 20250, 202-720-9509; Fax: 202-690-4374.

2) **Research Services:**
The Agricultural Research Service provides exporters with information, research, and consultants on a wide array of topics including shipping, storage, insect control, pesticide residues, and market disorders. Contact: Agricultural and Trade Analysis Division, U.S. Department of Agriculture, 14th and Independence Avenue, SW, Washington, DC 20250, 202-219-0700; Fax: 202-219-0759.

3) **Foreign Market Information:**
A special office serves as a single contact point within the Foreign Agriculture Service for agricultural exporters seeking foreign market information. The office also counsels firms which believe they have been injured by unfair trade practices. Contact: Trade Assistance and Promotion Office, U.S. Dept. of Agriculture, 14th and Independence Avenue, SW, Washington, DC 20250, 202-720-7420; Fax: 202-720-3229.

4)   Export Connections:
The AgExport Action Kit provides information which can help put U.S. exporters in touch quickly and directly with foreign importers of food and agricultural products. The services include trade leads, a *Buyer Alert* newsletter, foreign buyer lists, and U.S. supplier lists. All services are free. Contact: AgExport Connections, U.S. Department of Agriculture, Washington, DC 20250, 202-720-7103; Fax: 202-690-4374.

5)   Country Market Profiles:
Country-specific two to four page descriptions are available for 40 overseas markets for high value agricultural products. They provide market overview, market trends, and information on the U.S. market position, the competition, and general labeling and licensing requirements. Contact: Country Market Profiles, FAS Information Division, U.S. Department of Agriculture, Washington, DC 20250, 202-720-7420; Fax: 202-720-3229.

```
┌─────────────────────────────────────┐
│   Export Regulations, Licensing,     │
│        And Product Standards         │
└─────────────────────────────────────┘
```

Talk to ELVIS — Bureau of Export Administration (BXA)
BXA is responsible for controlling exports for reasons of national security, foreign policy, and short supply. Licenses on controlled exports are issued, and seminars on U.S. export regulations are held domestically and overseas.

Export license applications may be submitted and issued through computer via the Export License Application and Information Network (ELAIN). The System for Tracking Export License Application (STELA) provides instant status updates on license applications by the use of a touch-tone phone.

The Export Licensing Voice Information (ELVIS) is an automated attendant that offers a range of licensing information and emergency handling procedures. Callers may order forms and publications or subscribe to the *Office of Export Licensing (OEL) Insider Newsletter*, which provides regulatory updates. While using ELVIS, a caller has the option of speaking to a consultant.

Office of Export Licensing   202-482-4811
                             Fax: 202-482-3322
ELAIN   202-482-4811
STELA   202-482-2752
ELVIS   202-482-4811

The National Institute of Standards and Technology provides a free service which will identify standards for selling any product to any country in the world. This federal agency will tell you what the standard is for a given product or suggest where you can obtain an official copy of the standard.

National Center for Standards and
   Certification
National Institute of Standards and
   Technology
Building 411, Room A163
Gaithersburg, MD 20899   301-975-4040

```
┌─────────────────────────────────────┐
│        Cheap Office And              │
│    Conference Space Overseas         │
└─────────────────────────────────────┘
```

If you are travelling overseas on a business trip, you may want to look into renting office space and other services through the American Embassy. Depending on the country and the space available, the embassy can provide temporary office space for as low as $25 per day, along with translation services, printing, and other services. Meeting rooms, seminar or convention space along with promotion services, mailings, freight handling, and even catering may be available in many countries. Contact the Department of Commerce/US & FCS field office which is listed later in this chapter, or the appropriate country desk officer at the U.S. Department of Commerce in Washington, DC.

Other Services, Resources, And Databases

The following is a description of some other services and information sources that can be useful to anyone investigating overseas markets:

1) World Import/Export Statistics:

For the latest information on any product imported to or exported from any foreign country, contact: Foreign and U.S. Trade Reference Room, U.S. Department of Commerce, Room 2233, Washington, DC 20230, 202-482-4855.

2) Help In Selling To Developing Nations:

The U.S. Agency For International Development (AID) provides information to U.S. suppliers, particularly small, independent enterprises, regarding purchases to be financed with AID funds. U.S. small businesses can obtain special counseling and related services in order to furnish equipment, materials, and services to AID-financed projects. AID sponsors Development Technologies Exhibitions, where technical firms in the U.S. are matched up with those in lesser developed countries for the purpose of forming joint ventures or exploring licensing possibilities. AID provides loans and grants to finance consulting services that support project activities related to areas such as agriculture, rural development, health, and housing. Contact: Office of Business Relations, U.S. Agency for International Development, State Annex 14, Room 1200A, 320 21st St., NW, Washington, DC 20523, 703-875-1551.

3) Foreign Demographic Profiles:

The Government Printing office has a publication called the CIA *World Factbook*. Produced annually, this publication provides country-by-country data on demographics, economy, communications, and defense. The cost is $29 (GPO: 041-015-00173-6). Order by contacting Superintendent of Documents,

Government Printing Office, Washington, DC 20402; 202-512-1800.

4) Help With Selling Commodities Abroad:

The Foreign Agricultural Service is charged with maintaining and expanding export sales of U.S. agricultural commodities and products. Staff can provide information on foreign agricultural production, trade and consumption, marketing research including areas of demand for specific commodities in foreign countries, and analyses of foreign competition in agricultural areas. Other services include financing opportunities, contributing to export promotion costs, and testing market assistance. This office also handles U.S. representation to foreign governments and participates in formal trade negotiations. Contact: Foreign Agricultural Service, U.S. Department of Agriculture, 14th and Independence Ave., SW, Room 4647, South Building, Washington, DC 20250, 202-720-7420.

5) International Prices:

Export price indexes for both detailed and aggregate product groups are available on a monthly basis. Price trends comparisons of U.S. exports with those of Japan and Germany are also available. Contact: International Prices Division, Bureau of Labor Statistics, U.S. Dept. of Labor, 2nd Massachusetts Ave., NE, Room 3955, Washington, DC 20212, 202-606-7100.

6) Identifying Overseas Opportunities:

The International Trade Administration (ITA) of the Commerce Department assists American exporters in locating and gaining access to foreign markets. It furnishes information on overseas markets available for U.S. products and services, requirements which must be fulfilled, economic conditions in foreign countries, foreign market and investment opportunities, etc. Operations are divided into four major areas:

- **International Economic Policy:** promotes U.S. exports geographically by helping American businesses market products in various locations abroad and by solving the trade and investment problems they encounter. This office is staffed by Country Desk Officers knowledgeable in marketing and business practices for almost every country in the world. Contact: Office of International Economic Policy, ITA, U.S. Department of Commerce, Washington, DC 20230, 202-482-3022.

- **Export Administration:** supervises the enforcement provisions of the Export Administration Act, and administers the Foreign Trade Zone Program. Personnel in its export enforcement and its administration, policy, and regulations offices can offer technical advice and legal interpretations of the various export legislation which affect American businesses. Assistance in complying with export controls can be obtained directly from the Exporter Counseling Division within the Bureau of Export Administration (BXA) Office of Export Licensing in Washington, DC, 202-482-4811.

BXA also has four field offices that specialize in counseling on export controls and regulations:

Western Regional Office	714-660-0144
Northern California Branch Office	408-748-7450
Southern Branch Office	714-660-0144
New England Office	603-598-4300

- **Trade Development:** advises businesses on trade and investment issues, and promotes U.S. exports by industry or product classifications. Offices offer assistance and information on export counseling, statistics and trade data, licensing, trading companies, and other services. Contact: Office of Trade Development, ITA, U.S. Department of Commerce, Washington, DC 20230, 202-482-1461; Fax: 202-482-5697.

- **U.S. and Foreign Commercial Service:** provides information on government programs to American businesses, and uncovers trade opportunities for U.S. exporters. They also locate representatives and agents for American firms, assist U.S. executives in all phases of their exporting, and help enforce export controls and regulations. They operate through 47 district offices located in major U.S. cities and in 124 posts in 69 foreign countries. In addition, a valued asset of the U.S. and Foreign Commercial Services is a group of about 525 foreign nationals, usually natives of the foreign country, who are employed in the U.S. embassy or consulate and bring with them a wealth of personal understanding of local market conditions and business practices. U.S. exporters usually tap into these services by contacting the Department of Commerce/US & FCS field office in their state (listed later in this chapter), or Office of U.S. and Foreign Commercial Service, U.S. Department of Commerce, Washington, DC 20230; 1-800-USA-TRADE.

Or contact regional directors at:

Africa, Near East and Southeast Asia	202-482-4925
East Asia and Pacific	202-482-5251
Europe	202-482-5638
Western Hemisphere	202-482-5324
Japan	202-482-4527
FAX (Europe and Western Hemisphere)	202-482-3159
FAX (All others)	202-482-5179

7) **Latest News On Foreign Opportunities:** In addition to technical reports on foreign research and development, the National Technical Information Service (NTIS) sells foreign market airgrams and foreign press and radio translations. A free video is available explaining NTIS services. Contact: National Technical Information Service, U.S. Department of Commerce, 5285 Port Royal Rd., Springfield, VA 22161, 703-487-4650.

8) Planning Services for U.S. Exporters:
In its effort to promote economic development in Third World countries, the Trade and Development Program finances planning services for development projects leading to the export of U.S. goods and services. A free pamphlet is available that describes the planning services offered by the Trade and Development Program. To obtain a copy, contact: U.S. Trade and Development Program, Department of State, Room 309 SA-16, Washington, DC 20523-1602, 703-875-4357.

9) Terrorism Abroad:
Assistance is available to companies doing business abroad to assess current security conditions and risk in certain cities and countries which may pose a threat. Contact: Overseas Security Advisory Council (OSAC), U.S. Department of State, Washington, DC 20522-1003, 202-663-0533.

10) Trade Remedy Assistance Center:
The Center provides information on remedies available under the Trade Remedy Law. It also offers technical assistance to eligible small businesses to enable them to bring cases to the International Trade Commission. Contact: ITC Trade Remedy Assistance Center, U.S. International Trade Commission, 500 E St. SW, Washington, DC 20436, 202-205-2200.

11) International Expertise:
Staff in the following offices will prove helpful as information sources regarding the international scope of their respective subject areas:

Economics:
International Investment, Bureau of Economic Analysis, U.S. Dept. of Commerce, 1441 L St., NW, Washington, DC 20230, 202-606-9800.

Productivity and Technology Statistics:
Bureau of Labor Statistics, U.S. Dept. of Labor, 2 Massachusetts Ave., NE, #2150, Washington, DC 20212, 202-606-5600.

Investments and Other Monetary Matters:
Office of Assistant Secretary for International Affairs, U.S. Dept. of the Treasury, Room 3430, Washington, DC 20220, 202-622-0060.

European Lifestyles:
European Community Information Service, 2100 M St. NW, 7th Floor, Washington, DC 20037, 202-862-9500.

Population:
Barbara Boyle Torrey, Chief, Center for International Research, Bureau of Census, U.S. Department of Commerce, Room 205, Washington Plaza, Washington, DC 20233, 301-457-1403.

Population Reference Bureau, Inc., 1875 Connecticut Ave., NW, #520, Washington, DC 20009, 202-483-1100.

Country Development:
Inter-American Development Bank, 1300 NY Ave., NW, Washington, DC 20577, 202-623-1000.

International Monetary Fund, 700 19th St. NW, Washington, DC 20431, 202-623-7000.

World Bank, 1818 H St. NW, Washington, DC 20433, 202-477-1234.

12) National Trade Data Bank (NTDB):
This is a "one-stop" source for export promotion and international trade data collected by 17 U.S. government agencies. Updated each month and released on CD-ROM, the Data Bank enables a user with an IBM-compatible personal computer equipped with a CD-ROM reader to access over 100,00 trade documents. It contains the latest Census data on U.S. imports and exports by commodity and country; the complete Central Intelligence Agency (CIA) *World Factbook*; current market research reports compiled by the U.S. and Foreign and Commercial Service; the

complete Foreign Traders Index which has over 60,000 names and addresses of individuals and firms abroad interested in importing U.S. products; and many other data services. It is available for free at over 900 Federal Depository Libraries and can be purchased for $35 per disc or $360 for a 12-month subscription. Contact: Economics and Statistics Administration, U.S. Department of Commerce, Washington, DC 20230, 202-482-1986; Fax: 202-482-2164.

13) Global Demographics:

The Center for International Research at the Department of Commerce compiles and maintains up-to-date global demographic and social information for all countries in its International Data Base, which is accessible to U.S. companies seeking to identify potential markets overseas. Contact Systems Analysis and Programming Staff, 301-457-1403.

14) International Energy Database:

The Office of Fossil Energy forwards prospective energy-related leads to the Agency for International Development (AID) for inclusion in its growing trade opportunities database in an effort to reach an extended audience seeking energy-related trade opportunities. For more information on the Fossil Energy-AID Database contact: The Office of Fossil Energy, U.S. Department of Energy, 1000 Independence Ave. SW, Washington, DC 20585, 202-586-9680.

15) Product Info On 25 World Markets:

The Small Business Administration has an Export Information System (XIS), which are data reports providing specific product or service information on the top 25 world markets and market growth trends for the past five years. Contact: Office of International Trade, Small Business Administration, 409 Third St. SW, Washington, DC 20416, 202-205-6766.

16) On-Line Economic Bulletin Board (EBB):

This computer-based electronic bulletin board, is an online source for trade leads as well as the latest statistical releases from the Bureau of Census, the Bureau of Economic Analysis, the Bureau of Labor Statistics, the Federal Reserve Board, and other federal agencies. Subscribers pay an annual fee, plus cost per minute. Contact: EBB, Office of Business Analysis, U.S. Department of Commerce, Washington, DC 20230, 202-482-1986.

Now use your fax machine to get the latest economic, financial, and trade news available from the U.S. government. Just dial 1-900-786-2329 from your fax machine's touchtone telephone and follow the simple voice instructions. EBB/FAX™ stores the complete text of many government press releases and information files. The cost for this service is 65¢ per minute. Charges will appear on your regular phone bill and there are no registration fees. The list of files is updated every business day and service is available 24 hours a day, 7 days a week.

17) Free Legal Assistance:

The Export Legal Assistance Network (ELAN) is a nationwide group of attorneys with experience in international trade who provide free initial consultations to small businesses on export related matters. Contact: Export Legal Assistance Network, Small Business Administration, 409 Third St. SW, Washington, DC 20416, 202-778-3080; Fax: 202-778-3063.

18) Global Learning:

U.S. Department of Education, Business and International Education Programs. The business and international education program is designed to engage U.S. schools of business language and area programs, international study programs, public and private sector organizations, and U.S. businesses in a mutually productive relationship which will benefit the nation's future economic interest. Approximately $2.3 million annually is available to assist U.S. institutions of higher education to promote the nation's capacity for international understanding. Typical grantee activities include executive seminars, case studies, and export skill workshops. For more information contact: Center for International Education, U.S. Department of Education, 600 Independence Ave., SW, Washington, DC 20202; 202-401-9798.

19) Export Counseling — SCORE, ACE:
The Small Business Administration (SBA) can provide export counseling to small business exporters by retired and active business executives. Members of the Service Corps of Retired Executives (SCORE) and the Active Corps of Executives (ACE), with years of practical experience in international trade, assist small firms in evaluating their export potential and developing and implementing basic export marketing plans. For more information, contact your local SBA office listed in the government pages of your telephone book, or National SCORE Office, 1825 Connecticut Ave., NW, Suite 503, Washington, DC 20009; 800-634-0245; Fax: 202-705-7636.

20) Department of Energy — Office of International Affairs and Energy Emergencies:
The Department of Energy (DOE) promotes U.S. exports of energy goods, services, and technology primarily through participation in The Committee on Renewable Energy Commerce and Trade, and The Coal and Clean Technology Export Program. The following is a list of DOE's programs and the corresponding telephone numbers to call for more information.

Committee on Renewable Energy Commerce and Trade (CORECT): Through the concept of "one-stop shopping" potential exporters can receive comprehensive advice on potential markets, financing and information on export guidelines. Call the Office of Conservation and Renewable Energy, 202-586-8302; Fax: 202-586-1605.

Coal and Technology Export Program (CTEP): CTEP serves as a reservoir for international information on U.S. coal and coal technologies, as the Department of

Energy's intra-departmental coordinator, and as the USG inter-agency liaison for coal companies and technology firms. Call 202-586-7297.

The Export Assistance Initiative: This entity in the Bureau of International Affairs has been designed to help identify overseas opportunities for U.S. companies, identify and attempt to alleviate discriminatory trade barriers, and identify possible financing alternatives for U.S. companies. Call 202-586-1189.

21) Fax Retrieval Systems
A number of offices offer documents on demand, delivered directly to a fax machine 24 hours a day. These automated systems each have a menu of available documents which can be sent to a fax machine by dialing from a touch-tone phone and following directions. Below is a list of offices who offer this program:

Uruguay Round Hotline: This Fax retrieval system is located at the Trade Information Center and has information on the GATT agreement. Document #1000 is the menu of available information packets; 1-800-872-8723.

Eastern European Business Information Center (EEBIC): This Fax system has 5 main menus. Menu document #1000 has export and financing information. Document #2000 has a menu of documents relating to export and investment opportunities and upcoming trade events. A listing of Eastern European country information is available on document #3000. Documents #4000 and #5000 have information on the *Eastern Europe Business Bulletin*, and the *Eastern Europe Looks For Partners* publications; 202-482-5745.

Business Information Service for the Newly Independent States: There are 3 menus available through BISNIS. Menu number 1, document #0001 has trade and investment opportunities and trade promotion information. Menu number 2, document #0002 has industry and country specific information, and financing alternatives. Menu number 3, document #0003, has information on BISNIS publications; 202-482-3145.

Office of Mexico: The main menu for Mexico is document #0101. There is also a menu of labeling and standards requirements (document #8404). Information on documents relating to the certificate of origin and rules of origin under NAFTA is document #5000. A complete NAFTA tariff schedule is on document #6000; 202-482-4464.

Office of Canada: The main menu for Canada is document #0100. The number for the Canadian tariff schedule listed by Harmonized System tariff classification is document #0220; 202-482-3101.

Office of the Pacific Basin: The menu for the Pacific Basin system is document #1000. A listing of documents regarding Vietnam are available by requesting document #8600; 202-482-3875 or 202-482-3646.

Office of Africa, Near East, and South Asia: A list of documents covering the nations of the Near East is document #0100. Africa is #3000 and South Asian countries is #4000; 202-482-1064.

Overseas Private Investment Corporation: This system has information on OPIC project finance and political risk insurance programs; 202-336-8700.

22) International Visitors Program

Foreign individuals or groups are brought to the U.S. for about one month. The programs feature visits by business leaders and foreign government officials who have the opportunity to meet with their U.S. counterparts. Contact: William Codus, Office of Education/Voluntary Visitors, U.S. Information Agency, 202-619-5217; Fax: 202-205-0792.

Read All About It: Helpful Publications

Basic Guide to Exporting:

This publication outlines the sequence of steps necessary to determine whether to, and how to, use foreign markets as a source of profits. It describes the various problems which confront smaller firms engaged in, or seeking to enter, international trade, as well as the types of assistance available. It also provides a guide to appraising the sales potential of foreign markets and to understanding the requirements of local business practices and procedures in overseas markets. The booklet is available for $9.50 (GPO: 003-009-00604-0) from: Superintendent of Documents, U.S. Government Printing Office, Washington, DC 20402, 202-512-1800.

Exporter's Guide to Federal Resources for Small Business:

This free booklet describes the types of assistance available for small businesses interested in international trade opportunities. It is available from any of the Small Business Administration field offices or by contacting: Office of International Trade, U.S. Small Business Administration, 409 3rd St., SW, 6th Floor, Washington, DC 20416, 202-205-6720.

Commercial News USA:

This publication describes a free export promotion service that will publicize the availability of your new product to foreign markets, and test foreign market interest in your new product. There is a small fee. Contact: Marketing Programs Section,

Room 2106, U.S. Dept. of Commerce, Washington, DC 20230, 202-482-4918.

Export Programs: A Business Directory of U.S. Government Resources:

This guide provides an overview of U.S. government export assistance programs and contact points for further information and expertise in utilizing these programs. Contact: Trade Information Center, U.S. Department of Commerce, Washington, DC 20230, 1-800-872-8723.

Business America:

The principal Commerce department publication for presenting domestic and international business news. Each monthly issue includes a "how to" article for new exporters, discussion of U.S. trade policy, news of government actions that may affect trade, a calendar of upcoming trade shows, exhibits, fairs, and seminars. The annual subscription is $32 (GPO: 703-011-0000-4-W). Contact: Superintendent of Documents, Government Printing Office, Washington, DC 20402, 202-512-1800.

Key Officers of Foreign Service Posts: A Guide for Business Representatives:

Lists the names of key State and Commerce officers at U.S. embassies and consulates. Cost is $3.75 per copy. Contact: Superintendent of Documents, Government Printing Office, Washington, DC 20402, 202-512-1800.

Export Trading Company (ETC) Guidebook:

This Guidebook is intended to assist those who are considering starting or expanding exporting through the various forms of an ETC. The Guidebook will also facilitate your review of the ETC Act and export trading options and serve as a planning tool for your business by showing you what it takes to export profitably and how to start doing it. Cost is $11 (GPO: 003-009-00523-0). Contact: Superintendent of Docu-

ments, Government Printing Office, Washington, DC 20402, 202-512-1800.

Foreign Labor Trends:

Published by the Department of Labor, these are a series of reports, issued annually, that describe and analyze labor trends in more than 70 countries. The reports, which are prepared by the American Embassy in each country, cover labor-management relations, trade unions, employment and unemployment, wages and working conditions, labor and government, international labor activities, and other significant developments. Contact: Office of Foreign Relations, Room S 5006, 200 Constitution Ave., NW, Washington, DC 20210, 202-523-6257, 202-219-6257.

ABC's of Exporting:

This is a special issue of Business America which takes you step by step through the exporting process. It explains the federal agencies and how they can help, as well as providing a directory of export sources. This publication is free and is available by contacting: Trade Information Center, U.S. Department of Commerce, Washington, DC 20230, 1-800-872-8723.

Ag Exporter:

Monthly magazine published by the U.S. Department of Agriculture's Foreign Agricultural Service (FAS). The annual subscription cost is $17 (GPO: 701-027-00000-1). Contact: Superintendent of Documents, Government Printing Office, Washington, DC 20402; 202-512-1800.

AID Procurement Information Bulletin:

This publication advertises notices of intended procurement of AID-financed commodities. The subscription cost is free. Contact: USAID's Office of Small and Disadvantaged Business Utilization/ Minority Resource Center, Washington, DC 20523-1414; 703-875-1551.

The Government Printing Office (GPO) has many titles to choose from. For a listing, contact the GPO (listed below) by mail, or phone and ask for the Foreign Trade and Tariff Subject Bibliography (SB-123; 021-123-00405-1).

Government Printing Office
Superintendent of Documents
Washington, DC 20402
202-512-1800

U.S. Department of Commerce/ US & FCS Field Offices

Trade experts at these 64 offices advise companies on foreign markets.

Alabama
Birmingham: 950 22nd St., N, Room 707, 35203, 205-731-1331; Fax: 205-731-0076.

Alaska
Anchorage: 4201 Tudor Center Dr., World Trade Center, Suite 319, 99508-5916, 907-271-6237; Fax: 907-271-6242.

Arizona
Phoenix: 2901 North Central Ave., Phoenix Plaza, Suite 970, 85012, 602-640-2513; Fax: 602-640-2518.

Arkansas
Little Rock: 425 West Capitol Ave., TCBY Tower Building, Suite 700, 72201, 501-324-5794; Fax: 501-324-7380.

California
Los Angeles: 11000 Wilshire Blvd., Room 9200, 90024, 310-575-7104; Fax: 310-575-7220.
Long Beach: One World Trade Center, Suite 1670, 90831, 310-980-4550; Fax: 310-980-4561.
Newport Beach: 3300 Irvine Ave., Suite 305, 92660, 714-660-1688; Fax: 714-660-8039.
San Diego: 6363 Greenwich Drive, 92122, 619-557-5395; Fax: 619-557-6176.
San Francisco: 250 Montgomery St., 14th Floor, 94104, 415-705-2300; Fax: 415-705-2297.
Santa Clara: 5201 Great America Pkwy., Techmart Building, Suite 456, 95054, 408-970-4610; Fax: 408-970-4618.

Colorado
Denver: 1625 Broadway, Suite 680, 80202, 303-844-6623; Fax: 303-844-5651.

Connecticut
Hartford: 450 Main St., Room 610-B, 06103, 203-240-3530; Fax: 203-240-3473.

District of Columbia
Served by Baltimore, MD, U.S. Export Assistance Center.

Delaware
Served by Philadelphia, PA, District Office.

Florida
Miami: 5600 Northwest 36th St., Trade Port Building, 6th Floor, 33166, 305-526-7425; Fax: 305-526-7434.
Clearwater: 128 North Osceola Ave., 34615, 813-461-0011; Fax 813-449-2889.
Tallahassee: 107 W. Gaines St., Collins Bldg., Room 366G, 32399, 904-488-6469; Fax: 904-487-1407.

Georgia
Atlanta: 4360 Chamber-Dunwoody Road, Suite 310, 30341, 404-452-9101; Fax: 404-452-9105.
Savannah: 120 Barnard St., A-107, 31401, 912-652-4204; Fax: 912-652-4241.

Hawaii
Honolulu: 300 Ala Moana Blvd., Room 4106, Box 50026, 96850, 808-541-1782; Fax: 808-541-3435.

Idaho
Boise: 700 W. State St., Box 83720, Boise, 83720, 208-334-3857; Fax: 208-334-2361.

Illinois
Chicago: 55 W. Monroe, Xerox Center Suite 2440, 60603, 312-353-8040; Fax: 312-353-8120.
Rockford: 515 N. Court St., 61110-0247, 815-987-4347; Fax: 815-987-8122.

Indiana
Indianapolis: 11405 N. Pennsylvania St., Penwood One, Suite 106, Carmel, IN 46032, 317-582-2300; Fax: 317-582-2301.

Iowa
Des Moines: 210 Walnut St., Room 817, 50309, 515-284-4222; Fax: 515-284-4021.

Kansas
Wichita: 151 North Volutsia, 67214-4695, 316-269-6160; Fax: 316-683-7326.

Kentucky
Louisville: 601 W. Broadway, Room 636B, 40202, 502-582-5066; Fax: 502-582-6573.

Louisiana
New Orleans: 501 Magazine St., Hale Boggs Federal Building, Room 1043, 70130, 504-589-6546; Fax: 504-589-2337.

Maine
Augusta: 187 State St., Suite 59, 04333, 207-622-8249; Fax: 207-626-9156.

Maryland
Baltimore: 401 East Pratt St., World Trade Center, Suite 2432, 21202, 410-962-4539; Fax: 410-962-4529.

Massachusetts
Boston: World Trade Center, Suite 307, 02210, 617-424-5950; Fax: 617-424-5992.

Michigan
Detroit: 477 Michigan Ave., 1140 McNamara Bldg., 48226, 313-226-3650; Fax: 313-226-3657.
Grand Rapids: 300 Monroe NW, Room 408, 49503, 616-456-2411; Fax: 616-456-2695.

Minnesota
Minneapolis: 110 S. 4th St., Room 108, 55401, 612-348-1638; Fax: 612-348-1650.

Mississippi
Jackson: 201 W. Capitol St., Suite 310, 39201-2005, 601-965-4388 Fax: 601-965-5386.

Missouri
St. Louis: 8182 Maryland Ave., Suite 303, 63105, 314-425-3302; Fax: 314-425-3381.
Kansas City: 601 E. 12th St., Room 635, 64106, 816-426-3141; Fax: 816-426-3140.

Montana
Served by Boise, Idaho, Branch Office.

Nebraska
Omaha: 11133 O St., 68137, 402-221-3664; Fax: 402-221-3668.

Nevada
Reno: 1755 E. Plumb Lane, #152, 89502, 702-784-5203; Fax: 702-784-5343.

New Hampshire
Portsmouth (Boston, Massachusetts, District Office): 601 Spaulding Turnpike, Suite 29, 03801-2833, 603-334-6074; Fax: 603-334-6110.

New Jersey
Trenton: 3131 Princeton Pike Building 6, Suite 100, 08648, 609-989-2100; Fax: 609-989-2395.

New Mexico
Santa Fe: c/o Department of Economic Development, 1100 St. Francis Dr., 87503, 505-827-0350; Fax: 505-827-0263.

New York
Buffalo: 111 W. Huron St., Room 1312, Federal Building, 14202, 716-846-4191; Fax: 716-846-5290.
Rochester: 111 East Ave., 14604, 716-263-6480; Fax: 716-325-6505.
New York: 26 Federal Plaza, Room 3718, 10278, 212-264-0634; Fax: 212-264-1356.

North Carolina
Greensboro: 400 West Market St., Suite 400, 27401, 919-333-5345; Fax: 919-333-5158.

North Dakota
Served by Minneapolis, Minnesota, District Office.

Ohio
Cincinnati: 9504 Federal Building, 550 Main St., 45202, 513-684-2944; Fax: 513-684-3200.
Cleveland: 600 Superior Ave., Bank One Center, Suite 700, 44114, 216- 522-4750; Fax: 216-522-2235.

Oklahoma
Oklahoma City: 6601 Broadway Extension, Room 200, 73116, 405-231-5302; Fax: 405-841-5245.
Tulsa: 440 S. Houston St., Suite 505, 74127, 918-581-7650; Fax: 918-581-2844.

Oregon
Portland: Suite 242, One World Trade Center, 121 SW Salmon St., 97204, 503-326-3001; Fax: 503-326-6351.

Pennsylvania
Philadelphia: 660 American Ave., Suite 201, King of Prussia, PA 19406, 215-962-4980; Fax: 215-962-4989.
Pittsburgh: 1000 Liberty Ave., Room 2002, 15222, 412-644-2850; Fax: 412-644-4875.

Puerto Rico
San Juan: Room G-55 Federal Building, Chardon Ave. 00918, 809-766-5555; Fax: 809-766-5692.

Rhode Island
Providence: 7 Jackson Walkway, 02903, 401-528-5104; Fax: 401-528-5067.

South Carolina
Columbia: 1835 Assembly St., Suite 172, 29201, 803-765-5345; Fax: 803-253-3614.
Charleston: c/o Trident Technical College, Box 118067, CE-P, 66 Columbus St., 29423, 803-727-4051; Fax: 803-727-4052.

South Dakota
Served by Omaha, Nebraska, District Office.

Tennessee
Nashville: 404 James Robertson Pkwy., Suite 114, 37219, 615-736-5161; Fax: 615-736-2454.
Memphis: 22 N. Front St., Suite 200, 38103, 901-544-4137; Fax: 901-575-3510.

Texas
Dallas: 2050 N. Stemmons Freeway, Suite 170, Box 58130, 75258, 214-767-0542; Fax: 214-767-8240.
Austin: 410 E. 5th St., Suite 414A, Box 12728, 78711, 512-482-5939; Fax: 512-482-5940.
Houston: 1 Allen Center, Suite 1160, 500 Dallas 77002, 713-229-2578; Fax: 713-229-2203.

Utah
Salt Lake City: Suite 105, 324 S. State St., 84111, 801-524-5116; Fax: 801-524-5886.

Vermont
Montpelier: 109 State St., 4th Floor, 05609, 802-828-4508; Fax: 802-828-3258.

Virginia
Richmond: 704 E. Franklin St., 700 Center, Suite 550, 23219 804-771-2246; Fax: 804-771-2390.

Washington
Seattle: 3131 Elliott Ave., Suite 290, 98121, 206-553-5615; Fax: 206-553-7253.
Tri Cities: 320 N. Johnson St., Suite 350, Kennewick, WA 99336, 509-735-2751; Fax: 509-735-9385.

West Virginia
Charleston: 405 Capitol St., Suite 807, 25301, 304-347-5123; Fax: 304-347-5408.

Wisconsin
Milwaukee: 517 E. Wisconsin Ave., Room 596, 53202, 414-297-3473; Fax: 414-297-3470.

Wyoming
Served by Denver, Colorado, District Office.

State Government Assistance To Exporters

Last year state governments spent approximately $40,000,000 to help companies in their state sell goods and services overseas. This figure increased almost 50% over the previous two years. During the same period of time, federal monies devoted to maximizing companies' export capabilities remained virtually constant. This is another indicator of how the states are fertile sources of information and expertise for large and small businesses.

The underlying mission of these offices is to create jobs within their state. Usually their approach is to help companies develop overseas marketing strategies or to offer incentives to foreign companies to invest in their state. The major state trade development programs and services are outlined below.

1) **Marketing Research and Company Intelligence:**
All of the states can provide some degree of overseas marketing information. The level of detail will depend upon the resources of the state. Thirty-five states (except for California,

Hawaii, Idaho, Kansas, Maryland, Minnesota, Nebraska, Nevada, New Jersey, New York, South Dakota, Texas, Washington, West Virginia, and Wyoming) say they will do customized market studies for companies. Such studies are free or available for a small fee. For example, the Commonwealth of Virginia will do an in-depth market study for a company and charge $1,000. They estimate similar surveys done by the private sector cost up to $20,000. Virginia relies on MBA students and professors within the state university system who get credit for working on such projects.

Even if a state does not perform customized studies, the trade office within a Department of Economic Development will prove to be an ideal starting place for marketing information. Some states which do not undertake comprehensive studies for prospective exporters will do a limited amount of research for free. These offices can also point to outside sources as well as the notable resources at the federal level which may be able to assist. And those states with offices overseas also can contact these foreign posts to identify sources in other countries. Moreover, many of the offices have people who travel abroad frequently for companies and also work with other exporters. Such bureaucrats can be invaluable for identifying the exact source for obtaining particular market or company intelligence.

2) **Company and Industry Directories:**
Many states publish directories which are helpful to both exporters and researchers. Some states publish export/import directories which show which companies in the state are exporters and what they sell as well as which are importers and what they buy. Because many of the trade offices are also interested in foreign investment within their state, many publish directories or other reference sources disclosing which companies in their state are foreign owned, and by whom. Other state publications may include export service directories which list organizations providing services to exporters such as

banks, freight forwarders, translators, and world trade organizations. Some also publish agribusiness exporter directories, which identify agricultural-related companies involved in exporting.

3)   Free Newsletters:

All but four states (i.e., Florida, Kentucky, Ohio, and North Carolina) generate international newsletters or publish a special section within a general newsletter on items of interest to those selling overseas. These newsletters are normally free and cover topics like new trade leads, new rules and regulations for exports, and details about upcoming overseas trade shows. Such newsletters can also be a source for mailing lists for those whose clients include exporters. We haven't specifically investigated the availability of such lists, but remember that all states have a law comparable to the federal Freedom of Information Act which allows public access to government data.

4)   Overseas Contacts:

Finding a foreign buyer or an agent/distributor for a company is one of the primary functions of these state offices. How they do this varies from state to state. Many sponsor trade fairs and seminars overseas to attract potential buyers to products produced in their state. The more aggressive trade promotion offices may organize trade missions and escort a number of companies overseas and personally help them look for buyers or agents. Many will distribute a company's sales brochures and other literature to potential buyers around the world through their overseas offices. Some states work with the federal government and explore general trade leads and then try to match buyers with sellers. Others will cultivate potential clients in a given country and contact each directly.

5)   Export Marketing Seminars:

Many of the states conduct free or modestly priced seminars to introduce companies to selling overseas. Some of the courses are held in conjunction with the regional International Trade Administration office of the U.S. Commerce Department. The course may be general in nature, for example, *The Basics of Exporting*, or focused on specific topics such as *International Market Research Techniques*, *Letters of Credit*, *Export Financing*, or *How to do Business with Israel*.

6)   State Grants and Loans for Exporters:

Many states offer financial assistance for those wishing to export. Some states even provide grants (money you do not have to pay back) to those firms which cannot afford to participate in a trade mission or trade fair. This means that they provide money to those companies which are just trying to develop a customer base overseas. More typically the state will help with the financing of a sale through state-sponsored loans and loan guarantees, or assistance in identifying and applying for federal or commercial export financing.

7)   Trade Leads Databases:

Because these offices provide mostly services, there are not many opportunities for them to develop databases. However, their trade leads program is one area where a number of offices have computerized their information. These databases consist of the names and addresses along with some background information on those overseas companies which are actively searching or might be interested in doing business with companies within the state. The number of leads in such a system could range from several hundred to five or ten thousand. None of these states seem to have made such information available on machine readable formats to those outside the office. But, in light of state Freedom of Information statutes, it may be worth making a formal inquiry if you have an interest. The states which have computerized their trade leads include: Alabama, Arkansas, Arizona, California, Colorado, Connecticut, Delaware, Florida, Georgia, Hawaii, Illinois, Indiana, Iowa, Maine, Michigan, Maryland, Minnesota, Mississippi, Missouri, Nebraska, New Jersey, New York, North Carolina, North Dakota, Ohio, Oklahoma, Oregon, New Hampshire, Pennsylvania, Puerto Rico, Rhode Island, South Dakota, Tennessee, Texas, Utah, Virginia, Washington, West Virginia, and Wisconsin.

State International Trade Offices

The foreign cities in parentheses after the telephone number are those locations where the state maintains a trade office.

Alabama
International Development and Trade Division, Alabama Development Office, State Capitol, Montgomery, AL 36130, 205-242-0400, 800-248-0033; Fax: 205-242-0486 (Hanover, **Germany**; Seoul, **Korea**; Tokyo, **Japan**).

Alaska
International Trade Director, Office of International Trade, Dept. of Commerce and Economic Development, 3601 C St., Suite 798, Anchorage, AK 99503, 907-561-5585; Fax: 907-561-4557 (Tokyo, **Japan**; Seoul, **Korea**; Taipei, **Taiwan**).

Arizona
International Trade, Department of Commerce, 3800 N. Central, 15th Floor, Phoenix, AZ 85012, 602-280-1371; Fax: 602-280-1305 (Mexico City, **Mexico**; Tokyo, **Japan**; Taipei, **Taiwan**).

Arkansas
International Marketing, Arkansas Industrial Commission, One State Capitol Mall, Little Rock, AR 72201, 501-682-7690; Fax: 501-324-9856 (Brussels, **Belgium**; Tokyo, **Japan**; Taipei, **Taiwan**; Mexico City, **Mexico**).

California
California State World Trade Commission, 801 K St., Suite 1700, Sacramento, CA 95814, 916-324-5511; Fax: 916-324-5791 (Tokyo, **Japan**; London, **England**; Hong Kong; Frankfurt, **Germany**; Mexico City, **Mexico**; Taipei, **Taiwan**; Israel).

Export Development Office, 107 S. Broadway, Room 8039, Los Angeles, CA 90012, 310-590-5965.

Colorado
International Trade Office, Department of Commerce and Development, 1625 Broadway, Suite 680, Denver, CO 80202, 303-892-3850; Fax: 303-892-3820 (Tokyo, **Japan**; Seoul, **Korea**; London, **England**; Mexico City, **Mexico**).

Connecticut
International Division, Department of Economic Development, 865 Brook St., Rocky Hill, CT 06067, 203-258-4256; Fax: 203-529-0535 (Tokyo, **Japan**; Taipei, **Taiwan**; **Hong Kong**; Mexico City, **Mexico**).

Delaware
Delaware Development Office, International Trade Section, 820 French St., Carvel State Building, 3rd Floor, Wilmington, DE 19801, 302-577-6262; Fax: 302-577-3302.

District of Columbia
District of Columbia Office of International Business, 717 14th St., 11th Floor, NW, Washington, DC 20005, 202-727-1576; Fax: 202-727-1588.

Florida
Florida Department of Commerce, 366 Collins Building, Tallahassee, FL 32399-2000, 904-488-6124; Fax: 904-487-1407 (Toronto, **Canada**; Taipei, **Taiwan**; Seoul, **Korea**; Frankfort, **Germany**; Tokyo, **Japan**; London, **England**; Sao Paulo, **Brazil**; Mexico City, **Mexico**).

Georgia
Department of Industry, Trade and Tourism, Suite 1100, 285 Peachtree Center Ave., Atlanta, GA 30303, 404-656-3545; Fax: 404-651-6505 (Brussels, **Belgium**; Tokyo, **Japan**; Toronto, **Canada**; Seoul, **Korea**; Mexico City, **Mexico**).

Hawaii
International Services Branch, Department of Business and Economic Development, P.O. Box 2359, Honolulu, HI 96804, 808-587-2797; Fax: 808-587-2790.

Idaho
Economic Development, Department of Commerce, 700 W. State Street, Boise, ID 83720, 208-334-2470; Fax: 208-334-2783.

Illinois
International Business Division, Illinois Department of Commerce and Community Affairs, 100 W. Randolph St., Suite 3-400, Chicago, IL 60601, 312-814-7164; Fax: 312-814-6581 (Brussels, **Belgium**; **Hong Kong**; Tokyo, **Japan**; Warsaw, **Poland**; Mexico City, **Mexico**; Budapest, **Hungary**).

Illinois Export Council, 333 N. Michigan Ave., Chicago, IL 60601, 312-236-2162; Fax: 312-236-4625.

Indiana
International Trade Division, Department of Commerce, One North Capitol, Suite 700, Indianapolis, IN 46204, 317-232-3527; Fax 317-232-4146 (Tokyo, **Japan**; Mexico City, **Mexico**; Toronto, **Canada**; Taipei, **Taiwan**; Beijing, **China**; Seoul, **Korea**; **Netherlands**).

Iowa
International Marketing Division, Iowa Dept. of Economic Development, 200 East Grand Ave., Des Moines, IA 50309, 515-242-4743; Fax: 515-242-4918 (Frankfurt, **Germany**; Tokyo, **Japan**).

Kansas
Kansas Department of Commerce, 700 SW Harrison St., Suite 1300, Topeka, KS 66603, 913-296-4027; Fax: 913-296-5055 (Tokyo, **Japan**; Brussels, **Belgium**).

Kentucky
International Trade, Kentucky Office of Economic Development, 500 O St., #2300, Capitol Plaza, Frankfort, KY 40601, 502-564-7670; Fax 502-564-3256 (Tokyo, **Japan**; Brussels, **Belgium**).

Louisiana
Office of International Trade, P.O. Box 94185, Baton Rouge, LA 70804-9185, 504-342-4319; Fax: 504-342-5389 (Mexico City, **Mexico**; Taipei, **Taiwan**; **Netherlands**).

Maine
International and Economic Trade, Maine World Trade Commission, State House, Station 59, Augusta, ME 04333, 207-287-2656; Fax: 207-622-0234.

Maryland
Maryland International Division, World Trade Center, 401 East Pratt St., 7th Floor, Baltimore, MD 21202, 410-333-4295; Fax: 410-333-4302 (Brussels, **Belgium**; Yokohama, **Japan**; **Hong Kong**; Taipei, **Taiwan**).

Massachusetts
Office of International Trade and Investment, 100 Cambridge St., Room 1302, Boston, MA 02202, 617-367-1830; Fax: 617-227-3488 (Berlin, **Germany**).

Michigan
International Trade Division, International Trade Authority, Michigan Department of Commerce, P.O. Box 30105, Lansing, MI 48909, 517-373-1054; Fax: 517-335-2521 (Toronto, **Canada**; **Hong Kong**; Brussels, **Belgium**; Tokyo, **Japan**).

Minnesota
Minnesota Trade Office, 1000 World Trade Center, 30 E. 7th St., St. Paul, 55101, 612-297-4222; Fax: 612-296-3555 (Oslo, **Norway**; Stockholm, **Sweden**).

Mississippi
Department of Economic and Community Development, P.O. Box 849, Jackson, MI 39205, 601-359-6672; Fax: 601-359-3605 (Seoul, **Korea**; Tokyo, **Japan**; **Hong Kong**; Frankfort, **Germany**; Taipei, **Taiwan**).

Missouri
International Trade, Department of Economic Development, P.O. Box 118, Jefferson City, MO 65102, 314-751-4855; Fax: 314-751-7384 (Tokyo, **Japan**; Dusseldorf, **Germany**; Seoul, **Korea**; Taipei, **Taiwan**; Guadalajara, **Mexico**).

Montana
International Trade Office, Montana Department of Commerce, 1424 9th Ave., Helena, MT 59620, 406-444-3494; Fax: 406-444-2903 (Taipei, **Taiwan**; Kumamoto, **Japan**).

Nebraska
Department of Economic Development, 301 Centennial Mall South, P.O. Box 94666, Lincoln, NE 68509, 402-471-3111; Fax: 402-471-3778.

Nevada
Commission of Economic Development, Capital Complex, Carson, NV 89710, 702-687-4325; Fax: 702-787-4450.

New Hampshire
Office of International Commerce, Department of Resources and Economic Development, 601 Spaulding Turnpike, Suite 29, Portsmouth, NH 03801, 603-334-6074; Fax: 603-334-6110.

New Jersey
Division of International Trade, Department of Commerce and Economic Development, 28 West State St., 8th Floor, Trenton, NJ 08625, 609-633-3606; Fax: 609-633-3675 (Tokyo, **Japan**; London, **England**).

New Mexico
Trade Division, Economic Development, 1100 St. Francis Dr., Joseph Montoya Building, Santa Fe, NM 87503, 505-827-0307; Fax: 505-827-0263 (Mexico City, **Mexico**).

New York
International Division, Department of Commerce, 1515 Broadway, 51st Floor, New York Department of Economic Development, New York, NY 10036, 212-827-6100; Fax: 212-827-6279 (Tokyo, **Japan**; Wiesbaden, **Germany**; London, **England**; Milan, **Italy**; Ontario and Montreal, **Canada**; **Hong Kong**; Frankfurt, **Germany**).

North Carolina
International Division, Dept. of Commerce, 430 N. Salisbury St., Raleigh, NC 27611, 919-733-7193; Fax: 919-733-0110 (Dusseldorf, **Germany**; **Hong Kong**; Tokyo, **Japan**).

North Dakota
International Trade Specialist, Department of International Trade and Finance, 1833 E. Bismarck Expressway, Bismarck, ND 58504, 701-224-2810; Fax: 701-328-5320.

Ohio
International Trade Division, Department of Development, 77 S. High St., P.O. Box 1001, Columbus, OH 43216, 614-466-5017; 614-463-1540 (Brussels, **Belgium**; Tokyo, **Japan**; **Hong Kong**, Toronto, **Canada**).

Oklahoma
International Trade Division, Oklahoma Dept. of Commerce, 6601 Broadway Extension, Oklahoma City, OK 73116, 405-841-5220; Fax: 405-841-5245 (Frankfort, **Germany**; Seoul, **Korea**; Mexico City, **Mexico**; **Singapore**).

Oregon
International Trade Division, Oregon Economic Development Dept., #1 World Trade Center, Suite 300, 121 Salmon St., Portland, OR 97204, 503-229-5625; Fax: 503-222-5050 (Tokyo, **Japan**; Seoul, **Korea**; Taipei, **Taiwan**).

Pennsylvania
Dept. of Commerce, Office of International Trade, 464 Forum Building, Harrisburg, PA 17120, 717-783-5107; Fax: 717-234-4560 (Frankfurt, **Germany**; Tokyo, **Japan**; Brussels, **Belgium**; Toronto, **Canada**).

Puerto Rico
P.R. Dept. of Commerce, P.O. Box 4275, San Juan, PR 00936, 809-721-3290; Fax: 809-722-8477.

Rhode Island
International Trade Office, Department of Economic Development, 7 Jackson Walkway, Providence, RI 02903, 401-277-2601; Fax: 401-277-2102 (Mexico City, **Mexico**).

South Carolina
International Business Development, South Carolina State Department of Commerce, P.O. Box 927, Columbia, SC 29202, 803-737-0400; Fax: 803-737-0418 (Tokyo, **Japan**; Frankfort, **Germany**; Seoul **Korea**; **United Kingdom**).

South Dakota
South Dakota International Trade Center, Capitol Lake Plaza, Pierre, SD 57501, 605-773-5032.

Tennessee
Export Promotion Office, Department of Economic and Community Development, Rachel Jackson Building, 7th Floor, Nashville, TN 37219, 615-741-5870; Fax: 615-741-5829.

Texas
International Business Development Dept., Texas Department of Commerce, P.O. Box 12728, Austin, TX 78711, 512-320-0110; Fax: 512-320-9424 (Mexico City, **Mexico**; Frankfurt, **Germany**; Tokyo, **Japan**; Taipei, **Taiwan**).

Utah
Export Development Committee, Economic and Industrial Development Division, 324 S. State St., Salt Lake City, UT 84111, 801-538-3631 (Tokyo, **Japan**).

Vermont
International Business, Dept. of Economic Development, 109 State St., Montpelier, VT 05602, 802-828-3221; Fax: 802-828-3258.

Virginia
International Trade and Investment, 2 James Center, P.O. Box 798, Richmond, VA 23206, 804-371-8100; Fax: 804-371-8860 (Tokyo, **Japan**; Brussels, **Belgium**).

Washington
Domestic and International Trade Division, Department of Trade and Economic Development, 2001 Sixth Ave, 26th Floor, Seattle, WA 98121, 206-464-7143; Fax: 206-464-7222 (Tokyo, **Japan**; **Canada**).

West Virginia
West Virginia Development Office, Capitol Complex Bldg. 6, Room 525, Charleston, WV 25305, 304-558-2234; Fax: 304-558-1189 (Tokyo, **Japan**).

Wisconsin
Bureau of International Business Development, Department of Development, 123 W. Washington Ave., Madison, WI 53702, 608-266-1767; Fax: 608-266-5551 (Frankfurt, **Germany**; **Hong Kong**; Mexico City, **Mexico**; Toronto, **Canada**; Tokyo, **Japan**; Seoul, **Korea**; **South Korea**).

Wyoming
International Trade Division, Department of Commerce, 2301 Central Avenue, Cheyenne, WY 82002, 307-777-6412; Fax: 307-777-5840.

Overseas Travel: Business Or Pleasure

The following sources and services will be helpful to anyone who is on business or vacation in any foreign country:

1) **Arts America:**
The U.S. Information Agency assists qualified artists and performers in arranging private tours overseas. Its aim is to present a balanced portrayal of the American scene. Some of the past activities have included a major exhibition of American crafts shown in China, a modern dance company in the USSR, Spain, and Portugal, and a jazz ensemble in Nigeria, Senegal and Kenya. Contact: Program Manager, Office of the Arts in America, United States Information Agency, 301 4th St. SW, Room 568, Washington, DC 20547, 202-619-4779.

2) **Travel Overseas On Government Expense:**
The U.S. Speakers program will pay experts, who can contribute to foreign societies' understanding of the United States, to travel abroad and participate in seminars, colloquia, or symposia. Subjects relevant to the program include economics, international political relations, U.S. social and political processes, arts and humanities, and science and technology. To see if you qualify contact: U.S. Speakers, Office of Program Coordination and Development, U.S. Information Agency, 301 4th St. SW, Room 550, Washington, DC 20547, 202-619-4764.

3) **Citizens Arrested Overseas:**
The Arrest Unit at the State Department monitors arrests and trials to see that American citizens are not abused; acts as a liaison with family and friends in the United States; sends money or messages with written consent of arrestee; offers lists of lawyers; will forward money from the United States to detainee; tries to assure that your rights under local laws are

observed. The Emergency Medical and Dietary Assistance Program includes such services as providing vitamin supplements when necessary; granting emergency transfer for emergency medical care; and short-term feeding of two or three meals a day when arrestee is detained without funds to buy his or her own meals. Contact: Arrests Unit, Citizens Emergency Center, Overseas Citizens Service, Bureau of Consular Affairs, U.S. Department of State, 2201 C St. NW, Room 4811, Washington, DC 20520, 202-647-5225.

4) **Citizens Emergency Center:**
Emergency telephone assistance is available to United States citizens abroad under the following circumstances:

Arrests: 202-647-5225 (see details above)

Deaths: 202-647-5225; notification of interested parties in the United States of the death abroad of American citizens; assistance in the arrangements for disposition of remains.

Financial Assistance: 202-647-5225; repatriation of destitute nationals, coordination of medical evacuation of non-official nationals from abroad; transmission of private funds in emergencies to destitute United States nationals abroad when commercial banking facilities are unavailable (all costs must be reimbursed).

Shipping and Seamen: 202-647-5225; protection of American vessels and seamen.

Welfare and Whereabouts: 202-647-5225; search for nonofficial United States nationals who have not been heard from for an undue length of time and/or about whom there is special concern; transmission of emergency messages to United States nationals abroad. For other help contact: Overseas Citizen Services, Bureau of Consular Affairs, U.S. Department of State,

2201 C St. NW, Washington, DC 20520, 202-647-5225.

5) **Country Information Studies:**
For someone who wants more than what the typical travel books tell about a specific country, this series of books deals with more in-depth knowledge of the country being visited. Each book describes the origins and traditions of the people and their social and national attitudes, as well as the economics, military, political and social systems. For a more complete listing of this series and price information, contact: Superintendent of Documents, U.S. Government Printing Office, Washington, DC 20402, 202-512-1800.

6) **Foreign Country Background Notes:**
Background Notes on the Countries of the World is a series of short, factual pamphlets with information on the country's land, people, history, government, political conditions, economy, foreign relations, and U.S. foreign policy. Each pamphlet also includes a factual profile, brief travel notes, a country map, and a reading list. Contact: Public Affairs Bureau, U.S. Department of State, Room 4827A, 2201 C St. NW, Washington, DC 20520, 202-647-2518 for a free copy of *Background Notes* for the countries you plan to visit. This material is also available from the: Superintendent of Documents, U.S. Government Printing Office, Washington, DC 20402, 202-512-1800. Single copies cost from $1.50 to $56 for a set.

7) **Foreign Language Materials:**
The Defense Language Institute Foreign Language Center (DLIFC) has an academic library with holdings of over 100,000 books and periodicals in 50 different foreign languages. These materials are available through the national interlibrary loan program which can be arranged through your local librarian.

8) **Foreign Language Training:**
The Foreign Service Institute is an in-house educational institution for foreign service

officers, members of their families and employees of other government agencies. It provides special training in 50 foreign languages. Its instructional materials, including books and tapes, are designed to teach modern foreign languages. Instruction books must be purchased from Superintendent of Documents, U.S. Government Printing Office, Washington, DC 20402, 202-512-1800. Tapes must be purchased from the National Audiovisual Center, National Archive, NTIS, Springfield, VA, 22161, 1-800-788-6282 or 703-487-8400.

9) Free Booklets for Travelers:

The following booklets and guides are available free of charge:

Travel Information: Your Trip Abroad:

Contains basic information such as how to apply for a passport, customs tips, lodging information, and how American consular officers can help you in an emergency. Contact: Publications Distribution, Bureau of Public Affairs, U.S. Department of State, 2201 C St. NW, Room 5815A, Washington, DC 20520, 202-647-9859.

Customs Information:

Provides information about custom regulations both when returning to the U.S. as well as what to expect when traveling to different parts of the world. Contact: Customs Office, P.O. Box 7118, Washington, DC 20044.

Visa Requirements of Foreign Governments:

Lists entry requirements of U.S. citizens traveling as tourists, and where and how to apply for visas and tourist cards. Contact: Passport Services, Bureau of Consular Affairs, U.S. Department of State, 1425 K St. NW, Room G-62, Washington, DC 20524, 202-647-0518.

10) Passport Information:

A recorded telephone message provides general information on what is needed when applying for a U.S. passport. Call 202-647-0518. U.S. citizens and nationals can apply for passports at all passport agencies as well as those post offices and federal and state courts authorized to accept passport applications.

Government Auctions and
Surplus Property

Federal Auctions

Whether you're looking for a good bargain on equipment to furnish your home office, or whether you're interested in a low overhead business of buying government property and reselling it, all you need is here. Year round, the federal government offers hundreds of millions of dollars worth of property and goods -- from animals to real estate -- at remarkable prices. The Customs Service sells seized property -- jewelry, camera, rugs -- anything brought in from another country. The IRS auctions off everything imaginable -- boats, cars, businesses. The U.S. Postal Service sells unclaimed merchandise, including lots of books.

There is one story to inspire: a New Yorker bought surplus parachutes from the Pentagon and became a supplier selling clothesline cord. If you are looking for a business, try the Small Business Administration, which sells equipment and businesses it has acquired through foreclosure. Want a good deal on a house? U.S. Department of Housing and Urban Development offers repossessed homes -- sometimes for practically nothing -- on government fore-closures. There are also many people who go to the U.S. Postal Service auctions and buy bin loads of videos, CDs, and other goodies, and make nice money reselling them at flea markets.

Very few people know about these unique bargains because the federal government doesn't advertise them. Described below are 30 of Uncle Sam's Red Tag Specials. Contact the appropriate offices for more information. And remember, if you don't find what you want, stay at it. This is ongoing, and new merchandise and property are coming in all the time.

* Burros and Horses: Bureau of Land Management

Nevada State Office
Bureau of Land Management
U.S. Department of the Interior
850 Harvard Way
Reno, NV 89520-0006
702-785-6400
Fax: 702-673-6010

Or contact your local Bureau of Land Management office. The "Adopt-a-Horse" program is aimed at keeping wild herds at in the West at manageable levels, and allows individuals around the country to purchase a wild horse for $125 or a burro for $75. The animals usually have their shots. Aside from the purchase price you only need pay for shipping. If you live west of the Mississippi, call the Program Office above to find out which of the 12 adoption satellites are nearest you. Representatives of the BLM travel around the country, so you don't have to travel to Wyoming to participate. The only qualifications for adoption are that you have appropriate facilities to house the animal, that you are of legal age in your state, and that you have no record of offenses against animals. The horses and burros may not be used for any exploitative purposes such as rodeos or races, nor may they be re-sold. Upon adoption, you sign an agreement to that effect, and no title of ownership is given until one year after an adoption. Animals are usually from two to six years in age, and must be trained. The offices listed above have a brochure called *So You'd Like to Adopt a Wild Horse or Burro* on the "Adopt-a-Horse" program that gives more details.

Alaska
Alaska State Office, 222 W. 7th Ave., #13, Anchorage, AK 99513-7599; 907-271-5555.

Arizona
Phoenix District Office, 2015 W. Deer Valley Rd., Phoenix, AZ 85027; 602-780-8090.
Kingman Resource Area, 602-757-3161.

California
California State Office, Federal Building, Room E-2807, 2800 Cottage Way, Sacramento, CA 95825-1889; 916-979-2800.
Bakersfield District Office, 805-391-6049.
Ridgecrest, CA, 619-446-6064.
Susanville District Office, 916-257-5381.

Colorado
Canon City District Office, 3170 E. Main St., Canon City, CO 81212; 303-275-0631.

Idaho
Boise District Office, 3948 Development Ave., Boise, ID 83705-5389; 208-384-3300.

Montana, North Dakota, South Dakota
Montana State Office, 2222 N. 32nd St., Billings, MT 59107-6800; 406-255-2925.

Nevada
National Wild Horse and Burro Center, Palomino Valley, P.O. Box 3270, Sparks, NV 89432; 702-475-2222.

New Mexico, Kansas, Oklahoma, Texas
Oklahoma Resource Area, 221 N. Service Rd., Moore, OK 73160-4946; 405-794-9624.

Oregon, Washington
Burns District Office, HC74-12533, Highway 20 West, Hines, OR 97738; 503-573-4400.

Utah
Salt Lake City District Office, 2370 South 2300 West, Salt Lake City, UT 84119; 801-977-4300.

Wyoming, Nebraska
Rock Springs District Office, P.O. Box 1869, Highway 191 North, Rock Springs, WY 82902-1869; 307-382-5350.
Elm Creek, NE, 308-856-4498.

AL, AR, FL, GA, KY, LA, MS, NC, SC, TN, VA
Jackson District Office, 411 Briarwood Dr., Suite 404, Jackson, MS 39206; 601-977-5430.
Cross Plains, TN, 615-654-2180.

CT, DE, DC, IL, IN, IA, ME, MD, MA, MI, MN, MO, NH, NJ, NY, OH, PA, RI, VT, WV, WI
Milwaukee District Office, 310 W. Wisconsin Ave., Suite 225, Milwaukee, WI 53203.

* Christmas Trees, Seedling, Wooden Poles and Posts: Bureau of Land Management

U.S. Department of the Interior
Bureau of Land Management
Division of Forestry
1849 C Street, NW
Washington, DC 20240
202-653-8864
or
U.S. Forest Service (USDA)
202-208-3435; 202-205-1389

Contact your local Bureau of Land Management (BLM), U.S. Department of Interior. In the 11 Western states, the Bureau of Land Management has a program for obtaining low-cost Christmas trees from Federal lands. By contacting your local BLM office, you may obtain a permit for a nominal fee (usually $10) to cut a tree for your own use. You will be given a map with directions as to which are permissible areas for tree-cutting. Non-profit organizations may also qualify. Non-profit may get free use permits and cut larger amounts. Trees must be for their own use and may not be resold at fundraisers.

In addition, under the Minor Forest Products program, you may collect or cut specified small trees for use as poles or posts; or, you may obtain cactus or plant seedlings from areas of natural growth where there are abundant supplies -- again at a very low cost. These items are free for non-profit organizations for their own use. Permits for commercial usage may also be available. Cost depends on market value. Below are the addresses and phone numbers of Regional Bureau of Land Management Offices.

Alaska
222 W. 7th Ave. #13, Anchorage, AK 99513-5076; 907-271-5555.

Arizona
3707 N. 7th St., P.O. Box 16563, Phoenix, AZ 85011; 602-640-0504.

California
2800 Cottage Way, E-2841, Sacramento, CA 95825; 916-978-2835.

Colorado
2850 Youngfield St., Lakewood, CO 80215-7076; 303-239-3670.

Eastern States
7450 Ballston Blvd., Springfield, VA 22153; 703-440-1713.

Idaho
3380 Americana Terrace, Boise, ID 83706; 208-384-3014.

Montana
Granite Tower, 222 N. 32nd St., P.O. Box 36800, Billings, MT 59107-6800; 406-255-2913.

Nevada
850 Harvard Way, Reno, NV 89520-0006; 702-785-6586.

New Mexico
1474 Rodeo Road, P.O. Box 27115, Santa Fe, NM 87502-0115; 505-438-7514.

Oregon
1515 SW 5th Ave., P.O. Box 2965, Portland, OR 97208-2965; 503-952-6027.

Utah
324 South State Street, Suite 301, P.O. Box 45155, Salt Lake City, UT 84145-0155; 801-539-4021.

Wyoming
5353 Yellowstone Rd., P.O. Box 1828, Cheyenne, WY 82009; 307-775-6011.

* Federal Depository Insurance Corporation (FDIC)

Federal Depository Insurance Corporation
550 17th St. NW
Washington, DC 20429
202-393-8400
or
Office of Liquidations
1776 F Street NW
Washington, DC 20429
202-898-7343

The FDIC sells at auctions the furnishings and equipment of failed commercial banks. Consult the blue pages in your phone directory for the regional FDIC office nearest you. Each regional office handles their own personal property disposal. Professional auctioneers are contracted to auction off the accumulation of desks, calculators, chairs, computers and other furnishings that banks normally have. These auctions will be advertised in the auction section or classifieds of local newspapers.

The FDIC also holds open for offers costly commercial property and real estate. For a full catalog of these listings across the country, which also includes homes over $250,000 call 1-800-445-3683. They will send *The Liquidation Book* which is the marketing list that is most current. All the property the FDIC has to sell is in this book, but if you are interested in bidding on a house under $250,000, it is wise to ask them for the phone number of the FDIC sales office in your area that is in charge of selling them, and then contact them directly. About 97 percent of the listings in it are commercial offerings such as hotels, offices, and industries. Sales of commercial real estate are advertised nationally by the FDIC in such papers as *The Wall Street Journal.* Call for information on how to be placed on a mailing list.

* FHA Money May Be Waiting For You

Support Service Center
P.O. Box 23699
Washington, DC 20026-3699
HUD Locator   1-800-697-6967
                     202-708-1422

If you or someone in your family has successfully paid off a mortgage on a house, there may be money waiting for you at the U.S. Department of Housing and Urban Development (HUD). HUD oversees the Federal Housing Administration (FHA) which insures mortgages that your bank lends to house buyers. Each year FHA predicts how many people will default on their loans, and based on that prediction, they calibrate how much mortgage insurance home buyers will pay during that year. If it turns out that there are fewer loan defaults than FHA predicted, those borrowers that have continued to pay their mortgages have what are called "Mutual Mortgage Dividend" checks coming to them upon completion of the loan agreement. Call 703-235-8117 if you think you are due a one time mortgage insurance premium refund or a distributive share.

Another way you may qualify for an FHA insurance refund is to have taken out, say, a 30 year mortgage and paid the entire FHA insurance premium up front instead of in installments over the entire period of the loan. If you have completed the loan agreement in less than 30 years, you may have money coming back to you since you didn't use the insurance for the entire 30 years you've already paid for. In most cases, though, you have to carry a loan for at least 7 years to qualify for a dividend, and the longer you have a loan, the more likely it is that you will qualify for a dividend check.

In these cases where you prepay all of your mortgage insurance premium up front, your bank should let you know that you may eventually be eligible for a mutual mortgage refund upon fulfillment of the loan agreement. Also, after you have paid off your loan, your bank should notify HUD, who in turn should notify you if you have any refund coming, usually within six months. However, if HUD cannot locate you, they will add your name to a list of other individuals who cannot be located but have HUD money coming to them.

Through the Freedom of Information Act many individuals have gotten their hands on copies of this list from HUD and gone around the country tracking down the people and charging them fees to recover this HUD money. Depending on the size of the original loan, your dividend refund could be several thousand dollars, and since some of these "bounty hunters" may ask for up to 50% of the refund just for making a phone call that you could make yourself, you could be losing out on a substantial sum of money by letting them do it. In fact, all you have to do to get the same list the bounty hunters are using is to call 703-235-8117. The staff will mail to you an "information package" which contains the names of all the mortgagors in the state in which you reside (or request the list for), forms and basic information you would need to apply for a refund.

If you feel you may have money coming to you, or if a member of your family who took out a mortgage is now deceased and you are an heir,

try to locate the original loan contract number, and then make a few calls. To apply for a refund you will need the loan number and FHA case number, which you can find on the Recorded Deed of Purchase, kept at your local county courthouse.

* Firewood: U.S. Forest Service

U.S. Forest Service
Timber Management
U.S. Department of Agriculture
14th & Independence Ave. SW
Box 96090
Washington, DC 20090-6090
Operations and Technology Information
202-205-0855/0893

Contact your nearest National Forest Office (list below) to find out about the firewood program and to learn which national forest is near you. Also, ask these regional offices about firewood from state forestry organizations and private timber companies. Ask about availability of firewood before you make the trip. In any National Forest, you may pick up downed or dead wood for firewood for a nominal charge of $5 per cord, $10 minimum fee, after requesting a permit from the Forest of your choice. You may phone to request the permit, and must have it in your possession while collecting the wood. The Forest Service allows you to gather 2-10 cords worth of wood. Six cords are equal to 12 pick-up truck loads. Wood may not be collected for commercial purposes. All permits to cut wood are issued locally, so you must purchase permits directly from the district ranger. Regional offices do not sell permits.

Northern Region I
Federal Building, 200 East Broadway St., P.O. Box 7669, Missoula, MT 59807; 406-329-3316. Includes Northern Idaho and Montana.

Rocky Mountain Region II
740 Simms Ave., P.O. Box 25127, Lakewood, CO 80225; 303-275-5350. Includes Colorado, Nebraska, South Dakota, Eastern Wyoming.

Southwestern Region III
Federal Building, 517 Gold Ave. S.W., Albuquerque, NM 87102; 505-842-3306. Includes New Mexico, Arizona.

Intermountain Region IV
Federal Building, 324 25th St., Ogden, UT 84401; 801-625-5605. Includes Southern Idaho, Nevada, Utah, and Western Wyoming.

Pacific Southwest Region V
630 Sansome St., San Francisco, CA 94111; 415-705-2870. Includes California, Hawaii, Guam, Trust Territories of the Pacific Islands.

Pacific Northwest Region VI
333 SW First Avenue, P.O. Box 3623, Portland, OR 97208-3623; 503-326-3626. Includes Oregon and Washington. (Mt. Hood is the most popular national forest and may be sold out of permits. Call them in advance at 503-666-0700. Try also the state and private timber units at 503-326-2727 or the U.S. Forest Service at 503-326-2877 or 503-326-2957.)

Southern Region VIII
1720 Peachtree Rd. N.W., Atlanta, GA 30367; 404-347-4177. Includes Alabama, Arkansas, Florida, Georgia, Kentucky, Louisiana, Mississippi, North Carolina, Puerto Rico and the Virgin Islands, South Carolina, Tennessee, Texas, Virginia.

Eastern Region IX
310 West Wisconsin Ave., Room 500, Milwaukee, WI 53203; 414-297-3600. Includes Illinois, Indiana, Ohio, Michigan, Minnesota, Missouri, New Hampshire, Maine, Pennsylvania, Vermont, West Virginia, Wisconsin, and Fingerlakes section of New York.

Alaskan Region X
Federal Office Building, 709 West Ninth St., P.O. Box 21628, Juneau, AK 99802-1628; 907-586-8863. Abundance of wood results in extensive free-use permits.

* Homes: Department of Agriculture

Rural Housing and Community
 Development Service
14th & Independence Ave., SW
Room 5334-S
Washington, DC 20250
202-720-1474/1577

Contact your local Rural Housing and Community Development Service (formerly Farmers Home Administration FmHA) Office. There are 1900 around the country. The Rural Housing and Community Development Service, part of the Department of Agriculture, makes low-interest loans available to qualified applicants to purchase homes or farms in rural areas (among other things). Rural settings are small towns with a population under 10,000. Check to see if the locale you are interested in qualifies. Sometimes areas of up to 25,000 in

population are approved. Rural Housing and Community Development Service (RHCDS) is also charged with disposing of properties that are foreclosed. First, they make any necessary repairs to the properties, then offer them for sale to people who have the same qualifications as those applying for RHCDS loans (based on income, credit worthiness and other criteria). Eligible applicants also qualify to purchase the properties at special low RHCDS interest rates (as low as 1%). If no eligible applicants purchase a property, it is then put up for sale to the general public at competitive prices. If the property is not sold within 10 days, it may be reduced by 10%. Sales to the general public may be through RHCDS offices or through private real estate brokers. RHCDS "eligible applicants" must reside on the property purchased; but if no such eligible buyers are available, other buyers may use it for investment or rental purposes. A separate program applies for farms. This program is designed to serve people of modest income and good credit who don't have enough to make a down payment on a home. Credit evaluation is done on the most recent 12 months. Bankruptcy is not looked at after 36 months. The current loan budget is one-third of what is was in the 70's. This program is being changed to eventually act as insurers to guarantee loans from professional lenders. Applicants may work in a city if their home is rural. The address and telephone number for your local county office may be obtained by calling or writing the applicable state office listed below.

Alabama
Rural Housing and Community Development Service, Sterling Center, Office Building, 4121 Carmichael Rd., Suite 601, Montgomery, Al 36106-3683; 205-279-3400.

Alaska
Rural Housing and Community Development Service, 634 S. Bailey, Suite 103, Palmer, AK 99645; 907-745-2176.

Arizona
Rural Housing and Community Development Service, Phoenix Corporate Center, 3003 N. Central Ave., Suite 900, Phoenix, AZ 85012; 602-280-8700.

Arkansas
Rural Housing and Community Development Service, P.O. Box 2778, 700 W. Capitol, Little Rock, AR 72203; 501-324-6281.

California
Rural Housing and Community Development Service, 194 W. Main St., Suite F, Woodland, CA 95695-2915; 916-668-2000.

Colorado
Rural Housing and Community Development Service, 655 Parfet St., Room E100, Lakewood, CO 80215; 303-236-2801.

Delaware, Maryland
Rural Housing and Community Development Service, P.O. Box 400, 4611 S. DuPont Hwy., Camden, DE 19934-9998; 302-697-4300.

Florida
Rural Housing and Community Development Service, P.O. Box 147010, 4440 NW 25th Pl., Gainesville, FL 32614-7010; 904-338-3400.

Georgia
Rural Housing and Community Development Service, Stephens Federal Bldg., 355 E. Hancock Ave., Athens, GA 30610; 706-546-2162.

Hawaii
Rural Housing and Community Development Service, Federal Bldg., Room 311, 154 Waianuenue Ave., Hilo, HI 96720; 808-933-3000.

Idaho
Rural Housing and Community Development Service, 3232 Elder St., Boise, ID 83705; 208-334-1301.

Illinois
Rural Housing and Community Development Service, Illini Plaza, Suite 103, 1817 S. Neil St., Champaign, IL 61820; 217-398-5235.

Indiana
Rural Housing and Community Development Service, 5975 Lakeside Blvd., Indianapolis, IN 46278; 317-290-3100.

Iowa
Rural Housing and Community Development Service, 873 Federal Blvd., 210 Walnut St., Des Moines, IA 50309; 515-284-4663.

Kansas
Rural Housing and Community Development Service, P.O. Box 4653, 1200 SW Executive Dr., Topeka, KS 66604; 913-271-2700.

Kentucky
Rural Housing and Community Development Service, 771 Corporate Dr., Suite 200, Lexington, KY 40503; 606-224-7300.

Louisiana
Rural Housing and Community Development Service, 3727 Government St., Alexandria, LA 71302; 318-473-7920.

Maine
Rural Housing and Community Development Service, P.O. Box 405, 444 Stillwater Ave., Suite 2, Bangor, ME 04402-0405; 207-990-9106.

Massachusetts, Connecticut, Rhode Island
Rural Housing and Community Development Service, 451 West Street, Amherst, MA 01002; 413-253-4300.

Michigan
Rural Housing and Community Development Service, 3001 Coolidge Rd., Room 200, East Lansing, MI 48823; 517-337-6635.

Minnesota
Rural Housing and Community Development Service, 410 Farm Credit Service Bldg., 375 Jackson St., St. Paul, MN 55101-1853; 612-290-3842.

Mississippi
Rural Housing and Community Development Service, Federal Bldg., Suite 831, 100 W. Capitol St., Jackson, MS 39269; 601-965-4316.

Missouri
Rural Housing and Community Development Service, Parkdade Center, Suite 235, 601 Business Loop 70 West, Columbia, MO 65203; 314-876-0976.

Montana
Rural Housing and Community Development Service, Unit 1, Suite B, 900 Technology Blvd., Bozeman, MT 59715; 406-585-2580.

Nebraska
Rural Housing and Community Development Service, Federal Building, Room 308, 100 Centennial Mall N, Lincoln, NE 68508; 402-437-5551.

Nevada
Rural Housing and Community Development Service, 1390 S. Curry St., Carson City, NV 89703-5405; 702-887-1222.

New Jersey
Rural Housing and Community Development Service, Tarnsfield Plaza, Suite 22, 790 Woodlane Rd., Mt. Holly, NJ 08060; 609-265-3600.

New Mexico
Rural Housing and Community Development Service, Federal Building, Room 3414, 517 Gold Ave., SW, Albuquerque, NM 87102; 505-766-2462.

New York
Rural Housing and Community Development Service, The Galleries of Syracuse, 441 S. Salina St., Suite 357, Syracuse, NY 13202; 315-477-6400.

North Carolina
Rural Housing and Community Development Service, 4405 Bland Rd., Suite 260, Raleigh, NC 27609; 919-790-2731.

North Dakota
Rural Housing and Community Development Service, Federal Bldg., Room 208, 220 E. Rosser, P.O. Box 1737, Bismarck, ND 58502; 701-250-4781.

Ohio
Rural Housing and Community Development Service, Federal Bldg., Room 507, 200 N. High St., Columbus, OH 43215; 614-469-5606.

Oklahoma
Rural Housing and Community Development Service, 100 USDA, Suite 108, Stillwater, OK 74074; 405-742-1000.

Oregon
Rural Housing and Community Development Service, 101 SW Main, Suite 1410, Portland, OR 97204; 503-414-3300.

Pennsylvania
Rural Housing and Community Development Service, One Credit Union Place, Suite 330, Harrisburg, PA 17110-2996; 717-782-4476.

Puerto Rico
Rural Housing and Community Development Service, New San Juan Office Bldg., Room 01, 159 Carlos E. Chardon St., Hato Rey, PR 00918-5481; 809-766-5095.

South Carolina
Rural Housing and Community Development Service, Strom Thurmond Federal Bldg., Room 1007, 1835 Assembly St., Columbia, SC 29201; 803-765-5163.

South Dakota
Rural Housing and Community Development Service, Federal Bldg., Room 308, 200 Fourth St., SW, Huron, SD 57350; 605-352-1100.

Tennessee
Rural Housing and Community Development Service, 3322 West End Ave., Suite 300, Nashville, TN 37203-1071; 615-783-1300.

Texas
Rural Housing and Community Development Service, Federal Bldg., Suite 102, 101 South Main, Temple, TX 76501; 817-774-1301.

Utah
Rural Housing and Community Development Service, Wallace F. Bennett Federal Bldg., 125 S. State St., Room 5438, Salt Lake City, UT 84138; 801-524-4063.

Vermont, New Hampshire, Virgin Islands
Rural Housing and Community Development Service, City Center, 3rd Floor, 89 Main St., Montpelier, VT 05602; 802-828-6002.

Virginia
Rural Housing and Community Development Service, Culpeper Bldg., Suite 238, 1606 Santa Rosa Rd., Richmond, VA 23229; 804-287-1550.

Washington
Rural Housing and Community Development Service, Federal Bldg., Room 319, 301 Yakima St., P.O. Box 2427, Wenatchee, WA 98807; 509-664-0240.

West Virginia
Rural Housing and Community Development Service, 75 High St., Morgantown, WV 26505-7500; 304-291-4791.

Wisconsin
Rural Housing and Community Development Service, 4949 Kirschling Ct., Stevens Point, WI 54481; 715-345-7600.

Wyoming
Rural Housing and Community Development Service, Federal Bldg., Room 1005, 100 East B, P.O. Box 820, Casper, WY 82602; 307-261-5271.

* Homes: Department of Housing and Urban Development

Property Disposition Division
U.S. Department of Housing and Urban Development (HUD)
451 7th St. SW, Room 9172
Washington, DC 20410-4000
202-708-0740
HUD Locator   202-708-1422
Multi-Family Property Dispositions
                                     202-708-3343
Single-Family Property Dispositions
                                     202-708-0740

HUD homes are properties HUD owns as a result of paying the balance on foreclosed FHA insured home mortgages. Any qualified buyer can purchase a HUD home. Generally, your monthly mortgage payment should be no more than 29% of your monthly gross income. Many HUD homes require only a 3% down payment. You can move into some HUD homes with a $100 down payment. HUD will pay the real estate brokers commission up to the standard 6% of the sales price. HUD may also pay your closing costs. HUD homes are priced at fair market value. Consult your local newspapers for HUD listings; or, your regional HUD office, listed below; or, the real estate broker of your choice.

HUD's Property Disposition facilities are located within state offices and various coordinator's offices around the country. Contact your state office for details (see listing below). Frequently, HUD will advertise upcoming auctions of foreclosed properties in a local newspaper. The properties may be apartments, condominiums, or various kinds of single-family homes. The condition of these properties varies widely, including some that are little more than shells; and that, of course, affects the price. Some may be located in less than desirable neighborhoods; but others may end up being bargains, either as investments or personal residences. Bids are placed through private real estate brokers, who then submit them to HUD. Some offers for HUD homes are made to the seller and there may be negotiations. Offers for other HUD homes are done by bids placed during an "Offer Period." If you bid the full asking price, it may be accepted immediately. Otherwise, all the bids are opened at the close of the "Offer Period." The highest bidder wins. Contact the participating broker of your choice to show you the property and submit your bid. HUD broker contracted services are free to prospective buyers. Earnest money is a flat scaled fee ranging from $500-$2000 and must accompany the bid. Bidders must furnish their own financing. HUD stresses that properties sell "as is," so HUD will not make any repairs. It is up to a potential buyer to determine the value and condition, although the listings will state major problems.

Newspaper ads list houses that will be available for the next ten days, as well as others that did not sell in previous auctions. Listings include addresses, number of bedrooms and bathrooms, and suggested prices. Remember that HUD contracts are binding and non-negotiable: once your bid has won, there's no turning back. For a step by step buying guide to purchasing HUD owned homes, call the HUD Homeline, 1-800-767-4483, and request the brochure, *A Home of Your Own*. To learn about other programs at HUD that may be useful to you, call 202-708-0685.

Alabama
Heager Hill, State Coordinator, HUD-Alabama State Office, Beacon Ridge Tower, Suite 300, 600 Beacon Parkway West, Birmingham, AL 35209-3144; 205-290-7617.

Arizona
Terry Goddard, State Coordinator, HUD-Arizona State Office, Two Arizona Center, 400 N. 5th St., Suite 1600, Phoenix, AZ 85004-2361; 602-379-4434.

Arkansas
Bobbie J. (BJ) McCoy, Acting State Coordinator, HUD-Arkansas State Office, TCBY Tower, Suite 900,, 425 W. Capitol Ave.,, Little Rock, AR 72201-3488; 501-324-5401.

Alaska
Arlene Patton, State Coordinator, HUD-Alaska State Office, University Plaza Bldg., 949 E. 36th Ave., Suite 401, Anchorage, AK 99508-4135; 907-271-4170.

California
Arthur Agnos, Secretary's Representative, HUD-California State Office, Philip Burton Federal Bldg. and U.S. Courthouse, 450 Golden Gate Ave., P.O. Box 36003, San Francisco, CA 94102-3448; 415-556-4752.

Colorado
Anthony Hernandez, Secretary's Representative, HUD-Colorado State Office, 633 17th St., Denver, CO 80202-3607; 303-672-5448, ext. 1487.

Connecticut
Robert S. Donovan, Acting State Coordinator, HUD-Connecticut State Office, 330 Main St., Hartford, CT 06106-1860; 203-240-4523.

Delaware
David Sharbaugh, Acting State Coordinator, HUD-Delaware State Office, 824 Market St., Suite 850, Wilmington, DE 19801-3016; 302-573-6258.

District of Columbia
Jessica Franklin, State Coordinator, HUD-District of Columbia Office, Union Center Plaza, Phase II, 820 First St., NE, Suite 300, Washington, DC 20002-4205; 202-275-9206.

Florida
Jose Cintron, State Coordinator, Gables One Tower, 1320 S. Dixie Hwy., Coral Gables, FL 33146-2911; 305-662-4510.

Georgia
Davey L. Gibson, Secretary's Representative, HUD-Georgia State Office, Richard B. Russell Federal Bldg., 75 Spring St., SW, Atlanta, GA 30303-3388; 404-331-5136.

Hawaii
Gordon Y. Furutani, State Coordinator, HUD-Hawaii State Office, Seven Waterfront Plaza, 500 Ala Moana Blvd., Suite 500, Honolulu, HI 96813-4918; 808-522-8175.

Idaho
Gary Gillespie, Acting State Coordinator, HUD-Idaho State Office, Park IV, 800 Park Blvd., Suite 220, Boise, ID 83712-7743; 208-334-1991.

Illinois
Edwin Eisendrath, Secretary's Representative, HUD-Illinois State Office, Ralph Metcalfe Federal Bldg., 77 W. Jackson Blvd., Chicago, IL 60604-3507; 312-353-5680.

Indiana
William Shaw, State Coordinator, HUD-Indiana State Office, 151 N. Delaware St., Indianapolis, IN 46204-2526; 317-226-7606.

Iowa
William McNarney, State Coordinator, HUD-Iowa State Office, Federal Bldg., 210 Walnut St., Room 239, Des Moines, IA 50309-2155; 515-284-4512.

Kansas
Joseph O'Hern, Secretary's Representative, HUD-Kansas-Missouri State Office, Gateway Tower II, 400 State Ave., Room 200, Kansas City, KS 66101-2406; 913-551-5462.

Kentucky
State Coordinator, HUD-Kentucky State Office, 601 W. Broadway, P.O. Box 1044, Louisville, KY 40201-1044; 502-595-3607.

Louisiana
Jason Gamlin, State Coordinator, HUD-Louisiana State Office, Hale Boggs Federal Bldg., 9th Floor, 501 Magazine St., New Orleans, LA 70130-3099; 504-589-7200.

Maine
Richard Young, Acting State Coordinator, HUD-Maine State Office, 99 Franklin St., Bangor, ME 04401-4925; 207-945-0467.

Maryland
Harold Young, Acting State Coordinator, HUD-Maryland State Office, City Crescent Bldg., 10 S. Howard St., 5th Floor, Baltimore, MD 21201-2505; 410-962-2520.

Massachusetts
Mary Lou Crane, Secretary's Representative, HUD-Massachusetts State Office, Thomas P. O'Neill, Jr. Federal Building, 10 Causeway St., Room 375, Boston, MA 02222-1092; 617-565-5236.

Michigan
Regina F. Solomon, State Coordinator, HUD-Michigan State Office, Patrick V. McNamara Federal Bldg., 477 Michigan Ave., Detroit, MI 48226-2592; 313-226-7900.

Minnesota
Thomas Feeney, State Coordinator, HUD-Minnesota State Office, 220 Second St., South, Minneapolis, MN 55401-2195; 612-370-3288.

Mississippi
Thomas Cooper, Acting State Coordinator, HUD-Mississippi State Office, Dr. AH McCoy Federal Bldg., 100 W. Capitol St., Room 910, Jackson, MS 39269-1096; 601-965-4738.

Montana
Richard Brinck, State Coordinator, HUD-Montana State Office, Federal Office Bldg., Drawer 10095, 301 South Park, Room 340, Helena, MT 59626-0095; 406-449-5707.

Nebraska
Terry Gratz, State Coordinator, HUD-Nebraska State Office, Executive Tower Centre,, 10909 Mill Valley Rd., Omaha, NE 68154-3955; 402-492-3101.

Nevada
Paul Pradia, State Coordinator, HUD-Nevada State Office, Atrium Bldg., 333 N. Rancho Dr., Suite 700, Las Vegas, NV 89106-3714; 702-388-6500.

New Hampshire
David B. Harrity, State Coordinator, HUD-New Hampshire State Office, Norris Cotton Federal Bldg., 275 Chestnut St., Manchester, NH 03103-2487; 603-666-7681.

New Jersey
Diane Johnson, State Coordinator, HUD-New Jersey State Office, One Newark Center, 13th Floor, Newark, NJ 07102-5260; 201-622-7900, ext. 3102.

New Mexico
Michael R. Griego, State Coordinator, HUD-New Mexico State Office, 625 Truman St., NE, Albuquerque, NM 87110-6443; 505-262-6463.

New York
Diane Johnson, Acting Secretary's Representative, HUD-New York State Office, 26 Federal Plaza, New York, NY 10278-0068; 212-264-8068.

North Carolina
James Blackmon, State Coordinator, HUD-North Carolina State Office, Koger Bldg., 2306 W. Meadowview Rd., Greensboro, NC 27407-3707; 919-547-4001.

North Dakota
Keith Elliot, Acting State Coordinator, HUD-North Dakota State Office, Federal Bldg., 657 2nd Ave., North, P.O. Box 2483, Fargo, ND 58108-2483; 701-239-5136.

Ohio
Deborah C. Williams, State Coordinator, HUD-Ohio State Office, 200 N. High St., Columbus, OH 43215-2499; 614-469-7345.

Oklahoma
Katie Worsham, Acting State Coordinator, HUD-Oklahoma State Office, 500 Main St., Oklahoma City, OK 73102; 405-553-7400.

Oregon
Mark Pavolka, Acting State Coordinator, HUD-Oregon State Office, 400 SW 6th Ave., Suite 700, Portland, OR 97204-1632; 503-326-2561.

Pennsylvania
Karen A. Miller, Secretary's Representative, HUD-Pennsylvania State Office, The Wanamaker Bldg., 100 Penn Square East, Philadelphia, PA 19107-3390; 215-656-0600.

Puerto Rico
Maria Teresa Pombo, Acting State Coordinator, HUD-Caribbean Office, New San Juan Office Bldg., 159 Carlos E. Chardon Ave., San Juan, PR 00918-1804; 809-766-6121.

Rhode Island
Nancy Smith, State Coordinator, HUD-Rhode Island State Office, 10 Weybosset St., 6th Floor, Providence, RI 02903-3234; 401-528-5230.

South Carolina
Choice Edwards, State Coordinator, HUD-South Carolina State Office, Strom Thurmond Federal Building, 1835 Assembly Street, Columbia, SC 29201-2480; 803-765-5592.

South Dakota
Dwight Peterson, State Coordinator, HUD-South Dakota State Office, 2400 West 49th St., Suite I-201, Sioux Falls, SD 57105-6558; 605-330-4223.

Tennessee
Ginger Van Ness, State Coordinator, HUD-Tennessee State Office, 251 Cumberland Bend Dr., Suite 200, Nashville, TN 37228-1803; 615-736-5213.

Texas
Stephen Weatherford, Secretary's Representative, HUD-Texas State Office, 1600 Throckmorton, P.O. Box 2905, Fort Worth, TX 76113-2905; 817-885-5401.

Utah
John Milchick, State Coordinator, HUD-Utah State Office, 257 Tower, 257 East 200 South, Suite 550, Salt Lake City, UT 84111-2048; 801-524-5241.

Vermont
William Peters, Acting State Coordinator, HUD-Vermont State Office, Federal Building, 11 Elmwood Ave., Room 244, P.O. Box 879, Burlington, VT 05402-0879; 802-951-6290.

Virginia
Mary Ann Wilson, State Coordinator, HUD-Virginia State Office, The 3600 Centre, 3600 West Broad St., P.O. Box 90331, Richmond, VA 23230-0331; 804-278-4507.

Washington
Bob Santos, Secretary's Representative, HUD-Washington State Office, Seattle Federal Office Bldg., 909 First Ave., Suite 200, Seattle, WA 98104-1000; 206-220-5101.

West Virginia
Fred Roncaglione, State Coordinator, HUD-West Virginia State Office, 405 Capitol St., Suite 708, Charleston, WV 25301-1795; 304-347-7036.

Wisconsin
Delbert F. Reynolds, State Coordinator, HUD-Wisconsin State Office, Henry S. Reuss Federal Plaza, 310 W. Wisconsin Ave., Suite 1380, Milwaukee, WI 53203-2289; 612-370-3288.

Wyoming
William Garrett, Acting State Coordinator, HUD-Wyoming State Office, 4225 Federal Office Bldg., 100 East B St., P.O. Box 120, Casper, WY 82602-1918; 307-261-5252.

* Homes: H.O.P.E. 3

U.S. Department of Housing and Urban Development
Office of Community Planning and Development
Office of Affordable Housing Programs
451 7th St., S.W
Washington, DC 20410-7000
202-708-0324

The HUD Urban Homesteading Program has been replaced by the HOPE 3 Program. It is designed to provide homeownership for low income families and individuals. The funds will be distributed to the 10 HUD regions and awarded to local governments and non-profit organizations on a competitive bidding basis. It will generally provide down payment assistance for groups to acquire or rehabilitate affordable low income housing. Call your regional HUD office to find out who has been awarded grants, and then contact them directly to see what is available.

You qualify for housing help through HOPE 3 under the Low Income Family Housing Act if you are a first time homebuyer and are below 80% of the median income in your area. You may also qualify if you have not owned a home in 3 years. You must also meet the affordability criteria -- which requires that the cost of principal interest, taxes and insurance for the home comes to no more than 30% of your income. Since the program is new, the quality of public dissemination of information about these programs remains to be seen. These programs are instituted to help you, so don't be afraid to be persistent in asking for information about what HOPE 3 programs are available in your area from the Community Planning and Development Office at the Field or Regional HUD office nearest you.

To find out what the programs will provide and how to apply for a grant, contact John Garrity, DHUD, Office of Urban Rehabilitation, Room 7158, 451 Seventh Street, SW, Washington, DC 20410-7000, 202-708-0324 or look up the Monday, February 4, 1991 issue of the *Federal*

Register, Part X, DHUD, 24 CFR Subtitle A called *HOPE for Homeownership for Single Family Homes Program; Notice of Program Guidelines.*

* Homes: Veterans Administration

U.S. Veterans Administration (VA)
1120 Vermont Ave., NW
Washington, DC 20420
202-418-4270

Contact the local Veterans Administration Office in your state, or a real estate broker. Watch newspaper ads in local papers for listings of foreclosed properties. The "For Sale" signs on VA foreclosed properties are distinctive. The National Veterans Administration office in Washington, DC is not directly involved in handling the sales; for any inquiries you will be referred to a real estate broker or local VA office.

The Veterans Administration sells foreclosed properties through private real estate brokers. Properties are frequently advertised in local newspapers, giving information such as address, number of bedrooms and bathrooms, particular defects in the property, and price. Almost any real estate agent can show you the property. No broker has an exclusive listing for any of these properties. Local VA offices are the best source of information on the procedures involved in purchasing these properties. Regional offices publish lists of foreclosed properties with descriptions in multiple listing code and phone numbers to call about the property. In some cases, they will also directly send you lists of properties currently available in your area. These offices will mail out a list each time you write in a request, but unless you are a broker, they will not send the list for foreclosures to you on a monthly basis. You can, however, have the agent of your choice put on the mailing list. Others will not mail lists to you, but allow you to pick up the list from their office and/or will refer you to a broker. In either case, you must go through an agent to purchase the house, since they have the keys to the premises, and the

process is very much like a regular real estate transaction. The listing has the price on it the VA wants. It will also state if the VA is willing to entertain a lower price. Houses come "as is" with no guarantees, so it is important to inspect them carefully. Some are located in less than desirable neighborhoods, but there are bargains to be had as well. For the most part VA financed homes are mainstream suburban, not inner city. They are often found in neighborhoods located in economically hard hit areas -- such as the Southwest. Prices may drop on homes that are not sold in a certain period of time. VA financing is possible. Also, if you plan on VA financing, in cases of a tie, the other bidder gets priority for cash offers (pre-approved financing through a commercial lender.) You must state at the time of the bid whether you intend to use VA financing or have found your own.

There are two basic avenues to arrange financing. You can be pre-qualified by lenders and then go shopping. More commonly, the real estate broker you are working with will tell you what is available in the mortgage market. The usual way it works is that you find a broker, find a house, bid on it, wind the bid and then the broker helps you to find financing.

If you should win a bid on a VA foreclosed home but be unable to procure financing, some regional offices will put the home up for bid again. Others hold backup offers and will contact the next highest bidder if the original successful bidder is unable to complete the purchase. Most listings offer to sell financing at the current rate of interest for GI loans, even if the buyer is not a GI. A purchaser who is a GI can get these rates without using his GI benefits. Call the office listed above if you have questions. They will direct you to the appropriate department of your regional office. If you are a GI and wish to find out about a Certificate of Eligibility, whereby you can purchase a home worth up to $203,000 without a down payment, call 202-418-4270, ext. 3308 or your regional office. To discuss VA loan qualifications generally, call 202-827-1000 or your regional office.

Purchase is done through a sealed bidding process. Earnest money requirements are 1 percent of the purchase price, and are nonrefundable if the bid is accepted. This is a salvage program designed to recover what it can of the cost to the VA for purchasing the property, within a reasonable amount of time after foreclosure -- usually around 6 months.

* Miscellaneous Property: U.S. Customs Service

E.G.& G. Dynatrend
Attn: PAL
2300 Clarendon Blvd.
Suite 705
Arlington, VA 22201
703-351-7887
703-351-7880

E.G.& G. Dynatrend, under contract with the U.S. Customs Service, auctions forfeited and confiscated general merchandise, including vehicles, on a nationwide basis. Items include everything from vessels--both pleasure and commercial--to aircraft, machinery, clothes (in both commercial and individual quantities), jewelry, household goods, precious stones, liquor, furniture, high technology equipment, and infrequently, real estate. Public auctions and sealed and open bid methods are all used. Items are sold only by lot and number of items in a lot vary from one to many. You must bid on the entire lot.

The U.S. Customs Public Auction Line is 703-351-7887. Call it to subscribe to the mailing list of locations and dates of sales, to obtain general information about the custom sales program, dates of sales in your region or information about real estate sales. For $50 dollars per year you can subscribe to a mailing list of items to be auctioned nationwide; or you may subscribe to a list limited to one region of the country for $25. You will then receive fliers with descriptions of items available in upcoming auctions. There are two regions: states east of the Mississippi River, and states west of the Mississippi River. Send your name, address, telephone number, and a money order to the above address. Allow six to eight weeks for the first flier to arrive. The fliers will then arrive three weeks prior to the viewing period and will tell you when and where the items are available for inspection and details of auction procedures. Catalogs are also available a week before the sale with additional details. For sealed bids, a deposit in cashier's check for the total bid must be submitted along with the bid. Make the cashier's check payable to U.S. Customs Service/E.G.& G. Dynatrend, Agent. Indicate sale number on cashier's check and outside on the envelope.

U.S. Customs auctions are held every nine weeks in the following eight cities: Los Angeles, CA; Laredo, TX; Nogales, AZ; Miami, FL; Edinburg, TX; Houston, TX; Chula Vista, CA (San Diego, CA area); El Paso, TX; and Yuma, AZ. Other auctions are scheduled at different times at various other cities also.

* Miscellaneous Property: U.S. Department of Defense

The Defense Reutilization Marketing
  Service (DRMS)
Federal Center
74 N. Washington
Battle Creek, MI 49017-3092
616-961-7014
1-800-GOVT-BUY

Imagine what kinds of items are used, then discarded, by a government department as big as the Defense Department: literally everything from recyclable scrap materials and weapons accessories, to airplanes, ships, trains, and motor vehicles; to wood and metalworking machinery, agricultural equipment, construction equipment, communications equipment and medical, dental and veterinary supplies. Not to forget photographic equipment, chemical products, office machines, food preparation and serving equipment, musical instruments, textiles, furs, tents, flags, and sometimes live animals such as goats and horses. No activated items with military applications are included. Neither are real estate or confiscated items such as sports cars or luxury goods.

Goods sold are either surplus or not usable by other government agencies. First priority is given to designated groups which qualify for donations. The rest is then put up for public sale. By contacting the Defense Reutilization Marketing Service at the above address or telephone, you can receive a booklet called *How to Buy Surplus Personal Property* which explains what Department of Defense (DOD) has for sale and how to bid for it. The Defense Department also lists notices of Sealed Bid property sales in the Commerce Business Daily, available from the Superintendent of Documents, Government Printing Office, Washington, DC 20402-9325; 202-512-1800.

Sales are conducted by regional Defense Reutilization and Marketing Region (DRMR) sales offices which coordinate sales in their geographical area. Listed below are addresses and telephone numbers of the regional offices, which can direct you further as to exactly where items are physically sold. Local sales are by auction, spot bid, or on a retail basis. Auctions are held where there are relatively small quantities of a variety of items. Spot bids are made through forms submitted in the course of a sale - usually when the property is something with a high demand or interest. The retail sales offer small quantities at fixed, market-level prices. There are 180 retail sales outlets, on military bases.

Large quantities of goods are usually sold by sealed bid, which you submit by mail, along with a deposit, on a form you obtain in a catalog which describes the items. (You receive the catalogs once you are on the mailing list). Recyclable materials are sold through the Resource Recovery Recycling Program or through the Hazardous Property Program. Call the above listed number for further details. You

can be put on a mailing list to receive advance notice of DOD sales in your region, but if you don't make any bids after two notifications it will probably be removed unless you make an additional request to remain on the list. You can also be placed on a National Bidders List for sales throughout the country by contacting 1-800-222-DRMS. People under age 18 and members of the U.S. Armed Forces, including civilian employees, are not eligible to participate in these sales. This 800 number can also direct you to the retail sales outlet nearest you, and can give you other information on DRMS sales, including how to obtain a catalog.

Following are the Defense Reutilization and Marketing sales offices:

DRMR: Columbus, P.O. Box 500, Blacklick, OH 43004-0500, 614-692-2114. This region includes: MN, WI, MI, IA, NE, KS, MO, IL, IN, OH, WV, VA, DE, NJ, PA, , MD, CT, NY, RI, MA, ME, VT, NH, and District of Columbia

DRMR: Memphis, 2163 Airways Blvd., Memphis, TN 38114-0716, 901-775-4554. This region includes: TX, OK, AR, LA, MS, AL, TN, KY, GA, FL, SC, NC.

DRMR: Ogden, 500 W. 12 St., Building 2A1, Ogden, UT 84407-5001, 801-777-6557. This region includes: ND, SD, MT, WY, ID, UT, CO, AZ, NM, WA, OR, NV, CA.

You can also take advantage of DOD sales if you live outside the United States. The DOD booklet, *How to Buy Surplus Personal Property*, lists addresses for various regions in Europe and the Pacific.

* Miscellaneous Property: U.S. Postal Service
Claims and Inquiry Office
U.S. Postal Service
475 L'Enfant Plaza, S.W.
Washington, DC 20260-0001
202-636-1500
Vehicle Management Facility
202-832-0176
Contact the Mail Recovery Centers listed below for undeliverable goods; or your local Postmaster for Vehicle Maintenance Facilities and surplus property auctions. To receive

advance notice of the auctions you can write to a Mail Recovery Center and request that your name be put on the auction sales mailing list. To be on all of them, you must write to each one separately. Usually 10 days before the auction, you will be notified by postcard of the time, date and place. Viewing inspections are usually held 2 hours before the auction begins.

The Postal Service holds auctions of unclaimed merchandise which includes a wide range of property -- from electronic and household items -- to clothes, jewelry, linens, toys, all types of equipment, and lots of books. Sales are handled through the Mail Recovery Centers throughout the country listed below. However, any high value items such as art works, are sold at the New York auction. Contact your local Postmaster to ask about their auctions of surplus property and used vehicles. There are 225 post office vehicle maintenance facilities throughout the country. Their addresses and phone numbers are all listed at the back of the Zip Code Directory kept at post offices. The used vehicle sales can be good bargains, since the vehicles are somewhat fixed up, painted, and occasionally in good condition. Some jeeps, for instance, may sell for between $1200 and $1500. Recently a man bought 15 jeeps for $100 each at auction. Vehicles that do not sell off the storage lot are auctioned. Sometimes cars such as Pintos can be picked up for as little as $750. The sales conducted by the 225 Vehicle Maintenance Facilities around the country are usually fixed price sales, but 5 or 6 times per year auctions have been held at larger cities.

The mail recovery items are usually sold in lots of similar goods, with the volume or quantity varying widely. Prices depend on what the goods are and the number of people bidding at a particular auction. There may be a minimum bid required, such as $20; and often cash is the only acceptable payment. Bidders are responsible for removing the items purchased.

A flier for a Postal Service auction of unclaimed and damaged merchandise in St. Paul, Minnesota

advised that only those already on an established check register may pay by check; otherwise, cash is required. It also advised that potential bidders to bring their own containers -- boxes, crates, and bags -- for packing. The Postal Service in San Francisco, California, announced that books, jewelry, sound recordings, speakers, and cabinets, as well as miscellaneous merchandise would be available.

Eastern Region
U.S. Postal Service Mail Recovery Center, Room 531 A, 2970 Market St., Philadelphia, PA 19104-9652; 215-895-8140 (auction information and number to call to be notified by postcard of next upcoming auction). Includes Pennsylvania, Southern New Jersey, Maryland, Delaware, Ohio, Kentucky, Indiana, Virginia, West Virginia, North Carolina, and South Carolina.

Central Region
U.S. Postal Service Mail Recovery Center, 180 E. Kellogg St., Room 932, St. Paul, MN 55101-9607; 612-293-3083. Includes Minnesota, Michigan, Wisconsin, North Dakota, South Dakota, Nebraska, Iowa, Illinois, Northern New Jersey, New Hampshire, Maine, Vermont, Rhode Island, Massachusetts, Kansas, Missouri, Connecticut, and New York.

Southern Region
U.S. Postal Service Mail Recovery Center, 730 Great Southwest Parkway, Atlanta, GA 30336-2496; 404-344-1625. Includes Georgia, Florida, Louisiana, Tennessee, Arkansas, Mississippi, Oklahoma, part of Texas, Alabama, Mississippi, Virgin Islands, and Puerto Rico.

Western Region
U.S. Postal Service Mail Recovery Center, 390 Main St., 4th Floor, San Francisco, CA 94105-9602; 415-543-1826. Auctions are held at 228 Harrison St., San Francisco, CA. Includes: Alaska, Oregon, Idaho, California, Washington, Nevada, Utah, Arizona, New Mexico, part of Texas, Hawaii, Wyoming, Colorado, Montana, Guam, and Samoa.

* Miscellaneous Property: General Services Administration Property

Personal Property Sales Center
U.S. General Services Administration
1941 Jefferson Davis Hwy.
Arlington, VA 22202
703-305-7814/7240

Contact your local General Services Administration (GSA) office listed below. The GSA disposes of surplus property for most of the government agencies, and has items ranging from vehicles and scrap metals, to office furniture, office and industrial equipment, data processing equipment, boats, medical equipment, waste paper and computers; as well as aircraft, railroad equipment, agricultural equipment, textiles, food waste, photographic equipment, jewelry, watches, and clothing.

Some regional offices have no mailing list. Instead, there is a number they will give you to call that is a recorded message of all upcoming events. It will give the time, date, and location of the auction and type, such as warehouse, vehicles or office furniture. Other regions allow you to have your name placed on a mailing list to receive advance notices of auctions at no cost. Catalogs list the specific items and their condition. Sales are conducted as regular auctions, spot auctions (where bids are submitted on-the-spot in writing) and by sealed bid (written on a form and mailed in). For auctions and spot bids, you will have two days prior to the sale to view and inspect property, and one week prior for sealed bids. For sealed bid items you receive a catalog, once your are on the mailing list, describing the merchandise. If your region does not have a mailing list, you may pick up catalogs at the office or the sale. Announcements come out as property is accumulated, with March to October being the busiest period. The highest bidder wins in all cases.

Prices may range from way below wholesale for some items to close-to-market prices for others, especially automobiles and boats. Cars tend to be common American-made brands, such as Tempos, Citations, and Reliances. Cars are auctioned when they are three years old or have reached 60,000 miles, whichever occurs first, and are usually sold at a fair market price. Seized cars may be newer and of a foreign make. A Mercedes-Benz was recently sold at a National Capitol Region auction. Payment may be by cash, cashier's checks, money orders, traveler's checks, government, or credit union checks; but any personal or business checks must be accompanied by an Informal Bank Letter guaranteeing payment. Full payment must be made by the following day, and bidders are responsible for removal of all property. To bid in GSA auctions, you must register at the site and obtain a bidder number. Once you are on the bidders mailing list, you must bid at least once while receiving five mailings or your name will be removed from the list. Then you must contact the appropriate office again to continue receiving mailings.

Some listings for a GSA sale in Bismarck, North Dakota included the following items: miscellaneous kitchen equipment, meat slicers, coffee makers, cameras, film, binoculars, screens, paper, postage meter, nuts and bolts, typewriters, lettering set, mailboxes, lamps, and a streetlight.

For information about GSA auctions in your area, contact one of the regional offices listed below:

National Capitol Region (Washington DC and vicinity)
6808 Loisdale Rd., Building A, Springfield, VA 22150; 703-557-7785, or 703-557-7796, for a recording.

Region I (Boston)
GSA, Surplus Sales Branch, 10 Causeway St., Room 1079, Boston, MA, 02109; 617-565-7326, Auction Hotline Recording, 617-565-6045 or 800-755-1946.

Region II (New York)
GSA Surplus Sales Branch, 26 Federal Plaza, Room 20-116, New York, NY, 10078; 212-264-4824, or 212-264-4823, for a recording.

Region III (Philadelphia)
GSA Surplus Sales Branch, P.O. Box 40657, Philadelphia, PA 19107-3396; 215-656-3939 or 215-656-3400 for a recording.

Region IV (Atlanta)
GSA Surplus Sales Branch, Attn: 4PR, 401 West Peachtree St., Room 3015, Atlanta, GA 30365-2550; 404-331-0972, recording 404-331-5133 or 800-473-7836.

Region V (Chicago)
230 S. Dearborn St., Chicago, IL 60604; 312-353-6061 office, 800-755-1946 or 312-353-0246 hotline for a recorded announcement.

Region VI (Kansas)
GSA Surplus Sales Branch (6FB), 4400 College Blvd., Suite 175, Overland Park, KS 66211; 816-823-3700.

Region VII (Ft. Worth)
GSA Surplus Sales Branch (2PR), 819 Taylor St., Room 9A33, Ft. Worth, TX 76102-6105; 817-334-2352 or 800-833-4317, 817-334-2331 for a recorded announcement.

Region VIII (Denver)
GSA Surplus Sales Branch (7FBP-8), Denver Federal Center, Building 41, Room 253, P.O. Box 22506-DSC, Denver, CO 80225-0506; 303-236-7705 for recording or 303-236-7702.

Region IX (San Francisco)
GSA Surplus Sales Section 9PR, 525 Market St., 5th Floor, San Francisco, CA 94105; 415-744-5245 or 800-676-SALE for catalogs or mailing lists.

Region X (Washington)
GSA Surplus Sales Branch GSA Center (9PR-F), 400 15th St., SW, Room 1138, Auburn, WA 98001-6599; 206-931-7566 for a recording or 206-931-7547.

* Miscellaneous Property: Internal Revenue Service (IRS)

Office of Special Procedures
Internal Revenue Service
U.S. Department of the Treasury
1111 Constitution Ave., NW
Washington, DC 20224
202-622-6938

No information concerning auctions is available from this office. Contact your local district office to see if they maintain a mailing list to receive information on upcoming auctions. If not, this information can be found in your local newspaper. Check the classified section for a listing of IRS seized property to be sold. The listing will give phone number and details. The property sold by the IRS is seized from delinquent taxpayers rather than being used or surplus government property. Many kinds of merchandise are put up for auction, including real estate, vehicles, and office and industrial equipment. Sales are by both sealed bids and public auction. Regarding property sales, the IRS warns that land may still be redeemed by the original owner up to 180 days AFTER you, the bidder, purchase it at an auction; and therefore no deed is issued until this time period has elapsed. Buildings on land being sold by the IRS are NOT open for inspection by a potential buyer unless permission is granted by the taxpayer/owner.

Payment may be by cash, certified check, cashier's check, or money order. In some cases, full payment is required the day of the sale.

Otherwise, a 20% downpayment (or $200, whichever is greater) is needed to hold the property, with the balance due at a specified time from the date of the sale, not to exceed one month.

* Miscellaneous Property: U.S. Marshals Service

U.S. Marshals Service
Seized Assets Division
U.S. Department of Justice
600 Army-Navy Drive
Arlington, VA 22202
202-307-9237

Contact your local Sunday newspaper for auction notices in the legal section, or the nearest U.S. Marshals Office under U.S. Department of Justice. Usually the Marshals Office is located in the Federal Building of a city. The U.S. Marshals Service or a contracted commercial sales or auction service may handle disposal of the property. Sales are always listed every third Wednesday in *USA Today* newspaper.

In 1991, the Drug Enforcement Agency managed 1.4 billion dollars worth of property from convicted drug dealers. The U.S. Marshals Service, which holds crime-related property accumulated in Federal drug-related and other confiscations, auctions much of this off to the public through 94 offices around the country. Items sold include everything from entire working businesses, to cars, houses, copiers, jewelry, rare coin and stamp collections, apartment complexes, and restaurants. The government is not giving these properties away by any means, but bargains are possible as well as opportunities to purchase some exotic goodies. Confiscated viable businesses are managed by the Service until the time of the auction in order to keep up or increase the businesses' value.

Auctions are not scheduled regularly, but occur when items accumulate. Auctions may be conducted by private auctioneers or the Marshals Service itself. No mailing list is kept to notify you individually, and there is no national listing of items, since new properties are seized daily and adjudication of drug-related cases may take years. Payment at these auctions is by cash, certified check, or special arrangements when large amounts of money are involved. One note, the Marshals Service checks out people paying for large items with cash to make sure the government is not re-selling things to drug dealers. The Marshals Service also auctions off property seized by the Drug Enforcement Agency and the Federal Bureau of Investigation.

* Natural Resources Sales Assistance

Office of Liquidations
Small Business Administration (SBA)
409 Third Street SW, 8th Floor
Washington, DC 20416
1-800-827-5722
202-205-6500

The federal government sells surplus property and natural resources, such as timber. SBA works with government agencies which are selling the property and resources to assure that small businesses have an opportunity to buy a fair share of them. Occasionally natural resources that the federal government is releasing on the market are made available. Small fuel companies and producers may get the option to buy their fair share of federal government coal leases. The royalty oil program enables small and independent refineries to buy oil at valuations set by the federal government - which is in excess of spot market prices. Agricultural leases may be had for land on which to graze cattle or grow crops. This SBA program is designed to ensure that small businesses get their fair share of real and personal federal property put on the market. Don't expect bargains. To find out what SBA Natural Resources Sales Assistance programs are in your area, contact your nearest SBA office. For information on other SBA services, call 1-800-827-5722 (recorded listing from which you can order brochures.)

* Real Estate: General Services Administration Property Sales

General Services Administration (GSA)
Office of Real Estate Sales
Washington, DC 20406
1-800-GSA-1313

Call this toll-free number for national listing of properties and to receive a booklet describing the GSA real estate program. Then contact local GSA office for the area you are interested in. You can also obtain the list by calling the Property Disposal Division, 202-501-0067. The phone number of the local GSA office to contact will be provided on the list that is mailed to you free of charge upon request. If you have a computer equipped with a modem, you can access the Federal Real Estate Bulletin Board for information on real estate sales. Set you communications software to 8 data bits, no parity, and 1 stop bit. Dial 800-776-7872 or 202-501-6510.

* Real Estate: Small Business Administration (SBA)

U.S. Small Business Administration
Portfolio Management Division
409 Third Street, SW
Washington, DC 20416
202-205-6481
Recording from which to order brochures
1-800-827-5722

Contact your local SBA office located in 10 Regional Offices around the country, or any of the 68 District Offices. SBA does not maintain a mailing list. No district or regional SBA office is aware of what the other offices are offering. The SBA auctions off properties of people who have defaulted on home loan payments in SBA-sponsored programs. Listings of auctions are printed in local newspapers, usually in the Sunday edition in the classified section. Merchandise is identified as SBA property and sold by brokers, none of whom have the exclusive listing, or by private auctioneers. The auctioneers are chosen on a rotating basis. SBA attempts to sell to the highest bidder, but may reject a winning bid if too low. Sales are infrequent. Do not expect bargains. Items sold range from office furniture and equipment to buildings or entire bakeries, drycleaners, or other businesses. There may be parts or whole businesses available. The auctioneer may have an entire auction of SBA items, or a mixture of things from various sources. You may request to bid by sealed bid if you desire; and a deposit is required. Payment is by cash or certified check. If you are interested in certain categories of merchandise, you might want to be placed on the mailing list of one or more auctioneers who specialize in that particular type of item, such as farm equipment, for example. Since the SBA is often the guarantor of bank loans, SBA auctions are relatively infrequent and bargains are not easy to find. SBA Regional Offices follow:

Dallas: 8625 King George Dr., Dallas, TX 75235-3391; 214-767-7633

Kansas City: 328 8th St., Suite 307, Kansas City, MO 64105; 816-374-6380

Denver: 633 17th St., 7th Floor, Denver, CO 80202; 303-294-7186

San Francisco: 71 Stevenson St., 20th Floor, San Francisco, CA 94105-2939; 415-744-6402

Seattle: 1200 6th Ave., Suite 1805, Seattle, WA 98101-1128; 206-553-5676

Boston: 10 Causway, Room 812, Boston, MA 02222-1093; 617-565-8415

New York: 26 Federal Plaza, Room 3108, New York, NY 10278; 212-264-1450

King of Prussia: 475 Allendale Rd., Suite 201, King of Prussia, PA 19406; 610-962-3700

Atlanta: 1375 Peachtree St. N.E., 5th Floor, Atlanta, GA 30367-8102; 404-347-2797

Chicago: 300 South Riverside Plaza, Suite 1975 South, Chicago, IL 60606-6617; 312-353-5000

* Ships: Maritime Administration

U.S. Department of Transportation
Office of Ship Operations
Maritime Administration
400 7th St., SW, Room 7324
Washington, DC 20590
202-366-5111

When the government decides that a merchant ship is no longer needed or useable, it may put that ship up for sale by auction, through a sealed bid procedure. A ten percent deposit is required. It is sold to the highest bidder for its scrap value. Contact the above address to be put on the auction mailing list. When ships are available, you will receive descriptions of the ships and information on the bidding procedure.

* Timber Sales for Small Business

Government Contracting
Small Business Administration (SBA)
409 3rd St., SW, #8800
Washington, DC 20416
202-205-6470

The U.S. Government regularly sells timber from the federal forests managed by the U.S. Forest Service, Department of Agriculture, and the Bureau of Land Management, Department of Interior. On occasion, timber also is sold from federally-owned forests which are under the supervision of the Department of Defense, the Department of Energy, and the Tennessee Valley Authority, and the Department of the Interior. The SBA and these agencies work together to ensure full opportunity for concerns to bid on federal timber sales. SBA and the sales agencies jointly set aside timber sales for bidding by small concerns when it appears that, under open sales, small business would not obtain a fair share at reasonable prices. Contact your local SBA office for further specific information. It is listed in the blue pages of the telephone directory.

Donations To Non-Profit Organizations

* Art Exhibits

Smithsonian Institution
1100 Jefferson Dr., SW, Room 3146
Washington, DC 20560
202-357-3168
Fax: 202-357-4324

The Smithsonian can bring art to you, whether you live in a major metropolitan area or a rural one. The Smithsonian Institute Traveling Exhibition Service (SITES) sponsors approximately 65 different exhibits at any given time in museums and other locations around the country. The participation fee will range from $100 to $100,000. The exhibitions range from popular culture, to fine arts, photography, science, historical exhibits, or topics of interest to children. The collections are from other museums and institutions, and are most frequently sent to other museums, libraries, historic homes, or even schools and community centers. More than half the locations are in rural settings. SITES estimates that more than 11 million people view the exhibits it circulates in this program. The bigger exhibits that require special security arrangements go only to museums equipped to handle them. If interested, call the above number for the SITES *Updates* catalog.

* Books

Library of Congress
Exchange and Gift Division
1st and C Street, SE
Washington, DC 20540-4280
202-707-9511/9512

Government agencies, educational institutions, and other non-profit organizations may qualify to obtain free books from the U.S. Library of Congress. The books are largely technical and legal works, but from time to time contains entire collections from military installation lending libraries that have been closed. There is no way to tell what books will be available. Stock is constantly changing. Books are first offered on a competitive bidding basis. If they are not sold, they become available on a donation bidding basis. Commercial book dealers may compete in this bidding against non-profit organizations. The proceeds sustain the Book Preservation Program. Someone from the organization must choose which books are desired. He or she must have a letter from the organization or appropriate Congressional representative stating that the person it selected to choose the books acts for a non-profit organization. The Library will ship the books UPS at the organization's expense or the organization may supply the Library with pre-addressed franking labels. Congressional offices will help educational institutions such as universities and schools obtain these labels. Non-profit organizations may submit bids to purchase books. The Library will contact the organization if the bid is unacceptably low and give the bidder one chance to raise it. There is no limit on the number of books a group may order.

* Department of Housing and Urban Development (HUD)

HUD Library and Information Service
451 7th Street SW, Room 814
Washington, DC 20743

To find out about the over 100 programs HUD offers to assist low and moderate income housing groups and individuals, obtain *Programs of HUD* by calling 202-708-1420.

* Food and Surplus Commodities

USDA Food Distribution Programs
or Food Distribution Division
Food and Nutrition Service
3101 Park Center Drive, Room 503

Alexandria, VA 22302
703-305-2680

Non-profit groups with tax-exempt status may apply for surplus commodities held by the Agriculture Department, such as grain (usually flour), oils, and sometimes milk and cheese. The large quantities of surplus cheese and milk that existed a couple of years ago are largely depleted. The items available depend somewhat on which foods are currently in surplus. Contact your state distribution agency, frequently the state Department of Agriculture, Department of Education, or Administrative Services, or the above address.

* Foreign Gifts

General Services Administration
Crystal Mall Building #4
1941 Jefferson Davis Highway, Room 800
Washington, DC 20406
703-308-0745

Non-Presidential gifts worth over $200 from foreign countries to U.S. government agencies or their representatives may be displayed by the recipient in his government office, then purchased by him at an officially assessed value. If the gift is not purchased, it may end up in a State Surplus Property office, where the general public can get a chance to buy it. Watches and jewelry are commonly available, along with books, sculptures, and various artifacts. But the souvenir from Anwar Sadat to Jimmy Carter during the Middle East peace talks goes to the U.S. Archives and possibly later to the Jimmy Carter Library.

When gifts are reported to the GSA, they first go through the federal screening cycle. Federal agencies have the first chance to purchase items at retail value price. If none exercise that option, the recipient may purchase the item. If the item remains unsold, it enters the donation screening cycle. It may then be used for display purposes at state agencies such as libraries or museums. After that, it may be sold to the public at auction. At public auction, anyone can purchase the item. Non-profits have no special footing. Items are disposed of by GSA in basically the same way as other surplus and excess property.

Items desired by non-profit organizations should be requested through your local Surplus Property Office, which can then contact the GSA about a donation. You can find a list of foreign gifts given to government agencies published yearly in the *Federal Register*, State Department, Chief of Protocol, Washington, DC, 202-647-4169.

* Housing For The Homeless

Judy Breitman
Chief, Real Property Branch
Division of Health Facilities Planning
ORM/OM
Department of Health and Human Services
Parklawn Building, Room 17A-10
5600 Fishers Lane
Rockville, MD 20857
301-443-2265
Fax: 301-443-0084

The above will send you a helpful brochure entitled *Obtaining Federal Property for the Homeless: Questions and Answers About Federal Property Programs.* If you are part of a non-profit organization ministering to the homeless, the government is currently taking applications for eligible groups to receive excess or unused federal buildings or land for homeless people. The property is leased or deeded over. To find out what properties are available call the 24 hour hotline, 1-800-927-7588. Every Friday, *The Federal Register* (available from libraries or by subscription) will list which federal properties are available and where. The applying organization has 60 days after notice of property availability is published to submit a written expression of interest. It will then be sent an application packet and have 90 days after that to apply for the property. Criteria is outlined in *The Federal Register*. If you think your organization may qualify, call Public Health Service, 301-443-2265.

* Interagency Council on the Homeless

Office of Special Needs Assistance Programs
U.S. Department of Housing and Urban
Development
451 Seventh Street, SW, Room 7262

Washington, DC 20410
202-708-1480

This is a coordinating counsel of 16 different federal agencies, headed by the HUD Secretary. It works with state and local governments and private organizations on homeless-related efforts. Call for information on homeless activities. For information on financing rehabilitation or support services, contact HUD's Office of Special Needs Assistance Program at 202-708-4300.

Title V of the McKinney Act is the "Federal Surplus Property Program." You can call 1-800-927-7588 to get answers about the Title V Program and properties 24 hours per day. Under this program, federally owned surplus or unused property may be deeded, leased or made available on an interim basis at no cost to homeless providers such as states, local governments and non-profit organizations. To find out about eligible properties, ask to be put on the mailing list that tells you of properties in your area as they are published by contacting your nearest field HUD office.

* Miscellaneous Property

Director, Property Management Division
Office of Transportation and Property
 Management
Federal Supply Service
Washington, DC 20406
703-308-0745

Or contact your local State Office of Surplus Property. The General Services Administration (GSA) will donate items it handles to qualifying non-profit organizations which request it. Items are "as is" and range from tools, office machines, supplies and furniture, clothes, hardware, medical supplies to cars, boats, and planes. Your State Agency for Surplus Property, also called Office of Purchasing, Property Control, or General Services, makes the determination whether your group qualifies, then contacts the GSA to obtain it. There may be a charge of 2% of the value and a fee for handling and service. Groups eligible can include public agencies, and non-profit educational, public health, elderly, or homeless organizations.

* Tools for Schools

Federal Surplus Warehouse
1910 Darbytown Rd.
Richmond, VA 23231
804-236-3665

Qualifying nonprofit organizations and educational institutions can receive surplus federal property. Items available depend on what is in the warehouse at the time, which ranges from office furniture to industrial equipment. A completed application must first be submitted and approved. There are some stipulations, including a service charge based on the value of the merchandise. Contact this office for more information and an application.

* Travel Aboard An Icebreaker

Ice Operations Division
U.S. Coast Guard Headquarters
2100 2nd Street, SW
Washington, DC 20593
202-267-1450

The Coast Guard does not evaluates scientific projects to determine if they qualify. The group that qualifies as a primary user, because it is willing to pay for fuel and part of maintenance and helicopter costs on resupply trips, may send a scientist they select to ride along with one of the two Coast Guard Icebreakers that travel to the Arctic and Antarctica. At present, the National Science Foundation (4201 Wilson Blvd., Arlington, VA 22230, 703-306-1070) is the primary user. Other interested parties who wish to send scientists or observers, such as scientific or environmental groups must obtain the consent of the primary user for that trip. Most travelers are sponsored by government or educational organizations, but the Coast Guard is interested in any appropriate, professional project and will consider other applications as well. They can also be flexible on their itinerary to accommodate projects. Sometimes scientists on short missions may travel at no cost. In addition, special expeditions are commissioned, such as the one in 1992 by the U.S. Geological Survey. If interested, contact the primary user.

State Government Auctions

The following is a descriptive listing of state government offices which offer auctions or donations of surplus property.

Alabama

Alabama Surplus Property, P.O. Box 210487, Montgomery, AL 36121, 334-277-5866. Alabama auctions off a variety of items about three times per year, including office equipment, heavy machinery (such as milling machines and drill presses), and vehicles, including cars, trucks, boats, and tractors. Trailers, medical equipment, tires, dossiers, and lathes are also sold. The state advertises upcoming auctions in the classified section of local newspapers. Upon written request made to the above address, you can be put on a mailing list. You will then be notified 2 or 3 weeks in advance of each upcoming auction, but you won't receive a list of items. Lists of items can be picked up at the above office 2 days before the auction. Payment can be by cash, cashier's check, or personal check with a bank letter of credit. Items are available for viewing two days prior to the auction. No bids by mail.

Alaska

Surplus Property Management Office, 2400 Viking Dr., Anchorage, AK 99501, 907-279-0596. The Juno office is 907-465-2172. Call it for general information and mailing list information. Alaska's Division of General Services and Supply sells surplus office equipment, including furniture and typewriters, every Wednesday from 8:30 am to 3:30 pm in a garage sale fashion with prices marked for each item. For items costing over $1000, cash or cashiers checks are required. Vehicles, at various locations throughout the state, are sold during sealed bid or outcry auctions twice a year, in the spring and fall. Payment is by cashiers check after you have been notified of your winning bid.

Arizona

Office of Surplus Property, 1537 W. Jackson St., Phoenix, AZ 85007, 602-542-5701. About three times per year, usually in January, May, and September, Arizona auctions off everything from vehicles to miscellaneous office equipment and computers. Items are sold by lots rather than individually; and prices, especially cars, can be below blue book price, depending upon opening bids. Vehicles range from empty frames to Jaguars. A mailing list is maintained. You can have it sent to you for no charge. Individual cities and county governments in Arizona also hold their own surplus auctions.

Arkansas

State Marketing and Redistribution Office, 6620 Young Rd., Little Rock, AR 72209, 501-565-8645. Arkansas conducts both

sealed bid and retail, fixed price sales of surplus items. On Wednesdays, between 7:30 am and 3:00 pm, buyers may view and purchase items, which include office machines, tables, and tires, valued at under $500. Larger, more valuable items, including vehicles, medical equipment, mobile homes, and machine shop and automotive supplies, are sold by sealed bid. You can have your name placed on the mailing list for various categories such as computers, autos and miscellaneous equipment. You must bid three times to keep your name on the mailing list. The state also conducts sealed bids by mail. The bid fee is $1. No personal checks are accepted for sealed bids. All items are sold "as is," with no refunds or guarantees implied or stated.

California

State of California, Office of Fleet Administration, 1421 Richards Blvd., Sacramento, CA 95814, 916-327-9196 (recorded message), 916-327-2085.. Once a month on Wednesdays, the General Services Department of the state holds open bid auctions at Sacramento or Los Angeles State Garages of surplus automobiles previously owned by state agencies. Vehicles can be viewed from 8:30 am to 9:30 am. The auction begins at 9:30 am. Vehicles may include sedans, cargo and passenger vans, pick-ups (mostly American-made). Auctions are occasionally advertised in the newspapers. Minimum bid prices are set for exceptionally nice cars. Only state agency vehicles are sold. Payment is by cash, cashiers check, or certified check. Successful bidders have up to five working days to pay for and pick up the cars (the following Friday). Out-of-state checks are frowned upon. Prices vary greatly, and some vehicles have required minimum bids.

California Highway Patrol, Used Vehicle Sales Office, 3300 Reed Ave., W. Sacramento, CA 95605, 916-371-2270. Minimum bids are stated on a recorded telephone message (916-371-2284). The auction is by sealed bids which are opened at 3:00 pm daily; winners may be present or notified by telephone. Payment is by cashiers check, certified check, or, money order only -- no personal checks or cash accepted. Bids may be submitted and inspection is available between 8:00 am and 3:00 pm.

Colorado

Department of Correctional Industries, State Surplus Agency, 4200 Garfield Street, Denver, CO 80216, 303-321-4012. Several times a year, Colorado auctions off its surplus property, including motor vehicles. Auctions are pre-announced in newspaper ads, and a mailing list is also maintained. To be put on the mailing list, call the above number. The auctions of state property are held the third Thursday of every month. If you are on the mailing list, you will receive a notice the weekend before the auction with a brief description of the items. Non-profit organizations have first choice of state surplus items, which can include typewriters, desks, computers, file cabinets, hospital beds, and much more. Payment may be made by cash, money order or personal checks with two IDs.

Connecticut

60 State St. Rear, Wethersfield, CT 06109, 203-566-7018, or 203-566-7190. Items vary from day to day. Vehicles are auctioned separately 8 or 9 times per year, with ads in the 4 largest newspapers and on 2 radio stations giving advance notice. There is no mailing list. These auctions are usually on the second Saturday of the month. Vehicles may be viewed one hour prior to the auction. Buyers may also purchase a brochure with vehicle descriptions when they pay the $3 registration fee. You may go Monday-Friday, noon to 3:45 to view and purchase smaller items in their warehouse.

Delaware

Division of Purchasing Surplus Property, P.O. Box 299, Delaware City, DE 19706, 302-834-4550. Twice a year, in May and in September, Delaware publicly auctions off vehicles, office furniture, and other surplus or used property. Vehicles include school buses, paddle boats, vans, pick-up trucks, heavy equipment, and sedans. Prices depend on the condition of the item and how many people are bidding for it. Vehicles may be inspected prior to the auction. You may get on a mailing list to be advised of upcoming auctions. A flyer with information and conditions of payment will be sent to you.

District of Columbia

District of Columbia Dept. of Public Works, 5001 Shepard Parkway, SW, Washington, DC 20032, 202-645-4227. DC holds vehicle auctions every 1st and 3rd Tuesday of every month. Vehicles include cars, trucks, buses, ambulances, and boats. Inspection and viewing is available at 7:00 am, one hour prior to the 8:00 am open bid auction. $100 cash must be paid to attend the auction. Prices and conditions of vehicles vary greatly. No mailing list is kept. Auctions are posted 45 days in advance in the *Washington Times*. A $100 cash entry fee must be paid to attend an auction. This fee will be credited toward the purchase price, and is refunded if no car is purchased. Cars must be paid for in full at the auction by certified or cashier's check. Twice a year confiscated bikes and property found inside of cars go to auction.

Florida

Department of Management Services, Division of Motor Pool Bureau of Motor Vehicles, 813B Lake Bradford Rd., Tallahassee, FL 32304, 904-488-5178. Approximately once per month, somewhere in Florida, items are auctioned for the state. Descriptive information and viewing schedules are published in newspapers. Surplus items, including motorcars, heavy equipment and boats are sold. Automobile auctions take place anywhere from 7 to 15 times per year, with dates set 4 to 6 weeks in advance at various auction locations throughout the state. The auctions are advertised. Some industrial equipment is also included, along with various kinds of used and confiscated vans, trucks, and cars. Pleasure and fishing boats are also auctioned. Items may be viewed prior to the auction. Call 800-342-2666 (in state) to be placed on a mailing list.

Georgia

State of Georgia, Department of Administrative Services, Purchasing Division, Surplus Property Services, 1050 Murphy Avenue, SW, Atlanta, GA 30310, 404-756-4800. Georgia auctions vehicles, including sedans, wagons, trucks, vans, buses, and cement mixers. The state also auctions shop equipment, generators, typewriters, copiers, computers, tape recorders, and other office equipment, as well as audio-visual equipment, cameras, electronic equipment, and air conditioners. They keep a mailing list and also advertise the auctions in local newspapers. Merchandise may be inspected by pre-registered bidders two days before an auction. Vehicles may be started up, but not driven. For auctions, items are payable with cash only. Items must be paid for on the day of sale. Auctions are held every three months at different locations.

Hawaii

State Government Stock Control Department, 808-735-0348/0349. Hawaii does not conduct surplus sales at the state level. Federal public auctions are held by the Defense Reutilization Marketing Office, 808-474-2238.

Idaho

Division of Purchasing, 208-327-7465. In 1991 the Idaho state legislature dissolved centralized public auctions. Each state agency now holds its own auction or has a commercial auctioneer handle its surplus. If an agency decides to auction cars through sealed bids, it must advertise in 3 newspapers for 10 days. To find out if, when, and what an agency is disposing of through auction, contact that agency directly.

Illinois

Central Management Services, Division of Property Control, 1912 South 10 1/2 St., Springfield, IL 62707, 217-785-6903. Two or three times per year this office auctions vehicles and property. Auctions are held at the address listed above. Auctions are always held on Saturdays. Property includes office equipment, desks, chairs, typewriters, restaurant equipment, calculators, cameras, refrigerators, and filing cabinets. Scrap metal and equipment not easily moved are sold by sealed bid. The office maintains a mailing list which costs $20/year to subscribe. Notices of auctions and bids are mailed out 3 weeks prior to the auction. The auctions are also advertised in advance in local newspapers. All the cars auctioned have a minimum mileage of 75,000 miles and were driven by state employees. Prices vary widely, but below-market prices are available. Illinois auctions off vehicles by open bid auctions. (Confiscated cars are sold at federal auctions and may present greater possibility for a bargain.) Payment is made by cash, cashiers or certified check, or personal check with bank letter.

Indiana

State Surplus Property Section, 229 W. New York St., Indianapolis, IN 46202, 317-232-0134, warehouse; 317-232-1365, office. Indiana holds auctions as items accumulate through open cry auctions to the highest bidder. During the summer months, the state sells surplus from the Department of Transportation and the Department of Natural Resources. A mailing list is maintained. Auctions are advertised the first Thursday of every month in the *Indianapolis Star*. The auction date and selected auctioneer changes every year during July. Call the above office in May to obtain the new schedule. Sealed bids must contain 100% deposit. Payment is by cash, certified check, cashiers check, or money order. No personal checks or letters of credit are accepted. Items vary and are all state surplus.

Iowa

Department of Natural Resources, Wallace State Office Bldg., Des Moines, IA 50319, 515-281-5145. The Department of Natural Resources holds an auction when and if a sufficient number of items have accumulated, on the second Saturday of every May. Items disposed of include boats, fishing rods, tackle boxes, guns, and other fishing and hunting equipment, as well as office equipment. Payment is by cash or check with appropriate identification. There is no mailing list, but auctions are advertised in local newspapers.

Vehicle Dispatchers Garage, 301 E. 7th, Des Moines, IA 50319, 515-281-5121. The Vehicle Dispatchers Garage holds auctions, if there is sufficient accumulation, three to four times per year at 9:00 am on Saturdays. The state disposes of approximately 500 vehicles yearly through these auctions. They mostly sell patrol cars, pickups and trucks. All have at least 81,000 miles of travel on them, and prices vary widely. A deposit of $200 is required on the day of the sale, with full payment due by the following Wednesday. Payment may be made by cash or check with an accompanying letter of credit guaranteeing payment by the issuing institution. Viewing is possible Friday all day and Saturday morning prior to the sale. There is a mailing list. Auctions are advertised in the local papers.

Kansas

Kansas State Surplus Property, P.O. Box 19226, Topeka, KS 66619-0226, 913-296-2334, Fax: 913-296-7427. The State Surplus Property office sells sedans, snow plows, and everything they have, from staples to bulldozers. Property is first offered to other state agencies at set prices for 30 days. Whatever is left over is opened to public sale at the same prices. Prices tend to be competitive. Items are sold at set prices, with a catalog available containing descriptions of items and where they are located. Confiscated vehicles are not sold to the public. They are disposed of by county courthouses, usually to county agencies. To obtain copies of catalogs describing sealed bid items, write to the above address. It will be sent to you for 6 months, after which time your name will be purged unless you re-request it.

Kentucky

Kentucky Office of Surplus Property, 514 Barrett Ave., Frankfurt, KY 40601, 502-564-4836. Kentucky holds public auctions on Saturdays every two or three months. Items may include vehicles, desks, chairs, calculators, typewriters, file cabinets, tape recorders, electronic equipment, couches, beds, and lawnmowers, to name a few. Merchandise may be viewed the day before an auction. The office maintains a mailing list and also advertises upcoming auctions in local newspapers two to three weeks before the sale. Some items are auctioned by sealed bids. Property is payable by cash, certified check, or money order.

Louisiana

Division of Administration, Louisiana Property Assistance Agency, P.O. Box 94095, 1059 Brickyard Lane, Baton Rouge, LA 70804-9095, 504-342-6849. Public auctions are held on the second Saturday of every month at 9:00 am at 1502 North 17th St. Items may be viewed at the warehouse from 8:00 am to 4:30 pm the week before. Property sold ranges from medical and office equipment, to boats, shop equipment, typewriters, file cabinets, pinball machines, bicycles, televisions, adding machines, and chairs, and vehicles. All items are sold "as is" and "where is." Payment is required in full the day of the auctions, but no personal or company checks are accepted. In addition, all merchandise must be removed within five days after the sale. Auctions are conducted by a different auctioneer each year, depending on who wins the bid for the annual contract.

Maine

Office of Surplus Property, Station 95, Augusta, ME 04333, 207-287-5750. Five or six times per year, Maine publicly auctions off vehicles on the grounds of the Augusta Mental Health Institute. You must register to be able to bid. Vehicles may include police cruisers, pick-up trucks, snowmobiles, lawn mowers, and heavy equipment, such as large trucks, graders, and backhoes. Inspection is allowed between 7:30 am and 10:00 am the day of the auctions, which are always held on Saturdays. The impound yard opens at 7:00 am. Vehicles may be started up but not driven. Personal checks (local banks only), money orders, certified checks, and cash are all accepted. Exact date, place, and time of auctions are announced in local newspapers, but there is no mailing list. Payment is due for both vehicles and other items the day of the auction or sale.

Maryland

Maryland State Agency for Surplus Property, P.O. Box 122, 8037 Brock Bridge Rd., Jessup, MD 20794, 410-799-0440. Office furniture and the like are sold or donated to non-profit organizations or state agencies, and vehicles are sold to dealers only. The state maintains a warehouse for surplus property at the above address. After a certain length of time, items that do not go to non-profits or state agencies become available to the public at set prices at its retail store. Checks are acceptable up to $500.

Massachusetts

Massachusetts State Purchasing Agency, Department of Procurement and General Services, Surplus Property, One Ashburton Place, Room 1017, Boston, MA 02108, 617-727-7500. About six times per year, Massachusetts holds public auctions of surplus property. Bidders must register in the morning by filling out a card. The State Purchasing Agency places ads in The Boston Globe on the Sunday and Wednesday prior to each of the auctions, which are normally held on Saturdays. Vehicles are usually auctioned after about 60 or so accumulate. Vehicles sold include sedans, wagons, vans, and pick-ups with an average age of 7 years. The average car has over 100,000 miles. Conditions range from good to junk. Viewing is available the day before the auction from 9:00 am to 4:00 pm. Purchases are "as is". No start-ups allowed. The state does not auction other surplus property, in general, but occasionally special auctions are held for boats, parts from the Department of Public Works, and most recently, helicopters.

Michigan

State of Michigan, Department of Management and Budget, State Surplus Property, P.O. Box 30026, 12 Martin Luther King Blvd., Lansing, MI 48913, 517-335-8444. The state auctions off all kinds of office furniture, household goods, machinery, livestock, and vehicles, such as sedans, buses, trucks, and boats. Auctions are held at different locations for different categories of property. The State Surplus Property Office sends out yearly calendars with auction dates and information. Contact them at the above address to have it sent to you. Double check dates because additions or changes may occur. Auctions are also published in the local newspapers. Payment may be made by cash or check and should include the 6% state sales tax. No refunds are made. Inspections of merchandise are available either the day before from 8:00 am to 3:00 pm or the morning of an auction from 8:00 am to 9:30 am. Vehicles may be started but not driven. Auctions begin at 10:00 am. Items must be paid in full on the day of sale by cash or in state check. Buyer has 3 working days to remove the property.

Minnesota

Minnesota Surplus Operations Office, 5420 Highway 8, New Brighton, MN 55112, 612-639-4022; Hotline: 612-296-1056. The hotline is updated with any changes in the auction schedule. Minnesota holds about 15 auctions per year at different locations around the state. They sell vehicles such as old patrol cars, passenger cars, trucks, vans, and trucks, as well as heavy machinery, boats, snowmobiles and outboard motors. The state also auctions off furniture, office equipment, kitchen equipment, tools, and confiscated items such as vehicles, computers, jewelry, car stereos and radios, and other personal effects. Many of these items are sold under market price. You may be put on a mailing list to receive a calendar for the schedule of upcoming auctions for the year. Auctions are advertised in the locale where they occur by radio, TV, and in Minneapolis and St. Paul newspapers. Inspection of property is held from 8:00 am to 9:30 am, an hour and a half before the auction begins; and payment is by personal check for in-state residents, cash, or money order.

Mississippi

Department of Public Safety, Support Services, P.O. Box 958, Jackson, MS 39205, 601-987-1500. The state cars that are auctioned are mostly patrol cars, and only occasionally vans and other types of vehicles. State cars are usually wrecked or old. Most have at least 100,000 miles on them. Recent average prices have ranged from $1200 to $1500. The state is keeping cars longer, so less are being sold. These agency cars and others from the Department of Wildlife and Fisheries, military bases, Narcotics Division, and U.S. Marshal's Office -- which includes confiscated cars -- are auctioned the first Tuesday of every month by Mid South Auctions, 6655 N. State St., Jackson, MS 39213, 601-956-2700. Call to be put on the mailing list. Many car dealers as well as the public attend these auctions, so prices are competitive. Bargains are still possible. Payment must be in cash or cashiers check -- no personal checks. The balance is due the day of the auction. Cars are available a few days before the auction.

Missouri

State Of Missouri, Surplus Property Office, Materials Management Section, P.O. Drawer 1310, 117 N. Riverside Dr., Jefferson City, MO 65102, 314-751-3415. At various times throughout the year, Missouri holds regular public auctions every 6-8 weeks, as well as sealed bid auctions of merchandise located at various places in the state. The wide range of items include clothing, office equipment and vehicles. No confiscated or seized vehicles or other items are sold. You can be put on a mailing list to receive notices of upcoming auctions, plus they are advertised in local newspapers. For regular auctions, inspection is available the day before or on the day of the auction; and sealed bid items may be viewed two or three days before the deadline. Items may be sold by lot or individually. Payment may be made by cash or personal check.

Montana

Property and Supply Bureau, 930 Lyndale Ave., Helena, MT 59620-0137, 406-444-4514. Montana holds a vehicle auction once a year, of about 300 state vehicles. Contact the above to get on the mailing list. The auctions are by open cry and sealed bid. All items are from state surplus; nothing is seized or confiscated. These auctions are advertised in local newspapers prior to the auction. In addition, the state offers other property for sale each month on the second Friday of the month at set prices. The sales include items such as office supplies, computers, chairs, tables, and vehicles including trucks, vans, sedans, highway patrol cars, and more. Payment can be by cash, certified or business check, or bank check.

Nebraska

Nebraska Office of Administrative Services, Material Division, Surplus Property, P.O. Box 94901, Lincoln, NE 68509, 402-479-4890. Three or four times a year, Nebraska auctions off office furniture, computers, couches, and more. Separate auctions are held for vehicles and heavy equipment -- also about three or four times per year. Auctions are advertised in newspapers and on radio, and a mailing list is also kept. Sealed bids for property such as scrap iron, wrecked vehicles, guard posts, and tires are taken. Items are available for viewing two days prior to the auctions, which are held on Saturdays at 5001 S. 14th St. All items are sold "as is". Payment, which can be made by cash or check, must be in full on the day of the auction.

Nevada

Nevada Purchasing Division, Kinkead Bldg., Room 304 Capitol Complex, 209 E. Muzzer, Carson City, NV 89710, 702-687-4070. The sales and auction are located at the warehouse at 2250 Barnett Way, Reno, NV 89512. About once a year, Nevada holds a sale on the second Saturday in August of such items as calculators, desks, cabinets, tables and chairs. Office equipment is released for sale to the public at a set price. The sale is held to clear the warehouse, and is on a first come, first serve basis, with minimum prices to cover service and handling marked on the property. Very few vehicles are confiscated. Most are surplus turned in by other state agencies for resale. Vehicles and motorcycles are auctioned. Public auctions are not served by mailing lists but are advertised in the newspapers. You can be put on a mailing list to receive notice of sealed bid sales of 19 categories of merchandise, including heavy equipment, boats, and planes. Once you have requested to place your name on the mailing list, if you do not subsequently bid on two consecutive occasions, it will be removed. Payment is by cash or local check with proper I.D. No out of state checks accepted. For vehicles, you can put down a 5% deposit with 5 days to complete payment. The county, city and University of Nevada also advertise and hold public auctions.

New Hampshire

Office of Surplus Property 78 Regional Dr., Building 3, Concord, NH 03301, 603-271-2126. New Hampshire holds two auctions per year of vehicles and other equipment, such as office furniture and machines, and refrigerators. Vehicles, which include cruisers, pickups, vans, and sometimes confiscated vehicles may be viewed the day before the auction, while other merchandise can be viewed on the same day just before the auction. Vehicles may be started but not driven. A mailing list is maintained, and ads are also placed in local newspapers prior to the auctions. Acceptable payment includes cash and certified funds.

New Jersey

New Jersey Purchase and Property Distribution Center, CN-234, Trenton, NJ 08625-0234, 609-530-3300. New Jersey auctions used state vehicles such as vans, various types of compacts, and occasionally boats, buses and heavy equipment. Frequency of auctions depends on availability which currently averages once per month. Vehicles may be inspected and started up the day before the auction from 9:00 am to 3:00 pm. Payment is by cash, money order, or certified check. No personal checks. A 10% deposit is required to hold a vehicle. The successful bidder has 7 calendar days to complete payment and remove the vehicle by Friday. If an item is left after that, even if paid in full, a $20 per day storage fee is charged. After one week, the vehicle is forfeited. To be advised of auctions, put your name on the mailing list by writing the address above. Phone calls are not accepted. A recent vehicle auction in New Jersey offered a variety of Dodge and Chevy vehicles, ages ranging from three to thirteen years, with mileages from 50,000 to 130,000. Other surplus items are not put up for public auction, but are offered to other state agencies.

New Mexico

New Mexico Highway and Transportation Department, SB-2, 7315 Cerrillos Road, P.O. Box 1149, Santa Fe, NM 87504-1149, 505-827-5580. About once a year, on the last Saturday of September, New Mexico auctions off vehicles, including sedans, loaders, backhoes, snow removal equipment, pick-ups, vans, four-wheel drives, and tractors. They have some office equipment as well. The items come from state agencies. You may place your name on a mailing list to receive the exact date of the auction and descriptions of merchandise up for bidding. A public entity auction is held first. The published list of items to be publicly auctioned consists of what is left over. Everything is open auction; there are no sealed bids. Items may be inspected the day before the auction. Payment is by cash, checks with proper I.D., money orders, or cashier's checks. No credit cards.

Department of Public Safety, State Police Division, Attn: Major W.D. Morrow, P.O. Box 1628, Santa Fe, NM 87504; 505-827-9001. The above holds a public auction on the second Saturday in July at 4491 Cerrillos Road. Write the office above to be put on the mailing list. It is also advertised in local newspapers. Items sold include everything from calculators to cars. They come from seizures and surplus from other agencies. The vehicles may be viewed and started up the Friday before the auction. Payment may be by cash, money order, cashier's check or personal check with bank letter of guarantee.

New York

State of New York Office of General Service, Bureau of Surplus Property, Building #18, W.A. Harriman State Office Building Campus, Albany, NY 12226, 518-457-6335. The Office of General Services holds auctions continuously in locations around the state. The items are so numerous that the state finds it necessary to sell them by category. You can designate which categories you are interested in on the mailing list application. Items are sold as they become available. Sales are advertised one week in advance in local newspapers. These items include surplus and used office equipment, scrap material, agricultural items (even unborn cows). Most categories such as medical, photographic, institutional and maintenance equipment are sold through sealed bids, usually in lots of varying size. To participate in a sealed bid, you place your name on a mailing list for items in seven different categories, then make your bid by mail. Send the sealed bids to Bureau of Surplus Property Distribution, Building 18, State Office Building, Albany, NY 12226. The highest bidder wins and is notified by mail. Mailings give as much information as possible about the items being auctioned; but state officials stress that merchandise is sold "as is" and "where is". They advise viewing property in person before making a bid. A ten percent deposit is required with each sealed bid. Vehicles are sold by public auction and may include cars, trucks, buses, tractors, bulldozers, mowers, compressors, plows, sanders, and other highway maintenance and construction equipment. Large items are sold individually, and smaller equipment, such as chain saws, is more likely to be sold in lots. These auctions take place about 55 times per year. It is always possible that enough surplus may not accumulate to warrant an auction. The state warns that just because an auction is scheduled is no guarantee that it will occur. Payment may be made by certified check or cash. A ten percent deposit will hold a vehicle until the end of the day.

North Carolina

State Surplus Property, P.O. Box 33900, Raleigh, NC 27636-3900, 919-733-3889. North Carolina sells through sealed bids surplus state merchandise including vehicles and office equipment every Tuesday. Office equipment includes furniture, typewriters, desks, and chairs. For a fee of $15 you can be placed on a mailing list to receive weekly advisories of what is for auction, with a description of the item and its condition. Otherwise, if you visit the warehouse in person, you can pick up free samples of bid listings and look at lists of prices that items sold for in previous auctions. The warehouse is located on Highway 54 - Old Chapel Hill Road. Payment is by money order or certified check, and you have 15 days to pay for your merchandise and 15 days to pick it up. Items may be inspected two weeks before an auction from Monday to Friday between 8:00 am and 5:00 pm. On Tuesdays, the warehouse is closed between 1:00 pm and 3:00 pm when the bids are opened and the public is then invited to attend. The state may reject bids that are too low. Vehicles vary greatly in type and condition.

North Dakota

Surplus Property Office, P.O. Box 7293, Bismarck, ND 58507, 701-328-2273. Once a year, usually in August or September, the Office of Surplus Property auctions through open bidding surplus office furniture and equipment, as well as vehicles and scrap materials. The auction is advertised the two days before and merchandise may be viewed the morning of the auction. The auction is held at Igo Industrial Park. Cash, cashiers checks, or money orders are acceptable forms of payment. Personal or business checks are accepted only with a bank letter of credit.

Ohio

Office of State and Federal Surplus Property, 4200 Surface Road, Columbus, OH 43228, 614-466-5052. Ohio holds public auctions and sealed bid sales on a wide range of office machines and equipment, and furniture. There are no sealed bids on vehicles. No mailing list is maintained. Call or write for the information. When you attend an auction, you can fill out a label that will be used to notify you of the next auction. Vehicle auctions are held three to four times a year, depending on the amount accumulated. Inspections are available the day before. Vehicles may include sedans, trucks, vans, 4x4s, boats, mowers, tractors, and chain saws. No seized or confiscated items are sold. At the time of the auction, a 25% downpayment is required, with the balance due by the following Monday (auctions are held on Saturdays). For the sealed bid auctions, payment must be by money order or certified check.

Oklahoma

Central Purchasing, Dept. Central Services, B-4, State Capitol, Oklahoma City, OK 73105, 405-521-3046; general information only for public auctions, 405-521-3835; for general information and information on sealed bids, 405-521-2110. Oklahoma auctions vehicles as they accumulate. Vehicles often have from 80,000 to 120,000 miles on them and it is rare for a car to be rated as fair -- which means it is in running condition. They are usually bought by wholesalers. State agency cars are commonly sold, but occasionally seized or confiscated cars are sold. Agencies most likely to have auctions are: Department of Human Services (occasionally vehicles and other items, but they usually take their cars to public auctions); Wildlife Department (vehicles); Department of Public Safety (vehicles); and the Department of Transportation (vehicles). The Department of Transportation has four auctions per year. Vehicles are usually not in good condition. The state advises that you contact each agency separately for details. The auctions are not always advertised in newspapers, but some agencies, such as the Department of Transportation (405-521-2550) have mailing lists.

Oregon

Department of General Services, Surplus Property, 1655 Salem Industrial Drive NE, Salem, OR 97310, 503-378-4714 (Salem area). Oregon auctions both vehicles and other equipment, such as office furniture. Merchandise may include snow plows, horse trailers, computer equipment, desks, chairs, tires or shop equipment. Some items are in excellent condition, and bargains may be found. Items come from state agency surplus and confiscations. On rare occasions exotic items such as a Porsche and hot tub have been sold. Public sales are held every Friday at set prices. Sealed bid sales are held separately. The frequency of auctions depends on the amount of items to be disposed. The numbers of vehicles for sale is increasing. Cars are also sold every week at set prices. For info call the 24 hour information line that is always kept current, 503-373-1392, ext. 400. Ads are also placed on radio and in local newspapers in the areas where the auction will be held, giving the date and location of the auction. The procedure is to register and obtain a bidder number, which you hold up when you are making a bid. The forms may be obtained at the auction site. At the same time as you register, you must show some form of identification. The conditions and terms of sale are always listed. At the public sales if you pay by Mastercard or Visa, title is immediately released. You can also pay 10% down at the auction site and pay the balance at the office with Mastercard or Visa in 3 days. A mailing list is maintained.

Pennsylvania

General Services Department, Bureau of Vehicle Management, P.O. Box 1365, 2221 Forster Street, Harrisburg, PA 17105, 717-783-3132. About 10 times per year, depending on the number of cars accumulated, the DGS auctions off all kinds of vehicles. Many have mileages under 100,000, and ages commonly range from 1979 to 1986. There are about 200 cars at each auction. They are mostly used state agency cars that have been replaced, but up to 3 seized cars are also sold each year. An inspection period begins two weeks before an auction on Monday through Friday from 9:00 am to 5:00 pm at the storage facility located at 22nd & Forster Sts. in Harrisburg. Inspection period ends 2 days before the auctions. Each car has a form detailing its condition. It will state if the car must be towed. All cars are sold "as is". Cars are started up the day of the auction, which is open cry. If you request an application, you may have your name put on a mailing list for advance advisories of auctions for a period of six months. A $100 deposit is required (cash only) if you win a bid, with full payment due within five working days by cashier's check, certified check, or postal money order. No personal or company checks accepted.

Bureau of Supplies and Surplus, Department of General Services, P.O. Box 1365, 2221 Forster Street, Harrisburg, PA 17105, 717-787-4083. The Bureau of Supplies and Surplus of the General Services Department sells such items as mainframe computers and off-loading equipment, office furniture and machines, including typewriters, desks, chairs, sectional furniture, filing cabinets, copy machines, dictaphones, and calculators. This merchandise is first offered to other state agencies, then municipalities, and is then put up for public sale after five days. There is no mailing list for notification of upcoming auctions, but ads are placed in the local newspapers in the area where an auction will be held and in the *Pennsylvania Bulletin*. Property is sold at set prices. You may call to find out what items are currently for sale, or visit the warehouse which sells mostly office equipment such as computers, desks, chairs and file cabinets, between 10:00 am and 2:45 pm Monday through Friday.

Rhode Island

Department of Administration, Division of Purchase, 1 Capitol Hill, Providence, RI 02908, 401-277-2375. Rhode Island's Division of Purchase auctions off its surplus vehicles and office equipment, as well as other items, through sealed bid to a list of buyers who are usually in the business. Most of the cars sold have no plates and must be towed. They are sold primarily to wholesalers. Office equipment and supplies are primarily sold to suppliers. If the state ever does hold a public auction, it advertises two or three times in the local papers.

South Carolina

Surplus Property Office, Division of General Services, 1441 Boston Avenue, West Columbia, SC 29170, 803-822-5490. South Carolina sells items ranging from vehicles, to office and heavy equipment. Property is collected in monthly cycles and offered first to state agencies before being put up for sale to the public. No mailing list is kept for it, but you can visit the warehouse on 1441 Boston Ave., in West Columbia, which is open between 8:00 am and 4:30 pm Monday through Friday. Prices are tagged; there is no auction. Every 6 to 8 weeks, the General Services Division holds public auctions of items by lot for State, Federal, and Wildlife Department property. A mailing list is kept for advance advisories and property descriptions. There is a $15 fee, payable by check or money order, to receive the mailings annually. Items can be inspected two days prior to the sale. You are advised to make notes of the numbers of property you are interested in, then to check back to inquire if it is still available, since state agencies have first choice.

South Carolina Public Transportation Department, 1500 Shop Road, P.O. Box 191, Columbia SC 29202, 803-737-6635, for general information; 803-737-1488, for mailing list. About every five weeks, the South Carolina Department of Public Transportation holds auctions of its used and surplus vehicles, which include everything from patrol cars, trucks, and passenger cars, to highway equipment. To have your name put on a mailing list of upcoming auctions, call the number above. Payment is by cash, check or money order. Banking information will be requested for personal checks. Vehicles may be viewed from 9:00 am to 4:30 pm on the Tuesday before the auctions, which are always held on Wednesdays at 10 am. Vehicles are also available for viewing the day of the auction from 8 am - 10 am. You may start up the cars. The bidding is open. Usually about 100 cars are sold at each auction.

South Dakota

Bureau of Administration, State Property Management, 500 E. Capital, Pierre, SD 57501-3221, 605-773-4935. Twice a year, in the spring and fall, the Department of Transportation holds on its premises public auctions for office equipment and vehicles, including pick-ups. Most vehicles have over 85,000 miles on them and sell for well under market price. The cars usually sell for under $5000. Most are surplus or have been replaced at state agencies. A few are from seizures or confiscation. You may

visually inspect the vehicles prior to the auction, but you may not enter them. However, during the auction, the vehicles are started and demonstrated. Auctions and special sales are located wherever the most property has accumulated in the state. Call or write the above office to have your name put on the mailing list. There is no charge. Terms are up to the auctioneer. Title is released only after checks clear, or immediately if accompanied by a bank letter.

Tennessee

Department of General Services Property Utilization, 6500 Centennial Boulevard, Nashville, TN 37243-0543, 615-741-1711. Tennessee auctions surplus vehicles, and machinery of various kinds -- milling machines, lathes, welders, and metal working equipment. The vehicles are of all types, including dump trucks, pick-ups, sedans, and station wagons. Auctions are held in Jackson, Dandridge, Nashville, and Chattanooga when property accumulates. A mailing list is kept, and auctions are advertised in local newspapers. Items are available for inspection the day before the auction. Keys are in the car, and start ups are allowed. Register at no charge the morning of the auction. Payment can be in cash, cashier's checks, or certified check. The state also conducts sealed bids usually 12 times a year and most commonly on office furniture.

Texas

General Services Commission, P.O. Box 13047, Austin, TX 78711-3047, 512-463-3445. Every two months, Texas auctions off vehicles, office furniture and machines, and highway equipment. You must apply to be put on the mailing list, which will give you a brief description of items available at the next auction (call 512-463-3416). It will also tell you the location of the auction, which changes often. You may call the agency selling the property to arrange to inspect it; however, merchandise that is on site is available for inspection two hours before the auction. Items are mostly used state property, although some is confiscated as well. You must register to bid beforehand. Most registrations take place the day of the auction, beginning at 7:00 am. Payment on a winning bid is due at the end of the auction. Cash, cashiers check, certified check, money order, bank draft with Letter of Credit, or personal or company check with Letter of Credit are acceptable forms of payment. Items sold on site must be removed the day of the sale. For off-site items, 30 days are usually allowed for removal. Texas also holds sealed bid auctions, where you make a bid by mail. First, you indicate what category of property you are interested in, and they will send you bid forms and descriptions of items in that category. Sealed bid participants are notified by letter if winning bids and the exact amount due. Deposits for non-winners are returned. Also, each of the Texas state agencies hold local sales, for which each has its own mailing list and advertises in the local papers.

Utah

Utah State Surplus Office, 522 South 700 West, Salt Lake City, UT 84104, 801-533-5885. Utah auctions vehicles and office furniture, as well as heavy equipment, whenever property accumulates. Most items are sold by public auction, although sealed bid auctions are sometimes held as well. Mail-in bids are accepted if you can't attend in person. A 10% deposit is required. It is refunded unless you win the bid. Most of the public auctions are held in Salt Lake City at the address above, although some are occasionally held in other parts of the state. You may request your name be put on a mailing list to receive advance notice of auctions and a description of the items. Auctions are usually held on Saturdays. Property may be viewed the Thursday and Friday prior to an auction. Acceptable forms of payment are cash, cashier's check, and personal checks up to $100 with two forms of I.D. Checks over $100 must have a letter of guarantee from the bank. No business checks are accepted. Items must be removed and payments must be made in full on the day of the auction.

Vermont

Vermont Central Surplus Property Agency, RD #2, Box 520, Montpelier, VT 05602, 802-828-3394. Vermont sells low-priced surplus office furniture and machines on retail basis between 8:00 am and 4:00 pm Tuesday-Friday at the warehouse on Barre Montpelier Rd. Items include desks, chairs, file cabinets, and book shelves. Twice a year, vehicles, which may include police cruisers, dump trucks, and pick-ups, are sold by public auction, on a Saturday in late May and September. A mailing list is kept to advise you in advance of upcoming auctions. To have your name placed on it, contact the auctioneer. Local newspapers also advertise them. Vehicles may be inspected the Friday before an auction. The auctions are open bid, "as is", and "where is". There are no hold backs. The highest bid, even if it is far below market value, will take the item. A 25% deposit is due the day of the sale. The balance is due in 2 days, by the following Tuesday by 3:00 pm. Payment is up to the auctioneer, a private contractor. Usually, checks must be bank-certified, and a deposit is required to hold any vehicle not paid for in full the day of the auction.

Virginia

State Surplus Property, P.O. Box 1199, Richmond, VA 23209, 804-236-3666. Virginia auctions everything but land. It sells vehicles, office equipment and furniture, computers, tractors, bulldozers, dump trucks, pick-ups, and vans. Some of the cars are in good condition. Scrap metal, tires, and batteries are sold separately. Auctions may be held on any day of the week except Sunday. Sales are by both public auction and sealed bid. Agencies have the discretion to decide which way their surplus is sold. There may be sealed bid offerings every week, and as many as two auctions per week. Twice a year there are auctions for cars only. The rest are mixed. Items are occasionally seized, such as jewelry. Auction sites are at various locations around the state. You may call or write to place your name on a mailing list for both public auctions and sealed bid auctions. For sealed bid, there are usually 100 to 200 items available. Inspections are encouraged. They are allowed the day before the auction and again for a couple of hours on the day of the auction. For sealed bid items, you may call for more details on the items offered for sale or to make an appointment to inspect the items.

Washington

Office of Commodity Redistribution, 2805 C St. S.W., Building 5, Door 49, Auburn, WA 98001-7401, 206-931-3931, Fax: 206-931-3946. Washington holds auctions of used state vehicles, conducts "silent bids" (auctions where the bids are written rather than spoken), and also sells surplus materials by sealed bid (bids are placed through the mail) via catalogs. The vehicles are auctioned five times a year and include all kinds of used state conveyances, from patrol cars, to trucks and passenger cars, most having over 100,000 miles. There are few new luxury or confiscated type vehicles. The "silent bids" are held once a month, and include large quantities of office furniture sold by the pallet, with the exception of typewriters, which are sold individually. You may visit the warehouse to inspect the items beforehand. Payment may be made by cashiers check, money order, or cash, but no personal checks. For the sealed bids, you may request a catalog of merchandise, which includes everything from vehicles, to scrap material, office equipment, computers, clothes, cleaning fluids, tools, and pumps. Periodically the store at the central warehouse is open to the public where items may be purchased at set prices for cash. For any of these sales, you may request to be put on the mailing list at the address above.

West Virginia

West Virginia State Agency Surplus Property, 2700 Charles Ave., Dunbar, WV 25064, 304-766-2626. Contact the above to be put on the mailing list. Statewide sealed bids have a separate mailing list you must specifically request. For sealed bids, prospective buyers can inspect only by going to the site. Each month, West Virginia auctions such items as chairs, desks, telephones, computers, typewriters, office equipment and furniture, and other miscellaneous property, as well as vehicles. They are all auctioned at the same auction. The vehicles are in varying conditions. The auctions are always held on a Saturday. Inspection is available the week before the auction from 8:30 am to 4:30 pm. On auction day, the gate opens at 9:00 am. Miscellaneous property is sold until 12:00 noon. Then all the cars are sold. If time allows, any remaining miscellaneous property is auctioned. Payment may be by personal check, business check, or certified check, but no cash. Payment is due in full the same day. For sealed bids, payment is due 7-10 days after a bid has won.

Wisconsin

Wisconsin Department of Administration, P.O. Box 7880, Madison, WI 53707, 608-266-8024. The Department of Administration holds vehicle auctions approximately eight times a year -- usually with around 100 vehicles, including passenger vehicles, vans, trucks, and station wagons, all of different makes and models. Most are in running condition. Cars that need towing are rare and clearly designated. The vehicles are usually at least four years old, or have at least 70,000 miles on them. The auctions begin on Saturday at 10:00 am. Cars may be inspected the Friday before from 1:00 pm to 6:00 pm. The public may also inspect and start up the cars from 8:00 am to 10:00 am on the morning of the auction. Cars may be started but not driven. You may have your name placed on a mailing list for advance notice of auctions; however, the auctions are also advertised in local newspapers. There are no sealed bids. Payment is by cash, personal check, cashiers check, or money order. No credit cards. The full amount is due the day of the auction. Occasionally, if the auctioneer is consulted at pre-registration, a small delay for bank loan arrangements are pre-approved so that the prospective buyer can bid.

Wyoming

State Motor Pool, 723 West 19th Street, Cheyenne, WY 82002, 307-777-7247. Although it first donates most of its surplus property to other state agencies, Wyoming does auction its remaining surplus vehicles, which may include pick-ups, vans, sedans, and jeeps, and also tires. Although most have high mileage -- from 80,000 to 100,000 miles, the majority are dependable vehicles. You can have your name placed on a mailing list to receive advance notices of auctions, which are held when items accumulate. On the average, two or three auctions are held each year. The state also advertises in local newspapers. Inspection of the vehicles is available between 3:00 pm and 5:00 pm the Friday before the auction, which is usually held on Saturdays and begins at 10:00 am. No start ups are allowed. Anything known to be wrong with the car will be on the list handed out at the auction, or sent if you are on the mailing list. Payment depends on the auctioneer who is a private contractor. Usually, cash or check with proper I.D. are acceptable. Some cars go for well below market value, but others may bid up in price, depending on the mood of the crowd.

Franchising: How To Select
The Best Opportunity

Franchising: How To Select
The Best Opportunity

Franchising could be for you, according to a study conducted by Arthur Andersen & Company of 366 franchise companies in 60 industries reported that nearly 86% of all franchise operations opened in the previous five years were still under the same ownership; only 3% of these businesses were no longer in business. The U.S. Commerce Department reports that from 1971 to 1987, less than 5% of franchises were terminated on an annual basis. In contrast, a study conducted by the U.S. Small Business Administration from 1978 to 1988 found 62.2% of all new businesses were dissolved within the first six years of their operation, due to failure, bankruptcy, retirement, or other reasons. While we are sure you are beginning to entertain the idea of owning a new business, franchising is not risk free and needs to be entered into with a degree of caution. Therefore, you need to take measures to protect yourself. The following organizations and publications will help you find the right franchise for you.

Organizations

Federal Trade Commission (FTC)
Bureau of Consumer Protection
Division of Marketing Practices
Pennsylvania Avenue at 6th Street, NW
Washington, DC 20580
202-326-3128

Buying a franchise or a business opportunity may be appealing if you want to be your own boss, but have limited capital and business experience. However, without carefully investigating a business before you purchase, you may make a serious mistake. It is important to find out if a particular business is right for you and if it has the potential to yield the financial return you expect. A Federal Trade Commission (FTC) rule requires that franchise and business opportunity sellers provide certain information to help you in your decision. Under the FTC rule, a franchise or business opportunity seller must give you a detailed disclosure document at least ten business days before you pay any money or legally commit yourself to a purchase. This document gives 20 important items of information about the business, including: the names, addresses, and telephone numbers of other purchasers; the fully-audited financial statement of the seller; the background and experience of the business's key executives; the cost required to start and maintain the business; and the responsibilities you and the seller will have to each other once you buy. The disclosure document is a valuable tool that not only helps you obtain information about a proposed business, but assists you in comparing it with other businesses. If you are not given a disclosure document, ask why you did not receive one. Some franchise or business opportunity sellers may not be required to give you a disclosure document. If any franchise or business opportunity says it is not covered by the rule, you may want to verify it with the FTC, an attorney, or a business advisor. Even if the business is not required to give the document, you still may want to ask for the data to help you make an informed investment decision.

Some Important Advice From The FTC:

1. Study the disclosure document and proposed contracts carefully.

2. Talk to current owners. Ask them how the information in the disclosure document matches their experiences with the company. Visit the franchises to be sure they really exist. One group you should interview is those who have been in

business less than a year. Ask about the company's training program. Find out how long it took to break even and if the company's estimate of operating and working capital was accurate. The second group should be those in business for six years. Find out what kind of deal they got for the franchise and compare it to yours. There are strains in every franchise marriage. Find out what they are. Some franchises hire their own accountants to double check the franchises' accounting. When mistakes are made, it is often attributed to the franchise.

3. Investigate earnings claims. Earnings claims are only estimates. The FTC rule requires companies to have in writing the facts on which they base their earnings claims. Make sure you understand the basis for a seller's earnings claims.

4. Shop around: compare franchises with other available business opportunities. You may discover that other companies offer benefits not available from the first company you considered. The *Franchise Opportunities Handbook*, which is published annually by the Department of Commerce, describes thousands of companies that offer franchises. Contact other companies and ask for their disclosure documents. Then you can compare offerings.

5. Listen carefully to the sales presentation. Some sales tactics should signal caution. A seller with a good offer does not have to use pressure.

6. Get the seller's promises in writing. Any important promises you get from a salesperson should be written into the contract you sign.

7. Consider getting professional advice. You may want to get a lawyer, an accountant, or a business advisor to read the disclosure document and proposed contract to counsel you and help you get the best deal.

Although the FTC cannot resolve individual disputes, information about your experiences and concerns is vital to the enforcement of the Franchise and Business Opportunities Rule. The time to protect yourself is before you buy rather than after. Only fifteen states give you private rights to sue, and there is often a limited ability to recover. A franchiser knows your financial situation, and can often outwait you. Many franchise owners have no money left to hire a lawyer to try to recoup their losses. The FTC has two phone numbers of places you can call to ask for assistance. The Franchise Complaint Line, 202-326-2128, is staffed by a duty attorney and takes complaints about franchisers or disclosure requirements. The second number is:

FTC Franchise Rule Information Hotline
202-326-3220

Information on Federal Disclosure Requirements for Franchise and Business Opportunities ext.2

Information on Disclosure Statements for Specific Franchise and Business Opportunity Companies ext.3

Information on Complaints on File Against a Particular Franchise or Business Opportunity Venture ext.4

To Speak to an Attorney . . . . ext. 5

The following publications are available from the Federal Trade Commission Headquarters, 6th and Pennsylvania Ave., NW, Washington, DC 20850; 202-326-2502 voice/TDD:

Franchise and Business Opportunities -- a four-page guide about what to consider before buying a franchise.

The Franchise and Business Rule: Questions and Answers -- a one-page summary of the disclosure rule and penalties for infractions by the franchiser.

Franchise Rule Summary -- a seven-page, detailed technical explanation of the federal disclosure rule, which requires franchisers to furnish a document (with information on twenty topics) to the potential franchisee before a sale. This includes an explanation and description of the Uniform Franchise Offering Circular (UFOC) required in fourteen states.

State Agencies Administering Franchise Disclosure Laws

California (filing required)
Franchise Division, Department of Corporations, 1115 11th St., Sacramento, CA 95814; 916-445-7205.

Hawaii (filing required)
Franchise and Securities Division, State Department of Commerce, P.O. Box 40, Honolulu, HI 96813; 808-586-2722.

Illinois (filing required)
Franchise Division, Office of Attorney General, 500 South Second Street, Springfield, IL 62706; 217-782-4465.

Indiana (filing required)
Franchise Division, Office of Secretary of State, One N. Capitol St., Suite 560, Indianapolis, IN 46204; 317-232-6576.

Maryland (filing required)
Franchise Office, Division of Securities, 200 St. Paul Place, 20th Floor, Baltimore, MD 21202; 301-576-6360.

Michigan (notice required)
Antitrust and Franchise Unit, Office of Attorney General, 670 Law Building, Lansing, MI 48913; 517-373-7117.

Minnesota (filing required)
Franchise Division, Department of Commerce, 133 East Seventh St., St. Paul, MN 55101; 612-296-6328.

New York (filing required)
Franchise and Securities Division, State Department of Law, 120 Broadway, 23rd Floor, New York, NY 10271; 212-416-8211.

North Dakota (filing required)
Franchise Division, Office of Securities Commission, 600 East Boulevard, 5th Floor, Bismarck, ND 58505; 701-224-4712.

Oregon (no filing)
Corporate Securities Section, Department of Insurance and Finance, Labor and Industries Bldg., Salem, OR 97310; 503-378-4387.

Rhode Island (filing required)
Franchise Office, Division of Securities, 233 Richmond St., Suite 232, Providence, RI 02903; 401-277-3048.

South Dakota (filing required)
Franchise Office, Division of Securities, 910 E. Sioux Ave., Pierre, SD 57501; 605-773-4013.

Virginia (filing required)
Franchise Office, State Corporation Commission, 1300 E. Main St., Richmond, VA 23219; 804-371-9276.

Washington (filing required)
Franchise Office, Business License Services, State Securities Division, P.O. Box 648, Olympia, WA 98504; 206-753-6928.

Wisconsin (filing required)
Franchise Office, Wisconsin Securities Commission, P.O. Box 1768, Madison, WI 53701; 608-266-3364.

State Offices Administering Business Opportunity Disclosure Laws

California (filing required)
Consumer Law Section, Attorney General's Office, 1515 K St., Sacramento, CA 92101; 916-445-9555.

Connecticut (filing required)
Department of Banking, Securities Division, 44 Capitol Avenue, Hartford, CT 06106; 203-566-4560 ext. 8322.

Florida (filing required)
Department of Agriculture and Consumer Services, Room 110, Mayo Building, Tallahassee, FL 32301; 904-488-2221, 800-342-2176 (in-state only).

Georgia (no filing required)
Office of Consumer Affairs, No. 2 Martin Luther King Dr., Plaza Level, East Tower, Atlanta, GA 30334; 404-656-3790.

Indiana (filing required)
Consumer Protection Division, Attorney General's Office, 219 State House, Indianapolis, IN 46204; 317-232-6331.

Iowa (filing required)
Securities Bureau, Second Floor, Lucas State Office Building, Des Moines, IA 50319; 515-281-4441.

Kentucky (filing required)
Attorney General's Office, Consumer Protection Division, 209 St. Clair, Frankfort, KY 40601; 502-573-2200.

Louisiana (bond filing required)
Office of the Attorney General, Consumer Protection Division, 2610-A Woodale Blvd., Baton Rouge, LA 70804; 504-342-7900.

Maine (filing required)
Banking Bureau, Securities Division, State House, Station 121, Augusta, ME 04333; 207-582-8760.

Maryland (filing required)
Attorney General's Office, Securities Division, 200 St. Paul Pl., 20th Floor, Baltimore, MD 21202; 301-576-6360.

Michigan (notice required)
Consumer Protection Division, Department of the Attorney General, 670 Law Building, Lansing, MI 48913; 517-373-7117.

Minnesota (filing required)
Department of Commerce, Registration Division, 133 East 7th Street, St. Paul, MN 5501; 612-296-6328.

Nebraska (filing required)
Department of Banking and Finance, P.O. Box 95006, Lincoln, NE 68509; 402-471-2171, 402-471-3445.

New Hampshire (filing required)
Attorney General's Office, Consumer Protection Division, State House Annex, Concord, NH 03301; 603-271-3641.

North Carolina (filing required)
Department of Justice, Consumer Protection Division, P.O. Box 629, Raleigh, NC 27602; 919-733-3924.

Ohio (no filing required)
Attorney General's Office, Consumer Fraud and Crime Section, 25th Floor, State Office Tower, 30 East Broad Street, Columbus, OH 43266-0410; 614-466-8831, 800-282-0515 (in-state only).

Oklahoma (filing required)
Department of Securities, P.O. Box 53959, Oklahoma City, OK 73152; 405-235-0230.

South Carolina (filing required)
Secretary of State's Office, P.O. Box 11350, Columbia, SC 29211; 803-734-2169.

South Dakota (filing required)
Division of Securities, 910 E. Sioux Avenue, Pierre, SD 57501.

Texas (filing required)
Secretary of State's Office, Statutory Documents Section, P.O. Box 13563, Austin, TX 78711; 512-475-1769.

Utah (filing required)
Consumer Protection Division, 160 East 300 South, Salt Lake City, UT 84111; 801-530-6601.

Virginia (no filing required)
Consumer Affairs Office, 101 North 8th Street, Richmond, VA 23219; 804-786-0594, 800-451-1525 (in-state only).

Washington (filing required)
Department of Financial Institutions, Securities Division, P.O. Box 9033, Olympia, WA 98507-9033; 206-753-6928.

Publications

International Franchise Association (IFA)
1350 New York Avenue, NW
Washington, DC 20005
John Reynolds, Public Relations Officer
202-628-8000
Founded in 1960, the International Franchise Association (IFA) has more than 600 franchiser members, including thirty-five overseas. IFA members are accepted into the organization only after meeting stringent requirements regarding number of franchises, length of time in business, and financial stability. The IFA offers about twenty-five educational conferences and seminars yearly, including an annual convention and a legal symposium. There is a program on financing and venture capital designed to bring together franchisers and franchisees. Each year the association also sponsors several trade shows, open to the public, so that franchisers may attract potential franchisees. There is a library, and in the near future the Franchise Edge Data Base should be available for $49.95 offering informative information on 5,000 franchises. Information will also be available through Prodigy in the near future. For more information about Prodigy, call Scott Lehr at 202-662-0785. Ms. Holly Perkins, Public Relations Officer, will answer inquiries from the public and make referrals for speakers, courses, and resources on franchising.

The International Franchise Association publishes the following publications, which you can order by phone: 1-800-543-1038. For quick response regarding general information, membership information, educational programs, major conferences, international information, and CFE certification, you may contact the International Franchise Association's Fax-On-Demand Information Line at 202-628-3132.

To Help You Buy a Franchise
Answers to the 21 Most Commonly Asked Questions - $3
College of Franchise Knowledge - $49.95
50 Best Low-Investment,...Franchises - $12.95
Financing Your Franchise - $ 18.95
Franchise Bible - $ 19.95
Franchise Opportunities Guide - $ 15.00
The Franchise Survival Guide - $ 24.95
The Franchises: Dollars & Sense - $ 45.95
Franchising: The Inside Story - $ 20.00
Investigate Before Investing - $ 6.00
Tips and Traps When Buying a Franchise - $ 14.95

For Franchisees
Public Relations for the Franchisee - $ 21.00
Running a Successful Franchise - $ 29.95

To Help You Franchise Your Business

Between the Bumpa's - $ 22.50
Blueprint For Franchising A Business - $ 35.00
Complete Guide to Franchising in Canada - $ 30.00
Financial Strategies... - $ 25.00
The Franchise Option
    Hardcover - $ 30.00
    Softcover - $ 24.00
Franchising & Licensing - $ 32.00
Franchising in Europe - $ 28.50
Franchising--The How-To-Book - $ 12.50
The Guide to Franchising - $ 28.50
How To Be A Franchisor - $ 8.00
How To Franchise Internationally - $ 30.00
Restaurant Franchising - $ 46.95
Target Success - $ 5.95

For Franchisors

Franchise Relations Handbook - $ 35.00
Franchising: The Business Strategy... - $ 19.95
The Franchising Handbook - $ 75.00
How To Organize a Franchisee Advisory Council -
    $ 10.00
Multiple-Unit Franchising - $ 27.50
Wealth Within Reach - $ 20.00

Legal Information

Covenants Against Competition - $125.00
The Franchise Industry - $ 40.00
Franchise Legal Digest - $195.00
Franchise Sales Compliance Guide - $225.00
Franchising: Accounting, Auditing, Tax... - $ 95.00
Franchising Law: Practice & Forms - $335.00
International Franchising - $95.00

Audiocassettes, Videotapes, Disks

The Franchise Edge (Computer Disk) - $ 50.00
Franchising: A World of Opportunity (VHS) - $145.00
*Franchising: How To Be In Business For Yourself, Not
    By Yourself* (VHS) - $ 49.95
How To Make Franchising Work For You (Audio) -
    $ 35.00
IFA: A World Of Difference - $ 20.00
The National Franchise Mediation... (VHS) - $ 60.00
The New Entrepreneur (Audio) - $ 49.95

The New UFOC Guidelines (VHS) - $145.00
Opportunities In Franchising (Audio) - $ 35.00
Target Success (Audio set and workbook) - $ 39.95
Using The Media To Generate Leads (Audio) - $ 35.00

Reference Materials

Franchising in the Economy: 1991-1993 - $ 25.00
Franchisor/Franchisee Relations Survey - $ 5.00
The Future of Franchising... - $ 10.00
Glossary of Franchising Terms - $ 4.00
International Franchising: Selection... - $100.00
National Franchise Owner Study (Gallup) - $ 10.00
Franchising World magazine (price includes postage)
    Domestic - $ 12.00
    Canadian - $ 20.00
    Foreign - $ 39.00

Minority Business Development Agency
Department of Commerce
14th and Constitution Ave, NW
Washington, DC 20230   202-377-3237
The Minority Business Development Agency
(MBDA) can provide information to all
businesses, not just minority-owned businesses,
regarding franchising. They are the publishers
of *Franchise Opportunities Handbook*. A bible
of franchising information, this 336 page
directory has thousands of detailed listings of
companies, facts about the franchising
industry, guidance for investing in a franchise,
resource listings of helpful agencies and
organizations, and a bibliography. The cost is
$21.00; U.S. Government Printing Office,
Superintendent of Documents, Washington, DC
20420; 202-512-1800. MBDA has several
other free publications to assist people who are
interested in learning more about franchising.
They also answer questions regarding FTC
rules, major growth areas, how does a
franchise chain start, where do franchise sales
come from, and other general questions.

Top 30 Fastest Growing Franchise Companies

1. 7-Eleven Convenience Stores
2. Subway
3. Snap-On Tools
4. Matco Tools
5. McDonald's
6. Chem Dry Carpet Cleaning
7. Little Caesars Pizza
8. Burger King Corporation
9. Coverall North America Inc.
10. Mail Boxes Etc.
11. CleaNet USA Etc.
12. Jani-King
13. Dunkin' Donuts
14. Coldwell Banker Res. Affil., Inc.
15. Jazzercise Inc.
16. Tower Cleaning Systems
17. Miracle Ear
18. Play It Again Sports
19. GNC Franchising Inc.
20. Super 8 Models Inc.
21. Choice Hotels International
22. Jackson Hewitt Tax Services
23. Blimpie Corporation
24. Re/Max International
25. O.P.E.N. Cleaning Systems
26. Decorating Den
27. Baskin-Robbins USA Co.
28. Holiday Inn Worldwide
29. Superglass Windshield Repair
30. Hardee's

Did You Know?...

According to the International Franchise Association:

- A new franchise opens every 8 minutes of each business day.

- 1 of every 12 businesses is a franchise.

- By the year 2000 total franchise sales could reach $1 trillion dollars.

- Franchise sales account for 40.9% of all retail sales.

- In 1992, franchise chains created approximately 21,000 new business format franchises. In contrast, more than 220,000 new businesses failed last year, resulting in over 400,000 job losses.

- According to a 1991 Gallup Poll an overwhelming 94% of franchise owners say that they are successful. Seventy-five percent of franchise owners would do it again while, only 39% of Americans would repeat their job or business.

- Based on the Gallup Poll survey, the average total investment cost, including fees and any additional expenses, was $147,570. Fifty-six percent reported total investment cost under $100,000 while 26% reported total investment cost over $100,000.

- Based on the Gallup Poll survey, the average gross income before taxes of franchisees is $124,290. Forty-nine percent reported gross income of less than $100,000 and 37% reported gross income of more than $100,000.

For Women Only

For Women Only

Did you know that the recent surge in economic growth is actually being driven by small businesses that are in large part owned by women? That's right — women are starting businesses at **twice** the rate of men, and it's probably because women are finding that their dual careers as businesswomen and mothers are not being accommodated by big business very well at all. More and more, women are striking out on their own or with a partner that shares their same philosophy, and finding success on their own terms. Corporate America has held women as a group back long enough, and for that reason, women are launching their own businesses in unprecedented numbers.

When someone mentions the word "entrepreneur", most people conjure up the image of someone like Donald Trump smiling on the cover of some glossy business trade magazine. But these days chances are that smiling face will be decidedly more feminine looking than Donald's — it might be Donna's face, as in Donna Karan, who grew her apparel business into a million dollar money maker in just a few short years. As with men, hard work and commitment to make a business work are the ingredients women are using to create their own success, and not relying on others to hand it to them. Just look at some of these incredible statistics that the U.S. Small Business Administration has gathered on women business owners:

-   Over the last 15 years, the number of women-owned businesses has almost **doubled**.

-   In that same amount of time, the percentage of women-owned businesses increased by 10%, while those owned by men decreased by as much.

-   Over one-third of all businesses are now owned by women.

-   Women-owned businesses were awarded over $2 billion in federal prime contracts last year, compared to only $180 million about ten years ago, an increase of over ten fold.

-   75% of new businesses started by women succeed, compared to only 25% of those started by men.

Since most people in the U.S. actually work for small businesses, the government has been forced to take notice of these ever-increasing trends toward women-owned businesses. Chances are your new boss or CEO is going to be a woman, not someone like Lee Iacocca. Why else would the Small Business Administration (SBA) put a women's business ownership specialist at over 100 SBA offices across the country? You don't see the Small Business Administration bending over to help men out with special programs — anyone who reads the statistics can see who's going to be the most powerful group of emerging business owners over the next couple of decades.

As you'll see in this chapter, both the federal and state governments have created special programs to help women business owners compete and succeed.

* Small Business Administration Pilot Program

The Women's Pre-Qualified Loan Program is being tested for a year in Charlotte, North Carolina, and nine other cities nationwide. This program will give the Small Business Administration greater influence on the number of loans extended to women.

This program began on June 1, 1994. Through the program, women business owners can go directly to the Small Business Administration (SBA) for a loan guarantee review, instead of being required to go to a bank first. If the woman business owner qualifies, the SBA will issue a commitment letter that she can present as part of her loan application to a bank. If the bank approves the loan, the application is returned to the SBA for final review. The SBA's decision will be based on the ability of the woman business owner to pay back the loan.

Businesses must be 51% owned and operated by women to qualify for the lending program. Only Mecklenburg County businesses qualify for Charlotte's pilot program. The pilot women's program backs loans up to $250,000. The women's program backs loans up to $250,000, and will guarantee 90% of loans up to $155,000. Bigger loans will be backed 85%. There is no cap on the number of loans that will be processed through the pilot program.

Following the guidelines for the pilot program, women applicants will go to a "facilitator", who will screen applications for the SBA for a small fee. These fees have not been established as of this printing. The program is also being tested in Albuquerque, New Mexico; Chicago, Illinois; Columbus, Ohio; Helena, Montana; Montgomery, Alabama; Louisville, Kentucky; New Orleans, Louisiana; Salt Lake City, Utah; and San Francisco, California. While there is no way to monitor the number of women applicants who are rejected at the bank level under the existing system, the pilot program will work to improve that situation.

For more information, contact the Charlotte SBA office during business hours at 200 N. College St., Suite A2015, Charlotte, NC 28202; 704-344-6463.

* Fight Suppliers Who Won't Give You Credit

Public Reference Branch
Federal Trade Commission (FTC)
Washington, DC 20580
202-326-2222

Often women who have been divorced, have trouble establishing credit. And you need credit if you're going to run a business. The Federal Trade Commission (FTC) enforces the laws that prohibit creditors and credit bureaus from discriminating against women because of their sex or marital status, and they can send you the free publication, *Women and Credit Histories*. This pamphlet explains your credit rights under the law, how to get help in establishing your own credit, and what to do if you feel your credit application was unfairly denied.

* Grants, Loans and Loan Guarantees for Women Owned Businesses

Contact your state office of Economic Development located in your state capitol.
All federal money programs aimed at small business do not discriminate between women and non-women owned businesses. However, at the state level there are a number of specific money programs that are set aside only for women owned businesses. The programs vary from state to state and are changing all the time so it is best to check with your state Office of Economic Development in your state capital to insure you have the latest available information. Here is a listing for what a few states offer specifically for women entrepreneurs:

- Illinois has low interest loans up to $50,000
- Iowa has grants up to $25,000 and loan guarantees up to $40,000

- Louisiana has loans and loan guarantee programs up to $250,000
- Minnesota offers low interest loans for up to 50% of your project
- New York offers low interest loans from $20,000 to $500,000
- Wisconsin offers low interest loans for women owned businesses under $500,000 in sales

* Federal Government Set-Asides For Women Entrepreneurs

Contact your state office of Economic Development located in your state capitol

or

Superintendent of Documents
Government Printing Office
Washington, DC 20402
202-512-1800

Many federal government contracting offices are trying to insure that a certain percentage of their contracts go to women entrepreneurs. Most even have special offices that will help women entrepreneurs sell to their agencies. For help in selling your product or service to the government, contact your state Economic Development Office in your state capitol and obtain a copy of *Women Business Owners: Selling to the Federal Government*. It is available for $3.75 from the Government Printing Office.

* 15% Set-Aside for Women Entrepreneurs

Contact your state office of Economic Development located in your state capitol.

Not only is the federal government active in insuring that women get a fair share of government contracts, but many of the state governments are becoming involved. Some states, like California for example, have passed laws that force their state agencies to give at least 15% of their contracts to women and minority owned firms. Other states like Illinois, Iowa, Maine, Minnesota, Montana, New Jersey,

Oregon, and Washington are among those who are active in insuring that women obtain a fair share of state government contracts. Contact your state office of Economic Development to see how your business can take advantage of set-asides in your state.

* 28 States Offer Free Consulting To Women Only

Contact your state office of Economic Development located in your state capitol.

Although every state offers free help to any person wishing to start or expand a business in their state, there are 28 states that have set up special offices just for women entrepreneurs. As an example, Colorado established a women's clearinghouse which provides hands-on assistance with business planning, marketing, financing, and government contracts. They also hold seminars at 16 locations throughout the state. Ohio offers a wide range of free services including loan packaging and marketing research. Contact your state office of Economic Development to see what your state has to offer. If they don't have a "Women Only" office, don't let that stop you. It just means you'll have to share the help available with the men in your state.

* What To Do If You Suspect Your Bank Denied You Credit Because You Are a Woman or Divorced

Credit Practices Division
Federal Trade Commission
Washington, DC 20580
202-326-3758

Women looking for money to start up and run their businesses might run into lenders that discriminate against them simply because they are women or divorced. The Federal Trade Commission (FTC) enforces the Equal Credit Opportunity Act, which prohibits any creditor from denying credit to a consumer on the basis of sex or marital status. If you think you've been discriminated against by a lender, contact the Federal Trade Commission. While the Federal Trade Commission won't act on individual complaints, a number of complaints against the same lender may force them to investigate. If necessary, the Federal Trade Commission can take violators to court to get them to stop their illegal practices. If you want your complaint investigated and action taken immediately, contact one of the following agencies, depending on the type of lending institution involved:

National Banks
Comptroller of the Currency, Compliance Management, U.S. Department of the Treasury, Washington, DC 20219, 202-874-5000.

FDIC-Insured Banks
Division of Compliance and Consumer Affairs. 550 17th Street, NW, Room F-130, Washington, DC 20429, 202-898-3535.

Savings & Loans
Office of Thrift Supervision, U.S. Department of Treasury, 1700 G Street, NW, Washington, DC 20552, 202-906-6000.

State Banks
Contact your State Banking Commissioner.

* How To Select Quality Day Care For Your Child

County Cooperative Extension Service
6707 Groveton Dr.
Clinton, MD 20735
301-868-9410

If you're running your own small business or a business out of your home, you might need to consider finding good and reliable day care for your children to give you the time you need for your business. This office can send you a free copy of *How To Select Quality Day Care For Your Child,* which shows you what to look for in quality day care.

* How To Start a Child Care Business In Your Home

County Cooperative Extension Service
6707 Groveton Dr.
Clinton, MD 20735
301-868-9410

If you're interested in running a child care business out of your home, you'll need some necessary background information before you start. This office can send you a free copy of *Home-based Business: Child Care and Running a Child Care Business*, which includes information on such topics as record-keeping, registration and certification, rates to charge, advertising, and insurance. You'll also find a list of questions you should ask yourself, such as how suitable you are for the job, your feelings toward children, your physical stamina, your personal family life, and much more.

* Videos On Starting A Child Care Business

Contact your County Cooperative Extension Service listed under county government in your telephone book;

or

Video Production
Texas A & M University
107 Reed McDonald Building
College Station, TX 77843
409-845-2840
409-845-7800

Better Kid Care - Family Day Care Training is a 4-part video program in day care training. It includes the following topics: 1) Child Development, 2) Nutrition, 3) Health and Safety, and 4) Business Management. It is produced by the Texas Agricultural Extension Service and is available through their office (listed above) for a modest fee, or on a free loan basis through many County Cooperative Extension Service offices around the country. Call your local County Cooperative Extension Service for availability.

* How To Juggle The Stress of Your Business and Your Family

National Health Information Clearinghouse (NHIC)
P.O. Box 1133
Washington, DC 20013-1133
301-565-4167
1-800-336-4797

Trying to run a business can put a lot of added stress on you, your family, and your marriage, especially when business isn't going very well. The National Health Information Clearinghouse (NHIC) puts out a pamphlet entitled *Health-finder: Stress Information Resources* ($1), which lists and describes several government agencies and private organizations that offer publications and resources on work-related stress and stress management.

* Free Publications For Women Business Owners

Women's Bureau
Office of the Secretary
U.S. Department of Labor
200 Constitution Ave, NW
Washington, DC 20210
800-827-5355
202-219-6652

Are you interested in how many other women business owners there are in the U.S? How about what your chances are for climbing up through various management levels? If you're interested in finding out more about women in the workforce, including trends and future projections, you might find the following free publications informative:

Alternative Work Patterns
American Indian/Alaska Native Women Business Owners
Asian American Women Business Owners
Benefits to Employers Who Hire Women Veterans
Black Women Business Owners
Black Women in the Labor Force
Earning Differences Between Women and Men

Flexible Workstyles: A Look at Contingent Labor
Hispanic Origin Women Business Owners
State Maternity/Parental Leave Laws
Women Business Owners
Women in Management
Women in Skilled Trades
Women of Hispanic Origin in the Labor Force
Women on the Job: Careers in the Electronic Media
Women Who Maintain Families
Women With Work Disability
Women Workers: Outlook to 2005
Work and Family Resource Kit
Working Mothers and Their Children

* How To Get Start-Up Capital From Being Pregnant, Sexually Harassed, or From A Bad Shopping Experience

U.S. Customs Service
Fraud Division
Washington, DC 20229
1-800-BE-ALERT
or
Equal Employment Opportunity Commission (EEOC)
1801 L St., NW
Washington, DC 20570
1-800-669-4000
1-800-669-3362 (publications)

More people would quit what they're doing and start their own business if they had a small windfall of money to get them started. Here are two government programs that may turn a bad experience into the capital needed to begin a business.

As a business owner, there are times you may come across unscrupulous wholesalers who try to sell you some counterfeit products at cut-rate prices. Instead of risking your business by buying and reselling the bogus products, report the fraud to the U.S. Customs Service. If your complaint, which will be kept completely anonymous, leads to the seizure of counterfeit goods, you could receive a reward of up to $250,000, depending on the size of the case. What small business couldn't use some extra operating capital like that to keep it going?

So you want to start your own business because you've just been fired because you were pregnant, or wouldn't sleep with your boss to get a promotion? Before you go taking out any business loan, contact the Equal Employment Opportunity Commission (EEOC) and report how you think your former boss discriminated against you. The EEOC will investigate your complaint, and if they think there are grounds for prosecuting your former boss, they'll proceed with the case. If they prove the case, you could end up with enough money in back pay and other remedies to finance your own company.

* Health Insurance for Divorcees Who Start Their Own Business

Women Work
1625 K St NW, #300
Washington, DC 20006
202-467-6346

Under the new law, divorced and separated women and their children can continue to receive the same health insurance coverage they had before they were divorced or separated from their husbands at the group rate. The only difference is that they must pay the premium. This law applies to all private businesses that employ more than 20 people and to federal, state, and local government plans. Depending on the reason for displacement, you may be eligible to continue coverage for up to 36 months. You must contact the health plan within 60 days of the divorce or separation to indicate that you're electing to continue coverage. If the plan refuses to honor the law, contact your state's Insurance Commissioner, and they will investigate your complaint and get you the coverage to which you're entitled. For more information on this law, contact the Women Work at the above address.

* Meet Women Entrepreneurs In Your Neighborhood For Lunch

Office of Women's Business Ownership
U.S. Small Business Administration
409 3rd St., SW
Washington, DC 20416
202-205-6673

One of the biggest problems women entrepreneurs face is breaking into the "old boys" network of successful businessmen, and important opportunities can be lost without access to these kinds of connections. To help women interested in networking with other successful business people, the U.S. Small Business Administration has a new program that pairs up a woman who is just starting out with an experienced female Chief Executive Officer running the same kind of company. This business mentor can help the novice businesswoman make connections that might otherwise take her years to make on her own. Those interested in networking should also think about joining relevant professional associations, such as the National Association of Women Business Owners at 212-922-0465 or the National Association for Female Executives at 212-645-0770, or by contacting their local Chamber of Commerce.

* Seminars On How Women Can Sell to the Government

Office of Women's Business
U.S. Small Business Administration
409 3rd St., SW
Washington, DC 20416
202-205-6673

If you're not sure how to start doing business with the government, you might consider taking a seminar sponsored by the U.S. Small Business Administration on the procurement process. These seminars will give you a complete overview on what you'll need to know and do to get involved in bidding on and landing government business contracts. For information on when these seminars are scheduled in your area, contact the office above, or the Women's

Business Ownership Representative nearest you listed elsewhere in this chapter.

* Creative Financing for Women Entrepreneurs

Office of Women's Business Ownership
U.S. Small Business Administration
409 3rd St., SW
Washington, DC 20416
202-205-6673

One of the toughest parts of running a business is finding the capital resources to do it: MONEY. The Women's Business Ownership Office runs seminars on how women can use creative ways to locate financing if they've been turned down for loans by regular banks. For more information about these seminars, contact the office above or the Women's Business Ownership Representative nearest you listed elsewhere in this chapter.

* Free Mentors for New Women Entrepreneurs

Office of Women's Business Ownership
U.S. Small Business Administration
409 3rd St., SW
Washington, DC 20416
202-205-6673

How valuable would it be to your business to find a successful role model who's already gone through what's facing you as a female entrepreneur and who's willing to share her expertise with you at no charge? Through the Small Business Administration's Women's Network for Entrepreneurial Training (WNET)

you can be paired up with a successful mentor who will meet with you at least once a week for an entire year, allowing you to learn from her experience and begin networking with other successful business people. If you've had your business going for at least a year and have gross receipts of at least $50,000, you can qualify for the WNET program. For more information, contact the office above or the Women's Business Ownership Representative nearest you listed elsewhere in this chapter.

* Changing Laws to Help Women Business Owners

Congressional Caucus for Women's Issues
2471 Rayburn Building
Washington, DC 20515
202-225-6740

If you think that the climate for women business owners could be improved by passing a new law, you might think of sending your ideas to the Congressional Caucus for Women's Issues. This group keeps track of the issues most important to women across the country and introduces new legislation that can help meet those needs, including those of the community of women entrepreneurs. Recently, a new law was passed that allowed federal funding for U.S. Small Business Administration Demonstration Centers that specialize in offering counseling to women interested in starting and expanding businesses. Contact this office if you have any new ideas or would simply like them to send you information about the most recent legislation currently before Congress that concerns women business owners.

For Starters: Call Your Local
Women's Business Ownership Representative

Women entrepreneurs have special needs, and the U.S. Small Business Administration recognizes those needs. That's why they've added staff members who specialize in promoting women-owned businesses in the U.S. These Women's Business Ownership (WBO) Reps can help solve your unique business problems, such as how to network with other women business owners, where to find financial assistance on the state level, or how to get in on the lucrative government procurement programs, especially the ones that offer preferences to women-owned businesses. The WBO rep serving your area is your best starting place to help you cut through the red tape and direct you to free counseling and other valuable information sources.

Alabama

U.S. Small Business Administration, 2121 8th Ave., North, Suite 200, Birmingham, AL 35203-2398; 205-731-1334, Fax: 205-731-1404.

Alaska

U.S. Small Business Administration, 222 West 8th Ave., Room 67, Anchorage, AK 99513-7559; 907-271-4022, Fax: 907-271-4545.

Arizona

U.S. Small Business Administration, 2828 North Center, Suite 800, Phoenix, AZ 85004-1025; 602-640-2316, Fax: 602-640-2360.

U.S. Small Business Administration, 300 W. Congress St., Room 7-N, Tucson, AZ 85701-4459; 602-670-4759, Fax: 602-670-4763.

Arkansas

U.S. Small Business Administration, 2120 Riverfront, Suite 100, Little Rock, AR 72202; 501-324-5878, Fax: 501-324-5199.

California

U.S. Small Business Administration, 71 Stevenson St., San Francisco, CA 94105-2939; 415-744-6402, Fax: 415-744-6435.

U.S. Small Business Administration, 211 Main St., 4th Floor, San Francisco, CA 94105-1988; 415-744-6820, Fax: 415-744-6812.

U.S. Small Business Administration, 660 J St., Suite 215, Sacramento, CA 95814-2413; 916-551-1426, Fax: 916-551-1439.

U.S. Small Business Administration, 800 Front St., Room 4-S-29, San Diego, CA 92188-0270; 619-557-7252, Fax: 619-557-5894.

U.S. Small Business Administration, 901 W. Civic Center Dr., Suite 160, Santa Ana, CA 92703-2352; 714-836-2494, Fax: 714-836-2528.

U.S. Small Business Administration, 330 N. Brand Blvd., Suite 1200, Glendale, CA 91203-2304; 213-894-2956, Fax: 213-894-5665.

U.S. Small Business Administration, 2719 N. Air Fresno Dr., Suite 107, Fresno, CA 93727-1547; 209-487-5189, Fax: 209-487-5636.

U.S. Small Business Administration, 6477 Telephone Road, Suite 10, Ventura, CA 93003-4459; 805-642-1866, Fax: 805-642-9538.

U.S. Small Business Administration, 825 Bell Street, Suite 206, Sacramento, CA 95825; 916-978-4571, Fax: 916-978-4577.

Colorado

U.S. Small Business Administration, 999 18th St., Suite 701, Denver, CO 80202; 303-294-7186, Fax: 303-294-7153.

U.S. Small Business Administration, 721 19th St., Suite 426, Denver, CO 80202-2599; 303-844-3984, Fax: 303-844-6468.

Connecticut

U.S. Small Business Administration, 330 Main St., Hartford, CT 06106; 203-240-4700, Fax: 203-240-4659.

Delaware

U.S. Small Business Administration, 920 N. King St., Suite 412, Wilmington, DE 19801; 302-573-6295, Fax: 302-573-6060.

District of Columbia

U.S. Small Business Administration, 1111 18th St., NW, Washington, DC 20036; 202-634-1500, ext. 258.

U.S. Small Business Administration, 1110 Vermont Ave. NW, Suite 900, Washington, DC 20036; 202-606-4000, Fax: 202-606-4225.

Florida

U.S. Small Business Administration, 7825 Bay Meadows Way, Suite 100B, Jacksonville, FL 32256-7504; 904-443-1900, Fax: 904-443-1980.

U.S. Small Business Administration, 1320 S. Dixie Hwy., Suite 501, Coral Gables, FL 33146-2911; 305-536-5521, Fax: 305-536-4745.

U.S. Small Business Administration, 501 E. Polk Street, Suite 104, Tampa, FL 33602-3945; 813-228-2594, Fax: 813-228-2111.

U.S. Small Business Administration, 5601 Corporate Way, Suite 402, West Palm Beach, FL 33407-2044; 407-689-3922.

Georgia

U.S. Small Business Administration, 1720 Peachtree St., NW, Atlanta, GA 30309; 404-347-4749, Fax: 404-347-4745.

U.S. Small Business Administration, 1375 Peachtree St., NE, Atlanta, GA 30367; 404-347-2797, Fax: 404-347-2355.

U.S. Small Business Administration, One Baltimore Place, Suite 300, Atlanta, GA 30308; 404-347-3771, Fax: 404-347-3813.

U.S. Small Business Administration, 52 N. Main Street, Room 225, Statesboro, GA 30458; 912-489-8719.

Hawaii

U.S. Small Business Administration, 30 Ala Moana, Room 2213, Honolulu, HI 96850-4981; 808-541-2990, Fax: 808-541-2976.

Idaho

U.S. Small Business Administration, 1020 Main St., Suite 290, Boise, ID 83702-5745; 208-334-1696, Fax: 208-334-9353.

Illinois

U.S. Small Business Administration, 300 S. Riverdale, Room 1975S, Chicago, IL 60606; 312-353-5000, Fax: 312-353-3426.

U.S. Small Business Administration, 500 W. Madison St., Suite 1250, Chicago, IL 60661-2511; 312-353-4528, Fax: 312-886-5108.

U.S. Small Business Administration, 511 W. Capitol St., Suite 302, Springfield, IL 62704; 217-492-4416, Fax: 217-492-4867.

Indiana

U.S. Small Business Administration, 429 N. Pennsylvania St., Suite 100, Indianapolis, IN 46204; 317-226-7272, Fax: 317-226-7259.

Iowa

U.S. Small Business Administration, 373 Collins Rd., NE, Suite 100, Cedar Rapids, IA 52402-3147; 319-393-8630, Fax: 319-393-7585.

U.S. Small Business Administration, 210 Walnut St., Room 749, Des Moines, IA 50309; 515-284-4422, Fax: 515-284-4572.

Kansas

U.S. Small Business Administration, 100 E. English, Suite 510, Wichita, KS 67202; 316-269-6273, Fax: 316-269-6499.

Kentucky

U.S. Small Business Administration, 600 Dr. Martin Luther King, Jr. Pl., Room 188, Louisville, KY 40202; 502-582-5971, Fax: 502-582-5009.

Louisiana

U.S. Small Business Administration, 1661 Canal St., Suite 2000, New Orleans, LA 70112; 504-589-6685, Fax: 504-589-2339.

U.S. Small Business Administration, 500 Fammin St., Room 8A-06, Shreveport, LA 71101; 318-676-3196, Fax: 318-676-3214.

Maine

U.S. Small Business Administration, 40 Western Ave., Room 512, Augusta, ME 04330; 207-622-8378, Fax: 207-622-8277.

Maryland

U.S. Small Business Administration, 10 N. Howard St., Room 608, Baltimore, MD 21202; 410-962-4392, Fax: 410-962-1805.

Massachusetts

U.S. Small Business Administration, 155 Federal St., Boston, MA 02110; 617-451-2023, Fax: 617-565-8695.

U.S. Small Business Administration, 10 Causeway St., Room 265, Boston, MA 02222-1093; 617-565-5590, Fax: 617-565-5598.

U.S. Small Business Administration, 1550 Main St., Room 212, Springfield, MA 01103; 413-785-0268, Fax: 413-785-0267.

Michigan

U.S. Small Business Administration, 477 Michigan Ave., Room 515, Detroit, MI 48226; 313-226-6075, Fax: 313-226-4769.

U.S. Small Business Administration, 300 S. Front St., Marquette, MI 49885; 906-225-1108, Fax: 906-225-1109.

Minnesota

U.S. Small Business Administration, 100 N. 6th St., Suite 610, Minneapolis, MN 55403; 612-370-2324, Fax: 612-370-2303.

Missouri

U.S. Small Business Administration, 911 Walnut St., Kansas City, MO 64106; 816-426-3608, Fax: 816-426-5559.

U.S. Small Business Administration, 323 W 8th, Suite 501, Kansas City, MO 64106; 816-374-6706, Fax: 816-374-6759.

U.S. Small Business Administration, 815 Olive St., Suite 242, St. Louis, MO 63101; 314-539-6600, Fax: 314-539-3785.

U.S. Small Business Administration, 620 S. Glenstone, Suite 110, Springfield, MO 65802-3200; 417-864-7670, Fax: 417-864-4108.

Mississippi

U.S. Small Business Administration, One Hancock Plaza, Suite 1001, Gulfport, MS 39501-7758; 601-863-4449, Fax: 601-864-0179.

U.S. Small Business Administration, 101 W. Capitol St., Suite 400, Jackson, MS 39201; 601-965-4378, Fax: 601-965-4294.

Montana

U.S. Small Business Administration, 301 South Park Avenue, Room 528, Helena, MT 59626; 406-449-5381, Fax: 406-449-5474.

Nebraska

U.S. Small Business Administration, 11145 Mill Valley Rd., Omaha, NB 68154; 402-221-4691, Fax: 402-221-3680.

Nevada

U.S. Small Business Administration, 301 E. Stewart, Room 301, Las Vegas, NV 89125-2527; 702-388-6611, Fax: 702-388-6469.

U.S. Small Business Administration, 50 S. Virginia Street, Room 238, Reno, NV 89505-3216; 702-784-5268.

New Hampshire

U.S. Small Business Administration, 143 N. Main St., Suite 202, Concord, NH 03302-1257; 603-225-1400, Fax: 603-225-1409.

New Jersey

U.S. Small Business Administration, 60 Park Place, Newark, NJ 07102; 201-645-2434, Fax: 201-645-6265.

U.S. Small Business Administration, 2600 Mt. Ephurain Avenue, Camden, NJ 08104; 609-757-5183, Fax: 609-757-5335.

New Mexico

U.S. Small Business Administration, 625 Silver SW, Room 320, Albuquerque, NM 87102; 505-766-1870, Fax: 505-766-1057.

New York

U.S. Small Business Administration, 26 Federal Plaza, Room 31-08, New York, NY 10278; 212-264-1450, Fax: 212-264-0900.

U.S. Small Business Administration, 26 Federal Plaza, Room 3100, New York, NY 10278; 212-264-2454, Fax: 212-264-4963.

U.S. Small Business Administration, 100 S. Clinton St., Room 1071, Syracuse, NY 13260; 315-423-5383, Fax: 315-423-5370.

U.S. Small Business Administration, 333 E. Water St., Elmira, NY 14901; 607-734-8130, Fax: 607-733-4656.

U.S. Small Business Administration, 111 W. Huron St., Room 1311, Buffalo, NY 14202; 716-866-4301, Fax: 716-866-4418.

U.S. Small Business Administration, 35 Pinelawn Rd., Room 102E, Melville, NY 11747; 516-454-0750, Fax: 516-454-0769.

U.S. Small Business Administration, Corner of Clinton and Pearl, Room 815, Albany, NY 12207; 518-472-6300, Fax: 518-472-7138.

U.S. Small Business Administration, 100 State St., Room 410, Rochester, NY 14614; 716-263-6700, Fax: 716-263-3146.

U.S. Small Business Administration, 360 Rainbow Boulevard S, Niagara Falls, NY 14303; 716-282-4612, Fax: 716-282-1472.

U.S. Small Business Administration, 201 Varrick St., Suite 628, New York, NY 10014; 212-620-3722, Fax: 212-620-3730.

North Carolina

U.S. Small Business Administration, 200 N. College St., Suite A2015, Charlotte, NC 28202-2173; 704-344-6563, Fax: 704-344-6769.

North Dakota

U.S. Small Business Administration, 657 2nd Ave. North, Room 218, P.O. Box 3088, Fargo, ND 58102; 701-239-5131.

Ohio

U.S. Small Business Administration, 1111 Superior Ave., Suite 610, Cleveland, OH 44144-2507; 216-522-4180, Fax: 216-522-2038.

U.S. Small Business Administration, 2 Nationwide Plaza, Suite 1400, Columbus, OH 43215-2542; 614-469-6860, Fax: 614-469-2391.

U.S. Small Business Administration, 525 Vine St., Suite 870, Cincinnati, OH 45202; 513-684-2814, Fax: 513-684-3251.

Oklahoma

U.S. Small Business Administration, 200 NW 5th St., Suite 670, Federal Building, Oklahoma City, OK 73102; 405-231-4301, Fax: 405-231-4876.

Oregon

U.S. Small Business Administration, 222 SW Columbia Ave., Suite 500, Portland, OR 97201-6605; 503-326-2682, Fax: 503-326-2808.

Pennsylvania

U.S. Small Business Administration, 475 Allendale Square Rd., Suite 201, King of Prussia, PA 19406; 215-962-3700, Fax: 215-962-3743.

U.S. Small Business Administration, 475 Allendale Square Rd., Suite 201, King of Prussia, PA 19406; 215-962-3804, Fax: 215-962-3795.

U.S. Small Business Administration, 960 Penn Ave., Pittsburgh, PA 15222; 412-633-2780, Fax: 416-644-5446.

U.S. Small Business Administration, 100 Chestnut St., Room 309, Harrisburg, PA 17101; 717-782-3840, Fax: 717-782-4839.

U.S. Small Business Administration, 20 N. Pennsylvania Ave., Room 2327, Wilkes-Barre, PA 18702; 717-826-6497, Fax: 717-826-6287.

Rhode Island

U.S. Small Business Administration, 380 Westminister Mall, Providence, RI 02903; 401-528-4561, Fax: 401-528-4539.

South Carolina

U.S. Small Business Administration, 1835 Assembly St., Room 358, Columbia, SC 29201; 803-765-5376, Fax: 803-765-5962.

South Dakota

U.S. Small Business Administration, 101 S. Main Ave., Suite 101, Sioux Falls, SD 57102-0527; 605-330-4231, Fax: 605-330-4215.

Tennessee

U.S. Small Business Administration, 50 Vantage Way, Suite 201, Nashville, TN 37228-1550; 615-736-5881, Fax: 615-736-7232.

Texas

U.S. Small Business Administration, 10737 Gateway West, Suite 320, El Paso, TX 79902; 915-540-5676, Fax: 915-540-5636.

U.S. Small Business Administration, 606 N. Caranchua, Suite 1200, Corpus Christi, TX 78476; 512-888-3331, Fax: 512-888-3418.

U.S. Small Business Administration, 8625 King George Dr., Building C, Dallas, TX 75235-3391; 214-767-7633, Fax: 216-767-7870.

U.S. Small Business Administration, 9301 SW Freeway, Suite 550, Houston, TX 77074-1591; 713-773-6500, Fax: 713-773-6550.

U.S. Small Business Administration, 222 E. Van Buren St., Suite 500, Harlingen, TX 78550; 210-427-8533, Fax: 210-427-8537.

U.S. Small Business Administration, 1611 10th St., Suite 200, Lubbock, TX 79401; 804-743-7462, Fax: 804-743-7487.

U.S. Small Business Administration, 7400 Blanco Rd., Suite 200, San Antonio, TX 78216-4300; 210-229-4535, Fax: 210-229-4556.

U.S. Small Business Administration, 4300 Amom Carter Boulevard, Suite 114, Ft. Worth, TX 76155; 817-885-6500, Fax: 817-885-6500.

U.S. Small Business Administration, 819 Taylor Street, Room 8A-27, Ft. Worth, TX 76102; 817-334-3777, Fax: 214-767-0493.

U.S. Small Business Administration, 300 E. 8th Street, Room 520, Austin, TX 78701; 512-482-5258, Fax: 512-582-5290.

U.S. Small Business Administration, 505 E. Travis, Room 103, Marshall, TX 75670; 903-935-5257, Fax: 903-935-5258.

U.S. Small Business Administration, 4400 Amom Carter Blvd., Suite 10, Ft. Worth, TX 76155; 817-885-7600, Fax: 817-885-7616.

Utah

U.S. Small Business Administration, 125 S. State St., Suite 2237, Salt City, UT 84138-1195; 801-526-5804, Fax: 801-524-4160.

Vermont

U.S. Small Business Administration, 87 State St., Room 204, Montpelier, VT 05602; 802-828-4422, Fax: 802-828-4485.

Virginia

U.S. Small Business Administration, 400 N. 8th St., Room 3015, Richmond, VA 23240; 804-771-2400, Fax: 804-771-8018.

Washington

U.S. Small Business Administration, 2615 4th St., Room 440, Seattle, WA 98121; 206-553-5676, Fax: 206-553-4155.

U.S. Small Business Administration, 915 2nd Ave., Room 1792, Seattle, WA 98174-1088; 206-220-6520, Fax: 206-220-6570.

U.S. Small Business Administration, West 601 First Ave., Spokane, WA 99204-0317; 509-353-2800, Fax: 509-353-2829.

West Virginia

U.S. Small Business Administration, 168 W. Main St., Clarksburg, WV 26302; 304-623-5631, Fax: 304-623-0023.

U.S. Small Business Administration, 550 Eagan St., Room 309, Charleston, WV 25301; 304-347-5220, Fax: 304-347-5350.

Wisconsin

U.S. Small Business Administration, 212 E. Washington Ave., Room 213, Madison, WI 53703; 608-264-5261, Fax: 608-264-5541.

U.S. Small Business Administration, 310 W. Wisconsin Ave., Suite 400, Milwaukee, WI 53202; 414-297-3941, Fax: 414-297-1377.

Wyoming

U.S. Small Business Administration, 100 E. B St., Room 4001, Casper, WY 82602; 307-261-5761, Fax: 307-261-5499.

Local Woman-To-Woman Entrepreneur Help Centers

The U.S. Small Business Administration (SBA) has co-funded 19 Demonstration Centers across the country to assist women interested in starting up and expanding small businesses. What is unique about these programs is that most offer woman-to-woman, one-on-one counseling in all aspects of business, from employee relations, budgeting, and dealing with lenders, to legal, marketing, and accounting assistance. Unlike the help you might receive at an SBA office, these centers offer help by women exclusively for women. These non-profit centers are public/private-funded ventures, which means they will charge nominal fees for their services, although much less than you'd expect to pay for your own private business advisor.

California

American Woman's Economic Development Corp., 301 E. Ocean Blvd., Suite 1010, Long Beach, CA 90802; 213-983-3747, Fax: 213-983-3750.

West Co., A Women's Economic Self-Sufficiency Training Program, 413 N. State St., Ukiah, CA 95482; 707-462-2348.

West Co., A Women's Economic Self-Sufficiency Training Program, 333 C N. Franklin St., Fort Bragg, CA 95437; 707-964-7571.

Colorado

Mi Casa, Business Center for Women, 571 Galapago St., Denver, CO 80204; 303-573-1302, Fax: 303-573-0422.

District of Columbia

American Woman's Economic Development Corp., 2445 M St., NW, Room 490, P.O. Box 65644, Washington, DC 20035; 202-857-0091, Fax: 202-223-2775.

Georgia

YMCA of Greater Atlanta, 957 N. Highland Ave., NE, Atlanta, GA 30306; 404-872-4747.

Illinois

Women's Business Development Center, 8 S. Michigan Ave., Suite 400, Chicago, IL 60603; 312-853-3477, Fax: 312-853-0145.

Women's Business Development Center, SBDC/Joliet Junior College, 214 N. Ottawa, 3rd Floor, Joliet, IL 60431; 815-727-6544, ext. 1312.

Women's Business Development Center, Kankakee Community College. 4 Dearborn Square, Kankakee, Il 60901; 815-933-0375.

Women Business Owners Advocacy Program, SBDC/Rock Valley College, 1220 Rock St., Rockford, IL 61101; 815-968-4087.

Women's Economic Venture Enterprise, 229 16th St., Rock Island, IL 61201; 309-788-9793.

Indiana

Indiana Regional Minority Supplier Development Council, Inc., 300 E. Fall Creek Parkway, N.D., P.O. Box 44801, Indianapolis, IN 46244-0801; 317-923-2110.

Michigan

EXCEL! Women Business Owners Development Team, 200 Renaissance Ctr., Suite 1600, Detroit, MI 48243-1274; 313-396-3576.

EXCEL! Women Business Owners Development Team, 200 Ottawa NW, Suite 900, Grand Rapids, MI 49503-2465; 616-458-4783, Fax: 616-774-9081.

Minnesota

BI-CAP, Inc., Women in New Development WIND, P.O. Box 579, Bemidji, MN 56601; 218-751-4631, Fax: 218-751-8452.

Missouri

NAWBO of St. Louis, 911 Washington Ave., Suite 140, St. Louis, MO 63101; 314-621-6162.

New Mexico

Women's Economic Self-Sufficiency Team WESST Corp., 414 Silver Southwest, Albuquerque, NM 87102; 505-848-4760.

Women's Economic Self-Sufficiency Team WESST Corp., Taos County Economic Development Corp., P.O. Box 1389, Taos, NM 87571; 505-758-1161.

New York

American Woman's Economic Development Corp., 641 Lexington Ave., 9th Floor, New York, NY 10022; 212-688-1900, Fax: 212-688-2718.

Ohio

Ohio Coordinator, Melody Borchers, 614-466-4945.

Minority Female Entrepreneurship Program, Charles Christian, Director, 37 North High St., Columbus, OH 43215-3065; 614-225-6910, Fax: 614-469-8250.

Women's Economic Assistance Ventures (WEAV), Rosann Miller-Wethington, Executive Director, 105 West North College, P.O. Box 512, Yellow Springs, OH 45387; 513-767-2667, Fax: 513-767-1354.

Women's Entrepreneurial Growth Organization (WEGO), Barbara Lange, Director, 58 W. Center St., P.O. Box 544, Akron, OH 44309; 216-535-9346, Fax: 216-535-4523.

Women's Business Resource Program/Ohio University, Mary Ann McClure, Director, One President St., Athens, OH 45701; 614-593-0474, Fax: 614-593-1795.

Women Entrepreneurs, Inc., Joe-Ann Gibbons, Acting President/Director, 525 Vine St., 3rd Floor, Cincinnati, OH 45202; 513-684-0700.

Cleveland Women's Consortium, Michelle Spain, 1979 East 56th St., Cleveland, OH 44199; 216-881-8146.

Texas

Center for Women's Business Enterprise, 1200 Smith St., 2800 Citicorp Building, Houston, TX 77002; 713-658-0300.

Center for Women's Business Enterprise, 301 Congress Ave., Suite 1000, Austin, TX 78701; 512-476-7501, Fax: 512-476-2738.

Center for Women's Business Enterprise, 800 Interstate Bank Tower, Dallas, TX 75202; 214-855-7300, Fax: 214-855-7370.

Southwest Resource Development, 8700 Crownhill, Suite 700, San Antonio, TX 78209; 512-828-9034.

Center for Women's Business Enterprise, 8023 Vantage Dr., Suite 600, San Antonio, TX 78230; 512-377-2100.

Wisconsin

Women's Business Initiative Corp., 1020 N. Broadway, Milwaukee, WI 53202; 414-277-7004.

State Women Business Assistance Programs

The feds aren't the only ones noticing the emerging importance of female entrepreneurship in the U.S. Many states now have special programs to help new and expanding women-owned businesses get the special assistance they need to succeed. So far, almost half the states offer some kind of assistance to women business owners, from special set-aside programs to help women compete for lucrative government contracts, to nuts-and-bolts, one-on-one counseling, to special low-interest loan programs, such as the ones offered by Iowa and Louisiana.

It's important to keep in mind that just because your state doesn't currently have any special programs for women entrepreneurs, that doesn't mean that they won't in the near future. In fact, many states, like Florida and Utah, now have special women's business advocates in the state capitol to help bring the needs of women business owners to the attention of their legislators. This could mean new business programs for women offered in the future, so keep in touch with your state capitol to find out the status of these programs.

Alabama

Office of Minority Business Enterprise (OMBE)
Alabama Development Office
401 Adams Ave.
Montgomery, AL 36130
1-800-248-0033

The Office of Minority Business Enterprise (OMBE) helps women and minority entrepreneurs interested in starting or expanding their businesses prepare business plans and applications for SBA loans, fill out applications for state and federal procurement opportunities, and certify women- and minority-owned businesses to participate in the state purchasing programs.

Alaska

Minority Business Development Center
1577 C St., Suite 304
Anchorage, AK 99501
907-274-5400

The Minority Business Development Center provides management and financial consulting services including loan packaging, development, marketing, investment decisions, accounting systems, and other valuable business advice.

Bureau of Indian Affairs
Alaska Area Office
P.O. Box 25520
Juneau, AK 99802-5520
907-586-7103

Indian Business Development Grants: This program provides grants to assist in the development of Native-owned enterprise that will create jobs and other economic benefits for Alaska Native communities. Priority is given to rural business development projects. For profit businesses are eligible if they are at least 51% owned and operated by individual natives. Grants to individual natives range up to $100,000 with a minimum 75% match from private and/or public sector. The applicant must demonstrate that sufficient funding is not available from other sources.

Indian Loans for Economic Development: The program provides business management, and technical and financial assistance to individual natives and Native organizations for starting, expanding, or purchasing a business enterprise whose enterprise will create jobs and have other economic benefits. Priority is given to rural business development projects. Financial assistance is in the form of guaranteed or direct loans. 20% equity is required on loans and businesses must demonstrate economic feasibility.

Arizona

Arizona Business Connection
Arizona Department of Commerce
3800 N. Central, Suite 1400
Phoenix, AZ 85012
602-280-1480

This office serves as a clearinghouse of information to assist small businesses. One-on-one counseling is available.

Arkansas

Arkansas Industrial Development Commission
One State Capitol Mall
Little Rock, AR 72201
501-682-1060

The Minority Business Development Division provides business loan packaging, contract procurement assistance, bonding information, general business counseling, seminars, workshops, and referrals to other agencies.

Arkansas Industrial Development Commission
One State Capitol Mall

Little Rock, AR 72201
501-324-9043

The Small Business Division will do limited business research, limited inventor and manufacturer matching, and limited energy-efficient counseling and information.

California

Office of Small and Minority Business
Department of General Services
1808 14th St., Suite 100
Sacramento, CA 95814
916-322-5060

This office helps women-owned businesses interested in participating in the state's purchasing/contracting system, along with counseling, assistance, and protection for their interests.

Office of Civil Rights
Department of Transportation
1120 N St., Room 3400
Sacramento, CA 95814-5690
916-445-2276

This office offers women-owned businesses information on the certification necessary to participate in the state procurement program.

Colorado

Minority Business Office
Office of Business Development
1625 Broadway, Suite 1710
Denver, CO 80202
303-892-3840

The Women's Business Program acts as a resource clearinghouse for women business owners. They refer callers to the appropriate state and local offices that can provide them with the hands-on assistance they need, from business planning and marketing assistance to procurement programs and financing. The program also holds business planning seminars at 16 locations throughout the state.

Delaware

Minority Business Development Agency
800 French St., 6th Floor
Wilmington, DE 19801
302-571-4169

The agency assists minority businesses in the city of Wilmington by providing technical assistance, certificate of minority businesses, and workshops. They sponsor a Minority Business Trade Fair (the largest in the Northeast) once a year. The agency works with the Wilmington Economic Development Corporation to provide financing.

District of Columbia

Washington DC Minority Business
 Development Center
1133 15th St., NW, Suite 1120
Washington, DC 20005
202-785-2886

The center provides assistance in preparing business loans and loan proposals, management and technical assistance in the areas

of finance, business planning and operations, marketing, construction procurement services, and bid preparation. Services are provided at a subsidized rate.

Minority Business Opportunity Commission
2000 14th St., NW, Room 324
Washington, DC 20009
202-939-8780

The Minority Business Opportunity Commission (MBOC) is the District of Columbia government agency that certifies minority businesses eligible to participate in the Minority Business Sheltered Market Program and provides assistance in identifying procurement opportunities with the District government. The MBOC conducts seminars and workshops on District government and private sector contracting and publishes *Doing Business with the District — A How To Guide for Minority Participation.*

Florida

Florida Department of Transportation
Minority Programs Office
Hayden Burns Building, Room 260
Tallahassee, FL 32399-0450
904-488-3145

The office develops outreach programs to recruit and inform disadvantaged business enterprises about contracting opportunities with the Department of Transportation. It also has a business support component which assesses business needs for training and technical assistance. Specific programs include classroom training, on-the-job training, conferences, seminars, workshops, and proficiency standards attainment.

Minority Construction Program
Florida Board of Regents
Florida Education Center, Room 1601
Tallahassee, Fl 32399-1950
904-488-5251

This is a program to enhance minority participation in the State University System construction program. The goals of the Board of Regents are to achieve minority participation, to increase participation by minority architects and engineers, and to eliminate existing deterrents for the participation of socially and economically disadvantaged individuals and businesses. The board's long range goal is to achieve equitable distribution of contracts among all participants in the State University System.

Minority Business Office
Department of General Services
Knight Building
Koger Executive Center, Suite 201
2737 Centerview Dr.
Tallahassee, FL 32399-0100
904-487-0915

This office is responsible for certifying minority businesses to do business with the state and for maintaining a directory of these certified businesses. The directory is available to all state agencies.

Small and Minority Business Advocate
Florida Department of Commerce
Knight Building, #201

2737 Centerview Dr.
Tallahassee, FL 32399-0950
904-487-4698

The Small and Minority Business Advisory Council identifies the concerns and unique needs of small and minority owned businesses in Florida. It serves as a liaison between the business community, state agencies, and the legislature. It also serves as a review board for policies, procedures, and regulations as they relate to key issues of concern.

Georgia

Small and Minority Business Affairs
Georgia Department of Administrative Services
200 Piedmont Ave., SE
West Tower #1620
Atlanta, GA 30602
404-656-6315

The office assists small businesses in conducting business with state government, identification of coordinating offices in state agencies, and prerequisites.

The Minority Subcontractors Tax Credit is available to any company which subcontracts with a minority owned firm to furnish goods, property, or services to the state of Georgia. The credit is for 10% of the total amount of qualified payments to minority subcontractors during the tax year, but may not exceed $100,000 per year.

Minority Business Development Agency
401 W. Peachtree
Suite 1715
Atlanta, GA 30308
404-730-3300

Regional offices of the Minority Business Development Agency (of the U.S. Department of Commerce) manage a network of 25 local business assistance centers. At any of these centers a minority owner can get help with preparing a business loan package, securing sales, or solving a management problem. The centers maintain networks of local business development organizations, assist business people in the commercialization of technologies, and coordinate other federal agency activities which assist minority entrepreneurs.

Hawaii

Honolulu Minority Business Development Center
1132 Bishop St.
1st Hawaiian Tower #1000
Honolulu, HI 96813
808-531-6232

The center provides management and technical assistance to qualified ethnic minority individuals and firms in the areas of business and financial planning, contract procurement, marketing analyses, general management, bonding, office systems, and procedures.

Idaho

Disadvantaged Business Enterprise
110 North 27th St.
Boise, ID 83702
208-344-0150

This organization is funded by a federal grant. Its purpose is to assist women, minority, and disadvantaged business owners with the application process of becoming certified for federal government contracts.

Illinois

Small Business Advocate
Illinois Department of Commerce and Community Affairs
State of Illinois Center
100 W. Randolph St., Suite 3-400
Chicago, IL 60601
312-814-3540

The Small Business Advocate specializes in helping women, minorities, start-ups, and home-based business owners cut through the bureaucratic red tape and get the answers they need by offering information and expertise in dealing with various state, federal, and local agencies.

Small Business Assistance Bureau
Illinois Department of Commerce and Community Affairs
State of Illinois Center
620 E. Adams
Springfield, IL 62701
800-252-2923

The Women's Business Advocate offers programs to women entrepreneurs through a business calendar of events, which includes conferences at which business owners have an opportunity to network. The Advocate also maintains an extensive mailing list of women entrepreneurs. Through the Women's Business Development Center of The Neighborhood Institute, women business owners can get assistance in all phases of business development.

Under the Minority and Women Business Loan Program, women business owners can get long-term, fixed rate direct financing at below-market rates for loans from $5,000 to $50,000. One job must be created or retained for each $5,000 borrowed. Business owners can use the money for leasing or purchasing land and buildings, construction or renovation of fixed assets, purchase and installation of machinery and equipment, and working capital.

Under the Minority and Female Business Enterprise Program, Matchmaker Conferences are held to connect women business owners interested in landing government contracts with state and local purchasing agents.

Indiana

Small Business Development Center
Office of Minority and Women Business
    Development Division
One North Capitol
Indianapolis, IN 46204
317-264-2820

This office helps women- and minority-owned small businesses with all phases of development, from management and technical assistance, to contract bidding, procurement, educational seminars and training, and financial alternatives. As part of their Procurement Program, women- and minority-owned businesses receive help in seeking government services contracts.

Department of Economic Development
City of Fort Wayne
840 City-County Building
Fort Wayne, IN 46802
219-427-1127

The Minority Business Investment Program provides financial and management assistance to minority owned businesses in the Fort Wayne area.

Iowa

Targeted Small Business Program Manager
Department of Economic Development
200 E. Grand Ave.
Des Moines, IA 50309
515-242-4813

Under the Targeted Small Business Financial Assistance Program, women owned small businesses in Iowa can receive direct loans, loan subsidies, or grants of up to $25,000 and loan guarantees up to 75% of project, not to exceed $40,000 for start up and expansion.

Targeted Small Business
Iowa Department of Inspections and Appeals
Lucas Building, 2nd Floor
Des Moines, IA 50319-0083
515-281-7250

Under the Targeted Small Business Program, women and minority owned businesses can get help in getting certified as a targeted small business (any business 51% or more women or minority owned), and thereby become eligible for set-aside procurement programs sponsored by the state.

Kansas

Office of Minority Business
Existing Industry Development Division
Kansas Department of Commerce
700 SW Harrison
Topeka, KS 66603-3712
913-296-3805

This office helps women- and minority-owned businesses with the bidding procedures for public and private procurement opportunities in Kansas. They also offer management assistance to these businesses and help identify financial resources for them.

Kentucky

Office of Minority Affairs
State Office Building
501 High St.
Room 904
Frankfort, KY 40622
502-564-3601

This office certifies women- and minority-owned businesses interested in participating in the procurement program for state highway-related contracts.

Kentucky Cabinet for Economic Development
Capital Plaza Tower
Frankfort, KY 40601
502-564-2064

The Minority Business Division is a resource center for minority

business owners/managers. It identifies construction contracts, procurement opportunities, and offers training programs that address the business needs of the minority enterprises. It focuses on new job creation and job retention by serving existing minority businesses in the roles of ombudsman and expediter for business growth and retention.

Louisiana

Louisiana Economic Development Corporation
Department of Economic Development
P.O. Box 94185
Baton Rouge, LA 70804-9185
504-342-5675

Under the Minority and Women's Business Development Program, qualified women and minority owned businesses can receive loans or loan guarantees in amounts up to $250,000. This money can be used to finance construction, conversion, or expansions of business facilities, finance machinery, supplies, materials, or working capital line of credit. Direct loans are available when these businesses have been turned down by at least two financial institutions for a loan.

Division of Minority and Women's Business Enterprise
Department of Economic Development
P.O. Box 94185
Baton Rouge, LA 70804-9185
504-342-5373

This office offers women and minority owned businesses with one-on-one assistance and counseling on the state procurement and bidding process. They will direct these business owners to sources of management, technical, and financial assistance from state and federal government sources, as well as from the private sector. This office will also direct women and minority business owners to certain private sector industries in the state that have incentive programs to obtain goods and services from businesses owned by women or minorities, or which have franchise opportunities targeted for these group members.

Maine

Maine Department of Transportation
Division of Equal Opportunity
Employee Relations
State Station House
Augusta, ME 04333
207-289-3576

Under the Disadvantaged/Minority/Women Business Enterprise Program, women-owned businesses can get certification to obtain government contracts. This office helps business owners with the procurement procedures used to obtain government contracts.

Massachusetts

State Office of Minority and Women Business Assistance
Department of Commerce
100 Cambridge St.
Room 1305
Boston, MA 02202
617-727-8692

This office helps women and minority owned businesses get certified to participate in the state procurement programs.

Michigan

Targeted Services Division
Michigan Department of Commerce
4th Floor Law Building
P.O. Box 30225
Lansing, MI 48909
517-335-1835

This office runs Women Business Owners Services program which works largely as a referral service for women business owners. Business owners can also participate in special entrepreneurial education and procurement programs.

Minnesota

Department of Administration
Materials Management Division
112 Administrative Building
St. Paul, MN 55155
612-296-2600

This office certifies women-owned businesses to participate in the Small Business Program for procurement opportunities with the state. Once certified, a business earns a 6% preference on government contract bids.

Mississippi

Department of Economic and Community Development
P.O. Box 849
Jackson, MS 39205
601-359-3449

Under the Minority Business Enterprise Loan Program, women-owned businesses that show that they are economically disadvantaged are eligible to receive low-interest loans for up to 50% of a business project's cost.

Missouri

Council on Women's Economic Development & Training
1442 Aaron Court
P.O. Box 1684
Jefferson City, MO 65102
314-751-0810

The Council helps women small business owners through various programs, seminars, and conferences.

Missouri Department of Economic Development
P.O. Box 118
Jefferson City, MO 65102
314-751-3237

The Minority Business Assistance Program is designed to promote and encourage the development of minority owned businesses in Missouri. The program provides assistance in obtaining technical and financial assistance, education programs, minority advocacy, and networking with other programs and agencies.

The Missouri Council on Women's Economic Development and Training assists women in small business enterprises. The Council conducts programs, studies, seminars, and conferences. It promotes increased economic and employment opportunities through education, training, and greater participation in the labor force.

Montana

DBE Program Specialist
Civil Rights Bureau
Montana Department of Highways
2701 Prospect Ave.
P.O. 201001
Helena, MT 59620-1001
406-444-6331

The Disadvantaged Business Enterprise and Women Business Enterprise program certifies women owned businesses interested in bidding on and obtaining federal-aid highway construction contracts.

Nebraska

Office of Women's Business Ownership
Small Business Administration
11145 Mill Valley Rd.
Omaha, NE 68154
402-221-4691

The office directs Small Business Administration (SBA) programs to women business owners through special women's groups, seminars, networks, and other activities for women in the private sector.

Nevada

Nevada Commission on Economic Development
3770 Howard Hughes Parkway #295
Las Vegas, NV 89158
702-486-7282

This office provides assistance to women and minority business owners. Business opening kits are available. Links with financial services are also identified.

New Hampshire

Office of Business and Industrial Development
Division of Economic Development
172 Pembroke Rd.
P.O. Box 856
Concord, NH 03302-0856
603-271-2591

This office serves as a clearinghouse and referral center of programs for women and minority owned businesses.

New Jersey

Office of Women Business Enterprise
CN 835
Trenton, NJ 08625-0835
609-292-3862

This office helps businesswomen interested in opening, expanding, or buying a company.

Set-Aside and Certification Office
CN 835
Trenton, NJ 08625-0835
609-984-9835

This office helps women and minority owned businesses compete for government contracts by administering the New Jersey Unified Certification Program for Women and Minorities and the Set-Aside Program. Under the Set-Aside Program, women and minority owned businesses earn a preference on government contract bids.

Division of Development for Small Businesses and
    Women and Minority Businesses
CN 835
Trenton, NJ 08625-0835
609-292-3860

This office offers women and minority owned small businesses financial, marketing, procurement, technical, and managerial assistance.

New Mexico

Department of Economic Development and Tourism
Joseph Montoya Building
1100 St. Francis Dr., Room 2006
Santa Fe, NM 87503
505-827-0425

The Procurement Assistant Program educates business owners in all phases of government contracting, and provides comprehensive technical procurement counseling for obtaining defense, federal, state, and local government contracts. It offers training seminars (hands-on workshops), and offers small, minority and women owned businesses the opportunity to be entered into the annual New Mexico MSBPAP Business Directory.

New York

Division of Minority and Women's Business
Department of Economic Development
1 Commerce Plaza
Albany, NY 12245
518-474-6346
or
1515 Broadway, 52nd Floor
New York, NY 10036
212-827-6266

This office gives women and minority owned businesses consulting and technical assistance in obtaining benefits from state programs, with a focus on business financing. They also help these businesses get the proper certification to participate in the state procurement opportunities. Additionally, this office can help these business owners obtain federal government contracts.

New York Urban Development Corp.
Minority and Women Revolving Loan Fund
1515 Broadway
New York, NY 10036
212-930-0452

Women and minority owned industrial, commercial, service oriented, and start-up businesses can receive low interest loans. Retail businesses are evaluated on a case-by-case basis before they qualify. Loans range from $20,000 to $500,000 and may be used for construction, renovation, leasehold improvements, acquisition of land and buildings, acquisition of an ongoing business, establishment of a nationally recognized franchise outlet, machinery and equipment, and working capital.

North Carolina

North Carolina Minority Business Development Agency
430 N. Salisbury St.

Raleigh, NC 27603
919-571-4154

The agency provides information, referral, and support assistance to minority businesses. It offers technical referral assistance, procurement opportunities referral, management workshops and seminars, and coordination with other state and federal agencies.

North Dakota

Women Business Development Administration
Native American Business Development Administration
Department for Economic Development and Finance
1833 E. Bismarck Expressway
Bismarck, ND 58504
701-221-5300

These offices provide technical assistance in getting businesses started. Some of the services provided include location of funding and preparation of business plans.

Ohio

Minority Development Financing Commission
Ohio Department of Development
P.O. Box 1001
Columbus, OH 43266-0101
1-800-848-1300
614-466-4945

Under the Women's Business Resource Program, women can get help for start-up, expansion and management of their businesses. The program seeks to provide women with equal access to assistance and lending programs, and helps businesswomen locate government procurement opportunities. This office also acts as a statewide center of workshops, conferences, and Women's Business Owners statistics. All of the program's services are free. This office also publishes *Ohio Women Business Leaders*, a directory of women owned businesses in Ohio, along with other free publications.

Oklahoma

Oklahoma Department of Commerce
Small Business Division
P.O. Box 26980
Oklahoma City, OK 73126-0980
405-841-5227

Under the Women-Owned Business Assistance Program, businesswomen can get a variety of technical assistance, from business planning and marketing assistance, to financial information and government procurement practices.

The Minority Business Development Program provides support and assistance in the establishment, growth, and expansion of viable business enterprises. Counseling in the preparation of business plans and marketing strategies is available. The program also provides assistance for loan packaging, bid preparation, feasibility studies, and certification requirements.

Oregon

Office of Minority, Women & Emerging Small Businesses
155 Cottage St., NE
Salem, OR 97310

503-378-5651

This office certifies women owned, disadvantaged, and emerging small businesses, allowing them to participate in the state's targeted purchasing programs.

Pennsylvania

Bureau of Women's Business Development
Forum Building, Room 462
Harrisburg, PA 17120
717-787-3339

The Bureau offers women business owners one-on-one counseling and helps them get the information they need to solve their problems in developing a business. They also will refer women business owners to the appropriate state offices and agencies that can best help them with every kind of issue, from procurement assistance to developing business and financial strategies.

Rhode Island

Office of Minority Business Assistance
Department of Economic Development
7 Jackson Walkway
Providence, RI 02903
401-277-2601

This office certifies women and minority owned businesses under federal and state set-aside and goal programs and provides counseling assistance to these companies.

Tennessee

Office of Minority Business Enterprise
Department of Economic & Community Development
Rachel Jackson Building, 7th Floor
320 6th Ave. North
Nashville, TN 37219-5308
(in state) 1-800-342-8470
615-741-2545

This office offers information, advocacy, referral, procurement, and other services to minority businesses in the state. They publish a directory of minority businesses, offer conferences and seminars on topics useful to business owners, and serve as a clearinghouse of important information to minorities. They also match minority vendors with potential clients and help minorities identify and obtain procurement opportunities.

Utah

Small Business Administration
Salt Lake District Office
125 S. State St.
Salt Lake City, UT 84138
801-524-5800

The Women's Business Ownership Program offers a series of business training seminars and workshops for women business owners and for women who want to start their own small firms. This program provides a focus on business planning and development, credit, and procurement as it relates specifically to women and their businesses.

Vermont

Minority Assistance Program
City Hall, Room 32
Burlington, VT 05401
802-865-7177

This office provides technical assistance to women and minority business owners. Assistance is available in preparing business and marketing plans, as well as with tax preparation. A resource library is maintained, and a Minority Forum meeting is held monthly. The staff publishes a monthly newsletter covering topics of interest to minority business owners.

Washington

Office of Minority and Women's Business Enterprises
P.O. Box 41160
Olympia, WA 98504-1160
206-753-9693

This office helps women and minority owned businesses interested in participating in state contracting opportunities by moving them through the certification process. Once certified, businesses are eligible to receive a 5% preference when bidding competitively on goods and services purchased by the state. Upon request, businesses can be placed on bid lists maintained by individual agencies, education institutions, or contractors by contacting them directly.

Wisconsin

Women's Business Services
Department of Development
P.O. Box 7970
Madison, WI 53707
(in state) 1-800-435-7287
608-266-1018

The Women's Business Services offers assistance in gaining information about the state's loan programs available to women business owners. The office keeps track of the top 50 fastest growing and top 10 women owned business in Wisconsin. They also maintain a database of women owned businesses in the state.

Wisconsin Housing and Economic Development Authority
One South Pinckney St., #500
P.O. Box 1728
Madison, WI 53701-1728
608-266-0976

Under the Linked Deposit Loan Program, women or minority owned businesses with gross annual sales of less than $500,000 can qualify for low-rate loans. Loans are available under the prime lending rate for purchase or improvement of buildings, equipment, or land, but not for working capital. Business must be in manufacturing, retail trade, tourism, or agriculture packaging or processing.

Wisconsin Women Entrepreneurs
1126 S. 70th St., Suite 106
Milwaukee, WI 53214
414-475-2436

The office provides monthly programs, training, seminars, mentor committees, and a membership directory.

State Women's Business Advocates

These state funded offices provide technical support and referral services for planning financing, training, and other women's business issues.

Arizona

Ms. Hank Barnes, Director, Governor's Office of Women's Services, 1700 West Washington, #420, Phoenix, AZ 85007; 602-542-1755.

Mr. James Guyer, District Director, U.S. Small Business Administration, 2005 North Central Ave., 5th Floor, Phoenix, AZ 85004; 602-379-3737.

Arkansas

Ms. Mary Ann Campbell, CFP, Money Magic, Inc., 2923 Imperial Valley Dr., Little Rock, AR 72212; 501-277-6644.

California

Ms. Alice Flissinger, Office of Small and Minority Business, Department of General Services, 1808 14th St., Room 100, Sacramento, CA 95814; 916-322-5060.

Ms. Rieva Lesonsky, Editor-in-Chief, *Entrepreneurial Woman*, 2392 Morse Ave., Irvine, CA 92714; 714-261-2325.

Colorado

Ms. Dora D'Amico, Assistant Regional Administrator for Public Affairs and Communications, U.S. Small Business Administration, 999 18th St., Suite 701, Denver, CO 80202; 303-292-7033.

Ms. Charlotte Redden, Coordinator, Women's Business Program, Office of Business Development, 1625 Broadway, Suite 1710, Denver, CO 80202; 303-892-3840.

Connecticut

Ms. Katy Klarnet, Director of Public Relations, Connecticut Mutual Life Insurance Co., 140 Garden St., MS-G-26, Hartford, CT 06154; 800-234-2865; access code 1086, ext. 5073.

District of Columbia

Ms. Lindsey Johnson, Director, Office of Women's Business Ownership, U.S. Small Business Administration, 409 Third St., SW, Washington, DC 20416; 202-205-6673.

Illinois

Ms. Mollie Cole, Women's Business Advocate, Department of Commerce and Community Affairs, 100 West Randolph, Suite 3-400, Chicago, IL 60601; 312-814-6111.

Ms. Nancy Smith, Women's Business Ownership Coordinator, U.S. Small Business Administration, 230 South Dearborn St., Suite 510, Chicago, IL 60604; 312-353-4252.

Indiana

Ms. Betty McDonald, Programs Manager, Government Marketing Assistance Group, Indiana Department of Commerce, 1 North Capitol St., Suite 700, Indianapolis, IN 46204; 317-232-3393.

Louisiana

Ms. Angelisa Harris, Executive Director, Louisiana Dept. of Economic Development, Division of Minority and Women's Business Enterprise, P.O. Box 94185, Baton Rouge, LA 70804-9185; 405-841-5242.

Michigan

Kathleen Mechem, Director of Women Business Owner Services, Michigan Dept. of Commerce, 4th Floor Law Bldg., Box 30225, Lansing, MI 48909; 517-335-1835.

Minnesota

Ms. Tracy Thompson, Director, U.S. Small Business Development Center, Winona State University, Somsen Hall, Winona, MN 55987; 507-334-3965.

Nevada

Ms. Helen Myers, Director, Office of Small Business, State of Nevada, 2501 East Sahara, #304, Las Vegas, NV 89158; 702-486-4506.

Ohio

Ms. Melody K. Borchers, Manager, Women's Business Resource Program, Ohio Department of Development, 77 South High St., 28th Floor, Columbus, OH 43215; 614-466-4945.

Oklahoma

Ms. Marketia Head, Coordinator for Women-Owned Business Assistance Program, Department of Commerce, 6601 Broadway Extension, Oklahoma City, OK 73116; 405-841-5242.

Oregon

Ms. Diana McClelland, Co-Founder, The Foundation for Women Owned Businesses, 5031 East Foothills Rd., Lake Oswego, OR 97034; 503-790-7672.

Pennsylvania

Ms. Lenore Cameron, Exq., Director, Bureau of Women's Business Development, 462 Forum Building, Harrisburg, PA 17120; 717-787-3339.

Virginia

Ms. Anabel Gray, P.O. Box 3604, Lynchburg, VA 24503-0604; 804-528-9424.

Wisconsin

Ms. Saundra Herre, President, Herrewood Associates, 4101 Pennington, Racine, WI 53403; 414-554-8301.

Ms. Mary Strickland, Women's Business Services, Department of Development, 123 West Washington Ave., P.O. Box 7970, Madison, WI 53707; 608-266-0593.

Company Intelligence

How to Find Information On Any Company

When many researchers are doing investigations on companies they often rely only on two major information sources:

Public Companies = U.S. Securities and Exchange Commission Filings

Privately Held
Companies = Dun & Bradstreet Reports

Although many people still depend heavily on the Securities and Exchange Commission (SEC) and Dun & Bradstreet (D & B), these two resources have severe limitations. The Securities and Exchange Commission has information on approximately only 10,000 public companies in the United States. However, according to the IRS and the U.S. Bureau of the Census (both agencies count differently), there are between 5,000,000 and 12,000,000 companies in the country. So you can see that the SEC represents only a small fraction of the universe. Also, if you are interested in a division or a subsidiary of a public corporation and that division does not represent a substantial portion of the company's business, there will be no information on their activities on file at the SEC. This means that for thousands of corporate divisions and subsidiaries, it is necessary to look beyond the SEC.

D & B Won't Jail You
For Not Telling The Truth
But The Government Will

The problems with Dun & Bradstreet reports are more significant than the shortcomings of company filings at the SEC. The main drawback is that D & B reports have been established pri-

marily for credit purposes and are supposed to indicate the company's ability to pay its bills. Therefore, you will find information from current creditors about whether a business is late in its payments, which may or may not be a useful barometer to evaluate the company.

If there is additional financial information in these reports, you should also be aware of who in the company provides D & B with information and their motives. The information contained in these reports does not carry the legal weight of the company information registered with the Securities and Exchange Commission. If a company lies about any of the information it turns over to the SEC, a corporate officer could wind up in jail. Dun & Bradstreet, however, collects its information by telephoning a company and asking it to provide certain information voluntarily. The company is under no obligation to comply and, equally important, is under no obligation to D & B to be honest. Unlike the government, Dun & Bradstreet cannot prosecute.

If a competitor or someone was interested in acquiring Information USA, Inc., for example, the first likely step would be to obtain any financial data about this privately held company. In this hypothetical case, Information USA, Inc. might be interested in such a sale or perhaps want to impress the competition. Consequently, the information supplied to Dun & Bradstreet most likely would be the sanitized version which I would want outsiders to see. My only dilemma would be in remembering what half truths we told D & B last year so that our track record would appear consistent. However, Information USA, Inc. would not, and does not, play such games with its financial information filed with the Maryland Secretary of State.

This is why resourceful researchers are starting to appreciate the value of the thousands of non-traditional information sources such as public documents and industry experts.

Starting At The Securities And Exchange Commission

First find out whether the company you are gathering intelligence about is a public corporation. If it is, you should get your hands on copies of the company's Securities and Exchange Commission (SEC) filings. The fastest way to make this determination is to call:

Disclosure Inc.
5161 River Road Building 60
Bethesda, MD 20816
301-951-1300
800-638-8241

The price depends on which document you wish to have retrieved. The range is between $18 to $38 per document. If the company in question files with the Securities and Exchange Commission, the least you should do is to obtain a copy of the Annual Report, known as 10-K. This disclosure form will give you the most current description of the company's activities along with their annual financial statement.

Financial Statements In Addition To The Annual Report

In addition to the 10-K you may also want to see the company's most current financial statements by obtaining copies of all 10-Q's filed since their last 10-K. 10-Q's are basically quarterly financial statements which will bring you up-to-date since the last annual report.

The two other documents which may be of immediate interest are the 8-K's and the Annual Report to Stockholders. An 8-K will disclose

any major developments that have occurred since the last annual report, such as information about a takeover or major lawsuit. The Annual Report to Stockholders, the glossy quasi-public relations tool that is sent to all those who own stock in the company, can provide another component in assembling a company's profile. The most interesting item in this report, which is not included in the 10-K Annual Report, is the message from the president. This message often provides insights about the company's future plans.

Obtaining Copies of SEC Documents

The fastest way to get Securities and Exchange Commission (SEC) documents is through one of the many document retrieval companies which provide this service. In addition to the firm mentioned above, other companies that specialize in quickly obtaining corporate SEC filings include:

1) FACS Info Service, Inc.
157 Fisher Avenue
Eastchester, NY 10709
914-779-6900
Fax: 914-779-7038

2) Federal Document Retrieval, Inc.
   (Disclosure)
SEC Building
601 Indiana Ave., 8th Floor
Washington, DC 20001
202-347-2824

3) Research Information Services
717 D Street, NW
Washington, DC 20004
202-737-7111
Fax: 202-737-3324

4) Prentice Hall Legal and Financial Services
1090 Vermont Ave., NW, Suite 430
Washington, DC 20005
202-408-3120
Fax: 202-408-3142

5) Washington Service Bureau
   655 15th Street NW, Room 275
   Washington, DC 20005
   202-508-0600
   Fax: 202-508-0694

6) Washington Document Service
   400 7th Street NW, Suite 300
   Washington, DC 20001
   202-628-5200
   Fax: 202-626-7628

7) Vickers Stock Research Corp.
   600 S Street NW, Suite 504
   Washington, DC 20004
   202-626-4951

You can also go to one of the four major Securities and Exchange Commission Document Rooms to see any public filing. These reference rooms are located in Washington, DC, New York City, Chicago, and Los Angeles.

If the company headquarters or main office is located in the area served either by the Atlanta, Boston, Denver, Fort Worth, or Seattle regional offices, the 10-K and other documents can be examined at the appropriate SEC office. For the exact location of any of the regional offices mentioned contact:

Office of Public Affairs
U.S. Securities and Exchange Commission
450 5th Street NW, Stop 1-2
Washington, DC 20549
202-942-0020

One way to obtain free copies of these reports is to call the company and tell them you are a potential investor. Many public corporations are set up to respond to these inquiry.

Before you order any of these SEC filings, it is wise to ask for the total number of pages contained in each of the documents you want to obtain. Most of these document retrieval firms charge by the page, and no doubt, you don't want to be surprised if a company's amendment to its 10-K happens to run 500 pages in length.

Once you have obtained the SEC documents you can then explore the additional sources described below.

Clues At The State Level About Privately Held Companies Plus Divisions And Subsidiaries Of Public Corporations

The following sources are designed primarily to help you gather information on privately held companies or those divisions and subsidiaries of public corporations which are not contained in documents filed with the U.S. Securities and Exchange Commission. However, the sources described here will enhance your work in collecting data on all types of companies. If the company in question is not publicly owned, the next step is to turn your attention to the appropriate state government offices. All companies doing business in any state leave a trail of documentation there. The number of documents and the amount of detail vary widely depending upon the state regulations and the type of company.

One of the main reasons you should begin your search with the state government is that it may take longer to retrieve the information from the state offices than from other checkpoints which are described in this Section.

Puzzling Together Bits of Information

Remember that only the U.S. Securities and Exchange Commission documents provide you with information on your competitor or acquisition candidate. All other government documents are generated to comply with some law or policy, such as pollution control, consumer protection, or tax collection. Because of this, government bureaucrats who collect and analyze these documents have no idea just how valuable the information can be to you. Do not expect that the data contained in other government documents will be presented in a way that automatically will suit your particular needs. Furthermore, no single document will provide all the information about a corporate entity that you are seeking.

The strategy is to get any information you can because each piece might contribute to your overall information mosaic. Although a full profit and loss statement will be out of reach, the office of uniform commercial code can tell you to whom the company owes money and provide a description of the corporation's assets. The state office of corporations may not give you the total sales figure, but if the company's headquarter is out of state, it may tell you the corporation's total sales in that state and what percentage this is of its total. With a little bit of algebra you can estimate the total sales.

If it were as easy as making one phone call and getting complete financial information on any company, everyone would be doing it. Your competitive advantage lies in getting information that other people don't know about, or are too lazy to get.

In the event you intend to dig around at the state level, the following three offices are a must. They offer the biggest potential for the least amount of effort:

1) Office of Corporations

Every corporation, whether it is headquartered or has an office in a state, must file some information with a state agency. The corporations division or office of corporations usually is part of the office of the Secretary of State. When a company incorporates or sets up an office in the state, it must file incorporation papers, or something similar. This provides, at a minimum, the nature of the business, the names and addresses of officers and agents, and the amount of capital stock in the company. In addition to this registration, every company must file some kind of annual report. These annual reports may or may not contain financial data. Some states require sales figures, and others ask just for asset figures.

2) Office of Uniform Commercial Code

Any organization, and for that matter, any individual, which borrows money and offers an asset as collateral, must file within the state at the office of uniform commercial code. A filing is made for each loan and each of the documents is available to the public. To obtain these documents is a two step process. First, one must request a search to see if there are any filings for a certain company. The fee for a search is usually under $10. Such a search will identify the number of documents filed against the company. You then will have to request copies of each of these documents. The cost for each document averages only a few dollars. This office of uniform commercial code usually is located in, or near to, the same office of corporations.

3) State Securities Office

The U.S. Securities and Exchange Commission in Washington, DC regulates only those corporations which sell stock in their company across state lines. There is another universe of corporations which sells stock in their companies only within state lines. For such stock offerings, complete financial information is filed with the state securities regulator. These documents are similar to a those filed at the U.S. Securities and Exchange Commission. But, remember, that the documents vary from one state to the next and, equally important, the requirement of filing an annual report differs from state to state. Usually a telephone call to the office in charge can tell you whether a particular company has ever offered stock intrastate. If so, you are then in a position of getting copies of these filings. Usually the Secretary of State's office can refer you to the state's securities regulator.

Finding The Right State Office

Because of the multitude of differences between the 50 state governments, expect to make half a dozen calls before you locate the right office. Several starting places are described below with the simplest ones listed first.

1) State Government Operator
The AT&T information operator can give you the telephone number for the state government operator, and then in turn you can ask for the phone number of the specific government office.

2) State Department of Commerce
Now that every state is aggressively trying to get companies to expand or relocate to their state, these departments can serve as excellent starting points, because they are familiar with other government offices which regulate business. Many times these departments have established a "one-stop office" with a separate staff on call to help a business find whatever information it needs.

3) State Capital Library
By asking the state government operator to connect you to the state capital library, a reference librarian can identify the state agency which can best respond to your queries.

4) Directories
If you intend to dig around various state government offices on more than just an infrequent basis, you might consider purchasing a state government directory. Usually the state office of Administrative Services will sell you a directory, or you might want to contact the state bookstore. If you want to purchase a directory that covers all 50 states, consider:

State Executive Directory
Carroll Publishing Company
1058 Thomas Jefferson Street NW
Washington, DC 20007
202-333-8620
(Price is $135 per year plus shipping and handling.)

Tracking The Trail of Company Information In Other State Offices

The three offices described earlier are only the starting places for information on companies. There are dozens of other state agencies that are brimming with valuable bits of data about individual corporations; however, these sources require a bit more care because they can be used only under certain circumstances or require extra resourcefulness.

1) Utility and Cable TV Regulators
Utility companies are heavily regulated by state agencies, and as a result, there is a lot of financial and operational information that is accessible. Most people know that gas and electric companies fall into this category, but you may not be aware that this also applies to water companies, bus companies, rail systems, telephone companies, telecommunication companies, and cable TV operators.

2) Other State Regulators
State government is very similar to the federal government in that its function is to regulate many of the activities of the business community. In those states where state laws and enforcement are very effective, Uncle Sam relies on those states to enforce the federal laws. For example, the U.S. Food and Drug Administration will use the records from the state of New Jersey for information on pharmaceutical manufacturers instead of sending out its own team of federal data collectors. The U.S. Environmental Protection Administration will use state records in those states that have strict environmental statutes rather than using its own resources.

3) Financial Institutions
Banks, savings and loans, credit unions and other financial institutions all file information with the state bank regulator. Many of these organizations are also regulated by federal agencies so what you get from the state office often will be a copy of the form filed with the federal government.

4) Environment Regulators

Almost every state has an office which regulates pollutants in the air, water and ground. Such departments are similar to the U.S. Environmental Protection Agency in Washington, DC and monitor whether any new or old business is polluting the environment. If the company you are investigating has plans to build a new plant in the state, get ready to collect some valuable information. Before construction can begin, the company must file information with the state environmental protection agency. These documents will detail the size of the plant, what kind of equipment it will use, and how much this equipment will be used. With such information, other manufacturers in the same business can tell exactly what the capacity and estimated volume of the plant will be. Sometimes there will be three separate offices with authority over air, water or solid waste. Each will collect basically the same information, and they can be used, one against each other, to ensure that you get all the information you need.

5) Department of Commerce/Economic Development

As mentioned earlier, each state is now actively trying to attract and develop business development within the state. The state's office of economic development or department of commerce is normally charged with this responsibility. To attract business to the state, this agency has to know all about existing business throughout the state, which all translates into who is doing what, how successful they are, and how large the company is. At a minimum, the economic development office can probably provide you with information on the number of employees for a given company. They will also be aware what other government offices in the state keep records about the industry or company which interests you. The experts at this state agency are similar to the 100 industry analysts at the U.S. Department of Commerce and can serve as excellent resources for collecting government information on an industry.

6) State Government Contractors

Although many states are not accustomed to sharing information with researchers, you should be able to obtain details about any purchase the state makes. If the company in question sells to the state, you should get copies of their contracts. Just like the federal government which makes all this procurement information available, the state which spends public funds guarantees that the public has a right to know how the money is being spent. You may have to enforce your rights under the state law which is equivalent to the federal Freedom of Information Act.

7) Minority and Small Business

Many states maintain special offices which track minority firms and other small companies. These offices can be helpful by identifying these businesses and may also be able to tell you the size or products of a given business. The small business office and possibly a separate minority business division normally fall under the state department of commerce.

8) Attorney General

The state Attorney General's office is the primary consumer advocate for the state against fraudulent practices by businesses operating within the state. So, if the company you are investigating is selling consumer services or products, it would be worth the effort to check with this office. In some states the attorney generals have begun to concentrate on certain areas. For example, the office in Denver specializes in gathering information on companies selling energy saving devices, and the one in New York investigates companies with computerized databases which provide scholarship information.

9) Food and Drug Companies

Any company which produces, manufactures or imports either food or drug products is likely to come under the jurisdiction of the state food and drug agency. This office makes routine inspections of facilities and the reports are generally accessible; however, a Freedom of Information Act request is sometimes necessary.

County and Local Sources

County and local sources can prove to be the biggest bucket of worms as far as information sources go. Unlike state government offices where there are 50 varieties to choose from, there are over 5,000 different jurisdictions at the local level. Here are some basic checkpoints that can enhance your information gathering efforts.

Local Newspapers: Business Editors

The local newspaper can provide the best leads for anything you are investigating at the local level. It is perhaps the best source mentioned in this book. A well placed telephone call to the business editor or the managing editor, if there is not a business section, can prove to be most useful. In smaller towns, and even in suburbs of larger cities where there are suburban newspapers, a local business generates a good deal of news. A local reporter often knows the company like no one else in the country. The company executives usually are more open with the local media because they like to show off about how big they are, how much the company is growing, etc. A reporter is also likely to know company employees who can corroborate or refute the executive's remarks.

Ask the local newspaper if you can get copies of all articles written about the company in question. After you review them, call the reporter to see what additional information may be stored in his or her head.

Other Checkpoints

It is worth fishing for information in a number of other places, including agencies and private organizations.

1) Chamber of Commerce
Talking to someone on the research staff or the librarian can help you identify sources within the community about a company. A friendly conversation with Chamber executives can also provide insight into a company's financial position and strategies.

2) Local Development Authority
Many local communities, counties, and regional areas have established development authorities to attract business and industry to their area. They operate pretty much the same as the state department of economic development described above, and as a result, collect a large amount of data about the businesses in their area.

3) Local Courts
Civil and criminal court actions can provide excellent source material for company investigations. Perdue Chicken Company, a private corporation in Maryland, revealed its annual sales figures while fighting Virginia sales tax in the courts. A recent search revealed four financial-related suits filed against a large privately held political campaign fund raising firm in McLean, Virginia. If you are not in close proximity to the court, it may be worthwhile to hire a local freelance reporter or researcher. In most jurisdictions there are chronological indexes of both civil and criminal cases which are kept by the clerk of the court. These indexes record all charges or complaints made, the names of the defendants and plaintiffs in the event of civil cases, the date of the filing, the case number, and the disposition if one has been reached. Armed with the case number you can request to see the case files from the clerk.

Company Information At The Office Of Federal Regulators

The federal offices identified in the preceding section on market studies are also excellent sources for information on companies. Industry specialists within the federal government are likely to have information on companies or can refer you to other sources which may have just the information you need.

The 26 government agencies listed here are those that are involved with regulating industries and/or the companies within those industries. The information held at each federal office varies from agency to agency; however, most of the offices maintain financial or other information that most researchers would consider sensitive.

Airlines, Air Freight Carriers, and Air Taxis
Office of Community and Consumer Affairs, U.S. Department of Transportation, 400 7th Street SW, Room 10405, Washington, DC 20590l 202-366-2220/5957.

Airports
Airport Section, National Flight Data Center, Room 634, Federal Aviation Administration, ATM-612, 800 Independence Avenue SW, Washington, DC 20591; 202-267-9311.

Bank Holding Companies and State Members of the Federal Reserve System
Freedom of Information Act Office, Board of Governors of the Federal Reserve System, 20th Street and Constitution Avenue NW, Room B1122, Washington, DC 20551; 202-452-3684.

Banks, National
Communications Division, Comptroller of the Currency, 250 E St., SW, Washington, DC 20219; 202-874-4700.

Barge and Vessel Operators
Financial Analysis, Tariffs, Federal Maritime Commission, 800 N. Capitol St., NW, Washington, DC 20573; 202-523-5876.

Cable Television System Operators
Cable TV Branch, Federal Communications Commission, 1919 M Street NW, Room 416, Washington, DC 20554; 202-416-0856.

Colleges, Universities, Vocational Schools, and Public Schools
Office of Educational Research and Improvement, U.S. Department of Education, 555 New Jersey NW, Room 600, Washington, DC 20208-5530; 202-219-2050.

Commodity Trading Advisors
National Futures Association, 200 W. Madison St., Suite 1600, Chicago, IL 60606-3447, Attn: Compliance Dept.; 800-621-3570, Fax: 312-781-1467.

Consumer Products
Consumer Protection Division, U.S. Consumer Product Safety Commission, 200 St. Paul Place, Baltimore, MD 21202; 410-528-8662.

Electric and Gas Utilities and Gas Pipeline Companies
Federal Energy Regulatory Commission, 825 North Capitol Street NE, Room 9204, Washington, DC 20426; 202-208-0200.

Exporting Companies
Office of Export Trading Companies Affairs, U.S. Department of Commerce, 14th and Constitution Avenue, Room 1800, Washington, DC 20230; 202-482-5131.

Federal Land Bank and Production Credit Associations
Farm Credit Administration, 1501 Farm Credit Drive, McLean, VA 22102-5090; 703-883-4000.

Foreign Corporations
World Traders Data Report, U.S. Department of Commerce, Washington, DC 20230; 202-482-4204.

Government Contractors
Federal Procurement Data Center, General Services Administration, 7th and D Streets, SW, Room 5652, Washington, DC 20407; 202-401-1529.

Hospitals and Nursing Homes
National Center for Health Statistics, 6525 Belcrest Rd., Hyattsville, MD 20782; 301-436-8500.

Land Developers
Office of Interstate Land Registration, U.S. Department of Housing and Urban Development, 451 7th Street SW, Room 6262, Washington, DC 20410; 202-708-0502.

Mining Companies
Mine Safety and Health Administration, U.S. Department of Labor, 4015 Wilson Boulevard, Arlington, VA 22203; 703-235-1452.

Non-Profit Institutions
U.S. Internal Revenue Service, Freedom of Information Reading Room, 1111 Constitution Ave. NW, Room 1563, P.O. Box 388, Ben Franklin Station, Washington, DC 20044; 202-622-5164.

Nuclear Power Plants
Director, Office of Nuclear Reactor Regulation, U.S. Nuclear Regulatory Commission, Washington, DC 20555; 301-415-7163, 301-492-7000.

Pension Plans
Division of Inquiries and Technical Assistance, Office of Pension and Welfare Benefits Programs, U.S. Department of Labor, 200 Constitution Avenue NW, Room N5658, Washington, DC 20210; 202-219-8233.

Pharmaceutical, Cosmetic and Food Companies
Associate Commissioner for Regulatory Affairs, U.S. Food and Drug Administration, 5600 Fishers Lane, Room 14-90, Rockville, MD 20857; 301-443-1594.

Pesticide and Chemical Manufacturers
U.S. Environmental Protection Agency, Office of Pesticides and Toxic Substances, 401 M Street, SW (7101), Washington, DC 20460; 202-260-2902.

Radio and Television Stations
Mass Media Bureau, Federal Communications Commission, 1919 M Street NW, Room 302, Washington, DC 20554; 202-632-6485.

Railroads, Trucking Companies, Bus Lines, Freight Forwarders, Water Carriers, Oil Pipelines, Transportation Brokers, Express Agencies
U.S. Interstate Commerce Commission, 12th and Constitution Avenue NW, Room 4419, Washington, DC 20423; 202-927-7119.

Savings and Loan Associations
Office of Thrift Supervision, 1700 G Street NW, Washington, DC 20552; 202-906-6000.

Telephone Companies, Overseas Telegraph Companies, Microwave Companies, Public Land and Mobile Service
Common Carrier Bureau, Federal Communications Commission, 1919 M Street NW, Room 500, Washington, DC 20554; 202-632-6910.

Suppliers And Other Industry Sources

If all of the above sources fail to provide information you need on a given company, your last resort is to go directly into the industry and try to extract the information by talking with insiders.

Although your telephone is an essential and perhaps the best research tool, there are two other reference sources that will help you track down industry specialists:

1) **Trade Associations** are identified in *Encyclopedia of Associations* - (Gale Research Inc., Book Tower, 835 Penobscot Building, Detroit, MI 48277, 313-961-2242, 800-877-4253. For prepaid order, mail check for $395 for 1994 edition, $415 for 1995 edition to P.O. Box 71701, Chicago, IL 60694-1701);

2) **100 Industry Analysts** at the U.S. Department of Commerce. Government Industry Analysts who cover industries such as athletic goods, dairy products or truck trailers.

Your first step is to begin casting around for someone in the industry who knows about the company in question. When hunting for an expert, it is essential that you remain determined and optimistic about eventually finding one or several individuals who will be "information jackpots."

People who know their industry will be able to give you the details you need about any company (i.e., its size, sales, profitability, market strategies). These sources probably will not be able to give you the precise figure that is on the balance sheet or profit and loss statement, but they will offer a very educated guess which is likely to be within 10 to 20% of the exact figure. And usually this estimate is good enough for anyone to work with.

The real trick is finding the right people -- the ones who know. Talk to them and get them to share their knowledge with you.

Where Else To Look For Industry Experts

Industry experts are not concentrated in Washington, DC but are located all over the world, so you need to exercise some common sense to figure out where to find them. Here are some general guidelines.

1) Industry Observers
These are specialists on staff at trade associations, think tanks, and at the U.S. Department of Commerce and other government agencies. Anyone who concentrates on an industry has familiarity with the companies that comprise that industry.

2) Trade Magazines
You will find that there is at least one magazine which reports on every industry. The editors and reporters of these trade publications are also well acquainted with individual companies.

3) Suppliers

Most industries have major suppliers which must know about the industry they service and the companies within that industry. For example, the tire manufacturers anticipate every move among auto makers well before any other outsiders. Suppliers also have to know the volume of every manufacturer to whom they sell their product because of the obvious repercussions on the supplier's business. Every company is like this, even Information USA, Inc. We are basically a publisher, and if you talk to our printers, you would get a pretty good picture of exactly what we are doing.

Company Case Studies and Databases

1) Company Case Studies For As Little As $2 Each

Case studies of major and minor companies, as well as subsidiaries of public companies, can provide valuable competitive intelligence. These cases are identified in an $10 publication titled *Catalog of Teaching Materials*.

HBS Publications Division
Operations Department
Boston, MA 02163
617-495-6117
617-495-6006
Fax: 617-495-6985

2) Government and Commercial Databases

ABI/Inform, Disclosure, and Management Contents are just a few of the online databases which provide quick access to information about all types of companies. Additional leads for gathering intelligence about companies can be derived from diverse databases maintained by the U.S. government, many of which are identified in the *Federal Data Base Finder* (Information USA, Inc.).

Complete Financials On Franchising Companies

Franchising companies, whether public or privately held, must file detailed financial information in 14 different states. These state statutes create excellent opportunities for gathering competitive and marketing data as outlined below.

Inside Information

If the company of interest is a franchise organization, a great deal of financial information for their average franchisee is available in addition to their corporate profit and loss statements and balance sheets. A typical table of contents for a filing includes:

* biographical information on persons affiliated with the franchisor
* litigation
* bankruptcy
* franchisees' initial franchise fee or other initial payment
* other recurring or isolated fees and payments
* the franchisee's initial investment
* obligations of the franchisee to purchase or lease from designated sources
* obligations of the franchisee to purchase or lease in accordance with specifications or from approved suppliers
* financing arrangements
* obligations of the franchisor: other supervision, assistance or services
* territorial rights
* trademarks, service marks, trade names, logotypes and commercial symbols
* patents and copyrights
* obligation of the franchisee to participate in the actual operation of the franchise business
* restrictions on goods and services offered by the franchisee
* term, renewal, termination, repurchase, modification, assignment and related information

* agreements with public figures
* actual, average, projected or forecasted franchisee sales, profits and earnings
* information regarding franchises of the franchisor
* financial statements
* contracts
* standard operating statements
* list of operational franchisees
* estimate of additional franchised stores
* company-owned stores
* estimate of additional company-owned stores
* copies of contracts and agreements

Market Information and Franchising Trends

The franchise information packets often include information on the results of their market studies which establish the need for their product or service. These can provide valuable market information as well as forecasts for potential markets. Is the ice cream boom over? A quick check into Ben and Jerry's forecast for future stores will give you a clue of what the experts think.

Franchise companies are often the first to jump into current trends and fads in the U.S., for example, ice cream shops and diet centers. You can get an instant snapshot of such a trend by reviewing the marketing section of a franchise agreement.

Career Opportunities

If you ever wondered how much it would cost to open up your own bookstore, restaurant, video store, or most any other kind of venture, you can get all the facts and figures you need without paying a high-priced consultant or tipping your hand to your current employer. Just take a look at a franchise agreement from someone in a similar line of business. You can even discover the expected salary level.

New Business for Suppliers

If you are looking to sell napkins, Orange Julius or computer services to Snelling & Snelling, their franchise statements will disclose what kind of agreements they currently have with similar suppliers.

State Checkpoints for Franchising Intelligence

To obtain franchise agreements from the 14 states that require such disclosure, simply call one or more of the offices listed below and ask if a specific company has filed. Copies of the documentation are normally sent in the mail with a copying charge of $.10 to $.50 per page.

California
Department of Corporations, 1115 11th Street, Sacramento, 95814, 916-445-7205. Fee is 30 cents per page. Send blank check stating $25 limit. They will call with price for orders exceeding that amount.

Hawaii
Department of Commerce and Consumer Affairs, Business Registration Department, 1010 Richards Street, Honolulu, 96813, P.O. Box 40, Honolulu, 96810, 808-586-2730. Fee is 25 cents per page.

Illinois
Franchise Division, Office of Attorney General, 500 South Second Street, Springfield, 62704, 217-782-1090. Charge is a $40 flat fee per company franchise.

Indiana
Franchise Division, Secretary of State, 302 West Washington Street, Room E-111, Indianapolis, 46204, 317-232-0735. Fee is 10 cents per page plus handling charges.

Maryland
Assistant Attorney General, Maryland Division of Securities, 200 St. Paul Place, 21st Floor, Baltimore, 21202-2020, 410-576-6360. Maryland does not make copies. Suggests contacting Documents-To-Go, 800-879-4949.

Minnesota
Minnesota Department of Commerce, Enforcement Division, 133 East Seventh Street, St. Paul, 55101, 612-296-2594. Contact Ann Hagestad at 612-296-6328. Fee is 50 cents per page.

New York

Bureau of Investor and Protection Securities, New York State Department of Law, 120 Broadway, New York, 10271, 212-341-2200. Fee is 25 cents per page.

North Dakota

Franchise Examiner, North Dakota Securities Commission, 600 East Blvd., Fifth Floor, Bismarck, 58505, 701-224-2910. Documents are open for the public to inspect and copy, but this office does not provide copies as a service.

Oregon

Department of Insurance and Finance, Corporate Securities Section, Division of Finance and Corporate Securities, 21 Labor and Industries Bldg., Salem, 97310, 503-378-4387. Oregon does not keep franchise documents on file.

Rhode Island

Securities Section, Securities Division, 233 Richmond Street, Suite 232, Providence, 02903-4237, 401-277-3048. Special request form must be used. Fee is 15 cents per page copy and $15 an hour per search time.

South Dakota

Franchise Administrator, Division of Securities, State Capitol, Pierre, 57501, 605-773-4013. Fee is 50 cents per sheet.

Virginia

Franchise Section, Division of Securities and Retail Franchising, 1300 E. Main Street, Richmond, 23219, 804-371-9276. Fee is $.50 per page.

Washington

Department of Licensing, Securities Division, 405 Black Lake Blvd., SW, Olympia, 98507-9033, 206-753-6928. No charge for orders under 30 pages, then 10 cents for each page thereafter, plus tax.

Wisconsin

Franchise Investment Division, Wisconsin Securities Commission, PO Box 1768, 101 East Wilson Street, Madison, 53701, 608-266-3414/3364. Wisconsin does not provide copies of franchise agreements. One must come in person or hire private service.

Every Company Has to File With the State

State documents on 9,000,000 public and private companies have hit the computer age. Thirty states already offer online access to their files and others intend to follow suit within the next year. Computerized records are such a major issue with state officials who administer corporate division offices that they have placed online access on their annual convention agenda. Furthermore, 27 states will make their complete files available on magnetic tape, and, I should say, at bargain prices. And if you are not computerized, all but a few states offer free telephone research services. Here are a dozen ways to ferret out current information on companies:

- a list of companies by SIC code within a given state or county
- names and addresses of a company's officers and directors
- a list of all new companies incorporated in a given week or month
- the location of any company with a single phone call
- a mailing list of 300,000 companies for $100
- the availability of a given company name
- a complete list of non-profit organizations
- a list of companies by city, zip, date of incorporation, or size of capital stock
- a mailing list of limited partnerships
- a listing of companies on which a given individual is an officer or board member
- a listing of trademarks for a given state
- which companies in a given state are subsidiaries of a given company

Financial Data and Other Documents on File

Although there are variations, almost all states maintain the following documents for every company doing business in their state: Certificate of Good Standing; Articles of Incorporation; Reinstated Articles of Incorporation; Articles of Amendment; Articles of Merger; Articles of Correction; Articles of Dissolution; Certificate of Incorporation; Certificate of Authority; and Annual Report (which contains list of officers and directors).

All states require corporations to file the original Articles of Incorporation, a yearly annual report and amendments to the Articles of Incorporation. Clerks can provide you with certifications of good standing stating that the corporation has complied with the regulation to file a yearly annual report. A certificate of good standing does not assure financial stability, and is only a statement that the corporation has abided by the law. You may obtain a statement of name availability if you are searching for a name for your new corporation. Most states require prepayment for copies of documents. You can mail them a blank check stipulating the amount not to exceed a certain amount. You may want to call the phone information number for details before sending in your written request.

Only a few states require financial information in their annual reports. However, every state requires companies to list the value of the capital stock in their Articles of Incorporation. Some states, such as Massachusetts used to require financial data in the past, so it may be useful to request annual reports of previous years.

Data on Six Different Types of Companies

The types of companies required to file documents with the state include: Domestic Companies (those incorporated within the state), Foreign Companies (those incorporated in another state, but doing business in the state), Partnerships, Limited Partnerships, Non-Profit Organizations, Business Names (incorporated and non-incorporated firms). It should be emphasized here that all public and private companies as well as subsidiaries of public corporations are required to reveal this information.

Company Information Available in Numerous Formats

Each state provides information about corporations in some or all of the following formats:

1) Telephone, Mail and Walk-In Services:
Telephone information lines have been established in all but one state to respond to inquiries regarding the status of a specific corporation. New Jersey and North Dakota charge for phone service. The NJ Expedite Service allows you to receive information over the phone and charge the cost of the service to your credit card. Another option for New Jersey company information is to have it sent via Western Union's electronic mail service.

Telephone operators can verify corporate names, identify the resident agent and his address, the date of incorporation, the type of corporation (foreign, domestic, etc.), and the amount of capital stock. Often these operators can either take your request for documents on file pertaining to a corporation or they can refer you to the appropriate number. Names of officers and directors are never given over the phone. This information is usually contained in a company's annual report, copies of which can be requested by phone or letter.

These state telephone lines tend to be quite busy. It is not unusual for the larger offices of a corporation to answer over 1,200 inquiries a day. Persistence and patience are essential on your part. Requests for copies of documents usually require prepayment. You can mail them a blank check stipulating the amount not to exceed a certain amount. You may want to call the phone information number for details before sending in your written request.

Walk-in service, with access to all documents, is an option in every state. However, if you do not want to do the research yourself, almost every state can suggest private firms which will obtain the pertinent data for you.

2) Mailing Labels:
The following six states will print mailing labels of companies on file: Arizona, Idaho, Maine, New Mexico, Mississippi, and Nebraska. However, over half the states will sell you a computer tape of their files, from which mailing labels can be generated easily by a good mailhouse or service bureau.

3) Computer Tape Files:
Currently 27 states will provide you with magnetic tapes of their corporate files. The cost is very reasonable, and in many cases the state will require the user to supply blank tapes.

4) Custom Services:
Many of the states provide custom services with outputs ranging from computer printouts and magnetic tape files to statistical tables. Such services are a valuable way to obtain specific listings of corporations such all non-profit corporations or all companies within a given SIC code. Most states that offer this option compute cost by figuring time, programming time, and printing expense.

5) New Companies:
Almost all of the states offer some type of periodic listing of newly formed companies. As a rule, these can be purchased on a daily, weekly, or monthly subscription basis.

6) Microfiche and Microfilm:
Eleven of the states will also sell you copies of their documents on microfiche or microfilm at a nominal fee.

7) Online Access:

As mentioned earlier, thirty states now provide online access to their files, and other states are in the active planning stages. The states currently with online systems include:

Alabama, Alaska, Arizona, Arkansas, Colorado, Florida, Georgia, Hawaii, Idaho, Illinois, Indiana, Iowa, Kansas, Louisiana, Massachusetts, Michigan, Minnesota, Mississippi, Missouri, Nevada, New Mexico, North Carolina, Oklahoma, Pennsylvania, South Carolina, Texas, Utah, Virginia, and Vermont.

State Corporation Divisions

Alabama

Division of Corporation, Secretary of State, 4121 Carmichael Road, Montgomery, AL 36106 or P.O. Box 5616, Montgomery, AL 36103-5616, 205-242-5324; Selected Publications: *Guide to Incorporation.* Phone Information: 205-242-5324. Office is not completely computerized yet, but can do word search or partial name search by officer, incorporator, or serving agent. Copies of Documents on File: Available by written request for $1 per page plus $5 for certified copies. Mailing Labels: No. Magnetic Tape: No. Microfiche: No. New Corporate Listings: No. Custom Searches: Can do word search or partial name search. Online Access: Yes. Dial-up Program available. No fee for this pilot program. Contact Robina Jenkins, 205-242-5974. This office is in the process of being computerized. When fully on computer access, fee for online service may be charged. Number of Active Corporations on File: Figures not available.

Alaska

State of Alaska, Division of Banking, Securities and Corporation, Corporation Section, P.O. Box 110808, Juneau, AK 99811-0808, 907-465-2530. Selected Publications: *Establishing Business in Alaska* ($3), from State of Alaska, Division of Economic Development, P.O. Box 110808, Juneau, AK 99811-0808. Phone Information: 907-465-2530. Copies of Documents on File: Complete corporate record (Articles of Incorporation, annual report, amendments, etc.). Certified copies cost $20, list of Officers and Directors cost $1, Certificate of Status cost $25. Mailing Labels: No. Magnetic Tape: IBM- compatible. Copy of complete master file, excluding Officers and Directors is priced at $100. Hard copy directory is $65. Weekly supplements are an additional $5. Requester must supply blank tape. Microfiche: Yes. Complete file for $6. New Corporate Listings: No. Custom Searches: Available directly from them soon. Online Access: Yes. Contact Mike Monagle, 907-465-2530. Other: Printouts are available by corporation, SIC code, and zip code for $25 per list. Number of Active Corporations on File: 23,000.

Arizona

Arizona Corporations Division, Records Division, Secretary of State, 1200 W. Washington, Phoenix, AZ 85007 or P.O. Box 6019, Phoenix, AZ 85005, 602-542-3026. Selected Publications: Sample packet with forms and statutes mailed for $4. Guideline booklets will be available soon. Phone Information: 602-542-3026. Copies of Documents on File: Cost 50 cents per page, $5 for certified copies. Mailing Labels: No. Magnetic Tape: Master File $400, issued monthly. Requester must supply blank tape. Microfiche: All corporations statewide $75. New Corporate Listing: Monthly Listing of New Domestic Companies for $200 plus $200 for new foreign listings. Custom Searches: No. Can search by title or cross-reference by statutory agent only. Online Access: Yes. Available through Information America (800-235-4008), Dunn and Bradstreet and other commercial services. Number of Corporations on File: 100,000.

Arkansas

Secretary of State, Corporations Division, State Capitol Building, Room 058, Little Rock, AR 72201, 501-682-5151. Selected Publications: *Corporate Guide.* Phone Information: 501-682-5151. Copies of Documents on File: Call 501-371-3431 for copies at 50 cents a page plus $5 for certified copies. Mailing Labels: No. Magnetic Tape: Master file 2 cents per name. Microfiche: No. New Corporate Listing: Statistics only. Custom Searches: Categories include foreign, domestic, profit, and non-profit corporations. Cost: 2 cents per name, 50 cents per page. Online Access: Contact Philip Hoots at 501-682-3411. Number of Active Corporations on File: 1000,000.

California

Corporations, Supervisor of Records, Secretary of State, 1230 J Street Sacramento, CA 95814, 916-324-1485. Selected Publications: *Corporations Checklist Booklet.* Request must be in writing and cost is $5. Phone Information: Name Availability at 916-322-2387, Forms and Samples at 916-445-0620. Copies of Documents on File: Cost is $1 for first page, 50 cents for each additional page plus $5 for certified copies (written requests only). You must pay in advance or send check stating limit. Mailing Labels: No. Magnetic Tape: Yes. You must supply the tapes or be charged $24 for tape. Charges for making 22 tapes is $300. Contact Kevin Tibown. Categories: Active $521; Active Stock $427; Active Non-Stock $150; Active Non-Stock by Classification $150 per tape. Microfiche: No. Custom Searches: Computer generated listing of Active Stock ($17,030), Active Non-Stock ($422), Active Non-Stock by Classification $150 per list. Contact: Patricia Gastelum, Management Services Division, Information Systems Section, 1230 J Street, Suite 242, Sacramento, CA 95814, 916-322-0418. All orders must be submitted in writing. Basic cost of magnetic tape copy is $1.02 per 1,000 names. Basic cost of same run, for custom search, printed on paper, is $4.13 per 1,000 names. $150 minimum is applied to both. Online Access: No. Number of Corporations on File: 1,050,000.

Colorado

Corporate Division, Secretary of State, 1560 Broadway, Suite 200, Denver, CO 80202, 303-894-2251. Selected Publications: *Corporate Guide.* Copies of Documents on File: Cost is $1 a page, plus $5 for certification. Mailing Labels: No. Magnetic Tape: Available for $500 for complete set of five. Tapes must be purchased individually. Categories: Foreign and Domestic. Microfiche: Available at $1 a sheet (includes Summary of Master Computer File, total of 60-75 sheets - must be purchased in its entirety). New Corporate Listings: Reporting Service costs $200 a year. Weekly List of New Corporations. Written requests only. Custom Searches: Yes. Categories: Foreign and Domestic available on a cost recovery basis. The minimum fee is $50. Online Access: Available. Contact Patty Webb, 303-894-2200, ext. 300. Fee is $300 for 3 months or $1,000 per year. Number of Corporations on File: 235,000.

Connecticut

Office of Secretary of State, Division of Corporations, 30 Trinity Street, Hartford, CT 06106, 203-566-2448. Selected Publications: None, but to get a copy of *The Connecticut Law Book*, call 203-458-8000 or 203-741-3027. Phone Information: 203-566-8570. Copies of Documents on File: Fees are $20 for plain copy, $25 for certified. Written requests only. Mailing Labels: No. Magnetic Tape: Copy of master file $110. Requester must provide tapes. Microfiche: No. New Corporate Listing: No. Custom Searches: No. Online Access: Not at this time, but Southern New England Telephone (SNET) is working on a pilot program which should be available soon. Number of Corporations on File: 325,000.

Delaware

Delaware Department of State, Division of Corporations, Secretary of State, P.O. Box 898, Dover, DE 19903, 302-739-3073. Selected Publications: *Incorporating in Delaware*. Phone Information: 302-739-3073. Copies of Documents on File: Available at $1 per page plus $20 for certification, $100 for long forms of good standing. Contains all documents on the corporation. Requests may be faxed to 302-739-3812, but written requests are preferred. Requests must be paid for in advance. Call for number of pages. Documents filed prior to 1983 are not on computer and must be requested in writing. They offer Corporate Expedited Services (same day or 24-hour service) to file or retrieve certified documents. Additional fee is $20. You can pay by MasterCard or Visa and it is sent by Federal Express. Mailing Labels: No. Magnetic Tape: No. Microfiche: No. New Corporate Listings: Monthly New Corporation Listing. Fees are $10 per month which can be paid in advance for 6 months or a year. Contact Karen Scaggs. Custom Searches: Yes. Categories include foreign and domestic which are available on cost recovery basis. For manual search of foreign corporations, the fee is $30. Online Access: Not available. Number of Active Corporations on File: 212,000.

District of Columbia

Corporations Division, Consumer and Regulatory Affairs, 614 H Street, N.W., Room 407, Washington, DC 20001, 202-727-7278. Selected Publications: *Guideline and Instruction Sheet for Profit, Non-Profit, Foreign, or Domestic*. Phone Information: 202-727-7283. Copies of Documents on File: Available for $5 each (all copies certified). Mailing Labels: Will be available in near future. Profit and non-profit lists updated quarterly. Magnetic Tape: No. Microfiche: No. New Corporate Listings No. Custom Searches: Computer searches on agents are available. Online

Access: Possibly available in 1993. Number of Active Corporations on File: 40,000.

Florida

Division of Corporations, Secretary of State, PO Box 6327, Tallahassee, FL 32314, 904-487-6000. Selected Publications: *Copy of the Law Chapter 607* (corporate law). Forms included. (Publications on laws of non-profit corporations and limited partnerships also available.) Phone Information: 904-488-9000. Limit of up to 3 inquiries per call. No charge to receive hard copy of microfiche on the corporations. Copy of Documents on File: Available at $1 per page if you do it yourself. Written requests must be paid for advance: $1 for non-certified annual report; $10 for plain copy of complete file; $52.50 for any certified document including complete file. Microfiche: Yes. Contact Frank Reinhart or Ed Bagnell at Anacomp, 813-289-1608. Categories: Officers and Directors, Registered Agents and Domestic Corporations $250; Foreign, Non-Profit $85, Limited Partnerships $50, Trademarks $75 (addresses are included). Magnetic Tape: No. New Corporate Listings: No. Custom Searches: No. Online Access: Available on CompuServe, 800-848-8199. Address written request to Attn: Public Access, Division of Corporations, 904-487-6866. Ask for a CompuServe Intro-Pak. Charge for connect time is $24 per hour, plus $12.50 per hour additional corporate access fee. Both are prorated by time used. CompuServe can be contacted directly at South Eastern Information Systems, P.O. Box 6867, Tallahassee, FL 32314, Attn: Keith Meyer, 904-656-4500. As of February, 1992, Anacomp will handle. Contact Eileen Self, 904-487-6073 for service. Number of Active Corporations on File: 691,000.

Georgia

Division of Business Services and Regulation, Secretary of State, Suite 306, West Tower #2, Martin Luther King Drive, S.E., Atlanta, GA 30334, 404-656-2185. Selected Publications: None, but information package sent upon request. Phone Information: 404-656-2817. Copies of Documents on File: Available for at least a minimum of $10 and all copies certified. Bills will be sent for orders over $10. Mailing Labels: No. Magnetic Tape: Master file available for $600 a month if you supply the tape. Add $18 if they supply tape. Microfiche: No. New Corporate Listings: Quarterly Listing of New Corporations on magnetic tape. There are three lists which include Fulton County, the remainder of the state and foreign. Cost is $25 each. Send written requests to James Gullion. Custom Searches: No. Online Access: Available by subscription through Information America at 404-892-1800. Connect fee is $50. Access time is 55 cents per minute. Monthly service charge is $25-$55 per month depending on size of the firm. Number of Active Corporations on File: 200,000

Hawaii

Business Registration Division, Department of Commerce and Consumer Affairs, 1010 Richards Street, PO Box 40, Honolulu, HI 96810, 808-586-2727. Selected Publications: None. Phone Information: 808-586-2727. Copies of Documents on File: Available at 25 cents per page, plus 10 cents per page for certified copies. Expedited service available for $10 fee plus 25 cents per sheet, plus $1 per page. Mailing Labels: No. Magnetic Tape: No. Microfiche: No. New Corporate Listing: Weekly printout available but only for walk-ins. Custom Searches: No. Online Access: Available through FYI for no charge. Call 808-536-7133 (direct access number) or 808-586-1919. Number of Active Corporations on File: 45,000.

Idaho

Corporate Division, Secretary of State, Room 203, Statehouse, Boise, ID 83720, 208-334-2300. Selected Publications: *Idaho Corporation Law*. Phone Information: 208-334-2300. Copies of Documents on File: Available at 25 cents per page, $2 for certified copies. Mailing Labels: Very flexible and may be combined with custom search. Fee is $10 for computer base, 25 cents for first 100 pages, 10 cents for next 500 pages, and 5 cents per page thereafter. Magnetic Tape: Available for $20 per tape if you supply the tape. They will supply diskette for additional $10. Microfiche: Available for $10, 50 cents for each additional copy of same. Custom Searches: Available on basis of serving agent, profit, non-profit, type, status, state and jurisdiction. Very flexible. Same prices and categories apply to labels, microfiche and custom search. You supply the tapes or they will at cost. Contact Everett Wholers. New Corporate Listing: No, but published weekly in *The Idaho Business Review*. Online Access: Available through Data Share Program. Fee is $150 per year plus $18 per hour plus telephone line charges. Number of Active Corporations on File: 30,000.

Illinois

Corporations Division, Centennial Building, Room 328, Springfield, IL 62756, 217-782-6961. Selected Publications: *Guide for Organizing (Domestic, Non-profit, or Foreign)*. Phone Information: 217-782-7880. Copies of Documents on File: Available at $5 per page up to first 10 pages; 50 cents for each page thereafter. Fee is $10 for first 10 certified copies; 50 cents for each page thereafter. Mailing Labels: No. Magnetic Tape: Yes. Categories: Domestic and Foreign cost $1,500; Not-for-Profit cost $1,500. You must supply tape. Microfiche: Only condominiums list available for $150. New Corporate Listings: Daily list of newly formed corporations costs $318 per year; Monthly List priced at $180 per year. Custom Searches: No. Other: Certified List of Domestic and Foreign Corporations (Address of Resident Agent included) costs $38 for two volume set. Online Access: Available from Mead Data Central (LEXIS), 9393 Springboro Pike, P.O. Box 933, Dayton, OH 45401, Contact: Diane Fisher at 800-227-4908, ext. 6382. Cost is $500 per month. Number of Active Corporations on File: 240,000.

Indiana

Office of Corporation, Secretary of State, Room E018, 302 West Washington Street, Indianapolis, IN 46204, 317-232-6582. Selected Publications: *Indiana Corporation Guide*. Phone Information: 317-232-6576. Copies of Documents on File: Available at $1 per page and $15 to certify. May pay in advance or be billed. Mailing Labels: No. Magnetic Tape: No. Microfiche: No. New Corporate Listings: Daily Listing is published monthly for $20 a month. Custom Searches: No. Online Access: Available. Tapes made into computer database by Mead Data (LEXIS) at 800-634-9738 and by Information America 800-235-4008. Contact Bob Gardner at 317-232-6691. Number of Active Corporations on File: 200,000.

Iowa

Corporate Division, Secretary of State, Hoover State Office Building, Des Moines, IA 50319, 515-281-5204. Selected Publications: *Iowa Profit Corporations*. Phone Information: 515-281-5204. Copies of Documents on File: Available at $1 per page; certified copies cost $5. Mailing Labels: No. Magnetic Tape: Master file costs $165; detailed domestic profit $415; domestic non-profit $160 and requester must supply tape. Microfiche: No. New Corporate Listings: No. Custom Searches: Searches by Chapters of Incorporation (profit, non-profit, etc.) and or. Cost determined at time of request. Online Access: Available through Dial Up Program. Contact Allen Welsh at 515-281-8363. Cost is $150 per year, 30 cents per minute plus telephone charges. Number of Active Corporations on File: 97,000.

Kansas

Corporate Division, Secretary of State, Capitol Building, Second Floor, Topeka, KS 66612, 913-296-4564. Selected Publications: None. Will send out forms with instruction sheets. Phone Information: 913-296-4564. Copies of Documents on File: Available at 50 cents per page plus $7.50 for certified copies (written requests only). Must be paid for in advance. Mailing Labels: No. Magnetic Tape: Available. Master file costs $2,000. Microfiche: No. Other: Microfilm is available for $25 a roll plus $7.50 postage for up to 50 rolls. Master File on magnetic tape will be needed to use. Contact Cathy Martin. New Corporate Listings: No. Custom Searches: No. May be available in the future. Online Access: Available through Info Network Kansas, 913-296-5143. Number of Active Corporations on File: 66,000.

Kentucky

Corporate Division, Secretary of State, Room 154, Capitol Building, Frankfort, KY 40601, 502-564-2848. Selected Publications: *Rules and Laws Manual* ($8). Phone Information: 502-564-7336. Copies of Documents on File: Mail in request with payment. Call 502-564-7330 to obtain number of copies in advance. Cost is $1 per page; $5 plus $.50 per page for certified copies. Mailing Label: No. Magnetic Tape: Available for $250. Tape contains all profit and non-profit corporations on file. Microfiche: No. New Corporate Listings: Available for $50 a month. Custom Searches: No. Online Access: No, but is being considered. Number of Active Corporations on File: 80,000.

Louisiana

Corporate Division, Secretary of State, 3851 Essen Lane, Baton Rouge, LA 70809, 504-925-4704. Selected Publications: *Corporate Law Book* ($6). Phone Information: 504-925-4704. Copies of Documents on File: Available starting at $10 for certified articles. Cost for total file is $20. Mailing Label: No. Magnetic Tape: Available in the future. Microfiche: No. New Corporate Listing: Weekly Newsletter at no charge. (Requester must supply large pre-addressed envelope). Custom Searches: No. Online Access: Dial Up Access, 504-922-1475. Number of Active Corporations on File: 120,000.

Maine

Information and Report Section, Bureau of Corporations, Secretary of State, State House Station 101, Augusta, ME 04333,

207-287-4195. Selected Publications: *Guide to Completing Forms of Incorporation* (Blue Guide). Phone Information: 207-287-4195. Copies of Documents on File: Available for $2 per page, plus $5 for certified copies. Mailing Labels: No. Magnetic tape: No, but hope to have it in the near future. Contact Rebecca Wyke at 207-287-6308. Microfiche: No. New Corporate Listings: Monthly Corporations Listing costs $10. Contact Betsy at 207-289-4183. Custom Searches: No, but hope to have it in near future. Online Access: No. Number of Active Corporations on File: 40,000.

Maryland

Corporate Charter Division, Department of Assessments and Taxation, 301 W. Preston Street, Baltimore, Maryland 21201, 410-225-1330. Selected Publications: *Guide to Corporations*. Phone Information: 410-225-1330. Copies of Documents on File: Available for $1 per page, plus $6 for certified copies for walk-ins. If they make copy there is a $20 expediting fee. Mailing Labels: No. Magnetic Tape: Available for $250 weekly. Infrequent requests cost $425. Microfiche: No. New Corporate Listings: Monthly Corporate Computer Printout costs $25 a month. Custom Searches: Not at this time. Online Access: Hope to have in near future. Number of Active Corporations on File: 300,000.

Massachusetts

Corporate Division, Secretary of State, 1 Ashburton Place, Boston, MA 02108, 617-727-2850. Selected Publications: *Organizing a Business Corporation, Organizing a Non-Profit Corporation, When You Need Information About Corporations in Massachusetts, Choose a Name for Your Business, Compendium of Corporate Law* ($15). Phone Information: 617-727-2850. Copies of Documents on File: Available for 20 cents per page (send a minimum of 80 cents), $12 for certified copies. Mailing Labels: No. Magnetic Tape: Cost is $300 for copy of master file and record layout. Requester must supply tapes. Microfiche: No. New Corporate Listings: Semi-monthly Filings cost $15; Quarterly Filings cost $50; bi-weekly printout cost $15. Custom Searches: Available on a cost recovery basis. Online Access: Direct Access program. Cost is $149 annually. Connect time is 40 cents per minute. Number of Corporations on File: 375,000.

Michigan

Corporation Division, Corporation and Securities Bureau, Michigan Department of Commerce, PO Box 30054, 6546 Mercantile, Lansing, MI, 48909, 517-334-6302. Selected Publications: None. Phone Information: 517-334-6311. Copies of Documents on File: Available at a minimum of $6 for 6 pages or less, $1 for each page thereafter. Certified copies cost $10. (Request a price list.) Mailing Labels: No. Magnetic Tape: No. Microfiche: Available for $145. New Corporate Listings: Monthly Listing costs $90 per month. Custom Searches: No. Online Access: Available through Information America, 800-235-4008 or Mead Data, 313-259-1156. Number of Corporations on File: 251,000.

Minnesota

Corporate Division, Secretary of State, 180 State Office Building, St. Paul, MN 55155, 612-296-2803. Selected Publications: *Guide to Starting a Business in Minnesota*. Phone Information: 612-296-2803. Copies of Documents on File: Available for $3 per document, $8 for certified copies. Mailing Labels: Yes. Categories: Domestic, Limited Partnerships, Non-profits, Foreign, Foreign Limited, Foreign Non-profits, Trademarks, Business Trusts. Cost determined at time of request. Magnetic Tape: No. Microfiche: Available documents on file (Articles of Incorporation, annual reports, amendments) cost 21 cents sheet plus filing or retrieval fees. Paper copy of microfiche is $6 per corporation for complete file. $3 for articles of incorporation. New Corporate Listings: Daily Log costs 25 cents per page. Custom Searches: Available on a cost recovery basis. Categories same as for mailing labels. Online Access: Direct Access available for $50 annually plus transaction charge of $1 to $4. Number of Corporations on File: 194,500.

Mississippi

Office of Corporations, Secretary of State, PO Box 136, Jackson, MS 39205, 601-359-1350 or mailing address: 202 N. Congress, Suite 601, Jackson, MS 39201. Selected Publications: None. Phone Information: 601-359-1627. Copies of Documents on File: Available at $1 per page plus $10 for certified copies. Mailing Labels: No. Magnetic Tape: Available for $200 for set of 2. You are to supply tapes. Microfiche: No. New Corporate Listings: Monthly Listing costs $25. Custom Searches: Available to limited extent. Printout costs $2 per page. Online Access: Yes. $250 sign-up fee, plus flat monthly fee. $50 is monthly minimum for first 100 transactions. Contact Sheryl Crawford at 601-359-1548. Number of Active Corporations on File: 80,000. This office has converted to an automated system with advanced search capabilities.

Missouri

Corporate Division, Secretary of State, 301 High Street, PO Box 77, Jefferson City, MO 65102, 314-751-4194. Selected Publications: *Corporation Handbook*. Phone Information: 314-751-4153. Copies of Documents on File: Available at 50 cents per page plus $5 for certified copies. Send in written requests and they will bill. Mailing Labels: No. Magnetic Tape: Cost is between $100 and $200 for copy of master file. Contact Sara Welch at 314-751-5832. Microfiche: No. New Corporate Listings: Not usually, but can be set up on special request. Custom Searches: No. Online Access: Available through Mead Data Central (LEXIS), 9393 Springboro Pike, PO Box 933, Dayton, OH 45401, 513-865-6800; Prentice-Hall, Dunn and Bradstreet or Information America. Direct Dial Up access is available through the State Access Center. Contact John Bluma at 314-751-4780 or Sara Welch at 314-751-5832. Number of Active Corporations on File: 140,000.

Montana

Corporate Department, Secretary of State, Capitol Station, Helena, MT 59620, 406-444-3665. Selected Publications: None. Phone Information: 406-444-3665. Copies of Documents on File: Available for 50 cents per page; $2 for certification. Mailing Labels: No. Magnetic Tape: No. Microfiche: No. New Corporate Listings: No. Custom Searches: No, but can search by name of corporation only. Online Access: No. Number of Active Corporations on File: 33,000.

Nebraska

Corporate Division, Secretary of State, State Capitol, Lincoln, NE 68509, 402-471-4079. Selected Publications: None. Phone Information: 402-471-4079. Copies of Documents on File: Available for $1 per page, $10 for certified copies. Will bill for requests under $50. Mailing Labels: Available on a cost recovery basis. Can do for entire data base only. Contact Mr. Englert at 402-471-2554. Magnetic Tape: Available on a cost recovery basis. Also contact Mr. Englert. Microfiche: No. New Corporate Listings: Available upon request. Will set up for number of issues customer requests. $100 per issuance. Custom Searches: No. Online Access: No. Number of Active Corporations on File: 50,000

Nevada

Office of Corporations, Secretary of State, Capitol Complex, Carson City, NV 89710, 702-687-5203. Selected Publications: *Guidelines.* Phone Information: Corporate Status call 702-687-5105. Copies of Documents on File: Available for $1 per page, $10 for certified copies. Written request only, prepayment required (send a blank check stating limit). Mailing Labels: No. Magnetic Tape: Copy of master file available. Corporations takes 2 tapes which requester supplies. Cost per tape is $25. Microfiche: No. New Corporate Listings: Monthly Listing of New Corporations costs $25 a month. Custom Searches: Yes. Searches may be done by location of resident agent and other ways. Cost determined at time of request. Other: A three volume listing of corporations on file, in the "Alpha Listing", is published twice a year which includes names of active and inactive corporations but not addresses. Cost for set is $25. Contact Cindy Woodgate. Online Access: Dial Up Direct Access through subscription service. Your computer needs a communication pack and you must set up trust account from which $24.50 per hour, prorated by actual minutes used, will be deducted. For ID number and password, contact Cindy Woodgate. Number of Active Corporations on File: 60,000.

New Hampshire

Corporate Division, Secretary of State, State House, Room 204, Concord, NH 03301, 603-271-3244. Selected Publications: *How to Start a Business, New Hampshire Corporate Law.* Phone Information: 603-271-3246. Copies of Documents on File: Available for $1 per page, plus $5 for certified copies. Mailing Labels: No. Magnetic Tape: No. Microfiche: Complete listing of all registrations. No breakdown by type of entity (updated monthly). Annual Subscription costs $200. New Corporate Listings: Monthly Subscriber List costs $15 plus postage. Custom Searches: No. Other: Booklet listing all non-profit corporations is available for $45. Online Access: No. Number of Active Corporations on File: 33,000.

New Jersey

Commercial Recording Division, Secretary of State, 820 Bear Tavern Road, West Trenton, NJ 08628, (Mailing address: CN 308), 609-530-6400. Selected Publications: *Corporate Filing Packet.* Phone Information: General Information call 609-530-6405; Forms call 609-292-0013; Expedite Service call 609-984-7107. There is a charge for standard information, $5 look-up fee for each request plus $10 expedite fee. User may use VISA or Master Charge for payment. Answers available by phone, mail or Western Union Electronic Mail. Requests and answering copies may be done through Fax at 609-530-6433. Copies of Documents on File: Available for $10 plus $15 for certified copies. Mailing Labels: No. Magnetic Tape: No. Microfiche: No. New Corporate Listings: Monthly List of Corporations costs $100 per month. Custom Searches: Numerous search capabilities are available. Each request is reviewed on individual basis. Requester is billed for computer time. Online Access: No. Number of Active Corporations on File: 436,314.

New Mexico

State Corporation Commission, PO Drawer 1269, Santa Fe, NM 87504-1269, 505-827-4502. Selected Publications: None. Phone Information: 505-827-4504. Copies of Documents on File: Available for $1 per page, minimum $10, plus additional $25 for certified copies. Mailing Labels: No. Magnetic Tape: No. Microfiche: No. New Corporate Listings: Yes. Monthly listings available. Requester must send manilla self-addressed envelope. Online Access: Available through New Mexico Technet, 4100 Osuna N.E., Albuquerque, NM 87109, 505-345-6555. You may also pay the same charge as the State by purchasing it directly from the Corporation Division. They will bill you for usage monthly. Contact Mr. Salinas at 505-827-4502. Custom Searches: Yes. Categories: Corporate Name, Domestic or Foreign, Profit or Non-profit, Date of Incorporation, Active or Inactive, Identification Number, Amount of Capital Stock, Authorized Stock, Instrument file, Principal Office Address, Officers and Directors Names (includes addresses, Social Security numbers and titles), Name of Incorporators, Registered Agent and Office, Good Standing Status, Parent/Subsidiary Information. Call or put request in writing. Only a limited number of custom searches can be performed each month. Number of Active Corporations on File: over 100,000.

New York

New York State, Department of State, Division of Corporations, 162 Washington Avenue, Albany, NY 12231, 518-474-6200. Selected Publications: *Extract of Laws for Incorporating.* Phone Information: 518-474-6200. Copies of Documents on File: Available for $5 per document, $10 for certified copies. Mailing Labels: No. Magnetic Tape: No. Microfiche: No. New Corporate Listing: Report of Corporations is printed daily and mailed out every other day. It is available by subscription only for $125 per year, $75 for 6 months or $40 for 3 months. Online Access: Available in the near future. Number of Corporations on File: 1,200,000.

North Carolina

Division of Corporation, Secretary of State, 300 N. Salisbury Street, Raleigh, NC 27603-5909, 919-733-4201. Selected Publications: *North Carolina Business Corporation Guidelines, North Carolina's Non-profit Corporation Handbook.* Phone Information: 919-733-4201. Copies of Documents on File: Available for $1 per page, $5 for certified copies. Mailing Labels: No. Magnetic Tape: Available on cost recovery basis. To make a request, write Bonnie Elek. Categories: All active corporations, foreign, domestic, non-profit, and profit. Microfiche: No. New Corporate Listings: Available for $20 per month and issued in hard copy only. Custom Searches: Yes.

Categories: Type of Corporation, Professional Corporations, Insurance Corporations, Banks, and Savings and Loans. Not available for the type of business a corporation conducts. This may be available in the future. Online Access: Available. Number of Active Corporations on File: 180,000.

North Dakota

Corporation Division, Secretary of State, Capitol Building, 600 East Boulevard Avenue, Bismarck, ND 58505, 701-224-2905. Selected Publications: *North Dakota Business Corporation Act Statute*, $3. Phone Information: 701-224-4284. Copies of Documents on File: Search of records cost $5, four pages for $1, $10 for certified copies. Written or phone requests accepted. Requester will be billed for phone orders. Mailing Labels: No. Magnetic Tape: No. Microfiche: No. New Corporate Listings: Monthly Corporation List costs $10 per month. Custom Searches: No. Online Access: No, but may be available in the future. Number of Active Corporations on File: 22,500.

Ohio

Corporation Division, Secretary of State, 30 East Broad Street, 14th Floor, Columbus, OH 43266-0418, 614-466-3910. Selected Publications: *Corporate Checklist*. Phone Information: Corporate Status call 614-466-3910; Name Availability call 614-466-0590. Copies of Documents on File: Contact 614-466-1776. Available for $1 per page, $5 for certified copies. Mailing Labels: No. Magnetic Tape: Available for $125 for 6,250 corporation names, thereafter the cost is 2 cents per corporate name with a maximum of 25,000 names. Microfiche: No. New Corporate Listing: Call 614-466-8464. Weekly County-Wide Listing costs 25 cents per page, Weekly Statewide Listing costs 10 cents per page ($45 a month). Custom Searches: Yes. Categories: location (county), Foreign, Domestic, Profit, Non-Profit. Price structure is same as for Magnetic tape. Online Access: No. Number of Active Corporations on File: 400,000.

Oklahoma

Corporations, Secretary of State, 101 State Capitol Building, Oklahoma City, OK 73105, 405-521-3911. Selected Publications: *Forms and Procedures to Incorporate*. Phone Information: 900-820-2424 for record search. Charge is $3 per call. Copies of Documents on File: Available for $1 per page, $5 for certified copies. Mailing Labels: No. Magnetic Tape: $5 per tape which is supplied by requester. Microfiche: No. New Corporate Listings: Monthly Charter List costs $150 a month, plus Amendments $250 a month plus postage. Custom Searches: No. Online Access: Contact Beverly Curry at Information Systems, 404-892-1800. They purchase magnetic tape of Division's master file weekly to make a database which is complete except for new names. Number of Corporations on File (Active and Inactive): 224,159.

Oregon

Corporation Division, Department of Commerce, 255 Capitol St., NE, Suite 151, Salem, OR 97310-1327, 503-986-2200. Selected Publications: None. Phone Information: 503-986-2200. Copies of Documents on File: Available for $5 for all documents in a corporation's file except annual report. Annual reports are an additional $5. Certification fee is $15. Mailing Labels: No.

Magnetic Tape: Complete master file costs $200. Requester must provide tape. Microfiche: No. New Corporate Listings: Statistical Report of New Corporations is available for $15 per monthly issue, $150 per year. Custom Searches: Yes. Numerous categories with a minimum charge of $50. Online Access: Yes. Charges include $50 for hookup, $50 monthly fee, plus telephone charges and prorated computer time with a minimum $10 charge. Total minimum monthly cost is $80. Cost of average user is $100 per month. Mead Data, Information America and Dunn and Bradstreet also have database. Number of Active Corporations on File: 73,000.

Pennsylvania

Corporation Bureau, 308 N. Office Building, Harrisburg, PA 17120, 717-787-1997. Selected Publications: *Corporate Guide* (currently under revision). Phone Information: 717-787-1057. Copies of Documents on File: Available for $2 per page, $12 search fee, $28 for certified copies. Mailing Labels: No. Magnetic Tape: Copy of master file available for $900 per tape, Requester must supply 11 blank tapes. Microfiche: No. New Corporate Listings: County or area listing available for 25 cents per name. Custom Searches: Yes. Categories: Non-Profit, Domestic, Foreign, county location, Limited Partnerships, Fictitious name, Trademarks, Foreign Non-profits, Cooperatives, Professional Corporations 25 cents per name). Online Access: Available from Information America at 404-892-1800; Prentice-Hall, Legal and Financial Services at 518-458-8111; or Mead Data Central at 513-865-6800. Number of Corporations on File: 616,000.

Rhode Island

Corporations Division, Secretary of State, 100 North Main Street, Providence, RI 02903, 401-277-3040. Selected Publications: Instruction sheet, *The Rhode Island Law Book* ($10). Phone Information: 401-277-3040. Staff will look up two corporations per call. Copies of Documents on File: Available for 50 cents per page, $5 for certified sheet. Mailing Labels: No. Magnetic Tape: Available for $250 per tape. Requester supplies tape. They will put their database on disc. You supply 5 1/4 disc, MAG high density. Printouts cost 50 cents per page. There approximately 11 names per page. Microfiche: No. New Corporate Listings: Not usually provided. New corporate listings are published weekly in *The Providence Journal*, Sunday Business Section. Send a letter requesting weekly printouts. Custom Searches: No. Online Access: No. Number of Active Corporations on File: 90,000.

South Carolina

Division of Corporations, Secretary of State, PO Box 11350, Columbia, SC 29211, 803-734-2158. Selected Publications: None. Phone Information: 803-734-2158. Copies of Documents on File: Available for $1 for first page, 50 cents thereafter. $2 for plain charter and $4 for certified charter. Amendments are $1 per page thereafter and it costs $2 for certification. Mailing Labels: No. Magnetic Tape: No. Microfiche: No. New Corporate Listing: Special request only; contact Amy Hoskin at 803-734-2159. Custom Searches: No. Online Access: Yes. Available for $70 per month. Contact Bob Knight, Deputy Secretary. Number of Active Corporations on File: 250,000.

South Dakota

Corporate Division, Secretary of State, 500 East Capitol, Pierre, SD 57501, 605-773-4845. Selected Publications: None. Phone Information: 605-773-4845. Copies of Documents on File: Available for 50 cents per page plus $5 for certification. Mailing Labels: No. Magnetic Tape: No. Microfiche: No. New Corporate Listings: No. Custom Searches: No. Online Access: No. Number of Active Corporations on File: 30,000.

Tennessee

Office of Secretary of State, Services Division, Suite 1800, James K. Polk Building, Nashville, TN 37243-0306, 615-741-2286. Select Publications: None. Phone Information: 615-741-2286. Copies of Documents on File: Certified copies only are available for $10. Mailing Labels No. Magnetic Tape: Yes. Categories: All Corporations on file, Foreign, Domestic, Profit, Non-Profit, Banks, Credit Unions, Cooperative Associations. Charge of an additional $2 for each tape supplied. Cost, done on a cost recovery basis, is determined at time of request. Contact Mr. Thompson at 615-741-0584. Microfiche: No. New Corporate Listings: Monthly New Corporation Listing on a cost recovery basis of 25 cents per page, 8 names per page. Call 615-741-1111. Custom Searches: Yes. Categories: Same as for magnetic tape. Cost is same as for New Corporate Listing. Contact Mr. Thompson at 615-741-0584. Online Access: No. Number of Active Corporations on File: 100,000.

Texas

Corporation Section, Statute Filing Division, Secretary of State, PO Box 13697, Austin, TX 78711, 512-463-5586. Selected Publications: *Filing Guide to Corporations.* (Written requests only for a $15 fee.) Phone Information: 512-463-5555. Copies of Documents on File: Available for 85 cents for first page, 15 cents for each additional page. Certification is $5 plus $1 for each additional page. Invoices are sent for order not in excess of $100. Mailing Labels: No. Magnetic Tape: No. Microfiche: Names of officers and directors available. Cost determined at time of request. New Corporate Listings: Weekly Charter Update costs $27.50 per week. Custom Searches: No. Online Access: Available through Information America 404-892-1800. Contact Linda Gordon at 713-751-7900. Number of Active Corporations on File: 400,000.

Utah

Corporations and UCC, Division of Business Regulations, P.O. Box 45801, 160 East 300 South Street, Second Floor, Salt Lake City, UT 84145-0801, 801-530-4849. Selected Publications: *Going into Business, Doing Business in Utah, A Guide to Business Information.* Phone Information: 801-530-4849. Copies of Documents on File: Available for 30 cents a page plus $10 for certified copies. Mailing Labels: No. Magnetic Tape: Yes. Categories: Profit, Non-Profit, Foreign, Domestic. Cost includes computer time and programming fee. Microfiche: No. New Corporate Listing: Weekly New Corporation List 30 cents per page, New Doing Business As (DBA) List 30 cents per page. Custom Searches: Yes. Categories: Same as for Magnetic tape. Cost includes printing charge of 30 cents per page plus computer time and programming fee. Online Access: Available for $10 per month, 10 cents per minute. Contact Mya Eddy at 801-530-6643

about Data Share. Number of Active Corporations on File: 40,000.

Vermont

Corporate Division, Secretary of State, 109 State Street, Montpelier, VT 05602-2710, 802-828-2386. Selected Publications: *Doing Business in Vermont.* Phone Information: 802-828-2386. Copies of Documents on File: Available for $1 per page, $5 for certified copies. Send the $5 certification fee in advance. They will bill you for the copies. Mailing Labels: No. Magnetic Tape: Diskettes available for $6 - $10 plus 1 cent per name. Entire date base costs $250. Microfiche: No. New Corporate Listings: Yes. Monthly New Corporations and Trade names on diskette is $6 plus 1 cent per name. Total cost is never more than $15. Out-of-State Corporations, $50 for complete list. Custom Searches: Yes. Categories: Foreign, Domestic, Non-profits, by date of registration. Cost is 1 cent per name plus $6 to run list. Online Access: $10 per month, $.10 per minute. Contact: Betty Poulin. Number of Active Corporations on File: 24,000.

Virginia

Clerk of Commission, State Corporation Commission, Secretary of State, P.O. Box 1197, Richmond, VA 23209, street address: 1220 Bank Street, Richmond, VA 23219, 804-786-3672, Fax: 804-371-0118. Selected Publications: *Business Registration Guide.* Phone Information: 804-786-3733. Copies of Documents on File: Available for $1 per page, $3 for certified copies. Mailing Labels: No. Magnetic Tape: Possibly in the future. Microfiche: No. New Corporate Listings: No. Custom Searches: Yes. Categories: Foreign, Domestic, Non-profit, Professional corporation, Non-Stock, Public Service, Cooperatives. Available on cost recovery basis. Online Access: Available. Contact Betty Williams at 804-786-6703. Free while in pilot stage, then available on cost recovery basis. Number of Active Corporations on File: 160,000.

Washington

Corporate Division, Secretary of State, 2nd Floor Republic Bldg., 505 Union Ave, Mail Stop PM-21, Olympia, WA 98504, 206-753-7115. Selected Publications: *None.* Phone Information: 206-753-7115. Copies of Documents on File: Call 206-586-2061 to leave recorded message for document orders. Fees are $1 for the first page and 20 cents thereafter. Certification is $10. Mailing Labels: No. Magnetic Tape: No. Microfiche: Cost is $10 a month per set. New Corporate Listings: No except for statistical sheet. Custom Searches: No. Online Access: No. Number of Active Corporations on File: 145,000. This office is not computerized.

West Virginia

Corporate Division, Secretary of State, Room 139 West, State Capitol, Charleston, WV 25305, 304-342-8000. Selected Publications: *The Corporate Filings Requirements.* Phone Information: 304-342-8000. Copies of Documents on File: Available for 50 cents per page, $10 for certified copies. Mailing Labels: No. Magnetic Tape: No. Microfiche: No. New Corporate Listing: Monthly Report costs $5 a month or $50 per year. Custom Searches: Yes. Cost is $1 for first hour and $5 for every hour thereafter, prorated. Online Access: No. Number of Active Corporations on File: 39,000.

Wisconsin

Corporate Division, Secretary of State, PO Box 7846, Madison, WI 53707; Street address: 30 W. Mifflin St., 9th Floor, Madison, WI 53703, 608-266-3590. Selected Publications: *Chapter 180 Statutes Book ($5)*. Phone Information: 608-266-3590, Fax: 608-267-6813. Copies of Documents on File: For simple copy request must be in writing. Fee is $2. Faxed copies are 50 cents per page. Requests for certified copies may be phoned in. Fee is $10. Mailing Labels: No. Magnetic Tape: Available for $175. Address inquiries to Molly O'Connell. Microfiche: Yes. Monthly New Corporations costs $11 per month. New Corporate Listing: Yes (see microfiche entry). Minimum cost is $10 per week. Custom Searches: No. Online Access: No. Number of Active Corporations on File: 176,000.

Wyoming

Corporate Division, Secretary of State, State of Wyoming, Capitol Building, Cheyenne, WY 82002, 307-777-7311; Fax: 307-777-5339. Selected Publications: *Wyoming Business Corporation Act ($3)*. Phone Information: 307-777-7311. Copies of Documents on File: Available for 50 cents for first 10 pages then 15 cents per page, $3 for certified copies. Mailing Labels: No. Magnetic Tape: Yes. Categories: Trademarks, New Domestic, New Foreign. $18.76 per tape, customer must provide tape. Information cannot be used for solicitation. Submit written request with letter of purpose. Microfiche: Available for foreign and nonprofit corporations for $15. New Corporate Listings: Yes. $100 in state, $150 out of state. Also, you may be put on mailing list for weekly press release that appears in local journals, Business Section. Custom Searches: Yes. Categories: Trademarks 25 cents per name and address, New Domestic $120 or $80 if in-state request, New Foreign $120 or $80 if instate request. Limited capacity for other types of searches. Information cannot be used for solicitation. Submit written request with letter of purpose. Listing of all active profit corporation can be purchased for $25. Online Access: Will soon be available. Contact Jeanie Sawyer, 307-777-5334. Number of Active Corporations on File: 28,000.

Who Owes Money To Whom

Any public or private company, organization, and for that matter, individual, that borrows money and offers an asset as collateral, must file with the state at the Office of Uniform Commercial Code (UCC). A filing is made for each loan and each of the documents is available to the public. To obtain these documents is a two-step process. The first step is to request a search to see if there are any filings for a certain company. The fee for such a search usually is under $10. You will next want to request copies of each of these documents. The cost for each document averages only a few dollars. This Office of Uniform Commercial Code is part of the state government and usually is located near or in the same office as the Office of Corporations which falls under the Secretary of State.

The initial search of records will provide:
- the number of listings under one name;
- the file number for each of the listings;
- the date and time of filing; and
- the name and address of the debtor.

Each UCC filing will disclose:
- a description of the asset placed as collateral; and
- the name and address of the secured party.

This disclosure not only provides insights into the financial security of an individual or organization, but it can also give a picture of their assets. Remember, this information is available on any public or private company or individual. The next time your brother-in-law asks you for money for a new business venture, it probably is worth the investment of a few dollars for a UCC search to see whether your relative owes money to others.

Most states will ask if you would like certified or non-certified information. Certification means that they will stand by the accuracy of the information if it is used in a court or other legal proceeding. For most cases, business researchers will not need the extra procedure of certification.

Farm Loan Filings

The Food and Security Act of 1986 is a law that involves filings on crop and livestock loans. Not all states have adopted this law. However, those which have must set up an automated central filing system under the Office of Uniform Commercial Code. Many states have not adopted the law because of the expense involved in setting up the system. Under this system the office must be able to provide information on filings in 24 hours. The purpose of the system is to notify those who purchase crops from growers if the farmer has already offered that crop as collateral.

UCC Request Forms

Some states provide you with current information about recent filings over the telephone, but others will only accept your request on a standard UCC Form. Still others will respond if you send your request in writing but will give you a discount if your query is on an official UCC Form. Most states use UCC Form 11 for requesting information. Copies of UCC Forms for all 50 states are available by calling Forms, Inc. (800-854-1080). The cost for forms is as follows: 5 or less, $1 each; 6-49, $.75 each; 50-99, $.65 each; 100 and over, $.55 each.

Online Access

With online capabilities you can usually search by such categories as: personal or commercial debtor, type of amendments, name of secured party, name of assigned party, and type of collateral. The following states offer online access to their files: Alabama, Colorado, Florida, Illinois, Iowa, Kansas, Massachusetts, Mississippi, Montana, New Mexico, Nebraska, Oregon, Pennsylvania, South Carolina, South Dakota, Texas, Utah, Vermont, Washington, and Wyoming.

Exceptions

Louisiana is the only state that has not adopted the Uniform Commercial Code. Some parishes (counties) require filings. In Georgia these filings are maintained by the Clerk of the Superior Court.

Uniform Commercial Code Offices

Alabama

Uniform Commercial Code Division, Secretary of State, 4121 Carmichael Rd. Suite 200, Montgomery, AL 36106; 205-242-5231 (mailing address: P.O. Box 5616, Montgomery, AL 36103). Searches: Requests must be submitted in writing. The charge is $5 for name searches submitted on Alabama Form UCC-11, $7 for searches submitted by letter and $1 for each additional listing. Copies of Documents: Available for $1 per page. Farm Filings: Call 205-242-5231. List of new farm filings published every month. Regular printed listing is $25 per year for each collateral code. Microfiche listing is $15 per year for each collateral code. Online Access: Pilot Dial Up Program. Free. Does not show collateral. Contact: Robina Jenkins, 205-242-5136.

Alaska

Uniform Commercial Code Division, Central Filing System, 3601 C St., Suite 1140-A, Anchorage, AK 99503; 907-762-2104. Searches: Requests must be submitted in writing on an Alaska Form UCC-11. The charge is $15 per listing for copy search, $5 for information search. Information search only states whether an encumbrance exists and when it was filed. Copies of Documents: Available for $15 for all documents in a file (includes search fee.). File does not include lapsed documents. Farm Filings: Maintained by the District Recorder's Office.

Arizona

Uniform Commercial Code Department, Secretary of State, 7th Floor, 1700 W. Washington, Phoenix, AZ 85007; 602-542-6178. Searches: Requests must be submitted in writing on Arizona Form UCC-3 or UCC-11. The charge is $6 per name plus 50 cents per listing for copying fee. Fees must be paid in advance. Send blank check with stated limit or $6 and they will call you with the additional amount for copies. When they receive it they will release the documents. Copies of Documents: Available for 50 cents a page. Farm Filings: Maintained by the County Recorder.

Arkansas

Uniform Commercial Code, Secretary of State, State Capitol Building, Room 25, Little Rock, AR 72201; 501-682-5078. Searches: Requests must be submitted in writing in a letter or on a Arkansas Form UCC-11. The charge is $5 per debtor name. Copies of Documents: Available for $5 for the first three pages. Each additional page is $1. They will bill you for copies. Farm Filings: Maintained in this office. Same price and search request structure.

California

Uniform Commercial Code Division, Secretary of State, P.O. Box 1738, Sacramento, CA 95812 (street address: 1230 J Street, Sacramento, CA 95814); 916-445-8061. Searches: Request must be submitted in writing in a letter, on a California Form UCC-3 or Form UCC-11. Charge is $11 per name. One name per request only. For $30 a one name search will be conducted and all documents copied. Additional charges will be billed by invoice. Copies of Documents: Available for $1 for the first page and 50 cents for every additional page. All documents are certified. For additional gold seal certification, or to certify a file number, the fee is an additional $5. Farm Filings: If you do not find them at the state level, remember some are filed with the county government (there is no standard procedure in California).

Colorado

Uniform Commercial Code Division, Secretary of State, 1560 Broadway, Suite 200, Denver, CO 80202; 303-894-2200. Searches: A telephone information searches of two debtor's names (last four filings of each) is available at no cost. These searches are not certified. Written requests must be on a Form UCC-11 or it will not be processed. They prefer you send no money in and let them bill you. The charge is $25 for a search of one debtor name. A computer printout will be sent to verify the search if you do not want a copy search. Copies of Documents: Available for $1.25 per page. Farm Filings: Maintained at the County Court Recorder. Online Access: Call Patti Webb at 303-894-2200 ext. 300 for information on orientation classes for new accounts. They offer several subscription packages: 3 months for $300, or 1 year for $1000 with 15 minute access time each call; 1 year for $5000 with private telephone number, and 1 year for $10,000 with direct computer hookup, which allows user to connect as many as 8 computer terminals to the system.

Connecticut

Uniform Commercial Code Division, Secretary of State, 30 Trinity Street, Hartford, CT 06106; 203-566-4021. Searches: Request must be submitted in writing. The charge is $18 for request submitted on a Connecticut Form UCC-11. The charge for requests submitted by letter is $22. Copies of Documents: The charge for the first three pages is $5, each additional page is $3. Farm Filings: Maintained in this office. Use Connecticut Form UCC-a.

Delaware

Uniform Commercial Code Section, P.O. Box 793, John G. Townsend Building, Dover, DE 19903 (Street Address: Federal and Duke of York Street, Dover, DE 19901); 302-739-4279 (Choose 8 for UCC recorded message, choose 0 for a UCC service representative). Searches: Requests must be submitted in writing on UCC-11 Form. $10 per each debtor's name search. Copies of Documents: Available for $2 per page, $5 minimum. They will bill you. Farm Filings: Maintained by this office. This office is in the middle of being computerized. List of new filings in a particular category can be provided upon special request.

District of Columbia

Recorder of Deeds, 515 D Street NW, Washington, DC 20001; 202-727-5374. Searches: Requests must be submitted in writing. No special form required. The charge is $30 for each secured party. Must be paid in advance. Copies of Documents: Available for $2.25 per page, plus $2.25 for certification. Farm Filings: Maintained in this office. This office is computerized.

Florida

Uniform Commercial Code Division, Department of State, P.O. Box 5588, Tallahassee, FL 32314 (Street Address: 409 Gaines Street, Tallahassee, FL 32301); 904-487-6845. Searches: 904-487-6063. For printed verification a written request must be submitted on Florida Form UCC-11. Copies of Documents: Available for $20 per name. Farm Filings: Filings are maintained by the County Circuit Court. Online Access: UCC Division, 409 E. Gaines Street, Tallahassee, FL 32399; 904-487-6866. Write or call and they will send you an information booklet that describes the service they have available through CompuServe, 800-848-8199. The cost for online service is $24 per hour, plus $2 per month flat fee and other small fees charged by CompuServe.

Georgia

The State of Georgia does not maintain Uniform Commercial Code Filings. Contact the Clerk of Superior Court at the County level for these filings.

Hawaii

Uniform Commercial Code, Bureau of Conveyance, P.O. Box 2867, Honolulu, HI 96803; 808-587-0121. Searches: Requests must be submitted in writing on a Hawaii Form UCC-3 or any state's UCC-11. The search charge is $25 per debtor name, plus an additional 50 cents per listing. They will call you if there will be more charges for additional names found. Copies of Documents: Available for 50 cents per page. Farm Filings: Maintained by this office. Online Access: No.

Idaho

Secretary of State, Uniform Commercial Code Division, State House, Boise, ID 83720; 208-334-3191. Searches: Information may be requested by phone or in writing. The charge is $13 for phone requests and for written requests. An additional $1 is charged if the request is not submitted on an Idaho UCC-4 Form.

Charge for written requests submitted on UCC Form is $12. Copies of Documents: The charge for copying all documents involved in a search is $1. Farm Filings: A 24-hour Expedite Service is available for these filings. The charge is $17 for info search and $23 for copies. Online Access: Hopefully will be available in the future.

Illinois

Uniform Commercial Code Division, Secretary of State, Centennial Building, Room 30, 2nd and Edwards Street, Springfield, IL 62756; 217-782-7518. Searches: All requests must be in writing. Requests on non-standard forms will not be processed. Requests submitted on a Illinois Form UCC-11.7 are $10. Copies of Documents: The charge is 50 cents per page. Farm Filings: If you do not find them at the state level, remember, some are filed with the county government. (There is no standard procedure in Illinois.) Payment for searches and copies may be charged to VISA or Master Charge. Microfilm: Copies of all documents filed within the month are available on a subscription basis for $250 per month. Daily Computer Printout Listing: Available for $250 per month. Online Access: For information write the above office, or contact: Louise Blakley, 217-785-2235. A brochure explaining the system will be sent to you.

Indiana

Uniform Commercial Code Division, Secretary of State, 302 West Washington Street, Room E 018, Indianapolis, IN 46204; 317-232-6393. Searches: All searches must be requested in writing. An Indiana Form UCC-11 is preferred. The charge is $1 per debtor's name and 50 cents for each filing, and 50 cents per statement on the listing. All requests for searches received by Federal Express or Express Mail with return envelope are given a priority. Copies of Documents: The charge is 50 cents per page and $1 for certification. Farm Filings: If incorporated they are filed both at this office and the county recorder where the land is located. If the farm is not incorporated the filing is placed at the county recorder's office only. Online Access: Not available. This office has one of the quickest turnaround times in the nation but is not computerized.

Iowa

Uniform Commercial Code Division, Secretary of State, Second Floor, Hoover Building, Des Moines, IA 50319; 515-281-5204. Searches: Information may be requested by phone if you already have an established account, or in writing. The cost of a phone search is $5, plus $1 for a printout. The charge for a non-standard request is $6 and $5 for a request submitted on an Iowa Form UCC-11. Copies of Documents: The fee is $1 for each copy requested. All copies of liens are certified. Farm Filings: Maintained by this office. (Monthly updating may be obtained from Iowa Public Record Service, 515-223-1153.) Online Access: Available. Contact Allen Welsh, 515-281-8363. Cost is $150 per year, 30 cents per minute, plus telephone charges for dialup program.

Kansas

Uniform Commercial Code Division, Secretary of State, Second Floor, State Capitol, Topeka, KS 66612; 913-296-3650. Searches: Phone requests are accepted with VISA or MC or from those holding a prepaid account with the UCC. The charge for phone requests is $15 per name for verbal information and $5 for an order. The charge for written requests is $5. If staffing permits, all requests are filled within 24 hours. Copies of Documents: The charge is $1 per page. There is no additional charge for certification of name searches. They are always sent out certified. For file number searches, certification must be requested. Fee is 50 cents. Farm Filings: This office has handled farm filings since 1984. Filings prior to that year are maintained by the County Register of Deeds. Online Access: Available from Kansas Information Network with imaging capacity. Contact: Cathy. Other: Microfilm cost $25 per roll plus $7.50 for postage and handling, for up to 50 rolls. Total file has 42 rolls. New rolls, 4-5 monthly can be sent. Magnetic Tape: Master file costs $2,000. Updates are $15 weekly or $75 monthly.

Kentucky

Uniform Commercial Code Division, Office of Secretary of State, State Capitol Bldg., Capitol Avenue, Frankfort, KY 40601; 502-564-2848 Ext. 441. Searches: All searches of UCC filings must be conducted in person by requester or by outside agencies. Law firms or Kentucky Lender's Assistance, 606-278-6586 may do it for you. In addition to their fee, the UCC charges 10 cents per page for plain copies; $5 for certification and 50 cents for every page thereafter. Farm Filings: Filings are maintained by the County Circuit Court. Online Access: No.

Louisiana

The state of Louisiana has not adopted the Uniform Commercial Code. Filings may be maintained at the Parish (county) level.

Maine

Uniform Commercial Code Division, Secretary of State, State House Station 101, Augusta, ME 04333; 207-287-4177. Searches: All requests must be submitted in writing in a letter or on a Form UCC-11. State whether plain or certified copies are desired. Cost is $2 per page plus $10 for certification. Will bill. For expedited service an additional $5 fee guarantees a 24 hour turnaround time. Farm Filings: Maintained by this office. Online Access: No.

Maryland

Uniform Commercial Code Division, State Department of Assessments and Taxation, 301 West Preston Street, Baltimore, MD 21201; 410-225-1340. Searches: The State of Maryland does not conduct searches. They will provide a list of title companies that do provide that service. Some are: Hylinf Infoquest, 410-728-4990 and Harbor City Research, 301-539-0400. Copies cost $1 per page. Cost to certify a document is $6. Farm Filings: Maintained by this office. Online Access: No.

Massachusetts

Uniform Commercial Code Division, Secretary of State, Room 1711, 1 Ashburton Place, Boston, MA 02108; 617-727-2860. Searches: Requests must be submitted in writing on a Form UCC-11 (any state's form is acceptable). The charge is $5 for an information computer printout and $10 for computer printout with face page and up to 15 pages. They will call you if pages exceed this limit. All fees must be paid in advance. Requests sent

by Federal Express or Express Mail will be sent out same way with Air Bill, but all requests are processed in order received. No expediting service available. Copies of Documents: Charge is $2 per page and $3 for certification. Farm Filings: Maintained in Town Clerk's Office. Online Access: Available for $149 per year plus 40 cents per minute. Also carried by commercial services. Contact Richard Shipley, 617-729-5412.

Michigan

Uniform Commercial Code Section, P.O. Box 30197, Lansing, MI 48909-7697 (Mailing Address: 7064 Crowner Dr., Lansing, MI 48909); 517-322-1495. Searches: Telephone requests are handled on an expedite basis for already established accounts. The charge is an additional $25. You must have an account number with the UCC Section to obtain this service. The charge for requests submitted on non-standard forms are $6. Requests submitted on a Michigan Form UCC-11 is $3. Requests sent out by Federal Express or Express Mail are given priority, but all requests are processed in the order received. Copies of Documents: The charge is $1 per page and $1 for certification. Farm Filings: Filings are maintained by the County Recorder of Deeds. Online Access: No. Other: Microfilm available in contract basis for $50 per month. Format is not computer indexed. Write above address for details and contract.

Minnesota

Uniform Commercial Code Division, Secretary of State, 180 State Office Building, St. Paul, MN 55155; 612-296-2434. Searches: Requests must be submitted in writing and include a SASE. The charge for a request submitted on a Minnesota Form UCC-11 is $11. The charge for a request submitted on a non-standard form is $14. These charges include information on 5 listings and/or 5 copies. You will be billed if there are additional copies in excess of five. The charge for additional listings is 50 cents/listing. Copies of Documents: Available for 50 cents/page. Charge for certified copies is a $5 plus 50 cents for each page. Farm Filings: Available from the County Recorder of Deeds unless the debtor is a non-resident or a corporation and then they are filed with the UCC Division.

Mississippi

Uniform Commercial Code Division, Secretary of State, 202 N. Congress St., #601, Jackson, MS 39201; 601-359-1614. Searches: Phone information is available at no cost. Information available by phone is: approximate number of filings, secured party, file numbers, and date and time of filing. The charge for written requests submitted on Mississippi Form UCC-11 is $5. The charge for written requests submitted on non-standard forms is $10. Copies of Documents: Available for $2 a pages. Send initial $5 or $10 fee only. They will bill you for the exact amount of copies made. Farm Filings: Farm Filings are maintained by the above office. Other: Master list of all farm registrations available for $2040. Master list by type is $500 per crop. Online Access: Contact Cheryl Crawford, 601-359-1548. The cost is $250 per month plus 50 cents per transaction with minimum of 100 transactions. Service will be available as of 1/92. Will display name, address and collateral. Complete file microfilm available for $50 per roll.

Missouri

Uniform Commercial Code Division, Secretary of State, P.O. Box 1159, Jefferson City, MO 65102; 314-751-2360. Searches: Information searches will be given over the phone. These searches are not certified and are free of charge. (This service is not available on Mondays or the day after a holiday.) The charge for written requests is $8. Copies of Documents: Available for $8 per listing. The $8 fee covers the first 10 pages. Additional pages are 50 cents each. Farm Filings: Maintained by the County Recorder.

Montana

Uniform Commercial Code Bureau, Secretary of State, Capitol Station, Helena, MT 59620; 406-444-3665, Fax: 406-444-3926. Searches: Requests for searches will be accepted by phone. The charge if you have a prepaid account is $7, the same as for a written request. There are no restrictions on form in which you put written requests. Searches are conducted the day of the request for a $5 fee. Regular requests processed in 48 hours. Copies of Documents: Available for 50 cents a page. The charge for certification is $2. Farm Filings: Maintained in this office. For total listing of crop you are interested in, fill out a Buyer's Registration Form for crops you want on the list. Results can be done on paper or microfiche. Service is done on a cost recovery basis. Online Access: Contact Florence, 406-444-3665. She will send you an information brochure. The charge is $25 per month for unlimited use. Printed copies cost 50 cents each and are statutorily accepted documents.

Nebraska

Uniform Commercial Code Division, P.O. Box 95104, 301 Centennial Mall S., Lincoln, NE 68509; 402-471-4080. Searches: The charge for requests by phone is $1 per debtor's name. No verification is sent unless requested. If requested the charge for the printout is $3. The charge for written requests is $3. A computer printout containing a list of the filings is sent to the requester. Copies of Documents: Available for 50 cents per page. They will bill. Farm Filings: Maintained by the county government, but the above office will hooked up to all 93 countries and will do a search for you. The county will bill you directly for its service. Magnetic Tape: Available to large companies for $250 per month. Online Access: Available. Charge is $2 per inquiry. Contact Debbie Pester.

Nevada

Uniform Commercial Code Division, Secretary of State, Capitol Complex, Carson City, NV 89710; 702-687-5298. Searches: Only written requests for information will be accepted. The charge is $6 for a request submitted on a Nevada Form UCC-3, Form UCC-11 or any type of letter. For an additional $10 your request will be expedited. This fee must be paid with a separate check. Copies of Documents: Available for $1 per page and an additional $6 for certified copies. Farm Filings: Maintained at the office of the County Recorder. Online Access: No.

New Hampshire

Uniform Commercial Code Division, Secretary of State, State House, Room 204, Concord, NH 03301; 603-271-3276 or 271-3277. Searches: Requests must be submitted in writing by letter or on a Form UCC-11, and must contain a SASE in which requested documents will be mailed. Requests will not be processed without SASE enclosed. The charge for a request submitted on a New Hampshire Form UCC-11 is $5. The charge for a request submitted on a letter or non-standard form is $7. Copies of Documents: Available for 75 cents per file. Farm Filings: Maintained by this office. Microfiche: Available from New England Micrographics. Contact Nick Brattan, 603-625-1171. Online Access: No. This office is not computerized.

New Jersey

Uniform Commercial Code Division, State Department, State Capitol Building, CN303, Trenton, NJ 08625; 609-530-6426. Searches: Requests must be submitted in writing with exact name and address of debtor or on a New Jersey Form UCC-11 or a security agreement signed by the debtor. Payment must accompany request unless prepaid UCC account, Visa or MasterCard is used. Request may be Faxed, 609-530-0688. The charge is $25. Document is certified. Expedite Service is available for $5. The requester pays the express mail expense. Copies of Documents: Available for $1 per page. Farm Filings: Maintained by the county and the state. At the county level you will want to check with the County Recorder. Online Access: No.

New Mexico

Uniform Commercial Code Division, Bureau of Operations, Secretary of State, Executive Legislative Building, Room 400, Santa Fe, NM 87503; 505-827-3600. Searches: Certification is $8. Copies cost $1 per page. The State of New Mexico does not do searches, but they will provide you with a list of abstract companies that are authorized to do so. Call Bureau of Operations for list, 505-827-3608. Farm Filings: This office located at the same address with conduct a search for an Agricultural Eddective Financing Statement for $15. Contact Ben Vegil, 505-827-3609. They will follow-up the verbal report with a written statement. Online Access: Available through local services: Federal Abstracts, 505-982-5537, Lawyer's Title, 505-988-2333 and Capitol Documents, 505-984-2696. Also available from Dun and Bradstreet.

New York

Uniform Commercial Code Division, Secretary of State, P.O. Box 7021, Albany, NY 12225; 518-474-4763. Searches: Requests must be submitted in writing. For requests submitted on a New York Form UCC-11 the charge is $7. For requests submitted on non-standard forms the charge is $12. Copies of Documents: Available for $1.50 per page. Farm Filings: Maintained by both the state and the County Recorder. Online Access: No. Other: Microfiche available for $300 per month. Contact Virginia Cellery at 518-432-2733.

North Carolina

Uniform Commercial Code Division, Secretary of State, 300 N. Salisbury St., Raleigh, NC 27611; 919-733-4205. Searches: Requests must be submitted in writing. Signature for the requester is required, therefore make request on Form UCC-11 or North Carolina Form UCC-11. The charge is $8 per name. Search fee must be sent with request. All requests are handled within 24 hours of receipt. Copies of Documents: Available for $1 per page. Will bill. Farm Filings: Maintained by this office and County Recorder. Online Access: No, but will be available in the future. Other: Microfilm can be purchased for $50 per roll. New monthly listings generate about 2 rolls per month. Contact Judy Chapman.

North Dakota

Uniform Commercial Code Division, Secretary of State, Main Capitol Building, 600 Boulevard Avenue East, Bismarck, ND 58505; 701-224-3662. Searches: Requests may be phoned in or be submitted in writing preferably on a North Dakota UCC-11. Letters and nonstandard forms also accepted. The charge is $5. Copies of Documents: Available for $5 for the first three pages and $1 a page for additional pages. Farm Filings: The Central Notice staff will take requests for searches over the phone for crop and livestock filings. The charge is the same as above. Written requests are the same as stated above. Farm equipment and real estate filings are optional and were maintained by the state or the County Register of Deeds until 1/92. As of 1/92 the UCC and County Register of Deeds were hooked up to the same system. Online Access: No, but will be available in the future.

Ohio

Uniform Commercial Code Division, Secretary of State, 30 E. Broad Street, 14th Floor, Columbus, OH 43266-0418; 614-466-9316. Searches: Phone requests for information are not certified and are free of charge. Call 614-466-3623/3126. Limit is 3 requests per phone call. Written requests may be submitted on a non-standard letter form, Form UCC-11 or on an Ohio Form UCC-11. The charge is $9. It takes 6 months for these searches to be conducted. Expedite service is available for an additional $9. These requests are processed in 5 working days. Copies of Documents: Available for $1 per page. Farm Filings: Maintained by the County Recorder. Online Access: No.

Oklahoma

Uniform Commercial Code Office, Oklahoma County Clerk, 320 Robert S. Kerr, Room 105, Oklahoma City, OK 73102; 405-278-1521. Searches: Requests must be submitted in writing. The charge is $5. Copies of Documents: Available for $1 per page. Send $5 search fee with request. They will bill you for copies and call if amount is over $25. The charge for certification is $1. Farm Filings: Maintained by Secretary of State's Office, 405-521-2474. Online Access: No.

Oregon

Uniform Commercial Code Division, Secretary of State, 255 Capitol St., NE, Salem, OR 97310; 503-986-2200. Searches: Requests must be phoned in using Visa or MasterCard, charged to an established prepaid UCC account or submitted in writing by letter, or on Form UCC-11 or preferably on a Oregon Form UCC-25R. The charge is $5 per debtor's name. Copies of Documents: Available for $1 per page. Farm Filings: Maintained by this office. The charge for a search is $5 per name. Monthly reports by agricultural product code are available on microfilm or paper copy. For microfilm contact Micelle. Cost is $10 per reel weekly. Online Access: Available for $25 per month, plus 20 cents a minute for online use. Contact Michelle. Commercially available from Prentice Hall, 800-452-7856.

Pennsylvania

Uniform Commercial Code Division, Corporation Bureau, State Department, 308 N. Office Building, Harrisburg, PA 17120; 717-787-8712. Searches: Requests for searches must be paid in advance by check or money order only and submitted in writing on a Pennsylvania Form UCC-11. The charge is $12 per name search. $28 to certify. Must may in advance by check or money order. Copies of Documents: Available for $2 per page. Farm Filings: Maintained by this office. Online Access: Information America, 404-892-1800.

Rhode Island

Uniform Commercial Code Division, Secretary of State, 100 North Main Street, Providence, RI 02903; 401-277-2521. Searches: Requests must be submitted in writing. Same charge for request in letter form or on Form UCC-11. Call for number of pages. Requests will not be processed without payment in full. The charge is $5. Copies of Documents: Available for 50 cents per copy. Farm Filings: Maintained by the City Recorder of Deeds. Online Access: No.

South Carolina

Uniform Commercial Code Division, Secretary of State, P.O. Box 11350, Columbia, SC 29211; 803-734-2175. Searches: Requests must be submitted in writing on Form UCC-11, or preferably South Carolina Form UCC-4. Letters are not accepted. The charge is $5 per debtor name. No priority or expediting service. All requests done in the order received. Copies of Documents: Available for $2 for the first page, $1 for each page thereafter. Farm Filings: Maintained by County Recorder. Online Access: $70 monthly. Other: Microfilm from Archives is purchased by Dun and Bradstreet and may be purchased from the UCC division directly. Contact Thresha Southerland, 803-734-2176. One tape costs $50.

South Dakota

Central Filing System, Secretary of State, 500 E. Capitol, Pierre, SD 57501; 605-773-4422. Searches: Telephone information provided for no charge. Requests for searches are accepted from those with prepaid deposit accounts. Written requests are accepted on any UCC standard request form. The charge is $4. Fee for certification is $5. Copies of Documents: Available for 50 cents per page. They will bill you. Farm Filings: Maintained by this office. Online access at no charge is available. Online Access: Available by subscription. The system can be used by those with IBM compatible computers and Hayes compatible modems. Cost is $240 per year for 200 transactions and 10 cents per transaction thereafter.

Tennessee

Uniform Commercial Code Section, Secretary of State, J.K. Polk Building, 505 Deaderick St., Suite 1800, Nashville, TN 37219; 615-741-3276. Searches: Requests must be submitted in writing, preferably on a Tennessee Form UCC-11. Indicate if you want information or information plus copies. The charge is $10 even if the search shows no listing. Send the $10 fee with request. Copies of Documents: Available for $1 per copy. Do not send money with request. They will bill you. Requests sent with Express Mail envelopes will be sent the next day. All other requests take 3-4 days to process. Farm Filings: Maintained by this office and County Recorder. It is necessary to check with both offices. Online Access: No.

Texas

Uniform Commercial Code, Secretary of State, P.O. Box 13193, Austin, TX 78711-3193; 512-475-2705. Searches: The charge for a search requested by phone is $25. The charge for written requests submitted on Texas Form UCC-11 is $10. May Fax: 512-475-2812. The charge for written requests submitted on a letterhead or non-standard form is $25. Copies of Documents: Available for $1.50 per page with a $5 minimum charge. The charge for certification is an additional $5. Farm Filings: Maintained by the above office. Online Access: Available by Dialup Service. Cost is $3 per search, deducted from prepaid account. Contact Tina Whiteley, 512-475-2700.

Utah

Uniform Commercial Code Division, Business Regulation Department, 300 South Street, Second Floor, Salt Lake City, UT 84110; 801-530-6020. Searches: Written request may be on letter, UCC-11 or Utah Form UCC-2. The charge is $10 per debtor name. Copies of Documents: Available for 30 cents per page. Will bill. Certification: No additional charge. Document already certified. Farm Filings: Central Filings maintained these files. Phone requests are accepted. The charge is $10. Online Access: Available through Data-Share program on a subscription basis. The charge is $10 per month plus 10 cents per minute and telephone charges. Contact Mary Ann Saddler or Ted Wiggin at 801-530-6643.

Vermont

Uniform Commercial Code, Secretary of State, Montpelier, VT 05609 (Regular mail to: 109 State Street, Montpelier, VT 05609-1104; Fed Ex to: 94 Main Street, Montpelier, VT 05609); 802-828-2388. Searches: Requests for searches may be phoned in or submitted in writing. They will bill for phone requests. The charge is $5 per debtor name, plus 50 cents for an information sheet containing debtor's name, secured party, file number, and date and time filed. Copies of Documents: Available for $2 for 5" x 8" or $5 for 8 1/2" x 11" copies. Certification fee is $5. Farm Filings: Central Filings Section maintains these files. Contact the above address. The charges for searches is the same. Online Access: $10/month, $.10/minute.

Virginia

Uniform Commercial Code Division, State Corporation Commission, P.O. Box 1197, Richmond, VA 23209 (Street Address: 1220 Bank Street, Richmond, VA 23209); 804-786-3689. Searches: Requests for searches must be submitted in writing in a letter or Form UCC-11. The charge is $6 per debtor name. Copies of Documents: Available for $1 per page. There is

an additional charge of $6 for certification. Farm Filings: Maintained by this office and the County Recorder. Online Access: No.

Washington

Uniform Commercial Code Division, Department of Licensing, 405 Black Lake Blvd., Olympia, WA 98502 (Mailing Address: PO Box 9660, Olympia, WA 98507); 206-753-2523. Searches: Requests must be submitted in writing. Indicate if you want information or information and copies. The charge is $7 for all the listings of one debtor. Copies of Documents: Available for $12. This includes search fee, plus copies of all documents for one debtor. Farm Filings: Maintained in this office. Microfilm: Copies of each days filings are available for $6.50 per day plus shipping and handling fees. Online Access: Contact Darla Gehrke at 206-752-2523 for information on how to set up a prepaid account. Monthly minimum deposit is $200 from which $1 per minute online time and other fees are deducted.

West Virginia

Uniform Commercial Code Division, Secretary of State, 1900 Kanawha, Bldg. 1, Room 131W, Charleston, WV 25305-0770; 304-345-4000. Searches: Phone requests for information are accepted. The charge is $5. They will bill you. Written requests are preferred. The charge is $3 if Form UCC-11 is used, $5 for all others. Copies of Documents: Available for 50 cents per page. The charge for certification is $5. Farm Filings: Maintained by this office. Online Access: No.

Wisconsin

Uniform Commercial Code Division, Secretary of State, 30 West Mifflin St., Madison, WI 53703 (Mailing Address: P.O. Box 7847, Madison, WI 53707); 608-266-3087. Searches: Phone requests for information are accepted. The charge is $5 per filing. The charge for written requests is $5 per debtor name. Copies of Documents: Available for $1 per document. Certification certificate must be requested in writing and is an additional 50 cents. Farm Filings: Maintained by the County Register of Deeds. Other: Microfiche is available on a monthly basis. Contact Bonnie Fredrick at 608-266-3087.

Wyoming

Uniform Commercial Code, Secretary of State, State Capitol Building, Cheyenne, WY 82002; 307-777-5372. Searches: Phone requests for information are accepted for 2 debtor names. Requests may be Faxed to 307-777-5339. The charge is $5 for each name. The charge for written requests is the same. Copies of Documents: Available for 50 cents per page. Farm Filings: Maintained by this office and the County Recorder. Check both. Online Access: Available for $50 per month, plus telephone charges and usage fee. Minimum usage fee is $26 per month. Contact Jeanie Sawyer.

Companies That Only Sell Stock In One State

State Securities Offices Offer Company Information, Mailing List of Brokers and More

The offices of state security regulators offer financial data on thousands of companies which are not required to file with the U.S. Securities and Exchange Commission as well as the names, addresses, financial data, and consumer information on thousands of stockbrokers and broker-dealers.

State regulation of the sale of securities in the United States began in 1911 when the Kansas legislature passed the first securities law. North Carolina enacted a law the same year; Arizona and Louisiana did so in 1912. By 1919, 32 states had followed suit. Now, all states and the federal government have laws regulating the sale of corporate securities, bonds, investment contracts and stocks.

The reason for these laws is simple enough: they protect the public, unfamiliar with the intricacies of investing, against deceitful promoters and their often worthless stocks. This is the same type of function that the U.S. Securities and Exchange Commission performs in Washington, DC. The United States covers companies trading stocks across state boundaries, and the states cover companies trading stocks within their state. The laws -- called Blue Sky laws -- prevent speculative schemes "which have no more basis than so many feet of blue sky," according to the Commerce Clearing House Blue Sky Law Reports.

The Blue Sky Law is usually administered by each state's Securities Commission or Securities Division. Securities to be sold within a state must register with this office. If the issuer is a corporation, for example, it must submit the following information:

- articles of incorporation
- purpose of proposed business
- names and addresses of officers and directors
- qualifications and business history of applicant - detailed financial data

Each state, however, has numerous exemptions. Securities issued by national banks, savings and loan associations, non-profit organizations, public utilities, and railroads are usually exempt from the Blue Sky laws, as are securities listed on the stock exchange, those issued by companies registered with the U.S. Securities and Exchange Commission, and those issued by foreign governments with which the U.S. has diplomatic relations.

Securities offices also require broker-dealer firms, the agents (or sales representatives), and investments advisers wanting to work in the state to file applications.

Agents wanting to work in one or more states now apply for registration by filing with National Association of Securities Dealers' Central Registration Depository (CRD). To keep the CRD current, agents must submit all pertinent employment and application changes. All state securities offices are hooked up to the CRD through computer terminals and use them to monitor agents registered or applying to register in their jurisdictions as well as any complaints filed against individuals.

Most states will also use the system for registration of broker-dealer firms. Information kept in the repository will include registration applications, amendments to applications, complaints on file, and so forth. The purpose is to reduce the amount of paperwork for the states and to promote more uniformity.

The system is not set to accept broker-dealers' audited financial statements or annual reports so applicants will have to continue to file in the states requiring them. The broker-dealer phase of the CRD is now in operation. Several states are now trying to determine what, if any, information they will require broker- dealers to file with their securities divisions. Most of those states that have made a decision said they will continue to require annual financial reports to be filed with their offices.

Below are the names, addresses and telephone numbers for the state securities offices. Most of these offices will routinely provide information over the phone on whether specific companies, agents, or broker-dealers are registered in their states. Requests for more detailed information may have to be submitted in writing.

Securities Offices

Alabama
Securities Commission, 770 Washington Ave., Suite 570, Montgomery, AL 36130; 205-242-2984.

Alaska
Division of Banking, Securities and Corporations, Department of Commerce and Economic Development, State Office Building #94, P.O. Box 110807, Juneau, AK 99811-0807; 907-465-2521.

Arizona
Securities Division, Arizona Corporation Commission, 1200 West Washington St., Suite 201, Phoenix, AZ 85007; 602-542-4242.

Arkansas
Securities Department, Heritage West Building, Third Floor, 201 East Markham, Little Rock, AR 72201; 501-324-9260.

California
Securities Regulation Division, Department of Corporations, 3700 Wilshire Blvd., 6th Floor, Los Angeles, CA 90010; 213-736-2741.

Colorado
Division of Securities, Department of Regulatory Agencies, 1580 Lincoln, Suite 420, Denver, CO 80203; 303-894-2320.

Connecticut
Securities and Business Investments Division, Department of Banking, Securities and Business, 44 Capitol Ave., Hartford, CT 06106; 203-566-4560.

Delaware
Division of Securities, Department of Justice, 8th Floor, Civil Division, 820 North French St., Wilmington, DE 19801; 302-577-2515.

District of Columbia
Division of Securities, DC Public Service Commission, 450 5th St., NW, Suite 821, Washington, DC 20001; 202-626-5105.

Florida
Division of Securities and Investor Protection, Department of Banking and Finance, Office of Comptroller, The Capitol, LL-22, Tallahassee, FL 32399-0350; 904-488-9805.

Georgia
Business Services and Regulations, Office of Secretary of State, Suite 315 West Tower, Two Martin Luther King Dr., Atlanta, GA 30334; 404-656-2894.

Hawaii
Business Registration Division, Department of Commerce and Consumer Affairs, 1010 Richards St., PO Box 40, Honolulu, HI 96810; 808-586-2737.

Idaho
Securities Bureau, Department of Finance, 700 West State St., Boise, ID 83720-2700; 208-334-3684.

Illinois
Securities Department, Office of Secretary of State, 900 South Spring St., Springfield, IL 62704; 217-782-2256.

Indiana
Securities Division, Office of Secretary of State, 302 W. Washington, Room E-111, Indianapolis, IN 46204; 317-232-6681.

Iowa
Securities Bureau, Office of Commissioner of Insurance, Lucas State Office Building, 2nd Floor, Des Moines, IA 50319; 515-281-4441.

Kansas
Office of Securities Commissioner, 618 S. Kansas, 2nd Floor, Topeka, KS 66603-3804; 913-296-3307.

Kentucky
Division of Securities, Department of Financial Institutions, 477 Versailles Rd., Frankfort, KY 40601; 502-564-3390.

Louisiana
Securities Commission, 1100 Paydras Street, Suite #2250, New Orleans, LA 70163; 504-568-5515.

Maine
Securities Division, Bureau of Banking, Department of Professional and Financial Regulation, State House Station 121, Augusta, ME 04333; 207-582-8760.

Maryland
Division of Securities, Office of Attorney General, 200 St. Paul Place, 21st Floor, Baltimore, MD 21202-2020; 410-576-6360.

Massachusetts
Securities Division, Department of Secretary of State, 1719 John W. McCormack Building, One Ashburton Place, Boston, MA 02108; 617-727-3548.

Michigan
Corporation and Securities Bureau, Department of Commerce, 6546 Merchantile Way, Lansing, MI 48909; 517-334-6200.

Minnesota
Registration and Licensing Division, Department of Commerce, 133 East 7th Street, St. Paul, MN 55101; 612-296-4026.

Mississippi
Securities Division, Office of Secretary of State, P.O. Box 136, Jackson, MS 39205; 601-359-1350.

Missouri
Office of Secretary of State, 600 West Main, Jefferson City, MO 65101; 314-751-4136.

Montana
Securities Department, State Auditor's Office, 126 North Sanders, Room 270, Helena, MT 59620; 406-444-2040.

Nebraska
Bureau of Securities, Department of Banking and Finance, 1200 N Street, The Atrium #311, Lincoln, NE 68508; 402-471-3445.

Nevada
Securities Division, Office of Secretary of State, 1771 E. Flamingo Rd., Suite 212-B, Las Vegas, NV 89158; 702-486-6440.

New Hampshire
Department of State, Bureau of Securities Regulation, State House, Room 204, Concord, NH 03301-4989; 603-271-1463.

New Jersey
Bureau of Securities, 153 Halsey Street, 6th Floor, Newark, NJ 07101; 201-504-3600.

New Mexico
Securities Division, Regulation and Licensing Department, 725 St. Michaels Dr., P.O. Box 25101, Santa Fe, NM 87501; 505-827-7140.

New York
Bureau of Investor Protection and Securities, Department of Law, 120 Broadway, 23rd Fl., New York, NY 10271; 212-416-8200.

North Carolina
Securities Division, Department of State, 300 N Salisbury St., Suite 1000, Raleigh, NC 27603; 919-733-3924.

North Dakota
Office of Securities Commission, 600 E. Boulevard, 5th Floor, Bismarck, ND 58505; 701-224-3924.

Ohio
Division of Securities, Department of Commerce, 77 South High St, 22nd Fl., Columbus, OH 43266-0548; 614-644-7381.

Oklahoma
Department of Securities, 2401 North Lincoln Blvd., 4th Fl., Oklahoma City, OK 73152; 405-235-0230.

Oregon
Division of Finance and Corporate Securities, Department of Insurance and Finance, 21 Labor and Industries Bldg., Salem, OR 97310; 503-378-4387.

Pennsylvania
Securities Commission, Division of Licensing and Compliance, 1010 North Seventh St., 2nd Floor, Harrisburg, PA 17102-1410; 717-787-8061.

Rhode Island
Securities Division, Department of Business Regulation, 233 Richmond St., #232, Providence, RI 02903-4232; 401-277-3049.

South Carolina
Securities Division, Department of State, 1205 Pendelton St., #501, Columbia, SC 29201; 803-734-1087.

South Dakota
Division of Securities, Department of Commerce and Regulation, 118 W. Capitol, Pierre, SD 57501-2017; 605-773-4823.

Tennessee
Division of Securities, Department of Commerce and Securities, Volunteer Plaza, Suite 680, 500 James Robinson Pkwy., Nashville, TN 37243; 615-741-3187.

Texas
State Securities Board, 221 W. 6th Street, Suite 700, Austin, TX 78701; 512-474-2233.

Utah
Securities Division, Department of Business Regulation, P.O. Box 45808, Salt Lake City, UT 84145-0808; 801-530-6600.

Vermont

Securities Division, Department of Banking & Insurance, 89 Main Street, Drawer 20, Montpelier, VT 05600-3101; 802-828-3420.

Virginia

Division of Securities and Retail Franchising, State Corporation Commission, PO Box 1197, Richmond, VA 23209; 804-371-9051.

Washington

Securities Division, Department of Licensing, PO Box 9033, 405 Black Lake Blvd., SW, 2nd Floor, Olympia, WA 98507-9033; 206-753-6928.

West Virginia

Securities Division, State Auditor's Office, Room W-118, State Capitol, Charleston, WV 25305; 304-558-2257.

Wisconsin

Office of Commissioner of Securities, 101 East Wilson St., P.O. Box 1768, Madison, WI 53701; 608-266-3431.

Wyoming

Securities Division, Office of the Secretary of State, Capitol Building, Cheyenne, WY 82002; 307-777-7370.

State Licensing Offices

Buried within each state government are several, and sometimes dozens, of offices where individuals as well as business establishments must register in order to perform certain types of services and commercial activities. State laws require accountants, architects, concert promoters, employment agencies, podiatrists and numerous other professionals to register. The data derived from these regulatory boards provide unique opportunities for researchers and marketing executives to obtain demographic data, mailing lists and even competitive information.

Mailing Lists

Mailing lists offer the biggest potential from these offices. The unusual as well as the mundane are available in a variety of formats. Many of these lists are not accessible commercially, but you can get them from the states inexpensively and usually without restrictions. In other words, you can purchase a state list once, and use it over and over again. Commercial list brokers will never let you do this. Here is a sampling of available mailing lists:

- 1 cent per name for all dentists in Kentucky;
- Free directory of real estate agents in Arizona;
- $40 for a list of all nurses in Colorado;
- A mailing list of all contractors in Arkansas for $10;
- 2 cents per name for all swimming pool dealers in Florida;
- A listing of librarians in Georgia;
- 4 cents a name for all the psychologists in California;
- $100 for a computer tape of all accountants in Florida;

- $1.45 per 1,000 names for all medical practices in Illinois;
- Free list of all attorneys in Maine.

Almost every state provides mailing labels in the form of cheshire or pressure sensitive labels. In many cases, the charge is nominal.

Common Lists and Specialized Rosters

Every state maintains a variety of standard rosters. Some states keep as few as 20 lists and others have over 100. Names of licensed professionals and business establishments available from most every state include:

- medical professionals
- accountants
- real estate agents and brokers
- veterinarians
- barbers
- insurance agents
- architects
- nursing homes
- cosmetologists
- hearing aid dealers
- social workers
- lawyers

After reviewing the rundown of all 50 states and District of Columbia licensing boards, you will be amazed at the variety of lists that are within easy reach. In most cases you can obtain printouts for such licensed services as:

- burglar alarm contractors in Maine
- tow truck operations in Minnesota
- hat cleaners in Ohio
- ski areas in Michigan
- day care centers in New York

- security guards in New Hampshire
- outfitters in Colorado

Computer Tapes and Diskettes: Selections and Sorting Options

Many states can provide the information on magnetic tape and some are beginning to offer data on IBM PC compatible diskettes. Almost every state will allow you to select names by zip code or county whether the licensee is active or inactive. Some states will allow you to select certain demographic characteristics, such as years of formal education.

Markets and Demographics

With a little creativity and resourcefulness, the information at licensing boards can provide pertinent clues in formulating a market profile. For example, you can determine:

- which counties have the highest concentration of psychologists;
- what is the average number of years of schooling for real estate agents in certain zip codes;
- which zip codes have experienced the fastest growth for accountants for the past 10 years;
- the number of out-of-state licensed paralegals;
- which counties have the most podiatrists or veterinarians
- how many insurance agents there are in a given county.

Some states have the capability of performing historical analysis, while others will supply you with the raw data.

Competitive Intelligence

Depending upon the type of business you are investigating, pertinent competitive information may be ferreted from state licensing boards. For example, if you are a dentist, mobile home dealer, nursing home administrator or real estate broker, you could plot how many competitors you are up against in a given zip code or county. Or, you may be able to determine how many opticians work for an eye care chain, or tax consultants for a given tax preparer.

Organization of Licensing Boards

Approximately half of the states have a central office which is responsible for all licensed professions. For such states it is a relatively easy process to obtain information because it is all generated from a single source. However, the other states make this task difficult. Typically, each separate independent board maintains information for one profession. The only connection these agencies have to the state government is that their board members are appointed by the governor.

States With Restrictions

Some states have restrictions on the use of their lists of licensed professionals. California, District of Columbia, Hawaii, Louisiana, New Hampshire, North Dakota, and Oklahoma do not release information. Alabama and North Carolina will only release the number of professionals, not their names. Minnesota will only release information if action has been taken against a professional or business. And in Iowa, Montana, New York, and Rhode Island, the data may not be used for commercial purposes.

State Licensing Boards

Besides issuing licenses to professionals so they can do business, the following offices act as consumer watchdogs to make sure that those with licenses do business fairly and ethically. Not only will these offices investigate complaints against licensed professionals, they also have the ability to revoke or suspend the licenses if the professional repeatedly acts unprofessionally or unethically. Each state listing includes the professionals licensed in that state, including health professionals, along with their different licensing offices where noted.

Alabama

State Occupational Information Coordinating Community (SOICC), 401 Adams Ave., P.O. Box 5690, Montgomery, AL 36103-5690; 205-242-2990. Licensing boards and professions: accountants, aircraft personnel, architects, auctioneers, audiologists, speech pathologists, bar pilots, water transportation personnel, boxer and wrestler trainers, classroom teachers, coal mine foremen/mine electricians, cosmetologists, counselors, dentists, dental hygienists, chiropractors, doctors of medicine, physician's assistants, surgeon's assistants, school bus drivers, embalmer/funeral directors, engineer-in-training and professional engineers, land surveyors, fire fighters, foresters, general contractors, hearing aid specialists, heating and air conditioning contractors, insurance agents, interior designers, landscape architects, landscape horticulturist/planters, lawyers, pest control operators and fumigators, tree surgeons, law enforcement personnel, nurses, nursing home administrators, optometrists, pharmacists, physical therapists, physical therapist assistants, plumbers, podiatrists, polygraph examiners, psychologists, real estate brokers, security salespersons, social workers, veterinarians.

Alaska

Division of Occupational Licensing, Department of Commerce and Economic Development, State of Alaska, P.O. Box 110806, Juneau, AK 99811-0806; 907-465-2534. Licensing boards and professions: architects, engineers, land surveyors, audiologists, barbers and hairdressers, chiropractors, collection agencies, construction contractors, concert promoters, dental professionals, dispensing opticians, electrical administrators, geologists, guides, hearing aid dealers, marine pilots, physicians, morticians, naturopaths, nursing, nursing home administrators, optometrists, pharmacists, physical therapists, psychologists, public accountants, veterinarians.

Arizona

Arizona Department of Revenue, 1600 West Monroe, Phoenix, AZ 85007; 602-542-4576. Licensing boards and professions: pharmacists, physical therapists, podiatrists, psychologists, chiropractors, dentists, teachers, homeopathic specialists, veterinarians, medical examiners, radiologic technicians, naturopathic physicians, nurses, opticians, optometrists, osteopaths, barbers, cosmetologists, real estate brokers, contractors, technical registrators, insurance agents, physician assistants, nursing care administrators.

Arkansas

Governor's Office, State Capitol Building, Little Rock, AR 72201; 501-682-2345. Licensing boards and professions: architects, abstracters, accountants, barber examiners, funeral directors, contractors, cosmetologists, dental examiners, electricians, speech pathologists, audiologists, nurses, pharmacists, real estate brokers, veterinary engineers, land surveyors, athletic trainers, chiropractors, collection agencies, counselors, embalmers, foresters, landscape architects, manufactured home builders, physicians, opticians, optometrists, podiatrists, psychologists, sanitarians, social workers, soil classifiers, therapy technologists.

California

State of California, Department of Consumer Affairs, 400 R Street, Sacramento, CA 95814; 916-323-2191, or 800-344-9940 (toll-free in CA). Licensing boards professions: professional engineers, cosmetologists, fabric care technicians, physical therapists, medical quality assurance, physician's assistants, chiropractors, acupuncture specialists, accountants, psychologists, registered nurses, pharmacists, architects, funeral directors, embalmers, landscape architects, veterinarians, animal health technicians, home Furnishings decorators, collection and investigative agents, dentists, dental auxiliaries, barbers, behavioral scientists, optometrists, shorthand reporters, structural pest control operators, athletic trainers, vocational nurses, psychiatric technicians, osteopaths, electronic repair dealers, personnel services, geologists and geophysicists, dispensing opticians/contact lens examiners, respiratory care specialists, nursing home administrators, podiatrists, hearing aid dispensers, speech pathologists, audiologists, tax preparers.

Colorado

Department of Regulatory Agencies, State Services Building, 1560 Broadway, Suite 1550, Denver, CO 80202; 303-894-7855. Licensing Board/Professions: accountants, architects, barbers, cosmetologists, chiropractors, dentists, electricians, engineers, hearing aid dealers, insurance agents, land surveyors, mobile home dealers, nurses, nursing home administrators, optometrists, outfitters, pharmacists and pharmacies, physical therapists, physicians, plumbers, psychologists, realtors, ski lift operators, social workers, veterinarians.

Connecticut

Occupational Licensing Division, Department of Consumer Products, 165 Capitol Avenue, Hartford, CT 06106; 203-566-1107, or 800-842-2649 (toll-free in CT). Licensed Occupations: electricians, plumbers, heating and cooling specialists, well drillers, elevator installers, home improvement contractors, arborists, TV and radio repair specialists. Licensed Health Professions: Department of Health Services, 150 Washington St., Hartford, CT 06106; 203-566-7398. Physicians, dentists, optometrists, osteopaths, naturopaths, homeopaths, chiropractors, psychologists, registered nurses, licensed practical nurses, dental hygienists, registered physical therapists, hypertrichologists, audiologists, speech pathologists, podiatrists, hairdressers, barbers, embalmers, funeral directors, sewer installers/cleaners, registered sanitarians, nursing home administrators, hearing aid dealers, opticians, veterinarians, occupational therapists. Other Licensed Professions: Contact Professional Licensing Division, 165 Capitol Avenue, Room G1, Hartford, CT 06106, 203-566-1814: architects, landscape architects, engineers, engineers-in-training, land surveyors, pharmacists, patent medicine distributors, mobile manufactured home parks.

Delaware

Division of Professional Regulation, P.O. Box 1401, O'Neil Building, Dover, DE 19903; 302-739-4522. Complaints in writing only. Licensed Professionals: architects, accountants, landscape architects, cosmetologists, barbers, podiatrists, chiropractors, dentists, electricians, adult entertainment, physicians, nurses, real estate brokers, land surveyors, private employment agencies, athletic (wrestling and boxing), deadly weapons dealers, nursing home administrators, funeral directors, social workers, speech pathologists, hearing aid dealers, audiologists, psychologists, veterinarians, optometrists, occupational therapists, pharmacists, river boat pilots.

District of Columbia

Department of Consumer and Regulatory Affairs, 614 H Street NW, Room 108, Washington, DC 20001; 202-727-7080. Licensing Board/Professions: accountants, architects, barbers, cosmetologists, dentists, dieticians, electricians, funeral directors, physicians, nurses, nursing home administrators, occupational therapists, optometrists, pharmacists, physical therapists, plumbers, podiatrists, engineers, psychologists, real estate agents, refrigeration and air conditioning specialists, social workers, steam and other operating engineers, veterinarians.

Florida

Florida Department of Professional Regulation, 1940 N. Monroe St., Tallahassee, FL 32399-075; 904-488-6602. Licensing boards and professions: accountants, architects, barbers, chiropractors, cosmetologists, dentists, dispensing opticians, electrical contractors, professional engineers and land surveyors, landscape architects, funeral directors and embalmers, medical examiners, hearing aid dispensers, naturopathics, nursing home administrators, nurses, optometrists, osteopaths, pharmacists, pilot commissioners, podiatrists, psychologists, real estate brokers, veterinarians, acupuncture technicians, radiological health technicians, laboratory services, entomology specialists, emergency medical personnel.

Georgia

Examining Board Division, Secretary of State, 166 Pryor Street, SW, Atlanta, GA 30303; 404-656-3900. Licensing boards and professions: accountants, architects, athletic trainers, auctioneers, barbers, chiropractors, construction industry, cosmetologists, professional counselors, social workers, marriage and family therapists, dietitians, dentists, engineers, land surveyors, foresters, funeral directors/embalmers, geologists, hearing aid dealers and dispensers, landscape architects, librarians, physicians, nurses, nursing home administrators, occupational therapists, dispensing opticians, optometrists, pharmacists, physical therapists, podiatrists, polygraph testers, practical nurses, private detectives and security agencies, psychologists, recreation specialists, sanitarians, speech pathologists, audiologists, used car dealers, used motor vehicle dismantlers, rebuilders, and salvage dealers, veterinarians, water and wastewater treatment plant operators and laboratory analysts.

Hawaii

Office of the Director, Department of Commerce and Consumer Affairs, P.O. Box 3469, Honolulu, HI 96801; 808-586-2850.

Licensing boards and professions: accountants, acupuncture specialists, barbers, boxers, chiropractors, contractors, cosmetologists, dental examiners, detectives and guards, electricians and plumbers, elevator mechanics, engineers, architects, land surveyors, landscape architects, hearing aid dealers and fitters, massage specialists, physicians, motor vehicle Industry, motor vehicle repair technicians, naturopaths, nurses, nursing home administrators, dispensing opticians, optometrists, osteopaths, pest control operators, pharmacists, physical therapists, psychologists, real estate brokers, speech pathologists, audiologists, veterinarians, embalmers/funeral directors, collection agencies, commercial employment agencies, mortgage and collection servicing agents, mortgage brokers and solicitors, port pilots, time sharing and travel agents.

Idaho

State of Idaho, Department of Self-Governing Agencies, Bureau of Occupational Licenses, Owyhee Plaza, 1109 Main, #220, Boise, ID 83702; 208-334-3233. Licensing boards and professions: accountants, athletic directors, bartenders, engineers, land surveyors, dentists, geologists, physicians, architects, barbers, chiropractors, cosmetologists, counselors, dentists, environmental health specialists, hearing aid dealers and fitters, landscape architects, morticians, nursing home administrators, optometrists, podiatrists, psychologists, social workers, outfitters and guides, pharmacists, public works contractors, real estate brokers.

Illinois

State of Illinois, Department of Professional Regulations, 320 W. Washington, Third Floor, Springfield, IL 62786; 217-785-0800. Licensed professions: athletic trainers, architects, barbers, cosmetologists, chiropractors, collection agencies, controlled substance specialists, dentists and dental auxiliaries, polygraph testers, detectives, embalmers, funeral directors, land sales, land surveyors, physicians, nurses, nursing home administrators, occupational therapists, optometrists, pharmacists, physical therapists, podiatrists, boxing and wrestling, engineers, psychologists, accountants, real estate brokers and salespersons, roofing contractors, shorthand reporters, social workers, structural engineers, veterinarians.

Indiana

Indiana Professional Licensing Agency, Indiana Government Center S., 302 W. Washington Street, Room E-034, Indianapolis, IN 46204; 317-232-3997. Licensing boards and professions: accountants, architects, auctioneers, barbers, beauticians, boxers, engineers and land surveyors, funeral directors, plumbers, real estate agents, TV-radio and watch repair technicians. Licensed health professionals: Indiana Health Professional Bureau, One America Square #1020, Indianapolis, IN 46282; 317-232-2960 for the following medical specialties: chiropractors, dentists, health facility administrators, nurses, optometrists, pharmacists, sanitarians, speech pathologists, audiologists, psychologists, veterinarians, hearing aid dealers, podiatrists, physical therapists.

Iowa

Bureau of Professional Licensing, Iowa Department of Health, Lucas State Office Building, Des Moines, IA 50319; 515-281-4401. Licensed professionals: dietitians, funeral directors and embalmers, hearing aid dealers, nursing home administrators, optometrists, ophthalmology dispensers, podiatrists, psychologists, physical and occupational therapists, occupational therapist assistants, social workers, speech pathologists and audiologists, respiratory care therapists, barbers, cosmetologists, chiropractors, nurses, physicians, dentists, pharmacists, veterinarians. Other licensed professionals: Professional Licensing Regulation Division, Department of Commerce, 1918 SE Hulsizer, Ankeny, IA 50021; 515-281-7400: accountants, engineers and land surveyors, landscape architects, architects, real estate agents.

Kansas

Secretary of State, State Capitol, 2nd Floor, Topeka, KS 66612; 913-296-3489. Licensing boards: abstracters, accountants, adult home administrators, operating engineers, plumbers and pipefitters, carpenters, electrical workers, attorneys, barbers, cosmetologists, court reporters, dentists and dental auxiliaries, educators, emergency medical services, healing arts specialists, hearing aid dispensers, insurance agents, land surveyors, embalmers/funeral directors, nurses, optometrists, pharmacists, physical therapists, podiatrists, private schools, real estate agents, engineers, architects, landscape architects, veterinarians.

Kentucky

Division of Occupations and Professions, P.O. Box 456, Frankfort, KY 40602-0456; 502-564-3296. Licensing boards and professions: hearing aid dealers, nurses, private schools, psychologists, social workers, speech and audiologists. Other licensed professionals: Kentucky Occupational Information Coordinating Committee, 275 E. Main St., Two Center, Frankfort, KY 40621; 502-564-4258: accountants, agriculture specialists, architects, auctioneers, bar examiners, barbers, chiropractors, dentists, hairdressers, cosmetologists, emergency medical technicians Services, radiation and product safety specialists, insurance agents, medical licensure supervisors, natural resources and environmental protection specialists, nursing home administrators, ophthalmic dispensers, optometric examiners, pharmacists, physical therapists, podiatrists, polygraph examiners, professional engineers and land surveyors, real estate agents, veterinarians.

Louisiana

Department of Economic Development, 101 France St., (P.O. Box 94185), Baton Rouge, LA 70802; 504-342-3000. Licensing boards and professions: acupuncture assistants, adoption agencies, adult day care administrators, agricultural consultants, alcoholic beverages solicitors, ambulatory surgical centers, arborists, archaeological investigators, architects, auctioneers, barbers, beauticians, bedding and furniture upholsterers, beer distributors, blind business enterprise operators, blood alcohol analysts, embalmers/funeral directors, accountants, shorthand reporters, chiropractors, pesticide applicators, driving school instructors, sewage/construction contractors, cotton buyers, waste-salvage oil operators, cut flower dealers, dairy product retailers, day care centers, fuels dealers, dentists, drug manufacturers, egg marketers, electrolysis technicians, embalmers, emergency medical technicians, employment service agencies, family support counselors, grain dealers, hearing aid dealers, hemodialysis clinics, home health centers, horticulturists, independent laboratories, sewage system installers, insurance, landscape architects, nurses, lime manufacturers, liquefied gas distributors, livestock

dealers, maternity homes, mental and substance abuse clinics, midwives, nursing home administrators, nursery stock dealers, occupational therapists, optometrists, pesticide dealers, pharmacists, physical therapists, physicians, physicians, plant breeders, plumbers, podiatrists, solid waste processors, seafood distributors, psychologists, radiation therapists, radio and television repair technicians, radiologic technologists, real estate brokers, sanitarians, social workers, speech pathologists and audiologists, veterinarians, voice stress analysts.

Maine

Department of Professional and Financial Regulation, State House Station 35, Augusta, ME 04333; 207-582-8700. Licensing boards and professions: veterinarians, itinerant vendors, consumer credit protection services, insurance agents, athletic trainers, real estate agents, geologists and soil scientists, solar energy auditors, hearing aid dealers and fitters, accountants, arborists, barbers, commercial drivers, education instructors, speech pathologists and audiologists, auctioneers, electricians, funeral directors, foresters, dietitians, nursing home administrators, oil and solid fuel installers, substance abuse counselors, mobile home parks, river pilots, physical therapists, plumbers, psychologists, social workers, radiological technicians, occupational therapists, respiratory care therapists, nurses, dentists, chiropractors, osteopaths, podiatrists, physicians, engineers, attorneys.

Maryland

Division of Maryland Occupational and Professional Licensing, 501 St. Paul Pl., 9th Floor, Baltimore, MD 21202; 410-333-6209. Licensed professionals: architects, master electricians, engineers, foresters, hearing aid dealers, landscape architects, pilots, plumbers, land surveyors, public accountants, second hand dealers, precious metal and gem dealers, pawnbrokers, real estate agents and brokers, home improvement contractors, barbers and cosmetologists. Referral to the licensing agency for collection agencies, mortgage brokers and insurance agents can be provided by the office listed above. Other licensed professions: Boards and Commissions, Department of Health and Dental Hygiene, 4201 Patterson Ave., Baltimore, MD 21215; 410-764-4747: audiologists, chiropractors, dentists, dietitians, electrologists, medical examiners, morticians, nurses, nursing home administrators, optometrists, occupational therapists, pharmacists, physical therapists, podiatrists, professional counselors, psychologists, environmental sanitarians, speech pathologists, social workers, well drillers, water work and waste system operators.

Massachusetts

Division of Registration, 100 Cambridge St., Boston, MA 02202; 617-727-3074. Licensing boards and professions: electrologists, gas fitters, hairdressers, health officers, landscape architects, licensed practical nurses, nursing home administrators, optometrists, physician's assistants, podiatrists, pharmacists, plumbers, psychologists, real estate brokers, registered nurses, sanitarians, speech pathologists, audiologists, social workers, tv-repair technicians, physical therapists, occupational therapists, athletic trainers, architects, barbers, barber shops, certified public accountants, chiropractors, dental hygienists, dentists, dispensing opticians, pharmacies, electricians, embalmers, engineers, veterinarians, cosmetologists, and real estate appraisers.

Michigan

Michigan Department of License and Regulation, P.O. Box 30018, Lansing, MI 48909; 517-373-1870. Licensing board and professions: accountants, architects, barbers, athletic control (wrestlers and boxers), builders, carnival amusement rides, cosmetologists.

Minnesota

Office of Consumer Services, Office of Attorney General, 1400 NCL Tower, 445 Minnesota Street, St. Paul, MN 55101; 612-296-2331. Licensing boards and professions: abstracters, accountants, adjusters, alarm and communications contractors, architects, assessors, attorneys, auctioneers, bailbondsmen, barbers, beauticians, boiler operators, boxing related occupations, brokers, building officials, burglar installers, chiropractors, clergy, cosmetologists, dentists, dental assistants, dental hygienists, private detectives, electricians, energy auditors, engineers, financial counselors/financial planners, funeral directors/embalmers/morticians, hearing aid dispensers, insurance agents, investment advisors, landscape architects, land surveyors, midwives, notary publics, nursing home administrators, optometrists, osteopathic physicians, pawnbrokers, peace officers, pharmacists, physical therapists, physicians, surgeons, physician's assistants, high pressure pipefitters, plumbers, podiatrists, practical nurses, precious metal dealers, process servers, psychologists, real estate brokers, registered nurses, rehabilitation consultants, sanitarians, securities brokers, tax preparers, teachers, tow truck operators, transient merchants, veterinarians, water conditioning contractors and installers, water and waste treatment operators, water well contractors/explorers/engineers. Information will be released only if action has been taken against a professional or business.

Mississippi

Secretary of State, P.O. Box 136, Jackson, MS 39205; 601-359-3123. Licensing boards and professions: agricultural aviation pilots, architects, landscape architects, athletic trainers, funeral directors, chiropractors, dentists, physicians, nurses, nursing home administrators, optometrists, pharmacists, physical therapists, psychologists, veterinarians, barbers, cosmetologists, engineers and land surveyors, foresters, polygraph examiners, public accountants, public contractors, real estate agents, accountants, lawyers, dental hygienists, audiologists, embalmers, professional counselors, and speech pathologists.

Missouri

Division of Professional Registration, Department of Economic Development, 3605 Missouri Blvd., Jefferson City, MO 65109; 314-751-0293. Licensing boards and professions: accountants, architects/engineers/land surveyors, athletic trainers, barbers, chiropractors, cosmetologists, professional counselors, dentists, embalmers/funeral directors, healing arts specialists, employment agencies, hearing aid dealers/fitters, nurses, optometrists, podiatrists, pharmacists, real estate agents, veterinarians, insurance agents, nursing home administrators, lawyers, dental hygienists, physicians, physical therapists, speech pathologists and audiologists, psychologists.

Montana

Professional and Occupational Licensing, Business Regulation, Department of Commerce, 111 N. Jackson St., Helena, MT 5-9620; 406-444-3737. Licensing boards and professions: accountants, acupuncturists, architects, athletic trainers, barbers, beer distributors, chiropractors, cosmetologists, dental hygienists, dentists, denturists, electricians, electrologists, employment Agencies, engineers and land surveyors, hearing aid dispensers, insurance, landscape architects, lawyers, librarians, medical doctors, morticians, nurses, nursing home administrators, occupational therapists, operating engineers (boiler), optometrists, osteopathic physicians, pawnbrokers, physical therapists, plumbers, podiatrists, polygraph examiners, private investigators, psychologists, contractors, radiologic technologists, real estate brokers and salesmen, sanitarians, securities brokers and salesmen, social workers and counselors, speech pathologists and audiologists, taxidermists, tourist campground and trailer courts, veterinarians, water well drillers.

Nebraska

Bureau of Examining Boards, Nebraska Department of Health, P.O. Box 95007, Lincoln, NE 68509; 402-471-2115. Licensing boards and health professions: athletic trainers, advanced emergency medical technicians, audiologist/speech pathologists, cosmetologists, chiropractors, dentists/dental hygienists, embalmers/funeral directors, hearing aid dealers and fitters, pharmacists, podiatrists, optometrists, physical therapists, nurses, nursing home administrators, massage specialists, occupational therapists, professional counselors, psychologists, respiratory care specialists, social workers, sanitarians, veterinarians. For other licensing boards and professions, contact the NE state operator at 402-471-2311 to be connected with the board that licenses the following professions: accountants, engineers/architects, barbers, abstracters, appraisers, land surveyors, landscape architects.

Nevada

State of Nevada Executive Chamber, Capitol Complex, 1 E. Liberty Street, #311, Reno, NV 89501; 702-786-0231. Licensing boards and professions: accountants, architects, athletic trainers, audiologists and speech pathologists, barbers, chiropractors, contractors, cosmetologists, dentists, engineers and land surveyors, funeral directors and embalmers, hearing aid specialists, homeopaths, landscape architects, liquefied petroleum gas distributors, marriage and family counselors, physicians, naturopathic healing arts specialists, nurses, dispensing opticians, optometrists, oriental medicine, osteopaths, pharmacists, physical therapists, podiatrists, private investigators, psychologists, short-hand reporters, taxicab drivers, veterinarians.

New Hampshire

SOICC of New Hampshire, 64 B Old Sun Cook Rd., Concord, NH 03301; 603-228-9500. Licensing boards and professions: accountants, emergency medical technicians, engineers/architects/land surveyors, attorneys, auctioneers, insurance (bailbondsmen), barbers, cosmetologists, chiropractors, court reporters, dentists, drivers education Instructors, electricians, funeral directors/embalmers, engineers, physicians, private security guards, lobbyists, nurses, nursing home administrators, occupational therapists, optometrists, psychologists, pesticide control operators, pharmacists, plumbers, podiatrists, real estate agents, teacher agents, veterinarians, water supply and pollution control operators.

New Jersey

Director, Centralized Licensing for the Licensing Boards, Division of Consumer Affairs, 140 E. Front Street, Trenton, NJ 08625; 609-826-7150. Licensing boards and professions: accountants, architects, barbers, beauticians, dentists, electrical contractors, marriage counselors, plumbers, morticians, nurses, ophthalmic dispensing technicians, optometrists, pharmacists, physical therapists, professional engineers and landscape surveyors, professional planners, psychological examiners, shorthand reporters, veterinarians, public movers and warehousemen, acupuncture specialists, landscape architects, athletic trainers, hearing aid dispensers, chiropractors, opthomologists.

New Mexico

Regulation and Licensing Department, 725 St. Michael's Drive, P.O. Box 25101, Santa Fe, NM 87504; 505-827-7000. Licensing boards and professions: accountants, architects, athletic promoters, barbers, chiropractors, cosmetologists, dentists, engineers and land surveyors, landscape architects, physicians, nurses, nursing home administrators, occupational therapists, optometrists, osteopaths, pharmacists, physical therapists, podiatrists, polygraphers, private investigators, psychologists, realtors, thanatopractice, veterinarians.

New York

New York State Education Department, Division of Professional Licensing, Cultural Education Center, Empire State Plaza, Albany, NY 12230; 518-474-3852, or 800-342-3729 (toll-free in NY). Licensed professionals: acupuncturists, architects, audiologists, certified shorthand reporters, chiropractors, dentists, landscape architects, land surveyors, massage therapists, physicians, osteopaths, nurses, occupational therapists, ophthalmic dispensers, optometrists, pharmacists, physical therapists, podiatrists, engineers, psychologists, public accountants, social workers, speech pathologists, veterinarians.

North Carolina

North Carolina Center for Public Policy Research, P.O. Box 430, Raleigh, NC 27602; 919-832-2839. Licensing boards and professions: architects, auctioneers, barbers, boiler operators, accountants, chiropractors, cosmetologists, registered counselors, dental, electrical contractors, foresters, general contractors, hearing aid dealers and fitters, landscape architects, landscape contractors, marital and family therapists, physicians, navigators and pilots, morticians, nurses, nursing home administrators, opticians, optometrists, osteopaths, pesticide operators, pharmacists, physical therapists, plumbers and heating specialists, podiatrists, practicing psychologists, private protective services, professional engineers and land surveyors, public librarians, real estate, refrigeration technicians, sanitarians, social workers, speech and language pathologists, structural pest control operators, veterinarians, waste water treatment operators, water treatment facility operators.

North Dakota

North Dakota Legislative Council Library, 600 East Boulevard Avenue, Bismarck, ND 58505; 701-224-2916. Licensing boards and professions: abstracters, accountants, architects, athletic trainers, audiologists and speech pathologists, barbers, chiroprac-

tors, cosmetologists, dentists, dietitians, electricians, embalmers, emergency medical services, engineers and land surveyors, hearing aid dealers and fitters, massage therapists, physicians, nurses, nursing home administrators, occupational therapists, optometrists, pharmacists, physical therapists, plumbers, podiatrists, private investigators, private police security, psychologists, real estate agents, respiratory care specialists, social workers, soil classifiers, veterinarians, water well contractors.

Ohio

State of Ohio, Department of Administrative Services, Division of Computer Services, 30 East Broad St., 40th Floor, Columbus, OH 43215-0409; 614-466-2000. Licensed professionals: wholesale distributors of dangerous drugs, terminal distributors of dangerous drugs, pharmacists, accountants, barbers, barber shops, beauty shops, managing cosmetologists, cosmetologists, manicurists, architects, landscape architects, practical nurses, registered nurses, surveyors, engineers, surveyors, dentists, dental hygienists, osteopaths, physicians, podiatrists, chiropractors, midwives, embalmers, funeral directors, embalmer and funeral directors, hat cleaners, dry cleaners, public employment agencies, auctioneers, private investigators, auctioneers.

Oklahoma

Governor's Office, State Capitol, Oklahoma City, OK 73105; 405-521-2342 or State Information Operator, 405-521-2011. Licensing board and professions: accountants, real estate agents, physicians, foresters, medico-legals, nursing homes, nurses, optometrists, osteopaths, physicians, pharmacists, polygraph examiners, psychologists, shorthand reporters, social workers, speech pathologists, veterinarians, landscape architects, architects, chiropractors, cosmetologists, dentists, embalmers and funeral directors. For other licensed professionals, contact Occupational Licensing, OK State Health Department, 1000 North East, 10th Street, Oklahoma City, OK 73117; 405-271-5217: barbers, hearing aid dealers, electricians, water and waste treatment plant operators.

Oregon

Department of Economic Development, Small Business Advocates, 595 Cottage St. NE, Salem, OR 97310; 800-547-7842 or 800-233-3306 (toll-free in OR). Licensing boards and professions: accountants, architects, barbers and hairdressers, builders, contractors, collection agencies, debt consolidators, geologists, landscape architects, landscape contractors, and TV/radio service dealers, engineering examiners, fire marshals, insurance agents, maritime pilots, real estate agents, tax practitioners.

Pennsylvania

Bureau of Professional and Occupational Affairs, 618 Transportation and Safety Building, Harrisburg, PA 17120-2649; 717-787-8503, or 800-822-2113 (toll-free in PA). Licensing boards and professions: accountants, architects, auctioneers, barbers, cosmetology, funeral directors, landscape architects, professional engineers, real estate agents. For licensed health professions, contact Bureau of Professional and Occupational Affairs, Secretary of State, 618 Transportation and Safety Building, Harrisburg, PA 17120; 717-783-1400: dentists, physicians, nurses, nursing home administrators, occupational therapists, optometrists, osteopaths, pharmacists, physical therapists, podiatrists, psychologists, speech-language and hearing specialists, veterinarians, navigators.

Rhode Island
Rhode Island Occupational Information Coordinating Commission, 22 Hayes Street, Providence, RI 02908; 401-272-0830. Licensing boards and professions: nurses aides, psychologists, respiratory therapists, sanitarians, speech pathologists, veterinarians, physical therapists, plumbers, podiatrists, prosthetists, nurses, nursing home administrators, occupational therapists, opticians, optometrists, osteopaths, physician assistants, embalmers/funeral directors, hairdressers, cosmetologists, manicurists, massage therapists, physicians, midwives, acupuncturists, athletic trainers, audiologists, barbers, barber shops, chiropractors, dentists, dental hygienists, electrologist, architects, coastal resource management, engineers and land surveyors.

South Carolina
South Carolina State Library, 1500 Senate St., Columbia, SC 29201; 803-734-8666. Licensing boards and professions: accountants, architects, auctioneers, barbers, morticians, chiropractors, contractors, cosmetologists, dentists, engineers, environmental systems (well diggers), foresters, funeral services, landscape architects, physicians, nurses, nursing home administrators, occupational therapists, opticians, optometrists, pharmacists, physical therapists, professional counselors, marriage and family therapists, psychologists, real estate agents, sanitarians, home builder, social workers, speech pathologist/audiologists, veterinarians, athletic trainers (boxing and wrestling), geologists.

South Dakota
Department of Commerce and Regulation, 500 E. Capitol Ave., Pierre, SD 57501-5070; 605-773-3178. South Dakota Medical and Osteopath Examiners, 1323 S. Minnesota Avenue, Sioux Falls, SD 57105; 605-336-1965. Licensing boards and professions: physicians, osteopaths, physician's assistants, physical therapists, medical corporations, emergency technicians, abstracters, accountants, barbers, chiropractors, cosmetologists, electricians, engineers/architects, funeral directors, hearing aid dispensers, medical/osteopaths, nurses, nursing home administrators, optometrists, pharmacists, plumbers, podiatrists, psychologists, real estate agents, social workers, veterinarians.

Tennessee
Division of Regulatory Boards, Department of Commerce and Insurance, 500 James Robertson Parkway, Nashville, TN 37243; 615-741-3449. Licensing boards and professions: accountants, architects and engineers, auctioneers, barbers, collection services, contractors, cosmetologists, funeral directors and embalmers, land surveyors, motor vehicle salesmen and dealers, personnel recruiters, pharmacists, polygraph examiners, real estate. For other licensed health professionals, contact Division of Health Related Professions, Department of Health and Environment, 283 or 287 Plus Park Blvd Complex, Nashville, TN 37247-1010; 615-367-6220: dentists, dental hygienists, podiatrists, physicians, physician's assistants, osteopaths, optometrists, veterinarians, nursing home administrators, dispensing opticians, chiropractors, social workers, hearing aid dispensers, registered professional

environmentalists, marital and family counselors, speech pathology/audiologists, occupational and physical therapists, x-ray technicians, registered nurses, licensed practical nurses.

Texas
Texas Department of Commerce, 410 E. 5th Street, P.O. Box 12047, Austin, TX 78711-2728; 512-320-0110, or 800-888-0511 (toll-free in TX). Licensing boards and professions: accountants, architects, barbers, cosmetologists, morticians, educators, public safety, chiropractors, psychologists, dentists, real estate agents, engineers, veterinarians, insurance agents, land surveyors, landscape architects, fitting and dispensing of hearing aids, private investigators and private security agencies, polygraph, Vocational nurses, nursing home administrators, physicians, optometrists, structural pest control operators, pharmacists, physical therapists, plumbers, podiatrists, professional counselors, dietitians, speech-language pathology and audiology.

Utah
Division of Occupational and Professional Licensing, Department of Business Regulation, Heber M. Wells Building, 160 East 300 South, P.O. Box 45805, Salt Lake City, UT 84145-0805; 801-530-6628. Licensing boards and professions: accountants, architects, barbers, cosmetologists, electrologists, chiropractors, podiatrists, dentists, dental hygienists, embalmers, funeral directors, pre-need sellers, engineers, land surveyors, physicians, surgeons, Naturopaths, registered nurses, licensed practical nurses, nurse midwives, nurse anesthetists, nurse specialists, prescriptive practice specialist, IV therapists, optometrists, osteopaths, pharmacists, pharmacies, manufacturing pharmacies, shorthand reporters, veterinarians, health facility administrators, sanitarians, morticians, physical therapists, psychologists, clinical social workers, conduct research on controlled substance, marriage and family therapists, master therapeutic recreational specialists, speech pathologists, audiologists, occupational therapists, hearing aid specialists, massage therapists, massage establishments, acupuncture practitioners, physician assistants, dieticians, contractors.

Vermont
Division of Licensing and Registration, Secretary of State, Pavilion Office Building, Montpelier, VT 05609; 802-828-2363. Licensing boards and professions: accountants, architects, barbers, boxing control, chiropractors, cosmetologists, dentists, engineers, funeral directors/embalmers, land surveyors, medical board (physicians, podiatrists, real estate brokers, veterinarians, physical therapists, social workers, physician assistants, motor vehicle racing, nurses, nursing home administrators, opticians, optometrists, osteopaths, pharmacies, pharmacist, psychologists, private detectives, security Guards, radiological technicians.

Virginia
Virginia Department of Commerce, 3600 W. Broad St., Richmond, VA 23230; 804-367-8500. Licensed professions: accountants, architects, auctioneers, audiologists, barbers, boxers, contractors, commercial driver training schools, employment agencies, professional engineers, geologists, hairdressers, harbor pilots, hearing aid dealers and fitters, landscape architects, nursing home administrators, librarians, opticians, polygraph

examiners, private security services, real estate brokers, speech pathologists, land surveyors, water and wastewater works operators, wrestlers. For licensed health professions, contact receptionist, Health Professionals: 804-662-9900. The office listed above can provide you with phone numbers for the following licensing boards: dentists, funeral directors/embalmers, physicians, medical/legal assistants, nurses, optometrists, pharmacists, psychologists, professional counselors, social workers, veterinarians.

Washington

Department of Health, P.O. Box 47860, Olympia, WA 98504-7860; 206-586-4561. Licensed professions: acupuncturists, auctioneers, architects, barbers, camp club registration/salespersons, chiropractors, cosmetology schools/ instructors, cosmetologists, manicurists, collection agencies, debt adjusters/agencies, dentists, dental hygienists, drugless therapeutic-naturopaths, employment agencies/managers, professional engineers, engineers-in-training, land surveyors, engineering corporations/partnerships, escrow officers/agents, firearms dealers, embalmers, apprentice embalmers, funeral directors, funeral establishments, hearing aid dispensers/trainees, land development registration, landscape architects, massage operators, midwives, notary publics, nursing home administrators, occularists, occupational therapists, dispensing opticians, optometrists, osteopaths, osteopathic physician/ surgeon, osteopathic physician assistants, physicians, surgeons, physician's assistants, limited physician, podiatrists, practical nurses, psychologists, physical therapists, real estate (brokers, salespersons, corporations, partnerships, branch offices), land development representatives, registered nurses, timeshare registration and salespersons, veterinarians, animal technicians.

West Virginia

Administrative Law Division, Secretary of State, State Capitol, Charleston, WV 25305; 304-558-6000. Licensing boards and professions: accountants, architects, barbers, beauticians, chiropractors, dentists, and dental hygienists, embalmers and funeral directors, engineers, foresters, hearing-aid dealers, landscape architects, land surveyors, law examiners, physicians, practical nurses, registered nurses, nursing home administrators, occupational therapists, optometrists, osteopaths, pharmacists, physical therapists, psychologists, radiologic technicians, real estate agents, sanitarians, state water resources, veterinarians.

Wisconsin

Department of Regulation and Licensing, P.O. Box 8935, Madison, WI 53708; 608-266-7482. Licensed professions: accountants, animal technicians, architects, architects, engineers, barbers, bingo organizations, morticians, chiropractors, cosmetologists, distributors of dangerous drugs, dental hygienists, dentists, interior designers, private detectives, drug manufacturers, electrologists, professional engineers, funeral directors, hearing aid dealers/fitters, land surveyors, manicurists, physicians, surgeons, nurse midwives, registered nurses, licensed practical nurses, nursing home administrators, optometrists, pharmacists, physical therapists, physician's assistants, podiatrists, psychologists, raffle organizations, real estate brokers, beauty salons, electrolysis salons, veterinarians.

Wyoming

Governor's Office, State Capitol, Cheyenne, WY 82002; 307-777-7434. Licensing boards and professions: funeral directors and embalmers, health service administrators, buyers and purchasing agents, shorthand reporters, medical record technicians, accountants and auditors, claims adjusters, appraisers, engineers, architects, surveyors, interior designers and decorators, medical laboratory workers, dental laboratory technicians, opticians, radiological technicians, respiratory technicians, quality control inspectors, security salespeople, insurance agents, real estate agents, physicians, physician's assistants, chiropractors, pharmacists, occupational therapists, activity therapists, physical therapists, speech pathologist and audiologist, veterinarian, optometrist, dietitians, dentists, dental hygienists, registered nurses, licensed practical nurses, emergency medical technicians, nurse's aides, medical assistants, counselors, lawyers, legal assistants, cosmetologists and barbers.

State Company Directories

Market Info, Mailing Lists, Databases Available From State Company Directories

Would you like to know what kind of computing systems and software 24,000 manufacturing firms in California use? Or where to find out what materials 7,000 manufacturers in North Carolina need for their manufacturing processes? Or which of 2,700 manufacturers in Nevada have contracts with the federal government? You can get quick answers to these questions and more in the state directories of manufacturing companies.

These directories contain valuable information concerning what products are bought, sold, and distributed in each state. At the very least, each directory lists the companies' names, addresses, phone numbers, products, and SIC codes, and is cross- referenced by company name, location, and SIC code/product. So, if you want to find out which companies in Tennessee manufacture a certain type of electronic component and where they are located, all you have to do is look it up in the product index. If you want to find out what manufacturing firms are operating in a certain town or county, the geographic index will tell you. These directories can be invaluable for targeting new market areas, monitoring industry trends, developing more effective mailing lists, and much more.

The majority of these directories are put out by the individual state's Chamber of Commerce or Department of Economic Development, while private publishing firms compile and distribute the rest. The price and sophistication of these directories vary widely from state to state. While some, like Montana's, may offer only the basic information mentioned above, others, like the

Illinois directory, will also include key personnel, CEO, parent company, employment figures, import/export market, computer system used, and more. Prices range from $5 for Wyoming's directory, all the way to $165 for California's directory. Most of the prices listed below include shipping and handling, and state sales tax where applicable.

Many of these directories are also available in database formats and differ widely in cost. While there are some real bargains, such as Rhode Island's directory of 2,600 firms on diskette for $50, some, like Texas's of 18,000 firms, will cost you $1,000. Before ordering any of these databases, make sure that the software is compatible with your own system. Mailing labels for many of the directories are also available, and many states allow you to choose the companies you want for your mailing list on a cost per label basis.

List of State Company Directories

Alabama
Alabama Development Office, Research Division, State Capitol, 135 S. Union Street, Montgomery, AL 36130; 205-242-0400. $55. Listing of 6,500 companies includes name, address, phone, CEO, year established, employee figures, product lines, parent company, import/export, and SIC code. Cross-referenced by company name, location, product, parent company, international trade, and SIC code. Available on diskette. There is a $35 set up fee plus $.09 for each record. Entire state would be $600.

Alaska
Alaska Center for International Business, University of Alaska, 3211 Providence, Suite 203, Anchorage, AK 99508; 907-786-4300. *The Alaska Trade Directory*, a listing of 150 Alaska companies and industries that import or export, includes name, address, phone, CEO, key personnel, market area, product/service, and SIC code. Cross-referenced by company name and product/SIC code. Prices available on request.

Arizona

Phoenix Chamber of Commerce, Bank One Plaza, 201 N. Central, Suite 2700, Phoenix, AZ 85073; 602-254-5521. $75. Listing of 5,000 companies includes name, address, phone, CEO, employee figures, market area, products, and SIC code. Cross-referenced by company name, location, market area, and products/SIC code. Diskette format, $403.

Arkansas

Arkansas Industrial Development Foundation, P.O. Box 1784, Little Rock, AR 72203; 501-682-1121. $50. Listing of 2,500 companies includes name, address, phone, contact person, parent company, products, and SIC code. Cross-referenced by company name, location, and product/SIC code.

California

Database Publishing Company, 523 Superior Avenue, Newport Beach, CA 92663; 800-888-8434. $165. Listing of 24,000 companies includes name, address, phone, CEO, key personnel, sales volume, year established, parent company, products, computer brand used, import/export, employee figures, and SIC code. Cross- referenced by company name, location, products, and SIC code. Available on diskette for $975, book included.

Colorado

Business Research Division, University of Colorado, Campus Box 420, Boulder, CO 80309; 303-492-8227. $75. Listing of 4,700 companies includes name, address, phone, employee figures, market area, CEO, products, and SIC code. Cross-referenced by company name, location, and SIC code. Available in database format for $395. Mailing labels: $275/set. Prices may vary.

Connecticut

Connecticut Labor Department, Employment Security Division, Attn: Business Management, 200 Folly Brook Boulevard, Weathersfield, CT 06109; 203-566-3470. $24. The 1984 directory of 4,000 companies includes name, address, products, and SIC code. Cross-referenced by company name, location, products, and SIC codes. A quarterly updated listing is available for $7/year.

MacRae's Industrial Directories, 817 Broadway, 3rd Floor, New York, NY 10003; 800-622-7237. $129.50. Listing of 8,200 CT manufacturing firms includes name, address, phone, parent company, key personnel, employee figures, size, products, and SIC code. Cross-referenced by company name, location, and SIC code.

Delaware

Delaware State Chamber of Commerce, 1201 N. Orange Street, P.O. Box 671, Wilmington, DE 19899; 302-655-7221. $45 for state Chamber members; $55 for non-members. The directory of commerce and industry, listing over 5,600 companies, includes name, address, phone, CEO, employee figures, products/services, and SIC code. Cross-referenced by company name, location, and SIC code. Mailing labels: 25 cents/company.

Florida

Harris Publishing Company, 2057 Aurora Road, Twinsburg, OH 44087; 800-888-5900. $85. Listing of over 9,000 companies includes name, address, phone, CEO, employee figures, products, import/export, and SIC code. Cross-referenced by company name, location, and SIC code. Available on diskette, $325. Mailing labels: 10 cents per company, $150 per 1,000 names, 1,000 minimum.

Georgia

Georgia Department of Industry and Trade, Directory Section, P.O. Box 56706, Atlanta, GA 30343; 404-656-3619. $55. Listing of 8,000 companies includes name, address, phone, market area, parent company, key personnel, employee figures, year established, products, and SIC code. Cross-referenced by company name, location and SIC code.

Hawaii

Chamber of Commerce of Hawaii, 735 Bishop Street, Honolulu, HI 96813; 808-522-8800. $45. The current edition of over 150 companies includes name, address, phone, contact person, product, and SIC code. Cross-referenced by company name, location, and SIC code.

Idaho

Center for Business Development and Research, University of ID, Moscow, ID 83844-3227; 208-885-6611. The new directory of over 1,300 manufacturers will include name address, phone, CEO, product/service, contact person, import/ export, employee figures, and SIC code. Cross-referenced by company name, location, and SIC code. Diskette: PC compatible, cost available upon request.

Illinois

Harris Publishing Company, 2057 Aurora Road, Twinsburg, OH 44087; 800-321-9136. $145. Listing of over 20,000 companies includes name, address, phone, CEO, employee figures, computer brand used, year established, sales volume, product, and SIC code. Cross-referenced by company name, location, product, and SIC code. Diskette format, containing 9,000 companies with 20 or more employees, available for $325.

Indiana

Harris Publishing Company, 2057 Aurora Road, Twinsburg OH 44087; 800-321-9136. $98. Listing of over 8,000 companies includes name, address, phone, CEO, employee figures, year established, annual sales, computer brand used, products, and SIC code. Cross-referenced by company name, location, product, and SIC code. Diskette format, containing 6,000 companies with 10 or more employees, available for $295.

Iowa

Iowa Department of Economic Development, Research Section, 200 East Grand Avenue, Des Moines, IA 50309; 515-281-3925. $67. Listing of over 5,000 companies includes name, address, phone, CEO, purchasing agent, parent company, employee figures, product, and SIC code. Cross-referenced by company name, location, product, and SIC code. Available on diskette,

$299. Contact Harris Publishing, 2057 Aurora Road, Twinsburg, Oh 44087; 800-888-5900.

Kansas

Kansas Department of Commerce, 700 SW Harrison Street, Suite 1300, Topeka, KS 66603-3712; 913-296-3481. $40. Listing of 4,000 companies includes name, address, phone, contact person, parent company, employee figures, product, and SIC code. Cross-referenced by company name, location, product, and SIC code. Diskettes will be available in 1994.

Kentucky

Department of Economic Development, Maps and Publications, 133 Holmes Street, Frankfort, KY 40601; 502-564-4715. $30. Listing of 3,600 companies includes name, address, phone, CEO, year established, employee figures, products, and SIC code. Cross-referenced by company name, location, and SIC code.

Louisiana

Department of Economic Development, Commerce and Industry, P.O. Box 94185, Baton Rouge, LA 70804-9185; 504-342-5361. $55. Listing of 3,000 companies includes name, address, phone, CEO, purchasing agent, marketing area, import/export, products, and SIC code. Cross-referenced by company name, location, and SIC code. Database price available on request.

Maine

Maine Manufacturing Directory, Tower Publishing Company, 34 Diamond Street, P.O. Box 7220, Portland, ME 04112; 800-431-2665 in-state; 207-774-5361 out-of-state. $42.50. Listing of 2,200 companies includes name, address, phone, three contact persons, employee figures, gross sales, product, and SIC code. Cross-referenced by company name, location, and SIC code. Mailing labels: $55 for first 1,000, then 5 cents each. Diskettes, $225.

Maryland

Harris Publishing Company, 2057 Aurora Rd., Twinsburg, OH 44087; (800) 888-5900. $62. Listing of 2,500 companies includes name, address, phone, employee figures, year established, annual sales, products, key personnel, and SIC code. Divided into sections by company name, location, industry, import/ export, products, and SIC code. Mailing labels: $75 per 1,000 names, minimum charge $150. Diskette available for $249.

Massachusetts

George D. Hall Publishing Company, 50 Congress Street, Boston, MA 02109; 617-523-3745. $67.95 in-state; $56.95 out-of-state. Listing of 7,400 companies includes name, address, phone, CEO, sales volume, employee figures, products, and SIC code. Cross-referenced by company name, location, and product. Database format on diskette for any 3,000 companies available for $400. Mailing labels $225 minimum per 3,000; 6 cents/name.

Michigan

Harris Publishing Company, 2057 Aurora Road, Twinsburg, OH 44087; 800-321-9136. $145. Listing of 14,000 companies includes name, address, phone, CEO, employee figures, computer brands used, year established, products, and SIC code.

Cross-referenced by company name, location, product, and SIC code. Diskette format, containing 7,000 companies with 20 or more employees, available for $325.

Minnesota

National Information Systems, 4401 West 76th Street, Edina, MN 55435; 612-893-8308. $83.49. Listing of 9,000 companies includes name, address, phone, contact person, employee figures, sales volume, year established, products, and SIC code. Cross-referenced by company name, location, and product/SIC code.

Mississippi

Mississippi Department of Economic and Community Development, 1400 Walter Sillers Bldg., P.O. Box 849, Jackson, MS 39205; 601-359-3448. $50. Listing of 2,600 companies includes name, address, phone, CEO, key personnel, employee figures, parent company, products, international trade, and SIC code. Cross-referenced by company name, location, product, and SIC code. Available on diskette for $400, and $200 for yearly update.

Missouri

Harris Publishing Company, 2057 Aurora Road, Twinsburg, OH 44087; 800-321-9136. $97. Listing of 8,000 companies includes name, address, phone, CEO, employee figures, computer brand used, year established, product, and SIC code. Cross-referenced by company name, location, product, and SIC code. Diskette format, containing 4,800 companies with 10 or more employees, available for $299.

Montana

Department of Commerce, Business Assistance Division, 1424 9th Avenue, Helena, MT 59620; 406-444-3923. $20. Listing of 2,500 companies includes name, address, phone, owner, size classification, products, and SIC code. Cross- referenced by company name, location, product, and SIC code.

Nebraska

Nebraska Department of Economic Development, P.O. Box 94666, Lincoln, NE 68509; 402-471-3784. $40. Listing of 1,849 companies includes name, address, phone, CEO, parent company, employee figures, import/export, products, and SIC code. Cross-referenced by company name, location, and product/SIC code. Available on IBM compatible diskette for $150.

Nevada

Gold Hill Publishing Company, P.O. Drawer F, Virginia City, NV 89440; 702-847-0222. $109. Listing of 6,530 companies includes name, address, phone, parent company, CEO, key personnel, Fax #, square footage occupied, sales volume, products, import/ export, federal contracts, year established, years in NV, products, and SIC code. Cross-referenced by company name, location, and product/SIC code. Available on diskette for $400.

New Hampshire

Department of Resources and Economic Development, Industrial Development Office, 172 Pembroke Road, P.O. Box 1856, Concord NH 03302-1856; 603-271-2591. $47.50. Listing of

4,800 companies includes name, address, phone, CEO, ranking officers, year established, sales volume, import/export, products, and SIC code. Cross-referenced by company name, location, and product/SIC code. Available on IBM compatible diskette for $250/set of 4 + $4.74 postage and handling. To order, call Tower Publications, 800-969-8693.

New Jersey

Commerce Register, Inc., 190 Godwin Avenue, Midland Park, NJ 07432; 800-221-2172. $98.05. Listing of 11,000 companies includes name, address, phone, key personnel, sales volume, products, employee figures, square footage and acreage occupied, year established, SIC code, and bank, accountants, and law firms used. Cross-referenced by company name, location, and product/SIC code. Available on diskette for $155 minimum charge, depending on number of listings ordered.

New Mexico

Department of Economic Development, Joseph M. Montoya Building, 1100 St. Francis Dr., Santa Fe, NM 87503; 505-827-0300. $25. Listing of 1,800 companies includes name, address, phone, CEO, employee figures, products/ services, and SIC code. Cross-referenced by company name, location, and product/SIC code.

New York

MacRAE's Industrial Directories, 817 Broadway, 3rd Floor, New York, NY 10003; 800-622-7237. $135. Listing of 12,000 companies includes name, address, phone, key personnel, size classification, products, location, and SIC code. Diskette price, $400.

North Carolina

North Carolina Business Industry, Dept. D, P.O. Box 25249, Raleigh, NC 27611; 919-733-4151. $52.50. The new edition of 7,000 companies includes name, address, phone, CEO, year established, employee figures, parent company, import/export, product, and purchasing and product SIC codes. Cross-referenced by company name, location, parent company, product, products purchased, and import/export capabilities. Available on IBM magnetic tape database format for $1,000.

North Dakota

North Dakota Department of Economic Development and Finance, 1833 E. Bismarck Express, Bismarck, ND 58504; 701-224-2810. $50. Listing of over 600 companies includes name, address, phone, contact person, employee figures, products, and SIC code. Cross-referenced by company name, location, and product/SIC code. Diskette price $50.

Ohio

Harris Publishing Company, 2057 Aurora Road, Twinsburg, OH 44087; 800-321-9136. $145. Listing of 18,000 companies includes name, address, phone, CEO, employee figures, year established, annual sales, computer brand used, products, and SIC code. Cross-referenced by company name, location, product, and SIC code. Diskette format, containing 8,700 companies with 20 or more employees, available for $325.

Oklahoma

Oklahoma Department of Commerce, P.O. Box 26980, Marketing Division, Oklahoma City, OK 73126-0980; 405-843-9770, ext. 207. $40. Listing of 4,500 companies includes name, address, phone, owner's name, employee figures, product, and SIC code. Cross-referenced by company name, location, product, and SIC code.

Oregon

Oregon Economic Development Department, 775 Summer Street, NE, Salem, OR 97310; 503-986-0123. $75. Listing of 7,500 companies includes name, address, phone, employee figures, parent company, CEO, import/export, products, and SIC code. Cross-referenced by company name, product, and SIC code. Available in database formats and mailing labels at variable cost.

Pennsylvania

Harris Publishing Company, 2057 Aurora Road, Twinsburg, OH 44087; 800-321-9136. $145. Listing of 18,000 companies includes name, address, phone, CEO, employee figures, computer brand used, year established, products, and SIC code. Cross-referenced by company name, location, product, and SIC code. IBM compatible diskette format, containing 8,800 companies with 20 or more employees, available for $325.

Rhode Island

Department of Economic Development, Research Division, 7 Jackson Walkway, Providence, RI 02903; 401-277-2601. $10 for RI residents; $30 for non-residents. Listing of 2,600 companies includes name, address, phone, CEO, employee figures, parent company, products, and SIC code. Cross-referenced by company name, location, and SIC code. Available on IBM or MacIntosh compatible diskette for $50. Mailing labels: 5 cents per name.

South Carolina

State Development Board, P.O. Box 927, Columbia, SC 29202; 803-737-0400. Attn: Industrial Directory sales. $60. Listing of 3,200 companies includes name, address, phone, CEO, geographical location, purchasing agent, employee figures, product line, parent company, and SIC code. Cross-referenced by company name, location, product, and SIC code. Available on IBM compatible diskette for $500. Mailing labels: $50 set up fee, 10 cents per label.

South Dakota

Governor's Office of State Economic Development, Capitol Lake Plaza, Pierre, SD 57501; 605-773-5032. $35. Listing of 1,000 companies includes name, address, phone number, trade name, county, Fax number, marketing area, employee figures, CEO, purchasing agent, sales manager, products, and SIC code. Cross-referenced by company name, location, and SIC code. Mailing labels: $35/set.

Tennessee

M. Lee Smith Publishers and Printers, P.O. Box 198867, Arcade Station, Nashville, TN 37219; 615-242-7395. $68 in-state; $65 out-of-state. Listing of 5,300 companies includes name, address, phone, parent company, key personnel, employee figures, marketing area, computer brand used, products, and SIC code.

Available in database format, magnetic tape or diskette: $100 conversion fee, then $250 per 1,000 chosen. Mailing labels: $90 per 1,000. Diskette is available for $395. Diskette and book available for $345.

Texas

University of Texas, Bureau of Business Research, P.O. Box 7459, Austin, TX 78713-7459; 512-471-1616. $130. Two volume directory of 18,000 companies includes name, address, phone, key personnel, year established, sales volume, employee figures, market area, import/export, products, and SIC code. Volume 1 lists companies by name; volume 2 lists companies by product/SIC code. Available on diskette from $300 per section, or $1000 for entire state listing, 18,000 companies.

Utah

Utah Department of Community and Economic Development, 324 S. State St., Suite 500, Salt Lake City, UT 84111; 801-538-8700. $26. Listing of 2,600 companies includes name, address, phone, employee figures, products, and SIC code. Cross-referenced by company name and SIC code. Available in dBase 3 database format, high or low density diskettes. Prices may vary.

Vermont

Vermont Business Magazine, 2 Church Street, Burlington, VT 05401; 802-863-8038. $10 plus tax in-state; $15 out of state. Listing of 2,500 companies includes name, address, phone, geographical listing, plant location, CEO, parent company products trade names, products exported, employee figures, retail/mail order/or wholesale distribution, and SIC code. Cross-referenced by company name, location, and product/SIC code. Available on diskette for $300.

Virginia

Virginia Chamber of Commerce, 9 South 5th Street, Richmond, VA 23219; 804-644-1607. $78.38 in-state; $75 out-of-state. Listing of 4,000 companies includes name, address, phone, CEO, employee figures parent company, products, and SIC code. Cross-referenced by product, SIC code, county, and city.

Available in ASCII and ABCDIC magnetic tape database formats for $225. Mailing labels vary in price.

Washington

Database Publishing Company, 523 Superior Avenue, Newport Beach, CA 92663; 800-888-8434. $99. Listing of 4,100 companies includes name, address, phone, CEO, key personnel, sales volume, year established, parent company, products, computer brand used, employee figures, import/export, product, and SIC code. Cross-referenced by company name, location, products, and SIC code. Diskette available for $395. Mailing labels, $65/1,000.

West Virginia

Harris Publishing Company, 2057 Aurora Rd., Twinsburg, OH 44087; 800-321-9136. $49. Listing of 1,200 companies includes name, address, phone, CEO, employee figures, computer brand used, year established, products, and SIC code. Cross-referenced by company name, location, product, and SIC code. Diskette price, $249.

Wisconsin

WMC Service Corporation, P.O. Box 352, 501 East Washington Street, Madison, WI 53701-0352; 608-258-3400. $89.68/member, $131.88/non-member. Listing of 9,000 companies includes name, address, phone, CEO, year established, computer brand used, employee figures, parent company, Fax #, import/export, out-of-state affiliates, products, and SIC code. Cross-referenced by company name, location, product, and SIC code. Available on IBM compatible diskette $300/member, $450/non-member.

Wyoming

Department of Commerce, Division of Economic and Community Development, Barrett Bldg. 4 North, Cheyenne, WY 82002; 307-777-7284. $5 in-state, $15 out-of-state. Listing of 250 companies includes name, address, phone, CEO, market area, employee figures, product, and SIC code. Cross-referenced by company name, location, and SIC code. Diskette price $5 in-state, $15 out-of-state.

Company Background Reports
Free From Better Business Bureaus

If you are looking for information on a private or public company, and the company sells goods and services to consumers, you would be wise to check with the local Better Business Bureau in the city closest to the company's headquarters. A recent investigation into a patent research firm by our staff turned up a comprehensive report which outlined the company's activities, officers, claims and problems. For example, it revealed that the state of Wisconsin had filed a suit against the company. Moreover, it also outlined the company's response to the lawsuit.

The Better Business Bureaus (BBB) around the country provide this service **free** to consumers who may be interested in dealing with any given company. Simply call, and the local BBB will search its files for any information about the company in question. If the report is brief and straightforward, they will read it over the telephone. If it is more complex, like the report on the patent research company, a copy of it will be sent to you free of charge.

Listed below are the telephone numbers for the Better Business Bureaus in the U.S. and Canada.

Better Business Bureau Directory

Alabama
Birmingham	205-558-2222
Dothan	205-792-3804
Huntsville	205-533-1640
Mobile	205-433-5494/95
Montgomery	205-262-5606

Alaska
Anchorage	907-562-0704

Arizona
Phoenix	602-264-1721
Tucson	Inq. 602-662-7651
	Comp. 602-662-7654

Arkansas
Little Rock	501-664-7274

California
Bakersfield	805-322-2074
Colton	714-825-7280
Cypress	714-527-0680
Fresno	209-222-8111
Los Angeles	213-251-9696
Monterey	408-372-3149
Oakland	415-839-5900
Sacramento	916-443-6843
San Diego	619-281-6422
San Francisco	415-243-9999
San Jose	408-978-8700
San Mateo	415-696-1240
Santa Barbara	805-963-8657
Santa Rosa	707-577-0300
Stockton	209-948-4880/81

Colorado
Colorado Springs	719-636-1155
Denver	Inq. 303-758-2100
	Comp. 303-758-2212
Fort Collins	303-484-1348
Pueblo	719-542-6464

Connecticut
Fairfield	203-374-6161
Rocky Hill	203-529-3575
Wallingford	Inq. 203-269-2700
	Comp. 203-269-4457

Delaware
Wilmington	302-996-9200

District Of Columbia
Washington	202-393-8000

Florida
Clearwater	813-535-5522
Fort Myers	813-334-7331/7152
Jacksonville	904-721-2288
Maitland	407-660-9500
Miami	Inq. 305-625-0307
	Comp. 305-624-1302
New Port Richey	813-842-5459
Pensacola	904-433-6111
Port St. Lucie	407-878-2010
Tampa	813-875-6200
West Palm Beach	407-686-2200

Georgia

Albany	912-883-0744
Atlanta	404-688-4910
Augusta	404-722-1574
Columbus	404-324-0712/13
Macon	912-742-7999
Savannah	912-354-7521

Hawaii

Honolulu	808-942-2355

Idaho

Boise	208-342-4649
Idaho Falls	208-523-9754
Twin Falls	208-736-3971

Illinois

Chicago	Inq. 312-444-1188
	Comp. 312-346-3313
Peoria	309-688-3741
Rockford	815-963-2222

Indiana

Elkhart	219-262-8996
Evansville	812-473-0202
Fort Wayne	219-423-4433
Gary	219-980-1511
Indianapolis	317-637-0197
South Bend	219-277-9121

Iowa

Bettendorf	319-355-6344
Des Moines	515-243-8137
Sioux City	712-252-4501

Kansas

Topeka	913-232-0455
Wichita	316-263-3146

Kentucky

Lexington	606-259-1008
Louisville	502-583-6546

Louisiana

Alexandria	318-473-4494
Baton Rouge	504-926-3010
Houma	504-868-3456
Lafayette	318-981-3497
Lake Charles	318-433-1633
Monroe	318-387-4600
New Orleans	504-581-6222
Shreveport	318-221-8352

Maine

Portland	207-878-2715

Maryland

Baltimore	301-347-3990

Massachusetts

Boston	Inq. 617-426-9000
Hyannis	508)771-3022
Springfield	413-734-3114
Worcester	508-755-2548

Michigan

Grand Rapids	616-774-8236
Southfield	Inq. 313-644-1012
	Comp. 313-644-9136

Minnesota

Minneapolis/St. Paul	612-699-1111

Mississippi

Jackson	601-956-8282

Missouri

Kansas City	816-421-7800
St. Louis	Inq. 314-531-3300
Springfield	417-862-9231

Nebraska

Lincoln	402-467-5261
Omaha	402-346-3033

Nevada

Las Vegas	702-735-6900/1969
Reno	702-322-0657

New Hampshire

Concord	603-224-1991

New Jersey

Newark	201-642-INFO
Paramus	201-845-4044
Parsippany	201-334-5990
Toms River	201-270-5577
Trenton	201-588-0808
Westmont	609-854-8467

New Mexico

Albuquerque	505-884-0500
Farmington	505-326-6501
Las Cruces	505-524-3130

New York

Buffalo	716-856-7180
Farmingdale (Long Island)	516-420-0500
New York	212-533-7500
Rochester	716-546-6776
Syracuse	315-479-6635
Wappinger Falls	914-297-6550
White Plains	914-428-1230/31

North Carolina

Asheville	704-253-2392

Charlotte	704-332-7151
Greensboro	919-852-4240/41/42
Hickory	704-464-0372
Raleigh	919-872-9240
Winston-Salem	919-725-8348

Ohio

Akron	216-253-4590
Canton	216-454-9401
Cincinnati	513-421-3015
Cleveland	216-241-7678
Columbus	614-486-6336
Dayton	513-222-5825
Lima	419-223-7010
Mansfield	419-522-1700
Toledo	419-241-6276
Wooster	216-263-6444
Youngstown	216-744-3111

Oklahoma

Oklahoma City	Inq. 405-239-6081
	Inq. 405-239-6860
	Comp. 405-239-6083
Tulsa	918-492-1266

Oregon

Portland	503-226-3981

Pennsylvania

Bethlehem	215-866-8780
Lancaster	717-291-1151
Toll-Free York Co. Resident	846-2700
Philadelphia	215-496-1000
Pittsburgh	412-456-2700
Scranton	717-342-9129

Puerto Rico

San Juan	809-756-5400

Rhode Island

Warwick	Inq. 401-785-1212
	Comp. 401-785-1213

South Carolina

Columbia	803-254-2525
Greenville	803-242-5052
Myrtle Beach	803-497-8667

Tennessee

Blountville	615-323-6311
Chattanooga	615-266-6144
Knoxville	615-522-2552
Memphis	901-795-8771
Nashville	615-254-5872

Texas

Abilene	915-691-1533
Amarillo	806-358-6222
Austin	512-476-1616
Beaumont	409-835-5348
Bryan	409-823-8148/49
Corpus Christi	512-854-2892
Dallas	214-220-2000
El Paso	915-545-1212
Fort Worth	817-332-7585
Houston	713-868-9500
Lubbock	806-763-0459
Midland	915-563-1880
San Angelo	915-949-2989
San Antonio	512-828-9441
Tyler	214-581-5704
Waco	817-772-7530
Weslaco	512-968-3678
Wichita Falls	817-723-5526

Utah

Salt Lake City	801-487-4656

Virginia

Fredericksburg	703-786-8397
Norfolk	804-627-5651
(Peninsula area)	804-851-9101
Richmond	804-648-0016
Roanoke	703-342-3455

Washington

Kennewick	509-582-0222
Seattle	206-448-8888
Spokane	509-747-1155
Tacoma	206-383-5561
Yakima	509-248-1326

Wisconsin

Milwaukee	414-273-1600

Wyoming

None

International Bureaus

National Headquarters For Canadian Bureaus

Concord, Ontario	416-669-1248

Alberta

Calgary	403-258-2920
Edmonton	403-482-2341
Red Deer	403-343-3280

British Columbia

Vancouver	604-682-2711
Victoria	604-386-6348

Manitoba

Winnipeg	204-943-1486

New Brunswick
Saint John   709-658-1622

Newfoundland
St. John's   709-364-2222

Nova Scotia
Halifax   Inq. 902-422-6581
                                   Comp. 902-422-6582

Ontario
Hamilton   416-526-1111
Kitchener   519-579-3080
London   519-673-3222

Ottawa   613-237-4856
Toronto   416-766-5744
Windsor   519-258-7222

Quebec
Montreal   514-286-9281
Quebec   418-523-2555

Saskatchewan
Regina   306-352-7601

Israel
Tel Aviv   03-28-25-28

Market Studies, Demographics, and Statistics

Existing Market Studies

Finding information about a market, whether it is a comprehensive market study or a single fact or figure, seems to be one of the most common challenges for business researchers. And how one handles this problem can depend upon a number of variables, including time and money. Since it is virtually impossible to map out a research strategy for all possible circumstances, presented here is a collection of some obvious and not so obvious sources to help with such an effort. If you are under the gun to get the most information in the shortest amount of time, the good old telephone is the efficient method (refer to the section entitled *The Art of Getting A Bureaucrat To Help You*).

Traditional Published Sources

If you want to begin with traditional published sources, start with a local library that is oriented toward the business community. A nearby university with a business school or a large public library can be a good starting place. Many business libraries offer free or low-cost telephone research service. For example, the Brooklyn Public Library's Business Library (280 Cadman Plaza West, Brooklyn, NY 11201, 718-780-7800) will answer brief questions over the telephone and hold your hand in identifying information sources if you visit in person.

If you are not familiar with traditional published information sources, using the services of a research librarian can be an efficient way to get at exactly what is there that you need. If you are in a hurry, see what you can get over the telephone. If time is not critical, it will be worth visiting the library to become acquainted with local resources, because if these reference sources are not useful to you now, most likely

they will be in the future. Many of the questions we answer for clients at a rate of $100 an hour can be answered for free by a local reference librarian.

Computerized Data Bases And Data Sources

Currently there are an estimated 3,000 to 5,000 computerized data bases available to the public. Some publications which identify online data bases include:

1) *Data Base Directory Service* by Knowledge Industry Publications ($395, includes one year of monthly newsletters, a Directory available separately for $195, and a supplement published mid-year, *Data Base Alert*, from Knowledge Industry Publications, Inc., 701 Westchester Avenue, White Plains, NY 10604, 914-328-9157);

2) *Directory of Online Data Bases* by Gale Research, Inc., 835 Penobscot Bldg., Detroit, MI 48226, 1-800-877-4253. ($199 for two issues per year.)

3) *Directory of Portable Data Bases*, by Gale Research, Inc., 835 Penobscot Bldg., Detroit, MI 48226, 1-800-877-4253. ($99 for biannually issued subscription.)

Almost all major vendors maintain data bases which contain marketing information. A review of any of the four books cited above will help you pinpoint data bases which may be helpful, or you can call BRS, Dialog and other data base vendors directly. Some of the more popular data bases which contain marketing information on a wide variety of industries are basically indexes and abstracts of current trade and business periodicals. Included in this category are:

- ABI/INFORM
- Management Contents
- Predicasts
- NewsNet
- HARFAX Industry Data Sources

If you are a first time user of data bases, it may be wise to have someone else do your searching. Companies called Information Brokers are in this line of business. The best way to find such brokers is to contact your local reference librarian. They are in a good position to tell you what retrieval services exist locally.

If you have trouble with this method, you may find help by calling Dialog Information Services, Customer Service at 1-800-334-2564. This major data base vendor maintains a list of those organizations which provide this service. Dialog can narrow down your options according to what city you are in and what subjects you want searched. There is no charge for these referrals.

Be sure to inquire whether a nearby public, academic or specialized library performs online retrieval services. If they do, it is probably going to be much cheaper. For example, the Brooklyn Business Library will do **data base searches and charge only for direct out-of-pocket costs**. An information broker is likely to cost you three to four times more.

If you have a PC with a modem but have been reluctant to access the more complicated business data bases, you may want to contact EASYNET. This service offers simple and uniform access to over 850 data bases from 13 hosts worldwide, including most of the major business data bases. Your search is automatically intermediated by the Easynet Knowledge Gateway computer. Easynet covers most of the major business data bases. They have a set fee of $10 per search for a successful search. Some data bases have a surcharge and Easynet will let you know about them before the searches are made.

EASYNET/Telebase Systems, Inc.
435 Devon Park Dr., Suite 600
Wayne, PA 19087
1-800-EASYNET (modem number)
1-800-220-7616
215-293-4700

Refer to the section entitled *What's Good And Bad About Using Computers In The Information Age* for a more detailed discussion of the pros and cons of commercial online data bases.

Existing Market Studies

In order to find relevant market studies which have already been published, several checkpoints should be covered:

1) The data bases described above are likely to cover the news of currently released market studies.

2) Many industries have market research firms which specialize only in that industry. To identify these firms contact one or all of the following:

- an industry analyst at the U.S. Department of Commerce, Office of the Assistant Secretary for Trade Development at 202-482-1461;

- a specialist at an industry trade association (see *Encyclopedia of Associations* published by Gale Research Inc., 835 Penobscot Bldg., Detroit, MI 48226, 1-800-877-4253, available in most libraries);

- relevant trade magazines which can be identified by either one of the first two choices.

3) Contact those organizations which publish market studies on many industries, for example:

- Predicasts, 362 Lakeside Dr., Foster City, CA 94404, 1-800-321-6388, 415-378-5200;

- Frost and Sullivan, Inc., 106 Fulton Street, New York, NY 10038, 212-233-1080;

- Arthur D. Little Decision Resources, Bay Colony Corporate Center, 1100 Winter Street, Waltham, MA 02154, 617-487-3700;

- International Resource Development Inc., P.O. Box 1716, New Canaan, CT 06840, 203-966-2525;

- Creative Strategies Research International, 4633 Old Ironsides Drive, Suite 133, Santa Clara, CA 95054, 408- 748-3400; or

- BusinessCommunications Co. Inc., 25 Van Zant St., Norwalk, CT 06855, 203-853-4266;

4) Review the major data bases and publications which index available market studies for sale. These include:

- FINDEX: its data base or book identifies studies available from Wall Street investment firms and management consulting firms, contact: FIND/SVP, 625 Avenue of the Americas, 2nd Floor, New York, NY 10011, 212-645-4500. Call 1-800-346-3787 for a free catalogue or table of contents of Market Research Reports;

- INVESTEXT: its data base provides full text of research reports produced by Wall Street and regional investment banking companies. Contact: Thompson Financial Network, Investext, 11 Farnsworth Street, Boston, MA 02110, 617-345-2704, 1-800-662-7878; and

- Arthur D. Little/Online: provides access to the non- exclusive publications of Arthur D. Little Decision Resources and Arthur D. Little, Inc. Includes references and selected full-text items covering industry forecasts, strategic planning, company assessments, and emerging technologies. Contact: Arthur D. Little Decision Resources, Bay Colony Corporate Center, 1100 Winter Street, Waltham, MA 02154, 617-487-3700.

Market Studies From Associations

Many trade associations conduct market studies about their member organizations and/or industries. These reports may or may not be included in the data bases and other sources described above. It is worth contacting relevant associations directly to ensure that you have not missed an important report. To identify a relevant association use Gale's *Encyclopedia of Associations* (see reference above). This book is well indexed and available at most libraries. The proper association can normally be identified with a simple phone call to the reference desk or visit to a local library. If you cannot find what you need in this encyclopedia, the American Society of Association Executives may be of further help.

Information Central
American Society of Association Executives
1575 Eye Street, NW
Washington, DC 20005
202-626-2723

You should be aware that some associations will not sell their studies to non-members. However, there are some ways you can circumvent this problem.

1) Join the association; some memberships are relatively inexpensive.

2) Access thanks to antitrust laws; the association may be violating antitrust laws if it does not make the study available to non-members. This does not mean the organization cannot charge you a whole lot more than they do for its members. And, you must keep in mind that the ultimate action in pursuing this strategy is to take the association to court. But it is worth trying because many associations are very concerned about the antitrust laws, and simply mentioning that you are going to check with your legal counsel about possible antitrust violations may be enough to shake free the report.

If you want to investigate further about how an association may be violating antitrust laws, obtain a copy of *Association Law Handbook*, $65 for members, $80 for non-members, or *The Law of Associations*, $170 for members, $204 for non-members, or *Anti-Trust Procedures*, a compilation of anti-trust articles, $22 for members, $44 for non-members from American Society of Association Executives, plus $5.25 for regular UPS or first class postage and handling on all orders (see address above). This book explores association executives' worries and ways to avoid possible antitrust problems.

A $1,500 Market Study For Free

Many business researchers are unaware of the fact that if a high priced market study carries a copyright, like a Frost and Sullivan or Predicasts study, it may be **available for free** at the Library of Congress in Washington, DC. The Library receives two copies of all copyrighted material and usually adds these reports to its collection. The problem is that these companies are aware that people use the Library of Congress to see these studies and, as a result, they often wait for the last possible legal moment before filing their copyright. This can be 3 months or more after the study is published which means that it may take several more months before it gets into the collection.

Here are examples of how much money you can save by using this approach. Recently, we searched the Library of Congress catalog under "videotext" and found 39 reports, studies and publications, including the following:

- *Videotex & Teletex Markets* - a study published by Predicasts and for sale at $1,500; and

- *Advertising In The New Electronic Media* - a study available for $985 from International Resource Development.

Although both of these studies were about 10 years old, a recent review of the catalog showed that International Resource Development, Inc. alone, already had 20 new studies including:

- *Equipment Leasing in Europe*
- *Robot Vision Systems*
- *Speech Recognition and Voice Systems*
- *Microcomputer Educational Software for the Home*
- *Consumer Telephone Equipment*
- *High-Tech Drug Delivery Systems*
- *Uninterruptible Power Systems and Power Line Conditioning Equipment*

If you get to Washington, it will certainly be worth your time to visit the Library of Congress and discover market studies in your area of interest.

The Library is basically set up for visiting researchers, so it may be a bit more difficult, but not impossible, to see these studies if you do not come to Washington. However, you can arrange to obtain these studies through an interlibrary loan. The best way to do this is to identify the title of the study and then telephone the Reference Section at the Library of Congress to see if it is in their collection (telephone number noted below). If it is, then ask how to arrange an interlibrary loan. Any local library will also be happy to work with you on this matter.

If you do not know the title of a particular market study, it will be a bit harder to work remotely. The Library is not set up to do this sort of general reference work over the telephone. You can try calling the telephone reference number below to see what kind of assistance you can get to such an inquiry. If you do not get the help you need, call the office of your U.S. Representative or Senator (simply phone the Capitol Hill switchboard at 202-224-3121). What you should request is a list of Library of Congress holdings covering a specific subject area of interest. Requesting the titles of all Frost and Sullivan reports would not be of value because the publisher's name is not always an index term. **How successful you are at getting the Library to help may depend a lot on when you call and on how good you are at working with people over the telephone** (refer to the section entitled *The Art Of Getting A Bureaucrat To Help You*). Keep in mind that the Library is open weekdays 8:30 am until 9:30 pm Eastern standard time, Saturdays from 8:30 am to 5 pm, and Sundays from 1:00 pm to 5 pm.

> Telephone Reference Section
> Library of Congress
> Washington, DC 20540
> 202-707-5522 (general public)
> 202-707-2905 (news media queries)

The Library of Congress is not the only collection that contains copies of expensive market studies which can be viewed on sight or through an interlibrary loan. Practically every major federal agency has a library which collects studies in those fields within its mandate. The National Library of Medicine contains hundreds of market studies relating to health care; the U.S. Department of Energy has studies about the oil and gas industry; the U.S. Department of Defense maintains surveys of the aerospace industry, etc. If you cannot figure out which government agency is responsible for certain industries, either one of the following books can help:

1) *U.S. Government Manual*, ($21, Superintendent of Documents, U.S. Government Printing Office, Washington, DC 20402-9325, 202-783-3238); or

2) *Lesko's Info-Power*, by Matthew Lesko, ($39.95, 1994 Information USA), available at local bookstores and public libraries, or call 1-800-955-POWER.

If you don't have time to locate either of these books, the following free resources are designed to help you learn how the government can help you:

- The district or Washington office of your Member of Congress;

- Local Federal Information Center which is part of the General Services Administration, 410-722-9000; or

- Washington, DC Directory Assistance at 202-555-1212. These operators are equipped to identify phone numbers of major agencies.

Free Government Market Studies

The federal government serves as a major repository of market studies it generates. Not only are these reports likely to be available at very reasonable prices, such surveys also offer powerful information opportunities by virtue of the fact that most people are unaware of their availability. And, unlike market studies produced by commercial organizations which may invest 6 to 12 man-months on a project, a government sponsored effort is likely to represent several man-years worth of investment. The value for the money is unbeatable. The seven major government institutions which produce market studies are described below.

U.S. Congress

Each year the United States Congress conducts several thousand hearings which either analyze proposed legislation or oversee existing laws. In the same way that the government seems to affect every facet of our lives, the Congress seems to get involved in most every aspect of business. For instance, take the time when six franchise agreements from privately held companies became part of public testimony at hearings before the Senate Commerce Committee. Everyone in the industry said this information was proprietary and not available to anyone outside the companies in question.

In order to convince you of the broad range of areas probed by the Congress, listed below are a sampling of subject headings we recently found under the letter "M" in the index of bills for a recent session of Congress:

- Mail Order Business
- Major League Sports Community Protection
- Malpractice Insurance
- Malt Beverage Interbrand Competition
- Management Buyouts
- Management Consultants
- Management Information System
- Manganese
- Manufacturing Industries
- Marathon Running
- Marine Energy Resources
- Marketing of Farm Produce
- Materials Handling
- Meat Packing Industry
- Medical Corporations

An important aspect of a congressional hearing is that the committee in charge is usually very thorough in covering a subject. The best experts in the world normally present testimony or submit written comments. Committee staffers identify all available information sources and collect the latest research. Many times the committee will even commission a research study on the subject. Documentation from committee hearings normally exists in a number of formats which are described next.

1) **Published reports:** It often takes 6 months to one year after the date of the hearing before the report is published. Sometimes the printed committee or subcommittee hearings can be obtained free from the professional staffers or the full committee documents clerk. More popular transcripts on controversial subjects are frequently available for sale from the Government Printing Office (Superintendent of Documents, Washington, DC, 202-402-9325, 202-783-3238).

2) **Unedited transcripts:** Debates are published the following day in the *Congressional Record*. The Senate only has official reporters for debates. For unedited transcripts of Senate committee or subcommittee hearings, contact the committee to see what commercial transcription service they employed.

House committee transcripts, if available, are only available from the Office of Official Reporters to the House Committees, Room B-25, Cannon Building, Washington, DC 20515, 202-225-7187. Commercial reporting services are prohibited from transcribing and selling hearing transcripts. Transcripts are available from 1 to 10 working days after the hearing for $1.25 per page. The House Committees that allow transcripts of their hearings to be purchased are:

Agriculture
Budget
Education & Labor
Merchant Marines and Fisheries
Science, Space and Technology

Committees that sometimes make transcripts available for public purchase are:

Armed Services
DC Committee
Energy and Commerce
Small Businesses
Select Committee on Aging
Select Committee on Hunger

The remaining House committees do not publicly release transcripts of their hearings.

3) **Prepared testimony presented by witnesses:** These formal statements sometimes are made available before the hearing date, but usually a limited number of copies are distributed at the hearings. If you are trying to get this documentation and cannot wait until the hearing is printed, contact the committee or subcommittee staffer responsible for the hearing or call the witness directly to request a copy. These statements sometimes are made available before the hearing date and usually only a limited number of copies are distributed at the hearings. Both oral and written statements will comprise the published hearing record.

4) Studies commissioned by congressional committees: Such studies are usually conducted by the Congressional Research Service (CRS) of the Library of Congress. If copies are available, they can be obtained only through a Member of Congress. (More details about CRS reports are provided later in this Section.)

5) Formal comments about proposed legislation sent to the committee by interested parties, including government agencies: Such comments often are included in the published hearing and also are contained in the committee report on the bill. Moreover, they became part of the committee files and usually can be viewed in the committee office.

There are a number of options for finding out if hearings have been held on a specific topic. However, since there is no centralized list of all congressional hearings, you should expect to make a dozen or so calls.

1) Bill Status Office: 202-225-1772
This can be the fastest source because by accessing the LEGIS computerized data base, congressional staffers can tell you over the phone if legislation has been introduced on a specific topic. In addition to telling you which committees are working on the legislation, they can give you the status of a bill, who sponsored the measure, when it was introduced, and the status of similar bills. Although this congressional data base is limited because it does not cover investigative or "oversight" hearings, it is still quite inclusive since the information goes back to 1975. If a committee held a hearing on a subject because of proposed legislation, it is also likely to be responsible for oversight hearings on that subject. Telephone assistance is free and printouts are available for a $5 minimum, 20 cents per page. If you cannot easily arrange to have the printout picked up by messenger, you may want to ask your Representative or Senator's office to have it sent to you (and that way you can avoid the charge). Contact: Office of Legislative Information and Status, Ford House Office Building, 3rd & D Streets SW, Room 696, Washington, DC 20515.

2) Congressional Committees: 202-224-3121
Contacting a committee or subcommittee directly is another way to identify relevant hearings. However, the problem with this approach is that there are approximately 300 from which to choose. You must prepared to make a few calls before landing on target. The advantage to this method is that if the committee you call does not cover a particular subject area, it is usually very helpful in suggesting the appropriate committee. Keep in mind that the jurisdictions of many committees overlap, so it is necessary to check with all those committees when searching for valuable market information. If you do not get help, ask the Capitol Hill Switchboard at the number noted above to transfer you to the House or Senate Parliamentarian. These offices are very knowledgeable about the jurisdictions of all the committees. And, of course, you can also ask your Member of Congress to help identify the right committees.

3) Congressional Caucuses: 202-224-3121
The Steel Caucus, The Textile Caucus, and several dozen other "informal" study groups composed of House Members and Senators frequently produce reports on particular industries.

4) Congressional Information Service: 410-654-1550
This commercial firm indexes and provides copies of all published committee hearings. This service, *CIS Index*, has its limitations because some hearings are never published or are published a long time after the hearing has been held. Remember that copies of unpublished documentation can be obtained by using the methods described above. The complete service costs approximately $3,240 per year or $1,040 for the annual index. Most libraries are subscribers to this service. Contact: Congressional Information Service, Inc., 4520 East-West Highway, #800, Bethesda, MD 20814.

5) *The C.Q. Weekly Report*: 202-887-8500
Congressional Quarterly publishes *The C.Q. Weekly Report*, which lists all printed committee and subcommittee hearings. It contains an analysis of the week's current and pending legislative and political activity, including voting records and legislative, oversight and investigative activities released during the past week. Annual subscription is $1299 and it is also available online for $2,500 for 12 hours of online time. A hardbound *Almanac*, available for $295, is a compendium of a particular session's activity. To order, call 1-800-543-7793. Contact: Congressional Quarterly, Inc., 1414 22nd Street NW, Washington, DC 20037.

U.S. International Trade Commission

Part of the function of this agency is to study the volume of imports in comparison to domestic production and consumption. As a result, it produces close to 100 market studies each year on topics ranging from ice hockey sticks to clothespins. Some of the studies released recently include:

- Fresh Cut Flowers
- Malts and Starches
- Floor Coverings
- Body Supporting Garments
- Glass Mirrors
- Computers and Calculators
- Sewing Machines
- Loudspeakers
- Fork Lift Trucks
- Brooms and Brushes

If you are interested in publications produced prior to 1984, this office has the *Publications and Investigations of the United States Tariff Commission and the United States International Trade Commission* list. It is for in-house use only, but may be viewed at the Docket Room. This office will send you a free copy of *Lists of Selected Publications of the United States International Trade Commission*, which contains a list of reports that are now in print. You can also request to be placed on a list to be notified of future studies. Call 202-205-2000 to add your name to the mailing list. Free copies of any of the above publications can be ordered 24 hours a day, seven days a week by calling 202-205-1809 (recording), or contact:

Docket Room
Office of the Secretary
U.S. International Trade Commission
500 E Street SW, Room 112
Washington, DC 20436
202-252-1806/1807

Congressional Research Service: Reports

The Congressional Research Service (CRS) is an important research arm of the Library of Congress and conducts custom research for the Members of Congress on **any subject**. When a congressional committee plans hearings on a subject such as the insurance industry, often the Congressional Research Service will churn out a background report on the industry. Here are examples of some current studies which may be of interest to the business community:

- *Compensation in the Airline Industry*
- *Information Technology for Agriculture America*
- *Financial Innovations & Deregulation: Non-Bank Banks*
- *The Shrinking Market for Foreign Cars in Japan*
- *Wall Street Analysts' Reasons for the Decline in U.S.*
- *Production of Primary Petrochemicals*
- *Health Information Systems*
- *Attorney-Client Privilege*
- *Discount Brokerage of Securities: A Status Report*
- *Top Corporate Executive Compensation & Economic Performance*
- *Economic Statistics: Sources of Current Information*

- *Industrial Robots in the United States*
- *Domestic Crude Oil Production Projected to the Year 2000*

Free copies of these reports can be obtained only by contacting the Washington or district office of your Senator or Representative. The Congressional Research Service also publishes an index to all its reports. Although this *Index* is free, it can be difficult to obtain. If your legislator's office tells you they cannot get you an *Index*, ask to have a copy sent to the district office so you can review it at your Member's local office. Oddly enough, the reports are easier to get than the CRS Index. You can simply call your Member of Congress through the Capitol Hill Switchboard at 202-224-3121 or put your request in writing:

U.S. Senate
Washington, DC 20510

U.S. House of Representatives
Washington, DC 20515

**Congressional Research Service:
Current Issue Briefs**

Each day the Congressional Research Service updates over 400 studies, called Current Issue Briefs. These reports are designed to keep Members of Congress informed on timely topics. Listed below is a sampling of subjects covered.

- *Advertising of Alcoholic Beverages in the Broadcast Media*
- *CBS Takeover Attempts*
- *Greenmail and the Market for Corporate Control*
- *Backyard Satellite Earth Stations*
- *Commercial Banking Competition*
- *Genetic Engineering*
- *U.S. Automobile Industry: Issues and Statistics*
- *Foreign Investment in the U.S.: Trends and Impact*

- *Why Some Corporations Don't Pay Taxes*
- *Biotechnology*
- *Problems Facing U.S. Petroleum Refiners*
- *The Fortune 500: Name, Address, and Officers of the 500 Largest Industrial Corporations in the U.S.*

To receive a complete list of all Current Issue Briefs, you must contact the office of your Representative or Senator.

Every month the Congressional Research Service publishes *Update* which includes a list of new and updated issue briefs of current interest. Briefs that are no longer of intense public or congressional interest are listed in the *Archived Issue Briefs List*. These publications, along with copies of the Issue Briefs listed above, are available only by making arrangements through your Member of Congress in the same manner as described above.

**U.S. Commerce Department International
Trade Administration**

Each year the International Trade Administration (ITA) at the U.S. Department of Commerce investigates dozens of products from certain countries for possible violations of Anti-Dumping laws or the use of unfair subsidies under countervailing duty laws. These statutes have been established to protect domestic manufacturers from unfair foreign competition.

When the government conducts an investigation, the resulting file, that is open to public inspection, usually contains a complete report of the industry in question. The final determination of an investigation is published in *The Federal Register*. A few of the products the ITA has investigated since 1978 include:

- Butter Cookies
- Electric Golf Carts
- Iron Ore Pellets

- Ice Cream Sandwiches
- Moist Towelettes
- Motorcycle Batteries
- Photo Albums
- Electronic Tuners
- Ceramic Wall Tile
- Thin Sheet Glass

A complete listing of cases of industries studied by the ITA is available upon request. Copies of documentation from any of the above investigations are available for 10 cents per page if you make the copies yourself, 15 cents per page if they make the copies. However, this office is not set up to supply copies of files by mail and it is generally necessary to come in person or send someone on your behalf to get copies.

Central Records Unit
International Trade Administration
U.S. Department of Commerce
14th & Constitution Avenue NW
Room B-009
Washington, DC 20230
202-482-1248

General Accounting Office

The General Accounting Office (GAO) conducts special audits, surveys and investigations at the request of the U.S. Congress. It produces as many as 600 reports annually, many of which identify market opportunities. Below are just a few of their recent reports which have marketing potential.

- *Assessment of New Chemical Regulation Under the Toxic Substances Control Act*
- *Electronic Marketing of Agricultural Commodities*
- *SEC's Efforts to Find Lost and Stolen Securities*
- *Natural Gas Profit Data*
- *The U.S. Synthetic Fuels Corporation's Contracting With Individual Consultants*

- *Information on Historic Preservation Tax Incentives*
- *Licensing Data for Exports to Non-Communist Countries*
- *Disaster Assistance: Problems in Administering Payment for Nonprogram Crops*
- *Telecommunication Services: the 1991 Survey of Cable Television Rates and Services*
- *International Trade: Soviet Agricultural Reforms and the U.S. Government Response*
- *Foreign Assistance Aid: Energy Assistance and Global Warming*
- *Experience of Countries Using Alternative Motor Fuels*
- *Abandoned Mine Reclamation; Interior May Have Approved State Shift to Non-Coal Projects Prematurely*
- *Long Term Care Projected Needs of the Aging Baby Boom Generation*
- *Financial Markets: Computer Security at Five Stock Exchanges Need Strengthening*

The first copy of a report is available free of charge and additional copies can be obtained for $2 each. You can also receive a free annual index of available GAO reports, a free monthly catalog of current reports, and a free printout from a data base which contains all titles and document numbers. For further information or for any of the above contact the General Accounting Office. The pickup address is: Distribution Section, 700 4th Street NW, Room 1000, Washington, DC 20548; 202-512-6000. The mailing address is: General Accounting Office, Documents Center, P.O. Box 6015, East Gaithersburg, MD 20877. FAX requests to 301-258-4066.

Federal Trade Commission

Besides the antitrust activities of the U.S. Department of Justice, the Federal Trade Commission (FTC) also has the authority to investigate certain industries or companies for possible antitrust violations. Recent FTC investigations have targeted particular industries.

- Travel Industry
- Mail-Order Stamp Sales
- Motion Picture Industry
- Tuna Industry
- Bail Bond Industry
- Buying Clubs
- Business Opportunity Companies
- Hearing Aid Industry
- Dental Laboratories
- Fine Paper Industry

You can inquire to determine whether a specific company has been probed by the Commission. The investigation itself is confidential, but much results in documentation that is public record and available for 12 cents per page. Recent FTC reports and publications are:

- *The Business Guide to the Mail Order Rule*
- *The Impact of State Price and Entry Regulations on Intrastate Long Distance Telephone Rates*
- *How Should Health Claims for Food Be Regulated?*
- *Mergers in the U.S. Petroleum Industry*
- *General Equilibrium of the Analyses of the Welfare and Employment Effects on the U.S. Auto and Steel Industries*

The FTC will mail copies of reports they have on hand to you free of charge. Contact:

Public Reference Branch
Federal Trade Commission (FTC)
6th & Pennsylvania Avenue NW, Room 130
Washington, DC 20580
202-326-2222

Nine Federal Statistical Agencies

Everyone Is Selling Demographic Data That's Available Free

Almost everyone who sells demographic data is getting it from a public source and repackaging it for the convenience of the customer. A few years ago we were looking for demographic data on the use of health care facilities and were told by all the experts in the business that the Association of Blue Cross and Blue Shield Companies was the only place to obtain this data. After finally locating the office in the Association which produced this information, we were told it would cost us $50. At the time we were feeling a little poor, so we decided to check sources in the federal government. Soon we located an office at the Social Security Administration in Baltimore that actually collected the pertinent data which Blue Cross requested periodically. The statistician at the Social Security Administration said he would be happy to give us the data for free and, equally important, his information was more current than the data contained in the Blue Cross report because the Association had not yet asked him for the latest figures.

Many times it may be worth buying information from private firms, but there are times when it may not. In any case, you owe it to your organization to check on the availability of public demographic data from the primary non-commercial sources.

Nine Major Federal Statistical Agencies

The federal government is the place where you should definitely begin. Without a doubt it is the largest collector of demographic data in the world. Over $1 billion dollars are spent to amass the decennial census which counts all the noses and toilets in the country. Although budget cuts have reduced some federal data collection activities, more data still are generated by departments and agencies in Washington than you could imagine or could ever put to use. **Actually federal spending cutbacks have been more harmful to the dissemination of the information rather than the collection of demographic and statistical data.** Nowadays it is somewhat more difficult to determine what data are available and where to find it.

There are nine major federal statistical agencies which are listed below. Contact the ones you feel may be of some help in your data search. When you call, ask to speak to the data expert who concentrates on the specific issue you are investigating. If the expert tells you that his or her agency does not collect the exact data you require, remember that this government specialist probably can tell you who might have the information. These statisticians stay current by reading all pertinent journals and attending international conferences. Most likely they can tell you which organizations and individuals to contact.

Plotting The Baby Boom

Recently we were trying to obtain the forecast of births in the U.S., and in particular, first births (how many first born sons and daughters). The Bureau of the Census and the National Center for Health Statistics were very cooperative in giving us this data quickly. Equally helpful was a statistician at the Census Bureau who recommended an expert at the Urban Institute in Washington, DC who studied how much money parents spend on their children. A call to this expert produced a free report just published by the Institute, which showed that the average family spends over 50% more on their first child than they do on their second or third. This report, together with federal data on the boom in first births, proved to our client that the outlook for the baby products industry was on a large upswing.

The federal agencies noted here can probably provide much of the demographic data you need and also suggest sources elsewhere in the government as well as experts in the private sector.

1) Agriculture and Food Statistics
   National Agriculture Statistics Service
   Director, Estimates Division
   U.S. Department of Agriculture
   14th & Independence Avenue SW
   Washington, DC 20250
   202-720-3896

2) Economic and Demographic Statistics
   Bureau of the Census
   U.S. Department of Commerce
   Data User Service Division
   Customer Service
   Washington, DC 20233
   301-763-4100

3) Crime Statistics
   Uniform Crime Reporting Section
   Federal Bureau of Investigations (FBI)
   U.S. Department of Justice-GRB
   7th & D Streets, NW
   Washington, DC 20535
   202-324-5038

4) Economics-National, Regional and International
   Bureau of Economic Analysis
   U.S. Department of Commerce
   Washington, DC 20230
   202-523-0777

5) Education Statistics
   Office of Educational Research and Improvement

555 New Jersey Avenue NW, Room 300
Washington, DC 20208-5641
1-800-424-1616

6) Health Statistics
   National Center for Health Statistics
   U.S. Department of Health & Human Resources
   6525 Belcrest Road
   Hyattsville, MD 20782
   301-436-8500

7) Employment, Prices, Living Conditions, Productivity, and Occupational Safety and Health
   Bureau of Labor Statistics
   U.S. Department of Labor
   441 G Street NW
   Washington, DC 20212
   Information   202-606-7828
   Publications   202-606-7828, ext. 6

8) Import and Export Statistics
   World Trade Reference Room
   U.S. Department of Commerce
   Room 2233
   Washington, DC 20230
   202-482-2185

9) World Import and Export Statistics
   World Trade Statistics
   U.S. Department of Commerce
   Washington, DC 20230
   202-482-5242

Tips For Finding Federal Data

We have found that one of the best sources for identifying data in the federal government is a publication titled the *Statistical Abstract of the United States*. Do not expect to find the precise data you need in this book. What you will discover is an invaluable index to hundreds of data tables on literally thousands of subjects. Below each table is the name of the agency which produced the data. This means that if you are trying to locate how many left-handed monkeys there are in the United States, you can refer to the index under monkey and turn to the appropriate table. What you are likely to find is a table that contains data on all the monkeys in the country and not how many are left-handed. You can then look at the bottom of the table and see what office compiled the numbers. If you call the office directly, someone there can probably track down the information you need in their files (in this case of monkeys, it may be difficult). Remember this *Abstract* contains only a small fraction of data available from any government office, but it serves as an excellent starting point for identifying which federal office collects what kind of information. The latest edition can be purchased from the U.S. Government Printing Office (noted earlier).

Another way to uncover opportunities in the vast federal repository is to obtain a copy of the forms that are filled out in the data collection phase. For example, if you are selling toothpaste, you may see that those who completed the long census form in the last decennial census stated what kind of toothpaste they use. This may not be printed in any report offered by the Census Bureau, but that does not mean you cannot get this data. The Bureau can do a special search for you and charge you on a cost recovery basis. This is true with any federal agency. What you should do is request copies of the data collection forms for any survey you think may be of interest to you. If you are in a consumer-related business, you should at least get a copy of the long form used in the decennial census.

Hotlines For Monitoring
The Economy And Your Markets:
Listen To Tomorrow's News Today

Why wait for tomorrow's *Wall Street Journal* to find out the latest economic statistics that will affect your business? You can find out today by calling the U.S. Department of Commerce Hotline. This is the same message that the *Wall Street Journal* listens to before going to press. If you want to know when the best time is to convert your adjustable rate mortgage to a fixed rate mortgage, you don't have to wait until your mortgage banker gives you the information at the end of the month. You can plot the trends daily by calling the Mortgage Rate Hotline at the Federal National Mortgage Association. This is where your mortgage banker gets the information, and you can be a month ahead of him.

Banks and Savings and Loans, Information on Failed Banks
Federal Deposit Insurance Corporation
202-393-8400

Banks and Savings and Loans, Obtaining a Financial Statement on Your Bank
Federal Deposit Insurance Corporation
202-393-8400

Banks, Aggregate Reserves of Depository Institutions
Thursday, Federal Reserve Board
202-452-3206

Banks, Assets and Liabilities of Insured Domestically Chartered and Foreign Banks
Monday, Federal Reserve Board
202-452-3206

Benefits, Employment Costs
Middle of Month, Bureau of Labor Statistics
202-606-7828 ext. 4

Collective Bargaining Settlements in Private Industry
Middle of Month, Bureau of Labor Statistics
202-606-7828 ext. 5

Construction
Beginning of Month, Department of Commerce
202-393-4100

Consumer Price Index
Middle of Month, Bureau of Labor Statistics
202-606-7828 ext. 1

Credit, Consumer Installment
5th Working Day of Month; Federal Reserve Board
202-452-3206

Earnings, Hourly and Weekly
Beginning of Month; Bureau of Labor Statistics
202-606-7828 ext. 3

Earnings, Real
Middle of Month, Bureau of Labor Statistics
202-606-7828 ext. 5

Economic News
GNP, Trade Figures, Housing Starts, and Other Economic Figures, Department of Commerce
202-393-4100

Economic News Highlights
Department of Commerce
202-393-1847

Economic News Weekend Preview
Department of Commerce
202-393-4102

Employment Situation
Beginning of Month, Bureau of Labor Statistics
202-606-7828 ext. 3

Foreign Exchange Rates
Monday, and 1st of Month, Federal Reserve Board
202-452-3206

Foreign Trade
End of Month, Department of Commerce
202-393-4100

Gross National Product
End of Month, Department of Commerce
202-898-2451

Housing, New Home Sales
Beginning of Month, Department of Commerce
202-393-4100

Housing Starts
Middle of Month, Department of Commerce
202-393-4100

Hours Worked In A Week
Beginning of Month, Bureau of Labor Statistics
202-606-7828 ext. 3

Income, Personal
End of Month, Department of Commerce
202-898-2452

Industrial Production and Capacity Utilization
Middle of Month, Federal Reserve Board
202-452-3206

Interest Rates, Selected
Monday, Federal Reserve Board
202-452-3206

International Trade, Merchandise Trade
Middle of Month, Department of Commerce
202-898-2453

Inventories and Sales, Manufacturing and Trade
Middle of Month, Department of Commerce
202-393-4100

Market Studies, Demographics, and Statistics

Leading Economic Indicators
Beginning of Month, Department of Commerce
202-898-2450

Loans and Securities at All Commercial Banks
3rd Week of Month, Federal Reserve Board
202-452-3206

Merchandise Trade
Middle of Month, Department of Commerce
202-898-2453

Money Stock, Liquid Assets, and Debt Measures
Thursday, Federal Reserve Board
202-452-3206

Mortgage Rates, Adjustable Rate Information
Middle of Month, Federal Housing Finance Board
202-408-2940

Mortgage Rates, National Average Contract Rate For Purchase of Previous Occupied Homes By Combined Lenders
Middle of Month, Federal Housing Finance Board
202-408-2940

Mortgage Rates, 30-Year Fixed Rate Yields
Continually Updated, Federal National Mortgage Association
1-800-752-7020, 202-752-0471 ext. 3

Mortgage Rates, Fixed Intermediate Term Yields
Continually Updated, Federal National Mortgage Association
1-800-752-7020, 202-752-0471 ext. 4

Mortgage Rates, Adjustable Yields
Continually Updated, Federal National Mortgage Association
1-800-752-7020, 202-752-0471 ext. 5

Payroll for Industry
Beginning of Month, Bureau of Labor Statistics
202-606-7828 ext. 3

Personal Income and Outlays
End of Month, Bureau of Labor Statistics
202-606-7828

Plant and Equipment Expenditures
Middle of Month, Department of Commerce
202-898-2453

Producer Price Index
Middle of Month, Bureau of Labor Statistics
202-606-7828 ext. 2

Production and Capacity Utilization, Industrial
Middle of Month, Federal Reserve Board
202-452-3206

Productivity and Cost
Beginning of Month, Bureau of Labor Statistics
202-606-7828 ext. 5

Retail Trade, Advance Report for Previous Month
Middle of Month, Department of Census
202-393-4100

Salaries and Wages Information
Middle of Month, Bureau of Labor Statistics
202-606-7828 ext. 4

Sales and Inventories, Manufacturing and Trade
Middle of Month, Department of Commerce
202-393-4100

Treasury Bill Auction Results
Department of the Treasury
202-874-4400 ext. 221

Treasury Bill, Notice of Next Auction
Department of the Treasury
202-874-4400 ext. 211

Treasury Note and Bond Auction Results
Department of the Treasury
202-874-4400 ext. 222

Treasury Note and Bond, Notice of Next Auction
Department of the Treasury
202-874-4400 ext. 212

Treasury Securities, How To Purchase Notes, Bonds and Bills
Continually Updated, Department of the Treasury
202-874-4400 ext. 251

Unemployment Rates
Beginning of Month, Department of Labor Statistics
202-606-7828 ext. 3

Wholesale Trade
Middle of Month, Department of Commerce
202-393-4100

Wages and Salaries Information
Beginning of Month, Department of Labor Statistics
202-606-7828 ext. 4

State Data Centers

Approximately 1,300 organizations nationwide receive data from the U.S. Bureau of the Census and in turn disseminate the information to the public free of charge or on a cost recovery basis. These organizations are called state data centers and serve as ideal information sources for both local and national markets. The centers listed in this report are the major offices for each state. If you are looking for national markets, start with a center in your state. If you are searching for local market data, contact the center located in the relevant area.

Demographics and Target Market Identification

State data center offices are most frequently used for obtaining information on target markets. For instance, the Army and Navy used such services to identify which areas are populated with large numbers of teenagers in order to open recruiting offices and focus their advertising campaign. Avon door-to-door sales reps used state data center generated demographic maps to identify homes with highest potential. L.L. Bean relied on a center to determine large Hispanic populations for a special promotion of outdoor recreational products. These offices could provide current data including:

- The age distribution within a given county;
- Moving patterns for particular geographical areas;
- The number of wells and mobile homes in 85 counties;
- How many gravel pits in the state of Montana;
- Counties with the highest rate of illegitimate children;

- Analysis of why certain stores in an auto parts chain are doing better than others;
- Demographic profile of a person in need of child care;
- The top 25 markets by zip code;
- The number of male secretaries in a dozen contiguous counties.

Forecasting Future Markets

The biggest opportunities often lie in knowing the future of a market. Many of the state data centers have developed specific software for analyzing Census and other data to project growth of specific markets. Here is a sampling of what some centers can do:

- Population projections for every three years to the year 2020 (done by California center);
- State population changes by the year 2000;
- What year the white population will not be in the majority;
- The number of teenagers by the next century;
- Series of economic indicators for plotting future economic health in state (Oklahoma center provides such data).

Site Location

Another major area of interest is in providing information to companies considering relocating into a state. Because most states are aggressively trying to attract business, numerous customized services receive a high priority. Local centers can provide information such as the number of fast food restaurants in the area and the best location for another one. And some states, like Arkansas, have special site evaluation software which can manipulate Census data to show the demographic characteristics for market radiuses which are 2, 5 or 10 miles from a given site. Oklahoma and other states have free data sheets covering every community in their state which are loaded with specifics for choosing a location. Their reports contain data on:

- Distance from major cities
- Population: past and future
- Climate
- Municipal services
- Utilities
- Labor market analysis
- List of major manufacturers
- List of major employers
- Transportation
- Commercial services
- Major freight lines and truck terminals
- Educational facilities
- Financial institutions
- Tax structure
- Housing and churches
- Medical facilities
- Retail business in city
- Industrial financial assistance
- Water analysis report
- Recreational facilities
- Wholesale business in city
- Items deserving special consideration

Professional and Personal Relocation

The same services that are intended to help businesses relocate also can be useful to individuals and professionals. For example, if you are looking for a place to start an orthodontics practice, a local data center could determine which counties and cities have the most affluent families with young people -- a prime market for braces. Also, if you get an offer for a new job in another city, obtaining a data sheet on the local community like the one described above provides insight into the types

of housing, schools, churches, and recreational facilities available.

Business Proposals Plus
Loan and Grant Applications

If you are looking for money for either a grant, a loan or even venture money, data centers can provide the information needed for proposal writing. Grantors must have information such as what percent of people live below poverty line, and banks want to know current business patterns for a new enterprise when seeking a loan. These sorts of data can be obtained easily from these centers.

Level of Detail

Because the data centers use information from other sources in addition to the Bureau of Census, the level of detail will vary according to subject area as well as the state and office contacted. Much of the Census data can be provided at the state, county, city, census tract and block group level (which is normally even smaller than a zip code). Data according to zip code are also available for many categories of information. All states also have the public use micro data sample, which do not contain aggregate data, but actual questionnaire information filled out by respondents. They can be manipulated into any kind of special detail required.

Custom Work, Workshops
and Other Services

A lot of work performed by the data centers is customized in nature. The organizations collect data from other federal and state sources to enhance their Census information. Many have arrangements with other state data centers to send any computer file needed to do special analysis. This is how local centers can provide national information or inter-market comparisons. Some centers will even perform custom census projects for clients, which means raw data collection for market research.

Free and low cost workshops about services and information opportunities are sponsored in some areas for potential users. These workshops are important at the local level because in the past they were readily available from the Bureau of Census, but recent budget cuts have reduced their frequency and increased their price. Because of the centers' familiarity of census data, these offices are excellent starting places for almost any information search.

Formats

Data centers offer some of the most sophisticated formats you are likely to find from public organizations. They all provide computer tapes, off-the-shelf reports, custom reports from computer analysis, and quick answers over the telephone. Most are also set up to provide custom analysis and/or raw data on computer diskettes, and some -- like Ohio -- have developed a PC database from which they can generate standard reports and download onto diskettes. Colorado and other states are beginning to make data accessible online.

Prices

Although the U.S. government provides most of the data to these centers, the feds do not interfere with fee schedules. Most offices try to give out information free, but some charge on a cost recovery basis. Some states do not charge for the first so many pages of a report but charge a nominal fee for additional pages. Some say they have a minimum fee of $20 for customized computer runs. It is interesting that these centers sell you computerized data cheaper than the U.S. Bureau of the Census in Washington. In contrast to the Bureau's fee of $140, Illinois and Georgia only charge $50 for

a data tape file, and in Florida, the cost is $15 for a file.

In the dozens of interviews we conducted with these centers about the complicated market research reports they have provided to clients, the highest figure we found they ever charged was $2,000. That amount of money would buy virtually nothing from most marketing consultants.

State Data Centers

Below is a roster of data centers in all 50 states as well as the District of Columbia, Puerto Rico and Virgin Islands. Some of these Census Bureau information providers are based in state departments and agencies, universities, business colleges, and libraries. Each center listed below includes the name and phone number of the data expert.

Alabama

Center for Business and Economic Research, University of Alabama, P.O. Box 870221, Tuscaloosa, AL 34587-0221, Ms. Annette Walters, 205-348-6191.

Alabama Department of Economic and Community Affairs, Office of State Planning, P.O. Box 5690, 3465 Norman Bridge Road, Montgomery, AL 36103-5690, Mr. Parker Collins, 205-242-5493.

Alabama Public Library Service, 6030 Monticello Drive, Montgomery, AL 36130, Mr. Vince Thacker, 205-277-7330.

Alaska

Alaska State Data Center, Research and Analysis, Department of Labor, P.O. Box 25504, Juneau, AK 99802-5504, Ms. Kathryn Lizik, 907-465-6026.

Office of Management and Budget, Division of Policy, Pouch AD, Juneau, AK 99811, Mr. Jack Kreinheder, 907-465-3640.

Department of Education, Division of Libraries and Museums, Alaska State Library, Pouch G, Juneau, AK 99811, Ms. Patience Fredrickson, 907-465-2927.

Department of Community and Regional Affairs, Division of Municipal and Regional Assistance, P.O. Box BH, Juneau, AK 99811, Ms. Laura Walters, 907-465-4750.

Institute for Social and Economic Research, University of Alaska, 3211 Providence Drive, Anchorage, AK 99508, Mr. Jim Kerr, 907-786-7710.

Arizona

Arizona Department of Economic Security, Mail Code 045Z, 1789 West Jefferson Street, Phoenix, AZ 85007, Ms. Betty Jeffries, 602-542-5984.

Market Studies, Demographics, and Statistics

Center for Business Research, College of Business Administration, Arizona State University, Tempe, AZ, 85287, Mr. Tom Rex, 602-965-3961.

College of Business Administration, Northern Arizona University, Box 15066, Flagstaff, AZ 86011, Ms. Linda Stratton, 602-523-7313.

Research Library, Department of Library, Archives, and Public Records, 1700 West Washington, 2nd Floor, Phoenix, AZ 85007, Ms. Janet Fisher, 602-542-3701.

Division of Economic and Business Research, College of Business and Public Administration, University of Arizona, Tucson, AZ 85721, Ms. Pia Montoya, 602-621-2155.

Arkansas

State Data Center, University of Arkansas-Little Rock, 2801 South University, Little Rock, AR 72204, Ms. Sarah Breshears, 501-569-8530.

Arkansas State Library, 1 Capitol Mall, Little Rock, AR 72201, Ms. Mary Honeycutt-Leckie, 501-682-2864.

Research and Analysis Section, Arkansas Employment Security Division, P.O. Box 2981, Little Rock, AR 72203, Mr. Coy Cozart, 501-682-3159.

California

State Census Data Center, Department of Finance, 915 L Street, Sacramento, CA 95814, Ms. Linda Gage, Director, 916-322-4651, Mr. Richard Lovelady, 916-323-4141.

Sacramento Area COG, 106 K Street, Suite 300, Sacramento, CA 95816, Mr. Bob Faseler, 916-457-2264.

Association of Bay Area Governments, Metro Center, 8th and Oak Streets, P.O. Box 2050, Oakland, CA 94604-2050, Ms. Patricia Perry, 510-464-7937.

Southern California Association of Governments, 818 West 7th Street, 12th Floor, Los Angeles, CA 90017, Mr. Javier Minjares, 213-236-1800.

San Diego Association of Governments, First Federal Plaza, 401 B Street, Suite 800, San Diego, CA 92101, Ms. Karen Lamphere, 619-236-5300.

State Data Center Program, University of California-Berkeley, 2538 Channing Way, Berkeley, CA 94720, Ms. Ilona Einowski/Fred Gey, 510-642-6571.

Association of Monterey Bay Area Governments, 445 Reservation Road, Suite G, P.O. Box 838, Marina, CA 93933, Mr. Steve Williams, 408-883-3750.

Colorado

Division of Local Government, Colorado Department of Local Affairs, 1313 Sherman Street, Room 521, Denver, CO 80203, Ms. Rebecca Picaso, 303-866-2156.

Business Research Division, Graduate School of Business Administration, University of Colorado-Boulder, Boulder, CO 80309, Ms. Ginny Hayden, 303-492-8227.

Natural Resources and Economics, Department of Agriculture, Colorado State University, Fort Collins, CO 80523, Ms. Sue Anderson, 303-491-5706.

Documents Department, The Libraries, Colorado State University, Fort Collins, CO 80523, Ms. Suzanne Taylor, 303-491-1880.

Connecticut

Policy Development and Planning Division, Connecticut Office of Policy and Management, 80 Washington Street, Hartford, CT 06106-4459, Mr. Bill Kraynak, 203-566-8285.

Government Documents, Connecticut State Library, 231 Capitol Avenue, Hartford, CT 06106, Mr. Albert Palko, 203-566-4971.

Connecticut Department of Economic Development, Research, Planning, and Information Systems, 865 Brook Street, Rocky Hill, CT 06067-3405, Mr. Jeff Blodgett, 203-258-4219.

Capitol Region Council of Governments, 221 Main Street, Hartford, CT 06106, Ms. Barbara MacFarland, 203-522-2217.

Delaware

Delaware Development Office, 99 Kings Highway, P.O. Box 1401, Dover, DE 19903, Ms. Judy McKinney-Cherry, 302-739-4271.

College of Urban Affairs and Public Policy, University of Delaware, Graham Hall, Room 286, Academy Street, Newark, DE 19716, Mr. Ed Ratledge, 302-831-8406.

District of Columbia

Data Services Division, Mayor's Office of Planning, Room 570, Presidential Bldg., 415 12th Street, NW, Washington, DC 20004, Mr. Gan Ahuja, 202-727-6533.

Metropolitan Washington Council of Governments, 777 North Capitol Street, NE, Suite 300, Washington, DC 20002-4201, Mr. Robert Griffith/Ms. Carol Huskey, 202-962-3200.

Florida

Florida State Data Center, Executive Office of the Governor, REA/OPB, The Capitol, Room 1604, Tallahassee, FL 32399-0001, Ms. Valerie Jugger, 904-487-2814.

Center for the Study of Population, Institute for Social Research, 654 Bellemy Building, R-93, Florida State University, Tallahassee, FL 32306-4063, Dr. Ike Eberstein, 904-644-1762.

State Library of Florida, R.A. Gray Building, Tallahassee, FL 32399-0250, Ms. Lisa Close, 904-487-2651.

Bureau of Economic Analysis, Florida Department of Commerce, 107 West Gaines Street, 315 Collins Building, Tallahassee, FL 32399-2000, Mr. Nick Leslie, 904-487-2971.

Georgia

Division of Demographic and Statistical Services, Georgia Office of Planning and Budget, 254 Washington Street, SW, Room 640, Atlanta, GA 30334, Ms. Marty Sik, 404-656-0911.

Data Services, University of Georgia Libraries, 6th Floor, Athens, GA 30602, Dr. Hortense Bates, 404-542-0727.

Georgia Department of Community Affairs, Office of Coordinated Planning, 100 Peachtree Street, NE #1200, Atlanta, GA 30303, Mr. Keith Nelms, 404-656-3879.

Guam

Guam Department of Commerce, 590 South Marine Drive, Suite 601, 6th Floor GITC Building, Tamuning, Guam 96911, Mr. Peter R. Barcinas, 671-646-5841.

Hawaii

Hawaii State Data Center, Department of Business, Economic Development, and Tourism, 220 S. King Street, Suite 400, Honolulu, HI 96813, Mailing Address: P.O. Box 2359, Honolulu, HI 96804, Ms. Jan Nakamoto, 808-586-2493.

Information and Communication Services Division, State Dept. of Budget and Finance, Kalanimoku Building, 1151 Punchbowl Street, Honolulu, HI 96813, Ms. Joy Toyama, 808-568-1940.

Idaho

Idaho Department of Commerce, 700 West State Street, Boise, ID 83720, Mr. Alan Porter, 208-334-2470.

Institutional Research, Room 319, Business Building, Boise State University, Boise, ID 83725, Mr. Don Canning, 208-385-1613.

The Idaho State Library, 325 West State Street, Boise, ID 83702, Ms. Stephanie Kukay, 208-334-2150.

Center for Business Research and Services, Campus Box 8450, Idaho State University, Pocatello, ID 83209, Dr. Paul Zelus, 208-236-3049.

Illinois

Illinois Bureau of the Budget, William Stratton Building, Room 605, Springfield, IL 62706, Ms. Suzanne Ebetsch, 217-782-1381.

Census and Data Users Services, Department 4690, Research Services Bldg., Suite A, 4950 Illinois State University, Normal, IL 61790-4950, Dr. Roy Treadway/Dr. Del Ervin, 309-438-5946.

Center for Governmental Studies, Northern Illinois University, Social Science Research Bldg., DeKalb, IL 60115, Ms. Ruth Anne Tobias/Ms. Charlene Ceci, 815-753-0922/0934.

Regional Research and Development Services, Southern Illinois University at Edwardsville, P.O. Box 1456, Edwardsville, IL 62026-1456, Mr. Charles Kofron, 618-692-2278.

Chicago Area Geographic Information Study, Department of Geography, M/C 092, 1007 W. Harrison St., Room 2102, University of Illinois at Chicago, Chicago, IL 60607-7138, Mr. Jim Bash, 312-996-5274.

Northeastern Illinois Planning Commission, Research Services Department, 222 S. Riverside Plaza, Suite 1800, Chicago, IL 60606-6097, Max Dieber/Mary Cele Smith, 312-454-0400.

Indiana

Indiana State Library, Indiana State Data Center, 140 North Senate Avenue, Indianapolis, IN 46204, Mr. Ray Ewick, Director/Mr. Laurence Hathaway, 317-232-3733.

Indiana Business Research Center, Indiana University, School of Business, Bloomington, IN 47405, Dr. Morton Marcus, 812-855-5507.

Indiana Business Research Center, 801 W. Michigan, B.S. 4015, Indianapolis, IN 46202-5151, Ms. Carol Rogers, 317-274-2205.

Research Division, Indiana Department of Commerce, 1 North Capitol, Suite 700, Indianapolis, IN 46204, Mr. Robert Lain, 317-232-8959.

Iowa

State Library of Iowa, East 12th and Grand, Des Moines, IA 50319, Ms. Beth Henning, 515-281-4350.

Center for Social and Behavioral Research, University of Northern Iowa, Cedar Falls, IA 50614, Dr. Robert Kramer, 319-273-2105.

Census Services, Iowa State University, 320 East Hall, Ames, IA 50011, Dr. Willis Goudy, 515-294-8337.

Iowa Social Science Institute, University of Iowa, 345 Shaeffer Hall, Iowa City, IA 52242, Ms. Joyce Baker, 319-335-2371.

Census Data Center, Dept. of Education, Grimes State Office Building, Des Moines, IA 50319, Mr. Steve Boal, 515-281-4730.

Kansas

State Library, Room 343-N, State Capitol Building, Topeka, KS 66612, Mr. Marc Galbraith, 913-296-3296.

Division of the Budget, Room 152-E, State Capitol Building, Topeka, KS 66612, 913-296-0025.

Institute for Public Policy and Business Research, 607 Blake Hall, The University of Kansas, Lawrence, KS 66045-2960, Ms. Thelma Helyar, 913-864-3123.

Center for Economic Development and Business Research, Box 48, Wichita State University, Wichita, KS 67208, Ms. Janet Nickel, 316-689-3225.

Population and Research Laboratory, Department of Sociology, Kansas State University, Manhattan, KS 66506, Dr. Leonard Bloomquist, 913-532-5984.

Kentucky

Center for Urban and Economic Research, College of Business and Public Administration, University of Louisville, Louisville, KY 40292, Mr. Ron Crouch, 502-852-7990.

Governor's Office of Policy and Management, Capitol Annex, Room 201, Frankfort, KY 40601, Mr. Mike Mullins, 502-564-7300.

State Library Division, Department for Libraries and Archives, 300 Coffeetree Road, P.O. Box 537, Frankfort, KY 40601, Ms. Brenda Fuller, 502-875-7000.

Louisiana

Office of Planning and Budget, Division of Administration, P.O. Box 94095, 1051 N. 3rd Street, Baton Rouge, LA 70804, Ms. Karen Paterson, 504-342-7410.

Division of Business and Economic Research, University of New Orleans, Lake Front, New Orleans, LA 70148, Mr. Vincent Maruggi, 504-286-6980.

Division of Business Research, Louisiana Tech Univ., P.O. Box 10318, Ruston, LA 71272, Dr. Edward O'Boyle, 318-257-3701.

Reference Department, Louisiana State Library, P.O. Box 131, Baton Rouge, LA 70821, Ms. Virginia Smith, 504-342-4920.

Center for Life Course and Population Studies, Department of Sociology, Room 126, Stubbs Hall, Louisiana State University, Baton Rouge, LA 70803-5411, Mr. Charles Tolbert, 504-388-5359.

Center for Business and Economic Research, Northeast Louisiana University, Monroe, LA 71209, Dr. Jerry Wall, 318-342-1215.

Maine

Division of Economic Analysis and Research, Maine Department of Labor, 20 Union Street, Augusta, ME 04330, Mr. Raynold Fongemie, Director, Ms. Jean Martin, 207-287-2271.

Maine State Library, State House Station 64, Augusta, ME 04333, Mr. Gary Nichols, 207-287-5600.

Maryland

Maryland Department of State Planning, 301 West Preston Street, Baltimore, MD 21201, Mr. Robert Dadd/Ms. Jane Traynham, 410-225-4450.

Computer Science Center, University of Maryland, College Park, MD 20742, Mr. John McNary, 301-405-3037.

Enoch Pratt Free Library, Resource Center, Maryland Room, 400 Cathedral Street, Baltimore, MD 21201, Mr. Jeff Korman, 410-396-1789.

Small Business Development Center, 217 E. Redwood St., 10th Floor, Baltimore, MD 21202, Mr. Michael E. Long, 410-333-6996.

Massachusetts

Massachusetts Institute for Social and Economic Research, 128 Thompson Hall, University of Massachusetts, Amherst, MA 01003, Dr. Stephen Coelen, Director, 413-545-3460, Ms. Valerie Conti, 413-545-0176.

Massachusetts Institute for Social and Economic Research, Box 219, Saltonstall State Office Building, Room 1103, Boston, MA 02133, Mr. William Murray, 617-727-4537.

Cape Cod Community Library, Library/Learning Resource Center, Route 132, West Barnstable, MA 02668, Ms. Jeanmarie Fraser, 508-362-8638.

University of Massachusetts, Documents Library, 100 Morrissey Blvd., Boston, MA 02125, Ms. Frances Schlisinger, 617-287-5935.

Michigan

Michigan Information Center, Department of Management and Budget, Office of Revenue and Tax Analysis, P.O. Box 30026, Lansing, MI 48909, Mr. Eric Swanson, 517-373-7910.

MIMIC/Center for Urban Studies, Wayne State University, Faculty/Administration Bldg., 656 W. Kirby, Detroit, MI 48202, Kurt Metzger, 313-577-8996.

The Library of Michigan, Government Documents Service, P.O. Box 30007, 717 W. Allegan St., Lansing, MI 48909, Ms. F. Anne Diamond, 517-373-0640.

Minnesota

State Demographer's Office, Minnesota Planning, 300 Centennial Office Building, 658 Cedar Street, St. Paul, MN 55155, Mr. David Birkholz, 612-296-2557, Mr. David Rademacher, 612-297-3255.

Metropolitan Council Research, 230 East 5th Street, St. Paul, MN 55101, Mr. Chuck Ballantine, 612-291-8140.

Interagency Resource and Information Center, Department of Education, 501 Capitol Square Building, St. Paul, MN 55101, Ms. Patricia Tupper, 612-296-6684.

Mississippi

Center for Population Studies, The University of Mississippi, Bondurant Bldg., Room 3W, University, MS 38677, Dr. Max Williams, Director/Ms. Rachel McNeely, Manager, 601-232-7288.

Governor's Office of Federal-State Programs, Department of Community Development, 301 West Pearl Street, Jackson, MS 39203-3096, Mr. Jim Catt, 601-949-2219.

Division of Research and Information Systems, Department of Economic and Community Development, 1200 Walter Sillas Building, P.O. Box 849, Jackson, MS 39205, Mr. Bill Rigby, 601-359-2674.

Missouri

Missouri State Library, 600 W. Main Street, P.O. Box 387, Jefferson City, MO 65102, Ms. Kate Graf, 314-751-1823.

Missouri Small Business Development Centers, 300 University Place, Columbia, MO 65211, Terry Maynard, 314-882-0344.

Office of Administration, 124 Capitol Building, P.O. Box 809, Jefferson City, MO 65102, Mr. Ryan Burson, 314-751-2345.

Office of Computing, University of Missouri-St. Louis, 8001 Natural Bridge Road, Room 451 CCB, St. Louis, MO 63121, Dr. John Blodgett/Ms. Linda McDaniel, 314-553-6014.

Office of Social and Economic Data Analysis, University of Missouri-Columbia, 224 Lewis Hall, Columbia, MO 65211, Ms. Evelyn J. Cleveland, 314-882-7396.

Geographic Resources Center, University of Missouri-Columbia, 17 Stewart Hall, Columbia, MO 65211, Mr. Tim Haithcoat, 314-882-1404.

Montana

Census and Economic Information Center, Montana Department of Commerce, P.O. Box 200501, 1424 9th Avenue, Helena, MT 59620-0501, Ms. Patricia Roberts, 406-444-2896.

Montana State Library, 1515 East 6th Avenue, Capitol Station, Helena, MT 59620, Ms. Kathy Brown, 406-444-3004.

Bureau of Business and Economic Research, University of Montana, Missoula, MT 59812, Mr. Jim Sylvester, 406-243-5113.

Research and Analysis Bureau, Employment Policy Division, Montana Department of Labor and Industry, P.O. Box 1728, Helena, MT 59624, Ms. Cathy Shenkle, 406-444-2430.

Nebraska

Center for Public Affairs Research, Nebraska State Data Center, Peter Kiewit Conference Center, #232, University of Nebraska at Omaha, Omaha, NE 68182, Mr. Jerome Deichert, 402-595-2311/Mr. Tim Himberger, 402-554-4883.

Policy Research Office, P.O. Box 94601, State Capitol, Room 1319, Lincoln, NE 68509-4601, Ms. Prem L. Bansal, 402-471-2414.

Federal Documents Librarian, Nebraska Library Commission, The Atrium, 1200 North Street, Suite 120, Lincoln, NE 68508-2006, 402-471-2045.

The Central Data Processing Division, Dept. of Administration Services, 301 Centennial Mall S., Lower Level, P.O. Box 95045, Lincoln, NE 68509-5045, Mr. Jerry Douglas, 402-471-4862.

Nebraska Department of Labor, 550 S. 16th St., P.O. Box 94600, Lincoln, NE 68509-4600, Mr. Robert H. Shanahan, 402-471-2518.

Natural Resources Commission, 301 Centennial Mall South, P.O. Box 94876, Lincoln, NE 68509-4876, Mr. Mahendra Bansal, 402-471-2081.

Nevada

Nevada State Library, Capitol Complex, 100 Stewart Street, Carson City, NV 89710, Ms. Joan Kerschner/Ms. Patricia Deadder, 702-687-8327.

New Hampshire

Office of State Planning, 2-1/2 Beacon Street, Concord, NH 03301, Mr. Tom Duffy, 603-271-2155.

New Hampshire State Library, 20 Park Street, Concord, NH 03301-6303, Mr. John McCormick, 603-271-2060.

Office of Biometrics, University of New Hampshire, Pettee Hall, Durham, NH 03824, Mr. Owen Durgin, 603-862-3930.

New Jersey

New Jersey Department of Labor, Division of Labor Market and Demographic Research, CN 388-John Fitch Plaza, Trenton, NJ 08625-0388, Ms. Connie O. Hughes, Asst. Dir., 609-984-2593.

New Jersey State Library, U.S. Documents Office, 185 West State Street, CN 520, Trenton, NJ 08625-0520, Ms. Beverly Railsback, 609-292-6259.

CIT - Information Services, Princeton University, 87 Prospect Ave., Princeton, NJ 08544, Ms. Judith S. Rowe, 609-258-6052.

Center for Computer and Information Services, Rutgers University, CCIS-Hill Center, Busch Campus, P.O. Box 879, Piscataway, NJ 08854, Ms. Chris Jarocha-Ernst, 908-932-0265.

Rutgers University, Edward J. Bloustein School of Planning and Public Policy, Kilmer Campus, Lucy Stone Hall, B Wing, New Brunswick, NJ 08903, Dr. James Hughes, Assoc. Dean, 908-932-3822.

New Mexico

Economic Development Department, 1100 St. Francis Drive, Santa Fe, NM 87503, Ms. Laurie Moye, 505-827-0182.

New Mexico State Library, 325 Don Gaspar Avenue, P.O. Box 1629, Santa Fe, NM 87503, Ms. Laura Chaney, 505-827-3824.

Bureau of Business and Economic Research, University of New Mexico, 1920 Lomas NE, Albuquerque, NM 87131-6021, Mr. Kevin Kargacin, 505-277-6626, Mr. Bobby Leitch, 505-277-2216.

Department of Economics, New Mexico State Univ., Box 30001, Las Cruces, NM 88003, Dr. Kathleen Brook, 505-646-2112.

New York

Division of Policy and Research, Department of Economic Development, 1 Commerce Plaza, Room 905, 99 Washington Avenue, Albany, NY 12245, Mr. Robert Scardamalia, 518-474-1141.

Cornell University, CISER Data Archive, 201 Caldwell Hall, Ithaca, NY 14853, Ms. Ann Gray, 607-255-4801.

Nelson A. Rockefeller Institute of Government, 411 State Street, Albany, NY 12203, Michael Cooper, 518-443-5258.

New York State Library, 6th Floor, Cultural Education Center, Empire State Plaza, Albany, NY 12230, Ms. Mary Redmond, 518-474-3940.

Division of Equalization and Assessment, 16 Sheridan Avenue, Albany, NY 12210, Mr. Wilfred B. Pauquette, 518-474-6742.

North Carolina

North Carolina Office of State Planning, 116 West Jones Street, Raleigh, NC 27603-8003, Ms. Francine Stephenson, 919-733-3683.

Division of State Library, 109 East Jones Street, Raleigh, NC 27601-2807, Mr. Joel Sigmon, 919-733-3683.

Institute for Research in Social Science, University of North Carolina, Manning Hall CB 3355, Chapel Hill, NC 27599-3355, Mr. Ed Bachmann, 919-962-0512.

Center for Geographic Information, Office of State Planning, P.O. Box 27687, Raleigh, NC 27611, Ms. Karen Siderelis/Tim Johnson, 919-733-2090.

North Dakota

Department of Agricultural Economics, North Dakota State University, Morrill Hall, Room 224, P.O. Box 5636, Fargo, ND 58105, Dr. Richard Rathge, 701-237-8621.

Office of Intergovernment Assistance, State Capitol, 14th Floor, Bismarck, ND 58505, Mr. Jim Boyd, 701-224-2094.

Department of Geography, University of North Dakota, Grand Forks, ND 58202, Mohammad Hemmasi, 701-777-4246.

North Dakota State Library, Liberty Memorial Building, Capitol Grounds, Bismarck, ND 58505, Ms. Susan Pahlmeyer, 701-224-2490.

Northern Mariana Islands

Department of Commerce and Labor, Central Statistics Division, Saipan, Mariana Islands 96950, Mr. Juan Borja, 670-322-0874/0876.

Ohio

Ohio Data Users Center, Ohio Department of Development, P.O. Box 1001, 77 High Street, 27th Floor, Columbus, OH 43266-0101, Mr. Barry Bennett, 614-466-2115.

State Library of Ohio, 65 South Front Street, Columbus, OH 43215, Mr. Clyde Hordusky, 614-644-7051.

Cleveland State University, Northern Ohio Data and Information Service/The Urban Center, 1737 East Euclid Avenue, Room 45, Cleveland, OH 44115-9239, Mr. Mark Salling, 216-687-2209.

Ohio State University Library/ Census Data Center, 126 Main Library, 1858 Neil Avenue Mall, Columbus, OH 43210, Mr. Brian Martin, 614-292-6175.

University of Cincinnati, Southwest Ohio Regional Data Center, Institute for Policy Research, Mail Loc. 132, Cincinnati, OH 45221, Mr. Mark Carrozza, 513-556-5082.

Oklahoma

Oklahoma State Data Center, Oklahoma Department of Commerce, 6601 Broadway Extension, (Mailing address) P.O. Box 26980, Oklahoma City, OK 73126-0980, Mr. Jeff Wallace, 405-841-5184.

Oklahoma Department of Libraries, 200 NE 18th Street, Oklahoma City, OK 73105, Mr. Steve Beleu, 405-521-2502.

Center for Economic and Management Research, The University of Oklahoma, 307 W. Brooks, Norman, OK 73019, Mr. John McCraw, 405-325-2931.

Oregon

Oregon State Library, State Library Building, Salem, OR 97310, Mr. Craig Smith, 503-378-4277.

Center for Population Research and Census, School of Urban and Public Affairs, Portland State University, P.O. Box 751, Portland, OR 97207-0751, Mr. Ed Shafer/Ms. Maria Wilson-Figueroa, 503-725-5159.

Oregon Housing and Community Services Department, 1600 State Street, Suite 100, Salem, OR 97310-0161, Mr. Mike Murphy, 503-378-4730.

Geographic Information Systems, Department of Energy Building, 625 Marion Street NE, Salem, OR 97310, Mr. Kenneth C. Yingling, 503-378-4036.

Pennsylvania

Pennsylvania State Data Center, Institute of State and Regional Affairs, Pennsylvania State University at Harrisburg, 777 W. Harrisburg Pike, Middletown, PA 17057, Mr. Michael Behney, 717-948-6336.

Pennsylvania State Library, Forum Building, Harrisburg, PA 17105, Mr. John Geschwindt, 717-787-2327.

Puerto Rico

Puerto Rico Planning Board, Minillas Government Center, North Bldg., Avenida De Diego, P.O. Box 41119, San Juan, PR 00940-9985, Sr. Jose Jiminez, 809-728-4430.

Departmento de Educacion, P.O. Box 759, Hato Rey, PR 00919, Sra. Carmen Martinez, Sra. Nayada Pratts, 809-724-1046.

Universidad Intermaericana, Recinto de Guayama, P.O. Box 1559, Guayama, PR 00785, Angel Rivera, 809-864-2222.

Rhode Island

United Way of Rhode Island, 229 Waterman Street, Providence, RI 02906, Ms. Jane Nugent, 401-521-9000.

Rhode Island Department of State Library Services, 300 Richmond Street, Providence, RI 02903, Mr. Frank Iacona, 401-277-2726.

Social Science Data Center, Brown University, P.O. Box 1916, Providence, RI 02912, Mr. James McNally, 401-863-3459.

Rhode Island Department of Administration, Office of Municipal Affairs, One Capitol Hill, Providence, RI 02908-5873, Mr. Paul Egan, 401-277-6493.

Office of Health Statistics, Rhode Island Department of Health, 3 Capitol Hill, Providence, RI 02908, Dr. Jay Buechner, 401-277-2550.

Rhode Island Department of Education, 22 Hayes Street, Providence, RI 02908, Mr. James P. Karon, 401-277-3126.

Rhode Island Department of Economic Development, 7 Jackson Walkway, Providence, RI 02903, Mr. Vincent Harrington, 401-277-2601.

South Carolina

Division of Research and Statistical Services, South Carolina Budget and Control Board, Rembert Dennis Bldg. Room 425, Columbia, SC 29201, Mr. Bobby Bowers/Mr. Mike Macfarlane, 803-734-3780.

South Carolina State Library, P.O. Box 11469, Columbia, SC 29211, Ms. Mary Bostick, 803-734-8666.

South Dakota

Business Research Bureau, School of Business, University of South Dakota, 414 East Clark, Vermillion, SD 57069, Ms. DeVee Dykstra, 605-677-5287.

Documents Department, South Dakota State Library, 800 Governors Drive, Pierre, SD 57501-2294, Ms. Cheri Adams, 605-773-3131.

Labor Market Information Center, South Dakota Department of Labor, 420 S. Roosevelt, Box 4730, Aberdeen, SD 57402-4730, Mr. Phillip George, 605-622-2314.

Office of Administration Services, South Dakota Department of Health, 445 E. Capitol Avenue, Pierre, SD 57501-3185, Mr. John Jones, 605-773-3693.

South Dakota State University, Rural Sociology Department, Scobey Hall 226, Box 504, Brookings, SD 57007, Mr. Jim Satterlee, 605-688-4132.

Tennessee

Tennessee State Planning Office, John Sevier State Office Bldg., 500 Charlotte Ave., Suite 307, Nashville, TN 37243-0001, Mr. Charles Brown, 615-741-1676.

Center for Business and Economic Research, College of Business Administration, University of Tennessee, Room 100, Glocker Hall, Knoxville, TN 37996-4170, Ms. Betty Vickers, 615-974-5441.

Texas

State Data Center, Texas Department of Commerce, 9th and Congress Streets, (Mailing address) P.O. Box 12728, Capitol Station, Austin, TX 78711, Ms. Susan Tully, 512-320-9667.

Department of Rural Sociology, Texas A & M University System, Special Services Building, College Station, TX 77843-2125, Dr. Steve Murdock, 409-845-5115/5332.

Texas Natural Resources Information System (TNRIS), P.O. Box 13231, Austin, TX 78711, Mr. Charles Palmer, 512-463-8399.

Texas State Library and Archive Commission, P.O. Box 12927, Capitol Station, Austin, TX 78711, Ms. Diana Houston, 512-463-5455.

Utah

Office of Planning and Budget, State Capitol, Room 116, Salt Lake City, UT 84114, Ms. Linda Smith, 801-538-1550, Ms. Kirin McInnis, 801-538-1036.

University of Utah, Bureau of Economic and Business Research, 401 KDGB, Salt Lake City, UT 84112, Mr. Frank Hachman, 801-581-3353.

Department of Community and Economic Development, 324 South State Street, Suite 500, Salt Lake City, UT 84111, Mr. Doug Jex, 801-538-8897.

Department of Employment Security, 140 East 300 South, P.O. Box 11249, Salt Lake City, UT 84147-0249, Mr. Ken Jensen, 801-536-7813.

Vermont

Office of Policy Research and Coordination, Pavilion Office Building, 109 State Street, Montpelier, VT 05609, Ms. Cynthia Clancy, 802-828-3326.

Center for Rural Studies, University of Vermont, 207 Morrill Hall, Burlington, VT 05405-0106, Mr. Kevin Wiberg, 802-656-3201.

Vermont Department of Libraries, 109 State Street, Montpelier, VT 05609-0601, Ms. Sybil McShane, 802-828-3261.

Vermont Travel Department, 134 State Street, Montpelier, VT 05609, 802-828-3217.

Virginia

Virginia Employment Commission, 703 East Main Street, Richmond, VA 23219, Mr. Dan Jones, 804-786-8308.

Center for Public Service, University of Virginia, 918 Emmet Street North, Suite 300, Charlottesville, VA 22903-3491, Dr. Michael Spar, 804-982-5585.

Virginia State Library, Documents Section, 11th Street at Capitol Square, Richmond, VA 23219-3491, Mr. William R. Chamberlin, 804-786-2303.

Virgin Islands

University of the Virgin Islands, Eastern Caribbean Center, No. 2 John Brewer's Bay, Charlotte Amalie, St. Thomas, VI 00802, Dr. Frank Mills, 809-776-9200.

Virgin Islands Department of Economic Development, P.O. Box 6400, Charlotte Amalie, St. Thomas, VI 00801, Mr. Dan Inveen, 809-774-8784.

Washington

Forecasting Division, Office of Financial Management, 450 Insurance Bldg., Box 43113, Olympia, WA 98504-3113, Mr. George Hough, 206-586-2504.

Puget Sound Council of Govts., 216 1st Avenue South, Seattle, WA 98104, Neil Kilgren, 206-464-5355.

Social Research Center, Department of Rural Sociology, Washington State University, Pullman, WA 99164-4006, Dr. Annabel Kirschner-Cook, 509-335-4519.

Department of Sociology, Demographic Research Laboratory, Western Washington University, Bellingham, WA 98225, Mr. Lucky Tedrow, Director, 206-650-3176.

Department of Employment Security, LMEA, P.O. Box 46000, Olympia, WA 98504-6000, Gary Bodeutsch, 206-438-4804.

CSSCR, University of Washington, 145 Savery Hall, DK 45, Seattle, WA 98195, Fred Nick, 206-543-8110.

West Virginia

West Virginia Development Office, Research and Strategic Planning Division, Capitol Complex, Building 6, Room 553, Charleston, WV 25305, Ms. Mary C. Harless, 304-558-4010.

Reference Library, West Virginia State Library Commission, Science and Cultural Center, Capitol Complex, Charleston, WV 25305, Ms. Karen Goff, 304-348-2045.

Office of Health Services Research, WVU Health Science Center, Medical Center Drive, P.O. Box 9145, Morgantown, WV 26506-9145, Mr. Alex Lubman, 304-293-1086.

The Center for Economic Research, West Virginia University, 323 Business and Economic Building, Morgantown, WV 26506-6025, Dr. Tom Witt, Director/Mr. Randy Childs, 304-293-7832.

Wisconsin

Department of Administration, Demographic Services Center, 101 E. Wilson Street, 6th Floor, P.O. Box 7868, Madison, WI 53707-7868, Ms. Nadene Roenspies/Mr. Robert Naylor, 608-266-1927.

Applied Population Laboratory, Department of Rural Sociology, University of Wisconsin, 1450 Linden Drive, Room 316, Madison, WI 53706, Mr. Michael Knight, 608-265-3044.

Wyoming

Survey Research Center, University of Wyoming, P.O. Box 3925, Laramie, WY 82071, Mr. G. Fred Doll, 307-766-2931.

Department of Administration and Information, Economic Analysis Division, Emerson Building 327E, Cheyenne, WY 82002-0060, Mr. Steve Furtney/Mr. Wenlin Liu, 307-777-7504.

State Labor Information Centers

Alabama

Department of Industrial Relations, Research and Statistics Division, 649 Monroe St., Montgomery, AL 36130, 205-242-8855; Selected Publications: *Monthly Labor Market, Annual Average Labor Force, Occupational Trends*. Computer Readable Formats: No; Custom Research: Limited amount available free.

Alaska

Department of Labor, Research and Analysis, P.O. Box 25501, Juneau, AK 99802-5501, 907-465-4500; Selected Publications: *Economic Trends, Akcens Quarterly Newsletter, Career Guide, Industry-Occupation Outlook to 1994, Micro-Computer Occupational Information System (Micro-OIS), Wage Rates, Occupational Injury and Illness Information, Population Overview, Special Demographic Reports, Directory of Licensed Occupations, Residency Analysis of Alaska's Workers by Firm, Employment Insurance, Actuarial Study and Financial Handbook, State Salary Survey*. Computer Readable Formats: Limited availability; Custom Research: Limited amount available free.

Arizona

Department of Economic Security West, Research Administration, 1789 West Jefferson, Site Code 733A, Phoenix, AZ 85007, 602-542-3871; Selected Publications: *Arizona Economic Trends, Job Searchers Guide, Metro, Non-Metro Affirmative Action Planning Information, Applying for Government Jobs, Arizona Labor Market Newsletter, Arizona Occupational Employment Forecasts, Arizona Occupational Profiles, Employer Wage Survey, Helpful Hints for Job Seekers, Map of Major Employers*. Charge for special projects; all shelf publications are free.

Arkansas

Employment Security Department, Labor Market Information Section, P.O. Box 2981, Little Rock, AR 72203, 501-682-3197; Selected Publications: *Annual Planning Information, Annual Report, Annual Report of the Employment Security Division, Arkansas Labor Force Statistics, Covered Employment and Earnings, Interface Supply and Demand, Statistical Review, Current Employment Developments, Monthly Employment Trends, Monthly County Labor Market Information, Directory of Licensed Occupations, Job Hunters Guide to AR, Occupational Trends, Staffing Patterns*. Computer Readable Formats: Occupational trends on disk; Custom Research: A limited amount is available free.

California

Employment Development Department, Labor Market Information Division, 7000 Franklin Blvd., #1100, Sacramento, CA 95823, 916-262-2237; Selected Publications: *Annual Planning Information, California Labor Market Bulletin, Labor Market Information for Affirmative Action Programs, Labor Market Conditions in California, California Occupational Guides, Projections of Employment By Industry and Occupation*. Computer Readable Formats: Limited; Custom Research: Most everything is free.

Colorado

Department of Labor and Employment, Labor Market Information Section, 393 S. Harland Street, Lakewood, CO 80226; 303-937-4935; Selected Publications: *Affirmative Action Packets, Annual Planning Information Report, Colorado Springs Labor Force, Employment and Wages Quarterly, Occupational Employment Outlook Projection, Job Bank Wage Listing, Occupational Employment in Selected Industries, Quarterly Occupational Supply/Demand Outlook, Pueblo Labor Force, Occupational Supply and Demand, Denver, Boulder, Front Range, Western Slope, Occupational Employment Survey Publishing, Employment Projections*. Computer Readable Formats: No; Custom Research: Free on a limited basis.

Connecticut

Department of Labor, Office of Research and Information, 200 Folly Brook Blvd, Wethersfield, CT 06109-1114, 203-566-3472; Selected Publications: *Annual Report of the Commission of the Labor in Economy Work Force and Training Needs in Connecticut, Planning for the Future Publishing, Work Place 2000, Labor Situation, Labor Force Data, Annual Planning Information, The Occupational Outlook, New Manufacturing Firms* ($7 per year fee), *Occupations in Demand, Labor Market Review, Occupational Projections and Training Data*. Computer Readable Formats; No: Custom Research: Free.

Delaware

Labor Department, Occupational and Labor Market Information Office, P.O. Box 9029, University Office Plaza, Newark, DE 19714, 302-368-6962; Selected Publications: *Delaware Annual Brief, Delaware Monthly Digest, Delaware Jobs to 2005* $7.50, *Delaware Career Compass, Career Guidance-High School Information on Job Growth, ES202 Series, Occupational Wage Data-Government and Educational Services* (three year cycle), *Delaware Labor Supply and Demand: Occupational and Industrial Projections*. Computer Readable Formats: Inquire requested; Custom Research: Limited amount available free.

District of Columbia

Employment Services Department, Labor Market Information, Room 201, 500 C St., NW, Washington, DC 20001, 202-724-7214; Selected Publications: *Area Labor Summary, Labor Market*

Information for Affirmative Action Programs, Directory of 200 Major Employers, Annual Population Estimates By Census Tract; Computer Readable Formats: No; All shelf publications are free.

Florida

Department of Labor and Employment Security, Bureau of Labor Market Information, Suite 200, Hartman Building, 2012 Capital Circle, S.E., Tallahassee, FL 32399-2151, 904-488-1048; Selected Publications: *Affirmative Action Statistical Packets, Florida Employment Statistics, Florida Industry and Occupational Employment 1995, Florida Occupational Employment in Hospitals, Labor Force Summary, Labor Market Trends, Occupational Employment in Federal Government, Occupations Employment in the Finance, Insurance and Real Estate Industry, Occupational Employment in the Services Industry, Occupational Wage Surveys*. Computer Readable Formats: Bulletin board system for direct downloading.

Georgia

Department of Labor, Labor Information Systems, 148 International Blvd., NE, Atlanta, GA 30303, 404-656-3177; Selected Publications: *Area Labor Profiles, Civilian Labor Force Estimates, GA Employment and Earnings, GA Employment and Wages, GA Labor Market Trends, GA Occupational Employment, Civilian Labor Force Estimates, Data on Occupational Supply and Demand, Earnings by Industry and Area*. Computer Readable Formats: No; Custom Research: Charge for Large projects, all others free.

Hawaii

Labor Market and Employment Services Branch, Labor and Industrial Relations Dept., 830 Punchbowl St., Research Division, Honolulu, HI 96813, 808-586-8999; Selected Publications: *Labor Shortages in Agriculture, Demand Occupations, Occupations in Communication Industry, Job Hunters's Guide, Selected Wage Information, Unemployment Insurance Fact Book, Licensed Occupations, Occupational Employment Statistics, Occupational Illness and Injuries, Wage Rate, Workers Compensation, Characteristics of the Insured Unemployed, Employment and Payrolls, Labor Area News, Labor Force Information for Affirmative Action Programs*. Computer Readable Formats: No; Custom Research: Free.

Idaho

Department of Employment, Research and Analysis Bureau, 317 Main St., Boise, ID 83735, (208) 334-6469; Selected Publications: *LMI Directory, Idaho Monthly Employment Newsletter, Labor Forces in Idaho, Basic Economic Data, Annual Demographics Report, Affirmative Action Statistics, Area Employment Newsletter, Employment and Wages by Industry in Idaho*. Most everything is free, Fee for larger projects.

Illinois

Employment Security Bureau, Research and Analysis, 401 South State St., Chicago, IL 60605, 312-793-2316; Selected Publications: *Country Labor Force Summary-2000, Labor Market Review, Illinois at Work, Affirmative Action Information, Occupational Employment Statistics, Occupational Projections, Wage Survey, Where Workers Work, Illinois Employment*

Industrial Summary. Computer Readable Formats: No; Custom Research: Nominal fee.

Indiana

Employment Security Division, Labor Market Information, 10 N. Senate Ave., Indianapolis, IN 46209, 317-232-7701; Selected Publications: *Annual County Employment Patterns, Indiana Employment Review, Labor Force Estimates, Quarterly Covered Employment and Payrolls, Regional Economic Profiles, Occupational Employment Projections, Occupational Wage Surveys, Occupations In Demand, Hours and Earnings of Production Workers*. Computer Readable Formats: No; All shelf publications are free.

Iowa

Department of Employment Services, Labor Market Information Unit, 1000 E. Grand Ave., Des Moines, IA 50319, 515-281-8182; Selected Publications: *Condition of Employment Report/Analysis of the Iowa Market, Labor Market Information for Service Delivery Areas, State-Wide Wage Surveys, Labor Market Information for Affirmative Action Programs, Industry/Occupational Projections, Job Insurance Benefits, Iowa Occupational Planning Guide, Licensed Occupations, Labor Market Information Directory, Wages and Employment Covered by Employment Security, Affirmative Action Data for Iowa, Condition of Employment*. Computer Readable Formats: Electronic bulletin board; Custom Research: Free, nominal fee for larger projects.

Kansas

Department of Human Resources, Division of Employment and Training, Research and Analysis Section, 401 S.W. Topeka Blvd., Topeka, KS 66603, 913-296-5058; Selected Publications: *Occupational Staffing Patterns, Kansas Unemployment Insurance Claims, Monthly Labor Market Summary, Kansas Wage Survey, Affirmative Action Packet, Labor Market Review, Report on Employment-Hours and Earnings, Labor Force Estimates*. Computer Readable Formats: Limited; Custom Research: Charge for large projects, all others free.

Kentucky

Department for Employment Services, Research and Statistics, 275 E. Main St., CHR Bldg and Fl., Frankfort, KY 40601, 502-564-7976; Selected Publications: *Non-Agricultural Wage and Salary Employment, Kentucky Labor Market Newsletter, Estimate of Production Workers and Average Hours and Earnings, Labor Force Estimates, Occupational Outlook, Labor Area Summary, Labor Area Profile, Annual Planning Information, Affirmative Action, Labor Supply Estimates, Characteristics of Insured Unemployed, Average Covered Monthly Workers in Manufacturing by Industry Division and County, Total Wages by Industrial Division and County, Average Weekly Wages by Industrial Division and County*. Computer Readable Formats: No; Custom Research: Limited.

Louisiana

Department of Employment Security, Research and Statistics Unit, P.O. 94094, Baton Rouge, LA 70804-9094, 504-342-3141; Selected Publications: *Occupational Projections-1999-2000,*

Quarterly Employment and Wages, Annual Employment and Wages, Monthly Labor Market Information, Manpower for Affirmative Action, Annual Planning Report, Occupational Employment Statistics, Average Weekly Wage, LA Occupational Injuries and Illnesses. Computer Readable Formats: Limited; Custom Research: Limited amount available free.

Maine

Bureau of Employment Security, Division of Economic Analysis and Research, 20 Union St., Augusta, ME 04330-6826, 207-287-2271; Selected Publications: *Labor Market Digest Monthly, Maine Occupational Staffing Patterns in Hospitals-Government-Manufacturing/ Nonmanufacturing-Trade, Careers In Maine Woods.* Computer Readable Formats: Yes; Custom Research: Charge for larger projects, all others free.

Maryland

Department of Human Resources, Research and Analysis, Employment and Training, 1100 N. Eutaw St., Baltimore, MD 21201, 410-333-5007; Selected Publications: *Affirmative Action Data, Maryland Occupational Industrial Outlook, Civilian Labor Force Employment and Unemployment by Place of Residence, Claims Processed for Unemployment Insurance Benefits, Occupations in Maryland, Current Employment Statistics, Employment and Payrolls Covered by the Unemployment Insurance Law of Maryland, Zoned Employment and Unemployment Statistics, Industries in Maryland, Highlights of Maryland's Population Projections, Maryland Rural Manpower Report, Occupational Wage Information, Year in Review, Population and Labor Force in Maryland, A Profile: Services Industry in Maryland 1980-Present.* Computer Readable Formats: No. Customer Research: Limited amount available free.

Massachusetts

Division of Employment Security, Massachusetts Employment and Training Center, 19 Saniford Street, Charles F. Hurley Building, Boston, MA 02114, 617-626-6003; Selected Publications: *Planning Data: Massachusetts, Employment and Wages, Massachusetts Employment Review* (monthly), *Careers and Training in Allied Health, Career Choices in a Changing Economy.* Computer Readable Formats: Limited amount available free; Publications free when available.

Michigan

Employment Security Commission, Bureau of Research and Statistics, 7310 Woodward Ave., Detroit, MI 48202, 313-876-5439; Selected Publications: *Affirmative Action Information Report, Annual Planning Information, Claims Counter, Covered Employment Statistics, Monthly Labor Market Review, Occupational Employment Statistics Survey Publications, Occupations in Education, Occupational Wage Information, Michigan Regulated and Trade Industries, Occupational Projections and Training Data, Michigan Occupation/Industry Outlook 2000, Michigan Metropolitan Areas Occupation/Industry Outlook 2000, Michigan Non-metropolitan Areas Occupation/Industry Outlook 2000, Michigan Occupational Supply/Demand Report, Occupational Projections and Training Information for Michigan-OPTIM, Civilian Labor Force, Employment and Unemployment Estimates, Employment Hours*

and Earnings Estimates, Unemployment Insurance Program Statistics, Employment Trends, Hours and Earnings Trends, Production Worker Employee Trends 1982 to Present. Computer Readable Formats: Limited, electronic bulletin board; Custom Research: Limited amount available free.

Minnesota

Department of Jobs and Training, Research Office, 390 North Robert St., St. Paul MN 55101, 612-296-8716; Selected Publications: *Consumer Price Index, Career Bulletin, Employment Outlook by Region, Minnesota Wage Data by Industry and Area, Minnesota Employment Outlook to 1996, Minnesota Careers, MN Wage Data By Industry and Size of Firm, Employment and Wage Data By County, Minnesota Labor Market Review.* Computer Readable Format: Some data available via electronic bulletin board; Custom Research: Charge for large projects, all others free.

Mississippi

Employment Security Commission, Labor Market Information Department, P.O. Box 1699, Jackson, MS 39215-1699, 601-961-7424; Selected .PA Publications: *Guide to Labor Market Information, Annual Labor Force Averages, Annual Report, Employment and Job Openings 2005, Farm Income and Expenditures, Affirmative Action Programs, Monthly Labor Market Data, Labor Market Trends for Jackson Metro Area, Mississippi's Business Population, Occupational Employment and Job Openings by Unit of Analysis, Personal Income by Major Sources, Quarterly Labor Market Summary, Transfer Payments by Major Sources.* Computer Readable Formats: Yes, some publications available on diskettes; Customer Research: Limited amount available free.

Missouri

Division of Employment Security, Research and Analysis, P.O. Box 59, Jefferson City, MO 65104, 314-751-3602; Selected Publications: *Monthly Area Labor Trends, Labor Market Information for Affirmative Action Programs, Wages Paid in Selected Occupations, Employment Outlook.* Custom Research: Limited research available.

Montana

Department of Labor and Industry, Research and Analysis Bureau, P.O. Box 1728, Helena, MT 59624, 406-444-2430; Selected Publications: *Wage Surveys of the Private Sector, Wage Surveys of the Public Sector, Wage Surveys of Public Education, Quarterly Employment and Labor Force, Monthly Statistics in Brief, Annual Planning Information.* Computer Readable Formats: Forthcoming; Custom Research: Limited Amount available free.

Nebraska

Department of Labor, Labor Market Information, 550 South 16th St., Lincoln, NE 68509, 402-471-2600; Selected Publications: *Prairie/Farm and Ranch Profile, NE Labor Market Information Quarterly, Careers and Education in Nebraska, Monthly Labor Area Summary, Occupational Employment Statistics by Industry, Monthly Labor Force, Affirmative Action, Survey of Average Hourly Wage Rates, Occupational Newsletter.* Computer

Market Studies, Demographics, and Statistics

Readable Formats: No; Custom Research: Limited amount available for free.

Nevada

Employment Security Department, Employment Security Research Section, 500 E Third St., Carson City, NV 89713, 702-687-4550; Selected Publications: *Area Labor Review, Directory of Labor Market Information, Quarterly and Monthly Economic Update, Nevada Wage Survey, Occupational Projections, Job Finding Techniques.* Computer Readable Formats: Limited; Custom Research: Limited amount available free.

New Jersey

Labor Department, Labor Market Information Office, John Fitch Plaza CN056, Trenton, NJ 08625, 609-292-7376; Selected Publications: *Regional Labor Market Reviews, Regional Labor Market Newsletters, Compendium of New Jersey Wage Surveys, Employment and Economy Newsletter, Employment Trends, Economic Indicators Monthly.* Computer Readable Formats: Limited electronic bulletin board usage; Custom Research: Limited amount available free.

New Hampshire

Employment Security Department, Economic Analysis and Reports and Labor Market Information Bureau, 32 South Main St., Concord, NH 03301, 603-224-3311; Selected Publications: *Wage Survey, Vital Signs, Staffing Patterns in NH, Annual Report, Annual Planning Information, Annual Planning Information MSA's, Community Patterns NH, Economic Conditions, Employment and Wages by County, Employment and Wages MSA's, Employment and Wages by Planning Region, Fact Book: Cities and Towns, Firms By Size, Local Area Unemployment Statistics, NH Affirmative Action Data, NH Occupational Outlook 2005, Users Guide to Labor Market Information.* Computer Readable Formats: Call for availability and cost; Custom Research: Free.

New Mexico

Department of Employment Security, Economic Research and Analysis, P.O. Box 1928, Albuquerque, NM 87103, 505-841-8645; Selected Publications: *Covered Employment and Wages, Basic Concepts, Monthly Labor Market Review, Nonagricultural Wage and Salary Employment, Facts and Figures about New Mexico, Hours and Earnings Estimates, Albuquerque Small Employer Wage Survey, Jobs to 2000, Area Job Market Flyers, Large Employers in New Mexico by County.* Computer Readable Formats: Limited; Customer Research: Limited amount available for free.

New York

Department of Labor, Division of Research and Statistics, State Office Bldg. Campus #12, Albany, NY 12240, 518-457-3800; Selected Publications: *Statistics on Operations, Occupational Outlooks, Civilian Labor Force by Occupation, Selected Demographic Groups, Regular and Extended Benefits, State Unemployment Insurance, Collective Bargaining Settlements, Directory of Labor Unions and Employee Organizations in New York State Employment Review, Current Population Survey Data, Earnings and Hours in Selected Industries, The Job Seeker,* *Labor Area Summary Monthly Statistical Report, Labor Area Summary Quarterly Analytical Report, Labor Market Assessment: Occupational Supply and Demand, Occupational Brief, Occupational Projections, Occupational Employment Statistics, Occupational Guide, Occupational Needs, Occupation Licensed or Certified by New York State, Operations, Resident Employment Status of the Civilian Labor Force, Careers Exploration and Job Seeking, Total and Civilian Labor Force Summary, Selected Demographic Groups - NYS, Counties and SMSA's, Selected Labor Research Reports, Apprentice Training Hours and Earnings, Insured Employment and Payrolls, Local Area Unemployment Statistics, Non-Agricultural Wage and Salary Employment, Unemployment Insurance Operating Statistics.* Custom Research: Charge for large projects, all others free.

North Carolina

Employment Security Commission, Labor Market Information Division, P.O. Box 25903, Raleigh, NC 27611, 919-733-2936; Selected Publications: *Employment and Wages in NC Quarterly, Market Areas Newsletter, Past High School Intentions of NC Graduates by County, Occupational Trends: Year 2000: NC, NC Metro State Planning Regions A-F; G-L; M-R, NC Preliminary Civilian Labor Force Estimates, Active Job Applicants by County, Registered Applicants and Job Openings, Follow-Up Survey of NC High School Graduates by County, Wage Rates in Selected Occupations.* Computer Readable Formats: Forthcoming; Custom Research: Free, charge for larger projects.

North Dakota

Job Service, Research and Statistics, P.O. Box 5507, Bismarck, ND 58502, 701-224-3048; Selected Publications: *Occupational Supply/Demand Report, Employment and Wages, Monthly Labor Market Advisor, Occupations Wage Surveys and Benefits for Major Cities, Occupational Projections to 2000, Employment Surveys by Major City, Annual Planning Report.* Computer Readable Formats: No; Custom Research: Charge for large amounts, all others free.

Ohio

Bureau of Employment Services, Labor Market Information Division, 145 South Front St., Columbus, OH 43216, 614-466-4636; Selected Publications: *Employment and Unemployment Estimates, Covered Employment and Payroll, Trend Tables, Monthly Labor Market Review, County Labor Force Reports, Labor Force Estimates, Metropolitan Profile, Occupational Projections, Composition of Job Placements, Summary of Ohio Worker Training Program Activities.* Computer Readable Formats: Yes; Custom Research: Charge for large projects, all others free.

Oklahoma

Oklahoma Employment Security Commission, Economic Analysis, 2401 N. Lincoln Blvd., Oklahoma City, OK 73105, 405-557-7104; Selected Publications: *Labor Market Information, Manpower Information for Affirmative Action, Annual Report to the Governor, Handbook of Employment Statistics, County Employment and Wage Data, Occupational Wage Surveys.* Computer Readable Formats: Yes; Custom Research: Charge for large projects, all other free.

Oregon

Employment Division, Research and Statistics, 875 Union NE, Salem, OR 97311, 503-378-8656; Selected Publications: *Oregon Work Force at Risk, Dislocated Workers, Oregon Works, Affirmative Action Programs, Agricultural Employment, Average Weekly Earnings-Hours, Business and Employment Outlook, Monthly Local Labor Trends, Occupational Program Planning System, Oregon Wage Information.* Computer Readable Formats: No; Custom Research: Charge for large projects, all others free.

Pennsylvania

Department of Labor and Industry, Research and Statistics Division, 300 Capital Associates Bldg., Harrisburg, PA 17120-0034, 717-787-2114; Selected Publications: *Work Force 2000, Civilian Work Force Data by Labor Market Area of Residence, Annual Average Labor Force Data, Civilian Labor Force Series by Labor Market Area, PA Labor Market Areas Ranked on Basis of Rate of Unemployment, PA Unemployment Fact Sheet, Occupational Wage Surveys, Employment and Wages of Workers Covered by the PA Unemployment Compensation Law, Occupations Employment in Hospital Occupational Staffing Patterns for Selected Non-Manufacturing Industries, Affirmative Action Report, Labor Market Job Guides, PA's Microcomputer Occupational Information System* ($250), *Current Trends in Employment and Wages in PA Industries, PA Labor Force, Annual Planning Information Report, Hours and Earnings in Manufacturing and Selected Non-manufacturing Industries.* Computer Readable Formats: No; Custom Research: Charge for large projects, all others free.

Rhode Island

Department of Employment Security, Research and Statistics, 101 Friendship St., Providence, RI 02903, 401-277-3706; Selected Publications: *Occupational Projections 2000, Characteristics of Insured Unemployed, RI Employment Newsletter, Quarterly Labor Supply and Demand Report, Employment and Wages by City and Industry, Annual Planning Information, Manpower Information for Affirmative Action Programs, Employment In RI Hospitals.* Computer Readable Format: No; Custom Research: Free.

South Carolina

Employment Security Commission, Labor Market Information Division, P.O. Box 995, Columbia, SC 29202, 803-737-2660; Selected Publications: *Industrial Monographs, Wage Survey, Labor Market Review, Employment Trends, Occupational Projections 2005, Labor Force in Industry, Covered Employment and Wages in SC.* Computer Readable Formats: Limited; Custom Research: Charge for large projects, all others free.

South Dakota

Department of Labor, Labor Market Information Center, P.O. Box 4730, Aberdeen, SD 57402-4730, 605-622-2314; Selected Publications: *Labor Availability Studies, Labor Bulletin, Occupational Wage Information, Occupational Outlook Handbook, Employment and Earnings, Affirmative Action Package, Statewide Job Listings.* Computer Readable Formats: No; Custom Research: Limited amount available free.

Tennessee

Department of Employment Security, Research and Statistics Division, 11th Floor, James Robertson Parkway, Nashville, TN 37245-1040, 615-741-3639; Selected Publications: *Occupational Wage and Benefit Information, Minorities in Tennessee, Occupations in Demand, Licensed Occupations in Tennessee, Monthly Available Labor, Monthly Labor Force Summary, Commuting Patterns, Tennessee Employment Projections 2005, Tennessee Youth Report, Veterans in Tennessee, Women in the Labor Force, Tennessee High School Graduates.* Computer Readable Formats: Limited; Custom Research: Limited amount available free.

Texas

Texas Employment Commission, Economic Research and Analysis Dept., Room 208-T, TEC Building, Austin, TX 78778, 512-463-2616; Selected Publications: *Labor Force Estimates, Current Population Survey, Nonagricultural Wage and Salary Employment Estimates, Average Hours and Earnings Data, Employment and Wages by Industry and County, Affirmative Action Packets, Characteristics of the Insured Unemployed, Regional Reports, Labor Demand Projects by 2000, Occupational Employment Statistics.* Computer Readable Formats: Limited; Custom Research: Charge for large projects, all others free.

Utah

Utah Department of Employment Security, Labor Market Information Services, P.O. Box 45249, Salt Lake City, UT 84147, 801-536-7800; Selected Publications: *Annual Labor Market Report, Licensed Occupations in Utah, Utah Directory of Business and Industry.* Computer Readable Formats: On a limited basis. Custom Research: Free.

Vermont

Department of Employment and Training, Labor Market Information, P.O. Box 488, Montpelier, VT 05601, 802-229-0311; Selected Publications: *Occupation, Wage and Employment Survey, Job Openings, Affirmative Action Planning Data, Annual Planning Information, Combined Annual Report of DET and JTPA, Directory of Labor Market Information Employment and Earnings, Labor Market Area Bulletins, Vermont Labor Market, Employment and Wages Covered by Unemployment Insurance, Licensed Occupations in Vermont Mining and Quarrying, Construction, Unemployment Compensation Statistical Table, Vermont Economic and Demographic Profile Series.* Computer Readable Formats: No; Custom Research: Upon request, limited time available.

Virginia

Virginia Employment Commission, Labor Market and Demographics Analysis Section, P.O. Box 1358, Richmond, VA 23211, 804-786-8222; Selected Publications: *Guide to Establishing a Business, LMI Directory, Business Registration Guide, Work Force 2000, Labor Force by Sex and Minority Status, Commuting Patterns, Data on Public Schools, Economic Assumptions for the U.S. and VA, Economically Disadvantaged Data, Employment and Training Indicators, Employment and Wages in Establishments, Employment and Wages in VA,*

Monthly Labor Market Review, Wage Survey Selected Manufacturers Occupation, Licensed Occupations in VA, List of Employers By Size, State and County Veteran Population, Trends in Employment-Hours and Earnings, Quarterly Virginia Economic Indicators, Virginia Business Resource Directory. Computer Readable Formats: ALICE (Virginia based only); Custom Research: Limited for nominal fee.

Washington

Employment Security Group, Labor Market and Economic Analysis Branch, 605 Woodland Square Loop S.E., Lacey, WA 98503, mailing address P.O. Box 9046, Olympia, WA 98507-9046, 206-438-4804; Selected Publications: *Washington Labor Market, LMI Review, Annual Demographic Information, Area Wage Survey, Employment and Payrolls in Washington, Occupational Profiles and Projections.* Computer Readable Formats: Some; Custom Research: Large projects are charged on a contract basis.

West Virginia

Employment Security Department, Labor and Economic Research, 112 California Ave., Charleston, WV 25305, 304-558-2660; Selected Publications: *Affirmative Action, West Virginia Women in the Labor Force, Annual Planning Information, Metropolitan Statistical Areas Annual Planning Information, Job Training Partnership Act, West Virginia County Profiles, WV Economic Summary, Employment and Earnings Trends, Insured Workers Summary, Occupational Projections, Veterans Report, Wage Survey, Directory of Publications, Licensed Occupations in West Virginia.* Computer Readable Formats: Forthcoming; Custom Research: Limited amount available free.

Wisconsin

Department of Industry, Labor and Human Relations, Employment and Training Library, P.O. Box 7944, Madison, WI 53707, 608-267-9613; Selected Publications: *LMI: A Reference Guide of WI Publications, Labor Market Planning Information, Taxes Due Covered by Wisconsin U.C. Law, Wisconsin Projections 1988-2000, Affirmative Action Data, Career Connection, Monthly Wisconsin Economic Indicators, Civilian Labor Force Estimates, Consumer Price Index, Employment and Wages, Wage Survey, Covered Employment By Size of Industry and County, Wisconsin Employment Picture, Wisconsin Works, Inform Bi-Monthly.* Computer Readable Formats: Some; Custom Research: Charge for large projects.

Wyoming

Employment Security Commission, Research and Analysis, P.O. Box 2760, Casper, WY 82602, 307-265-6732; Selected Publications: *Manufacturing and Hospitals, Wyoming's Annual Planning Report, Wyoming's Covered Employment and Wage Data, Labor Force Trends, Affirmative Action Package.* Computer Readable Format: No; Custom Research: Limited amount available.

State Statistical Abstracts

For years researchers have been aware of the importance of keeping around the latest edition of the *Statistical Abstract of the United States* (available for $32 in paperback and $38 in hardback from Superintendent of Documents, U.S. Government Printing Office, P.O. Box 371954, Pittsburgh, PA 15250-7954, 202-512-1800). Now if you are interested in local or regional opportunities, trends, or markets, every state government offers their own *State Statistical Abstract* or something comparable. Most of the states produce their abstract on an annual basis.

Tables and graphs are used to illustrate the performance of the economy. Where comparisons can be made, state, regional, and national data can be compared. Market analysts, businesses and researchers will find the following kinds of information in a statistical abstract:

- how many of Fortune magazine's top 500 companies have manufacturing plants in the state;
- the number of jobs directly or indirectly related to exports;
- largest sources of personal income;
- number of people employed in agricultural/non-agricultural jobs;
- how a state ranks in population and land size;
- number of acres of forest land;
- number of airports, number privately owned;
- number of registered aircraft;
- changes in population-age distribution;
- percentage of 17- and 18 year olds graduating from high school;
- number of state universities, vocational schools;
- number of vehicle registrations;

- crime rates; and
- traffic fatalities.

Similar to the *Statistical Abstract of the U.S.* in providing important data in charts and tables, these state abstracts offer important leads to more detailed sources of information. Although the specific charts and tables may not offer the exact detail of data you require on a particular topic, they will identify the offices which generate this type of information. By contacting the specific office, you are likely to get the precise data you require. They can't publish everything they have in a single statistical abstract, but they can dig the information out of their files for you.

State Statistical Abstracts

Alabama
Alabama Department of Economic and Community Affairs, P.O. Box 25037, Montgomery, AL 36125-0347; 205-242-8672. Publication: *County Data Book* ($12).

Alaska
Alaska Department of Labor, Research and Analysis, P.O. Box 25501, Juneau, AK 99802; 907-465-4500, Publications: *Employment and Earnings Report, Statistical Quarterly* (free).

Arizona
Arizona Department of Economic Security Research Administration, P.O. Box 6123, Phoenix, AZ 85007; 602-542-3871. Publication: *Labor Market Information-Annual Planning Information* (free).

Arkansas
Arkansas Industrial Development Commission, 1 State Capitol Mall, Little Rock, AR 72201; 501-682-1121. Publication: *Arkansas Statistical Abstract 94'*.

California
Department of Finance, 915 L St., 8th Floor, Sacramento, CA 95814; 916-322-2263. Publication: *California Statistical Abstract* (free).

Colorado

State Planning and Budget, Room 114, 2000 E. Colfax St., Denver, CO 80203; 303-866-3386. Publication: *Economic Perspective* (free).

Connecticut

Office of Policy and Management, Budget and Financial Management Div., 80 Washington St., Hartford, CT 06106; 203-566-8342. Publication: *Economic Report of the Governor* (free).

Delaware

Delaware Economic Development Office, State of Delaware, Executive Dept., 99 Kings Highway, P.O. Box 1401, Dover, DE 19903; 302-739-4271. Publication: *Data Book 94'* ($25).

District of Columbia

Office of Policy and Program Evaluation, Room 208, District Building 1350, Pennsylvania Ave., NW, Washington, DC 20004; 202-727-6979. Publication: *Indices* ($21).

Florida

University Presses of Florida, 15 NW 15th St., Gainesville, FL 32611; 904-392-1351. Publication: *Florida Statistical Abstract* ($29.95), *A Statistical Abstract* ($10 or more).

Hawaii

State of Hawaii, Business and Economic Development, P.O. 2359, Honolulu, HI 96804, Attention: Library; 808-586-2424. Publication: *State of Hawaii Data Book* (($8).

Idaho

Secretary of State, P.O. Box 83720, Boise, ID 83720-0080; 208-334-2852. Publication: *Idaho Blue Book* ($10).

Illinois

University of Illinois, Bureau of Economic and Business Research, 1206 S. 6th St., 428 Commerce West, Champaign, IL 61820; 217-333-2330. Publication: *Illinois Statistical Abstract* ($40).

Indiana

Indiana University Press, 601 N. Morton St., Bloomington, IN 47404; 812-855-5507. Publication: *The Indiana Fact Book* ($39.95 plus $3 shipping and handling).

Iowa

Iowa Department of Economic Development, 200 East Grand Ave., Des Moines, IA 50309; 515-242-4700. Publication: *Statistical Profile of Iowa* (free).

Kansas

Department of Commerce and Housing, 700 SW Harrison St., Suite 100, Topeka, KS 66603-3712; 913-296-3481. Publication: *Kansas Facts and Statistics.*

Kentucky

Cabinet for Economic Development, 133 Holmes St. Frankfort,

KY 40601; 502-564-4715. Publication: *Maine Statistical Summary* (free).

Maryland

Department of Economic and Employment Development, 217 East Redwood, 11th Floor, Baltimore, MD 21202; 410-333-6953. Publication: *Statistical Abstract* ($40).

Massachusetts

MISER/State Data Center, University of Massachusetts, 128 Thompson Hall, Amherst, MA 01003. Publication: *1990 Census of Population and Housing* (summary tape file #3) $15.

Michigan

University of Michigan Press, P.O. 1104, Ann Arbor, MI 48106; 313-764-4392. Publication: *Michigan Statistical Abstract* ($50).

Minnesota

Department of Trade and Economic Development, Business Division, St. Paul, MN 5501-2146; 612-297-2353. Publication: *Compare Minnesota* (free).

Mississippi

Mississippi State University, Business and Community Development Division, 500 Metro Square, 121 7th Place, East, Mississippi State, MS 39762; 601-325-3817. Publication: *Mississippi Statistical Abstract* ($35).

Missouri

University of Missouri, B&PA Research Center, 10 Professional Building, Columbia, MO 65211; 314-882-4805. Publication: *Statistical Abstract* ($25).

Montana

Department of Commerce, Census and Economic Information Center, 1424 9th Ave., Helena, MT 59620-0501. Publication: *County Data Base* ($20 for a complete copy or $4 per section).

Nebraska

Department of Economic Development, Research Division, P.O. Box 94666, Lincoln, NE 68509; 402-471-3111. Publication: *Nebraska Statistical Handbook* (approximately $12.50).

Nevada

Vital Statistics, 505 East King St., Carson City, NV 89710; 702-687-4480. Publication: *Statistical Abstract* (free).

New Jersey

New Jersey Department of Labor, Publication Unit, CN056, Trenton, NJ 08625-0056; 609-633-6434. Publication: *Monthly New Jersey Economic Indicators.*

New Mexico

Economic Development Department, 1100 St. Francis Drive, Santa Fe, NM 87503; 505-827-1734. Service: "One Stop Shop", an on-line database offering a variety of information, 1-800-283-2638 (free).

New York

Rockefeller Institute of Government, 411 State St., Albany, NY 12203-1003; 518-443-5522. Publication: *New York Statistical Yearbook* ($50 plus $4 shipping and handling).

North Carolina

State Planning Office, State Library, 116 W. Jones St., Raleigh, NC 27603; 919-733-3270. Publication: *North Carolina State Statistical Abstract* (1991 is the last hard copy available. This information is now on an on-line data base which can be accessed via LINK. The state library charges a $3.50 access fee plus .05 cents per page).

North Dakota

The Bureau of Business and Economic Research, College of Business and Public Administration, Box 8369, Univ. of North Dakota, Grand Forks, ND 58202; 701-777-3353. Publication: *North Dakota Statistical Abstract* ($4 to cover shipping and handling). The last edition is 1987; although there has been interest in an update, the funding has not been available.

Ohio

Ohio of Strategic Research, Ohio Department of Development, P.O. Box 1001, Columbus, OH 43216-1001; 1-800-848-1300 ext. 2116. Publication: *County Profiles* ($50).

Oklahoma

University of Oklahoma, CEMR (Center for Economic and Management Research), College of Business Administration, 307 W. Brooks St., Room 4, Norman OK 73019; 405-325-2931. Publication: *Statistical Abstract* ($22).

Oregon

Economic Development Department, 775 Summer St., Salem, OR 97310; 503-986-0118. Publication: *Oregon Economic Profile* ($3.50).

Pennsylvania

State Data Center, State University at Harrisburg, Capitol, Middletown, PA 17057. Publication: *Statistical Abstract* ($40).

Rhode Island

Department of Economic Development, 7 Jackson Walkway, Providence, RI 02903; 401-277-2601. Publication: *Annual Economic Trend Series* (free).

South Carolina

Division of Research and Statistical Services, 1000 Assembly St., Rembert C. Dennis Building, Suite 425, Columbia, SC 29201; 803-734-3793. Publication: *South Carolina Statistical Abstract* ($30 your choice of hard copy or disk).

South Dakota

Business Research Bureau, School of Business, The University of South Dakota, 414 East Clark St., Vermillion, SD 57069-2390; 605-677-5287. Publication: *South Dakota Community Abstract* ($25, 1993 available).

Tennessee

University of Tennessee, Center for Business and Economic Research, S. 100 Glocker Hall, College of Business Administration, Knoxville, TN 37996; 615-974-5441. Publication: *Tennessee State Statistical Abstract* ($36 plus shipping and handling).

Texas

Department of Commerce, Research and Planning Division, State Data Center, P.O. Box 12728, Austin, TX 78711; 512-463-1166. Publication: *The Texas Almanac* is available in bookstores.

Utah

Office of Planning and Budget, Room 116, State Capitol Building, Salt Lake City, UT 84114; 801-538-1027. Publication: *Economic Report to the Governor* ($15).

Vermont

Vermont Department of Employment and Training, Office of Labor Market Information, P.O. Box 488, Montpelier, VT 05601-0488; 802-828-4202. State labor market information publications are available upon request at no charge. Publications: *Annual Planning Information, Annual Report, Projections to 2000.*

Virginia

Cooper Center for Public Service, 918 Emmet North, Suite 300, Charlottesville, VA 22903; 804-982-5522. Publication: *Virginia Statistical Abstract* ($42.50 plus $4 shipping and handling).

Washington

Office of the Forecast Council, Evergreen Plaza, Room 300, Mail Stop 0912, Olympia, WA 98504; 206-586-6785. Publication: *Economic and Revenue Forecast for Washington State* ($4.50 per issue in state, $9 per issue out of state or you can subscribe annually for $18 and $36, respectively).

West Virginia

Chamber of Commerce, Research and Strategic Planning, P.O. Box 2789, Charleston, WV 25330; 304-342-1115.

Wisconsin

Wisconsin Department of Development, 123 West Washington Ave., P.O. Box 7970, Madison, WI 53707; 608-266-1018. Publications: *Biennial Report--Wisconsin Department of Development, Community Profiles* (Specify Community), *Wisconsin Economic Profile.*

Wyoming

Division of Economic Analysis, Room 327E, Emerson Building, Cheyenne, WY 82002-0060; 307-777-7504. Publications: *The Wyoming Data Handbook* (free), *The Equality State Almanac.*

State Forecasting Agencies

State planning offices can provide vast quantities of local market information, demographic data, and company intelligence--more than you would believe possible. Every state has a bureau equivalent to a planning office to assist the Governor in charting future economic change. Of course, the quantity of information varies from one state to the next as does the sophistication in methods of gathering and analyzing data. However, most information is generated to support decision making for policies and legislative initiatives which will affect the current and future status of the state economy. These blueprints for the future usually include plans for attracting new businesses and industries as well as improving the quality of housing, education and transportation.

It should be noted that there is a wide disparity in the research and strategic focus of these state planning offices. The position of this function within the state bureaucratic structure often provides clues about the scope of its mission. In most states this forecasting operation is housed in the Department of Economic Development or in a separate policy office under the Governor's office. However, in our survey of all fifty states, we discovered this crucial function in unexpected places. In South Carolina, for example, there is a special Commission on the Future within the Lieutenant Governor's office, and in Texas, a comparable office falls under the jurisdiction of the state comptroller.

Business Expansion and Economic Outlook

If you currently do business in a state or intend to establish a business there, it would be wise to learn about the Governor's long-term strategy. Keep in mind that no one is more concerned about the state's future than this elected official. If your company sells to farmers, inquire at the planning office about the Governor's agricultural policies. If your firm relies on high tech complementary business, see whether there is a plan to attract high tech companies. Or, if you are interested in consumer markets, be aware of demographic projections conducted by the planning agency for the state as well as for specific regions and counties. Many states appear to be charting future population patterns on a regular basis as is evident with the sampling of publications noted here.

Georgia: *Total Population: 1980, 1990; Projection 2000, 2010*
Nebraska: *Nebraska Statistical Handbook*
New Hampshire: *New Hampshire Population Projections*
New Jersey: *Annual Economic Forecast*
South Carolina: *Commission on the Future*
Utah: *Utah: 2000*

Demographics and Market Studies

Most of these offices are aware of the current demographic situation within their state. They also continually monitor the major industries in the state as well as emerging industries. Their data are usually derived from a combination of federal, state and locally generated information. Sometimes these offices are part of the state data center program run by the U.S. Bureau of the Census. Demographic studies as well as state statistical abstracts are readily available.

Arizona: *Community Profiles*
Minnesota: *Counties & Townships Demographics Estimates Survey*
North Dakota: *Demographics*

Oklahoma: *County Profiles*
Utah: *Utah Economic and Demographic Profiles*
Wisconsin: *Community Economic Profiles*

These state planning offices often produce in-depth market studies on diverse topics, for example:

Arizona: *Economic Impact Study of Major League Baseball Team on State of Arizona*
Michigan: *Michigan Products*
Missouri: *The Missouri Advantage for Plastics and Metal Industries*
Nebraska: *Profit Opportunities in Nebraska for Manufacturers of Pet Food*
New York: *Canadian Investment in Northern New York--Some Empirical Observations*

Company Information and Industry Directories

Many of these offices are responsible for maintaining information on the companies which are located within their state. It is not unusual for the state to collect the following data on every manufacturer and corporation:

- Name of company;
- Address and telephone number;
- Names of principal officers;
- Types of products or services produced;
- Number of employees; and
- Sales estimate.

You stand to learn more about a company, especially its financial picture, if the business in question received some type of economic assistance from the state. After all, once a company takes taxpayer money, the public has a right to know. There is a number of companies that fall into this category. We have received a list of over 100 firms which obtained financial assistance from Pennsylvania in a single year.

Other handy resources available from many state planning offices are company directories. Many

of them concentrate on one industry sector.

Kansas: *Kansas Minority Business*
Montana: *The Montana Manufacturers Directory*
Oregon: *Directory of Oregon Wood Products Manufacturers*
South Dakota: *Directory of Manufacturers and Processors*
Wisconsin: *Business Help Directory*
Wyoming: *Directory of Manufacturing and Mining*

Databases and Special Services

Because these planning agencies share their forecasts and statistical data with other offices with the state government, often the data are readily available to the public, usually for free or on a cost recovery basis. Already many have established customized databases, some of which permit direct online access. Examples include:

- Delaware's online information available on real-estate and census;

- Florida's nine public access databases and customized research requests;

- Oklahoma's Oklahoma Resources Integrated General Information Network System; and

- Utah's OPB online database (current publications and census information).

State Planning Offices

The address and telephone numbers are included for the primary planning offices in each state as well as the District of Columbia. The publications listed with the office do not represent the entire universe of hardcopy data available. These titles are included only when the office is capable of providing us with a current listing. There are states which have publication, but do not have any sort of a catalog. For those states you must request data under specific topic headings.

Alabama
Alabama Department of Economic and Community Affairs, P.O. Box 25037, Montgomery, AL 36125-0347; 205-242-8672. Publication: *Annual Report.*

Market Studies, Demographics, and Statistics

Alaska

State Planning Office, Division of Policy, Commerce and Economic Development, Office of Management and Budget, P.O. AM, Juneau, AK 99811; 907-465-2500.

Arizona

Arizona Department of Commerce, 3800 N. Central, Suite 1500, Phoenix, AZ 85012; 602-280-1300. *1994 Governor's Report on Affordable Housing, Arizona Federal Labor Standards Handbook, Arizona Housing Resource Directory, Arizona Housing Trust Fund Program Summary, Community Development Block Grant Procurement and Contracting Handbook, Community Development Block Grant Program Guide* ($5), *Comprehensive Housing Affordability Strategy FY 1994* ($10), *HOME Program Summary, Housing Rehabilitation Manual, Low Income Housing Tax Credit Allocation Plan, Office of Housing and Infrastructure Development Program Information, Twenty Questions About Community Development Block Grants, Economic Impact Study of Major League Baseball Team on State of Arizona* (Deloitte-Touche) ($20), *Business Assistance Center Promotional Brochure, Business Connection Information Packet, Guide to Establishing a Business in Arizona, Strategic Plan* (Volume 1) ($18), *Advisory/Expert Reports* (Volume II) ($70), *Townhall/Public Forum Reports* (Volume III) ($25), *Strategic Assessment* (Volume IV) ($20), *Strategic Assessment: Regional Data* (Volume V) ($15), *Strategic Framework* (Volume VI) ($10), a complete set of all six documents ($135), *GSPED Information Packets, GSPED News* (Newsletter), *Annual Report, The Arizona Advantage, Arizona Community Profiles* (by community, annual) (145 in all - $18 with binder - $15 without binder), *Arizona Growth Report, Relocation Information Packet, Student Facts Packet of Information Especially for Students, Arizona: Our Brand Means Business, Arizona Statistical Review, Doing Business in Indian Country, Arizona Directory of Exporters* (annual) ($35 for book $100 for diskette), *Arizona Exports, Arizona High Technology Directory* (call the Kelland Corporation at 948-3198 - annual $55), *Arizona International Business Resource Guide* (annual $15), *Financial Resources for Business Development, Arizona State Clearinghouse Procedures, Federal Funding Guide* (bi-weekly), *Federal Grants and Contracts, Federal Monitor* (bi-monthly), *Local/State Funding Report, Reviewer Bi-Weekly, Arizona Economic Development Directory* (semi-annually $2.50), *Arizona Newsletter* (quarterly), *Board of Adjustment Handbook, Common Questions about Planning Newsletter* (quarterly), *Community Guide to Preparing a Housing Plan* ($9), *EconDB Newsletter* (quarterly), *Economic Development & Community Assessment Database* (EconDB) software available on disk in Windows and DOS version), *Facilitators Handbook* ($2), *General and Comprehensive Plan, Guidelines for Organizing a Chamber* ($8), *Guide to the Mainstreet Program* (annual), *The Lonely Guy's Handbook* (a compilation of handy material for new executive directors $10), *Planning and Developing Laws in Arizona, Planning and Zoning Handbook* ($25), *The Planning Commission Basics, A Planning Guide to Tourism Development for Rural Areas* ($3), *Public Meetings, Rural Resource Directory* ($3), *Town Hall Workbook* ($5), Film in Arizona Hotline, 602-280-1389, *Film in Arizona Products and Services Manual, Apartment Guide to Saving Energy and Money, "Arizona Build"*

1992-93 Directory, Arizona Energy News (quarterly), *Arizona Energy Patterns and Trends 1960-1990* ($3), *Arizona Quarterly Energy Data Report, Award-winning Energy Conscious Community Projects, Bright Ideas Series: Energy and the Environment/Photovoltaic- Solar Energy/Recycling/Shading and Landscaping for Energy Efficiency/Solar Cookers, Consumer Rights, DriveWise, DriveWise Glove Compartment Card, Energy Checklist, Energy Checklist for Commercial Buildings, Energy Dollar Flow Analysis for the State of Arizona 1990, Energy Policy in Arizona: A Plan for Sustainable Development 1990, How to Reduce Your Energy Costs, Just Conserve It! Fact Sheets, Money, Energy and the Manufactured Home, Public Policy Update, Starting at Home: Recycling to Protect Our Environment, The Solar Electric Option* ($1), *Sunsmart: An Energy Handbook for Desert Dwellers, Your Guide to the Arizona Corporation Commission.*

Arkansas

Office of Industrial Development, State of Arkansas, #1 Capitol Mall, Little Rock, AR 72201; 501-682-1121. Publication: *Annual Report.*

California

Commission on Economic Development, State of California, State Capital, Room 1028, Sacramento, CA 95814; 916-324-5065. Publications: *Guide for Entrepreneurs, Department of Finance-Statistical Forecasting, Guide to Business Resources-The Climate's Right, Los Angeles-Economics, Trade and Commerce-Small Business Centers* (916-322-1394).

Colorado

Colorado Department of Personnel, 1313 Sherman St., Denver, CO 80203; 303-866-2321. Publication: *Stateline.* Other Services: Community Profiles Database, covering 63 counties and 260 municipalities. More information on demographics can be obtained from State of Colorado, Division of Local Government, Department of Local Affairs, Room 521, Denver, CO 80203; 303-866-2156.

Connecticut

Connecticut Department of Economic Development, Research Department, 865 Brook St., Rocky Hill, CT 06067; 203-258-4288. Publications: *Annual Report, Connecticut Economic Forecast, New England Economic Projections* (includes all 6 states).

Delaware

Delaware Economic Development Office, State of Delaware, Executive Department, 99 Kings Highway, P.O. Box 1401, Dover, DE 19903; 302-739-4271. Publications: *Data Book 94'* (will not be revised, $25), *Comparison of Estimated State and Local Family Tax Burdens, Small Business Start-Up Guide, Procurement Guide.* Call 302-739-4204 for a copy of the 3 year Capital Budget Plan. Other Services: Business Research Section maintains an extensive library of data resources and responds to requests for economic, demographic and travel information. Selective online access available to computerized real estate file. Online census information is available. A computerized hotel reservation system is also available.

District of Columbia

D.C. Office of Planning, 415 12th St., NW, Washington, DC 20004; 202-727-6492. Publications: *Census Tract Map* (large $2), *Census Tract Map* (small $1), *STFI Census Data* (single ward, single tract or city $1.50/8 wards and city $10), *1990 Census Tract/Block Population and Housing Units Data Book* ($10), *1990 Census: Social, Economic and Housing Characteristics/STF-3* (District of Columbia and each ward/book $30, set of tables for one indicator plus map $4), *Socio/Economic Indicators* (book by census tract $15, set of tables for one indicator plus map $3), *Monograph 1 - Population and Housing Unit Changes 1980 to 1990* ($7.50), *Monograph 2 - Population, Household and Household Characteristics: 1990* ($12), *Monograph 3 - Senior Population 1990 Census* ($10), *Monograph 4 - Youth Population 1990 Census* ($10), *Monograph 5 - Hispanic Population 1990 Census* ($10), *District of Columbia Street Address Directory by Street, Census Tract and Ward* ($30), *Chinatown Design Guidelines Study/December 1989* ($5), *Comprehensive Plan Generalized Land Use Map 1* ($5), *Comprehensive Plan for the National Capital/District Elements* ($5), *D.C. Law 8-129 District of Columbia Comprehensive Plan Amendments Act of 1989* ($5), *Draft Ward Plan/by Ward January 1992* ($5), *Implementing the District Elements of the Comprehensive Plan for the National Capital Fiscal Years 1990-1991 Fifth Edition* ($15), *Comprehensive Plan Planning Report/August 1983* ($15), *A Living Downtown for Washington, D.C./April 1981* ($6), *Downtown D.C.: Recommendations for the Downtown Plan/Mayor's Downtown Committee - July 1982* ($9), Photocopies ($.10 per image).

Florida

Bureau of Economic Analysis, Florida Department of Commerce, Division of Economic Development, Tallahassee, FL 32399-2000; 904-487-2971. Publications: *Florida and the Other Forty-Nine, County Comparisons, Profile of the Florida Visitor*. A 5-year Agency Strategic Plan can be obtained by calling 904-487-2156. Special Services: Five public access databases and customized research requests; 904-488-4255.

Georgia

Office of Planning and Budget, Demographic and Statistical Services, 254 Washington St., SW, Atlanta, GA 30334-8500; 404-656-3820. Publications: *The Georgia State: Attachment A* - Population projections by age, sex, and race for 2000 for all Georgia counties, *Attachment B* - Population projections by age, sex, and race for 2010 for all Georgia, *Attachment C* - 1990 Census by age, sex and race for all Georgia counties, *Attachment 1* - Civilian Labor Force Estimates, Georgia Department of Labor (monthly, annually), *Attachment 2* - Total Population: 1980, 1990; Projections: 2000, 2010, *Attachment 3* - 1992 Population Estimates by County, U.S. Census Bureau, *Attachment 4* - Personal & Per Capita Income by County (1992) from "Survey of Current Business", BEA, *Attachment 5* - State Data Center Program, Georgia, U.S. address list, *Attachment 6* - 1990 Census Population totals by county and incorporated place, *Attachment 7* - 1990 & 1980 Census counts and comparisons by county, *Attachment 8* - 1990 Census counts by race for Georgia cities, *Attachment 10* - Public Law 94-171 totals and age 18 and over by county, *Attachment 11* - 1990 and 1980 census counts and comparisons by place, *Attachment 12* - 1990 Census tract population by race, housing units by MSA, *Attachment 13* - 1990 Census counts by CCD, *Attachment 14* - 1990 Census STF 1A by county, MSA, and selected cities, *Attachment 15* - 1990 Census STF 1A, Tables 1-18 (in file cabinet), *Attachment 16* - 1990 Census STF 1A by age, race, sex, and Hispanic origin for Georgia counties, *Attachment 17* - 1980 and 1990 Census counts for all states, *Attachment 18* - 1990 PL94-171 Block data by county (in library), *Attachment 20* - 1990 Census STF 1A 15 page profile by state, county, MSA, RDC, place, census tract, *Attachment 21* - 1990 Census per capita income, median family income, median household income, *Attachment 22* - MSA Counties, 1993, *Attachment 23* - Poverty characteristics, 1990 Census, *Attachment 27* - "Georgia Descriptions in Data" order form, STF 1A, STF 3A order forms, *Attachment 28* - Georgia Population 1970, 1980, *Attachment 31* - Per capita income, 1979-92, BEA, *Attachment 34* - Provisional estimates of households for counties, July 1, 1988, *Attachment 38* - Housing units authorized by building permits, (monthly, annually), *Attachment 40* - County estimates for 1970 through 1980, *Attachment 41* - Population of Incorporated Places 1960-1080 from "Number of Inhabitants", *Attachment 42* - DEA Regional Economic Projections for MSAs (1990 & 2000) projected), *Attachment 44* - Regional Development Center contacts and map, executive directors, counties in each RDC, *Attachment 45* - Map of Georgia counties, MSAs, *Attachment 47* - BEA projections 2040.

Hawaii

Department of Business, Economic Development and Tourism, 220 S. King St., Honolulu, HI 96813; 808-586-2406. Publications: *Facts and Figures, State and Economic Report, Annual Report of Hawaii, Starting a Business in Hawaii*.

Idaho

Department of Commerce, Economic Development, Room 108, State Capital, Boise, ID 83720; 208-334-2470. Publications: *Economic Development Agenda, Operating a Business, Agencies That Help Businesses*.

Illinois

Illinois Department of Commerce and Community Affairs, 620 East Adams St., Springfield, IL 62701; 217-782-3233. Publication: *Annual Report* (free).

Indiana

Indiana Economic Development Council, One North Capitol Ave., Suite 425, Indianapolis, IN 46204-2224; 317-631-0871, Fax: 317-231-7067. Publications: *Annual Report: Indiana Economic Development Council, Inc., An Assessment of Indiana's Competitive Position in Business Recruitment* ($1), *An Assessment of Indiana's Competitive Position in Business Recruitment* ($5), *Best Practice in Business Attraction and Indigenous Development* ($2.50), *Business Climate and Quality of Life in Indiana: Survey of Leading Hoosier Firms* ($2.50), *Building Foundations for Growth: Financing Infrastructure in Indiana During the 1990s* ($2.50), *Business Education Partnerships: How They Work in Indiana, The Corporation for Science and Technology 1982-1990: A Mid-Course Review of*

Indiana's Lead Technology Development Initiative of the 1980's ($15), *Corporate Profile: Indiana Economic Development Council, Inc., A Discussion of Market-Based Approaches to Workforce Training in Indiana* ($4.50), *Economic Development* ($2.50), *The Employment Service Sector in Indiana: Key Strategic Issues for the '90s* ($4.50), *The Effectiveness of Tax Incentives in Economic Development* ($2.50), *Economic Development Program Profiles* ($10), *Finance "Tool Box" Reference Guide* ($10), *Food Processing Industries in Indiana* ($5), *Governor's Initiative in Economic Development* ($5), *Growing Indiana's Wood Products Industry: The Competitive Challenge* ($6), *Hoosier Horizons: 1992 Assessment of the Indiana Economy, Hoosier Horizons: 1992 Assessment of the Indiana Economy, Indiana Small Business Expansion Through Capital Availability* ($2), *Infrastructure Investment: A Key to Growth of the Hoosier Economy* ($2), *Investing IN Indiana* (free summary), *Investing IN Indiana 1994* ($20), *KREDA Update 1993* ($2.50), *Lifelines to Rural Indiana: The Role of Telecommunications in Rural Economic Development 1991*, (4.50), *The New Localism*, Entrepreneurial Economy Review 1991, *1994 Economic Report to the Governor: Changes and Challenges in Workforce Development, Urban Development*, Entrepreneurial Economy Review, *Rural Development: What is Known and Where Might We Go With It* ($2.50, *SWOT Analysis for Indiana's Strategic Economic Development Planning Process 1992* ($4.50), *Southern Indiana Grows 1993* ($2.50), *A Sector-Based Approach for Economic Development Indiana Business Review 1993* ($1), *Towards an Investment-Led Approach to Economic Development in the Midwest 1992* ($2.50).

Iowa

Iowa Dept. of Economic Development, 200 East Grand Ave., Des Moines, IA 50309; 515-242-4700. Publications: *Iowa Economic Forecast Quarterly, The Digest, Statistical Profile of Iowa.*

Kansas

Department of Commerce and Housing, 700 SW Harrison St., Suite 100, Topeka, KS 66603-3712; 913-296-3481. Publications: *Guide to Starting a Business in Kansas*, ("Steps to Success") 1991 edition $2.50), *Data for Site Selection* (Kansas Data Book $5), *Business Climate Review, Business Assistance Resource Directory* (1993 edition), *Kansas Minority Business Directory* (1994 edition), *Kansas Housing Services Directory* (1994 edition), *Directory of Kansas JobShops* (1988 edition), *Kansas Association Directory* (1991 edition), *Kansas International Trade Resource Directory* (1990 edition), *Kansas Companies Who Export Directory* (1992 edition), *Kansas Aerospace Directory* (1990 edition), *Kansas Agribusiness Directory* (1990 edition), *Kansas Facts and Stats, KDOC&H Annual Report, Trade Show Assistance Program, Workforce Training Programs, Kansas PRIDE Program Annual Report, Existing Industry Development, Community Development Information* (1993 edition), *Export Financing, Minority & Women-Owned Business, Venture Capital, Helping Kansas Companies, Kansas Housing, Kansas Housing Profile, Kansas Comprehensive Housing Affordability Strategy, Kansas Mortgage Savers Program, "Kansas!" Magazine, Stories with a Common Thread, Developing Kansas, Kansas Main Street, Kansas Pride Program* (bi-monthly newsletter), *Rooftops.*

Center for Economic Development and Business Research, 2nd Floor, Devlin Hall, W. Frank Barton School of Business, Wichita State University, Wichita, KS 67260-0121; 316-689-3225. Publications: *Business & Economic Report, Kansas Economic Indicators.*

The University of Kansas, Institute for Public Policy and Business Research, 607 Blake Hall, Lawrence, Kansas 66045-2960. Publication: *Kansas Business Review.*

Kentucky

Center for Business and Economic Research, 302 Mathews Building, University of Kentucky, Lexington, KY 40506-0047; 606-257-7675. Publication: *Annual Economic Report.*

Louisiana

State Planning Office, Division of Administration, 1051 North Riverside Mall, Baton Rouge, LA 70804; 504-342-7410.

Maine

Department of Economic and Community Development, State House Station 59, Augusta, ME 04333; 207-287-2656. Also, Data Census Manager, 20 Union Street, Augusta, ME 04330-6827; 207-287-2271.

Maryland

Office of Research, Department of Economic and Employment Development, 217 E. Redwood Street, Baltimore, MD 21202; 410-333-6947, Publications: *The Economic Impact of Horseracing Industry on the Economy of Maryland, The Impact of Defense Spending on the Maryland Economy, The Impact of the Preakness Celebration '90 in Maryland, The Impact of the Christopher Columbus Center of Marine Research and Exploration, The Impact of the National Aquarium in Baltimore City, The Impact of Savage River State Forest in Maryland, The Economic and Fiscal Impacts of the US Canoe and Kayak Team Olympic Trials, The Economic and Fiscal Impacts from the Construction and Operations of the Oriole Park at Camden Yards, The Economic and Fiscal Impacts of Baltimore Orioles' 1992 Season In Maryland, 1992 Update--Christopher Columbus Center of Marine Research and Exploration, The Economic Impact of Baltimore Area Chemical Establishments, The Economic Impact of Maryland Insurance Industry, The Economic and Fiscal Impacts of Electric Vehicle Drivetrain Production in Maryland, The Economic and Fiscal Impacts of NIH in Maryland and the United States, Maryland Economic Outlook, Maryland International Business Report, Maryland Economic Indicators, Reports on Manufacturing, and Workers' Compensation.*

Massachusetts

Executive Office of Economic Affairs, One Ashburton Place, Room 2101, Boston, MA 02108; 617-727-1130.

Michigan

Michigan Jobs Commission, Customer Assistance and Research Services, 201 N. Washington Sq., Lansing, MI 48913; 517-373-4600. Publications: *Michigan: The Location of Choice, Welcome to Michigan, Michigan Overview, Michigan's Business Services,*

Michigan's Commitment to Advanced Technology, Michigan's Education System, Michigan's Energy Costa and Availability, Michigan's Labor Force Characteristics, Michigan's Strategic Access to Markets and Suppliers, Michigan's Transportation Infrastructure, Review of Michigan Taxes, A, Questions and Answers on Michigan's Single Business Tax, A Review of Michigan Taxes: The Impact of Proposal A, 16-State Tax Comparison Tables, Tax Comparison: Michigan Vs. Ontario, State Tax Comparison Services--Michigan vs. (any of the following) Arkansas, California, Connecticut, Florida, Georgia, Illinois, Indiana, Kentucky, Minnesota, Missouri, New Jersey, New York, North Carolina, Ohio, Pennsylvania, South Carolina, Tennessee, Texas, Wisconsin, Michigan and Ontario Industrial Comparison, D&B Top 100 Companies Based on Annual Sales, D&B Top 500 Companies Based on Annual Sales, Michigan Products, Economic Growth Report 1992, Economic Performance & Condition of Michigan's MSA's 1989, Employment Trends in Michigan's Large & Small Firms, Michigan Community Indicators-1991, Michigan Business Activity Quarterly Report, Michigan Economic Update, Michigan Economic News, Michigan Economy, Michigan Export Data, Michigan Gross State Product, Michigan's Rural Lower Peninsula, Michigan Personal Income Growth, Small Business Questions & Answers, University of Michigan Mid-Year Review & Economic Forecast for 1992 to 1994, Automotive Update, Electronic Component Industry Report, GM Willow Run Suppliers Survey Results, Michigan Office Furniture Industry, Michigan Plastics Industry Update, Michigan Service Industry, Michigan Manufacturing Statistics, State Manufacturing Statistics for the following States: Arkansas, Georgia, Illinois, Indiana, Kentucky, Minnesota, Missouri, New York, North Carolina, Ohio, Pennsylvania, South Carolina, Tennessee, Texas and Wisconsin covering the following industries: Chemical Products, Electric/Electronic Equipment, Fabricated Metals, Food Products, Furniture, Instruments, Lumber/Wood, Machinery, Paper Products, Primary Metals, Printing/Publishing, Rubber & Plastics, Transportation Equipment, United States and Michigan Industry Profiles, Agriculture, Auto Parts, Financial Services & Insurance, Food Processing, High Technology, Machine Tool, Motor Vehicle, Pollution Control, Steel, United States and Michigan Industry Profiles, Biotech, Chemical & Allied Products, Medical Instruments, Office Furniture, Plastics, Service, Wholesale Trade.

Minnesota

Minnesota State Planning Agency, Office of Strategic and Long-Range Planning, 300 Centennial Building, 658 Cedar St., St. Paul, MN 55155; 612-296-3985. Publications: *A Cut Above: Criminal Justice Cost* (line item), *School Enrollment Growth* (line item), *Counties/Payroll and Employment Growth* (line item), *Welfare Migration* (line item), *Children's Services Report Card, Minnesota Milestones: 1993 Progress Report, A Cut Above: Minnesota's National Rankings, Tomorrow's Households: Trends and Issues, Children's Services Report Card* (online from DATANET), *Conversations About the Future* ($3), *Redefining Progress: Working Toward a Sustainable Future* ($15), *Troubling Perceptions: 1993 Minnesota Crime Survey, Minnesota's National Rankings, A Shared Vision--State Level Governance Options for Children and Family Services, Achieving Inclusive Policy Projects: A Guide to Success, Action for*

Children Listen '94 Brochure, Action for Children Kids Conference, Agency Style Guide, Budget 2001 Line Item Overall Design, Budget 2001: Government Salaries Line Item, Budget 2001: Welfare Migration Line Item, Child Poverty in Minnesota Population Note, Child Poverty in Minnesota: Trends and Issues, Children's Services Report Card (available in hard-copy or online from DATANET), *Collaborative Grants Prevention and Intervention Funding Brochure Collaborative Grants Prevention and Intervention Manual, Counties and Townships Demographics Estimates Survey, Syberstate: Minnesota on the Information Superhighway, Doing Things Better--Innovation, Cooperation and Quality, EPPL-7 Licensing Brochure, Government Ethics Report, Growth Management Full Report--Phase 1, Kids Can't Wait Progress Report, Labor Force Projections* (Demography Series Report #4), *Media Mailing List/Faxing List, Minnesota Milestones Progress Report Card, Minnesota Planning Logo* (Electronic File), *MOAPPP Third Annual Conference--4/18, Narcotics Task Force Report, Redefining Progress: Working Toward a Sustainable Future, Tomorrow's Households: The Next 30 Years* (Demography Series Report #3), *Troubling Perceptions: 1993 Minnesota Crime Survey, Action for Children Newsletter* (monthly-fax), *EQB MONITOR* (bi-weekly newsletter), *Fresh Facts: Emerging Issues and Vital Trends* (6 times/year-fax), *MOAPP Monitor: Teen Pregnancy Prevention* (Quarterly newsletter), *Population Notes* (Newsletter), *A Changing Population: The Next 30 Years* (Demography Series Report #1), *A Question of Balance: Managing Growth and the Environment, District Data Book: Minnesota Legislative Districts 1993, Making the Connection: Linking Housing, Jobs and Transportation, Minnesota Gambling 1993, Minnesota Multi-jurisdictional Narcotic Task Force Program 1992 Report, Minnesota's Changing Counties: The Next 30 Years* (Demography Series Report #2), *Population and Household Estimates 1992* (Available on Diskette), *State of Diversity: A Plan of Action for Minnesota, State of Diversity Resource Guide, What Can I Do To Prevent Harm To Children.*

Mississippi

Department of Economic and Community, P.O. Box 849, Jackson, MS 39205; 601-359-3449. Publications: *Annual Report, Newsletter, Overview Brochure.*

Missouri

Department of Economic Development, State of Missouri, P.O. Box 118, 301 W. High, Room 770, Jefferson City, MO 65102-0118; 314-751-4241, 800-523-1434.

Community Development Block Grants (CDBG Program): 314-751-4146. Publications: *On the Block* (newsletter), *Community Development Block Grant Programs Annual Competition Guidelines and Application.*

Community Programs: 314-751-4849. Publications: *Awards in Review, Missouri Community Betterment, Surveying Community Attitudes, Elements of Economic Development, Role of the Economic Developer, Rural Communities Economic Assistance Application, Missouri Main Street Program Brochure, Main Street Missouri--The First Three Years, CDBG Downtown Revitalization Guidelines and Application, Community Solid*

Waste Management, Attracting New Enterprises, Assisting Local Enterprises, Creating New Enterprises, Capturing Outside Wealth, Capturing Local Wealth, Rural Economic and Community Development Catalog.

Finance: 314-751-0717. Publications: *Action Fund Guidelines and Application, Industrial Infrastructure Guidelines and Application, Loan Guarantee Application (MEDEIB), Single Issue Tax Exempt IRB General Information and Application, Missouri Economic Development Export and Infrastructure Board (MEDEIB) Tax Credit Application, Spec Building Guidelines and Application, Neighborhood Improvement District, Finance Programs Available in Missouri.*

High Technology: 314-751-5095. Publications: *High Technology Companies in Missouri, Missouri Business Modernization and Technology Corporation Annual Report, Small Business Innovation Research (SBIR) Resource Guide, SBIR Program Brochures, Venture Capital Companies in Missouri.*

Business Development: 314-751-4999. Publications: *Missouri Export Credit Insurance, Missouri International Trade Directory, Export Development Office (EDO), Foreign Investment Directory, Joint Venture Opportunities, Department of Commerce Commercial News, United Kingdom Investment in Missouri, Canadian Investment in Missouri, Japanese Investment in Missouri, German Investment in Missouri, European Investment in Missouri.*

National: 314-751-9045. Publications: *The Missouri Advantage, Helping Missouri Business Prosper.*

Research and Planning: 314-751-3674. Publications: *Basics of Economic Development, Community Fact Book--A Guide for Missouri Communities, Community Profiles, DED Annual Report, Economic Development Laws, Executive Planning Summary, Language of Economic Development, Missouri Facts and Figures, Missouri Directory of Manufacturers* (this directory must be ordered from Harris Publishing Co., Twinsburg, Ohio 800-888-5900), *New and Expanding Industry Annual Report, The Missouri Advantage for Automotive Industry, The Missouri Advantage for Communication Industry, The Missouri Advantage for Electronics, The Missouri Advantage for Food Industry, The Missouri Advantage for Office, Research, and Distribution Facilities, The Missouri Advantage for Plastics and Metals Industries.*

Business Information Programs: 314-751-4982, 800-523-1434. Publications: *Starting a New Business in Missouri, MEDIS Quick Reference Manual, Missouri Product Finder Brochure and Registration Form, MEDIS Brochure, Industrial Land Site Registration Form, Industrial Building Registration Form, Home-based Business Literature, Demographics Book and Disk, Missouri Product Finder Directory, MBAC Card, MSCL Business Start-up Handouts, Publications and Brochures, Spec/Shell Building Survey.*

Tax Benefits: 314-751-6835. Publications: *New/Expanded Business Facility and Enterprise Zone Tax Benefits Application, Small Business Incubator Tax Credit Application, Neighborhood*

Assistance Program Tax Credit Application, Development and Reserve Fund; Export Finance; Infrastructure Fund Tax Credit Application, Seed Capital Tax Credit Application, Taxes--The Missouri Advantage, Nine Tax Benefit Programs--The Missouri Advantage, New/Expanded Business Facility and Enterprise Zone Tax Laws, Enterprise Zone Contact List, Enterprise Zone Map, Research Tax Credit Application (effective 1/1/94).

Montana
Business Assistance Division, Department of Commerce, State of Montana, 1424 9th Ave., Helena, MT 59620; 406-444-3923. Publications: *The Montana Manufacturers Directory* ($25), *The Montana Exporters Guide, The Made in Montana Products Directory, The "Business Finance Under the Big Sky", The "Montana Statewide Training Calendar", SBDC Newsletter.*

Nebraska
Nebraska Department of Economic Development, 301 Centennial Mall South, P.O. Box 94666, Lincoln, NE 68509; 402-471-3111, 1-800-426-6505. Publications: *Nebraska Statistical Handbook* ($15), *Nebraska Directory of Manufacturers* ($50), *Nebraska Development News* (newsletter), *NCIP* (Nebraska Community Improvement Program, newsletter).

Nevada
Commission on Economic Development, State of Nevada, Capitol Complex, Carson City, NV 89710; 702-687-4325. Publications: *Focus 2000, Nevada Progress, Nevada Business Guide, Nevada Industrial Directory.*

New Hampshire
Office of State Planning, State of New Hampshire, Executive Dept., 2 1/2 Beacon St., Concord, NH 03301; 603-271-2155.

Data Management Publications: *Current Estimates and Trends in New Hampshire's Housing Supply, New Hampshire Population Projections-Total Population for Cities and Towns; 1990-2015* (five year increments), *OSP Program Handbook; 1993, 1993 Population Estimates of New Hampshire Cities and Towns, A BRIEF LOOK* (an introductory profile of state data, amenities and characteristics, 1993), *Full and Part-Time Employment by Major Industry for U.S., N.H. and N.H Counties 1986-1991, New Hampshire Population Projections for Counties by Age and Sex 1994, Selected Economic Characteristics of NH Municipalities, 1990 Census, Statistical Profile of NH 1970-1990.*

Policy and Administration Publications: *Federal Register Report, Annual Federal Assistance Report* (published twice monthly), *New Hampshire Intergovernmental Review Process* (annual), *Legislative Update* (weekly), *Legislative Session Final Report.*

GIS Publications: *NH GRANIT Data Catalog* (June 1993), *NH GRANIT Users Guide* (October 1992), *GIS Handbook for Municipalities* (August 1994).

Water Protection Assistance Program Publications: *Municipal Guide to Wetland Protection, A Summary of the Plan for the Squam Lakes Watershed* (1991), *Local Land Use Management Techniques for Water Resources Protection and Geographic*

Inventory Procedures (January 1992), *Model Health Ordinances to Implement a Wellhead or Groundwater Protection Program, State Development Plan* (1994), *State Development Plan Economic Trends Analysis* (1994), *Model Shoreland Protection Ordinance* (April 1994).

Municipal and Regional Assistance Publications: *Planning and Land Use Regulation* (annual $5.25), *The Board of Adjustment in New Hampshire: A Handbook for Local Officials* (1994 $5), *Status of Municipal Planning and Land Use Regulations in New Hampshire* (annual 1994), *The Handbook of Subdivision Review* (1988 with 1994 amendments), *OSP Technical Bulletins 1-10.*

Recreation Planning Publications: *Municipal Recreation and Conservation Budget Survey* (1991), *Public Access Plan for New Hampshire's Lakes, Ponds, and Rivers* (1991), *Outdoor Recreation Action Program* (1990-1991), *New Hampshire Wetlands Priority Plan, 1994, New Hampshire Outdoors* (1994-1998 SCORP), *Land Protection and the Tax Advantages for New Hampshire Land Owners*, Second Edition (1987), *Land Protection for NH Communities and Conservation Organizations* (1985).

New Jersey

Office of Economic Analysis, State of New Jersey, 1 West State St., Trenton, NJ 08625; 609-292-2568. Publications: *Economic Report of the Governor-Annual, Economic Forecast-Annual.*

New Mexico

Economic Development Department, 1100 St. Francis Drive, Santa Fe, NM 87503; 505-827-1734. Service: "One Stop Shop", an online data base with various information (free).

New York

The Nelson A. Rockefeller Institute of Government, 411 State St., Albany, New York 12203-1003; 518-443-5522. Publications: *Rockefeller Institute Publications List, Attrition Versus Layoffs: How to Estimate the Costs of Holding Employees on Payroll When Savings are Needed* ($2), *Background Data on the Implementation of the 1985 Albany Strategic Plan: Task Force on Downtown, Government Finances and Services, Housing and Community Development, Business Opportunities and Employment* (free), *Building the Twentieth Century Public Works Machine* ($2), *Canadian Investment in New York State: Appalachia or a Haven for Foreign Investors?* ($3), *Canadian Investment in Northern New York: Some Empirical Observations* ($2), *Capital Cities: Challenges and Opportunities* ($5), *Case for Tax-Exempt Bond Financing of Mortgages: The Rich Get Richer But The Poor Get Houses* ($2), *Citizen Participation in Government Decision Making: The Toxic Waste Threat at Love Canal, Niagara Fall, New York* ($2), *Citizen Surveys as Citizen Participation Mechanisms, Development of Local Discretionary Authority* ($2), *Diagnosing and Planning for the Learning Disabled: The Relationship Between State Policies and Services* ($3), *Differences Among States in the Impact of the Recession* ($20), *Diversification Into Long Term Care: A New Opportunity for Hospitals?* ($2), *Economic Growth and Development on Long Island* ($2), *Economic Recovery of New York: When and How?* (free), *Economic Restructuring and the Politics of Land/Use Planning in NYC* ($2), *Expanding the Economic Pie* ($3),

Feasibility Study for Establishing a New York State Research and Development Center for Hazardous Waste Management (Includes Executive Summary) ($10), *Federal Role in State Fiscal Stress* ($20), *Free Trade for New York: The Economic Impact of the Canada-US Free Trade Agreement on NYS* ($3), *Governing the Empire State: An Insider's Guide* ($9.95), *Governor and the Attorney General in New York* ($3), *Gubernatorial-Legislative Relations in New York State* ($2), *Hard Truths/Tough Choices: An Agenda for State and Local Reform* (call 518-443-5825), *Impact of State Human Resource Policy on New York's Economic Development* ($3), *Legislative Appropriation of Federal Grants in New York* ($2), *Legislative Initiative in Budgeting Reform: New York's Key Item Reporting Systems* ($5), *New York State Project 2000: Prevention Policies for At-Risk Children* (1989/$10), *New York State Project 2000: Report on Electricity* (1986/$10), *New York State Project: Report on Corrections and Criminal Justice* (1986/$10), *New York State Project 2000: Report on Economic Development* (1986/$10), *New York State Project 2000: Report on Economic Structure* (1986/$10), *New York State Project 2000: Report on Housing* (1988/$10), *New York State Project 2000: Report on Long-Term Care* (1986/$10), *New York State Project 2000: Report on Population* (1986/$10), *New York State Project 2000: Report on Science and Technology* (1986/$10), *New York State Project 2000: Report on Water Resources* (1986/$10), *North Country Successes: Case Studies of Successful Entrepreneurs in the ANCA Region* ($3), *Partnership to Progress, Realizing Albany's Future* ($5), *Perspectives on Budgeting in New York* ($3), *Probable Effects of Introducing a Sectional Fare System into the NYC Subway* ($2), *Profile of a Recession: The New York Experience in the Early 1990's* ($3), *Promotion, Policies and Programs* ($3), *Public Service and the Future* (free), *Reorganization of New York State Government in the Twentieth Century* ($2), *Report on the Local Government Restructuring Project of the Nelson A. Rockefeller Institute of Government* (free), *Rethinking State and Local Economic Development Strategies* (free), *Revenue Estimation in New York State: Technique, Politics, or Luck?* ($5), *Role of State Tax Incentives in Attracting and Retaining Business* ($3), *State Fiscal Briefs* (call for more information, $15 each), *Structural Changes, Employment and Pay Trends: Shaping Federal Staffing Issues in the New York Region* ($3), *Study of the Nonprofit Sector in New York State: Its Size, Nature and Economic Impact* ($15), *Technology and the Research Environment of the Future: The Impact of the Information Science Revolution on the Research Environment of the Future* ($3), *Toward a Better Partnership: the Nonprofit Sector and State Government in NYS* ($5), *Toward the Implementation of the 21 Alcoholic Beverage Law in NYS* ($5), *Toward Integrating the Electricity Production of Hydro Quebec and the NY Power Pool* ($2).

North Carolina

Business and Industry Development, 116 Jones St., Raleigh, NC 27603-8003; 919-733-4151. Publications: *Department of Commerce-Community Profiles, General Information Business Climate.*

North Dakota

North Dakota Research Department, Office of the Governor, Bismark, ND 58505; 701-328-5300. Publications: *Statistical*

Study-North Dakota University, Planning Report, Demographics, Directory of North Dakota Manufacturers.

Ohio
State of Ohio, Department of Development, Office of Strategic Research, P.O. Box 1001, Columbus, OH 43216; 614-466-2116. Publication: *Annual Report.*

Oklahoma
Oklahoma Department of Commerce, Research and Planning Division, 6601 Broadway, P.O. Box 26980, Oklahoma City, OK 73126-0980; 405-843-9770, 800-879-6552. Publications: *Directory.*

Census/Data Center: 405-841-5184. Publications: *Demographic State of the State.* Services: Census data requests, census maps, demographic/population research, Geographic Information System (GIS). Oklahoma Resources Integrated General Information Network System is a free, online computerized bulletin board system; Oklahoma City calling area 325-5883, Washington, D.C. area 800-765-6552, out-of-state 405-325-5883 (ORIGINS), population projections/estimates, population requests, TIGER (Topologically Integrated Geographic Encoding and Referencing System (geographic digital database).

Data Management Team: 405-841-5183. Publications: *Community Profiles, County Profiles, Fortune 500 List* (Oklahoma), *Major Employers Report, Manufacturer's Directory, New and Expanded Manufacturers, Real Estate Database, State Data, Union Election Results.*

Economic Analysis Team: 405-841-5178. Publications: *Analysis of Capital Spending Plans, Annual MISER Census Export by State, Capital Investment Trends in Industry, Construction/Real Estate Reports, Consumer Price Index/Cost of Living, County Business Patterns, Economic Forecasts & Impact Analysis, Economic and Policy Research, Economic Trends, Federal Government Statistical Releases, Forecast Data, HUD Median Family Income, Income and Employment Data, Industry Reports, Micro IMPLAN* (software), *Oklahoma Business & Industry Survey, Quarterly Economic Indicators, Targeted Industries.*

Policy and Planning Team: 405-841-5148. Publications: *Business Plan/Program Performance, Oklahoma Futures, Planning Assistance, Policy Research and Analysis, Winning the Race to the Future-Oklahoma 2007, Building a Better Oklahoma* (5-year plan), *Strategic Economic Development Plan* (also known as The 5-Year Plan), *Current Realities.*

Oregon
Oregon Economic Development Department, 775 Summer St., NE, Salem, OR 97310; 503-373-1290 (contact this office unless another phone number is given). Publications: *A Summary of Oregon Taxes* (Oregon Department of Revenue), *Business Referral List* (Small Business Program, 503-373-1241), *Challenge the Future* (Key Industries Section, 503-378-2286), *Executive Summary, Oregon Travel and Tourism* (Tourism Division, 503-373-1270), *Job Training Partnership, Key Industry Profiles* (Key Industries Section, 503-378-2286), *The Official*

Oregon Travel Guide (Tourism Division, 503-373-1270), *Oregon, Oregon Fact Sheets, Oregon Film & Video Industry Relocation Packet* (Film & Video Office, 503-373-1232), *Oregon Film Locations Brochure* (Film & Video Office, 503-373-1232), *Oregon Helping Oregon* (Key Industries Section, 503-378-2286), *Oregon's Largest Employers 1992, Regulatory Research Project: Gasoline Service Stations in Oregon* (Small Business Program, 503-373-1241), *A Plan for the Tourism Industry* (503-373-1270, $5), *Annual Economic Impact Report for Oregon Travel* (503-373-1270, $10), *Directory of Oregon Manufacturers* (printed version for $75 or diskette for $200), *Directory of Oregon Wood Products Manufacturer* ($25), *Doing Business in Oregon* (0-10 copies free, 11+ copies $1.50 each plus shipping and handling), *Economic Profile of Oregon* ($3.50), *Ad Conversion Studies* ($10), *Helping Oregon Export* ($10), *Oregon County Economic Indicators* ($3.50), *Oregon International Trade Directory*, 1990-91 edition ($15), *Oregon Travel and Tourism Visitor Profile* ($15), *Travel Industry Employment in Oregon: 1991* ($10).

Pennsylvania
Pennsylvania Department of Commerce, 433 Forum Bldg., Harrisburg, PA 17120; 717-783-1132. Publication: *Leaders in Economic Development.*

South Carolina
Commission on the Future of South Carolina, Office of Lieutenant Governor, P.O. Box 142, Columbia, SC 29202; 803-734-2080.

South Dakota
Governor's Office of Economic Development, Capitol Lake Plaza, 711 Wells Ave., Pierre, SD 57501-3369; 605-773-5032. Publication: *Economic Development Programs of Manufacturers and Processors* ($45).

Tennessee
Department of Economic and Community Development, 32-Sixth Ave., North, Rachel Jackson Bldg., Nashville, TN 37219; 615-741-1888.

Texas
Comptroller of Public Accounts, LBJ State Office Building, Austin, TX 78774; 512-463-4000. Publications: *Annual Financial Report, 1988-1989 Biennial Revenue Estimate, 1988-1989 Biennial Budget Estimate, Taxes and Texas: A National Survey on Alternatives and Comparisons, Texas Fees-Putting a Price on State Services, Quarterly Survey of Business Expectations in Texas, Sales and Franchise Tax Exemptions, Decontrolling Natural Gas-The Impact on Texas Prices and Tax Revenue, The High Finance of Higher Education, The Petroleum Industry and the Texas Sales Tax.*

Utah
Governor's Office of Planning and Budget, 116 State Capitol, Salt Lake City, Utah 84114; 801-538-1027, Fax: 801-538-1547. Publications: *Executive Budget Recommendations, Budget Summary, Utah Data Guide Newsletter, Economic and Demographic Projections, Utah Economic and Demographic Profiles, Utah Demographic Report, 1990 Census Briefs, Utah*

Migration Database: Sources, Methods, Limitations and Analysis 1994, Utah State and Local Government Fiscal Impact Model Working Paper Series: 1994, Utah Local Government Fiscal Database: An overview and Evaluation, June 1994 ($10), *Utah Ski Data Base 1994, Utah in the Global Economy 1993, Utah State Senate Districts: Economic and Demographic Characteristics, Higher Education Enrollment in Utah: A Demographic Perspective of Growth, Rural Utah Tourism Report 1992, Tourism Infrastructure Inventories for Mountainland, Bear River, Central and Southeastern Multi-County District 1992, Utah's Defense Economy 1992, Environment and Development in Rural Utah 1992, Water Development in Utah 1992, Utah Ski Database 1991, Utah State and Local Government Fiscal Benefit-Cost Model* (1990), *Technical Report on the Economic Analysis of the Brighton Ski Area Master Plan* (1991), *Historic Analysis of Property Taxes* (1980 Update), *Impact of Lake Powell Tourism on State and Local Tax Revenues* (1989), *Analysis of Demand for Recreation Uses in the Wasatch Front Canyons* (1988), *Migration in Utah* (1988), *Historic Analysis of Public Education Expenditures* (1987), *Historic Analysis of Property Taxes* (1986), *Economic Issues of Wilderness* (1986), *The Impacts of the Gramm-Rudman-Hollings Deficit Reduction Act* (1986), *The Importance of the Agricultural Industry in Utah* (1984), *Social and Economic Impact Analysis: Utah-Southwestern Utah Coal Environmental Impact Statement* (1983), *The Economic Issues Surrounding the Vitro Remedial Action Alternatives* (1983), *Final Socio-economic Technical Report: Utah Basin Synfuels Development* (1983), *The Economic and Demographic Impacts of the Intermountain Power Project* (1982), *Utah: 2000* (1980), *Energy: 2000* (1980), *The Planning Project Newsletter, State Planning Report, Economic Report to the Governor* ($15), *State Economic Coordinating Committee, The Impact of Tax Limitation in Utah* (1987), *State Mandates Study, Utah Advisory Commission on Intergovernmental Relations, The First Four Years: July 1987 - June 1991, State of Utah Comprehensive Annual Financial Report, Going Into Business In Utah, Poverty in Utah* (1985), *Utah Directory of Business and Industry, Utah Export Directory, Utah Facts, Affirmative Action Information, Annual Report of Job Service Activities, Labor Market Information Reports, Occupations In Demand, Helpful Hints for Job Seekers, Utah Labor Market Report, Utah Job Outlook for Occupations, Utah Directory of Business and Industry, Employment & Wages - By Size of Firm* (1989), *Hard at Work: Women in the Utah Labor Force* (1989), *Licensed Occupations in Utah, Utah's Career Guide, Utah Workforce 2000, Utah's Labor Force Characteristics, Crime in Utah, Utah Marriage and Divorce, Utah Vital Statistics, Fall Enrollment Report of Utah School Districts, Data Book, Utah Energy Statistical Abstract, Annual Report, Statistical Study of Assessed Valuations, Utah Statistics of Income, Gross Taxable Retail Sales and Purchases, New Car and Truck Sales, Initial Tax Burdens on Business and Households in Ten Western States: 1984-1985, Utah Construction Report Newsletter, Statistical Abstract of Utah, Utah Economic and Business Review Newsletter, Research Briefs, Research Reports, Statistical Review of Government in Utah, State Local Government in Utah 1992, Regional Planning Projections, Surveillance of Land Use and Socio-economic Characteristics, Economic Outlook, Office of Job Training Career Decisions Survey, Panel Survey of Migration History and Intentions Among Utahns, Follow-up Survey of Utah Exporters to Pacific Rim Countries, Survey of Utah Farmers and Economic Effects of the 1988 Drought, Survey of the Canyon Master Plan, Survey of Salt Lake City Residents on Earthquake Preparedness, Survey of Utah Exporters to Pacific Rim Countries, Omnibus Survey of Utah Households, Survey of University of Utah Students: Financing, Satisfaction, Plans for the Future, Time-Use Patterns Among One- and Two-Parent Households, School-Age Children's View of the Future, Survey of Utah Communities to Assess Impact of Changes in Long Distance Rates on Consumers, Survey of Utahns to Assess Attitudes About Wilderness Designations, Socio-demographic Survey of Residents in Southeastern Utah, Health Interview Survey of Utah, Panel Survey of Utah Households, Satisfaction with Primary Care in Rural Utah, Perceptions of the Quality of Life Among Elderly Viewed by the Elderly, by Adult Children of the Elderly, and by General Practitioners, Olympic Survey Results, Survey of Health Services Utilization Patterns and Mental Health Help-Seeking Behavior, Nuclear Waste Survey, Cost of Living Index, American Demographics* magazine, *Business Economics - The Journal of the National Association of Business Economists, Economic Report of the President, John Naisbitt's Trend Letter, Salt Lake Area Keeping Score, State Bond Prospectuses, State Policy Data Book: 1985-1990, U.S.G.S. Topographical Maps, Utah Business* magazine, *Utah Spectrum, News on Multiple-Use Management* (BLM newsletter), *Western Blue Chip Economic Forecast* (Arizona State University). OPB Online Database provides current publications and Census information that can be downloaded to a personal computer. Call 801-538-1550 for more information.

Vermont

Office of Policy Research and Coordination, Pavillion Office Building, 109 State St., Montpelier, VT 05602; 802-828-3326. Services and Responsibilities: Monitor trends and anticipate the impact of evolving technologies such as telecommunications, provide staff for the Governor's Council of Economic Advisors, Data on Vermont's Economy.

Virginia

Governor's Office, Department of Economic Development, 901 East Byrd, Richmond, VA 23219; 804-371-8263.

Washington

Washington State, Community Trade and Economic Development, Office of Financial Management, 9th and Columbia Bldg., P.O. Box 48300, Olympia, WA 98504-8300; 306-753-5617. Publication: *1993 Washington State Data Book.*

West Virginia

Research and Strategic Planning, Department of Industrial and Community Development, 1900 Washington St., East Building 6, Room 904, Charleston, WV 25305; 304-558-4010.

Wisconsin

Wisconsin Department of Development, 123 West Washington Ave., P.O. Box 7970, Madison, WI 53707; 608-266-1018. Publications: *Business Tax Chronology, Business Help Directory, Biennial Report--Wisconsin Department of Development (DOD), Community Economic Profiles* (Specify Community), *Community*

Preparedness Manual, County Economic Profiles (Specify Community), *Doing Business and Living in Wisconsin, Financing Alternatives* ($2), *Financial Resources Available to Wisconsin Businesses: A Quick Reference Guide, Going Into Business in Wisconsin: An Entrepreneur's Guide, High Technology Companies in Wisconsin* ($4), *Industrial Revenue Bond Report, Key Media Contracts* ($3.50), *Local Development Organizations, New Industries and Plant Expansions, Starting A Business? Here's Help!, Technical Resources Available to Wisconsin Businesses and Communities, Technology Resources Available to Wisconsin Businesses* ($3.50), *Wisconsin Economic Profile,*

Wisconsin Highway Map, Wisconsin: The Resourceful State, Worker's Compensation Insurance Rates: A Four-State Comparison.

Wyoming

Economic Development and Stabilization Board, 2301 Central Ave., Barrett Building, 4th Floor North, Cheyenne, WY 82002; 307-777-7284. Publications: *Wyoming Directory of Manufacturing and Mining, Wyoming Financial Assistant Programs, Mineral Yearbook.*

State Division of Motor Vehicles

Mailing lists galore and plentiful market research data derived from state motor vehicle departments offer the potential for increasing your bottom line. Did you ever want to know how many 40-year old males in Boston wear contact lenses, or perhaps obtain the names and addresses of all Arizonians who own Cadillacs? Well, it is within the realm of possibility.

Believe it or not, those long lines that drive us crazy when registering a car or renewing a driver's license have a bright side. Each person in line turns over to the state a wealth of information about him or herself. This data -- name, address, age, physical characteristics, and buying patterns -- are the stuff of which customer lists, market studies, and demographic analyses are made. While states charge you for this information, it will cost a fraction of what you would spend if you hired some sharp marketing consultant to unearth the data.

Take the example of my friend, Ron, a mechanic for expensive foreign cars in Wilmington, Delaware. One day Ron got tired of watching his boss laugh all the way to the bank and decided he wanted to open a shop of his own. Through the state he was able to obtain printouts of all owners of Audis, BMWs, and Mercedes in his area. Armed with this information, Ron ultimately was able to obtain a small business loan, open a shop, and now is making more than I'd care to admit.

Many states maintain files not only on autos, but also on boats and recreational vehicles. This data can be of further help in targeting potential customers. It doesn't take business brilliance to deduce that a person living in Palm Beach, who owns several high-ticket imported cars and has a 37-foot Hatteras yacht, is a potential customer for a home security company.

Many states will sort through their driver's license database by age and sex for an additional charge and provide a listing, for example, of all females between the ages of 18 and 45 years living in a particular district. If you are launching a magazine aimed at working women, this is priceless marketing intelligence. The same holds true for older persons who have special senior citizen identifiers and for young males who are eligible for the Selective Service.

This data is used in countless ways by researchers for compiling statistics on health issues, and of course, used by the government for manufacturer recalls or warranty programs, and emission studies. Insurance companies, financial institutions, and other businesses thrive on this cross-sectioning of the body public.

Information derived from a state's automobile owner registration master file is usually available in two formats -- magnetic tape or computer printouts. Most states prefer sending you a tape for larger files, while printouts are allowed for shorter sorts. In addition, some states offer mailing labels for an additional charge.

The most likely sorting options include: an entire state file; all vehicles within a county; vehicle type (2-door, 4-door, 4-wheel drive) by state or county; and vehicle make or year by state or county.

Driver's license information can usually be extracted to provide: name and license number (only); name, license number, and address; and a variety of other factors regarding age or sex. All states charge for this information, usually per 1,000 entries plus a set-up fee, but the potential for increasing your profits by using this valuable data will far outweigh the costs.

There are a few states which do not release this data for commercial purposes. These are Alabama, Connecticut, Georgia, Hawaii, Indiana, Kansas, New Jersey, New Mexico, New York, Oklahoma, Pennsylvania, Rhode Island, and South Dakota. Arkansas, California, Montana, Nebraska, North Carolina, Utah, Virginia are the states which will not divulge driver's license information, but will turn over vehicle registration files. Wyoming will give you driver's license information, but will not turn over vehicle registration files. That leaves 29 states which are wide open.

Motor Vehicle Offices

Alabama

Drivers: Alabama Department of Public Safety, Drivers License Division, P.O. Box 1471, Montgomery, AL 36272; 205-242-4400. This data is not released for commercial purposes.

Registration: Alabama Department of Revenue, Motor Vehicle Division, P.O. Box 327640, Montgomery, AL 36312-7630; 205-242-9000. This data is not released for commercial purposes.

Arizona

Drivers: Arizona Motor Vehicles Division, 1801 W. Jefferson St., Phoenix, AZ 85007; 602-255-7567. Request must be in writing with complete name, license number and date of birth. The cost is $3 for a 39 month check, $5 for a 5 year check.

Registration: Arizona Motor Vehicles Division, 1801 W. Jefferson St., Room 230M, Phoenix, AZ 85007; 602-255-7567. Database: Arizona Owners - contains owner's name and address plus make, model, year, tag and license numbers for 1,655,833 cars and 875,000 other vehicles. Services: A mailing list is available for $3,500, or a computer tape can be purchased and data sorted by name and address. Tape cost is $30 per 1,000 names received.

Arkansas

Drivers: Arkansas Office of Motor Vehicle Registration, P.O. Box 1272, Little Rock, AR 72203; 501-682-7060. Services: license information is protected under the Privacy Act. A release must be signed by a driver before that data can be released. Ths cost is $1 per request.

Registration: Arkansas Office of Motor Vehicle Registration, P.O. Box 1272, Little Rock, AR 72203; 501-682-7060. Database: Arkansas Automobile Owners - contains owner's name and address plus make, model, year and license number for over 15

million automobiles and approximately 300,000 million other vehicles including motorcycles and boats. Services: No data tapes are released. Records are open for public inspection at the office only.

California

Drivers: Department of Motor Vehicles, P.O. Box 944247, Sacramento, CA 94269; 916-657-6555. This data is not released for commercial purposes.

Registration: Department of Motor Vehicles, P.O. Box 944240, MS-D-146, Sacramento, CA 94244-2470. Database: California Automobile Owners - contains owner's name and address as well as make, model, year, tag and license numbers of 16.5 million automobiles and 631,000 motorcycles. Services: This file must be purchased in its entirety (i.e., information of all motorcycles and registration records for automobiles) The cost is approximately $100 per 1,000 names.

Colorado

Drivers: Colorado Motor Vehicle Division, Traffic Records, 140 W. 6th Ave., #104, Denver, CO 80204; 303-572-5601. Database: Colorado Drivers - contains name, address, license number of 3,167,570 drivers. It is available in two files: provisional and adult permits. Services: One time single run only of name, address and license number. The cost is $35 per 1,000 names with a $1,000 minimum plus $5 set-up fee.

Registration: Colorado Motor Vehicle Division, Traffic Records, 140 W. 6th Ave., #103, Denver, CO 80204; 303-623-9463. Database: Colorado Owners - contains name and address only. Services: One time single run of name, address and license number only. The cost is $25 per 1,000 names with a $1,000 minimum.

Connecticut

Drivers and Registration: Connecticut State Department of Motor Vehicles, 60 State Street, Wethersfield, CT 06109; 203-566-3830. This data is not released for commercial purposes.

Delaware

Drivers: Delaware Motor Vehicles Division, P.O. Box 698, Dover, DE 19903; 302-739-4461. Database: Delaware Drivers - provides name, address, height, weight and other drivers license information except hair color of 494,035 drivers. Services: Some ready-made programs available. Any additional programming requires additional charges. Prices are available upon request.

Registration: Delaware Motor Vehicle Division, P.O. Box 698, Dover DE 19903; 302-739-4461. Database: Delaware Owners - provides owner's name and address along with make, model, year, title number, and expiration date of 580,849 registered cars, motorcycles or trucks. Services: A data tape can be purchased with sorting of reportable variables for $375 plus $11 per 1,000 names.

District of Columbia

Drivers: District of Columbia, Department of Public Works Information Office, 301 C St., NW, Room 1025, Washington, DC 20001; 202-727-6761. Database: District of Columbia Drivers - contains name, address, suspensions, sex, height, weight, type of permit, license number, expiration dates, and restrictions of 800,000 drivers. Services: Computer tapes and printouts available. Data can be sorted by categories but not recommended. Cost is $1,700.

Registration: District of Columbia, Department of Public Works Information Office, 301 C St., NW, Room 1025, Washington, DC 20001; 202-727-1159. Database: District of Columbia Owners - contains owner's name, address, make, model, year, tag number, and registration number of 263,290 vehicles. Services: Computer tape is available. The data can be sorted. The cost varies depending on the information requested.

Florida

Drivers: Florida Highway Safety and Motor Vehicles Department, Neil Kirkman Building, Tallahassee, FL 32301; 904-488-6710. Database: Florida Drivers - contains name, address, and date of birth of over 12 million drivers. Services: No sorting is available. A computer tape or printout can be obtained for $.45 per second.

Registration: Florida Highway Safety and Motor Vehicles Department, Neil Kirkman Building, Tallahassee, FL 32301; 904-488-6710. Database: Florida Automobile Owners - provides owner's name and address plus make, model, year, tag number and class code for 7 million cars and 5 million other vehicles. Services: No sorting is available. The data is available on a computer tape or printout. Cost is $1.60 per second.

Georgia

Drivers: Motor Vehicle Records, 959 E. Confederate Ave., Atlanta, GA 30316; 404-624-7487. Data is not released.

Registration: Motor Vehicle Division, Trinity Washington Bldg., Atlanta, GA 30334; 404-656-4156. This data is not released for commercial purposes.

Hawaii

Drivers and Registration: Division of Motor Vehicles and Licenses, 2455 S. Beretainia St., Honolulu, HI 96814; 808-973-2700. Data is not released.

Idaho

Drivers: Idaho Transportation Department, Economics and Research Section, P.O. Box 7129, Boise, ID 83707-1129; 208-334-8741. Database: Idaho Drivers - provides name, address, sex, date of birth, license type, expiration date, and county of residence of approximately 1,000,000 drivers. Services: Data may be selected by sex, age or range of ages, and county of residence. The cost is $75 plus computer charges (this varies depending on size of the file, sorts, etc.) and shipping charges.

Registration: Idaho Transportation Department, Economics and Research Section, P.O. Box 7129, Boise, ID 83707-1129; 208-334-8741. Database: Idaho Owners - provides registered owner, address, make, model, year, issue and expiration dates of approximately 1,300,000 records. Services: Data can be selected by registration type, and/or county of residence. The cost is $75 plus computer charges (varies depending on the size of the file, sorts, etc.) and shipping charges. Computer tape or printouts are available.

Illinois

Drivers: Illinois Secretary of State, Drivers Services Division, 2701 S. Dirksen Parkway, Springfield, IL 62723; 217-782-1978. Database: Illinois Drivers - contains name, address, sex, make, model, and year of over 6 million passenger cars and over 2 million other vehicles. Services: Data can be sorted by various categories and provided on a computer tape for $200 plus $20 per 1,000 names, or on a printout for $.50 per page (15,000 names or less).

Registration: Illinois Secretary of State, Centennial Building, Room 114, Springfield, IL 62756; 217-782-0029. Database: Illinois Automobile Owners - provides owner's name and address, make, model and year of over 6 million passenger cars and over 2 million other vehicles. Services: Complete records are available. Data can be sorted by various categories. Computer tapes available for $200 plus $20 per 1,000; computer printouts for $.50 per page (15,000 names or less).

Indiana

Drivers and Registration: Indiana Bureau of Motor Vehicles, 100 N. Senate Ave., Indianapolis, IN 46204; 317-232-2798. This data is not released for commercial purposes.

Iowa

Drivers: Iowa Department of Transportation, Drivers Services, Lucas State Office Building, Des Moines, IA 50319; 515-244-8725. Database: Iowa Drivers - provides name, address, date of birth, height, weight, restrictions, issue and expiration dates, license number, and restrictions of 2.5 million drivers. Services: Data is listed in order by license number. Data cannot be sorted. Computer tapes are available for $370 (tapes must be provided by requester).

Registration: Iowa Department of Transportation, Office of Vehicle Registration, P.O. Box 9204, Des Moines, IA 50306-9204; 515-237-3182. Database: Iowa Automobile Owners - provides complete description of vehicle for 4.2 million cars and other vehicles. Services: Data tapes available for $.39 per thousand names plus $14 for each tape, computer time charge for sorts and a $20 set up fee.

Kansas

Drivers: Topeka Drivers License Bureau, 37th and Burlingame, Topeka, KS 66609; 913-266-7380. This data is not released for commercial purposes.

Market Studies, Demographics, and Statistics

Registration: Topeka Drivers License Bureau, 37th and Burlingame, Topeka, KS 66609; 913-266-3621. This data is not released for commercial purposes.

Kentucky

Drivers: Kentucky Transportation Cabinet, Division of Driver Licenses, State Office Bldg., 501 High St., Frankfort, KY 40622; 502-564-4864. Database: Kentucky Drivers - provides name, address, and date of birth of over 2.4 million drivers. Services: Data can be sorted by various categories. Computer tapes or printouts are available for $.01 per name plus $510 for programming and computer costs.

Registration: Kentucky Transportation Cabinet, Division of Motor Vehicle Licenses, State Office Building, Room 205, Frankfort, KY 40622; 502-564-5301. Database: Kentucky Automobile Owners - provides owner's name and address along with make, model and year for over 2 million vehicles. Services: Data can be sorted by various categories. Computer tapes and printouts available for $.02 per name plus programming costs ($510). Mailing labels can be purchased for $3.50 per 1,000 plus programming costs.

Louisiana

Drivers: Louisiana Department of Public Safety and Corrections, P.O. Box 66614, Baton Rouge, LA 70896; 504-925-6146. Database: Louisiana Drivers - provides name, address, height, weight, sex, date of birth of 2.7 million drivers. Services: Computer tapes and printouts are available. Data can be sorted by variables. Cost is $.03 per name plus $500.

Registration: Louisiana Department of Public Safety and Corrections, P.O. Box 66614, Baton Rouge, LA 70896; 504-925-6146. Database: Louisiana Owners - provides owner's name, address, make, model and year, date of acquisition, color, new or used for 4.5 million vehicles. Services: Computer tapes and printouts are available for $.03 per record and $500.

Maine

Drivers: Maine Motor Vehicle Division, 101 Hospital Street, Station 29, Augusta, ME 04333; 207-287-5553. Database: Maine Drivers - provides name, address, date of birth, and sex of 800,000 drivers. Services: Data available on computer tape or printouts Mailing labels are available for an extra charge. The cost depends on the type of search and the amount of time involved.

Registration: Maine Motor Vehicle Division, 101 Hospital Street, Station 29, Augusta, ME 04333; 207-287-5553. Database: Maine Automobile Owners - contains owner's name and address, date of birth as well as make, model, year, identification number for 700,000 registered vehicles. Services: Data can be sorted by variables and can be purchased on computer tape, printouts or mailing labels. Cost available on request.

Maryland

Drivers: Maryland Motor Vehicle Administration, 6601 Ritchie Highway, Room 200, Glen Burnie, MD 21062; 410-768-7665. Database: Maryland Drivers - contains name, address, date of birth, height, weight, and identification number of over 2 million drivers. Services: Data can be sorted by variables and is available on computer tape for $500 (non-refundable).

Registration: Maryland Motor Vehicle Administration, 6601 Ritchie Highway, Room 200, Glen Burnie, MD 21062; 410-768-7665. Database: Maryland Automobile Owners - provides owner's name and address along with make, manufacturer, and year for nearly 3 million passenger cars and 3 million other vehicles. Some insurance information is included such as company and policy number. The cost is available upon request.

Massachusetts

Drivers: Massachusetts Registry of Motor Vehicles, 100 Nashua Street, Boston, MA 02114; 617-727-3716. Database: Massachusetts Automobile Drivers - provides name, address, and Social Security number of 4 million drivers. Services: Data can be sorted by all variables except sex. The cost is $1,000 for the first 1,000 names and $40 per 1,000 records thereafter. Data is available on computer tape or printout (for less than 30,000 names).

Registration: Massachusetts Registry of Motor Vehicles, 100 Nashua Street, Boston, MA 02114; 617-727-3716. Database: Massachusetts Automobile Owners - contains owner's name and address along with make, model and year of 5 million vehicles. Services: Sorting of data is available, for instance, by particular insurance company the owner carries. The cost is $1,000 for the first 1,000 names and $40 per 1,000 records thereafter. Data is available on computer tape or printout (for less than 30,000 names).

Michigan

Drivers: Michigan Systems Programming Division, 7064 Crowners Drive, Lansing, MI 48918; 517-322-1624. Database: Michigan Drivers - provides names, address, date of birth, and sex of 6,447,174 drivers. Services: Data may be selected by sex, date of birth, county, state, city, and zip code at a cost of $64 per 1,000 names versus $16 per 1,000 names unsorted. There is a $500 minimum charge. Data can be purchased on computer tape or printout. It is also available in limited amount on disk. The cost is available upon request.

Registration: Michigan Department of State, Data Processing Division, 7064 Crowners Drive, Lansing, MI 48918; 517-322-1584. Database: Michigan Automobile Owners - provides owner's name and address with year, license number, make and model of 5,234,916 passenger cars and 2,261,688 other vehicles. Services: The cost for sorting is $64 per 1,000 names versus $16 per 1,000 unsorted names. There is a $500 minimum charge. Data can be purchased on computer tape or printout. The cost is available upon request.

Minnesota

Drivers: Minnesota Department of Public Safety, Driver/Vehicle Services Division, Transportation Building, 395 John Ireland Blvd., St. Paul, MN 55155; 612-297-2442. Database: Minnesota Drivers - provides name, address, and sex of 3.3 million drivers. Services: Data can be sorted; there is an extra fee if more information is required. Data is available on printout or computer tape or mailing labels for $8 to $10 per name with a $500 minimum. Custom programming cost varies depending on complexity of request.

Registration: Minnesota Department of Public Safety, Driver/Vehicle Services Division, Transportation Building, 395 John Ireland Blvd., St. Paul, MN 55155; 612-297-2442. Database: Minnesota Automobile Owners - contains owner's name and address along with make, model and year for 3.2 million cars and 2.1 million other vehicles. Services: Certain data can be sorted. Data is available on computer tape or printout. There is a $500 minimum plus $8 per 1,000 names.

Mississippi

Drivers: Mississippi Department of Public Safety/Data Processing, P.O. Box 958, Jackson, MS 39205; 601-987-1212. Database: Mississippi Drivers - contains name, address, date of birth, race and sex of over 1,924,696 drivers. Services: Data cannot be sorted. The entire file must be purchased for $250 plus $20 per reel.

Registration: Mississippi State Tax Commission Network, P.O. Box 960, Room 220, Jackson, MS 39205; 601-359-1117. Database: Mississippi Automobile Owners - provides a complete file, including owner's name and address, make, model, year of 1.6 million registered vehicles. Services: Data can be sorted and made available on computer tape or printout. Cost varies according to the search done. Mailing labels are available for an extra charge.

Missouri

Drivers: Missouri Department of Revenue, Information Services Bureau, P.O. Box 41, Jefferson City, MO 65105; 314-751-4600. Database: Missouri Drivers - contains name, address, sex, date of birth, height, weight, eye color, restrictions, license number, class, and county of 3.4 million drivers. Services: Data available on computer tape or printouts for $.18 per 50,000 records. Process fee is $85.26 and programming fee is $28.75 per hour. Mailing labels available for an extra charge ($2 per 1,000).

Registration: Missouri Department of Revenue, Information Services Bureau, P.O. Box 41, Jefferson City, MO 65105; 314-751-5486. Database: Missouri Owners - provides name and address of registered owners plus make, model, year, number of cylinders, type of fuel, license number, license expiration date, and year for over 4.2 million cars and 3.4 million other vehicles. Services: Data available on computer tape or printout. Cost: $.18 per 50,000 records. Process fee is $85.26 and programming fee is $28.75 per hour. Mailing labels available for an extra fee of $2 per 1,000.

Montana

Drivers: Drivers Services, 303 North Roberts, Helena, MT 59620; 406-444-3275. Data is not released.

Registration: Montana Motor Vehicle Division, 925 Main St., Deer Lodge, MT 59722; 406-846-1423. Database: Montana Automobile Owners - provides owner's name and address along with year, make, model, body, color, serial number, second owner for over one million registered vehicles. Services: Data available on computer tape and printout. The cost is $300 for the first 10,000 names and $30 per 1,000 names thereafter on tape or disk. Cost for each additional 1,000 names on printout is $40.

Nebraska

Drivers: Nebraska Department of Motor Vehicles, P.O. Box 94789, Lincoln, NE 68509; 402-471-3909. This data is not released for commercial purposes.

Registration: Nebraska Department of Motor Vehicles, P.O. Box 94789, Lincoln, NE 69509; 402-471-3909. Database: Nebraska Automobile Owners - provides listing by make, model, and year which includes owner's name and address for 856,000 passenger cars and 650,000 other vehicles. Services: Data can be provided on computer tape and printout for $12 per 1,000 with a $500 minimum.

Nevada

Drivers: Nevada Department of Motor Vehicles, 555 Wright Way, Carson City, NV 89711; 702-687-5505. Database: Nevada Drivers - provides name, address, date of birth, height, weight, for more than one million drivers. Services: Data can be sorted by county, zip code, date of birth and make of car. Data available on computer tape or printout (up to 1,000,000 names). Mailing labels available for an extra fee. Cost is $2,500 for the entire file or $15 per 1,000 for a partial listing.

Registration: Nevada Department of Motor Vehicles, 555 Wright Way, Carson City, NV 89711; 702-687-5505. Database: Nevada Owenrs - provides owner's name, address along with make, model and year for one million registered vehicles. Data may be selected by county, zip code and make of car. Services: Computer tape is available for $2,500 or portions prorated $15 per thousand. A printout is available for up to 1,000,000 records. Data is also available on mailing labels. (Prices are subject to change.)

New Hampshire

Drivers: New Hampshire Department of Safety, Data Processing, 10 Hazen Drive, Concord, NH 03305; 603-271-2314. Database: New Hampshire Drivers - consists of name, address, physical characteristics, Social Security number, class of license, issue and expiration date, and restriction of 843,000 drivers. Services: Data can be sorted by sex or age. Data provided on computer tape or printout. Prices vary, depending on data requested and size of the file.

Registration: New Hampshire Department of Safety, Data Processing, 10 Hazen Drive, Concord, NH 03305; 603-271-2314. Database: New Hampshire Owners - contains owner's name and address along with make, model and year for 815,628 passenger cars and 517,606 other vehicles. Services: Data can be sorted by zip code, model or make. Data available on computer tape or printout (extra charge). Fees vary depending on request. Entire file available on microfiche for $50.

New Jersey

Drivers and Registration: Motor Vehicle Services, Certified Information Unit, CN142, Trenton, NJ 08666; 609-292-4102. This data is not released for commercial purposes.

New Mexico

Drivers and Registration: New Mexico Taxation and Revenue Department, Motor Vehicle Division, P.O. Box 1028, Santa Fe, NM 87504-1028; 505-827-2294. Data is not released.

New York

Drivers: New York State Department of Motor Vehicles, Data Preparation, Empire State Plaza, Albany, NY 12202; 518-473-5595. This data is not released for commercial purposes.

Registration: State Department of Motor Vehicles, Empire State Plaza, P.O. Box 2650, Room 433, Albany, NY 12202; 518-473-5595. This data is not released for commercial purposes.

North Carolina

Drivers: Transportation Data Service Center, Century Center, Building B, 1020 Birchridge Rd., Raleigh, NC 27610; 919-250-4204. This data is not released for commercial purposes.

Registration: Transportation Data Service Center, Century Center, Bldg. B, 1020 Birchridge Rd., Raleigh, NC 27610; 919-250-4204. Database: North Carolina Automobile Owners - provides owner's name and address, second owner's name, make, model, year, plate classification, license number and weight of vehicle for 5.5 million registered vehicles. Services: Data can be sorted by model, year, make, county, zip code and other variables. Cost is $250 for the first 5,000 records and $20 per 1,000 records thereafter.

North Dakota

Drivers: North Dakota Drivers License and Traffic Safety Division, 608 East Boulevard Avenue, Bismarck, ND 58505-0700; 701-224-2601. Database: North Dakota Drivers - provides name, address, date of birth, and license number of 450,000 drivers. Services: Special sort/extraction is available. The cost is $9 per 1,000 names with a $250 minimum. Mailing labels are also available for an extra fee.

Registration: North Dakota Department of Transportation, Motor Vehicle Service Division, 608 E. Boulevard, Bismarck, ND

58505; 701-224-2725. Database: North Dakota Automobile Owners - contains owner's name and address along with make, model and year of 369,010 passenger cars and 391,968 other vehicles. Services: Data can be sorted by variables and provided on computer printout tape for $50 plus $40 per 1,000 names. Mailing labels available for an extra fee.

Ohio

Drivers: Ohio Bureau of Motor Vehicles, Data Services, P.O. Box 16520, Columbus, OH 43266-0020; 614-752-7695. Database: Ohio Drivers - includes name, address, sex, date of birth, height, weight, hair color, eye color, zip code, and some restrictions for over 7.4 million registered drivers. Services: Data can be sorted by variables. Data is available on computer tape for $.75 per record. Mailing labels are $.08 each.

Registration: Ohio Bureau of Motor Vehicles, Data Services, P.O. Box 16520, Columbus, OH 43266-0020; 614-752-7695. Database: Ohio Automobile Owners - provides owner's name, address, make, model, year, license number, and expiration date for over 9 million registered vehicles. Services: Data can be sorted by variables. Available on computer tape or printout at $.75 per record. Mailing labels provided for $.08 each.

Oklahoma

Drivers and Registration: Oklahoma Tax Commission, Motor Vehicle Division, 2501 N. Lincoln Blvd., Oklahoma City, OK 73194; 405-521-3217. Data tapes are not sold. Individual records can be requested for $1 each.

Oregon

Drivers: Oregon Department of Transportation, Motor Vehicle Division, 1905 Lana Ave., NE, Salem, OR 97314; 503-945-5259. Database: Oregon Drivers - contains name, address, sex, age, and date of birth for over 2 million drivers. Services: Data can be sorted and provided on computer tape for $180 or printout for $180 for full file.

Registration: Oregon Department of Transportation, Motor Vehicle Division, 1905 Lana Ave., NE, Salem, OR 97314; 503-945-5259. Database: Oregon Automobile Owners - contains owner's name and address along with make, model and year for over two million registered vehicles. Services: Data can be selected by variables. Data is also available on computer tape or printout for $180.

Pennsylvania

Drivers and Registration: Bureau of Drivers License Information, Box 58691, Harrisburg, PA 17106; 717-787-2158. This data is not released for commercial purposes.

Rhode Island

Drivers and Registration: Department of Motor Vehicles, State Office Building, Providence, RI 02903; 401-277-2064. This data is not released for commercial purposes.

South Carolina

Drivers: South Carolina Highway Department, Public Transportation, P.O. Box 1498, Columbia, SC 29216-0028; 803-251-2940. Database: South Carolina Drivers - provides name, address, date of birth, license number, and restrictions for 1.8 million drivers. Services: Data may be sorted by last name, zip code, tag number as well as automobile and/or motorcycles for 100,000 records. Computer tapes or printouts are available for $1,200.

Registration: South Carolina Highway Department, Public Transportation, P.O. Box 1498, Columbia, SC 29216-0028; 803-251-2940. Database: South Carolina Automobile Owners - contains name and address of 700,000 registered vehicles along with make, year and serial number. Services: Data may be sorted by last name, county, city, state, insurance information and tag number as well as automobile and/or motorcycles. Requests must be in writing. Prices are available upon written request.

South Dakota

Drivers and Registration: Division of Motor Vehicles, 118 W. Capitol St., Pierre, SD 57501; 605-773-3545. Data is not released.

Tennessee

Drivers: Department of Safety Information System, 150 Forter Ave., Nashville, TN 37210; 615-251-5322. Database: Tennessee Drivers - contains name, address, date of birth, sex and physical characteristics of approximately 3.5 million drivers. Services: Data can be sorted by category. Computer tapes, printouts and mailing labels are available for a minimum $500 plus $.10 per record.

Registration: Department of Safety Information Systems, 150 Forter Ave., Nashville, TN 37210; 615-741-3945. Database: Tennessee Automobile Owners - contains owner's name, address, model, make, year and tag number of approximately 4 million vehicles. Services: Computer tapes, printouts and mailing labels available for $300 minimum, plus $100 set up fee plus $20.05 per 1,000 names. (Prices subject to change.)

Texas

Drivers: Texas Department of Public Safety, Attn: L.I. and V.I., P.O. Box 4087, Austin, TX 78773; 512-465-2000. Database: Texas Drivers - provides name, address, date of birth, and license number for over 1.3 million drivers. Services: Data can be sorted by category. Data provided on computer tape for $30,000 for the entire file, or $2.25 per 1,000.

Registration: Texas Department of Transportation, Division of Motor Vehicles, 40th and Jackson, Austin, TX 78779-0001; 512-465-7531. Database: Texas Automobile Owners - contains owner's name and address along with make, model, year, previous owner, and lien holder for 14 million vehicles. Services: Sorting is not available. Data available on computer tape for $4,000 plus $.30 per 1,000 written records.

Utah

Drivers: Department of Public Safety, Drivers License Division, 4501 S. 2700 West, 3rd Floor, P.O. Box 30560, Salt Lake City, UT 84130-0560; 801-965-4437. This data is not released for commercial purposes.

Registration: Utah State Tax Commission, Data Processing, 160 E. 300 South St., Salt Lake City, UT 84134; 801-538-8309. Database: Utah Automobile Owners - provides owner's name and address along with make, model and year for 1.9 million vehicles. Services: Data can be sorted and made available on computer tape for $300 to $400.

Vermont

Drivers: Vermont Department of Motor Vehicles, 120 State St., Montpelier, VT 05603; 802-828-2020. Database: Vermont Drivers - contains name, address, physical characteristics, license number and date of birth for 427,512 drivers. Services: Full identification must be provided in order to obtain information (company or corporation). Cost is $4 for each record up to 4 records.

Registration: Vermont Department of Motor Vehicles, 120 State Street, Montpelier, VT 05603; 802-828-2020. Database: Vermont Automobile Owners - provides owner's name and address along with make, model and year for 327,016 passenger cars and 207,684 other vehicles. Services: Must provide vehicle identification to obtain information. Cost is $4 for each record.

Virginia

Drivers: Dealer and Information, P.O. Box 7412, Richmond, VA 23269; 804-367-0538. Data is not released.

Registration: Dealer and Information, P.O. Box 7412, Richmond, VA 23269,; 804-367-0538. Services: If you provide the license number or registration number, they will provide the information. Initial fee of $3,000 plus $5 per record.

Washington

Drivers: Department of Licensing, Highways/Licensing Building, P.O. Box 3090, Olympia, WA 98507; 206-753-6961. Database: Washington Drivers - provides name, date of birth and address of registered drivers. Services: Sorting is available. A written request is required and an agreement must be signed. Each program is custom made. The charge is $3,680 plus tax.

Registration: Department of Licensing, Highways/Licenses Building, Olympia, WA 98507; 206-753-6950. Database: Washington Automobile Owners - contains owner's name, address, make, model, year and class of vehicle. Services: Data can be sorted alphabetically by owner's name, address, make, model, year and class of vehicle. It can be sorted alphabetically by owner's name, state or county. A written request is required and an agreement must be signed. Each program is custom made. The charge is $3,680 plus tax.

West Virginia

Drivers: West Virginia Department of Motor Vehicles, Bldg. #3, Room 113, Charleston, WV 25317; 304-558-2723. Database: West Virginia Drivers - provides name, address, height, weight, race, sex, and date of birth for 1.4 million drivers. Services: Data can be sorted and provided on computer tape or printout. Cost is $5,040.

Registration: West Virginia Department of Motor Vehicles, Bldg. #3, Room 113, Charleston, WV 25317; 304-558-2723. Database: West Virginia Automobile Owners - contains owner's name and address along with make, model and year of 1.4 million passenger cars and 246,000 other vehicles. Services: Data can be sorted and provided on computer tape or printout for $5,040.

Wisconsin

Drivers: Wisconsin Department of Transportation, 4802 Sheybogan Ave., P.O. Box 7918, Madison, WI 53711; 608-266-2353. Database: Wisconsin Drivers - provides an alphabetical list of name, address, date of birth, sex and drivers record for 4.5 million drivers. Services: Data available on computer tape for $2,200.

Registration: Wisconsin Department of Transportation, 4802 Sheybogan Ave., P.O. Box 7911, Madison, WI 53707-7911; 608-266-2353. Database: Wisconsin Owners- provides owner's name and address plus make, model and year of 2.3 million passenger cars and 1.7 million other vehicles. Services: Data cannot be sorted. Entire file must be purchased on computer tape for $2,200.

Wyoming

Drivers: Wyoming Department of Transportation, Attn: Driver Control, P.O. Box 1708, Cheyenne, WY 82003; 307-777-4710. Database: Wyoming Drivers - provides name, address, date of birth, Social Security number, status, expiration, and issuance date for 500,000 drivers. Services: Cost for magnetic tape: $1 per record with a $100 minimum. All requests must be approved by the Commission.

Registration: Wyoming Department of Transportation, Licensing Station, 5300 Bishop Blvd., Cheyenne, WY 82009; 307-777-4810. Data is not released.

How Do I
Take Care of the Kids?

How Do I
Take Care Of The Kids?

Will your home-based business run a little better if you have free day care for your kids? If so, you should check out the government programs in this section that will actually give you money and help to make that happen. And if you're not worried about day care for yourself, you may be interested in using these programs to start a home-based day care business.

Twenty-seven year old Robvato Gray — mother of four children — had been on welfare since the age of 18 and had lived in government housing for 8 years. She received food stamps and $184 per month from AFDC.

Wanting to better herself, she started to provide child care for mothers at $25 per week. Soon she began to realize that she was providing the same quality care that centers in her area were, but getting only about one-third of the money.

She began checking into government programs and began to participate in a program where the government paid Day Care Home Providers weekly to watch the children of welfare recipients, while mothers worked. The program also gives the day care provider money on a monthly basis to provide food for the children. Additionally she got a government grant through a neighborhood center to purchase $1000 worth of toys for the children she watched.

By increasing her weekly fee to about $75, Robvato not only increased her income from $104 per month to $4000 per month, but increased her self esteem. She has been off welfare for a year and a half, has two homes and two vehicles. The inspiration of this success has led her to start a janitorial business, as well as to give speeches and to train other women on AFDC to become self-sufficient.

Families all over the country are taking advantage of government programs to help them find affordable day care for their little ones. What follows is a list of starting places to help you make your dreams come true.

* Let Every Child Get A Head Start
Administration For Children and Families
U.S. Dept. of Health and Human Services
Head Start Bureau
Washington, DC 20201
202-205-8572

Each year, almost one million children from low-income families enter school for the first time, and many have health problems and a lack of self confidence. The Head Start Program addresses the needs of low-income preschool children, and provides educational, social, medical, dental, nutrition, and mental health services. In 1993, Head Start had 36,300 classrooms serving 721,268 children. In order to qualify to enroll a child in a Head Start program, a parent must meet certain income guidelines (in 1993 a family of 3 could earn $11,890), and parent involvement is encouraged. The U.S. Department of Health and Human Services awards grants to local public agencies, private non-profit organizations and school systems for the purpose of operating Head Start programs at the community level. To locate a Head Start Program near you contact your local board of education or department of social services (look in the blue pages of your phone book) or contact the office listed above.

* Money For Child Care Or Even To Start A Day Care Center
Division of Child Care
Administration for Children, Youth, and Families

U.S. Dept. of Health and Human Services
200 Independence Ave., SW
Room 352G
Washington, DC 20201
202-690-6782

Child care issues should not be a stumbling block for people who want to start a training program or continue their education. This program emphasizes the role of parents in choosing the care that best meets their family's child care needs. Parents may choose from a variety of child care providers, including center-based, family child care and in-home care, care provided by relatives, and sectarian child care providers. You can even **get money to start a day care center.** Federal funds are available to States, Indian Tribes, and Territories to provide grants, contracts, and certificates for child care services for low-income families with a parent who is working or attending a training or education program. Funding is also provided to improve the availability and quality of child care and for early childhood development and before- and after-school services. For information on how to take advantage of this program in your state and to find out eligibility requirements, contact your State agency listed below, or the main office listed above.

Child Care and Development Block Grant State Lead Agencies

Alabama
Frances Arnold, Assistant Director for Day Care, Division of Family and Children Services, Alabama Department of Human Resources, 50 Ripley St., Montgomery, AL 36130; 205-242-1425, Fax: 205-242-0939.

Alaska
Jan Brewer, Child Care Programs Coordinator, Alaska Department of Community and Regional Affairs, 333 W. 4th Ave., Suite 220, Anchorage, AK 99501-2341; 907-269-4676, Fax: 907-269-4520.

Arizona
Bruce Liggett, Program Administrator, Arizona Department of Economic Security, Box 6123, Phoenix, AZ 85005-6123; 602-542-4248, Fax: 602-542-4197.

Arkansas
Jimmy Fields, Administrator, Management Services Unit, Arkansas Department of Human Services, Division of Children and Family Services, P.O. Box 1437, Slot 626, Little Rock, AR 72203-1437; 501-682-8757, Fax: 501-682-8666.

California
Janet Poole, Administrator, Child Development Division, California State Department of Education, 560 J St., Suite 220, Sacramento, CA 95814-4785; 916-322-4240, Fax: 916-323-6853.

Colorado
Grace Hardy, Manager, Office of Child Care Services, Colorado Department of Social Services, 1575 Sherman St., Denver, CO 80203-1714; 303-866-5958, Fax: 303-866-2704.

Connecticut
Randy Wong, Child Care Coordinator, Connecticut Dept. of Social Services, 1049 Asylum Ave., Hartford, CT 06105-2431; 203-566-5889, Fax: 203-566-7613.

Delaware
Dave Loughery, Social Services Administrator, Delaware Department of Health and Social Services, P.O. Box 906, New Castle, DE 19720; 302-577-4439, Fax: 302-577-4405.

District of Columbia
Pamela Ellison, Early Childhood Development Specialist, Office of Early Childhood Development, 717 14th St., NW, Suite 730, Washington, DC 20005; 202-727-1839, Fax: 202-727-9709.

Florida
Sandi Harris, Chief, Child Care Services, Florida Department of Health and Rehabilitative Services, 1317 Windwood Blvd., Building 7, Tallahassee, FL 32399-0700; 904-488-4900, Fax: 904-488-9584.

Georgia
Frenda A. Norwood, Human Services Program Specialist, Family Support Unit, Division of Family and Children Services, Georgia Department of Human Resources, Two Peachtree St., NW, Suite 12-400, Atlanta, GA 30383; 404-657-3438, Fax: 404-657-3489.

Guam
Diana Calvo, Bureau of Economic Security, Guam Department of Public Health and Social Services, Room 242, Route 10, Manqilao, Guam 96923; 671-734-7286.

Hawaii
Elisabeth Chun, Program Specialist, Governor's Office of Children and Youth,, P.O. Box 3044, Honolulu, HI 96802; 808-586-0133, Fax: 808-586-0122.

Idaho
Jana Jones, Director, Idaho Office for Children, Office of the Governor, State House, 1109 Main St., Lower Level, Boise, ID 83720-2651; 208-334-2651, Fax: 208-334-3267.

Illinois
Sue Howell, Chief, Office of Child Development, Illinois Department of Child and Family Services, 406 E. Monroe St., Mail Station 55, Springfield, IL 62701-1498; 217-524-2480, Fax: 217-785-2454.

Indiana
James Hmurovich, Indiana Family and Social Services Administration, Division of Family and Children, 402 W. Washington St., Room W341, P.O. Box 7083, Indianapolis, IN 46207-7083; 317-232-1144, Fax: 317-232-7948.

Iowa
Rosemary Norlin, Federal Day Care Program Manager, Iowa Department of Human Services, Hoover State Office Building, Des Moines, IA 50319-0114; 515-281-8166, Fax: 215-281-4597.

Kansas
Karen Juola, Coordinator of Child Care Services, Kansas Dept. of Social and Rehabilitation Services, 300 SW Oakley, West Hall, Topeka, KS 66606; 913-296-3742, Fax: 913-296-6960.

Kentucky
Cliff Jennings, Manager, Management and Evaluation Branch, Department for Social Services, Cabinet for Human Resources, 275 E. Main St., 6W, Frankfort, KY 40621; 502-564-6750, Fax: 502-564-2467.

Louisiana
William Ludwig, Deputy Secretary, Louisiana Department of Social Services, P.O. Box 3776, Baton Rouge, LA 70821; 504-342-6712, Fax: 504-342-8636.

Maine
Jeanette Talbot, Federal Grants Manager, Office of Child Care Coordination, Maine Department of Human Services, 221 State St., Augusta, ME 04333-0011; 207-287-5060, Fax: 207-626-5555.

Maryland
Barbara Smith-Hamer, Director of Child Care Administration, Maryland Department of Human Resources, 2701 N. Charles St., Baltimore, MD 21218; 410-554-0410, Fax: 410-554-0448.

Massachusetts
Janet L. George, Undersecretary for Human Services, Massachusetts Executive Office of Health and Human Services, One Ashburton Place, Room 1109, Boston, MA 02108; 617-727-0077, Fax: 617-727-1396.

Michigan
David Berns, Director, Office of Children's Services, Michigan Department of Social Services, 235 S. Grand Ave., P.O. Box 3037, Lansing, MI 48909; 517-335-6159.

Minnesota
Linda Foster, Director, Child Care Fund, Minnesota Department of Human Services, 444 Lafayette Rd., St. Paul, MN 55155-3832; 612-296-0179.

Mississippi
Ronnie McGinnis, Director, Office for Children and Youth, Mississippi Department of Human Services, P.O. Box 352, Jackson, MS 39205-0352; 601-359-4555, Fax: 601-359-4422.

Missouri
Doris Hall Ford, Deputy Director for Income Maintenance, Division of Family Services, Missouri Department of Social Services, P.O. Box 88, Jefferson City, MO 65103; 314-751-3124, Fax: 314-526-4837.

Deborah Word, The Child Care Unit, Department of Health, P.O. Box 570, Jefferson City, MO 65102; 314-751-4279, Fax: 314-526-2969.

Montana
Boyce Fowler, CCDBG Administrator, Montana Dept. of Family Services, P.O. Box 8005, Helena, MT 59604; 406-444-5900, Fax: 406-444-5956.

Nebraska
Deborah Mabry-Strong, Director, Child Care and Development, Nebraska Department of Social Services, P.O. Box 95026, Lincoln, NE 68509-5026; 402-471-9451, Fax: 402-471-9449.

Nevada
Gerald Allen, CCDBG Coordinator, Nevada Department of Human Resources, 505 E. King St., Carson City, NV 89710; 702-687-4730, Fax: 702-687-4733.

New Hampshire
Carol G. Mooney, Child Care Coordinator, New Hampshire Department of Health and Human Services, Commissioner's Office, 6 Hazen Dr., Concord, NH 03301; 603-271-4343, Fax: 603-271-4232.

New Jersey
Terry Castro, Chief, Bureau of Policy and Standards Development, New Jersey Department of Human Services, 3 Quakerbridge Plaza, CN 716, Trenton, NJ 08625; 609-588-2282, Fax: 609-588-7240.

New Mexico
Jacqueline Lowe, Bureau Chief, Child Care Bureau, Department of Children, Youth and Families, P.O. Drawer 5160, Room 377, Santa Fe, NM 87502-5160; 505-827-7499, Fax: 505-827-9978.

New York
Christina Hay, Director, Bureau of Early Childhood Services, New York State Department of Social Services, 40 N. Pearl St., 11B, Albany, NY 12243; 518-474-9324, Fax: 518-474-9617.

North Carolina
Barbara Spaulding, Program Development Coordinator, North Carolina Department of Human Resources, P.O. Box 29553, Raleigh, NC 27603-0553; 919-571-4848, Fax: 919-571-4918.

North Dakota
John Opp, Director of AFDC Division, Office of Economic Assistance, North Dakota Department of Human Services, State Capitol - Judicial Wing, 600 E. Boulevard Ave., Bismarck, ND 58505; 701-224-4009, Fax: 701-224-2359.

Northern Mariana Islands
Timothy Thornburg, Federal Projects Coordinator, CNMI Department of Community and Cultural Affairs, CNMI Public School System, P.O. Box 1370 CK, Saipan, MP 98950; 670-322-6405, Fax: 670-322-4056.

Ohio
Joel Rabb, Chief, Bureau of Child Care, Ohio Department of Human Services, 65 E. Broad St., 5th Floor, Columbus, OH 43215; 614-466-1043, Fax: 614-466-0164.

Oklahoma
Prins Ella Anderson, Administrator of CCDBG, Office of Child Care, Oklahoma Dept. of Human Services, P.O. Box 25352, Oklahoma City, OK 73125; 405-521-3561, Fax: 405-528-4786.

Oregon
Janis Elliot, Child Care Coordinator, Department of Human Resources, Human Resources Bldg., 4th Floor, 500 Summer St., NE, Salem, OR 97310-1012; 503-373-7282, Fax: 503-378-6484.

Palau
Irung Ikeda, Child Care Program Developer, Palau Community Action Agency, P.O. Box 3000, Koror, Palau 96940; 690-488-1170, Fax: 680-488-1169.

Pennsylvania
Kathryn Holod, CCDBG Administrator, Bureau of Child Day Care Services, Office of Children, Youth and Families, Pennsylvania Dept. of Public Welfare, Box 2675, Harrisburg, PA 17105; 717-787-8691, Fax: 717-787-7753.

Puerto Rico
Mario Rosado Acevedo, Ph.D., Executive Director, Puerto Rico Office of Child Services and Community Development, Office of the Governor, Ponce de Leon Ave., Call Box 15091, San Juan, PR 00902; 809-721-2245, Fax: 809-723-1113.

Rhode Island
Barbara A. Gianola, Chief, Office of Child Care, Rhode Island Department of Human Services, 275 Westminster St., 5th Floor, Providence, RI 02903; 401-464-3415, Fax: 401-464-1876.

South Carolina
Dottie Garvey, Deputy Bureau Chief, Interagency Coordination, South Carolina Health and Human Services Finance Commission, P.O. Box 8206, Columbia, SC 29202; 803-253-6154, Fax: 803-253-6152.

South Dakota
Bobbi Brown, Program Administrator, Child Care Services, South Dakota Dept. of Social Services, 700 Governors Dr., Pierre, SD 57501-2291; 605-773-4766, Fax: 605-773-4855.

Tennessee
Janet Camp, Director, Day Care Services, Tennessee Dept. of Human Services, Citizens Plaza - 14th Floor, 400 Deaderick St., Nashville, TN 37248; 615-741-7130, Fax: 615-741-4165.

Texas
Charlotte Brantley, Director, CCDBG Program, Texas Department of Human Services, Client Self-Support Services, P.O. Box 149030, Austin, TX 78714-9030; 512-450-4179, Fax: 512-450-3864.

Utah
Cathie Pappas, Program Specialist, Child Care, Office of Family Support, Utah Department of Human Services, P.O. Box 45500,

Salt Lake City, UT 84145-0500; 801-538-3976, Fax: 801-538-4212.

Vermont
Christopher J. Mulvaney, Federal Programs Administrator, Vermont Department of Social and Rehabilitation Services, 103 S. Main St., Waterbury, VT 05671-2401; 802-241-2120, Fax: 802-241-2980.

Virginia
Mary Ellen Verdu, Director, Virginia Council on Child Day Care and Early Childhood Programs, Washington Building, Suite 1116, 1100 Bank St., Richmond, VA 23219; 804-371-8603, Fax: 804-371-6570.

Virgin Islands
Judy Richardson, Virgin Islands Dept. of Human Services, Knud Hansen Complex, Bldg. A, 1303 Hospital Ground, Charlotte Amalie, VI 00802; 809-774-0930, Fax: 809-774-3466.

Washington
Karen Tvedt, Chief, Office of Child Care Policy, Washington Department of Social and Health Services, P.O. Box 45710, Olympia, WA 98504-5710; 206-586-6066, Fax: 206-586-1040.

West Virginia
Kay Tilton, Director, Day Care and Licensing, DHHR/Bureau of Social Services, Bldg. 6, Room B-850, State Capitol Complex, Charleston, WV 25305; 304-558-7980, Fax: 304-558-8800.

Wisconsin
David Edie, Director, Office of Child Care and Social Services, Wisconsin Department of Health, 1 W. Wilson St., Madison, WI 53705; 608-266-6946, Fax: 608-264-6750.

Wyoming
Ken Kaz, CCDBG Administrator, Wyoming Dept. of Family Services, Hathaway Building, 2300 Capitol Ave., Cheyenne, WY 82002-0490; 307-777-7561, Fax: 307-777-7747.

* More Child Care Help Close To Home

See state by state listing below

The Federal government gives money to the States, who then in turn give money to local organizations to provide child care services. Sometimes it is difficult to track the money, but one way is to contact your local Department of Human Services. They can let you know what programs are available to you in your area, as well as direct you to other programs and resources you can use. Many have established special programs, such as Child Care Management Services or Child Care Resource Centers to help you locate appropriate services. Look for the Department of Human Services in the blue pages of your phone book under your county's listings. If you have trouble locating the number, contact your State office which is listed below.

State Day Care Offices

Alabama
State Department of Health, Office of Day Care, 50 Ripley St., Montgomery, AL 36130; 205-242-1425.

Alaska
Department of Community and Regional Affairs, Division of Community and Rural Development, Childcare Programs, 333 W. 4th Ave., Suite 220, Anchorage, AK 99501-2341; 907-269-4670.

Arizona
Department of Social Services, DES, 1789 W. Jefferson, Phoenix, AZ 85007; 602-542-0238.

Arkansas
State Department of Health and Human Services, Day Care Eligibility Section, P.O. Box 1437, Slot 604, Little Rock, AR 72203; 501-682-8754.

California
California Childcare Resource and Referral Network, 111 New Montgomery St., San Francisco, CA 94105; 415-882-0234.

Colorado
State Department of Health, Office of Social Services, Child Care Licensing, 1575 Sherman St., Denver, CO 80203; 303-866-5958.

Connecticut
Department of Public Health and Addiction Services, Day Care Licensing Division, 150 Washington St., Hartford, CT 06457; 203-566-2575.

Connecticut does not have a centralized number for childcare assistance or information. Each county has an individual department of social services which provides referrals. For the social service agency closest to you, contact the United Way's Resource and Referral Information line at 800-505-1000.

Delaware
Department of Health and Human Services, Office of Day Care Eligibility, 1624 Jessup St., Wilmington, DE 19802; 302-577-3101.

District of Columbia
Department of Human Services, Office of Resource and Referral, 2121 Decatur Place, NW; Washington, DC 20008; 202-387-0002.

Florida
Florida does not have a centralized number for childcare assistance or information. Each county has an individual department of social services which provides referrals. For the social service agency closest to you contact: Big Ben Community Coordinated Childcare, Office of Resource and Referral, 203 Appalachia Parkway, Suite 209, Tallahassee, FL 32301; 904-878-0636.

Georgia
State Department of Health, Child Care Licensing Unit, 2 Peach Tree St., NW, 20th Floor, Atlanta, GA 30303-3167; 404-657-5562.

Hawaii
State Department of Human Services, Child Care Licensing Division, 33 S. King St., Rm. 500, Honolulu, HI 96813; 808-586-7090.

Idaho
Idaho does not have a centralized number for childcare assistance or information. Each county has an individual department of social services which provides referrals. For the social service agency closest to you contact: Child Care Connection, 950 N. Cole Rd., Boise, ID 83704; 208-322-4453.

Illinois
State Department of Health, Children and Family Services Division, 500 S. 6th St. Rd., Springfield, IL 62703; 217-786-6830.

Indiana
State Department of Health, Division of Family and Children, Bureau of Child Development, 402 W. Washington St., Room 386, Indianapolis, IN 46204-2739; 317-232-7097.

Iowa
State Department of Health, Human Services Division, Adult, Children and Family Services, Hoover State Office Building, 5th Floor, Des Moines, IA 50319; 515-281-6074.

Kansas
Department of Social and Rehabilitative Services, Employment Preparation Services, Child Care Eligibility Division, P.O. Box 1424, Topeka, KS 66601; 913-296-1396.

Kentucky
Department of Social Services, Child Care Services Branch, 275 E. Main St., 6 West, Frankfort, KY 40621; 502-564-2524.

Louisiana
Department of Social Services, Childcare Assistance Program, State Office, P.O. Box 91193, Baton Rouge, LA 70821-9193; 504-342-9108.

Maine
Bureau of Child and Family Services, 221 State St., Station 11, Augusta, ME 04333; 207-287-5060.

Maryland
Department of Human Resources, Child Care Administration - Licensing Division, 311 W. Saratoga St., Baltimore, MD 21201; 410-767-7801.

How Do I Take Care of the Kids?

Massachusetts
Department of Social Services, Child Care Unit, 24 Farnsworth St., Boston, MA 02210; 617-727-0900.

Michigan
Department of Social Services, Office for Young Children, 5303 S. Cedar St., P.O. Box 30161, Lansing, MI 48909; 517-887-4319.

Minnesota
State Department of Health, Resources for Childcaring, 450 N. Syndicate St., Suite 5, St. Paul, MN 55104; 612-641-0305.

Mississippi
Department of Human Services, Child Care Express, P.O. Box 352, Jackson, MS 39205; 601-359-4544 or 800-877-7882.

Missouri
State Department of Health, Department of Maternal Child and Family Health, Child Care Licensing Division, P.O. Box 570, Jefferson City, MO 65102; 314-751-6172.

Montana
State Department of Health, Division of Family Services, Child Care Licensing, P.O. Box 8005, Helena, MT 59624; 406-444-5900.

Nebraska
Department of Social Services, Child Care Division, 1050 N St., Lincoln, NE 68508; 402-471-7000.

Nevada
Child Care Resource Council, 1090 S. Rock Boulevard, Reno, NV 89502; 702-856-6210.

New Hampshire
Department of Health and Human Services, Office of Data Management, 6 Hazen Dr., Concord, NH 03301; 800-852-3345, Ext. 4271 or 4379.

New Jersey
Department of Health, Division of Youth and Family Services, Child Care Licensing, CN 717, Trenton, NJ 08625-0717; 609-292-9220.

New Mexico
Department of Health, Child Care Licensing Division, P.O. Drawer 5760, Santa Fe, NM 87502; 505-827-7684.

New York
State Department of Health, Social Services Division, Albany Regional Office, Child Care Licensing Bureau, 40 N. Pearl St., 3 City Square, 1st Floor, Albany, NY 12243; 518-432-2763.

North Carolina
State Department of Health, Child Development Division, Child Care Licensing, P.O. Box 29553, Raleigh, NC 27626; 919-662-4499.

North Dakota
State Department of Health, Children and Family Services, Child Care Licensing Unit, 600 E. Blvd. Ave., Bismarck, ND 58505; 701-224-4809.

Ohio
State Department of Human Services, Bureau of Child Care Services, 65 E. State St., 5th Fl., Columbus, OH 43215; 614-466-1043.

Oklahoma
State Department of Human Services, Office of Information and Referral, P.O. Box 25352, 2400 N. Lincoln, Oklahoma City, OK 73125; 405-521-2778.

Oregon
State Department of Health, Child Care Licensing, Child Care Division, 875 Union St., NE, Salem, OR 97311; 503-378-3178.

Pennsylvania
State Department of Health, Day Care Licensing Division, Central Region, DPW Complex #2, Lanco Lodge, Harrisburg, PA 17125; 717-772-7078.

Rhode Island
To obtain a listing of child care providers contact: Department of Children, Youth and Families, 610 Mt. Pleasant Ave., Providence, RI 02908; 401-277-4741. To find out whether you qualify for assistance contact: Department of Human Services, Child Care Assistance, 275 W. Minister St., Providence, RI 02903; 401-277-1337.

South Carolina
To obtain a listing of day care centers contact: State Department of Social Services, Child Care Licensing Division, P.O. Box 1520, Room 520, Columbia, SC 29202-1520; 803-734-5740. To find out whether or not you qualify for assistance, contact the ABC Voucher Program at 800-476-0199.

South Dakota
Department of Social Services, Child Care Services, Child Care Licensing Division, 700 Governor's Dr., Pierre, SD 57501; 605-773-4766.

Tennessee
State Department of Health, Day Care Licensing Division, 400 Dedrick St., Nashville, TN 37248; 615-741-7129.

Texas
Department of Human Services, Child Care Services, P.O. Box 149030, Austin, TX 78714-9030; 512-450-4179.

Utah
Department of Human Services, Office of Child Care Assistance, 1385 S. State St., Salt Lake City, UT 84115; 801-468-0077.

Vermont
Department of Social and Rehabilitative Services, Childcare Services Division, 103 S. Main St., Waterbury, VT 05761-2401; 802-241-2158.

Virginia
To obtain a listing of child care facilities contact: Department of

Social Services, Child Care Licensing Division, 1604 Santa Rosa Rd., With Bldg., Suite 130, Richmond, VA 23229; 804-662-9743. To find out whether or not you qualify for child care assistance, contact your local county Department of Social Services or Richmond's Department of Social Services at 804-692-1730.

Washington
Child Care Action Service, Office of Child Care Resource and Referral, P.O. Box 446, Olympia, WA 98507-0446; 206-754-0810.

West Virginia
Department of Health and Human Resources, Office of Social Services, Bldg. 6, Rm. 850, State Capital, Charleston, WV 25305; 304-558-7980.

Wisconsin
State Department of Health and Social Services, Child Care Licensing Division, 3601 Memorial Dr., Madison, WI 53704; 608-243-2400.

Wyoming
State Department of Family Services, Office of Child Care Licensing, Hathaway Bldg., Cheyenne, WY 82002-0490; 307-777-6848.

* Child Care Money For Those On Or Just Off AFDC

Office of Family Assistance
Administration for Children and Families
U.S. Department of Health and Human Services
370 L'Enfant Promenade, SW, Fifth Floor
Washington, DC 20447
202-401-9294

For those who are struggling to work, but the cost of child care is making you wonder if the effort is worth it, take heart. There is an Aid To Families With Dependent Children (AFDC) At-Risk Care Program which permits States to provide child care to low-income families who are not receiving AFDC, need child care in order to work, and would otherwise be at risk of becoming eligible for AFDC. There are also funds for AFDC recipients (Title IV-A Child Care) to allow them to pursue employment or work training, as well as transitional funds to assist those recently off AFDC. The central point of administration of these programs are with state welfare agencies. In this way state agencies, which also have the responsibility for

providing welfare, employment, and related services under the Job Opportunities and Basic Skills Training (JOBS) program, can coordinate child care with these services. States may not be using the title "At-Risk Care Program, or Title IV-A Child Care" so make sure you explain your situation clearly and state that you need child care assistance. There is a list of state lead agencies below, who may be able to assist you in locating a local source who received child care monies.

IV-A Child Care Directors

Alabama
Carolyn Tidwell, Child Day Care Coordinator, Division of Family and Child Services, Department of Human Resources, 50 N. Ripley St., Montgomery, AL 36130; 205-242-1435.

Alaska
Patti Palmer, IV-A Child Care Coordinator, Department of Health and Social Services, Division of Public Assistance, P.O. Box 110640, Juneau, AK 99811-0640; 907-465-5842.

Arizona
Bruce Liggett, Program Manager, Child Care Administration, Box 6123, Phoenix, AZ 85005-6123; 602-542-4248.

Arkansas
George Montgomery, Manager, Project Success, Dept. of Human Services, Division of Economic and Medical Services, P.O. Box 1437, Slot 1230, Little Rock, AR 72203; 501-682-8277.

Debbie Hopkins, Director, Day Care Eligibility Unit, Dept. of Human Services, Division of Children and Family Services, P.O. Box B1437, Slot 604, Little Rock, AR 72203; 501-682-8763.

California
Bruce Wagstaff, Chief, Employment and Immigration Program Bureau, Department of Social Services, M/X 6-700, 744 P St., Sacramento, CA 95814; 916-657-2367.

Colorado
Grace Hardy, Director, Office of Child Care Services, Department of Social Services, 1575 Sherman St., Denver, CO 80203-1714; 303-866-5958.

Connecticut
Randy Wong, Child Care Team Leader, Department of Social Services, 1049 Asylum Ave., Hartford, CT 06105; 203-566-4204.

Delaware
Mary Ann Daniels, Chief Social Services Administrator, Delaware Health and Social Services, Division of Social Services, CT Building, P.O. Box 906, New Castle, DE 19720; 302-577-4454.

District of Columbia
Ann McWilliams, Child Care Coordinator, Department of Human Services, Room 820, 605 G St., NW, Washington, DC 20001; 202-727-6929.

Florida
Sandi Harris, Chief of Child Care, Department of Health and Rehabilitative Services, 2811 International Blvd., Tallahassee, FL 32301; 904-488-4900.

Albertine McDaniel, Assistant Secretary for Economic Services, Department of Health and Rehabilitative Services, 1317 Winewood Blvd., Tallahassee, FL 32399-0700; 904-488-3271.

Georgia
Delores Woodward, Chief, Family Support Unit, Division of Family and Children Services, 2 Peachtree St., NW, Atlanta, GA 30303; 404-657-3436.

Guam
Jesse S. Catahay, Chief, Human Services Administration, Division of Public Welfare, Department of Public Health and Social Services, P.O. Box 2816, Agana, Guam 96910; 011-671-784-7015.

Hawaii
Gary Kemp, JOBS Administrator, Self-Sufficiency and Support Services Division, Pacific Building, Suite 90, 1001 Bishop St., Honolulu, HI 96813; 808-586-7054.

Idaho
Kathy James, Acting Bureau Chief, Bureau of Family Self Support, Division of Family and Community Services, Tower Building, 7th Floor, 450 W. State St., Boise, ID 83710; 208-334-6618.

Illinois
Michele Piel, Director, Child Care and Development Branch, 624 S. Michigan Ave., 2nd Floor, Chicago, IL 60606; 312-793-3610.

Indiana
Sandra Henschen, AFDC Program Manager, Department of Public Welfare, 402 W. Washington, Room W363, Indianapolis, IN 46204; 317-232-4919.

Iowa
Don Kassar, Chief, Bureau of Individual and Family Support, Department of Human Services, Hoover State Building, 5th Floor, Des Moines, IA 50319; 515-281-3186.

Kansas
Karen Juola, Coordinator of Children's Services, Department of Social and Rehabilitation Services, Smith Wilson Building, 300 SW Oakley, Topeka, KS 66606; 913-296-3742.

Kentucky
Tom Johnson, Administrator, Cabinet for Human Resources, 275 E. Main St., 6th Floor, Frankfort, KY 40601.

Louisiana
Sandra Whitfield, Assistance Payments Director, Department of Social Service, Office of Family Support, 618 Main St., Baton Rouge, LA 70801; 504-342-4051.

Linda Beavais, Director (ARCC), Child Care Assistance Program, Department of Social Service, P.O. Box 91193, Baton Rouge, LA 70821; 504-342-9109.

Maine
Rose Masure, AFDC Program Manager, Bureau of Income Maintenance, Department of Human Services, State House Station 11, Augusta, ME 04333-0011; 207-289-3624.

Maryland
Barbara Smith-Hamer, Director, Child Care Administration, Department of Human Resources, 311 W. Saratoga St., 1st Floor, Baltimore, MD 21201; 410-333-3042.

Massachusetts
Rod Southwick, Program Manager, Massachusetts JOBS, Child Care, Department of Public Welfare, 600 Washington St., Boston, MA 02111; 617-348-5938.

Michigan
JoAnne Nagy, Acting Director, Child Day Care Services, Department of Social Services, P.O. Box 30037, Lansing, MI 48909; 517-373-9204.

Minnesota
Linda Foster, Children's Services, Department of Human Services, 444 Lafayette Dr., St. Paul, MN 55155-3832; 612-296-2030.

Mississippi
Ms. Ronnie McGinnis, Director, Office for Children and Youth, Department of Human Services, P.O. Box 352, Jackson, MS 39205-0352; 601-359-4551.

Missouri
Greg Vadner, Deputy Director of Income Maintenance, Division of Family Services, P.O. Box 88, Jefferson City, MO 65103-0088; 314-751-3124.

Montana
Linda Briese, Child Care Coordinator, Department of Social and Rehabilitative Services, Division of Family Assistance, P.O. Box 4210, Helena, MT 59604; 406-444-1828.

Nebraska
Margaret Hall, Administrator, Public Assistance Division, Department of Social Services, P.O. Box 95026, Lincoln, NE 68509-5026; 402-471-9264.

Nevada
Jackie Chaney, Chief, Benefit Services, State Welfare Division, 2527 N. Carson St., Carson City, NV 89710; 702-687-4834.

New Hampshire
Arthur Chicaderis, Administrator, Bureau of Employment and Support Services, Office of Economic Services, Dept. of Health and Human Services, 6 Hazen Dr., Concord, NH 03301; 603-271-4249.

New Jersey
David Hines, Child Care Director, Division of Family Development, Statewide Operations, CN 716, 6 Quakerbridge Plaza, Trenton, NJ 08625; 609-588-2159.

New Mexico
Marise McFadden, Project Forward Program Manager, Income Support Division, Human Services Department, P.O. Box 2348, Santa Fe, NM 87504-2348; 505-827-7262.

Jacky Lowe, Child Care Bureau Chief, Preventive Services Division, Department of Children, Youth and Families, P.O. Drawer 5160, Santa Fe, NM 87502; 505-827-4033.

New York
Joanne Friedell, Director, Bureau of Early Childhood Services, Section 11B, Department of Social Services, 40 N. Pearl St., Albany, NY 12243; 518-474-9633.

North Carolina
Kay Fields, Chief, Public Assistance Section, Division of Social Services, Room 1021, Albemarle Building, 325 N. Salisbury St., Raleigh, NC 27603; 919-733-7831.

North Dakota
Sue Satterthwaite, Administrator, Child Care Assistance Program, Office of Economic Assistance, State Capitol, Judicial Wing, 600 E. Boulevard Ave., Bismarck, ND 58505-0250; 701-224-4603.

Ohio
Kathleen Capps, Acting Chief, Bureau of Child Care, Child Care and Family Services, 65 E. State, 5th Floor, Columbus, OH 43215; 614-466-1043.

Oklahoma
Charlesetta Combs, Program Supervisor, Day Care Unit, Income Support, Department of Human Services, P.O. Box 25352, Oklahoma City, OK 73125; 405-521-3432.

Oregon
Judy Johnson, IV-A Child Care Coordinator, Department of Human Relations, Adult and Family Services Division, Second Floor, 500 Summer St., NE, Salem, OR 97310; 503-945-6806.

Pennsylvania
Nancy Norcross, Director of Child Care and Family Support, Bureau of Employment and Training, Dept. of Public Welfare, P.O. Box 2675, Harrisburg, PA 17105-2675; 717-787-1684.

Puerto Rico
Lydia Rivera, IV-A Child Care Administrator, Department of Social Services, Family Services Program, Isla Grande, Building #10, P.O. Box 11398, Santurce, PR 00910; 809-723-2127.

Rhode Island
Joseph Dean, Administrator, Office of Child Care, Division of Community Services, Department of Human Services, 600 New Londen Ave., Cranston, RI 02920; 401-464-3071.

South Carolina
Hiram Spain, Director, Work Support Program, Dept. of Social Services, P.O. Box 1520, Columbia, SC 29202; 803-737-5916.

South Dakota
Dennis Pelkofer, AFDC Program Administrator, Department of Social Services, Kneip Building, 700 Governor's Dr., Pierre, SD 57501-2291; 605-773-4678.

Bobbie Brown, Program Administrator, Department of Social Services, Office of Child Care Services, 700 Governor's Dr., Pierre, SD 57501-2291.

Tennessee
Janet Camp, Director of Day Care Services, Department of Human Services, 400 Deaderick St., Citizens Plaza Building, 14th Floor, Nashville, TN 37248-9600; 615-741-7130.

Wanda Moore, Director of JOBSWORK, Department of Human Services, 400 Deaderick St., Citizens Plaza Building, Nashville, TN 37219; 615-741-6953.

Texas
Charlotte Brantley, Unit Leader, Child Care Services, Department of Human Services, P.O. Box 149030, Austin, TX 78714-9030; 512-450-4179.

Utah
Helen Thatcher, Assistant Director, Office of Family Support, Department of Human Services, 120 N. 200 W., Suite 325, Salt Lake City, UT 84103-0500; 801-538-3964.

Vermont
Edward Cafferty, Program Chief, Reach-Up Program, Department of Social Welfare, 103 S. Main St., Waterbury, VT 05676; 802-241-2811.

Christopher J. Mulvaney, Federal Programs Administrator, Dept, of Social and Rehabilitative Services, 103 S. Main St., Waterbury, VT 05676; 802-241-2120.

Virginia
Ben Greenberg, Child Day Care Program Manager, Department of Social Services, Theater Row Building, 730 E. Broad St., Richmond, VA 23219-1849; 804-692-1298.

Virgin Islands
Verna Garcia, Department of Human Services, Administrator of Volunteer and Special Programs, 11A and 11B Golden Rock, Christiansteed, St. Croix USVI 00820; 809-773-2323.

Washington
Dori Shoji, Program Manager, Dept. of Social and Health Services, Division of Income Assistance, P.O. Box 4500, Olympia, WA 98504-5400; 206-438-8278.

West Virginia
Kay Tilton, Director of Licensing and Day Care, Bureau of Human Resources, Capitol Complex, Building 6, Room 850B, Charleston, WV 25305; 304-558-7980.

Wisconsin
Dave Edie, Director, Office of Child Care, 1 W. Wilson St., Madison, WI 53707; 608-266-6946.

Wyoming
Ellen Sevall, Program Consultant, Department of Family Services, Hathaway Building, Room 372, Cheyenne, WY 82002-0490; 307-777-6848.

* Comprehensive Child Development Centers

Administration for Children and Families
P.O. Box 1182
Washington, DC 20013
202-205-8566

Children don't have to wait to be preschoolers to take advantage of government programs. The Comprehensive Child Development Program is a five-year demonstration program that provides intensive comprehensive support services to children from birth to entrance into elementary school. They also provide support services to parents and other household family members in locating training and employment opportunities, in securing adequate health care, nutrition assistance, and housing. Currently, there are over 30 programs in existence. Contact one of the programs listed below to learn more about eligibility requirements and application procedures.

Comprehensive Child Development Program Directory of Grantees

Cohort I Grantees
Region I
Project AFRIC, Dimock Community Health Center, 55 Dimock St., Richards Building, Roxbury, MA 02119; 617-442-1113, Fax: 617-445-0091.

Windham County Family Support Program, Brattleboro Town School District, 218 Canal St., Brattleboro, VT 05301; 802-254-3742, Fax: 802-254-3750.

Region II
Project CHANCE, 136 Lawrence St., Suites 3A & B, Brooklyn, NY 11201; 718-330-0845, Fax: 718-330-0846.

Region III
Parent Child Resource Center, Edward C. Mazique Parent Child Center, Inc., 1719 13th St., NW, Washington, DC 20009; 202-462-3375, Fax: 202-939-8696.

Family Start, Friends of the Family, Inc., 2225 N. Charles St., Baltimore, MD 21218; 410-366-1288, Fax: 410-366-2273.

Family Foundations, Community Human Services, 1811 Boulevard of the Allies, Pittsburgh, PA 15219; 412-281-3511, Fax: 412-281-3254.

Region IV
T.I.P.P. (Toddlers, Infants, Preschoolers, and Parents), Dade County Community Action Agency, 1325 NW 71st St., Miami, FL 33147; 305-694-TIPP, 547-4800, Fax: 305-694-2712.

Operation Family, Community Action Council, P.O. Box 11610, (Street Address: 913 Georgetown St., 40511), Lexington, KY 40576; 606-233-4600, Fax: 606-244-2219.

Tennessee CAREs, Bureau of Educational Research and Services, Tennessee State University, 330 Tenth Ave. N., Nashville, TN 37203-3401; 615-251-1540, Fax: 615-251-1530.

Region V
Project Focus, Grand Rapids Child Guidance Clinic, 1309 Madison, SE, Grand Rapids, MI 49506; 616-243-8240, Fax: 616-243-8554.

West CAP Full Circle Project, 525 Second St., P.O. Box 308, Glenwood City, WI 54013-0308; 715-265-4271, Fax: 715-265-7031.

Region VI
Project Family, P.O. Box 120, (Street Address: 4208 Frazier Pike), College Station, AR 72053; 501-490-1929, Fax: 501-320-4264.

City of Albuquerque CCDP, Albuquerque Department of Community Services, Office of Child Development, 1701 4th St., SW, Albuquerque, NM 87102; 505-768-6080, Fax: 505-768-6031.

Primero Los Ninos, La Clinica de Familia, 225 E. Idaho, La Mission Pl. #26, Las Cruces, NM 88005; 505-526-2007, Fax: 505-525-9121.

Avance CCDP, Avance-San Antonio, Inc., 435 S. San Darfo, San Antonio, TX 78237; 210-431-6640, Fax: 210-431-6607.

ShareCare Program, Day Care Association of Fort Worth and Tarrant County, 121 N. Rayner, Ft. Worth, TX 76111; 817-831-8115, Fax: 817-831-7439.

Region VII
Mid-Iowa Community Action, 212 W. Ingledue, Marshalltown, IA 50158; 515-752-7162, 515-754-1520, Fax: 515-752-9724.

Project Eagle, Gateway Centre, Tower 2, Suite 1001, Fourth and State Avenues, Kansas City, KS 66101; 913-281-2648, Fax: 913-281-2680.

Region VIII
Family Futures, Attn: Project Director, 3801 Martin Luther King, Jr. Blvd., Denver, CO 80205; 303-355-2008, Fax: 303-331-0248.

Little Hoop Community College, P.O. Box 269, (Street Address: 1st St.), Ft. Totten, ND 58335; 701-766-4070, Fax: 701-766-4077.

Community-Family Partnership Project, Center for Persons with Disabilities, UMC 6800, Logan, UT 84322-6800; 801-797-2008, Fax: 801-750-2044.

Region IX
Conocimiento, Southwest Human Development, Inc., 202 E. Earll, Suite 140, Phoenix, AZ 85012-2636; 602-266-5976, Fax: 602-274-8952.

Enrich, Venice Family Clinic, 604 Rose Ave., Venice, CA 90291; 310-314-7320, Fax: 310-314-7641.

Region X
Families First, Children's Home Society of Washington, P.O. Box 1997, (Street Address: 4338 Auburn Way N.; 98002), Auburn, WA 98071; 206-854-0700, Fax: 206-852-3119.

Cohort II Grantees
Region III
Philadelphia Child Guidance Center, 4025 Chestnut St., Philadelphia, PA 19104; 215-243-3180, Fax: 215-243-2892.

Region IV
UPLIFT, Inc. CCDP, 400A W. Whittington St., Greensboro, NC 27406; 910-333-2525, Fax: 910-333-6315.

Village Partnership Project, 555 Reidville Rd., Spartanburg, SC 29306; 803-594-6762, Fax: 803-594-6767.

Civitan International Research Center, University of Alabama at Birmingham, P.O. Box 313, UAB Station, Birmingham, AL 35924-0017.
or
370 Sparks Building, 1720 7th Ave. S., Birmingham, AL 35233-0017; 205-934-1093, Fax: 205-975-2380.

Region V
Family Service and Visiting Nurse Association, 550 Front St., Alton, IL 62002-0250; 618-463-8904, Fax: 618-463-5959.

Lessie Bates Davis Neighborhood House, Family Development Center, 1045 State St., East St. Louis, IL 62205; 618-875-2211, Fax: 618-875-2241.

Personal Best, Chestnut Health Systems, 702 W. Chestnut St., Bloomington, IL 61701; 309-827-6027, ext. 3402.

Proviso Family Services (Service Delivery Agency), 500 Washington St., Maywood, IL 60153; 708-343-8690.

Springfield Urban League (Service Delivery Agency), 1225 E. Lawrence, Springfield, IL 62703; 217-528-0893, Fax: 217-528-0897.

Region IX
The Ark, SHIELDS for Families Project, Inc., 11705 Deputy Yamamoto Place, Suite A, Lynwood, CA 90262.
or
1721 E. 120th St., Los Angeles, CA 90059; 213-357-6930, Fax: 213-569-1979.

Hope Street Family Center, UCLA Department of Pediatrics, Child Development, 300 UCLA Medical Plaza, Los Angeles, CA 90024-7033; 310-794-7658, Fax: 310-206-4215.

Oakland Birth to School Project - CCDP, East Bay Perinatal Council, 10 Eastmont Mall, Suite 200, Oakland, CA 94605; 510-635-8112, Fax: 510-635-8401.

Region X
N.E.W. Family Coalition, EWU Center for Health Research, Mail Stop 56, Cheney, WA 99004.
or
West 407 Riverside, Suite 421, Spokane, WA 99201; 509-359-4208, Fax: 509-359-6639.

Northwest Washington Rural Resources, 320 N. Main, Colville, WA 99114; 509-684-8421.

* Ease Some Of Your Employees Concerns

Work and Family Clearinghouse
Women's Bureau
U.S. Department of Labor
200 Constitution Ave., NW
Washington, DC 20210
800-827-5335

Finding reliable, affordable day care is never easy, but companies are finding that providing on-site day care keeps employees happier and profits on the rise. The Work and Family Clearinghouse publishes the Work and Family Resource Kit which helps employers understand the range of family needs emerging in the work place and options such as flextime and job sharing. The Clearinghouse can even refer you to companies similar to your own to see how they operate these innovative programs, and the benefits they have received. For your free copy contact the office listed above.

* Get Up To $2,287 In Credits Or Refunds

Internal Revenue Service
Information Line
800-829-1040

Take advantage of some of the perks the IRS gives to those who have children. If you have a job, earn less than $23,050 (1993 figure), and have a child living with you, you could be eligible for the Earned Income Credit (EIC). This Credit reduces the amount of tax you owe, and is intended to offset some of the increases in living expenses and social security taxes. The EIC is comprised of three different credits:

basic, health insurance, and extra credit for a child born in the tax year. You could qualify for up to $1,434 from the basic credit, $465 from the health insurance credit, and $388 for the extra credit for a child born in the year. Get a copy of Publication 596 which explains the form you need to file and eligibility.

* Get A Kid, Get A Credit

Internal Revenue Service
Information Line
800-829-1040

You may be able to take a credit if you pay someone to care for your dependent who is under age 13, your disabled dependent, or your disabled spouse, so that you can work. For purposes of the credit, "disabled" refers to a person physically or mentally not capable of self-care. Request Publication 503 Child and Dependent Care Expenses which outlines the credit, as well as explains the tax rules covering benefits paid under an employer-provided dependent care assistance plans.

* Child Care While You Train

Employment and Training Administration
U.S. Department of Labor
Office of Worker Readjustment Programs
200 Constitution Ave., NW, Room N-4469
Washington, DC 20210
202-219-5577

If you have been laid off from work and are not likely to return to the same employer, you may be considered a dislocated worker. Dislocated workers are those who have been laid off from a job due to factory down-sizing, reorganization, trade issues, military down-sizing, and more. There are many services available to dislocated workers through the Title III Program which provides for retraining and readjustments for these workers. Some local providers cover the cost of child care while you retrain for another job. To become eligible for these services, you must contact your local State Employment Services office or the Job Training Partnership

Act office (look in the blue pages of your phone book). If you are part of any government training program, make sure to ask if child care or transportation costs are covered. In many instances, there are some funds available. The following programs also may offer childcare:

Job Corps
U.S. Department of Labor
200 Constitution Ave., NW, Room N4510
Washington, DC 20210
202-219-5556

Job Training Partnership Act
U.S. Department of Labor
200 Constitution Ave., NW, Room N5426
Washington, DC 20210
202-219-5305

Indian and Native American Job Training Program
U.S. Department of Labor
200 Constitution Ave., NW, Room 4643
Washington, DC 20210
202-219-8502

* Workplace Literacy

National Workplace Literacy Program
U.S. Department of Education
ED/OVAE/DNP/SPB
400 Maryland Ave., SW
Switzer Building, Room 4512
Washington, DC 20202
202-205-5977

In order to improve the literacy rate for adults, many literacy programs are being started in the workplace. These programs teach basic skills that can result in new or continued employment, career advancement, or increased productivity for workers. Money is available for projects to improve literacy skills, adult secondary education services, and even to provide education counseling, transportation, and non-working hours child care services to adult workers while they participate in the program. To learn more about the grant application process or to learn what programs exist in your state, contact the office listed above.

* Check Out Day Care Before You Sign Up Junior

See state by state listing below

We don't trust our kids with just anyone, so how do you check out a day care before you enroll your child? Each state has a different type of licensing procedure and requirements, so you can contact your state office listed below to learn more about what is required of day care facilities (many states require that facilities which operate out of people's homes also be licensed). In addition, some states have special offices where you can register a complaint concerning a day care establishment, as well as learn whether complaints are already on file regarding a particular facility.

Day Care Licensing Offices

The following offices are starting places for finding out who in the state government licenses day care centers.

Alabama
State Department of Health, Office of Day Care, 50 Ripley St., Montgomery, AL 36130; 205-242-1425.

Alaska
Department of Health and Human Services, Office of Day Care Licensing, 10002 Glacier Highway, Juneau, AK 99801; 907-790-3221.

Arizona
State Department of Health, Office of Child Care Licensing, 1647 E. Morton St., Phoenix, AZ 85020; 602-255-1272.

Arkansas
State Department of Health and Human Services, Child Care Licensing Unit, P.O. Box 840, Slot 4400, Little Rock, AR 72203; 501-682-2309.

California
State Department of Health, Office of Social Services, Day Care Licensing Unit, 8745 Fulsom Blvd., Suite 200, Sacramento, CA 95826; 916-387-4530.

Colorado
State Dept. of Health, Office of Social Services, Child Care Licensing, 1575 Sherman St., Denver, CO 80203; 303-866-5958.

Connecticut
Department of Public Health and Addiction Services, Day Care Licensing Division, 150 Washington St., Hartford, CT 06457; 203-566-2575.

Delaware
Department of Health and Human Services, Office of Child Care Licensing, DSCYF, 1825 Falkland Rd., Wilmington, DE 19805; 302-633-2702.

District of Columbia
Department of Social Services, Consumer and Regulatory Affairs, SFRA/SSFD, Room 1035, 614 H St., NW, Washington, DC 20001; 202-727-7226.

Florida
Department of Health and Human Resources, Children and Family Services, Day Care Licensing Division, 2811 A Industrial Plaza Dr., Tallahassee, FL 32320; 904-488-4900.

Georgia
State Dept. of Health, Child Care Licensing Unit, 2 Peachtree St., NW, 20th Floor, Atlanta, GA 30303-3167; 404-657-5562.

Hawaii
State Dept. of Human Services, Child Care Licensing Division, 33 S. King St., Room 500, Honolulu, HI 96813; 808-586-7090.

Idaho
State Dept. of Health, Boise City Clerk's Office, Child Care Licensing Unit, P.O. Box 500, Boise, ID 83701; 208-384-3710.

Illinois
State Department of Health, Children and Family Services Division, Child Care Licensing Unit, 1001 N. Walnut St., Springfield, IL 62702; 217-785-2688.

Indiana
State Department of Health, Division of Family and Children, Child Care Licensing Unit, 402 W. Washington St., Room W364, Indianapolis, IN 46204; 317-233-5414.

Iowa
State Department of Health, Human Services Division, Child Care Licensing Department, Hoover State Office Building, 5th Floor, Des Moines, IA 50319; 515-281-6074.

Kansas
Kansas Department of Health and Environment, Child Care Licensing Division, Mills Building, Room 400C, 900 SW Jackson, Topeka, KS 66612-1290; 913-296-1270.

Kentucky
State Department of Health, Department of Social Services, Child Care Licensing Unit, 275 E. Main St., Frankfort, KY 40621; 502-564-2800.

Louisiana
State Department of Health, Child Care Licensing Division, P.O. Box 3078, Baton Rouge, LA 70821; 504-922-0015.

Maine
Bureau of Child and Family Services, 221 State St., Station 11, Augusta, ME 04333; 207-287-5060.

Maryland
Department of Human Resources, Child Care Administration, Licensing Division, 311 W. Saratoga St., Baltimore, MD 21201; 410-767-7854.

Massachusetts
State Department of Health, Office of Children, Day Care Licensing Division, 1 Ashburton Place, Boston, MA 02108; 617-727-8900.

Michigan
State Department of Health, Child Care Licensing Division, Suite 121, Grand Tower Building, P.O. Box 30037, Lansing, MI 48909; 517-373-8300.

Minnesota
State Department of Health, Child Care Licensing Unit, 50 W. Kellogg Blvd., St. Paul, MN 55102; 612-266-2400.

Mississippi
Mississippi State Department of Health, Child Care Division, P.O. Box 1700, Jackson, MS 39215-1700; 601-960-7613.

Missouri
State Department of Health, Department of Maternal Child and Family Health, Child Care Licensing Division, P.O. Box 570, Jefferson City, MO 65102; 314-751-6172.

Montana
State Dept. of Health, Division of Family Services, Child Care Licensing, P.O. Box 8005, Helena, MT 59604; 406-444-5900.

Nebraska
State Department of Health, Child Care Licensing Division, 2200 St. Mary's Ave., Lincoln, NE 68502; 402-441-8023.

Nevada
State Department of Health, Day Care Licensing Division, 711 E. 5th St., Carson City, NV 89710; 702-687-5911.

New Hampshire
State Department of Health and Human Service, Child Care Licensing Unit, 6 Hazen Dr., Health and Human Services Building, Concord, NH 03301; 603-271-4685.

New Jersey
Department of Health, Division of Youth and Family Services, Child Care Licensing, CN 717, Trenton, NJ 08625-0717; 609-292-9220.

New Mexico
Department of Health, Child Care Licensing Division, P.O. Drawer 5760, Santa Fe, NM 87502; 505-827-7684.

New York
State Department of Health, Social Services Division, Albany Regional Office, Child Care Licensing Bureau, 40 N. Pearl St., 3 City Square, 1st Floor, Albany, NY 12243; 518-432-2763.

North Carolina
State Department of Health, Child Development Division, Child Care Licensing, P.O. Box 29553, Raleigh, NC 27626; 919-662-4499.

North Dakota
State Department of Health, Children and Family Services, Child Care Licensing Unit, 600 E. Blvd. Ave., Bismarck, ND 58505; 701-224-4809.

Ohio
State Department of Health, Children and Family Services, Child Care Licensing Division, 65 E. State St., 5th Floor, Columbus, OH 43215; 614-466-3438.

Oklahoma
State Department of Human Services, P.O. Box 25352, Oklahoma City, OK 73125; 405-521-3646.

Oregon
State Department of Health, Child Care Licensing, Child Care Division, Employment Department, Salem, OR 97311; 503-378-3178.

Pennsylvania
State Department of Health, Day Care Licensing Division, Central Region, DPW Complex #2, Lanco Lodge, Harrisburg, PA 17125; 717-772-7078.

Rhode Island
Department of Children, Youth and Families, Child Care Licensing Division, 10 Davo Square, Providence, RI 02903; 401-277-4741.

South Carolina
State Department of Social Services, Child Care Licensing Division, P.O. Box 1520, Room 520, Columbia, SC 29202-1520; 803-734-5740.

South Dakota
Department of Social Services, Child Care Services, Child Care Licensing Division, 700 Governor's Dr., Pierre, SD 57501; 605-773-4766.

Tennessee
State Department of Health, Day Care Licensing Division, 400 Dedrick St., Nashville, TN 37248; 615-741-7129.

Texas
State Department of Health, P.O. Box 149030, Austin, TX 78714-9030; 512-450-3260.

Utah
Department of Human Services, Office of Child Care Licensing, 120 North, 200 West, #317, Salt Lake City, UT 84103; 801-538-4242.

Vermont
Department of Licensing, Child Care Licensure, 103 S. Main St., Montpelier, VT 05761-2401; 802-241-2158.

Virginia
State Department of Health, Child Care Licensing Division, 730 Broad St., Richmond, VA 23219; 804-692-1700.

Washington
Office of Child Care Policy, Child Care Licensing Division, DSHS, P.O. Box 1366, Olympia, WA 98507; 206-664-3843.

West Virginia
Department of Health and Human Resources, Office of Social Services, Building 6, Room 850, State Capital, Charleston, WV 25305; 304-558-7980.

Wisconsin
State Department of Health and Social Services, Child Care Licensing Division, 3601 Memorial Dr., Madison, WI 53704; 608-243-2400.

Wyoming
State Dept. of Family Services, Office of Child Care Licensing, Hathaway Building, Cheyenne, WY 82002; 307-777-6595.

* Money To Let You Hit The Books

Contact:

Your College Admissions Office

In a survey of colleges around the country, it was discovered that over a thousand community colleges and 4 year colleges and universities provide child care for free or reduced costs. Most operate on a sliding fee scale, and offer a variety of services with some offering hot lunches and infant care. These child care centers are frequently staffed with preschool and early education students to provide them training while taking care of your child. Talk to the admission officer at schools which you are considering to learn if they offer this benefit, the cost of service with your income, and even if there is waiting list.

* JOBS For You

Office of Family Assistance
Administration for Children and Families
370 L'Enfant Promenade, SW
Washington, DC 20447
202-401-4534

Are you on public assistance, but would like to be working? JOBS (Jobs Opportunities and Basic Skills) Training Program is a state and federally funded program which provides education and training for public assistance recipients along with the necessary support services to help you find quality jobs. You can take part in basic math and reading skills classes, job training programs, and even on-the-job training. JOBS is required to provide or reimburse you for transportation and other work-related expenses, as well as offer child care for those who need it. Child care is subsidized for parents, so that they may choose the best child care provider for the child. Payment rates are set by the State, and the care must meet certain standards. Contact your local Aid to Families with Dependent Children (AFDC) office, or contact the State JOBS Coordinator for information on the JOBS program nearest you.

Jobs Program Directory

Alabama
Office of Work and Training Services, Public Assistance Division, S. Gordon Persons Building, 50 Ripley Street, Montgomery, AL 36130; 205-242-1950.

Alaska
Division of Public Assistance, Dept. of Health and Social Service, P.O. Box 110640, Juneau, AK 99811-0640; 907-465-3347.

Arizona
Dept. of Economic Security, P.O. Box 6123, Site Code 8011, Phoenix, AZ 85005; 602-542-6310.

Arkansas
Department of Human Services, P.O. Box 1437, Little Rock, AR 72203; 501-682-8375.

California
Department of Social Services, 744 P Street M/S 6-700, Sacramento, CA 95814; 916-657-1878.

Colorado
Department of Social Services, 1575 Sherman Street, Denver, CO 80203; 303-866-2643.

Connecticut
Department of Income Maintenance, 110 Bartholomew Avenue, Hartford, CT 06106; 203-566-4204.

Delaware
Division of Social Services, P.O. Box 906, New Castle, DE 19720; 302-577-4451.

District of Columbia
Department of Human Services, 33 N Street NE, Washington, DC 20001; 202-727-1293.

How Do I Take Care of the Kids?

Florida
Dept. of Health and Rehabilitative Services, 1317 Winewood Boulevard, Tallahassee, FL 32399-0700; 904-487-2380.

Maine
Maine Department of Human Services, Statehouse Station #11, 32 Winthrop St., Augusta, ME 04333; 207-289-3106.

Maryland
Department of Human Resources, 311 W. Saratoga Street, Room 745, Baltimore, MD 21201; 410-333-0028.

Massachusetts
Department of Public Welfare, 600 Washington St., Boston, MS 02111; 617-348-5931.

Michigan
Department of Social Services, 300 South Capitol Ave., Suite 501, Lansing, MI 48909; 517-373-7382.

Minnesota
Department of Human Services, 444 Lafayette Road, St. Paul, MN 55155; 612-296-5482.

Mississippi
Department of Human Services, 421 W. Pascagoula, Jackson, MS 29302; 601-960-4279.

Missouri
Division of Family Services, 72728 Plaza Drive, P.O. Box 88, Jefferson City, MO 65103; 314-751-3124.

Montana
Department of Social and Rehabilitation Services, P.O. Box 4210, Helena, MT 59604; 406-444-4540.

Nebraska
Department of Social Services, 301 Centennial Mall South, 5th Floor, P.O. Box 95026, Lincoln, NE 68509; 402-471-3121.

Nevada
Nevada State Welfare Division, Capitol Complex, 2527 North Carson Street, Carson City, NV 89710; 702-687-4143.

New Hampshire
New Hampshire Department of Health and Human Services, 6 Hazen Drive, Concord, NH 03301-6521; 603-271-4249.

New Jersey
Department of Human Services, CN 716, Trenton, NY 08625; 609-588-2401.

New Mexico
New Mexico Human Services Department, P.O. Box 2348, Santa Fe, NM 87500; 505-827-4429.

New York
New York Department of Social Services, 40 North Pearl Street, Albany, NY 12243; 518-473-8744.

North Carolina
Department of Human Resources, 325 North Salisbury Street, Raleigh, NC 27611; 919-733-2873.

North Dakota
Department of Human Services, State Capitol, New Wing, 3rd Floor, Bismarck, ND 58505; 701-224-4001.

Ohio
Department of Human Services, State Office Tower, 31st Floor, 30 East Broad Street, Columbus, OH 43266-0423; 614-466-3196.

Oklahoma
Department of Human Services, P.O. Box 25352, Oklahoma City, OK 73125; 405-521-3646.

Oregon
Adult and Family Services Division, Human Resource Bldg., 2nd Floor, Salem, OR 97310-1013; 503-945-6115.

Pennsylvania
Department of Public Welfare, P.O. Box 2675, Harrisburg, PA 17105; 717-787-8613.

Puerto Rico
SOSEDF, Isla Grande, Building #0, Santurce, PR 00910; 809-722-2863.

Rhode Island
Department of Human Services, 600 New London Avenue, Cranston, RI 02920; 401-464-2423.

South Carolina
Department of Social Services, P.O. Box 1520, Columbia, SC 29202; 803-252-6338.

South Dakota
Department of Social Services, Richard F. Kneip Building, Pierre, SD 57501; 605-773-3493.

Tennessee
Department of Human Services, 12th Floor, 400 Deadericks, Nashville, TN 37219; 615-741-6953.

Texas
Department of Human Services, Mail Code 521E, P.O. Box 2960, Austin, TX 78769; 512-450-3011.

Utah
Department of Human Services, 120 North 200 West, Salt Lake City, UT 84145-0500; 801-538-3973.

Vermont
Department of Social Welfare, State Office Building, 103 South Main Street, Waterbury, VT 05676; 802-241-2800.

Virgin Islands
Department of Human Services, P.O. Box 550, Barbele Plaza South, St. Thomas, VI 00801; 809-774-4673.

Virginia
Department of Social Services, 8007 Discovery Drive, Richmond, VA 23288; 804-662-9032.

Washington
Department of Social and Health Services, P.O. Box 45400, Olympia, WA 98504-5400; 206-438-8350.

West Virginia
Department of Health and Human Services, Building 6, State Office Complex, Charleston, WV 25305; 304-558-8834.

Wisconsin
Dept. of Health and Social Services, P.O. Box 7935, 1 West Wilson St., Room 350, Madison, WI 53707-7935; 608-266-3035.

Wyoming
Dept. of Family Services, Hathaway Building, Room 347, 2300 Capitol Ave., Cheyenne, WY 82002-0710; 307-777-6849.

* Money For Employers In Appalachia

Executive Director
Appalachian Regional Commission
1666 Connecticut Ave., NW
Washington, DC 20235
202-884-7700

If you own a business in the Appalachian region and are having trouble recruiting employees, maybe you should consider offering a child care program. The Appalachian Regional Commission offers grants to companies to assist them in providing child care services to their employees. Grants can cover technical assistance, operating, construction, renovation, and equipment, and can cover up to 80% of the total cost. There are 399 eligible counties including some in Alabama, Georgia, North Carolina, Kentucky, Maryland, Mississippi, New York, Ohio, Pennsylvania, South Carolina, Tennessee, Virginia, and all of West Virginia. Contact the Appalachian Regional Commission for more information about this program.

* Give Everyone An Even Start

Compensatory Education Programs
U.S. Department of Education
Office of Elementary and Secondary
  Education
400 Maryland Ave., SW
Washington, DC 20202
202-401-1692

If someone you know is in need of training in learning to read and they also have a child under 7, they may be able to participate in the Even Start Program. Even Start is designed to provide family centered education programs that involve parents and children. It includes instructional programs that promote adult literacy, train parents to support the educational growth of their children, and help children to succeed in school. Transportation to the program is offered, as is child care for the periods when parents are in the program. To be eligible parents must reside in an elementary school area served by Chapter 1, which is for areas with a predominance of lower-income residents. Even Start is often offered by community-based organizations, local education agencies, and others. The Office listed above can provide you with information on Even Start Programs near you, as well as provide you with information on Even Start Programs for Migrant Education and Indian Tribes.

* Child Care Help From Your State

Office of Community Services
Division of State Assistance
370 L'Enfant Promenade, SW
Washington, DC 20447
202-401-9344

In order to give States the freedom to choose what particular services they need, the Federal government provides the Social Services Block Grant (Title XX). This allows each State to provide social services which best suit the needs of the individuals residing in the State. Examples of funded services include child day care, protective and emergency services for children and adults, homemaker and chore services, information and referral, adoption, foster care, counseling, and transportation. To find out what services are provided in your State contact your State Department of Social Services.

Social Services Block Grant State Contacts

Alabama
Mr. Charles G. Cleveland, Commissioner, Department of Human Resources, S. Gordon Persons Bldg., 50 Ripley Street, Montgomery, AL 36130; 205-242-1160.

Alaska
Theodore A. Mala, M.D., MPH, Commissioner, Department of Health and Social Services, P.O. Box 110601, Juneau, AK 99811-0601; 907-465-3030.

American Samoa
Fuala'Au H. Tamate, Director, Social Services Division, Department of Human Services, Pago Pago, AS 96799; 684-633-2696.

Arizona
Ms. Linda J. Blessing, Director, Department of Economic Security, 1717 West Jefferson, Phoenix, AZ 85007; 602-542-4702.

Arkansas
Mr. Tom Dalton, Director, Arkansas Department of Human Services, Donaghey Building - Suite 326, 7th and Maine Street, P.O. Box 1437, Little Rock, AR 72203-1437; 501-682-8650.

California
Ms. Eloise Anderson, Director, California Department of Social Services, 744 P Street - Mail Station 17-11, Sacramento, CA 95814; 916-657-2598.

Colorado
Ms. Karen Beye, Executive Director, Department of Social Services, 1575 Sherman Street, Denver, CO 80203-1714; 303-866-5800.

Connecticut
Ms. Patricia Giardi, Acting Commissioner, Department of Social Services, 25 Sigourney Street, Hartford, CT 06106-5033; 203-424-5008.

Delaware
Ms. Carmen Nazario, Secretary, Delaware Department of Health and Social Services, 1901-N. Dupont Highway, New Castle, DE 19720; 302-577-4500.

District of Columbia
Mr. Vincent C. Gray, Director, D.C. Department of Human Services, 801 North Capitol Street, N.E., Washington, DC 20002; 202-279-6002.

Florida
Mr. James Towey, Secretary, Department of Health and Rehabilitative Services, 1323 Winewood Boulevard, Tallahassee, FL 32399-0700; 904-488-7721.

Georgia
James G. Ledbetter, Ph.D., Commissioner, Georgia Department of Human Resources, 47 Trinity Avenue, S.W., Atlanta, GA 30334-5600; 404-656-5680.

Guam
Leticia V. Espaldon, M.D., Director, Department of Public Health and Social Services, P.O. Box 2816, Agana, GU 96910; 011-671-734-7269.

Hawaii
Ms. Wihona E. Rubin, Director, Hawaii State Department of Social Services and Housing, P.O. Box 339, Honolulu, HI 96809; 808-548-6260.

Idaho
Mr. Jerry L. Harris, Director, Idaho Department of Health and Welfare, State House, 450 West State Street, Boise, ID 83720-5450; 208-334-5500.

Illinois
Mr. Robert Wright, Director, Illinois Department of Public Aid, Harris Bldg. II, 100 South Grand Avenue - East, Springfield, IL 62762; 217-782-6716.

Indiana
Mr. Jeff Richardson, Secretary, Family & Social Services Administration, 150 North West Market Street, P.O. Box 7083, Indianapolis, IN 46207-7083; 317-233-4456, 1-800-545-7763.

Iowa
Mr. Charles M. Palmer, Director, Department of Human Services, Hoover State Office Building, E. 13th and Walnut, Des Moines, IA 50319; 515-281-5452.

Kansas
Ms. Donna Whiteman, Secretary, Department of Social and Rehabilitation Services, Docking State Office Building, 915 Harrison Street, Room 603-N, Topeka, KS 66612; 913-296-3271.

Kentucky
Ms. Peggy Wallace, Commissioner, Department of Social Services, 275 E. Main Street, 6th Floor W, Frankfort, KY 40621; 502-564-4650.

Louisiana
Mrs. Gloria Bryant-Banks, Secretary, Department of Social Services, P.O. Box 3776, 755 Third St., North, Room 228, Baton Rouge, LA 70821; 504-342-0286.

Maine
Ms. Jane Sheehan, Commissioner, Department of Human Services, 221 State Street, Augusta, ME 04333; 207-289-2736.

Maryland
Mr. Luther Starnes, Secretary, Department of Human Resources, 311 West Saratoga Street, Baltimore, MD 21201; 410-767-7109.

Massachusetts
Ms. Linda K. Carlisle, Commissioner, Department of Social Services, 24 Farnsworth Street, Boston, MA 02114; 617-727-0900 Ext. 202.
and
Mr. Charles H. Crawford, Commissioner, Massachusetts Commission for the Blind, 88 Kinston Street, Boston, MA 02111-2227; 617-727-5550, ext. 4503.

Michigan
Mr. Gerald H. Miller, Director, Michigan Department of Social Services, 235 South Grand Avenue, P.O. Box 30037, Lansing, MI 48909; 517-373-2000.

Minnesota
Ms. Natalie Haas-Steffen, Commissioner, Minnesota Department of Human Services, 444 Lafayette Road, St. Paul, MN 55155-3815; 612-296-2701.

Mississippi
Mr. Gregg Phillips, Interim Executive Director, Department of Human Services, 421 West Pascagoula Street, Jackson, MS 39203; 601-960-4250.

Missouri
Mr. Gary J. Stangler, Director, Department of Social Services, Broadway State Office Building, P.O. Box 1527, Jefferson City, MO 65102-1527; 314-751-4815.

Montana
Peter S. Blouke, Ph.D., Director, Department of Social and Rehabilitation Services, P.O. Box 4210, Helena, MT 59604; 406-444-5622.

Nebraska
Ms. Mary Dean Harvey, Director, Nebraska Department of Social Services, 301 Centennial Mall, South, P.O. Box 95026, 5th Floor, Lincoln, NE 68509-5026; 402-471-3121.

Nevada
Mr. Scott M. Craigie, Director, Department of Human Resources, 505 E. King Street, Room 600 - Kinkead Building, Carson City, NV 89710; 702-687-4733.

New Hampshire
Harry H. Bird, M.D., Commissioner, Department of Health and Human Services, 6 Hazen Drive, Concord, NH 03301-6505; 603-217-4334.

New Jersey
Mr. William Waldman, Commissioner, New Jersey Department of Human Services, Capital Place 1 CN-700, Trenton, NJ 08625; 609-292-3717.

New Mexico
Mr. Wayne Powell, Secretary, Department of Children, Youth and Families, P.O. Drawer 5160, Santa Fe, NM 87502; 505-827-7602.

New York
Mr. Michael J. Dowling, Commissioner, New York State Department of Social Services, 40 North Pearl Street, Albany, NY 12243-0001; 518-474-9475.

North Carolina
Ms. Mary K. Deyampert, Director, Division of Social Services, Department of Human Resources, 325 North Salisbury Street, Raleigh, NC 27603; 919-733-3055.

North Dakota
Ms. Yvonne M. Smith, Associate Director, Office of Field Services and Program Development, North Dakota Department of Human Services, 600 E. Boulevard Avenue, Bismarck, ND 58505-0265; 701-224-4050.

Northern Marianas
Mr. Jesse B. Pangelinan, Director, Department of Community and Cultural Affairs, Saipan, Mariana Islands 96950; 670-322-9366.

Ohio
Mr. Arnold R. Tompkins, Director, Ohio Department of Human Services, 30 East Broad Street - 32nd Floor, Columbus, OH 43266-0423; 614-466-6282.

Oklahoma
Mr. Benjamin Demps, Jr., Director, Department of Human Services, P.O. Box 25352, Oklahoma City, OK 73125; 405-521-3646.

Oregon
Mr. Kevin W. Concannon, Director, Oregon Department of Human Resources, 500 Summer Street, Salem, OR 97310; 503-378-3033.

Pennsylvania
Ms. Karen Snider, Secretary, Pennsylvania Department of Public Welfare, Room 333, Health and Welfare Building, Harrisburg, PA 17120; 717-787-2600.

Puerto Rico
Mrs. Carmen L. Rodriquez de Rivera, Secretary, Puerto Rico Department of Social Services, P.O. Box 11398, Santurce, PR 00910; 809-725-4511.

Rhode Island
Mr. Robert J. Fallon, Director, Department of Human Services, Aime J. Forand State Office Bldg., 600 New London Avenue, Cranston, RI 02920; 401-464-2121.

South Carolina
Eugene A. Laurent, Ph.D., Executive Director, State Health & Human Services Finance Commission, P.O. Box 8206, Columbia, SC 29202-8206; 803-253-6100.

South Dakota
Mr. James Ellenbecker, Secretary, Department of Social Services, Richard Kneip Building, 700 Governor's Drive, Pierre, SD 57501; 605-773-3165.

Tennessee
Mr. Robert A. Grunow, Commissioner, Department of Human Services, Citizens Plaza Building, 400 Deaderick Street, Nashville, TN 37219; 615-741-3241.

Texas
Mr. Burton Raiford, Commissioner, Texas Department of Human Services, 701 W. 51st Street, P.O. Box 149030, Austin, TX 78714-9030; 512-450-3011.

Utah
Mr. Kerry D. Steadman, Executive Director, Utah Department of Social Services, 120 North - 200 West, P.O. Box 45500, Salt Lake City, UT 84145-0500; 801-538-4001.

Vermont
Mr. Cornelius D. Hogan, Secretary, Agency of Human Services, 103 South Main Street, Waterbury, VT 05676; 802-241-2220.

Virginia
Ms. Carol A. Brunty, Commissioner, Department of Social Services, Blair Building, 8007 Discovery Drive, Richmond, VA 23229-8699; 804-662-1900.

Virgin Island
Mrs. Juel C. Rhymer, Commissioner, Department of Social Welfare, P.O. Box 539, St. Thomas, VI 00801; 809-774-0930.

Washington
Ms. Jean Soliz, Secretary, Washington Department of Social and Health Services, Mail Stop OB 44, Olympia, WA 98503; 206-753-3395.

West Virginia
Mr. Harry A. Burgess, Director, W.V. Office Of Social Services, Building 6, Room 850, Capitol Complex, Charleston, WV 25305; 304-558-8800.

Wisconsin
Mr. Gerald Whitburn, Secretary, Wisconsin Department of Health and Social Services, 1 West Wilson Street, Room 650, Madison, WI 53707; 608-266-9622.

Wyoming
Mr. George Lovato, Director, Department of Family Services, 2300 Capital Ave, 3rd Floor, Cheyenne, WY 82002; 307-777-7561.

More Free Help for Your Home-Based Business

More Free Help
For Your Home-Based Business

The government has hundreds of information sources and assistance programs that home-based business owners can use, just like the fat cats do, to cut costs and increase their profits. For example: Why spend hundred of dollars hiring a lawyer to explain the trade laws that might apply to your business when you can talk to a legal expert at the Federal Trade Commission about them for the price of a phone call? Why pay for expensive crime insurance from a private carrier to protect your home office, when you might be able to get the same coverage from the federal government for a fraction of the cost? Why hire a high-priced specialist who will promise to find you customers, when the government can help you do it for free?

Not only can the government help you start and run your home-based business, they can even help you furnish it at bargain basement prices. By attending government surplus property auctions, you can get all the office furniture, computer equipment, and filing cabinets you need for pennies on the dollar. The Department of Defense, for example, has auctioned off office chairs for $10 and desks for $25.

The government is likely to have all the money, help and information you will ever need for running your home-based business and what's great about these resources is that they're free. All the Fortune 500 companies relay on government programs and information sources for succeeding in their business and you can too.

* Free Home-Based Business Start Up Guide
Office of Business Development & Marketing
Small Business Administration
Washington, DC 20416
202-205-6665

The SBA has put together a free pamphlet for those who are thinking about starting their own small business out of their homes: *How To Start A Home-Based Business*. This guide is part of the SBA's *Focus On The Facts* series of publications, which also includes information on raising capital, business planning, marketing, pricing, and exporting.

* How to Write Off Your Car and Home, and Summer Vacation As a Business Expense
Taxpayer Services
Internal Revenue Service
U.S. Department of the Treasury
1111 Constitution Ave., NW
Room 2422
Washington, DC 20224
800-424-3676

One advantage to owning a home-based business is being able to write off car expenses related to your job. For more information on guidelines for writing off your car, get a free copy of *Business Use Of A Car* (#917) explains the expenses you may deduct for the use of your car in your home-based business. And a copy of *Business Use Of Your Home* (#587) can help you decide if you qualify to deduct certain expenses for using part of your home for your business. Deductions for the business use of a home computer are also discussed. The IRS will also show you how to piggy back a vacation onto your business travel. *Travel, Entertainment, and Gift Expenses* (#463) explains what expenses you may deduct for business-related travel, meals, entertainment, and gifts for your business, along with the reporting and recordkeeping requirements for these expenses.

* Free Videos on How To Start a Business In Your Home

Office of Business Development & Marketing
Small Business Administration (SBA)
409 3rd St., SW
Washington, DC 20416
202-205-6743
or
Oklahoma State University
Agricultural Communications
111 Public Information Building
Stillwater, OK 74078
405-744-3737

The SBA has produced a home video specially geared toward home-based business owners. *Home-Based Business: A Winning Blueprint* takes you through many of the steps necessary to a successful home-based business, from setting up your home office and networking strategies, to avoiding isolation and building the right kind of image for your company. You can purchase it for $39.00 from the following address: SBA, "Success s", Dept. A, P.O. Box 30, Denver, CO 80202-0030. You can review the video for free for 30 days before you decide to purchase. Contact the office listed above in Washington, D.C.

Home-Based Business Basics shows potential business owners how to do market research, handle finances, cope with legal problems, do promotions and juggle family relationships. The film is produced by a member of the County Cooperative Extension service and is available on a free loan basis at your local county cooperative extension service offices throughout the country. Call your local operator for your nearest office. Or you can purchase the film for $30 direct from the producer listed above.

* Is Your Advertising Legal?

Advertising Practices Division
Federal Trade Commission
6th & Pennsylvania Ave., NW
Washington, DC 20580
202-326-3131

Attracting new customers through advertising is an important part of a successful business, but you'll want to do it fairly and honestly. This division of the FTC can provide you with information about how to comply with the law and avoid making deceptive advertising claims.

* Is Your Office Asbestos and Radon Free?

Office of Information and Public Affairs
Consumer Product Safety Commission
Washington, DC 20207
800-638-2772
or
Radon Division (ANR-464)
Office of Radon Programs
U.S. Environmental Protection Agency
401 M St., SW
Washington, DC 20460
800-SOS-RADON; 202-475-9605

If you've set your office up in your basement, you might be exposing yourself to hazardous asbestos insulation. To find out more about home asbestos and eliminating its hazards, contact the CPSC for a free copy of *Asbestos in the Home*. Setting up office in the basement may also make yourself vulnerable to the effects of radon gas, which often enter homes through cracks in the basement floors. To get more information on the radon risks in your area, how to test for radon, and how to protect your home, contact the EPA office above. They can send you free radon publications, along with the number of a radon expert in your state.

* Keep Up To Date On The Cheapest Way To Send Out Mail

Business Mailer Updates
P.O. Box 999
Springfield, VA 22150-0999
or
Marketing Department
Regular Mail Services Division
U.S. Postal Service
475 L'Enfant Plaza, SW
Washington, DC 20260-6336
202-268-6965

When you do business through the mail, you need to keep up on rate and classification changes when they occur. The Postal Service puts out, *Memo To Mailers*, a free monthly publication to keep you posted of any of these changes, along with other relevant postal news. To be put on the mailing list, write to the above address, or for more information about the *Memo*, contact: Communications Department, U.S. Postal Service, 475 L'Enfant Plaza, SW, Washington, DC 20260; 202-268-6874.

Part of having a successful home-based business is knowing how to use the mail service effectively. To help you better prepare your mail for sending, the Marketing Department of the Postal Service has put together a free booklet, *A Guide To Business Mail Preparation*. This booklet gives you information on addressing for automation, postnet bar codes, and FIM patterns, all of which prepares your mail to be processed more efficiently, economically, and accurately, which makes for happier customers.

* How Business Reply Mail Can Bring You New Customers
Rates and Classification Department
U.S. Postal Service
475 L'Enfant Plaza
Washington, DC 20260
202-268-5316

If you use the mail a lot in your business to solicit customers, you might look into using business reply mail. Under this service, you guarantee to pay the postage for all replies returned to you at the regular first class rate plus a business reply fee. To use this service, you have to pay a small annual permit charge. Contact this office for more information on setting up this service for your business mailings.

* Free Tax Consulting By The Experts
Internal Revenue Service
1111 Constitution Ave, NW
Washington, DC 20224
800-424-1040

or
Your Local IRS Office

Why pay big money to a tax attorney or accountant when you can get better information for free? Many entrepreneurs believe that you will get a more favorable answer by hiring your own expert than you would if you call the IRS, but this has not shown to be the case. The law is the law, and private studies show that your chances of saving money on your tax bill is no greater whether you go to the IRS or to a high priced consultant for help. The problem is that most people don't know how to call the IRS to get the right answer. If the person at the IRS hotline seems a little unsure of their answer or if you just want another opinion, ask the IRS person to have a specialist call you back. Within a day or two you will get a call from an IRS expert who specializes in your question. They will take as much time as you need to make sure that you get all the deductions you are entitled to.

* Free Help To Start a Home-Based Tax Preparation Business
Volunteer and Education Branch
Taxpayer Service Division
Internal Revenue Service
U.S. Dept. of Treasury
1111 Constitution Ave, NW
Room 1315
Washington, DC 20224
202-566-4904

If you want to start your own tax preparation business you don't have to pay H&R Block or some other commercial organizations $200 to take a course. You can take a free course from the best experts in the work, the IRS. Many times these courses are given by IRS auditors and this is how you really learn the inside secrets on how to avoid the wrath of the IRS computer. Courses are available every year during the Fall. In return for free training you are required to volunteer a few hours of your time during one tax season to help others prepare their returns. The rest of your time you can charge for preparing tax returns. The IRS also offers free small business workshops which assist entrepreneurs in understanding their tax obligations.

* Make Sure Your Computer Screen Isn't Hazardous To Your Health

Information & Consumer Affairs
Occupational Safety and Health
  Administration
U.S. Department of Labor
Washington, DC 20210
202-523-8148

People who run home-based businesses often spend many hours sitting in front of their computer screens doing work. If you're one of these people, you should be aware of what the U.S. Department of Labor has discovered about the hazardous of display terminals. The following two relevant publications are available free from OSHA: *Display Terminals* and *Working Safely with Display Terminals*.

* Getting The Most Out Of Your Home Computer

SBA Publications
P.O. Box 46521
Denver, CO 80201

Setting up the right computer system is very important for many home-based businesses. The SBA has a couple of publications to help you out with computer problems:

How To Get Started With A Small Business Computer. Helps you forecast your computer needs, evaluate the alternatives and select the right computer system for your business. (MP14) $2. Make check payable to the U.S. Small Business Administration.

* Free Help In Setting Up Your Own Complaint Handling System

Marketing Practices Division
Federal Trade Commission
6th & Pennsylvania Ave., NW
Washington, DC 20580
202-326-3128

A successful business knows how to keep consumers coming back, even after they've complained about a product or service. They way they do this is by establishing a fair and effective system of resolving customer complaints quickly and inexpensively. The FTC works to promote such procedures among businesses, and they will provide you with information to help you develop an effective consumer complaint process for your business.

* How To Handle Salesmen Who Come To Your Home

Enforcement Division
Federal Trade Commission
6th & Pennsylvania Ave., NW
Washington, DC 20580
202-326-3034

If your home-based business gets sales people coming to your door trying to sell you items you can't really decide if you want, you should be aware of the FTC's *Cooling-Off Rule*, which requires sellers to give consumers notice of their three-day cancellation rights. For more information about the *Cooling Off Rule*, including a free pamphlet that describes the law, contact the FTC.

* Free Seminars On Starting A Business At Home

Contact your County Cooperative Extension Service listed under county government in your telephone book

Most counties in the U.S. have Cooperative Extension Services that can provide you with information on how to start up and run a home-based business. Many can provide you with free publications, while others may even run free workshops or seminars on home-based business-- it all depends on what your county Extension Service is doing. Most of these Services put out free newsletters that describe upcoming events, such as workshops, along with articles that might be of interest to you as a home-based business owner. Contact your Cooperative Extension Service to be put on their mailing list and for more information about their home-based business resources.

* Get Your Credit Fixed For Free

Contact your County Cooperative Extension Service listed under county government in your telephone book
or
Consumer Credit Counseling Service
8701 Georgia Ave
Silver Spring, MD 20910
301-589-5600
800-338-CCCS

Can't get a business loan because you have bad credit? Don't spend hundred of dollars to a credit repair clinic to tell you how to do it, contact your county's Cooperative Extension Service. These Services routinely run money and budgeting workshops at no charge that can show you how to fix your credit problems and pay off your bills more efficiently. If your county Cooperative Extension Service doesn't hold money workshops, you might consider contacting the Consumer Credit Counseling Service, which runs non-profit counseling services across the country, including in your state. Call them at 800-338-CCCS for the service nearest you.

* Cheap Crime Insurance for Your Business Equipment

Federal Crime Insurance
P.O. Box 6301
Rockville, MD 20850
800-638-8780
301-251-1660

If your home is burglarized, your home-based business could suffer large losses, such as expensive computer and telephone equipment. Residents in 13 states are eligible for a federal crime insurance program that actually subsidizes the cost of insurance to you. This means cheaper insurance premiums because the federal government is paying part of the bill for you. The following states and territories participate: AL, CA, CT, DE DC, FL, GA, IL, KS, MD, NJ,

NY, PA, RI, TN, and Puerto Rico and the Virgin Islands. Contact this office for more information about the program and an application.

* The Best Way To Keep Your Customers

Office of Consumer Affairs
U.S. Department of Commerce
Washington, DC 20230
202-482-5001

Finding customers is only half the story of a successful business; you also need to know how to keep them once you have them. And to do that you need to know how to develop good customer relations through honest and effective advertising, warranties, product safety, and complaint handling procedures. Contact this office for more information on these subjects, along with getting free copies of the following publications from their series of *Consumer Affairs Guides For Business*:

Advertising, Packaging, and Labeling
Product Warranties and Servicing
Managing Consumer Complaints
Credit And Financial Issues
Consumer Product Safety

This office can also provide you with information about local small business conferences based on these consumer affairs issues.

* Choosing Day Care for Work-At-Home Families

County Cooperative Extension Service
6707 Groveton Dr.
Clinton, MD 20735
301-868-9410

If you're running your own small business or a business out of your home, you might need to consider finding good and reliable day care for your children to give you the time you need for your business. This office can send you a free copy of *How To Select Quality Day Care For Your Child*, which shows you what to look for in day care.

* How The Law Protects You If You Don't Pay Your Bills

Credit Practices Division
Federal Trade Commission
6th & Pennsylvania Ave., NW
Washington, DC 20580
202-326-3758

If you're thinking of starting a debt collection agency, you'll need to know what the law says you can and cannot do to collect a debt for a client. The FTC can provide you with information on the *Fair Debt Collection Practices Act*, which prohibits debt collectors from engaging in unfair, deceptive, or abusive practices, such as overcharging, harassment, and disclosing consumers' debts to third parties. If you're being harassed by a debt collection agency, the FTC would like to hear about it.

* Free Legal Help On The Best Way To Treat Your Employees

Employment Standards Administration
U.S. Department of Labor, Room C4325
Washington, DC 20210
202-219-8743

One of the reasons people want to run their own businesses is that they don't like working for unfair and abusive bosses. To make sure that you don't turn into one of them, you'll need to know the federal laws that protect your employees' rights. The following free publications from the ESA will give you a good introduction to those labor laws:

Employer's Guide to Compliance with Federal Wage-Hour Laws
Federal Minimum Wage and Overtime Pay Standards
Handy Reference Guide to the Fair Labor Standards Act
Highlights of Computing Overtime Pay Under the FLSA
How the Federal Wage and Hour Laws Applies to Holidays
Employment of Apprentices
Employment of Messengers
Making EEO and Affirmative Action Work

Also see *Labor Laws and Small Business* below for more information on this subject.

* How To Get People and Companies Who Owe You Money To Pay Up

- Local Postmaster of the U.S. Postal Service
    Call the information operator for the city in question
- State Division of Motor Vehicles
    Call your state government operator in your state capitol
- State Attorney General Office
    Call your state government operator in your state capitol
- State Office of Uniform Commercial Code
    Call your state government operator in your state capitol
- State Office of Corporations
    Call your state government operator in your state capitol

Before you pay an attorney big money to help you collect a bad debt, there are a number of government offices you can turn to that will help you get your money for free or for just a few dollars.

If you are looking for an individual who moved, contact the U.S. Postal Service and the state Division of Motor Vehicles. The Post Office in the city of the last know address of your deadbeat friend will give you their forwarding address and charge you only $1.00. This information is kept at most Post Offices for 18 months. And for a few dollars, almost every state government will give you the address of anyone from their file of driver licenses. Almost everyone has a drivers license.

If a business owes you money, a letter to the Attorney General in the state where the business is headquartered can easily shake lose your money. Most Attorney General offices will send the business an official letter of inquiry, and this is enough to scare any legitimate businessperson into paying their bills.

Another effective method is to use the information in government offices to shame a business into paying their bill. The Office of Corporations in every state capitol will give you the name and address of all the officers of any businesses in their state. And the state Office of Uniform Commercial Code will give you the names of all the other people this business owes money to. It is a law that anytime a business, or individual, borrows money and puts up an asset as collateral, the information is filed at the Office of Uniform Commercial Code. When you send a letter asking someone for payment, you can send copies of the letter to all these other people. And what is most effective, is that the people listed as officers of most small businesses are friend and relatives of the owner, and it can be very embarrassing for a business owner to have them know how unfairly they are treating you.

* Free Accounting Help

Contact your State Department of Economic Development Office for the Small Business Development Center near you

Accountants are expensive, especially if your small business, like most, don't have a lot of working capital to throw around. Instead of going out and hiring your own personal accountant, contact your local SBDC. Many of these centers have accounting experts who will sit down with you and help you develop your own accounting and recordkeeping systems. They can also help you work through any accounting problems that you might run into. If you don't have an SBDC near you, contact your nearest Small Business Administration Office-- they work with the Service Corps of Retired Executives (SCORE) whose members can also provide you with free accounting assistance and advice.

* Entrepreneur Quiz

Superintendent of Documents
Government Printing Office
Washington, DC 20402
202-512-1800

For $2.00, GPO will send you a copy of *Starting and Managing a Business from Your Home*,

which contains a questionnaire to help you decide if you have the right kind of personality to be a successful entrepreneur and home-based business owner. Also included are descriptions of products and services to help you start your own home-based business, such as business planning, recordkeeping, taxes, and insurance.

* What You Need To Know When Selling Food and Medical Products

Small Business Coordinator
Food and Drug Administration
5600 Fishers Lane, Room 15-61
Rockville, MD 20857
301-827-3430

If you are going to be selling any food or drug products as part of your business, you'll need to know how to comply with the FDA's packaging and labeling regulations for these products. This office can explain FDA procedures and help you comply with their rules. Contact them for a free copy of *A Small Business Guide to the FDA*, which will give you an overview of the small business compliance program.

* How To Pick A Work-At-Home Franchise

Bureau of Consumer Protection
Federal Trade Commission
6th and Pennsylvania Ave, NW
Washington, DC 20580
202-326-3128
or
International Franchising Association
1350 New York Ave, NW
Washington, DC 20005
202-628-8000
or
Your State Franchising Office

Just because you want to run a business out of your home, doesn't mean that you're not in a position to consider owning a franchise. Owning a franchise can mean you already have name recognition and advertising done for you. Of course, Pizza Hut isn't going to let you run a business out of your home, but others might, like lawn care companies, leak detection services, upholstery cleaners, commercial office cleaners, maid services, sewer and drain cleaning services, and many more.

The Federal Trade Commission will send you a number of free publications that will tell you what you need to know before buying a franchise. The International Franchise Association also has a number of publications on this topic, but they charge a small fee.

There are a number of state governments that require franchisors who are selling franchises in their state to file detailed background information on their company which is made available to the public. Call your state capitol operator to see if your state has such requirements, or call the Federal Trade Commission and they will tell you which states you can contact to get this information.

* Check If You And Your Employees Are Safe Working In Your Home
Information & Consumer Affairs
Occupational Safety and Health
  Administration
U.S. Department of Labor
Washington, DC 20210
202-219-4667

Depending on what your small business is, you might be faced with potential health and safety concerns, anything from indoor air quality to stiff joints from typing too much. OSHA has put out a series of free publications of interest to small businesses to help you remedy or avoid potential health and safety problems: *Handbook For Small Businesses, General Industry Digest, Construction Industry Digest,* and *Consultation Services For Employers.*

* Free Inspections of Your Home for Health And Safety Hazards
National Institute for Occupational Safety
  and Health
4676 Columbia Parkway

Cincinnati, OH 45226
800-356-4674

The National Institute for Occupational Safety and Health (NIOSH) is responsible for conducting research to make the nation's workplaces healthier and safer by responding to urgent requests for assistance from employers, employees, and their representatives where imminent hazards are suspected. They conduct inspections, laboratory and epidemiologic research, publish their findings, and make recommendations for improved working conditions. They will also inspect any workplace for free if three employees sign a form alleging that the environment may be dangerous. Employees have the option of keeping anonymous. If any of the following applies to you, NIOSH can provide you with more information:

Do you use a video display terminal most of the day?

Are you concerned about the chemicals you are using in your dry cleaning?

Do you have tingling in your hands (carpal tunnel syndrome)?

Do you use a jackhammer most of the day and are now finding that your fingers are no longer sensitive to heat or cold?

Do you do the same motion again and again, such as on an assembly line?

Do you feel your job is causing you mental stress?

Are you having trouble hearing?

* How To Choose The Best Health Insurance Coverage
Office of Business Development &
  Marketing
Small Business Administration
409 3rd St., SW
Washington, DC 20416
202-205-6743
Or
National Health Information Clearinghouse
  Hotline
P.O. Box 1133
Washington, DC 20013-1133

301-565-4167
800-336-4797

Owning your own business means that you no longer will have your health insurance taken care of the way it was when you worked for somebody else. To help you figure out the best way to find a health insurance plan best suited to your needs, the SBA has produced a free publication that's part of their *Focus on the Facts* series called *Small Business Health Insurance*. This publication covers such topics as indemnity, managed care, selecting a plan, and self insurance. Contact this office for your free copy.

How To Get Free Health Care If You Can't Afford Health Insurance

Public Health Service
Health Resource and Services Administration
U.S. Department of Health and Human
  Services
Rockville, MD 20857
800-492-0359 (in MD)
800-638-0742

If you can't afford health insurance and you meet certain income requirements, you may be eligible to receive free medical care under the Hill-Burton law. Under this law, hospitals and other health facilities that receive federal funding for construction and modernization must provide certain medical services at no charge to those who can't afford to pay. By calling the toll-free number above, you can find out which hospitals in your area are participating in this program, along with income eligibility requirements. If your home-based business is your only source of income, and it's making little or no profit, you may in fact be eligible for free health care.

* How Labor Laws Affect Your Small Business

Office of Small and Disadvantaged Business
  Utilization
U.S. Department of Labor
200 Constitution Ave., NW, Room C-2318
Washington, DC 20210
202-219-9148

Just because you run a small or home-based business doesn't mean you don't have to obey federal labor laws like larger companies do. To find out what laws apply to your small business regarding such topics as wages, overtime, pensions, and health and safety, contact this office for a free copy of the booklet, *Major Laws Administered by the U.S. Department of Labor Which Affect Small Business*. You should also contact your state's labor department to find out what state laws you should know about.

* Should You Lease Or Buy A Car For Your Business

Consumer Information Center
Pueblo, CO 81009

As a small business owner, you might have to decide whether it's better for you to lease or buy a car for the business. Using plain english, the *Consumer Guide To Vehicle Leasing* will give you an explanation of the advantages and disadvantages of buying and leasing a car, and show you how to decide what's best for you. It's available for $.50 from the Consumer Information Center.

* Get Legal Help at Little or No Cost

Contact your State Department of Economic Development Office for the Small Business Development Center near you

Many Small Business Development Centers offer free or low-cost legal advice concerning laws that you might run up against in running your small business. And since most small businesses, especially home-based businesses, have very little working capital to throw around, the last thing you want to do is spend what you do have on an expensive lawyer. They can help you with legal questions like:

When should you form a corporation?
Can my employer sue me if I take some of his business with me?

Before getting your own personal, and expensive, lawyer, contact a Small Business

Development Center and see if they can give you the legal advice you need without having to spend a lot of money.

* Legal Advice On Trade Laws
Public Reference Branch
Federal Trade Commission
Washington, DC 20580
202-326-2222

If you're not sure what business laws may apply to your new business, contact the FTC's Public Reference Branch. If you let them know what kind of business you're thinking of running, they'll be able to direct you to an expert at the FTC who specializes in the laws that you might need to know. They can send you copies of the regulations and help you comply with them. The following laws may apply to your small business. The FTC experts and their direct phone numbers are included:

Mail Order Rule, which requires companies to ship purchases made by mail when promised or give consumers option to cancel order for a refund. Elaine Kolish, 202-326-3042.

Care Labeling Rule, which requires manufacturers of textile clothing and fabrics to attach care label instructions. Steve Ecklund, 202-326-3034.

Unordered Merchandise Statute, which permits consumers to keep, as a free gift, unordered merchandise they receive through the U.S. mail. Vada Martin, 202-326-3002.

Cooling-Off Rule, which gives consumers three days to cancel sales for $25 or more made away from the seller's place of business. Brent Mickum, 202-326-3132.

Games of Chance in the Food Retailing and Gasoline Industries Rule, which requires disclosure of odds of winning prizes, the random distribution of winning prize pieces, and publication of winners' names. 216-522-4210.

Magnuson-Moss Act, which requires warranty information to be made available to consumers before making a purchase. 202-326-3128.

Holder-In-Due-Course Rule, which gives consumers certain protection when goods they buy on credit are not satisfactory. 202-326-3758.

* Avoid Mail Fraud Through The Mail
Public Affairs Branch
Postal Inspection Service
U.S. Postal Service
475 L'Enfant Plaza, SW
Washington, DC 20260
202-268-4293
or
Enforcement Division
Federal Trade Commission
6th & Pennsylvania Ave., NW
Washington, DC 20580
202-326-2996

Since many home-based businesses do business through the mail, you should be aware of the ways some con artists use the mail to steal from you. To help you, the Postal Service publishes the free booklet, *Postal Crime Prevention: A Business Guide*, which shows business owners how to protect themselves. It includes information on different types of mail fraud, check cashing precautions, guidelines for mailroom security, bombs in the mail, and other problems with mail-related crime.

If you receive merchandise through the mail that you did not order, you can keep it as a gift. Find out your rights by contacting the Federal Trade Commission and obtaining a free copy of the *Unordered Merchandise Statute*.

* Have The Government Find You Customers
Contact your State Office of Economic Development to locate a Small Business Development Center near you
or

- State Government Offices
    Contact your State Government Operator located in your state capitol

    or

- Federal Government Offices
    Call your local U.S. Government Federal Information Center listed in your telephone directory or call the main Federal Information Center at 301-722-9000.

The government has what is indisputably the best marketing information in the world, and all the Fortune 500 companies use it to make their millions. If Citicorp uses government information to decide the best place to put up a new branch bank or for getting a list of rich people to sell trust services to, you can use the same sources to decide the best place to market a home improvement business or to get a mailing list of all the women in your neighborhood who are over 150 pounds to sell them a new diet product.

There are three basic starting places for tapping into all this huge marketing information. The best place to get free, or very-low-cost marketing consulting help is at your local Small Business Development Center (SBDC). These offices will sit down with you and help you work out the specifics on who your market is and how to reach them.

State governments offer a wide variety of market information. The division of Motor Vehicles sell information from drivers licenses and motor vehicle registrations. With this you can identify all the rich single men over 6 feet tall in your zip code. You can also get listings of doctors, lawyers, real estate agents, and even delicatessens from state licensing and regulatory offices. Or your state Census Data Center can identify those zip codes most likely to have young children who can afford orthodontist work. Your state government operator in your state capitol can help you locate the specific office that may be able to help you.

Federal government offices spend hundreds of millions of dollars on marketing information

rarely used by entrepreneurs. The U.S. Dept. of Agriculture can give you information on the market for thousands of products, including house plants, diets, aquaculture, and even bull sperm. The U.S. Department of Commerce can give you the latest information on hundreds of products, including golf balls, computers, toys, or biotechnology. And the U.S. International Trade Administration provides marketing information on items like video games, mushrooms, and broom handles. Your local U.S. Government, Federal Information Center can help you locate the specific office that can help you.

* The Government Will Sell Your Service or Product In Other Countries

- State Office of International Marketing
    Contact your State Office of Economic Development located in your state capitol

Don't hire a high-priced international marketing consultant if you want to see if your product or service has any opportunity of being a success in another country. Both state a federal governments are very active in offering free and low cost assistance to small businesses who wish to take advantage of markets overseas. There are programs that will provide you with free market studies for your product in any country in the world. Other programs will have embassy officials who will locate local businesses who are willing to sell your product or service in that country, and programs that will provide you with financing to sell your products overseas.

* Find A Free Government Expert On Any Topic

- Federal Government Offices
    Call your local U.S. Government Federal Information Center listed in your telephone directory or call the main Federal Information Center at 301-722-9000

It is estimated that there are approximately 700,000 experts in the federal government, each spending their careers studying some aspect of business that entrepreneurs can tap into. If you are looking for expertise on how to sell a new t-shirt idea, you can call the government's underwear expert at the U.S. International Trace Commission. This expert gets paid over $60,000 a year to study the t-shirt business, and if you treat her properly, she is available to you for the price of a telephone call. You are never going to find a private consultant who will know as much as this government expert. In fact, if you were to hire a private marketing consultant, they'd probably call a government expert to find the answer that they turn around and charge you big bucks for! You may be interested in the pasta expert at the Department of Commerce if you have a new pasta product. Or the 900 number expert at the Federal Communication Commission if you're planning to start your own Love Line.

* What Are The Rules If You Sell Your Products Through The Mail?

Enforcement Division
Federal Trade Commission
6th & Pennsylvania Ave., NW
Washington, DC 20580
202-326-2996

Since many home-based businesses do business through the mail, you'll need to be aware of the FTC's *Mail Order Rule*, which requires companies to ship purchases made by mail when promised or to give consumers the option to cancel their order for a refund. For more information on the rule and how it might apply to your business, contact the FTC.

* Free Marketing Help

Contact your State Office of Economic Development to locate a Small Business Development Center near you

Finding out if there's a market for your products or services is the most critical part of planning a successful business. This process includes having to analyze your competition, suppliers, and new customers. The SBA can hook you up with experts through the Service Corps of Retired Executives (SCORE) who can provide you with free advice on how to develop and execute an effective marketing plan. Don't spend a lot of money you don't have on a marketing "expert" you heard of or found in the telephone book--get it done for free through an expert at your SBA office.

* How To Set Up A Pension Plan For One Employee

Superintendent of Documents
Government Printing Office
Washington, DC 20402
202-512-1800

If you hire permanent employees, you might be interested in finding out how to set up a pension plan for them. To do this, you'll need to know more about the pension laws. For $1.50, GPO will send you a copy of *Simplified Employee Pensions: What Small Businesses Need to Know*, a publication specially geared toward small business owners. For more general information about the pension laws, the following office will send you a list of their free pension publications: Division of Public Information, Pension and Welfare Benefits Administration, U.S. Department of Labor, Washington, D.C. 20210; 202-219-8921.

* 80% Discount on Office Equipment and Supplies

U.S. General Services Administration
18th & F Sts., NW
Washington, DC 20405
410-796-8899

If you need office furniture, typewriters, computers, wastebaskets, postage meters, paper clips--practically anything you could possibly imagine--for your home-based business, but don't have much money to spend on it, the federal government might be your best buy. The General Services Administration is the federal government's housekeeper--they keep track of what supplies the government needs and doesn't need to run properly. Anything they don't need, such as overstock of office furniture and equipment, is auctioned off at rock-bottom prices. Auctions are held at GSA regional offices throughout the U.S. This office can put you on a mailing list to notify you of upcoming auctions, or you can contact the GSA office nearest you:

Atlanta
GSA, Surplus Sales Branch, 75 Spring St. SW, Atlanta, GA 30303; 404-331-0972.

Boston
GSA, Surplus Sales Branch, 10 Causeway St., 9th Floor, Boston, MA; 617-565-7316.

Chicago
GSA, 230 S. Dearborn St., Chicago, IL 60604; 312-353-6061.

Denver
GSA, Surplus Supply Branch, Denver Federal Center, Building 41, Denver, CO 80225; 303-236-7705.

Fort Worth
GSA, Surplus Sales Branch, 819 Taylor St., Ft. Worth, TX 76102; 817-334-2351.

Kansas
GSA, Surplus Sales Branch, 6F BPS 4400, College Blvd., Suite 175, Overland, KS 66211.

New York
GSA, Surplus Sales Branch, 26 Federal Plaza, Room 20-2016, New York, NY 10278; 212-264-4824.

Philadelphia
GSA, Surplus Sales Branch, 9th & Market Sts., Philadelphia, PA 19107; 215-597-SALE.

San Francisco
GSA, Surplus Sales Branch, 525 Market St., 32nd Floor, San Francisco, CA 94105; 415-974-9189.

Washington State
GSA, Surplus Sales Branch, GSA Center, Auburn, WA 98002; 206-931-7562.

Washington, D.C.
GSA, 6808 Loisdale Rd., Bldg. A, Springfield, VA 22150; 703-557-7785.

What follows is a small list of other federal agencies that sell office furniture and supplies at auctions. Contact them for further information:

Internal Revenue Service	800-829-1040
U.S. Postal Service	202-268-2000
U.S. Customs Service	405-357-9194
Dept. of Defense	616-961-7331
U.S. Marshals Service	202-307-9237

* How To Protect Yourself From Office Supply Sales Schemes

Marketing Practices Division
Federal Trade Commission
6th & Pennsylvania Ave., NW
Washington, DC 20580
202-326-3128

One of the ways small businesses can lose money is by becoming the victims of office supply sales schemes, where your company gets billed for supplies that you never ordered or received, and you don't find out until after your check is cashed. If you think you've been the victim of such a scheme or would like information about how con artists run them, contact the FTC.

* How To Package and Label Your Products According To The Law

Enforcement Division
Federal Trade Commission
6th and Pennsylvania Ave., NW
Washington, DC 20580
202-326-3042

If you're producing and selling any consumer product, you need to be aware of the *Fair Packaging and Labeling Act*, which requires consumer commodities to be accurately labeled to describe the product's identity and net quantity. For more information on how this law might apply to your products, contact the FTC.

* How To Price Your Product So You Make The Most Money

SBA Publications
P.O. Box 30
Denver, CO 80201-0030
202-205-6666

You've got a good product or service but don't know how much you should sell it for. The SBA's publication, *Pricing Your Products And Services Profitably (FM13)*, tells you how to do it, and includes various pricing techniques and when to use them. Price: $2.

* How To Make Your Product Safe For Your Customers

Office of Information and Public Affairs
Consumer Product Safety Commission
Washington, DC 20207
800-638-2772

You might think that the product you're making or selling in your home-based business is great, but it needs to meet certain government safety standards before you can sell it. The CPSC publishes three free publications that will explain those standards to you:

Retailers Guide
Guide for Manufacturers, Distributors, and Retailers
Guide for Retailers

It's important that you know and follow their guidelines, because if a consumer is hurt from using your product, the CPSC has the authority to force you to recall it and correct the problem.

* How To Raise Money

Office of Business Development & Marketing
Small Business Administration
409 3rd St., SW
Washington, DC 20416
202-205-6743

Raising money to run your business is as basic a task as their is to be successful. As part of its Focus on the Facts series, the SBA has put together a free publication titled How to Raise Money for a Small Business. This free fact sheet outlines the basics of raising money, where to find it, borrowing it, types of business loans, how to write a loan proposal, and SBA financial programs. Contact this office for a copy.

* How To Set Up A Self-Employed Retirement Plan

Taxpayer Services
Internal Revenue Service
U.S. Department of the Treasury
1111 Constitution Ave., NW, Room 2422
Washington, DC 20224
800-829-1040

This IRS office can provide you with a free copy of Self-Employed Retirement Plans (#560), which discusses retirement plans (Keogh plans) for self-employed individuals, such as those running home-based businesses, and certain partners in partnerships. These retirement plans allow the self-employed to put away a certain amount of their earnings each year into a tax free account retirement account.

* Free Consultants (SCORE)

Contact your local U.S. Small Business Administration (SBA) office
or
SBA Hotline   800-827-5722

SCORE members work with local SBA offices to provide small business owners with free advice and assistance on all kinds of problems that you might run into in your day-to-day work, such as problems in accounting, marketing, business planning, and so on. Contact your local Small Business Administration office for more information on how SCORE might help you out with your special business needs.

* Free Videos Show How To Start Or Expand A Small Business

Office of Business Development & Marketing
Small Business Administration
409 3rd St., SW
Washington, DC 20416
202-205-6666

The SBA has five VHS tapes that are helpful to business owners who are trying to develop marketing, promotional, and business plans. You can purchase these from the above address, or you can request a copy to review for 30 days free of charge.

Marketing: Winning Customers With A Workable Plan. Offers a step-by-step approach on how to write the best possible marketing plan for your business. Explains the best methods for determining customer needs, how to identify and develop a working profile for potential customers and much more. $30.00

The Business Plan: Your Roadmap To Success. Teaches the essentials of developing a business plan that will help lead you to capital, growth, and profitability. Tells what to include, what to omit, and how to get free help from qualified . $30.00

Promotion: Solving The Puzzle. Shows you how to coordinate advertising, public relations, direct mail, and trade shows into a successful promotional strategy that targets new customers, increases sales, and saves you money. $39.00

Home-Based Business: A Winning Blueprint. This practical program examines the essentials of operating within a productive and profitable home-based business - from designing your home office and avoiding isolation to networking strategies and building an image that gets you taken seriously. $39.

Basics of Exporting. This videotape shows you how to open doors to international markets. This tape provides information on: getting your goods overseas, payment mechanisms, selling and distributing overseas, international marketing, and sources of financial assistance. $39.

* Hotline Helps Entrepreneurs Handle The Stress of Small Business
National Health Information Clearinghouse
P.O. Box 1133
Washington, DC 20012
800-336-4797; 301-565-4167

Trying to run a business out of your home can put a lot of added stress on you, your family, and marriage, especially when business isn't going very well. NHIC puts out a pamphlet titled *Healthfinder: Stress Information Resources*, which lists and describes several government agencies and private organizations that offer publications and resources on work-related stress and stress management. It's available for $1.00.

* Get A Tax Break For Hiring and Training New Employees
Employment Training Administration
Office of Public Affairs
U.S. Department of Labor, Room S-2322
Washington, DC 20210
202-219-8743

If your business employs certain types of people, such as dislocated workers or workers who have lost their jobs because of competition, your business may qualify for a federal tax credit. This Targeted Jobs Tax Credit allows businesses to write off from these taxes a portion of the salaries they pay to these special workers. This federal tax credit program is run on the state and local levels, and to find out specific information on eligibility requirements, contact your state Department of Labor or local private industry council. If you are interested in participating in this program, these offices can locate workers for you and help you through the paperwork.

This Targeted Jobs Tax Credit program can be used in conjunction with another program under the Job Training Partnership Act where the government will pay part of your employee's salary if you meet certain eligibility requirements and provide on-the-job training, such as computer or carpentry skills to the employee. Under this program, you need to hire certain disadvantaged employees, such as the handicapped, the economically disadvantaged, minorities, and the like. The office above can send you free copies of fact sheets on the Job Training Partnership Act and the Targeted Jobs Tax Credit Program.

* Tax Information For Home-Based Businesses
Taxpayer Services
Internal Revenue Service
U.S. Department of the Treasury

1111 Constitution Ave., NW, Room 2422
Washington, DC 20224
800-424-3676

Depending on the size and nature of your home-based business, there may be a lot of information you'll need to know about your federal tax responsibilities. The IRS puts out a whole series of free publications that explain the current tax laws to help you better understand them. The titles, along with brief descriptions and ordering numbers, are listed below.

Accounting Periods and Methods (#538) explains which accounting periods and methods can be used for figuring federal taxes, and how to apply for approval to change from one period or method to another.

Bankruptcy And Other Debt Cancellation (#908) explains the income tax aspects of bankruptcy and discharge of debt for individuals and small businesses.

Business Expenses (#535) discusses such expenses as fringe benefits, rent, interest, taxes, insurance, and employee benefit plans. It also explains the choice to capitalize certain business expenses; amortization and depletion; and the circumstances in where expenses are and are not deductible.

Business Use Of A Car (#917) explains the expenses you may deduct for the use of your car in your home-based business.

Business Use Of Your Home (#587) can help you decide if you qualify to deduct certain expenses for using part of your home for your business. Deductions for the business use of a home computer are also discussed.

Circular E, Employer's Tax Guide (#15) explains what you'll need to know if you employ others as part of your home-based business.

Condemnations and Business Casualties and Thefts (#549) explains how to deduct for casualties and thefts to your business property, such as when your business computer is stolen during a robbery.

Depreciation (#534) tells you how to calculate and how to write off the depreciated value of property and equipment associated with your home-based business.

Earned Income Credit (#596) discusses who may receive the earned income credit, and how to figure and claim the credit.

Educational Expenses (#508) explains how, if you take educational courses related to your home-based business, you can deduct these expenses from your taxes.

Examination of Returns, Appeal Rights, and Claims for Refund (#556) is helpful if your tax return is examined by explaining the procedures for the examination of items of partnership income, deduction, gain, loss, and credit.

Interest Expense (#545) tells you how to deduct interest payments on loans you take out to run your home-based business.

Moving Expenses (#521) explains how you can deduct moving expenses when you relocate home-based business as you move.

Sales and Other Dispositions of Assets (#544) explains how to figure gain and loss on such transactions as trading or selling an asset used in a business, along with the tax results of different types of gains and losses.

Self-Employed Retirement Plans (#560) discusses retirement plans (Keogh plans) for self-employed individuals, such as those running home-based businesses, and certain partners in partnerships.

Self-Employment Tax (#533) explains the self-employment tax (i.e., social security tax) that self-employed, home-based business owners must pay.

Tax Guide for Small Business (#334) explains the federal tax laws that apply to businesses, including the four major forms of business organizations--sole proprietorships, partnerships, corporations, and S corporations--along with the tax responsibilities for each.

Tax Information For Direct Sellers (#911) gives you helpful information if your home-based business involves "direct selling," that is, selling products to others on a person-to-person basis, such as door-to-door sales, sales parties, or by appointment in your home.

Tax Information on Corporations (#542) tells you what you need to know if you incorporate your home-based business.

Tax Information on Partnerships (#541) tells you what you'll need to know if you run your home-based business as a partnership.

Tax Information On S Corporations (#589) explains how corporations are taxed under subchapter S of the tax code.

Taxpayers Starting A Business (#583) shows sample records that a small business can use if it operates as a sole proprietorship. Records like these will help you prepare complete and accurate tax returns and make sure you pay only the tax you owe. It also discusses the taxpayer identification number that you must use, information returns you may have to file, and the kinds of business taxes you may have to pay.

Travel, Entertainment, and Gift Expenses (#463) explains what expenses you may deduct for business-related travel, meals, entertainment, and gifts for your business, along with the reporting and recordkeeping requirements for these expenses.

* Is Your Name Legal?

Trademark Search Library
Patent and Trademark Office
U.S. Department of Commerce

2011 Jefferson Davis Hwy., Room 2C08
Arlington, VA 22202
703-557-4636

Before you decide to name your new business something like Disneyland or Nutrisystem, it might be a good idea to find out if someone else already owns the trademark on the name. All registered trademarks, logos, and slogans are filed in the Trademark Search Library, and you can visit the library to research the name you want to use for your business. If you can't get to the library yourself, you can find a professional trademark specialist to hire do the search for you by looking in the telephone directory. The library staff will not do a search for you if you haven't formally applied for a trademark. However, if you do apply for a trademark, the library will tell you if the name is already taken, and if it isn't, they'll award you the trademark. Contact this office for more information on researching and applying for a trademark.

* Pay Fair

Wage and Hour Division
Fair Labor Standards
U.S. Department of Labor
200 Constitution Ave.
Washington, DC 20210
202-219-4907

Don't be caught in a pay dispute. You can learn the ins and outs of paying your employees a fair wage simply by calling the Wage and Hour Division. They can explain the rules governing minimum wage and who qualifies for time-and-a-half pay and when. This Division can even send you written material which provides more detailed information.

* How Much Should You Pay For A Typist With 2 Years Experience

Bureau of Labor Statistics
U.S. Department of Labor
Washington, DC 20210
202-606-7800
or
Your State Department of Labor

When you run a small business, you need to

know how much to pay your employees and how much to charge for your services based on average wage rates in your area of the country. The Bureau of Labor Statistics (BLS) has compiled the following *Area Wage Surveys* for major industries across the country. BLS also publishes an annual white-collar wage study, *Professional, Administrative, Technical, and Clerical Survey*. Contact this office or your Local Department of Labor Office located in your state capitol.

* What's The Law If Your Business Offers a Warranty

Marketing Practices Division
Federal Trade Commission
6th & Pennsylvania Ave., NW
Washington, DC 20580
202-326-3128

If you're selling a product with a warranty, you should know about the *Magnuson-Moss Warranty Act*, which requires you to make warranty information available to consumers before making a purchase, and to honor your warranty obligations. To find out more about this law and how to comply with it, contact the Federal Trade Commission (FTC).

* Do You Need A Permit For Running A Business Out of Your Home?

Contact your local Business council
Depending on what your home-based business is, you might need to get zoning permits to run your business at home. Local zoning laws exist so that residential neighborhoods aren't overrun by traffic created by having daily business going on in the area. This is especially true is a business has a steady flow of customers showing up to buy things. Your local business council will be able to tell you if your business will require a zoning permit.

* Home-Based Child Care Business

County Cooperative Extension Service
6707 Groveton Dr.

Clinton, MD 20735
301-868-9410

If you're interested in running a child care business out of your home, you'll need some background information before you start. This office, or the Cooperative Extension Service in your own county, can send you free copies of *A Home-based Business: Child Care* and *Running A Child Care Business*, which include information on such topics as record keeping, registration and certification, rates to charge, advertising, and insurance. You'll also find a list of questions you should answer about how suitable you are for the job, such as your feelings toward children, your physical stamina, your personal family life, and much more.

* Videos On Starting A Child Care Business

Contact your County Cooperative Extension Service listed under county government in your telephone book
or
Video Production
Texas A & M University
107 Reed McDonald Bldg.
College Station, TX 77843
409-845-2840

Better Kid Care - Family Day Care Training is a 4 part video program in day care training. It includes the following topics: 1) Child Development, 2) Nutrition, 3) Health and Safety, and 4) Business Management. It is produced by the Texas Agricultural Extension Service and is available through their office listed above for a modest fee or on a free loan basis through many County Cooperative Extension Service offices around the country.

* Free Legal Help Before You Buy A Franchise

Federal Trade Commission
Bureau of Consumer Protection
Division of Enforcement
Pennsylvania Ave at 6th Street, NW
Washington, DC 20580

Franchise Rule Information Hotline
202-326-3220
Franchise Complaint Line
202-326-3128
According the U.S. Federal Trade Commission (FTC) there are no accurate data available to prove that franchisees have a lower failure rate then new businesses. So when it a franchise salesman tries to make you believe otherwise, check him out at the FTC. If you buy a lemon, only 15 states give you private rights to sue and there is often a limited ability to recover. A franchiser knows your financial situation, and can often outwait you. Many franchisees have no money left to hire a lawyer to try to recoup their losses. The FTC has two telephone numbers you can call to ask for assistance. The Franchise Complaint Line is staffed by a duty attorney and takes complaints about franchisers. The second if the Franchise Rule Hotline which will tell you how to investigate a franchiser and will let you consult with a franchise attorney.

* Hotlines For Checking Out Business Opportunities Scams

Contact your State Business Opportunity Office located in your state capitol
or
Contact your State Attorney General Office located in your state capitol
You won't make a million dollars working from home and anyone who promises you that is lying to you. Actually, anyone who promises that you will make a lot of fast money in any kind of business is probably lying to you. You should check out any kind of "business opportunity" salesman, and you can do it for free. Twenty two states have Business Opportunity Laws and have establishes special offices that will help you check out the claims any salesman makes to you and punish wrongdoers.

California	916-445-9555
Colorado	203-566-4560
Florida	904-488-2221
	800-342-2176

Georgia	404-656-3790
Indiana	317-232-6331
Iowa	515-281-4441
Kentucky	502-573-2200
Louisiana	504-342-7900
Maine	207-582-8760
Maryland	410-576-6360
Michigan	517-373-7117
Minnesota	612-296-6328
Nebraska	402-471-2171
New Hampshire	603-271-3641
North Carolina	919-733-3924
Ohio	614-466-8831
	800-282-0515
Oklahoma	405-235-0230
South Carolina	803-734-2169
South Dakota	605-773-4013
Texas	512-475-1769
Utah	801-530-6601
Virginia	804-786-0594
	800-451-1525
Washington	206-753-6928

If your state is not included in this list contact the office of your State Attorney General located in your state capitol.

* Is Your Client Sexually Harassing You

Equal Employment Opportunity Commission
1801 L St., NW
Washington, DC 20507
800-669-3362
You can't have your client investigated by the government for discrimination based on sex, age, race, religion, color national origin with way you can if they are your employer or boss. But, if you do encounter such behavior you can do your part in letting them know that they would be violating federal laws if you were their employee. The office above will provide you with all the free legal advice and literature you need. And for your friends who are still employees, give them this number. This is also the office that will come out and investigate sexual harassment charges.

* Government Loans To Start Your Own Energy Conservation Business

Contact your state Economic Development Office in your state capitol

or

Your Local Small Business Administration Office

The Small Business Administration has established a separate funding program to assist entrepreneurs who provide energy production and conservation services for others. This can include engineering, architectural, consulting or other professional services specializing in specific energy measures. The funding may be in the form of direct loans or loan guarantees and can be as high as $750,000. They can be used for start-up or expansion purposes. Ask about Energy Business Loan Guarantees.

* Free Government Study Shows That Plants Eliminate 90% of Office Pollution

NASA Library
Bldg. 1100, Room 517A
Stennis Space Center, MS 39529
601-688-3244

A recent NASA study called, *Interior Landscape Plants for Indoor Air Pollution Abatement* shows that indoor plants are not only aesthetically pleasing but are also healthier. Most house plants are very effective at removing chemicals from the air and can clean up to 90% of your indoor air pollution. This report is free.

* Help For Your Company To "Buy Green"

Resource Conservation and Recovery Act
Environmental Protection Agency
401 M St., SW,
Washington, DC 20460
202-260-9327

Your company can support recycling by examining your purchase orders to determine what items can be substituted with recycled products. Is your paper made from recycled paper? Your state recycling office may be able to direct you to vendors in your area who carry recycled products. The Resource Conservation and Recovery Act office has a free publication titled *Procurement Guidelines for Buying Recycled Products*, which provides guidance in making the switch to green.

* Free Hotline Helps You Save Your Energy Dollars

Energy and Renewable Energy Clearinghouse
U.S. Dept. of Energy
P.O. Box 3048
Merrifield, VA 22116
800-428-2525

The U.S. Dept. of Energy supports the Energy and Renewable Energy Clearinghouse (EREC), which can answer any question you have concerning energy conservation and renewable energy sources, such as solar energy. They try to get you to be as specific as possible with your questions, so they can better tailor the packets of information they send you. They can answer questions regarding the maintenance of your heating/cooling systems, adding insulation, or passive solar design (which is a good idea for people to consider when constructing a new building). They also have a staff of commercialization specialists who work with small energy business or inventors. They provide help in identifying funding sources, answer patent and licensing questions, assist with business plans, and offer marketing suggestions. There is a two to four week turnaround time, so plan ahead. Some of the help they provide includes helping a financial analyst determine if she should approve funding of a cogeneration project (where steam and electricity are simultaneously produced from a single source). EREC provides information on cogeneration, how it works, and other instances of its use. EREC also provided a wind energy company with marketing information for their product. They encouraged the company to write to energy related publications to get their product editorial coverage, and even provided the company with the names and addresses.

* Hotline Helps You Save On Your Trash Bill

Resource Conservation and Recovery Act
  Hotline
Environmental Protection Agency
401 M St, SW
Washington, DC 20460
703-920-9810
800-424-9346

Recycling not only can reduce the amount of trash being sent to landfills, but can be cost-effective too. It is easy to start simple recycling programs and help is close by. Each state has a recycling office that can give you advice, direction, and information regarding the establishment of recycling efforts. Help varies from state to state but can include recycling literature to distribute to employees, lists of people who will haul away scrap paper, and speakers who will come to your business to educate your employees on recycling. The RCRA Hotline also has several free publications on recycling including: *Recycle* - provides basic information on recycling; and *Recycling Works* - explains the recycling process and takes you through examples of programs in various states.

* Free Health Inspection of Your Workplace

National Institute for Occupational Safety
  and Health
4676 Columbia Parkway
Cincinnati, OH 45226
800-356-4674

The National Institute for Occupational Safety and Health (NIOSH) is responsible for conducting research to make the nation's workplaces healthier and safer by responding to urgent requests for assistance from employers, employees, and their representatives where imminent hazards are suspected. They conduct inspections, laboratory and epidemiologic research, publish their findings, and make recommendations for improved working conditions. They will inspect any workplace for free, if three employees sign a form stating that the environment may be dangerous. Employees

have the option of keeping anonymous. If any of the following applies to you, NIOSH can provide you with more information:

Do you use a video display terminal most of the day?
Are you concerned abut the chemicals you are using in your dry cleaning?
Do you have tingling in your hands (carpal tunnel syndrome)?
Do you use a jackhammer most of the day and are now finding that your fingers are no longer sensitive to heat or cold?
Do you do the same motion again and again, such as on an assembly line? You could be at risk for repetitive motion-associated trauma.
Do you feel your job is causing you mental stress?
Are you having trouble hearing?

* Free Help To Make Your Company A Safe And Healthy Place To Work

Occupational Safety and Health
  Administration
U.S. Dept. of Labor
200 Constitution Ave, NW
Washington, DC 20210
202-219-7266

The Occupational Safety and Health Administration was created to encourage employers and employees to reduce workplace hazards and to implement new, or improve existing, safety and health programs. They provide research on innovative ways of dealing with these problems, maintain a recordkeeping system to monitor job related injuries and illnesses, and develop standards and enforce them, as well as establish training programs.

If you are concerned about the health and safety of your employees, and are having trouble establishing a safe workplace, OSHA will provide free and confidential consultation assistance.

If you have been working hard to clean up your employees' work space, and have reduced the number of injuries occurring on the job, you can be eligible for a Voluntary Protection Program award certificate.

If you are responsible for training your employees on how to work safely in a variety of situations, you can have assess to over 65 high quality, low-cost, training videos.

If you are interested in the safety record of another company, OSHA can provide you with the entire range of inspection data, including who, what, when, where and why companies are inspected and the violations that were found (Contact: Office of Management Data Systems, 202-219-7008).

If you want to take a class to learn more about how to make your workplace safe and healthy for your employees, OSHA has courses covering areas such as electrical hazards, machine guarding, ventilation and ergonomics (Contact: Safety and Health Training Institute, 708-297-4810).

An extensive list of publications is available including:
Controlling Electrical Hazards
Asbestos Standards for the Construction Industry
Hand and Power Tools
Grain Handling
Hearing Conservation
Respiratory Protection
Working Safely with Video Display Terminals
Workplace Health Programs

* Will Your Employees Get Carpal Tunnel Syndrome?

National Institute for Occupational Safety and Health
4676 Columbia Parkway
Cincinnati, Ohio 45226
800-356-4674

Carpal Tunnel Syndrome is a tingling sensation in the hands and fingers and can be caused or aggravated by repeated twisting or awkward postures, particularly when combined with high force. The population at risk includes persons employed in such industries or occupations as construction, food preparation, clerical work, product fabrication and mining. The National Institute for Occupational Safety and Health provides free information on this syndrome including the latest developments in research, preventive recommendations, and bibliographies.

* Are Your Video Display Terminals Making Your Employees Sick?

National Institute for Occupational Safety and Health
4676 Columbia Parkway
Cincinnati, OH 45226
800-356-4674

Over one million people each day sit down to work in front of a computer terminal, imputing and outputting information. There have been concerns about its effect on people's eyesight, its effects on pregnant women, and its potential for causing carpal tunnel syndrome. The National Institute for Occupational Safety and Health offers a free booklet describing the latest research covering all these issues.

* Free Research For Employee's Health Problems

National Health Information Center
ODPHP
P.O. Box 1133
Washington, DC 20013
301-565-4167
800-336-4797

U.S. businesses have begun implementing health education/promotion programs at worksite to help keep employees healthy and to help contain long-term health care costs. Simultaneously, groups of local businesses throughout the country have established coalitions for the purpose of implementing plans to reduce health care costs. Many of these groups view worksite health promotion programs, such as physical fitness, stress management, weight control, smoking cessation, nutrition, and drug and alcohol awareness, as an effective strategy that will contribute to achieving their goals. The National Health Information Center can provide you with publications and brochures on a wide variety of health topics, and can refer you to organizations who can help you set up programs at your place of business. This could be a one day event to test for high blood pressure, a blood donation program, free speakers, or more extensive health promotion programs.

* Cheap Office And Conference Space Overseas

Trade Information Center
U.S. Department of Commerce
Washington, DC 20230
800-USA-TRADE

If you are travelling overseas on a business trip, you may want to look into renting office space and other services through the American Embassy. Depending on the country and the space available, the embassy can provide temporary office space for as low as $25.00 per day, along with translation services, printing and other services. Meeting rooms, seminar or convention space along with promotion services, mailings, freight handling, and even catering may be available in many countries. Contact the field ITA office which is listed later in this chapter or the appropriate country desk officer at the U.S. Department of Commerce in Washington, DC.

* Free Legal Help If You Get Audited

Volunteer and Education Branch
Taxpayer Service Division
Internal Revenue Service
U.S. Department of the Treasury
1111 Constitution Ave., NW, Room 1315
Washington, DC 20224
202-566-6352

Under this program, law and graduate accounting school students are given special permission to practice before the IRS on behalf of taxpayers who cannot afford professional help. Volunteers are needed to help with the

clinic operations or to serve as Student Tax Clinic Directors. Students work under the direction of their professors to handle legal and technical problems. Your local taxpayer education coordinator will inform you of tax clinics in your area.

* Fight The IRS For Free

Problem Resolution Staff
Assistant to the Commissioner
Taxpayer Ombudsman
Internal Revenue Service
U.S. Department of the Treasury
1111 Constitution Ave., NW
Washington, DC 20224
202-566-4948
800-829-1040

A major goal of the Problem Resolution Program (PRP) is to solve tax problems that have not been resolved through normal procedures. PRP represents the interests and concerns of taxpayers within the IRS and seeks to prevent future problems by identifying the root causes of such problems. Each IRS district, service center and regional office has a Problem Resolution Officer (PRO). In resolving problems and protecting taxpayer rights, PROs have authority to intervene to assure IRS actions are correct and appropriate. Effective January 1, 1989, authority to issue Taxpayer Assistance Orders (TAOs) was granted to the Taxpayer Ombudsman. This authority was delegated to the Problem Resolution Officers, as field representatives of the Ombudsman. TAOs may be issued when, in the judgement of the Ombudsman or PRO, a taxpayer is suffering, or is about to suffer a significant hardship as a result of an IRS action or inaction. A TAO can order the function that is handling the taxpayer's case to take appropriate steps to relieve the hardship. The order can also suggest alternative actions to resolve the case. Requests for such relief may be made by taxpayers, their representatives, or by IRS employees on behalf of taxpayers. Contact the IRS toll-free information number regarding tax questions, and ask for Problem Resolution assistance.

* Find Out IF There Is Legislation That Will Affect Your Business

LEGIS
Office of Legislative Information
House Office Building Annex 2
2nd & D Streets, SW, Room 696
Washington, D.C. 20515
202-225-1772

The Bill Status Office can tell you within seconds the latest action on any federal legislation. Every bill and resolution for the current session as well as all House and Senate legislation dating back to 1975 are contained in LEGIS, a computerized database. When you call, it is best to give a key word or phrase (i.e., product liability, hazardous waste) which will help the congressional aides search LEGIS. This office can provide such detailed information as:

Have any bills been introduced covering a given topic?
Who is the sponsor of the bill?
How many cosponsors are there?
When was it introduced?
Which committees have the bills been referred to?
Have any hearings been held?
Has there been any floor action?
Has a similar bill been introduced in the other chamber?
Has there been any action on the other side of the Hill?
Have the House and Senate agreed to a compromise bill?
Has the bill been sent to the White House?
Has the President signed or vetoed the bill?
What is the PL (public law) number?

Telephone assistance is free, and printouts from LEGIS are available for $.20 per page but must be picked up at the Bill Status Office. However, by making arrangements with your Representative's or Senator's office, you can avoid this nominal charge and also have the printout mailed to your home or office.

Free Experts

Free Help in Finding A Free Expert

Not only is the world full of experts who are willing to help resolve your information problems for free, there are organizations whose mission it is to put you in touch with these experts. Here is a list of some of these clearinghouses arranged by subject area. Don't forget to use the Experts Chapter which includes the name and phone number of experts by keyword from aquaculture to zinc. Remember that these experts spend their lives studying specific areas and are waiting to help you for free as long as you treat them right.

* Agriculture and Commodities

Office of Public Affairs, Room 413A
U.S. Department of Agriculture
Washington, DC 20250
202-720-4623

A staff of research specialists are available to provide specific answers or direct you to an expert in any agricultural-related topic.

National Agricultural Library
10301 Baltimore Boulevard
Beltsville, MD 20705-2351
301-504-5755

This library serves as an information clearinghouse.

National Agricultural Statistics Service
U.S. Department of Agriculture, NAS
14th & Independence Avenue SW
Room 4117
South Building
Washington, DC 20250
202-720-3896

The Agricultural Statistics Service (ASS) provides contacts for agricultural production, stocks, prices and other data.

* Arts and Entertainment

Performing Arts Library
John F. Kennedy Center
Washington, DC 20566
202-707-6245

This center which works jointly with the Library of Congress offers reference services on any aspect of the performing arts.

* Best and Worst Industries and Companies

U.S. Department of Commerce
Washington, DC 20230
202-482-2000

Over 100 analysts monitor all the major industries in the U.S. and the companies within these industries ranging from athletic products to truck trailers.

Office of Industries
U.S. International Trade Commission
500 E Street SW
Room 504
Washington, DC 20436
202-205-3296

Experts analyze impact of world trade on U.S. industries ranging from audio components to x-ray apparatus.

* Business Advice

Roadmap Program
U.S. Department of Commerce
14th and Constitution Avenue NW
Washington, DC 20230
202-482-3176

Roadmap Program provides reference services on all aspects of commerce and business.

Library
U.S. Department of Commerce
14th and Constitution Avenue NW
Washington, DC 20230
202-482-5511
This library also provides reference services on all aspects of business.

* Country Experts

Country Officers
U.S. Department of State
2201 C Street NW
Washington, DC 20520
202-647-4000
Hundreds of experts are available to provide current political, economic, and other background information on the country they study. Call to ask for number of specific country officer.

U.S. Department of Commerce
International Trade Administration
Washington, D.C. 20230
202-482-2000
Teams of experts from these regions can provide information on marketing and business practices for every country in the world.

Agricultural and Trade Analysis Division
Economics Research Service
U.S. Department of Agriculture
14th and Independence Ave.
Washington, DC 20005-4788
202-720-8732
This office provides information on agricultural-related aspects of foreign countries.

Foreign Agricultural Services
Information Division
U.S. Department of Agriculture
14th and Independence Avenue, SW
Washington, DC 20250
202-720-9461
The Foreign Agricultural Service (FAS) provides data on world crops, agricultural policies, and markets.

Division of International Minerals
Bureau of Mines
U.S. Department of Interior
810 7th Street, NW, MS 5205
Washington, DC 20241
202-501-9666
Foreign country experts monitor all aspects of foreign mineral industries.

* Crime

National Criminal Justice Reference Service
National Institute of Justice
Box 6000
Rockville, MD 20850
301-251-5500
Database and reference service provide bibliographies and expertise free or sometimes for a nominal fee.

Uniform Crime Reporting Section
Federal Bureau of Investigation
U.S. Department of Justice
409 7th St., NW
Washington, DC 20535
202-324-3000
Statistics are available on eight major crimes against person and property.

* Demographics, Economic and Industry Statistics

Data Users Service Division
Bureau of the Census
Customer Service
Washington, DC 20233
301-763-4100
Staff will guide you to the billions of dollars worth of taxpayer supported data.

* Economics: National, Regional and International

Bureau of Economic Analysis
U.S. Department of Commerce
Washington, DC 20230
202-523-0777
This is the first place to call for economic data.

* Education

Office of Educational Research and
  Improvement
U.S. Department of Education
555 New Jersey Ave., NW
Washington, DC 20208-1235
202-708-5366

A network of 16 information clearinghouses that identify literature, experts, audiovisuals, funding, etc.

Educational Information Branch
Department of Education/OERI
555 New Jersey Avenue, NW
Washington, DC 20208
1-800-424-1616

Hotline provides referrals to other information sources on any aspect of education.

* Energy

National Energy Information Center
U.S. Department of Energy
1F048 Forrestal Building
1000 Independence Ave., SW
Washington, DC 20585
202-586-8800

This office provides general reference services on Department of Energy data.

Conservation and Renewable Energy
Inquiry and Referral Service
P.O. Box 8900
Silver Spring, MD 20907
1-800-523-2929

Free help on how to save energy as well as information on solar, wind, or any other aspect of renewable energy.

U.S. Department of Energy
Office of Scientific and Technical
  Information
P.O. Box 62
Oak Ridge, TN 37831
615-576-1301

This office provides research and other information services on all energy related topics.

* Health

ONHIC
National Health Information Center
PO Box 1133
Washington, DC 20013-1133
1-800-336-4797
301-565-4167 in MD

For leads to both public and private sector health organizations, research centers and universities.

National Center for Health Statistics
U.S. Department of Health and Human
  Services
6525 Belcrest Rd., Room 1064
Presidential Building
Hyattsville, MD 20782
301-436-8500

This clearinghouse can provide data on any aspect of health.

* Housing

Library and Information Services Center
U.S. Department of Housing and Urban
  Development
451 7th Street SW
Washington, DC 20410
202-708-2370

This library provides information on all aspects of housing and staff will direct you to a program which meets your needs.

* Import and Export Statistics

Foreign Trade Reference Room
U.S. Department of Commerce
14th and Constitution Ave., NW
Washington, DC 20230
202-482-2185

This library can provide data on many aspects of U.S. trade.

* Metals and Minerals

Division of Mineral Commodities (Domestic)
Bureau of Mines
U.S. Department of the Interior

810 7th Street, NW
Washington, DC 20241
202-501-9450

Dozens of commodity specialists collect, analyze, and disseminate information on the adequacy and availability of the mineral base for the national economy.

* Prices, Employment, Productivity And Living Conditions Statistics

U.S. Department of Labor
Bureau of Labor Statistics
Washington, DC 20212
202-606-7828

There are subject specialists in such areas as plant closings, labor force projections, producer price indexes, work stoppages.

* World Import and Export Statistics

World Trade Statistics
U.S. Department of Commerce
Room 2233, Herbert Hoover Building
14th and Constitution Ave.
Washington, DC 20230
202-482-5242

This is place for numbers concerning most country's trade.

General Sources

These three offices are the places to get help in locating experts in government as well as the private sector and trade associations.

* Associations

Information Central
American Society of Association Executives
1575 Eye Street NW
Washington, DC 20005
202-626-2723

If you cannot find a relevant association after referring to *Gale's Encyclopedia of Associations* (which is available in most libraries) this organization will help find the right one.

* Government Experts

Federal Information Center
P.O. Box 600
Cumberland, MD 21501-0600
301-722-9000

Centers are located throughout the country and the staff will find you an expert in the government on most any topic.

* Technical Research

Science and Technology Division
Reference Section, Library of Congress
1st and Independence, SE
Washington, DC 20540
202-707-5639

This reference section offers both free and fee-based reference and bibliographic services.

State Starting Places For Finding Experts

If you have trouble locating the exact office you need from the listings elsewhere in the book, this is the section for you. The first place you should start is with State Information Offices listed below. The operators at these offices are normally trained to handle information requests from people who don't know where to go within the state bureaucracy. If you are not successful, try either or both of the other offices listed.

Governor's Office

Because the responsibilities of various state offices often overlap, it may be helpful to begin your data search by contacting the state governor's office. While every state has a central switchboard to field inquiries regarding state business, the number is usually helpful only if you already know which agency is responsible for gathering and interpreting the information you are after. If you are hazy in this regard, the state governor's office will certainly know the appropriate agency department and, if you are lucky, even the name of the special contact person to call.

State Library

A vast amount of research information is available from the state library. After all, it is the official repository of state agency documents and the first place to start if you want to do all of the footwork yourself. In addition, most state libraries also shelve copies of federal government documents and publications.

State libraries are paid for with tax dollars and are open to the public. Collections usually include state legal codes, state historical documents, archival records, genealogy type information, business and economic records, statistical abstracts and annual reports.

In each library these is generally a government information person who can provide telephone and personal assistance to researchers. In addition, there is often a staff specialist to help with statistical questions.

The following is a list of state operators, librarians, and governor's offices.

State Information and Governor's Offices

Alabama
State Information: 205-242-8000

Governor's Office: Office of the Governor, Statehouse, 11 South Union St., Montgomery, AL 36130; 205-242-7100.

State Library: Alabama Public Library Service, 6030 Monticello Drive, Montgomery, AL 36130; 205-277-7330.

Alaska
State Information: 907-465-2111

Governor's Office: Office of the Governor, P.O. Box 110001, Juneau, AK 99811; 907-465-3500.

State Library: Libraries and Museums, P.O. Box 110571, Juneau, AK 99811-0571; 907-465-2920.

Arizona
State Information: 602-542-4900

Governor's Office: Office of Office of the Governor, 1700 West Washington St., Phoenix, AZ 85007; 602-542-4331.

State Library: Department of Library Archives and Public Records, State Capitol, Room 442, 1700 W. Washington, St., Phoenix, AZ 85007; 602-542-4159.

Arkansas

State Information: 501-682-3000

Governor's Office: Office of the Governor, State Capitol Building, Room 250, Little Rock, AR 72201; 501-682-2345.

State Library: Arkansas State Library, 1 Capitol Mall, Little Rock, AR 72201; 501-682-1527.

California

State Information: 916-322-9900

Governor's Office: Office of the Governor, State Capitol, Sacramento, CA 95814; 916-445-2841.

State Library: California State Library, Library and Courts Building, Sacramento, CA 95814; 916-654-0261.

Colorado

State Information: 303-866-5000

Governor's Office: Office of the Governor, 136 State Capitol Building, Denver, CO 80203-1792; 303-866-2471.

State Library: Colorado State Library, 201 East Colfax Ave., Denver, CO 80203; 303-866-4799.

Connecticut

State Information: 203-240-0222

Governor's Office: Office of the Governor, Executive Chambers, Room 202, Hartford, CT 06106; 203-566-4840.

State Library: Connecticut State Library, 231 Capitol Ave., Hartford, CT 06115; 203-566-3056.

Delaware

State Information: 302-739-4000

Governor's Office: Office of the Governor, Tatnall Bldg., William Penn Street, Dover, DE 19901; 302-739-4101.

State Library: Delaware State Library, 43 South DuPont Highway, Dover, DE 19901; 302-739-4748.

District of Columbia

Information: 202-727-1000

Mayor's Office: Executive Office of the Mayor, 441 4th NW, Room 1100, 1 Judiciary Square, Washington, DC 20001; 202-727-2980.

Central Library: Martin Luther King, Jr. Memorial Library, 901 G St. NW, Washington, DC 20001; 202-727-1101.

Florida

State Information: 904-488-1234

Governor's Office: Office of the Governor, The Capitol, Tallahassee, FL 32399-0001; 904-488-4441.

State Library: Florida State Library, R.A. Gray Building, 500 Bruno St., Tallahassee, FL 32399; 904-487-2651.

Georgia

State Information: 404-656-2000

Governor's Office: Office of the Governor, 203 State Capitol, Atlanta, GA 30334; 404-656-1776.

State Library: Georgia State Library, 156 Trinity Ave, Atlanta, GA 30303; 404-656-2462.

Hawaii

State Information: 808-548-6222

Governor's Office: Office of the Governor, State Capitol, Honolulu, HI 96813; 808-548-5420.

State Library: Hawaii State Library, 478 South King St., Honolulu, HI 96813; 808-548-4775.

Idaho

State Information: 208-334-2411

Governor's Office: Office of the Governor, State House, Boise, ID 83720; 208-334-2100.

State Library: Idaho State Library, 325 West State St., Boise, ID 83720; 208- 334-5124.

Illinois

State Information: 217-782-2000

Governor's Office: Office of the Governor, State Capitol, Springfield, IL 62706; 217-782-6830.

State Library: Illinois State Library, 300 S. 2nd Street, Springfield, IL 62701; 217-782-7848.

Indiana

State Information: 317-232-1000

Governor's Office: Office of the Governor, State House, 100 N. Capitol Ave. Indianapolis, IN 46204; 317-232-4567.

State Library: Indiana State Library, 140 North Senate, Indianapolis, IN 46204; 317-232-3675.

Iowa

State Information: 515-281-5011

Governor's Office: Office of the Governor, State Capitol, Des Moines, IA 50319; 515-281-5211.

State Library: Iowa State Library, East 12th and Grand Streets, Des Moines, IA 50319; 515-281-4118.

Kansas

State Information: 913-296-0111

Governor's Office: Office of the Governor, State House, Topeka, KS 66612; 913-296-3232.

State Library: Kansas State Library, State House, Topeka, KS 66612; 913-296-3296.

Kentucky

State Information: 502-564-3130

Governor's Office: Office of the Governor, State Capitol Building, Frankfort, KY 40601; 502-564-2611.

State Library: Kentucky State Library, 700 Capitol Ave., #200, Frankfort, KY 40601-3489; 502-564-4848.

Louisiana

State Information: 504-342-6600

Governor's Office: Office of the Governor, P.O. Box 94004, Baton Rouge, LA 70804; 504-342-7015.

State Library: Louisiana State Library, P.O. Box 131, Baton Rouge, LA 70821; 504-342-4923.

Maine

State Information: 207-582-9500

Governor's Office: Office of the Governor, State House Station 1, Augusta, ME 04333; 207-287-3531.

State Library: Maine State Library, State House, Station 83, Augusta, ME 04333; 207-287-5600.

Maryland

State Information: 410-974-2000

Governor's Office: Office of the Governor, State House, Annapolis, MD 21404; 410-974-3901.

State Library: Maryland State Archives, Hall of Records, 350 Rowe Boulevard, Annapolis, MD 21404; 410-974-3914.

Massachusetts

State Information: 617-722-2000

Governor's Office: Office of the Governor, State House, Boston, MA 02133; 617-727-3600.

State Library: 341 State Street, Boston, MA 02133; 617-727-2590.

Michigan

State Information: 517-373-1837

Governor's Office: Office of the Governor, State Capitol Building, Lansing, MI 48913; 517-373-3400.

State Library: Michigan State Library, 717 W. Allegan, Lansing, MI 48909; 517-373-5400.

Minnesota

State Information: 612-296-6013

Governor's Office: Office of the Governor, 130 State Capitol, St. Paul, MN 55155; 612-296-3391.

State Library: Legislative Reference Library, State Office Building, St. Paul, MN 55155; 612-296-3398.

Mississippi

State Information: 601-359-1000

Governor's Office: Office of the Governor, P.O. Box 139, Jackson, MS 39205; 601-359-3150.

State Library: Department of Archives and History Library, P.O. Box 571, Jackson, MS 39205; 601-359-6850.

Missouri

State Information: 314-751-2000

Governor's Office: Office of the Governor, State Capitol, P.O. Box 720, Jefferson City, MO 65102-0720; 314-751-3222.

State Library: Missouri State Library, P.O. Box 387, Jefferson City, MO 65102-0387; 314-751-3615.

Montana

State Information: 406-444-2511

Governor's Office: Office of the Governor, State Capitol, Helena, MT 59620; 406-444-3111.

State Library: Montana State Library, 1515 East 6th Ave., Helena, MT 59620; 406-444-3115.

Nebraska

State Information: 402-471-2311

Governor's Office: Office of the Governor, State Capitol, P.O. Box 94848, Lincoln, NE 68509-4848; 402-471-2244.

State Library: Nebraska State Library, P.O. Box 98910, Lincoln, NE 68509-8910; 402-471-3189.

Nevada

State Information: 702-687-5000

Governor's Office: Office of the Governor, State Capitol Bldg., Carson City, NV 89710; 702-687-5670.

State Library: Nevada State Library, 100 Sewart St., Carson City, NV 89710; 702-687-5160.

New Hampshire

State Information: 603-271-1110

Governor's Office: Office of the Governor, State House, Concord, NH 03301; 603-271-2121.

State Library: New Hampshire State Library, 20 Park St., Concord, NH 03301; 603-271-2394.

New Jersey

State Information: 609-292-2121

Governor's Office: Office of the Governor, 125 West State St., State House, Trenton, NJ 08625; 609-292-6000.

State Library: New Jersey State Library, State House Annex, CN 520, Trenton, NJ; 609-292-6220.

New Mexico

State Information: 505-827-4011

Governor's Office: Office of the Governor, State Capitol Building, Santa Fe, NM 87503; 505-827-3000.

Governor's Office: State Library: New Mexico State Library, 325 Don Gaspar, Santa Fe, NM 87503; 505-827-3800.

New York

State Information: 518-474-2121

Governor's Office: Office of the Governor, State Capitol, Albany, NY 12224; 518-474-5355.

State Library: New York State Library, Empire State Plaza, Madison Avenue, Albany, NY 12230; 518-474-5355.

North Carolina

State Information: 919-733-1110

Governor's Office: Office of the Governor, State Capitol, Raleigh, NC 27603; 919-733-5811.

State Library: North Carolina State Library, 109 East Jones St., Raleigh, NC 27611; 919-733-2570.

North Dakota

State Information: 701-224-2000

Governor's Office: Office of the Governor, State Capitol, Bismarck, ND 58505; 701-224-2200.

State Library: North Dakota State Library, State Capitol, Bismarck, ND 58505; 701-224-2490.

Ohio

State Information: 614-466-2000

Governor's Office: Office of the Governor, State House, Columbus, OH 43215; 614-466-3555.

State Library: Ohio State Library, 65 South Front St., Columbus, OH 43266; 614-644-7061.

Oklahoma

State Information: 405-521-1601

Governor's Office: Office of the Governor, 212 State Capitol, Oklahoma City, OK 73105; 405-521-2342.

State Library: Oklahoma State Library, 200 N.E. 18th St., Oklahoma City, OK 73105; 405-521-2502.

Oregon

State Information: 503-378-3131

Governor's Office: Office of the Governor, 254 State Capitol, Salem, OR 97310; 503-378-3100.

State Library: Oregon State Library, State Library Building, Salem, OR 97310; 503-378-4274.

Pennsylvania

State Information: 717-787-2121

Governor's Office: Office of the Governor, 225 Main Capitol Bldg., Harrisburg, PA 17120; 717-787-5962.

State Library: Pennsylvania State Library, P.O. Box 1601, Harrisburg, PA 17105; 717-787-5718.

Rhode Island

State Information: 401-277-2000

Governor's Office: Office of the Governor, 222 State House, Providence, RI 02903; 401-277-2080.

State Library: Rhode Island State Library, Room 208, State House, Providence, RI 02903; 401-277-2473.

South Carolina

State Information: 803-734-1000

Governor's Office: Office of the Governor, P.O. Box 11369, Columbia, SC 29211; 803-734-9818.

State Library: South Carolina State Library, P.O. Box 11469, Columbia, SC 29225; 803-734-8666.

South Dakota

State Information: 605-773-3011

Governor's Office: Office of the Governor, State Capitol, Pierre, SD 57501; 605-773-3212.

State Library: South Dakota State Library, 500 E. Capitol, Pierre, SD 57501; 605-773-3131.

Tennessee

State Information: 615-741-3011

Governor's Office: Office of the Governor, State Capitol, Nashville, TN 37219; 615-741-2001.

State Library: Tennessee State Library, 403 7th Ave. North, Nashville, TN 37243; 615-741-2764.

Texas

State Information: 512-463-4630

Governor's Office: Office of the Governor, P.O. Box 12428, Austin, TX 78711; 512-463-2000.

State Library: Texas State Library, P.O. Box 12927, Austin, TX 78711; 512-463-5455.

Utah

State Information: 801-538-3000

Governor's Office: Office of the Governor, Room 210, State Capitol, Salt Lake City, UT 84114; 801-538-1000.

State Library: Utah State Library, 2150 South 300 West, Suite 16, Salt Lake City, UT 84115; 801-466-5888.

Vermont

State Information: 802-828-1110

Governor's Office: Office of the Governor, 109 State Street, Montpelier, VT 05609-0101; 802-828-3333.

State Library: Vermont State Library, 109 State Street, Montpelier, VT 05609-0601; 802-828-3261.

Virginia

State Information: 804-786-0000

Governor's Office: Office of the Governor, P.O. Box 1475, Richmond, VA 23212; 804-786-2211.

State Library: Virginia State Library, 11th St and Capitol Square, Richmond, VA 23219; 804-786-8929.

Washington

State Information: 206-753-5000

Governor's Office: Office of the Governor, Legislative Building, Olympia, WA 98504; 206-753-6780.

State Library: Washington State Library, Capitol Campus, Mail Stop AJ-11, Olympia, WA 98504; 206-753-5590.

West Virginia

State Information: 304-558-3456

Governor's Office: Office of the Governor, Main Capitol Complex, Charleston, WV 25305; 304-558-2000.

State Library: West Virginia State Library, Cultural Center, Charleston, WV 25305; 304-558-2041.

Wisconsin

State Information: 608-266-2211

Governor's Office: Office of the Governor, 115 E. Capitol, Madison, WI 53702; 608-266-1212.

State Library: State Historical Society, 816 State St., Madison, WI 53706; 608-264-6534.

Wyoming

State Information: 307-777-7011

Governor's Office: Office of the Governor, State Capitol, Cheyenne, WY 82002; 307-777-7434.

State Library: Wyoming State Library, Supreme Court Building, 23rd and Capitol, Cheyenne, WY 82002; 307-777-7283.

11,500 Free Industry, Economic, and Demographic Experts

You may have heard of the "seven-phone call rule" for tracking down an expert who will help you for free. Well, now you can throw that phrase out the window. With this handy list of 11,500 government experts you are likely to find the right subject specialist in only ONE phone call.

Do you have a new idea to revolutionize the crayon market? Shetty Sundar at the U.S. International Trade Commission has spent her career analyzing this market. Want to know how many women-owned businesses there are in the United States? Contact Elaine Emanuel at the Bureau of Census and she will give you the official data. You'll find 60 bureaucrats listed in this chapter who are experts in computers and

the computer industry. You will also find experts on sewing machines, eggs, fish nets, and robots. Remember each of these professionals has devoted his or her life work to studying a specific area and will share their knowledge without charging a penny **just as long as you treat them right.** (Refer to the *How To Start a Home-Based Business* chapter, specifically "The Art of Getting a Bureaucrat to Help You" and "Case Study: Jelly Beans", for guidance on how to deal with bureaucrats.)

The abbreviations for the federal agency which precede an expert's telephone number are spelled out below. If you have trouble with a telephone number, after all, numbers change all the time, simply contact the agency directly.

AARP =	American Association of Retired Parents, 601 E Street, NW, Washington, DC 20049
ABLEDATA =	ABLEDATA, 8455 Colesville Road, Suite 935, Silver Spring, MD 20910
ACCESS =	The Access Group, 1776 Peachtree Road, NW, Atlanta, GA 30309
ACTIS =	AIDS Clinical Trials Information Service, P.O. Box 6421, Rockville, MD 20849
ACYF =	Administration for Children and Youth and Families, HHS, 901 D St., SW, Washington, DC 20447
ADEAR =	Alzheimer's Disease Education and Referral (ADEAR) Center, P.O. Box 8250, Silver Spring, MD 20907
AGRI =	National Agriculture Statistics Service, U.S. Department of Agriculture, 14th and Independence Avenue, SW, Washington, DC 20250
AHCPR =	Agency for Health Care Policy and Research, HHS, 2101 East Jefferson St., Ste. 501, Rockville, MD 20852
AHCPR =	AHCPR Clearinghouse, P.O. Box 8547, Silver Spring, MD 20907
AID =	Agency for International Development, 2201 C Street NW, Washington, DC 20523
AIDS =	AIDS Action Committee of Massachusetts, 131 Clarendon Street, Boston, MA 02116
ALM =	ALM International (American Leprosy Missions), One ALM Way, Greenville, SC 29601
ALSA =	Amyotrophic Lateral Sclerosis Association, 21021 Ventura Boulevard, Suite 321, Woodland Hills, CA 91364
AMC =	AMC Cancer Information and Counseling Line, 1600 Pierce Street, Denver, CO 80214
AOA =	Administration on Aging, HHS, 330 Independence Avenue, Washington, DC 20201
ASH =	Assistant Secretary for Health, HHS, 200 Independence Avenue, SW, Room 719-H, Hubert Humphrey Bldg., Washington, DC 20201
ATSDR =	Agency for Toxic Substances and Disease Registry, HHS, 1600 Clifton Rd., NE, Mail Stop 828, Atlanta, GA 30333
BEHCETS =	American Behcet's Association Inc.,P.O. Box 54963, Minneapolis, MN 55454
BEIB =	Biomedical Engineering and Instrumentation Branch, NIH, 9000 Rockville Pike, Bldg. 13, Bethesda, MD 20892
BHCDA =	Bureau of Health Care Delivery and Assistance, HHS, 5600 Fishers Lane, Room 7-05, Rockville, MD 20857
BJSCONTA =	U.S. Department of Justice, 10th and Constitution Avenue, NW, Washington, DC 20530
CC =	Clinical Center, NIH, 9000 Rockville Pike, Bldg. 10, Bethesda, MD 20892
CDC =	Centers for Disease Control, HHS, Room 2067, Bldg. 1, Atlanta, GA 30333
CENSUS =	Data Users Service Division, Customer Service, Bureau of Census, U.S. Department of Commerce, Washington, DC 20233
CNTYCOM =	Country Desk Officers, International Trade Administration, U.S. Department of Commerce, Washington, DC 20230
CNTYMINE =	Bureau of Mines, U.S. Department of Interior, 810 7th St., NW, Washington, DC 20241
CNTY STATE =	United States Department of State, 2201 C St., NW, Washington, DC 20520
COMMERCE =	Industry Experts, Public Affairs, International Trade Administration, U.S. Department of Commerce, Washington, DC 20230

CPSC =	Consumer Product Safety Commission, 4330 East West Highway, Bethesda, MD 20814
CUSTOMS =	U.S. Customs Service, Department of the Treasury, Customs Information Exchange, U.S. Customhouse, Code 20437, 6 World Trade Center, New York, NY 10048
DAS =	Division of Administrative Services, NIH, Building 1, 9000 Rockville Pike, Bethesda, MD 20892
DC =	District of Columbia
DCRT =	Division of Computer Research and Technology, NIH, 9000 Rockville Pike, Bethesda, MD 20892
DEO =	Division of Equal Opportunity, NIH, 9000 Rockville Pike, Bldg. 31, Bethesda, MD 20892
DMCH =	Division of Maternal and Child Health, HHS, 5600 Fishers Lane, Rockville, MD 20857
DN =	Division of Nursing, HHS, 5600 Fishers Lane, Rockville, MD 20857
DOT =	Department of Transportation, 400 7th Street, SW, Washington, DC 20590
DPCS =	Division of Primary Care Services, HHS, 5600 Fishers Lane, Rockville, MD 20857
DPM =	Division of Personnel Management, NIH, 9000 Rockville Pike, Bldg. 1, Bethesda, MD 20892
DRG =	Division of Research Resources, NIH, 9000 Rockville Pike, Bldg. 31, Bethesda, MD 20892
DRR =	Division of Research Resources, NIH, 9000 Rockville Pike, Bldg. 31, Bethesda, MD 20892
DRS =	Division of Research Services, NIH, 9000 Rockville Pike, Bldg. 12, Room 4007, Bethesda, MD 20892
ECONOMICS =	Bureau of Economic Analysis, U.S. Department of Commerce, Washington, DC 20230
EPA =	Environmental Protection Agency, 401 M St., Washington, DC 20460
EX-IM Bank =	Export - Import Bank, 811 Vermont Avenue, NW, Washington, DC 20571
FAA =	Federal Aviation Administration, 800 Independence Avenue, SW, Washington DC 20591
FAES =	Foundation for Advanced Education in the Sciences, Inc., NIH, One Cloister Court, Building 60, Suite 230, Bethesda, MD 20814-1460
FCC =	Federal Communications Commission, 1919 M St., NW, Room 734, Washington, DC 20554-0001
FDA =	Food and Drug Administration, HHS, 5600 Fishers Lane, Room 1505 Parklawn Bldg., Rockville, MD 20857
FHWA =	Federal Highway Administration, 400 7th Street, SW, Washington, DC 20590
FIC =	Fogarty International Center, NIH, 9000 Rockville Pike, Bldg. 38, Bethesda, MD 20892
FRA =	Federal Railroad Administration, 400 7th Street, SW, Washington, DC 20590
FRS =	Federal Reserve System, Twentieth Street and Constitution Avenue, NW, Washington, DC 20551
FS =	Forest Service, U.S. Department of Agriculture, Auditors Building, 201 14th Street, S.W., Washington, DC 20250
FWS =	Fish and Wildlife Service, Department of the Interior, 1849 C Street, N.W., Washington, DC 20240
FTC =	Federal Trade Commission, 6th St. and Pennsylvania Avenue, NW, Washington, DC 20580
GAO =	Government Accounting Office, 441 G Street, NW, Washington, DC 20548
HCFA =	Health Care Financing Administration, HHS, 200 Independence Avenue, SW, Room 435-H, Hubert Humphrey Bldg., Washington, DC 20201
HHS =	Regional Directors, Health and Human Services, Room 638-E, Hubert Humphrey Bldg., 200 Independence Avenue, SW, Washington, DC 20201
HHSREG =	Regional Directors, Health and Human Services, Room 638-E, Hubert Humphrey Bldg., 200 Independence Avenue, SW, Washington, DC 20201
HRSA =	Health Resources and Services Administration, HHS, 5600 Fisher Lane, Room 1443, Parklawn Bldg., Rockville, MD 20857
IHS =	Indian Health Service, HHS, Room 6-35, Parklawn Bldg., Rockville, MD 20857
IG =	Inspector General, Office of, HHS, 330 Independence Avenue, SW, Room 5259, HHS Cohen Bldg., Washington, DC 20201
LABOR =	Bureau of Labor Statistics, U.S. Department of Labor, 2 Massachusetts Avenue, NW, Washington, DC 20212
MAPB =	Medical Arts and Photography Branch, 9000 Rockville Pike, Bldg. 10, Bethesda, MD 20892
MD =	Maryland
MINES =	Division of Mineral Commodities, U.S. Department of Interior, 810 7th St., NW, Washington, DC 20241
NAPARE =	National Center for Perinatal Addiction, Research and Education, 200 North Michigan Avenue, Suite 300, Chicago, IL 60601
NAL =	National Agricultural Library, Beltsville, MD 20705
NASA =	National Aeronautics and Space Administration, Washington, DC 20546
NCDB =	National Center for Drugs and Biolgics, NIH, 9000 Rockville Pike, Bldg. 29, Bethesda, MD 20892
NCHS =	National Center for Health Statistics, HHS, 6525 Bellcrest Rd., Hyattsville, MD 20782
NCI =	National Cancer Institute, NIH, 9000 Rockville Pike, Bldg. 31, Bethesda, MD 20892
NCNR =	National Center for Nursing Research, NIH, 9000 Rockville Pike, Bldg. 31, Bethesda, MD 20892
NEA =	National Endowment for the Arts, 1100 Pennsylvania Avenue, N.W., Washington DC 20506
NEH =	National Endowment for the Humanities, 1100 Pennsylvania Avenue, N.W., Washington, DC 20506
NEI =	National Eye Institute, NIH, 9000 Rockville Pike, Bldg. 31, Bethesda, MD 20892
NEIC =	National Energy Information Center, Energy Information Administration, Department of Energy, E1-231, Forrestal Bldg., Washington, DC 20585
NHLBI =	National Heart, Lung, and Blood Institute, NIH, 9000 Rockville Pike, Bldg. 31, Bethesda, MD 20892
NHTSA =	National Highway Traffic Safety Administration, 400 7th Street, SW, Washington, DC 20590
NIA =	National Institute on Aging, NIH, 9000 Rockville Pike, Bldg. 31, Bethesda, MD 20892
NIAID =	National Institute of Allergy and Infectious Diseases, NIH, 9000 Rockville Pike, Bldg. 31, Bethesda, MD 20892
NIAMS =	National Institute of Arthritis and Musculoskeletal and Skin Diseases, 9000 Rockville Pike, Bldg. 31, Bethesda, MD 20892
NICHD =	National Institute of Child Health and Human Development, NIH, 9000 Rockville Pike, Bldg. 31, Bethesda, MD 20892
NIDA =	National Institute on Drug Abuse, HHS, 5600 Fishers Lane, Rockville, MD 20857
NIDDK =	National Institute of Diabetes and Digestive and Kidney Diseases, NIH, 9000 Rockville Pike, Bldg. 31, Bethesda, MD 20892
NIDR =	National Institute of Dental Research, NIH, 9000 Rockville Pike, Bldg. 31, Bethesda, MD 20892
NIEHS =	National Institute of Environmental Health Sciences, NIH, Research Triangle Park, NC 27709

Free Experts

NIGMS =	National Institute of General Medical Sciences, NIH, 5333 Westbard Avenue, Room 926, Bethesda, MD 20892
NIH =	National Institutes for Health, 9000 Rockville Pike, Bldg 1, Room 126, Bethesda, MD 20892
NIMH =	National Institute of Mental Health, NIH, 5600 Fishers Lane, Rockville, MD 20857
NINDS =	National Institute of Neurological Disorders and Stroke, 9000 Rockville Pike, Bldg. 31, Bethesda, MD 20892
NIST =	National Institute of Standards and Technology, Gaithersburg, MD 20899
NRC =	United States Nuclear Regulatory Commission, 11555 Rockville Pike, Rockville, MD 30852
NLM =	National Library of Medicine, 8600 Rockville Pike, Bethesda, MD 20894
NTSB =	National Transportation Safety Board, 490 L'Enfant Plaza, SW, Washington DC 20594
OB =	Office of Biologics, NIH, 9000 Rockville Pike, Bldg. 29, Bethesda, MD 20892
OCA =	Office of Consumer Affairs, HHS, 1620 L St., NW, Ste. 700, Washington, DC 20036
OC =	Office of Communications, NIH, 9000 Rockville Pike, Bldg. 1, Bethesda, MD 20892
OCR =	Office for Civil Rights, HHS, 300 Independence Avenue, SW, Room 5044, HHS Cohen Bldg., Washington, DC 20201
OD =	Office of the Director, NIH, 9000 Rockville Pike, Bldg. 1, Bethesda, MD 20892
OERT =	Office of Extramural Research and Training, NIH, P.O. Box 12233, Research Triangle Park, NC 27709
OHDS =	Office of Human Development Services, HHS, 200 Independence Avenue, SW, Washington DC 20201
OPIC =	Overseas Private Investment Corporation, 1100 New York Avenue, NW, Washington, DC 20527
OPM =	Office of Personnel Management, 1900 E Street, NW, Washington, DC 20415
OPRR =	Office for Protection from Research Risks, NIH, 9000 Rockville Pike, Bldg. 31, Bethesda, MD 20892
ORS =	Office of Research Services, NIH, 9000 Rockville Pike, Bldg. 1, Bethesda, MD 20892
PEC =	Peace Corps, 1990 K St., NW, Washington, DC 20526
PHS =	Public Health Service, HHS, Office of Communication, 200 Independence Avenue, SW, Washington, DC 20201
PTO =	Patent and Trademark Office, Crystal Mall 1, 1911 Jefferson Davis Highway, Arlington, VA 22202
SAMHSA =	Substance Abuse and Mental Health Service Administration, 5600 Fishers Lane, Rockville, MD 20857
SBA =	Small Business Administration, 409 third Street, SW, Washington, DC 20416
SEC =	United States Securities and Exchange Commission, 450 5th Street, NW, Washington, DC 20549
SSA =	Social Security Administration, 6401 Security Blvd., Room 932, Altmeyer Bldg., Baltimore, MD 21235
SSAREG =	Public Information Contacts, Social Security Administration, 6401 Security Blvd., Room 932, Altmeyer Bldg., Baltimore, MD 21235
TRADREP =	Office of the U.S. Trade Representative, 600 17th St., NW, Washington, DC 20506
Treasury =	Department of the Treasury, 1500 Pennsylvania Avenue, NW, Washington, DC 20220
USITC =	Office of Industries, U.S. International Trade Commission, 500 E. St., SW, Washington, DC 20436
UMD =	University of Maryland, University of Maryland-College Park, College Park, MD 20742
USCG =	United States Coast Guard, 2100 2nd Street, SW, Washington, DC 20593
USIA =	United States Information Agency, 301 4th Street, SW, Washington, DC 20547
UVA =	University of Virginia, Office of Television News, Booker House, PO Box 9018, Charlottesville, VA 22906-9018
VA =	Virginia
VIC =	Visitor Information Center, NIH, 9000 Rockville Pike, Bldg.10, Bethesda, MD 20892
VRP =	Veterinary Resources Program, NIH, 9000 Rockville Pike, Bldg. 14, Bethesda, MD 20892
World Bank =	World Bank, 1818 H Street, NW, Washington DC 20433

Addresses for Non-abbreviated Organizations

Advocacy Center for the Elderly and Disabled, 210 O'Keefe Avenue, Suite 700, New Orleans, LA 70112

Aeronational, P.O. Box 538, Washington, PA 15301

Air Ambulance America, 5804 Sunset Drive, Miami, FL 33156

Al-Anon, Alateen Family Group, P.O. Box 862, Midtown Station, New York, NY 10018

Alcohol and Drug Helpline, 4578 Highland Drive, Salt Lake City, UT 84117

Alcohol Rehab for the Elderly, P.O. Box 267, Hopedale, IL 61747

Alliance of Genetic Support Groups, 35 Wisconsin Circle, Suite 440, Chevy Chase, MD 20815

Alzheimer's Association, 919 N. Michigan Ave., Suite 1000, Chicago, IL 60611

American Academy of Allergy and Immunology, 611 East Wells Street, Milwaukee, WI 53202

American Academy of Facial Plastic and Reconstructive Surgery, 1101 Vermont Avenue, Suite 304, NW, Washington, DC 20005

American Academy of Family Physicians, 8880 Ward Pkwy., Kansas City, MO 64114

American Association of Kidney Patients, 100 S. Ashley Dr., Suite 280, Tampa, FL 33602

American Board of Medical Specialists, 47 Perimeter Center East, Suite 500, Atlanta, GA 30346

American Cancer Society, 1599 Clifton Road, NE, Atlanta, GA 30329

American Chiropractic Association, 1701 Clarendon Blvd., Arlington, VA 22209

American College of Legal Medicine, 611 East Wells St., Milwaukee, WI 53202

American College of Physicians, Independence Mall West, Sixth Street at Race, Philadelphia, PA 19106

American Council on Alcoholism, 5024 Campbell Boulevard, Suite H, Baltimore, MD 21236

American Council of the Blind (ACB), 1155 15th Street, Suite 720, NW, Washington, DC 20005

American Diabetes Association, 1660 Duke Street, Alexandria, VA 22314

American Foundation for the Blind, 15 West 16th Street, New York, NY 10011

American Heart Association, 415 North Charles Street, P.O. Box 17025, Baltimore, MD 21203

American Heart Association Stroke Connection, 7272 Greenville Avenue, Dallas, TX 75231

American Institute for Preventive Medicine, 30445 Northwestern Highway, Suite 350, Farmingham Hills, MI 48334

American Kidney Fund, 6110 Executive Blvd, Suite 1010, Rockville, MD 20852

American Liver Foundation Hepatitus Hotline, 1425 Pompton Avenue, Cedar Grove, NJ 07009

American Lupus Society, 3914 Del Arno Blvd., Suite 922, Torrance, CA 90503

American Mental Health Counselors Association, 5999 Stevenson Avenue, Alexandria, VA 22304

American Osteopathic Association, 142 East Ontario Street, Chicago, IL 60611

American Paralysis Association, 500 Morris Avenue, Springfield, NJ 07081

American Parkinson's Disease Association, 60 Bay Street, Suite 401, Staten Island, NY 10301

American Social Health Association, P.O. Box 13827, Research Triangle Park, NC 27709

American Society for Dermatologic Surgery, 930 Meachum, Schaumburg, IL 60173

American Society for Psychoprophylaxis in Obstetrics (ASPO/Lamaze), 1200 19th Street, Suite 300, NW, Washington, DC 20036

American Society of Plastic and Reconstructive Surgeons, 444 East Algonquin Road, Arlington Heights, IL 60005

American Speech-Language-Hearing Association Consumer Hotline, 10801 Rockville Pike, Kensington, MD 20852

American Trauma Society, 8903 Presidential Parkway, Suite 512, Upper Marlboro, MD 20772

Ankylosing Spondylitis Association, 511 North La Cienga, Suite 216, Los Angeles, CA 90048

Aplastic Anemia Foundation of America, P.O. Box 22689, Baltimore, MD 21201

Arthritis Consulting Service, 4620 North State Road 7, Suite 206, Ft. Lauderdale, FL 33319

Arthritis Foundation, 1314 Spring Street NW, Atlanta, GA 30309

Association of American Physcians and Surgeons, 1601 North Tucson Boulevard, Suite 9, Tucson, AZ 85716

Association of Surgical Technologists, 7108 S. Alton Way, Englewood, CO, 80112

Asthma and Allergy Foundation of America, 1125 15th Street, Suite 502, NW, Washington, DC 20005

Atrial Fibrillation (AF) Hotline, 625 N. Michigan Ave., Chicago, IL 60611

Back Pain Hotline, 3801 West 15th Street, Plano, TX 75075

Batten Disease Support and Research Association, 2600 Parsons Ave., Colombus, OH 43207

Be Healthy Inc., 51 Saltrock Road, Baltic, CT 06330

Better Hearing Institute Hearing Helpline, 5021-B Backlick Rd., Annandale, VA 22003

Blind Children's Center, 4120 Marathon St., P.O. Box 29159, Los Angeles, CA 90029

Blinded Veterans Association, 477 H Street, NW, Washington DC 20001

Bowman Gray School of Medicine, Epilepsy Information Service, Medical Center Boulevard, Winston-Salem, NC 27157

Braille Institute, 741 North Vermont Avenue, Los Angeles, CA 90029

Candlelighters Childhood Cancer Foundation, 7910 Woodmont Avenue, Suite 400, Bethesda, MD 20814

CDC National AIDS Clearinghouse, P.O. Box 6003, Rockville, MD 20849

Chemical Information Referral Center, 2501 M St., NW, Washington, DC 20037

Child Find of America, P.O. Box 277, New Paltz, NY 12561

Child Help USA, 6463 Independence Avenue, Woodland Hills, CA 91367

Child Research, 155 Plan Way, Warwick, RI 02886

Children's Craniofacial Association, 10210 North Central Expressway, Suite 230, Dallas, TX 75231

Children's Hospice International, 700 Princess Street, Alexandria, VA 22314

Chronic Fatigue and Immune Dysfunction Syndrome Association (CFIDS), P.O. Box 220398, Charlotte, NC 28222

Cleft Palate Foundation, 1218 Grandview Avenue, Pittsburgh, PA 15211

Coast Guard Hotline, 2100 Second Street, SW, Washington, DC 20593

Cocaine Anonymous, 3740 Overland Avenue, Suite G, Los Angeles, CA 90034

Contact Lens Manufacturers Association, 421 King St., Suite 224, Alexandria, VA 22314

Cooley's Anemia Foundation, 29-09 26th Avenue, Flushing, NY 11354

Cornelia de Lange Syndrome Foundation, 60 Dyer Ave., Collinsville, CT 06022

Covenant House, 346 West 17th Street, New York, NY 10011

Crohn's and Colitis Foundation of America, 386 Park Avenue South, 17th Floor, New York, NY 10016-8804

Cystic Fibrosis Foundation, 6931 Arlington Road, Bethesda, MD 20814

Deafness Research Foundation, Nine E. 38th St., 7th Fl., New York, NY 10016

Delaware Divison of Aging, Department of Health and Social Services, 1901 North Dupont Highway, New Castle, DE 19720

Inspector General's Hotline, P.O. Box 17303, Baltimore, MD 29303

Devereux Foundation, 19 South Waterloo Road, Devon, PA 19333

Edna Gladney Center, 2300 Hemhill, Fort Worth, TX 76110

Eldercare Locator, 1112 16th Street, Suite 100, NW, Washington, DC 20036

Endometriosis Association, P.O. Box 92187, Milwaukee, WI 53202

Epilepsy Foundation of America, 4351 Garden City Dr., Suite 406, Landover, MD 20785

Foundation Center Customer Service, 79 Fifth Ave. at 16th St., New York, NY 10003

French Foundation for Alzheimer's Research, 11620 Wilshire Boulevard, Suite 820, Los Angeles, CA 90025

AID Atlanta, 1438 West Peachtree Street, NW, Atlanta, GA 30309

Good Samaritan Project Teen, 3030 Walnut Street, Kansas City, MO 64108

Grief Recovery Helpline, 8306 Wilshire Blvd., Suite 21A, Beverly Hills, CA 90211

Guide Dog Foundation for the Blind, 371 E. Jericho Turnpike, Smithtown, NY 11787

Health Education Resource Organization (HERO), 101 West Read Street, Suite 825, Baltimore, MD 21201

Health Insurance Association of America, 1025 Connecticut Avenue, NW, Washington, DC 20036

Hearing Helpline, P.O. Box 1840, Washington, DC 20013

Heart Information Service, Texas Heart Institute, P.O. Box 20345, Houston, TX 77225

Heartspring, 2400 Jardine Drive, Witchita, KS 67219

Help for Incontinent People, P.O. Box 544, Union, SC 23979

Hemophilia and AIDS/HIV Network for the Dissemination of Information (HANDI), 110 Greene Street, Suite 406, New York, NY 10012

Higher Education and Adult Training for People With Handicaps Resource Center, One Dupont Circle, Suite 800, Washington, DC 20036

Hill-Burton Free Hospital Care Hotline, Rockville, MD 20857

Histiocytosis Association of America, 609 New York Road, Glassboro, NJ 08028

Human Growth Foundation, 7777 Leesburg Pike, Suite 202S, Falls Church, VA 22043

Huntington's Disease Society of America, 140 West 22nd Street, Sixth Floor, New York, NY 10011

Immune Deficiency Foundation, 3565 Ellicott Mills Drive, Unit B-2, Ellicott City, MD 21044

International Hearing Society, 20361 Middlebelt Road, Livonia, MI 48152

Job Accommodation Network, West Virginia University, 918 Chestnut Ridge Road, P.O. Box 6080, Morgantown, WV 26506

Just Say No International, 2101 Webster Street, Suite 1300, Oakland, CA 94612

Juvenile Diabetes Foundation, 432 Park Avenue South, 16th Floor, New York, NY 10016

Kevin Collins Foundation for Missing Children, Box 590473, San Francisco, CA 94159

Kidsrights, 10100 Park Cedar Drive, Charlotte, NC 28210

La Leche League International, P.O. Box 1209, Franklin Park, IL 60131

Leukemia Society of America, 600 Third Ave., 4th Floor, New York, NY 10016

Little People of America, P.O. Box 9897, Washington, DC 20016

Living Bank (Organ Donation), P.O. Box 6725, Houston, TX 77265

Lupus Foundation of America, 4 Research Pl., Suite 180, Rockville, MD 20850

Lyme Disease Foundation, One Financial Plaza, Hartford, CT 06103

Medic Alert Foundation International, 2323 Colorado, Turlock, CA 95381

Medical Awareness Association, 3421 M St. NW, Suite 303, Washington, DC 20007

MEDICARE Issues Hotline, 200 Independence Ave., SW, Washington, DC 20201

Meniere's Network of the Ear Foundation at Baptist Hospital, 2000 Church Street, Box 111, Nashville, TN 37236

Missing Children Help Center, 410 Ware Blvd., Suite 400, Tampa, FL 33619

Mother Against Drunk Driving, 511 East John Carpenter Freeway, Suite 700, Irving, TX 75062

Myasthenia Gravis Foundation, 222 S. Riverside Plaza, Suite 1540, Chicago, IL 60606

National Abortion Federation, 1436 U St., Suite 103, NW, Washington, DC 20009

National Adoption Center, 1500 Walnut St., Suite 701, Philadelphia, PA 19102

National Alliance of Blind Students, 1155 15th Street, Suite 720, NW, Washington, DC 20005

National Association for the Craniofacially Handicapped, P.O. Box 11082, Chattanooga, TN 37401

National Association for the Education of Young Children, 1509 16th Street, NW, Washington, DC 20036

National Association for Parents of the Visually Impaired, P.O. Box 317, Watertown, MA 02272

National Association of People with AIDS (NAPWA), P.O. Box 18345, Washington, DC 20036

National Association of Radiation Survivors, P.O. Box 278, Live Oak, CA 95953

National Center for Missing and Exploited Children, 2101 Wilson Boulevard, Suite 550, Arlington, VA 22201

National Center for Stuttering, 200 East 33rd Street, New York, NY 10016

National Center for Vision and Aging, The Lighthouse, 111 E. 59th St., New York, NY 10022

National Center for Youth with Disabilities (NCYD), University of Minnesota, 420 Delaware Street, SE, Minneapolis, MN 55455

National Child Abuse Hotline, Box 630, Hollywood, CA 90028

Childwatch, P.O. Box 1368, Jackson, MI 49204

National Clearinghouse on Family Support and Children's Mental Health, Portland State University, P.O. Box 751, Portland, OR 97202

National Cocaine Hotline, P.O. Box 100, Summit, NJ 07902

National Council on Aging, 409 Third Street, SW, Washington, DC 20024

National Council on Alcoholism and Drug Dependence Hopeline, 12 West 21st Street, Suite 700, New York, NY 10010

National Council on Child Abuse and Family Violence, 1155 Connecticut Avenue, Suite 300, NW, Washington, DC 20036

National Criminal Justice Reference Service, P.O. Box 6000, Rockville, MD 20850

National Dairy Council, 10255 West Higgins, #900, Rosemont, IL 60018

National Domestic Violence Hotline, P.O. Box 463100, Mt. Clemens, MI 48043

National Down Syndrome Congress, 1605 Chantilly Dr., Suite 250, Atlanta, GA 30324

National Down Syndrome Society, 666 Broadway, New York, NY 10012

National Easter Seal Society, 70 East Lake Street, Chicago, IL 60601

National Eye Care Project, P.O. Box 9688, San Francisco, CA 94101

National Eye Research Foundation, 910 Skokie Blvd., #207A, Northbrook, IL 60062

National Fire Protection Association, Batterymarch Park, Quincy, MA 02269

National Foundation for Depressive Illness, P.O. Box 2257, New York, NY 10116

National Fragile X Foundation, 1441 York Street, Suite 215, Denver, CO 80206

National Gaucher Foundation, 11140 Rockville Pike, Suite 350, Rockville, MD 20852

National Head Injury Foundation, 1176 Massachusetts Avenue, Suite 100, NW, Washington, DC 20036

National Headache Foundation, 5252 North Western Avenue, Chicago, Il 60625

National Health Information Center, P.O. Box 1133, Washington, DC 20013

National Hearing Aid Society, 20361 Middlebelt Road, Livonia, MI 48152

National Hospice Organization, 1901 N. Moore St., Suite 901, Arlington, VA 22209

National Information Center for Children and Youth with Handicaps, P.O. Box 1492, Washington, DC 20013

National Information Center for Orphan Drugs and Rare Diseases, P.O. Box 1133, Washington, DC 20013

National Institute for Rehabilitation Engineering, P.O. Box T, Hewitt, NJ 07421

National Jewish Center for Immunology and Respiratory Medicine, Lung Line, 1400 Jackson Street, Denver, CO 80206

National Kidney Foundation, 30 East 33rd, New York, NY 10016

National Lymphedema Network, 2211 Post St., Suite 404, San Francisco, CA 94115

National Marrow Donor Program, 3433 Broadway Street, NE, Suite 400, Minneapolis, MN 55413

National Mental Health Association Information Center, 1021 Prince Street, Alexandria, VA 22314

National Multiple Sclerosis Society (NMSS), 733 Third Avenue, Sixth Floor, New York, NY 10017

National Neurofibromatosis Foundation (NNF), 120 Wall St., New York, NY 10005

National Organization for Albinism and Hypopigmentation, 1530 Locust St., #29, Philadelphia, PA 19102

National Organization for Rare Disorders, P.O. Box 8923, New Fairfield, CT 06812

National Organization on Disability (NOD), 910 16th Street, NW, Suite 600, Washington, DC 20006

National Parkinson Foundation, 1501 NW Ninth Ave., Miami, FL 33136

National Pesticide Telecommunications Network, Texas Tech University, Thompson Hall, Room S129, Lubbock, TX 79430

National Psoriasis Foundation, 6600 SouthWest 92nd Avenue, Suite 300, Portland, OR 97223

National Center for Bioethics Literature, Georgetown University, Washington, DC 20057

National Rehabilitation Information Center, 8455 Colesville Road, Suite 935, Silver Spring, MD 20910

National Resource Center on Child Abuse and Neglect, 63 Inverness Drive East, Englewood, CO 80112

National Resource Center on Homelessness and Mental Illness, 262 Delaware Avenue, Delmar, NY 12054

National Retinitis Pigmentosa Foundation, 1401 Mount Royal Avenue, Fourth Floor, Baltimore, MD 21217

National Reye's Syndrome Foundation, Inc., P.O. Box 829, Bryan, OH 43506

National Runaway Switchboard, 3080 North Lincoln, Chicago, IL 60657

National Safety Council, 1121 Spring Lake Drive, Itasca, Il 60613

National Second Surgical Opinion Program, Helath Care Financing Administration, 200 Indepdendence Avenue, SW, Washington, DC 20201

National Spinal Cord Injury Association, 545 Concord Ave., Cambridge, MA 02138

National Stroke Association, 8480 East Orchard Road, Suite 1000, Englewood, CO 80111

National Tuberous Sclerosis Association, 8000 Corporate Drive, Suite 120, Landover, MD 20785

New England Center for Headache, 778 Long Ridge Road, Stamford, CT 06902

North American Riding for the Handicapped (NARHRA), P.O. Box 33150, Denver, CO 80233

Nutrition Information Service, University of Alabama at Birmingham, Webb Building, Room 447, UAB Station, Birmingham, AL 35294

Occupational Hearing Service, Dial A Hearing Screen Test, P.O. Box 1880, Media, PA 19063

Office of Minority Health Resource Center, P.O. Box 37337, Washington, DC 20013

Orton Dyslexia Society, Chester Building, Suite 382, 8600 La Salle Road, Baltimore, MD 21286

Parkinson's Disease Foundation, Columbia-Presbyterian Medical Center, 650 West 168th Street, New York, NY 10032

Pennsylvannia Department of Health, Office of Drug and Alcohol Programs, Health and Welfare Building, Room 929, Sixth and Commonwealth, Harrisburg, PA 17120

People's Medical Society, 462 Walnut Street, Allentown, PA 18102

Planned Parenthood Federation of America, 810 Seventh Ave., New York, NY 10019

Polycystic Kidney Disease Research foundation, 922 Walnut Street, Suite 411, Kansas City, MO 64106

Prevention Blindness America, 500 E. Remington Rd., Schaumburg, IL 60173

Primary Care Management Systems, 224 East Clara Street, Port Hueneme, CA 93041

Project Inform, 1965 Market Street, Suite 220, San Francisco, CA 94103

R P Foundation Fighting Blindness, 1401 Mount Royal Avenue, Fourth Floor, Baltimore, MD 21217

Runaway Hotline, P.O. Box 12428, Austin, TX 78711

Rural Information Center Health Service, 10301 Baltimore Avenue, Room 304, Bletsville, MD 20705

Safe Sitter, 1500 North Ritter Avenue, Indianapolis, IN 46219

Sarcoidosis Family Aid and Research Foundation, P.O. Box 22868, Newark, NJ 07101

Self-Help Network of Kansas, Witchita State University, 1845 Fairmont, Campus Box 34, Witchita, KS 67260

Shrine Hospital Referral Line, 2900 Rocky Point Drive, Tampa, FL 33607

Sickle Cell Disease Association of America, Inc., 3345 Wilshire Boulevard, Suite 1106, Los Angeles, CA 90010

Simon Foundation, 3621 Thayer Street, Evanstown, IL 60201

Sjogren's Syndrome Association, 3201 West Evans Drive, Phoenix, AZ 85023

Sound Options, Inc., 917 Pacific Avenue, Suite 608, Tacoma, WA 98402

Spina Bifida Association of America, 45900 MacArthur Boulevard, Suite 250, Washington, DC 20007

Spinal Cord Injury Hotline, 2201 Argonne Drive, Baltimore, MD 21218

Sturge-Weber Foundation, P.O. Box 460931, Aurora, CO 80046

Sudden Infant Death Syndrome Alliane, 10500 Little Patuxent Parkway, Suite 420, Colombia, MD 21044

TOUGHLOVE, P.O. Box 1069, Doylestown, PA 18901

Tourette Syndrome Association (TSA), 42-40 Bell Boulevard, Bayside, NY 11361

Tripod Grapevine, 2901 North Keystone Street, Burbank, CA 91504

United Cerebral Palsy Association, Inc., 1522 K Street, NW, Suite 1112, Washington, DC 20005

United Leukodystrophy Foundation, 2304 Highland Drive, Sycamore, IL 60178

Unitde Network for Organ Sharing (UNOS), P.O. Box 13770, Richmond, VA 23225

United Ostomy Association, 36 Executive Park, Suite 120, Irvine, CA 92714

United Sclerodema Foundation, P.O. Box 399, Watsonville, CA 95077

USP Pratitioners Reporting Network, 12601 Twinbrook Pkwy., Rockville, MD 20852

Vietnam Veterans Agent Orange Victims, P.O. Box 2465, Darien, CT 06820

Visiting Nurses Association of America, 3801 East Florida Avenue, Suite 900, Denver, CO 80210

Wisconsin Clearinghouse (Drug and alcohol prevention educational materials and publications), University of Wisconsin, P.O. Box 1468, Madison, WI 53701

Women's Sports Foundation Information and Referral Service, Eisenhower Park, East Meadow, NY 11554

YMCA of the USA, 101 North Wacker, Chicago, IL 60606

Y-Me National Breast Cancer Organization, 212 West Van Buren, Fourth Floor, Homewood, IL 60607

Embassy

Afghanistan, Republic of, 2341 Wyoming Avenue, NW, Washington, DC 20008

Albania, Republic of, 1511 K Street, NW, Suite 1010, Washington, DC 20005

Algeria, Democratic & Popular Republic of, 2118 Kalorama Road, NW, Washington, DC 20008

Angola, Republic of, 1899 L Street, NW, Suite 400, Washington, DC 20036

Antigua and Barbuda, Suite 4M, 3400 International Dr., NW, Washington, DC 20008

Argentine Republic, 1600 New Hampshire Avenue, NW, Washington, DC 20009

Armenia, Republic of, 1660 L Street, NW, Suite 210, Washington, DC 20036

Australia, 1601 Massachsetts Avenue, NW, Washington, DC 20036

Austria, 3524 International Court, NW, Washington, DC 20008

Azerbaijan, Republic of, 927 15th Street, Suite 700, Washington, DC 20005

Bahamas, Commonwealth of The, 2220 Massachusetts Avenue, NW, Washington, DC 20008

Bahrain, State of, 3502 International Drive, NW, Washington, DC 20008

Bangladesh, People's Republic of, 2201 Wisconsin Ave., NW, Washington, DC 20007

Barbados, 2144 Wyoming Avenue, NW, Washington, DC 20008

Belarus, Republic of, Suite 1619, New Hampshire Ave., NW, Washington, DC 20009

Belgium, 3330 Garfield Street, NW, Washington, DC 20008

Belize, 2535 Massachusetts Avenue, NW, Washington, DC 20008

Benin, Republic of, 2737 Cathedral Avenue, NW, Washington, DC 20008

Bolivia, 3014 Massachusetts Avenue, NW, Washington, DC 20008

Bosnia and Herzegovina, 1707 L Street, Suite 760, NW, Washington, DC 20036

Botswana, Republic of, 3400 International Drive, Suite 7M, NW, Washington, DC 20008

Brazil, 3006 Massachusetts Avenue, NW, Washington, DC 20008

Brunei, State of Brunei Darussalam, 2600 Virginia Avenue, Suite 300, NW, Washington, DC 20037

Bulgaria, Republi of, 1621 22d Street, NW, Washington, DC 20008

Burkina Faso, 2340 Massachusetts Avenue, NW, Washington, DC 20008

Burundi, Republic of, 2233 Wisconsin Ave., Suite 212, NW, Washington, DC 20007

Cameroon, Republic of, 2349 Massachusetts Ave., NW, Washington, DC 20008

Canada, 501 Pennsylvania Avenue, NW, Washington, DC 20001

Cape Verde, Republic of, 3415 Massachusetts Ave., NW, Washington, DC 20007

Central African Republic, 1618 22d Street, NW, Washington, DC 20008

Chad, Republic of, 2002 R Street, NW, Washington, DC 20009

Chile, 1732 Massachusetts Avenue, NW, Washington, DC 20036

China, People's Republic of, 2300 Connecticut Ave., NW, Washington, DC 20008

Colombia, 2118 Leroy Place, NW, Washington, DC 20008

Comoros, Federal and Islamic Republic of the, 336 E 45th, 2nd Floor, New York City, NY 10017

Congo, Republic of, 4891 Colorado Avenue, NW, Washington, DC 20011

Costa Rica, 2114 South Street, NW Washington, DC 20008

Czech Republic, 3900 Spring of Freedom Street, NW, Washington, DC 20008

Denmark, 3200 Whitehaven Street, NW, Washington, DC 20008

Djibouti, Republic of, 1156 15th Street, Suite, 515, NW, Washington, DC 20005

Dominican Republic, 1715 22d Street, NW, Washington DC 20008

Ecuador, 2535 15th Street, NW, Washington, DC 20009

Egypt, Arab Republic of, 3521 International Court, NW, Washington, DC 20008

El Salvador, 2308 California Street, NW, Washington, DC 20008

Equatorial Guinea (temporary), 57 Magnolia Avenue, Mt. Vernon, NY 10553

Eriteria, State of, 910 17th Street, Suite 400, NW, Washington, DC 20006

Estonia, 1030 15th Street, Suite 1000, NW, Washington, DC 20005

Ethiopia, 2134 Kalorama Road, NW, Washington, DC 20008

Fiji, Republic of, 2233 Wisconsin Ave., Suite 240, NW, Washington, DC 20007

Finland, 3301 Massachusetts Avenue, NW, Washington, DC 20008

France, 4101 Reservoir Road, NW, Washington, DC 20007

Gabonese Republic, 2233 Wisconsin Ave., Suite 200, NW, Washington, DC 20007

Gambia, 1155 - 15th Street, Suite 1000, NW, Washington, DC 20005

Georgia, Republic of (temporary), 1511 K St., Suite 424, NW, Washington, DC 20005

Germany, Federal Republic of, 4645 Reservoir Rd., NW, Washington, DC 20007

Ghana, 3512 International Drive, NW, Washington, DC 20008

Greece, 2221 Massachusetts Avenue, NW, Washington, DC 20008

Grenada, 1701 New Hampshire Avenue, NW, Washington, DC 20009

Guatemala, 2220 R Street, NW, Washington, DC 20008

Guinea, Republic of, 2112 Leroy Place, NW, Washington, DC 20008

Guinea-Bissau, Republic of, 918 16th Street, NW, Washington, DC 20006

Guyana, 2490 Tracy Place, NW, Washington, DC 20008

Haiti, Republic of, 2311 Massachusetts Avenue, NW, Washington, DC 20008

Holy See, The Apostolic Nunciature, 3339 Massachusetts Avenue, NW, Washington, DC 20008

Honduras, 3007 Tilden Street, NW, Washington, DC 20008

Hungary, Republic of, 3910 Shoemaker Street, NW, Washington, DC 20008

Iceland, 2022 Connecticut Avenue, NW, Washington, DC 20008

India, 2107 Massachusetts Avenue, NW, Washington, DC 20008

Indonesia, Republic of, 2020 Massachusetts Ave., NW, Washington, DC 20036

Ireland, 2234 Massachusetts Avenue, NW, Washington, DC 20008

Israel, 3514 International Drive, NW, Washington, DC 20008

Italy, 1601 Fuller Street, NW, Washington, DC 20009

Jamaica, 1520 New Hampshire Avenue, NW, Washington, DC 20036

Japan, 2520 Massachusetts Avenue, NW, Washington, DC 20008

Jordon, Hashemite Kingdom of, 3504 International Dr., NW, Washington, DC 20008

Kazakhstan, Republic of, 3421 Massachusetts Ave., NW, Washington, DC 20008

Kenya, Republic of, 2249 R Street, NW, Washington, DC 20008

Korea, 2450 Massachusetts Avenue, NW, Washington, DC 20008

Kyrgyzstan, Kyrgz Republic, 1511 K St., Suite 706, NW Washington, DC 20005

Laos, Lao People's Democratic Republic, 222 S St., NW, Washington, DC 20008

Latvia, 4325 17th Street, NW, Washington, DC 20011

Lebanon, 2560 28th Street, NW, Washington, DC 20008

Lesotho, Kingdom of, 2511 Massachusetts Avenue, NW, Washington, DC 20008

Liberia, Republic of, 5201 16th Street, NW, Washington, DC 20011

Lithuania, Republic of, 2622 16th Street, NW, Washington, DC 20009

Luxembourg, 2200 Massachusetts Avenue, NW, Washington, DC 20008

Madagascar, Democratic Republic of, 2374 Massachusetts Avenue, NW, Washington, DC 20008

Malawi, 2408 Massachusetts Avenue, NW, Washington, DC 20008

Malaysia, 2401 Massachusetts Avenue, NW, Washington, DC 20008

Mali, Republic of, 2130 R Street, NW, Washington, DC 20008

Malta, 2017 Connecticut Avenue, NW, Washington, DC 20008

Marshall Islands, Republic of, 2433 Massachusetts Avenue, NW, Washington, DC 20008

Mauritania, Islamic Republic of, 2129 Leroy Place, NW, Washington, DC 20008

Mauritius, 4301 Connecticut Avenue, Suite 441, NW, Washington, DC 20008

Mexico, 1911 Pennsylvania Avenue, Suite 441, NW, Washington, DC 20006

Micronesia, Federated States of, 1725 N Street, NW, Washington, DC 20036

Moldova, Republic of, 1511 K Street, Suite 329, NW, Washington, DC 20005

Mongolia, 2833 M Street, NW, Washington, DC 20007

Morocco, Kingdom of, 1601 21st Street, NW, Washington, DC 20009

Mozambique, Republic of, 1990 M St., Suite 570, NW, Washington, DC 20036

Myanmar, Union of, 2300 S Street, NW, Washington, DC 20008

Nambia, Republic of, 1605 New Hampshire Avenue, NW, Washington, DC 20009

Nepal, 2131 Leroy Place, NW, Washington, DC 20008

Netherlands, 4200 Wisconsin Ave., NW, Washington, DC 20016

New Zealand, 37 Observatory Circle, NW, Washington, DC 20008

Nicaragua, 1627 New Hampshire Avenue, NW, Washington, DC 20009

Niger, Republic of, 2204 R Street, NW, Washington, DC 20008

Nigeria, Federal Republic of, 1333 16th street, NW, Washington, DC 20036

Norway, 2720 34th Street, NW, Washington, DC 20008

Oman, Sultanate of, 2535 Belmont Road, NW, Washington, DC 20008

Pakistan, 2315 Massachusetts Avenue, NW, Washington, DC 20008

Iranian Interests Section, 2209 Wisconsin Avenue, NW, Washington, DC 20007

Panama, Republic of, 2862 McGill Terrace, NW, Washington, DC 20008

Papua New Guinea, 1615 New Hampshire Avenue, NW, Washington, DC 20008

Paraguay, 2400 Massachusetts Avenue, NW, Washington, DC 20008

Peru, 1700 Massachusetts Avenue, NW, Washington, DC 20036

Phillipines, 1600 Massachusetts Avenue, NW, Washington, DC 20036

Poland, Republic of, 2640 16th Street, NW, Washington, DC 20009

Portugal, 2125 Kalorama Road, NW, Washington, DC 20008

Qatar, State of, 600 New Hampshire Ave., Suite 1180, NW, Washington, DC 20037

Romania, 1607 23rd Street, NW, Washington, DC 20008

Russia, Federation, 2650 Wisconsin Avenue, NW, Washington, DC 20007

Rwanda, Republic of, 1714 New Hampshire Ave., NW, Washington, DC 20009

Saint Kitts and Nevis, 2100 M Street, Suite 608, NW, Washington, DC 20037

Saint Lucia, 2100 M Street, Suite 309, NW, Washington, DC 20037

Sant Vincent and the Grenadines, 1717 Massachusetts Avenue, Suite 102, NW, Washington, DC 20036

Saudia Arabia, 601 New Hampshire Avenue, NW, Washington, DC 20037

Senegal, Republic of, 2112 Wyoming Avenue, NW, washington, DC 20008

Seychelles, Republic of, 820 Second Ave., Suite 900F, New York City, NY 10017

Sierre Leone, 1701 19th Street, NW, Washington, DC 20009

Singapore, Republic of, 3501 International Place, NW, Washington, DC 20009

Slovakia, Republic of, 2201 Wisconsin Avenue, Suite 380, NW, Washington, DC 20007

Slovenia, Republic of, 1525 New Hampshire Ave., NW, Washington, DC 20036

South Africa, 3051 Massachusetts Avenue, NW, Washington, DC 20008

Spain, 2375 Pennsylvania Avenue, NW, Washington, DC 20037

Sri Lanka, Democratic Socialist Rep. of, 2148 Wyoming Avenue, NW, Washington, DC 20008

Sudan, Republic of, 2210 Mssachusetts Avenue, NW Washington, DC 20008

Suriname, Republic of, 4301 Connecticut Avenue, Suite 108, NW, Washington, DC 20008

Swaziland, Kingdom of, 3400 International Drive, NW, Washington, DC 20008

Sweden, 1501 M Street, NW, Washington, DC 20005

Switzerland, 2900 Cathedral Avenue, NW, Washington, DC 20008

Syrian Arab Republic, 2215 Wyoming Avenue, NW, Washington, DC 20008

Tanzania, United Arab Republic of, 2139 R Street, NW, Washington, DC 20008

Thailand, 2300 Kalorama Road, NW, Washington, DC 20007

Togo, Republic of, 2208 Massachusetts Avenue, NW, Washington, DC 20008

Trinidad and Tobago, Republic of, 1708 Massachusetts Avenue, NW, Washington, DC 20036

Tunisia, 1515 Mssachusetts Avenue, NW, Washington, DC 20005

Turkey, Republic of, 1714 Massachusetts Avenue, NW, Washington, DC 20036

Turkmenstein, Republic of, 1511 K St., Suite 412, NW, Washington, DC 20005

Uganda, Republic of, 5909 16th Street, NW, Washington, DC 20011

Ukraine, 3350 M Street, NW, Washington, DC 20007

United Arab Emirates, 3000 K Street, Suite 600, NW, Washington, DC 20007

United Kingdom and Northern Ireland, 3100 Massachusetts Avenue, NW, Washington, DC 20008

Uruguay, 1918 F Street, NW, Washington, DC 20006

Uzbekistan, Republic of, 1511 K Street, Suite 600, NW, Washington, DC 20007

Venezuela, Republic of, 1099 30th Street, NW, Washington, DC 20007

Western Samoa, 820 Second Avenue, Suite 800, New york City, NY 10017

Yemen, Republic of, 2600 Virginia Ave., Suite 705, NW, Washington, DC 20037

Yugoslavia, 2410 California Street, NW, Washington, DC 20008

Zaire, Republic of, 1800 New Hampshire Avenue, NW, Washington, DC 20009

Zambia, Republic of, 2419 Massachusetts Avenue, NW, Washington, DC 20008

Zimbabwe, Republic of, 1608 New Hampshire Ave., NW, Washington, DC 20009

Experts

A

Abaca....Cook, Lee USITC 202-205-3471
Abetalipoproteinemia....Staff NHLBI 301-496-4236
Abortion (Research Relating to)....Staff NICHD 301-496-5133
Abortion (Research Relating to)....Staff CDC 404-639-3286
Abortion (Research Relating to)....Staff NCHS 301-436-8500
Abortion/Surveillance Data....Sims, Anne CDC 404-639-3286
Abortion....Staff National Abortion Federation 800-772-9100
Above Ground Storage Tanks....Staff EPA 202-260-1130
Abrasion (Corneal)....Staff NEI 301-496-5248
Abrasive Products....Presbury, Graylin COMMERCE 202-482-5158
Abrasive....DeSapio, Vincent USITC 202-205-3435
Abrasives, Natural....Austin, Gordon MINES 202-501-9388
Abrasives, Manmade....Austin, Gordon MINES 202-501-9388
Abrasives....Bell, Mark L. PTO 703-308-3823
ABS resins....Misurelli, Denby USITC 202-205-3362
Absences from Work, Empl/Unempl Statistics....Staff LABOR 202-606-6378
Abuse of Processing-Non-Hearing (audio)....Staff FCC 202-418-2780
Abuse of Process-Non-Hearing....Staff FCC 202-418-1600
Abuse Liability....Staff NIDA 301-496-5248
Abuse Liability....Mona Brown NIDA 301-443-6245
Access....Staff FCC 202-418-1595
Accessories....Weiss, Martin CUSTOMS 212-466-5881
Accident Statistics....Staff CDC 404-329-3286
Accident Statistics....Staff NCHS 301-496-8500
Accident Prevention and the Elderly....Staff NIA 301-496-1752
Accounting Services....Bedore, James USITC 202-205-3424
Accounting Issues....Staff FCC 202-418-0800
Accounting and Related Issues....Lee, Ronald CENSUS 301-763-5435
Accounting....Chittum, J. Marc COMMERCE 202-482-0345
Accreditation (Health Professions)....Staff HRSA/BHPr 301-443-3376
Accreditation (Nurse Training)....Staff HRSA/BHPr 301-443-5786
Acetal resins....Misurelli, Denby USITC 202-205-3362
Acetates....Michels, David USITC 202-205-3352
Acetic acid....Michels, David USITC 202-205-3352
Acetone....Michels, David USITC 202-205-3352
Acetoricinoleic acid ester....Johnson, Larry USITC 202-205-3351
Achondroplasia....Staff NICHD 301-496-5133
Achondroplasia....Staff NIAMS 301-496-8188
Acid, oleic....Randall, Rob USITC 202-205-3366
Acid, stearic....Randall, Rob USITC 202-205-3366
Acid Rain....Jordy, George NEIC 301-903-2971
Acid Rain....Staff EPA 202-233-9150
Acidosis....Staff NICHD 301-496-5133
Acids, inorganic....Trainor, Cynthia USITC 202-205-3354
Acne (Cystic)....Staff NIAMS 301-496-8188
Acne....Staff NIAMS 301-496-8188
Acoustic Neuroma....Staff NIDCD 301-296-7243
Acoustic Neuroma....Staff NINDS 301-496-5751
Acoustics....Gellner, Michael L. PTO 703-308-1436
Acquired Immune Deficiency Syndrome (AIDS)....Staff PHS 800-342-2437
Acquired Immune Deficiency Syndrome (AIDS)....Staff NCI 301-496-5583
Acquired Immune Deficiency Syndrome (AIDS)....Staff NIAID 301-496-5717
Acquisitions, Land....Staff FWS 202-358-2200
Acquisitions....Staff FCC 202-418-0930
Acromegaly....Staff NIDDK 301-496-3583
Acrylates....Michels, David USITC 202-205-3352
Acrylic resins....Misurelli, Denby USITC 202-205-3362
Acrylonitrile....Michels, David USITC 202-205-3352
ACTH, Excessive Secretion....Staff NHLBI 301-496-4236
Actinide Chemistry....Marianelli, Robert NEIC 301-903-5808
Activated carbon....Randall, Bob USITC 202-205-3366
Acupuncture (Animal Studies)....NIDA 301-443-6245
Acupuncture....Staff NINDS 301-496-5751
Acute Leukemia....Staff NCI 301-496-5583
Acute Hemorrhagic Conjunctivitis....Staff NEI 301-496-5248
Acute Puncture (Animal Studies)....Staff NIDA 301-443-6245
Acyclic plasticizers....Johnson, Larry USITC 202-205-3351

ADA for Economic Development....Sclater, Jeanne SBA 202-205-6552
Adaption to Clinical Illness....NINR 301-496-0207
Adding Machines....Baker, Scott USITC 202-205-3386
Addison's Disease....Staff NIDDK 301-496-3583
Addressing machines....Baker, Scott USITC 202-205-3386
Adenoma of the Thyroid....Staff NIDDK 301-496-3583
Adherence to Therapeutic Regimens....Staff NINR 301-496-0207
Adhesive Bonding....Simmons, David A. PTO 703-308-1972
Adhesives/Sealants....Prat, Raimundo COMMERCE 202-482-0128
Adhesives....Jonnard, Aimison USITC 202-205-3350
Adipic acid esters....Johnson, Larry USITC 202-205-3351
Adjudication....Gaskins, Carla Justice Stat 202-508-8546
Adjudication....Langan, Patrick Justice Stat 202-616-3490
Administration, Director, Office of....Burke, Sally NLM 301-496-6491
Administrative Law Judges....Parker, Lewis, F. FTC 202-326-3632
Administrative Law Judges....Jones, Shirley J. FTC 202-326-3634
Administrative Law Judges....Timony, James P. FTC 202-326-3635
Administrative Law Judges....Cabell, Henry B. FTC 202-326-3642
Administrative Law Judges....Harriger, Patricia A. FTC 202-326-3626
Administrative Systems Training....Staff OD/DPM 301-496-6211
Administrative Procedure Act....Staff FCC 202-418-1720
Admission (Health Professions Schools)....Staff BHPr 301-443-3376
Admission Procedures (Patient)....Staff CC 301-496-4891
Admissions (Patient)....Staff CC 301-496-3315
Adolescence....Staff NIMH 301-443-4513
Adolescence....Staff NICHD 301-496-5133
Adolescent Drug Use....Brown, Mona NIDA 301-443-6245
Adolescent Pregnancy....Staff NICHD 301-496-5133
Adolescent Pregnancy....Sheeran, Patrick NICHD 301-594-4004
Adoption....Kharfen, Michael ACF 202-401-9215
Adoption....Staff National Adoption Center 800-862-3678
Adrenal Gland....Staff NIDDK 301-496-3583
Adrenal Insufficiency....Staff NICHD 301-496-5133
Adrenoleukodystrophy....Staff NINDS 301-496-5751
Adrenomyeloneuropathy....Staff NINDS 301-496-5751
Adult Education....Staff FAES 301-496-7976
Advanced Industrial Concepts....Gunn, Marvin NEIC 202-586-2826
Advanced Solid Rocket Motor....Staff NASA 205-544-5041
Advanced Studies....Staff FIC 301-496-2516
Advanced Technology....Uriano, G.A. NIST 301-975-5187
Advanced Training (Registered Nurse)....Staff BHPr 301-443-5786
Advanced TV-General Engineering....Staff FCC 202-418-2190
Advanced TV-Legal....Staff FCC 202-418-2130
Advertising services....Evans, Katherine USITC 202-205-3407
Advertising Questions....Staff FCC 202-418-1430
Advertising....Frederick, Eliot COMMERCE 202-482-1134
Advertising....Zanot, Eric J. UMD 301-405-2429
Advisory Committees....Staff OD 301-496-2123
Adynamia....Staff NINDS 301-496-5751
Aerodynamic Research....Staff NASA 804-864-6123
Aeroelasticity Research....Staff NASA 804-864-6123
Aeronautics Research....Staff NASA 804-864-6123
Aeronautics....Jordan, Charles PTO 703-308-0918
Aeronautics....Koehler, Keith NASA 804-824-1579
Aeronautics....Rachul, Lori NASA 216-433-8806
Aeronautics....Whitehead, Robert NASA 202-358-2693
Aerospace, Aircraft and Parts Industry Group....Roycroft, John C. SEC 202-942-1960
Aerospace Financing Issues....Jackson, Jeff COMMERCE 202-482-6234
Aerospace Industry Analysis....McDonald, Eric COMMERCE 202-482-1237
Aerospace Industry Data....McDonald, Eric COMMERCE 202-482-1237
Aerospace Market Promo.....Largay, Tony COMMERCE 202-482-6236
Aerospace Information and Analysis....McDonald, Eric COMMERCE 202-482-1237
Aerospace Market Development....Largay, Tony COMMERCE 202-482-6236
Aerospace Policy and Analysis....Bender, Juliet COMMERCE 202-482-1233
Aerospace Technology....Ellis, Linda NASA 216-433-2900
Aerospace Trade Policy Issues....Bender, Juliet COMMERCE 202-482-1233
Aerospace Trade Promo....Bender, Juliet COMMERCE 202-482-1233

Aerospace - Marketing Support....Pederson, Heather COMMERCE 202-482-1228

Aerospace - Space Programs....Farner, Peter COMMERCE 202-482-2232

Aerospace - Space Marketing Support....Pederson, Heather COMMERCE 202-482-6239

Affiliate Transactions....Staff FCC 202-418-0850

Affiliates, Domestic....Nardolilli, Pamela FRS 202-452-3289

Affiliates, Foreign....Clubb, Christopher FRS 202-452-3778

Afghanistan/Minerals....Kuo, Chin Cnty Mines 202-501-9693

Afghanistan (Kabul)....Staff Cnty State 202-647-9552

Afghanistan.....Mohabbat, Yar Mohammad Cnty Embassy 202-234-3770

Afghanistan....Azizian, Abdul Aziz Cnty Embassy 202-234-3770

Afghanistan....Gilman, Timothy Cnty Commerce 202-482-2954

Afghanistan....Hutchings, Dayna Cnty Export-Import Bank 202-565-3737

Afghanistan....Sayeh, Antoinette M. Cnty World Bank 202-473-4719

Afghanistan....VanRenterghem, Cynthia Cnty Treasury 202-622-0343

Afghanistan....Winchester, Rebecca Cnty USIA 202-619-6528

Africa...Jones, Walter OPIC 202-336-8654

AG Indexes with options....Fichert, David CFT 312-353-3181

Agammaglobulinemia....Staff NIAID 301-496-5717

Agar agar....Jonnard, Aimison USITC 202-205-3350

Age and Sex (U.S.)....Staff CENSUS 301-457-2397

Age Search (Access to Personal Census Records)....Staff CENSUS 301-457-1167

Age-Related Muscular Degeneration....Staff NEI 301-496-5248

Ageism....Staff NIA 800-222-2225

Agenesis of the Corpus Callosum....Staff NINDS 301-496-5751

Agent Orange....Sims, Anne CDC 404-639-3286

Agent Orange victims....Staff Vietnam Veterans Agent Orange Victims 800-521-0198

Ageusia....Staff NIDCD 301-496-7243

Agglomerating machinery....Greene, William USITC 202-205-3405

Aging-Related Maculopathy....Staff NEI 301-496-5248

Aging, Administration on....Benson, William AOA 202-619-0556

Aging and vision....Staff The Lighthouse 800-334-5497

Aging (Mental Health)....Staff NIMH 301-443-4513

Aging, National Institute on....Torres-Gil, Fernando AOA 301-401-4634

Aging....Sprott, Richard L. FAES 301-496-4996

Aging....Staff NIA 301-496-1752

Aging....Staff National Council on the Aging 800-424-9046

Agnogenic Myeloid Metoplasia....Staff NHLBI 301-496-4236

Agreements--Collective Bargaining/Public File....Cimini, Michael LABOR 202-606-6275

Agribusiness, Major Proj.....Bell, Richard COMMERCE 202-482-2460

Agricultural Affairs/trade matters....Early, Suzanne US Trade Rep 202-395-6127

Agricultural Chemicals....Maxey, Francis P. COMMERCE 202-482-0128

Agricultural Credit....Walraven, Nicholas 202-452-2655

Agricultural Finances - Cash Receipts....Williams, Roberts Agri 202-219-0804

Agricultural Finances - Cash Receipts....Dixon, Connie Agri 202-219-0805

Agricultural Finances - Costs and Returns....Dismukes, Robert Agri 202-219-0840

Agricultural Finances - Costs and Returns....Morehart, Mitch Agri 202-219-0801

Agricultural Finances - Credit and Financial Markets....Ryan, Jim Agri 202-219-0798

Agricultural Finances - Credit and Financial Markets....Sullivan, Pat Agri 202-219-0719

Agricultural Finances - Credit and Financial Markets-World....Baxter, Tim Agri 202-219-0708

Agricultural Finances - Credit and Financial Markets....Stam, Jerry Agri 202-219-0892

Agricultural Finances - Farm Real Estate Taxes....DeBraal, Peter Agri 202-219-1011

Agricultural Finances - Farm, Annual....Strickland, Roger Agri 202-219-0807

Agricultural Finances - Farm Household....Bentley, Susan 202-219-0931

Agricultural Finances - Future Markets....Heifner, Richard Agri 202-219-0868

Agricultural Finances - Futures Markets - Crops....Plato, Gerry Agri 202-501-6763

Agricultural Finances - Income - Farm Forecast....McElroy, Bob Agri 202-219-0802

Agricultural Finances - Prices, Parity and Indexes-Received....Vanderberry, Herb Agri 202-720-5446

Agricultural Finances - Prices, Parity and Indexes - Paid....Kleweno, Doug Agri 202-720-4214

Agricultural Finances - Prices, Parity and Indexes....Milton, Bob Agri 202-720-3570

Agricultural Finances - Production Costs - Livestock....Shapouri, H. Agri 202-219-1491

Agricultural Finances - Production Costs - Sweeteners....Clauson, Annette Agri 202-219-0890

Agricultural Finances - Production Costs - Sweeteners....Buzzanell, Peter Agri 202-219-0888

Agricultural Finances - Production Costs....Kleweno, Doug Agri 202-720-4214

Agricultural Finances - Production Costs - Crops....Dismukes, Robert Agri 202-219-0840

Agricultural Finances - Production Costs - Dairy....Matthews, Ken Agri 202-219-0710

Agricultural Finances - Subsidies....Mabbs-Zeno, Carl Agri 202-219-0631

Agricultural Finances - Subsidies....Nelson, Fred Agri 202-219-0695

Agricultural Finances - Taxes....Durst, Ron Agri 202-219-0897

Agricultural Finances - Wages and Labor....Oliveira, Victor Agri 202-219-0033

Agricultural Finances....Hacklander, Duane Agri 202-219-0798

Agricultural Finances....Morehart, Mitch Agri 202-219-0801

Agricultural Lands....Staff FWS 703-358-1744

Agricultural Machinery....Fravel, Dennis USITC 202-205-3404

Agricultural Machinery....Weining, Mary COMMERCE 202-482-4708

Agricultural Subsidies....Johnson, Jim Agri 202-219-0001

Agricultural Trade and Marketing Information Center....Lassanyi, Mary NAL 301-504-5509

Agriculture, Crop Statistics....Hutton, Linda CENSUS 301-763-8569

Agriculture, Data Requirements and Outreach....Wilson, Ewen CENSUS 301-763-8555

Agriculture, Farm Economics....Liefer, James A. CENSUS 301-763-8514

Agriculture, General Information....Staff CENSUS 800-523-3215

Agriculture, Guam....Hoover, Kent CENSUS 301-763-8564

Agriculture Issues....Harman, John W. GAO 202-512-5138

Agriculture, Livestock Statistics....Hutton, Linda CENSUS 301-763-8569

Agriculture, No. Marianas....Hoover, Kent CENSUS 301-763-8564

Agriculture, Puerto Rico....Hoover, Kent CENSUS 301-763-8564

Agriculture, State - Virginia, Richmond....Bass, R. Agri 804-786-3500

Agriculture, State - West Virginia, Charleston....Loos, Dave Agri 304-558-2217

Agriculture, State - Alabama, Montgomery....Kleweno, Dave Agri 334-279-3555

Agriculture, State - Alaska, Palmer....Brown, D.A. Agri 907-745-4272

Agriculture, State - Arizona, Phoenix....Sherman, W. M. Agri 602-288-8850

Agriculture, State - Arkansas, Little Rock....Klugh, B.F. Agri 501-324-5145

Agriculture, State - California, Sacramento....Tippett, H.J. Agri 916-498-5161

Agriculture, State - Colorado, Lakewood....Hudson, C.A. Agri 303-236-2300

Agriculture, State - Delaware, Dover....Feurer, T.W. Agri 302-736-4811

Agriculture, State - Florida, Orlando....Freie, R.L. Agri 407-648-6013

Agriculture, State - Georgia, Athens....Snipes, L.E. Agri 404-546-2236

Agriculture, State - Hawaii, Honolulu....Martin, D.A. Agri 808-973-2907

Agriculture, State - Idaho, Boise....Gerhardt, D.G. Agri 208-334-1507

Agriculture, State - Illinois, Springfield....Clampet, J.L. Agri 217-492-4295

Agriculture, State - Indiana, West Lafayette....Gann, R.W. Agri 317-494-8371

Agriculture, State - Iowa, Des Moines....Sands, J. Agri 515-284-4340

Agriculture, State - Kansas, Topeka....Bryam, T.J. Agri 913-233-2230

Agriculture, State - Kentucky, Louisville....Williamson, D. D. Agri 502-582-5293

Agriculture, State - Louisiana, Baton Rouge....Frank, A.D. Agri 504-922-1362

Agriculture, State - Maryland, Annapolis....West, M.B. Agri 410-841-5740

Agriculture, State - Michigan, Lansing....Fedewa, D.J. Agri 517-377-1831

Agriculture, State - Minnesota, St. Paul....Hunts, M. Agri 612-296-2230

Agriculture, State - Mississippi, Jackson....Gregory, T. Agri 601-965-4575

Agriculture, State - Missouri, Columbia....Walsh, P.A. Agri 314-876-0950

Agriculture, State - Montana, Helena....Stringer, M. Agri 406-449-5303

Agriculture, State - Nebraska, Lincoln....Dobbs, B. Agri 402-437-5541

Agriculture, State - Nevada, Reno....Owens, M. J. Agri 702-784-5584

Agriculture, State - New Jersey, Trenton....Battaglia, R.J. Agri 609-292-6385

Agriculture, State - New Mexico, Las Cruces....Gore, C.E. Agri 505-522-6023

Agriculture, State - New England - Concord, NH....Davis, A.R. Agri 603-224-9639

Agriculture, State - New York, Albany....Schooley, R.E. Agri 518-457-5570

Agriculture, State - North Carolina, Raleigh....Murphy, R.M. Agri 919-856-4394

Agriculture, State - North Dakota, Fargo....Beard, L. W. Agri 701-239-5306

Agriculture, State - Ohio, Columbus....Ramey, J.E. Agri 614-469-5590

Agriculture, State - Oklahoma, Oklahoma City....Beloyed, D. Agri 405-525-9226

Agriculture, State - Oregon, Portland....Rowley, H. K. Agri 503-326-2131

Agriculture, State - Pennsylvania, Harrisburg....Evans, W.C. Agri 717-787-3904

Agriculture, State - South Carolina, Columbia....Graham, R. Agri 803-765-5333

Agriculture, State - South Dakota, Sioux Falls....Ranek, J.C. Agri 605-330-4235

Agriculture, State - Tennessee, Nashville....Danekas, G. Agri 615-781-5300

Agriculture, State - Texas, Austin....Findley, D. S. Agri 512-482-5581

Agriculture, State - Utah, Salt Lake City....Gneiting, D.J. Agri 801-524-5003

Agriculture, State - Washington, Tumwater....Hasslen, D.A. Agri 360-902-1940

Agriculture, State - Wisconsin, Madison....Pratt, L.H. Agri 608-224-4848

Agriculture, State - Wyoming, Cheyenne....Coulter, R.W. Agri 307-772-2181

Agriculture/trade matters....Kaska, Edward US Trade Rep 202-395-3320

Agriculture, Virgin Islands....Hoover, Kent CENSUS 301-763-8564

Agriculture....Rosine, John FRS 202-452-2971

Agroforestry....Huke, Susan FS 202-235-9461

Aid to Families with Dependent Children (AFDC)....Kharfen, Michael ACF 202-401-9215

AID ATLANTA....Staff Georgia Dept. of Health 800-551-2728

AIDS (Acquired Immune Deficiency Syndrome)....Arthur, Lawrence PHS 202-690-5471

AIDS and IV drug abuse....Brown, Mona NIDA 301-443-6245

AIDS Clinical Trials....Staff ACTIS 800-874-2572

AIDS Dementia....Staff NINDS 301-496-5751

AIDS Drugs....Staff Project Inform 800-334-7422

AIDS Education at Work....Staff AIDS Action Committee of Massachusetts 800-669-0696

AIDS/HIV....Waller, Robert CDC 404-639-2928

AIDS, Neurological Symptoms or Effects of....Staff NINDS 301-496-5751

AIDS, Neurological Symptoms or Effects of....Staff NIDCD 301-496-7243

AIDS, Pediatric....Staff NICHD 301-496-5133

AIDS, Research Facilities....Staff NCRR 301-594-7938

AIDS...Staff Good Samaritan Project Teen 800-234-8336

AIDS....Staff NAPWA 800-673-8538

AIDS....Staff NCI 301-496-5583

AIDS....Staff NIAID 301-496-5717

AIDS....Staff PHS Hotline 800-342-2437

Air and Radiation....Staff EPA 202-260-7400

Air and Energy Policy Division....Staff EPA 202-260-5490

Air Compressors, Gas....McDonald, Edward COMMERCE 202-482-2107

Air Conditioners....Francke, Eric CUSTOMS 212-466-5669

Air conditioners....Mata, Ruben USITC 202-205-3403

Air Conditioning Equipment....Bell, Richard COMMERCE 202-482-3509

Air Division....Staff EPA 202-260-7606

Air Enforcement Division....Staff EPA 202-564-2260

Air Environmental Laws....Wallo, Andrew NEIC 202-586-4996

Air Gas Compressors, Trade Promo.....Heimowitz, Leonard COMMERCE 202-482-0558

Air/Ground Communication...Johnson, Nathaniel FAA 202-287-7027

Air Pollution Training....Staff EPA 919-541-2401

Air Pollution Control Equipment....Jonkers, Loretta COMMERCE 202-482-0564

Air Pollution and Respiratory Health....Etzel, Ruth CDC 404-488-7320

Air Quality (Outdoor Cities)....Staff EPA 202-260-1023

Air Quality Planning and Standards....Staff EPA 202-541-5615

Air Quality Management Division....Staff EPA 202-541-0886

Air Risc Hotline....Staff EPA 919-541-0888

Air Taxi....Hakala, Katherine M FAA 202-267-8086

Air Traffic Control Equipment (Market Support)....Smerkanich, Audrey COMMERCE 202-482-6235

Air Traffic Rules....Matthews, Reginald FAA 202-267-8783

Air Traffic....Pollard, William FAA 202-267-3666

Air transportation services....Lahey, Kathleen USITC 202-205-3409

Air Transportation Services....Lahey, Kathleen USITC 202-205-3409

Airborne Science and Applications....Staff NASA 415-604-3934

Aircraft Accident Investigation....Rawson, John D FAA 202-267-8190

Aircraft and Aircraft Engines, Trade Promo.....Smerkanich, Audrey COMMERCE 202-482-6235

Aircraft and Aircraft Engines, Market Support....Pederson, Heather COMMERCE 202-482-6239

Aircraft Auxiliary Equipment, Market Support....Pederson, Heather COMMERCE 202-482-1228

Aircraft Certification Service....McSweeney, Thomas E FAA 202-267-8235

Aircraft Engines, Trade Promo.....Smerkanich, Audrey COMMERCE 202-482-6235

Aircraft Fuel Economy Research....Rachul, Lori NASA 216-433-8806

Aircraft Noise Abatement Research....Rachul, Lori NASA 216-433-8806

Aircraft Operating Problems Research....Koehler, Keith NASA 804-824-1579

Aircraft Parts, Trade Promo/Aux Equipment....Smerkanich, Audrey COMMERCE 202-482-6235

Aircraft Parts, Market Support....Smerkanich, Audrey COMMERCE 202-482-6235

Aircraft Propulsion....Rachul, Lori NASA 216-433-8806

Aircraft Radio Licenses-Technical Questions....Staff FCC 202-418-0680

Aircraft Radio Licenses-General Questions....Staff FCC 800-322-1117

Aircraft Reliability Research....Rachul, Lori Ann NASA 216-433-8806

Aircraft Testing....Staff NASA 804-864-3314

Aircraft....Dicerbo, Mario CUSTOMS 212-466-5672

Aircraft....Andersen, Peder USITC 202-205-3409

Airlines....Alford, Eugene COMMERCE 202-482-5071

Airport Equipment, Trade Promo....Smerkanich, Audrey COMMERCE 202-482-6235

Airport Equipment, Market Support....Smerkanich, Audrey COMMERCE 202-482-6235

Airports, Ports, Harbors, Major Projects....Smith, Jay COMMERCE 202-482-4642

Airport Safety....Mudd, Leonard E FAA 202-267-3053

Airway Facilities Training Program....Kruger, Mike FAA 202-366-7400

Airway facilities....Archilla, Joaquin FAA 202-267-8181

Al-Anon....Staff Alateen Family Group Hotline 800-344-2666

Alarms, burglar and fire....Scott, Baker USITC 202-205-3386

Alaska Joint Board....Staff FCC 202-418-0830

Albania....Altheim, Stephen Cnty Treasury 202-622-0125

Albania....Amick, Jack Peace Corps 202-606-3548

Albania....Corwin, Elizabeth Cnty USIA 202-619-5055

Albania....Dawson, Kathleen Cnty Treasury 202-622-5815

Albania....Dilja, Lubin Cnty Embassy 202-223-4942

Albania....Keller, Jeremy Cnty Commerce 202-482-4915

Albania....LeMaster, Cheryl Peace Corps 202-606-3547

Albania....Staff Cnty State 202-647-3747

Albania....Stillwell, Carol Cnty TDA 703-875-4357

Albania....Varallyay, Julius G. Cnty World Bank 202-473-7210

Albania....Waxman-Lenz, Roberta Cnty Export-Import Bank 202-565-3742

Albania....Xheph, Mustafa Cnty Embassy 202-223-4942

Albania\Minerals....Steblez, Walter Cnty Mines 202-501-9672

Albinism (Eyes)....Staff NEI 301-496-5248

Albinism....Staff National Organization for Albinism and Hypopigmentation 800-473-2310

Albright's Syndrome....Staff NIDDK 301-496-3583

Albright's Syndrome....Staff NICHD 301-496-5133

Albright's Syndrome....Staff NIAMS 301-496-8188

Albums (autograph, photograph)....Twarok, Chris USITC 202-205-3314

Alcohol Abuse and Alcoholism, National Institute on....Miller, Diane NIAAA 301-443-3860

Alcohol and Aging....Staff NIAAA 301-443-3860

Alcohol and Cancer....Staff NCI 301-496-5583

Alcohol and Cancer....Staff NIAAA 301-443-3860

Alcohol and Aging....Staff NCADI 301-468-2600

Alcohol and Aging....Staff NIA 301-496-1752

Alcohol, elderly....Alcohol Rehab for the Elderly 800-354-7089

Alcohol Fuels....Costello, Raymond NEIC 202-586-8072

Alcohol Fuels....Russell, John NEIC 202-536-8053

Alcohol Fuels....Staff NEIC 202-586-9920

Alcohol, oleyl....Randall, Rob USITC 202-205-3366

Alcohol....Alcohol and Drug Helpline 800-821-4357

Alcohol....Staff NAPARE 800-638-2229

Alcohol....Staff NCADI 301-468-2600

Alcohol....Staff NIAAA 301-443-3860

Alcohol....Staff Office of Alcohol and Drug Programs 800-932-0912

Alcoholic Beverages....Kenney, Cornelius COMMERCE 202-482-2428

Alcoholic beverage labeling....Staff ATF 202-927-7777

Alcoholic beverage permits....Staff ATF 202-927-8100

Alcoholism prevention....Staff Wisconsin Clearinghouse 800-322-1468

Alcoholism....Staff NIAAA 301-443-3860

Alcoholism....Staff NCADI 301-468-2600

Alcoholism....Staff American Council on Alcoholism 800-527-5344

Alcoholism....Staff National Council on Alcoholism and Drug Dependence Hopeline 800-622-2255

Alcohols, polyhydric, fatty acids....Land, Eric USITC 202-205-3349

Alcohols....Michels, David USITC 202-205-3352

Aldehydes....Brady, Thomas CUSTOMS 212-466-5747

Aldehydes....Michels, David USITC 202-205-3352

Aldosteronism....Staff NHLBI 301-496-4236

Alexander's Syndrome....Staff NINDS 301-496-5751

Algeria/Minerals....Michalski, Bernadette Cnty Mines 202-501-9699

Algeria (Algiers)....Staff Cnty State 202-647-4680

Algeria....Belkadi, Mouloud Cnty Embassy 202-265-2800

Algeria....Bencherif, Hadji Osmane Cnty Embassy 202-265-2800

Algeria....Clement, Claude/Cerone, Chris Cnty Commerce 202-482-1860

Algeria....Early, Evelyn Cnty USIA 202-619-6528

Algeria....El Baroudy, Samia Cnty World Bank 202-473-2370

Algeria....Imam, Fahmila Cnty Export-Import Bank 202-565-3738

Algeria....Mandel, Pamela Cnty AID 202-663-2617
Algeria....VanRenterghem, Cynthia Cnty Treasury 202-622-0343
Alien Restricted Permits....Staff FCC 202-418-2780
Aliferis, Peter V. GAO 202-512-4707
Alkali metals....Connant, Kenneth USITC 202-205-3346
Alkaloids....Nesbitt, Elizabeth USITC 202-205-3355
Alkaptonuria....Staff NHLBI 301-496-4236
Alkylating Agents....Staff NCI 301-496-5583
Allergic Rhinitis....Staff NIAID 301-496-5717
Allergic Diseases....Kaliner, Michael A. FAES 301-496-9314
Allergies (Eyes)....Staff NEI 301-496-5248
Allergies....Staff NIAID 301-496-5717
Allergies....Staff American Academy of Allergy and Immunology 800-822-2762
Allergy and Infectious Diseases, National Inst. of....Randall, Patricia NIH 301-496-5717
Allergy....Staff Asthma and Allergy Foundation of America 800-727-8462
Allied Health Professions....Staff HRSA/BHPr 301-443-3376
Allocations FM....Staff FCC 202-418-2180
Almaty....Eighmy, Thomas Cnty AID 202-647-6920
Almonds....Burket, Stephen USITC 202-205-3318
Alopecia....Staff NIAMS 301-496-8188
Alpaca....Shelton, Linda USITC 202-205-3457
Alpers Syndrome....Staff NINDS 301-496-5751
Alpha-1-antitrypsin Deficiency (liver)....Staff NIDDK 301-654-3810
Alpha-1-antitrypsin Deficiency (lung)....Staff NHLBI 301-496-4236
Alternate energy....Foreso, Cynthia USITC 202-205-3348
Alternate Fuels Statistics....Geidl, John NEIC 202-254-5570
Alternate Long Distance Service Providers....Staff FCC 202-418-1544
Alternate Dispute Resolution....Staff FCC 202-418-0960
Alternative Farming Systems Information Center....Gates, Jane NAL 301-504-5724
Alternative Fuels Data Center....Eberhardt, James NEIC 202-586-9837
Alternative Fuels....Ferrell, John NEIC 202-586-8072
Alternative Medicine....Staff OD 301-402-2466
Alternative Motor Fuels....Bower, Marc NEIC 202-586-3891
Altitude....Staff NHLBI 301-496-4236
Alumina....Conant, Kenneth USITC 202-205-3346
Aluminum compounds....Greenblatt, Jack USITC 202-205-3353
Aluminum Extrud. Alum Rolling....Cammarota, David COMMERCE 202-482-5157
Aluminum Forgings, Electro....Cammarota, David COMMERCE 202-482-5157
Aluminum Sheet, Plate/Foil....Cammarota, David COMMERCE 202-482-5157
Aluminum....McNay, Deborah USITC 202-205-3425
Aluminum....Plunkert, Patricia MINES 202-501-9419
Alumni (NIH)....Staff FAES 301-530-0567
Alveolar Bone (Regeneration/Resorption)....Staff NIDR 301-496-4261
Alveolar Microlithiasis....Staff NHLBI 301-496-4236
Alveolar Proteinosis....Staff NHLBI 301-496-4236
Alzheimer's Disease....Staff NINDS 301-496-5751
Alzheimer's Disease....Staff NIDCD 301-496-7243
Alzheimer's Disease....Staff NIA 301-496-1752
Alzheimer's Disease....Staff NIMH 301-443-4513
Alzheimer's Disease....Staff Alzheimer's Association 800-272-3900
Alzheimer's Disease....Staff ADEAR 800-438-4380
Alzheimer's Research....Staff French Foundation for Alzheimer's Research 800-477-2243
AM Antennas, Directional....Staff FCC 202-418-2660
AM Stereo....Staff FCC 301-725-1585
AM Technical Standards Applications....Staff FCC 202-418-2660
Amateur (Ham) Radio-Antenna Ordinance Preemption....Staff FCC 202-418-0680
Amateur (Ham) Radio-Application forms....Staff FCC 800-322-1117
Amateur (Ham) Radio-Compliance....Staff 202-418-0680
Amateur (Ham) Radio-Engineering....Staff FCC 202-418-0680
Amateur (Ham) Radio-Exam Availability....Staff FCC 202-418-0680
Amateur (Ham) Radio-Forfeitures....Staff FCC 202-418-0680
Amateur (Ham) Radio-General....Staff FCC 800-322-1117
Amateur (Ham) Radio-Interference to TV/Phone etc....Staff FCC 202-418-1170
Amateur (Ham) Radio-Operating Questions....Staff FCC 202-418-0680
Amateur (Ham) Radio-Reciprocal Licenses....Staff FCC 800-322-1117
Amateur (Ham) Radio-Revocations....Staff FCC 202-418-0680
Amateur (Ham) Radio-Status....Staff 800-322-1117
Amateur (Ham) Radio-Status Licenses....Staff FCC 800-322-1117
Amateur (Ham) Radio-Technical....Staff FCC 202-418-0680
Amaurotic Idiocy....Staff NINDS 301-496-5751

Ambergris....Land, Eric USITC 202-205-3349
Ambiguous Genitalia....Staff NICHD 301-496-5133
Amblyopia....Staff NEI 301-496-5248
Ambulance and Rescue Squads....Staff FCC 717-337-1212
Ambulance....Staff Air Ambulance of America 800-262-8526
Ambulance....Staff Aeronational (air ambulance transport) 800-245-9987
Ambulatory Patient Centers....Staff CC 301-496-3141
Amebiasis....Staff NIAID 301-496-5717
American Disability Act(ADA)....Staff FCC 202-418-0190
American fisheries products....Corey, Roger USITC 202-205-3327
American Nurses' Association....Staff NIH 816-474-5720
American Sign Language....Staff NIDCD 301-496-7243
Amides, fatty acids of (surface-active agents)....Land, Eric USITC 202-205-3349
Amides....Michels, David USITC 202-205-3352
Amines, fatty acids of (surface-active agents)....Land, Eric USITC 202-205-3349
Amines....Michels, David USITC 202-205-3352
Amino acids....Michels, David USITC 202-205-3352
Amino Acid Disorders....Staff NICHD 301-496-5133
Amino nitrogen....Hollrah, Glen H. PTO 703-308-4552
Ammonia....Trainor, Cynthia USITC 202-205-3354
Ammonium nitrate, fertilizer....Trainor, Cynthia USITC 202-205-3354
Ammonium nitrate, fuel-sensitized...Johnson, Larry USITC 202-205-3351
Ammonium nitrate, non-explosive or non-fertilizer....Greenblatt, Jack USITC 202-205-3353
Ammonium phosphate....Greenblatt, Jack USITC 202-205-3353
Ammonium sulfate....Greenblatt, Jack USITC 202-205-3353
Ammunition....Jordan, Charles PTO 703-308-0918
Ammunition....Luther, Dennis USITC 202-205-3498
Amniocentesis....Staff NICHD 301-496-5133
Amphetamines....Staff NIDA 301-443-6245
Amplifiers....Puffert, Douglas USITC 202-205-3402
Amplifiers....Sherman, Thomas USITC 202-205-3389
Amusement games....Millin, Vincent PTO 703-308-1065
Amusement devices....Love, John PTO 703-308-0873
Amyloid Polyneuropathy....Staff NINDS 301-496-5751
Amyloidosis (cardiac)....Staff NHLBI 301-496-4236
Amyloidosis....Staff NIDDK 301-654-4415
Amyloidosis....Staff NEI 301-496-5248
Amyloidosis....Staff NIAMS 301-496-8188
Amyotonia Congenita....Staff NINDS 301-496-5751
Amyotrophic Lateral Sclerosis....Staff NIDCD 301-496-7243
Amyotrophic Lateral Sclerosis....Staff NINDS 301-496-5751
Amyotrophic Lateral Sclerosis....Staff ALSA 800-782-4747
Anabolic Steroids....Staff NIDA 301-443-6245
Analgesic-Associated Nephropathy....Staff NIDDK 301-654-4415
Analgesics....Nesbitt, Elizabeth USITC 202-205-3355
Analog computational computers....Envall, Roy PTO 703-305-9706
Analysis and Data, Producer Price Indexes....Howell, Craig LABOR 202-606-7704
Analysis....Clark, Stephen FRS 202-452-3752
Analytical Chemistry....Staff NIGMS 301-496-7301
Analytical chemistry....Housel, James PTO 703-308-4027
Analytical Instruments....Nealon, Marquarite COMMERCE 202-482-3411
Analytical Instrument (Trade Promo)....Manzolino, Frank COMMERCE 202-482-2991
Anaphylaxis....Staff NIAID 301-496-5717
Anaplasia....Staff NCI 301-496-5583
Andalusite....DeSapio, Vincent USITC 202-205-3435
Andean Affairs....Lenzy, Karen US Trade Rep 202-395-5190
Andorra....Staff Cnty State 202-647-1412
Anemia (Hemolytic and Aplastic)....Staff NHLBI 301-496-4236
Anemia (Hemolytic and Aplastic)....Staff NCI 301-496-5583
Anemia....Staff NIDDK 301-496-3583
Anencephaly....Staff NINDS 301-496-5751
Anesthesiology (Dental)....Staff NIDR 301-496-4261
Anesthesiology....Staff NIGMS 301-496-7301
Aneurysm (Brain or Spinal)....Staff NINDS 301-496-5751
Aneurysm....Staff NHLBI 301-496-4236
Angelman's Disease....Staff NINDS 301-496-5751
Angina Pectoris....Staff NHLBI 301-496-4236
Angioedema....Staff NIAID 301-496-5717
Angiography....Staff NHLBI 301-496-4236
Angioplasty....Staff NHLBI 301-496-4236
Angles, shapes, and sections (steel)....Kaplan, Stephanie USITC 202-205-3436
Angola (Luanda)....Staff Cnty State 202-647-8434

Angola/Minerals....Mobbs, Philip Cnty Mines 202-501-9674
Angola....Daniels, Gussie Cnty AID 202-647-4328
Angola....Holm-Olsen, Finn Cnty Commerce 202-482-4228
Angola....Kotze, Joan Cnty Treasury 202-622-0333
Angola....Maybury-Lewis, Anthony Cnty Export-Import Bank 202-565-3739
Angola....Patel, Praful C. Cnty World Bank 202-473-4250
Angola....Patricio, Jose Goncalves Martins Cnty Embassy 202-785-1156
Angola....Schwartz, Larry Cnty USIA 202-619-6904
Angola....Silva, Jose Maria Cnty Embassy 202-785-1156
Angora....Shelton, Linda USITC 202-205-3457
Anguilla....Brooks, Michelle Cnty Commerce 202-482-2527
Anguilla....Wilkins, Michele Cnty Export-Import Bank 202-565-3743
Aniline Dyes (and Cancer)....Staff NCI 301-496-5583
Animal Bedding....Staff OD/DL 301-496-1160
Animal (Caging, Housing, Watering)....Staff NCRR 301-594-7933
Animal Colonies and Models (Special)....Staff DRR 301-594-7933
Animal Feeds....Conte, Ralph CUSTOMS 212-466-5759
Animal feeds....Pierre-Benoist, John USITC 202-205-3320
Animal Food....Staff OD/DL 301-496-1160
Animal Genetics....Staff NCRR 301-496-5255
Animal Health....Staff NCRR 301-496-4463
Animal husbandry....Love, John PTO 703-308-0873
Animal husbandry....Mancene, Gene PTO 703-308-2696
Animal Husbandry....Staff NCRR 301-496-2527
Animal Models for Aging Research....Staff NIA 301-496-1752
Animal Nutrition....Staff NCRR 301-496-4481
Animal oil, fats, greases....Reeder, John USITC 202-205-3319
Animal Research (Intramural)....Staff OD/DC 301-496-8740
Animal Research (Intramural)....Staff NCRR 301-594-7938
Animal Research....Staff OD/DC 301-496-8740
Animal Research....Staff NCRR 301-594-7938
Animal Resources Program....Staff NCRR 301-594-7938
Animal Sanitation....Staff OD/ORS 301-496-2960
Animal Welfare Information Center....Larson, Jean NAL 301-504-5215
Animal Welfare Policy....Staff OPRR 301-496-7163
Animal Welfare....Staff NIDA 301-443-6245
Animal Welfare....Staff NCRR 301-594-7938
Animal Welfare....Staff OD/DC 301-496-8740
Animals: Guide for the Care and Use of Lab Animals....Staff NCRR 301-594-7938
Aniridia....Staff NEI 301-496-5248
Ankylosing Spondylitis....Staff Ankylosing Spondylitis Association 800-777-8189
Ankylosing Spondylitis....Staff NIAMS 301-496-8188
Anorexia Nervosa....Staff NIMH 301-496-4513
Anorexia Nervosa....Staff NICHD 301-496-5133
Anosmia....Staff NIDCD 301-496-7243
Anosmia....Staff NINDS 301-496-5751
Anoxia....Staff NHLBI 301-496-4236
ANSI Committee 63....Staff FCC 301-725-1585
Antarctica/Minerals....Doan, David Cnty Mines 202-501-9678
Antenatal Diagnosis....Staff NICHD 301-496-5133
Antenna measurements....Repjar, Andrew G. NIST 303-497-5703
Antenna Structures and Towers....Staff FCC 800-322-1117
Antenna Survey....Staff FCC 800-322-1117
Antenna....Kitzmiller, John USITC 202-205-3387
Antennas....Hajec, Donald PTO 703-308-4075
Anthracite....Foreso, Cynthia USITC 202-205-3348
Anthrax....Staff NIAID 301-496-5717
Anti-inflammatory agents....Nesbitt, Elizabeth USITC 202-205-3355
Anti-infective agents....Nesbitt, Elizabeth USITC 202-205-3355
Antialphatrypsin....Staff NIDDK 301-496-3583
Antibiotics....Staff NIAID 301-496-5717
Anticoagulant Drugs....Staff NHLBI 301-496-4236
Anticonvulsants....Nesbitt, Elizabeth USITC 202-205-3355
Antidiuretic Hormone....Staff NHLBI 301-496-4236
Antidiuretic Hormone....Staff NIDDK 301-496-3583
Antigens....Nucker, Christine M PTO 703-308-4028
Antigua/Barbuda....Brooks, Michelle Cnty Commerce 202-482-2527
Antigua and Barbuda (St. John's)....Staff Cnty State 202-647-2621
Antigua/Minerals....Torres, Ivette Cnty Mines 202-501-9670
Antigua....Lewis, Patrick Albert Cnty Embassy 202-362-5211
Antigua....Marcus, Anthony Cnty Treasury 202-622-1218
Antigua....Nallari, Raj R. Cnty World Bank 202-473-8697
Antigua....Prosper, Debbie Cnty Embassy 202-362-5211

Antigua....Wilkins, Michele Cnty Export-Import Bank 202-565-3743
Antihistamines....Nesbitt, Elizabeth USITC 202-205-3355
Antimetabolites....Staff NCI 301-496-5583
Antimony compounds....Greenblatt, Jack USITC 202-205-3353
Antimony....Carlin, James Jr., MINES 202-501-9426
Antimony....Lundy, David USITC 202-205-3439
Antipyretics....Nesbitt, Elizabeth USITC 202-205-3355
Antiques....Mushinske, Larry CUSTOMS 212-466-5739
Antiques....Spalding, Josephine USITC 202-205-3498
Antisocial Behavior....Staff NIMH 301-496-4513
Antithrombin III Deficiency....Staff NHLBI 301-496-4236
Antitrust Laws....Nardolilli, Pamela FRS 202-452-3289
Antiviral drug products....Boring, Daniel L. FAES 301-594-5029
Antiviral Substances....Staff NIAID 301-496-5717
Anxiety Disorders....Staff NIMH 301-496-4513
Aorta....Staff NHLBI 301-496-4236
Aortic Valve....Staff NHLBI 301-496-4236
Aortic Insufficiency/Stenosis....Staff NHLBI 301-496-4236
Aortitis....Staff NHLBI 301-496-4236
Apes and Monkeys (Medical Research)....Staff NCRR 301-594-7938
Aphakia....Staff NEI 301-496-5248
Aphasia (due to Stroke)....Staff NINDS 301-496-5751
Aphasia....Staff NIDCD 301-496-7243
Aphasia....Staff NINDS 301-496-5751
Aphthous Stomatitis-Recurrent....Staff NIDR 301-496-4261
Aplastic Anemia....Staff Aplastic Anemia Foundation of America 800-747-2820
Aplastic Anemia....Staff NHLBI 301-496-4236
Apparatus, Filtering/Purifying....Francke, Eric CUSTOMS 212-466-5669
Apparel and Textiles Industry Group....Owings, Christopher SEC 202-942-1900
Apparel, Body Supporting....Burtnik, Brian CUSTOMS 212-466-5880
Apparel, Food and Raw Materials, Intl. Price Ind....Frumkin, Rob LABOR 202-606-7106
Apparel, Knit Wearing: Men's....Ryan, Mary CUSTOMS 212-466-5877
Apparel, Knit Wearing: Boys'....Ryan, Mary CUSTOMS 212-466-5877
Apparel, Leather....Weiss, Martin CUSTOMS 212-466-5881
Apparel, Miscellaneous....DeGaetano, Angela CUSTOMS 212-466-5540
Apparel, Plastic Wearing....Weiss, Martin CUSTOMS 212-466-5881
Apparel, Women's Woven Wearing....Schiazzano, Patricia CUSTOMS 212-466-5866
Apparel, Woven Wearing: Men's....Shea, Gerard CUSTOMS 212-466-5878
Apparel, Woven Wearing: Boys'....Shea, Gerard CUSTOMS 212-466-5878
Apparel....Dulka, William COMMERCE 202-482-4058
Appeals....Staff FCC 202-418-1740
Appliances, Small....Smyth, James CUSTOMS 212-466-2084
Appliances....Duvall, Steven SEC 202-942-1950
Application Status-All Private Radio....Staff FCC 800-322-1117
Application Status-AM....Staff FCC 202-418-2670
Application Status-FM....Staff FCC 202-418-2730
Application Status-TV....Staff FCC 202-418-1630
Applications Fraud-Cellular....Staff FCC 202-418-1320
Applications Fraud-Private Radio....Staff FCC 202-418-0620
Appraisals, Land....Staff FWS 703-358-1713
Apraxia (speech)....Staff NIDCD 301-496-7243
Apraxia....Staff NIDCD 301-496-7243
Apraxia....Staff NINDS 301-496-5751
Aquaculture Information Center....McVey, Eileen NAL 301-504-5558
Aquaculture....Harvey, Dave Agri 202-219-0085
Aquaculture....Little, Robert Agri 202-720-6147
Aquaculture....Moore, Joel Agri 202-720-3244
Aquaculture....Staff FWS 703-358-1715
Aquatic Species Management....Staff FWS 703-358-1710
Aquatic Resource Education....Staff FWS 703-358-2156
Arachnoid Cyst....Staff NINDS 301-496-5751
Arachnoiditis....Staff NINDS 301-496-5751
Aran Duchenne Spinal Muscular Dystrophy....Staff NINDS 301-496-5751
Arboretum, National Library....Fernandez, Katya NAL 202-245-4538
ARC (AIDS-Related Complex)....Staff NIAID 301-496-5717
ARC Injection....Staff Project Inform 800-334-7422
Arch Glazing Petition....Giles, Ken CPSC 301-504-0580
Archaeology Research....Staff NEH 202-606-8210
Archaeology....Staff FWS 703-358-1786
Architecture Services....Polly, Laura USITC 202-205-3408
Architecture, Urban Planning....Beatley, Timothy UVA 904-924-6459
Architecture....Bowler, Alyssa PTO 703-305-9702

Architecture....Harris, William M. UVA 804-924-6450
Area Measurement....Hirschfeld, Don CENSUS 301-457-1099
Argentina (Buenos Aires)....Staff Cnty State 202-647-2401
Argentina/Minerals....Velasco, Pablo Cnty Mines 202-501-9677
Argentina....Granillo Ocampo, Raul Enrique Cnty Embassy 202-939-6400
Argentina....Hagerstrom, Mark V. Cnty World Bank 202-473-9208
Argentina....Jaureguiberry, Nora L. Cnty Embassy 202-939-6400
Argentina....Leeb, Howard Cnty USIA 202-619-5867
Argentina....Mye, Randolph Cnty Commerce 202-482-1548
Argentina....Neil, Jeff Cnty Treasury 202-622-1268
Argentina....Prevot, Babette Cnty AID 202-647-4359
Argentina....Wilkins, Michele Cnty Export-Import Bank 202-565-3743
Argon....Conant, Kenneth USITC 202-205-3346
Armenia....Carlen, James Cnty Treasury 202-622-0122
Armenia....Kreslins, Dagnija Cnty AID 202-736-4317
Armenia....Levine, Richard Cnty MINES 202-501-9682
Armenia....Nanagulian, Rouben Robert Cnty Embassy 202-628-5766
Armenia....O'Keefe, Monica Cnty USIA 202-619-5057
Armenia....Ruhl, Onno Cnty World Bank 202-458-9119
Armenia....Shugarian, Rouben Robert Cnty Embassy 202-628-5766
Armenia....Staff Cnty State 202-647-8671
Armenia....Stillwell, Carol Cnty TDA 703-875-4357
Armenia....Viksnins, Helen Peace Corps 202-606-5517
Armenia....Waxmen-Lenz, Roberta Cnty Export-Import Bank 202-565-3742
Armenia....Wootton, Nicholas Peace Corps 202-606-5519
Arms....Luther, Dennis USITC 202-205-3497
Arnold-Chiari Malformations....Staff NINDS 301-496-5751
Arrhythmias....Staff NHLBI 301-496-4236
Arsenic compounds....Greenblatt, Jack USITC 202-205-3353
Arsenic....Conant, Kenneth USITC 202-205-3346
Arsenic....Loebenstein, Roger MINES 202-501-9416
Art, works of....Spalding, Josephine USITC 202-205-3498
Art Services....Staff NCRR 301-496-2868
Arteriosclerosis (Cerebral)....Staff NINDS 301-496-5751
Arteriosclerosis....Staff NHLBI 301-496-4236
Arteriovenous Malformations (Cerebral and Spinal)....Staff NINDS 301-496-5751
Arteritis (eyes)....Staff NEI 301-496-5248
Arthritis and Musculoskeletal and Skin Dis., Nat'l Ins....Raab, Connie NIH 301-496-8118
Arthritis Information Clearinghouse....Staff NIAMS 301-495-4484
Arthritis....Staff Arthritis Foundation 800-283-7800
Arthritis....Staff Arthritis Consulting Services 800-327-3027
Arthritis....Staff NIAMS 301-496-8188
Arthritis....Staff NIA 301-496-1752
Arthrogryposis Multiplex Congenita....Staff NIAMS 301-496-8188
Arthrogryposis Multiplex Congenita....Staff NIAMS 301-496-8188
Arthroscopy....Staff NIAMS 301-496-8188
Article carriers....Recia, Henry PTO 703-308-1382
Article dispensing....Olszewski, Robert PTO 703-308-2588
Article handling....Huppert, Michael PTO 703-308-1107
Artificial Blood Vessels....Staff NHLBI 301-496-4236
Artificial flowers of man-made fibers....Cook, Lee USITC 202-205-3471
Artificial flowers....Spalding, Josephine USITC 202-205-3498
Artificial Heart Valves....Staff NHLBI 301-496-4236
Artificial Heart....Staff NHLBI 301-496-4236
Artificial Insemination....Staff NICHD 301-496-5133
Artificial Intelligence Research....Staff NASA 713-483-5111
Artificial Intelligence....Montgomery, Shelagh COMMERCE 202-482-0571
Artificial Intelligence....Staff NLM 301-496-9300
Artificial Joints....Staff NIAMS 301-496-8188
Artificial Lung....Staff NHLBI 301-496-4236
Artificial mixtures of fatty substances....Randall, Rob USITC 202-205-3366
Artificial Pancreas....Staff NIDDK 301-496-3583
Artificial Skin....Staff NIGMS 301-496-7301
Aruba/Minerals....Rabchevsky, George Cnty Mines 202-501-9680
Aruba....Brooks, Michelle Cnty Commerce 202-482-2527
Aruba....Marcus, Anthony Cnty Treasury 202-622-1218
Aruba....Wilkins, Michele Cnty Export-Import Bank 202-565-3743
Asbestos Action Program (Technical Questions)....Staff EPA 202-260-3904
Asbestos and Cancer....Staff NCI 301-496-5583
Asbestos and the Workplace....Sims, Anne CDC 404-639-3286
Asbestos/Cement Products....Pitcher, Charles COMMERCE 202-482-0132
Asbestos Clearinghouse....Staff EPA 800-368-5888
Asbestos Ombudsman Clearinghouse/Hotline....Staff EPA 800-368-5888

Asbestos Ombudsman and Small Business Clearinghouse....Staff EPA 703-305-5938
Asbestos Publications....Staff EPA 202-554-1404
Asbestos....Virta, Robert MINES 202-501-9384
Asbestos....White, Linda USITC 202-205-3427
Asbestosis....Staff NHLBI 301-496-4236
Asbestosis....Staff CDC/NIOSH 404-639-3286
ASEAN....Paine, George Cnty Commerce 202-482-3877
Ashgabat....Eighmy, Thomas Cnty AID 202-647-6920
Asia/trade matters....Lund, Christina US Trade Rep 202-395-6813
Asia/trade matters....Cassidy, Robert US Trade Rep 202-395-3430
Asia/trade matters....Byrons, Wendy C. US Trade Rep 202-395-3900
Asia....Greenberg, Richard OPIC 202-336-8616
Asparagus....McCarty, Timothy USITC 202-205-3324
Aspartame, Neurological Effects of....Staff NINDS 301-496-5751
Asperger's Syndrome....Staff NINDS 301-496-5751
Aspergillosis....Staff NIAID 301-496-5717
Asphalt, Natural....Solomon, Cheryl C. MINES 202-501-9393
Asphalt....White, Linda USITC 202-205-3427
Asphyxia....Staff NINDS 301-496-5751
Aspirin Allergy....Staff NIAID 301-496-5717
Aspirin-Myocardial Infarction Study (AMIS)....Staff NHLBI 301-496-4236
Assembly Equipment....Abrahams, Edward COMMERCE 202-482-0312
Assessment and Management of Side Effects of Disease Treatments....Staff NINR 301-496-0207
Assessment and Management of Symptoms NINR 301-496-0207
Assistant Commissioner, Compensation Levels and Trnd....MacDonald, Kathleen M. LABOR 202-606-6302
Assistant Commissioner, Consumer Prices and Price Index....Greenlef, Joan LABOR 202-606-6952
Assistant Commissioner, Empl/Unempl. Stats, Curr. Empl. An....Bregger, John E. LABOR 202-606-6388
Assistant Commissioner, Empl/Unempl. Stats, Fed/State....Vacant LABOR 202-606-6500
Assistant Commissioner, Industry Prices and Pr. Index....Vacant LABOR 202-606-7700
Assistant Commissioner, Intl. Price Indexes....Reut, Katrina LABOR 202-606-7100
Assistant Commissioner, Safety, Health and Work. Cond....Eisenberg, William M. LABOR 202-606-6304
Assisted Circulation....Staff NHLBI 301-496-4236
Assistive Devices....Staff NIDCD 301-496-7243
Associate Commissioner, Compensation and Work. Cond....Vacant LABOR 202-606-6300
Associate Commissioner, Empl/Unempl Stats....Plewes, Thomas J. LABOR 202-606-6400
Associate Commissioner, Employment Projections....Kutscher, Ronald LABOR 202-606-5700
Associate Commissioner, Prices and Living Cond.....Dalton, Kenneth LABOR 202-606-6960
Associate Commissioner, Productivity and Technology.....Dean, Edwin R. LABOR 202-606-5600
Asthma....Staff Asthma and Allergy Foundation of America 800-727-8462
Asthma....Staff NIAID 301-496-5717
Asthma....Staff NHLBI 301-496-4236
Astigmatism....Staff NEI 301-496-5248
Astronaut appearances....Clary, Tawna NASA 202-358-1718
Astronaut Training....Staff NASA 713-483-5111
Astronomy Research....Gundy, Cheryl NASA 301-338-4707
Astronomy....Chevalier, Roger A. UVA 804-924-7494
Astrophysical Research....Katz, Jessie NASA 301-286-5566
Asymmetric Septal Hypertrophy (ASH)....Staff NHLBI 301-496-4236
AT & T Price Caps....Staff FCC 202-418-1520
Ataxia Telangiectasia....Staff NINDS 301-496-5751
Ataxia Telangiectasia....Staff NCI 301-496-5583
Ataxia....Staff NINDS 301-496-5751
Atelectasis....Staff NHLBI 301-496-4236
Atherosclerosis (Effect on Vision)....Staff NEI 301-496-5248
Atherosclerosis (Cerebral)....Staff NINDS 301-496-5751
Atherosclerosis....Staff NHLBI 301-496-4236
Athetosis....Staff NINDS 301-496-5751
Athlete's Foot....Staff NIAID 301-496-5717
Athlete's Heart....Staff NHLBI 301-496-4236
Athletic equipment....Witherspoon, Ricardo USITC 202-205-3496

Atmospheric Science Research....Staff NASA 804-864-6122

Atmospheric and Indoor Air Programs....Staff EPA 202-233-9140

Atomic Physics....Wiese, W.L. NIST 301-975-3200

Atomic Safety and Licensing Board....Cotter, Paul NRC 301-415-7450

Atomic Vapor Laser Isotope Separation Plant...Lowe, Owen W. NEIC 301-903-5161

Atopic Dermatitis....Staff NIAMS 301-496-8188

Atopic Dermatitis....Staff NIAID 301-496-5717

Atrial Fibrillation....Staff AF Hotline 800-423-1925

Atrial Fibrillation....Staff NHLBI 301-496-4236

Atrophy....Staff NINDS 301-496-5751

Attention Deficit Disorder....Staff NINDS 301-496-5751

Attention Deficit Disorder....Staff NICHD 301-496-5133

Attention Deficit Disorder....Staff NIMH 301-443-4513

Attribution of Ownership of Mass Media Licenses....Staff FCC 202-418-1630

Auction Hotline....Staff FCC 202-418-1400

Auctions....Staff FCC 202-418-1400

Audio components....Puffert, Douglas USITC 202-205-3402

Audio systems....Kuntz, Curt PTO 703-305-4708

Audio Visual Services....Siegmund, John COMMERCE 202-482-4781

Audiology (Clinical Center patients)....Staff CC 301-496-5368

Audiovisual Material (For Health Prof. Education)....Staff NLM 301-496-6095

Audiovisual Materials (Nursing)....Staff HRSA/BHPr 301-443-5786

Auditory System....Staff NIDCD 301-496-7243

Audits....Staff FCC 202-418-0820

Augmentative Devices....Staff NIDCD 301-496-7243

Aural Rehabilitation....Staff NIDCD 301-496-7243

Australia (Canberra)....Staff Cnty State 202-647-9691

Australia....Bouck, Gary (Bus.)/Golike, William (Policy) Cnty Commerce 202-482-2471

Australia....Coyne, Bruce J. Cnty Embassy 202-797-3000

Australia....Demeter, Katalin Cnty World Bank 202-458-4661

Australia....Imam, Fahmila Cnty Export-Import Bank 202-565-3738

Australia....Jabbs, Theodore Cnty USIA 202-619-5836

Australia....Lyday, Travis Cnty Mines 202-501-9695

Australia....Russell, Donald Eric Cnty Embassy 202-797-3000

Australia....Vacant Cnty Treasury 202-622-0166

Austria (Vienna)....Staff Cnty State 202-647-1484

Austria/Minerals....Plachy, Josef Cnty Mines 202-501-9673

Austria....Combs, Philip Cnty Commerce 202-482-2920

Austria....Gosnell, Peter Cnty Export-Import Bank 202-565-3733

Austria....Lemaistre, Alice Cnty USIA 202-619-6184

Austria....Mackour, Oscar Cnty Treasury 202-622-0145

Austria....Stift, Desiree Cnty Embassy 202-895-6700

Austria...Tuerk, Helmet Cnty Embassy 202-895-6700

Autism....Staff NICHD 301-443-5133

Autism....Staff NIMH 301-443-4513

Autism....Staff NINDS 301-496-5751

Auto Industry Affairs Parts/Suppliers....Reck, Robert O. COMMERCE 202-482-1418

Auto Industry Affairs....Keitz, Stuart COMMERCE 202-482-0554

Auto Parts/Suppliers (Trade Promotions)....White, John C. COMMERCE 202-482-0671

Autoimmune Disease....Staff NIAID 301-496-5717

Autoimmune Disease....Staff NIAMS 301-496-8188

Automated Clearinghouse....Young, Florence FRS 202-452-3955

Automatic Teller Machine Theft....Kaplan, Carol Justice Stat 202-307-0759

Automation (Laboratory Apparatus and Processes)....Staff NCRR/BEIB 301-496-4426

Automobile - Catalytic Converters....Staff EPA 202-233-9090

Automobile Emissions- Recalls....Staff EPA 202-233-9260

Automobile Emissions....Staff EPA 202-260-7647

Automobile - Imports....Staff EPA 202-233-9660

Automobile Loans....Luckett, Charles FRS 202-452-2925

Automobile Parts....Topolansky, Adam USITC 202-205-3394

Automobile Warranty Information....Staff EPA 202-233-9100

Automobiles....Desoucey, Robert CUSTOMS 212-466-5667

Automobiles....Hagey, Michael USITC 202-205-3392

Automotive and other Vehicles Industry Group....Daly, James M. SEC 202-942-1800

Autonomic drugs....Nesbitt, Elizabeth USITC 202-205-3355

Auxiliary Antennas/Transmitters-AM....Staff FCC 202-418-2660

Auxiliary Antennas/Transmitters-FM....Staff FCC 202-418-2740

Auxiliary Antennas/Transmitters-TV FCC 202-418-1630

Availability of Nursing Resources-Quality Patient Care....Staff NINR 301-496-0207

Avascular Necrosis....Staff NIAMS 301-496-8188

Average Retail Food Prices--Monthly, CPI....Cook, William LABOR 202-606-6988

Average Retail Prices and Indexes of Fuels and Utilities.....Adkins, Robert LABOR 202-606-6985

Average Retail Prices and Indexes, Motor Fuels Only....Chelena, Joseph LABOR 202-606-6982

Aversives....Giles, Ken CPSC 301-504-0580

Aviation and Helicopter Services....Alford, Eugene COMMERCE 202-482-5071

Aviation, International....Gretch, Paul DOT 202-366-2423

Aviation Licenses....Staff FCC 717-337-1212

Aviation Medicine....Jordon, Jon L FAA 202-267-3535

Aviation Safety Analysis....Bermingham, Barry DOT 202-366-4466

Aviation Safety Information....Edwards, Carolyn FAA 202-366-5995

Aviation Safety....Huettner, Charles FAA 202-267-9613

Aviation safety....Loeb, Bernie NTSB 202-382-6610

Avionics Marketing....Pederson, Heather COMMERCE 202-482-2835

Avionics Testing....Deason, Billie A. NASA 713-483-5111

Azerbaijan....Adoteye, Philip C. Cnty World Bank 202-473-5509

Azerbaijan....Carlen, James Cnty Treasury 202-622-0122

Azerbaijan....Kreslins, Dagnija Cnty AID 202-736-4317

Azerbaijan....Kurbanov, Fakhratdin Cnty Embassy 202-842-0001

Azerbaijan....Levine, Richard Cnty MINES 202-501-9682

Azerbaijan....O'Keefe, Monica Cnty USIA 202-619-5057

Azerbaijan....Pashayev, Hafiz Mir Jalal Cnty Embassy 202-842-0001

Azerbaijan....Staff Cnty State 202-647-8671

Azerbaijan....Waxmen-Lenz Cnty Export-Import Bank 202-565-3742

Azides....Johnson, Larry USITC 202-205-3351

Azo chemistry....Lee, Mary PTO 703-308-4546

B

B-19 Infection (Human Parvovirus)....Staff NICHD 301-496-5133

Baby Bottle Tooth Decay....Staff NIDR 301-496-4261

Baby carriages, strollers, and parts....Abrahamson, Dana USITC 202-205-3430

Baby Walkers....Tyrrell, Elaine CPSC 301-504-0580

Baccalaureate Nursing Schools....Staff HRSA/BHPr 301-443-6333

Back Pain....Staff Back Pain Hotline 800-247-2225

Back Problems....Staff NIAMS 301-496-8188

Back Problems....Staff NINDS 301-496-5751

Bacterial Endocarditis....Staff NHLBI 301-496-4236

Bacterial Meningitis....Staff NIAID 301-496-5717

Bacterial Meningitis....Staff NIDCD 301-496-7243

Bacteriologic Media....Staff OD/ORS 301-496-6017

Bacteriology....Staff NIAID 301-496-5717

Bags or sacks....Cook, Lee USITC 202-205-3471

Bags....Gorman, Kevin CUSTOMS 212-466-5893

Bahamas (Nassau)....Staff Cnty State 202-647-2621

Bahamas/Minerals....Rabchevsky, George Cnty Mines 202-501-9670

Bahamas....Carey, Sheila Gweneth Cnty Embassy 202-319-2660

Bahamas....Donaldson, Timothy Baswell Cnty Embassy 202-319-2660

Bahamas....Head, Alfred Cnty USIA 202-619-6835

Bahamas....Hume, Susan Cnty World Bank 202-473-2407

Bahamas....Marcus, Anthony Cnty Treasury 202-622-1218

Bahamas....Siegelman, Mark Cnty Commerce 202-482-5880

Bahamas....Wilkins, Michele Cnty Export-Import Bank 202-565-3743

Bahrain (Manama)....Staff Cnty State 202-647-6572

Bahrain/Minerals....Michalski, Bernadette Cnty Mines 202-501-9699

Bahrain....Abdulkader, Mohammed Ibrahim Cnty Embassy 202-342-0741

Bahrain....Abdulla, Muhammad Abdul Ghaffer Cnty Embassy 202-342-0741

Bahrain....Clement, Claude Cnty Commerce 202-482-5545

Bahrain....Farah, Ahmed Cnty World Bank 202-473-2649

Bahrain....Maybury-Lewis Anthony Cnty Export-Import Bank 202-565-3739

Bahrain....Mercer, Dorothy Cnty Treasury 202-622-0184

Bahrain....Vacant Cnty USIA 202-619-6528

Bail (Federal)....Kaplan, Carol Justice Stat 202-307-0759

Bakery Products....Janis, William V. COMMERCE 202-482-2250

Balance of Payments, Chief....Bach, Christopher L., ECONOMIC 202-606-9545

Balance (Normal and Disordered)....Staff NIDCD 301-496-7243

Balkin States....Staff Cnty Commerce 202-482-2645

Ball Bearings....Reise, Richard COMMERCE 202-482-3489

Balls, sports and play....Witherspoon, Ricardo USITC 202-205-3496
Baltic Republics....Altheim, Stephen Cnty Treasury 202-622-0125
Baltic States....Staff Cnty State 202-647-3187
Baltics....Visknins, Helen Peace Corps 202-606-5517
Baltimore Longitudinal Study of Aging....Staff NIA 410-558-8139
Baltimore Longitudinal Study of Aging....Staff NIA 301-496-1752
Bamboo....Hoffmeier, Bill USITC 202-205-3321
Bandages, impregnated w/ medicinals....Randall, Rob USITC 202-205-3366
Banding, Bird....Staff FWS 703-358-0205
Bangladesh/Minerals....Kuo, Chin Cnty Mines 202-501-9693
Bangladesh (Dhaka)....Staff Cnty State 202-647-9552
Bangladesh....Frederick, David Cnty AID 202-647-5863
Bangladesh....Hutchings, Dayna Cnty Export-Import Bank 202-565-3737
Bangladesh....Kabir, Humayun Cnty Staff Embassy 202-342-8372
Bangladesh....Lowenstein, Linda Cnty World Bank 202-458-0428
Bangladesh....McCoy, Ethel Cnty Treasury 202-622-0336
Bangladesh....Simmons, John Cnty Commerce 202-482-2954
Bangladesh....Swaleheen, Mushfiq Us Cnty Embassy 202-342-8372
Bangladesh....Winchester, Rebecca Cnty USIA 202-619-6528
Bank Acquisitions....Simon, David FRS 202-452-3611
Bank credit Cards....Hurt, Adrienne FRS 202-452-2412
Bank for International Settlements....Siegman, Charles FRS 202-452-3308
Bank Rates on Business loans....English, William FRS 202-736-5645
Banking, International....Frankel, Allen FRS 202-452-3578
Banking services....Melly, Chrisopher USITC 202-205-3461
Banking services.... USITC 202-205-3436
Banking....Shuman, John COMMERCE 202-482-3050
Bankruptcy Reorganizations....Berman, Michael A. SEC 202-942-0810
Banks Industry Group....Tow, A. Richard SEC 202-942-1760
Banks....Staff SEC 202-942-7040
Barbados/Minerals....Rabchevsky, George Cnty Mines 202-501-9670
Barbados....Blackman, Courtney N. Cnty Embassy 202-939-9200
Barbados....Brooks, Michelle Cnty Commerce 202-482-2527
Barbados....Clarke, Roy Cnty Embassy 202-939-9200
Barbados....Head, Alfred Cnty USIA 202-619-6835
Barbados....Marcus, Anthony Cnty Treasury 202-622-1218
Barbados....Scoseria, Carmen C. Cnty World Bank 202-473-8677
Barbados....Staff Cnty State 202-647-2130
Barbados....Wilkins, Michele Cnty Export-Import Bank 202-565-3743
Barbasco....Wanser, Stephen USITC 202-205-3363
Barbiturates....Nesbitt, Elizabeth USITC 202-205-3355
Barbiturates....Staff NIDA 301-443-6245
Barbuda/Minerals....Torres, Ivette Cnty Mines 202-501-9680
Barbuda....Lewis, Patrick Albert Cnty Embassy 202-362-5211
Barbuda....Marcus, Anthony Cnty Treasury 202-622-1218
Barbuda....Nallari, Raj R. Cnty World Bank 202-473-4250
Barbuda....Prosper, Debbie Cnty Embassy 202-362-5211
Barge Freight Index....Schambach, Duane CFT 312-353-9022
Barite....Johnson, Larry USITC 202-205-3351
Barite....Searls, James, P. MINES 202-501-9407
Barium carbonate....Johnson, Larry USITC 202-205-3351
Barium compounds....Greenblatt, Jack USITC 202-205-3353
Barium pigments....Johnson, Larry USITC 202-205-3351
Barium sulfate....Johnson, Larry USITC 202-205-3351
Barium....Lundy, David USITC 202-205-3439
Barlow's Syndrome (Mitral Valve Prolapse)....Staff NHLBI 301-496-4236
Barrettes....Burns, Gail USITC 202-205-2501
Bars (steel)....Kaplan, Stephanie USITC 202-205-3436
Bartter's Syndrome....Staff NHLBI 301-496-4236
Basal Cell....Staff NCI 301-496-5583
Basic Energy Sciences....Staff NEIC 301-903-3081
Basic Paper and Board Mfg....Branley, Gary COMMERCE 202-482-0375
Basic Research....Staff NIGMS 301-496-7301
Basketwork, wickerwork, related products....Hoffmeier, Bill USITC 202-205-3321
Bathing caps....Jones, Jackie USITC 202-205-3466
Bathing caps....Hamey, Amy USITC 202-205-3465
Bathroom facilities....Recia, Henry PTO 703-308-1382
Batten Disease....Staff Battan Disease Support and Research Association 800-448-4570
Batten's Disease....Staff NINDS 301-496-5751
Battered Spouses....Staff NIMH 301-443-4513
Battered Spouses....Staff Hot-Line 301-654-1881
Batteries, Storage....Larrabee, David COMMERCE 202-482-0607
Batteries....Curran, David CUSTOMS 212-466-4680

Batteries....Eaton, Russell NEIC 202-586-0205
Batteries....Polly, Laura USITC 202-205-3408
Battery manufacturing....Hearn, Brian E. 703-308-2552
Battery-Driven Vehicles....Alpaugh, Richard NEIC 202-586-1477
Bauxite, Alumina, Prim Alum....Cammarota, David COMMERCE 202-482-5157
Bauxite calcined....White, Linda USITC 202-205-3427
Bauxite for metal....McNay, Deborah USITC 202-205-3425
Bauxite....Sehnke, Errol D. MINES 202-501-9421
Bay rum or bay water....Land, Eric USITC 202-205-3349
BCG (Bacillus Calmette-Guerin)....Staff NCI 301-496-5583
Beads, articles of....Witherspoon, Ricardo USITC 202-205-3489
Beads....Witherspoon, Ricardo USITC 202-205-3489
Beans, ex oilseed....McCarty, Timothy USITC 202-205-3324
Bearings, ball and roller....Polly, Laura USITC 202-205-3408
Bearings....Riedl, Karl CUSTOMS 212-466-5493
Bechet's Disease (eyes)....Staff NEI 301-496-5248
Becker's Muscular Dystrophy....Staff NINDS 301-496-5751
Bed Wetting....Staff NICHD 301-443-5133
Bed Wetting....Staff NIDDK 301-654-4415
Bedding....Hansen, John CUSTOMS 212-466-5854
Bedding....Sweet, Mary Elizabeth USITC 202-205-3455
Beds....Cuomo, Peter PTO 703-308-0827
Beef....Ludwick, David USITC 202-205-3329
Beepers-Common Carrier....Staff FCC 202-418-1330
Beepers-Private Carrier Paging and Microwave....Staff FCC 202-418-0620
Beer....Harney, Amy USITC 202-205-3465
Behavioral and Social Sciences....Staff NICHD 301-496-6832
Behavioral and Social Sciences....Staff NIMH 301-443-4513
Behavioral Pharmacology....Staff NIDA 301-443-6245
Behavioral Therapy....Staff NIDA 301-443-6245
Behcet's Disease (Neurological Effects of)....Staff NINDS 301-496-5751
Behcet's Disease (Systemic)....Staff NIDR 301-496-4261
Behcet's Disease (Systemic)....Staff NIAMS 301-496-8188
Behcet's....Staff American Behcet's Association Inc. 800-723-4238
Belarus....Carlen, James Cnty Treasury 202-622-0122
Belarus....Garg, Prabhat Cnty World Bank 202-473-2171
Belarus....Gontcharenok, Vladimir Cnty Embassy 202-986-1604
Belarus....Levine, Richard Cnty MINES 301-501-9682
Belarus....Martynov, Serguei Nikolaevich Cnty Embassy 202-986-1604
Belarus....McCleod, Evelyn Cnty AID 202-736-7646
Belarus....O'Keefe, Monica Cnty USIA 202-619-5057
Belarus....Staff Cnty State 202-647-6764
Belarus....Waxman-Lenz, Roberta Cnty Export-Import Bank 202-565-3742
Belgium (Brussels)....Staff Cnty State 202-647-6592
Belgium/Minerals....Zajac, William Cnty Mines 202-501-9671
Belgium....Adam, Andre Cnty Embassy 202-333-6900
Belgium....Bensimon, Simon Cnty Commerce 202-482-5041
Belgium....Gosnell, Peter Cnty Export-Import Bank 202-565-3733
Belgium....Holloway, Barbara Cnty Treasury 202-622-0098
Belgium....Kulla, Morgan Cnty USIA 202-619-6853
Belgium....Lepage, Christian Cnty Embassy 202-333-6900
Belize/Minerals....Velasco, Pablo Cnty Mines 202-501-9677
Belize (Belize City)....Staff Cnty State 202-647-3381
Belize....Brooks, Michelle Cnty Commerce 202-482-2527
Belize....Cambell, Edward Cnty AID 202-647-4105
Belize....Erlandson, Barbara Peace Corps 202-606-3624
Belize....Haylock, Claude Bromwell Cnty Embassy 202-332-9636
Belize....John Herrman Cnty TDA 703-875-4357
Belize....Lindo, Dean R. Cnty Embassy 202-332-9636
Belize....Neil, Jeff Cnty Treasury 202-622-1268
Belize....Opstein, Sally Cnty USIA 202-619-5864
Belize....Scoseria, Carmen C. Cnty World Bank 202-473-8677
Belize....Wilkins, Michele Cnty Export-Import Bank 202-565-3743
Bell's Palsy....Staff NINDS 301-496-5751
Belting and Hose....Prat, Raimundo COMMERCE 202-482-0128
Belting, industrial....Cook, Lee USITC 202-205-3471
Belting of rubber or plastics (for machinery)....Misurelli, Denby USITC 202-205-3362
Belts, apparel: Leather....Jones, Jackie USITC 202-205-3466
Belts, apparel: Other mens and boys....Sweet, Mary Elizabeth USITC 202-205-3455
Belts, apparel: Other womens and girls....Sweet, Mary Elizabeth USITC 202-205-3455
Bemiconductor Prod. Equipment....Andrews, Michael COMMERCE 202-482-2795

Benign Prostatic Hyperplasia....Staff NIDDK 301-654-4415
Benign Congenital Hypotonia....Staff NINDS 301-496-5751
Benign Mucosal Pemphigoid....Staff NIAMS 301-496-8188
Benin (Cotonou)....Staff Cnty State 202-647-1540
Benin/Minerals....Mobbs, Philip Cnty Mines 202-501-9679
Benin....Baily, Jess Cnty USIA 202-619-5900
Benin....Barber, Ed Cnty Treasury 202-622-1730
Benin....Bezek, Jill Cnty TDA 703-875-4357
Benin....Brown, Arthur Peace Corps 202-606-3237
Benin....Guidi, Kouassi Cnty Embassy 202-232-6656
Benin....Henke, Debra Cnty Commerce 202-482-5149
Benin....Maybury-Lewis Anthony Cnty Export-Import Bank 202-565-3739
Benin....Moreno-Herrero, Bianca Cnty World Bank 202-473-9178
Benin....Swift, Gail Peace Corps 202-606-3136
Benin....Tonoukouin, Lucien Edgar Cnty Embassy 202-232-6656
Bensenoid intermediates, miscellaneous....Matusik, Ed USITC 202-205-3356
Bentonite....DeSapio, Vincent USITC 202-205-3435
Benzene....Raftery, Jim USITC 202-205-3365
Benzenoid plastics....Misurelli, Denby USITC 202-205-3362
Benzenoid varnishes....Johnson, Larry USITC 202-205-3351
Benzenoid paints....Johnson, Larry USITC 202-205-3351
Benzenoid plasticizers....Johnson, Larry USITC 202-205-3351
Benzo(a)pyrene....Staff NCI 301-496-5583
Benzodiazepines....Staff NIDA 301-443-6245
Benzoic acid....Matusik, Ed USITC 202-205-3356
Berger's Disease....Staff NIDDK 301-654-4415
Beriberi (Nutritional)....Staff NIDDK 301-496-3583
Beriberi (Neurological)....Staff NINDS 301-496-5751
Bermuda/Minerals....Rabchevsky, George Cnty Mines 202-501-9670
Bermuda (Hamilton)....Staff Cnty State 202-647-8027
Bermuda....Brooks, Michelle Cnty Commerce 202-482-2527
Bernard-Soulier Syndrome....Staff NIDDK 301-496-3583
Beryllium compounds....Greenblatt, Jack USITC 202-205-3353
Beryllium....Kramer, Deborah A. MINES 202-501-9394
Beryllium....Lundy, David USITC 202-205-3439
Beryllium....Males, Barbara COMMERCE 202-482-0606
Best's Disease....Staff NEI 301-496-5248
Beta-thalassemia (Cooley's Anemia)....Staff NHLBI 301-496-4236
Betatron....Staff NCI 301-496-5583
Beverages, Alcoholic....Harney, Amy USITC 202-205-3465
Beverages, Alcoholic....Maria, John CUSTOMS 212-466-5730
Beverages Industry Group....Roycroft, John C. SEC 202-942-1960
Beverages, Non-alcoholic....Dennis, Alfred USITC 202-205-3316
Beverages....Kenney, Cornelius COMMERCE 202-482-2428
Bhutan/Minerals....Wu, John Cnty Mines 202-501-9697
Bhutan....Gilman, Timothy Cnty Commerce 202-482-2954
Bhutan....Gradisher, Thomas Cnty USIA 202-619-5529
Bhutan....Hutchings, Dayna Cnty Export-Import Bank 202-565-3737
Bhutan....McCoy, Ethel Cnty Treasury 202-622-0336
Bhutan....Nicholaws, Peter Cnty World Bank 202-458-0420
Bhutan....Staff Cnty State 202-647-2141
Bicycles and parts....Seastrum, Carl USITC 202-205-3493
Bicycles....Desoucey, Robert CUSTOMS 212-466-5667
Bicycles....Tyrrell, Elaine CPSC 301-504-0580
Bicycles....Vanderwolf, John COMMERCE 202-482-0348
Bilateral Agreements....Staff FIC 301-496-5903
Biliary Cirrhosis....Staff NIDDK 301-496-3583
Bilirubinemia....Staff NICHD 301-496-5133
Billed Party Preference....Staff FCC 202-418-1594
Billfolds....Seastrum, Carl USITC 202-205-3493
Billiard cloth....Cook, Lee USITC 202-205-3471
Billing and Collections....Staff FCC 202-418-1995
Binge Eating....Staff NIMH 301-496-443-4513
Binocular Vision....Staff NEI 301-496-5248
Binswanger's Disease....Staff NINDS 301-496-5751
Bio-related Chemistry....Staff NIGMS 301-496-7301
Bio-related Chemistry....Staff NIGMS 301-496-7301
Biochemical genetics....Gottesman, Susan FAES 301-496-3524
Biochemistry Instrumentation....Staff NCRR 301-594-7938
Biochemistry....Litchen, Michael J. FAES 301-496-3393
Biodegradable Plastics....Staff EPA 202-260-5649
Bioethics Literature....Staff National Center for Bioethics Literature 800-633-3849
Bioethics of Clinical Decisionmaking....Staff NINR 301-496-0207
Bioethics....Bonkovsky, Frederick O. FAES 301-496-2429

Biofeedback....Staff NHLBI 301-496-4236
Biofeedback....Staff NIMH 301-443-4513
Biofuels....Morrer, Richard NEIC 202-586-9315
Biogasoline....Moorer, Richard NEIC 202-586-9315
Biohazard Control....Staff OD/ORS 301-496-2960
Biohazard Identification....Staff OD/ORS 301-496-2960
Biohazards (Cancer Research)....Staff NCI 301-496-5583
Biological Community Profiles....Staff FWS 703-358-1715
Biological Information Services....Goshorn, Jeanne C. NLM 301-496-1131
Biological Models and Materials Resources Program....Staff NCRR 301-594-7906
Biology....Block, Gene D. UVA 804-924-3606
Biomedical Communications....Staff NLM 301-496-6308
Biomedical Computer Centers....Staff NCRR 301-496-5411
Biomedical Engineering....Staff NIGMS 301-496-7301
Biomedical Engineering....Staff NCRR/BEIB 301-496-4741
Biomedical Information Services....Spann, Melvin L. NLM 301-496-1131
Biomedical Research Training and Fellowships....Staff NIGMS 301-496-7301
Biomedical Research Training and Fellowships....Staff DRG 301-594-7248
Biomedical Research Technology Program....Staff NCRR 301-593-7934
Biomedical Research Support Program....Staff NCRR 301-594-7947
Biomedical Research Technology Programs....Staff NCRR 301-594-7934
Biometrics....Huque, Mohammad FAES 301-443-4594
Bioorganic Chemistry....Kirk, Kenneth L. FAES 301-496-2619
Biophysics....Staff NIGMS 301-496-7301
Biopsy....Staff NCI 301-496-5583
Biotechnology Information Center....Dobert, Raymond NAL 301-504-5947
Biotechnology Information....Staff NLM 301-496-2475
Biotechnology, Trade Promo....Kimmel, Edward COMMERCE 202-482-3640
Biotechnology....Arakaki, Emily COMMERCE 202-482-0128
Biotechnology....Levin, Morris FAES 301-405-1056
Biotechnology....Moore, Mike PTO 703-308-4474
Biotechnology....Powell, L.J. NIST 301-975-2627
Bipolar Disorder....Staff NIMH 301-443-4513
Bird meat....Newman, Douglas USITC 202-205-3328
Birth Defects and Genetic Diseases....Erickson, David J. CDC 404-488-7160
Birth Defects and Developmental Disabilities....Adams, M. J. CDC 404-488-7150
Birth Defects (Developmental)....Staff NICHD 301-496-5133
Birth Defects (Neurological)....Staff NINDS 301-496-5751
Birth defects....Staff Cornelia de Lange Syndrome Foundation 800-223-8355
Birth Place....Hansen, Kristin CENSUS 301-457-2454
Birth Weight....Staff NICHD 301-496-5133
Birth....Staff NICHD 301-496-5133
Bishkek....Eighmy, Thomas Cnty AID 202-647-6920
Bismuth compounds....Greenblatt, Jack USITC 202-205-3353
Bismuth....Brown, Robert Jr. MINES 202-501-9577
Bismuth....Lundy, David USITC 202-205-3439
Bituminous coal....Foreso, Cynthia USITC 202-205-3348
Black Lung Disease....Gambino, Phil SSA 410-965-8904
Black Lung Disease....Sims, Anne CDC 404-639-3286
Black Holes....Staff NASA 410-338-4514
Black powder....Johnson, Larry USITC 202-205-3351
Blankets....Sweet, Mary Elizabeth USITC 202-205-3455
Blasting caps....Johnson, Larry USITC 202-205-3351
Blastomycosis....Staff NIAID 301-496-5717
Bleaching machines....Greene, William USITC 202-205-3405
Blepharitis....Staff NEI 301-496-5248
Blepharospasm....Staff NINDS 301-496-5751
Blepharospasm....Staff NEI 301-496-5248
Blind (Rehabilitation and Research)....Staff NEI 301-496-5248
Blind students....Staff National Adoption Center 800-424-8666
Blind....ACB 800-424-8666
Blind....Staff American Foundation for the Blind 800-232-5463
Blindness....Staff R P Foundation Fighting Blindness 800-683-5555
Blindness....Staff Blind Children's Center 800-222-3566
Blindness....Staff Prevent Blindness America 800-331-2020
Blindness....Staff Blinded Veterans Association 800-669-7079
Bloch-Sulzberger Syndrome (Neurological Effects)....Staff NINDS 301-496-5751
Blood Brain Barrier....Staff NINDS 301-496-5751
Blood Cells....Staff NHLBI 301-496-4236
Blood Coagulation....Staff NHLBI 301-496-4236
Blood Diseases....Staff NHLBI 301-496-4236
Blood Donations....Staff CC 301-496-1048
Blood Fractions....Staff NHLBI 301-496-4236
Blood Groups....Staff NHLBI 301-496-4236

Blood Plasma....Staff NHLBI 301-496-4236
Blood Plasma....Staff FDA/NCDB/OB 301-496-4396
Blood Pressure....Staff NHLBI 301-496-4236
Blood Resources (National)....Staff NHLBI 301-496-4236
Blood Substitutes....Staff NHLBI 301-496-4236
Blood Vessels....Staff NHLBI 301-496-4236
Blouses....Sweet, Mary Elizabeth USITC 202-205-3455
Blowers and Fans....Jonkers, Loretta COMMERCE 202-482-0564
Blowers....Riedl, Karl CUSTOMS 212-466-5493
Boat Building, Major Proj.....Vanderwolf, John COMMERCE 202-482-0348
Boat Radios....Staff FCC 202-418-0680
Boats, Craft....Vanderwolf, John COMMERCE 202-482-0348
Boats, Pleasure....Vanderwolf, John COMMERCE 202-482-0348
Boats, Pleasure....Lahey, Kathleen USITC 202-205-3409
Boats....Wholey, Patrick CUSTOMS 212-466-5668
Body Weight....Staff NIDDK 301-496-3583
Body-supporting garments, includes corset/brassieres....Sundar, Shetty USITC 202-205-3486
Boilers....Francke, Reic CUSTOMS 212-466-5669
Boilers....Fravel, Dennis USITC 202-205-3404
Bolivia (La Paz)....Staff Cnty State 202-647-3076
Bolivia/Minerals....Velasco, Pablo Cnty Mines 202-501-9677
Bolivia....Anne McKinney Cnty TDA 703-875-4357
Bolivia....Clapham, Lizzie Peace Corps 202-606-3499
Bolivia....Davis, Janice Peace Corps 202-606-3198
Bolivia....Epstein, Sharon Cnty AID 202-647-4358
Bolivia....Hunt, Rebecca Cnty Commerce 202-482-2521
Bolivia....Iwase, Noriko Cnty World Bank 202-473-0137
Bolivia....Jarvis, Catherine Cnty USIA 202-619-5867
Bolivia....Lopez, Miguel Antonio Cnty Embassy 202-483-4410
Bolivia....Neil, Jeff Cnty Treasury 202-622-1268
Bolivia...R. Petricevic, Andres Cnty Embassy 202-483-4410
Bolivia....Wilkins, Michele Cnty Export-Import Bank 202-565-3743
Bolivian Hemorrhagic Fever....Staff NIAID 301-496-5717
Bolting cloth....Cook, Lee USITC 202-205-3471
Bolts....Brandon, James USITC 202-205-3433
Bonds, Technical Information....Decorleto, Donna FRS 202-452-3956
Bone, articles of....Spalding, Josephine USITC 202-205-3498
Bone black....Johnson, Larry USITC 202-205-3351
Bone char....Randall, Rob USITC 202-205-3366
Bone Disorders....Staff NIAMS 301-496-8188
Bone Marrow Transplantation....Staff NIAID 301-496-5717
Bone Marrow Transplantation....Staff NHLBI 301-496-4236
Bone Marrow Transplantation....Staff NCI 301-496-5583
Bone Marrow Failure....Staff NHLBI 301-496-4236
Bone marrow....Staff National Marrow Donor Program 800-654-1247
Book Store (Clinical Center)....Staff FAES 301-496-5274
Bookbinding machinery....Lusi, Susan USITC 202-205-3400
Books (Export Promo)....Kimmel, Edward COMMERCE 202-482-3640
Books-Information-NIH Library....Staff NCRR 301-496-2184
Books-Information-NIH Library....Staff NLM 301-496-6095
Books....Abramowitz, Carl CUSTOMS 212-466-5733
Books....Lofquist, William S. COMMERCE 202-482-0379
Books....Twarok, Chris USITC 202-205-3314
Borax....Greenblatt, Jack USITC 202-205-3353
Borderline Personality Disorder....Staff NIMH 301-443-4513
Boric acid....Trainor, Cynthia USITC 202-205-3354
Boron compounds....Greenblatt, Jack USITC 202-205-3353
Boron....Greenblatt, Jack USITC 202-205-3353
Boron....Lyday, Phyllis A. MINES 202-501-9405
Bosnia....Alkalaj, Sven Cnty Embassy 202-833-3612
Bosnia...Dzirlo, Sakir Cnty Embassy 202-833-3612
Bosnia....Staff Cnty State 202-736-7677
Bosnia....Steblez, Walter Cnty MINES 202-501-9672
Bosnia-Herce....Waxman-Lenz Roberta Cnty Export-Import Bank 202-565-3742
Bosnia-Herzegovina....Fraile-Ordonez, Maria Cnty World Bank 202-473-4838
Bosnia-Herzegovina....Altheim, Stephen Cnty Treasury 202-622-0125
Bosnia-Herzegovina....Corwin, Elizabeth Cnty USIA 202-619-5055
Botswana/Minerals....Antonides, Lloyd Cnty Mines 202-501-9686
Botswana (Gaborone)....Staff Cnty State 202-647-8433
Botswana....Bowler, Gina Peace Corps 202-606-3644
Botswana....Fox, Russell Peace Corps 202-606-3645
Botswana....Holm-Olsen, Finn Cnty Commerce 202-482-4228
Botswana....Lane, Bernard Cnty AID 202-647-4228

Botswana....Maybury-Lewis Anthony Cnty Export-Import Bank 202-565-3739
Botswana....Moorad, Mustaq Ahmed Cnty Embassy 202-244-4990
Botswana....Patel, Praful C. Cnty World Bank 202-473-4250
Botswana....Rauch, Margie Cnty Treasury 202-622-0251
Botswana....Schwartz, Larry Cnty USIA 202-619-6904
Botswana....Sebele, Botseletse Kingsley Cnty Embassy 202-244-4990
Botswana....Younge, Nathan Cnty TDA 703-875-4357
Bottles, pails and dishes, of rubber of plastics....Raftery, Jim USITC 202-205-3365
Botulism....Staff NIAID 301-496-5717
Boundaries of Legal Areas, State Boundary Certifica....Sobel, Joel CENSUS 301-457-1099
Boundaries of Legal Areas, Boundary Changes....Goodman, Nancy CENSUS 301-457-1099
Bowel Diseases, Inflammatory....Staff NIDDK 301-496-5583
Bowen's Disease....Staff NCI 301-496-5583
Brachial Plexus Injuries....Staff NINDS 301-496-5751
Bradycardia....Staff NHLBI 301-496-4236
Braids, other....Shelton, Linda USITC 202-205-3457
Braille....Staff Braille Institute 800-272-4553
Brain Banks....Staff NINDS 301-496-5751
Brain Injury....Staff NINDS 301-496-5751
Brain Tumor....Staff American Brain Tumor Association 800-886-2282
Brain Tumor....Staff NIDCD 301-496-7243
Brain Tumor....Staff NINDS 301-496-5751
Brain Tumor....Staff NCI 301-496-5583
Brain....Staff NIMH 301-443-4513
Brain....Staff NINDS 301-496-5751
Brake systems...Oberleitner, Robert PTO 703-308-3569
Brakes....Oberleitner, Robert PTO 703-308-3569
Brass....Lundy, David USITC 202-205-3439
Brazil (Brasilia)....Staff Cnty State 202-647-9407
Brazil/Minerals....Gurmendi, Alfredo Cnty Mines 202-501-9681
Brazil....de Araujo, Fredrico Cesar Cnty Embassy 202-745-2700
Brazil....Farris, Larry Cnty Commerce 202-482-3871
Brazil....Flecha De Lima, Paulo-Tarso Cnty Embassy 202-202-745-2700
Brazil....Korff, Michael Cnty USIA 202-619-6835
Brazil....Marcus, Anthony Cnty Treasury 202-622-1218
Brazil....Maybury-Lewis Anthony Cnty Export-Import Bank 202-565-3739
Brazil....Parel, Chris Cnty World Bank 202-473-3918
Brazil....Prevot, Babette Cnty AID 202-647-4359
Bread and other baked goods....Schneider, Greg USITC 202-205-3326
Breast Cancer....Staff Y-Me National Breast Cancer Association 800-221-2141
Breast Cancer....Staff NCI 301-496-5583
Breast Implants....Staff FDA 800-532-4440
Breast Milk....Staff NICHD 301-496-5133
Breeder reactor....Greenblatt, Jack USITC 202-205-3353
Brick, ceramic....White, Linda USITC 202-205-3427
British Indian Ocean Territories (BIOT)....Staff Cnty State 202-647-8913
British Pound with options....Lang, Dawn M. CFT 312-353-9018
Broadcast News....Barkin, Steve UMD 301-405-2412
Broadcast services (Radio, Television)....Staff OD/OC 301-496-5895
Broadcasting Satellites....Staff FCC 202-418-1610
Broadcasting services....Huthoefer, Lori USITC 202-205-3303
Broiler with options....Fichert, David CFT 312-353-3181
Bromine....Conant, Kenneth USITC 202-205-3346
Bromine....Lyday, Phyllis A. MINES 202-501-9405
Bronchiectasis....Staff NHLBI 301-496-4236
Bronchitis (Chronic)....Staff NHLBI 301-496-4236
Brooms....Burns, Gail USITC 202-205-2501
Brucellosis....Staff NIAID 301-496-5717
Brunei/Minerals....Wu, John Cnty Mines 202-501-9697
Brunei (Bandar Seri Begawan)....Staff Cnty State 202-647-3276
Brunei....Abdul Latif, Hali Jaya bin Cnty Embassy 202-342-0159
Brunei....Cung, Raphael Cnty Commerce 202-482-3877
Brunei....Gilroy, Meg Cnty USIA 202-619-5836
Brunei....Imam, Fahmila Cnty Export-Import Bank 202-565-3738
Brunei....Shelton, Alison Cnty Treasury 202-622-0354
Brunei....Sukaimi, Janeh Cnty Embassy 202-342-0159
Brushes....Brownchweig, Gilbert CUSTOMS 212-466-5744
Brushes....Burns, Gail USITC 202-205-2501
Bruxism....Staff NIDR 301-496-4261
Bubonic Plague....Staff NIAID 301-496-5717
Buckets....Staff CPSC 301-504-0580

Buckles....Brandon, James USITC 202-205-3433

Budget Issues....Psner, Paul L. GAO 202-512-9573

Budget Issues....Irving, Paul L. GAO 202-512-9573

Buerger's Disease (Thromboangiitis Obliterans)....Staff NHLBI 301-496-4236

Builders Hardware....Williams, Franklin COMMERCE 202-482-0132

Builders' Wares....Burtnik, Brian CUSTOMS 212-466-5880

Building boards....Hoffmeier, Bill USITC 202-205-3321

Building components (wood)....Hoffmeier, Bill USITC 202-205-3321

Building Environment....Hill, James E. NIST 301-975-5851

Building Materials and Construction....Pitcher, Charles B. COMMERCE 202-482-0132

Building Materials, Trade Policy....Pitcher, Charles COMMERCE 202-482-0132

Building materials....Frohnsdorff, Geoffrey J. NIST 301-975-6706

Building Materials....Frohnsdorff, G.J. NIST 301-975-6706

Buildings, Energy Efficient....Kapus, Theodore NEIC 202-586-9123

Bulbar Palsy....Staff NINDS 301-496-5751

Bulbs (lamps)....Cutchin, John USITC 202-205-3396

Bulgaria (Sofia)....Staff Cnty State 202-647-0310

Bulgaria/Minerals....Steblez, Walter Cnty Mines 202-501-9672

Bulgaria....Amick, Jack Peace Corps 202-606-3548

Bulgaria....Amick, Jack Peace Corps 202-606-3548

Bulgaria....Botoucharova, Snejana Damianova Cnty Embassy 202-387-7969

Bulgaria....Gallagher, Tricia Cnty Treasury 202-622-0117

Bulgaria....Keller, Jeremy Cnty Commerce 202-482-4915

Bulgaria....Kraske, Huda Cnty World Bank 202-473-3564

Bulgaria....LeMasters, Cheryl Peace Corps 202-606-3547

Bulgaria....Petkov, Latchezar Cnty Embassy 202-387-7969

Bulgaria....Stillwell, Carol Cnty TDA 703-875-4357

Bulgaria....Waxman-Lenz, Roberta Cnty Export-Import Bank 202-565-4742

Bulimia....Staff NICHD 301-496-5133

Bulimia....Staff NIMH 301-443-4513

Bulletin Boards....Staff FCC 202-418-0940

Bulletin Board....Staff CENSUS 301-457-2310

Bullous Pemphigoid....Staff NIAMS 301-496-8188

Bunker "C" fuel oil....Foreso, Cynthia USITC 202-205-3348

Buprenorphine....Staff NIDA 301-443-6245

Bureau of Competition - Accounting....Broberg, Evelyn S. FTC 202-326-2569

Bureau of Competition - Accounting....Painter, David T. FTC 202-326-2574

Bureau of Competition - Accounting....Rowe, Ronald Baylor FTC 202-326-2610

Bureau of Competition - Accounting....Steffen, Boris J. FTC 202-326-2573

Bureau of Competition - Administration....Baumgartner, Phillip A. FTC 202-326-2546

Bureau of Competition - Administration....Foster, Patricia A. FTC 202-326-2852

Bureau of Competition - Administration....Kennedy, Chandra FTC 202-326-2547

Bureau of Competition - Administration....Kereszturi, Joyce A. FTC 202-326-2541

Bureau of Competition - Administration....McGraw, Jeanne M. FTC 202-326-2565

Bureau of Competition - Administration....Onley, Essie FTC 202-326-2544

Bureau of Competition - Administration....Shelton, Joyce A. FTC 202-326-2856

Bureau of Competition - Administration....Salters, Willie FTC 202-326-2561

Bureau of Competition - Compliance.....Clayborne, Delores M. FTC 202-326-2152

Bureau of Competition - Compliance....Baruch, Roberta S. FTC 202-326-2861

Bureau of Competition - Compliance....Davidson, Kenneth FTC 202-326-2863

Bureau of Competition - Compliance....Ducore, Daniel P. FTC 202-326-2526

Bureau of Competition - Compliance....Eckhaus, Joseph FTC 202-326-2665

Bureau of Competition - Compliance....Gill, Pamela A. FTC 202-326-2765

Bureau of Competition - Compliance....Lawler, Stewart FTC 202-326-3181

Bureau of Competition - Compliance....Libby, Kenneth A. FTC 202-326-2694

Bureau of Competition - Compliance....Ortiz, Rafael A. FTC 202-326-2672

Bureau of Competition - Compliance....Patel, Chirag FTC 202-326-2824

Bureau of Competition - Compliance....Piotrowski, Elizabeth A. FTC 202-326-2623

Bureau of Competition - Compliance....Rohlck, Eric C. FTC 202-326-2681

Bureau of Competition - Compliance....Schenoff, Anne K. FTC 202-326-2031

Bureau of Competition - Compliance....Scott, Pauline FTC 202-326-2670

Bureau of Competition - Compliance....Seymour, Jane R. FTC 202-326-2678

Bureau of Competition - Compliance....Strong, Arthur FTC 202-326-3478

Bureau of Competition - Compliance....Von Nirschel, David FTC 202-326-3213

Bureau of Competition - Compliance....Williams, Tonya FTC 202-326-2054

Bureau of Competition - Compliance....Youngwood, Gordon FTC 202-326-2808

Bureau of Competition - Gen. Lit. (Assoc and Business).....Lomax, Joan C. FTC 202-326-2901

Bureau of Competition - Gen. Lit. (Assoc and Business)....Catt, Malcolm L. FTC 202-326-2911

Bureau of Competition - Gen. Lit. (Assoc and Business)....Cox, Kent FTC 202-326-2058

Bureau of Competition - Gen. Lit. (Assoc and Business)....Boynton, Evelyn B. FTC 202-326-2737

Bureau of Competition - Gen. Lit. (Assoc and Business).....Veney, Wanda M. FTC 202-326-2895

Bureau of Competition - Gen. Lit. (Assoc and Business)....McCartney, P. Abbott FTC 202-326-2695

Bureau of Competition - Gen. Lit. (Assoc and Business)....Oppenheim, Martha H. FTC 202-326-2941

Bureau of Competition - Gen. Lit. (Assoc and Business)....Hoagland, John R. FTC 202-326-2893

Bureau of Competition - Gen. Lit. (Assoc and Business)....Draluck, Jonathan FTC 202-326-2564

Bureau of Competition - Gen. Lit. (Assoc and Business)....McNeely, Michael FTC 202-326-2904

Bureau of Competition - Gen. Lit. (Assoc and Business).....Marks, Randall FTC 202-326-2571

Bureau of Competition - Gen. Lit. (Assoc and Business)....Zimmerman, Seth B. FTC 202-326-2914

Bureau of Competition - Gen. Lit. (Assoc.and Business)....Harcketts, J. Dennis FTC 202-326-2783

Bureau of Competition - Gen. Lit. (Energy and Food)....Skubel, Marmichael O. FTC 202-326-2611

Bureau of Competition - Gen. Lit. (Energy and Food)....Wilensky, Steven FTC 202-326-2650

Bureau of Competition - Gen. Lit. (Energy and Food)....Washington, Norris FTC 202-326-2606

Bureau of Competition - Gen. Lit. (Energy and Food)....Frumin, Jill M. FTC 202-326-2758

Bureau of Competition - Gen. Lit. (Energy and Food)....Jones, Robert FTC 202-326-2740

Bureau of Competition - Gen. Lit. (Energy and Food)....Krulla, Rhett R. FTC 202-326-2608

Bureau of Competition - Gen. Lit. (Energy and Food)....Henning, Renee S. FTC 202-326-2621

Bureau of Competition - Gen. Lit. (Energy and Food)....Hershey, Micheline FTC 202-326-2191

Bureau of Competition - Gen. Lit. (Energy and Food)....Schneider, Marc FTC 202-326-2062

Bureau of Competition - Gen. Lit. (Energy and Food)....Dodson, Beverly A. FTC 202-326-2939

Bureau of Competition - Gen. Lit. (Energy and Food)....Licker, Naomi FTC 202-326-2851

Bureau of Competition - Gen. Lit. (Energy and Food)....Fishkin, James FTC 202-326-2663

Bureau of Competition - Gen. Lit. (Energy and Food)....Petrizzi, Maribeth FTC 202-326-2615

Bureau of Competition - Gen. Lit. (Energy and Food)....Salemi, Constance M. FTC 202-326-2643

Bureau of Competition - Gen. Lit. (Energy and Food)....Lipson, Frank FTC 202-326-2617

Bureau of Competition - Gen. Lit. (Energy and Food)....Nolan, Arthur J. FTC 202-326-2770

Bureau of Competition - Gen. Lit. (Energy and Food)....Tovsky, Robert S. FTC 202-326-2634

Bureau of Competition - Gen. Lit. (Energy and Food)....Silver, Daniel FTC 202-326-3102

Bureau of Competition - Gen. Lit. (Energy and Food)....McDonald, Carol E. FTC 202-326-2616

Bureau of Competition - Gen. Lit. (Energy and Food)....Shapiro, Barbara K. FTC 202-326-2633

Bureau of Competition - Gen. Lit. (Energy and Food)....Villavicencio, Alice M. FTC 202-326-3155

Bureau of Competition - Gen. Lit. (Energy and Food)....Richman, Peter FTC 202-326-2563

Bureau of Competition - Gen. Lit. (Energy and Food)....Proctor, Barbara FTC 202-326-2630

Bureau of Competition - Gen. Lit. (Energy and Food)....Liedquist-Scott, Philo FTC 202-326-2631

Bureau of Competition - Gen. Lit. (Energy and Food)....Schildkraut, Marc G. FTC 202-326-2622

Bureau of Competition - Gen. Lit. (Energy and Food)....Lawrence, Jo Ann FTC 202-326-2642

Bureau of Competition - Gen. Lit. (Energy and Food)....Joseph, Anthony Low FTC 202-326-2910

Bureau of Competition - Gen. Lit. (Energy and Food)....Johnson, Dennis F. FTC 202-326-2712

Bureau of Competition - Gen. Lit. (Health Care)....Hilder, Elizabeth FTC 202-326-2545

Bureau of Competition - Gen. Lit. (Health Care)....Jones, Patricia Y. FTC 202-326-2942

Bureau of Competition - Gen. Lit. (Health Care)....Narrow, David M. FTC 202-326-2744

Bureau of Competition - Gen. Lit. (Health Care)....Greene, Stephanie FTC 203-326-2925

Bureau of Competition - Gen. Lit. (Health Care)....Moreland, Judith A. FTC 202-326-2776

Bureau of Competition - Gen. Lit. (Health Care)....White, Christine FTC 202-326-3707

Bureau of Competition - Gen. Lit. (Health Care)....Maxwell, Sally L. FTC 202-326-2674

Bureau of Competition - Gen. Lit. (Health Care)....Brazille, Lorraine FTC 202-326-2059

Bureau of Competition - Gen. Lit. (Health Care)....Schwartz, Allison FTC 202-326-2926

Bureau of Competition - Gen. Lit. (Health Care)....Osnowitz, Steve FTC 202-326-2746

Bureau of Competition - Gen. Lit. (Health Care)....Pender, David FTC 202-326-2549

Bureau of Competition - Gen. Lit. (Health Care)....Allen, Patricia FTC 202-326-3176

Bureau of Competition - Gen. Lit. (Health Care)....Bissegger, Michael R. FTC 202-326-2154

Bureau of Competition - Gen. Lit. (Health Care)....Voss, Oscar M. FTC 202-326-2750

Bureau of Competition - Gen. Lit. (Health Care)....Blumenreich, Linda FTC 202-326-2751

Bureau of Competition - Gen. Lit. (Health Care)....Tucker, Deborah FTC 202-326-2766

Bureau of Competition - Gen. Lit. (Health Care)....Bellack, George R. FTC 202-326-2763

Bureau of Competition - Gen. Lit. (Health Care)....Davis, Rendell A., Jr. FTC 202-326-2894

Bureau of Competition - Gen. Lit. (Health Care)....Connelly-Draper, Molly FTC 202-326-2760

Bureau of Competition - Gen. Lit. (Health Care)....Langley, Stephanie FTC 202-326-2944

Bureau of Competition - Gen. Lit. (Health Care)....Gibbs, Garry FTC 202-326-2767

Bureau of Competition - Gen. Lit. (Health Care)....Friedman, Alan J. FTC 202-326-2742

Bureau of Competition - Gen. Lit. (Health Care)....Horoschak, Mark J. FTC 202-326-3688

Bureau of Competition - Gen. Lit. (Health Care)....Schorr, Gary FTC 202-326-3063

Bureau of Competition - Gen. Lit. (Health Care)....Brownman, Joseph S. FTC 202-326-2605

Bureau of Competition - Gen. Lit. (Health Care)....Bruno, Marian FTC 202-326-2846

Bureau of Competition - Gen. Lit. (Health Care)....Clark-Coleman, Sheila FTC 202-326-2759

Bureau of Competition - Gen. Lit. (Health Care)....Meier, Markus FTC 202-326-2781

Bureau of Competition - Gen. Lit. (Mergers)....Scribner, John E. FTC 202-326-3271

Bureau of Competition - Gen. Lit. (Mergers)....Weber, John C. FTC 202-326-2829

Bureau of Competition - Gen. Lit. (Mergers)....Woodard, Carolyn FTC 202-326-2706

Bureau of Competition - Gen. Lit. (Non-Mergers)....Waldeck, Cecelia FTC 202-326-3669

Bureau of Competition - Gen. Lit. (Non-Mergers)....Mills, Karen FTC 202-326-2052

Bureau of Competition - Gen. Lit. (Non-Mergers)....Sockwell, Stephen W., Jr. FTC 202-326-2950

Bureau of Competition - Gen. Lit. (Non-Mergers)....Seesel, John H. FTC 202-326-2702

Bureau of Competition - Gen. Lit. (Non-Mergers)....Hahm, Kevin K. FTC 202-326-2306

Bureau of Competition - Gen. Lit. (Non-Mergers)....Stevens, Peer L. FTC 202-326-3154

Bureau of Competition - Gen. Lit. (Non-Mergers)....Hackley, Jacqueline FTC 202-326-2729

Bureau of Competition - Gen. Lit. (Non-Mergers)....Abrahamsen, Dana FTC 202-326-2906

Bureau of Competition - Gen. Lit. (Non-Mergers)....Spriggs, Valicia A. FTC 202-326-2839

Bureau of Competition - Gen. Lit. (Non-Mergers)....Kinzelman, Gregory FTC 202-326-2073

Bureau of Competition - Gen. Lit. (Non-Mergers)....Antalics, Michael FTC 202-326-2821

Bureau of Competition - Gen. Lit. (Non-Mergers)....Bloom, Morris A. FTC 202-326-2707

Bureau of Competition - Gen. Lit. (Non-Mergers)....Nolan, Paul FTC 202-326-2770

Bureau of Competition - Gen. Lit. (Non-Mergers)....Costilo, L. Barry FTC 202-326-2024

Bureau of Competition - Gen. Lit. (Non-Mergers)....Inglefield, David L. FTC 202-326-2637

Bureau of Competition - Gen. Lit. (Non-Mergers)....Menna, Mark FTC 202-326-2722

Bureau of Competition - Gen. Lit. (Non-Mergers)....Cook, Robert FTC 202-326-2771

Bureau of Competition - Gen. Lit. (Non-Mergers)....Riddell, Stephen FTC 202-326-2721

Bureau of Competition - Gen. Lit. (Non-Mergers)....Gray, Jessica FTC 202-326-3342

Bureau of Competition - Gen. Lit. (Non-Mergers)....Johnson, Joyce FTC 202-326-2576

Bureau of Competition - Gen. Lit. (Non-Mergers)....Parker, Patrice FTC 202-326-2837

Bureau of Competition - Gen. Lit. (Non-Mergers)....Nagata, Ernest A. FTC 202-326-2714

Bureau of Competition - Gen. Lit. (Non-Mergers)....Cunningham, Linda FTC 202-326-2638

Bureau of Competition - Gen. Lit. (Non-Mergers)....Moscatelli, Catharine FTC 202-326-2749

Bureau of Competition - Gen. Lit. (Non-Mergers)....Dagen, Richard FTC 202-326-2628

Bureau of Competition - Gen. Lit. (Non-Mergers)....Easterling, Wallace W. FTC 202-326-2936

Bureau of Competition - Gen. Lit. (Non-Mergers)....Lanning, William FTC 202-326-3361

Bureau of Competition - Gen. Lit. (Non-Mergers)....Cole, Judith A. FTC 202-326-2693

Bureau of Competition - Gen. Lit. (Non-Mergers)....Doyle, Robert W., Jr. FTC 202-326-2819

Bureau of Competition - Gen. Lit. (Non-Mergers)....Dugan, John, F. FTC 202-326-2715

Bureau of Competition - Gen. Lit. (Non-Mergers)....Barnes, Rosenna FTC 202-326-2796

Bureau of Competition - Gen. Lit. (Non-Mergers)....McDuffie, Lourine FTC 202-326-2735

Bureau of Competition - General Litigation (Mergers)....Levy, Richard A. FTC 202-326-2814

Bureau of Competition - General Litigation (Mergers)....Brooks, Sylvia M. FTC 202-326-2682

Bureau of Competition - General Litigation (Non-Mergers)....Forster, Mary C. FTC 202-326-2212

Bureau of Competition - General Litigation....Malester, Ann B. FTC 202-326-2682

Bureau of Competition - General Litigation....Elmore, Ernest FTC 202-326-3109
Bureau of Competition - General Litigation....Miller, Anne E. FTC 202-326-2806
Bureau of Competition - General Litigation....Feldman, Dawn FTC 202-326-2064
Bureau of Competition - General Litigation....Jex, Elizabeth FTC 202-326-3273
Bureau of Competition - General Litigation....Berg, Karen E. FTC 202-326-2960
Bureau of Competition - General Litigation....Bernstein, Steven K. FTC 202-326-2423

Bureau of Competition - General Litigation....Moskowitz, Lenore H. FTC 202-326-2779

Bureau of Competition - General Litigation....Mendel, Jacqueline FTC 202-326-2603

Bureau of Competition - General Litigation....Stephenson, Patricia FTC 202-326-2877

Bureau of Competition - General Litigation....Triggs, Casey FTC 202-326-2804

Bureau of Competition - General Litigation....Tahyar, Benjamin FTC 202-326-2889

Bureau of Competition - General Litigation.....Blunt, Deborah M. FTC 202-326-2145

Bureau of Competition - General Litigation....Wilkinson, Laura FTC 202-326-2830

Bureau of Competition - General Litigation....Pettee, Susan P. FTC 202-326-2826

Bureau of Competition - General Litigation....Holden, James FTC 202-326-2963

Bureau of Competition - General Litigation....Pickett, Robert FTC 202-326-2682

Bureau of Competition - General Litigation....Moiseyev, Michael FTC 202-326-3106

Bureau of Competition - General Litigation....Higgins, Claudia R. FTC 202-326-2682

Bureau of Competition - General Litigation....Heydenreich, Melissa FTC 202-326-2543

Bureau of Competition - International Antitrust....Parisi, John J. FTC 202-326-2133

Bureau of Competition - International Antitrust....Karlsson, Paul FTC 202-326-2566

Bureau of Competition - International Antitrust....Feuillan, Jacques C. FTC 202-326-2379

Bureau of Competition - International Antitrust....Schimpff, Kirsten M. FTC 202-326-2731

Bureau of Competition - Mergers....Berman, Jacqueline FTC 202-326-3769

Bureau of Competition - Mergers....Bush, Michele B. FTC 202-326-2619

Bureau of Competition - Mergers....Faulk, Linda M. FTC 202-326-2822

Bureau of Competition - Mergers....Foreman, Elaine FTC 202-326-2531

Bureau of Competition - Mergers....Koberstein, Nicholas R. FTC 202-326-2743

Bureau of Competition - Mergers....Mahan, Carrie FTC 202-326-3680

Bureau of Competition - Mergers....Perez, Christina FTC 202-326-2048

Bureau of Competition - Mergers....Piercy, Carey FTC 202-326-2962

Bureau of Competition - Mergers....Taylor, Pamela FTC 202-326-2237

Bureau of Competition - Mergers....Waldman, Craig A. FTC 202-326-2602

Bureau of Competition - Mergers...Martin, Lisa FTC 202-326-2888

Bureau of Competition - Office of the Director....Clark, Barbara A. FTC 202-326-2562

Bureau of Competition - Office of the Director....Greenbaum, Joan S. FTC 202-326-2629

Bureau of Competition - Office of the Director....Green, Geoffrey FTC 202-326-2641

Bureau of Competition - Office of the Director....Egan, James C., Jr. FTC 202-326-2886

Bureau of Competition - Office of the Director....Arquit, Kevin J. FTC 202-326-2556

Bureau of Competition - Office of the Director....White, Roxanne FTC 202-326-4954

Bureau of Competition - Office of the Director....Winslow, Walter T., Jr. FTC 202-326-2560

Bureau of Competition - Office of the Director....Steptoe, Mary Lou FTC 202-326-2584

Bureau of Competition - Office of the Director....Taylor, Mildred E. FTC 202-326-2553

Bureau of Competition - Office of the Director....Whitener, Mark D. FTC 202-326-2845

Bureau of Competition - Office of the Director....Baer, William J. FTC 202-326-2952

Bureau of Competition - Office of the Director....Rowe, Ronald A. FTC 202-326-2610

Bureau of Competition - Policy and Evaluation....Morse, Howard FTC 202-326-2949

Bureau of Competition - Policy and Evaluation....Mongoven, James F. FTC 202-326-2879

Bureau of Competition - Policy and Evaluation....Cariaga, Frances P. FTC 202-326-2882

Bureau of Competition - Policy and Evaluation....Doying, William A.E. FTC 202-326-2582

Bureau of Competition - Policy and Evaluation....Averitt, Neil W. FTC 202-326-2885

Bureau of Competition - Policy and Evaluation....Hadley, Benjamin FTC 202-326-2598

Bureau of Competition - Premerger Notification.....Moss, Betty W. FTC 202-326-3650

Bureau of Competition - Premerger Notification....Ovuka, Nancy M. FTC 202-326-2609

Bureau of Competition - Premerger Notification....Epps, Melea R.C. FTC 202-326-2705

Bureau of Competition - Premerger Notification....Cohen, Victor FTC 202-326-2849

Bureau of Competition - Premerger Notification....Hancock, Thomas F. FTC 202-326-2946

Bureau of Competition - Premerger Notification....Kaplan, Jeffrey FTC 202-326-2943

Bureau of Competition - Premerger Notification....Horton, Renee A. FTC 202-326-2842

Bureau of Competition - Premerger Notification....Choslovsky, Jonathan FTC 202-326-2639

Bureau of Competition - Premerger Notification....Rubenstein, Hy David FTC 202-326-2887

Bureau of Competition - Premerger Notification....Smith, Richard B. FTC 202-326-2850

Bureau of Competition - Premerger Notification....Sipple, John M., Jr. FTC 202-326-2862

Bureau of Competition - Premerger Notification....Sharpe, Patrick FTC 202-326-2848

Bureau of Competition - Premerger Notification....Schechter, William I. FTC 202-326-3119

Bureau of Competition - Premerger Notification....Peay, Sandra M. FTC 202-326-2844

Bureau of Competition....Krauss, Joseph FTC 202-326-2713

Bureau of Consumer Affairs - Advertising Practices....Bloom, Jeffrey I. FTC 202-326-3327

Bureau of Economics - Antitrust....Ferguson, James M. FTC 202-326-3386

Bureau of Economics - Antitrust....Saltzman, Harold E. FTC 202-326-3459

Bureau of Economics - Antitrust....Wu, Lawrence FTC 202-326-2229

Bureau of Economics, Director's Office....Wise, Michael O. FTC 202-326-3344

Bureau of Economics - Office of the Director....Painter, Susan FTC 202-326-3370

Bureau of Economics - Policy Analysis....Person, Brenda W. FTC 202-326-2554

Burkina Faso....Foster, Whitney P. Cnty World Bank 202-473-4653

Burkina Faso....Maybury-Lewis Anthony Cnty Export-Import Bank 202-565-3739

Burkina Faso....Baily, Jess Cnty USIA 202-619-5900

Burkina Faso....Kotze, Joan Cnty Treasury 202-622-0333

Burkina Faso....Ouedraogo, Gaetan R. Cnty Embassy 202-332-5577

Burkina Faso....Ouedraogo, Oulemayne Cnty Embassy 202-332-5377

Burkina Faso (Ouagadougou)....Staff Cnty State 202-647-2791

Burkina Faso....Michelini, Philip Cnty Commerce 202-482-4388

Burkina Faso/Minerals....Mobbs, Philip Cnty Mines 202-501-9679

Burkina....Saulters, Willie Cnty AID 202-647-6039

Burkitt's Lymphoma....Staff NCI 301-496-5583

Burma/Minerals....Wu, John Cnty Mines 202-501-9697

Burma (Myanmor)....Dwight, Lawrence Cnty Treasury 202-622-0356

Burma (Myanmar)...Paine, George Cnty Commerce 202-482-3877

Burma (Rangoon)....Staff Cnty State 202-647-7108

Burma....Camp, Bea Cnty USIA 202-619-5837

Burma....Ntahomvukiye, Severin Cnty Embassy 202-342-2574

Burma....Respess, Rebecca Cnty TDA 703-875-4357

Burn care for children....Staff Shriners Hospital Referral Line 800-237-5055

Burn Research....Staff NIGMS 301-496-7301

Burning Mouth Syndrome....Staff 301-496-4261

Bursitis....Staff NIAMS 301-496-8188

Burundi (Bujumbura)....Staff Cnty State 202-647-3139

Burundi/Minerals....Antonides, Lloyd Cnty Mines 202-501-9686

Burundi....Barber, Ed Cnty Treasury 202-622-1730

Burundi....Goode, Sachiko Peace Corps 202-606-3695

Burundi....Henning, Herman Cnty USIA 202-619-5926

Burundi....Irabahinyuje-Sakubu, Beatrice Cnty Embassy 202-3422574

Burundi....Lloyd, Linda Cnty AID 202-647-9809

Burundi....Maybury-Lewis Anthony Cnty Export-Import Bank 202-565-3739

Burundi....Michelini, Philip Cnty Commerce 202-482-4388

Burundi....Wilhelm, Vera A. Cnty World Bank 202-473-4366

Buses....Hagey, Michael USITC 202-205-3392

Business Administration....Allen, Brandt R. UVA 804-924-4842

Business Cycle Indicators....Statistical Indicators Staff ECONOMIC 202-606-5366

Business Data Centers....Staff CENSUS 301-457-1305

Business Establishment List, Empl/Unempl. Stats....Searson, Michael LABOR 202-606-6469

Business Forms....Bratland, Rose Marie COMMERCE 202-492-0380

Business/Industry Data Centers....Staff CENSUS 301-457-2580

Business Initiatives....Harrison, Monika SBA 202-205-6665

Business Investment...Funk, Charles CENSUS 301-763-2542

Business Licenses....Staff FCC 717-337-1212

Business Opportunities, Small and Disadvantaged Utilization....Staff HUD 202-708-1428

Business Opportunities....Staff FCC 202-416-0934

Business Outlook, Chief....Vacant ECONOMIC 202-606-5365

Business Radio....Staff FCC 717-337-1212

Business Statistics, Business Owners' Characterist....McCutcheon, Donna CENSUS 301-457-2568

Business Statistics, County Business Patterns....Hanczaryk, Paul CENSUS 301-457-2580

Business Statistics, Minority Businesses....McCutcheon, Donna CENSUS 301-457-2568

Businesses, Disadvantaged....Smith, Gloria NEIC 202-586-7377

Businesses, Minority-Owned....Smith, Gloria NEIC 202-586-7377

Businesses, Women-Owned....Smith, Gloria NEIC 202-586-7377

Butadiene....Raftery, Jim USITC 202-205-3365

Butane....Land, Eric USITC 202-205-3349

Butter....Ludwick, David USITC 202-205-3329

Buttons....Shildneck, Ann USITC 202-205-3499

Butyl alcohol....Michels, David USITC 202-205-3352

Butyl benzyl phthalate....Johnson, Larry USITC 202-205-3351

Butyl oleate....Johnson, Larry USITC 202-205-3351

Butyl rubber....Misurelli, Denby USITC 202-205-3362

Butyl stearate....Johnson, Larry USITC 202-205-3351

Butylene....Raftery, Jim USITC 202-205-3365

Bypass Surgery....Staff NHLBI 301-496-4236

Byssinosis (Brown Lung Disease)....Staff NHLBI 301-496-4236

C

C.A.R.....Maybury-Lewis, Anthony Cnty Export-Import Bank 202-565-3739

Cable-Aeronautical Radio....Staff FCC 202-416-0903

Cable Broadcasting....Siegmund, John COMMERCE 202-482-4781

Cable Equipment Capability....Staff FCC 202-416-0903

Cable Forms....Staff FCC 202-416-0919

Cable-Franchising Authority....Staff FCC 202-416-0940

Cable-General Inquiries Western U.S.....Staff FCC 202-416-0953

Cable-General Inquiries Southern U.S.....Staff FCC 202-416-0860

Cable-General Inquiries Central U.S.....Staff FCC 202-416-0876

Cable-General Inquiries Northeastern U.S.....Staff FCC 202-416-0859

Cable Leakage Index....Staff FCC 202-416-0903

Cable-Signal Leakage....Staff FCC 202-416-0903

Cable-Small Systems Hotline....Staff FCC 202-416-0818

Cable Special Relief Petitions....Staff FCC 202-416-0903

Cable System Files....Staff FCC 202-416-0921

Cable-Technical Standards....Staff FCC 202-416-0903

Cable Television Franchising....Staff FCC 202-416-0940

CAD/CAM/CAE Software....Swann, Vera A. COMMERCE 202-482-0396

Cadastral Surveys....Staff FWS 703-358-1713

Cadmium....Kuck, Peter MINES 202-501-9436

Cadmium....Lundy, David USITC 202-205-3439

Caffeine and its compounds....Nesbitt, Elizabeth USITC 202-205-3355

Calcium carbonate....Johnson, Larry USITC 202-205-3351

Calcium carbonate....Tepordei, Valentin V. MINES 202-501-9392

Calcium compounds....Greenblatt, Jack USITC 202-205-3353

Calcium pigments....Johnson, Larry USITC 202-205-3351

Calcium sulfate....Johnson, Larry USITC 202-205-3351

Calcium....Greenblatt, Jack USITC 202-205-3353

Calcium....Miller, Michael MINES 202-501-9409

Calculators....Baker, Scott USITC 202-205-3386

Calculus....Staff NIDR 301-496-4261

Calendaring machines....Lusi, Susan USITC 202-205-3400

Calender of Events....Staff OD/OC 301-496-2266

California MTC (Manufacturing Technology Center)....Chernesky, John J. NIST 310-353-3060

Call Signs Allocation....Staff FCC 202-418-1680

Call Signs - Availability Only....Staff FCC 202-418-0270

Call Signs Block Allocation....Staff FCC 202-653-8126

Call Signs - Radio....Staff FCC 202-418-1680

Call Signs - TV....Staff FCC 202-418-1680

Calligraphy....Staff FWS 202-208-4111

Calling Card....Staff FCC 202-418-1530

Cambodia/Minerals...Lyday, Travis Cnty Mines 202-501-9695

Cambodia....Camp, Bea Cnty USIA 202-619-5837

Cambodia....Imam, Fahmila Cnty Export-Import Bank 202-565-3738

Cambodia....Pho, Hong-Phong B. Cnty Commerce 202-482-3877

Cambodia....Respess, Rebecca Cnty TDA 703-875-4357

Cambodia....Sanaka, Yoshio Cnty World Bank 202-458-0628

Cambodia....Schneider, Todd Cnty Treasury 202-622-0335

Cambodia....Staff Cnty State 202-647-3133

Cameos....Witherspoon, Ricardo USITC 202-205-3489

Cameras....Kiefer, Barbara CUSTOMS 212-466-5685

Cameroon (Yaounde)....Staff Cnty State 202-647-1707

Cameroon/Minerals....Dolley, Thomas Cnty Mines 202-501-9690

Cameroon....Barber, Ed Cnty Treasury 202-622-1730

Cameroon....Bezek, Jill Cnty TDA 703-875-4357

Cameroon....Henke, Debra Cnty Commerce 204-482-5149

Cameroon....Henning, Herman Cnty USIA 202-619-5926

Cameroon....Jordon, Kim Peace Corps 202-606-3097

Cameroon....Khouzam, Magda Cnty World Bank 202-473-4701

Cameroon....Maybury-Lewis Anthony Cnty Export-Import Bank 202-565-3739

Cameroon....Mendouga, Jerome Cnty Embassy 202-265-8790

Cameroon....Ndzengue, Pierre Cnty Embassy 202-265-8790

Cameroon....Trouba, Larry Peace Corps 202-606-3998

Cameroon....Vandergriff, Teresa Cnty AID 202-647-9207

Camphor....Randall, Rob USITC 202-205-3366

Canada (Ottawa)....Staff Cnty State 202-647-2170

Canada/Minerals....Heydari, Michael Cnty Mines 202-501-9688

Canada/trade matters....Burckey, Claude US Trade Rep 202-395-3412

Canada....Chretien, Raymond A.J. Cnty Embassy 202-682-1740

Canada....Don, Jonathan Cnty Commerce 202-482-3101

Canada....Gosnell, Peter Cnty Export-Import Bank 202-565-3733

Canada....Kulla, Morgan Cnty USIA 202-619-6853

Canada....Pascoe, Pat Cnty Treasury 202-622-0093

Canada....Wright, Robert Cnty Embassy 202-265-8790

Canadian Dollar with options....Bice, David CFT 312-353-7880

Canavan's Disease....Staff NINDS 301-496-5751

Cancer and Aging....Staff NIA 301-496-1752

Cancer and Aging....Staff NCI 301-496-5583

Cancer Control Program....Staff NCI 301-496-5583

Cancer Information Service....Staff NCI 800-422-6237

Cancer Institute, National....Nealon, Eleanor NIH 301-496-6631

Cancer Institute, National....Newman, Patricia NIH 301-496-6641

Cancer Prevention....Sunnarborg, Katharyn CDC 404-488-5080

Cancer (Reproductive Tract)....Staff NICHD 301-496-5133

Cancer (Reproductive Tract)....Staff NCI 301-496-5583

Cancer Research....Staff NCI 301-496-5583

Cancer....Staff ACS 800-227-2345

Cancer....Staff AMC Cancer Information and Counseling Line 800-525-3777

Cancer....Staff CIC 800-4-CANCER

Candida....Staff NIDR 301-496-4261

Candida....Staff NIAID 301-496-5717

Candidiasis....Staff NIAID 301-496-5717

Candidiasis....Staff NIDR 301-496-4261

Candles....Brownchweig, Gilbert CUSTOMS 212-466-5744

Candles....Randall, Rob USITC 202-205-3366

Candy....Maria, John CUSTOMS 212-466-5730

Canes....Spalding, Josephine USITC 202-205-3498

Canker Sores....Staff NIDR 301-496-4261

Canned Goods....Williams, Janis COMMERCE 202-482-2250

Canoes....Lahey, Kathleen USITC 202-205-3409

Capacitors....Malison, Andrew USITC 202-205-3391

Capacitors....Reynolds, Bruce A. PTO 703-308-3305

Capacitors....Vacant CUSTOMS 212-466-5673

Cape Verde....Radisic, Gradimir Cnty World Bank 202-473-7539

Cape Verde....Hutchings, Dayna Cnty Export-Import Bank 202-565-3737

Cape Verde....Baily, Jess Cnty USIA 202-619-5900

Cape Verde....Vandergriff, Teresa Cnty AID 202-647-9207

Cape Verde....Barber, Ed Cnty Treasury 202-622-1730

Cape Verde....Younge, Nathan Cnty TDA 703-875-4357

Cape Verde....Santon, Corentino, Virgilio Cnty Embassy 202-965-6820

Cape Verde....Barbosa, Jose Eduardo Cnty Embassy 202-965-6820

Cape Verde....Michelini, Philip Cnty Commerce 202-482-4388

Cape Verde....Mitchell, Willis Peace Corps 202-606-3708

Cape Verde (Praia)....Staff Cnty State 202-647-1596

Cape Verde Islands/Minerals....Mobbs, Philip Cnty Mines 202-501-9679

Capital Flows, International....Stekler, Lois FRS 202-452-3716

Capital Measurement, Productivity Research...Harper, Michael LABOR 202-606-5603

Capital Punishment....Greenfeld, Lawrence Justice Stat 202-616-3281

Capitation Grants for Health Professions Schools....Staff HRSA/BHPr 301-443-6880

Capitation Grants for Nurse Training....Staff HRSA/BHPr 301-443-5786

Caprolactam monomer....Matusik, Ed USITC 202-205-3356

Caps....Hamey, Amy USITC 202-205-3465

Caps....Jones, Jackie USITC 202-205-3466

Captioning....Staff NIDCD 301-496-7243

Carbohydrate products....Robinson, Douglas PTO 703-308-2897

Carbohydrates....Breneman, Bruce PTO 703-308-3324

Carbon activated....Randall, Bob USITC 202-205-3366

Carbon and graphite electrodes....Cutchin, John USITC 202-205-3396

Carbon black....Johnson, Larry USITC 202-205-3351

Carbon Black....Prat, Raimundo COMMERCE 202-482-0128

Carbon dioxide....Conant, Kenneth USITC 202-205-3346

Carbon disulfide....Conant, Kenneth USITC 202-205-3346

Carbon Products....Brownchweig, Gilbert CUSTOMS 212-466-5744

Carbon tetrachloride....Michels, David USITC 202-205-3352

Carbon....Johnson, Larry USITC 202-205-3351

Carboxylic acids....Michels, David USITC 202-205-3352

Carboxymethyl cellulose salts (surface active)....Land, Eric USITC 202-205-3349

Carcalon (Krebiozen)....Staff NCI 301-496-5583

Carcinogen Assessment....Staff EPA 202-260-3814

Carcinogen....Staff NCI 301-496-5583

Carcinogenesis....Donovan, Paul J. FAES 301-846-1245

Carcinoma....Staff NCI 301-496-5583

Card cases....Seastrum, Carl USITC 202-205-3493

Cardiac Arrest....Staff NHLBI 301-496-4236

Cardiac Disease....Staff NHLBI 301-496-4236

Cardiac Pacemakers....Staff NHLBI 301-496-4236

Cardiomegaly....Staff NHLBI 301-496-4236

Cardiomyopathy (Hypertrophic, Dilated)....Staff NHLBI 301-496-4236

Cardiomyoplasty....Staff NHLBI 301-496-4236

Cardiopulmonary Resuscitation (CPR)....Staff NHLBI 301-496-4236

Cardiovascular Disease....Staff NHLBI 301-496-4236

Cardiovascular drugs....Nesbitt, Elizabeth USITC 202-205-3355

Cardioversion....Staff NHLBI 301-496-4236

Carditis....Staff NHLBI 301-496-4236

Career Criminals....Langan, Patrick Justice Stat 202-616-3490

Career Criminals....Greenfeld, Lawrence Justice Stat 202-616-3281

Careers in Nursing....Staff DRR 301-443-5786

Caregiving and Older People....Staff NIA 301-496-1752

Caribbean Basin....Dowling, Jay Cnty Commerce 202-482-1648

Caribbean Development Bank....Nallari, Raj R. 202-473-8697

Caribbean Primate Research Center....Staff NCRR 301-594-7933

Caribbean....Allgeir, Peter US Trade Rep 202-395-6135

Caries....Staff NIDR 301-496-4261

Carotid Artery Disease....Staff NHLBI 301-496-4236

Carpal Tunnel Syndrome....Staff NIAMS 301-496-8188

Carpal Tunnel Syndrome....Staff NINDS 301-496-5751

Carpets....Sweet, Mary Elizabeth USITC 202-205-3455

Carrier Identification Codes....Staff FCC 202-202-0940

Carrier Common Line Charge...Staff FCC 202-418-1595

Carrots....McCarty, Timothy USITC 202-205-3324

Carrying Cases....Gorman, Kevin CUSTOMS 212-466-5893

Cartography....Staff FWS 703-358-1713

Case....Swann, Vera COMMERCE 202-482-0396

Casein....Randall, Rob USITC 202-205-3366

Cash registers....Baker, Scott USITC 202-205-3386

Castile soap....Land, Eric USITC 202-205-3349

Casting machines....Greene, William USITC 202-205-3405

Castleman's Disease....Staff NHLBI 301-496-4236

Cat Cry Syndrome (Cri Du Chat)....Staff NICHD 301-496-5133

Cat Scratch Fever....Staff NIAID 301-496-5717

Catalytic compositions....Beck, Shrive PTO 703-308-3808

Catalytic Converters....Staff EPA 202-233-9020

Cataplexy....Staff NINDS 301-496-5751

Cataract....Staff NEI 301-496-5248

Catheterization (Cardiac or Heart)....Staff NHLBI 301-496-4236

Cathode-Ray tubes....Kitzmiller, John USITC 202-205-3387

Cattle (Feeder) with options....Fichert, David CFT 312-353-3181

Cattle with options....Fichert, David CFT 312-353-3181

Caulking compounds....Johnson, Larry USITC 202-205-3351

Caulks....Johnson, Larry USITC 202-205-3351

Caustic potash....Conant, Kenneth USITC 202-205-3346

Caustic soda....Conant, Kenneth USITC 202-205-3346

Caymans....Brooks, Michelle Cnty Commerce 202-482-2527

CB Radio-General Licensing....Staff FCC 800-322-1117

CB Radio Service....Staff FCC 202-418-0680

CB Radio-Technical Questions....Staff FCC 202-418-0680

CD Players....Dicerbo, Mario CUSTOMS 212-466-5672

CD-ROM....Staff CENSUS 301-457-1234

CDC Information Center....Kennedy, Joan U. CDC 404-639-1601

CDC Information Center (Database).... CDC 404-639-1718

CEA (Carcinoembryonic Antigen)....Staff NCI 301-496-5583

Cedar leaf....Land, Eric USITC 202-205-3349

Celiac Disease....Staff NIDDK 301-496-3583

Celiac Disease....Staff NIAID 301-496-5717

Cell Aging....Staff NIA 301-496-1752

Cell Bank....Staff NIGMS 301-496-7301

Cell Biology....Staff NIGMS 301-496-7301

Cellular Function....Staff NIGMS 301-496-7301

Cellular General....Staff FCC 202-418-1310

Cellular Immunology....Finerty, John FAES 301-496-7815

Cellular Mobile Radio....Staff FCC 202-418-1310

Cellular Structure....Staff NIGMS 301-496-7301

Cellular Telephone Fraud....Staff FCC 804-441-6472

Cellular Unserved Areas....Staff FCC 202-418-1320

Cellular Unserved Areas....Staff FCC 202-418-1320

CellularVision....Staff FCC 202-418-0871

Cement compositions....Bell, mark L. PTO 703-308-3823

Cement, hydraulic....White, Linda USITC 202-205-3427

Cement Plants, Major Proj.....Brandes, Jay COMMERCE 202-482-3352

Cement....Clifton, James R. NIST 301-975-6707

Cement...Pitcher, Charles COMMERCE 202-482-0132

Cement....Solomon, Cheryl C. MINES 202-501-9393

Cements, dental....Randall, Rob USITC 202-205-3366

Cements of rubber, vinyl, etc.....Jonnard, Aimison USITC 202-205-3350

CENDATA....Staff CENSUS 301-457-1214

Census and You (Monthly Newsletter)....Tillman, Neil CENSUS 301-457-1221

Census and You (Monthly Newsletter)....Morton, Jackson CENSUS 301-457-1221

Census Awareness (Regional Offices)....Staff CENSUS 301-457-2032

Census Catalog....McCall, John CENSUS 301-457-1221

Census Customer Service Fax Number....Staff CENSUS 301-457-4714

Census Geographic Concepts....Staff CENSUS 301-457-1099

Census History....Solomon, Les CENSUS 301-457-1167

Census of Retail Trade, Virgin Islands....Hoover, Kent CENSUS 301-763-8564

Census of Retail Trade, Puerto Rico....Hoover, Kent CENSUS 301-763-8564

Census of Retail Trade, Guam....Hoover, Kent CENSUS 301-763-8564

Census of Selected Service Industries, Virgin Isl....Hoover, Kent CENSUS 301-763-8564

Census of Selected Service Industries, Puerto Rico....Hoover, Kent CENSUS 301-763-8564

Census of Selected Service Industries, Guam....Hoover, Kent CENSUS 301-763-8564

Census of Wholesale Trade, Virgin Islands....Hoover, Kent CENSUS 301-763-8564

Census of Wholesale Trade, Guam....Hoover, Kent CENSUS 301-763-8564

Census of Wholesale Trade, Puerto Rico....Hoover, Kent CENSUS 301-763-8564

Census Personnel Locator....Staff CENSUS 301-457-4608

CENTAM....Staff Cnty State 202-647-3381

Centenarians....Staff NIA 301-496-1752

Center for Hazardous Materials Hotline....Staff EPA 800-334-2467

Centers for Disease Control....Staff CDC 404-329-3291

Centers of Population....Hirschfeld, Don CENSUS 301-457-1099

Central African Republic....Michelini, Philip Cnty Commerce 202-482-4388

Central African Republic (Bangui)....Staff Cnty State 202-647-1707

Central African Republic....Cohen, Ellen Cnty World Bank 202-473-4463

Central African Republic....Gaba, N'dinga Cnty Embassy 202-483-7800

Central African Republic/Minerals....Dolley, Thomas Cnty Mines 202-501-9690

Central African Republic....Henning, Herman Cnty USIA 202-619-5926

Central African Republic....Koba, Henry Cnty Embassy 202-483-7800

Central African Republic....Palghat, Kathy Cnty Treasury 202-622-0332

Central African Republic....Bezek, Jill Cnty TDA 703-875-4357
Central Auditory Processing Disorders....Staff NIDCD 301-496-7243
Central Core Disease....Staff NINDS 301-496-5751
Central Europe/trade matters....Novelli, Catherine US Trade Rep 202-395-4620
Central Europe....Brereton, Barbara OPIC 202-336-8617
Central Storeroom....Staff OD/DL 301-496-9156
Centrifuges....Greene, William USITC 202-205-3400
Ceramic construction articles....White, Linda USITC 202-205-3427
Ceramic Gas Turbines....Sebestyen, Thomas NEIC 202-586-8012
Ceramic sanitary fixtures....Fulcher, Nancy USITC 202-205-3434
Ceramic table, kitchen articles....McNay, Deborah USITC 202-205-3425
Ceramics (Advanced)....Shea, Moira COMMERCE 202-482-0128
Ceramics Machinery....Shaw, Eugene COMMERCE 202-482-3494
Ceramics....Freiman, Stephen W. NIST 301-975-6119
Ceramics....Freiman, S.W. NIST 301-975-6119
Ceramics....Kalkines, George CUSTOMS 212-466-5794
Cereal breakfast foods....Schneider, Greg USITC 202-205-3326
Cereal grains....Pierre-Benoist, John USITC 202-205-3320
Cerebellar Arteriovenous Malformations....Staff NINDS 301-496-5751
Cerebellar Arteriosclerosis....Staff NINDS 301-496-5751
Cerebellar Ataxia....Staff NINDS 301-496-5751
Cerebellar Lesions....Staff NINDS 301-496-5751
Cerebral Death....Staff NINDS 301-496-5751
Cerebral Degeneration....Staff NINDS 301-496-5751
Cerebral Palsy....Staff NIDCD 301-496-7243
Cerebral Palsy....Staff United Cerebral Palsy Associations, Inc. 800-872-5827
Cerebral Palsy....Staff NINDS 301-496-5751
Cerebrotendious Xanthomatosis....Staff NINDS 301-496-5751
Cerebrovascular Disease....Staff NINDS 301-496-5751
Cerium compounds....Greenblatt, Jack USITC 202-205-3353
Cerium....DeSapio, Vincent USITC 202-205-3435
Ceroid Lipofuscinosis....Staff NINDS 301-496-5751
Certificates of Deposit....Reid, Brian FRS 202-452-3589
Certifications-Equipment Authorization....Staff FCC 301-725-1585
Cervical Disorders (Non-Malignancy)....NICHD 301-496-5133
Cervical Spine Disorders....Staff NIAMS 301-496-8188
Cesium compounds....Greenblatt, Jack USITC 202-205-3353
Cesium....Reese, Robert G., Jr. MINES 202-501-9413
Chad (N'Djamena)....Staff Cnty State 202-647-1707
Chad/Minerals....Dolley, Thomas Cnty Mines 202-501-9690
Chad....Cisse, Amadou B. Cnty World Bank 202-473-3345
Chad....Favitsou-Boulandi, Lemaye Cnty Embassy 202-462-4009
Chad....Henning, Herman Cnty USIA 202-619-5926
Chad....Kotze, Joan Cnty Treasury 202-622-0333
Chad....Mahamat-Saleh, Ahmat Cnty Embassy 202-462-4009
Chad....Michelini, Philip Cnty Commerce 202-482-4388
Chad....Saulters, Willie Cnty AID 202-647-6039
Chad....Trouba, Larry Peace Corps 202-606-3998
Chad....Waxman-Lenz, Roberta Cnty Export-Import Bank 202-565-3742
Chad....Younge, Nathan Cnty TDA 703-875-4357
Chagas' Disease....Staff NIAID 301-496-5717
Chain, of base metal....Kaplan, Stephanie USITC 202-205-3436
Chairman's Office.....Hamill, James C., Jr. FTC 202-326-2107
Chairs....Spalding, Josephine USITC 202-205-3498
Chalazion....Staff NEI 301-496-5248
Chalk (pigment grade)....Johnson, Larry USITC 202-205-3351
Chalks....Seastrum, Carl USITC 202-205-3493
Channel black....Johnson, Larry USITC 202-205-3351
Chaparral Tea....Staff NCI 301-496-5583
Chaplains (Hospital)....Staff CC 301-496-3407
Character Qualifications....Staff FCC 202-428-1600
Characteristics of Injuries and Illnesses, Comp. Wk....Biddle, Elyce LABOR 202-606-6170
Charcoal Broiling of Meat....Staff NCI 301-496-5583
Charcot-Marie-Tooth Disease....Staff NINDS 301-496-5751
Charge Syndrome....Staff NICHD 301-496-5133
Check controlled....Huppert, Michael PTO 703-308-1107
Check-writing machines....Scott, Baker USITC 202-205-3386
Chediak-Higashi Syndrome....Staff NIAID 301-496-5717
Cheese....Ludwick, David USITC 202-205-3329
Chelation Therapy (For Arterios., Hemosiderosis)....Staff NHLBI 301-496-4236
Chemical and Petroleum Branch....Staff EPA 919-541-5673
Chemical and Physical Hazards....Kapolka, Robert J. CDC 404-639-3147
Chemical compositions....Lieberman, Paul PTO 703-308-2523

Chemical Elements....Brady, Thomas CUSTOMS 212-466-4769
Chemical elements....Conant, Kenneth USITC 202-205-3346
Chemical Emergency Preparedness and Prevention....Staff EPA 202-260-8600
Chemical gas purification processes....Lewis, Michael M. PTO 703-308-2535
Chemical Hazards....Staff OD/ORS 301-496-2960
Chemical Information Services....Hazard, George F. NLM 301-496-1131
Chemical Kinetics....Lias, S. NIST 301-975-2562
Chemical Measurement Techniques....Patrinus, Aristides NEIC 301-903-3251
Chemical pathology....Copeland, Edmund FAES 301-594-7154
Chemical Plants, Major Proj.....Haraguchi, Wally COMMERCE 202-482-4877
Chemical Reactors....Warden, Robert PTO 703-308-2920
Chemical safety....Staff CPSC 301-504-0580
Chemical Sciences....Marianelli, Robert NEIC 301-903-5808
Chemical Spills National Response Center....Staff EPA 202-426-2675
Chemical Spills....Staff FWS 202-208-2148
Chemicals and Allied Products....Kelly, Michael COMMERCE 202-482-0128
Chemicals Industry Group....Tow, A. Richard SEC 202-942-1760
Chemicals (Technical and Non-Technical Questions)....Staff EPA 202-260-3850
Chemicals....Elkins, John Customs 202-482-7020
Chemicals....Shaw, Eugene COMMERCE 202-482-3494
Chemistry of hydrocarbons....Beck, Shrive PTO 703-308-3808
Chemotherapy (Cancer)....Staff NCI 301-496-5583
Chemotherapy (Effect on Teeth)....Staff NIDR 301-496-4261
Chesapeake Bay Program....Staff EPA 410-267-0061
Chicken pox....Staff NIAID 301-496-5717
Chief Economist, BEA....Triplett, Jack E. ECONOMIC 202-606-9603
Child abnormalities....Staff Human Growth Foundation 800-451-6434
Child Abuse and Neglect....Kharfen, Michael ACF 202-401-9215
Child abuse....Staff National Child Abuse Hotline 800-422-4453
Child Abuse....Staff National Resource Center on Child Abuse and Neglect 800-227-5242
Child Abuse....Staff OHDS/ACYF 301-205-8646
Child Abuse...Staff National Council on Child Abuse and Family Violence 800-222-2000
Child Care Information (Preschool)....Staff NIH 301-496-5144
Child Care, Population....Bachu, Amara CENSUS 301-457-2416
Child Care, Population....O'Connell, Martin CENSUS 301-457-2416
Child Development....Staff OHDS/ACYF 301-775-7782
Child Exploitation....Burgasser, George C. Justice 202-514-5780
Child Find....Staff Child Find of America 800-I-AM-LOST
Child Help....Staff Child Help USA 800-422-4453
Child Neglect....Staff National Resource Center on Child Abuse and Neglect 800-227-5242
Child Rearing....Staff NIMH 301-443-4513
Child safety....Staff CPSC 301-504-0580
Child....Staff Child Reach 800-556-7918
Childbirth....Staff NICHD 301-496-5133
Childbirth....Staff HRSA/BHCDA/DMCH 301-443-2170
Childhood Malignancies....Staff NCI 301-496-5583
Childhood Mental Illness....Staff NIMH 301-443-4515
Childhood Progressive Dementia....Staff NINDS 301-496-5751
Children with disabilities born to Vietnam Veterans....Staff Access Group 800-821-8580
Children (Gifted)....Staff NIMH 301-443-4515
Children's Attitudes Towards Aging....Staff NIA 301-496-1752
Children's Inn (NIH)....Staff 301-496-5672
Children's Mental Health....Staff Family Support and Children's Mental Health 800-628-1696
Children's TV Enforcement....Staff FCC 202-418-1630
Children's TV Renewal....Staff FCC 202-418-1630
Childwatch....Staff National Child Safety Council 800-222-1464
Chile/Minerals....Velasco, Pablo Cnty Mines 202-501-9677
Chile....Augusto, Suzana Campos Cnty World Bank 202-473-9096
Chile....Biehl, John Cnty Embassy 202-785-1746
Chile....Clapham, Lizzie Peace Corps 202-606-3499
Chile....Davis, Janice Peace Corps 202-606-3198
Chile....Geiser, Barbara Cnty Treasury 202-622-1271
Chile....John Herrman Cnty TDA 703-875-4357
Chile....Leeb, Howard Cnty USIA 202-619-5867
Chile....Montes, Joaquin Cnty Embassy 202-785-1746
Chile....Prevot, Babette Cnty AID 202-647-4359
Chile....Staff Cnty State 202-647-2407
Chile....Turner, Randy Cnty Commerce 202-482-1703
Chile....Wilkins, Michele Cnty Export-Import Bank 202-565-3743

Chilean Affairs....Early, Jane US Trade Rep 202-395-5190
Chimpanzee Breeding and Research Program....Staff NCRR 301-594-7938
China Affairs....Stites, Richard Cnty USIA 202-619-5839
China/Minerals....Tse, Pui-Kwan Cnty Mines 202-501-9696
China, People's Republic of (Beijing)....Staff Cnty State 202-647-6300
China (policy analyst)....Siegal, Byron US Trade Rep 202-395-5070
China (policy planning)....Weisel, Barbara US Trade Rep 202-395-5070
China/trade matters....Lee, Sands US Trade Rep 202-395-3900
China/trade matters....Lehr, Deborah US Trade Rep 202-395-5050
China/trade matters....Cantilina, Amy US Trade Rep 202-395-5050
China....Daoyu, Li Cnty Embassy 202-328-2500
China....Dong, Buming Cnty Embassy 202-328-2501
China....Dwight, Lawrence Cnty Treasury 202-622-0356
China....Frye, Lisa Peace Corps 202-606-0956
China....Huston, Christy Peace Corps 202-606-0970
China....Hutchings, Dayna Cnty Export-Import Bank 202-565-3737
China....Respess, Rebecca Cnty TDA 703-875-4357
China....Rix, David C. Cnty World Bank 202-458-5517
China....Tsui, Tom C. Cnty World Bank 202-458-0432
Chinaware articles....McNay, Deborah USITC 202-205-3425
Chinaware....Bratland, Rosemarie COMMERCE 202-482-0380
Chinaware....Kalkines, George CUSTOMS 212-466-5794
Chiropractic Association....Staff ACA 800-327-1129
Chlamydial Infections....Staff NIAID 301-496-5717
Chlorides, nonmetallic....Conant, Kenneth USITC 202-205-3346
Chlorine....Conant, Kenneth USITC 202-205-3346
Chlorofluorocarbons....Michels, David USITC 202-205-3352
Chlorofluorocarbons (CFC)....Staff EPA 202-233-9410
Chloroform....Michels, David USITC 202-205-3352
Chocolate....Gallagher, Joan USITC 202-205-3317
Chocolate....Maria, John CUSTOMS 212-466-5730
Cholera....Staff NIAID 301-496-5717
Cholesteatoma....Staff NIDCD 301-496-7243
Cholesterol....Staff NHLBI/IC 301-251-1222
Chondromalacia....Staff NIAMS 301-496-8188
Chondrosarcoma....Staff NCI 301-496-5583
Chordoma....Staff NCI 301-496-5583
Choriocarcinoma....Staff NCI 301-496-5583
Chorionic Villus Sampling (CVS)....Staff 301-496-5133
Choroiditis....Staff NEI 301-496-5248
Christmas Island/Minerals....Lyday, Travis Cnty Mines 202-501-9695
Christmas Decorations....Rauch, Theodore CUSTOMS 212-466-5892
Chrome pigments....Johnson, Larry USITC 202-205-3351
Chromium compounds....Greenblatt, Jack USITC 202-205-3353
Chromium....Papp, John F. MINES 202-501-9438
Chromium....Presbury, Graylin COMMERCE 202-482-5158
Chromium....Yost, Charles USITC 202-205-3432
Chronic Bronchitis....Staff NHLBI 301-496-4236
Chronic Disease Prevention....Byers, Tim CDC 404-488-5099
Chronic Disease Nutrition....Byers, Tim E. CDC 404-488-5099
Chronic EBV....Staff NIAID 301-496-5717
Chronic Fatigue Syndrome....Staff NIAID 301-496-5717
Chronic Fatigue Syndrome....Staff CFIDS 800-442-3437
Chronic Fatigue Syndrome....Staff NINDS 301-496-5751
Chronic Fatigue Syndrome....Staff NIMH 301-443-4513
Chronic Granulomatous Disease....Staff NIAID 301-496-5717
Chronic Hepatitis with Rheumatic Disease....Staff NIAMS 301-496-8188
Chronic Infections....Staff NIAID 301-496-5717
Chronic Myelogenous Leukemia....Staff NCI 301-496-5583
Chronic Obstructive Lung Disease (COPD)....Staff NHLBI 301-496-4236
Chronic Obstructive Lung Disease (COPD)....Staff NCNR 301-496-0526
Churg-Strauss Syndrome....Staff NIAID 301-496-5717
Cicatricial Pemphigoid....Staff NEI 301-496-5248
Cigarette Lighters....Maruggi, Al CPSC 301-504-0580
Cigarette Safety....Kaplan, Kathy CPSC 301-504-0580
Cigarettes, Research....Staff NCI 301-496-5583
Cigars and cigarettes....Harney, Amy USITC 202-205-3465
Cigars and cigarettes holders....Burns, Gail USITC 202-205-2501
Cigars and cigarettes lighters....Burns, Gail USITC 202-205-2501
Cinchona bark alkaloids and their salts....Nesbitt, Elizabeth USITC 202-205-3355
Cincinnati - Regional Office....Moore, William GAO 513-684-7125
Cinnamon oil (essential oil)....Land, Eric USITC 202-205-3349
Circulation/Circulatory System....Staff NHLBI 301-496-4236
Circumcision....Staff NICHD 301-496-5133

Cirrhosis....Staff NIDDK 301-496-3583
Cirrhosis....Staff NIAAA 301-443-3860
Citizens' Agreements....Staff FCC 202-418-1430
Citizenship....Staff CENSUS 301-457-2403
Citral...Land, Eric USITC 202-205-3349
Citrates....Michels, David USITC 202-205-3352
Citric acid....Michels, David USITC 202-205-3352
Citrus fruits....Dennis, Alfred USITC 202-205-3316
Civet....Land, Eric USITC 202-205-3349
Civil Aircraft Agreement....Bender, Juliet COMMERCE 202-482-4222
Civil Aviation Security....Flynn, Cathal FAA 202-267-9863
Civil Aviation Security Operations....Osmus, Lynne FAA 202-267-8537
Civil Aviation....Alford, Eugene COMMERCE 202-482-5071
Civil Cases (Federal)....Kaplan, Carol Justice Stat 202-307-0759
Civil Engineering....Demetsky, Michael J. UVA 804-924-6362
Civil Money Penalties....Holtz, Judy IG 202-619-1142
Clackerballs....Tyrell, Elaine CPSC 301-504-0850
Class A Power Increase Applications....FCC 202-418-2720
Classification System, Standard Industrial, Em/Un....Bennott, William LABOR 202-606-6474
Classification....Hartman, Frank CENSUS 301-763-7182
Classified electrical applications....Tarcza, Thomas C. PTO 703-308-1689
Classified mechanical applications....Jordan, Charles PTO 703-308-0918
Claudication....Staff NHLBI 301-496-4236
Clays....DeSapio, Vincent USITC 202-205-3435
Clays....Virta, Robert MINES 202-501-9384
Clean Lakes Program....Staff EPA 202-260-5904
Clean LAN/Waste Lan Hotline....Staff EPA 703-908-2066
Cleaners, under 10 lbs each....Randall, Rob USITC 202-205-3366
Cleaning apparatus....Recia, Henry PTO 703-308-1382
Cleaning machinery....Jackson, Georgia USITC 202-205-3399
Cleaning machines (textile)....Greene, William USITC 202-205-3405
Cleaning....Bedore, James USITC 202-205-3424
Cleaning....Goldberg, Gerald PTO 703-308-5443
Cleanwater Act....Staff EPA 202-260-5700
Clearances (News Releases)....Staff OD/OC 301-496-2535
Clearing Houses, Automated....Young, Florence FRS 202-452-3955
Clearinghouse for Census Data Services....Staff CENSUS 301-457-1305
Cleft Lip....Staff NIDR 301-496-4261
Cleft Palate....Staff Cleft Palate Foundation 800-242-5338
Cleft Palate....Staff NIDR 301-496-4261
Climate Change Division....Staff EPA 202-260-8825
Clinical Center (Reception and Information Desk)....Staff CC 301-496-3141
Clinical Electives for Medical Students at Clinical Center....Staff CC 301-496-2427
Clinical Information System (CLINFO)....Staff NCRR 301-594-7945
Clinical Medicine (Animals)....Staff NCRR 301-496-1076
Clinical Pathology....Staff CC 301-496-5668
Clinical Research Applications of Computer Technology.....Staff NCRR 301-594-7938
Clinical Research Centers....Staff NCRR 301-594-7945
Clinical Research....Staff CC 301-496-4891
Clocks....Luther, Dennis USITC 202-205-3497
Clocks....Schwartz, Stanley CUSTOMS 212-466-5895
Closure fasteners....Cuomo, Peter PTO 703-308-0827
Closures, stoppers, seals, lids, caps, rubber or plastic....Trainor, Cynthia USITC 202-205-3354
Clotting Disorders....Staff NHLBI 301-496-4236
Clove oil (essential oil)....Land, Eric USITC 202-205-3349
CMV Retinitis....Staff NEI 301-496-5248
CO/Fuel Gas Detectors....Staff Reuben CPSC 301-504-0580
Coal and Minerals....Staff FWS 703-358-2183
Coal and Electricity....Como, Anthony NEIC 202-586-5935
Coal Exports....Rasmussen, Joghn COMMERCE 202-482-1466
Coal Exports....Yancik, Joseph J. COMMERCE 202-482-1466
Coal Related Securities....Chavez, Carlos SEC 202-942-2970
Coal Statistics....Geidl, John NEIC 202-254-5570
Coal-tar pitch....Foreso, Cynthia USITC 202-205-3348
Coal tar, crude....Foreso, Cynthia USITC 202-205-3348
Coal Technology Export Program....Swink, Denise NEIC 202-586-0559
Coal, Technology....Vacant NEIC 202-586-1650
Coal Workers' Pneumoconiosis (Black Lung Disease)....Staff NHLBI 301-496-4236
Coal....Biggerstaff, Margie NEIC 202-586-3867

Coal....Foreso, Cynthia USITC 202-205-3348

Coal....Karsteter, Dorothy NEIC 202-586-4216

Coarctation of the Aorta....Staff NHLBI 301-496-4236

Coast Station Licenses....Staff FCC 717-337-1212

Coast Station Rules and Hearings....Staff FCC 202-632-7175

Coastal Anadromous Fish....Staff FWS 703-358-1718

Coastal Barrier Coordination....Staff FWS 703-358-2183

Coastal Barrier Research....Staff FWS 703-358-1710

Coated fabric apparel....Jones, Jackie USITC 202-205-3466

Coated Garments: Boys'....Raftery, William CUSTOMS 212-466-5851

Coated Garments: Women's....Raftery, William CUSTOMS 212-466-5851

Coated Garments: Men's....Raftery, William CUSTOMS 212-466-5851

Coating compositions....Bell, Mark L. PTO 703-308-3823

Coating elements....Hafer, Robert PTO 703-308-2674

Coating machines....Greene, William USITC 202-205-3405

Coats, Women's Knit....Crowley, Michael CUSTOMS 212-466-5852

Coats' Disease....Staff NEI 301-496-5248

Cobalt compounds....Greenblatt, Jack USITC 202-205-3353

Cobalt....Lundy, David USITC 202-205-3439

Cobalt....Presbury, Graylin COMMERCE 202-482-5158

Cobalt....Shedd, Kim B. MINES 202-501-9420

Cobalt....Staff NCI 301-496-5583

Cocaine....Staff Cocaine Anonymous 800-347-8998

Cocaine....Staff National Cocaine Hotline 800-262-2463

Cocaine....Staff NIDA 301-443-6245

Cochlear Implant....Staff NIDCD 301-496-7243

Cockayne's Syndrome....Staff NIA 301-496-1752

Cocks and valves....Mata, Ruben USITC 202-205-3403

Cocoa....Gallagher, Joan USITC 202-205-3317

Coffee and Tea....Gray, Fred Agri 202-219-0888

Coffee....Maria, John CUSTOMS 212-466-5730

Coffee....Schneider, Greg USITC 202-205-3326

Cogan's Syndrome....Staff NEI 301-496-5248

Cogeneration Energy Systems....Walter, Donald NEIC 202-586-2090

Cognition....Staff NICHD 301-496-5133

Cognition....Staff NIMH 301-443-4513

Coin Distribution....Epps, James FRS 202-452-2222

Coin handling....Huppert, Michael PTO 703-308-1107

Coin purses....Seastrum, Carl USITC 202-205-3493

Coinage....Epps, James FRS 202-452-2222

Coke for fuel....Foreso, Cynthia USITC 202-205-3348

Coke, calcined (non-fuel)....White, Linda USITC 202-205-3427

Cold Storage....Lange, John Agri 202-720-0585

Coley's Mixed Toxins....Staff NCI 301-496-5583

Colitis....Staff Crohn's and Colitis Foundation of America 800-932-2423

Colitis....Staff NIDDK 301-496-3583

Collagen Disease....Staff NIAMS 301-496-8188

Collagen Disease....Staff NHLBI 301-496-4236

Collagen/Collagenase....Staff NIDR 301-496-4261

Collapsed Lung....Staff NHLBI 301-496-4236

Collective Bargaining Agreements Analysis....Cimini, Michael LABOR 202-606-6275

Collective Bargaining Settlements, Major, Comp/Wk....Devine, Janice M. LABOR 202-606-6276

Collective Bargaining--Public File, Agreements....Cimini, Michael LABOR 202-606-6275

Colombia (Bogota)....Staff Cnty State 202-647-3023

Colombia/Minerals....Rabchevsky, George Cnty Mines 202-501-9670

Colombia....Jarvis, Catherine Cnty USIA 202-619-5867

Colombia....Lleras, Carlos Cnty Embassy 202-387-8338

Colombia....Parkinson, Katherine Cnty Treasury 202-622-5292

Colombia....Pizano Salazar, Diego Cnty Embassy 202-387-8338

Colombia....Schneider, John Cnty AID 202-647-4365

Colombia....Wallentin, Eduardo Cnty World Bank 202-473-5600

Colombia....Wilkins, Michele Cnty Export-Import Bank 202-565-3743

Color Blindness (Deficiency)....Staff NEI 301-496-5248

Colorectal Neoplasms....Staff NCI 301-496-5583

Coloring Matter....Joseph, Stephanie CUSTOMS 212-466-5768

Colostomy....Staff NIDDK 301-654-3810

Columbia....Moore, Paul Cnty Commerce 202-482-1659

Columbium....Cunningham, Larry D. MINES 202-501-9443

Columbium....Lundy, David USITC 202-205-3439

Columbium....Presbury, Graylinn, C. COMMERCE 202-482-5158

Coma....Staff NINDS 301-496-5751

Combs....Brownchweig, Gilbert CUSTOMS 212-466-5744

Combs....Burns, Gail USITC 202-205-2501

Commerce....DeMong, Richard F. UVA 804-924-3227

Commercial Aircraft (Trade Policy)....Bender, Juliet COMMERCE 202-482-4222

Commercial Development of Space....Norwood, Robert NASA 202-358-2320

Commercial/Indus Refrig....Bell, Richard COMMERCIAL 202-482-5126

Commercial Lighting Fixtures....Bodson, John COMMERCE 202-482-0681

Commercial Operator Licenses....Staff FCC 202-418-0680

Commercial Operators....Staff FCC 202-418-0680

Commercial Printing....Lofquist, William COMMERCE 202-482-0379

Commercial Printing....Lofquist, William COMMERCE 202-482-0379

Commercial Radio Operator Licensing....Staff FCC 202-418-0680

Commercial Radio apps.- Gen. Radiotelephone operator....Staff FCC 202-418-0680

Commercial Radio apps.- Global Maritime FCC 202-418-0680

Commercial Radio apps.- Radar Endorsement....Staff FCC 202-418-0680

Commercial Radio apps.- Radio Telegraph licenses....Staff FCC 202-418-0680

Commercial Radio apps.- Restricted Permit....FCC 202-418-0680

Commercial Rulings....Durant, John Customs 202-482-6990

Commercial Space Ventures....Norwood, Robert NASA 202-358-2320

Commissioned Officer Information....Staff OD/DPM 301-496-4212

Commissioner, Special Assistant to Office of....Barkume, Anthony J. LABOR 202-606-7808

Commissioner, Special Assistant to Office of....Parks, William LABOR 202-606-7807

Commissioner's Office - Azcuenaga, Mary L....Buek, Alexandra P. FTC 202-326-2145

Commissioner's Office - Azcuenaga, Mary L.....Heim, Joan L. FTC 202-326-2145

Commissioner's Office - Azcuenaga, Mary L.....Parrish, Pearl D. FTC 202-326-2145

Commissioner's Office - Azcuenaga, Mary L.....Jeter, LaJuan J. FTC 202-326-2145

Commissioner's Office - Azcuenaga, Mary L.....Bokat, Karen G. FTC 202-326-2912

Commissioner's Office - Azcuenaga, Mary L.....Warden, John B. FTC 202-326-2145

Commissioner's Office - Chairman's Office....Anderson, Rita D. FTC 202-326-2109

Commissioner's Office....Yao, Dennis A. FTC 202-326-2171

Commissioner's Office....Simmons, Gwendolynn FTC 202-326-2172

Commissioner's Office....Steiger, Janet D. FTC 202-326-3400

Commissioner's Office, Mary Azcuenaga....Pahl, Thomas B. FTC 202-326-2145

Commissioner's Office....Engle, Mary Koelbel FTC 202-326-3161

Commissioner's Office - Office of the Chairman....Rosenfeld, Dana FTC 202-326-2113

Commissioner's Office - Office of the Chairman....Bond, Ronald S. FTC 202-326-3424

Commissioner's Office - Owen, Deborah K.....Eisenstat, Philip FTC 202-326-2157

Commissioner's Office - Pitofsky, Robert....Etchison, Glenda L. FTC 202-326-3401

Commissioner's Office....Pitofsky, Robert FTC 202-326-2100

Commissioner's Office....Starek, Roscoe B., III FTC 202-326-2150

Commissioner's Office - Starek, Roscoe B., III....Armendariz, Rebecca FTC 202-326-2124

Commissioner's Office - Starek, Roscoe B., III....Cook, Barbara A. FTC 202-326-2150

Commissioner's Office - Starek, Roscoe B., III....Davis, Megan Wagner FTC 202-326-2127

Commissioner's Office - Starek, Roscoe B., III....Norris, Catherine FTC 202-326-2123

Commissioner's Office - Steiger, Janet D.....Anderson, Emily FTC 202-326-2109

Commissioner's Office - Steiger, Janet D.....Armstrong, Katherine FTC 202-326-3250

Commissioner's Office - Steiger, Janet D.....Miles, Elizabeth D. FTC 202-326-2108

Commissioner's Office - Steiger, Janet D.....Conn, David FTC 202-326-2114

Commissioner's Office - Steiger, Janet D.....Cohen, William E. FTC 202-326-2110

Commissioner's Office - Steiger, Janet D.....Crist, Sandy FTC 202-326-2105

Commissioner's Office - Steiger, Janet D.....Vedova, Holly K. FTC 202-326-3237

Commissioner's Office - Steiger, Janet D.....White, Robert S. FTC 202-326-2102

Commissioner's Office - Varney, Christine....Labuda, Laurie FTC 202-326-3315

Commissioner's Office - Yao, Dennis A.....Thompson, Patricia V. FTC 202-326-2169

Commissioner's Office - Yao, Dennis A.....Harris, LaVerne H. FTC 202-326-2170
Commissioner's Office - Yao, Dennis A.....Vecchi, Christa Van Anh FTC 202-326-3166
Commissioner's Office - Yao, Dennis A.....Corley, Derry L. FTC 202-326-2168
Commissioner's Office - Yao, Dennis A.....Murphy, R. Dennis FTC 202-326-3524
Commissioner's Office - Yao, Dennis A.....Dahdouh, Thomas FTC 202-326-2263
Commissioner's Office - Yao, Dennis A.....DeSanti, Susan S. FTC 202-326-2167
Commodity and Programs and Policies - Crops....Evans, Sam Agri 202-219-0840
Commodity Flow Survey....Fowler, John CENSUS 301-457-2108
Common Cold....Staff NIAID 301-496-5717
Commonwealth of Independent States....Levine, Richard Cnty Mines 202-501-9685
Commonwealth of Independent States....Staff Peace Corps 202-606-3973
Commonwealth of Independent States....Staff Cnty State 202-647-9559
Commonwealth of Independent States....Staff Peace Corps 202-606-3973
Communicable and Infectious Diseases....Staff NIAID 401-496-5717
Communicable and Infectious Diseases....Staff CDC 404-639-3534
Communication Human (Disorders)....Staff NIMH 401-443-4513
Communication Human (Disorders)....Staff NINDS 401-496-5751
Communication Human (Disorders)....Staff NIDCD 401-496-7243
Communication Human (Normal)....Staff NIDCD 301-496-7243
Communications Industry Group....Owings, Christopher SEC 202-942-1900
Communications Office....lachance, Janice R. OPM 202-606-1800
Communications....Combs, William SBA 202-205-6606
Communications....Stillman, Rona B. GAO 202-512-6412
Communications....Stillman, Rona B. GAO 202-512-6412
Community Affairs....Loney, Glenn FRS 202-452-3585
Community Corrections and Detention....Clark, John R. Justice Stat 202-514-8585
Community Development....England-Joseph, Judy GAO 202-512-7631
Community Energy Systems....Gunn, Marvin E. NEIC 202-586-2826
Community Health Centers....Staff HRSA 301-443-3376
Community of License Changes AM....Staff FCC 202-418-2660
Community of License Changes FM....Staff FCC 202-418-2180
Community of License Changes TV....Staff FCC 202-418-2180
Community Planning and Development....Staff HUD 202-708-0270
Community Reinvestment Act....Soboeiro, John FRS 202-452-3838
Community Services Program....Kharfen, Michael ACF 202-401-9215
Commuter Aircraft....Hakala, Katherine M FAA 202-267-8086
Commuting, Population....Boertein, Celia CENSUS 301-457-2454
Commuting....Salopek, Phil CENSUS 301-457-2454
Comoros (Moroni)....Staff Cnty State 202-647-6473
Comoros/Minerals....Antonides, Lloyd Cnty Mines 202-501-9674
Comoros....Barber, Ed Cnty Treasury 202-622-1730
Comoros....Bezek, Jill Cnty TDA 703-875-4357
Comoros....Eap, Pisei Phlong Cnty World Bank 202-473-4364
Comoros....Imam, Fahmila Cnty Export-Import Bank 202-565-3738
Comoros....Larsen, Mark Cnty USIA 202-619-4894
Comoros....Schmitz, Virginia Peace Corps 202-606-3334
Comoros....Walkins, Chandra Cnty Commerce 202-482-4564
Comparative Renewals AM/FM Stations....Staff FCC 202-418-2780
Comparative Renewals TV Stations....Staff FCC 202-418-1630
Comparative Medicine Program....Staff NCRR 301-594-7933
Compensation Administration....Mikowicz, Jerome OPM 202-606-2858
Compensation and Working Conditions, Asst. Commis.....Vacant LABOR 202-606-6300
Compensation and Working Conditions, Employee Ben.....Staff LABOR 202-606-6222
Compensation and Working Conditions, Employer Costs....Rogers, Brenda LABOR 202-606-6206
Compensation and Working Conditions, Industry injuries and illness....Staff LABOR 202-606-6180
Compensation and Working Conditions, Recorded Message....24-hour hotline LABOR 202-606-7828
Compensation and Working Conditions, Supp. Data....Biddle, Elyce LABOR 202-606-6170
Compensation and Working Conditions, Supp. Data....Biddle, Elyce LABOR 202-606-6170
Compensation and Working Conditions, Work Injury Report Surveys....Jackson, Ethel LABOR 202-606-6167
Compensation Levels and Trends, Asst. Commis.....MacDonald, Kathleen M. LABOR 202-606-6302
Competitive Bidding....Staff FCC 202-418-2030
Competitiveness Issues....Mendelowitz, Allan I. 202-512-5889
Complaints by Investors....Staff SEC 202-942-7040

Complaints Telephone (consumer)....Staff FCC 202-632-7553
Composites, Advanced....Manion, James COMMERCE 202-482-5157
Composting (Yardwaste and Municipal Solid Waste)....Staff EPA 703-308-7258
Compulsory Treatment (Drug Abuse)....Staff NIDA 301-443-6245
Computational Molecular Biology....Staff DRCT 301-496-1141
Computational Aerodynamics....Farrar, Diane NASA 415-604-3934
Computer and Communication Systems, Director of....Bennett, Harry D. NLM 301-496-1351
Computer and DP Services....Inoussa, Mary COMMERCE 202-482-5820
Computer and DP Services....Atkins, Robert G. COMMERCE 202-482-4781
Computer applications....Teska, Kevin PTO 703-305-9704
Computer Consulting....Adkins, Robert COMMERCE 202-482-4781
Computer control systems....Envall, Roy PTO 703-305-9706
Computer Crime....Kaplan, Carol Justice Stat 202-307-0759
Computer/data processing services....Bringe, Julie USITC 202-205-3390
Computer, Midrange....Woods, Clay COMMERCE 202-482-3013
Computer, Personal....Miles, Timothy O. COMMERCIAL 202-482-2990
Computer, Personal....Woods, R. Clay COMMERCE 202-482-3013
Computer, Portable....Hoffman, Heidi M. COMMERCE 202-482-0569
Computer Professional Services....Atkins, Robert COMMERCE 202-482-4781
Computer, Super....Streete, Jonathan P. COMMERCE 202-482-0480
Computer Systems and Services, Chief....Doyle, James P. ECONOMIC 202-606-9909
Computer systems...Harvey, Jack PTO 703-305-9704
Computerized Search Services....Staff NIH 301-496-6095
Computerized Search Services....Staff NCRR/NIH Library 301-496-1156
Computers and Business Equipment, Office of....Inoussa, Mary COMMERCE 202-482-5820
Computers in Medical Research....Staff DCRT 301-496-6203
Computers in Medical Research....Staff NCRR 301-594-7934
Computers Industry Group...Duvall, Steven C. SEC 202-942-1900
Computers, Midrange....Hoffman, Heidi M. COMMERCE 202-482-2053
Computers, Trade Promo.....Fogg, Judy A. COMMERCE 202-482-4936
Computers, Workstations....Sirceter, Jonathan COMMERCE 202-482-0480
Computers....Stillman, Rona B. GAO 202-512-6412
Concrete and products....White, Linda USITC 202-205-3427
Concrete....Clifton, James R. NIST 301-975-6707
Condensate, lease....Foreso, Cynthia USITC 202-205-3348
Conductors....Cutchin, John USITC 202-205-3396
Conductors....Picard, Leo PTO 703-308-0538
Conduit....Cutchin, John USITC 202-205-3396
Conduits....Curran, David CUSTOMS 212-466-5680
Conduits....Recia, Henry PTO 703-308-1382
Condyloma....Staff NIAID 301-496-5717
Confectionery Products....Kenney, Cornelius COMMERCE 202-482-2428
Confectionery....Gallagher, Joan USITC 202-205-3317
Confidentiality and Privacy Issues....Gates, Jerry CENSUS 301-457-2516
Confidentiality of Data....Kaplan, Carol Justice Stat 202-307-0759
Congenital Abnormalities....Staff NEI 301-496-5248
Congenital Abnormalities....Staff NINDS 301-496-5751
Congenital Abnormalities....Staff NICHD 301-496-5133
Congenital Adrenal Hyperplasia....Staff NIDDK 301-496-3583
Congenital Adrenal Hyperplasia....Staff NICHD 301-496-5133
Congenital Heart Disease....Staff NHLBI 301-496-4236
Congenital Infections....Staff NIAID 301-496-5717
Congestive Heart Failure....Staff NHLBI 301-496-4236
Congo (Brazzaville)....Staff Cnty State 202-647-3139
Congo/Minerals....Dolley, Thomas Cnty Mines 202-501-9690
Congo....Boussoukou-Boumba, Pierre Damien Cnty Embassy 202-726-0825
Congo....Henke, Debra Cnty Commerce 202-482-5149
Congo....Henning, Herman Cnty USIA 202-619-5926
Congo....Maybury-Lewis, Anthony Cnty Export-Import Bank 202-565-3739
Congo....Palghat, Kathy Cnty Treasury 202-622-0332
Congo....Sachika, Goode Peace Corps 202-606-3695
Congo....Wilson, Michael Cnty World Bank 202-473-4714
Congo....Younge, Nathan Cnty TDA 703-875-4357
Congressional Affairs....Staff CENSUS 301-457-2171
Congressional Districts, Boundaries....Ramirez, Lourdes CENSUS 301-457-1099
Congressional Districts, Address Locations....Staff CENSUS 301-457-1050
Congressional Districts, Component Areas....Ramirez, Lourdes CENSUS 301-457-1099
Congressional Inquiries....Staff SEC 202-942-0014
Congressional Relations Office....Hall, Dorian J. FTC 202-326-2195
Congressional Relations....Kando, Carol A. FTC 202-326-3152

Conjunctivitis....Staff NEI 301-496-5248

Connective Tissue Diseases....Staff NIAMS 301-496-8188

Consensus Development Conferences....Staff OD/OMAR 301-496-1143

Conservation....Staff NEIC 202-586-8800

Constipation and Aging....Staff NIA 301-496-1752

Constipation....Staff NIDDK 301-654-3810

Construction and Forestry, PPI, Prices/Lv. Cond....Davies, Wanda LABOR 202-606-7713

Construction, Domestic....MacAuley, Patrick COMMERCE 202-482-0132

Construction, Machinery....Heimowitz, L. COMMERCE 202-482-0558

Construction Machinery....Heimowitz, L. COMMERCE 202-482-0558

Construction paper....Rhodes, Richard USITC 202-205-3322

Construction Permit Extensions AM....Staff FCC 202-418-2670

Construction Permit Extensions FM....Staff FCC 202-418-2710

Construction Permit Extensions TV....Staff FCC 202-418-1630

Construction services....Polly, Laura USITC 202-205-3408

Construction Statistics, Census/Industry Surveys....Kristoff, James CENSUS 301-457-2813

Construction Statistics, Constr Authorzd by Bldg Permit....Hoyle, Linda CENSUS 301-457-4641

Construction Statistics, New Residential, Charact....Berman, Steve CENSUS 301-457-4666

Construction Statistics, New Residential, Sales....Berman, Steve CENSUS 301-457-4666

Construction Statistics, New Residential, House Complet....Fondelier, David CENSUS 301-457-4703

Construction Statistics, New Residential, In Select MSA....Jacobson, Dale CENSUS 301-457-4666

Construction Statistics, New Residential, Housing Start....Fondelier, David CENSUS 301-457-4703

Construction Statistics, Residential Alterations....Huesman, Joe CENSUS 301-457-1605

Construction Statistics, Residential Repairs....Huesman, Joe CENSUS 301-457-1605

Construction Statistics, Value New Constr Put in Place....Roff, Joe CENSUS 301-457-1605

Consulting services....DeSapio, Vincent USITC 202-205-3435

Consumer Affairs, Energy Affairs....Gauldin, Michael NEIC 202-586-5373

Consumer Affairs (all press inquiries)....Freidlander, Bernice OCA 202-395-7904

Consumer Affairs Compliance....Loney, Glenn FRS 202-452-3585

Consumer Assistance....Staff FCC 202-418-0190

Consumer Complaints about Financial Institutions....Whitehead, Myrna L FRS 202-452-3693

Consumer Expenditure Survey....Dopkowski, Ron CENSUS 301-457-3914

Consumer Expenditure Survey, Prices, Data Tapes....Passero, William LABOR 202-606-6900

Consumer Expenditure Survey, Prices and Liv. Cond....Jacobs, Eva LABOR 202-606-6900

Consumer Expenditure Survey, Surv. Data and Tapes....Passero, William LABOR 202-606-6900

Consumer Expenditure Survey, Surv. Oper., Pr/Lv.....Dietz, Richard LABOR 202-606-6872

Consumer Goods....Bodansky, Harry COMMERCE 202-482-5783

Consumer Price Indexes, Avg. Ret. Pr., Fuels and Util.....Adkins, Robert LABOR 202-606-6985

Consumer Price Indexes, Avg. Retail Food Pr--Mo.....Cook, William LABOR 202-606-6988

Consumer Price Indexes, Pr/Lv. Con, Data Diskettes....Gibson, Sharon LABOR 202-606-6968

Consumer Price Indexes, Prices and Living Cond.....Jackman, Patrick LABOR 202-606-6952

Consumer Price Indexes, Prices and Living Cond.....Jackman, Patrick LABOR 202-606-6952

Consumer Price Indexes, Prices and Living Conditions....Staff LABOR 202-606-7000

Consumer Price Indexes, Recorded CPI Detail....24-Hour Hotline LABOR 202-606-7828

Consumer Prices and Price Indexes, Asst. Comm....Greenlef, Joan LABOR 202-606-6952

Consumer Protection Bureau - Advertising Practices....Jones, Deitra FTC 202-326-3151

Consumer Protection Bureau - Advertising Practices....Ostheimer, Michael FTC 202-326-2699

Consumer Protection Bureau - Advertising Practices....Renant, Danielle FTC 202-326-3247

Consumer Protection Bureau - Advertising Practices....Kolish, Elaine D. FTC 202-326-3042

Consumer Protection Bureau - Advertising Practices....Johnson, Barbara J. FTC 202-326-3149

Consumer Protection Bureau - Advertising Practices....Hoppock, Theodore H. FTC 202-326-3087

Consumer Protection Bureau - Advertising Practices....Momin, Karim C. FTC 202-326-2418

Consumer Protection Bureau - Advertising Practices....Fremont, Laura FTC 202-326-2649

Consumer Protection Bureau - Advertising Practices....Greisman, Lois C. FTC 202-326-3404

Consumer Protection Bureau - Advertising Practices....Guelzow, Lynn F. FTC 202-326-2386

Consumer Protection Bureau - Advertising Practices....Kopchik, Lisa B. FTC 202-326-3139

Consumer Protection Bureau - Advertising Practices....Pulley, Samichie K. FTC 202-326-3147

Consumer Protection Bureau - Advertising Practices....Warder, Nancy S. FTC 202-326-3048

Consumer Protection Bureau - Advertising Practices....Rusk, Michelle K. FTC 202-326-3148

Consumer Protection Bureau - Advertising Practices....Rosso, Rosemary FTC 202-326-2174

Consumer Protection Bureau - Advertising Practices....Skidmore, Patricia A. FTC 202-326-3050

Consumer Protection Bureau - Advertising Practices....Bank, Kevin M. FTC 202-326-2675

Consumer Protection Bureau - Advertising Practices....Murray, Joanna C. FTC 202-326-3256

Consumer Protection Bureau - Advertising Practices....Levin, Toby M. FTC 202-326-3156

Consumer Protection Bureau - Advertising Practices....Maher, Anne FTC 202-326-2987

Consumer Protection Bureau - Advertising Practices....Mazis, Michael B. FTC 202-326-2613

Consumer Protection Bureau - Advertising Practices....Fink, Duane E. FTC 202-326-3145

Consumer Protection Bureau - Advertising Practices....Fair, Lesley A. FTC 202-326-3081

Consumer Protection Bureau - Advertising Practices....Ashford, LaToya C. FTC 202-326-3467

Consumer Protection Bureau - Advertising Practices....Cohn, Susan FTC 202-326-3053

Consumer Protection Bureau - Advertising Practices....Johnson, Barbara J. FTC 202-326-3149

Consumer Protection Bureau - Advertising Practices....Priesman, Phillip FTC 202-326-2484

Consumer Protection Bureau - Advertising Practices....Evans, Janet M. FTC 202-326-2125

Consumer Protection Bureau - Advertising Practices....Watts, Marianne R. FTC 202-326-3074

Consumer Protection Bureau - Advertising Practices....Thomas, Sheri FTC 202-326-3398

Consumer Protection Bureau - Advertising Practices....Wilkenfeld, Judith D. FTC 202-326-3150

Consumer Protection Bureau - Advertising Practices....Peeler, C. Lee FTC 202-326-3090

Consumer Protection Bureau - Advertising Practices....Winston, Joel FTC 202-326-3153

Consumer Protection Bureau - Advertising Practices....Knight, Sydney FTC 202-326-2162

Consumer Protection Bureau - Advertising Practices....Dahl, Brian A. FTC 202-326-3182

Consumer Protection Bureau - Advertising Practices....Davidson, Michael FTC 202-326-2454

Consumer Protection Bureau - Advertising Practices....Forbes, Georgianna A. FTC 202-326-3183

Consumer Protection Bureau - Advertising Practices....Del Borello, Michael FTC 202-326-3051

Consumer Protection Bureau - Advertising Practices....Colbert, Lynne J. FTC 202-326-3571

Consumer Protection Bureau - Advertising Practices....Cleland, Richard FTC 202-326-3088

Consumer Protection Bureau - Advertising Practices....Dershowitz, Michael FTC 202-326-3158

Consumer Protection Bureau - Advertising Practices....Axelroad, Benjamin FTC 202-326-3008

Consumer Protection Bureau - Consumer and Bus. Educ.....Vawter, Irene FTC 202-326-3268

Consumer Protection Bureau - Consumer and Bus. Educ....Holz, Dawne FTC 202-326-3087

Consumer Protection Bureau - Consumer and Bus. Educ.....Shanoff, Carolyn FTC 202-326-3270

Consumer Protection Bureau - Consumer and Bus. Educ.....Tressler, Colleen P. FTC 202-326-2368

Consumer Protection Bureau - Credit Practices....Cohen, Stephen FTC 202-326-3222

Consumer Protection Bureau - Credit Practices....Brinckerhoff, Clarke FTC 202-326-3208

Consumer Protection Bureau - Credit Practices....Credle, Lillie R. FTC 202-326-2975

Consumer Protection Bureau - Credit Practices....Lamb, Cynthia S. FTC 202-326-3001

Consumer Protection Bureau - Credit Practices....Wilmore, Sandra FTC 202-326-3169

Consumer Protection Bureau - Credit Practices....Sellers, Evelyn FTC 202-326-3226

Consumer Protection Bureau - Credit Practices....Morris, Lucy Eggersten FTC 202-326-3295

Consumer Protection Bureau - Credit Practices....Silverman, Steven D. FTC 202-326-2460

Consumer Protection Bureau - Credit Practices....Hansberry, Grace A. FTC 202-326-3236

Consumer Protection Bureau - Credit Practices....Nixon, Judith M. FTC 202-326-3173

Consumer Protection Bureau - Credit Practices....Isaac, Ronald G. FTC 202-326-3231

Consumer Protection Bureau - Credit Practices....Acuff, Victoria R. FTC 202-326-2773

Consumer Protection Bureau - Credit Practices....Kane, Thomas E. FTC 202-326-2304

Consumer Protection Bureau - Credit Practices....Reynolds, Carole L. FTC 202-326-3230

Consumer Protection Bureau - Credit Practices....Keller, Christopher W. FTC 202-326-3159

Consumer Protection Bureau - Credit Practices....D'Entremont, Donald FTC 202-326-2736

Consumer Protection Bureau - Credit Practices....Chang, Nina FTC 202-326-2708

Consumer Protection Bureau - Credit Practices....Cohen, Stephen L. FTC 202-326-3222

Consumer Protection Bureau - Credit Practices....Taylor, Brenda A. FTC 202-326-3125

Consumer Protection Bureau - Credit Practices....Medine, David FTC 202-326-3224

Consumer Protection Bureau - Credit Practices....Twohig, Peggy FTC 202-326-3210

Consumer Protection Bureau - Credit Practices....Yates, Valerie FTC 202-326-3494

Consumer Protection Bureau - Credit Practices....Carroll, Millicent FTC 202-326-2696

Consumer Protection Bureau - Credit Practices....Childs, Beverly R. FTC 202-326-3174

Consumer Protection Bureau - Credit Practices....Baheri, Leila M. FTC 202-326-5610

Consumer Protection Bureau - Credit Practices....Brown, Connie FTC 202-326-3212

Consumer Protection Bureau - Credit Practices....Taylor, Carletta D. FTC 202-326-3225

Consumer Protection Bureau - Credit Practices....Barrios, Jarrett FTC 202-326-3183

Consumer Protection Bureau - Credit Practices....Wahl, Hughes E. FTC 202-326-2999

Consumer Protection Bureau - Education....Jones, Michael J. FTC 202-326-2421

Consumer Protection Bureau - Enforcement....Boyle, Terrence J. FTC 202-326-3016

Consumer Protection Bureau - Enforcement....Brewer, Joel N. FTC 202-326-2967

Consumer Protection Bureau - Enforcement....Cowen, Jonathan FTC 202-326-2533

Consumer Protection Bureau - Enforcement....Dingfelder, Justin FTC 202-326-3017

Consumer Protection Bureau - Enforcement....Dublin, Brenda J. FTC 202-326-2976

Consumer Protection Bureau - Enforcement....Easton, Robert E. FTC 202-326-3029

Consumer Protection Bureau - Enforcement....Ecklund, Stephen C. FTC 202-326-2841

Consumer Protection Bureau - Enforcement....Feinstein, Jeffrey E. FTC 202-326-2372

Consumer Protection Bureau - Enforcement....Frankle, Janice Podoll FTC 202-326-3022

Consumer Protection Bureau - Enforcement....Frisby, Robert FTC 202-326-2098

Consumer Protection Bureau - Enforcement....Graybill, Dean C. FTC 202-326-3284

Consumer Protection Bureau - Enforcement....Kelly, Deborah H. FTC 202-326-3003

Consumer Protection Bureau - Enforcement....Koman, Joseph J., Jr. FTC 202-326-3014

Consumer Protection Bureau - Enforcement....Lewis, Ronald D. FTC 202-326-2985

Consumer Protection Bureau - Enforcement....Martin, Vada L. FTC 202-326-3002

Consumer Protection Bureau - Enforcement....Massie, Thomas D. FTC 202-326-2982

Consumer Protection Bureau - Enforcement....McMurtrey, Nathan FTC 202-326-2308

Consumer Protection Bureau - Enforcement....Metrinko, Peter FTC 202-326-2104

Consumer Protection Bureau - Enforcement....Mickum, George B. FTC 202-326-3132

Consumer Protection Bureau - Enforcement....Mills, James G. FTC 202-326-3035

Consumer Protection Bureau - Enforcement....Pate, Jeffrey FTC 202-326-2305

Consumer Protection Bureau - Enforcement....Phillips, Joyce D. FTC 202-326-3041

Consumer Protection Bureau - Enforcement....Purcell, Adam FTC 202-326-2038

Consumer Protection Bureau - Enforcement....Rodriguez, Edwin FTC 202-326-3147

Consumer Protection Bureau - Enforcement....Sacks, Ruth S. FTC 202-326-3033

Consumer Protection Bureau - Enforcement....Sciacca, Michael FTC 202-326-2305

Consumer Protection Bureau - Enforcement....Tatum, Barbara FTC 202-326-2978

Consumer Protection Bureau - Enforcement....Thomas, Beverly J. FTC 202-326-2938

Consumer Protection Bureau - Enforcement....Toufexis, Rose FTC 202-326-3011

Consumer Protection Bureau - Enforcement....Vecellio, Constance M. FTC 202-326-2966

Consumer Protection Bureau - Enforcement....Welther, Michael S. FTC 202-326-2038

Consumer Protection Bureau - Enforcement....Wilenzick, Marc B. FTC 202-326-2442

Consumer Protection Bureau - Enforcement....Wright, Janet FTC 202-326-2980

Consumer Protection Bureau - Marketing Practices....D'Mara, Jeffries FTC 202-326-2264

Consumer Protection Bureau - Marketing Practices....Stone, Christopher FTC 202-326-3138

Consumer Protection Bureau - Marketing Practices....Ireland, Robert S. FTC 202-326-3114

Consumer Protection Bureau - Marketing Practices....Shetty, Vaishali FTC 202-326-2149

Consumer Protection Bureau - Marketing Practices....Jennings, Carol FTC 202-326-3010

Consumer Protection Bureau - Marketing Practices....Hile, Allen FTC 202-326-3122

Consumer Protection Bureau - Marketing Practices....Harrington, Eileen FTC 202-326-3127

Consumer Protection Bureau - Marketing Practices....Kresses, Mamie FTC 202-326-2070

Consumer Protection Bureau - Marketing Practices....Hodapp, Lawrence FTC 202-326-3105

Consumer Protection Bureau - Marketing Practices....Singer, John Andrew FTC 202-326-3234

Consumer Protection Bureau - Marketing Practices....Tregillus, Craig FTC 202-326-2970

Consumer Protection Bureau - Marketing Practices....Torok, David FTC 202-326-3075

Free Experts

Consumer Protection Bureau - Marketing Practices....Quaresima, Richard A. FTC
202-326-3130

Consumer Protection Bureau - Marketing Practices....Reznek, Sarah FTC
202-326-2213

Consumer Protection Bureau - Marketing Practices....Pitofsky, Sally Forman FTC
202-326-3318

Consumer Protection Bureau - Marketing Practices....Shikiar, Robert FTC
202-326-3009

Consumer Protection Bureau - Marketing Practices....Luehr, Paul H. FTC
202-326-2236

Consumer Protection Bureau - Marketing Practices....Guerard, Collot FTC
202-326-3338

Consumer Protection Bureau - Marketing Practices....Haynes, William L. FTC
202-326-3107

Consumer Protection Bureau - Marketing Practices....Howard, Patricia S. FTC
202-326-2321

Consumer Protection Bureau - Marketing Practices....Howard, Myra FTC
202-326-2047

Consumer Protection Bureau - Marketing Practices....Grant, Elizabeth FTC
202-326-3299

Consumer Protection Bureau - Marketing Practices....Feinstein, Mary S. FTC
202-326-3064

Consumer Protection Bureau - Marketing Practices....Schwanke, Marianne K. FTC
202-326-3165

Consumer Protection Bureau - Marketing Practices....Banks, Nicole O. FTC
202-326-2264

Consumer Protection Bureau - Marketing Practices....Danielson, Carole I. FTC
202-326-3115

Consumer Protection Bureau - Marketing Practices....Modell, Shira D. FTC
202-326-3116

Consumer Protection Bureau - Marketing Practices....Rowan, Thomas P. FTC
202-326-3129

Consumer Protection Bureau - Marketing Practices....Toporoff, Steven FTC
202-326-3135

Consumer Protection Bureau - Marketing Practices....Morris, Beverly M. FTC
202-326-3260

Consumer Protection Bureau - Marketing Practices....Salsburg, Daniel FTC
202-326-3032

Consumer Protection Bureau - Marketing Practices....Kupchyk, Areta L. FTC
202-326-2014

Consumer Protection Bureau - Marketing Practices....Johnson, Delores M. FTC
220-326-3124

Consumer Protection Bureau - Marketing Practices....Norton, Lawrence FTC
202-326-3126

Consumer Protection Bureau - Marketing Practices....Vera, Martha W. FTC
202-326-3096

Consumer Protection Bureau - Marketing Practices....Hudging, Iona FTC
202-326-2927

Consumer Protection Bureau - Marketing Practices....Cook, John M. FTC
202-326-2056

Consumer Protection Bureau - Marketing Practices....Cohn, Thomas A. FTC
202-326-3532

Consumer Protection Bureau - Marketing Practices....Howerton, Kent C. FTC
202-326-3013

Consumer Protection Bureau - Office of Director....Hutchins, Clovia FTC
202-326-3215

Consumer Protection Bureau - Office of Director....Grossman, Beth M. FTC
202-326-3019

Consumer Protection Bureau - Office of Director....Maronick, Thomas J. FTC
202-326-2291

Consumer Protection Bureau - Office of Director....Jung, Louise R. FTC
202-326-2989

Consumer Protection Bureau - Office of Director....Broder, Betsy FTC
202-326-2968

Consumer Protection Bureau - Office of Director....Chung, Jock K. FTC
202-326-2984

Consumer Protection Bureau - Office of Director....Parnes, Lydia B. FTC
202-326-2676

Consumer Protection Bureau - Office of Director....Legal, Sharon V. FTC
202-326-3240

Consumer Protection Bureau - Office of Director....Bernstein, Jodie FTC
202-326-3430

Consumer Protection Bureau - Office of Director....Morris, Lee Willis FTC
202-326-3312

Consumer Protection Bureau - Office of Director....Enright, Maureen FTC
202-326-3160

Consumer Protection Bureau - Office of Director....Brown, Gloria FTC
202-326-3047

Consumer Protection Bureau - Operations....Bow, Kimberley D. FTC
202-326-3252

Consumer Protection Bureau - Operations....Branch, Nicole FTC 202-326-2086

Consumer Protection Bureau - Operations....Burruss, James S., Jr. FTC
202-326-3261

Consumer Protection Bureau - Operations....Clark, Randal S. FTC 202-326-3685

Consumer Protection Bureau - Operations....Cossette, Darlene M. FTC
202-326-3255

Consumer Protection Bureau - Operations....Mandak, Dondra M. FTC
202-326-3246

Consumer Protection Bureau - Operations....Miller, Sylvia FTC 202-326-3258

Consumer Protection Bureau - Operations....Moten, Verletta FTC 202-326-6252

Consumer Protection Bureau - Operations....Peterson, Mark D. FTC 202-326-3731

Consumer Protection Bureau - Operations....Solomon, Tsione FTC 202-326-3251

Consumer Protection Bureau - Operations....Tharrington, Nicole L. FTC
202-326-2416

Consumer Protection Bureau - Operations....Tufts, Tamar FTC 202-326-2411

Consumer Protection Bureau - Service Industry....Sheer, Alain FTC 202-326-3321

Consumer Protection Bureau - Service Industry....Breslauer, Alan D. FTC
202-326-2430

Consumer Protection Bureau - Service Industry....Osinbajo, Deborah A. FTC
202-326-3316

Consumer Protection Bureau - Service Industry....Gordimer, Douglas FTC
202-326-3003

Consumer Protection Bureau - Service Industry....Hippsley, Heather FTC
202-326-3285

Consumer Protection Bureau - Service Industry....Katz, Michael A. FTC
202-326-3123

Consumer Protection Bureau - Service Industry....Friedman, Robert D. FTC
202-326-3297

Consumer Protection Bureau - Service Industry....Owens, Denise FTC
202-326-3277

Consumer Protection Bureau - Service Industry....Bowie, Darren FTC
202-326-2018

Consumer Protection Bureau - Service Industry....Jones, Elaine FTC 202-326-3622

Consumer Protection Bureau - Service Industry....Spiegel, David R. FTC
202-326-3281

Consumer Protection Bureau - Service Industry....Stevenson, Hugh FTC
202-326-3511

Consumer Protection Bureau - Service Industry Practices....Bash, Eric FTC
202-326-2892

Consumer Protection Bureau - Service Industry....Spiro, Daniel A. FTC
202-326-3288

Consumer Protection Bureau - Service Industry....Lamberton, Peter W. FTC
202-326-3274

Consumer Protection Bureau - Service Industry....Mooradian, Jeffrey FTC
202-326-3086

Consumer Protection Bureau - Service Industry....Aliza, Ben FTC 202-326-2905

Consumer Protection Bureau - Service Industry....Toone, Cassandra L. FTC
202-326-3276

Consumer Protection Bureau - Service Industry....Kinscheck, Renate FTC
202-326-3283

Consumer Protection Bureau - Service Industry Pract....Crowley, John A. FTC
202-326-3280

Consumer Protection Bureau - Service Industry....Rothchild, John FTC
202-326-3307

Consumer Protection Bureau - Service Industry....Wagner, Connie FTC
202-326-3309

Consumer Protection Bureau - Service Industry....Dolan, James Reilly FTC
202-326-3292

Consumer Protection Bureau - Service Industry....Chambers, Sylvia J. FTC
202-326-3286

Consumer Protection Bureau - Service Industry....Williams, Gwendolyn C. FTC
202-326-3311

Consumer Protection Bureau - Service Industry Practices.....Daynard, Matthew
FTC 202-326-3291

Consumer Protection Bureau - Service Industry....Abdullah, Raouf FTC
202-326-3024

Consumer Protection Bureau - Service Industry....Gurwitz, Stephen FTC
202-326-3272

Consumer Protection Bureau - Service Industry....Kelly, Richard F. FTC 202-326-3304

Consumer Protection Bureau - Service Industry Prac....Michaels, Jason J. FTC 202-326-2239

Consumer Protection Bureau - Service Industry....Jones-Thompson, Gwendolyn L. FTC 202-326-3305

Consumer Protection Bureau - Service Industry Prac....Mills, Sondra FTC 202-326-2673

Consumer Protection Bureau - Service Industry....Fields, Mary C. FTC 202-326-3098

Consumer Protection Bureau - Service Industry....Lesemann, Dana FTC 202-326-3146

Consumer Protection Bureau - Service Industry....Gross, Walter, III FTC 202-326-3319

Consumer Protection Bureau - Service Industry....Fix, David FTC 202-326-3298

Consumer Protection Bureau - Service Industry Practices....Chua, Michele FTC 202-326-3248

Consumer Protection Bureau....Jackson, Howard R. FTC 202-326-3170

Consumer Protection Bureau....Brody, Jay D. FTC 202-326-2419

Consumer Protection Bureau....Bertrand, Jenna R. FTC 202-326-2823

Consumer Protection Bureau....Lefevre, John F. FTC 202-326-3209

Consumer Protection Bureau....Blickman, Neil J. FTC 202-326-3038

Consumer Protection Bureau....Bonanno, Peter FTC 202-326-2495

Consumer Protection, Business Education....Jansen, Bonnie FTC 202-326-2988

Contact lens....Staff Contact Lens Manufacturers Association 800-343-5367

Contact Lenses....Staff NEI 301-496-5248

Containers Industry Group....Duvall, Steven SEC 202-942-1950

Containers, of base metal....Fulcher, Nancy USITC 202-205-3434

Containers (of wood)....Hoffmeier, Bill USITC 202-205-3321

Containment Systems....Barrett, Richard J. NRC 301-415-3627

Contaminants, Environmental....Staff FWS 703-358-2148

Contest Giveaway....Staff FCC 202-418-1430

Continental Shelf, Outer....Staff FWS 202-358-2183

Continuous Ambulatory Peritoneal Dialysis (CAPD)....Staff NIDDK 301-654-4415

Contraception....Staff NICHD 301-496-5133

Contraceptives....Cruzan, Susan FDA 301-443-3285

Contraceptives....Staff NICHD 301-496-5133

Contract Policy....Staff OD/OA 301-496-6014

Contractors, Building Materials and Related Services....Duvall, Steven SEC 202-942-1950

Control levers....Cuomo, Peter PTO 703-308-0827

Conventional Fossil Fuel Power (Major Projects)....Dollison, Robert COMMERCE 202-482-2733

Conventions, Exhibits....Dickinson, Joanne CENSUS 301-457-1191

Converted Paper Prod....Stanley, Gary COMMERCE 202-482-0375

Converters....Greene, William USITC 202-205-3405

Conveyors....Olszewski, Robert PTO 703-308-2588

Cook Islands....Respess, Rebecca Cnty TDA 703-875-4357

Cook Islands....Berghage, Jeff Peace Corps 202-606-1098

Cook Islands....Staff Cnty State 202-647-3546

Cooley's Anemia....Staff Cooley's Anemia Foundation 800-221-3571

Cooley's Anemia....Staff NHLBI 301-496-4236

Cooperative Forestry....Liu, Karen FS 202-205-1378

Copper Wire Mills....Mains, Barbara COMMERCE 202-482-0606

Copper compounds....Greenblatt, Jack USITC 202-205-3353

Copper/Brass Mills....Mains, Barbara COMMERCE 202-482-0606

Copper....Edelstein, Daniel MINES 202-501-9415

Copper....Lundy, David USITC 202-205-3439

Copra and coconut oil....Reeder, John USITC 202-205-3319

Cor Pulmonale....Staff NHLBI 301-496-4236

Cordage machines....Greene, William USITC 202-205-3405

Cordage....Konzet, Jeffrey CUSTOMS 212-466-5885

Cordless Telephone....Staff FCC 202-653-6288

Cork and cork products....Hoffmeier, Bill USITC 202-205-3321

Corn with options....Amato, David CFT 312-353-9025

Corn, field....Reeder, John USITC 202-205-3319

Corneal Disorders....Staff NEI 301-496-5248

Corneal Transplantation....Staff NEI 301-496-5248

Cornelia deLange Syndrome....Staff NICHD 301-496-5133

Coronary Artery Surgery Study (CASS)....Staff NHLBI 301-496-4236

Coronary Angioplasty....Staff NHLBI 301-496-4236

Coronary Artery Disease....Staff NHLBI 301-496-4236

Coronary Bypass....Staff NHLBI 301-496-4236

Coronary Disease....Staff NHLBI 301-496-4236

Corporate Filings....Staff SEC 202-942-8090

Corporate Financial Audits....Gramling, Robert W. GAO 202-512-9406

Corrections - Community....Baunach, Phyllis Jo Justice Stat 202-307-0361

Corrections - General....Baunach, Phyllis Jo Justice Stat 202-307-0361

Corrections - General....Beck, Allen Justice Stat 202-616-3277

Corrections - General....Greenfeld, Lawrence Justice Stat 202-616-3281

Corrections - General....Innes, Christopher Justice Stat 202-724-3121

Corrections - General....Kane, Patrick R. Justice Stat 202-307-3226

Corrections - General....Kline, Susan Justice Stat 202-724-3118

Corrections - General....Stephan, James Justice Stat 202-616-3289

Corrections....Beck, Allen Justice Stat 202-616-3277

Corrections....Innes, Christopher Justice Stat 202-724-3121

Corrections....Staff Justice Stat 202-307-3106

Corrections....Greenfeld, Lawrence Justice Stat 202-616-3281

Corrections....Baunach, Phyllis Jo Justice Stat 202-307-0361

Corrosion Inhibition....Warden, Robert PTO 703-308-2920

Corrosion....Ricker, Richard E. NIST 301-975-6023

Corundum-Emery....Austin, Gordon MINES 202-501-9388

Cosmetic and Toiletry Preparations....Joseph, Stephanie CUSTOMS 212-466-5768

Cosmetic Allergy....Staff FDA 202-205-4231

Cosmetic creams....Land, Eric USITC 202-205-3349

Cosmetics (Export Promo)....Kimmel, Ed COMMERCE 202-482-3460

Cosmetics, perfumery, toilet preparations....Land, Eric USITC 202-205-3349

Cosmetics....Bailey, John E. FDA 202-205-4530

Cost Allocation Models....Staff FCC 202-418-0810

Cost of Capital Audits....Staff FCC 202-418-0850

Cost of Crime - General....Rand, Michael Justice Stat 202-616-3494

Cost of Crime - General....Lindgren, Sue Justice Stat 202-307-0760

Cost of Crime - To Government....Lindgren, Sue Justice Stat 202-307-0760

Cost of Crime - To Victims....Klaus, Patsy Justice Stat 202-307-0776

Cost-of-Living Abroad, Productivity and Technology....Capdevielle, Patricia LABOR 202-606-5654

Costa Rica....Stanton, Dan Peace Corps 202-606-3620

Costa Rica...Wilkins, Michele Cnty Export-Import Bank 202-565-3743

Costa Rica....Opstein, Sally Cnty USIA 202-619-5864

Costa Rica....Vandenbos, James Cnty AID 202-647-9541

Costa Rica....Bayly, Rachel Cnty Treasury 202-622-1266

Costa Rica....Quintanilla, Rosalinda Cnty World Bank 202-473-7673

Costa Rica....Picado, Sonia Cnty Embassy 202-234-2945

Costa Rica....Silva, Carlos Cnty Embassy 202-234-2945

Costa Rica....Davis, Janice Peace Corps 202-606-3198

Costa Rica....Siegelman, Mark Cnty Commerce 202-482-5680

Costa Rica (San Jose)....Staff Cnty State 202-647-3518

Costa Rica/Minerals....Rabchevsky, George Cnty Mines 202-501-9670

Costochondritis....Staff NIAMS 301-496-8188

Costume Jewelry, Trade Promo....Beckham, R. COMMERCE 202-482-5478

Cote D'Ivoire....Maybury-Lewis Anthony Cnty Export-Import Bank 202-565-3739

Cote d'Ivoire....Palghat, Kathy Cnty Treasury 202-622-0332

Cote D'Ivoire....van Trotsenburg, Axel Cnty World Bank 202-473-6794

Cote D'Ivoire....Koumoue, Koffi Moise Cnty Embassy 202-797-0300

Cote d'Ivoire....Bezek, Jill Cnty TDA 703-875-4357

Cote D'Ivoire....Akeo, Severin Mathias Cnty Embassy 202-797-0300

Cote d'Ivoire (Abidjan)....Staff Cnty State 202-647-1540

Cote d'Ivoire (Ivory Coast)....Dolley, Thomas Cnty Mines 202-501-9690

Cotton Seed Oil....Janis, William V. COMMERCE 202-482-2250

Cotton - World....Whitton, Carolyn Agri 202-219-0826

Cotton....Latham, Roger Agri 202-720-5944

Cotton....Meyer, Leslie Agri 202-219-0840

Cotton....Skinner, Robert Agri 202-219-0840

Cotton....Sweet, Mary Elizabeth USITC 202-205-3455

Cottonseed and cottonseed oil....Reeder, John USITC 202-205-3319

Council of Europe....Staff Cnty State 202-647-1708

Counseling (Drug Abuse)....Staff NIDA 301-443-6245

Counterfeit Notes...Cameron, Jon FRS 202-452-2220

Country Exposure Reports....Adams, Sarah FRS 202-452-2634

County Business Patterns....Hanczaryk, Paul CENSUS 301-457-2580

County and City Data Books....Cevis, Wanda CENSUS 301-457-1166

Courier Services....Elliot, Fred COMMERCE 202-482-1134

Court Appeals....Gaskins, Carla Justice Stat 202-508-8546

Court Appeals....Langan, Patrick Justice Stat 202-616-3490

Court Appeals....Lindgren, Sue Justice Stat 202-307-0760

Court Case Processing Time....Gaskins, Carla Justice Stat 202-508-8546

Court Case Processing Time - Federal....Kaplan, Carol Justice Stat 202-307-0759
Court Caseload....Gaskins, Carla Justice Stat 202-508-8546
Court Caseload...Langan, Patrick Justice Stat 202-616-3490
Court Organization....Gaskins, Carla Justice Stat 202-508-8546
Court Organization...Langan, Patrick Justice Stat 202-616-3490
Courts....Gaskins, Carla Justice Stat 202-508-8546
Courts....Langan, Patrick Justice Stat 202-616-3490
Coxsackie Virus (Hand-Food and Mouth Disease)....Staff NIAID 301-496-5717
Coxsackie Virus (Hand-Foot and Mouth Disease)....Staff NICHD 301-496-5133
Cranes....Greene, William USITC 202-205-3405
Craniofacial, children....Staff Children's Craniofacial Association 800-535-3643
Craniofacial Malformations....Staff NIDR 301-496-4261
Craniofacially handicapped....Staff National Association for the Craniofacially Handicapped 800-332-2373
Crayons....Seastrum, Carl USITC 202-205-3493
Creams, cosmetic....Land, Eric USITC 202-205-3349
Cretinism....Staff NIDDK 301-496-3583
Creutzfeldt-Jakob Disease....Staff NINDS 301-496-5751
Cri Du Chat (Cat Cry Syndrome)....Staff NICHD 301-496-5133
Crib Death (SIDS)....Staff NICHD 301-496-5133
Crib Toys....Tyrrell, Elaine CPSC 301-504-0580
Crigler-Najar Syndrome....Staff NIDDK 301-654-3810
Crime and the Elderly....Staff NIA 301-496-1752
Crime and the Elderly....Staff NIA 301-496-1752
Crime and Drug Abuse....Staff NIDA 301-443-6245
Crime Incidence, Rates, and Trends....Chaiken, Jan Justice Stat 202-307-0765
Crime Incidence, Rates, and Trends....Klaus, Patsy Justice Stat 202-307-0776
Crime Incidence, Rates, and Trends....Rand, Michael Justice Stat 202-616-3494
Crime Incidence, Rates, and Trends....Taylor, Bruce Justice Stat 202-616-3498
Crime, Location of....Kinderman, Charles Justice Stat 202-616-3489
Crime Measurement Methods....Taylor, Bruce Justice Stat 202-616-3498
Crime Measurement Methods....Rand, Michael Justice Stat 202-616-3494
Crime Measurement Methods....Kinderman, Charles Justice Stat 202-616-3489
Crime, organized....Singer, Laura S. SEC 202-942-4542
Crime, organized....Zelinsky, Yuri SEC 202-942-4846
Crime, Population...Hoff, Gail CENSUS 301-457-3925
Crime Prevention Measures....Staff Justice Stat 202-466-6272
Crime Seasonality....DeBarry, Marshall Justice Stat 202-616-3489
Crime Severity....Klaus, Patsy Justice Stat 202-307-0776
Crime Types: Federal, Bank Robbery, Computer....Scalia, John Justice Stat 202-616-3276
Crime Types: Homicide....White, Paul Justice Stat 202-307-0771
Crime Types: Homicide....Zawitz, Marianne Justice Stat 202-616-3499
Crime Types: Rape, Robbery, Assault, Theft....Klaus, Patsy Justice Stat 202-307-0776
Crime Types: Rape, Robbery, Assault, Theft....Harlow, Caroline Justice Stat 202-307-0757
Crime Types: Rape, Robbery, Assault, Theft....Rand, Michael Justice Stat 202-616-3494
Criminal Defendants - Federal....Kaplan, Carol Justice Stat 202-307-0759
Criminal Defendants....Gaskins, Carla Justice Stat 202-508-8546
Criminal Defendants....Langan, Patrick Justice Stat 202-616-3490
Criminal History Data Quality....Kaplan, Carol Justice Stat 202-307-0759
Criminal Justice Agencies....Lindgren, Sue Justice Stat 202-307-0760
Criminal Justice Expenditure and Employment....Lindgren, Sue Justice Stat 202-307-0760
Criminal Justice....Staff NCJRS 800-851-3420
Crisis Intervention....Staff Primary Care Management Systems 800-444-9999
Critical Care Medicine Department....Staff CC 301-496-9565
Croatia....Altheim, Stephen Cnty Treasury 202-622-0125
Croatia....Corwin, Elizabeth Cnty USIA 202-619-5055
Croatia....Cosic, Kresimir Cnty Embassy 202-588-5899
Croatia....Elwan Ann E. Cnty World Bank 202-473-2435
Croatia....Sarcevic, Peter A. Cnty Embassy 202-588-5899
Croatia....Staff Cnty State 202-736-7361
Croatia....Waxman-Lenz, Roberta Cnty Export-Import Bank 202-565-3742
Croatia...Rabchevsky, George Cnty MINES 202-501-9670
Crohn's disease....Staff Crohn's and Colitis Foundation of America 800-932-2423
Crohn's Disease....Staff NIAID 301-496-5717
Crohn's Disease....Staff NIDDK 301-654-3810
Crop Protection....Staff FWS 703-358-2043
Cross Interest Policy....Staff FCC 202-418-2130
Cross Ownership TV/Cable....Staff FCC 202-416-0856
Cross-Eye....Staff NEI 301-496-5248

Crude cresylic acid....Foreso, Cynthia USITC 202-205-3348
Crude Oil...Linville, Bill NEIC 918-337-4375
Crude Oil....Heath, Charles NEIC 202-586-6860
Crude petroleum....Foreso, Cynthia USITC 202-205-3348
Crushing machines....Greene, William USITC 202-205-3405
Cryofibrinogenemia....Staff NHLBI 301-496-4236
Cryoglobulinemia....Staff NHLBI 301-496-4236
Cryolite....White, Linda USITC 202-205-3427
Cryosurgery (Eyes)....Staff NEI 301-496-5248
Cryosurgery....Staff NCI 301-496-5583
Cryptococcosis....Staff NIAID 301-496-5717
Cryptosporidiosis....Staff NIAID 301-496-5717
Cuba (Havana)....Staff Cnty State 202-647-9272
Cuba/Minerals....Rabchevsky, George Cnty Mines 202-501-9681
Cuba....Marcus, Anthony Cnty Treasury 202-622-1218
Cuba....Shumake, Josie Cnty USIA 202-619-5864
Cuba....Siegelman, Mark Cnty Commerce 202-482-5680
Cuba...Wilkins, Michele Cnty Export-Import Bank 202-565-3743
Cucumbers....McCarty, Timothy USITC 202-205-3324
Cued Speech.....Staff NIDCD 301-496-7243
Culm....Foreso, Cynthia USITC 202-205-3348
Cupric oxide....Conant, Kenneth USITC 202-205-3346
Cuprous oxide....Conant, Kenneth USITC 202-205-3346
Current Analysis of U.S. Export and Import Price Ind....Vachris, Michelle LABOR 202-606-7155
Current Business Analysis....Fox, Douglas R. ECONOMIC 202-606-9683
Current Business Statistics....Statistical Series Staff ECONOMIC 202-606-9607
Current-Carrying Wiring Devices....Whitley, Richard A. COMMERCE 202-482-0682
Current Employment Analysis, Assist. Comm. Empl/Unempl....Bregger, John E. LABOR 202-606-6388
Current Wage Developments, Comp. and Working Cond....Cimini, Michael LABOR 202-606-6275
Curtains....Sweet, Mary Elizabeth USITC 202-205-3455
Cushing's Syndrome....Staff NICHD 301-496-5133
Cushing's Syndrome....Staff NIDDK 301-496-3583
Cushing's Syndrome....Staff NINDS 301-496-5751
Cushing's Syndrome....Staff NHLBI 301-496-4236
Cushions....Spalding, Josephine USITC 202-205-3498
Customer Service....Staff CENSUS 301-457-4100
Cut flowers....Burket, Stephen USITC 202-205-3318
Cut Flowers....Conte, Ralph CUSTOMS 212-466-5759
Cutis Laxa....Staff NHLBI 301-496-4236
Cutlery....Bello, Felix USITC 202-205-3120
Cutlery...Bratland, Rosemarie COMMERCE 202-482-0380
Cutlery....Preston, Jacques CUSTOMS 212-466-5488
Cutting machines textile....Greene, William USITC 202-205-3405
Cyclic Idiopathic Edema....Staff NHLBI 301-496-4236
Cyclitis....Staff NEI 301-496-5248
Cyprus (Nicosia)....Staff Cnty State 202-647-6113
Cyprus/Minerals....Mobbs, Philip Cnty Mines 202-501-9679
Cyprus....Corro, Ann Cnty Commerce 202-482-3945
Cyprus....Hutchings, Dayna Cnty Export-Import Bank 202-565-3737
Cyprus....Jacovides, Andrew Cnty Embassy 202-462-5772
Cyprus....Mehra, Suman Cnty World Bank 202-473-2247
Cyprus....Miltiadou, Miltos Cnty Embassy 202-462-5772
Cyprus....Santoro, Eugene Cnty USIA 202-619-6582
Cyprus....VanRenterghem, Cynthia Cnty Treasury 202-622-0343
Cystic Fibrosis....Staff Cystic Fibrosis Foundation 800-344-4823
Cystic Fibrosis (Pancreas)....Staff NIDDK 301-496-3583
Cystic Acne....Staff NIAMS 301-496-8188
Cystinosis....Staff NICHD 301-496-5133
Cystinuria....Staff NIDDK 301-654-4415
Cystitis....Staff NIDDK 301-654-4415
Cytology....Staff NCI 301-496-5583
Cytomegalic Inclusion Disease....Staff NIDCD 301-496-7243
Cytomegalic Inclusion Disease....Staff NINDS 301-496-5751
Cytomegalovirus (Congenital)....Staff NHLBI 301-496-4236
Cytomegalovirus (Congenital)....Staff NEI 301-496-5248
Cytomegalovirus (Congenital)....Staff NICHD 301-496-5133
Cytomegalovirus (Congenital)....Staff NIAID 301-496-5717
Czech Republic....Waxman-Lenz, Roberta Cnty Export-Import Bank 202-565-3742
Czech Republic....Gallagher, Tricia Cnty Treasury 202-622-0117
Czech Republic....Hewer, Ulrich Albert Cnty World Bank 202-473-2279

Czech Republic....Bazala, Razvigor Cnty USIA 202-619-5055
Czech Republic....Ann Lien Cnty TDA 703-875-4357
Czech Republic....Lockwood, Jennifer Peace Corps 202-606-3607
Czech Republic....Schiel, Russell Peace Corps 202-606-3606
Czech Republic....Mowrey, Mark Cnty Commerce 202-482-4915
Czech....Vancura, Petr Cnty Embassy 202-363-6316
Czech....Zantovsky, Michael Cnty Embassy 202-363-6315
Czechoslovakia/Minerals....Steblez, Walter Cnty Mines 202-501-9672
Czechoslovakia (Prague)....Staff Cnty State 202-647-1457

D

D-Mark with options....Bice, David CFT 312-353-7880
D'Jibouti....Watkins, Chandra Cnty Commerce 202-482-4564
Dairy Products - Milk, Ice Cream, etc.....Buckner, Dan Agri 202-720-4448
Dairy Products - Milk, Ice Cream, etc.....Miller, Jim Agri 202-219-0770
Dairy Products - Milk, Ice Cream, etc.....Short, Sara Agri 202-219-0769
Dairy products....Ludwick, David USITC 202-205-3329
Dairy Products....Janis, William V. COMMERCE 202-482-2250
Dairy....Staff National Dairy Council 800-426-8271
Dam Safety....Staff FWS 703-358-1719
Dance....Moyeda, Cynthia NEA 202-682-5435
Dance....Sonntag, Doug NEA 202-682-5000
Dandy-Walker Syndrome....Staff NINDS 301-496-5751
Dangerous drugs....Van Vliet, Theresa Justice 202-514-0917
Darier's Disease....Staff NIAMS 301-496-8188
Data Acquisition Systems....Brown, Dwayne NASA 202-358-1726
Data and Tapes, Consumer Expend. Survey, Prices....Passero, William LABOR 202-606-6900
Database management systems....Black, Thomas PTO 703-305-9707
Database Management....Staff DCRT 301-496-6256
Database Services....Inoussa, Mary COMMERCE 202-482-5820
Databases (Bibliograpic Information)....Staff NLM 301-496-6095
Data Diskettes, Employment Projections....Bowman, Charles LABOR 202-606-5702
Data Diskettes and Tapes, State and Area Labor Force....Marcus, Jessie LABOR 202-606-6392
Data Diskettes, Consumer Price Indexes, Pr/Lv. Con....Gibson, Sharon LABOR 202-606-6968
Data Diskettes and Tapes, Empl. and Wages, Empl/Unempl....Buso, Michael LABOR 202-606-6499
Data Diskettes, Prices and Living Conditions....Rosenberg, Elliott LABOR 202-606-7728
Data processing services....Xavier, Neil USITC 202-205-3450
Data processing machines....Bringe, Julie USITC 202-205-3390
Data Processing Services....Atkins, Robert G. COMMERCE 202-482-4781
Data Tapes, Industry-Occup. Matrix, Empl. Proj.....Turner, Delores LABOR 202-606-5730
Data Tapes, Productivity and Technology....Kriebel, Bertram LABOR 202-606-5606
Day Care....Kharfen, Michael ACF 202-401-9215
Daytime Broadcasting....Staff FCC 202-418-2660
Deafness, National Institute of....Allen, Marin NIH 301-496-7243
Deafness....Staff Deafness Research Foundation 800-535-3323
Deafness....Staff NIDCD 301-496-7243
Death and Dying....Staff NIA 301-443-1752
Death and Dying....Staff NIMH 301-443-4515
Decalcomanias (decals)....Twarok, Chris USITC 202-205-3314
Decennial Census, 1990 Counts f/Current Boundaries....Miller, Joel CENSUS 301-457-1099
Decennial Census, Content and Tabula, Program Design....Berman, Patricia CENSUS 301-457-3960
Decennial Census, Content, General....Berman, Patrica A. CENSUS 301-457-3960
Decennial Census, Content, General....Paez, Al CENSUS 301-457-3995
Decennial Census, Count Information....Staff CENSUS 301-457-2933
Decennial Census, Count Information....Staff CENSUS 301-457-2131
Decennial Census, Count Questions, 1990 Census...Kobilarcik, Ed CENSUS 301-457-3994
Decennial Census, Demographic Analysis....Robinson, Gregg CENSUS 301-457-2103
Decennial Census, Housing Data, Special Tabuls. of....Bonnette, Robert CENSUS 301-763-8553
Decennial Census, Litigation....Gregg, Valerie CENSUS 301-457-4102

Decennial Census, Population Data, Special Tab. of....Cowan, Rosemarie CENSUS 301-457-2408
Decennial Census, Post-Enumeration Surveys....Hogan, Howard CENSUS 301-457-2665
Decennial Census, Publications, General....Hemming, Robert CENSUS 301-457-4130
Decennial Census, Publications, General....Hemming, Robert CENSUS 301-457-4130
Decennial Census, Reapportionment....Turner, Marshall CENSUS 301-457-4039
Decennial Census, Redistricting....Turner, Marshall CENSUS 301-457-4039
Decennial Census, Sampling Methods....Woltman, Henry CENSUS 301-457-4199
Decennial Census, Tabulations, General....Porter, Gloria CENSUS 301-457-4019
Decennial Census, Tabulations, General....Stark, Billie CENSUS 301-457-4158
Decennial Census, User-Defined Area Program....Quasney, Adrienne CENSUS 301-457-3819
Decennial Management....Miskusa, Susan CENSUS 301-457-2933
Decennial Planning Division....LaMacchia, Robert CENSUS 301-457-1022
Decibel Information....Staff NIDCD 301-496-7243
Decontamination (Radioactive Spills)....Staff OD/ORS 301-496-2254
Decontamination....Staff OD/ORS 301-496-2960
Decubitus Ulcers....Staff NIAMS 301-496-8188
Decubitus Ulcers....Staff NIA 301-496-1752
Deep Vein Thrombosis....Staff NHLBI 301-496-4236
Deep Space Communications Complex....Wood, Alan S. NASA 818-354-5011
Defense Audit....Connor, David M. GAO 202-512-9095
Defense Energy Programs....Reis, Victor NEIC 202-586-2177
Degenerative Joint Disease....Staff NIAMS 301-496-8188
Degenerative Basal Ganglia Disease....Staff NINDS 301-496-5751
Deglutition....Staff NIDR 301-496-4261
Dejerine-Sottas Disease....Staff NINDS 301-496-5751
Delayed Puberty....Staff NICHD 301-496-5133
Delivery devices....Olszewski, Robert PTO 703-308-2588
Delivery of Nursing Care....Staff NINR 301-496-0207
Dementia....Staff NIMH 301-443-4513
Dementia....Staff NINDS 301-496-5751
Dementia....Staff NIA 301-496-1752
Demographic Programs, Statistical Research....Waite, Preston CENSUS 301-457-4287
Demographic Studies, Center for....Wetzel, James R. CENSUS 301-457-4076
Demography of Aging....Staff NIA 301-496-1752
Demography....Staff NICHD 301-496-5133
Demyelinating Diseases....Staff NINDS 301-496-5751
Dengue....Staff NIAID 301-496-5717
Denmark/Minerals....Zajac, William Cnty Mines 202-501-9671
Denmark (Copenhagen)....Staff Cnty State 202-647-5669
Denmark....Dyvig, Peter Cnty Embassy 202-234-4300
Denmark....Gosnell, Peter Cnty Export-Import Bank 202-565-3733
Denmark....Holloway, Barbara Cnty Treasury 202-622-0098
Denmark....Hoppe, Christian Cnty Embassy 202-234-4300
Denmark....Kendall, Maryanne Cnty Commerce 202-482-3254
Denmark....Rankin-Galloway, Honore Cnty USIA 202-619-5283
Dental Amalgams....Staff NIDR 301-496-4261
Dental Assistants (Education)....Staff HRSA/BHPr 301-443-1173
Dental Care Programs (Aged, Handicapped, Prepaid)....Staff HRSA 301-443-6853
Dental cements....Randall, Rob USITC 202-205-3366
Dental Diseases/Disorders....Staff NIDR 301-496-4261
Dental Implants....Staff NIDR 301-496-4261
Dental materials....Tesk, John A. NIST 301-975-6799
Dental Research, National Institute of....Jacquet, Brent NIH 301-496-6705
Dental Restorative Materials....Staff NIDR 301-496-4261
Dental Sealants....Staff NIDR 301-496-4261
Dental X-rays....Staff NIDR 301-496-4261
Dentistry....Mancene, Gene PTO 703-308-2696
Dentobacterial Plaque Infection....Staff NIDR 301-496-4261
Dentures....Staff NIDR 301-496-4261
Depression and Aging....Staff NIMH 301-443-4513
Depression and Aging....Staff NIA 301-496-1752
Depression....Staff National Foundation for Depressive Illness 800-248-4344
Depression....Staff NIMH 301-443-4513
Depth Perception....Staff NEI 301-496-5248
Deputy Director BEA....Landefeld, Steven ECONOMIC 202-606-9602
Deputy Commissioner, Office of....Barron, William G. LABOR 202-606-7802
Dermatitis Herpetiformis....Staff NIAMS 301-496-8188
Dermatological agents....Nesbitt, Elizabeth USITC 202-205-3355

Dermatology....Staff American Society for Dermatologic Surgery 800-441-2737
Dermatology....Staff NIAMS 301-496-8188
Dermatology....Staff NCI 301-496-5583
Dermatomyositis....Staff NIAMS 301-496-8188
Dermatomyositis....Staff NINDS 301-496-5751
Dermographism....Staff NIAID 301-496-5717
DES (Diethylstilbestrol)....Staff NCI 301-496-5583
DES (Diethylstilbestrol)....Staff NICHD 301-496-5133
DES (Diethylstilbestrol)....Staff FDA 301-443-3170
Desalination/Water Reuse....Wheeler, Frederica COMMERCE 202-482-3509
Design Services....Staff NCRR 301-496-5566
Designer Drugs....Staff NIDA 301-443-6245
Detergents....Joseph, Stephanie CUSTOMS 212-466-5768
Detergents....Land, Eric USITC 202-205-3349
Developmental Disabilities and Birth Defects....Adams, M.J., Jr. CDC 404-488-7150
Developmental Disabilities....Kharfen, Michael ACF 202-401-9215
Developmental Disorders....Staff NIDCD 301-496-7243
Developmental Disorders....Staff NINDS 301-496-5751
Developmental Disorders....Staff NICHD 301-496-5133
Developmental Endocrinology....Chrousos, George P. FAES 301-496-5800
Developmental Endocrinology....Chrousos, George FAES 301-496-4686
Developmentally Disabled....Staff Devereux Foundation 800-345-1292
Devic's Syndrome....Staff NINDS 301-496-5751
Dextrine....Randall, Rob USITC 202-205-3366
Di(2-ethylhexyl) adipate....Johnson, Larry USITC 202-205-3351
Di(2-ethylhexyl) phthalate....Johnson, Larry USITC 202-205-3351
Diabetes and Aging (Type 1 and Type 2)....Staff NIA 301-654-3327
Diabetes and Aging (Type 1 and Type 2)....Staff NIDDK 301-654-3327
Diabetes (And Arteriosclerosis)....Staff NHLBI 301-496-4236
Diabetes and Gum Disease....Staff NIDR 301-496-4261
Diabetes and Pregnancy....Staff NICHD 301-496-5133
Diabetes Clearinghouse....Staff NIDDK 301-654-3327
Diabetes, Digestive and Kidney Disorders, Nat'l Inst....Singer, Betsy NIH 301-496-3583
Diabetes Insipidus....Staff NIDDK 301-654-3327
Diabetes (Juvenile)....Staff NIDDK 301-654-3327
Diabetes Mellitus....Staff NIDDK 301-654-3327
Diabetes with Insulin Allergy or Resistance....Staff NIAID 301-496-5717
Diabetes with Insulin Allergy or Resistance....Staff NIDDK 301-654-3327
Diabetes....Staff American Diabetes Association 800-232-3472
Diabetes....Staff Juvenile Diabetes Foundation 800-223-1138
Diabetes....Taylor, Simeon FAES 301-496-2596
Diabetic Eye Disease....Staff NIDDK 301-654-3327
Diabetic Eye Disease....Staff NEI 301-496-5248
Diabetic Neuropathy....Staff NINDS 301-496-5751
Diabetic Neuropathy....Staff NIDDK 301-654-3327
Diabetic Retinopathy....Staff NEI 301-496-5248
Diabetic Retinopathy....Staff NIDDK 301-654-3327
Diagnostic Laboratories for Animal Disease....Staff NCRR 301-594-7933
Diagnostic Radiology....Staff CC 301-496-7700
Dial-a-Porn Complaints....Staff FCC 202-632-7553
Dialysis, Kidney....Staff NIDDK 301-654-4415
Diamond, Industrial....Prebury, Graylin COMMERCE 202-482-5158
Diamond....Austin, Gordon MINES 202-501-9388
Diamond-Blackfan Syndrome....Staff NHLBI 301-496-4236
Diamonds....DeSapio, Vincent USITC 202-205-3435
Diarrheal Illnesses....Staff NIAID 301-496-5717
Diarrheal Illnesses....Staff NIDDK 301-654-3810
Diathermy Approval....Staff FCC 301-725-1585
Diatomite....Taylor, Harold MINES 202-501-9754
Diatomite....White, Linda USITC 202-205-3427
Dictation machines....Puffert, Douglas USITC 202-205-3402
Diego Garcia....Staff Cnty State 202-647-6453
Dietary Restriction....Staff NIA 301-496-1752
Diethylstilbestrol (DES)....Staff NCI 301-496-5583
Diethylstilbestrol (DES)....Staff FDA 301-443-3170
Diethylstilbestrol (DES)....Staff NICHD 301-496-5133
Diffuse Sclerosis....Staff NINDS 301-496-5751
Digestive Diseases Clearinghouse....Staff NIDDK 301-654-3810
Digestive Diseases....Staff NIDDK 301-654-3810
Digital communications....Olms, Douglas W. PTO 703-305-4703
Digital communications....Chin, Stephen PTO 703-305-4714
Digital computers....Envall, Roy PTO 703-305-9706

Digital data error correction....Envall, Roy PTO 703-305-9706
Digital Device Measurements....Staff FCC 301-725-1585
Dijbouti...Larsen, Mark Cnty USIA 202-619-4894
Dijbouti...McKoy, Ethel Cnty Treasury 202-622-0336
Dilsobutylene....Raftery, Jim USITC 202-205-3365
Dilsodecyl phthalate....Johnson, Larry USITC 202-205-3351
Dinnerware of ceramic....McNay, Deborah USITC 202-205-3425
Dioctyl phthalates....Johnson, Larry USITC 202-205-3351
Diphtheria....Staff NIAID 301-496-5717
Diploma Schools of Nursing....Staff HRSA/BHPr 301-443-5786
Direct Mail...Elliot, Fred COMMERCE 202-482-1134
Director, Office of the....Lindberg, Donald A. NLM 301-496-6221
Director, BEA....Carson, Carol S. ECONOMIC 202-606-9600
Director's Office - Information Services....Brill, Kendra J. FTC 202-326-2607
Director's Office....Rich, Jessica FTC 202-326-2148
Disabilities....Staff NOD 800-248-2253
Disability Benefits, Social Security....Gambino, Phil SSA 410-965-8904
Disabled....Staff ABLEDATA 800-227-0126
Disabled....Staff Advocacy Center for the Elderly and Disabled 800-960-7705
Disaster Assistance....Kulik, Bernard SBA 202-205-6734
Disc Drives, Diskettes....Valverde, Daniel COMMERCE 202-482-0573
Discoid Lupus Erythematosus....Staff NIAMS 301-496-8188
Discouraged Workers, Empl./Unempl. Stats....Hamel, Harvey LABOR 202-606-6378
Discouraged Workers, Employment Statistics....Hamel, Harvey LABOR 202-606-6378
Disease Information Hotline.... CDC 404-332-4555
Disease Prevention....Staff NINR 301-496-0207
Disequilibrium....Staff NIDCD 301-496-7243
Disinfection....Staff OD/ORS 301-496-2960
Displaced Workers, Empl/Unempl Statistics....Gardner, Jennifer LABOR 202-606-6378
Disposal (Animal Waste, Dead Animal, Infect. Materials)....Staff OD/ORS 301-496-2960
Distillate fuel oil....Foreso, Cynthia USITC 202-205-3348
Distilled Water....Staff OD/ORS 301-496-2960
Distribution services....Luther, Dennis USITC 202-205-3497
Diuretics....Staff NHLBI 301-496-4236
Diurnaldystonia....Staff NINDS 301-496-5751
Diverticulitis....Staff NIDDK 301-654-3810
Diverticulosis....Staff NIDDK 301-654-3810
Divorce Statistics....Staff CDC 301-436-8500
Dizziness....Staff NIDCD 301-496-7243
Dizziness....Staff NINDS 301-496-5751
Djibouti, Republic of (Djibouti)....Staff Cnty State 202-647-5684
Djibouti/Minerals....Antonides, Lloyd Cnty Mines 202-501-9686
Djibouti....Bouraleh, Issa Daher Cnty Embassy 202-331-0270
Djibouti....Hutchings, Dayna Cnty Export-Import Bank 202-565-3737
Djibouti....Morin, Denyse E. Cnty World Bank 202-473-9732
Djibouti....Olhaye, Roble Cnty Embassy 202-331-0270
DMSO (Dimethylsulfoxide)....Staff NCI 301-496-5583
DMSO (Dimethylsulfoxide)....Staff FDA/NCDB 301-443-1016
DNA Chemistry....Reeder, Dennis NIST 301-975-3128
DNA....Staff NIGMS 301-496-7301
DNA....Staff OD/OSPL 301-496-9838
Docket Information....Staff FCC 202-418-1740
Docket Information Court of Appeals....Staff FCC 202-418-1770
Docket Information FCC Adjudicatory Proceedings....Staff FCC 202-418-1780
Docket Information Supreme Court....Staff FCC 202-418-1770
Doll carriages, stroller, and parts....Abrahamson, Dana USITC 202-205-3430
Dolls....Abrahamson, Dana USITC 202-205-3430
Dolls....Hodgen, Donald COMMERCE 202-482-3346
Dolls....Wong, Alice CUSTOMS 212-466-5538
Dolomite, dead burned....DeSapio, Vincent USITC 202-205-3435
Domestic Oil Reserves Statistics....Petersen, Jimmie NEIC 202-586-6401
Domestic Violence....Staff Michigan Coalition Against Domestic Violence 800-333-7233
Domestic Violence....Langan, Patrick Justice Stat 202-616-3490
Domestic Violence....Rand, Michael Justice Stat 202-616-3494
Domestic Violence....Klaus, Patsy Justice Stat 202-307-0776
Dominica (Roseau)....Staff Cnty State 202-647-2130
Dominica/Minerals....Rabchevsky, George Cnty Mines 202-501-9670
Dominica....Brooks, Michelle Cnty Commerce 202-482-2527
Dominica....Marcus, Anthony Cnty Treasury 202-622-1218

Dominica....Nallari, Raj R. Cnty World Bank 202-473-8697

Dominica....Watty, Edward I. Cnty Embassy 202-334-6781

Dominica....Wilkins, Michele Cnty Export-Import Bank 202-565-3743

Dominican Republic....Wilkins, Michele Cnty Export-Import Bank 202-565-3743

Dominican Republic....Parkinson, Katherine Cnty Treasury 202-622-5292

Dominican Republic....Quehl, Scott Cnty World Bank 202-473-8652

Dominican Republic....Head, Alfred Cnty USIA 202-619-6835

Dominican Republic... Cnty TDA 703-875-4357

Dominican Republic....Ariza, Jose Del Carmen Cnty Embassy 202-332-6280

Dominican Republic....Suro, Dario Cnty Embassy 202-332-6280

Dominican Republic....Soto, Rodrigo Cnty Commerce 202-482-5680

Dominican Republic....Almaguer, Antoinette Peace Corps 202-606-3322

Dominican Republic....Menyhart, Krista Peace Corps 202-606-3323

Dominican Republic (Santo Domingo)....Staff Cnty State 202-647-2620

Dominican Republic/Minerals....Rabchevsky, George Cnty Mines 202-501-9670

Down Syndrome....Staff National Down Syndrome Society 800-221-4602

Down Syndrome....Staff National Down Syndrome Congress 800-232-6372

Down Syndrome....Staff NICHD 301-496-5133

Down apparel....Jones, Jackie USITC 202-205-3466

Draperies....Sweet, Mary Elizabeth USITC 202-205-3455

Drawing instruments....Roth, Jordon USITC 202-205-3467

Dresses....Crowley, Michael CUSTOMS 212-466-5852

Dresses....Sweet, Mary Elizabeth USITC 202-205-3455

Dressing machines (textile)....Greene, William USITC 202-205-3405

Drilling Mus/Soft Compounds....Vacant COMMERCE 202-482-0564

Drink-preparing machines...Jackson, Georgia USITC 202-205-3399

Drinking Water Branch....Staff EPA 202-260-5526

Drinking Water Standards....Staff EPA 202-260-7575

Drinking and Cancer....Staff NCI 301-496-5583

Drug Abuse, in Workplace....Brown, Mona NIDA 301-443-6245

Drug Abuse, National Institute on....Brown, Mona NIDA 301-443-6245

Drug Abuse, Prenatal....Brown, Mona NIDA 301-443-6245

Drug Abuse Treatment....Hurley, Joan NIDA 301-443-6549

Drug Abuse Treatment....Staff NIDA 301-443-6549

Drug Allergy....Staff NIAID 301-496-5717

Drug Enforcement Administration....Staff DEA 202-307-1000

Drug Hemolytic Anemia....Staff NIDDK 301-496-3583

Drug prevention....Staff Wisconsin Clearinghouse 800-322-1468

Drug Purpura....Staff NIDDK 301-496-3583

Drug Research Survey....Staff NIDA 301-443-6245

Drug Resistance....Staff NIAID 301-496-5717

Drug Test Guidelines....Brown, Mona NIDA 301-443-6245

Drugs and Aging....Staff NIA 301-496-1752

Drugs and Drug Labeling: AIDS Drugs....Williams, Bradford FDA 301-443-3285

Drugs and Drug Labeling....Lecos, Chris FDA 202-205-4144

Drugs and Drug Labeling: Generic....Sporn, Douglas FDA 301-594-0340

Drugs and Drug Labeling: Orphan Drugs....Cruzan, Susan FDA 301-443-3285

Drugs and Drug Labeling: Over-the Counter....Weintraub, Michael FDA 301-594-1924

Drugs and Drug Labeling: Prescription Drugs, Biologic....Fazzari, Frank FDA 301-594-2073

Drugs and Drug Labeling: Women's Issues (Drugs)....Staff FDA 301-443-3285

Drugs and Prisoners....Stephan, James Justice Stat 202-616-3289

Drugs and Prisoners....Baunach, Phyllis Jo Justice Stat 202-307-0361

Drugs (Cancer)....Staff NCI 301-496-5583

Drugs (Cardiac)....Staff NHLBI 301-496-4236

Drugs (Eyes)....Staff NEI 301-496-5248

Drugs - General....Lindgren, Sue Justice Stat 202-307-0760

Drugs Industry Group....Daly, James M. SEC 202-942-1800

Drugs, natural....Nesbitt, Elizabeth USITC 202-205-3355

Drugs, synthetic....Nesbitt, Elizabeth USITC 202-205-3355

Drugs (Use and Abuse)....Staff NIDA 301-443-6245

Drugs....Alcohol and Drug Helpline 800-821-4357

Drugs....Hurt, William COMMERCE 202-482-0128

Drugs....Staff NAPARE 800-638-2229

Drugs....Staff National Council on Alcoholism and Drug Dependence Hopeline 800-622-2255

Drugs....Staff HUD Drug Information and Strategy Clearinghouse 800-955-2232

Drugs....Staff Office of Drug and Alcohol Programs 800-932-0912

Drunk driving....Staff MADD 800-438-6233

Drunk Driving....Zawitz, Marianne Justice Stat 202-616-3499

Dry Edible Beans....Budge, Arvin Agri 202-720-4285

Dry Edible Beans....Plummer, Charles Agri 202-219-0009

Dry Edible Beans....Lucier, Gary Agri 202-219-0884

Dry Eyes....Staff NEI 301-496-5248

Dry-cleaning machines....Jackson, Georgia USITC 202-205-3399

Drying machines....Jackson, Georgia USITC 202-205-3399

Duchenne Muscular Dystrophy....Staff NINDS 301-496-5751

Duchenne Muscular Dystrophy....Staff NIAMS 301-496-8188

Duck Stamps....Staff FWS 202-208-4354

Dumping Toxic Waste....Staff EPA 202-260-1024

Dumping vehicles....Huppert, Michael PTO 703-308-1107

Dupuytren's Contracture....Staff NIAMS 301-496-8188

Dupuytren's Contracture....Staff NINDS 301-496-5751

Durable Consumer Goods....Ellis, Kevin M. COMMERCE 202-482-1176

Dushanabe....Eighmy, Thomas Cnty AID 202-647-6920

Dust Inhalation Diseases (Pneumonoconioses)....Staff FDA 301-443-3170

Dust Inhalation Diseases (Pneumonoconioses)....Staff NHLBI 301-496-4236

Dust Inhalation Diseases (Pneumonoconioses)....Staff CDCW/NIOSH 404-639-3286

Dwarfism....Staff Little People of America 800-243-9273

Dwarfism....Staff NICHD 301-496-5133

Dyeing machines....Greene, William USITC 202-205-3405

Dyeing....Lieberman, Paul PTO 703-308-2552

Dyes....Wanser, Stephen USITC 202-205-3363

Dynamite....Johnson, Larry USITC 202-205-3351

Dysarthia....Staff NIDCD 301-496-7243

Dysarthria....Staff NINDS 301-496-5751

Dysautonomia....Staff NINDS 301-496-5751

Dysentery....Staff NIAID 301-496-5717

Dysfluency....Staff NIDCD 301-496-7243

Dysgeusia....Staff NIDCD 301-496-7243

Dysgraphia....Staff NINDS 301-496-5751

Dyskinesia....Staff NINDS 301-496-5751

Dyslexia....Staff Orton Dyslexia Society 800-222-3123

Dyslexia....Staff NIMH 301-443-4513

Dyslexia....Staff NINDS 301-496-5751

Dyslexia....Staff NICHD 301-496-5133

Dyslexia....Staff NIDCD 301-496-7243

Dysmenorrhea....Staff NICHD 301-496-5133

Dysphagia....Staff NIDCD 301-496-7243

Dyspnea....Staff NHLBI 301-496-4236

Dyspraxia (Speech)....Staff NIDCD 301-496-7243

Dyspraxia....Staff NINDS 301-496-5751

Dystonia Musculorum Deformans (Torsion Dystonia)....Staff NINDS 301-496-5751

Dystonia....Staff NINDS 301-496-5751

Dystonia....Staff NIDCD 301-496-7243

E

E. Caribbean....Brooks, Michelle Cnty Commerce 202-482-4464

E.Q. Guinea....Maybury-Lewis, Anthony Cnty Export-Import Bank 202-565-3739

Ear Infection....Staff NIDCD 301-496-7243

Ear Wax....Staff NIDCD 301-496-7243

Earnings, Employment and Earnings Publication....Green, Gloria LABOR 202-606-6376

Earnings, Foreign Countries, Productivity and Tech.....Capdevielle, Patricia LABOR 202-606-5654

Earnings, Population Survey....Mellor, Earl LABOR 202-606-6378

Earnings Publication....Green, Gloria LABOR 202-606-6376

Earnings, Real--News Release, Empl/Unempl. Stats....Hiles, David LABOR 202-606-6547

Ears....Staff Meniere's Network of the Ear Foundation 800-545-4327

Earth-moving machines....Polly, Laura USITC 202-205-3408

Earth Observing System (EOS)....Staff NASA 301-286-5566

Earthenware, articles of....McNay, Deborah USITC 202-205-3425

Earthenware....Bratland, Rosemarie COMMERCE 202-482-0380

Earthenware....Kalkines, George CUSTOMS 212-466-5794

Earthquake Engineering....Lew, H.S. NIST 301-975-6061

East Caribbean....Almaguer, Antoinette Peace Corps 202-606-3322

Easter Seal....Staff National Easter Seal Society 800-221-6827

Eastern Caribbean....Feingold, David Cnty AID 202-647-4106

Eastern Europe....Brereton, Barbara OPIC 202-336-8617

Eastern Europe/trade matters....Underwood, Jennifer US Trade Rep 202-395-4620

Eastern European Health Scientist Exchange Program....Staff FIC 301-496-4784

Eating Disorders....Staff NIMH 301-443-4513

Eaton-Lambert Myasthenic Syndrome....Staff NINDS 301-496-5751

ECG....Staff NHLBI 301-496-4236

Echocardiography....Staff NHLBI 301-496-4236

Eclampsia/Preeclampsia....Staff NICHD 301-496-5133

Ecological Effects Branch....Staff EPA 202-305-7347

Econometrics, Ass't to Director....Hirsch, Albert A. ECONOMIC 202-606-9627

Economic Accounts, Associate Director for National....Parker, Robert P. ECONOMIC 202-606-9607

Economic Census Products....Zeisset, Paul CENSUS 301-457-4116

Economic Development....Forbes, Patricia SBA 202-205-6657

Economic Growth/Empl Proj, Associate Commissioner....Kutscher, Ronald LABOR 202-606-5700

Economic Growth/Empl Proj, Data Diskettes....Bowman, Charles LABOR 202-606-5702

Economic Growth/Empl Proj, Economic Growth Proj....Saunders, Norman LABOR 202-606-5723

Economic Growth/Empl Proj, Ind-Occpl Empl Matrix....Turner, Delores LABOR 202-606-5730

Economic Growth/Empl Proj, Labor Force Projection....Fullerton, Howard LABOR 202-606-5711

Economic Growth/Empl Proj, Occupational Projections....Rosenthal, Neal LABOR 202-606-5701

Economic Growth/Empl Proj, Occupational Outlook Hand....Pilot, Michael LABOR 202-606-5703

Economic Growth/Empl Proj, Occupational Outlook Quarterly....Staff LABOR 202-606-5707

Economic Impact Studies....Atkinson, William J. SEC 202-942-8020

Economic Programs, Statistical Research....Monsour, Nash J. CENSUS 301-457-4978

Economic Projections, Employment Projections....Saunders, Norman LABOR 202-606-5723

Economics Bureau - Antitrust....Brogan, Robert D. FTC 202-326-3508

Economics Bureau - Antitrust....Callison, Elizabeth FTC 202-326-3521

Economics Bureau - Antitrust....Coate, Malcolm FTC 202-326-3351

Economics Bureau - Antitrust....Creswell, Jay S., Jr. FTC 202-326-3519

Economics Bureau - Antitrust....Dobson, Douglas C. FTC 202-326-3465

Economics Bureau - Antitrust....Fisher, Alan A. FTC 202-326-3516

Economics Bureau - Antitrust....Gessler, Kevin O. FTC 202-326-2306

Economics Bureau - Antitrust....Gessler, Geary A. FTC 202-326-3463

Economics Bureau - Antitrust....Gladieux, Jennifer FTC 202-326-3507

Economics Bureau - Antitrust....Glasner, David FTC 202-326-3345

Economics Bureau - Antitrust....Griffith, Carolyn FTC 202-326-3450

Economics Bureau - Antitrust....Gulyn, Peter FTC 202-326-2194

Economics Bureau - Antitrust....Harmon, Bernadette D. FTC 202-326-3449

Economics Bureau - Antitrust....Hoskin, Daniel FTC 202-326-3372

Economics Bureau - Antitrust....Howell, John M. FTC 202-326-3456

Economics Bureau - Antitrust....Iosso, Thomas FTC 202-326-2720

Economics Bureau - Antitrust....Iosso, Ilona FTC 202-326-3355

Economics Bureau - Antitrust....John, Tammy FTC 202-326-3462

Economics Bureau - Antitrust....Layher, William N. FTC 202-326-3515

Economics Bureau - Antitrust....Levinson, Robert FTC 202-326-3517

Economics Bureau - Antitrust....Levinson, Robert FTC 202-326-3517

Economics Bureau - Antitrust....Levy, Roy FTC 202-326-3353

Economics Bureau - Antitrust....Ludwick, Richard FTC 202-326-2246

Economics Bureau - Antitrust....Martin, Fred FTC 202-326-3514

Economics Bureau - Antitrust....Nelson, Steven R. FTC 202-326-3523

Economics Bureau - Antitrust....Patterson, Margaret A. FTC 202-326-3472

Economics Bureau - Antitrust....Pegram, William M. FTC 202-326-3336

Economics Bureau - Antitrust....Pidano, Charles FTC 202-326-3454

Economics Bureau - Antitrust....Rodriguez, Armando FTC 202-326-3616

Economics Bureau - Antitrust....Sacher, Seth B. FTC 202-326-2606

Economics Bureau - Antitrust....Silvia, Louis FTC 202-326-3471

Economics Bureau - Antitrust....Simpson, John D. FTC 202-326-3451

Economics Bureau - Antitrust....Tatem, Lewis FTC 202-326-3373

Economics Bureau - Antitrust....Wadbrook, Clare FTC 202-326-3420

Economics Bureau - Antitrust....Wagner, Curtis FTC 202-326-3348

Economics Bureau - Antitrust....Williams, Mark FTC 202-326-3374

Economics Bureau - Antitrust....Zichterman, Elizabeth C. FTC 202-326-3410

Economics Bureau - Consumer Protection....Braman, Susan FTC 202-326-3163

Economics Bureau - Consumer Protection....Lean, David F. FTC 202-326-3480

Economics Bureau - Consumer Protection....Mulholland, Joseph FTC 202-326-3378

Economics Bureau - Consumer Protection....Boorstein, Randi M. FTC 202-326-3482

Economics Bureau - Consumer Protection....Daniel, Lisa M. FTC 202-326-3394

Economics Bureau - Consumer Protection....Silversin, Louis FTC 202-326-3385

Economics Bureau - Consumer Protection....Hertzendorf, Mark FTC 202-326-2768

Economics Bureau - Consumer Protection....VanderNat, Peter FTC 202-326-3518

Economics Bureau - Consumer Protection....Wells, Pamela L. FTC 202-326-3371

Economics Bureau - Consumer Protection....Lacko, James FTC 202-326-3387

Economics Bureau - Consumer Protection....Cox, Carolyn FTC 202-326-3434

Economics Bureau - Consumer Protection....Small, Helen W. FTC 202-326-3375

Economics Bureau - Consumer Protection....Anderson, Keith B. FTC 202-326-3428

Economics Bureau - Consumer Protection....Pappalardo, Janis K. FTC 202-326-3380

Economics Bureau - Consumer Protection....Butters, Gerald R. FTC 220-326-3393

Economics Bureau - Consumer Protection....Porter, Russell FTC 202-326-3460

Economics Bureau - Economic Policy Analysis....Ippolito, Pauline M. FTC 202-326-3477

Economics Bureau - Economic Policy Analysis....Stansel, James C. FTC 202-326-3481

Economics Bureau - Economic Policy Analysis....Reiffen, David FTC 202-326-2027

Economics Bureau - Economic Policy Analysis....Kelly, Kenneth H. FTC 202-326-3358

Economics Bureau - Economic Policy Analysis....Daniel, Tim FTC 202-326-3520

Economics Bureau - Economic Policy Analysis....Barnes, Davina G. FTC 202-326-3346

Economics Bureau - Economic Policy....Koopmans, Reinout M. FTC 202-326-3497

Economics Bureau - Economic Policy Analysis....Breen, Denis A. FTC 202-326-3447

Economics Bureau - Economic Policy Analysis....Kim, Andrew FTC 202-326-3363

Economics Bureau - Economic Policy Analysis....Hilke, John C. FTC 202-326-3483

Economics Bureau - Economic Policy Analysis....Yangh, Jun Cheol FTC 202-326-2057

Economics Bureau - Economic Policy Analysis....Kiely, Eileen FTC 202-326-3382

Economics Bureau - Economic Policy Analysis....Morkre, Morris E. FTC 202-326-3365

Economics Bureau - Economic Policy Analysis....Vita, Mike FTC 202-326-3493

Economics Bureau - Economic Policy Analysis....Wellford, Charissa FTC 202-326-3020

Economics Bureau - Economic Policy Analysis....Grawe, Oliver FTC 202-326-3445

Economics Bureau - Economics Policy Analysis....Yi, Seong Gu FTC 202-326-3368

Economics Bureau - European Assistance....Kneuper, Robert FTC 202-326-3469

Economics Bureau - General Counsel Brashears, Nicole K. FTC 202-326-2455

Economics Bureau - Office of the Director....Johnson, Janice C. FTC 202-326-3332

Economics Bureau - Office of the Director....Brown,Mary FTC 202-326-3429

Economics Bureau - Office of the Director....Carpenter, Lynn J. FTC 202-326-3390

Economics Bureau - Office of the Director....Harris, Kyle FTC 202-326-3399

Economics Bureau - Office of the Director....Altrogge, Phyllis D. FTC 202-326-3464

Economics Bureau - Office of the Director....Baker, Jonathon FTC 202-326-2930

Economics Bureau - Office of the Director....Deyak, Timothy FTC 202-326-3379

Economics Bureau - Office of the Director....Samuels, Carolyn FTC 202-326-3412

Economics Bureau - Office of the Director....Meadows, Chrystal E. FTC 202-326-3489

Economics Bureau - Office of the Director....Richards, Karin F. FTC 202-326-2601

Economics Bureau - Office of the Director....Rosano, William V. FTC 202-326-3422

Economics Bureau - Office of the Director....Farber, Leslie FTC 202-326-3510

Economics Bureau - Office of the Director....Roberts, Gary FTC 202-326-2937

Economics Bureau - Office of the Director....Pautler, Paul A. FTC 202-326-3357

Economics Bureau - Office of the Director....Williams, Cheryl G. FTC 202-326-3418

Economics Bureau - Office of the Director....Treakle, Coletta A. FTC 202-326-3481

Economics Bureau - Policy....Breen, Denis A. FTC 202-326-3447

Economics Bureau....Schumann, Lawrence FTC 202-326-3359
Economics Bureau....Ward, Michael R. FTC 202-326-2096
Economics....Elzinga, Kenneth G. UVA 804-924-6752
Economizers....Fravel, Dennis USITC 202-205-3404
Ectodermal Dysplasias....Staff NIAMS 301-496-8188
Ectodermal Dysplasias....Staff NIDR 301-496-4261
Ectopic Hormones....Staff NIDDK 301-496-3583
Ectopic Pregnancy....Staff NICHD 301-496-5133
Ecuador (Quito)....Staff Cnty State 202-647-3338
Ecuador/Minerals....Velasco, Pablo Cnty Mines 202-501-9677
Ecuador....Bayly, Rachel Cnty Treasury 202-622-1266
Ecuador....Clapham, Lizzie Corps 202-606-3499
Ecuador....Davis, Janice Peace Corps 202-606-3198
Ecuador....Epstein, Sharon Cnty AID 202-647-4358
Ecuador....Hentschel, Jesko S. Cnty World Bank 202-458-1936
Ecuador....Jarvis, Catherine Cnty USIA 202-619-5867
Ecuador....John Herrman Cnty TDA 703-875-4357
Ecuador....Moore, Paul Cnty Commerce 202-482-1659
Ecuador....Salvador, Gonzalo Cnty Embassy 202-234-7200
Ecuador....Teran-Teran, Edgar Cnty Embassy 202-234-7200
Ecuador...Wilkins, Michele Cnty Export-Import Bank 202-565-3743
Eczema....Staff NIAID 301-496-5717
Eczema....Staff NIAMS 301-496-8188
Edema....Staff NHLBI 301-496-4236
Edible gelatin....Jonnard, Aimison USITC 202-205-3350
Edible preparations....Schneider, Greg USITC 202-205-3326
Education and Curriculum Support Projects....Jackson, Dorothy CENSUS 301-457-1210
Education, Environmental....Staff FWS 703-358-1786
Education Facilities, Major Proj.....White, Barbara COMMERCE 202-482-4160
Education (Nursing)....Staff HRSA/BHPr/DN 301-443-5786
Education Programs....Stephens, Richard NEIC 202-586-2366
Education Services....Evans, Katherine USITC 202-205-3407
Education....Bunker, Linda K. UVA 804-924-0740
Education....Gibbs, Anette UVA 804-924-3880
Education....Morra, Linda G. GAO 202-512-7014
Education....Rhile, Howard G. GAO 202-512-6418
Education....Staff National Association for the Education of Young Children 800-424-2460
Educational Attainment, Empl/Unempl. Stats....Staff LABOR 202-606-6378
Educational Attainment, Employment Statistics....Staff LABOR 202-606-6378
Educational devices....Mancene, Gene PTO 703-308-2696
Educational Programs....Frank Owens NASA 202-358-1110
Educational Programs....Richardson, Deborah NAL 301-504-5779
Educational/Training....Chandorsekara,A. COMMERCE 202-482-1318
Eggs....Newman, Douglas USITC 202-205-1318
Egypt, Arab Republic of (Cairo)....Staff Cnty State 202-647-1228
Egypt/Minerals....Dolley, Thomas Cnty Mines 202-501-9690
Egypt....El Sayed, Ahmed Maher Cnty Embassy 202-244-4319
Egypt....Hoppenbrouwer, Laurens M. Cnty World Bank 202-473-2716
Egypt....Hutchings, Dayna Cnty Export-Import Bank 202-565-3737
Egypt....McKoy, Ethel Cnty Treasury 202-622-0336
Egypt....Ramzy, Ezzeldin Cnty Embassy 202-244-5131
Egypt....Sams, Thomas/Wright, Corey Cnty Commerce 202-482-1860
Egypt....Squire, Margo Cnty USIA 202-619-5529
Egypt....Vacant Cnty AID 202-663-2610
Ehlers-Danlos Syndrome....Staff NIAMS 301-496-8188
Eisenmenger's Syndrome....Staff NHLBI 301-496-4236
EKG....Staff NHLBI 301-496-4236
El Salvador....Wilkins, Michele Cnty Export-Import Bank 202-565-3743
El Salvador....Parkinson, Katherine Cnty Treasury 202-622-5292
El Salvador....Barrett, Kathleen Cnty AID 202-647-9535
El Salvador....Opstein, Sally Cnty USIA 202-619-5864
El Salvador....Fluckiger, Stefan Cnty World Bank 202-473-0093
El Salvador....Anne McKinney Cnty TDA 703-875-4357
El Salvador....Sol, Ana Cristina Cnty Embassy 202-265-9671
El Salvador....Soler, Ana Vilma Cnty Embassy 202-265-9672
El Salvador/Minerals....Velasco, Pablo Cnty Mines 202-501-9677
El Salvador (San Salvador)....Staff Cnty State 202-647-3681
El Salvador....Lee, Helen Cnty Commerce 202-482-2528
Elastic fabrics....Shelton, Linda USITC 202-205-3457
Elastomers....Misurelli, Denby USITC 202-205-3362
Eldercare....Staff Eldercare Locator 800-677-1116
Eldercare....Staff Sound Options, Inc. 800-628-7649

Elderly, alcohol....Alcohol Rehab for the Elderly 800-354-7089
Elderly (Drug Abuse)....Staff NIDA 301-443-6245
Elderly Victims....Klaus, Patsy Justice Stat 202-307-0776
Elderly....Staff Advocacy Center for the Elderly and Disabled 800-960-7705
Elec/Power Gen/Transmission and Dist Eqt (Trade Pro)....Kostalas, Anthony COMMERCE 202-482-2390
Electric and Hybrid Propulsion Systems....Barber, Kenneth NEIC 202-586-2198
Electric and Nuclear Power....Welch, Thomas NEIC 202-586-8800
Electric and Nuclear Power....Jeffers, William NEIC 202-586-8800
Electric charge systems....Pellinen, David PTO 703-308-0538
Electric Energy Statistics....Hutzler, Mary NEIC 202-586-2222
Electric heating....Reynolds, Bruce A. PTO 703-308-3305
Electric Industrial Apparatus Nec....Bodson, John COMMERCE 202-482-0681
Electric Machinery and Trans., Producer Price Index....Yatsko, Ralph LABOR 202-606-7745
Electric-Magnetic Field Technical Questions....Staff EPA 202-260-9640
Electric Networks....Brewer, Robert H. NEIC 202-586-2828
Electric photocopying....Grimely, Arthur PTO 703-308-1373
Electric resistance heating devices....Reynolds, Bruce A. PTO 703-308-3305
Electric sound and visual signalling apparatus....Baker, Scott USITC 202-205-3386
Electric Vehicles....Barber, Kenneth NEIC 202-586-2198
Electric welding....Reynolds, Bruce A. PTO 703-308-3305
Electrical Articles....Curan, David CUSTOMS 212-466-4680
Electrical Engineering....Papantoni-Kazakos, Panayota UVA 804-924-6102
Electrical housings for mounting assemblies....Picard, Leo PTO 703-308-0538
Electrical Industry....Daly, James M. SEC 202-942-1800
Electrical measuring....Weider, Kenneth PTO 703-305-4707
Electrical music tone generation....Shoop, William M. PTO 703-308-3103
Electrical Power Plants, Major Proj.....Dollison, Robert COMMERCE 202-482-2733
Electrical safety....Staff CPSC 301-504-0580
Electrical Structures....Curan, David CUSTOMS 212-466-4680
Electrical switches and arc suppression....Pellinen, David PTO 703-308-0538
Electrical systems and devices, protection....Pellinen, David PTO 703-308-0538
Electrical testing....Chilcot, Richard PTO 703-305-4716
Electrical testing....Weider, Kenneth PTO 703-305-4707
Electrical Vol Standards....Staff CPSC 301-504-0580
Electricity Transmission....Brewer, Robert NEIC 202-586-2828
Electricity Transmission, Health Effects of....Brewer, Robert NEIC 202-586-2828
Electricity....Petersons, Oskars NISt 301-975-2400
Electricity....Sugg, William COMMERCE 202-482-1466
Electrocardiogram....Staff NHLBI 301-496-4236
Electrochemical processes....Niebling, John F. PTO 703-308-3325
Electrochemical products....Niebling, John F. PTO 703-308-3325
Electroheological fluids....Lieberman, Paul PTO 703-308-2552
Electromagnetic control systems....Pellinen, David PTO 703-308-0538
Electromagnetic fields....Newell, Allen C. NIST 303-497-3131
Electromagnets...Picard, Leo PTO 703-308-0538
Electromechanical appliances....Jackson, Georgia USITC 202-205-3399
Electron Physics....Clark, C.W. NIST 301-975-3709
Electron Microscopy....Staff DRS/BEIB 301-496-2599
Electron Microscopy....Staff NIDR 301-496-4261
Electron Microscopy....Staff NCRR 301-496-5545
Electronic Components/Prod and Test Eqt, Trade Promo.....Ruffin, Marlene COMMERCE 202-482-0570
Electronic Database Services....Inoussa, Mary COMMERCE 202-482-5820
Electronic Equipment Marketing....Staff FCC 202-418-1170
Electronic Fund Transfer Crime....Kaplan, Carol Justice Stat 202-307-0759
Electronic Industry....Daly, James M. SEC 202-942-1800
Electronic, (Legislation)....Donnelly, Margaret COMMERCE 202-482-5466
Electronic Prod. and Test.....Ruffin, Marlene COMMERCE 202-482-0570
Electronic Prod. and Test (Export Promo)....Ruffin, Marlene COMMERCE 202-482-0570
Electronic technology....Puffert, Douglas USITC 202-205-3402
Electronic tubes....Malison, Andrew USITC 202-205-3391
ElectroOptical Instruments, Trade Promo.....Manzolillo, Franc COMMERCE 202-482-2991
Electrophotography....McCarnish, Marion PTO 703-308-3961
Electrothermic appliances....Jackson, Georgia USITC 202-205-3399
Elementary and Secondary Education Programs....Staff NEH 202-606-8377
Elements, chemical....Conant, Kenneth USITC 202-205-3346
Elephantiasis....Staff NIAID 301-496-5717
Elevators, Moving Stairways....Weining, Mary COMMERCE 202-482-4708

Elevators....Greene, William USITC 202-205-3405
Elevators....Olszewski, Robert PTO 703-308-2588
Eligibility Criteria (Grants)....Staff DRG 301-594-7248
Embolism....Staff NHLBI 301-496-4236
Embroidery machines....Greene, William USITC 202-205-3405
Emergency Broadcast System....Staff FCC 202-418-1220
Emergency Medical Services....Staff FCC 717-337-1212
Emergency Plan. and Community Right-to-Know Hotline....Staff EPA 800-535-0202
Emergency Response....Brockman, Kenneth E. NRC 301-415-7482
Emigration....Fernandez, Edward CENSUS 301-457-2103
Emission Standards....Staff EPA 919-541-5571
Emissions Standards Division....Staff EPA 919-541-5571
Emotionally Handicapped....Staff Devereux Foundation 800-345-1292
Emphysema....Staff NHLBI 301-496-4236
Empl/Unempl Stats, (ES202), Empl/Wgs Ind....Bush, Joseph LABOR 202-606-6492
Empl/Unempl Stats, Assistant Commis.....Plewes, Thomas J. LABOR 202-606-6400
Empl/Unempl Stats, Benchmarks....Getz, Patricia LABOR 202-606-6521
Empl/Unempl Stats, Business Establishment List....Searson, Michael LABOR 202-606-6469
Empl/Unempl Stats, Curr. Empl. An, Assistant Commis.....Bregger, John E. LABOR 202-606-6388
Empl/Unempl Stats, National Data, Data Diskettes....Staff LABOR 202-606-6551
Empl/Unempl Stats, Occl Empl/Unempl, Occpl Empl Sv...Johnson, Lawrence LABOR 202-606-6517
Empl/Unempl Stats, State Data, Demographic Charact....Biederman, Edna LABOR 202-606-6392
Empl/Unempl Stats, Std Occupational Classification....McElroy, Michael LABOR 202-606-6516
Empl/Unempl Stats, Std Industrial Classification....Bennott, William LABOR 202-606-6474
Empl/Unempl Stats, Unempl Ins Stats, Establ Record....Cimini, Michael LABOR 202-606-6275
Empl/Unempl Stats, Unempl Ins Stats, Claimant Data....Terwilliger, Yvonne LABOR 202-606-6392
Empl.and Wages, Empl/Unempl, Data Diskettes and Tapes....Buso, Michael LABOR 202-606-6499
Employee Assistance Programs (Drug- Related)....Staff NIDA 301-443-6245
Employee Benefit Survey, General Info., Comp./Wk. Con....Staff LABOR 202-606-6222
Employee Benefit Survey, Health and Life Insur.....Blostin, Allan LABOR 202-606-6240
Employee Benefit Survey, Retirement and Capital Acc....Houff, James LABOR 202-606-6238
Employee Benefits, Compensation and Working Condition....Staff LABOR 202-606-6199
Employee Relations....Marks, Marjorie OPM 202-606-2920
Employer Costs for Employee Comp, Comp and Working....Rogers, Brenda LABOR 202-606-6199
Employment Analysis, Current, Assist. Comm. Empl/Unempl....Bregger, John E. LABOR 202-606-6388
Employment and Earnings Period. Empl/Unempl. Stats....Green, Gloria LABOR 202-606-6376
Employment and Unempl. Stats. Earnings, Pop. Survey....Mellor, Earl LABOR 202-606-6378
Employment and Unempl. Stats, Longitud. Data/Gr.Flow....Horvath, Francis LABOR 202-606-6345
Employment and Unempl. Stats., Mass Layoff Stats.....Siegel, Lewis LABOR 202-606-6404
Employment and Unempl. Stats., Minimum Wage Data....Haugen, Steve LABOR 202-606-6378
Employment and Unempl. Stats., Multiple Jobholders....Stinson, John LABOR 202-606-6373
Employment and Unempl. Stats, Older Workers....Rones, Philip LABOR 202-606-6378
Employment and Unempl. Stats, Part-time Workers....Nardone, Thomas LABOR 202-606-6378
Employment and Unempl. Stats, States Est. Surv. Data....Podgornik, Guy LABOR 202-606-6534
Employment and Unempl. Stats., States Est. Surv.....Shipp, Kenneth LABOR 202-606-6519
Employment and Unempl. Stats, Working Poor....Herz, Diane LABOR 202-606-6378

Employment and Unempl. Stats, Flexitime and Shift....Mellor, Earl LABOR 202-606-6378
Employment and Unempl. Stats, Labor Force Data Disk....Marcus, Jessie LABOR 202-606-6392
Employment and Unempl. Stats, Est. Surv.....Seifert, Mary Lee LABOR 202-606-6552
Employment, Area Data....Shipp, Kenneth LABOR 202-606-6519
Employment Cost Index, Comp. and Working Cond.....Shelly, Wayne LABOR 202-606-6206
Employment Information....Whitford, Richard OPM 202-606-2605
Employment Projections, Assistant Commis.....Kutscher, Ronald LABOR 202-606-5700
Employment Projections, Data Diskettes....Bowman, Charles LABOR 202-606-5702
Employment Projections, Economic Growth....Saunders, Norman LABOR 202-606-5723
Employment Projections, Productivity and Technology....Franklin, James LABOR 202-606-5709
Employment Projections, Productivity and Technology....Fullerton, Howard LABOR 202-606-5711
Employment Requirements Tables, Productivity and Tech....Franklin, James LABOR 202-606-5709
Employment Statistics....Palumbo, Thomas CENSUS 301-763-8574
Employment Stats, Area Data, Employment....Shipp, Kenneth LABOR 202-606-6519
Employment Stats, Area Data, Demog Charact....Biederman, Edna LABOR 202-606-6392
Employment Stats, Curr Empl Anal., Assist. Commis.....Bregger, John E. LABOR 202-606-6388
Employment Stats, Discouraged Workers....Hamel, Harvey LABOR 202-606-6378
Employment Stats, Displaced Workers....Horvath, Francis LABOR 202-606-6345
Employment Stats, Dropouts....Cohany, Sharon LABOR 202-606-6378
Employment Stats, Earn Stats, Qrtly Empl and Wage....Bush, Joseph LABOR 202-606-6492
Employment Stats, Earnings Publication....Green, Gloria LABOR 202-606-6376
Employment Stats, Educational Attainment....Staff LABOR 202-606-6376
Employment Stats, Employment Publication....Green, Gloria LABOR 202-606-6376
Employment Stats, Family Charactr of Labor Force....Hayghe, Howard LABOR 202-606-6378
Employment Stats, Ind Earn Stats, Mthly Payr Surv....Seifert, Mary Lee LABOR 202-606-6552
Employment Stats, Ind Empl Stats, Mthly Payr Surv....Seifert, Mary Lee LABOR 202-606-6552
Employment/Unempl Stats, Associate Commissioner....Plewes, Thomas J. LABOR 202-606-6400
Employment/Unempl Stats, Machine Readable Data....Green, Gloria LABOR 202-606-6376
Employment/Unempl Stats, Minorities....Cattan, Peter LABOR 202-606-6378
Employment/Unempl Stats, Older Workers....Rones, Philip LABOR 202-606-6378
Employment/Unempl Stats, Permanent Plant Closings....Siegel, Lewis LABOR 202-606-6404
Employment/Unempl Stats, Permanent Mass Layoffs....Siegel, Lewis LABOR 202-606-6404
Employment/Unempl Stats, Real Earnings, News Release....Hiles, David LABOR 202-606-6547
Employment/Unempl Stats, State Data, Employment....Shipp, Kenneth LABOR 202-606-6519
Employment/Unempl Stats, Students....Cohany, Sharon LABOR 202-606-6378
Employment/Unempl Statistics, Trends....Staff LABOR 202-606-6378
Employment/Unempl Stats, Veterans....Cohany, Sharon LABOR 202-606-6378
Employment/Unempl Stats, Women....Hayghe, Howard LABOR 202-606-6378
Employment/Unempl Stats, Work-life Estimates....Horvath, Francis LABOR 202-606-6345
Employment....Morra, Linda G. GAO 202-512-7014
Employment....Palumbo, Thomas CENSUS 301-763-8574
Enamel....Staff NIDR 301-496-4261
Enamels....Johnson, Larry USITC 202-205-3351
Encephalitides....Staff NINDS 301-496-5751
Encephalitis Lethargica....Staff NINDS 301-496-5751
Encephalitis....Staff NIAID 301-496-5717
Encephalitis....Staff NINDS 301-496-5751
Encephalomyelitis....Staff NINDS 301-496-5751
Encopresis....Staff NIDDK 301-654-3810

Encopresis....Staff NICHD 301-496-5133

End Stage Renal Disease....Staff NIDDK 301-496-3583

Endangered Species Bulletins, Tech.....Staff FWS 703-358-2166

Endangered Species....Staff FWS 703-358-1710

Endangered Species Listing....Staff FWS 703-358-2171

Endangered Species Permits....Staff FWS 703-358-2104

Endangered Species Recovery Plans....Staff FWS 703-358-2171

Endocarditis....Staff NHLBI 301-496-4236

Endocardium....Staff NHLBI 301-496-4236

Endocrine Gland....Staff NICHD 301-496-5133

Endocrinologic Muscle Disease....Staff NINDS 301-496-5751

Endocrinology of Aging....Staff NIA 301-496-1752

Endocrinology (Sexual Development)....Staff NICHD 301-496-5133

Endocrinology....Staff NIDDK 301-496-3583

Endodontics....Staff NIDR 301-496-4261

Endometriosis....Staff Endometriosis Association 800-992-3636

Endometriosis....Staff NICHD 301-496-5133

Energy and Environ. Sys.....Greer, Damon COMMERCE 202-482-5456

Energy Assist. Block Grant/For Low Income Families....Kharfen, Michael ACF 202-401-9215

Energy Assist. Block Grant/For Low Income Families....Staff ACF 202-401-9215

Energy Biosciences Research....Rabson, Robert NEIC 301-903-2873

Energy, Commodities....Oddenino, Charles L. COMMERCE 202-482-1466

Energy, Commodities....Yancik, Joseph J. COMMERCE 202-482-1466

Energy Conservation Programs....Staff FWS 703-358-1719

Energy Conservation....Freedman, Karen NEIC 202-586-8800

Energy Conservation....Staff J. NEIC 800-523-2929

Energy Demand Policy....Staff NEIC 202-586-4444

Energy Efficient Buildings....Oliver, Robert NEIC 202-586-9127

Energy Efficient Buildings....Kapus, Theodore NEIC 202-586-9123

Energy Industry Group....Owings, Christopher SEC 202-942-1900

Energy Information Statistics....Bishop, Yvonne NEIC 202-254-5419

Energy Information Statistical Standards....Bishop, Yvonne NEIC 202-254-5419

Energy, International....Melick, William FRS 202-452-2296

Energy Inventions....Staff NEIC 202-586-1479

Energy Issues....Rezendes, Victor S. GAO 202-512-3841

Energy Management Education....Stephens, Richard NEIC 202-586-8949

Energy Markets Short-Term Forecasting....Staff NEIC 202-586-1441

Energy Pollutant Research....Krey, Philip W. NEIC 212-620-3616

Energy, Producer Price Index....Caswell, Maria LABOR 202-606-7722

Energy-Related Business Assistance....Everett, George NEIC 800-428-2525

Energy-Related Inventions and Innovations....Staff NEIC 202-586-1479

Energy-Related Inventions Program (ERIP)....Staff NEIC 202-586-1479

Energy-Related Inventions Program....Lewett, P. NIST 301-975-5504

Energy, Renewable....Davis, Michael J. NEIC 202-586-9220

Energy, Renewable....Ervin, Christine COMMERCE 202-482-0556

Energy, Solar....Burch, Gary NEIC 202-586-8121

Energy statistics....Miller, Renee NEIC 202-254-5507

Energy Supply Policy....Coburn, Leonard NEIC 202-586-5667

Energy Technical Assistance....Bowes, Ronald NEIC 202-586-5517

Energy....Tsao, Che Sheung FRS 202-452-3898

Enforcement Operations....Hess, Frederick Justice 202-514-3684

Enforcement....Walton, Steve Customs 202-927-1600

Engine Design....Sebestyen, Thomas NEIC 202-586-8012

Engineering (Biomedical)....Staff DCRT 301-496-1111

Engineering (Biomedical)....Staff NIGMS 301-496-7301

Engineering (Biomedical)....Staff NCRR 301-496-4426

Engineering/Construction Services, Trade Promo.....Mc Auley COMMERCE 202-482-0132

Engineering resins....Misurelli, Denby USITC 202-205-3362

Engineering services....Polly, Laura USITC 202-205-3408

Engines....Anderson, Peder USITC 202-205-3388

Engines....Vacant CUSTOMS 212-466-5673

Enteritis...Staff NIDDK 301-654-3810

Enterprise Statistics....Salyers, Eddie CENSUS 301-763-7234

Enterprise Statistics....Staff CENSUS 301-763-7234

Entertainment Industries....Siegmund, John COMMERCE 202-482-4701

Entertainment services....R-Archila, Laura USITC 202-205-3488

Environment, Safety and Health Concerns....Gilbertson, Mark NEIC 202-586-5042

Environment services....Bedore, James USITC 202-205-3424

Environmental Affairs....Bond, Michael OPIC 202-336-8613

Environmental Carcinogens....Staff NCI 301-496-5583

Environmental Contaminants....Staff FWS 703-358-2148

Environmental Control....Staff OD/ORS 301-496-3537

Environmental control....Vacant PTO 703-308-0101

Environmental Coordination....Staff FWS 703-358-2183

Environmental Crimes....Sarachan, Ronald Justice 202-272-9875

Environmental Economics, Chief....Rutledge, Gary L. ECONOMIC 202-606-5350

Environmental Education....Staff FWS 703-358-1786

Environmental Education....Staff EPA 202-260-4965

Environmental Enforcement....Cruden, John C. Justice 202-514-1604

Environmental Hazards and Health Effects....Ngi, Eric CDC 404-488-7350

Environmental Health Sciences, Nat'l Institute of....Lee, Christopher A. NIH 919-541-3819

Environmental Health, National Center for....Jackson, Richard J. CDC 404-488-7000

Environmental Health....Staff NIEHS 919-541-3345

Environmental Issues - General Information Hotline....Staff EPA 800-759-4372

Environmental Mutagenesis....Staff NIEHS 919-541-3345

Environmental Pollution...Staff NIDCD 301-496-7243

Environmental Protection Issues....Guerro, Peter F. GAO 202-512-6111

Environmental Requirements for Laboratory Animals....Staff OD 301-496-1357

Environmental Review....Newberry, Scott F. NRC 301-415-1183

Environmental Safety....Staff OD/ORS 301-496-3537

Environmental Sciences....Allen, Ralph O. UVA 804-982-4922

Environmental Standards and Requirements....Staff FCC 202-418-1700

Environmental Statistics and Information....Staff EPA 202-260-2680

Environmental Teratology....Staff NIEHS 919-541-3345

Environmental Toxicology....Zeeman, Maurice G. FAES 202-260-1237

Environmental Trade Promo.....Mack, Midred COMMERCE 202-482-0516

Enzymes...Nesbitt, Elizabeth USITC 202-205-3355

Eosinophilic Granuloma of the Lung....Staff NHLBI 301-496-4236

Eosinophilic Syndrome....Staff NIAID 301-496-5717

EPA Action Line....Staff EPA 800-223-0425

EPA Journal....Staff EPA 202-260-6643

EPA Recycling Program....Staff EPA 202-260-4928

Epidemic Aid/Disease Outbreaks....Sims, Anne CDC 404-639-3286

Epidemiology of Aging....Staff NIA 301-496-1752

Epidemiology/Biostatistics....Hirsch, Robert FAES 202-994-7778

Epidemiology....Anello, Charles FAES 301-443-4227

Epidemiology....Diehl, Scott R. FAES 301-295-1671

Epidemiology....Friedman, Lawrence M. FAES 301-496-2533

Epidemiology....Stewart, John CDC 404-639-3629

Epidermodysplasis Verruciformis....Staff NIAMS 301-496-8188

Epidermolysis Bullosa....Staff NIAMS 301-496-8188

Epiglottitis...Staff NIAID 301-496-5717

Epikeratophakia....Staff NEI 301-496-5248

Epilepsy....Chandler, Jerry L. FAES 301-496-1846

Epilepsy....Epilepsy Foundation of America 800-332-1000

Epilepsy....Staff Epilepsy Information Service 800-642-0500

Epilepsy....Staff NINDS 301-496-5751

Epistaxis (Nosebleed)....Staff NHLBI 301-496-4236

Epoxides....Michels, David USITC 202-205-3352

Epoxidized ester....Johnson, Larry USITC 202-205-3351

Epoxidized linseed oils....Johnson, Larry USITC 202-205-3351

Epoxidized soya oils....Johnson, Larry USITC 202-205-3351

Epoxy polymers....Bleutge, John PTO 703-308-2363

Epoxy resins....Misurelli, Denby USITC 202-205-3362

Epstein-Barr Syndrome....Staff NIAID 301-496-5717

Epstein-Barr Virus....Staff NIAID 301-496-5717

Equal Employment Opportunity Compliance....Patrick, Erline SBA 202-205-6750

Equal Employment Opportunity....Staff OD/DEO 301-496-6301

Equatorial Guinea....Barber, Ed Cnty Treasury 202-622-1730

Equatorial Guinea....Wilson, Michael J. Cnty World Bank 202-473-4714

Equatorial Guinea....Henning, Herman Cnty USIA 202-619-5926

Equatorial Guinea....Biyogo Nsue, Teodoro Cnty Embassy 919-738-9584

Equatorial Guinea (Malabo)....Staff Cnty State 202-647-1707

Equatorial Guinea....Jefferson, Deborah Peace Corps 202-606-3709

Equatorial Guinea....Mitchell, Willis Peace Corps 202-606-3708

Equatorial Guinea....Michellini, Philip Cnty Commerce 202-482-4388

Equatorial Guinea/Minerals....Dolley, Thomas Cnty Mines 202-501-9690

Equipment Authorization Certification....Staff FCC 301-725-1585

Equipment leasing....Bedore, James USITC 202-205-3424

Equipment Measurement Authorization....Staff FCC 301-725-1585

ERIP (Energy-Related Inventions Program)....Staff NEIC 202-586-1479

Eritica....McKoy, Ethel Cnty Treasury 202-622-0336

Eritrea....Antonides, Lloyd Cnty MINES 202-501-9686

Eritrea....Berhe, Arefaine Cnty Embassy 202-429-1991

Eritrea....Ggani, Ejaz Cnty World Bank 202-473-4819
Eritrea....Hutchings, Dayna Cnty Export-Import Bank 202-565-3737
Eritrea....Kahsai, Amdemicael Cnty Embassy 202-429-1991
Eritrea....Staff Cnty State 202-647-6485
Eritrea....Thorman, Peter Cnty AID 202-647-7986
Erythema Elevatum Diutinum....Staff NIAMS 301-496-8188
Erythema Multiforme....Staff NIAID 301-496-5717
Erythema Nodosum....Staff NIAID 301-496-5717
Erythroblastosis Fetalis....Staff NICHD 301-496-5133
Erythrocytes (Red Blood Cells)....Staff FDA/NCDB 301-496-3556
Erythrocytes (Red Blood Cells)....Staff NHLBI 301-496-4236
Erythromelalgia....Staff NHLBI 301-496-4236
Erythropoietin....Staff NHLBI 301-496-4236
Esophageal Disorders....Staff NIDDK 301-654-3810
Esophagus, Carcinoma....Staff NCI 301-496-5583
Esotropia....Staff NEI 301-496-5248
Essential oils....Land, Eric USITC 202-205-3349
Essential Hypertension....Staff NHLBI 301-496-4236
Establishment Survey, Data Disk.....Podgornik, Guy LABOR 202-606-6534
Establishment Survey, Emp/Unemp.....Shipp, Kenneth LABOR 202-606-6519
Establishment Survey, National, Empl/Unempl.....Seifert, Mary Lee LABOR 202-606-6552
Establishment Survey, Natl., Indus. Classif. Empl/Unempl....Getz, Patricia LABOR 202-606-6521
Establishment Survey, States and Areas, Data Diskette....Podgornik, Guy LABOR 202-606-6534
Establishment Survey, States and Areas, Empl/Unemp....Shipp, Kenneth LABOR 202-606-6519
Esters, fatty-acid, of polyhdric alcohols....Land, Eric USITC 202-205-3349
Esters....Lee, May PTO 703-308-4546
Estimates and Incidence/Industry Injuries and Illness....Staff LABOR 202-606-6180
Estonia....Altheim, Stephen Cnty Treasury 202-622-0125
Estonia....Ann Lien Cnty TDA 703-875-4357
Estonia....Ilves, Toomes Hendrik Cnty Embassy 202-789-0320
Estonia....Jovanovic, Djordje Cnty World Bank 202-473-4070
Estonia....Kross, Eerik-Niiles Cnty Embassy 202-789-0320
Estonia....Levine, Richard Cnty Mines 202-501-9682
Estonia....Robinson, Susan Cnty USIA 202-619-6853
Estonia....Staff Cnty State 202-647-3187
Estonia....Viksnins, Helen Peace Corps 202-606-5517
Estonia....Waxman-Lenz, Roberta Cnty Export-Import Bank 202-565-3742
Estonia....Wootton, Nicholas Peace Corps 202-606-5519
Estrogen Therapy....Staff NIA 301-496-1752
Estrogen Replacement Therapy....Staff NIA 301-496-1752
Estrogen Replacement Therapy....Staff NIAMS 301-496-8188
Estrogen Replacement Therapy....Staff NICHD 301-496-5133
Estrogen Replacement Therapy....Staff NCI 301-496-5583
Estrogen Replacement Therapy....Staff FDA 301-443-3170
Ethane....Land, Eric USITC 202-205-3349
Ethanol....Brady, Thomas CUSTOMS 212-466-5747
Ethanolamines....Michels, David USITC 202-205-3352
Ethers, fatty-acid, of polyhydric alcohols....Land, Eric USITC 202-205-3349
Ethers....Brady, Thomas CUSTOMS 212-466-4769
Ethers....Michels, David USITC 202-205-5747
Ethics....NCHGR 301-402-0911
Ethiopia/Minerals....Antonides, Lloyd Cnty Mines 202-501-9686
Ethiopia (Addis Ababa)....Staff Cnty State 202-647-6485
Ethiopia....Adugna, Fisseha Cnty Embassy 202-234-2282
Ethiopia....Gebhart, George E. Cnty World Bank 202-473-7502
Ethiopia....Gebre-Christos, Berhane Cnty Embassy 202-234-2281
Ethiopia....Hutchings, Dayna Cnty Export-Import Bank 202-565-3737
Ethiopia....Larsen, Mark Cnty USIA 202-619-4894
Ethiopia....McKoy, Ethel Cnty Treasury 202-622-0336
Ethiopia....Pryor, Jeanne Cnty AID 202-647-7988
Ethiopia....Watkins, Chandra Cnty Commerce 202-482-4564
Ethyl alcohol (ethanol) for nonbeverage use....Michels, David USITC 202-205-3352
Ethylene dibromide....Michels, David USITC 202-205-3352
Ethylene glycol....Michels, David USITC 202-205-3352
Ethylene oxide....Michels, David USITC 202-205-3352
Ethylene-propylene rubber....Misurelli, Denby USITC 202-205-3362
Ethylene....Raftery, Jim USITC 202-205-3365
Eurasia/trade matters....Novelli, Catherine US Trade Rep 202-395-4620

Eurodollars with options....SIA Manasses CFT 312-353-9027
Europe/trade matters....Marcich, Chris US Trade Rep 202-395-4620
Europe/trade matters....Kaska, Edward US Trade Rep 202-395-3320
European Affairs/trade matters....Mowrey, Mark US Trade Rep 202-395-4620
European Assistance....Moore, Erroll FTC 202-326-2071
European Communities....Staff Cnty State 202-647-1708
European Community....Ludolph, Charles Cnty Commerce 202-482-5276
European Economic Community (EEC)....Staff Cnty State 202-647-1708
European Economic Community....Staff Cnty State 202-647-1708
European Free Trade Association (EFTA)...Staff Cnty 202-647-2395
European Services....Kaska, Edward US Trade Rep 202-395-3320
European Space Agency....Staff Cnty State 202-647-2395
European union....Currie, James Cnty Embassy 202-862-9500
European Union....Van AGT, Andreas Cnty Embassy 202-862-9500
Evaluation and Incident Investigation....Rubin, Stuart D. NRC 301-415-7480
Ewing's Sarcoma....Staff NCI 301-496-5583
Ex Parte Rules....Staff FCC 202-418-1740
Ex Parte Rules....Staff FCC 202-418-1720
Excimer Laser (Eye)....Staff NEI 301-496-5248
Executive Director's Office....Wiggs, Barbara B. FTC 202-326-2196
Executive Director's Office....Lustic, Barbara FTC 202-326-2088
Executive Director's Office....Blumenthal, Don M. FTC 202-326-2255
Executive Director's Office....Woods, James M. FTC 202-326-2232
Executive Director's Office....Hunter, Nancy L. FTC 202-326-2202
Executive Director's Office....Holland, Peggy FTC 202-326-3426
Executive Director's Office....Giffin, James M. FTC 202-326-2209
Executive Director's Office....Zytnick, Joseph FTC 202-326-2224
Executive Director's Office....Walton, Robert, III FTC 202-326-2205
Executive Director's Office....Straight, Rosemarie FTC 202-326-2207
Executive Director's Office - Starek, Roscoe B. III....Yi, Seoung Gu FTC 202-326-2127
Executive Director's Office....Miller, Sula FTC 202-326-2199
Executive Director's Office....Kelsey, Teresa J. FTC 202-326-2196
Executive Director's Office....Pham, Tuan FTC 202-326-2241
Executive Director's Office....Proctor, Alan FTC 202-326-2204
Executive Director's Office - Automated Systems....Mills, Mark C. FTC 202-326-3214
Exec. Director's Office - Automated Systems....Momeni, Ali FTC 202-326-2232
Exec. Director's Office - Automated Systems....Morris, Derrick FTC 202-326-2116
Exec. Director's Office - Automated Systems....Johnson, Loretta FTC 202-326-3624
Exec. Director's Office - Automated Systems....Barnes, Doug FTC 202-326-2269
Exec. Director's Office - Automated Systems....Feldmann, Lester A. FTC 202-326-2216
Exec. Director's Office - Automated Systems....Frank, F. Michael FTC 202-326-2217
Exec. Director's Office - Automated Systems....Lewis, Matthew FTC 202-326-2791
Exec. Director's Office - Automated Systems....Johnson, Gracie E. FTC 202-326-2211
Exec. Director's Office - Automated Systems....Pulliam, Denise M. FTC 202-326-2508
Exec. Director's Office - Automated Systems....Chambers, Michael D. FTC 202-326-2379
Exec. Director's Office - Automated Systems....DeVaughn, Willetta FTC 202-326-2233
Exec. Director's Office - Automated Systems....Condor, Karen FTC 202-326-3402
Exec. Director's Office - Automated Systems....Chmielewski, Richard FTC 202-326-2402
Exec. Director's Office - Automated Systems....Greynolds, Mark C. FTC 202-326-2290
Exec. Director's Office - Automated Systems....Lynch, Dennis FTC 202-326-2840
Exec. Director's Office - Automated Systems....Krupinski, Robert FTC 202-326-2231
Exec. Director's Office - Automated Systems....Edwards, Kathleen N. FTC 202-326-2240
Exec. Director's Office - Automated Systems....Anthony, Edward M. FTC 202-326-3527
Exec. Director's Office - Automated Systems....Dawson, Curtis FTC 202-326-2036
Exec. Director's Office - Automated Systems....Hales, Gregory E. FTC 202-326-2795
Exec. Director's Office - Automated Systems....Williams, Ken FTC 202-326-2082

Exec. Director's Office - Automated Systems....Massey, Karla FTC 202-326-3570

Exec. Director's Office - Automated Systems....St. Claire, Susan L. FTC 202-326-2227

Exec. Director's Office - Automated Systems....Pascoe, George FTC 202-326-3405

Exec. Director's Office - Automated Systems....Rougeau, Brian FTC 202-326-2952

Exec. Director's Office - Automated Systems....Lou, Linda FTC 202-326-2994

Exec. Director's Office - Automated Systems....Luhrs, Rick FTC 202-326-2404

Exec. Director's Office - Automated Systems....Lucas, Lionel FTC 202-326-2166

Exec. Director's Office - Automated Systems....Snyder, I. Michael FTC 202-326-2298

Exec. Director's Office - Automated Systems....Llewellyn, David W. FTC 202-326-3639

Exec. Director's Office - Automated Systems....Vermillion, Bonnie FTC 202-326-2226

Exec. Director's Office - Automated Systems....Overholt, Roberta FTC 202-326-2228

Exec. Director's Office - Automated Systems....Pitt, Julia K. FTC 202-326-2445

Exec. Director's Office - Automated Systems....Enger, Craig C. FTC 202-326-2898

Exec. Director's Office - Automated Systems....Enger, Erik L. FTC 202-326-2238

Exec. Director's Office - Automated Systems....Robertson, Diana FTC 202-326-2230

Executive Director's Office - Automated Systems....Smith, Jeff M. FTC 202-326-2529

Executive Director's Office - Automated Systems....Sheriff, Jennifer L. FTC 202-326-2913

Executive Director's Office - Automated Systems....Nguyen, Minh FTC 202-326-2604

Executive Director's Office - Budget and Finance....Hendershot, Alec R. FTC 202-326-3334

Executive Director's Office - Budget and Finance....Thorpe, Wilhelmina FTC 202-326-2219

Executive Director's Office - Budget and Finance....Fielding, Parcellena FTC 202-326-2312

Executive Director's Office - Budget and Finance....Smith, Virginia FTC 202-326-2784

Executive Director's Office - Budget and Finance....Delacruz, Margaret A. FTC 202-326-2322

Executive Director's Office - Budget and Finance....Thompson, Carl M. FTC 202-326-2337

Executive Director's Office - Budget and Finance....Simms, Anthony FTC 202-326-2325

Executive Director's Office - Budget and Finance....Haynes, Donna M. FTC 202-326-2327

Executive Director's Office - Budget and Finance....Arnold, Richard D., II FTC 202-326-2314

Executive Director's Office - Budget and Finance....Rodriguez, Lenore FTC 202-326-2190

Executive Director's Office - Budget and Finance....Farmer, Melissa S. FTC 202-326-2251

Executive Director's Office - Budget and Finance....Savell, Toby Sunshine FTC 202-326-2422

Executive Director's Office - Budget and Finance....Feggins, Payne D. FTC 202-326-2315

Executive Director's Office - Budget and Finance....Hailes, Gail E. FTC 202-326-2318

Executive Director's Office - Budget and Finance....Spriggs, Shari FTC 202-326-2339

Executive Director's Office - Budget and Finance....Hodge, Denise D. FTC 202-326-2324

Executive Director's Office - Budget and Finance....Reinertson, Diane L. FTC 202-326-2051

Executive Director's Office - Budget and Finance....Murphy, Jon FTC 202-326-2328

Executive Director's Office - Budget and Finance....Woodson, Louise V. FTC 202-326-3301

Executive Director's Office - Budget and Finance....Lancaster, Dorothy M. FTC 202-326-2488

Executive Director's Office - Budget and Finance....McLaughlin, Narvarius W. FTC 202-326-2329

Executive Director's Office - Information Management....Baella, Thomas FTC 202-326-2384

Executive Director's Office - Information Management....De La Cruz, Dexter FTC 202-326-2432

Executive Director's Office - Information Management....Jennings, Bruce FTC 202-326-2383

Executive Director's Office - Information Management....Knott, Margie FTC 202-326-2833

Executive Director's Office - Information Management....Ottie, Denise B. FTC 202-326-2381

Executive Director's Office - Information Mangement....Brown, Gregory FTC 202-326-3697

Executive Director's Office - Information Services....Adams, Bonita FTC 202-326-2528

Executive Director's Office - Information Services....Ajibawo, Abiola S. FTC 202-326-2530

Executive Director's Office - Information Services....Bacon, Geraldine G. FTC 202-326-2380

Executive Director's Office - Information Services....Baella, Thomas G. FTC 202-326-2031

Executive Director's Office - Information Services....Barber, Lisa FTC 202-326-2947

Executive Director's Office - Information Services....Barsant, Adolph FTC 202-326-2250

Executive Director's Office - Information Services....Blades, Donna L. FTC 202-326-3005

Executive Director's Office - Information Services....Bolden, Sandra B. FTC 202-326-2406

Executive Director's Office - Information Services....Booker, Lance FTC 202-326-2523

Executive Director's Office - Information Services....Borlase, Michele FTC 202-326-2302

Executive Director's Office - Information Services....Carter-Johnson, Jean FTC 202-326-2405

Executive Director's Office - Information Services....Chambers, Dewayne W. FTC 202-326-3036

Executive Director's Office - Information Services....Conrad, Jean FTC 202-326-2378

Executive Director's Office - Information Services....Cunningham, Jack FTC 202-326-2387

Executive Director's Office - Information Services....Curtin, Frank FTC 202-326-2280

Executive Director's Office - Information Services....Douglass, Franklin S. FTC 202-326-2376

Executive Director's Office - Information Services....Eperson, Patricia C. FTC 202-326-2420

Executive Director's Office - Information Services....Golden, Keith G. FTC 202-326-2410

Executive Director's Office - Information Services....Hammonds, Estelle FTC 202-326-2388

Executive Director's Office - Information Services....Harewood, Stanley M. FTC 202-326-3028

Executive Director's Office - Information Services....Hermingstyne, Dawn A. FTC 202-326-2878

Executive Director's Office - Information Services....Hutchins, Barry FTC 202-326-2373

Executive Director's Office - Information Services....Hynes, Barbara A. FTC 202-326-2389

Executive Director's Office - Information Services....Johnson, Dana FTC 202-326-2431

Executive Director's Office - Information Services....Johnson, Phyllis A. FTC 202-326-2507

Executive Director's Office - Information Services....Kennedy, Patty FTC 202-326-2013

Executive Director's Office - Information Services....Kuykendall, Eunice, Jerusha E. FTC 202-326-2413

Executive Director's Office - Information Services....Leonard, Lynne C. FTC 202-326-3684

Executive Director's Office - Information Services....Long, Marcus D. FTC 202-326-2660

Executive Director's Office - Information Services....Maisel, Theodore A. FTC 202-326-2415

Executive Director's Office - Information Services....Moore, Joyce M. FTC 202-326-3018

Executive Director's Office - Information Services....Moynahan, Eileen FTC 202-326-2449

Executive Director's Office - Information Services....Pierce, Marilyn S. FTC 202-855-1000

Executive Director's Office - Information Services....Reese, Genevieve E. FTC 202-326-2409

Executive Director's Office - Information Services....Titzer, Kristine L. FTC 202-326-2407

Executive Director's Office - Information Services....Tucker, Francenia FTC 202-326-3037

Executive Director's Office - Information Services....Woodson, Margaret B. FTC 202-326-2417

Executive Director's Office - Library....Sullivan, R. Elaine FTC 202-326-2385

Executive Director's Office - Personnel....Allen, Gelinda A. FTC 202-326-2876

Executive Director's Office - Personnel....Axelrod, Harold FTC 202-326-2790

Executive Director's Office - Personnel....Berry, Chrishania R. FTC 202-326-2363

Executive Director's Office - Personnel....Carter, Carole A. FTC 202-326-2550

Executive Director's Office - Personnel....Caton, Kathleen FTC 202-326-2342

Executive Director's Office - Personnel....Cooper, Erica FTC 202-326-2021

Executive Director's Office - Personnel....Crayton, Erika L. FTC 202-326-2022

Executive Director's Office - Personnel....Davis, Elliot FTC 202-326-2022

Executive Director's Office - Personnel....Harris, Barbara A. FTC 202-326-2428

Executive Director's Office - Personnel....Holmes, Ann FTC 202-326-2345

Executive Director's Office - Personnel....Kotecki, Naldyne FTC 202-326-2427

Executive Director's Office - Personnel....La Veille, Monica FTC 202-326-2361

Executive Director's Office - Personnel....McCoy, Catherine M. FTC 202-326-2358

Executive Director's Office - Personnel....Miller-Duncan, Glenda FTC 202-326-2367

Executive Director's Office - Personnel....Schwarz, Mae FTC 202-326-2341

Executive Director's Office - Personnel....Skipper, Brenda FTC 202-326-2365

Executive Director's Office - Personnel....Smith, Del FTC 202-326-2357

Executive Director's Office - Personnel....Smith, Jhana FTC 202-326-2384

Executive Director's Office - Personnel....Steinberg, Sharon FTC 202-326-2364

Executive Director's Office - Personnel....Yates, Diedra M. FTC 202-326-2354

Executive Director's Office - Procurement and Gen. Services.....Moore, David L. FTC 202-326-2277

Executive Director's Office - Procurement and Gen. Services.....Hutcherson, Willie S. FTC 202-326-2297

Executive Director's Office - Procurement and Gen. Services.....Vogt, Eric FTC 202-326-2259

Executive Director's Office - Procurement and Gen. Services....Greulich, Sherron FTC 202-326-2271

Executive Director's Office - Procurement and Gen. Services.....Moore, Francenia K. FTC 202-326-2872

Executive Director's Office - Procurement and Gen. Services.....Justice, Julius FTC 202-326-2275

Executive Director's Office - Procurement and Gen. Services.....Hymon, James F. FTC 202-326-3736

Executive Director's Office - Procurement and Gen. Services....Lorette, Barbara D. FTC 202-326-2260

Executive Director's Office - Procurement and Gen. Services....Clayborne, Charles FTC 202-326-2272

Executive Director's Office - Procurement and Gen. Services....Elliott, George T. FTC 202-326-2278

Executive Director's Office - Procurement and Gen. Services.....Wheeler, Bruce FTC 202-326-2270

Executive Director's Office - Procurement and Gen. Services.....Wells, Ernest L. FTC 202-326-2248

Executive Director's Office - Procurement and Gen. Services....Enos, Mary Ann FTC 202-326-2266

Executive Director's Office - Procurement and Gen. Services.....Goines, Russell E. FTC 202-326-2267

Executive Director's Office - Procurement and Gen. Services....Vasser, Robert M. FTC 202-326-2245

Executive Director's Office - Procurement and Gen. Services....Brewer, Ronald L. FTC 202-326-2243

Executive Director's Office - Procurement and Gen. Services....Walker, William FTC 202-326-2343

Executive Director's Office - Procurement and Gen. Services....Dickerson, William F. FTC 202-326-3735

Executive Director's Office - Procurement and Gen. Services....Woods, Donna K. FTC 202-326-2296

Executive Director's Office - Procurement and Gen. Services....Armstead, Gloria FTC 202-326-2262

Executive Director's Office - Procurement and Gen. Services....Bolden, Skipp D. FTC 202-326-2273

Executive Director's Bureau - Procurement and Gen. Services....Rice, Melvin L. FTC 202-326-2297

Executive Director's Office - Procurement and Gen Services....Royster, Lawrence D., Sr. FTC 202-326-2251

Executive Director's Office - Procurement and Gen. Services....Wilson, Ricardo M. FTC 202-326-2261

Executive Director's Office - Procurement and Gen. Services....Hayes, Ronald FTC 202-326-3734

Executive Director's Office - Procurement and Gen. Services....Green, Theresa Y. FTC 202-326-2243

Executive Director's Office - Procurement and Gen. Services.....Simpson, Flossie I. FTC 202-326-2297

Executive Director's Office - Procurement and Gen. Services.....Sefchick, Jean FTC 202-326-2258

Executive Director's Office - Procurement and Gen. Services....Gillette, Brian K. FTC 202-326-2253

Executive Director's Office - Procurement and Gen. Services.....Meritt, Claude O., Jr. FTC 202-326-2286

Exercise Physiology....Staff NIAMS 301-496-8188

Exercise and Aging....Staff NIA 301-496-1752

Exercise and the Heart....Staff NHLBI 301-496-4236

Exercising devices....Apley, Richard PTO 703-308-0305

Exercising devices...Love, John PTO 703-308-0873

Exhibits, Conventions....Dickinson, Joanne CENSUS 301-457-1191

Exhibits and Publications (Printing)....Beckwith, Frances NLM 301-496-6308

Exotic Fish....Staff FWS 703-358-1718

Exotic Species....Staff FWS 703-358-1718

Exotropia....Staff NEI 301-496-5248

Expanded Interconnection....Staff FCC 202-418-1576

Expanded Band AM....Staff FCC 202-418-2670

Experimental Aerodynamics....Staff NASA 415-604-5000

Experimental Aerodynamics....Mewhinney, Michael NASA 415-604-3937

Experimental Allergic Encephalomyelitis (EAE)....Staff NINDS 301-496-5751

Experimental Immunology....O'Shea, John FAES 301-496-6026

Explosive devices....Jordan, Charles PTO 703-308-0918

Explosives....Johnson, Larry USITC 202-205-3351

Explosives....Kramer, Deborah MINES 202-501-9394

Explosives....Maxey, Francis P. COMMERCE 202-482-0128

Explosives....Preston, Jacques CUSTOMS 212-466-5488

Export and Import Price Indexes, Curr. Anal.....Vachris, Michelle LABOR 202-606-7155

Export Trading Company Affairs....Muller, George COMMERCE 202-482-5131

Exposure Assessment Group....Staff EPA 202-260-8909

Extramural Associates Program....Staff OD/OERT 301-496-9728

Extrapyramidal Disorders....Staff NINDS 301-496-5751

Eye Banks....Staff NEI 301-496-5248

Eye Care....Staff NEI 301-496-5248

Eye Diseases....Staff NEI 301-496-5248

Eye Exercises....Staff NEI 301-496-5248

Eye Health Education Program....Staff NEI 301-496-5248

Eye Institute, National....Stein, Judith NIH 301-496-5248

Eye (Radiation and Ultra Violet Effect)....Staff FDA/NCDRH 301-594-2205

Eye (Statistics)....Staff NCHS 301-436-8500

Eye Strain....Staff NEI 301-496-5248

Eye....Staff National Eye Care Project 800-222-3937

Eye....Staff National Eye Research Foundation 800-621-2258

Eyeglasses....Johnson, Christopher USITC 202-205-3488

Eyeglasses....Staff NEI 301-496-5248

F

FAA Clearance EMI Problems....Staff FCC 202-418-2780

Fabric folding machines....Greene, William USITC 202-205-3405

Fabricated Metal Construction Materials....Williams, Franklin COMMERCE 202-482-0132

Fabrics: billiard cloth....Cook, Lee USITC 202-205-3471

Fabrics: bolting cloth....Cook, Lee USITC 202-205-3471

Fabrics, Coated or Laminated....Barth, George CUSTOMS 212-466-5884

Fabrics: coated....Cook, Lee USITC 202-205-3471

Fabrics: elastic....Shelton, Linda USITC 202-205-3457

Fabrics, embroidered....Konzet, Jeffrey CUSTOMS 212-466-5885

Fabrics: embroidered....Shelton, Linda USITC 202-205-3457

Fabrics: impression....Shelton, Linda USITC 202-205-3457

Fabrics, knit....Konzet, Jeffrey CUSTOMS 212-466-5885
Fabrics: knit....Shelton, Linda USITC 202-205-3457
Fabrics: narrow....Shelton, Linda USITC 202-205-3457
Fabrics, nonwoven....Barth, George CUSTOMS 212-466-5884
Fabrics: nonwoven....Sussman, Donald USITC 202-205-3470
Fabrics: oil cloths....Cook, Lee USITC 202-205-3471
Fabrics: tapestry, woven....Shelton, Linda USITC 202-205-3457
Fabrics, Technical....Barth, George CUSTOMS 212-466-5884
Fabrics: tire....Cook, Lee USITC 202-205-3471
Fabrics: tracing cloth....Cook, Lee USITC 202-205-3471
Fabrics: Tufted....Shelton, Linda USITC 202-205-3457
Fabrics, Woven....Tytelman, Alan CUSTOMS 212-466-5896
Fabrics, woven: cotton....Shelton, Linda USITC 202-205-3457
Fabrics, woven: glass....McNay, Deborah USITC 202-205-3425
Fabrics, woven: jute....Cook, Lee USITC 202-205-3471
Fabrics, woven: manmade fibers....Shelton, Linda USITC 202-205-3457
Fabrics, woven: pile....Shelton, Linda USITC 202-205-3457
Fabrics, woven: silk....Shelton, Linda USITC 202-205-3457
Fabrics: woven, wool....Shelton, Linda USITC 202-205-3457
Fabry's Disease....Staff NICHD 301-496-5133
Fabry's Disease....Staff NINDS 301-496-5751
Fabry's Disease....Staff NHLBI 301-496-4236
Facial Surgery....Staff American Academy of Facial Plastic and Reconstructive Surgery 800-332-3223
Facial Neuralgia (Tic Douloureux)....Staff NINDS 301-496-5751
Facilities Management....Bass, Robert C. FTC 202-326-2265
Facilities Management....Lampkins, Gladys M. FTC 202-326-2307
Facilities Management....Alston, Jerome FTC 202-326-2301
Facilities Management....Morris, Patrick A. FTC 202-326-2309
Facilities Management....Singleton, Frieda FTC 202-326-2580
Facilities Management....Morris, J. Wayne FTC 202-326-2310
Facsimile (FAX)--Wire....Staff FCC 202-326-2625
Facsimile....Coles, Edward L. PTO 703-305-4712
Factory Automation Systems....Bloom, Howard NIST 301-975-3508
FAES (Foundation for Adv. Educa. in the Sciences)....Staff FAES 301-496-7976
Fainting (Syncope)....Staff NHLBI 301-496-4236
Fair Credit Billing Act....Hurt, Adrienne FRS 202-452-2412
Fair Credit Reporting Act....Gell, Jane FRS 202-452-3667
Fair Housing Act....Loney, Glenn FRS 202-452-3585
Fair Housing and Equal Opportunity....Staff HUD 202-708-3735
Fairness Doctrine Enforcement....Staff FCC 202-418-1440
Falconry....Staff FWS 703-358-1821
Falls and Frailty....Staff NIA 301-496-1752
Familial Ataxia Telangiectasia....Staff NCI 301-496-5583
Familial Ataxia Telangiectasia....Staff NINDS 301-496-5751
Familial Dysautonomia (Riley-Day Syndrome)....Staff NINDS 301-496-5751
Familial Hypercholesterolemia....Staff NHLBI 301-496-4236
Familial Hypertension....Staff NHLBI 301-496-4236
Familial Mediterranean Fever....Staff NIAMS 301-496-8188
Familial Periodic Paralysis....Staff NINDS 301-496-5751
Familial Spastic Paraparesis....Staff NINDS 301-496-5751
Families....Staff CENSUS 301-457-2394
Family and Aging....Staff NIA 301-496-1752
Family Characteristics of Labor Force....Hayghe, Howard LABOR 202-606-6378
Family Issues....Lewis, Terry ACYF 202-205-8102
Family Medicine Training....Staff HRSA/BHPr 301-443-1467
Family Nursing Practitioner....Staff HRSA/BHPr 301-443-6333
Family Physicians....Staff American Academy of Family Physicians 800-274-2237
Family Planning (Research)....Staff NICHD 301-496-5133
Family Planning....Staff ASH 301-594-4008
Family Planning....Staff NCNR 301-496-0526
Family Size....Staff NICHD 301-496-5133
Family support....Staff Family Support and Mental Health 800-628-1696
Family Violence....Staff National Council on Child Abuse and Family Violence 800-222-2000
Family....Staff Family Care Givers Alliance 800-445-8106
Fanconi's Anemia....Staff NHLBI 301-496-4236
Fans....Mata, Ruben USITC 202-205-3403
Farm Bill....Staff FWS 703-358-2043
Farm Machinery....Weining, Mary COMMERCE 202-482-4708
Farm Population....Dahmann, Don CENSUS 301-457-2413
Farmlands....Staff FWS 703-358-2043
Farms and Land - Farm Numbers....Ledbury, Dan Agri 202-720-1790
Farms and Land - Farm Output and Productivity....Douvelis, George Agri 202-219-0840

Farms and Land - Farm Real Estate....Beach, Doug Agri 202-219-0443
Farms and Land - Foreign Land Ownership....DeBraal, Peter Agri 202-219-1011
Farms and Land - Land Ownership and Tenure....Wunderlich, Gene Agri 202-219-0427
Farms and Land - Land Use....Daugherty, Arthur Agri 202-219-0424
Farms and Land - World....Urban, Francis Agri 202-219-0717
Farsightedness....Staff NEI 301-496-5248
Fasteners (Industrial)....Reise, Richard COMMERCE 202-482-3489
Fasteners (Nails, Screws, Etc.)....Fitzgerald, John CUSTOMS 212-466-5492
Fasteners....Cuomo, Peter PTO 703-308-0827
Fats and Oils...Janis, William V. COMMERCE 202-482-2250
Fats and vegetable oils and their products....Reeder, John USITC 202-205-3319
Fatty acid amides....Land, Eric USITC 202-205-3349
Fatty acid esters of polyhydric alcohols....Land, Eric USITC 202-205-3349
Fatty acid quaternary ammonium salts (surface act)....Land, Eric USITC 202-205-3349
Fatty acids....Randall, Rob USITC 202-205-3366
Fatty alcohols of animal or vegetable origin....Randall, Rob USITC 202-205-3366
Fatty and Aromatic Substances....Joseph, Stephanie CUSTOMS 212-466-5768
Fatty ethers of animal or vegetable origin....Randall, Rob USITC 202-205-3366
Fatty substances derived from animal, marine, veg....Randall, Rob USITC 202-205-3366
Fear of Crime....Rand, Michael Justice Stat 202-616-3494
Fear of Crime....Lindgren, Sue Justice Stat 202-307-0760
Fear of Crime....Klaus, Patsy Justice Stat 202-307-0776
Feather products....Spalding, Josephine USITC 202-205-3498
Feathers....Steller, Rose USITC 202-205-3323
Febrile Convulsions....Staff NINDS 301-496-5751
Febrile Seizures....Staff NICHD 301-496-5133
Federal Energy Regulatory Commission....Schaffer, Rebecca NEIC 202-208-0004
Federal Information Center....Staff 800-347-1997
Federal Justice....Kaplan, Carol Justice Stat 202-307-0759
Federal Reserve Bulletin....Dykes, S Ellen FRS 202-452-3952
Federal Reserve Regulatory Service....Lahm, Diana FRS 202-452-3547
Federal Reserve System Publications....Kyles, Linda FRS 202-452-3244
Federal Tax Deposits....Bermudez, Michael FRS 202-452-3954
Feed Grains - Corn, Sorghum, Barley, Oats - World....Morgan, nancy Agri 202-501-8511
Feed Grains - Corn, Sorghum, Barley, Oats....Riley, Peter Agri 202-501-8512
Feed Grains - Corn, Sorghum, Barley, Oats....Van Lahr, Charles Agri 202-720-7369
Feed Grains - Corn, Sorghum, Barley, Oats....Dowdy, William Agri 202-720-3843
Feeds, animal....Pierre-Benoist, John USITC 202-205-3320
Fees General....Staff FCC 202-418-0192
Fees Private Radio...Staff FCC 800-322-1117
Fees Regulatory....Staff FCC 202-418-0192
Feldspar....Potter, Michael J. MINES 202-501-9387
Feldspar....White, Linda USITC 202-205-3427
Fellowships and Training in Laboratory Animal Medicine and Science....Staff NCRR 301-594-7933
Fellowships for Research Training in Nursing....Staff NINR 301-496-0207
Fellowships for Research Training in Toxicology....Staff NIEHS 919-755-4022
Female Offenders - Federal....Kaplan, Carol Justice Stat 202-307-0759
Female Offenders....Conley, Joyce Justice Stat 202-633-2214
Female Victims....Klaus, Patsy Justice Stat 202-307-0776
Fencing, Metal....MacAuley, Patrick COMMERCE 202-482-0132
Ferments....Nesbitt, Elizabeth USITC 202-205-3355
Ferricyanide blue...Johnson, Larry USITC 202-205-3351
Ferrites....Cutchin, John USITC 202-205-3396
Ferroalloys Products....Presbury Greylin COMMERCE 202-482-5158
Ferroalloys....Houck, Gerald MINES 202-501-9439
Ferroalloys....Yost, Charles USITC 202-205-3432
Ferrocerium....Johnson, Larry USITC 202-205-3351
Ferrocyanide blue....Johnson, Larry USITC 202-205-3351
Ferrous Scrap...Bell, Charles COMMERCE 202-482-0608
Fertility/Births....Bachu, Amara CENSUS 301-457-2416
Fertility/Births....O'Connell, Martin CENSUS 301-457-2416
Fertility Drugs....Staff NICHD 301-496-5133
Fertility....Staff NICHD 301-496-5133
Fertilizers....Brownchweig, Gilbert CUSTOMS 212-466-5744
Fertilizers....Maxey, Francis P. COMMERCE 202-482-0128
Fertilizers....Trainor, Cynthia USITC 202-205-3354
Fetal Alcohol Syndrome....Staff NIAAA 301-443-3860
Fetal Alcohol Syndrome....Staff NICHD 301-496-5133

Fetal Alcohol Syndrome Prevention....Hymbaugh, Karen CDC 404-488-7370

Fetal Development (Drug Effects)....Staff NIDA 301-443-6245

Fetal Monitoring....Staff NICHD 301-496-5133

Fetus....Staff NICHD 301-496-5133

Fever Blisters....Staff NIDR 301-496-4261

Fever....Staff NIAID 301-496-5717

Fiber Optic Devices....Bovernick, Rodney PTO 703-305-3594

Fibers....Konzet, Jeffrey CUSTOMS 212-466-5885

Fibers: abaca....Cook, Lee USITC 202-205-3471

Fibers: alpaca....Steller, Rose USITC 202-205-3323

Fibers: angora....Steller, Rose USITC 202-205-3323

Fibers: camel hair....Steller, Rose USITC 202-205-3323

Fibers: cashmere....Steller, Rose USITC 202-205-3323

Fibers: cotton....Sweet, Mary Elizabeth USITC 202-205-3455

Fibers: flax....Cook, Lee USITC 202-205-3471

Fibers: jute....Cook, Lee USITC 202-205-3471

Fibers: manmade....Shelton, Linda USITC 202-205-3457

Fibers: silk....Shelton, Linda USITC 202-205-3457

Fibers: sisal and henequen....Cook, Lee USITC 202-205-3471

Fibers: wool....Steller, Rose USITC 202-205-3323

Fibrillation....Staff NHLBI 301-496-4236

Fibrin....Randall, Rob USITC 202-205-3366

Fibrinolysis....Staff NHLBI 301-496-4236

Fibroid Tumors....Staff NICHD 301-496-5133

Fibromuscular Dysplasia....Staff NHLBI 301-496-4236

Fibromuscular Hyperplasia....Staff NIAMS 301-496-8188

Fibromyalgia....Staff NIAMS 301-496-8188

Fibrositis....Staff NIAMS 301-496-8188

Fibrotic Lung Diseases....Staff NHLBI 301-496-4236

Fibrous Dysplasia....Staff NINDS 301-496-5751

Fibrous Dysplasia....Staff NIAMS 301-496-8188

Field Enforcement Actions...Staff FCC 202-418-1170

Fifth Disease....Staff NIAID 301-496-5717

Fiji/Minerals....Lyday, Travis Cnty Mines 202-501-9695

Fiji (Suva)....Staff Cnty State 202-647-3546

Fiji....Berghage, Jeff Peace Corps 202-606-1098

Fiji....Davies, Irene Cnty World Bank 202-458-2481

Fiji....Harmnam, Judy Cnty Embassy 202-337-8320

Fiji....Imam, Fahmila Cnty Export-Import Bank 202-565-3738

Fiji....Jabbs, Theodore Cnty USIA 202-619-5836

Fiji....Nacuva, Pita Kewa Cnty Embassy 202-337-8320

Fiji....Respess, Rebecca Cnty TDA 703-875-4357

Fiji....Shelton, Alison Cnty Treasury 202-622-0354

Filariasis....Staff NIAID 301-496-5717

Filberts....Burket, Stephen USITC 202-205-3318

File management systems....Black, Thomas PTO 703-305-9707

Filling apparatus....Recia, Henry PTO 703-308-1382

Film (photographic)....Baker, Scott USITC 202-205-3386

Film, plastics....Misurelli, Denby USITC 202-205-3362

Film....Brownchweig, Gilbert CUSTOMS 212-466-5744

Films, Wildlife Video....Staff FWS 202-205-5611

Filters/Purifying Equipment....Wheeler, Fredrica COMMERCE 202-482-3509

Finance and Management Ind.....Candilis, Wray O. COMMERCE 202-482-0339

Finance....Goerl, Vincette L. 202-927-0600

Financial Assistance....Cox, John R. SBA 202-205-6490

Financial Industry Group....Roycroft, John C. SEC 202-942-1960

Financial Interest....Staff FCC 202-418-2130

Financial Management Policies....Hill, John W. GAO 202-512-8549

Financial Management....Hill, John W. GAO 202-512-8549

Financial services....Melly, Christopher USITC 202-205-3461

Financial Syndication....Staff FCC 202-418-2130

Finders Preference...Staff FCC 800-322-1117

Fine/industrial arts....Zarfus, Lou PTO 703-305-3260

Fine arts....Shooman, Ted PTO 703-305-3170

Finland (Helsinki)....Staff Cnty State 202-647-5669

Finland/Minerals....Plachy, Jozef Cnty Mines 202-501-9673

Finland....Gosnell, Peter Cnty Export-Import Bank 202-565-3733

Finland....Holloway, Barbara Cnty Treasury 202-622-0098

Finland....Kendall, Maryanne Cnty Commerce 202-482-3254

Finland....Polho, Aapo Cnty Embassy 202-298-5800

Finland....Rankin-Galloway, Honore Cnty USIA 202-619-5283

Finland....Valtasaari, Jukka Cnty Embassy 202-298-5800

Fire extinguishers....Mitchell, David PTO 703-308-0361

Fire Management....Staff FWS 202-208-2595

Fire Protection....Cowart, Everett CDC 404-639-3148

Fire protection....Staff National Fire Protection Association 800-344-3555

Fire Research Laboratory....Wright, R.N. NIST 301-975-5900

Fire Safety Engineering....Fowell, A. NIST 301-975-6863

Fire safety....Staff CPSC 301-504-0580

Fire Science....Gann, R.G. NIST 301-6866

Fire....Staff FCC 717-337-1212

Firearm licenses....Staff ATF 404-679-5040

Far East....Staff GAO 808-541-1250

Firearms importing....Staff ATF 202-927-8320

Firearms....Jordan, Charles PTO 703-308-0918

Firearms....Luther, Dennis USITC 202-205-3497

Firearms....Preston, Jacques CUSTOMS 212-466-5488

Firewood....Hoffmeier, Bill USITC 202-205-3321

Fireworks....Johnson, Larry USITC 202-205-3351

Fireworks....Staff CPSC 301-504-0580

First aid kits....Randall, Rob USITC 202-205-3366

Fish and Wildlife Service....Staff EPA 202-208-5634

Fish and Wildlife Law Enforcement....Staff FWS 703-358-1949

Fish and Wildlife Reference Service....Staff FWS 703-358-2156

Fish and Wildlife News....Staff FWS 202-208-5634

Fish Broodstock Program....Staff FWS 703-358-1715

Fish Conservation and Management Act....Staff 703-358-1715

Fish Control Chemicals....Staff FWS 703-358-1715

Fish Culture Information....Staff FWS 703-358-1715

Fish Disease Diagnosis/Control....Staff FWS 703-358-1715

Fish Diseases/Research....Staff FWS 703-358-1715

Fish, Exotic....Staff FWS 703-358-1718

Fish Habitat Research....Lennartz, Michael R. FS 202-205-1524

Fish Hatcheries....Staff FWS 703-358-1715

Fish Health Centers....Staff FWS 703-358-1715

Fish Husbandry....Staff FWS 703-358-1715

Fish Law Enforcement....Staff FWS 703-358-1949

Fish nets and netting....Cook, Lee USITC 202-205-3471

Fish Nets and Nettings....Barth, George CUSTOMS 212-466-5884

Fish oils....Reeder, John USITC 202-205-3319

Fish Propagation....Staff FWS 703-358-1715

Fish Stocks....Staff FWS 703-358-1715

Fish....Conte, Ralph CUSTOMS 212-466-5759

Fish....Corey, Roger USITC 202-205-3327

Fisheries, Major Proj.....Bell, Richard COMMERCE 202-482-2460

Fishery Information Systems....Staff FWS 703-558-1861

Fishing on Refuges....Staff FWS 703-358-2043

Fishing tackle....Witherspoon, Ricardo USITC 202-205-3489

Flags....Cook, Lee USITC 202-205-3471

Flares....Johnson, Larry USITC 202-205-3351

Flashlights....Cutchin, John USITC 202-205-3396

Flat glass and products....Lukes, James USITC 202-205-3426

Flat goods....Seastrum, Carl USITC 202-205-3493

Flat goods....Gorman, Kevin CUSTOMS 212-466-5893

Flat panel displays....Malison, Andrew USITC 202-205-3391

Flaxseed and linseed oil....Reeder, John USITC 202-205-3319

Flight Control Research....Witherspoon, John NASA 804-864-6170

Flight Research Programs....Lovato, Nancy NASA 805-258-3448

Flight Services....Whatley, David FAA 202-267-9090

Flight simulating machines....Andersen, Peder USITC 202-205-3388

Flight Simulation Research....Hutchison, Jane NASA 415-604-4968

Flight Standards....Accardi, Thomas C FAA 202-267-8237

Floaters....Staff NEI 301-496-5248

Floating structures....Lahey, Kathleen USITC 202-205-3409

Floor coverings, textile....Sweet, Mary Elizabeth USITC 202-205-3465

Floor Coverings....Hansen, John CUSTOMS 212-466-5854

Flooring (wood)....Hoffmeier, Bill USITC 202-205-3321

Floppy Baby (Nemaline Myopathy)....Staff NINDS 301-496-5751

Floral waters....Land, Eric USITC 202-205-3349

Floriculture....Johnson, Doyle Agri 202-501-7949

Floriculture....Rogers, Latham Agri 202-720-5944

Flour (grain)....Pierre-Benoist, John USITC 202-205-3320

Flour....Vacant COMMERCE 202-482-2428

Flower and foliage: artificial, other....Spalding, Josephine USITC 202-205-3498

Flower and foliage: preserved, other....Spalding, Josephine USITC 202-205-3498

Flowers, Artificial....Rauch, Theodore CUSTOMS 212-466-5892

Flowers....Janis, William V. COMMERCE 202-482-2250

Flu and Older People....Staff NIA 301-496-1752

Flu...Staff NIAID 301-496-5717
Fluid conveying....Mitchell, David PTO 703-308-0361
Fluid Power....McDonald, Edward COMMERCE 202-482-0680
Fluorescein Angiography....Staff NEI 301-496-5248
Fluoridation....Reeves, Thomas CDC 404-639-8377
Fluoridation....Staff CDC 404-639-8377
Fluoridation....Staff NIDR 301-496-4261
Fluoride Research....Staff NIDR 301-496-4261
Fluorine....Conant, Kenneth USITC 202-205-3346
Fluorocarbons....Michels, David USITC 202-205-3352
Fluorosis....Staff NIDR 301-496-4261
Fluorspar....DeSapio, Vincent USITC 202-205-3435
Fluorspar....Miller, Michael MINES 202-501-9409
Fluxes....Michaels, David USITC 202-205-3352
FM Antennas, Directional....Staff FCC 202-418-2740
FM Application Status....Staff FCC 202-418-2730
FM Blanketing Interference...Staff FCC 202-418-2740
FM Boosters Legal....Staff FCC 202-418-1690
FM Boosters Technical....Staff FCC 202-418-1690
FM Technical Standards....Staff FCC 202-418-2740
FM Translators Legal/Policy....Staff FCC 202-418-1690
FM Translators Technical....Staff FCC 202-418-1690
Foams....Kight, John PTO 703-308-2453
Fogarty Scholars....Staff FIC 301-496-4161
Fogarty Publications....Staff FIC 301-496-2075
Foil, metal: aluminum....Yost, Charles USITC 202-205-3432
Foil, metal: other....Lundy, David USITC 202-205-3439
Folk Arts....Sheehy, Daniel NEA 202-682-5449
Food Additives/Dyes....Corwin, Emil FDA 202-205-4144
Food Additives....Staff FDA 301-205-4144
Food and Nutrition Information Center....Facinoli, Sandy NAL 301-504-5414
Food and Chemicals, Prices/Lv. Cond....Hippen, Roger LABOR 202-606-7715
Food, Apparel, and Raw Materials, Intl. Price Ind.....Frumkin, Rob LABOR 202-606-7106
Food - Food Assistance and Nutrition....Smallwood, Dave Agri 202-219-1265
Food - Food Assistance ....Smallwood, Dave Agri 202-219-1265
Food - Food Away From Home....Price, Charlene Agri 202-501-6765
Food - Food Consumption....Putnam, Judy Agri 202-501-7413
Food - Food Demand and Expenditures....Blaylock, James Agri 202-219-0900
Food - Food Demand and Expenditures....Haidacher, Richard Agri 202-219-0868
Food - Food Demand and Expenditures (World)....Stallings, Dave Agri 202-219-0708
Food - Food Manufacturing and Retailing....Handy, Charles Agri 202-219-0859
Food - Food Manufacturing....Gallo, Tony Agri 202-219-1260
Food - Food Policy (World)....Westcott, Paul Agri 202-219-0840
Food - Food Policy - World....Lynch, Loretta Agri 202-219-0689
Food - Food Policy....Kuhn, Betsey Agri 202-219-0409
Food - Food Policy....Smallwood, Dave Agri 202-219-1265
Food - Food Safety and Quality....Roberts, Tanya Agri 202-219-0857
Food - Food Safety and Quality....Unnevehr, Laurian Agri 202-219-0400
Food - Food Wholesaling....Epps, Walter Agri 202-219-0866
Food Grains - Rice....Kerestes, Daniel Agri 202-720-9526
Food Grains - Wheat....Allen, Ed Agri 202-219-0831
Food Grains - Wheat....Siegenthaler, Vaughn Agri 202-720-8068
Food Industry Group....Daly, James M. SEC 202-942-1800
Food Issues....Harman, John W. GAO 202-512-5138
Food Labeling....Corwin, Emil FDA 202-205-4144
Food - Marketing Margins and Statistics....Haidacher, Richard Agri 202-219-0870
Food - Marketing Margins and Statistics....Dunham, Denis Agri 202-219-0870
Food - Marketing Margins and Statistics....Elitzak, Howard Agri 202-219-1254
Food - Marketing Margins and Statistics....Handy, Charles Agri 202-219-0866
Food-preparing machines....Jackson, Georgia USITC 202-205-3399
Food - Price Spreads (Meat)....Duewer, Larry Agri 202-219-0712
Food Prices and Consumer Index....Clauson, Annette Agri 202-501-6552
Food Prices and Consumer Price Index....Elitzak, Howard Agri 202-219-1254
Food Prices Retail, Consumer Expenditure Survey....Cook, William LABOR 202-606-6988
Food Products Machinery....Shaw, Gene COMMERCE 202-482-3494
Food, Raw Materials, and Apparel, Intl. Price Ind....Frumkin, Rob LABOR 202-606-7106
Food - Retailing....Kaufman, Phil Agri 202-219-0728
Food Retailing....Kenney, Cornelius COMMERCE 202-482-2428
Food safety....Karstadt, Myra FAES 202-332-9110
Food....Elkins, John Customs 202-482-7020

Foot Disorders....Staff NIAMS 301-496-8188
Footwear with Uppers of Rubber, Plastic or Leather....Foley, Richard CUSTOMS 212-466-5890
Footwear....Byron, James E. COMMERCE 202-482-4034
Footwear....Shildneck, Ann USITC 202-205-3499
Forbearance (Nondominant)....Staff FCC 202-418-1573
Forecasting Prison Populations....Staff Justice Stat 202-307-7703
Foreign Banks with U.S. Branches....O'Day, Kathleen FRS 202-452-3786
Foreign Born Population....Staff CENSUS 301-457-2403
Foreign Countries--Hourly Compensation Costs...Capdevielle, Patricia LABOR 202-606-5654
Foreign Countries, Labor Force and Unemployment....Sorrentino, Constance LABOR 202-606-5654
Foreign Countries--Prices, Prod. and Tech.....Godbout, Todd LABOR 202-606-5654
Foreign Countries--Productivity, Unit Labor Costs....Neef, Arthur LABOR 202-606-5654
Foreign Exchange Markets....Smith, Ralph W FRS 202-452-3712
Foreign Exchange Rates....Decker, Patrick J FRS 202-452-3314
Foreign Governments....Duvall, Steven SEC 202-942-1950
Foreign Language Education....Staff NEH 202-606-8373
Foreign Margin Stock List....Wolffrum, Margaret A FRS 202-452-2781
Foreign Medical Students....Shaffer, Sylvia HRSA 301-443-3376
Foreign Missions....Picard, James Customs 202-646-5056
Foreign Official Reserves....Smith, Ralph FRS 202-452-3712
Foreign Patents....Dell'Orto, Kathleen PTO 703-308-3278
Foreign Program Distribution....Staff FCC 202-418-2780
Foreign Radio Ownership....Staff FCC 202-418-2780
Foreign Scientists Assistance....Staff FIC 301-472-6166
Foreign Securities Margin Requirements....Holz, Scott FRS 202-452-2781
Foreign Service....Klang, Gordon OPM 202-606-0961
Foreign Trade Data Services....Staff CENSUS 301-457-3041
Foreign Trade Data Services....Higbee, Reba CENSUS 301-457-3041
Foreign Trade, Shippers Export Declaration....Blyweiss, Hal CENSUS 301-457-1086
Foreign Trade, U.S.....Morisse, Kathryn A FRS 202-452-3773
Foreign trade zones....Burns, Gail USITC 202-205-2501
Foreign Trust Activities....Vinnedge, Donald R FRS 202-452-2717
Foreign TV Ownership....Staff FCC 202-418-1630
Forest Diseases....Smith Richard S. FS 202-205-1532
Forest Fire Sciences....Donoghue, Linda R. FS 202-205-1561
Forest Insects....Powell, Janine FS 202-205-1532
Forest Products, Domestic Construction....Kristensen, Chris COMMERCE 202-482-0384
Forest Products, Trade Policy....Stanley, Gary COMMERCE 202-482-0375
Forest Products....Stanley, Gary COMMERCE 202-482-0375
Forest Products....Vacant FS 202-205-1565
Forest Protection....Staff FWS 703-358-2043
Forest Radio Service....Staff FCC 717-337-1212
Forest Recreation and Urban Forestry....Ewert, Alan FS 202-205-1092
Forestry and Construction, Prices and Living Cond....Davies, Wanda LABOR 202-606-7714
Forestry and Construction, Prices and Living Cond.....Davies, Wanda LABOR 202-606-7714
Forestry Atmospheric Deposition Research....Dunn, Paul H. FS 202-205-1524
Forestry Ecosystem Research....Ruark, Gregory FS 202-205-1524
Forestry, Global Change Research....Niebla, Elvia E. FS 202-205-1561
Forestry, Land Reclamation....Duscher, Karl FS 202-205-1244
Forestry, Lands and Resource Information....Holmes, Chris FS 202-205-1006
Forestry, Mineral Materials....Marshall, Steve FS 202-205-1246
Forestry, Oil and Gas Analysis....Holm, Melody FS 303-236-9376
Forestry, Pesticide Use....Staff FS 202-205-1600
Forestry, Soils Program....Avers, Peter FS 202-205-0977
Forestry, Solid Leasable Minerals....Kurcaba FS 202-205-1239
Forestry, Water Rights Program....Glasser, Steve FS 202-205-1475
Forestry, Water Rights....Glasser, Steve FS 202-205-1475
Forestry Wetlands Research....Ryan, Douglas FS 202-205-1524
Forfeiture....Zawitz, Marianne Justice Stat 202-616-3499
Forged-steel grinding balls....Polly, Laura USITC 202-205-3408
Forgings Semifinished Steel....Bell, Charles COMMERCE 202-482-0608
Fork-lift trucks....Polly, Laura USITC 202-205-3408
Formaldehyde....Michels, David USITC 202-205-3352
Fossil Energy....Siegal, Linda NEIC 202-586-6660
Fossil Fuel Power Generation, Major Proj.....Dollison, Robert COMMERCE 202-482-2733

Foster Care....Kharfen, Michael ACF 202-401-9215
Foundation....Staff Foundation Center Customer Service 800-424-9836
Foundry Equipment....Kemper, Alexis COMMERCE 202-482-5956
Foundry Industry....Bell, Charles COMMERCE 202-482-0608
Foundry products....Bello, Felix USITC 202-205-3120
Fracture Healing....Staff NIAMS 301-496-8188
Fragile X Syndrome....Staff National Fragile X Foundation 800-688-8765
Fragile X Syndrome....Staff NICHD 301-496-5133
France/Minerals....Newman, Harold R. Cnty Mines 202-501-9669
France (Paris)....Staff Cnty State 202-647-1412
France....Andreani, Jacques Cnty Embassy 202-944-6000
France....Gosnell, Peter Cnty Export-Import Bank 202-565-3733
France....Mikalis, Elana Cnty Commerce 202-482-6008
France....Seifkin, David Cnty USIA 202-619-6582
France....Vacant Cnty Treasury 202-622-0166
France....Villemur, Patrick Cnty Embassy 202-944-6000
Franchising services....Melly, Christopher USITC 202-205-3461
Fraud Hotline, HUD....Staff HUD 800-347-3735
Fraud, Scientific....Staff OASH/ORI 301-443-3400
Fraud, Waste and Abuse-Investigations, Audits....Holtz, Judy IG 202-619-1149
Fraud....Herera, Maria Customs 202-927-1510
Free Trade Area of the Americas (FTAA)....Lenzy, Karen US Trade Rep 202-395-5190
Freedom of Information Act General....Staff FCC 202-418-0210
Freedom of Information, Office of....Leathers, Laura CDC 404-639-2388
Freedom of Information Office....Christian, Darlene PHS 301-443-5252
Freedom of Information....Staff OD/DC 301-496-5633
French Guinea/Minerals....Gurmendi, Alfredo Cnty Mines 202-501-9681
French Antilles....Staff Cnty State 202-647-2620
French Polynesia....Staff Cnty State 202-647-3546
Freon (chlorofluorocarbons)....Michels, David USITC 202-205-3352
Friedreich's Ataxia....Staff NINDS 301-496-5751
Friends of the Clinical Center....Staff FOCC/CC 301-402-0193
Frohlich's Syndrome (Adiposogenital Dystrophy)....Staff NICHD 301-496-5133
Frohlich's Syndrome (Adiposogenital Dystrophy)....Staff NIDDK 301-496-3583
Frohlich's Syndrome (Adiposogenital Dystrophy)....Staff NINDS 301-496-5751
Frozen Fruits, Vegetables and Specialties....William, Janis V. COMMERCE 202-482-2250
Fructose....Randall, Rob USITC 202-205-3366
Fruit, edible, ex citrus....Frankel, Lee USITC 202-205-3315
Fruits and Vegetables....Hopartd, Stanley CUSTOMS 212-466-5760
Fruits and Tree Nuts....Bertelsen, Diane Agri 202-219-0884
Fruits and Tree Nuts....Hintzman, Kevin Agri 202-720-5412
Fruits and Tree Nuts....Shields, Dennis Agri 202-219-0884
Fruits and Tree Nuts - Tree Nuts....Johnson, Doyle Agri 202-219-0884
Fuchs' Dystrophy....Staff NEI 301-496-5248
Fuel Cycle Safety and Safeguards....Burnett, Robert F. NRC 301-415-7212
Fuel, jet....Foreso, Cynthia USITC 202-205-3348
Fuel oil, bunker "C"....Foreso, Cynthia USITC 202-205-3348
Fuel oil, navy special....Foreso, Cynthia USITC 202-205-3348
Fuel oil (nos. 1, 2, 3, 4, 5, 6)....Foreso, Cynthia USITC 202-205-3348
Fuels and Chemical Analysis....Staff EPA 313-668-4557
Fuels and Utilities Index, Monthly....Adkins, Robert LABOR 202-606-6985
Fuels and Utilities Retail Prices, Consumer Price Index....Adkins, Robert LABOR 202-606-6985
Fulminates....Johnson, Larry USITC 202-205-3351
Fumes (Hazardous)....Staff OD/ORS 301-496-2960
Functional fluids....Lieberman, Paul PTO 703-308-2552
Fund Raising...Staff FCC 202-418-1720
Fungal Infections....Staff NIAID 301-496-5717
Fungal Diseases (Eyes)....Staff NEI 301-496-5248
Funnel Chest (Pectus Excavatum)....Staff NHLBI 301-496-4236
Fur and furlike apparel....Hamey, Amy USITC 202-205-3465
Fur and furlike apparel....Jones, Jackie USITC 202-205-3466
Fur Goods....Byron, James E. COMMERCE 202-482-4034
Furfural....Michels, David USITC 202-205-3352
Furnace black....Johnson, Larry USITC 202-205-3351
Furnaces....Francke, Reic CUSTOMS 212-466-5669
Furnaces....Mata, Ruben USITC 202-205-3403
Furnaces....Staff CPSC 301-504-0580
Furnishings....Hansen, John CUSTOMS 212-466-5854
Furniture....Hodgen, Donald COMMERCE 202-482-3346
Furniture....Mushinske, Larry CUSTOMS 212-466-5739
Furniture....Spalding, Josephine USITC 202-205-3498

Furskins....Steller, Rose USITC 202-205-3323
Fuse/Burn....Giles, Ken CPSC 301-504-0580
Fused Alumina, (Abrasive)....Austin, Gordon MINES 202-501-9388
Fuses: Blasting....Johnson, Larry USITC 202-205-3351
Fuses: electrical....Malison, Andrew USITC 202-205-3391
Fusion Energy....Greenblatt, Jack USITC 202-205-3353
Fusion Energy....Davies, Anne NEIC 301-903-4941
Fusion Plasma....Crandall, David NEIC 301-903-4596
Futures Trading....Homer, Laura FRS 202-452-2781
Fuzzy Logic....Montgomery, Sheila COMMERCE 202-482-0397

G

G. Bissaue....Fossum, Linnea Peace Corps 202-606-3708
G6PD Deficiency....Staff NHLBI 301-496-4236
Gabon (Libreville)....Staff Cnty State 202-647-3139
Gabon/Minerals....Mobbs, Philip Cnty Mines 202-501-9679
Gabon....Boundoukou-Latha, Paul Cnty Embassy 202-797-1000
Gabon....Henke, Debra Cnty Commerce 202-482-5149
Gabon....Henning, Herman Cnty USIA 202-619-5926
Gabon....Jefferson, Deborah Peace Corps 202-606-3709
Gabon....Maybury-Lewis Anthony Cnty Export-Import Bank 202-565-3739
Gabon....Mitchell, Willis Peace Corps 202-606-3708
Gabon....Nguembi, Fidele Moussavou Cnty Embassy 202-797-1000
Gabon....Palghat, Kathy Cnty Treasury 202-622-0332
Gabon....Wilson, Michael J. Cnty World Bank 202-473-4714
Gabon....Younge, Nathan Cnty TDA 703-875-4357
Galactorrhea....Staff NIDDK 301-496-3583
Galactosemia....Staff NICHD 301-496-5133
Galactosemia....Staff NINDS 301-496-5751
Galactosemia....Staff NIDDK 301-496-3583
Galileo Flight Project....Wilson, James NASA 818-354-5011
Gallbladder....Staff NIDDK 301-654-3810
Gallium....Kramer, Deborah A. MINES 202-501-9394
Gallium....Lundy, David USITC 202-205-3439
Gallstones....Staff NIDDK 301-654-3810
Gambia, The (Banjul)....Staff Cnty State 202-647-4567
Gambia/Minerals....Dolley, Thomas Cnty Mines 202-501-9690
Gambia....Baily, Jess Cnty USIA 202-619-5900
Gambia....Barber, Ed Cnty Treasury 202-622-1730
Gambia....Bezek, Jill Cnty TDA 703-875-4357
Gambia....Bowler, Gina Peace Corps 202-606-3644
Gambia....Brown, Edward K. Cnty World Bank 202-473-4834
Gambia....Dibba, Aminatta Cnty Embassy 202-785-1399
Gambia....Fox, Russell Peace Corps 202-606-3644
Gambia....Hutchins, Dayna Cnty Export-Import Bank 202-565-3737
Gambia....Michelin, Philip Cnty Commerce 202-482-4388
Gambia....Niec, Rebecca Cnty AID 202-647-9206
Gambia....Tunkara, Kemo Cnty Embassy 202-785-1379
Gambling problem....Staff National Council on Problem Gambling 800-522-4700
Game animals....Steller, Rose USITC 202-205-3323
Games and Childrens' Vehicles....Hodgen, Donald COMMERCE 202-482-3346
Games....Abrahamson, Dana USITC 202-205-3430
Games....McKenna, Thomas CUSTOMS 212-466-5475
Gaming Enforcement....Staff FCC 202-418-1430
Gamma Ray Observatory....Shannon, Ernie NASA 301-286-6256
Gamma Ray Observatory....Staff NASA 301-286-8102
Garage Door Openers--Licenses....Staff FCC 717-337-1212
Garage Door Operators....Staff CPSC 301-504-0580
Garnet....Austin, Gordon MINES 202-501-9388
Garters and suspenders....Sweet, Mary Elizabeth USITC 202-205-3455
Gas generators....Fravel, Dennis USITC 202-205-3404
Gas Industry Group....Daly, James M. SEC 202-942-1800
Gas oil....Foreso, Cynthia USITC 202-205-3348
Gas-operated metalworking appliances....Fravel, Dennis USITC 202-205-3404
Gas Reserves Statistics....Lique, Diane NEIC 202-586-6090
Gas Vol Standards....Staff CPSC 301-504-0580
Gaseous Diffusion Plants (GDP)....Alexander, James NEIC 615-576-0885
Gases, Greenhouse....Patrinus, Aristides NEIC 301-903-5348
Gaskets/Gasketing Materials....Reiss, Richard COMMERCE 202-482-3489
Gasoline, Retail Prices....Chelena, Joseph LABOR 202-606-6982
Gasoline....Foreso, Cynthia USITC 202-205-3348
Gastric Hypersecretion....Staff NIDDK 301-654-3810

Gastrinoma....Staff NIDDK 301-654-3810
Gastritis....Staff NIDDK 301-654-3810
Gastrointestinal Disorders....Staff NIDDK 301-654-3810
Gastrointestinal Tract Diseases....Staff NIDDK 301-654-3810
GATT....Hasha, Gene Agri 202-219-0818
Gaucher's Disease....Staff National Gaucher Foundation 800-925-8885 Head
Injuries....Staff National Head Injury Foundation 800-444-6443
Gaucher's Disease....Staff NINDS 301-496-5751
Gauze, impregnated with medicinals....Randall, Rob USITC 202-205-3366
Gaza....Roberts, Nigel Cnty World Bank 202-473-2241
GBF/DIME System....Staff CENSUS 301-457-1305
Gears....Riedl, Karl CUSTOMS 212-466-5493
Gelatin, articles of....Spalding, Josephine USITC 202-205-3498
Gelatin, edible....Jonnard, Aimison USITC 202-205-3350
Gelatin, inedible....Jonnard, Aimison USITC 202-205-3350
Gelatin, photographic....Jonnard, Aimison USITC 202-205-3350
Gelatin....Brownchweig, Gilbert CUSTOMS 212-466-5744
Gem Stones....Austin, Gordon MINES 202-501-9388
Gems....DeSapio, Vincent USITC 202-205-3435
Gemstones, imitation....Witherspoon, Ricardo USITC 202-205-3489
Gen. Indus. Mach. Nec, Exc 35691....Shaw, Eugene COMMERCE 202-482-2204
GenBank (Genetic Sequence Data Bank)....Staff NLM 301-496-2475
Gene Mapping....Staff NCHGR 301-402-0911
Gene Therapy...Staff NHLBI 301-496-4236
Gene Therapy....Staff NCI 301-496-5583
Gene Therapy....Staff OD/OSPL 301-496-9838
General Agreement on Trade and Tariffs (GATT)....Klein, Cecelia US TradeRep
202-395-3063
General Aviation Aircraft (Market Support)....Green, Ron COMMERCE
202-482-4228
General Clinical Research Centers Program....Staff NCRR 301-594-7945
General Counsel.....Plyler, Joyce FTC 202-326-2155
General Counsel....Vidas, Sandra M. FTC 202-326-2456
General Counsel's Office....Ballard, Sonia D. FTC 202-326-2669
General Forms...Staff FCC 202-418-0210
General Information - Environmental Issues Hotline....Staff EPA 800-759-4372
General Information....Staff CENSUS 301-457-4100
General Information....Staff FCC 202-418-0190
General Litigation (Assoc. and Business Practices)....Abrahamsen, Dana FTC
202-326-2906
General Litigation (Assoc. and Business Practices)....Alexander, Janice FTC
202-326-2891
General Litigation (Health Care)....Allen, Patricia A. FTC 202-326-3176
General Litigation....Lord, Terry Justice 202-514-1026
General, Medical Sciences, National Institute of....Dieffenbach, Ann NIH
301-496-7301
General Mobile Radio Service General....Staff FCC 800-322-1117
General Mobile Radio Service Technical....Staff FCC 202-418-0680
General Mobile Licenses....Staff FCC 717-337-1212
General Mobile Radio Service....Staff FCC 717-337-1212
Generator Sets/Turbines (Major Proj)....Dollison, Robert C0MMERCE
202-482-2733
Generators....Cutchin, John USITC 202-205-3396
Genetic counseling....Biesecker, Barbara B. FAES 301-496-3979
Genetic Pancrea. Involv. not due to Cystic Fibrosis....Staff NIDDK 301-496-3583
Genetics, Animal Monitoring....Staff NCRR 301-496-9188
Genetics, Developmental....Adhya, Sankar L. FAES 301-496-2495
Genetics of Aging....Staff NIA 301-496-1752
Genetics....Bale, Sherri J. FAES 301-402-2679
Genetics....Francomano, Clair FAES 301-402-8255
Genetics....Staff Alliance of Genetic Support Groups 800-336-4363
Genetics....Staff NIGMS 301-496-7301
Genetics....Staff NIDCD 301-496-7243
Genetics....Staff NIDR 301-496-4261
Genetics....Staff NINDS 301-496-5751
Genetics....Staff NICHD 301-496-5133
Genital Warts....Staff NIAID 301-496-5717
Genital Herpes....Staff NIAID 301-496-5717
Genome....Staff NCHGR 301-402-0911
Geology....Goodell, Grant UVA 804-4-0559
Geometrical instruments....Goldberg, Gerald PTO 703-308-5443
Geophysical Phenomena Research....Staff NASA 415-604-3937
Geophysical Research....Shannon, Ernie 301-286-6256
Georgia....Carlen, James Cnty Treasury 202-622-0122

Georgia....Djaparidze, Tedo Cnty Embassy 202-393-5959
Georgia....Hall, Christopher L. Cnty World Bank 202-473-4418
Georgia....Kreslins, Dagnija Cnty AID 202-736-4317
Georgia....Levine, Richard Cnty Mines 202-501-9682
Georgia....Makharadze, Gueorgui Cnty Embassy 202-393-5959
Georgia....Skipper, Thomas Cnty USIA 202-619-5057
Georgia....Staff Cnty State 202-647-8671
Georgia....Waxmen-Lenz, Roberta Cnty Export-Import Bank 202-565-3742
Geoscience Research....Coleman, James NEIC 301-903-5822
Geothermal Energy....Jelacic, Al 202-586-5340
Geothermal Loan Guarantee Program....Staff NEIC 202-586-1539
Geriatric Medicine....Staff NIA 301-496-1752
Geriatric Psychiatry....Staff NIA 301-496-1752
Geriatric Psychiatry....Staff NIMH 301-443-4515
Geriatrics....Dutta, Chhanda FAES 301-496-1033
Geriatrics....Staff NIA 301-496-1752
German Measles (Rubella)....Staff NIAID 301-496-5717
Germanium oxides....Conant, Kenneth USITC 202-205-3346
Germanium....Lundy, David USITC 202-205-3439
Germanium....Schnecke, Errol MINES 202-501-9421
Germany, East/Minerals....Zajac, William Cnty Mines 202-501-9671
Germany....Chrobog, Juergen Cnty Embassy 202-298-4000
Germany....Fisher, Brenda Cnty Commerce 202-482-2435
Germany....Gosnell, Peter Cnty Export-Import Bank 202-565-3733
Germany....Kloepfer, Joan Cnty Commerce 202-482-2841
Germany....Larsen, John Commerce 202-482-2434
Germany....Lemaistre, Alice Cnty USIA 202-619-6184
Germany....Mackour, Oscar Cnty Treasury 202-622-0145
Germany....Matussek, Thomas Cnty Embassy 202-298-4000
Germany....Staff Cnty State 202-647-2005
Germfree Rodents....Staff NCRR 301-496-5255
Gerontology....Staff NIA 301-496-1752
Gerson Method....Staff NCI 301-496-5583
Gerstmann's Syndrome....Staff NICHD 301-496-5133
Gestation....Staff NICHD 301-496-5133
Ghana (Accra)....Staff Cnty State 202-647-1596
Ghana/Minerals....van Oss, Hendrik Cnty Mines 202-501-9687
Ghana....Brown, Arthur Peace Corps 202-606-3137
Ghana....Effah-Apenteng, Nana Cnty Embassy 202-686-4520
Ghana....Henke, Debra Cnty Commerce 202-482-5149
Ghana....Maybury-Lewis Anthony Cnty Export-Import Bank 202-565-3739
Ghana....Najm, Fauzia Cnty World Bank 202-473-4981
Ghana....O'Neal, Adrienne Cnty USIA 202-619-6904
Ghana....Palghat, Kathy Cnty Treasury 202-622-0332
Ghana....Spio-Garbrah, Ekwow Cnty Embassy 202-686-4520
Ghana....Swift, Gail Peace Corps 202-606-3136
Ghana....Wilburn, Adolph Cnty AID 202-647-9339
Ghana....Younge, Nathan Cnty TDA 703-875-4357
Giant Cell Arteritis....Staff NEI 301-496-5248
Giardiasis....Staff NIAID 301-496-5717
Gibraltar....Staff Cnty State 202-647-8027
Giftware (Export Promo)....Beckham, Reginald COMMERCE 202-482-5478
Gigantism....Staff NIDDK 301-496-3583
Gilbert's Syndrome....Staff NIDDK 301-496-3583
Gilles de la Tourette's Disease....Staff NINDS 301-496-5751
Gingivitis....Staff NIDR 301-496-4261
Glace fruit and vegetable substances....Frankel, Lee USITC 202-205-3315
Glands....Staff NIDDK 301-496-3583
Glass articles, nspf....Lukes, James USITC 202-205-3426
Glass containers....Lukes, James USITC 202-205-3426
Glass fiber....Lukes, James USITC 202-205-3426
Glass, Flat....Williams, Franklin COMMERCE 202-482-0132
Glass (flat)....Lukes, James USITC 202-205-3426
Glass yarn....Lukes, James USITC 202-205-3426
Glass....Bunin, Jacob CUSTOMS 212-566-5796
Glassblowing....Staff NCRR/BEIP 301-496-5195
Glassware (Issue and Washing)....Staff OD/ORS 301-496-4595
Glassware....Bratland, Rosemarie COMMERCE 202-482-0380
Glassware....McNay, Deborah USITC 202-205-3425
Glassworking machines....Fravel, Dennis USITC 202-205-3404
Glaucoma....Staff NEI 301-496-5248
Glazing compounds....Johnson, Larry USITC 202-205-3351
Gliomas....Staff NINDS 301-496-5751
Global Change Division....Staff EPA 202-233-9190

Global Change (service issues)....Wright, Janet NAL 202-720-3434

Global Changes (technical issues)....Rand, Roberta NAL 301-504-6684

Global Climate Change....Galas, David J. NEIC 301-903-3251

Global Commodity Outlook....Whitton, Carolyn Agri 202-219-0825

Globoid Cell Leukodystrophy....Staff NINDS 301-496-5751

Glomerulonephritis....Staff NIDDK 301-654-4415

Gloves (Work)....Byron, James E. COMMERCE 202-482-4034

Gloves....Burtnik, Brian CUSTOMS 212-466-5880

Gloves....Jones, Jackie USITC 202-205-3466

Glucose Intolerance....Staff NIDDK 301-654-3327

Glue, articles of....Spalding, Josephine USITC 202-205-3498

Glue, of animal or vegetable origin....Jonnard, Aimison USITC 202-205-3350

Glue size....Jonnard, Aimison USITC 202-205-3350

Glue....Brownchweig, Gilbert CUSTOMS 212-466-5744

Gluten Intolerance....Staff NIDDK 301-654-3810

Glycerine....Michels, David USITC 202-205-3352

Glycogen Storage Disease....Staff NICHD 301-496-5133

Glycogen Storage Disease....Staff NIDDK 301-496-3583

Glycols....Michels, David USITC 202-205-3352

Glycoside products....Robinson, Douglas PTO 703-308-2897

Goats....Steller, Rose USITC 202-205-3323

Goiter....Staff NIDDK 301-496-3583

Gold compounds....Greenblatt, Jack USITC 202-205-3353

Gold with options....Rosenfeld, David CFT 312-353-9026

Gold....Lucus, John M. MINES 202-501-9417

Gold....McNay, Deborah USITC 202-205-3425

Golf equipment....Witherspoon, Ricardo USITC 202-205-3496

Gonads....Staff NICHD 301-496-5133

Gonorrhea....Staff NIAID 301-496-5717

Goodpasture's Syndrome....Staff NIDDK 301-496-3583

Goodpasture's Syndrome....Staff NHLBI 301-496-4236

Gout....Staff NIAMS 301-496-8188

Government and Foreign Affairs....Cooper, Alice H. UVA 804-924-4660

Government and Foreign Affairs....Abraham, Henry J. UVA 804-924-3958

Government and Foreign Affairs....Jordan, David C. UVA 804-924-3298

Government Business Operations Issues....Gadsby, J. William GAO 202-512-8387

Government Contracting....Dumaresq, Thomas SBA 202-205-6460

Government-Press Relations, Broadcast Journalism....Holman, Ben UMD 301-405-2420

Government-Press relations....Hiebert, Ray E. UMD 301-405-2419

Government, Productivity in, Prod. and Tech.....Forte, Darlene J. LABOR 202-606-5621

Government....Galbraith, Karl D. ECONOMIC 202-606-9778

Governments, Criminal Justice Statistics....Stevens, Alan CENSUS 301-457-1550

Governments, Employment....Wulf, Henry CENSUS 301-457-1486

Governments, Federal Expenditure Data....McArthur, Robert CENSUS 301-457-1565

Governments, Finance....Wulf, Henry CENSUS 301-457-1486

Governments, Governmental Organization....Kellerman, David CENSUS 301-457-1586

Governments, Operations Support and Analysis....Fanning, William CENSUS 301-457-1515

Governments, Taxation....Wulf, Henry CENSUS 301-457-1486

Graduate Courses....Staff FAES 301-496-7976

Grain Dust Project....Cheney, Sheldon NAL 301-504-4204

Grain Mill Products....Janis, William V. COMMERCE 202-482-2250

Grain products, milled....Reeder, John USITC 202-205-3319

Grain....Conte, Ralph CUSTOMS 212-466-5759

Grains....Pierre-Benoist, John USITC 202-205-3320

Granite....White, Linda USITC 202-205-3427

Grant Application Kits....Staff DRG 301-594-7248

Grants and Awards (General)....Staff DRG 301-594-7248

Grants and Awards (Statistics)....Staff 301-594-7248

Grants Associates Program....Staff OD/OERT 301-496-1736

Grants (Medical Libraries)....Staff NLM 301-496-4221

Granulocytopenia....Staff NIDDK 301-496-3583

Granulomatous Diseases....Staff NIAID 301-496-5717

Grape Cure....Staff NCI 301-496-5583

Grapefruit oil (essential oil)....Land, Eric USITC 202-205-3349

Graphite....Taylor, Harold A. MINES 202-501-9754

Graphite....White, Linda USITC 202-205-3427

Grasslands....Staff FWS 703-358-2043

Grateful Med (Software for Information Retrieval)....Staff NLM 301-496-6308

Grave's Disease (Eye Complications)....Staff NEI 301-496-5248

Grave's Disease (General Information)....Staff NIDDK 301-496-3583

Grease, lubricating....Foreso, Cynthia USITC 202-205-3348

Great Lakes Fisheries....Staff FWS 703-358-1718

Great Lakes MTC (Manufacturing Technology Center)....Sutherland, George H. NIST 216-432-5300

Greece (Athens)....Staff Cnty State 202-647-6113

Greece/Minerals....Zajac, William Cnty Mines 202-501-9671

Greece....Corro, Ann Cnty Commerce 202-482-3945

Greece....Holloway, Barbara Cnty Treasury 202-622-0098

Greece....Hutchings, Dayna Cnty Export-Import Bank 202-565-3737

Greece....Kokossis, Constantin Cnty Embassy 202-939-5800

Greece....Santoro, Eugene Cnty USIA 202-619-6582

Greece....Tsilas, Loucas Cnty Embassy 202-939-5800

Greenhouse Gases....Patrinus, Aristides NEIC 301-903-3251

Greenland/Minerals....Zajac, William Cnty Mines 202-501-9672

Greenland....Staff Cnty State 202-647-5669

Greensand....Searls, James P. MINES 202-501-9407

Greeting Cards....Bratland, Rose Marie COMMERCE 202-482-0380

Grenada (St. George's)....Staff Cnty State 202-647-2621

Grenada....Brooks, Michelle Cnty Commerce 202-482-2527

Grenada....Marcus, Anthony Cnty Treasury 202-622-1218

Grenada....Modeste, Denneth Cnty Embassy 202-265-2561

Grenada....Nallari, Raj R. Cnty World Bank 202-473-8697

Grenada....Rabchevsky, George Cnty Mines 202-501-9670

Grenada....Wilkins, Michele Cnty Export-Import Bank 202-565-3743

Grenadines....Layne, Kingsley Cnty Embassy 202-462-7806

Grenadines....Marcus, Anthony Cnty Treasury 202-622-1218

Grenadines....Nallari, Raj R. Cnty World Bank 202-473-8697

Grenadines....Norris, Cecily A. Cnty Embassy 202-462-7846

Grief...Staff Grief Recovery Hotline 800-445-4808

Grinding machines....Greene, William USITC 202-205-3405

Ground fish....Corey, Roger USITC 202-205-3327

Ground Water and Drinking Water....Staff EPA 202-250-5543

Ground Water Exploration and Development....Wheeler, Frederica COMMERCE 202-482-3509

Ground Water Protection....Staff EPA 202-260-7077

Group Quarters, Population....Smith, Denise CENSUS 301-457-2378

Growth and Development....Staff NICHD 301-496-5133

Growth Hormone Deficiency....Staff NIDDK 301-496-3583

Growth Hormone Deficiency....Staff NICHD 301-496-5133

Guadeloupe (Basse-Terre)....Staff Cnty State 202-647-2620

Guadeloupe/Minerals....Rabchevsky, George Cnty Mines 202-501-9670

Guadeloupe....Brooks, Michelle Cnty Commerce 202-482-2527

Guatemala (Guatemala City)....Staff Cnty State 202-647-1145

Guatemala/Minerals....Velasco, Pablo Cnty Mines 202-501-9677

Guatemala....Anne McKinney Cnty TDA 703-875-4357

Guatemala....Bayly, Rachel Cnty Treasury 202-622-1266

Guatemala....Berz, Cristina N. Cnty World Bank 202-473-3901

Guatemala....Erlandson, Barbara Peace Corps 202-606-3624

Guatemala....Lee, Helen Cnty Commerce 202-482-2527

Guatemala....Mulet, Edmond Cnty embassy 202-745-4952

Guatemala....Opstein, Sally Cnty USIA 202-619-5864

Guatemala....Toriello, Magdalena Cnty Embassy 202-745-4953

Guatemala....Vandenbos, James Cnty AID 202-647-9541

Guatemala....Wilkins, Michele Cnty Export-Import Bank 202-565-3743

Guest Researchers (Foreign)....Staff FIC 301-496-6166

Guide dog....Staff Guide Dog Foundation for the Blind 800-548-4337

Guide for the Care and Use of Laboratory Animals....Staff NCI 301-496-5545

Guide to Grants and Contracts....Staff OD 301-496-1789

Guides....Young, Gary CENSUS 301-457-1221

Guillain-Barre Syndrome (Polyneuritis)....Staff NINDS 301-496-5751

Guinea Bissau....Barber, Ed Cnty Treasury 202-622-1730

Guinea Bissau....Cabral, Alfredo Lopes Cnty Embassy 202-872-4222

Guinea Bissau....Younge, Nathan Cnty TDA 703-875-4357

Guinea Bissau....Garcia, Ligia Maria Cnty Embassy 202-265-6901

Guinea Bissau (Bissau)....Staff Cnty State 202-647-4567

Guinea Bissau....Michelin, Philip Cnty Commerce 202-482-4388

Guinea Bissau....Baily, Jess Cnty USIA 202-619-5900

Guinea Bissau....Edwards, Jennifer R. Cnty World Bank 202-473-4875

Guinea Bissau....Waxman-Lenz, Roberta Cnty Export-Import Bank 202-565-3742

Guinea Bissau....Wickman, Cam Cnty AID 202-647-6335

Guinea Bissau/Minerals....Dolley, Thomas Cnty Mines 202-501-9690

Guinea (Conakry)....Staff Cnty State 202-647-3407

Guinea/Minerals....Izon, David Cnty Mines 202-501-9674

Guinea....Ansoumane, Camara Cnty Embassy 202-483-9420

Guinea....Baily, Jess Cnty USIA 202-619-5900

Guinea....Barber, Ed Cnty Treasury 202-622-1730

Guinea....Bezek, Jill Cnty TDA 703-875-4357

Guinea....Esposito, Dina Cnty AID 202-647-7887

Guinea....Martinez, Carmen Cnty World Bank 202-473-4734

Guinea....Michelin, Philip Cnty Commerce 202-482-4388

Guinea....Trouba, Larry Peace Corps 202-606-3695

Guinea....Waxman-Lenz, Roberta Cnty Export-Import Bank 202-565-3742

Guinea...Barry, Elhadj Boubacar Cnty Embassy 202-483-9420

Gulf Corporation Council....Staff Cnty State 202-647-6562

Gum Disease....Staff NIDR 301-496-4261

Gums and resins....Reeder, John USITC 202-205-3319

Gun cotton....Johnson, Larry USITC 202-205-3351

Gun tracing....Staff ATF 304-274-4100

Gunpowder....Johnson, Larry USITC 202-205-3351

Guns and Ammunition....Vanderwolf, John COMMERCE 202-482-0348

Gut, articles of....Spalding, Josephine USITC 202-205-3498

Gut; catgut, whip gut, oriental gut, and wormgut....Ludwick, David USITC 202-205-3329

Guyana (Georgetown)....Staff Cnty State 202-647-2621

Guyana/Minerals....Doan, David Cnty Mines 202-501-9678

Guyana....Boonma, Sawai Cnty World Bank 202-473-3058

Guyana....Brooks, Michelle Cnty Commerce 202-482-2527

Guyana....Feingold, David Cnty AID 202-647-4106

Guyana....Ishmael, Mohammed Ali Odeen Cnty Embassy 202-265-6900

Guyana....John Herrman Cnty TDA 703-875-4357

Guyana....Korff, Michael Cnty USIA 202-619-6835

Guyana....Marcus, Anthony Cnty Treasury 202-622-1218

Guyana....Wilkins, Michele Cnty Export-Import Bank 202-565-3743

Gynecological Research....Nelson, Lawrence FAES 301-496-4686

Gynecology....Staff NICHD 301-496-5133

Gynecomastia....Staff NICHD 301-496-5133

Gynecomastia....Staff NIDDK 301-496-3583

Gypsum board....Hoffmeier, Bill USITC 202-205-3321

Gypsum....Austin, Gordon MINES 202-501-9388

Gypsum....White, Linda USITC 202-205-3427

Gyrate Atrophy....Staff NEI 301-496-5248

H

Habeas Corpus....Kaplan, Carol Justice Stat 202-307-0759

Habitat Management....Staff FWS 703-358-1718

Habitat Models....Staff FWS 703-358-1710

Habitat Resources Research....Staff FWS 703-358-1710

Hafnium....Gambogi, Joseph MINES 202-501-9390

Hafnium....Lundy, David USITC 202-205-3439

Hailey's Disease....Staff NIDDK 301-496-3583

Hair, articles of.... USITC 202-205-3498

Hair curlers, nonelectric....Burns, Gail USITC 202-205-3501

Hair Loss....Staff NIAMS 301-496-8188

Hair Ornaments....Brownchweig, Gilbert CUSTOMS 212-466-5744

Hair ornaments....Burns, Gail USITC 202-205-2501

Hair Spray....Staff FDA 301-245-1061

Hair Testing (Drug Abuse)....Staff NIDA 301-443-6245

Hair....Steller, Rose USITC 202-205-3323

Haiti/Minerals....Rabchevsky, George Cnty Mines 202-501-9678

Haiti (Port-au-Prince)....Staff Cnty State 202-736-4707

Haiti....Almaguer, Antoinette Peace Corps 202-606-3322

Haiti....Casimir, Jean Cnty Embassy 202-332-4090

Haiti....Fluckiger, Stefan Cnty World Bank 202-473-0093

Haiti....Geiser, Barbara Cnty Treasury 202-622-1271

Haiti....Head, Alfred Cnty USIA 202-619-6835

Haiti....Joseph, Louis Harold Cnty Embassy 202-332-4092

Haiti....Siegelman, Mark Cnty Commerce 204-482-5680

Haiti....Wilkins, Michele Cnty Export-Import Bank 202-565-3743

Halides, nonmetallic....Conant, Kenneth USITC 202-205-3346

Hallervorden-Spatz Disease....Staff NINDS 301-496-5751

Hallucinogens....Staff NIDA 301-443-6245

Halogenated hydrocarbons....Michels, David USITC 202-205-3352

Halogens....Conant, Kenneth USITC 202-205-3346

Hand/Edge Tools Ex Mach TI/Saws....Abrahams, Edward COMMERCE 202-482-0312

Hand, Foot, and Mouth Disease....Staff NIAID 301-496-5717

Hand Saws, Saw Blades....Abrahams, Edward COMMERCE 202-482-0312

Hand tools: household....Brandon, James USITC 202-205-3433

Hand tools with self-contained motor....Cutchin, John USITC 202-205-3396

Hand tools: other....Brandon, James USITC 202-205-3433

Hand Tools....Birnbaum, Melvyn CUSTOMS 212-466-5487

Hand-Schueller-Christian Syndrome....Staff NHLBI 301-496-4236

Handbags....Byron, James E. COMMERCE 202-482-4034

Handbags....Gorman, Kevin CUSTOMS 212-466-5893

Handbags....Seastrum, Carl USITC 202-205-3493

Handbook, Occupational Outlook, Empl. Projections....Pilot, Michael LABOR 202-606-5703

Handicapped Discrimination....Haynes, Marcella OCR 202-619-0671

Handicapped (severely)....Staff National Institute for Rehabilitation Engineering 800-736-2216

Handicapped....Staff ABLEDATA 800-227-0126

Handicapped....Staff NARHA 800-369-7433

Handicapped....Staff National Information Center for Children and Youth with Handicaps 800-695-0285

Handkerchiefs....Hamey, Amy USITC 202-205-3465

Handkerchiefs....Jones, Jackie USITC 202-205-3466

Handwork yarns: cotton....Warlick, William USITC 202-205-3459

Handwork yarns: manmade fibers....Warlick, William USITC 202-205-3459

Handwork yarns: wool....Shelton, Linda USITC 202-205-3457

Hansen's Disease....Staff NIAID 301-496-5717

Happy Puppet Syndrome....Staff NINDS 301-496-5751

Harada's Disease....Staff NEI 301-496-5248

Harassing Telephone Calls....Staff FCC 202-632-7553

Hard Surfaced Floor Coverings....McCauley, Patrick COMMERCE 202-482-0132

Hard-to-Reach Populations....Staff NIDA 301-443-6245

Hardboard....Hoffmeier, Bill USITC 202-205-3321

Hardening of the Arteries....Staff NHLBI 301-496-4236

Hashimoto's Disease....Staff NIDDK 301-496-3583

Hashimoto's Disease....Staff NHLBI 301-496-4236

Hats....Hamey, Amy USITC 202-205-3465

Hats....Jones, Jackie USITC 202-205-3466

Hay Fever....Staff NIAID 301-496-5717

Hay....Baker, Allen Agri 202-219-0839

Hay....Tice, Thomas Agri 202-219-0840

Hazard Screening....Giles, Ken CPSC 301-504-0580

Hazardous Chemical Spills....Staff FWS 703-358-2148

Hazardous materials....Chipkevich, Bob NTSB 202-382-6585

Hazardous Materials....Eldridge, K USCG 202-267-1577

Hazardous Site Evaluation....Staff EPA 202-603-8850

Hazardous Substances Information Office....Siegel, Sidney NLM 301-496-5022

Hazardous Substances Information....Staff NLM 301-496-1131

Hazardous substances....DeBerry, Elizabeth FAES 301-496-5022

Hazardous Waste Cleanups....Staff EPA 703-603-8710

Hazardous Waste Disposal Unit....Staff EPA 202-307-8833

Hazardous Waste Disposal....Lytle, Jill NEIC 202-586-0370

Hazardous Waste Enforcement - General....Staff EPA 703-412-9810

Hazardous Waste Ombudsman Hotline....Staff EPA 800-262-7937

Hazardous Waste Publications....Staff EPA 703-603-8710

Hazardous Waste Spills - Emergency Response....Staff EPA 202-260-9361

Hazardous Waste - Superfund....Staff EPA 703-412-9810

Hazardous Waste Transporting Generating or Permits....Staff EPA 202-233-9160

Hazardous Wastes....Staff 404-639-0615

Head Injury....Staff NINDS 301-496-5751

Head Injury....Staff NIDCD 301-496-7243

Head Lice (Pediculosis)....Staff NIAID 301-496-5717

Head Start...Kharfen, Michael ACF 202-401-9215

Headache....Staff NINDS 301-496-5751

Headaches....Staff New England Center for Headache 800-245-0088

Headaches....Staff National Headache Foundation 800-843-2256

Headwear....Hamey, Amy USITC 202-205-3465

Headwear....Jones, Jackie USITC 202-205-3466

Headwear....Weiss, Martin CUSTOMS 212-466-5881

Health and Environmental Research....Patterson, Elsie NEIC 301-903-2987

Health and Life Insurance, Comp. and Working Condition....Blostin, Allan LABOR 202-606-6240

Health and medical services....Johnson, Christopher USITC 202-205-3488

Health care industry advancements....Staff Medical Awareness Association 800-899-0005

Health Care - Nurse....Brooke, Joan FTC 202-326-2120

Health Care Policy and Research, Agency for....Gaus, Clifton R. AHCPR 301-594-6662

Health Care Policy and Research, Agency for....Gaus, Clifton R. AHCPR 301-594-6662

Health Care Resources....Shaffer, Sylvia HRSA 301-443-3376

Health Care Technology....Holohan, Thomas AHCPR 301-594-4023

Health Care....Staff Agency for Health Care Policy and Research Clearinghouse....Staff 800-358-9295

Health Effects Division....Staff EPA 202-305-7351

Health Effects of Electricity Transmission....Brewer, Robert NEIC 202-586-2828

Health Expenditures (U.S. Totals)....Hardy, Robert HCFA 202-966-3206

Health Financing Issues....Ratner, Jonathan GAO 202-512-7107

Health Information Programs Development, Dir. of....Siegel, Elliot R. NLM 301-496-8834

Health Maintenance Organizations (HMOs)....Hardy, Robert HCFA 202-966-3206

Health Manpower Education....Staff HRSA/BHPr 301-827-3365

Health Policy, Office of....Staff EPA 202-260-5900

Health Professionals....Staff HRSA/BHPr 301-827-3365

Health Professions and Health Profession Loans....Staff HRSA 301-827-3365

Health Promotion and Disease Prevention....Stoiber, Susanne ASH 202-205-0152

Health Promotion and Disease Prevention....Sims, Anne CDC 404-639-3286

Health Promotion....Staff NINR 301-496-0207

Health Services Research Information....Cahn, Marjorie NLM 301-496-0176

Health Statistics, National Center for....Sandra, Smith NCHS/CDC 301-436-7551

Health Surveys....Mangold, Robert CENSUS 301-457-3879

Health....Francis, Simon COMMERCE 202-482-2697

Health....Staff National Health Information Center 800-336-4797

Health....Staff American Social Health Association 800-227-8922

Health....Staff HHS Hotline 800-368-5779

Healthy Start....McCann, Thurma HRSA 301-443-0543

Hearing Aid....Staff International Hearing Society 800-521-5247

Hearing impaired....Staff Tripod Grapevine 800-352-8888

Hearing Impaired....Staff Hearing Helpline 800-424-8576

Hearing Loss and Aging....Staff NIA 301-496-1752

Hearing Loss and Aging....Staff NINDS 301-496-5751

Hearing Loss and Aging....Staff CC 301-496-5368

Hearing....Staff Occupational Hearing Service 800-222-3277

Hearing....Staff Hearing Helpline 800-327-9355

Hearing....Staff American Speech-Language-Hearing Association Consumer Helpline 800-638-8255

Hearing....Staff National Hearing Aid Society 800-521-5247

Hearing....Staff NINDS 301-496-5751

Hearing....Staff NIDCD 301-496-7243

Heart Attacks....Staff NHLBI 301-496-4236

Heart Block....Staff NHLBI 301-496-4236

Heart Disease....Staff NHLBI 301-496-4236

Heart-Lung Machines....Staff NHLBI 301-496-4236

Heart, Lung and Blood Inst.....Bellicha, Terry NIH 301-496-4236

Heart Murmurs....Staff NHLBI 301-496-4236

Heart Pacemaker....Staff NHLBI 301-496-4236

Heart Transplantation....Staff NHLBI 301-496-4236

Heart Valves....Staff NHLBI 301-496-4236

Heart....Staff American Heart Association 800-242-8721

Heart....Staff Heart Information Service 800-292-2221

Heat-insulating articles....DeSapio, Vincent USITC 202-205-3435

Heat process equipment....Lusi, Susan USITC 202-205-2334

Heat-Resistant Materials....Staff NASA 804-864-6120

Heat Stroke and Aging....Staff NIA 301-496-1752

Heat Tapes....Staff CPSC 301-504-0580

Heat Treating Equipment....Kemper, Alexis COMMERCE 202-482-5956

Heating Equipment Ex. Furnaces....Bodson, John COMMERCE 202-482-3509

Heavy Metals (Cadmium, Zinc, Mercury)....Staff NIEHS 919-541-3345

Helicopter Services....Johnson, C. William COMMERCE 202-482-5012

Helicopters, Market Support....Smarkanich, Audrey COMMERCE 202-482-2835

Helicopters (Trade Promo)....Vacant COMMERCE 202-482-1228

Helicopters....Green, Ron COMMERCE 202-482-4222

Heliotropin....Land, Eric USITC 202-205-3349

Helium, Division of Helium Field Operations....Leachman, William D. MINES 806-376-2604

Helium....Conant, Kenneth USITC 202-205-3346

Helpline (Workplace, Drug-Related)....Staff NIDA 301-443-6245

Hemangiomas....Staff NHLBI 301-496-4236

Hematology....Finlayson, John FAES 301-496-5544

Hemiplegia....Staff NINDS 301-496-5751

Hemochromatosis....Staff NHLBI 301-496-4236

Hemodialysis....Staff NIDDK 301-654-4415

Hemoglobin Genetics....Staff NIDDK 301-496-3583

Hemoglobinopathies....Staff NIDDK 301-496-3583

Hemolytic Anemia....Staff NHLBI 301-496-4236

Hemolytic Anemia....Staff NIDDK 301-496-3583

Hemolytic Disease (Newborn)....Staff NICHD 301-496-5133

Hemolytic Disease (Newborn)....Staff NHLBI 301-496-4236

Hemophilia and AIDS....Staff HANDI 800-424-2634

Hemophilia....Staff NHLBI 301-496-4236

Hemophilus Influenzae....Staff NIAID 301-496-5717

Hemorrhagic Diseases....Staff NHLBI 301-496-4236

Hemorrhagic Diseases....Staff NIDDK 301-496-3583

Hemorrhoids....Staff NIDDK 301-654-3810

Hemorrhoids....Staff NHLBI 301-496-4236

Hemosiderosis....Staff NHLBI 301-496-4236

Henoch-Schonlein Purpura....Staff NIAID 301-496-5717

Henoch-Schonlein Purpura....Staff NICHD 301-496-5133

Hepatitis (Treatment of Acute or Chronic)....Staff NIAID 301-496-5717

Hepatitis (Treatment of Acute or Chronic)....Staff NIDDK 301-654-3810

Hepatitis....Margolis, Harold CDC 404-639-2339

Hepatitis....Staff American Liver Foundation Hepatitis Hotline 800-223-0179

Hepatitis....Staff NIAID 301-496-5717

Hepatitis....Staff NIDDK 301-496-3583

Herbicide-Fungicides....Staff EPA 202-305-6250

Herbicides....Hollrah, Glen H. PTO 703-308-4552

Heredity and Cancer....Staff NCI 301-496-5583

Hereditary Angioedema....Staff NIAID 301-496-5717

Hereditary Cerebellar Ataxia....Staff NINDS 301-496-5751

Hereditary Emphysema....Staff NHLBI 301-496-4236

Hereditary Hemorrhagic Telangiectasia....Staff 301-496-4236

Hereditary Movement Disorders....Staff NINDS 301-496-5751

Hereditary Nervous System Tumors....Staff NINDS 301-496-5751

Hereditary Spastic Paraplegia....Staff NINDS 301-496-5751

Hereditary Spherocytosis....Staff NHLBI 301-496-4236

Heritable Disorders of Connective Tissue....Staff NIAMS 301-496-8188

Heritable Disorders of Connective Tissue....Staff NHLBI 301-496-4236

Hernias (Abdominal, Bladder)....Staff NIDDK 301-654-3810

Herniated Disc....Staff NIAMS 301-496-8188

Heroin....Staff NIDA 301-443-4265

Herpes (Nervous System Involvement)....Staff NINDS 301-496-5751

Herpes Simplex (Eye Effects)....Staff NEI 301-496-5248

Herpes Simplex Virus (Oral Lesions)....Staff NIDR 301-496-4261

Herpes Simplex Virus (Type II)....Staff NIAID 301-496-5717

Herpes Zoster (Shingles)....Staff NINDS 301-496-5751

Herpes Zoster-Varicella Infections....Staff NIAID 301-496-5717

Herzegovina....Alkalaj, Sven Cnty Embassy 202-833-3612

Herzegovina....Dzirlo, Sakir Cnty Embassy 202-833-3613

Herzegovina....Steblez, Walter cnty MINES 202-501-9672

Heterocyclic Compounds....Brady, Thomas CUSTOMS 212-466-5747

Hiatal Hernia....Staff NIDDK 301-496-3583

Hiccups....Staff NHLBI 301-496-4236

Hide cuttings....Trainor, Cynthia USITC 202-205-3354

Hides....Steller, Rose USITC 202-205-3323

High Alpha Technology....Staff NASA 805-866-8569

High Blood Pressure....Staff NIA 301-496-1752

High Blood Pressure....Staff NHLBI 301-496-4236

High-Density Lipoproteins (HDL)....Staff NHLBI 301-496-4236

High Energy Fuel Research....Rachul, Lori NASA 216-443-8806

High School Program for Minorities....Staff NCRR 301-594-7947

High School Senior Survey....Staff NIDA 301-443-4265

High Tech Trade, U.S. Competitiveness....Hatter, Victoria L. COMMERCE 202-482-3895

High Voltage Electron Microscopy....Staff NCRR 301-594-7934

High Voltage Electron Microscopy....Staff NCRR 301-594-7934

High Voltage Transmission Lines....Klunder, Kurt NEIC 202-586-2826

Highway Advisory Radio....Staff FCC 202-418-0620

Highway Institute, National....Shrieves, George M FHWA 703-285-2770

Highway Safety....Bennett, Clark FHWA 202-366-1153

Highway safety....Osterman, Joseph NTSB 202-382-6854

Highway Statistics....Walsh, William NHTSA 202-366-1503

Hill-Burton Health Facilities....Shaffer, Sylvia HRSA 301-443-3376

Hip Replacement....Staff NIAMS 301-496-8188

Hirsutism....Staff NIAMS 301-496-8188

Hispanic and Other Ethnic Population Statistics....Staff CENSUS 301-457-4100
Histiocytosis....Staff Histiocytosis Association of America 800-548-2758
Histiocytosis....Staff NHLBI 301-496-4236
Histiocytosis....Staff NCI 301-496-5583
Histoplasmosis (Eye)....Staff NEI 301-496-5248
Histoplasmosis....Staff NIAID 301-496-5717
Historical Medical Prints and Photographs....Staff NLM 301-496-5961
Historical Prints and Photographs....Keister, Lucinda NLM 301-496-5961
Historical statistics....Staff CENSUS 301-457-1166
Historical Statistics....Staff CENSUS 301-457-1166
History of Medicine....Teigen, Philip NLM 301-496-5405
History of Medicine....Staff NLM 301-496-5405
History of NIH....Staff OD/OC 301-496-6610
History....Braun, Herbert UVA 701-924-6397
HIV/AIDS....Jaffe, Harold W. CDC 404-639-2000
HIV immunoassays....Nucker, Christine M PTO 703-308-4028
HIV Infection....Staff NCI 301-496-5583
HIV Infection....Staff NIAID 301-496-5717
HIV Injection....Staff Project Inform 800-334-7422
HIV: Oral Complications....Staff NIDR 301-496-4261
Hives....Staff NIAID 301-496-5717
Hoarseness....Staff NIDCD 301-496-7243
Hoaxes-Broadcast....Staff FCC 202-418-1430
Hodgkin's Disease....Staff NCI 301-496-5583
Hogs (live) with options....Prentice, Jon CFT 312-353-8647
Hogs....Newman, Douglas USITC 202-205-3328
Hoists/Overhead Cranes....Wiening, Mary COMMERCE 202-482-4708
Holy See....Cacciavillan, Most Reverend Agostino Cnty Embassy 202-333-7121
Home and Community Based Care (Medicaid)....Hardy, Robert HCFA 202-966-3206
Home Care, Nursing Home Care, Hospital Care....Staff NCNR 301-496-0526
Home furnishings....Sweet, Mary Elizabeth USITC 202-205-3455
Home Health Care....Hardy, Robert HCFA 202-966-3206
Home Mortgage Disclosure....Wood, John C FRS 202-452-2412
Home safety....Staff CPSC 301-504-0580
Homeless Population....Taeuber, Cynthia CENSUS 301-457-2378
Homeless youth....Staff Covenant House 800-999-9999
Homeless....Kharfen, Michael ACF 202-401-9215
Homeless....Staff HUD 202-708-1480
Homeless....Staff NIDA 301-443-4265
Homelessness....Staff National Resource Center on Homelessness and Mental Illness 800-444-7415
Homocystinuria....Staff NHLBI 301-496-4236
Homocystinuria....Staff NICHD 301-496-5133
Honduras/Minerals....Rabchevsky, George Cnty Mines 202-501-9670
Honduras (Tegucigalpa)....Staff Cnty State 202-647-4980
Honduras....Anne McKinney Cnty TDA 703-875-4357
Honduras....Baier, Kraig Cnty AID 202-647-9555
Honduras....Bowyer, Nicolette Cnty World Bank 202-473-8724
Honduras....Flores Bermudez, Roberto Cnty Embassy 202-966-7702
Honduras....Lee, Helen Cnty Commerce 202-482-2528
Honduras....Lostumbo, Julie Peace Corps 202-606-3620
Honduras....Murray, Mandy Peace Corps 202-606-3321
Honduras....Opstein, Sally Cnty USIA 202-619-5864
Honduras....Parkinson, Katherine Cnty Treasury 202-622-5292
Honduras....Rodezno-Fuentes, Salvador Cnty Embassy 202-966-2604
Honduras....Wilkins, Michele Cnty Export-Import Bank 202-565-3743
Honey - Prices....Schuchardt, Rick Agri 220-720-7737
Honey - Prod.....Kruchten, Tom Agri 202-690-4870
Honey....Hoff, Fred Agri 202-219-0883
Hong Kong/Minerals....Tse, Pui-Kwan Cnty Mines 202-501-9696
Hong Kong/trade matters....Cantilina, Amy US Trade Rep 202-395-5050
Hong Kong....Hutchings, Dayna Cnty Export-Import Bank 202-565-3737
Hong Kong....Dwight, Lawrence Cnty Treasury 202-622-0356
Hong Kong....Bakar, Sheila Cnty Commerce 202-482-3932
Hong Kong....Staff Cnty State 202-647-6300
Hoof, articles of....Spalding, Josephine USITC 202-205-3498
Hoofs, crude....Ludwick, David USITC 202-205-3329
Hooks and eyes....Brandon, James USITC 202-205-3433
Hormone Distribution....Staff NIDDK 301-496-3583
Hormones and Cancer....Staff NCI 301-496-5583
Hormones (Sex)....Staff NICHD 301-496-5133
Hormones....Nesbitt, Elizabeth USITC 202-205-3355
Hormones....Staff NIDDK 301-496-3583

Horn, crude....Ludwick, David USITC 202-205-3329
Horn, articles of....Spalding, Josephine USITC 202-205-3498
Horology....Shoop, William M. PTO 703-308-3103
Horse Racing Programming and Advertising....Staff FCC 202-418-0200
Horses....Steller, Rose USITC 202-205-3323
Horticultural machinery....Fravel, Dennis USITC 202-205-3404
Hose and Belting....Prat, Raimundo COMMERCE 202-482-0128
Hose, industrial....Cook, Lee USITC 202-205-3471
Hose, of rubber or plastics....Misurelli, Denby USITC 202-205-3362
Hoses....Mazzola, Joan CUSTOMS 212-466-5880
Hosiery....Linkins, Linda USITC 202-205-3469
Hospice Care....Staff NIA 301-496-1752
Hospice Care....Staff NCI 301-496-5583
Hospice....Hardy, Robert HCFA 202-966-3206
Hospice....Staff National Hospice Organization 800-658-8898
Hospice....Staff Children's Hospice International 800-242-4453
Hospice...Staff Hospice Education Institute 800-331-1620
Hospital Administrators....Staff HRSA/BHPr 301-443-2134
Hospital-Based Schools of Nursing....Staff HRSA/BHPr 301-443-2134
Hospital Care Statistics....Pokras, Robert CDC 301-436-7125
Hospital care....Staff Hill-Burton Free Hospital Care Hotline 800-638-0742
Hospital Infections....Staff NIAID 301-496-5717
Hotel and Restaurant Eq., Export Promo.....Kimmel, Edward K. COMMERCE 202-482-3640
Hotels and Motels....Sousane, J. Richard COMMERCE 202-482-4582
Hotline (Fraud and Abuse)....Holtz, Judy IG 202-619-1142
Hourly Compensation Costs, Foreign Countries....Capdevielle, Patricia LABOR 202-606-5654
Household Appliances....Harris, John M. COMMERCE 202-482-1178
Household Articles, Metal....Smyth, James CUSTOMS 212-466-2084
Household Articles Plastic....Rauch, Theodore CUSTOMS 212-466-5892
Household Estimates for States and Counties....Staff CENSUS 301-457-2465
Household Furniture....Hodgen, Donald COMMERCE 202-482-3346
Household Hazardous Waste....Staff EPA 202-260-5649
Household Wealth....Eller, T.J. CENSUS 301-763-8578
Households Touched by Crime....Rand, Michael Justice Stat 202-616-3494
Housewares....Beckham, Reginald COMMERCE 202-482-5478
Housing, American Housing Survey....Montfort, Edward CENSUS 301-763-8551
Housing and Real Estate Industry....Parratt, Shelley SEC 202-942-1840
Housing and Urban Development. Major Proj.....White, Barbara COMMERCE 202-482-4160
Housing, Components of Inventory Change Survey....Williams, Barbara CENSUS 301-763-8551
Housing Construction....Cosslett, Patrick COMMERCE 202-482-5125
Housing, Decennial Census....Bonnette, Robert CENSUS 301-763-8553
Housing, Income Statistics....Staff CENSUS 301-763-8576
Housing, Indian....Staff HUD 202-708-0950
Housing, Information....Bonnette, Robert CENSUS 301-763-8553
Housing Issues....England-Joseph, Judy GAO 202-512-7631
Housing, Market Absorption....Smoler, Anne CENSUS 301-763-8165
Housing, Multifamily....Staff HUD 202-708-2495
Housing, New York City Housing and Vacancy Survey....Fronczek, Peter CENSUS 301-763-8165
Housing, Public....Staff HUD 202-708-0950
Housing, Single Family....Staff HUD 202-708-3175
Housing, Vacancy Data....Collis, Robert CENSUS 301-763-8165
Housing....Staff HUD 800-245-2691
Howard Hughes Medical Institute....Staff 301-215-8500
Hubble Space Telescope (HST)....Katz, Jesse NASA 301-286-5566
Hubble Space Telescope....Villard, Ray NASA 301-338-4514
HUD Fraud Hotline....Staff HUD 800-347-3735
Human Development....Staff NICHD 301-443-5133
Human Genetic Mutant Cell Repository....Staff NIGMS 301-496-7301
Human Papilloma Virus (HPV)....Staff NCI 301-496-5583
Human Papilloma Virus (HPV)....Staff NIAID 301-496-5717
Humane Transport of Fish and Wildlife....Staff FWS 703-358-2095
Hungary (Budapest)....Staff Cnty State 202-647-3238
Hungary/Minerals....Steblez, Walter Cnty Mines 202-501-9671
Hungary....Ann Lien Cnty TDA 703-875-4357
Hungary....Banklaki, Gyorgy Cnty Embassy 202-362-6730
Hungary....Bazala, Razvigor Cnty USIA 202-619-5055
Hungary....Hewer, Ulrich Albert Cnty World Bank 202-473-2279
Hungary....Horvath, Gabor Cnty Embassy 202-362-6730
Hungary....Jackson, Juhan Cnty Treasury 202-622-0766

Hungary....Lockwood, Jennifer Peace Corps 202-606-3607
Hungary....Scheil, Russell Peace Corps 202-606-3606
Hungary....Touhey, Brian Cnty Commerce 202-482-4915
Hungary....Waxman-Lenz, Roberta Cnty Export-Import Bank 202-565-3742
Hunt's Disease....Staff NINDS 301-496-5751
Hunter Education Programs....Staff FWS 703-358-2156
Hunter's Syndrome....Staff NIDDK 301-496-3583
Hunting and Fishing Survey, National....Staff FWS 703-358-2156
Hunting, Refuges....Staff FWS 703-358-2043
Huntington's Disease....Staff Huntington's Disease Society of America 800-345-4372
Huntington's Disease....Staff NINDS 301-496-5751
Hurler's Syndrome....Staff NIDDK 301-496-3583
Hurler's Syndrome....Staff NICHD 301-496-5133
Hyaline Membrane Disease....Staff NICHD 301-496-5133
Hyaline Membrane Disease....Staff NHLBI 301-496-4236
Hybrid....Envall, Roy PTO 703-305-9706
Hydranencephaly....Staff NINDS 301-496-5751
Hydraulics....Riedl, Karl CUSTOMS 212-466-5493
Hydrazine....Conant, Kenneth USITC 202-205-3346
Hydro Power Plants, Major Proj.....Dollison, Robert COMMERCE 202-482-2733
Hydrocarbon Geoscience Research....Hochoheiser, Bill NEIC 202-586-5614
Hydrocarbons....Brady, Thomas CUSTOMS 212-466-5747
Hydrocarbons....Raftery, Jim USITC 202-205-3365
Hydrocephalus....Staff NICHD 301-496-5133
Hydrocephalus....Staff NINDS 301-496-5751
Hydrochloric acid....Trainor, Cynthia USITC 202-205-3354
Hydroelectric Energy....Loose, Ronald NEIC 202-586-5348
Hydroelectric Power Projects....Staff FWS 703-358-2183
Hydroelectric Power....Loose, Ronald NEIC 202-586-5348
Hydrofluoric acid....Trainor, Cynthia USITC 202-205-3354
Hydrogen....Conant, Kenneth USITC 202-205-3346
Hydroxides, inorganic....Conant, Kenneth USITC 202-205-3346
Hygienists (Education)....Staff HRSA/BHPr 301-443-6837
Hyperactivity....Staff NINDS 301-496-5751
Hyperactivity....Staff NIMH 301-443-4513
Hyperactivity....Staff NICHD 301-496-5133
Hyperacusis....Staff NIDCD 301-496-7243
Hyperbaric Chamber - UMD Shock Trauma Center....Staff 410-328-8869
Hyperbaric Oxygenation....Staff NHLBI 301-496-4236
Hyperbilirubinemia....Staff NIDDK 301-496-3583
Hyperbilirubinemia....Staff NICHD 301-496-5133
Hypercalcemia....Staff NIDDK 301-496-3583
Hypercalciuria....Staff NIDDK 301-496-3583
Hypercholesterolemia....Staff NHLBI 301-496-4236
Hyperglycemia....Staff NIDDK 301-496-3583
Hyperkeratosis....Staff NIAMS 301-496-8188
Hyperlipidemia....Staff NHLBI 301-496-4236
Hyperlipoproteinemia....Staff NHLBI 301-496-5343
Hyperparathyroidism....Staff NIDDK 301-496-3583
Hyperpyrexia (heat stroke/heat exhaustion)....Staff NIA 301-496-1752
Hypersensitivity Pneumonitis....Staff NIAID 301-496-5717
Hypersonic Engines....Staff NASA 804-864-3305
Hypersonic Aircraft....James, Donald G. NASA 415-604-3935
Hypertension....Staff NCNR 301-496-0526
Hypertension....Staff NHLBI 301-496-4236
Hyperthermia (heat stroke/heat exhaustion)....Staff NIA 301-496-1752
Hyperthermia....Staff NCI 301-496-5583
Hyperthyroidism....Staff NIDDK 301-496-3583
Hypertriglyceridemia....Staff NHLBI 301-496-4236
Hypertrophic Cardiomyopathy....Staff NHLBI 301-496-4236
Hyperuricemia....Staff NIDDK 301-496-3583
Hyperventilation....Staff NHLBI 301-496-4236
Hypnotics....Nesbitt, Elizabeth USITC 202-205-3355
Hypobetalipoproteinemia....Staff NHLBI 301-496-4236
Hypocomplementemic Glomerulonephritis....Staff NIAID 301-496-5717
Hypogammaglobulinemia....Staff NHLBI 301-496-4236
Hypogeusia Hereditary Deafness....Staff NIDCD 301-496-7243
Hypoglycemia....Staff NIDDK 301-496-3583
Hypoglycemia....Staff NHLBI 301-496-4236
Hypogonadism....Staff NICHD 301-496-5133
Hypogonadism....Staff NIDDK 301-496-3583
Hypokalemia....Staff NHLBI 301-496-4236
Hypokalemic Periodic Paralysis....Staff NINDS 301-496-5751

Hypolipoproteinemia....Staff NIDDK 301-496-3583
Hypoparathyroidism....Staff NIDDK 301-496-3583
Hypopigmentation....Staff National Organization for Albinism and Hypopigmentation 800-473-2310
Hypopituitarism....Staff NIDDK 301-496-3583
Hypoplastic Anemia....Staff NHLBI 301-496-4236
Hyposmia....Staff NIDCD 301-496-7243
Hypospadias....Staff NICHD 301-496-5133
Hypotension....Staff NHLBI 301-496-4236
Hypothalamus....Staff NICHD 301-496-5133
Hypothalamus....Staff NIDDK 301-496-3583
Hypothermia (Accidental)....Staff NIA 301-496-1752
Hypothyroidism, Goitrous....Staff NIA 301-496-3583
Hypotonia....Staff NINDS 301-496-5751
Hypoventilation....Staff NHLBI 301-496-4236
Hypoxia....Staff NHLBI 301-496-4236
Hypsarrhythmia....Staff NINDS 301-496-5751

I

Ice (Methamphetamine)....Staff NIDA 301-443-4265
Iceland Disease....Staff NINDS 301-496-5751
Iceland/Minerals....Plachy, Jozef Cnty Mines 202-501-9673
Iceland (Reykjavik)....Staff Cnty State 202-647-5669
Iceland....Benediktsson, Elinor Cnty Embassy 202-265-6653
Iceland....Gosnell, Peter Cnty Export-Import Bank 202-565-3733
Iceland....Holloway, Barbara Cnty Treasury 202-622-0098
Iceland....Jonsdottir Ward, Margaret Cnty Embassy 202-265-6654
Iceland....Kendall, Maryanne Cnty Commerce 202-482-3254
Iceland....Rankin-Galloway, Honore Cnty USIA 202-619-5283
Ichthyosis....Staff NIAMS 301-496-8188
Idiopathic Autonomic Insufficiency....Staff NHLBI 301-496-4236
Idiopathic Hypertrophic Subaortic Stenosis (IHSS)....Staff NHLBI 301-496-4236
Idiopathic Infantile Arterial Calcification....Staff NHLBI 301-496-4236
Idiopathic Inflammatory Myopathy....Staff NINDS 301-496-5751
Idiopathic Osteoporosis....Staff NIAMS 301-496-8188
Idiopathic Pulmonary Fibrosis....Staff NHLBI 301-496-4236
Idiopathic Thrombocytopenic Purpura (ITP)....Staff NHLBI 301-496-4236
Idiopathic Thrombocytopenic Purpura (ITP)....Staff NIDDK 301-496-3583
IGE....Staff NIAID 301-496-5717
IGE....Staff NIAID 301-496-5717
Ignition equipment....Topolansky, Adam USITC 202-205-3394
Ileitis....Staff NIDDK 301-654-3810
Image analysis....Moore, David K. PTO 703-305-4706
Image Processing....Staff DCRT 301-496-2250
Image Processing....Staff DCRT 301-496-7963
Imaging (Brain)....Staff NINDS 301-496-5751
Imaging....Staff NCRR 301-594-7934
Imaging....Staff NCRR 301-496-4741
Immigration (Legal/Undocumented)....Frenandez, Edward CENSUS 301-457-2103
Immigration....Staff ACF 202-401-9215
Immune Deficiency....Immune Deficiency Foundation....Staff 800-296-4433
Immune Deficiency Diseases....Staff NIAID 301-496-5717
Immunization, Disease....Orenstein, Walter A. CDC 404-639-8200
Immunization....Sims, Anne CDC 404-639-3286
Immunizations (Foreign Travel)....Staff CDC 404-639-3286
Immunoassays and other binding assays....Scheiner, Toni PTO 703-308-3983
Immunogens....Nucker, Christine M PTO 703-308-4028
Immunology (Cancer)....Staff NCI 301-496-5583
Immunology....Staff American Academy of Allergy and Immunology 800-822-2762
Immunology....Staff Lung Line 800-222-5864
Immunology....Staff NIAID 301-496-5717
Immunotherapy (Cancer)....Staff NCI 301-496-5583
Impaired Health Professionals....Staff NIDA 301-443-6245
Implantable Defibrillator....Staff NHLBI 301-496-4236
Implants, Lens....Staff NEI 301-496-5248
Impotence....Staff NIDDK 301-654-4415
Impotence....Staff NIMH 301-443-4515
In vivo diagnostics....Hollrah, Glen H. PTO 703-308-4552
In Vitro Fertilization....Staff NICHD 301-496-5133
Inactive Waste Site Cleanup....Duffy, Leo P. NEIC 202-586-7710
Inactive Waste Site Management....Duffy, Leo P. NEIC 202-586-7710

Inappropriate Antidiuretic Hormone Syndrome....Staff NHLBI 301-496-4236

Inborn Errors of Metabolism....Staff NHLBI 301-496-4236

Inborn Errors of Metabolism....Staff NICHD 301-496-5133

Inborn Errors of Metabolism....Staff NINDS 301-496-5751

Inborn Errors of Metabolism....Staff NICHD 301-496-5133

Inborn Heart Defects....Staff NHLBI 301-496-4236

Incapacitation....Greenfeld, Lawrence Justice Stat 202-616-3281

Incapacitation....Langan, Patrick Justice Stat 202-616-3490

Incident Response....Congel, Frank NRC 301-415-7476

Incidental Radiation Devices....Staff FCC 202-653-6288

Incinerators....Staff EPA 703-308-8434

Income Security Issues....Ross, Jane GAO 202-512-7215

Incontinence....Staff Simon Foundation 800-237-4666

Incontinence....Staff NIDDK 301-654-4415

Incontinence....Staff NIA 301-496-1752

Incontinent people....Staff Help for Incontinent People 800-252-3337

Incontinentia Pigmenti....Staff NINDS 301-496-5751

Independent States/trade matters....Underwood, Jennifer US Trade Rep 202-395-4620

Index Medicus....Staff NLM 301-496-6308

Indexes of Fuels and Utilities, Monthly....Adkins, Robert LABOR 202-606-6985

India/Minerals....Lyday, Travis Cnty Mines 202-501-9695

India (New Delhi)....Staff Cnty State 202-647-2141

India/trade matters....Ruzicka, Rick US Trade Rep 202-395-6813

India....Gradisher, Thomas Cnty USIA 202-619-5529

India....Hardy, Nancy Cnty AID 202-647-6967

India....Hutchings, Dayna Cnty Export-Import Bank 202-565-3737

India....Nickel, William C. Cnty World Bank 202-458-0336

India....Quinn, Lois Cnty Treasury 202-622-0092

India....Ray, Siddhartha Cnty Embassy 202-939-7000

India....Sibal, Kanwal Cnty Embassy 202-939-7000

India....Simmons, John/Crown, John/Gilman, Tim Cnty Commerce 202-482-2954

Indian Fisheries Resources/Treaties....Staff FWS 703-358-1718

Indian Health....Kendrick, Tony IHS 301-44-3593

Indian Health....Trujillo, Michael IHS 301-443-1083

Indian Housing....Staff HUD 202-708-0950

Indian Hunting, Migratory Birds....Staff FWS 703-358-1714

Indian Resources....Meshorer, Hank Justice 202-272-4111

Indian Wildlife Assistance....Staff FWS 703-358-1718

Indians - Administration for Native Americans....Kharfen, Michael ACF 202-401-9215

Indigent Defense....Gaskins, Carla Justice Stat 202-508-8546

Indium....Brown, Robert Jr. MINES 202-501-9577

Indium....Lundy, David USITC 202-205-3439

Indo-China....Vermillion, James Cnty AID 202-647-4528

Indonesia (Jakarata)....Staff Cnty State 202-647-3276

Indonesia/Minerals....Kuo, Chin Cnty Mines 202-501-9693

Indonesia....Freeman, Kay Cnty AID 202-647-4507

Indonesia....Garrity, Moique P. Cnty World Bank 202-473-4952

Indonesia....Gilroy, Meg Cnty USIA 202-619-5836

Indonesia....Goddin, Karen Cnty Commerce 202-482-3877

Indonesia....Imam, Fahmila Cnty Export-Import Bank 202-565-3738

Indonesia....Rahman, Talaat Cnty TDA 703-875-4357

Indonesia....Shelton, Alison Cnty Treasury 202-622-0354

Indonesia....Siregar, Arifin Mohamad Cnty Embassy 202-775-5200

Indonesia....Sukarna, Muchamad Cnty Embassy 202-775-5200

Indoor Air Division, National Program....Staff EPA 202-233-9030

Indoor Air Division....Staff EPA 202-233-9030

Indoor Air Quality....Persily, Andrew K. NIST 301-975-6418

Induced Movement Disorders....Staff NINDS 301-496-5751

Industrial arts....Word, A. Hugo PTO 703-305-3171

Industrial ceramics....DeSapio, Vincent USITC 202-205-3435

Industrial Chemicals and Cancer....Staff NCI 301-496-5583

Industrial Chemicals (Effects on Human Health)....Staff NIEHS 919-541-3345

Industrial Chemicals....Hurt, William A. COMMERCE 202-482-0128

Industrial Classification, Est. Surv., Natl. Emp/Unemp....Getz, Patricia LABOR 202-606-6521

Industrial diamonds....DeSapio, Vincent USITC 202-205-3435

Industrial Drives/Gears....Reiss, Richard COMMERCE 202-482-3489

Industrial electric furnaces....Reynolds, Bruce A. PTO 703-308-3305

Industrial/fine arts....Douglas, Alan PTO 703-305-3255

Industrial gases....Conant, Kenneth USITC 202-205-3346

Industrial Gases....Hurt, William COMMERCE 202-482-0128

Industrial Hygiene....Gaunce, Jean A. CDC 404-639-3415

Industrial Hygiene....Staff OD/ORS 301-496-2960

Industrial licenses....Staff FCC 717-337-1212

Industrial Minerals, Assistant Branch Chief....Morse, D. MINES 202-501-9402

Industrial Minerals, Assistant Branch Chief....Mozian, Z. MINES 202-501-9396

Industrial Minerals, Chief, Branch of....Barsotti, Aldo F. MINES 202-501-9399

Industrial Organic Chemicals....Hurt, William COMMERCE 202-482-0128

Industrial Prices and Price Indexes, Asst. Commis....Staff LABOR 202-606-7700

Industrial Process Controls....Bodson, John COMMERCE 202-482-0681

Industrial Process Controls....Nealon, Marguerite COMMERCE 202-482-0411

Industrial Productivity....Swink, Denis NEIC 202-586-9232

Industrial Solid (Non Hazardous) Waste....Staff EPA 202-260-4807

Industrial Structure....Davis, Lester A. COMMERCE 202-482-4924

Industrial Technology Transfer....Sisson, Kurt NEIC 202-586-6750

Industrial Trucks....Wiening, Mary COMMERCE 202-482-4608

Industry and Commodity Classification....Kristoff, James CENSUS 301-457-2813

Industry Data Centers....Rowe, John CENSUS 301-457-1305

Industry - Occupational Employment Matrix....Turner, Delores LABOR 202-606-5730

Industry Projections and Economic Growth, Empl. Pro....Bowman, Charles LABOR 202-606-5702

Industry/trade matters....Phillips, Don 202-395-5656

Industry Wage Surveys, Comp. and Work. Conditions....Staff LABOR 202-606-6245

Inedible gelatin....Jonnard, Aimison USITC 202-205-3350

Inertial Confinement Fusion....Davies, Nelia NEIC 301-903-4941

Infant Formula....Corwin, Emil FDA 202-205-4144

Infant Mortality/"Health Start"....Smith, Sandra CDC 301-436-7135

Infant Mortality/"Healthy Start"....Shaffer, Sylvia HRSA 301-443-3376

Infant Mortality....Staff NCHS 301-436-8500

Infant Mortality....Staff CDC 404-488-5141

Infant Mortality....Staff NICHD 301-496-5133

Infant Nutrition....Staff NICHD 301-496-5133

Infant placement....Staff Edna Gladney Center 800-452-3639

Infant Suffocation....Tyrrell, Elaine CPSC 301-504-0580

Infantile Muscular Atrophy....Staff NIAMS 301-496-5751

Infantile Muscular Atrophy....Staff NINDS 301-496-5751

Infantile Spinal Muscular Atrophy....Staff NINDS 301-496-5751

Infants (Care)....Staff HRSA 301-443-6600

Infants' accessories or apparel....Sweet, Mary Elizabeth USITC 202-205-3455

Infections....Staff NIAID 301-496-5717

Infectious Arthritis....Staff NIAMS 301-496-8188

Infectious Eye Disease....Staff NEI 301-496-5248

Infectious Materials (Disposal)....Staff OD/ORS 301-496-2960

Infectious Mononucleosis....Staff NIAID 301-496-5717

Infectious Wastes....Staff EPA 202-260-8551

Infertility....Staff NICHD 301-496-5133

Inflammatory Bowel Disease....Staff NIAID 301-496-5717

Inflammatory Bowel Disease....Staff NIDDK 301-496-3583

Inflatable Articles....McKenna, Thomas CUSTOMS 212-466-5475

Influenza....Sims, Anne CDC 404-639-3286

Influenza....Staff NIAID 301-496-5717

Infomercials....Staff FCC 202-418-1430

Information Centers Branch....Frank, Robyn NAL 301-504-5414

Information Industries....Inoussa, Mary C. COMMERCE 202-482-5820

Information Programs....Pindell, Alvetta NAL 301-504-5204

Information Retrieval Services....Staff NLM 301-496-6095

Information Retrieval Services....Staff NCRR/NIH Library 301-496-1156

Information Services, Chief,....DiCesare, Constance LABOR 202-606-5887

Information services....Huthoefer, Lori USITC 202-205-3303

Information Specialists, Publ. and Special Studies....Staff LABOR 202-606-7828

Infraction Reports--International....Staff FCC 202-653-8138

Infrared Astronomy....Hutchison, Jane NASA 415-604-4968

Ingot molds....Greene, William USITC 202-205-3405

Inhalants....Staff NIDA 301-443-6245

Inherited Blood Abnormalities....Staff NHLBI 301-496-4236

Inherited Blood Abnormalities....Staff NIDDK 301-496-3583

Inherited Metabolic Disorders....Staff NIDDK 301-496-3583

Inherited Neurologic Abnormalities....Staff NINDS 301-496-5751

Injunctions....Staff FCC 202-632-7112

Injuries (Eye)....Staff NEI 301-496-5248

Injury Prevention and Control....Rosenberg, Mark L. CDC 404-488-4690

Ink powders....Johnson, Larry USITC 202-205-3351

Ink....Brownchweig, Gilbert CUSTOMS 212-466-5744

Inks....Johnson, Larry USITC 202-205-3351

Inland Fish and Reservoirs....Staff FWS 703-358-1710

Innovation....Levinson, Terry NEIC 202-586-1479

Inorganic acids....Trainor, Cynthia USITC 202-205-3354

Inorganic Chemicals....Hurt, William COMMERCE 202-482-0128

Inorganic compounds and mixtures....Greenblatt, Jack USITC 202-205-3353

Inorganic Compounds and Mixtures....DiMaria, Joseph CUSTOMS 212-466-4769

Inorganic compounds....Lewis, Michael M. PTO 703-308-2535

Inorganic hydroxides....Conant, Kenneth USITC 202-205-3346

Inorganic oxides....Conant, Kenneth USITC 202-205-3346

Inorganic Pigments....Kostallas, Anthony COMMERCE 202-482-0128

Inorganic silicon compounds....Chaudhuri, Olik PTO 703-308-2546

Insanity Defense....Baunach, Phyllis Jo Justice Stat 202-307-0361

Insect-Borne Infections....Staff NIAID 301-496-5717

Insect Stings Allergy....Staff NIAID 301-496-5717

Insecticide-Rodenticides....Staff EPA 703-305-5200

Insects, Forest....Lyon, Robert FS 202-205-1532

Insomnia....Staff NIMH 301-443-4513

Inspector General Whistle Blower Hotline....Staff EPA 800-424-4000

Institutional Conservation Methods....Volk, Robert NEIC 202-586-8034

Instrument Development....Staff DRS/BEIB 301-496-4741

Instrument Development....Staff NCRR 301-496-4741

Instrument Research....Staff NCRR 301-594-7934

Instruments: controlling....Moller, Ruben USITC 202-205-3495

Instruments: dental....Johnson, Christopher USITC 202-205-3488

Instruments, Drafting....Losche, Robert CUSTOMS 212-466-5670

Instruments: drawing....Roth, Jordon USITC 202-205-3467

Instruments Industry Group....Owings, Christopher SEC 202-942-1900

Instruments: mathematical calculating....Roth, Jordon USITC 202-205-3467

Instruments, Measuring and Controlling....Riedl, Karl CUSTOMS 212-466-5493

Instruments: measuring or checking....Moller, Ruben USITC 202-205-3495

Instruments: medical....Johnson, Christopher USITC 202-205-3488

Instruments: musical....Witherspoon, Ricardo USITC 202-205-3489

Instruments, Navigational....Losche, Robert CUSTOMS 212-466-5670

Instruments: navigational....Roth, Jordon USITC 202-205-3467

Instruments: surgical....Johnson, Christopher USITC 202-205-3488

Instruments: surveying....Roth, Jordon USITC 202-205-3467

Instruments: testing....Moller, Ruben USITC 202-205-3495

Insulation....MacAuley, Patrick COMMERCE 202-482-0132

Insulators, ceramic....Cutchin, John USITC 202-205-3396

Insulators....Picard, Leo PTO 703-308-0538

Insulinomas....Staff NIDDK 301-496-3583

Insurance Claimants (Unempl). Empl/Unempl.Stats.....Terwilliger, Yvonne LABOR 202-606-6392

Insurance Industry Group....Duvall, Steven SEC 202-942-1950

Insurance Programs....Flynn, William OPM 202-606-0600

Insurance....Bedore, James USITC 202-205-3424

Insurance....Health Insurance Association of America....Staff 800-635-1271

Insurance....McAdam, Bruce COMMERCE 202-482-0348

Integrity (Scientific)....Staff OASH/ORI 301-443-3400

Intellectual Development....Staff NICHD 301-496-5133

Intellectual Property Rights, Services....Siegmund, John E. COMMERCE 202-482-4781

Inter-Government Affairs....Staff FCC 202-418-1900

Interconnection....Staff FCC 202-418-1576

Interest Bearing Notes....Montecalvo, Alyssa FRS 202-452-3471

Interest Rate, Foreign....Decker, Patrick FRS 202-452-3314

Interest Rate, Domestic....Culbreth, Leonard FRS 202-452-2853

Interest on Deposits....Ireland, Oliver FRS 202-452-3625

Interest on Federal Reserve Notes....Evans, Gregory L FRS 202-453-3945

Interest on Savings Account....Reid, Brian FRS 202-452-3589

Interference-General....Staff FCC 202-418-0190

Interferon....Staff NCI 301-496-5583

Interferon....Staff NIAID 301-496-5717

Interindustry Economics, (Acting Chief)....Maley, Leo C. ECONOMIC 202-606-9634

Intermittent Claudification....Staff NHLBI 301-496-4236

International Activities, Fish and Wildlife....Staff FWS 703-358-1754

International Activities....Glickman, Marianne NEA 202-682-5422

International Activities....Staff FIC 301-496-1415

International Affairs, NASA....Rahn, Debra NASA 202-358-1639

International Affairs....Browning, Douglas M. Customs 202-927-0400

International Affairs....Kelley, Joseph E. GAO 202-512-4128

International Affairs....Proctor, George W. Justice 202-514-0000

International, Analysis-US Transact's w/Unaffil Foreigners....DiLullo, Anthony J. ECONOMIC 202-606-9558

International, Analysis of US Transact-Unaffiliated Foreigner....Whichard, Obie G. ECONOMIC 202-606-9890

International, Annual Surveys-US Transact's w/Unaffil Foreigners....Emond, Christopher J. ECONOMIC 202-606-9826

International Audit Organization....Kelley, Joseph GAO 202-512-4128

International Aviation....Bauerlein, Joan W FAA 202-267-3213

International Aviation....Gretch, Paul DOT 202-366-2423

International, Benchmark Survey-US Transact's w/Unaffil For.....Kozlow, Ralph ECONOMIC 202-606-9853

International, Capital Expend. of Major-Owned Foreign Affil.....Fahim-Nadir, Mahnaz ECONOMIC 202-606-9828

International Conferences....Staff FIC 301-496-2516

International Coordination and Liason...Staff FIC 301-496-4784

International Crime Data....Kalish, Carol Justice Stat 202-307-0235

International Economics, Associate Director....Pollack, Gerald A. ECONOMIC 202-606-9602

International Economics, Balance of Payments....Bach, Christopher L. ECONOMIC 202-606-9545

International Economics, Current Account Estimates....Bach, Christopher ECONOMIC 202-606-9545

International Economics, Current Account Analysis....DiLullo, Anthony J. ECONOMIC 202-606-9558

International Economics, Special Analysis....Lawson, Ann ECONOMIC 202-606-9462

International Energy Analysis....Pumphrey, David NEIC 202-586-6832

International Fellowship Programs....Staff FIC 301-496-1653

International Finance....Mendelowitz, Allan I. GAO 202-512-5889

International, For. Dir US Invest. - New Investment Surv.....Cherry, Joseph ECONOMIC 202-606-9817

International, For. Dir US Invest. New Investment Surv Anal....Fahim-Nadir, Mahnaz ECONOMIC 202-606-9828

International, Foreign Dir. US Invest, Benchmark and Annual Anal....Mataloni, Raymond D. ECONOMIC 202-606-9867

International, Foreign Dir. US Invest, Benchmark and Annual Surv....Galler, David H. ECONOMIC 202-606-9835

International, Foreign Military Sales....Atherton, Daniel ECONOMIC 202-606-9593

International Forestry....Sirmon, Jeff M. FS 202-205-1650

International, Government Transactions....Bach, Christopher ECONOMIC 202-606-9545

International Health Activities....Vogel, Linda ASH 301-443-1774

International Health....Davis, Joe H. CDC 404-639-2101

International Information Center....Sutton, Cynthia FRS 202-452-3411

International Investment, Chief....Barker, Betty L. ECONOMIC 202-606-9805

International Liaison....Kenney, James B FAA 202-267-3719

International Major Projects....Thibeault, Robert COMMERCE 202-482-5225

International, Merchandise Trade....Murad, Howard ECONOMIC 202-606-9572

International, Multinat'l Corps, Analysis of Activities....Mataloni, Raymond J. ECONOMIC 202-606-9867

International Operations....Staff COMMERCE 202-482-0300

International Patent Documentation....Auton, Gary PTO 703-305-5122

International Policy....Staff FCC 202-418-1460

International Price Indexes, Assist. Commiss.....Reut, Katrina LABOR 202-606-7100

International Price Indexes, Food, Raw Matls, Appl....Frumkin, Rob LABOR 202-606-7106

International Price Indexes, Machinery....Costello, Brian LABOR 202-606-7107

International Price Indexes, Revision, Pr/Lv.Cond.....Reut, Katrina LABOR 202-606-7100

International, Private Capital Transactions....Scholl, Russell B. ECONOMIC 202-606-9579

International Programs, Director....Vacant NLM 301-496-6481

International Programs....Cutrell,John FHA 202-366-0111

International, Quarterly and Annual Balance of Payments Data....Fouch, Gregory G. ECONOMIC 202-606-5577

International, Quarterly and Annual Balance of Payments Anal....Fouch, Gregory G. ECONOMIC 202-606-5577

International Research and Awards....Staff FIC 301-496-1653

International Research....Staff NEH 202-606-8204

International Statistics, Africa....Rowe, Patricia CENSUS 301-457-1358

International Statistics, Asia....Rowe, Patricia CENSUS 301-457-1358

International Statistics, China, People's Republic....Harbaugh, Christina CENSUS 301-457-1360

International Statistics, Europe....Stanecki, Karen CENSUS 301-457-1406

International Statistics, International Data Base....Johnson, Peter CENSUS 301-457-1403

International Statistics, Latin America....Rowe, Patricia CENSUS 301-457-1358

International Statistics, North America....Rowe, Patricia CENSUS 301-457-1358

International Statistics, Oceania....Rowe, Patricia CENSUS 301-457-1358

International Statistics of Common Carriers....Staff FCC 202-418-0940

International Statistics, Soviet Union....Stanecki, Karen CENSUS 301-457-1406

International Statistics, Women in Development....Rowe, Patricia CENSUS 301-457-1358

International Studies Program....Staff FIC 301-496-2516

International Thermonuclear Experimental Reactor...James, Thomas R. NEIC 301-903-5378

International Trade Compliance....Seidel, Stuart P. Customs 202-482-6920

International Trade....Fisher, Irene SBA 202-205-6720

International Trade....Mendelowitz, Allan I GAO 202-512-5889

International Transportation and Trade....Levine, Arnold DOT 202-366-4368

International Transportation....Watts, Patricia ECONOMIC 202-606-9589

International Travel....Bolyard, Joan E. ECONOMIC 202-606-9550

International, US Direct Investment Abroad, Analysis....Zeile, William ECONOMIC 202-606-9893

International, US Direct Invest. Abroad, Payments Data Bal.....New, Mark W. ECONOMIC 202-606-9875

International, US Direct Invest. Abroad, Benchmark and Annual Sur....Walker, Patricia G. ECONOMIC 202-606-9889

International Visitor Program....Salisbury, Diane DOD 703-614-6543

International Visitors Program....Vandrovec, Gene CENSUS 301-457-2816

International Visitors Program....Pane Pinto, Nina CENSUS 301-457-2816

International...Staff FCC 202-418-0680

Internet information....Staff CENSUS 301-457-1242

Interplanetary Space Probes....Brown, Dwayne C. NASA 202-358-1726

Interstate Land Sales Registration....Staff HUD 202-708-0502

Interstitial Cystitis....Staff NIDDK 301-654-4415

Interstitial Lung Diseases....Staff NHLBI 301-496-4236

Interstitial Nephritis....Staff NIDDK 301-654-4415

Intestinal Malabsorption Syndrome....Staff NIDDK 301-654-3810

Intracranial Aneurysm....Staff NINDS 301-496-5751

Intraocular Lenses....Staff NEI 301-496-5248

Intrauterine Growth Retardation....Staff NICHD 301-496-5133

Introduced Species, Fish and Wildlife....Staff FWS 703-358-1718

Inventions, Energy-Related....Staff NEIC 202-586-1479

Investigations....Staff FCC 202-418-1170

Investigative Programs....DeVaughn, Stephen Customs 202-9271500

Investment in Plant and Equipment....Hansen, Kenneth CENSUS 301-457-4755

Investment Management....Muir, S. Cassin COMMERCE 202-482-0346

Investment....Stillman, Robert SBA 202-205-6510

Iodine....Conant, Kenneth USITC 202-205-3346

Iodine....Lyday, Phillis A. MINES 202-501-9405

Ionizing Radiation....Coursey, B.M. NIST 301-975-5584

Ionosphere....Staff FCC 202-653-8166

Iran/Minerals....Heydari, Michael Cnty Mines 202-501-9688

Iran....Austin, Ken Cnty Treasury 202-622-0174

Iran....Fitzgerald-Wilks, Kate/Thanos, Paul Cnty Commerce 202-482-1860

Iran....Hutchings, Dayna Cnty Export-Import Bank 202-565-3737

Iran....Staff Cnty State 202-647-6111

Iran....Vaurs, Rene Cnty World Bank 202-473-5034

Iran....Winchester, Rebecca Cnty USIA 202-619-6528

Iraq (Baghdad)....Staff Cnty State 202-647-5692

Iraq/Minerals....Antonides, Lloyd Cnty Mines 202-501-9686

Iraq....Austin, Kim Cnty Treasury 202-622-0174

Iraq....Hutchings, Dayna Cnty Export-Import Bank 202-565-3737

Iraq....Macgregor, John Cnty World Bank 202-473-7311

Iraq....Sams, Thomas/Wright, Corey Cnty Commerce 202-482-1860

Iraq....Vacant Cnty USIA 202-619-6528

Iraqi....Al-Tai, A.M. Cnty Embassy 202-483-7500

Iraqi....Hamed, Fadhel H. Cnty Embassy 202-483-7500

Ireland (Dublin)....Staff Cnty State 202-647-6585

Ireland/Minerals....Newman, Harold R. Cnty Mines 202-501-9669

Ireland....Collins, Michael Cnty Embassy 202-462-3939

Ireland....Fitzpatrick, Boyce Cnty Commerce 202-482-2177

Ireland....Gallagher, Dermot A. Cnty Embassy 202-462-3939

Ireland....Gosnell, Peter Cnty Export- Import Bank 202-565-3733

Ireland....Kulla, Morgan Cnty USIA 202-619-6853

Ireland....Mackour, Oscar Cnty Treasury 202-622-0145

Iridocyclitis....Staff NEI 301-496-5248

Iritis....Staff NEI 301-496-5248

Iron and Steel....Houck, Gerald MINES 202-501-9439

Iron and Steel Scrap....Houck, Gerald MINES 202-501-9439

Iron and Steel Slag....Solomon, Cheryl S. MINES 202-501-9393

Iron blues....Johnson, Larry USITC 202-205-3351

Iron compounds....Greenblatt, Jack USITC 202-205-3353

Iron Deficiency Anemia....Staff NIDDK 301-496-3583

Iron Deficiency Anemia....Staff NHLBI 301-496-4236

Iron Ore....Kirk, William S. MINES 202-501-9430

Iron ore....MacKnight, Peg USITC 202-205-3431

Iron oxide pigments....Potter, Michael MINES 202-501-9387

Irrigation, Major Proj.....Weining, Mary COMMERCE 202-482-4608

Irritable Bowel Syndrome....Staff NIDDK 301-654-3810

Isador....Staff NCI 301-496-5583

Ischemia....Staff NHLBI 301-496-4236

Ischemic Heart Disease....Staff NHLBI 301-496-4236

Isinglass....Jonnard, Aimison USITC 202-205-3350

Islet Cell Hyperplasia....Staff NIDDK 301-496-3583

Islet Cell Transplants....Staff NIDDK 301-496-3583

Isobutane....Raftery, Jim USITC 202-205-3365

Isobutylene....Raftery, Jim USITC 202-205-3365

Isocyanates....Kight, John PTO 703-308-2453

Isoprene....Raftery, Jim USITC 202-205-3365

Isopropyl myristate....Johnson, Larry USITC 202-205-3351

Isotope Production....Erb, Donald NEIC 301-903-5338

Isotopes....Staff NCI 301-496-5583

Israel/Minerals....Izon, David Cnty Mines 202-501-9674

Israel (Tel Aviv)....Staff Cnty State 202-647-3672

Israel....Gur, Shlomo Cnty Embassy 202-364-5500

Israel....Hughes, Elizabeth Cnty Treasury 202-622-0183

Israel....Hutchings, Dayna Cnty Export-Import Bank 202-565-3737

Israel....Rabinovich, Itamar Cnty Embassy 202-364-5500

Israel....Slatterry, John Cnty AID 202-663-2613

Israel....Thanos, Paul Cnty Commerce 202-482-1860

Israel....Winton, Donna Cnty USIA 202-619-6528

Italy/Minerals....Newman, Harold Cnty Mines 202-501-9669

Italy (Rome)....Staff Cnty State 202-647-3746

Italy....Biancheri, Boris Cnty Embassy 202-328-5500

Italy....Fagiolo, Boris Cnty Embassy 202-328-5500

Italy....Fitzpatrick, Boyce Cnty Commerce 202-482-2177

Italy....Gosnell, Peter Cnty Export-Import Bank 202-565-3733

Italy....Holloway, Barbara Cnty Treasury 202-622-0098

Italy....Santoro, Eugene Cnty USIA 202-619-6582

ITFS Legal Policy....Staff FCC 202-418-1610

ITFS Technical Application....Staff FCC 202-418-1610

IVDS Application Status....Staff FCC 800-322-1117

IVDS Auction Information....Staff FCC 202-418-0660

IVDS Auction Winners....Staff FCC 202-418-0660

Ivory, articles of....Spalding, Josephine USITC 202-205-3498

Ivory Coast/Minerals....van Oss, Hendrik Cnty Mines 202-501-9687

Ivory Coast....Michelini, Philip Cnty Commerce 202-482-4388

Ivory Coast....Wickman, Cam Cnty AID 202-647-6335

Ivory Coast....Baily, Jess Cnty USIA 202-619-5900

Ivory Coast....Palghat, Kathy Cnty Treasury 202-622-0332

Ivory, tusks....Ludwick, David USITC 202-205-3329

J

Jackets: mens and boys....Sweet, Mary Elizabeth USITC 202-205-3455

Jackets: womens and girls....Sweet, Mary Elizabeth USITC 202-205-3455

Jails, Inmates, and Crowding....DeWitt, Charles Justice Stat 202-307-2942

Jails, Inmates, and Crowding....Greenfeld, Lawrence Justice Stat 202-616-3281

Jails, Inmates, and Crowding....Stephan, James Justice Stat 202-616-7273

Jails, Inmates, and Crowding....Baunach, Phyllis Jo Justice Stat 202-307-0361

Jakob-Creutzfeldt Disease....Staff NINDS 301-496-5751

Jamaica (Kingston)....Staff Cnty State 202-647-2620

Jamaica/Minerals....Rabchevsky, George Cnty Mines 202-501-9670

Jamaica....Almaguer, Antoinette Peace Corps 202-606-3322

Jamaica....Anne McKinney Cnty TDA 703-875-4357

Jamaica....Bayly, Rachel Cnty Treasury 202-622-1266

Jamaica....Bernal, Richard Leighton Cnty Embassy 202-452-0660

Jamaica....Bryan, Basil Keith Cnty Embassy 202-452-0660

Jamaica....Cambell, Edward Cnty AID 202-647-4105

Jamaica....Head, Alfred Cnty USIA 202-619-6835
Jamaica....Nallari, Raj Cnty World Bank 202-473-8697
Jamaica....Siegelman, Mark Cnty Commerce 202-482-5680
Jamaica....Wilkins, Michele Cnty Export-Import Bank 202-565-3743
Jams and Jellies....William, Janis COMMERCE 202-482-2250
Jams, jellies, and marmalades....Frankel, Lee USITC 202-205-3315
Jansky-Bielschowsky Disease....Staff NINDS 301-496-5751
Japan/Minerals....Wu, John Cnty Mines 202-501-9697
Japan (policy analyst)....Siegal, Byron US Trade Rep 202-395-5070
Japan (policy planning)....Weisel, Barbara US Trade Rep 202-395-5070
Japan/trade matters....Burns, David US Trade Rep 202-395-5050
Japan/trade matters....Sands, Lee US Trade Rep 202-395-3900
Japan/trade matters....Wolff, Derek US Trade Rep 202-395-3900
Japan (Tokyo)....Staff Cnty State 202-647-3152
Japan....Gosnell, Peter Cnty Export-Import Bank 202-565-3733
Japan....Hashimoto, Hiroshi Cnty Embassy 202-939-6700
Japan....Kuriyama, Takakazu Cnty Embassy 202-939-6700
Japan....Leslie, E./Kennedy, E./Christian, A. Cnty Commerce 202-482-2425
Japan....Loevinger, David G. Cnty Treasury 202-622-0159
Japan....Spector, Brooks Cnty USIA 202-619-5838
Japan....Wolff, Derek US Trade Rep 202-395-5070
Japanese Yen with options....Bice, David CFT 312-353-7880
Jerusalem....Winton, Donna Cnty USIA 202-619-6528
Jet fuel....Foreso, Cynthia USITC 202-205-3348
Jewelry, Export Promo.....Beckham, Reginald COMMERCE 202-482-5478
Jewelry....Harris, John M. COMMERCE 202-482-1178
Jewelry....Schwartz, Stanley CUSTOMS 212-466-5895
Jewelry....Witherspoon, Ricardo USITC 202-205-3489
Job Vacancy Stats, Employment Statistics....Butani, Shail LABOR 202-606-6400
Joint Replacement....Staff NIAMS 301-496-8188
Jordan (Amman)....Staff Cnty State 202-647-1022
Jordan/Minerals....Dolley, Thomas Cnty Mines 202-501-9690
Jordan....Hughes, Elizabeth Cnty Treasury 202-622-0174
Jordan....Hutchings, Dayna Cnty Export-Import Bank 202-565-3737
Jordan....Macgregor, John Cnty World Bank 202-473-7311
Jordan....Mufti, Faris Sh. Cnty Embassy 202-966-2664
Jordan....Slatterry, John Cnty AID 202-663-2613
Jordan....Tarawneh, Fayez A. Cnty Embassy 202-966-2664
Jordan....Winton, Donna Cnty USIA 202-619-6528
Jordan....Wright, Corey/Samms, Thomas Cnty Commerce 202-482-1860
Joseph's Disease....Staff NINDS 301-496-5751
Joubert Syndrome....Staff NINDS 301--496-5751
Journal, EPA....Staff EPA 202-260-6643
Journal Information....Staff NCRR/NIH Library 301-496-2184
Journal Information....Staff NLM 301-496-6095
Journalism research methods....Newhagan, John D. UMD 301-405-2417
Judges....Gaskins, Carla Justice Stat 202-508-8550
Judges....Langan, Patrick Justice Stat 202-616-3490
Judiciary....Gaskins, Carla Justice Stat 202-508-8550
Judiciary....Langan, Patrick Justice Stat 202-616-3490
Juices, fruit....Dennis, Alfred USITC 202-205-3316
Juices, vegetable....Dennis, Alfred USITC 202-205-3316
Juices....Maria, John CUSTOMS 212-466-5730
Jurisdictional Separations...Staff FCC 202-418-0830
Just Say No....Staff Just Say No International 800-258-2766
Justice Issues....Rabkin, Norman J. GAO 202-512-8777
Juvenile Corrections....Baunach, Phyllis Jo Justice Stat 202-307-0361
Juvenile Corrections....Kline, Susan Justice Stat 202-724-3118
Juvenile Delinquency....Staff NIMH 301-443-4513
Juvenile Diabetes....Staff NIDDK 301-654-3327
Juvenile Mascular Degeneration....Staff NEI 301-496-5248
Juvenile Rheumatoid Arthritis....Staff NIAMS 301-496-8188
Juvenile Spin. Musc. Atrophy (Kug.-Wel. Disease)....Staff NINDS 301-496-5751
Juveniles - General....Lindgren, Sue Justice Stat 202-307-0760
Juxtaglomerular Hyperplasia (Bartter's Syndrome)....Staff NHLBI 301-496-4236

K

Kanner's Syndrome....Staff NINDS 301-496-5751
Kaolin....DeSapio, Vincent USITC 202-205-3435
Kaposi's Sarcoma....Staff NCI 301-496-5583
Kawasaki Disease....Staff CDC 401-639-3286
Kawasaki Disease....Staff NIAID 301-496-5717

Kawasaki Disease....Staff NHLBI 301-496-4236
Kazakhstan....Eighmy, Thomas Cnty AID 202-647-6920
Kazakhstan....Essenbaev, Mara T. Cnty Embassy 202-333-4507
Kazakhstan....Konishi, Motoo Cnty World Bank 202-458-0507
Kazakhstan....Levine, Richard Cnty Mines 202-501-9682
Kazakhstan....Resnick, Bonnie Cnty Treasury 202-622-0108
Kazakhstan....Rossate, Julie Peace Corps 202-606-3040
Kazakhstan....Shamson, Tanya Cnty TDA 703-875-4357
Kazakhstan....Skipper, Thomas Cnty USIA 202-619-5057
Kazakhstan....Souleimenov, Touleoutai Cnty Embassy 202-333-4504
Kazakhstan....Staff Cnty State 202-647-6869
Kazakhstan....Waxman-Lenz, Roberta Cnty Export-Import Bank 202-565-3742
Kearns-Sayre Syndrome....Staff NINDS 301-496-5751
Keloid....Staff NIAMS 301-496-8188
Kenya/Minerals....Izon, David Cnty Mines 202-501-9692
Kenya (Nairobi)....Staff Cnty State 202-647-6479
Kenya....Bezek, Jill Cnty TDA 703-875-4357
Kenya....Kipkorir, Benjamin Edgar Cnty Embassy 202-387-6101
Kenya....Kotze, Joan Cnty Treasury 202-622-0333
Kenya....Larsen, Mark Cnty USIA 202-619-4894
Kenya....Magnus, Charles Cnty World Bank 202-473-4154
Kenya....Maybury-Lewis, Anthony Cnty Export-Import Bank 202-565-3739
Kenya....Muriithi, Geoffrey K. Cnty Embassy 202-387-6101
Kenya....Schmitz, Virginia Peace Corps 202-606-3334
Kenya....Terry, Carlton Cnty AID 202-647-5584
Kenya....Watkins, Chandra Cnty Commerce 202-482-4564
Keratitis....Staff NEI 301-496-5248
Keratoconus....Staff NEI 301-496-5248
Keratomileusis....Staff NEI 301-496-5248
Keratoplasty....Staff NEI 301-496-5248
Keratosis....Staff NIAMS 301-496-8188
Kerosene....Foreso, Cynthia USITC 202-205-3348
Ketones....Michels, David USITC 202-205-3352
Key cases....Seastrum, Carl USITC 202-205-3493
Keyboards....Peng, John PTO 703-305-4945
Kidney Dialysis....Hardy, Robert HCFA 220-690-6145
Kidney Disease....Staff Polycystic Kidney Disease Research Foundation 800-753-2873
Kidney Fund....Staff American Kidney Fund 800-638-8299
Kidney Patients....Staff AAKP Patients 800-749-2257
Kidney Stones....Staff NIDDK 301-654-4415
Kidney, Urology Clearinghouse....Staff NIDDK 301-468-6345
Kidney....Staff National Kidney Foundation 800-622-9010
Kidney....Staff NIDDK 301-654-4415
Kidsrights....Staff Kidsrights 800-892-5437
Kienback's Disease....Staff NIAMS 301-496-8188
Kiribati (Gilbert Islands)/Minerals....Lyday, Travis Cnty Mines 202-501-9695
Kiribati (Tarawa)....Staff Cnty State 202-647-3546
Kiribati....Rahman, Talaat Cnty TDA 703-875-4357
Kiribati....Davies, Irene Cnty World Bank 202-458-2481
Kiribati....Imam, Fahmila Cnty Export-Import Bank 202-565-3738
Kiribati....Shelton, Alison Cnty Treasury 202-622-0354
Kitchen Cabinets....Wise, Barbara COMMERCE 202-482-0375
Kleine-Levin Syndrome....Staff NINDS 301-496-5751
Klinefelter's Syndrome....Staff NICHD 301-496-5133
Knee Replacement....Staff NIAMS 301-496-8188
Knitting machines....Greene, William USITC 202-205-3405
Knotted Netting....Konzet, Jeffrey CUSTOMS 212-466-5885
Koch Antitoxins....Staff NCI 301-496-5583
Korea, North and South....Staff Cnty State 202-647-7717
Korea, North/Minerals....Kuo, Chin Cnty Mines 202-501-9693
Korea, South/Minerals....Kuo, Chin Cnty Mines 202-501-9693
Korea....Ban, Ki Moon Cnty Embassy 202-524-9273
Korea....Donius, Jeffrey/Duvall, Dan Cnty Commerce 202-482-4390
Korea....Park, Kun Woo Cnty Embassy 202-524-9273
Korea....Schneider, Todd Cnty Treasury 202-622-0335
Korea....Shetty, Sundhir Cnty World Bank 202-458-1939
Korea....Spector, Brooks Cnty USIA 202-619-5838
Korea-North....Imam, Fahmila Cnty Export-Import Bank 202-565-3738
Korea-South....Imam, Fahmila Cnty Export-Import Bank 202-565-3738
Krabbe's Disease....Staff NINDS 301-496-5751
Krebiezen (Carcalon)....Staff NCI 301-496-5583
Krgyz Republic....Eighmy, Thomas Cnty AID 202-647-6920
Kryrgyzstan....Skipper, Thomas Cnty USIA 202-619-5057

Kugelberg-Welander Disease (Juv. Spi. Mus. Atoph.)....Staff NINDS 301-496-5751

Kuru....Staff NINDS 301-496-5751

Kuwait (Kuwait)....Staff Cnty State 202-647-6562

Kuwait/Minerals....Michalski, Bernadette Cnty Mines 202-501-9699

Kuwait....Al-Sabah, Mohammed Sabah Al-Salim Cnty Embassy 202-966-0702

Kuwait....Al-Saif, Salah Hamdan Cnty Embassy 202-966-0702

Kuwait....Austin, Ken Cnty Treasury 202-622-0174

Kuwait....Farah, Ahmed Cnty World Bank 202-473-2649

Kuwait....Vacant Cnty USIA 202-619-6528

Kuwait....Wright, Corey/Sams, Thomas Cnty Commerce 202-482-1680

Kuwait...Maybury-Lewis, Anthony Cnty Export-Import Bank 202-565-3739

Kyanite-Mullite....Potter, Michael J. MINES 202-501-9387

Kyanite....DeSapio, Vincent USITC 202-205-3435

Kyphosis....Staff NIAMS 301-496-8188

Kyrghyzstan....Koff, Allison S. Cnty TDA 703-875-4357

Kyrghyzstan....Russate, Julie Peace Corps 202-606-3040

Kyrgyz Republic....Cooke, Nancy J. Cnty World Bank 202-473-8727

Kyrgyzstan....Chukin, Almas Cnty Embassy 202-347-3732

Kyrgyzstan....Levine, Richard Cnty Mines 202-501-9682

Kyrgyzstan....Omuraliev, Jumgalbek O. Cnty Embassy 202-347-3732

Kyrgyzstan....Resnick, Bonnie Cnty Treasury 202-622-0108

Kyrgyzstan....Staff Cnty State 202-647-6859

Kyrgyzstan....Waxman-Lenz, Roberta Cnty Export-Import Bank 202-565-3742

L

La Leche....Staff La Leche League International 800-525-3243

Labels....Cook, Lee USITC 202-205-3471

Labor Composition, Multifactor Productivity, Hrs.....Rosenblum, Larry LABOR 202-606-5606

Labor Force and Unemployment, Foreign Countries....Sorrentino, Constance LABOR 202-606-5654

Labor Force Data, Data Disk and Tapes....Marcus, Jessie LABOR 202-606-6392

Labor Force Data, Machine-readable data, Empl/Un....Green, Gloria LABOR 202-606-6376

Labor Force Projections....Fullerton, Howard LABOR 202-606-5711

Labor Force, State and Area Tapes and Diskettes....Marcus, Jessie LABOR 202-606-6392

Labor Management Relations....Foley, Phyllis G. OPM 202-606-2930

Laboratory Animals....Staff NCRR 301-496-2527

Laboratory Animals....Staff NCRR 301-496-5545

Laboratory devices....Aziz, Kaiser J. FAES 301-594-3084

Laboratory Glassware....Staff OD/ORS 301-496-4595

Laboratory Instruments, Trade Promo.....Manzalillo, Frank COMMERCE 202-482-2991

Laboratory Instruments....Nealon, Marguerite COMMERCE 202-482-3411

Labyrinthine Hydrops....Staff NIDCD 301-496-7243

Labyrinthitis....Staff NINDS 301-496-5924

Labyrinthitis....Staff NIDCD 301-496-7243

Lace....Cook, Lee USITC 202-205-3455

Lace....Konzet, Jeffrey CUSTOMS 212-466-5885

Lacemaking machines....Greene, William USITC 202-205-3405

Lacings....Cook, Lee USITC 202-205-3455

Lacquers....Johnson, Larry USITC 202-205-3351

Lacrimal Glands....Staff NEI 301-496-5248

Lactation....Staff NICHD 301-496-5133

Lactose Intolerance....Staff NIDDK 301-654-3810

Lactose....Randall, Rob USITC 202-205-3366

Laetrile....Staff NCI 301-496-5583

Lakes....Wanser, Stephen USITC 202-205-3363

Lamb....Steller, Rose USITC 202-205-3323

Laminar Flow Rooms....Staff OD/ORS 301-496-2960

LAMM (Heroin Treatment)....Staff NIDA 301-443-6245

Lamp black....Johnson, Larry USITC 202-205-3351

Lamps (bulbs)....Cutchin, John USITC 202-205-3396

Lamps....Kalkines, George CUSTOMS 212-466-5794

Land Acquisition....Kollins, William J. Justice 202-272-6776

Land and Space Based Remote Sensing Instruments....Staff NASA 804-864-6170

Land and Water Conservation Fund....Staff FWS 703-358-1713

Land Disposal....Staff EPA 202-260-4687

Land Disposition, Fish and Wildlife....Staff FWS 703-358-1713

Land Fields....Staff EPA 202-260-4687

Land Mobile Frequent Assignment Techniques....Staff FCC 717-337-1411

Land Mobile Radio Service (Private)-Legal....Staff FCC 202-418-0620

Land Mobile Service (Private)-General....Staff FCC 800-322-1117

Land Resource Usage and Analysis....Staff FWS 703-358-1706

Land Transportation....Staff FCC 717-337-1212

Land vehicles....Focarino, Margaret PTO 703-308-0885

Langerhans-Cell Granulomatosis....Staff NHLBI 301-496-4236

Language and journalism....McAdams, Katherine C. UMD 301-405-2423

Language Development....Staff NINDS 301-496-5924

Language Development....Staff NIDCD 301-496-7243

Language Development....Staff NICHD 301-496-5133

Language....Staff American Speech-Language-Hearing Association Consumer Helpline 800-638-8255

Language....Staff CENSUS 301-457-2464

Language....Staff NINDS 301-496-5924

Language....Staff NIDCD 301-496-7243

Laos/Minerals....Lydays, Travis Cnty Mines 202-501-9694

Laos (Vientiane)....Staff Cnty State 202-647-3133

Laos....Camp, Bea Cnty USIA 202-619-5837

Laos....Imam, Fahmila Cnty Export-Import Bank 202-565-3738

Laos....Pho, Hong-Phong B. Cnty Commerce 202-482-3875

Laos....Phommachanh, Hiem Cnty Embassy 202-332-6416

Laos....Respess, Rebecca Cnty TDA 703-875-4357

Laos....Schneider, Todd Cnty Treasury 202-622-0335

Laos....Soukhathivong, Seng Cnty Embassy 202-332-6417

Laryngeal Nodules....Staff NIDCD 301-496-7243

Laryngectomy....Staff NIDCD 301-496-7243

Laryngitis....Staff NIDCD 301-496-7243

Laser Angioplasty....Staff NHLBI 301-496-4236

Laser (Cancer Surgery)....Staff NCI 301-496-5583

Laser Energy Conversion Techniques....Staff NASA 804-864-6122

Laser (Tatoo Removal/Dermatology)....Staff 301-496-8188

Laser Treatment (Eyes)....Staff NEI 301-496-5248

Lasers, Trade Promo.....Manzolilo, Frank COMMERCE 202-482-2991

Lasers....Bovernick, Rodney PTO 703-305-3594

Lassa Fever....Staff NIAID 301-496-5717

Latin America....Greenberg, Richard OPIC 202-336-8616

Latin America/trade matters....Frechette, Myles US Trade Rep 202-395-6135

Latvia....Altheim, Stephen Cnty Treasury 202-622-0125

Latvia....Ann Lien Cnty TDA 703-875-4357

Latvia....Jovanovic, Djordje Cnty World Bank 202-473-4070

Latvia....Kalnins, Ojars Erikas Cnty Embassy 202-726-8213

Latvia....Levine, Richard Cnty Mines 202-501-9682

Latvia....Robinson, Susan Cnty USIA 202-619-6853

Latvia....Staff Cnty State 202-647-3187

Latvia....Upmacis, Ints Cnty Embassy 202-726-8214

Latvia....Viksnins, Helen Peace Corps 202-606-5517

Latvia....Waxman-Lenz, Roberta Cnty Export-Import Bank 202-565-3742

Latvia....Wooton, Nicholas Peace Corps 202-606-5519

Launch Vehicles....Brown, Dwayne C. NASA 202-453-8956

Laundry machines....Jackson, Georgia USITC 202-205-3399

Laurence-Moon-Bardet-Biedl Syndrome....Staff NINDS 301-496-5751

Law Enforcement....Saunders, Norman T USCG 202-267-0977

Law Enforcement....Harris, Daniel C. GAO 202-512-8720

Law Enforcement, Prosecution and Courts - State....Manson, Donald Justice Stat 202-616-3491

Lawn and Garden Equipment....Hodgen, Donald COMMERCE 202-482-3348

Layoff Statistics, Empl/ Unempl. Stats.....Siegel, Lewis LABOR 202-606-6404

Lead Based Paints....Staff CDC 404-639-3286

Lead compounds....Greenblatt, Jack USITC 202-205-3353

Lead Encephalopathy....Staff NINDS 301-496-5751

Lead for pencils....Seastrum, Carl USITC 202-205-3493

Lead pigments...Johnson, Larry USITC 202-205-3351

Lead Poisoning Anemia....Staff NHLBI 301-496-4236

Lead Poisoning Prevention....Giles, Ken CPSC 301-504-0580

Lead Poisoning Prevention....Forney, David B. CDC 404-488-7330

Lead Poisoning....Grigg, Bill PHS 202-690-6867

Lead Poisoning....Staff NIEHS 919-541-3345

Lead Poisoning....Staff CDC 404-639-3286

Lead Products....Larrabee, David COMMERCE 202-482-0607

Lead....Smith, Gerald MINES 202-501-9431

Lead....White, Linda USITC 202-205-3427

Learning Center for Interactive Technology....Staff NLM 301-496-6280

Learning Disabilities....Staff NIDCD 301-496-7243

Learning Disabilities....Staff NIMH 301-443-4513
Learning Disabilities....Staff NINDS 301-496-5751
Learning Disabilities....Staff NICHD 301-496-5133
Lease condensate....Foreso, Cynthia USITC 202-205-3348
Leasing Equipment and Vehicles....Uzella, Elinore COMMERCE 202-482-4654
Leather apparel....Hamey, Amy USITC 202-205-3465
Leather apparel....Jones, Jackie USITC 202-205-3466
Leather footwear parts....Shildneck, Ann USITC 202-205-3499
Leather, Producer Price Index....Paik, Soon LABOR 202-606-7714
Leather Products....Byron, James E. COMMERCE 202-482-4034
Leather Tanning....Byron, James E. COMMERCE 202-482-4034
Leather....Steller, Rose USITC 202-205-3323
Lebanon (Beirut)....Staff Cnty State 202-647-6148
Lebanon/Minerals....Michalski, Bernadette Cnty Mines 202-501-9699
Lebanon....Hoppenbrouwer, Laurens M. Cnty World Bank 202-473-2716
Lebanon....Maalouf, Massoud Cnty Embassy 202-939-6300
Lebanon....Slatterry, John Cnty AID 202-663-2613
Lebanon....Tabbarah, Riad Cnty Embassy 202-939-6300
Lebanon....VanRenterghem, Cynthia Cnty Treasury 202-622-0343
Lebanon....Winton, Donna Cnty USIA 202-619-6528
Lebanon....Wright, Corey/Sams, Thomas Cnty Commerce 202-482-1860
Lebanon...Hutchings, Dayna Cnty Export-Import Bank 202-565-3737
Leber's Disease....Staff NEI 301-496-5248
Left Ventricular Assist Device (LVAD)....Staff NHLBI 301-496-4236
Legal Medicine....Staff American College of Legal Medicine 800-433-9137
Legal Services....Huthoefer, Lori USITC 202-205-3303
Legal Services....Chittum, J. Marc. COMMERCE 202-482-0345
Legg-Perthes Disease....Staff NIAMS 301-496-8188
Legionella Pneumophila....Staff CDC 404-639-3286
Legionella Pneumophila....Staff NIAID 301-496-5717
Legionnaire's Disease....Staff CDC 404-639-3286
Legionnaire's Disease....Staff NIAID 301-496-5717
Legislation....Gregg, Valerie CENSUS 301-457-4102
Legislation....Jones, Thomas CENSUS 301-457-2512
Legislative Affairs....Staff FCC 202-418-1900
Legislative Information....Staff OD/DLA 301-496-3471
Legislative Reviews...Clark, David L. GAO 202-512-9489
Legislative Reviews....Cark, David L. GAO 202-512-9489
Leigh's Disease (Subacute Necrotizing Encephal.)....Staff NINDS 301-496-5751
Leishmaniasis....Staff NIAID 301-496-5717
Leisure (resorts) Industry Group....Roycroft, John C. SEC 202-942-1960
Lemon oil (essential oil)....Land, Eric USITC 202-205-3349
Lennox-Gastaut Syndrome....Staff NINDS 301-496-5751
Lens Implants....Staff NEI 301-496-5248
Lens....Staff NEI 301-496-5248
Lenses....Johnson, Christopher USITC 202-205-3488
Leprosy....Staff ALM International 800-537-7679
Leprosy....Staff NIAID 301-496-5717
Lesch-Nyhan Disease....Staff NIMH 301-443-4513
Lesch-Nyhan Disease....Staff NIDDK 301-496-3583
Lesch-Nyhan Disease....Staff NINDS 301-496-5751
Lesotho/Minerals....Mobbs, Philip Cnty Mines 202-501-9679
Lesotho (Maseru)....Staff Cnty State 202-647-8434
Lesotho....Barber, Ed Cnty Treasury 202-622-1730
Lesotho....Bulane, Eunice M. Cnty Embassy 202-797-5533
Lesotho....Holm-Olsen, Finn Cnty Commerce 202-482-4228
Lesotho....Jones, Donald Peace Corps 202-606-3246
Lesotho....Khabele, Moliehi Cnty Embassy 202-797-5534
Lesotho....Kohlman, Mark Peace Corps 202-606-3247
Lesotho....Lane, Bernard Cnty AID 202-647-4228
Lesotho....Maybury-Lewis, Anthony Cnty Export-Import Bank 202-565-3739
Lesotho....Patel, Praful C. Cnty World Bank 202-473-4250
Lesotho....Schwartz, Larry Cnty USIA 202-619-6904
Lesotho....Younge, Nathan Cnty TDA 703-875-4357
Letterer-Siwe Syndrome....Staff NHLBI 301-496-4236
Leukemia....Staff Leukemia Society of America 800-955-4572
Leukemia....Staff NCI 301-496-5583
Leukoaraiosis....Staff NINDS 301-496-5751
Leukodystrophy....Staff United Leukodystrophy Foundation 800-728-5483
Leukodystrophy....Staff NINDS 301-496-5751
Leukoencephalopathy....Staff NINDS 301-496-5751
Leukoplakia....Staff NIDR 301-496-4261
Levulose....Randall, Rob USITC 202-205-3366
Liberia/Minerals....Izon, David Cnty Mines 202-501-9674

Liberia (Monrovia)....Staff Cnty State 202-647-1658
Liberia....Blackett, Konah K. Cnty Embassy 202-723-0437
Liberia....Maybury-Lewis, Anthony Cnty Export-Import Bank 202-565-3739
Liberia....Michelini, Philip/Cerone, Chris Cnty Commerce 202-482-4388
Liberia....Morlu, John S. Cnty Embassy 202-723-0437
Liberia....O'Neal, Adrienne Cnty USIA 202-619-6904
Liberia....Palghat, Kathy Cnty Treasury 202-622-0332
Liberia....Wright, Minnie Cnty AID 202-647-8288
Liberia...Tallroth, Nils Borje Cnty World Bank 202-473-4876
Librarians Office....Staff NCRR/NIH 301-496-2447
Library (DCRT)....Staff DCRT 301-496-1658
Library (National Library of Medicine)....Staff NLM 301-496-6095
Library (NIH)....Staff NCRR/NIH 301-496-1156
Library Services....Staff NCRR/NIH Library 301-496-2447
Library Tours....Staff NCRR/NIH Library 301-496-1156
Library - Toxic Substances....Staff EPA 202-260-3944
Library....Staff CENSUS 301-763-5042
Libya/Minerals....Dolley, Thomas Cnty Mines 202-501-9690
Libya (Tripoli)....Staff Cnty State 202-647-4674
Libya....Clement, Claude Cnty Commerce 202-482-5545
Libya....Early, Evelyn Cnty USIA 202-619-6528
Libya....El Baroudy, Samia Cnty World Bank 202-473-2370
Libya....Hutchings, Dayna Cnty Export-Import Bank 202-565-3737
Libya....VanRenterghem, Cynthia Cnty Treasury 202-622-0343
Lice....Staff NIAID 301-496-5717
License Renewal....Newberry, Scott F. NRC 301-415-1183
Licenses-Cellular....Staff FCC 202-418-1320
Licenses (Common Carrier Mobile Services)....Staff FCC 202-418-1330
Licenses, Federal Permits....Staff FWS 703-358-2183
Lichen Planus....Staff NIAMS 301-496-8188
Lichen Planus....Staff NIDR 301-496-4261
Liechtenstein....Gosnell, Peter Cnty Export-Import Bank 202-565-3733
Liechtenstein....Staff Cnty State 202-647-1484
Life Cycle....Staff NIA 301-496-1752
Life Expectancy....Staff NIA 301-496-1752
Life Extension....Staff NIA 301-496-1752
Life Insurance and Health, Comp. and Working Cond.....Blostin, Allan LABOR 202-606-6240
Life on Other Planets....Staff NASA 415-604-3934
Life Review....Staff NIA 301-496-1752
Life Sciences Research....Staff NASA 713-438-5111
Lifeline....Staff FCC 202-418-0940
Light oil....Foreso, Cynthia USITC 202-205-3348
Light Water Reactor Safety....McGaff, David NEIC 301-903-5447
Lighting equipment....Cutchin, John USITC 202-205-3396
Lighting Fixtures....Kalkines, George CUSTOMS 212-466-5794
Ligninsulfonic acid and its salts....Land, Eric USITC 202-205-3349
Lignite....Foreso, Cynthia USITC 202-205-3348
Limb Lengthening....Staff NIAMS 301-496-8188
Lime....Miller, Michael MINES 202-501-9409
Lime....White, Linda USITC 202-205-3427
Limestone....White, Linda USITC 202-205-3427
Linear Accelerator....Staff NCI 301-496-5583
Linear Marketing....Staff FCC 214-235-3369
Link Up America....Staff FCC 202-418-0940
Lipid Research Clinics....Staff NHLBI 301-496-4236
Lipid Storage Diseases....Staff NINDS 301-496-5751
Lipid Transport Disorders....Staff NHLBI 301-496-4236
Lipidemia....Staff NHLBI 301-496-4236
Lipidosis....Staff NINDS 301-496-5751
Lipoma....Staff NIAMS 301-496-8188
Lipoproteins....Staff NHLBI 301-496-4236
Liquefied natural gas (LNG)....Land, Eric USITC 202-205-3349
Liquefied petroleum gas (LPG)....Land, Eric USITC 202-205-3349
Liquefied refinery gas (LRG)....Land, Eric USITC 202-205-3349
Liquid Metal Reactors (LMR)....Rosen, Sol NEIC 301-903-3218
Liquid purification....Dawson, Robert A. PTO 703-308-2340
Liquid Waste....Staff OD/ORS 301-496-2960
Liquid Waste (Radioactive)....Staff OD/ORS 301-496-2254
Lissencephaly....Staff NINDS 301-496-5751
Lister Hill Center....Staff NLM 301-496-6308
Listeriosis....Staff NIAID 301-496-5717
Literature of journalism....Paterson, Judith UMD 301-405-2425
Literature....Bradford, Gigi NEA 202-682-5451

Lithium compounds....Greenblatt, Jack USITC 202-205-3353
Lithium stearate....Randall, Rob USITC 202-205-3366
Lithium....Conant, Kenneth USITC 202-205-3346
Lithium....Ober, Joyce A. MINES 202-501-9406
Lithuania.....Levine, Richard Cnty Mines 202-501-9682
Lithuania....Altheim, Stephen Cnty Treasury 202-622-0125
Lithuania....Ann Lien Cnty TDA 703-875-4357
Lithuania....Edintas, Alfonsas, Cnty Embassy 202-234-5860
Lithuania....Lee, Barbara Wingate Cnty World Bank 202-473-7084
Lithuania....Paslauskas, Jonas Cnty Embassy 202-234-5860
Lithuania....Robinson, Susan Cnty USIA 202-619-6853
Lithuania....Staff Cnty State 202-647-5669
Lithuania....Viksnins, Helen Peace Corps 202-606-5517
Lithuania....Waxman-Lenz, Roberta Cnty Export-Import Bank 202-565-3742
Lithuania....Wooton, Nicholas Peace Corps....202-606-5519
Liver....Staff NIDDK 301-654-3810
Livestock - Cattle and Sheep....Gustafson, Ron Agri 202-219-0360
Livestock - Cattle....Groskurth, Dean Agri 202-720-3040
Livestock Damage Control....Staff FWS 703-358-1718
Livestock - Hogs....Fuchs, Doyle Agri 202-720-3106
Livestock - Hogs....Reed, Steve Agri 202-219-0828
Livestock - Sheep....Simpson, Linda Agri 202-720-3578
Livestock - World....Gustafson, Ron Agri 202-219-0360
Livestock - World....Shagam, Shayle Agri 202-219-0765
Living Arrangements, Population....Saluter, Arlene CENSUS 301-457-2465
LNG Plants (Major Proj)....Brandes, Jay COMMERCE 202-482-3352
Loa-loa....Staff NIAID 301-497-5717
Local Exchange Competition....Staff FCC 202-418-1595
Local Government Radio....Staff FCC 717-337-1212
Local Market Agreements....Staff FCC 202-418-1680
Locked-In Syndrome....Staff NINDS 301-496-5751
Locks and Keys....Staff OD/ORS/Locksmith 301-496-3507
Locks....Cuomo, Peter PTO 703-308-0827
Locks....Smyth, James CUSTOMS 212-466-2084
Loeffler's Syndrome....Staff NIAID 301-496-5717
Logs, rough....Hoffmeier, Bill USITC 202-205-3321
Logs, Wood....Wise, Barbara COMMERCE 202-482-0375
Long-Term Care and Alternatives....Hardy, Robert HCFA 202-690-6145
Longevity (Statistics)....Staff NIA 301-496-1752
Longevity (Statistics)....Staff NCHS 301-436-8500
Longitudinal Data/Gross Flows, Empl/Unempl. Stats.....Horvath, Francis LABOR 202-606-6345
Lotteries....Staff FCC 202-418-1430
Lou Gehrig's Disease....Staff NINDS 301-496-5751
Loud Commercials Enforcement....Staff FCC 202-418-1430
Loudspeakers....Puffert, Douglas USITC 202-205-3402
Low Back Pain (Sciatica)....Staff NINDS 301-496-5751
Low Back Pain....Staff NIAMS 301-496-8188
Low Birth Weight....Staff NICHD 301-496-5133
Low Blood Pressure....Staff NHLBI 301-496-4236
Low-Density Lipoproteins (LDL)....Staff NHLBI 301-496-4236
Low Energy Nuclear Research....Hendrie, David NEIC 301-426-1698
Low fuming brazing rods....Lundy, David USITC 202-205-3439
Low-Income Weatherization Assistance....Staff NEIC 202-586-2204
Low Vision Aids....Staff NEI 301-496-5248
Lowe Syndrome (Oculocerebrorenal)....Staff NICHD 301-496-5133
Lowe's Syndrome....Staff NEI 301-496-5248
Lowest Unit Charge....Staff FCC 202-418-1440
LPTV-Application Status...Staff FCC 202-1650
LPTV-Assignments....Staff FCC 202-418-1650
LPTV-Lotteries....Staff FCC 202-418-1640
LPTV-Renewals....Staff FCC 202-418-1640
LPTV-Sales....Staff FCC 202-418-1650
LPTV-Technical....Staff FCC 202-418-1640
LSD....Staff NIDA 301-443-6245
Lube fittings....Fravel, Dennis USITC 202-205-3404
Lubricating oil....Foreso, Cynthia USITC 202-205-3348
Lubricating grease....Foreso, Cynthia USITC 202-205-3348
Luggage....Byron, James E. COMMERCE 202-482-4034
Luggage....Gorman, Kevin CUSTOMS 212-466-5893
Luggage....Seastrum, Carl USITC 202-205-3493
Lumber with options....Rosenfeld, Donald CFT 312-353-9026
Lumber....Hoffmeier, Bill USTIC 202-205-3321
Lumber....Wise, Barbara COMMERCE 202-482-0375

Lunar Landing Research Vehicle....Hunley, Dil NASA 805-358-3447
Lunar Landing Research Vehicle....Martin, Cam NASA 805-258-3448
Lunar Samples Research....Staff NASA 713-483-5111
Lung Cancer....Staff NCI 301-496-5583
Lung Disease (Asbestosis)....Staff NIEHS 919-541-3345
Lung Disease (Infectious/Allergenic)....Staff NIAID 301-496-5717
Lung Disease (Non-infec., Non-aller., Non-tumor.)....Staff NHLBI 301-496-4236
Lung Disease (Tumorous/Cancerous)....Staff NCI 301-496-5583
Lupus Erythematosus....Staff NIAID 301-496-5717
Lupus Erythematosus....Staff NINDS 301-496-5751
Lupus Erythematosus....Staff NIAMS 301-496-8188
Lupus....Staff American Lupus Society 800-331-1802
Lupus....Staff Lupus Foundation of America 800-558-0121
Luxembourg (Luxembourg)....Staff Cnty State 202-647-6557
Luxembourg/Minerals....Zajac, William Cnty Mines 202-501-9671
Luxembourg....Bensimon, Simon Cnty Commerce 202-482-5401
Luxembourg....Berns, Alphonse Cnty Embassy 202-265-4171
Luxembourg....Gosnell, Peter Cnty Export-Import Bank 202-565-3733
Luxembourg....Holloway, Barbara Cnty Treasury 202-622-0098
Luxembourg....Kulla, Morgan Cnty USIA 202-619-6853
Luxembourg....Munchen, Jean-Paul Cnty Embassy 202-265-4171
Lyme Arthritis/Lyme Disease....Staff NIAMS 301-496-8188
Lyme Arthritis/Lyme Disease....Staff NIAID 301-496-5717
Lyme disease....Staff Lyme Disease Foundation 800-886-5963
Lymphadenopathy Syndrome (LAD)....Staff NIAID 301-496-5717
Lymphangiomyomatosis....Staff NHLBI 301-496-4236
Lymphedema....Staff National Lymphedema Network 800-541-3259
Lymphedema....Staff NCI 301-496-5583
Lymphoblastic Lymphosarcoma....Staff NCI 301-496-5583
Lymphocytopenia....Staff NHLBI 301-496-4236
Lymphoma....Staff NCI 301-496-5583
Lymphosarcoma....Staff NCI 301-496-5583

M

Macao/trade matters....Cantilina, Amy US Trade Rep 202-395-5050
Macao....Hutchings, Dayna Cnty Export-Import Bank 202-565-3737
Macao....Matheson, JeNelle Cnty Commerce 202-482-2462
Macaroni and other alimentary pastes....Schneider, Greg USITC 202-205-3326
Macau....Staff Cnty State 202-647-6300
Macedonia....Corwin, Elizabeth Cnty USIA 202-619-5055
Macedonia....Jackson, Juhan Cnty Treasury 202-622-0766
Macedonia....Kraske, Huda Cnty World Bank 202-473-3564
Macedonia....Staff Cnty State 202-647-0757
Macedonia....Steblez, Walter Cnty Mines 202-501-9672
Macedonia....Waxman-Lenz, Roberta Cnty Export-Import Bank 202-565-3742
Machine Belts and Clothing....Barth, George CUSTOMS 212-466-5884
Machine-readable Data, Labor Force Data, Empl/Unempl....Green, Gloria LABOR 202-606-6376
Machine Tool Accessories....Abrahams, Edward COMMERCE 202-482-0312
Machinery, Agricultural....Wholey, Patrick CUSTOMS 212-466-5668
Machinery, Excavating....Wholey, Patrick CUSTOMS 212-466-5668
Machinery, Heavy Industrial....Horowitz, Alan CUSTOMS 212-466-5494
Machinery Industry Group....Duvall, Steven SEC 202-942-1950
Machinery, International Price Indexes, Prices and Liv. Cond....Costello, Brian LABOR 202-606-7107
Machinery, International Price Indexes....Costello, Brian LABOR 202-606-7107
Machinery, Office and Textile....Brodbeck, Arthur CUSTOMS 212-466-5490
Machinery, Prices and Living Conditions....Alterman, William LABOR 202-606-7108
Machinery, Printing....Francke, Eric CUSTOMS 212-466-5669
Machinery....Amernick, Marvin Customs 202-482-7030
Machines: agricultural or horticultural....Fravel, Dennis USITC 202-205-3404
Machines and machinery: adding....Baker, Scott USITC 202-205-3386
Machines and machinery: addressing....Baker, Scott USITC 202-205-3386
Machines and machinery: agglomerating....Greene, William USITC 202-205-3405
Machines and machinery: agricultural or horticultural....Fravel, Dennis USITC 202-205-3404
Machines: bookbinding....Lusi, Susan USITC 202-205-2334
Machines: calculators....Baker, Scott USITC 202-205-3386
Machines: cash registers....Baker, Scott USITC 202-205-3386
Machines: casting machines....Greene, William USITC 202-205-3405
Machines: checkwriting....Baker, Scott USITC 202-205-3386
Machines: cleaning (heat process equipment)....Lusi, Susan USITC 202-205-2334

Malta....Borg Oliver De Puget, Albert Cnty Embassy 202-462-3611
Malta....Emmett, Annemarie Peace Corps 202-606-3196
Malta....Gosnell, Peter Cnty Export-Import Bank 202-565-3733
Malta....Grima Baldacchino, Vanessa Cnty Embassy 202-462-3612
Malta....Jill Bezek Cnty TDA 703-875-4357
Malta....McLaughlin, Robert Cnty Commerce 202-482-3748
Malta....Santoro, Eugene Cnty USIA 202-619-6582
Malta....Schildwachter, Christy Peace Corps 202-606-3196
Malta....VanRenterghem, Cynthia Cnty Treasury 202-622-0343
Malta....Vaurs, Rene Cnty World Bank 202-473-5034
Malts....Pierre-Benoist, John USITC 202-205-3320
Mammals, Marine....Staff FWS 703-358-1718
Mammography....Staff NCI 301-496-5583
Management consulting....Chittum, J. Marc COMMERCE 202-482-0345
Management consulting services....DeSapio, Vincent USITC 202-205-3435
Manganese compounds....Greenblatt, Jack USITC 202-205-3334
Manganese....Fulcher, Nancy USITC 202-205-3434
Manganese....Jones, Thomas S. MINES 202-501-9428
Manganese....Presbury, Graylin COMMERCE 202-482-5158
Mania....Staff NIMH 301-443-4513
Manifold Business Forms....Bratland, Rose Marie COMMERCE 202-482-0380
Manmade fiber....Dulka, William COMMERCE 202-482-4058
Manmade fibers....Freund, Kimberlie USITC 202-205-3456
Manmade fibers....Shelton, Linda USITC 202-205-3457
Manmade fibers....Warlick, William USITC 202-205-3459
Manned Flight....Phelps, Patti NASA 407-867-4444
Mantles....Vacant USITC 202-205-3343
Manufacturers, Nondurables....Zampogna, Michael CENSUS 301-457-4810
Manufacturers Operations Division....Staff EPA 202-233-9240
Manufacturers, Prod Data, Nondurables, Census/Annual Svy....Zampogna, Michael CENSUS 301-457-4810
Manufacturers, Prod Data, Durables, Census/Annl Svy....Hansen, Kenneth CENSUS 301-457-4755
Manufacturers, Prod Data, Nondurables, Cur Indrl Rp....Flood, Thomas CENSUS 301-457-2589
Manufacturers, Special Topics, Concentration....Hait, Andy CENSUS 301-457-4769
Manufacturers, Special Topics, Inventories....Menth, Kathy CENSUS 301-457-4832
Manufacturers, Special Topics, Monthly Shipments....Menth, Kathy CENSUS 301-457-4832
Manufacturers, Special Topics, Orders....Menth, Kathy CENSUS 301-457-4832
Manufacturers, Special Topics, Pollution Abatement....Champion, Elinor CENSUS 301-457-4701
Manufacturers, Special Topics, Research/Develop Capa....Champion, Elinor CENSUS 301-457-4701
Manufacturing, Durables (Census/Annual Survey)....Hansen, Kenneth CENSUS 301-457-4755
Manufacturing Extension Partnership (MEP)....Nanzetta, Phil NIST 301-975-5020
Manufacturing Industry Group....Parratt, Shelley SEC 202-942-1840
Manufacturing Technology Centers....Carr, K NIST 301-975-4676
Maple Syrup Urine Disease....Staff NIDDK 301-496-3583
Maps, 1980 Census Map Orders....Baxter, Leila CENSUS 812-288-3192
Maps, 1990 Census....Staff CENSUS 301-457-4100
Maps, Cartographic Operations....Staff CENSUS 301-457-4100
Maps, Computer Mapping....Broome, Fred CENSUS 301-457-1056
Marble, breccia, and onyx....White, Linda USITC 202-205-3427
MARC (Minority Access to Research Careers)....Staff NIGMS 301-496-7301
Marfan's Syndrome....Staff NHLBI 301-496-4236
Marfan's Syndrome....Staff NEI 301-496-5248
Marfan's Syndrome....Staff NIAMS 301-496-8188
Margarine....Janis, William V. COMMERCE 202-482-2250
Marijuana (Effect on Glaucoma)....Staff NEI 301-496-5248
Marijuana (In Urine)....Staff NIDA 301-443-6245
Marine Inspections Investigations....Staff FCC 202-418-1170
Marine Insurance....Johnson, C. William COMMERCE 202-482-5012
Marine Investigation....Gibson, Larry USCG 202-267-1430
Marine Mammal Research....Staff FWS 703-358-1718
Marine Mammals....Staff FWS 703-358-1718
Marine Pollution Control....Staff EPA 202-260-8448
Marine Radio Exemptions....Staff FCC 202-418-0680
Marine Radio....Staff FCC 202-418-0680
Marine Recreational Equipment, Export Promo.....Beckham, Reginald COMMERCE 202-482-5478

Marine Resources....Kilbourne, James C. Justice 202-272-4421
Marine Safety Evaluation....Sheek, Steve USCG 202-267-1417
Marine Safety Center....Walsh, Thomas USCG 202-366-3877
Marine safety....Murtagh, Marjorie NTSB 202-382-6860
Marine Services....Staff FCC 717-337-1212
Marital Characteristics of Labor Force....Hayghe, Howard LABOR 202-606-6378
Marital Status....Saluter, Arlene CENSUS 301-457-2465
Maritime Services....Lahey, Kathleen USITC 202-205-3409
Maritime Shipping....Johnson, C. William COMMERCE 202-482-5012
Marker (Cancer)....Staff NCI 301-496-5583
Marketing Promo., Basic Ind.....Trafton, Donald R. COMMERCE 202-482-2493
Marketing Rules....Staff FCC 301-725-1585
Marketing....Gethers, Sandra Customs 202-482-6980
Marketing....Morin, Bernard A. UVA 804-924-3477
Marriage Statistics....Heuser, Robert CDC 301-436-8954
Mars Exploration....Ulrich, Peter B. NASA 202-358-0315
Marsh Land....Staff FWS 703-358-2043
Marshall Islands...Imam, Fahmila Cnty Export-Import Bank 202-565-3738
Marshall Islands...Shelton, Alison Cnty Treasury 202-622-0354
Marshall Islands...Davies, Irene Cnty World Bank 202-458-2481
Marshall Islands...Rahman, Talaat Cnty TDA 703-875-4357
Marshall Islands...Jefferson, Mary Peace Corps 202-606-1038
Marshall Islands, De Brum, Banny Cnty Embassy 202-234-5414
Marshall Islands....Kendall, Wilfred I Cnty Embassy 202-234-5414
Marshall Islands (Majuro)....Staff Cnty State 202-647-0108
Martinique/Minerals....Rabchevsky, George Cnty Mines 202-501-9670
Martinique (Fort-de-France)....Staff Cnty State 202-647-2620
Martinique....Brooks, Michelle Cnty Commerce 202-482-2527
Mary Woodard Lasker Center for Health, Education and Research....Staff 301-951-6700
Mass Layoff Statistics, Empl/Unempl. Stats.....Siegel, Lewis LABOR 202-606-6404
Mass Layoff Statistics, Employment/Unemployment....Siegel, Lewis LABOR 202-606-6404
Mass Layoffs, Employment Statistics....Siegel, Lewis LABOR 202-606-6404
Mass media and society....Stepp, Jr., Carl UMD 301-405-2428
Mass Spectrometers....Staff NCRR 301-594-7934
Mastectomy....Staff NCI 301-496-5583
Mastication....Staff NIDR 301-496-4261
Mastocytosis....Staff NIAID 301-496-5717
Matches....Johnson, Larry USITC 202-205-3351
Materials, Advanced....DeSapio, Vincent COMMERCE 202-482-3435
Materials Reliability....McHenry, H.I. NIST 303-497-3268
Maternal and Child Health....Vacant HRSA 301-443-3376
Maternal and Child Nutrition....Wong, Faye L. CDC 404-488-5099
Maternal Drug Use....Staff NIDA 301-443-6245
Maternity home....Staff Edna Gladney Center 800-452-3639
Mathematical Modeling....Staff DCRT 301-496-1121
Mattresses....Spalding, Josephine USITC 202-205-3498
Mauritania/Minerals....Michalski, Bernadette Cnty Mines 202-501-9699
Mauritania (Nouakchott)....Staff Cnty State 202-647-3407
Mauritania....Carrere, Noel Cnty World Bank 202-473-7213
Mauritania....Early, Evelyn Cnty USIA 202-619-6528
Mauritania....Hanson, Julie Peace Corps 202-606-3004
Mauritania....Iyahi, Ismail Ould Cnty Embassy 202-232-5700
Mauritania....McKoy, Ethel Cnty Treasury 202-622-0336
Mauritania....Posner, Mara Cnty Commerce 202-482-4388
Mauritania....Saulters, Willie Cnty AID 202-647-6039
Mauritania....Waxman-Lenz, Roberta Cnty Export-Import Bank 202-565-3742
Mauritania....Younge, Nathan Cnty TDA 703-875-4357
Mauritania...Diaw, Amadou Cnty Embassy 202-232-5700
Mauritius (Port Louis)....Staff Cnty State 202-647-6473
Mauritius/Minerals....Antonides, Lloyd Cnty Mines 202-501-9686
Mauritius....Akpa, Emmanuel Cnty World Bank 202-473-4367
Mauritius....Barber, Ed Cnty Treasury 202-622-0336
Mauritius....Dhalladoo, Israhyananda Cnty Embassy 202-244-1492
Mauritius....Imam, Fahmila Cnty Export-Import Bank 202-565-3738
Mauritius....Larsen, Mark Cnty USIA 202-619-4894
Mauritius....Neewoor, Anund Priyay Cnty Embassy 202-244-1491
Mauritius....Watkins, Chandra Cnty Commerce 202-482-4564
MBS resins....Misurelli, Denby USITC 202-205-3362
McArdle's Disease....Staff NICHD 301-496-5133
McArdle's Disease....Staff NIDDK 301-496-3583
McArdle's Disease....Staff NINDS 301-496-5751

Measles Encephalitis....Staff NINDS 301-496-5751

Measles Immunization....Staff CDC 404-639-8225

Measles....Staff NIAID 301-496-5717

Meat and Dairy Products....Conte, Ralph CUSTOMS 212-466-5759

Meat, inedible....Ludwick, David USITC 202-205-3329

Meat Products....William, Janis COMMERCE 202-482-2250

Meat....Staff Hotline Agriculture 800-535-4555

Mechanical and Aerospace Engineering....Jacobson, Ira D. UVA 804-924-6217

Mechanical Power Transmission Eqmt. Nec.....Reise, Richard COMMERCE 202-482-3489

Mechanical registers....Gellner, Michael L. PTO 703-308-1436

Mechanical safety....Staff CPSC 301-504-0580

Meconium Aspiration Syndrome....Staff NICHD 301-496-5133

Media Arts....O'Doherty, Brian NEA 202-682-5452

Media (Bacteriologic)....Staff OD/ORS 301-496-6017

Media Inquiries....Staff FCC 202-418-0500

Medic Alert....Staff Medic Alert Foundation 800-432-5378

Medicaid....Hardy, Robert HCFA 202-966-3206

Medicaid....Scanlon, William GAO 202-512-4561

Medical apparatus....Johnson, Christopher USITC 202-205-3488

Medical Care for Aged....Staff NIA 301-496-1752

Medical Devices....Cruzan, Susan FDA 301-443-3285

Medical Facilities, Major Proj.....Haraguchi, Wallace COMMERCE 202-482-4877

Medical Fraud/Quackery....Adams, Betsy FDA 301-443-4177

Medical Informatics....Staff NLM 301-496-9300

Medical Information System (MIS)....Staff CC 301-496-7946

Medical Instruments, Trade Promo.....Keen, George B. COMMERCE 202-482-2010

Medical Instruments....Fuchs, Michael COMMERCE 202-482-0550

Medical Instruments....Preston, Jacques CUSTOMS 212-466-5488

Medical materials....Tesk, John A. NIST 301-975-6799

Medical Nuclear Safety....Cool, Donald NRC 301-415-7197

Medical Photography....Staff NCRR/MAPB 301-496-5995

Medical School Grants....Staff HRSA 301-443-1433

Medical Scientist Training Program....Staff NIGMS 301-496-7301

Medical Specialists....Staff American Board of Medical Specialists 800-776-2378

Medical Staff Fellowship Training Program....Staff CC 301-496-2427

Medical Statistics....Flegal, Katherine CDC 301-436-7075

Medical Subject Headings....Schuyler, Peri L. NLM 301-496-1495

Medical Waste....Staff EPA 202-260-8551

Medical Waste....Staff EPA 202-260-8551

Medically Underserved Areas....Vacant HRSA 301-443-3376

Medicare....Hickman, Peter HCFA 202-690-5950

MEDICARE...Staff HCFA 800-638-6833

Medicine for the Public (Lect., Videos, Booklets)....Staff CC 301-496-2563

Medicine, Legal....Staff American College of Legal Medicine 800-433-9137

Medicine, National Library of...Lindberg, David 301-496-6221

Mediterranean Fever....Staff NIAMS 301-496-8188

Mediterranean Fever....Staff NIAID 301-496-5717

Mediterranean/trade matters....Marcich, Chris US Trade Rep 202-395-4620

Mediterranean/trade matters....Richards, Timothy US Trade Rep 202-395-3320

Mediterranean/trade matters....Jones, Chris US Trade Rep 202-395-3320

Mediterranean/trade matters....Marcich, Christopher US Trade Rep 202-395-4620

Medlars/Medline....Staff NLM 301-496-6193

Meige's Syndrome (Facial Dystonia)....Staff NIDCD 301-496-7243

Meige's Syndrome (Facial Dystonia)....Staff NINDS 301-496-5751

Melamine resins....Misurelli, Denby USITC 202-205-3362

Melamine....Michels, David USITC 202-205-3352

Melanoma....Staff NEI 301-496-5248

Melanoma....Staff NCI 301-496-5583

MELAS....Staff NINDS 301-496-5751

Melkerson's Syndrome....Staff NINDS 301-496-5751

Memory Loss....Staff NIA 301-496-1752

Memory....Staff NIMH 301-443-4513

Memory....Staff NINDS 301-496-5751

Meniere's Disease....Staff NINDS 301-496-5751

Meniere's Disease....Staff NIDCD 301-496-7243

Meningitis....Perkins, Bradley CDC 404-639-2215

Meningitis....Staff NIAID 301-496-5717

Meningitis....Staff NINDS 301-496-5751

Meningocele....Staff NICHD 301-496-5133

Meningocele....Staff NINDS 301-496-5751

Meningococcal Meningitis....Staff NIAID 301-496-5717

Menkes' Disease....Staff NINDS 301-496-5751

Menopause....Staff NIA 301-496-1752

Menstruation....Staff NICHD 301-496-5133

Mental Health and Aging....Staff NIA 301-496-1752

Mental Health and Aging....Staff NIMH 301-443-4513

Mental health....Baron, David A. FAES 301-496-4588

Mental Health....Staff American Mental Health Counselors Association 800-326-2642

Mental Health....Staff National Mental Health Association Information Center 800-969-6642

Mental Illness....Staff National Resource Center on Homelessness and Mental Illness 800-444-7415

Mental Retardation (PCMR)....Kharfen, Michael ACF 202-401-9215

Mental Retardation....Staff NICHD 301-496-5133

Mentally handicapped....Staff Devereux Foundation 800-345-1292

Menthol....Land, Eric USITC 202-205-3349

Mercury compounds....Greenblatt, Jack USITC 202-205-3353

Mercury, Fluorspar....Manion, James J. COMMERCE 202-482-5157

Mercury in Fish....Staff EPA 202-208-5634

Mercury Poisoning....Staff NINDS 301-496-5751

Mercury....Conant, Kenneth USITC 202-205-3346

Mercury....Jasinski, Stephen MINES 202-501-9418

Mergers and Acquisitions....Staff FCC 202-632-4887

Metabolic Disorders....Staff NIDDK 301-496-3583

Metabolic (Nervous System)....Staff NINDS 301-496-5751

Metabolism (Inborn Errors)....Staff NINDS 301-496-5751

Metabolism (Inborn Errors)....Staff NICHD 301-496-5133

Metachromatic Leukodystrophy....Staff NINDS 301-496-5751

Metal Articles....Birnbaum, Melvyn CUSTOMS 212-466-5487

Metal Building Products....Williams, Franklin COMMERCE 202-482-0132

Metal Cookware....Harris, John COMMERCE 202-482-0380

Metal Cutting Machine Tools....Bratland, Rosemarie COMMERCE 202-482-0380

Metal Cutting Tools Fr Mach Tools....Vacant COMMERCE

Metal Foils....Fitzgerald, John CUSTOMS 212-466-5492

Metal Forming Machine Tools...Pilaroscia, Megan COMMERCE 202-482-0609

Metal Metabolism....Staff NIDDK 301-496-3583

Metal Powders....Malos, Barbara COMMERCE 202-482-0606

Metal Producers Industry Group...Parratt, Shelley SEC 202-942-1840

Metal rolling mills....Fravel, Dennis USITC 202-205-3404

Metal working machines....Fravel, Dennis USITC 202-205-3404

Metallurgy-alloys....Sillbaugh, Jan H PTO 703-308-3829

Metallurgy Research....Thomas, Iran NEIC 301-903-3426

Metallurgy....Pugh, E.N. NIST 301-975-5960

Metallurgy....Pugh, E. Neville NIST 301-975-5960

Metals and Mining Industry Group....Tow, A. Richard SEC 202-942-1760

Metals, Assistant Branch Chief....Butterman, W. MINES 202-501-9425

Metals, Assistant Branch Chief....Sibley, S.F. MINES 202-501-9344

Metals, Chief, Branch of....Makar, Harry MINES 202-501-9432

Metals, Prices and Living Conditions....Kazanowski, Edward LABOR 202-606-7735

Metals, Secondary....Cammarota, David COMMERCE 202-482-5157

Metals....Amernick, Marvin Customs 202-482-7030

Metals....Fitzgerald, John CUSTOMS 212-466-5492

Metalworking Equipment Nec.....McGibbon, Patrick COMMERCE 202-482-0314

Metalworking....Pilarosca, Megan COMMERCE 202-482-0609

Metastases....Staff NCI 301-496-5583

Metastic Tumors (Central Nervous System)....Staff NINDS 301-496-5751

Meteorological instruments....Roth, Jordon USITC 202-205-3467

Meteorological Research....Staff John NASA 301-286-1584

Methacrylates....Michels, David USITC 202-205-3352

Methadone....Staff NIDA 301-443-6245

Methamphetamine and Heavy Metal Contamination....Staff NIDA 301-443-6245

Methane....Land, Eric USITC 202-205-3349

Methane....Moorer, Richard NEIC 202-586-9315

Methanol....Joseph, Stephanie CUSTOMS 212-466-5768

Methodology, Prices and Living Conditions....Rosenberg, Elliott LABOR 202-606-7728

Methyl alcohol (methanol)....Michels, David USITC 202-205-3352

Methyl ethyl ketone....Michels, David USITC 202-205-3352

Methyl oleate....Johnson, Larry USITC 202-205-3351

Methylene Chloride....Giles, Ken CPSC 301-504-0580

Metropolitan Areas (MSA's), Population....Fitzsimmons, James CENSUS 301-457-2422

Metropolitan Areas....Fitzsimmons, James CENSUS 301-457-2422

Mexican Affairs....Melle, John US Trade Rep 202-395-3412

Mexican Affairs....Amirthanayagam, Aruna US Trade Rep 202-395-3412

Mexico (Mexico, D.F.)....Staff Cnty State 202-647-9894

Mexico/Minerals....Heydari, Michael Cnty Mines 202-501-9688

Mexico/trade matters....Roh, Charles US Trade Rep 202-395-5663

Mexico....De Lara-Rangel, Salvador Cnty Embassy 202-728-1600

Mexico....Herzog, Jesus Silva Cnty Embassy 202-728-1600

Mexico....Hill, Derek Cnty Treasury 202-622-1269

Mexico....Prevot, Babette Cnty AID 202-647-4359

Mexico....Ricks, Shawn Cnty Commerce 202-482-0300

Mexico....Shumake, Josie Cnty USIA 202-619-5864

Mexico....Swannack-Nunn, Susan Cnty World Bank 202-458-2472

Mexico....Wilkins, Michele Cnty Export-Import Bank 202-565-3743

Mica....Hedrick, James MINES 202-501-9412

Mica....Presbury, Graylin COMMERCE 202-482-5158

Mica....White, Linda USITC 202-205-3427

Mice (Genetic Resource)....Staff NCRR 301-496-5255

Microanalysis Science....Velapoldi, RA NIST 301-975-3917

Microbiological Monitoring....Staff OD/ORS 301-496-2960

Microbiology....Garges, Susan FAES 301-496-1019

Microcephaly....Staff NINDS 301-496-5751

Microcephaly....Staff NICHD 301-496-5133

Micronesia....Imam, Fahmila Cnty Export-Import Bank 202-565-3738

Micronesia....Lukan, James Leo Cnty Embassy 202-223-4383

Micronesia....Marehalau, Jesse B. Cnty Embassy 202-223-4383

Micronesia....Shelton, Alison Cnty Treasury 202-622-0354

Micronesia....Staff Cnty State 202-647-0108

Microorganisms Control....Staff OD/ORS 301-496-2960

Microphones....Puffert, Douglas USITC 202-205-3402

Microscopes....Johnson, Christopher USITC 202-205-3488

Microtrach....Staff NHLBI 301-496-4236

Microtropia....Staff NEI 301-496-5248

Microvascular Angina....Staff NHLBI 301-496-4236

Microvascular Surgery....Staff NINDS 301-496-5751

Mid-America MTC (Manufacturing Technology Center)....Clay, Paul E. NIST 913-649-4333

Middle East/trade matters....Jones, Chris US Trade Rep 202-395-3320

Middle East....Jones, Walter OPIC 202-336-8654

Middle Ear Infections....Staff NINDS 301-496-5751

Middle Ear Infections....Staff NIDCD 301-496-7243

Midwest MTC (Manufacturing Technology Center)....Taback, Michael NIST 313-769-4377

Migraine (Headache)....Staff NINDS 301-496-5751

Migrant Health....Shaffer, Sylvia HRSA 301-443-3376

Migration, Current Statistics....Hansen, Kristin CENSUS 301-457-2454

Migratory Bird Research....Staff FWS 703-358-1713

Mild Retardation Prevention.... CDC 404-488-7370

Military Lands, Wildlife....Staff FWS 703-358-1718

Military Operations....Gebicke, Mark E. GAO 202-512-5140

Milk Intolerance....Staff NIDDK 301-654-3810

Milk....Ludwick, David USITC 202-205-3329

Millinery ornaments....Spalding, Josephine USITC 202-205-3498

Millwork....Williams, Franklin COMMERCE 202-482-0132

Minamata Disease (Mercury Poisoning)....Staff NINDS 301-496-5751

Mineral Based Cons. Materials, Asphalt....Pitcher, Charles B. COMMERCE 202-482-0132

Mineral Based Const. Mats., Clay....Pitcher, Charles B. COMMERCE 202-482-0132

Mineral Based Const. Mats., Concrete....Pitcher, Charles B. COMMERCE 202-482-0132

Mineral Based Cons. Mats., Gypsum....Pitcher, Charles B. COMMERCE 202-482-0132

Mineral Based Cons. Mats., Stone....Pitcher, Charles B. COMMERCE 202-482-0132

Mineral Industries....Horning, Patricia CENSUS 301-457-4680

Mineral Metabolism....Staff NIDDK 301-496-3583

Mineral oil....Foreso, Cynthia USITC 202-205-3348

Mineral salts....Randall, Rob USITC 202-205-3366

Mineral substances, miscellaneous....Lundy, David USITC 202-205-3439

Mineral wool....White, Linda USITC 202-205-3427

Minerals (and Vitamins)....Staff NHLBI 301-496-4236

Minerals in the World Economy/Minerals....Kimbell, Charles Cnty Mines 202-501-9659

Minerals, Non-Metallic....Bunin, Jacob CUSTOMS 212-566-5796

Minimal Brain Dysfunction....Staff NINDS 301-496-5751

Minimal Brain Dysfunction....Staff NIMH 301-443-4513

Minimum Wage Data, Empl/Unempl. Stats.....Haugen, Steve LABOR 202-606-6378

Minimum Wage Data, Employment/Unemployment....Haugen, Steve LABOR 202-606-6378

Mining Industry Group....Tow, A. Richard SEC 202-942-1760

Mining Machinery, Trade Promo....Zanetakos, George COMMERCE 202-482-0552

Mining Machinery....McDonald, Edward COMMERCE 202-482-0680

Mining machines....Polly, Laura USITC 202-205-3408

Mining....Polly, Laura USITC 202-205-3408

Mining....Staff FCC 717-337-1212

Mink....Kruchten, Tom Agri 202-690-4870

Minorities (Drug Data)....Staff NIDA 301-443-6245

Minorities, Empl./ Unempl. Stats.....Cattan, Peter LABOR 202-606-6378

Minority Access to Research Careers (MARC)....Staff NIGMS 301-496-7301

Minority Aging....Staff NIA 301-496-1752

Minority Biomedical Research Support (MBRS)....Staff NIGMS 301-496-7301

Minority Health....Simpson, Clay E. ASH 301-443-5084

Minority Health....Staff Minority Health Resource Center 800-444-6472

Minority High School Student Research Apprentices....Staff NCRR 301-594-7947

Minority Institutions Program....Staff NCRR 301-594-7944

Minority Owned Businesses....Strang, Valerie CENSUS 301-763-5726

Minority Ownership Policies....FCC 202-418-2130

Mirror Fusion Systems....Brewer, Robert NEIC 202-586-2828

Misarticulation....Staff NIDCD 301-496-7243

Miscellaneous animal products....Ludwick, David USITC 202-205-3329

Miscellaneous articles of pulp and paper....Rhodes, Richard USITC 202-205-3322

Miscellaneous benzenoid intermediates....Matusik, Ed USITC 202-205-3356

Miscellaneous fish products....Corey, Roger USITC 202-205-3327

Miscellaneous products....Spalding, Josephine USITC 202-205-3498

Miscellaneous Reimbursable....Godoy, Francisco FTC 202-326-3757

Miscellaneous Textile and Related Articles....Gualario, Vito CUSTOMS 212-466-5886

Miscellaneous vegetable products....Pierre-Benoist, John USITC 202-205-3320

Miscellaneous wood products....Hoffmeier, Bill USITC 202-205-3321

Misconduct (Scientific)....Staff OASH/ORI 301-443-3400

Missing Children....Staff Kevin Collins Foundation for Missing Children 800-272-0012

Missing Children....Staff Missing Children Help Center 800-875-5437

Mitochondrial Myopathies....Staff NINDS 301-496-5751

Mitral Valve....Staff NHLBI 301-496-4236

Mixed Connective Tissue Disease....Staff NIAMS 301-496-8188

Mixtures (artificial) of fatty substances....Randall, Rob USITC 202-205-3366

Mixtures of inorganic compounds....Greenblatt, Jack USITC 202-205-3353

Mixtures of organic compounds....Michels, David USITC 202-205-3352

Mobile Homes....Cosslett, Patrick COMMERCE 202-482-5125

Mobius Syndrome...Staff NINDS 301-496-5751

Moccasins....Shildneck, Ann USITC 202-205-3499

Model Airplanes....Staff FCC 717-337-1212

Model Rocket Motors....Staff CPSC 301-504-0580

Models (Animal)....Staff NCRR 301-594-7933

Models (Mathematical)....Staff NCRR 301-496-5771

Models (Non-Mammalian)....Staff NCRR 301-594-7906

Models (Radio Controlled)-Cars....Staff FCC 202-418-0680

Models (Radio Controlled)-Planes....Staff FCC 202-418-0680

Models....Abrahamson, Dana USITC 202-205-3430

Modular High Temperature Reactors....Rosen, Sol NEIC 301-903-1642

Molasses....Vacant USITC 202-205-3454

Molders' boxes, forms, and patterns....Greene, William USITC 202-205-3405

Molding....Francke, Eric CUSTOMS 212-466-5669

Molding....Woo, Jay PTO 703-308-3793

Moldings, wooden....Hoffmeier, Bill USITC 202-205-3321

Moldova....Leanca, Iurie Cnty Embassy 202-783-3012

Moldova....Levine, Richard Cnty Mines 202-501-9682

Moldova....McCleod, Evelyn Cnty AID 202-736-7646

Moldova....Rebecca Respess Cnty TDA 703-875-4357

Moldova....Ruhl, Omno Cnty World Bank 202-458-9119

Moldova....Skipper, Thomas Cnty USIA 202-619-5057

Moldova....Staff Cnty State 202-647-8671

Moldova...Tau, Nicolae Cnty Embassy 202-783-3012

Moldova...Carlen, James Cnty Treasury 202-622-0122

Moldova...Waxman-Lenz, Roberta Cnty Export-Import Bank 202-565-3742

Molecular Beam Epitaxy....Comas, James NIST 301-975-2061

Molecular Biology....Davies, David R. FAES 301-496-4295
Molecular Biology....Staff NIGMS 301-496-7301
Molecular Biology....Staff NIDA 301-443-6245
Molecular Cardiology....Adelstein, Robert S. FAES 301-496-1865
Molecular Genetics....Staff NIGMS 301-496-7301
Molecular Pharmacology....Kohn, Kurt W. FAES 301-496-5941
Molecular Physics....Suenram, R. NIST 301-975-2377
Molybdenum compounds....Greenblatt, Jack USITC 202-205-3932
Molybdenum....Blossom, John MINES 202-501-9435
Molybdenum....DeSapio, Vincent USITC 202-205-3435
Molybdenum....Presbury, Graylin COMMERCE 202-482-5158
Monaco....Staff Cnty State 202-647-2633
Money Laundering.....Greenberg, Theodore S. Justice 202-514-1758
Mongolia/Minerals....Wu, John Cnty Mines 202-501-9697
Mongolia/trade matters....Cantilina, Amy US Trade Rep 202-395-5050
Mongolia....Dawagiv, Luvsandorj Cnty Embassy 202-333-7117
Mongolia....Frye, Lisa Peace Corps 202-606-0970
Mongolia....Hahm, Hongjoo J. Cnty World Bank 202-458-2346
Mongolia....Howell, Charles Cnty AID 202-647-4515
Mongolia....Huston, Christine Peace Corps 202-606-0970
Mongolia....Hutchings, Dayna Cnty Export-Import Bank 202-565-3737
Mongolia....Narankuu, Khalzhuu Cnty Embassy 202-333-7117
Mongolia....Respess, Rebecca Cnty TDA 703-875-4357
Mongolia....Schneider, Todd Cnty Treasury 202-622-0335
Mongolia....Staff Cnty State 202-647-6300
Mongolia....Vacant Cnty Commerce 202-482-2462
Mongolism (Down Syndrome)....Staff NICHD 301-496-5133
Monitoring Station Protection....Staff FCC 202-418-1210
Monoclonal Gammopathy....Staff NHLBI 301-496-4236
Monofilaments, manmade....Shelton, Linda USITC 202-205-3457
Mononucleosis....Staff NIAID 301-496-5717
Monorails....Wiening, Mary COMMERCE 202-482-4708
Monosodium glutamate....Land, Eric USITC 202-205-3349
Monserrat/Minerals....Rabchevsky, George Cnty Mines 202-501-9670
Monthly Labor Review, Exec. Ed., Public and Spec Stud....Fisher, Robert W. LABOR 202-606-5903
Monthly Product Announcement....Kilbride, Mary CENSUS 301-457-1221
Montserrat....Brooks, Michelle Cnty Commerce 202-482-2527
Moon Exploration....Keegan, Sarah NASA 703-271-5591
Morocco/Minerals....Dolley, Thomas Cnty Mines 202-501-9690
Morocco (Rabat)....Staff Cnty State 202-647-4675
Morocco....Benaissa, Mohamed Cnty Embassy 202-462-7979
Morocco....Clement, Claude/Cerone, Chris Cnty Commerce 202-482-2527
Morocco....Early, Evelyn Cnty USIA 202-619-6528
Morocco....Emmett, Annemarie Peace Corps 202-606-3196
Morocco....Imam, Fahmila Cnty Export-Import Bank 202-565-3738
Morocco....Mandel, Pamela Cnty AID 202-663-2617
Morocco....Schildwachter, Christy Peace Corps 202-606-3196
Morocco....Schneider, Todd Cnty Treasury 202-622-0335
Morocco....Stillwell, Carol Cnty TDA 703-875-4357
Morocco....Tourougui, Abdelhamid Cnty Embassy 202-462-7982
Morocco....Vaurs, Rene Cnty World Bank 202-473-5034
Mortality Rates (Cancer)....Staff NCI 301-496-5583
Mortality Statistics....Rosenbery, Harry CDC 301-436-8884
Mortgage Backed Securities....Lang, Dawn M. CFT 312-353-9018
Mortgages Industry Group....Roycroft, John C. SEC 202-942-1960
Motion pictures....Gellner, Michael L. PTO 703-308-1436
Motion pictures....R-Archila, Laura USITC 202-205-3411
Motion Pictures....Seigmund, John COMMERCE 202-482-4781
Motion Sickness....Staff NIDCD 301-496-7243
Motor Carrier Standards....Scapellato, James E FHWA 202-366-1790
Motor Carrier....Staff FCC 717-337-1212
Motor Carriers....Rea, Samuel W P FHWA 202-366-1724
Motor control systems....Shoop, William M. PTO 703-308-3103
Motor Fuels, Only, Avg. Ret. Prices and Indexes....Chelena, Joseph LABOR 202-606-6982
Motor Neuron Disease....Staff NINDS 301-496-5751
Motor oil....Foreso, Cynthia USITC 202-205-3348
Motor transportation services....Lahey, Kathleen USITC 202-205-3409
Motor vehicle bodies....Mitchell, David PTO 703-308-0361
Motor vehicle wheels....Mitchell, David PTO 703-308-0361
Motor vehicles: armored vehicles....Polly, Laura USITC 202-205-3408
Motor Vehicles Auto Ind. Affairs....Warner, Albert COMMERCE 202-482-0669
Motor vehicles: buses....Hagey, Michael USITC 202-205-3392

Motor vehicles: fork-lift/self-propelled trucks....Hagey, Michael USITC 202-205-3392
Motor vehicles: passenger autos....Hagey, Michael USITC 202-205-3392
Motor vehicles: snowmobiles....Polly, Laura USITC 202-205-3408
Motor vehicles: tractors, extruck tractors....Fravel, Dennis USITC 202-205-3404
Motor vehicles: trucks (includes truck tractors)....Hagey, Michael USITC 202-205-3392
Motor vehicles....Focarino, Margaret PTO 703-308-0885
Motor vehicles....Kashnikow, Andres PTO 703-308-1137
Motor Vehicles....Warner, Albert T. COMMERCE 202-482-0669
Motorcycles....Desoucey, Robert CUSTOMS 212-466-5667
Motorcycles....Topolansky, Adam USITC 202-205-3394
Motorcycles....Vanderwolf, John COMMERCE 202-482-0348
Motors: electric....Bodson, John COMMERCE 202-482-0681
Motors: electric....Cutchin, John USITC 202-205-3396
Motors: non-electric....Andersen, Peder USITC 202-205-3388
Motors....Smyth, James CUSTOMS 212-466-2084
Movement Disorders....Staff NINDS 301-496-5751
Moya-Moya Disease....Staff NINDS 301-496-5751
Mozambique (Maputo)....Staff Cnty State 202-647-8433
Mozambique/Minerals....van Oss, Hendrik Cnty Mines 202-501-9687
Mozambique....Cossa, Berta Celestino Cnty Embassy 202-293-7146
Mozambique....Holm-Olsen, Finn Cnty Commerce 202-482-4228
Mozambique....Imam, Fahmila Cnty Export-Import Bank 202-565-3738
Mozambique....Mendelson, Deborah Cnty AID 202-647-2965
Mozambique....Patricio, Hipolito Periera Zozimo 202-293-7146
Mozambique....Pomerantz, Phyllis R. Cnty World Bank 202-473-7170
Mozambique....Rauch, Margie Cnty Treasury 202-622-0251
Mozambique....Schwartz, Larry Cnty USIA 202-619-6904
MPTP (New Heroin)....Staff NIDA 301-443-6245
Mucolipidoses....Staff NINDS 301-496-5751
Mucopolysacchardios....Staff NINDS 301-496-5751
Mucopolysacchardios....Staff NIDDK 301-496-3583
Mucopolysacchardiosis....Staff NIAMS 301-496-8188
Mufflers (apparel)....Hamey, Amy USITC 202-205-3465
Mufflers (apparel)....Jones, Jackie USITC 202-205-3466
Multi-Infarct Dementia....Staff NIA 301-496-1752
Multi-Infarct Dementia....Staff NINDS 301-496-5751
Multifactor Productivity, Labor Composition, Hrs.....Rosenblum, Larry LABOR 202-606-5606
Multifamily Housing....Staff HUD 202-708-2495
Multilateral trade negotiations....Lavoral, Warren US Trade Rep 202-395-3324
Multiple Basal Cell Carcinoma....Staff NCI 301-496-5583
Multiple Myeloma....Staff NCI 301-496-5583
Multiple Ownership Rules Radio....Staff FCC 202-418-2780
Multiple Ownership Rules TV....Staff FCC 202-418-1630
Multiple Personality Disorder...Staff NIMH 301-443-4513
Multiple Risk Factor Intervention Trial....Staff NHLBI 301-496-4236
Multiple Sclerosis....Staff NINDS 301-496-5751
Multiple Sclerosis....Staff NMSS 800-344-4867
Multiple Sclerosis....Staff NIDCD 301-496-7243
Multiple Warts....Staff NCI 301-496-5583
Multiplex communications....Olms, Douglas W. PTO 703-305-4703
Multiply-handicapped children....Staff Heartspring 800-835-1043
Mumps....Staff NIAID 301-496-5717
Munchausen's Syndrome...Staff NIMH 301-443-4513
Muni Bonds with options....SIA Manasses CFT 312-35-39027
Municipal Solid Waste Management....Staff EPA 703-308-7258
Municipal Solid Waste Management - Combustion....Staff EPA 703-308-8254
Municipal Waste....Sisson, Kurt D. NEIC 202-586-6750
Murmurs (Heart)....Staff NHLBI 301-496-4236
Muscle Disorders....Staff NINDS 301-496-5751
Muscle Disorders....Staff NIAMS 301-496-8188
Muscle Wasting....Staff NIAMS 301-496-8188
Muscle Wasting....Staff NINDS 301-496-5751
Muscular Atrophy....Staff NINDS 301-496-5751
Muscular Atrophy....Staff NIAMS 301-496-8188
Muscular Dystrophy....Staff NINDS 301-496-5751
Muscular Fatigue....Staff NINDS 301-496-5751
Musculoskeletal Fitness....Staff NIAMS 301-496-8188
Museums and Historic Orgns. Projects....Staff NEH 202-606-8284
Museum of Medical Research....Staff OD/OC 301-496-6610
Mushrooms....McCarty, Timothy USITC 202-205-3324
Music....Gellner, Michael L. PTO 703-308-1436

Music....Handy, D. Antoinette NEA 202-682-5445
Music....Siegmund, John COMMERCE 202-482-4781
Musical instruments, accessories....Witherspoon, Ricardo USITC 202-205-3489
Musical instruments, parts....Witherspoon, Ricardo USITC 202-205-3489
Musical Instruments....Kalkines, George CUSTOMS 212-466-5794
Musical Instruments....Harris, John COMMERCE 202-482-1178
Musk, grained or in pods....Land, Eric USITC 202-205-3349
Mutual Funds....Muir, S. Cassin COMMERCE 202-482-0349
Mutual Recognition Agreements....Staff FCC 301-725-1585
Myanmar....Brideau-Hall, Rebecca Cnty World Bank 202-458-0517
Myanmar....Imam, Fahmila Cnty Export-Import Bank 202-565-3738
Myanmar....Sein, Paw Lwin Cnty Embassy 202-332-9045
Myanmar....U Thaung, Daw May Kyi Sein Cnty Embassy 202-332-9044
Myasthenia Gravis....Staff Myasthenia Gravis 800-541-5454
Myasthenia Gravis....Staff NINDS 301-496-5751
Mycobacterial Infections....Staff NIAID 301-496-5717
Mycoplasma....Staff NIAID 301-496-5717
Mycosis Fungoides....Staff NCI 301-496-5583
Mycotoxins....Staff NIEHS 919-541-3345
Myelodysplastic Syndromes....Staff NCI 301-496-5583
Myelodysplastic Syndromes....Staff NHLBI 301-496-4236
Myelofibrosis....Staff NHLBI 301-496-4236
Myelofibrosis....Staff NCI 301-496-5583
Myeloma....Staff NCI 301-496-5583
Myeloproliferative Disorders....Staff NHLBI 301-496-4236
Myocardial Infarction....Staff NHLBI 301-496-4236
Myocardium....Staff NHLBI 301-496-4236
Myoclonus....Staff NINDS 301-496-5751
Myofascial Pain Syndrome....Staff NIAMS 301-496-8188
Myopia....Staff NEI 301-496-5248
Myositis Ossificans....Staff NIAMS 301-496-8188
Myositis....Staff NIAMS 301-496-8188
Myositis....Staff NINDS 301-496-5751
Myotonia Atrophica....Staff NINDS 301-496-5751
Myotonia Atrophica....Staff NIAMS 301-496-8188
Myotonia Congenita....Staff NINDS 301-496-5751
Myotonia Congenita....Staff NIAMS 301-496-8188
Myotonia Congenita....Staff NICHD 301-496-5133
Myotonia Dystrophica....Staff NINDS 301-496-5751
Myotonia....Staff NIAMS 301-496-8188
Myths on Aging....Staff NIA 301-496-1752

N

NAFTA....Reba, Maria Customs 202-927-1488
Nails....Yost, Charles USITC 202-205-3442
Naltrexone....Staff NIDA 301-443-6245
Namibia/Minerals....Heydari, Michael Cnty Mines 202-501-9688
Namibia....Bezek, Jill Cnty TDA 703-875-4357
Namibia....Daniels, Gussie Cnty AID 202-647-4328
Namibia....Holm-Olsen, Finn Cnty Commerce 202-482-4228
Namibia....Isaack, Japhet Cnty Embassy 202-986-0540
Namibia....Jones, Donald Peace Corps 202-606-3246
Namibia....Kohlman, Mark Peace Corps 202-606-3247
Namibia....Kolomoh, Tuliameni Cnty Embassy 202-986-0540
Namibia....Maybury-Lewis, Anthony Cnty Export-Import Bank 202-565-3739
Namibia....Patel, Praful C. Cnty World Bank 202-473-4250
Namibia....Rauch, Margie Cnty Treasury 202-622-0251
Namibia....Schwartz, Larry Cnty USIA 202-619-6904
Namibia....Staff Cnty State 202-647-9429
Naphtha....Foreso, Cynthia USITC 202-205-3348
Naphthalene (refined)....Matusik, Ed USITC 202-205-3356
Napkins, cloth....Sweet, Mary Elizabeth USITC 202-205-3455
Narcolepsy....Staff NINDS 301-496-5751
Narcotics....Van Vliet, Theresa Justice 202-514-0917
Narrow fabrics....Shelton, Linda USITC 202-205-3457
NASA Engineering....Rachul, Lori NASA 216-433-8806
NASA Innovation....Paules, Granville NASA 202-358-0706
NASA Mission Safety....Brown, Dwayne C. NASA 202-358-1726
NASA Science and Engineering Labs....Staff NASA 205-544-9492
NASA Scientific Balloon Program....Koehler, Keith NASA 804-824-1579
NASA Sounding Rocket Program....Koehler, Keigh NASA 804-824-1579
NASA Tethered Satellite....Staff NASA 205-544-9492

Natality, Marriage and Divorce Statistics....Heuser, Robert CDC 301-436-8954
Natality Statistics....Heuser, Robert CDC 301-436-8954
National Air Data Branch....Staff EPA 919-541-5582
National Air Toxic Information Clearinghouse....Staff EPA 919-541-0850
National, Business Cycle Indicators....Webb, Michael ECONOMIC 202-606-5590
National Cancer Program....Staff NCI 301-496-5583
National, Capital Consumption....Shelby, Herman ECONOMIC 202-606-9721
National, Capital Expenditures....Moylan, Carol ECONOMIC 202-606-9711
National, Capital Stock....Musgrave, John C. ECONOMIC 202-606-9721
National Center for Biotechnology Information....Staff NLM 301-496-2475
National Cholesterol Education Program....Staff NHLBI 301-496-0554
National, Composite Indexes....Robinson, Charles S. ECONOMIC 202-606-4500
National, Computer Price Index....Sadee, Nadia ECONOMIC 202-606-9736
National, Construction....Lane, Lance ECONOMIC 202-606-9726
National, Corporate Profits and Taxes....Petrick, Kenneth A. ECONOMIC 202-606-9738
National Crime Survey - Data Tapes....Taylor, Bruce Justice Stat 202-616-3498
National Crime Survey - Data Tapes....Rand, Michael Justice Stat 202-616-3494
National Crime Survey - Data Tapes....DeBerry, Marshall Justice Stat 202-307-0775
National Crime Survey - General....DeBerry, Marshall Justice Stat 202-307-0775
National Crime Survey - General....Dodge, Richard Justice Stat 202-616-3485
National Crime Survey - General....Harlow, Caroline Justice Stat 202-307-0757
National Crime Survey - General....Klaus, Patsy Justice Stat 202-307-0776
National Crime Survey - General....Rand, Michael Justice Stat 202-616-3494
National Crime Survey - General....Taylor, Bruce Justice Stat 202-616-3498
National Crime Survey - Redesign....Dodge, Richard Justice Stat 202-616-3485
National Crime Survey - Redesign....Taylor, Bruce Justice Stat 202-616-3498
National Crime Survey - Supplements....Kindermann, Charles Justice Stat 202-616-3489
National Crime Survey....DeBarry, Marshall Justice Stat 202-307-0775
National Crime Survey....Rand, Michael Justice Stat 202-616-3494
National Crime Survey....Taylor, Bruce Justice Stat 202-616-3498
National, Cyclically-Adjusted Budget....Michael Webb ECONOMIC 202-606-5590
National, Depreciation....Shelby, Herman ECONOMIC 202-606-9721
National, Disposable Personal Income....Lally, Paul ECONOMIC 202-606-9743
National, Dividends....Petrick, Kenneth A. ECONOMIC 202-606-9738
National, Employee Benefit Plans....Lally, Paul ECONOMIC 202-606-9743
National, Employee Compensation....Lally, Paul ECONOMIC 202-606-9743
National Environmental Policy Act....Staff FCC 202-418-1700
National Environmental Policy Act (NEPA)....Rudy, Gregory NEIC 202-586-2177
National, Environmental Studies....Rugledge, Gary L. ECONOMIC 202-606-5350
National Establishment Survey, Empl/Unempl....Seifert, Mary Lee LABOR 202-606-6552
National Establishment Survey, Indust. Classif. E/Un....Getz, Patricia LABOR 202-606-6521
National Exchange Carrier Association Policy....Staff FCC 202-418-0940
National Eye Health Education Program (NEHEP)....Staff NEI 301-496-5248
National, Farm Output, Product, and Income....Smith, George ECONOMIC 202-606-9746
National, Federal Govt., Contributions and Transfers....Tsehaye, Benyam ECONOMIC 202-606-5591
National, Federal Govt Defense Purchases of Goods and Services....Galbraith, Karl D. ECONOMIC 202-606-9793
National, Federal Govt Nondefense Purchases-Goods and Services....Labella, Ramen ECONOMIC 202-606-5593
National, Federal Govt., Receipts and Expenditures....Dobbs, David T. ECONOMIC 202-606-9776
National Fish Hatchery System....Staff FWS 703-358-1715
National Forest System....Reynolds, Gary FS 202-205-1523
National, GNP by Industry....Yuskavage, Robert ECONOMIC 202-606-5307
National, GNP, Computer Tapes, Disks and Printouts....Barnes, Phyllistine ECONOMIC 202-606-9700
National, GNP, Current Estimates....Mannering, Virginia H. ECONOMIC 202-606-9732
National, Gross Private Domestic Investment....Moylan, Carol ECONOMIC 202-606-9711
National Health Issues....Nadel, Mark V. GAO 202-512-7119
National Health Service Corps....Shaffer, Sylvia HRSA 201-443-3376
National High Blood Pressure Education Program....Staff NHLBI 301-496-0554
National Household Survey....Staff NIDA 301-443-6245
National Hunting and Fishing Survey....Staff FWS 703-358-2156
National Income and Wealth, Auto Output....McCully, Clint ECONOMIC 202-606-9735

National Income and Wealth, Chief....Donahoe, Gerald F. ECONOMIC 202-606-9715

National Information Center....Hannan, Maureen FRS 202-452-3618

National Information Infrastructure....Staff FCC 202-418-0940

National, Input-Output Annual Tables....Horowitz, Karen ECONOMIC 202-606-5587

National, Input-Output, Benchmark Tables...Planting, Mark A. ECONOMIC 202-606-5586

National, Input-Output Tables, Computer Tapes, Disks and Print....Clark, Vanessa ECONOMIC 202-606-5307

National, Input-Output Tables, Goods-Producing Industry....Bonds, Belinda ECONOMIC 202-606-5586

National, Input-Output Tables, Services Producing Industry....Lawson, Ann ECONOMIC 202-606-5586

National Institute of Corrections....Thigpen, Morris L. Justice 202-307-3106

National, Interest Income and Payments....Schuster, Mary Kate ECONOMIC 202-606-9740

National, Inventories....Wasshausen, David B. ECONOMIC 202-606-9752

National, Inventory/Sales Ratios....Wasshausen, David B. ECONOMIC 202-606-9752

National, Methodology....Beckman, Barry A. ECONOMIC 202-606-9662

National, National Income....Taub, Leon ECONOMIC 202-606-9722

National, Net Exports....Krincek, Corrine ECONOMIC 202-606-9729

National Oral Health Information Clearinghouse: A Resource for Special Care Patients....Staff NIDR 301-402-7364

National, Output Measures....Ehemann, Christian ECONOMIC 202-606-9717

National Partnership Clearinghouse....Staff OPM 202-606-2940

National, Personal Consumption Expenditures, Autos....Johnson, Everette P. ECONOMIC 202-606-9725

National, Personal Consumption Expenditures, Other Goods....Key, Greg ECONOMIC 202-606-9727

National, Personal Consumption Expenditures, Prices....McCully, Clint ECONOMIC 202-606-9735

National, Personal Consumption Expenditures, Services....Myung, Han ECONOMIC 202-606-9719

National, Personal Consumption Expenditures....McCully, Cling ECONOMIC 202-606-9735

National, Personal Income....Lally, Paul ECONOMIC 202-606-9743

National Pesticides Survey....Staff EPA 202-260-7570

National Pesticides Telecommunications Network....Staff EPA 800-858-7378

National, Plant and Equipment Expenditures....Crawford, Jeffrey W. ECONOMIC 202-606-9713

National Pollutant Discharge Elimination System....Staff EPA 703-821-4823

National, Pollution Abatement and Control Spending....Rutledge, Gary L. ECONOMIC 202-606-5350

National Pregnancy and Health Survey....Staff NIDA 301-443-6245

National, Price Measures (Fixed-Weighted)....Hook, Mimi W. ECONOMIC 202-606-9723

National, Producers' Durable Equipment....Crawford, Jeffrey W. ECONOMIC 202-606-9713

National Projections, States and Metro. Areas....Sullivan, David ECONOMIC 202-606-5594

National, Proprietors' Income, Nonfarm....Abney, Willie J. ECONOMIC 202-606-9701

National Radon Hotline....Staff EPA 800-767-7236

National, Rental Income....McBride, Denise ECONOMIC 202-606-9733

National Research Service Awards....Staff DRG 301-594-7248

National, Residential Construction....Lane, Lance ECONOMIC 202-606-9726

National, Savings....Donahoe, Gerald F. ECONOMIC 202-606-9715

National Security Analysis....Davis, Richard A. GAO 202-512-3504

National Services Information Centers.... CENSUS 301-763-1384

National, State and Local Govt, Purchases of Goods and Services.....Peters, Donald L. ECONOMIC 202-606-5594

National, State and Local Govt., Receipts and Expend.....Sullivan, David F. ECONOMIC 202-606-5594

National, Statistical Series....Young, Mary D. ECONOMIC 202-606-9677

National, Structures....Lane, Lance ECONOMIC 202-606-9726

National, UN and OCED System of National Accounts....Seskin, Eugene ECONOMIC 202-606-9744

National, Wages and Salaries....Schlitzer, Tracey D. ECONOMIC 202-606-9763

National, Wealth Estimates....Herman, Shelby ECONOMIC 202-606-9721

Native American Affairs....Stamps, Quanah SBA 202-205-6552

NATO (North Atlantic Treaty Organization)....Staff Cnty State 202-736-7299

Natural gas liquids (NGL)....Land, Eric USITC 202-205-3349

Natural Gas....Altman, Paula NEIC 202-586-8800

Natural Gas....Cogan, Jonathan NEIC 202-586-8800

Natural Gas....Gillett, Tom COMMERCE 202-482-1466

Natural gas....Land, Eric USITC 202-205-3349

Natural Gas....Tomaszewski, Clifford NEIC 202-586-9482

Natural pearls....Witherspoon, Ricardo USITC 202-205-3489

Natural resins....Kight, John PTO 703-308-2453

Natural resources and Related Equipment....Daly, James M. SEC 202-942-1800

Natural Resources...Duffus, James GAO 202-512-7756

Natural rubber...Misurelli, Denby USITC 202-205-3362

Natural, Synthetic Rubber....Raymundo, PRAT COMMERCE 202-482-0128

Nauru/Minerals....Lyday, Travis Cnty Mines 202-501-9695

Nauru....Imam, Fahmila Cnty Export-Import Bank 202-565-3738

Nauru....Staff Cnty State 202-647-3546

Nauru...Shelton, Alison Cnty Treasury 202-622-0251

Naval Reactor Propulsion....Staff NEIC 412-476-7200

Navigation, Air or Water....Staff FCC 202-632-7175

Navigation Safety....Staff Coast Guard Hotline 800-368-5647

Navigational instruments....Jordon, Roth USITC 202-205-3467

Navy special fuel oil....Foreso, Cynthia USITC 202-205-3348

Nearsightedness....Staff NEI 301-496-5248

Neckties....Sweet, Mary Elizabeth USITC 202-205-3455

Nemaline Myopathy (Floppy Baby)....Staff NINDS 301-496-5751

Neonatal Adaptation....Staff NICHD 301-496-5133

Neonatal Asphyxia....Staff NINDS 301-496-5751

Neonatal Respiratory Distress Syndrome...Staff NHLBI 301-496-4236

Neoplasms (Trophoblastic)....Staff NCI 301-496-5583

Nepal (Kathmandu)....Staff Cnty State 202-647-1450

Nepal/Minerals....Wu, John Cnty Mines 202-501-9697

Nepal....Dhungana, Basudev Prasad Cnty Embassy 202-667-4550

Nepal....Gilman, Timothy Cnty Commerce 202-482-2954

Nepal....Hutchings, Dayna Cnty Export-Import Bank 202-565-3737

Nepal....Paudel, Yug Nath S. Cnty Embassy 202-667-4550

Nepal....Phillips, Scott Peace Corps 202-606-1053

Nepal....Prennushi, Giovanna Cnty World Bank 202-473-2641

Nepal....Respess, Rebecca Cnty TDA 703-875-4357

Nepal....VanRenterghem, Cynthia Cnty Treasury 202-622-0343

Nepal....Winchester, Rebecca Cnty USIA 202-619-6528

Nepheline Syenite....Potter, Michael J. MINES 202-501-9387

Nephritis....Staff NIDDK 301-654-4415

Nephrocalcinosis....Staff NIDDK 301-654-4415

Nephrolithiasis....Staff NIDDK 301-654-4415

Nephrotic Syndrome....Staff NIDDK 301-654-4415

Nerve Damage....Staff NINDS 301-496-5751

Netherlands Antille....Wilkins, Michele Cnty Export-Import Bank 202-565-3743

Netherlands Antilles....Brooks, Michelle Cnty Commerce 202-482-2527

Netherlands Antilles (Curacao)....Staff Cnty State 202-647-2620

Netherlands Antilles/Minerals....Rabchevsky, George Cnty Mines 202-501-9670

Netherlands/Minerals....Zajac, William Cnty Mines 202-501-9671

Netherlands (The Hague)....Staff Cnty State 202-647-6557

Netherlands....Bensimon, Simon Cnty Commerce 202-482-5401

Netherlands....Gosnell, Peter Cnty Export-Import Bank 202-565-3733

Netherlands....Hamer, Alphons C.M. Cnty Embassy 202-244-5300

Netherlands....Holloway, Barbara Cnty Treasury 202-622-0098

Netherlands....Jacobovits De Szeged, Adriaann Pieter Roetert Cnty Embassy 202-244-5300

Netherlands....Kulla, Morgan Cnty USIA 202-619-6853

Nettings: fish....Cook, Lee USITC 202-205-3471

Nettings: other....Sweet, Mary Elizabeth USITC 202-205-3455

Neural Prostheses...Staff NINDS 301-496-5751

Neural Stimulation....Staff NINDS 301-496-5751

Neural Stimulation....Staff NIDCD 301-496-7243

Neural Tube Defects....Staff NICHD 301-496-5133

Neural Tube Defects....Staff NINDS 301-496-5751

Neuralgia....Staff NINDS 301-496-5751

Neuritis (Peripheral Neuropathy)....Staff NINDS 301-496-5751

Neuro-Ophthalmology....Staff NEI 301-496-5248

Neuroaxonal Dystrophy....Staff NINDS 301-496-5751

Neurobiology (Drug-Related)....Staff NIDA 301-443-6245

Neuroblastoma....Staff NEI 301-496-5248

Neurochemistry....Quarles, Richard FAES 301-496-6647

Neuroendocrinology....Bondy, Caroline FAES 301-496-6664

Neurofibromatosis (von Recklinghausen's)....Staff NINDS 301-496-5751

Neurofibromatosis (von Recklinghausen's)....Staff NIDCD 301-496-7243

Neurofibromatosis....Staff NNF 800-323-7938

Neurogenic Arthropathy....Staff NINDS 301-496-5751

Neurogenic Disability (Mouth and Pharynx)....Staff NIDR 301-496-4261

Neurologic Disease....Staff NINDS 301-496-5751

Neurological Disorders and Stroke, Nat'l Inst. of....Emr, Marian NIH 301-496-5924

Neurology....Grafman, Jordan FAES 301-496-0220

Neuromuscular Disease....Staff NINDS 301-496-5751

Neuromyelitis (Devic Syndrome)....Staff NINDS 301-496-5751

Neuromyopathies....Staff NINDS 301-496-5751

Neuromyositis....Staff NINDS 301-496-5751

Neuronal Ceroid Lupofuscinoses....Staff NINDS 301-496-5751

Neuropathies....Staff NINDS 301-496-5751

Neuropharmacology....Staff NINDS 301-496-5751

Neuroscience....Staff NINDS 301-496-5751

Neuroscience....Staff NIMH 301-443-4513

Neurosclerosis....Staff NINDS 301-496-5751

Neurosyphilis....Staff NINDS 301-496-5751

Neurotoxicity....Staff NINDS 301-496-5751

Neurotoxicity..Staff NIDA 301-443-6245

Nevis....Irish, John P. Cnty Embassy 202-686-2636

New Caledonia/Minerals....Lyday, Travis Cnty Mines 202-501-9695

New Caledonia....Staff Cnty State 202-647-3546

New Drug Synthesis and Chemistry of Drugs....Staff NIDA 301-443-6245

New Releases....Staff OD/OC 301-496-2535

New Zealand/Minerals....Lyday, Travis Cnty Mines 202-501-9695

New Zealand (Wellington)....Staff Cnty State 202-647-9691

New Zealand....Bouck, Gary (Bus.)/Golike, William (Policy) Cnty Commerce 202-482-3647

New Zealand....Cooper, Fiona Ruth Cnty Embassy 202-328-4800

New Zealand....Imam, Fahmila Cnty Export-Import Bank 202-565-3738

New Zealand....Jabbs, Theodore Cnty USIA 202-619-5836

New Zealand....Mackour, Oscar Cnty Treasury 202-622-0145

New Zealand....Wood, L. John Cnty Embassy 202-328-4800

Newborn....Staff NICHD 301-496-5133

News Gathering and Publishing....Staff FCC 717-337-1212

Newspaper management....Kenney, Alisa V. UMD 301-405-2427

Newspapers....Bratland, Rose Marie COMMERCE 202-482-0380

Newsprint....Twarok, Chris USITC 202-205-3314

NFA Firearms....Staff ATF 202-927-8340

Nicaragua (Managua)....Staff Cnty State 202-647-2205

Nicaragua/Minerals....Rabchevsky, George Cnty Mines 202-501-9670

Nicaragua....Bowyer, Nicolette L. Cnty World Bank 202-473-8724

Nicaragua....Dowling, Jay Cnty Commerce 202-482-1648

Nicaragua....Eckerson, David Cnty AID 202-647-9551

Nicaragua....Erlandson, Barbara Peace Corps 202-606-3624

Nicaragua....John Herrman Cnty TDA 703-875-4357

Nicaragua....Marcus, Anthony Cnty Treasury 202-622-1218

Nicaragua....Mayorga-Cortes, Roberto Genaro Cnty Embassy 202-939-6570

Nicaragua....Opstein, Sally Cnty USIA 202-619-5864

Nicaragua....Wilkins, Michele Cnty Export-Import Bank 202-565-3743

Nicaragua....Wong-Valle, Jorge Cnty Embassy 202-939-6570

Nickel compounds....Greenblatt, Jack USITC 202-205-3353

Nickel Products....Presbury, Graylin COMMERCE 202-482-0575

Nickel....Kuck, Peter H. MINES 202-501-9436

Nickel....Lundy, David USITC 202-205-3439

Nicotine...Staff NIDA 301-443-6245

Niemann-Pick Disease....Staff NINDS 301-496-5751

Niemann-Pick Disease....Staff NEI 301-496-5248

Niger/Minerals....Izon, David Cnty Mines 202-501-9674

Niger (Niamey)....Staff Cnty State 202-647-2791

Niger....Baily, Jess Cnty USIA 202-619-5900

Niger....Cisse, Amadou Cnty World Bank 202-473-4652

Niger....Michelini, Philip Cnty Commerce 202-482-4388

Niger....Palghat, Kathy Cnty Treasury 202-622-0332

Niger....Posner, Mara Peace Corps 202-606-3004

Niger....Sangare, Moussa Cnty Embassy 202-483-4227

Niger....Seydou, Adamou Cnty Embassy 202-483-4224

Niger....Waxman-Lenz, Roberta Cnty Export-Import Bank 202-565-3742

Niger....Werlin, Louise Cnty AID 202-647-8125

Niger....Younge, Nathan Cnty TDA 703-875-4357

Nigeria (Abuja)....Staff Cnty State 202-647-1597

Nigeria/Minerals....Izon, David Cnty Mines 202-501-9674

Nigeria....Bezek, Jill Cnty TDA 703-875-4357

Nigeria....Bowler, Gina Peace Corps 202-606-3644

Nigeria....Denton, Hazel Cnty World Bank 202-473-4895

Nigeria....Fox, Russell Peace Corps 202-606-3645

Nigeria....Henke, Degra Cnty Commerce 202-482-5149

Nigeria....Kazaure, Zubair Mahmud Cnty Embassy 202-986-8400

Nigeria....Maybury-Lewis, Anthony Cnty Export-Import Bank 202-565-3739

Nigeria....O'Neal, Adrienne Cnty USIA 202-619-6904

Nigeria....Onah, Adoga Cnty Embassy 202-986-8400

Nigeria....Palghat, Kathy Cnty Treasury 202-622-0332

Nigeria....Woodruff, Neil Cnty AID 202-647-6321

Night Blindness....Staff NEI 301-496-5248

Nightwear....DeGaetano, Angela CUSTOMS 212-466-5540

Nikkei with options....Fedinets, Robert P. CFT 312-353-9016

Nitric acid....Trainor, Cynthia USITC 202-205-3354

Nitriles....Lee, Mary PTO 703-308-4546

Nitrites....Michels, David USITC 202-205-3352

Nitrites....Staff NIDA 301-443-6245

Nitrogen Compounds....Joseph, Stephanie CUSTOMS 212-466-5768

Nitrogen....Cantrell, Raymond MINES 202-501-9411

Nitrogen....Conant, Kenneth USITC 202-205-3346

Nitrogenous fertilizers....Trainor, Cynthia USITC 202-205-3354

Nitrosamines....Staff NCI 301-496-5583

Niue....Berhage, Jeff Peace Corps 202-606-1098

Niue....Rahman, Talaat Cnty TDA 703-875-4357

Nobel Prize....Staff NIGMS 301-496-7301

Noise Information....Staff EPA 202-260-4996

Noise....Staff NIDCD 301-496-7243

Noise....Staff NINDS 301-496-5751

Non-alcoholic Beverages....Manogue, Robert COMMERCE 202-482-2428

Non-bank Acquisitions....Greene, D Christopher FRS 202-452-2263

Non-benzenoid resins....Misurelli, Denby USITC 202-205-3362

Non-cash Collections....DeCorleto, Donna FRS 202-452-3956

Non-commercial Educational Stations-FM Apps.....Staff FCC 202-418-2710

Non-current Carrying Wiring Devices....Bodson, John COMMERCE 202-482-0681

Non-durable Goods....Simon, Leslie B. COMMERCE 202-482-0341

Non-electric Machinery, Prices and Living Cond.....Dickerson, Bryandt LABOR 202-606-7744

Non-electric motors and engines....Andersen, Peder USITC 202-205-3388

Non-energy Related Inventions Program....Lewett, G.P. NIST 301-975-5504

Non-enumerated products....Spalding, Josephine USITC 202-205-3498

Non-Farm Proprietors' Income and Employment....Levine, Bruce ECONOMIC 202-606-9260

Non-ferrous Foundries....Bell, Charles COMMERCE 202-482-0608

Non-ferrous Metals....Cammorota, David COMMERCE 202-482-5157

Non-Game Wildlife....Staff FWS 703-358-1718

Non-Hodgkins Malignant Lymphoma....Staff NCI 301-496-5583

Non-infectious Chemical Agents (Eff. on Human Hea.)....Staff NIEHS 919-541-3345

Non-metallic article shaping....Silbaugh, Jan H PTO 703-308-3829

Non-metallic elements....Lewis, Michael M. PTO 703-308-2535

Non-metallic Minerals Nec....Manion, James J. COMMERCE 202-482-0575

Non-residential Constr (Domestic)....MacAuley, Patrick COMMERCE 202-482-0132

Non-Toxic Shot....Staff FWS 703-358-1714

North America Affairs....Weiss, David US Trade Rep 202-395-3412

North American Numbering Plan....Staff FCC 202-418-0940

Northeast MTC (Manufacturing Technology Center)....Tebbano, Mark NIST 518-283-1010

Norwalk Agent....Staff NIAID 301-496-5717

Norway/Minerals....Plachy, Josef Cnty Mines 202-501-9673

Norway (Oslo)....Staff Cnty State 202-647-5669

Norway....Devlin, James Cnty Commerce 202-482-4414

Norway....Gosnell, Peter Cnty Export-Import Bank 202-565-3743

Norway....Klepsvik, Karsten Cnty Embassy 202-333-6000

Norway....Mackour, Oscar Cnty Treasury 202-622-0145

Norway....Rankin-Galloway, Honore Cnty USIA 202-619-5283

Norway....Vibe, Kjeld Cnty Embassy 202-333-6000

Nosebleed (Epistaxis)....Staff NHLBI 301-496-4236

Notes, Counterfeit....Cameron, Jon FRS 202-452-2220

Notes, Technical Information....Decorleto, Donna FRS 202-452-3956

Notes, Treasury....DeCorleto, Donna FRS 202-452-3956

Nuclear Energy Institute....Davis, Edward NEIC 202-484-2660

Nuclear Energy Statistics....Geidl, John NEIC 202-254-5570

Nuclear Energy....Greenblatt, Jack USITC 202-205-3353
Nuclear Enforcement....Lieberman, James NRC 301-415-2741
Nuclear Facility Safety....Pearson, Orin NEIC 202-586-2407
Nuclear Fusion....Davies, Anne NEIC 301-903-4941
Nuclear (Heart Pacemaker)....Staff NHLBI 301-496-4236
Nuclear Magnetic Resonance Spectrometers....Staff NCRR 301-594-7934
Nuclear Magnetic Resonance....Becker, Edwin D. FAES 301-496-1024
Nuclear Material Safety and Safeguards....Paperiello, Carl J. NRC 301-415-7800
Nuclear Medicine Department....Staff CC 301-496-6455
Nuclear Physics....Hendrick, David NEIC 301-903-3613
Nuclear Power Plants....Werner, Thomas NEIC 301-903-3773
Nuclear Power Plants, Major Proj.....Dollison, Robert COMMERCE 202-482-2733
Nuclear Power Projects....Staff FWS 703-358-2183
Nuclear Reactor Regulation....Russell, William T. NRC 301-415-1270
Nuclear Reactors....Duraiswamy, Sam NRC 301-415-7364
Nuclear Safety Issues....Black, Richard NEIC 301-903-0102
Nuclear Safety Regulations....Rollow, Thomas NEIC 202-586-2407
Nuclear Waste....Major, Richard K. NRC 301-415-7366
Nuclear Weapons Stockpiles....Ford, John NEIC 301-903-3782
Number Research, Price and Index, Pr/Lv. Cond....Zieschang, Kimberly LABOR 202-606-6573
Numerical Controls Fr. Mach. Tools....Pilaroscia, Megan COMMERCE 202-482-0609
Numerical controls....Malison, Andrew USITC 202-205-3391
Nursery Trade Catalogs....Ho, Judith NAL 301-504-5876
Nurses....Staff Visiting Nurse Association of America 800-426-2547
Nursing Department....Staff CC 301-496-5661
Nursing Homes and Care....Staff HRSA 301-443-3376
Nursing Homes....Hardy, Robert HCFA 301-966-3206
Nursing Homes....Staff NIA 301-496-1752
Nursing Interventions....Staff NINR 301-496-0207
Nursing Research, National Center for....Pollin, Geraldine NIH 301-496-0207
Nursing Research, National Center for....McBride, Esther NIH 301-496-0207
Nursing Systems....Staff NCNR 301-496-0526
Nutrition and Aging....Staff NIA 301-496-1752
Nutrition and Cancer....Staff NCI 301-496-5583
Nutrition, Cancer Research....Staff American Institute for Cancer Research
Nutrition Hotline 800-843-8114
Nutrition, Maternal and Child....Wong, Faye L. CDC 404-488-5099
Nutrition Research Coordination....Staff OD 301-496-9281
Nutrition....Hubbard, Van S. FAES 301-594-7573
Nutrition....Meyers, Linda ASH 202-205-9007
Nutrition....Staff Nutrition Information Service 800-231-3438
Nutrition....Staff NICHD 301-496-5133
Nutrition....Staff HRSA/DMCH 301-443-4026
Nutrition....Staff NIDDK 301-496-3583
Nutrition....Stoiber, Suzanne ASH 202-205-0152
Nutrition....Trowbridge, Frederick L. CDC 404-488-5090
Nutritional Statistics....Kuczmarski, Robert CDC 301-436-7072
Nuts, Bolts, Washers....Reise, Richard COMMERCE 202-482-3489
Nuts, Edible....Burket, Stephen USITC 202-205-3318
Nuts, Edible....Janis, William V. COMMERCE 202-482-2250
Nuts....Conte, Ralph CUSTOMS 212-466-5759
Nystagmus....Staff NEI 301-496-5248

O

Oakum....Cook, Lee USITC 202-205-3471
Oats with options....Gore, Philip CFT 312-886-3044
Obesity in Children....Staff NHLBI 301-496-4236
Obesity in Children....Staff NICHD 301-496-5133
Obesity....Staff NIDDK 301-496-3583
Obesity....Staff NHLBI 301-496-4236
Obesity....Staff NIMH 301-496-4513
Obscene Broadcasts....Staff FCC 202-418-1430
Obscenity....Burgasser, George C. Justice 202-514-5780
Obsessive-Compulsive Disorder...Staff NIMH 301-443-4513
Occupation Statistics....Priebe, John/Masumura, Wilfred CENSUS 301-763-8574
Occupational Data/Current Survey, Empl/Unempl.St.....Staff LABOR 202-606-6378
Occupational Diseases....Staff CDC/NIOSH 404-639-3286
Occupational Lung Disease....Staff NHLBI 301-496-4236
Occupational Medicine....Gebus, George NEIC 301-903-7385

Occupational Mobility, Occup. Data, Empl/Unempl. Data....Rones, Philip LABOR 202-606-6378
Occupational Outlook Handbook, Employment Proj.....Pilot, Michael LABOR 202-606-5703
Occupational Outlook Quarterly, Empl. Proj.....Fountain, Melvin LABOR 202-606-5707
Occupational Projections....Rosenthal, Neal LABOR 202-606-5701
Occupational Safety and Health, National Institute for....Sims, Anne CDC 404-639-3286
Occupational Safety and Health....Poster, Diane CDC 404-639-3061
Occupational Safety....Gibbs, Roy NEIC 301-903-4343
Ocean Biological Experiments....Koehler, Keith NASA 802-824-1579
Ocean Energy....Loose, Ronald NEIC 202-586-5348
Ocean Physics Research....Koehler, Keith NASA 804-824-1579
Ocean Shipping....Johnson, William C. COMMERCE 202-482-5012
Ocean Thermal Energy....Loose, Ronald NEIC 202-586-5348
Oceania/trade matters....Stillman, Betsy US Trade Rep 202-395-6813
Oceans and Coastal Protection Division....Staff EPA 202-260-1952
Oceans and Watersheds....Staff EPA 202-260-7166
Ocular Hypertension....Staff NEI 301-496-5248
Oculocraniosomatic Neuromuscular Disease....Staff NINDS 301-496-5751
Odor....Staff NIDCD 301-496-7243
Odor....Staff NINDS 301-496-5751
Odoriferous Compounds....Joseph, Stephanie CUSTOMS 212-466-5768
Odoriferous or aromatic substances....Land, Eric USITC 202-205-3349
Offal....Ludwick, David USITC 202-205-3329
Offender-based Transaction Statistics....Manson, Donald Justice Stat 202-616-3491
Offender-based Transaction Statistics....Langan, Patrick Justice Stat 202-616-3490
Offenders - Federal....Kaplan, Carol Justice Stat 202-307-0759
Offenders, Female....Baunach, Phyllis Jo Justice Stat 202-307-0361
Offenders, Female - Federal....Kaplan, Carol Justice Stat 202-307-0759
Offenders....Baunach, Phyllis Jo Justice Stat 202-307-0361
Offenders....Beck, Allen Justice Stat 202-616-3277
Offenders....Greenfeld, Lawrence Justice Stat 202-616-3281
Offenders....Stephan, James Justice Stat 202-616-7273
Office copying machines....Baker, Scott USITC 202-205-3386
Office Equipment Industry Group....Duvall, Steven SEC 202-942-1950
Office machines....Baker, Scott USITC 202-205-3386
Office of Congressional Relations....Leslie, Louise M. FTC 202-326-2195
Office of Congressional Relations....Prendergast, William B. FTC 202-326-2195
Office of Congressional Relations....Hall, Dorian J. FTC 202-326-2186
Office of Consumer and Competition Advocacy....Laney, Veronica FTC 202-326-2249
Office of inspector General-Audits....Staff FCC 202-418-0470
Office of Inspector General-Complaints....Staff FCC 202-418-0470
Office of Inspector General-Investigations....Staff FCC 202-418-0470
Office of Inspector General....Staff FCC 202-418-0470
Office of Inspector General....Trzeciak, Adam R. FTC 202-326-2435
Office of Inspector General....Treitsch, Dennis R. FTC 202-326-2581
Office of Inspector General....Zirkel, Frederick J. FTC 202-326-2800
Office of Inspector General....Williams, Joyce E. FTC 202-326-2313
Office of Public Affairs....Mack, Brenda A. FTC 202-326-2182
Office of Public Affairs....Leslie, John T. FTC 202-326-2178
Office of Public Affairs....Shaipro, Howard FTC 202-326-2176
Office of Public Affairs....Farrell, Claudia FTC 202-326-2181
Office of Public Affairs....Elder, Donald FTC 202-326-2181
Office of the Commissioner....Azcuenaga, Mary L. FTC 202-326-2145
Office of the Executive Director....Milton, Kathleen FTC 202-326-3253
Office of the General Counsel....Rittner, Kathleen FTC 202-326-2498
Office of the General Counsel....Rowan, Michael FTC 202-326-2489
Office of the General Counsel....Coleman, Jill E. FTC 202-326-2414
Office of the General Counsel....Kane, Maryanne S. FTC 202-326-2450
Office of the General Counsel....Levine, Joanne L. FTC 202-326-2474
Office of the General Counsel....Freedman, Bruce G. FTC 202-326-2464
Office of the General Counsel....DeLuca, Nancy F. FTC 202-326-2440
Office of the General Counsel....Etheridge, Monica M. FTC 202-326-2666
Office of the General Counsel....Dooley, Frederick E. FTC 202-326-2443
Office of the General Counsel....DuPree, Scott E. FTC 202-326-2479
Office of the General Counsel....Fields, Kwasi A. FTC 202-326-2452
Office of the General Counsel....DeMille-Wagman, Lawrence FTC 202-326-2448
Office of the General Counsel....Winerman, Marc L. FTC 202-326-2451
Office of the General Counsel....Wagman, Lawrence FTC 202-326-2448
Office of the General Counsel....Goosby, Consuella M. FTC 202-326-2486
Office of the General Counsel....Greenfield, Gary M. FTC 202-326-2753

Office of the General Counsel....Cummins, Jerold D. FTC 202-326-2471

Office of the General Counsel....Golden, William P. FTC 202-326-2494

Office of the General Counsel....Murphy, John T. FTC 202-326-2457

Office of the General Counsel....Crockett, Elaine FTC 202-326-2453

Office of the General Counsel....Isenstadt, Ernest J. FTC 202-326-2473

Office of the General Counsel....Spears, James M. FTC 202-326-2480

Office of the General Counsel....Worthy, Betty J. FTC 202-326-2459

Office of the General Counsel....White, Christian S. FTC 202-326-2476

Office of the General Counsel....Hurwitz, James D. FTC 202-326-2847

Office of the General Counsel....Dawson, Rachel Miller FTC 202-326-2463

Office of the General Counsel....Kaye, Ira S. FTC 202-326-2426

Office of the General Counsel....Neal, Valary FTC 202-326-2066

Office of the General Counsel....Orlans, Melvin H. FTC 202-326-2475

Office of the General Counsel....Shaffer, Jay C. FTC 202-326-2557

Office of the General Counsel....Pressley, Doris P. FTC 202-326-2916

Office of the General Counsel....Lewis, Tina M. FTC 202-326-2465

Office of the General Counsel....Polydor, Cheryl L. FTC 202-326-2279

Office of the General Counsel....Melman, Leslie R. FTC 202-326-2478

Office of the General Counsel....Shonka, David C. FTC 202-326-2436

Office of the General Counsel....Miller, Rachel Dawson FTC 202-326-2463

Office of the General Counsel....Tang, Alexander FTC 202-326-2447

Office of the Secretary.....Felder, Clayrine K. FTC 202-326-2153

Office of the Secretary....Ashe, Maurice FTC 202-326-2516

Office of the Secretary....Berman, Benjamin I. FTC 202-326-2513

Office of the Secretary....Bradley, Tasha FTC 202-326-3347

Office of the Secretary....Carson, Diane B. FTC 202-326-2515

Office of the Secretary....Clark, Donald S. FTC 202-326-2514

Office of the Secretary....Donohue, Richard C. FTC 202-326-3112

Office of the Secretary....Dowdle, Walter D. FTC 202-326-2505

Office of the Secretary....Foster, Elizabeth M. FTC 202-326-2187

Office of the Secretary....Liebman, Marvin FTC 202-326-2069

Office of the Secretary....Lofty, Bernita V. FTC 202-326-3117

Office of the Secretary....Pierce, Diane E. FTC 202-326-2519

Office of the Secretary....Plummer, C. Landis FTC 202-326-2520

Office of the Secretary....Reynolds, Ronald H. FTC 202-326-2521

Office of the Secretary....Stephen, David FTC 202-326-2512

Office of the Secretary....Tanner, Trina A. FTC 202-326-2517

Office of the Secretary....Thielen, John J. FTC 202-326-2506

Office of the Secretary....Tinker, Wallace FTC 202-326-2192

Office of the Secretary....Williams, Linda A. FTC 202-326-2515

Office of the Secretary....Wood, Dolores A. FTC 202-326-2518

Offshore Radio Telecommunications Service....Staff FCC 202-653-5560

Oil and Gas Development and Refining, Maj. Proj.....Miles, Max COMMERCE 202-482-0679

Oil and Gas (Fuels Only)....Gillett, Tom COMMERCE 202-482-1466

Oil and Gas Leasing on Fish and Wildlife Refuges....Staff FWS 703-358-2183

Oil and Gas Statistics....Peterson, Jimmie NEIC 202-586-6401

Oil and Hazardous Material Spills....Staff EPA 202-267-2675

Oil and Hazardous Material Spills Response Hotline....Staff EPA 800-424-8802

Oil Field Machinery, Trade Promo.....Miles, Max COMMERCE 202-482-0679

Oil Field Machinery....Vacant COMMERCE 202-482-0680

Oil Industry Group....Daly, James M. SEC 202-942-1800

Oil, lubricating....Foreso, Cynthia USITC 202-205-3348

Oil Pollution....Staff EPA 703-603-8707

Oil Shale, Major Proj.....Bell, Richard COMMERCE 202-482-2460

Oil Shale Reserves Management....Furiga, Richard NEIC 202-586-4410

Oil Spills - Emergency Response Division....Staff EPA 800-424-8802

Oil Spills....Staff FWS 703-358-2148

Oil, Used....Staff EPA 703-603-8707

Oilcloth....Cook, Lee USITC 202-205-3471

Oils, Animal and Vegetable....Maria, John CUSTOMS 212-466-5730

Oils, essential....Land, Eric USITC 202-205-3349

Oilseeds - Soybeans, Sunflowers....Sanford, Scott 202-501-8550

Oilseeds - Soybeans, Sunflowers....Ash, Mark Agri 202-219-0838

Oilseeds - Soybeans, Sunflowers - World....Castaneda, Jaime Agri 202-219-0826

Oilseeds - Soybeans, Sunflowers....Kerestes, Dan Agri 202-270-9526

Oilseeds....Reeder, John USITC 202-205-3319

Older Drivers....Staff NIA 301-496-1752

Older Women....Staff NIA 301-496-1752

Older Workers, Empl/Unempl. Stats.....Rones, Philip LABOR 202-606-6378

Oleic acid ester....Johnson, Larry USITC 202-205-3351

Oleic acid....Randall, Rob USITC 202-205-3366

Oleyl alcohols....Randall, Rob USITC 202-205-3366

Olivopontocerebellar Atrophy....Staff NINDS 301-496-5751

Oman/Minerals....Michalski, Bernadette Cnty Mines 202-501-9699

Oman (Muscat)....Staff Cnty State 202-647-6571

Oman....Al-Dhahab, Abdulla Moh'd Aqueel Cnty Embassy 202-387-1980

Oman....Al-Rawas, Ghazi Said Cnty Embassy 202-387-1981

Oman....Konigshofer, Friedrich Cnty World Bank 202-473-2988

Oman....Mabury-Lewis, Anthony Cnty 202-565-3739

Oman....Mercer, Dorothy Cnty Treasury 202-622-0184

Oman....Thanos, Paul Cnty Commerce 202-482-1860

Oman....Vacant Cnty USIA 202-619-6528

Oman....Vacant Cnty AID 202-663-2620

On Site Contractor Employees....Saunders, Paristina FTC 202-326-2243

On Site Contractor Employees....Hallman, Kevin J. FTC 202-326-2243

On Site Contractor Employees....Lathern, Ronald C. FTC 202-326-2290

On Site Contractor Employees....Gardner, Kevin P. FTC 202-326-2243

On Site Contractor Employees....Cassagnol, Pascale FTC 202-326-2088

On Site Contractor Employees....Baxter, Robert L., II FTC 202-326-2243

Onchocerciasis....Staff NEI 301-496-5248

Onchocerciasis....Staff NIAID 301-496-5717

Oncology....Staff NCI 301-496-5583

One-Way Paging and Signaling....Staff FCC 202-653-8157

Online Information Retrieval Services....Staff NCRR/NIH Library 301-496-1156

Online Information Retrieval Services....Staff NLM 301-496-6095

Open Network Architecture....Staff FCC 202-418-1571

Ophthalmia Neonatorum....Staff NEI 301-496-5248

Ophthalmic Congenital and Genetic Disease....Staff NEI 301-496-5248

Ophthalmic....Johnson, Christopher USITC 202-205-3488

Ophthalmology Research....Staff NEI 301-496-5248

Oppenheim's Disease (Amyotonia Congenita)....Staff NINDS 301-496-5751

Optic Atrophy....Staff NEI 301-496-5248

Optic Neuritis....Staff NEI 301-496-5248

Optic....Tarcza, Thomas C. PTO 703-308-1689

Optical communication....Chilcot, Richard PTO 703-305-4716

Optical elements....Johnson, Christopher USITC 202-205-3488

Optical Equipment....Kiefer, Barbara CUSTOMS 212-466-5685

Optical goods....Johnson, Christopher USITC 202-205-3488

Optical measuring....Chilcot, Richard PTO 703-305-4716

Optical Physics....Clark, C.W. NIST 301-975-3709

Optical testing....Chilcot, Richard PTO 703-305-4716

Optics....Gellner, Michael L. PTO 703-308-1436

Optometry Research....Staff NEI 301-496-5248

Oral Cancer....Staff NCI 301-496-5583

Oral Cancer....Staff NIDR 301-496-4261

Oral Contraceptives....Staff NICHD 301-496-5133

Oral Health....Marianos, Donald W. CDC 404-488-4452

Oral Surgery-Intravenous Sedation....Staff NIDR 301-496-4261

Orange oil (essential oil)....Land, Eric USITC 202-205-3349

Ordering Info (Computer Software, Publications)....Customer Services Staff CENSUS 301-457-4100

Ores....Fitzgerald, John CUSTOMS 212-466-5492

Organ Donation....Staff UNOS 800-243-6667

Organ donation....Staff Living Bank 800-528-2971

Organ Donations (Eyes)....Staff NEI 301-496-5248

Organ Transplants....Braslow, Judy HRSA 301-443-7577

Organ Transplants/Medicare, Medicaid Funding....Hardy, Robert HCFA 202-966-3206

Organic acids....Michels, David USITC 202-205-3352

Organic Analytical Research....May, Willie E. NIST 301-975-3108

Organic Brain Syndrome...Staff NINDS 301-496-5751

Organic Brain Syndrome....Staff NINDS 301-496-5751

Organic Chemicals....Kelly, Michael COMMERCE 202-482-0128

Organization for Economic Cooperation and Develop.....Staff Cnty State 202-647-2469

Organized Crime....Coffey, Paul E. Justice 202-514-3594

Organo-metallic compounds....Michels, David USITC 202-205-3352

Organo-Sulfur Compounds....Winters, William CUSTOMS 212-466-5747

Original Telephone and Telephone Plant Cost....Staff FCC 202-632-3772

Orotic Aciduria....Staff NIDDK 301-654-4415

Orphan drugs....Staff National Information Center for Orphan Drugs and rare Diseases 800-456-3505

Orphan Drugs....Haffner, Marlene FDA 301-443-4903

Orphan Drugs....Staff FDA 301-443-4903

Orphan Drugs....Staff NINDS 301-496-5751

Orphan Drugs....Staff OD 301-402-4336

Orthodontics....Staff NIDR 301-496-4261

Orthognathic Surgery....Staff NIDR 301-496-4261
Orthokeratology....Staff NEI 301-496-5248
Orthopedic care for children...Staff Shriners Hospital Referral Line 800-237-5055
Orthopedic Disorders....Staff NIAMS 301-496-8188
Orthopedic Implants....Staff NIAMS 301-496-8188
Orthopedics instruments....Apley, Richard PTO 703-308-0305
Orthostatic Hypotension....Staff NINDS 301-496-5751
Orthostatic Hypotension....Staff NHLBI 301-496-4236
Orthotics....Staff NIAMS 301-496-8188
Osgood-Schlatter Disease...Staff NIAMS 301-496-8188
Osler-Weber-Rendu Syndrome....Staff NHLBI 301-496-4236
Ossein....Jonnard, Aimison USITC 202-205-3350
Osteitis Deformans....Staff NIAMS 301-496-8188
Osteoarthritis with Age....Staff NIA 301-496-1752
Osteoarthritis....Staff NIA 301-496-1752
Osteoarthritis....Staff NIAMS 301-496-8188
Osteochondrosis...Staff NIAMS 301-496-8188
Osteogenesis Imperfecta....Staff NICHD 301-496-5133
Osteogenesis Imperfecta....Staff NIAMS 301-496-8188
Osteogenesis....Staff NIAMS 301-496-8188
Osteogenic Sarcoma....Staff NCI 301-496-5583
Osteomalacia....Staff NIAMS 301-496-8188
Osteomyelitis....Staff NIAMS 301-496-8188
Osteonecrosis....Staff NIAMS 301-496-8188
Osteopathic Medicine....Staff American Osteopathic Association 800-621-1773
Osteoporosis with Age....Staff NIAMS 301-496-8188
Osteoporosis....Staff NICHD 301-496-5133
Osteoporosis....Staff NIAMS 301-496-8188
Osteosclerosis (Osteopetrosis)....Staff NICHD 301-496-5133
Osteosclerosis (Osteopetrosis)....Staff NIAMS 301-496-8188
Ostomy....Staff United Ostomy Association 800-826-0826
Ostomy....Staff NIDDK 301-654-3810
OTC (over-the-counter margin stock list)....Wolffrum, Margaret FRS 202-452-2781
Otitis Media....Staff NIDCD 301-496-7243
Otitis Media....Staff NIAID 301-496-5717
Otitis Media....Staff NICHD 301-496-5133
Otosclerosis....Staff NIDCD 301-496-7243
Otosclerosis....Staff NINDS 301-496-5751
Ototoxic Drugs....Staff NIDCD 301-496-7243
Outdoor Air - Cities....Staff EPA 202-260-5575
Outdoor Lightning Fixtures....Bodson, John COMMERCE 202-482-0681
Outdoor Power (Export Promo)....Hodgen, Donald COMMERCE 202-482-3346
Outer Continental Shelf....Staff FWS 703-358-2183
Ovarian Cancer....Staff NCI 301-496-5583
Ovens....Mata, Ruben USITC 202-205-3403
Oviduct....Staff NICHD 301-496-5133
Ovulation....Staff NICHD 301-496-5133
Ovum....Staff NICHD 301-496-5133
Oxalosis and Hyperoxaluria....Staff NIDDK 301-654-3810
Oxides, inorganic....Conant, Kenneth USITC 202-205-3346
Oxygen....Conant, Kenneth USITC 202-205-3346
Oxygenators (Artificial Lungs)....Staff NHLBI 301-496-4236
Ozone - Stratospheric....Staff EPA 919-541-5526

P

Pacemaker (Cardiac/Heart)....Staff NHLBI 301-496-4236
Pacemakers....Cruzan, Susan FDA 301-443-3285
Pacific Islands (General)....Staff Cnty State 202-647-3546
Pacific Islands....Bouck, Gary (Bus.)/Golike, William (Policy) Cnty Commerce 202-482-2471
Pacific Nations....Jabbs, Theodore Cnty USIA 202-619-5836
Pacific/trade matters....Lake, Charles US Trade Rep 202-395-3900
Pacific/trade matters....Cassidy, Robert US Trade Rep 202-395-3430
Pacific/trade matters....Lund, Christina US Trade Rep 202-395-6813
Packages....Goldberg, Gerald PTO 703-308-5443
Packaging Machinery....Shaw, Gene COMMERCE 202-482-3494
Packaging machines....Jackson, Georgia USITC 202-205-3399
Paget's Disease of Bone (Osteitis Deformans)....Staff NIAMS 301-496-8188
Paget's Disease of the Skin....Staff NCI 301-496-5583
Paging--One Way....Staff FCC 717-337-1212
Pain and the Elderly....Staff NIA 301-496-1752

Pain (Cancer Related)....Staff NCI 301-496-5583
Pain (Oral-Facial)....Staff NIDR 301-496-4261
Pain (Pharmacology)....Staff NIDA 301-443-6245
Pain....Staff NINDS 301-496-5751
Pain....Staff NIDR 301-496-1752
Paint rollers....Burns, Gail USITC 202-205-2501
Paint sets, artist's....Johnson, Larry USITC 202-205-3351
Paint....Brownchweig, Gilbert CUSTOMS 212-466-5744
Paintings....Mushinske, Larry CUSTOMS 212-466-5739
Paints/Coatings....Prat, Raimundo COMMERCE 202-482-0128
Paints....Johnson, Larry USITC 202-205-3351
Pajamas....Sweet, Mary Elizabeth USITC 202-205-3455
Pakistan (Islamabad)....Staff Cnty State 202-647-9823
Pakistan/Minerals....Kuo, Chin Cnty Mines 202-501-9693
Pakistan....Fardoust, Shahrokh Cnty World Bank 202-473-3049
Pakistan....Ghazanfar, Agha Cnty Embassy 202-939-6200
Pakistan....Gilman, Timothy Cnty Commerce 202-482-2954
Pakistan....Hutchings, Dayna Cnty Export-Import Bank 202-565-3737
Pakistan....Kiranbay, Carol Cnty AID 202-647-6967
Pakistan....Lodhi, Maleeha Cnty Embassy 202-939-6200
Pakistan....Ordonez, Miguel Peace Corps 202-606-3118
Pakistan....VanRenerghem, Cynthia Cnty Treasury 202-622-0343
Pakistan....Winchester, Rebecca Cnty USIA 202-619-6528
Palau (Koror)....Staff Cnty State 202-647-0108
Palau....Imam, Fahmila Cnty Export-Import Bank 202-565-3738
Palau....Lyday, Travis Cnty Mines 202-501-9695
Palestine....Hughes, Elizabeth Cnty Treasury 202-622-0174
Palm oil....Reeder, John USITC 202-205-3319
Palmitic acid esters....Johnson, Larry USITC 202-205-3351
Palpitation....Staff NHLBI 301-496-4236
Palsy, Cerebral....Staff NINDS 301-496-5751
Palsy, Progressive Supranuclear....Staff NINDS 301-496-5751
Panama/Minerals....Rabchevsky, George Cnty Mines 202-501-9670
Panama (Panama City)....Staff Cnty State 202-647-4986
Panama....Anne McKinney Cnty TDA 703-875-4357
Panama....Arias, Ricardo Alberto Cnty Embassy 202-483-1407
Panama....Berz, Cristina Cnty World Bank 202-473-3901
Panama....Geiser, Barbara Cnty Treasury 202-622-1271
Panama....Lee, Helen Cnty Commerce 202-482-2528
Panama....Lostumbo, Julie Peace Corps 202-606-3620
Panama....Murray, Mandy Peace Corps 202-606-3321
Panama....Shumake, Josie Cnty USIA 202-619-5864
Panama....Suescam Alfaro, Alfredo Cnty Embassy 202-483-1407
Panama....Wilkins, Michele Cnty Export-Import Bank 202-565-3743
Pancreatic Diseases....Staff NIDDK 301-654-3810
Panencephalitis....Staff NINDS 301-496-5751
Panic Disorder...Staff NIMH 301-443-4513
Pantyhose....Shetty, Sundar USITC 202-205-3486
Pantyhose....DeGaetano, Angela CUSTOMS 212-466-5540
Pap Smear....Staff NCI 301-496-5583
Paper and Board Packaging....Stanley, Gary COMMERCE 202-482-0375
Paper and Paper Products....Abromowitz, Carl CUSTOMS 212-466-5733
Paper Industries Machinery....Abrahams, Edward COMMERCE 202-482-0312
Paper Industry Group....Owings, Christopher SEC 202-942-1900
Paper machines....Lusi, Susan USITC 202-205-2334
Paper, products of....Twarok, Chris USITC 202-205-3314
Paper....Rhodes, Richard USITC 202-205-3322
Paper....Stanley, Gary COMMERCE 202-482-0375
Paperboard machines....Lusi, Susan USITC 202-205-2334
Paperboard, products of....Twarok, Chris USITC 202-205-3314
Paperboard....Rhodes, Richard USITC 202-205-3322
Papermakers' felts....Cook, Lee USITC 202-205-3471
Papermaking materials....Rhodes, Richard USITC 202-205-3322
Papillomavirus and Cancer....Staff NCI 301-496-5583
Papillomavirus....Staff NIAID 301-496-5717
Papua New Guinea....Imam, Fahmila Cnty Export-Import Bank 202-565-3738
Papua New Guinea....Jabbs, Theodore Cnty USIA 202-619-5836
Papua New Guinea....Schneider, Todd Cnty Treasury 202-622-0335
Papua New Guinea....Hamidian-Rad, Pirouz Cnty World Bank 202-473-4879
Papua New Guinea....Respess, Rebecca Cnty TDA 703-875-4357
Papua New Guinea....Ekivaki-Seruvatu, Alofa Cnty Embassy 202-745-3680
Papua New Guinea....Watangia, Kepas Isimel Cnty Embassy 202-745-3680
Papua New Guinea....Nagle, Douglas Peace Corps 202-606-3290
Papua New Guinea....Schell, Russell Peace Corps 202-606-3231

Papua New Guinea....Lee, Allison Peace Corps 202-606-0983
Papua New Guinea/Minerals....Lyday, Travis Cnty Mines 202-501-9695
Papua New Guinea (Port Moresby)....Staff Cnty State 202-647-3546
Parachutes....Andersen, Peder USITC 202-205-3388
Paraguay (Asuncion)....Staff Cnty State 202-647-2296
Paraguay/Minerals....Gurmendi, Alfredo Cnty Mines 202-501-9681
Paraguay....Anne McKinney Cnty TDA 703-875-4357
Paraguay....Augusto, Suzana C. Cnty World Bank 202-473-9096
Paraguay....Erlandson, Barbara Peace Corps 202-606-3499
Paraguay....Geiser, Barbara Cnty Treasury 202-622-1271
Paraguay....Gonzalez, Federico A. Cnty Embassy 202-483-6961
Paraguay....Leeb, Howard Cnty USIA 202-619-5867
Paraguay....Mye, Randolph Cnty Commerce 202-482-1548
Paraguay....Prevot, Babette Cnty AID 202-647-4359
Paraguay....Prieto, Jorge G. Cnty Embassy 202-483-6960
Paraguay....Ross, Rebecca Peace Corps 202-606-3575
Paraguay....Wilkins, Michele Cnty Export-Import Bank 202-565-3743
Paralysis Agitans....Staff NINDS 301-496-5751
Paralysis, Periodic....Staff NINDS 301-496-5751
Paralysis....Staff American Paralysis Association 800-225-0292
Paramedical Training....Staff HRSA/BHPr 301-443-5794
Paramyotonia Congenita....Staff NINDS 301-496-5751
Paranoia....Staff NIMH 301-443-4513
Paraosmia....Staff NIDCD 301-496-7243
Paraplegia....Staff NINDS 301-496-5751
Parasitic Disease....Staff NIAID 301-496-5717
Parasitic Diseases....Staff CDC 404-488-7760
Parasitology....Staff NIAID 301-496-5717
Parathyroid Disorders....Staff NIDDK 301-496-3583
Parenthood....Staff Planned Parenthood Federation of America 800-230-7526
Parenting....Staff Positive Pregnancy and Parenting Fitness 800-433-5523
Parents of Visually Impaired....Staff National Association for Parents of the Visually Impaired 800-562-6265
Paris Air Show....Staff COMMERCE 202-482-2835
Parkinson's Disease....Staff American Parkinson's Disease Association 800-223-2732
Parkinson's Disease....Staff 800-457-6676
Parkinson's Disease....Staff National Parkinson foundation 800-327-4545
Parkinson's Disease....Staff NINDS 301-496-5751
Parkinson's Disease....Staff NIDCD 301-496-7243
Parkinsonism-Dementia....Staff NINDS 301-496-5751
Parole and Parolees....Greenfeld, Lawrence Justice Stat 202-616-3281
Parole and Parolees....Huggins, M. Wayne Justice Stat 202-307-3106
Paroxysmal Atrial Tachycardia (PAT)....Staff NHLBI 301-496-4236
Paroxysmal Nocturnal Hemoglobinuria....Staff NIAID 301-496-5717
Paroxysmal Nocturnal Hemoglobinuria....Staff NHLBI 301-496-4236
Pars Planitis....Staff NEI 301-496-5248
Part-time Workers, Employment/Employment....Nardone, Thomas LABOR 202-606-6378
Particle Beams....Wood, Robert NEIC 301-903-5535
Particle board....Hoffmeier, Bill USITC 202-205-3321
Party favors....Abrahamson, Dana USITC 202-205-3430
Parvovirus Infections....Staff NIAID 301-496-5717
Passenger autos, trucks, and buses....Hagey, Michael USITC 202-205-3392
Pasta....Manogue, Robert COMMERCE 202-482-2428
Patents, Fish and Wildlife....Staff FWS 703-358-1938
Pathogen-Free Mice and Rats....Staff NCRR 301-496-5255
Pathology....Elin, Ronald J. FAES 301-496-5668
Patient Activities Department....Staff CC 301-496-2276
Patient Dumping....Holtz, Judy IG 202-619-1142
Patient Emergency Fund...Staff CC 301-496-2381
Patient Referrals...Staff CC 301-496-4891
Paving Materials, Asphalt....McCauley, Patrick COMMERCE 202-482-0132
Paving Materials, Concrete....Pitcher, Charles COMMERCE 202-482-0132
Pay Telephone Compensation....Staff FCC 202-418-0960
PC-MATLAB....Staff DCRT 301-496-1122
PC-MLAB....Staff DCRT 301-402-1942
PC-MLAB...Staff DCRT 301-496-1122
PCBs (Polychlorinated Biphenyl) Chem. Regulations....Staff EPA 202-260-3933
PCP...Staff NIDA 301-443-6245
PCS-Auctions Hotline....Staff FCC 202-418-1400
Peanuts - World....McCormick, Ian Agri 202-219-0840
Peanuts....Burket, Stephen USITC 202-205-3318
Peanuts....Ropel, Stephen Agri 202-720-8843

Peanuts....Sanford, Scott Agri 202-219-0835
Pearl essence....Johnson, Larry USITC 202-205-3351
Pearls....Witherspoon, Ricardo USITC 202-205-3489
Peat moss....Trainor, Cynthia USITC 202-205-3354
Peat....Cantrell, Raymond MINES 202-501-9411
Pectin....Janis, William V. COMMERCE 202-482-2250
Pectin....Jonnard, Aimison USITC 202-205-3350
Pectus Excavatum (Funnel Chest)....Staff NHLBI 301-496-4236
Pedodontics....Staff NIDR 301-496-4261
Peer Review Organizations (PROs)....Hardy, Robert HCFA 202-966-3206
Peer Review Orgs./Sanctions....Holtz, Judy IG 202-619-1142
Peer Review Process (Grants)....Staff DRG 301-594-7248
Pelizaeous-Merzbacher Disease....Staff NINDS 301-496-5751
Pelvic Inflammatory Disease....Staff NIAID 301-496-5717
Pemphigoid (Ocular)....Staff NEI 301-496-5248
Pemphigoid....Staff NIAMS 301-496-8188
Pemphigus Vulgaris....Staff NIAMS 301-496-8188
Pencils/Pens, etc.....Vanderwolff, John COMMERCE 202-482-0348
Pencils....Seastrum, Carl USITC 202-205-3493
Pencils....Smyth, James CUSTOMS 212-466-2084
Penicillin....Nesbitt, Elizabeth USITC 202-205-3355
Pens....Smyth, James CUSTOMS 212-466-2084
People/China....McCall, Laura Cnty Commerce 202-482-3583
People/China....McQueen, Cheryl Cnty Commerce 202-482-3932
People with handicaps....People with Handicaps Resource Center 800-544-3284
People....Staff People's Medical Society 800-624-8773
Peptic Ulcers....Staff NIDDK 301-654-3810
Perchloroethylene....Michels, David USITC 202-205-3352
Percutaneous Transluminal Coronary Angioplasty...Staff NHLBI 301-496-4236
Perfumery, cosmetics, and toilet preps....Land, Eric USITC 202-205-3349
Periarteritis Nodosa....Staff NIAID 301-496-5717
Periarteritis Nodosa....Staff NHLBI 301-496-4236
Pericardial Tamponade....Staff NHLBI 301-496-4236
Pericarditis....Staff NHLBI 301-496-4236
Pericardium....Staff NHLBI 301-496-4236
Perilymph Fistula....Staff NIDCD 301-496-7243
Perinatal Biology....Staff NICHD 301-496-5133
Periodic Paralysis....Staff NINDS 301-496-5751
Periodicals Reading Room....Krug, Patricia NAL 301-504-5204
Periodicals....Bratland, Rose Marie COMMERCE 202-482-0380
Periodontal Diseases....Staff NIDR 301-496-4261
Peripheral Nerve Tumor....Staff NINDS 301-496-5751
Peripheral Neuropathy (Neuritis)...Staff NINDS 301-496-5751
Peripheral Vascular Disease....Staff NHLBI 301-496-4236
Perlite....Bolen, Wallace P. MINES 202-501-9389
Permit Information, Fish and Wildlife....Staff FWS 703-358-2104
Pernicious Anemia....Staff NIDDK 301-496-3583
Peroneal Muscular Atrophy....Staff NINDS 301-496-5751
Peroxides and Acetals....Brady, Thomas CUSTOMS 212-466-5747
Peroxides, inorganic....Conant, Kenneth USITC 202-205-3346
Personal leather goods....Seastrum, Carl USITC 202-205-3493
Personality....Staff NIMH 301-443-4513
Persons with disabilities....Staff Job Accommodation Network 800-526-7234
Pertussis....Staff NIAID 301-496-5717
Peru (Lima)....Staff Cnty State 202-647-3360
Peru/Minerals....Gurmendi, Alfredo Cnty Mines 202-501-9681
Peru....Entwistle, Janet K. Cnty World Bank 202-473-0130
Peru....Hunt, Rebecca Cnty Commerce 202-482-2521
Peru....Jarvis, Catherine Cnty USIA 202-619-5867
Peru....Luna, Ricardo V. Cnty Embassy 202-833-9860
Peru....Parkinson, Katherine Cnty Treasury 202-622-5292
Peru....Quesada, Luis Cnty Embassy 202-833-9869
Peru....Schneider, John Cnty AID 202-647-4365
Peru....Wilkins, Michele Cnty Export-Import Bank 202-565-3743
Pesticide Hotline....Staff EPA 806-743-3095
Pesticide Information....Staff EPA 202-305-5919
Pesticide Monitoring Programs, National....Staff FWS 703-358-2148
Pesticide Monitoring....Staff FWS 703-358-2148
Pesticides and Toxic Substances....Staff EPA 202-235-5300
Pesticides and Toxic Enforcement....Staff EPA 202-260-4544
Pesticides Information Center....Staff EPA 202-305-5919
Pesticides....Hollrah, Glen H. PTO 703-308-4552
Pesticides....Reilly, Cornelius CUSTOMS 212-466-5770
Pesticides....Staff National Pesticide Telecommunications Network 800-858-7378

Pesticides....Staff NIEHS 919-541-3345
Pesticides....Wanser, Stephen USITC 202-205-3363
Pet animals (live)....Steller, Rose USITC 202-205-3323
Pet Food....Manogue, Robert COMMERCE 202-482-2428
Pet Products (Export Promo)....Kimmel, Edward K. COMMERCE 202-482-3640
Petrochemicals Plants, Major Proj.....Max, Miles COMMERCE 202-482-0679
Petrochemicals, Cyclic Crudes....Kelly, Michael COMMERCE 202-482-0128
Petrochemicals....Kelly, Michael COMMERCE 202-482-0128
Petroleum, Crude and Refined Products....Gillett, Tom COMMERCE 202-482-1466
Petroleum (Ground Level)....Staff EPA 919-541-5526
Petroleum Offshore Drilling....Staff FCC 717-337-1212
Petroleum Products Markets....Cook, John NEIC 202-586-5214
Petroleum Statistics....Heath, Charles NEIC 202-586-6860
Petroleum....Brady, Thomas CUSTOMS 212-466-5747
Petroleum....Christian, Trisha NEIC 202-586-8800
Petroleum....Foreso, Cynthia USITC 202-205-3348
Petroleum....Withrow, Leola NEIC 202-586-8800
Peyronie's Disease....Staff NIDDK 301-654-4415
Phacoemulsification....Staff NEI 301-496-5248
Pharmaceuticals....Reilly, Cornelius CUSTOMS 212-466-5770
Pharmaceuticals....Hurt, William COMMERCE 202-482-0128
Pharmacology Information System (PROPHET)....Staff NCRR 301-594-7934
Pharmacology Research Associate Training Program....Staff NIGMS 301-496-7301
Pharmacology/Toxicology....Staff NIGMS 301-496-7301
Pharmacology/Toxicology....Staff NIEHS 919-541-3345
Pharynx....Staff NIDR 301-496-4261
Phenois....Kight, John PTO 703-308-2453
Phenol....Matusik, Ed USITC 202-205-3356
Phenolic resins....Misurelli, Denby USITC 202-205-3362
Phenylketonuria (PKU)....Staff NICHD 301-496-5133
Pheochromocytema....Staff NHLBI 301-496-4236
Philippines (Manila)....Staff Cnty State 202-647-1221
Philippines/Minerals....Lyday, Travis Cnty Mines 202-501-9695
Philippines....Basilio, Antonio I. Cnty Embassy 202-467-9300
Philippines....Camp, Bea Cnty USIA 202-619-5837
Philippines....Imam, Fahmila Cnty Export-Import Bank 202-565-3738
Philippines....Khan, Shamina Cnty World Bank 202-458-2895
Philippines....Paine, George Cnty Commerce 202-482-3875
Philippines....Philip, Scott Peace Corps 202-606-1053
Philippines....Quinn, Lois Cnty Treasury 202-622-8014
Philippines....Rabe, Raul Ch. Cnty Embassy 202-467-9300
Philippines....Rahman, Talaat Cnty TDA 703-875-4357
Phlebitis....Staff NHLBI 301-496-4236
Phlebothrombosis....Staff NHLBI 301-496-4236
Phobias....Staff NIMH 301-496-4513
Phonograph and parts....Puffert, Douglas USITC 202-205-3402
Phonograph records....Puffert, Douglas USITC 202-205-3402
Phonographic equipment....Puffert, Douglas USITC 202-205-3402
Phonographs....Puffert, Douglas USITC 202-205-3402
Phosphate Rock....Cantrell, Raymond MINES 202-501-9411
Phosphatic fertilizers....Trainor, Cynthia USITC 202-205-3354
Phosphoric acid esters....Johnson, Larry USITC 202-205-3351
Phosphoric acid....Trainor, Cynthia USITC 202-205-3354
Phosphorous esters....Lee, Mary PTO 703-308-4546
Phosphorus compounds....Conant, Kenneth USITC 202-205-3346
Phosphorus....Trainor, Cynthia USITC 202-205-3354
Photocells....Malison, Andrew USITC 202-205-3391
Photocoagulation....Staff NEI 301-496-5248
Photocopy Services....Staff NIH Library/DRS 301-496-2983
Photocopying apparatus....Baker, Scott USITC 202-205-3386
Photocopying....Gellner, Michael L. PTO 703-308-1436
Photographic chemicals....Wanser, Stephen USITC 202-205-3363
Photographic Equipment and Supplies....Watson, Joyce COMMERCE 202-482-0574
Photographic film: scrap....Baker, Scott USITC 202-205-3386
Photographic film: waste....Baker, Scott USITC 202-205-3386
Photographic gelatin....Jonnard, Aimison USITC 202-205-3350
Photographic supplies....Baker, Scott USITC 202-205-3386
Photographs (Historical)....Staff NLM 301-496-5961
Photographs....Twarok, Chris USITC 202-205-3314
Photography....Gellner, Michael L. PTO 703-308-1436
Photography....Staff NCRRR 301-496-5995

Photovoltaics....Rannels, James E. NEIC 202-586-1720
PHS Commissioned Corps....Griss, William ASH 202-690-6867
Phthalic acid esters....Johnson, Larry USITC 202-205-3351
Phthalic anhydride....Matusik, Ed USITC 202-205-3356
Physical Environment. Agents (Effect on Hum. Hea.)....Staff NIEHS 919-541-3345
Physical Fitness and Sports, President's Council on....Perlmutter, Sandy ASH 202-272-3421
Physical Mapping....Staff NCHGR 301-402-0911
Physician's Assistant....Staff HRSA/BHPr 301-443-5794
Physicians....Staff Association of American Physicians and Surgeons 800-635-1196
Physicians...Staff American College of Physicians 800-523-1546
Physics....McCarthy, James UVA 701-924-6783
Physiology....Staff NIGMS 301-496-7301
Pi-Mesons (Cancer Treatment)....Staff NCI 301-496-5583
Pi-Mesons (Cancer Treatment)....Staff NCI 301-496-5583
Pick's Disease....Staff NIA 301-496-1752
Pick's Disease....Staff NINDS 301-496-5751
Pickwickian Syndrome....Staff NHLBI 301-496-4236
Pig iron....MacKnight, Peg USITC 202-205-3431
Pigmented Villonodular Synovitis....Staff NIAMS 301-496-8188
Pigments, inorganic....Johnson, Larry USITC 202-205-3351
Pigments, organic....Wanser, Stephen USITC 202-205-3363
Pigments....Bell, Mark L. PTO 703-308-3823
Pigments....Brownchweig, Gilbert CUSTOMS 212-466-5744
Pillow blocks....Fravel, Dennis USITC 202-205-3404
Pillowcases....Sweet, Mary Elizabeth USITC 202-205-3455
Pillows....Spalding, Josephine USITC 202-205-3498
Pinball machines....Abrahamson, Dana USITC 202-205-3430
Pinene....Michels, David USITC 202-205-3352
Pink Eye....Staff NEI 301-496-5248
PinWorms....Staff NIAID 301-496-5717
Pipe, of rubber or plastics....Misurelli, Denby USITC 202-205-3362
Pipeline safety...Jackson, Larry NTSB 202-382-0670
Pipelines (Major Promo)....Miles, Max COMMERCE 202-482-0679
Pipes, tobacco....Burns, Gail USITC 202-205-2501
Pitch from wood....Randall, Rob USITC 202-205-3366
Pituitary Tumors....Staff NICHD 301-496-5133
Pituitary Tumors....Staff NIDDK 301-496-3583
Pituitary Tumors....Staff NINDS 301-496-5751
Pityriasis Rubra Pilaris....Staff NIAMS 301-496-8188
Pityriasis....Staff NIAMS 301-496-8188
PKU (Phenylketonuria)....Staff NICHD 301-496-5133
PL-480 Program...Staff FIC 301-496-1653
Placenta....Staff NICHD 301-496-5133
Plant Closings Statistics....Siegel, Lewis LABOR 202-606-6404
Plant Genome Information Center....McCarthy, Susan NAL 301-504-6613
Plants, live....Burket, Stephen USITC 202-205-3318
Plants....Conte, Ralph CUSTOMS 212-466-5759
Plaque (Dental)....Staff NIDR 301-496-4261
Plasma Cell Cancer....Staff NCI 301-496-5583
Plaster products....White, Linda USITC 202-205-3427
Plastic Construction Products, Most....Williams, Franklin COMMERCE 202-482-0132
Plastic Materials....Raimundo, Prat COMMERCE 202-482-0128
Plastic processes....Silbaugh, Jan H PTO 703-308-3829
Plastic Products Machinery....Robinson, Raymond COMMERCE 202-482-0610
Plastic Products....Prat, Raimundo COMMERCE 202-482-0128
Plastic Sheet....Mazzola, Joan CUSTOMS 212-466-5880
Plastic Surgeons....Staff American Society of Plastic and Reconstructive Surgeons 800-635-0635
Plastic wood....Johnson, Larry USITC 202-205-3351
Plasticizers....Johnson, Larry USITC 202-205-3351
Plastics, Biodegradable....Staff EPA 703-308-7259
Plastics products....Raftery, Jim USITC 202-205-3365
Plastics....Misurelli, Denby USITC 202-205-3362
Platelet Abnormalities....Staff NIDDK 301-496-3583
Platelet Requests....Staff CC 301-496-3608
Platelet Requests....Staff NCI 301-496-5583
Platelet Requests....Staff NHLBI 301-496-4236
Plateletpheresis Center....Staff CC 301-496-4321
Platinum compounds....Greenblatt, Jack USITC 202-205-3353
Platinum Group Metals....Trease, Robert Jr. MINES 202-501-9413

Platinum group metals....McNay, Deborah USITC 202-205-3425
Platinum....Rosenfeld, David CFT 312-353-9026
Pleasure boats....Lahey, Kathleen USITC 202-205-3409
Pleurisy....Staff NHLBI 301-496-4236
Plumbing Fixtures and Fittings....Shaw, Robert COMMERCE 202-482-0132
Plumbing Fixtures....Pitcher, Charles COMMERCE 202-482-0132
Plutonium....Greenblatt, Jack USITC 202-205-3353
Plywood/Panel Products....McNamara, Kathy COMMERCE 202-482-0375
Plywood....Hoffmeier, Bill USITC 202-205-3321
PMS (Premenstrual Syndrome)....Staff NIMH 301-443-4515
PMS (Premenstrual Syndrome)....Staff NICHD 301-496-5133
Pneumococcal Infections....Staff NIAID 301-496-5717
Pneumoconioses (Dust Inhalation Disease)....Staff NHLBI 301-496-4236
Pneumocystis Carinii....Staff NIAID 301-496-5717
Pneumonia and Older People....Staff NIA 301-496-1752
Pneumonia....Staff NIAID 301-496-5717
Pneumothorax....Staff NHLBI 301-496-4236
Point-of-Use Water Treatment....Vacant COMMERCE 202-482-3509
Point-to-Point Microwave Common Carrier....Staff FCC 202-634-1706
Poison Control Ctrs.....Staff VA 202-625-3333
Poison Control Ctrs.....Staff MD 800-492-2414
Poison Control Ctrs.....Staff DC 202-625-3333
Poison Control Ctrs.....Staff MD 410-528-7701
Poison Ivy....Staff NIAID 301-496-5717
Poland/Minerals....Steblez, Walter Cnty Mines 202-501-9671
Poland (Warsaw)....Staff Cnty State 202-647-4139
Poland....Ann Lien Cnty TDA 703-875-4357
Poland....Azemien, Susan Cnty Treasury 202-622-2887
Poland....Horvai, Andras Cnty World Bank 202-473-3046
Poland....Jaroszynski, Andrzej Cnty Embassy 202-234-3801
Poland....Kozminski, Jerzy Cnty Embassy 202-234-3800
Poland....Lockwood, Jennifer Peace Corps 202-606-3607
Poland....Robinson, Susan Cnty USIA 202-619-6853
Poland....Schiel, Russell Peace Corps 202-606-3606
Poland....Waxman-Lenz, Roberta Cnty Export-Import Bank 202-565-3742
Poland....Zuck, Audrey Cnty Commerce 202-482-4915
Pole Attachments....Staff FCC 202-634-1861
Police Statistics....Manson, Donald Justice Stat 202-616-3491
Police Statistics....White, Paul Justice Stat 202-307-0771
Polioencephalitis (Cerebral Poliomyelitis)....Staff NINDS 301-496-5751
Poliomyelitis....Staff NIAID 301-496-5717
Polishes under 10 lbs each....Randall, Rob USITC 202-205-3366
Political campaign agendas in US and Britain....Gurevitch, Michael UMD 301-405-2418
Pollen Allergy....Staff NIAID 301-496-5717
Pollution (Air, Waste, Water)....Staff EPA 202-260-7606
Pollution Abatement Reporting....Staff FWS 703-358-1719
Pollution Control Equipment....Jonkers, Loretta COMMERCE 202-482-0564
Pollution Funds Center....Sheehan, Daniel USCG 703-235-4720
Pollution Prevention Division....Staff EPA 202-260-3557
Pollution Prevention Policy....Staff EPA 202-260-8621
Polyarteritis....Staff NHLBI 301-496-4236
Polycarbonate resins....Misurelli, Denby USITC 202-205-3362
Polychondritis....Staff NIAMS 301-496-8188
Polycystic Kidney Disease....Staff NIDDK 301-654-4415
Polycystic Ovary Syndrome....Staff NICHD 301-496-5133
Polycythemia (Vera)....Staff NHLBI 301-496-4236
Polycythemia (Vera)....Staff NCI 301-496-5583
Polyester resins....Misurelli, Denby USITC 202-205-3362
Polyesters....Kight, John PTO 703-308-2453
Polyethylene terephthalate (PET) resins....Misurelli, Denby USITC 202-205-3362
Polyethylene....Misurelli, Denby USITC 202-205-3362
Polyhydric alcohols, fatty acids of, animal/veg....Land, Eric USITC 202-205-3349
Polyhydric alcohols of polysaccharides and rare....Randall, Rob USITC 202-205-3366
Polyhydric alcohol....Michels, David USITC 202-205-3352
Polyisoprene rubber....Misurelli, Denby USITC 202-205-3362
Polymers....Misurelli, Denby USITC 202-205-3362
Polymers....Smith, L.E. NIST 301-975-6762
Polymyalgia Rheumatica....Staff NIAMS 301-496-8188
Polymyositis....Staff NINDS 301-496-5751
Polymyositis....Staff NIAMS 301-496-8188
Polyneuritis (Guillain-Barre Syndrome)....Staff NINDS 301-496-5751
Polyostotic Fibrous Dysplasia (Albright's Syndr.)....Staff NIAMS 301-496-8188

Polypropylene....Misurelli, Denby USITC 202-205-3362
Polyps and Cancer....Staff NCI 301-496-5583
Polyps, Colon....Staff NIDDK 301-496-3583
Polyps, Colon....Staff NCI 301-496-5583
Polysaccharides....Randall, Rob USITC 202-205-3366
Polysiloxanes....Bleutge, John PTO 703-308-2363
Polystyrene resins....Misurelli, Denby USITC 202-205-3362
Polysulfides....Bleutge, John PTO 703-308-2363
Polyurethane resins....Misurelli, Denby USITC 202-205-3362
Polyvinyl alcohol resins....Misurelli, Denby USITC 202-205-3362
Polyvinyl chloride....Misurelli, Denby USITC 202-205-3362
Pompe's Disease....Staff NIDDK 301-496-3583
Pompe's Disease....Staff NINDS 301-496-5751
Poor, Working, Employment/Unemployment Statistics....Herz, Diane LABOR 202-606-6378
Population, Age and Sex (States, Counties)....Staff CENSUS 301-457-2422
Population, Aging....Kinsella, Kevin CENSUS 301-457-1371
Population, Apportionment....Staff CENSUS 301-457-2381
Population, Citizenship....Staff CENSUS 301-457-2403
Population, Commuting....Boertein, Celia CENSUS 301-457-2454
Population, Consumer Expenditure Survey....Hoff, Gail CENSUS 301-457-3925
Population, Crime....Hoff, Gail CENSUS 301-457-3925
Population, Disability....McNeil, Jack CENSUS 301-763-8300
Population Dynamics and Problems....Staff NICHD 301-496-5133
Population Ecology, Fish and Wildlife....Staff FWS 703-358-1710
Population, Education....Staff CENSUS 301-457-2464
Population, Estimates....Staff CENSUS 301-457-2422
Population, General Information....Staff CENSUS 301-457-2422
Population, Group Quarters....Smith, Denise CENSUS 301-457-2378
Population Health Studies....Goldsmith, Robert NEIC 301-903-5926
Population, Homeless....Clark, Annette CENSUS 301-457-2378
Population Information....Staff CENSUS 301-457-2422
Population, Language....Staff CENSUS 301-457-2464
Population, Longitudinal Surveys....Higgins, Sarah CENSUS 301-457-3801
Population, National Estimates....Staff CENSUS 301-457-2422
Population, National Surveys....Staff CENSUS 301-457-2422
Population, Outlying Areas....Levin, Michael CENSUS 301-457-2327
Population, Place of Birth....Hansen, Kristin CENSUS 301-457-2454
Population, School District Data....Ingold, Jane CENSUS 301-457-2408
Population, State and Outlying Areas Estimates....Staff CENSUS 301-457-2422
Population, State Projections....Staff CENSUS 301-457-2422
Population Survey (Current), Earnings, Empl/Unempl.....Mellor, Earl LABOR 202-606-6378
Porcelain Electrical Supplies, Part....Whitley, Richard A. COMMERCE 202-482-2213
Pork bellies with options....Prentice, Jon CFT 312-353-8647
Pork....Newman, Douglas USITC 202-205-3328
Porphuria....Staff NHLBI 301-496-4236
Porphyria....Staff NIAMS 301-496-8188
Porphyria....Staff NIDDK 301-654-3810
Port Safety....Sabol, Albert USCG 202-267-0489
Port Security....Sabol, Albert USCG 202-267-0489
Portugal (Lisbon)....Staff Cnty State 202-647-1412
Portugal/Minerals....Newman, Harold R. Cnty Mines 202-501-9669
Portugal....Double, Mary Beth Cnty Commerce 202-482-4508
Portugal....Feliz-Alves, Rui Cnty Embassy 202-328-8610
Portugal....Gosnell, Peter Cnty Export-Import Bank 202-565-3733
Portugal....Guimaraes, Fernando Andresen Cnty Embassy 202-328-8610
Portugal....Holloway, Barbara Cnty Treasury 202-622-0098
Portugal....Seifkin, David Cnty USIA 202-619-6582
Portugal....Szaszkiewicz, Barbara Cnty World Bank 202-473-4374
Position Emission Tomography....Wood, Robert NEIC 301-903-5355
Positional Vertigo....Staff NIDCD 301-496-7243
Positron Emission Tomography....Staff NINDS 301-496-5751
Postage-franking machines....Baker, Scott USITC 202-205-3386
Postal Services....Staff OD/DAS (Mailroom) 301-496-5651
Postdoctoral Fellowships....Staff DRG 301-594-7248
Postdoctoral Fellowships....Staff OD/OERT 301-496-1963
Postherpetic Neuralgia....Staff NINDS 301-496-5751
Postnatal Care....Staff NICHD 301-496-5133
Postpartum Depression....Staff NIMH 301-443-4513
Postpolio Muscular Atrophy....Staff NINDS 301-496-5751
Postpolio Syndrome....Staff NINDS 301-496-5751
Postural Hypotension....Staff NHLBI 301-496-4236

Potash....Searls, James P. MINES 202-501-9407
Potash....Trainor, Cynthia USITC 202-205-3354
Potassic fertilizers....Trainor, Cynthia USITC 202-205-3354
Potassium and sodium salts from coconut and other oils....Land, Eric USITC 202-205-3349
Potassium chloride....Trainor, Cynthia USITC 202-205-3354
Potassium compounds....Greenblatt, Jack USITC 202-205-3353
Potassium (Content of Foods)....Staff NHLBI 301-496-4236
Potatoes....Budge, Arvin Agri 202-720-4285
Potatoes....Lucier, Gary Agri 202-219-0117
Potatoes....McCarty, Timothy USITC 202-205-3324
Potatoes....Plummer, Charles Agri 202-219-0009
Pottery....Bratland, Rosemarie COMMERCE 202-482-0380
Pottery....McNay, Deborah USITC 202-205-3425
Poultry - Broilers, Turkeys, Eggs....Milton, Madison Agri 202-219-1192
Poultry - Broilers, Turkeys, Eggs....Christensen, Lee Agri 202-219-0714
Poultry - Broilers, Turkeys, Eggs - World....Witucki, Larry Agri 202-219-0766
Poultry - Broilers, Turkeys and Eggs....Little, Robert Agri 202-720-6147
Poultry - Broilers, Turkeys, Eggs....Krutchen, Tom Agri 202-690-4870
Poultry - Broilers, Turkeys and Eggs....Moore, Joel Agri 202-720-3244
Poultry Products....Hodgen, Donald A. COMMERCE 202-482-3346
Poultry....Newman, Douglas USITC 202-205-3328
Poultry....Staff Hotline Agriculture 800-535-4555
Poverty Statistics, Current Surveys....Staff CENSUS 301-763-8578
Powder, smokeless....Johnson, Larry USITC 202-205-3351
Powered-Lift Technology....Waller, Peter NASA 415-604-3938
Prader-Willi Syndrome....Staff NICHD 301-496-5133
Precious Metal Jewelry....Harris, John M. COMMERCE 202-482-1178
Precious stones....DeSapio, Vincent USITC 202-205-3435
Precocious Puberty....Staff NICHD 301-496-5133
Predator Control, Fish and Wildlife....Staff FWS 703-358-1718
Preemption of State Laws....Staff FCC 202-418-1720
Prefabricated Buildings, Metal....Williams, Franklin COMMERCE 202-482-0132
Prefabricated Buildings, Wood....Cosslett, Patrick COMMERCE 202-482-0132
Pregnancy and Infant Health....Atrash, Hani K. CDC 404-488-5147
Pregnancy....Staff NAPARE 800-638-2229
Pregnancy....Staff Positive Pregnancy and Parenting Fitness 800-433-5523
Pregnancy....Staff NICHD 301-496-5133
Pregnancy....Staff NCNR 301-496-0526
Prematurity....Staff NICHD 301-496-5133
Prenatal Care....Staff NICHD 301-496-5133
Prenatal Nutrition....Staff NICHD 301-496-5133
Prepared Meats....Manogue, Robert COMMERCE 202-482-2428
Presbycusis/Hearing and Aging....Staff NIA 301-496-1752
Presbycusis/Hearing and Aging....Staff NINDS 301-496-5751
Presbycusis/Hearing and Aging....Staff NIDCD 301-496-7243
Presbycusis....Staff NIDCD 301-496-7243
Presbycusis....Staff NINDS 301-496-5751
Presbyopia....Staff NEI 301-496-5248
Prescription Drug Abuse...Staff NIDA 301-443-6245
Presenile Dementia....Staff NINDS 301-496-5751
Presenile Dementia....Staff NIMH 301-443-4513
Presenile Dementia....Staff NIA 301-496-1752
Preservation and Access Program....Pindell, Alvetta NAL 301-504-5204
Press Information....Staff CENSUS 301-457-2974
Pretrial Release and Crime - Federal....Kaplan, Carol Justice Stat 202-307-0759
Prevention Research (Drug Abuse)...Staff NIDA 301-443-6245
Preventive Health Block Grant....Sims, Anne CDC 404-639-3286
Preventive Medicine....Staff American Institute for Preventive Medicine 800-345-2476
Price Caps....Staff FCC 202-418-1520
Price and Index Number Research, Prices/Lv. Cond....Zieschang, Kimberly LABOR 202-606-6573
Price Indexes (Consumer) Prices and Liv. Cond.....Jackman, Patrick LABOR 202-606-6952
Price Indexes, International, Assist. Commiss.....Reut, Katrina LABOR 202-606-7100
Prices, Foreign Countries, Prod. and Technol.....Godbout, Todd LABOR 202-606-5654
Prices/Living Conds, Assist. Commis.....Dalton, Kenneth LABOR 202-606-6960
Prices/Living Conds, Assist. Commis, Consumer Price Index....Greenlef, Joan LABOR 202-606-6950
Prices/Living Conds, Assist. Commis, Consumer Prices....Greenlef, Joan LABOR 202-606-6950

Prices/Living Conds, Associate Commissioner....Dalton, Kenneth LABOR 202-606-6960
Prices/Living Conds, Consumer Expenditure Survey Data....Passero, William LABOR 202-606-6900
Prices/Living Conds, Consumer Expenditure Survey Operations....Dietz, Richard LABOR 202-606-6872
Prices/Living Conds, Consumer Expenditure Survey Tapes....Passero, William LABOR 202-606-6900
Prices/Living Conds, Consumer Expenditure Survey....Jacobs, Eva LABOR 202-606-6900
Prices/Living Conds, Consumer Expenditure Survey....Jacobs, Eva LABOR 202-606-6900
Prices/Living Conds, Consumer Price Indexes....Jackman, Patrick LABOR 202-606-6952
Prices/Living Conds, Consumer Price Indexes....Staff LABOR 202-606-7000
Prices/Living Conds, CPI, Data Diskettes....Gibson, Sharon LABOR 202-606-6968
Prices/Living Conds, CPI Recorded Detail....24-Hour Hotline LABOR 202-606-7828
Prices/Living Conds, Data Diskettes....Rosenberg, Elliott LABOR 202-606-7728
Prices/Living Conds, Data Diskettes....Rosenberg, Elliott LABOR 202-606-7728
Prices/Living Conds, Dept. Store Inventory....Gibson, Sharon LABOR 202-606-6968
Prices/Living Conds, Electric machinery and Transpor....Yatsko, Ralph LABOR 202-606-7747
Prices/Living Conds, Estd Retail Food Price, Mthly....Cook, William LABOR 202-606-6988
Prices/Living Conds, Food, Raw Matls, Apprl....Frumkin, Rob LABOR 202-606-7106
Prices/Living Conds, Forestry and Construction....Davies, Wanda LABOR 202-606-7714
Prices/Living Conds, Index Number Research Studies....Zieschang, Kimberly LABOR 202-606-6573
Prices/Living Conds, Indexes, Fuels, Mthly....Adkins, Robert LABOR 202-606-6985
Prices/Living Conds, Indexes, Utils, Mthly....Adkins, Robert LABOR 202-606-6985
Prices/Living Conds, Intl Price Indexes....Reut, Katrina LABOR 202-606-7100
Prices/Living Conds, Intl. Pr., Machinery....Costello, Brian LABOR 202-606-7107
Prices/Living Conds, Intl. Prices, Revision....Reut, Katrina LABOR 202-606-7100
Prices/Living Conds, Leather....Paik, Soon LABOR 202-606-7714
Prices/Living Conds, Machinery....Alterman, William LABOR 202-606-7108
Prices/Living Conds, Metals....Kazanowski, Edward LABOR 202-606-7735
Prices/Living Conds, Non-electric mach.....Dickerson, Bryandt LABOR 202-606-7744
Prices/Living Conds, Non-electric Machinery....Dickerson, Bryandt LABOR 202-606-7744
Prices/Living Conds, PPI, Forestry....Davies, Wanda LABOR 202-606-7714
Prices/Living Conds, PPI, Current Analysis....Howell, Craig LABOR 202-606-7705
Prices/Living Conds, Price Research Studies....Zieschang, Kimberly LABOR 202-606-6753
Prices/Living Conds, Producer Price Indexes....Tibbetts, Thomas LABOR 202-606-7700
Prices/Living Conds, Recorded CPI Summary....24-Hour quickline LABOR 202-606-6994
Prices/Living Cond., Recorded PPI Detail....24-hour hotline LABOR 202-606-7828
Prices/Living Conds, Retail Prices, Fuels, Mthly....Adkins, Robert LABOR 202-606-6985
Prices/Living Conds, Retail Prices, Gasoline....Chelena, Joseph LABOR 202-606-6982
Prices/Living Conds, Retail Prices, Utils, Mthly....Adkins, Robert LABOR 202-606-6985
Prices/Living Conds, Services....Gerduk, Irwin LABOR 202-606-7748
Prices/Living Conds, Statistical Methods....Hedges, Brian LABOR 202-606-6897
Prices/Living Conds, Textiles....Paik, Soon LABOR 202-606-7714
Prices/Living Conds, Transportation Equipment....Yatsko, Ralph LABOR 202-606-7747
Primary Biliary Cirrhosis....Staff NIDDK 301-654-3810
Primary Lateral Sclerosis....Staff NINDS 301-496-5751
Primary Ovarian Failure....Staff NICHD 301-496-5133
Primary Plastics....Reilly, Cornelius CUSTOMS 212-466-5770
Primate Research Centers Program....Staff NCRR 301-496-5175
Primate Research....Staff NCRR 301-594-7938

Prime mover dynamo plants....Pellinen, David PTO 703-308-0538

Prime Time Access Rule...Staff FCC 202-418-2130

Principe....Blackwell, Gloria Peace Corps 202-606-3998

Principe....Edwards, Jennifer R. Cnty World Bank 202-473-4875

Principe....Swezey, Virginia Peace Corps 202-606-3998

Printed circuit boards....Malison, Andrew USITC 202-205-3391

Printed matter....Twarok, Chris USITC 202-205-3314

Printed Matter....Abramowitz, Carl CUSTOMS 212-466-5733

Printing devices....Burr, Edgar PTO 703-308-0979

Printing and Publishing....Lofquist, William COMMERCE 202-482-0379

Printing ink....Johnson, Larry USITC 202-205-3351

Printing machines (textiles)....Greene, William USITC 202-205-3405

Printing machines....Lusi, Susan USITC 202-205-2334

Printing Trades Machines/Equipment....Robinson, Raymond COMMERCE 202-482-0610

Printing Trade Services....Lofquist, William COMMERCE 202-482-0379

Prisoner Surveys, National Prisoner Statistics....Hoff, Gail CENSUS 301-457-3925

Prisons, Prisoners, and Crowding....Greenfeld, Lawrence Justice Stat 202-616-3281

Prisons, Prisoners, and Crowding....Stephan, James Justice Stat 202-616-7273

Prisons, Prisoners, and Crowding....Huggins, Wayne M. Justice Stat 202-307-3106

Prisons, Prisoners, and Crowding....Baunach, Phyllis Jo Justice Stat 202-307-0361

Prisons, Prisoners, and Crowding....Beck, Allen Justice Stat 202-616-3277

Prisons, Prisoners, and Crowding....Innes, Christopher Justice Stat 202-724-3121

Privacy and Security of Data....Kaplan, Carol Justice Stat 202-307-0759

Private Carriers Communications....Staff FCC 717-337-1212

Private Coast Stations....Staff FCC 202-418-0680

Private Operational Fixed Services....Staff FCC 717-337-1212

Private Security....Zawitz, Marianne Justice Stat 202-616-3499

Privatization of Corrections....Lindgren, Sue Justice Stat 202-307-0760

Prize Giveaway....Staff FCC 202-418-1430

Probation and Probationers....Greenfeld, Lawrence Justice Stat 202-616-3281

Procaine....Staff NIA 301-496-1752

Process Control Instruments, Trade Promo.....Manzolilo, Frank COMMERCE 202-482-2991

Process Control Instruments....Nealon, Margaret COMMERCE 202-482-3411

Process Measurements....Rosasco, GJ NIST 301-975-2609

Procurement Services....Staff OD/ORS 301-496-3181

Producer Price Indexes, Analysis and Data....Howell, Craig LABOR 202-606-7704

Producer Price Indexes, Analysis and Data....Howell, Craig LABOR 202-606-7704

Producer Price Indexes, Electric Machinery and Trans....Yatsko, Ralph LABOR 202-606-7747

Producer Price Indexes, Forestry and Construction....Davies, Wanda LABOR 202-606-7713

Producer Price Indexes, Metals....Kazanowski, Edward LABOR 202-606-7735

Producer Price Indexes Prices/Living Cond.....Tibbetts, Thomas LABOR 202-606-7700

Producer Price Indexes, Textiles and Leather....Paik, Soon LABOR 202-606-7714

Product defects....Staff USP Practitioners Reporting Network 800-487-7776

Product manufacturing....Envall, Roy PTO 703-305-9706

Product safety....Staff CPSC 301-504-0580

Product safety....Staff CPSC 800-638-2772

Productivity and Technology, Assist. Commis.....Dean, Edwin R. LABOR 202-606-5600

Productivity and Technology, Associate Commissioner....Dean, Edwin R. LABOR 202-606-5600

Productivity and Technology, Compensation, For. Countries....Capdevielle, Patricia LABOR 202-606-5654

Productivity and Technology, Cost-of-Living Abroad....Capdevielle, Patricia LABOR 202-606-5654

Productivity and Technology, Data Diskettes....Fulco, Lawrence J. LABOR 202-606-5604

Productivity and Technology, Data Tapes....Kriebel, Bertram LABOR 202-606-5606

Productivity and Technology, Data Tapes....Kriebel, Bertram LABOR 202-606-5606

Productivity and Technology, Earnings, Foreign Countries....Capdevielle, Patricia LABOR 202-606-5654

Productivity and Technology, Employment Projections....Franklin, James LABOR 202-606-5709

Productivity and Technology, Employment Requirement Tbls....Franklin, James LABOR 202-606-5709

Productivity and Technology, For Countries, Other Econ In....Neef, Arthur LABOR 202-606-5654

Productivity and Technology, Foreign Countries, Labor For....Sorrentino, Constance LABOR 202-606-5654

Productivity and Technology, Foreign Countries, Productivity....Neef, Arthur LABOR 202-606-5654

Productivity and Technology, Foreign Countries, Unemployment....Sorrentino, Constance LABOR 202-606-5654

Productivity and Technology, Productivity and Costs-News Release....Fulco, Lawrence J. LABOR 202-606-5604

Productivity and Technology, Productivity in Government....Forte, Darlene J. LABOR 202-606-5621

Productivity and Technology, Productivity Research....Harper, Michael LABOR 202-606-5603

Productivity and Technology, Productivity Trends Federal Govt....Ardolini, Charles W. LABOR 202-606-5618

Productivity and Technology, Tech Trends, Major Ind....Riche, Richard LABOR 202-606-5626

Productivity in Government, Productivity and Tech.....Forte, Darlene J. LABOR 202-606-5621

Productivity, Multifactor, Labor Composition, Hrs.....Rosenblum, Larry LABOR 202-606-5606

Productivity Research, Capital Measurement, Pr/Tch....Harper, Michael LABOR 202-606-5603

Productivity Trends in Selected Industries....Ardolini, Charles W. LABOR 202-606-5618

Productivity Trends in Selected Ind. and Fed. Gov't....Ardolini, Charles W. LABOR 202-606-5618

Productivity, Unit Labor Costs, Foreign Countries....Neef, Arthur LABOR 202-606-5654

Professional Services....Staff OPM 202-606-4400

Professional services....Xavier, Neil USITC 202-205-3450

Progeria....Staff NIA 301-496-1752

Progestins and Progesterone....Staff NICHD 301-496-5133

Progestins and Progesterone....Staff HRSA/DMCH 301-443-4026

Progressive Cerebral Degeneration....Staff NINDS 301-496-5751

Progressive Dementia in Children....Staff NINDS 301-496-5751

Progressive Infantile Spinal Muscular Atrophy....Staff NINDS 301-496-5751

Progressive Leukodystrophy....Staff NINDS 301-496-5751

Progressive Multifocal Leukoencephalopathy....Staff NINDS 301-496-5751

Progressive Muscular Atrophy....Staff NINDS 301-496-5751

Progressive Supranuclear Palsy....Staff NINDS 301-496-5751

Progressive Systemic Sclerosis....Staff NINDS 301-496-5751

Progressive Systemic Sclerosis....Staff NIAMS 301-496-8188

Project LASER Volunteer Programs....Widenhofer, Karen NASA 205-544-3234

Project LASER Discovery Lab....Armstrong, Pat NASA 205-544-1798

Projections, Labor Force, Employment Projections....Fullerton, Howard LABOR 202-606-5711

Projections, Occupational, Empl. Proj.....Rosenthal, Neal LABOR 202-606-5701

Projectors (photographic)....Baker, Scott USITC 202-205-3386

Propagation Research, Fish and Wildlife....Staff FWS 703-358-1710

Propane....Land, Eric USITC 202-205-3349

Property Utilization....Staff OD/OL 301-496-4247

Propulsion Systems....Brogan, John NEIC 202-586-1477

Propylene glycol....Michels, David USITC 202-205-3352

Propylene oxide....Michels, David USITC 202-205-3352

Propylene....Raftery, Jim USITC 202-205-3365

Prosecution....Gaskins, Carla Justice Stat 202-508-8550

Prosecution....Langan, Patrick Justice Stat 202-616-3490

Prostaglandins....Staff NICHD 301-496-5133

Prostaglandins....Staff NHLBI 301-496-4236

Prostate Enlargement....Staff NIDDK 301-654-4415

Prostate/Hyperplasia of the Prostate....Staff NIDDK 301-654-4415

Prostate/Hyperplasia of the Prostate....Staff NIA 301-496-1752

Prostatitis....Staff NIDDK 301-654-4415

Prosthesis (Hearing)....Staff NIDCD 301-496-7243

Prostheses (Heart and Blood Vessel)....Staff NHLBI 301-496-4236

Prostheses (Orthotics)....Staff NIAMS 301-496-8188

Prosthetic devices....Green, Randall PTO 703-308-2912

Prosthetic devices....Staff NINDS 301-496-5751

Prosthodontics....Staff NIDR 301-496-4261

Protection of Human Subjects...Staff OD/OPRR 301-496-7005

Protein Abnormalities with Neurologic Disease....Staff NINDS 301-496-5751

Protein C and S....Staff NHLBI 301-496-4236

Protein Engineering....Staff DCRT 301-496-1100

Prurigo Nodularis....Staff NIAMS 301-496-8188

Pseudogout....Staff NIAMS 301-496-8188
Pseudohypoparathyroidism....Staff NIDDK 301-496-3583
Pseudomonas Infections....Staff NIAID 301-496-5717
Pseudosenility....Staff NIA 301-496-1752
Pseudotumor Cerebri....Staff NINDS 301-496-5751
Pseudotumor Cerebri....Staff NEI 301-496-5248
Pseudoxanthoma Elasticum....Staff NHLBI 301-496-4236
Psittacosis....Staff NIAID 301-496-5717
Psoriasis....Staff National Psoriasis Foundation 800-248-0886
Psoriasis....Staff NIAMS 301-496-8188
Psoriatic Arthritis....Staff NIAMS 301-496-8188
Psychology....Allen, Joseph P. UVA 804-982-4727
Psychology....McCarty, Richard UVA 804-924-4730
Psychoneuroimmunomodulation....Staff NINDS 301-496-5751
Psychopathology....Staff NIDA 301-443-6245
Psychopharmacology....Staff NIMH 301-443-4513
Psychoprophylaxis....Staff American Society for Psychoprophylaxis in Obstetrics 800-368-4404
Psychotherapeutic agents....Nesbitt, Elizabeth USITC 202-205-3355
Psychotherapy/Counseling....Staff NIDA 301-443-6245
Psychotic Episodes....Staff NIMH 301-443-4513
Pterygium....Staff NEI 301-496-5248
Ptosis....Staff NEI 301-496-5248
Public Affairs, Office of....Sims, Anne CDC 404-639-3286
Public Affairs Office....Murfy, Alexander FTC 202-326-2180
Public Affairs....Corlett, Cleve E. GAO 202-512-4800
Public Affairs....Hayden, Elizabeth A. NRC 301-415-8200
Public Coast Stations....Staff FCC 202-418-0680
Public Defense....Gaskins, Carla Justice Stat 202-508-8550
Public File Requirements AM/FM/TV....Staff FCC 202-418-1430
Public Health and Safety....Ziemer, Paul NEIC 202-586-6151
Public Health Issues....Nadel, Mark V. GAO 202-512-7119
Public Health System....Nicola, Ray CDC 404-639-1904
Public Health....Fintor, Lou FAES 301-496-5410
Public Housing....Staff HUD 202-708-0950
Public Information, Director, Office of....Mehnert, Robert NLM 301-496-6308
Public Information, Fish and Wildlife Service....Staff FWS 202-208-5634
Public Information Office - Atlanta....Mull, Daryl SSAREG 404-331-0612
Public Information Office - Boston....Czarnowski, Kurt SSAREG 617-565-2881
Public Information Office - Chicago....Mahler, Mary SSAREG 312-353-7092
Public Information Office, Chief....Mohn, Ingrid A. ECONOMIC 202-606-9900
Public Information Office - Dallas....O'Neil, Dee SSAREG 214-767-4191
Public Information Office - Denver....Taylor, Peter SSAREG 303-844-4441
Public Information Office - Kansas City....Nolker, Bud SSAREG 816-426-6191
Public Information Office - New York....Clark, John SSAREG 212-264-2500
Public Information Office - Philadelphia....Edward, Dana SSAREG 215-597-3747
Public Information Office - San Francisco....Walker, Leslie SSAREG 415-744-4664
Public Information Office - Seattle....Farrell, Dan SSAREG 206-615-2660
Public Information Office....Kendrick, Tony IHS 301-443-3593
Public Information Office....Velez, Larry OCR 202-619-1587
Public Information Office....Grigg, Bill ASH 202-690-6867
Public Information Office....Holtz, Judy IG 202-619-1142
Public Information Office....Gambino, Phil SSA 410-965-8904
Public Information Office....Kharfen, Michael ACF 202-401-9215
Public Information Office....Helsing, James SAMHSA 301-443-8956
Public Information Center....Staff EPA 202-260-2080
Public Information Office....Murry, Kevin AHCPR 594-1364
Public Information Office....Hardy, Robert HCFA 301-966-3206
Public Information Office....Shaffer, Sylvia HRSA 202-443-3376
Public Information Office....O'Hara, James FDA 301-443-1130
Public Information....Maulsby, Richard PTO 703-305-8341
Public inquiries....Moye, Melba D. NTSB 202-382-6787
Public inquiries....Staff DOD 703-697-5737
Public Opinion About Crime....Zawitz, Marianne Justice Stat 202-616-3499
Public Opinion About Crime....Lindgren, Sue Justice Stat 202-307-0760
Public relations, magazine journalism....Grunig, Larissa A. UMD 301-405-2431
Public relations theory and techniques....Zerbinos, Eugenia UMD 301-405-2430
Public Relations....Grunig, James E. UMD 301-405-2416
Public relations....Vacant USITC 202-205-3410
Public Services Division....Lacroix, Eve-Marie NLM 301-496-5501
Public Surveys, Fish and Wildlife Service....Staff FWS 703-358-1730
Public Transportation Systems....Vacant FTA 202-366-4995
Public Use, Fish and Wildlife Hatcheries....Staff FWS 703-358-1715

Public Use, Fish and Wildlife Refuges....Staff FWS 703-358-1786
Public-Use Microdata Samples....Campbell, Carmen CENSUS 301-457-1139
Publication Clearance...Staff OD/OC 301-496-4143
Publication Grants....Staff NLM 301-496-6131
Publications and Special Studies, Assoc. Com....Klein, Deborah P. LABOR 202-606-5900
Publications Information, Public. and Spec. Studies....Staff LABOR 202-606-7828
Publications (Inquiries) and NLM Photos/Slides....Beckwith, Frances NLM 301-496-6308
Publications Office, Recorded Current....24-Hour Hotline LABOR 202-606-7828
Publications Office, Press Officer....Hoyle, Kathryn LABOR 202-606-5902
Publications Office, TDD (Telecom. Device for Deaf)....TDD LABOR 202-606-5897
Publications....Colby, Lloyd SEC 202-942-4040
Publishing Industry Group....Roycroft, John C. SEC 202-942-1960
Publishing....Lofquist, William COMMERCE 202-482-0379
Puerto Rico....Siegelman, Mark Cnty Commerce 202-482-5680
Pulleys....Fravel, Dennis USITC 202-205-3404
Pulmonary Alveolar Proteinosis....Staff NHLBI 301-496-4236
Pulmonary Angiomyomatosis....Staff NHLBI 301-496-4236
Pulmonary Diseases (Infectious/Allergenic)....Staff NIAID 301-496-5717
Pulmonary Diseases (Non-Inf., Non-All., Non-Tum.)....Staff NHLBI 301-496-4236
Pulmonary Diseases (Tumorous/Cancerous)....Staff NCI 301-496-5583
Pulmonary Edema....Staff NHLBI 301-496-4236
Pulmonary Embolism....Staff NHLBI 301-496-4236
Pulmonary Emphysema....Staff NHLBI 301-496-4236
Pulmonary Fibrosis....Staff NHLBI 301-496-4236
Pulmonic Stenosis....Staff NHLBI 301-496-4236
Pulp, articles of....Rhodes, Richard USITC 202-205-3322
Pulp machines....Lusi, Susan USITC 202-205-2334
Pulp Mills, Major Proj.....Miles, Max COMMERCE 202-482-0679
Pulpmills....Stanley, Gary COMMERCE 202-482-0375
Pulpwood....Hoffmeier, Bill USITC 202-205-3321
Pumice....Bolen, Wallace P. MINES 202-501-9389
Pumice....White, Linda USITC 202-205-3427
Pumps, air and vacuum....Mata, Ruben USITC 202-205-3403
Pumps, liquid....Mata, Ruben USITC 202-205-3403
Pumps, Pumping Eqmt....Vacant COMMERCE 202-482-0680
Pumps, Valves, Comp (Trade Promo.)....Zanetakos, George COMMERCE 202-482-0552
Pumps....Riedl, Karl CUSTOMS 212-466-5493
Pure Red Cell Aplasia....Staff NHLBI 301-496-4236
Purpara....Staff NHLBI 301-496-4236
Purpura....Staff NIDDK 301-654-4415
Purpura....Staff NIAMS 301-496-8188
Putty...Johnson, Larry USITC 202-205-3351
Puzzles....Abrahamson, Dana USITC 202-205-3430
Pyelonephritis....Staff NIDDK 301-654-4415
Pyorrhea....Staff NIDR 301-496-4261
Pyrethrum....Wanser, Stephen USITC 202-205-3363
Pyridine....Foreso, Cynthia USITC 202-205-3348

Q

Qatar (Doha)....Staff Cnty State 202-647-6572
Qatar/Minerals....Izon, David Cnty Mines 202-501-9674
Qatar....Al-Khari, Ali Saad Cnty Embassy 202-338-0111
Qatar....Al-Thani, Sheikh Abdulrahman bin Saud Cnty Embassy 202-338-0111
Qatar....Konigshofer, Friedrich Cnty World Bank 202-473-2988
Qatar....Mercer, Dorothy Cnty Treasury 202-622-0184
Qatar....Thanos, Paul Cnty Commerce 202-482-1870
Qatar....Vacant Cnty USIA 202-619-6528
Quadriplegia....Staff NINDS 301-496-5751
Quality Control--Common Carrier....Staff FCC 202-418-1500
Quantum Physics....Leone, S.R. NIST 303-497-6807
Quanum Metrology....Deslaattes, R.D. NIST 301-975-4841
Quarantine, Disease....Perez, Tony D. Charles R. CDC 404-639-8107
Quarterly Financial Report....Lee, Ronald CENSUS 301-763-5435
Quarterly, Occupational Outlook, Empl. Proj.....Rosenthal, Neal LABOR 202-606-5701
Quartz Crystal....Austin, Gordon MINES 202-501-9388
Quartzite....White, Linda USITC 202-205-3427

Quasars....Staff NASA 205-544-0034
Quatar....Mabury-Lewis Anthony Cnty Export-Import Bank 202-565-3739
Quaternary ammonium salts, fatty acids....Land, Eric USITC 202-205-3349
Quebracho....Wanser, Stephen USITC 202-205-3363
Quill, articles of....Spalding, Josephine USITC 202-205-3498
Quilts....Sweet, Mary Elizabeth USITC 202-205-3455

R

Rabies....Staff NIAID 301-496-5717
Race Statistics....Staff CENSUS 301-457-2453
Racing shells....Hagey, Michael USITC 202-205-3392
Racketeering....Coffey, Paul E. Justice 202-514-3594
Radar apparatus....Kitzmiller, John USITC 202-205-3387
Radial Keratotomy....Staff NEI 301-496-5248
Radiant energy systems....Dzierzynski, Paul PTO 703-308-4822
Radiation, Effect on Eyes....Staff NEI 301-496-5248
Radiation, Effect on Teeth....Staff NIDR 301-496-4261
Radiation Environmental Laws....Wallo, Andrew NEIC 202-586-4996
Radiation, Nervous System....Staff NINDS 301-496-5751
Radiation, Nonionizing....Staff OD/ORS 301-496-2960
Radiation, Nonionizing....Staff NIEHS 919-541-3345
Radiation Programs, Office of....Staff EPA 202-233-9320
Radiation Protection....Staff D. CDC 404-639-3147
Radiation Questions....Staff EPA 202-233-9280
Radiation Safety Badges....Staff OD/ORS 301-496-2254
Radiation Safety Officer....Staff NIH 301-496-2254
Radiation Safety (Radio. Spills, Lab. Surveys)....Staff OD/ORS 301-496-5774
Radiation Safety....Cruzan, Susan FDA 301-443-3285
Radiation Safety....Staff FDA 301-594-4752
Radiation Studies Division....Staff EPA 202-233-9340
Radiation Studies....Smith, James M. CDC 404-488-7040
Radiation survivors....Staff National Association of Radiation Survivors 800-798-5102
Radiation....Staff NCI 301-496-5583
Radio and TV Broadcast Eqpmt....Siegmund, John COMMERCE 202-482-4781
Radio apparatus and parts....Kitzmiller, John USITC 202-205-3387
Radio Control Radio Service....Staff FCC 202-418-0680
Radio Industry....Owings, Christopher SEC 202-942-1900
Radio navigational apparatus....Kitzmiller, John USITC 202-205-3387
Radio Noise....Staff FCC 301-725-1585
Radio Ownership Regulations (Broadcast)....Staff FCC 202-418-2780
Radio receivers....Kitzmiller, John USITC 202-205-3387
Radio....Tarcza, Thomas C. PTO 703-308-1689
Radioactive Materials (Shipping and Receiving)....Staff OD/ORS 301-496-2254
Radioactive Waste Disposal....Lytle, Jill NEIC 202-586-0370
Radioactive Waste Disposal at NIH (Solid and Liquid)....Staff OD/ORS 301-496-2254
Radiolocation--Industrial....Staff FCC 717-337-1212
Radiometric Physics....Parr, A.C. NIST 301-975-3739
Radionuclide Techniques in CV Diagnosis....Staff NHLBI 301-496-4236
Radios....Dicerbo, Mario CUSTOMS 212-466-5672
Radioscope Power Systems....Lane, Robert NEIC 301-903-4362
Radiotelephone Equipment....Staff FCC 301-725-1585
Radiotherapy (Cancer)....Staff NCI 301-496-5583
Radium....Staff NCI 301-496-5583
Radon Division....Staff EPA 202-233-9370
Radon Information....Staff EPA 202-233-9370
Radon Publications....Staff EPA 202-260-9370
Rags....Cook, Lee USITC 202-205-3471
Rail, locomotives....Lahey, Kathleen USITC 202-205-3409
Railroad Development....McQueen, James T FRA 202-366-9660
Railroad Equipment....Wholey, Patrick CUSTOMS 212-466-5668
Railroad Safety Analysis....Leeds, John G FRA 202-366-9186
Railroad Safety....Fine, Bruce FRA 202-366-0895
Railroad safety....Lauby, Robert NTSB 202-382-6845
Railroad Services....Wolfe, Claudia COMMERCE 202-482-5086
Railroads Industry Group....Parratt, Shelley SEC 202-942-1840
Railroads (Major Proj)....Smith, Jay L COMMERCE 202-482-4642
Railroads....Staff FCC 717-337-1212
Railway equipment....Oberleitner, Robert PTO 703-308-2569
Railway rolling stock.:..Lahey, Kathleen USITC 202-205-3409
Railway switches....Huppert, Michael PTO 703-308-1107

Railways, spring devices....Oberleitner, Robert PTO 703-308-3569
Railway track....Huppert, Michael PTO 703-308-1107
Rain Forests....Martin, R. Michael FS 703-235-1676
Rainwear....Shetty, Sundar USITC 202-205-3457
Ramsey Hunt Syndrome....Staff NINDS 301-496-5751
Ramsey Hunt Syndrome....Staff NIDCD 301-496-7243
Range Research....Lennartz, Michael R. FS 202-205-1524
Rape....Baldwin, Elaine NIMH 301-443-4536
Rare diseases....Staff National Organization for Rare Disorders 800-999-6673
Rare diseases....Staff National Information Center for Orphan Drugs and Rare Diseases 800-456-3505
Rare Diseases....Staff OD 301-496-1454
Rare Disorders (Neurological)....Staff NINDS 301-496-5751
Rare-earth metals....Conant, Kenneth USITC 202-205-3346
Rare-earth compounds....Greenblatt, Jack USITC 202-205-3353
Rare Earths....Hedrick, James B. MINES 202-501-9412
Rare saccharides....Randall, Rob USITC 202-205-3366
Rattan....Hoffmeier, Bill USITC 202-205-3321
Raw Materials, Food, and Apparel, Intl. Price Ind.....Frumkin, Rob LABOR 202-606-7106
Raynaud's Disease....Staff NHLBI 301-496-4236
Raynaud's Syndrome....Staff NIAMS 301-496-8188
RCRA/Superfund (OUST Hotline)....Staff EPA 800-424-9346
RCRA Information Hotline....Staff EPA 415-744-2074
Reactor Analysis....Rosenthal, Jack E. NRC 301-415-7488
Reactor Controls....Boger, Bruce NRC 301-415-1004
Reactor Radiation....Rowe, J.M. NIST 301-975-6210
Reactor Radiation....Rowe, Michael J. NIST 301-975-6210
Reading Development....Staff NICHD 301-496-5133
Reading Development....Staff NIDCD 301-496-7243
Reading Development....Staff NINDS 301-496-5751
Reading Disorders....Staff NINDS 301-496-5751
Reading Disorders....Staff NIDCD 301-496-7243
Reading Disorders....Staff NICHD 301-496-5133
Reading Disorders....Staff Dept. of Education 202-245-8707
Real Earnings--News Release, Empl/Unempl. Stats....Hiles, David LABOR 202-606-6547
Real Estate and Housing Industry....Parratt, Shelley SEC 202-942-1840
Reasonable Access....Staff FCC 202-418-1440
Recalls (Automobile Emissions)....Staff EPA 202-233-9240
Recalls (drugs)....Adams, Betsy FDA 301-443-3285
Recalls (food)....Corwin, Emil FDA 202-205-4144
Receptacles....Sewell, Paul T PTO 703-308-2126
Recidivism....Beck, Allen Justice Stat 202-616-3277
Recidivism....Greenfeld, Lawrence Justice Stat 202-616-3281
Recidivism....Shipley, Bernard Justice Stat 202-307-7703
Recombinant DNA Activity....Staff OD 301-496-9838
Recombinant DNA....Staff NIAID 301-496-5717
Recombinant DNA....Staff NIGMS 301-496-7301
Reconstituted crude petroleum....Foreso, Cynthia USITC 202-205-3348
Reconstructive Surgeons....Staff American Society of Plastic and Reconstructive Surgeons 800-635-0635
Reconstructive Surgery....Staff American Academy of Facial Plastic and Reconstructive Surgery 800-332-3223
Record Retention Requirement...Staff FCC 202-418-0210
Recorded CPI Detail, Prices and Living Cond.....24-Hour Hotline LABOR 202-606-7828
Recorded Messages, Compensation and Working Condition....24-hour hotline LABOR 202-606-7828
Records Imaging Processing System....Staff FCC 202-418-0293
Records, tapes and recording media....Puffert, Douglas USITC 202-205-3402
Recovery Plans, Endangered Species....Staff FWS 703-358-2183
Recreation, Fish and Wildlife Recreation....Staff FWS 703-358-1715
Recreation, Refuges....Staff FWS 703-358-1786
Recreational Equipment, Export Promo.....Beckham, Reginald COMMERCE 202-482-5478
Rectifiers....Vacant CUSTOMS 212-466-5673
Recurrent Fever....Staff NIAID 301-496-5717
Recurrent Pyogenic Infections....Staff NIAID 301-496-5717
Recycling (General Issues)....Staff EPA 202-260-6261
Recycling Program (EPA)....Staff EPA 703-308-8300
Red Blood Cells (Erythrocytes)....Staff NHLBI 301-496-4236
Red Blood Cells (Erythrocytes)....Staff FDA/NCDB 301-496-3556
Reeling machines....Greene, William USITC 202-205-3405

Refarming of Shared Spectrum....Staff FCC 202-418-0620
Reference and Users Service....Kulp, Leslie NAL 301-504-6875
Reference Center....Staff FCC 202-418-0270
Reference Desk....Staff NAL 301-504-5479
Reference Services....Staff NCRR/NIH Library 301-496-2184
Reference Services...Staff NLM 301-496-6095
Reflex Sympathetic Dystrophy Syndrome....Staff NIAMS 301-496-8188
Reflux Nephropathy....Staff NIDDK 301-496-3583
Refractive Errors....Staff NEI 301-496-5248
Refractories....DeSapio, Vincent USITC 202-205-3435
Refractory Anemia....Staff NHLBI 301-496-4236
Refractory glass....Bell, Mark L. PTO 703-308-3823
Refractory Products....Duggan, Brian COMMERCE 202-482-0610
Refrigerants....Lieberman, Paul PTO 703-308-2552
Refrigeration equipment....Mata, Ruben USITC 202-205-3403
Refrigeration....Francke, Eric CUSTOMS 212-466-5669
Refrigeration....Radebaugh, Ray NIST 303-497-3710
Refsum's Disease....Staff NINDS 301-496-5751
Refugee Resettlement....Kharfen, Michael ACF 202-401-9215
Regeneration (CNS)...Staff NINDS 301-496-5751
Regional Affairs, Western Hemisphere....Eppler, Dale US Trade Rep 202-395-5190
Regional, BEA Economic Areas....Trott, Jr., Edward A. ECONOMIC 202-606-9231
Regional Director - Atlanta....Ford-Roegner, Patricia HHSREG 404-331-2442
Regional Director - Boston....Johnston, Philip HHSREG 617-565-1500
Regional Director - Chicago....Weiss, Elaine HHSREG 312-353-5160
Regional Director - Dallas....Montoya, Patricia HHSREG 214-767-3301
Regional Director - Denver....Carey, Margaret HHSREG 303-844-3372
Regional Director - Kansas City....Steele, Kathleen HHSREG 816-426-2821
Regional Director - New York....Greene, Alison HHSREG 212-264-4600
Regional Director - Philadelphia....Yeakel, Lynn H. HHSREG 215-596-6492
Regional Director - San Francisco....Phelon, Ronald W. FTC 415-744-7920
Regional Director - San Francisco....Grantland, Johnson HHSREG 415-556-6746
Regional Director - Seattle....McBride, Patricia HHSREG 206-615-2010
Regional, Disposable Personal Income....Brown, Robert ECONOMIC 202-606-9246
Regional, Dividends, Interest and Rental Income....Jolley, Charles A. ECONOMIC 202-606-9257
Regional Economic Analysis, Chief....Kort, John R. ECONOMIC 202-606-9221
Regional Economic Measurement, Chief....Knox, Hugh ECONOMIC 202-606-9605
Regional, Economic Situation, Current....Friedenberg, Howard L. ECONOMIC 202-606-9216
Regional Economics, Associate Director....Knox, Hugh W. ECONOMIC 202-606-9605
Regional Economics, Associate Director....Knox, Hugh W. ECONOMIC 202-606-9605
Regional Enteritis....Staff NIDDK 301-654-3810
Regional, Farm Proprietors' Income and Employment....Zavrel, James M. ECONOMIC 202-606-9290
Regional, Gross State Product Estimates....Staff ECONOMIC 202-606-4500
Regional Medical Libraries....Staff NLM 301-496-4777
Regional, Methodology....Bailey, Wallace K. ECONOMIC 202-606-9254
Regional Office -....Cooper, Joanne FTC 202-326-2257
Regional Office - ....Dowdy, Lemuel W. FTC 202-326-2981
Regional Office - ....Wallace, Cheryl J. FTC 202-326-3712
Regional Office - Atlanta....Alphin, Katherine B. FTC 404-347-7520
Regional Office - Atlanta....Bolen, Ida FTC 404-347-7046
Regional Office - Atlanta....Brennan, Virginia FTC 404-347-7540
Regional Office - Atlanta....Carlone, Ralph GAO 404-679-1800
Regional Office - Atlanta....Couillou, Chris M. FTC 404-347-7517
Regional Office - Atlanta....Davis, Paul K. FTC 404-347-7524
Regional Office - Atlanta....Foster, Andrea FTC 404-347-7516
Regional Office - Atlanta....House, Nicole L. FTC 404-347-7541
Regional Office - Atlanta....Kirtz, Harold E. FTC 404-347-7522
Regional Office - Atlanta....Laitsch, Ronald E. FTC 404-347-7535
Regional Office - Atlanta....Liebes, Cinday A. FTC 404-347-7514
Regional Office - Atlanta....Ozburn, Chris Edmonds FTC 404-347-7515
Regional Office - Atlanta....Powell, Saundra FTC 404-347-4836
Regional Office - Atlanta....Rohrer, James T. FTC 404-347-7534
Regional Office - Atlanta....Schanker, Barbara S. FTC 404-347-7518
Regional Office - Atlanta....Staff CENSUS 404-730-3833
Regional Office - Atlanta....Taylor, Mark FTC 404-347-7512

Regional Office - Atlanta....Walton, Doris P. FTC 404-347-7532
Regional Office - Atlanta....Whittaker, Ingrid FTC 404-347-7536
Regional Office - Atlanta....Williams, Addie L. FTC 404-347-7510
Regional Office - Boston....Arleo, Jonathon FTC 617-424-5960
Regional Office - Boston....Barry, Daniel FTC 617-424-5960
Regional Office - Boston....Block, Paul G. FTC 617-424-5960
Regional Office - Boston....Bolton, Barbara E. FTC 617-424-5960
Regional Office - Boston....Caverly, Andrew FTC 617-424-5960
Regional Office - Boston....Cooper, Gary S. FTC 617-424-5960
Regional Office - Boston....Dugan, John T. FTC 617-424-5960
Regional Office - Boston....Gray, Jessica D. FTC 617-424-5960
Regional Office - Boston....Greenberg, Sara FTC 617-424-5960
Regional Office - Boston....Haley, Mary G. FTC 617-424-5960
Regional Office - Boston....Harrington, Diane J. FTC 617-424-5960
Regional Office - Boston....Hughes, Thomas M. FTC 617-424-5960
Regional Office - Boston....Keniry, David I., Jr. FTC 617-424-5960
Regional Office - Boston....Morse, Phoebe D. FTC 617-424-5960
Regional Office - Boston...Ols, John M. GAO 617-565-7555
Regional Office - Boston....Robertson, Terry L. FTC 617-424-5960
Regional Office - Boston....Staff CENSUS 617-424-0510
Regional Office - Boston....Wood, Kristie FTC 617-424-5960
Regional Office - Boston....Wood, Pamela J. FTC 617-424-5960
Regional Office - Charlotte....Staff CENSUS 704-371-6142
Regional Office - Chicago....Baker, Steven C. FTC 312-353-8156
Regional Office - Chicago....Damtoft, Russel W. FTC 312-353-3771
Regional Office - Chicago....Daniels, Janice A. FTC 312-353-7178
Regional Office - Chicago....DiGiulio, Barbara A. FTC 312-353-7178
Regional Office - Chicago....Dodge, Karen D. FTC 312-353-4448
Regional Office - Chicago....Franczyk, Nicholas J. FTC 312-353-7957
Regional Office - Chicago....Fuller, Catherine R. FTC 312-353-5576
Regional Office - Chicago....Genda, Christine M. FTC 312-353-5261
Regional Office - Chicago....Hallerud, John C. FTC 312-353-5575
Regional Office - Chicago....Hughes, Timothy T. FTC 312-353-4431
Regional Office - Chicago....Krause, Alan E. FTC 312-353-4441
Regional Office - Chicago....Luke, John H. GAO 312-220-7600
Regional Office - Chicago....McGrew, Theresa M. FTC 312-353-5532
Regional Office - Chicago....Miller, Michael T. FTC 312-353-5260
Regional Office - Chicago....Olson, Mary E. FTC 312-353-4427
Regional Office - Chicago....Russell, Thomas J. FTC 312-353-4523
Regional Office - Chicago....Smith, Michele FTC 312-353-5045
Regional Office - Chicago....Staff CENSUS 708-562-1740
Regional Office - Chicago....Tortorice, Mary E. FTC 312-353-4435
Regional Office - Chicago....Williams, Vassoria L. FTC 312-353-4426
Regional Office - Chicago....Wronka, Kathleen F. FTC 312-353-4442
Regional Office - Cleveland....Amdur, Ilene FTC 216-522-4210
Regional Office - Cleveland....Balster, Steven W. FTC 216-574-2425
Regional Office - Cleveland....Broyles, Phillip FTC 216-522-4217
Regional Office - Cleveland....Doubrava, Brenda W. FTC 216-574-2426
Regional Office - Cleveland....Greene, Willie L. FTC 216-574-2427
Regional Office - Cleveland....Griffiths, Stephanie M. FTC 216-574-2428
Regional Office - Cleveland....Hessoun, Bonnie T. FTC 216-574-2429
Regional Office - Cleveland....Lerner, Louis L. FTC 312-353-5528
Regional Office - Cleveland....Mendenhall, John M. FTC 216-574-2432
Regional Office - Cleveland....Milgrom, Michael FTC 216-574-2433
Regional Office - Cleveland....Pirrone, Jaclyn S. FTC 216-574-2434
Regional Office - Cleveland....Plottner, David V. FTC 216-574-2435
Regional Office - Cleveland....Powell, Catherine F. FTC 216-574-2436
Regional Office - Cleveland....Rose, Michael B. FTC 216-574-2437
Regional Office - Cleveland....Sternlicht, Melissa FTC 216-522-4210
Regional Office - Cleveland....Stewart, Douglas FTC 216-574-2429
Regional Office - Cleveland....Vantusko, Mary Jo. FTC 216-522-4208
Regional Office - Cleveland....Williams, Brinley H. FTC 216-574-2439
Regional Office - Cleveland....Zeman, Gerald C. FTC 216-522-2440
Regional Office - Dallas....Arthur, Susan E. FTC 214-767-5517
Regional Office - Dallas....Black, Michael R. FTC 202-326-3457
Regional Office - Dallas....Blackman, Claire R. FTC 214-767-5503
Regional Office - Dallas....Donsky, Robin L. FTC 214-767-5503
Regional Office - Dallas....Elliott, James E. FTC 214-767-5509
Regional Office - Dallas....Garcia, Ernestina FTC 214-767-5503
Regional Office - Dallas....Golder, James R. FTC 214-767-5508
Regional Office - Dallas....Gosha-Nelson, Jannette FTC 214-767-5503
Regional Office - Dallas....Griggs, W. David FTC 214-767-5510
Regional Office - Dallas....Hickman, Joseph L. FTC 214-767-5503
Regional Office - Dallas....Kennedy, Gary D. FTC 214-767-5512

Regional Office - Dallas....Lenamond, Leslee A. FTC 214-767-5503
Regional Office - Dallas....Malmberg, Kristin L. FTC 214-767-5513
Regional Office - Dallas....McCowan, Curtistene S. FTC 214-767-5503
Regional Office - Dallas....Morgan, Maridel S. FTC 214-767-5503
Regional Office - Dallas....Peterson, Robert A. GAO 214-777-5700
Regional Office - Dallas....Shepherd, Judith A. FTC 214-767-5510
Regional Office - Dallas....Spears, Debby H. FTC 214-767-5503
Regional Office - Dallas....Staff CENSUS 214-767-7105
Regional Office - Dallas....Weart, Steven E. FTC 214-767-5516
Regional Office - Denver....Brew, Thomas J. GAO 303-572-7317
Regional Office - Denver....Carter, Thomas B. FTC 214-767-5518
Regional Office - Denver....Charter, Janice FTC 303-844-2868
Regional Office - Denver....Cole, Pamela M. FTC 303-844-2255
Regional Office - Denver....Cramer, Norman FTC 303-844-2275
Regional Office - Denver....Dahnke, Jeffrey FTC 303-844-2254
Regional Office - Denver....Farrand, Kelli A. FTC 303-844-2276
Regional Office - Denver....Gomez, Cynthia FTC 303-844-3082
Regional Office - Denver....Huff, Jan FTC 303-844-3590
Regional Office - Denver....Keese, Deborah C. FTC 303-844-2276
Regional Office - Denver....Kessler, Jonathan FTC 303-844-2276
Regional Office - Denver....Kraus, Loretta FTC 303-844-2273
Regional Office - Denver....Naylor, Sharon L. FTC 303-844-3576
Regional Office - Denver....Nickerson, Eric FTC 303-844-3584
Regional Office - Denver....Palmquist, Elizabeth FTC 303-844-2274
Regional Office - Denver....Staff CENSUS 303-969-7750
Regional Office - Denver....Wild, Claude C., III FTC 303-844-3571
Regional Office - Detroit....Staff CENSUS 313-259-1875
Regional Office - Kansas City....Staff CENSUS 913-551-6711
Regional Office - Kansas City....Watts, James R. GAO 913-384-7418
Regional Office - Los Angeles....Farias, Eliana R. FTC 310-235-7890
Regional Office - Los Angeles....Stock, Linda M. FTC 310-235-7896
Regional Office - Los Angeles....Harris, Robbie R. FTC 310-235-7890
Regional Office - Los Angles....Staff CENSUS 818-904-6339
Regional Office - Los Angeles....Willis, Elizabeth M. FTC 310-575-7971
Regional Office - Los Angeles....Willins, Paul K. FTC 310-235-7968
Regional Office - Los Angeles....Ell, Victor GAO 213-346-8045
Regional Office - Los Angeles....Syta, Thomas J. FTC 310-235-7879
Regional Office - Los Angeles....Staples, Greg FTC 310-235-7990
Regional Office - Los Angeles....Jacobs, John D. FTC 310-235-6602
Regional Office - Los Angeles....Smart, Bret S. FTC 310-235-7975
Regional Office - Los Angeles....Roark, Paul R. FTC 310-235-7870
Regional Office - Los Angeles....Frauens, Sue L. FTC 310-235-6140
Regional Office - Los Angeles....Guler, Ann M. FTC 310-235-7966
Regional Office - Los Angeles....Sekovich, Dale S. FTC 310-235-7572
Regional Office - Los Angeles....Donaldson, Nancy D. FTC 310-235-7890
Regional Office - Los Angeles....Deitch, Russell S. FTC 310-235-7965
Regional Office - Los Angeles....French, Kathy S. FTC 310-575-6138
Regional Office - Los Angeles....Dawson, Darlene FTC 310-235-7974
Regional Office - Los Angeles....McKown, Raymond E. FTC 310-235-7962
Regional Office - New York....Bloom, Michael J. FTC 212-264-1201
Regional Office - New York....D'Amato, Donald G. FTC 212-264-1223
Regional Office - New York....Au, Alice FTC 212-264-1210
Regional Office - New York....Loughnan, Alan FTC 212-264-1232
Regional Office - New York....Oteri, Patricia FTC 212-264-9804
Regional Office - New York....Goldsmith, Harriet S. FTC 212-264-1208
Regional Office - New York....McLean, Rhonda J. FTC 212-264-1211
Regional Office - New York....Roth, Marc S. FTC 212-264-8855
Regional Office - New York....Fischman, Ethel B. FTC 212-264-4688
Regional Office - New York....Waldman, Ronald FTC 212-264-1242
Regional Office - New York....Lopez, Digna FTC 212-264-0716
Regional Office - New York....Lipkowitz, Eugene FTC 212-264-1230
Regional Office - New York....Eichen, Robin E. FTC 212-264-1250
Regional Office - New York....Staff CENSUS 212-264-4730
Regional Office - New York....Paynter, Carole FTC 212-264-1225
Regional Office - New York....DiFilippi, Anna GAO 212-264-0962
Regional Office - New York....Chandrika, Kapadia FTC 212-264-1205
Regional Office - Norfolk....Stevens, Joe B. GAO 804-552-8112
Regional Office - San Francisco....Badger, Linda K. FTC 415-744-7920
Regional Office - San Francisco....Aguilar, Lisa FTC 415-744-7920
Regional Office - San Francisco....Harris, Lisa A. FTC 415-744-7920
Regional Office - San Francisco....Newmann, David M. FTC 415-744-7920
Regional Office - San Francisco....Phelon, Ronald FTC 415-744-7920
Regional Office - San Francisco....Weigand, John FTC 415-744-7920
Regional Office - San Francisco....Steinitz, Sidney FTC 202-326-3282

Regional Office - San Francisco....Kauffman, Craig D. FTC 415-744-7920
Regional Office - San Francisco....Gold, Matthew FTC 415-744-7920
Regional Office - San Francisco....Sodergren, Harold G. FTC 415-744-7920
Regional Office - San Francisco....O'Brien, Kerry FTC 415-744-7920
Regional Office - San Francisco....McCormick, Thomas P. GAO 415-904-2200
Regional Office - San Francisco....Kundig, Sylvia J. FTC 415-744-7920
Regional Office - San Francisco....Klurfeld, Jeffrey A. FTC 415-744-7920
Regional Office - San Francisco....Stone, Ralph E. FTC 415-744-7920
Regional Office - San Francisco....Wright, Gerald E. FTC 415-744-7920
Regional Office - San Francisco....Steiner, Jerome M., Jr. FTC 415-744-7920
Regional Office - San Francisco....Wodinsky, Erika R. FTC 415-744-7920
Regional Office - Seattle....Benfield, Mary T. FTC 206-220-6350
Regional Office - Seattle....Brook, Randall H. FTC 206-220-6350
Regional Office - Seattle....Decker, Kathryn FTC 206-220-6350
Regional Office - Seattle....Durham, Eleanor FTC 206-220-6350
Regional Office - Seattle....Fournier, Dean A. FTC 206-220-6350
Regional Office - Seattle....France, Laureen FTC 206-220-6350
Regional Office - Seattle....Harwood, Charles A. FTC 206-220-6350
Regional Office - Seattle....Hensley, Patricia A. FTC 206-220-6350
Regional Office - Seattle....Kirkwood, John B. FTC 206-220-6350
Regional Office - Seattle....Lipinsky, Joseph FTC 206-220-6350
Regional Office - Seattle....Meissner, James K. GAO 206-287-4810
Regional Office - Seattle....Nielsen, Kathryn C. FTC 206-220-6350
Regional Office - Seattle....Samter, Nadine S. FTC 206-220-6350
Regional Office - Seattle....Schroeder, Robert J. FTC 206-220-6350
Regional Office - Seattle....Schuller, Stella A. FTC 206-220-6350
Regional Office - Seattle....Silveira, Robert FTC 206-220-6350
Regional Office - Seattle....Staff CENSUS 206-728-5314
Regional Office - Seattle....Stansell, Maxine FTC 206-220-6350
Regional Office - Seattle....Thorleifson, Tracy S. FTC 206-220-6350
Regional Office - Seattle....Woods, K. Shane FTC 206-220-6350
Regional Office - Seattle....Zerbe, Richard O. FTC 206-220-6350
Regional Office - Seattle....Zweibel, George J. FTC 206-220-6350
Regional, Personal Income and Employment, Counties....Hazan, Linnea ECONOMIC 202-606-9254
Regional, Personal Income and Employment, Metro Area....Hazan, Linnea ECONOMIC 202-606-9254
Regional, Personal Income and Employment, States....Hazan, Linnea ECONOMIC 202-606-9254
Regional, Projections-States and Metropolitan Areas....Pigler, Carmen C. ECONOMIC 202-606-9227
Regional, Requests for Pers. Income and Employment Data....Information System Staff ECONOMIC 202-606-5360
Regional, Shift-Share Analysis....Kort, John R. ECONOMIC 202-606-9221
Regional, State Ecometric Modeling....Lienesch, C. Thomas ECONOMIC 202-606-9223
Regional, State Quarterly Personal Income....Whiston, Isabelle B. ECONOMIC 202-606-4500
Regional, Transfer Payments....Brown, Robert ECONOMIC 202-606-4500
Regional, Wage and Salary Income and Employment....Carnevale, Sharon ECONOMIC 202-606-9247
Registers....Hajec, Donald PTO 703-308-4075
Regulators....Topolansky, Adam USITC 202-205-3394
Regulatory and International Safeguards....Sherr, Theodore S. NRC 301-415-7218
Regulatory Flexibility Act....Staff FCC 202-418-1720
Rehabilitation Medicine Department....Staff CC 301-496-4733
Rehabilitation....Staff National Rehabilitation Information Center 800-346-2742
Rehabilitation....Staff NIA 301-496-1752
Reiter's Syndrome....Staff NIAMS 301-496-8188
Relays....Curran, David CUSTOMS 212-466-5680
Reliability and Risk Assessment....Baranowsky NRC 301-415-7493
Religious Studies....Childress, James F. UVA 701-924-3741
Remission....Staff NCI 301-496-5583
Remote Control Rules....Staff FCC 202-2190
Remote Sensing Techniques....Sullivan, Nancy NASA 601-688-3341
Remote Sensor Systems....Koehler, Keith NASA 804-824-1579
Renal Artery Stenosis....Staff NHLBI 301-496-4236
Renal Disorders in Children....Staff NIDDK 301-654-4415
Renal Glycosuria....Staff NIDDK 301-654-4415
Renal Hypertension....Staff NIDDK 301-654-4415
Renal Tubular Acidosis....Staff NIDDK 301-654-4415
Renal Vascular Disease....Staff NIDDK 301-654-4415
Renewable Energy Conversion....Staff NEIC 800-528-2929
Renewable Energy Equipment....Garden, Les COMMERCE 202-482-0556

Renewable Energy Resources....King, Marion NEIC 202-586-8800
Renewable Energy Resources....Freedman, Karen NEIC 202-586-8800
Renewable Energy...Davis, Michael J. NEIC 202-586-9220
Renewals Radio....Staff FCC 202-418-2780
Renewals TV....Staff FCC 202-418-1630
Renovascular Hypertension....Staff NHLBI 301-654-4415
Rental (Scientific)....Staff DRS 301-496-4131
Reporting Crime to Police....Harlow, Caroline Justice Stat 202-307-0757
Reproductive Disorders....Staff NICHD 301-496-5133
Rescue Squads....Staff FCC 717-337-1212
Research Aircraft....Brown, Dwayne C. NASA 202-358-1726
Research and Development....Price, James B. COMMERCE 202-482-4781
Research Career Development....Staff DRG 301-594-7248
Research (ethical issues)....Staff OD/OERT 301-496-7005
Research Grants....Staff DRG 301-594-7248
Research Industry Group....Owings, Christopher SEC 202-942-1900
Research Training....Staff DRG 301-594-7248
Research Training....Staff NIGMS 301-496-7301
Residence Adjustment...Zabronsky, Daniel ECONOMIC 202-606-4500
Residential Lighting Fixtures....Bodson, John COMMERCE 202-482-0681
Residual fuel oil....Foreso, Cynthia USITC 202-205-3348
Resistors....Josephs, Irwin CUSTOMS 212-466-5673
Resistors....Malison, Andrew USITC 202-205-3391
Resistors...Reynolds, Bruce A. PTO 703-308-3305
Resorts Industry Group....Roycroft, John C. SEC 202-942-1960
Resorts (leisure)....Roycroft, James M. SEC 202-942-1960
Resource Conservation and Reclamation Act (RCRA)....Traceski, Thomas NEIC 202-586-2481
Resources for Research....Staff NCRR 301-594-7938
RESPA (real estate settlement procedures act)....Goodman, Sheilah FRS 202-452-3667
Respiratory devices....Burr, Edgar PTO 703-308-0979
Respiratory Diseases (Infectious/Allergenic)....Staff NIAID 301-496-5717
Respiratory Diseases (Non-In., Non-All., Non-Tum.)....Staff NHLBI 301-496-4236
Respiratory Diseases (Tumorous/Cancerous)....Staff NCI 301-496-5583
Respiratory Diseases....Anderson, Larry CDC 404-639-3596
Respiratory Distress Syndrome...Staff NHLBI 301-496-4236
Respiratory medicine....Staff Lung Line 800-222-5864
Respiratory Syncytial Virus....Staff NIAID 301-496-5717
Restless Leg Syndrome....Staff NINDS 301-496-5751
Retail Trade, Advance Monthly Sales....Piencykoski, Ronald CENSUS 301-457-2713
Retail Trade, Annual Sales....Piencykoski, Ronald CENSUS 301-457-2713
Retail Trade, Census....Staff CENSUS 301-457-2687
Retail Trade, Monthly Trade Report....True, Irving CENSUS 301-457-2706
Retail Trade, Monthly Inventories....Piencykoski, Ronald CENSUS 301-457-2713
Retail Trade....Burroughs, Helen COMMERCE 202-482-1542
Retailing Industry Group....Tow, A. Richard SEC 202-942-1960
Retinal Degeneration....Staff NEI 301-496-5248
Retinal Detachment....Staff NEI 301-496-5248
Retinal Diseases....Dudley, Peter A. FAES 301-496-5884
Retinal Diseases....Staff NEI 301-496-5248
Retinal Vascular Disease....Staff NEI 301-496-5248
Retinitis Pigmentosa....Staff National Retinitis Pigmentosa Foundation 800-683-5555
Retinitis Pigmentosa....Staff NEI 301-496-5248
Retinoblastoma....Staff NEI 301-496-5248
Retinopathies....Staff NEI 301-496-5248
Retired persons....Staff AARP 800-424-2277
Retirement and Capital Acc, Employee Benefit Survey....Houff, James LABOR 202-606-6238
Retirement Programs....Titus, Frank D. OPM 202-606-0300
Retirement....Staff NIA 301-496-1752
Rett's Syndrome....Staff NINDS 301-496-5751
Reunion/Minerals....Antonides, Lloyd Cnty Mines 202-501-9686
Reunion....Staff Cnty State 202-647-2453
Reye's Syndrome....Staff National Reye's Syndrome Foundation, Inc. 800-233-7393
Reye's Syndrome....Staff NINDS 301-496-5751
Rh Factor....Staff NHLBI 301-496-4236
Rhabdomyosarcoma and Undifferentiated Sarcomas....Staff NCI 301-496-5583
Rhenium....Blossom, John W. MINES 202-501-9435
Rhenium....Lundy, David USITC 202-205-3439

Rheumatic Fever....Staff NIAID 301-496-5717
Rheumatic Heart....Staff NHLBI 301-496-4236
Rheumatoid Arthritis....Staff NIAMS 301-496-8188
Rhinitis....Staff NIAID 301-496-5717
Rhodium compounds....Greenblatt, Jack USITC 202-205-3353
Ribbons: inked....Cook, Lee USITC 202-205-3471
Ribbons: other....Shelton, Linda USITC 202-205-3457
Ribbons: typewriter....Shelton, Linda USITC 202-205-3457
Rice Milling....Manogue, Robert COMMERCE 202-482-2428
Rice with options....Sepsey, Judy CFT 312-353-9025
Rice...Reeder, John USITC 202-205-3319
Ricinoleic acid esters...Johnson, Larry USITC 202-205-3351
Rickets, Vitamin-D Resistant....Staff NIDDK 301-496-3583
Rickettsial Diseases....Staff NIAID 301-496-5717
Riding crops....Spalding, Josephine USITC 202-205-3498
Riding Mowers....Staff CPSC 301-504-0580
Rifles....Luther, Dennis USITC 202-205-3497
Right-of-Way....Orski, Barbara K FHWA 202-366-0342
Riley-Day Syndrome....Staff NINDS 301-496-5751
Ringworm....Staff NIAID 301-496-5717
River Blindness....Staff NIAID 301-496-5717
River Blindness....Staff NEI 301-496-5248
Roads, Railroads, Mass Trans (Major Proj)....Smith, Jay L. COMMERCE 202-482-4642
Robot Metrology....Goodwin, Kenneth R. NIST 301-975-3421
Robotics Research....Staff NASA 713-483-8693
Robots...Pilaroscia, Megan COMMERCE 202-482-0609
Rocky Mountain Spotted Fever....Staff NIAID 301-496-5717
Rods, plastics....Misurelli, Denby USITC 202-205-3362
Roller Bearings....Reise, Richard COMMERCE 202-482-3489
Rolling machines, except metal....Lusi, Susan USITC 202-205-2334
Rolling Mill Machinery....Green, William COMMERCE 202-482-3405
Rollings mills, metal....Fravel, Dennis USITC 202-205-3401
Romania (Bucharest)....Staff Cnty State 202-647-4272
Romania/Minerals....Stebion, Walter Cnty Mines 202-501-9672
Romania....Amick, Jack Peace Corps 202-606-3548
Romania....Anne McKinney Cnty TDA 703-875-4357
Romania....Bazala, Razvigor Cnty USIA 202-619-5055
Romania....Botez, Mihail Horia Cnty Embassy 202-332-4846
Romania....Green, Pam Cnty Commerce 202-482-4915
Romania....Jackson, Juhan Cnty Treasury 202-622-0766
Romania....LeMaster, Cheryl Peace Corps 202-606-3547
Romania....Mateescu, Radu Cnty Embassy 202-332-4848
Romania....Szaszkiewicz, Barbara Cnty World Bank 202-473-4374
Romania....Waxman-Lenz, Roberta Cnty Export-Import Bank 202-565-3742
Roofing, Asphalt....Franklin, William COMMERCE 202-482-0132
Root Caries....Staff NIDR 301-496-4261
Rope....Cook, Lee USITC 202-205-3471
Rosemary oil (essential oil)....Land, Eric USITC 202-205-3349
Rotary Ablation...Staff NHLBI 301-496-4236
Rotavirus....Staff NIAID 301-496-5717
Rouges....Land, Eric USITC 202-205-3349
Rubber and Plastic Articles....Mazzola, Joan CUSTOMS 212-466-5880
Rubber, natural....Misurelli, Denby USITC 202-205-3362
Rubber Products....Prat, Raimundo COMMERCE 202-482-0128
Rubber Sheet....Mazzola, Joan CUSTOMS 212-466-5880
Rubber, Synthetic and Natural....Joseph, Stephanie CUSTOMS 212-466-5768
Rubber, synthetic....Misurelli, Denby USITC 202-205-3362
Rubber....Prat, Raimundo COMMERCE 202-482-0128
Rubbers....Kight, John PTO 703-308-2453
Rubella....Staff NIAID 301-496-5717
Rubeola....Staff NIAID 301-496-5717
Rubidium....Reese, Jr., Robert MINES 202-501-9413
Rugs....Hansen, John CUSTOMS 212-466-5854
Rugs....Sweet, Mary Elizabeth USITC 202-205-3455
Rule Questions....Staff FCC 202-418-0680
Runaway Youth/Homeless....Kharfen, Michael ACF 202-401-9215
Runaways....Staff Runaway Hotline 800-231-6946
Runaways....Staff National Runaway Switchboard 800-621-4000
Runaways....Staff National Runaway Switchboard 800-621-4000
Rural Aged....Staff NIA 301-496-1752
Rural Development - Agric. and Community Linkages....Schluter, Gerald Agri 202-219-0785
Rural Development - Business and Industry....Bernat, Andrew Agri 202-219-0539

Rural Development - Community Development....Sears, David Agri 202-219-0546

Rural Development - Credit and Financial Markets....Sullivan, Pat Agri 202-219-0721

Rural Development - Employment...Parker, Tim Agri 202-219-0541

Rural Development - Employment...Swaim, Paul Agri 202-219-0553

Rural Development - Local Government Finance....Reeder, Richard Agri 202-219-0551

Rural Development - Policy....Reeder, Richard Agri 202-219-0551

Rural Development....McGranahan, David Agri 202-219-0533

Rural Development....Long, Dick Agri 202-219-0530

Rural Health...Human, Jeffrey HRSA 301-443-0835

Rural Health....Staff Rural Information Health Service 800-633-7701

Rural Information Center...John, Patricia NAL 301-504-5372

Rural Residence....Staff CENSUS 301-457-1200

Russia...Cavanagh, Stacy Peace Corps 202-606-3974

Russia...Fabrizio, Lynn Cnty Commerce 202-482-0988

Russia....Koff, Allison S. Cnty TDA 703-875-4357

Russia....Levine, Richard Cnty Mines 202-501-9682

Russia...Luhmann, Eric OPIC 202-336-8621

Russia....MacManus, Joseph Cnty USIA 202-619-5057

Russia...McGrew, Wes Cnty Treasury 202-622-2876

Russia...Moore, Anne Peace Corps 202-606-3973

Russia....Olive, Marsha M. Cnty World Bank 202-473-7331

Russia....Staff Cnty State 202-647-9806

Russia....Vorontsov, Yuli M. Cnty Embassy 202-298-5700

Russia....Waxman-Lenz, Roberta Cnty Export-Import Bank 202-565-3742

Russia....Westin, Richard Cnty World Bank 202-473-8261

Russia....Whittle, Dennis B. Cnty World Bank 202-473-8518

Russia...Baldwin, Pamela Cnty AID 202-736-4627

Russian Wheat Aphids Project....Olson, Wayne NAL 301-504-5204

Rwanda (Kigali)....Staff Cnty State 202-647-3139

Rwanda/Minerals....Antonides, Lloyd Cnty Mines 202-501-9686

Rwanda....Barber, Ed Cnty Treasury 202-622-1730

Rwanda....English, Linda K. Cnty World Bank 202-473-5049

Rwanda...Henning, Herman Cnty USIA 202-619-5926

Rwanda...Lloyd, Linda Cnty AID 202-647-9809

Rwanda....Maybury-Lewis, Anthony Cnty Export-Import Bank 202-565-3739

Rwanda....Michelini, Philip Cnty Commerce 202-482-4388

Rwanda....Mutaboba, Joseph W. Cnty Embassy 202-232-2882

S

S-Franc with options....Bice, David CFT 312-35-37880

S&P 500 Index with options....Fedinets, Robert P. CFT 312-353-9016

S&P MidCap400 Index with options....Fedinets, Robert P. CFT 312-353-9016

Saccharin....Land, Eric USITC 202-205-3349

Saddlery and Harness Products....Byron, James COMMERCE 202-482-4034

Safe Drinking Water Hotline....Staff EPA 800-426-4791

Safes....Cuomo, Peter PTO 703-308-0827

Safety Equipment, Trade Promo.....Umstead, Dwight COMMERCE 202-482-2410

Safety Glasses...Staff OD/ORS 301-496-2960

Safety, Health and Work. Cond, Asst. Commiss.....Eisenberg, William M. LABOR 202-606-6304

Safety, Navigation....Staff Coast Guard Hotline 800-368-5647

Safety Program...Staff OD/ORS 301-496-1357

Safety recommendations....Sweedler, Barry M. NTSB 202-382-6810

Safety....Schulman, Lawrence FTA 202-366-4052

Safety....Staff National Safety Council 800-621-7619

Salicin....Randall, Rob USITC 202-205-3366

Saliva....Staff NIDR 301-496-4261

Salivary System Diseases....Staff NIDR 301-496-4261

Salmonella Infections....Staff NIAID 301-496-5717

Salmonellosis and Turtles....Staff CDC 404-639-3286

Salt....Greenblatt, Jack USITC 202-205-3353

Salt....Kostick, Dennis S. MINES 202-501-9410

Salts, inorganic....Greenblatt, Jack USITC 202-205-3353

Salts, organic....Michels, David USITC 202-205-3352

Sampling Methods, Current Programs....Waite, Preston J. CENSUS 301-457-4287

San Marino....Gosnell, Peter Cnty Export-Import Bank 202-565-3733

San Marino....Staff Cnty State 202-647-2453

SAN resins....Misurelli, Denby USITC 202-205-3362

Sanction of Health Providers....Holtz, Judy IG 202-619-1142

Sand and Gravel, Construction....Bolen, Wallace MINES 202-501-9389

Sand and Gravel, Industrial....Bole, Wallace MINES 202-501-9389

Sand....White, Linda USITC 202-205-3427

Sandals....Shildneck, Ann USITC 202-205-3499

Sanitation....Staff OD/ORS 301-496-2960

Santavuori Disease....Staff NINDS 301-496-5751

Sao Tome....Maybury-Lewis, Anthony Cnty Export-Import Bank 202-565-3739

Sao Tome....Edwards, Jennifer R. Cnty World Bank 202-473-4875

Sao Tome....Henning, Herman Cnty USIA 202-619-5926

Sao Tome....Younge, Nathan Cnty TDA 703-875-4357

Sao Tome....Jefferson, Deborah Peace Corps 202-606-3709

Sao Tome....Willis, Mitchell Peace Corps 202-606-3708

Sao Tome and Principe....Barber, Ed Cnty Treasury 202-622-1730

Sao Tome and Principe....Michelini, Philip Cnty Commerce 202-482-4388

Sao Tome and Principe....Staff Cnty State 202-647-3139

Sao Tome and Principe/Minerals....Dolley, Thomas Cnty Mines 202-501-9690

Saphenous Vein Bypass Grafts....Staff NHLBI 301-496-4236

Saran....Misurelli, Denby USITC 202-205-3362

Sarcoidosis....Sarcoidosis Family Aid and Research Foundation 800-223-6429

Sarcoidosis....Staff NIAID 301-496-5717

Sarcoidosis....Staff NHLBI 301-496-4236

Sarcoidosis....Staff NEI 301-496-5248

Sarcoma of Bone and Soft Tissue....Staff NCI 301-496-5583

Sarcoma....Staff NCI 301-496-5583

Sardines....Corey, Roger USITC 202-205-3327

Satellite Communications....Rachul, Lori NASA 216-433-8806

Satellite Design....Staff NASA 301-286-5566

Satellite Spread Spectrum....Staff FCC 301-725-1585

Satellite Testing....Staff NASA 301-286-1584

Satellite Tracking....Staff NASA 301-286-1584

Satellites, Communications....Cooper, Patricia COMMERCE 202-482-4466

Satin white...Johnson, Larry USITC 202-205-3351

Saudi Arabia....Maybury-Lewis, Anthony Cnty Export-Import Bank 202-565-3739

Saudi Arabia....Vacant Cnty USIA 202-619-6528

Saudi Arabia....Curry, David Cnty Treasury 202-622-2140

Saudi Arabia....Ahmad, Mirza Qamar Cnty World Bank 202-473-2652

Saudi Arabia....Kattan, Ahmed A. Cnty Embassy 202-342-3800

Saudi Arabia....Bin Sultan, His Royal Highness Prince Bandar Cnty Embassy 202-342-3800

Saudi Arabia....Cerone, Christopher/Clement, Claude Cnty Commerce 202-482-1860

Saudi Arabia/Minerals....Michalski, Bernadette Cnty Mines 202-501-9699

Saudi Arabia (Riyadh)....Staff Cnty State 202-647-7550

Sausages....Ludwick, David USITC 202-205-3329

Saving and Loans Industry Group....Tow, A. Richard SEC 202-942-1760

Scabies....Staff NIAID 301-496-5717

Scales....Lusi, Susan USITC 202-205-2334

Scandium....Hedrick, James B. MINES 202-501-9412

Scars....Staff NIAMS 301-496-8188

Scarves....Hamey, Amy USITC 202-205-3465

Scarves....Jones, Jackie USITC 202-205-3466

Schilder's Disease....Staff NINDS 301-496-5751

Schistosomiasis....Staff NIAID 301-496-5717

Schizophrenia....Staff NIMH 301-443-4513

Scholars-in-Residence....Staff FIC 301-496-4161

School District Data...Ingold, Jane CENSUS 301-457-2408

Schwanoma....Staff NCI 301-496-5583

Sciatica....Staff NINDS 301-496-5751

Sciatica....Staff NIAMS 301-496-8188

Science and Technology Research Programs....Staff NEH 202-606-8210

Science Issues....Rezendes, Victor S. GAO 202-512-3841

Scientific Computing Resource Center....Staff DCRT 301-402-3488

Scientific Information Center....Rosicky, Henry PTO 703-308-0808

Scientific Instruments, Trade Promo.....Manzolilo, Frank COMMERCE 202-482-2991

Scientific Literature....Brown, Maxine PTO 703-308-4473

Scientific Measurement/Control Equipment....Nealon, Marguerite COMMERCE 202-482-3411

Scientific Visualization....Fowler, Howland NIST 301-975-2703

Scleroderma....Staff United Scleroderma Foundation 800-722-4673

Scleroderma....Staff NIAMS 301-496-8188

Scleroderma....Staff NHLBI 301-496-4236

Sclerosis, Multiple....Staff NINDS 301-496-5751

Sclerosis....Staff NINDS 301-496-5751

Sclerotherapy....Staff NHLBI 301-496-4236

Scoliosis....Staff NIAMS 301-496-8188
SCOR (Specialized Centers of Research)....Staff NHLBI 301-496-4236
Scrap cordage....Cook, Lee USITC 202-205-3471
Screening machines....Greene, William USITC 202-205-3405
Screw Machine Products....Reise, Richard COMMERCE 202-482-3489
Screws, Washers....Reise, Richard COMMERCE 202-482-3489
Screws....Brandon, James USITC 202-205-3433
Sculptures....Mushinske, Larry CUSTOMS 212-466-5739
Seabirds....Staff FWS 703-358-1821
Sealing machinery....Lusi, Susan USITC 202-205-2334
Seasonal Adjustment Methodology, Empl/Unempl. Stats....McIntire, Robert LABOR 202-606-6345
Seat belts....Cook, Lee USITC 202-205-3471
Sebacic acid esters....Johnson, Larry USITC 202-205-3351
Securities industries....Melly, Christopher USITC 202-205-3461
Security and Commodity Brokers....Muir, S. Cassin COMMERCE 202-482-0349
Security Interests in a License....Staff FCC 202-418-2130
Sedatives (Hypnotics)....Staff NIDA 301-443-6245
Sedatives....Nesbitt, Elizabeth USITC 202-205-3355
Seed Trade Catalogs....Ho, Judith NAL 301-504-5876
Seeds, field and garden....Pierre-Benoist, John USITC 202-205-3320
Seeds, oil-bearing....Reeder, John USITC 202-205-3319
Seeds, spice....Schneider, Greg USITC 202-205-3326
Seeds....Conte, Ralph CUSTOMS 212-466-5759
Segawa's Dystonia....Staff NINDS 301-496-5751
Selenium compounds....Greenblatt, Jack USITC 202-205-3353
Selenium....Conant, Kenneth USITC 202-205-3346
Selenium....Jasinski, Stephen MINES 202-501-9418
Self-Help....Staff Self-Help Network of Kansas 800-445-0116
Self-Help....Staff TOUGHLOVE 800-333-1069
Self Protection, Justifiable Use of Force....Zawitz, Marianne Justice Stat 202-616-3499
Semiconductor device manufacturing....Hearn, Brian E. PTO 703-308-2552
Semiconductor devices....James, Andrew PTO 703-308-4894
Semiconductor stock materials....Hearn, Brian E. PTO 703-308-2552
Semiconductors....Josephs, Irwin CUSTOMS 212-466-5673
Semiconductors....Malison, Andrew USITC 202-205-3391
Semiconductors....Roark, Robin COMMERCE 202-482-3090
Senegal (Dakar)....Staff Cnty State 202-647-2865
Senegal/Minerals....Dolley, Thomas Cnty Mines 202-501-9690
Senegal....Baily, Jess Cnty USIA 202-619-5900
Senegal....Bezek, Jill Cnty TDA 703-875-4357
Senegal....Boccara, Bruno Cnty World Bank 202-473-4689
Senegal....Gueye, Silcarneyni Cnty Embassy 202-234-0541
Senegal....Hutchings, Dayna Cnty Export-Import Bank 202-565-3737
Senegal....Michelini, Philip Cnty Commerce 202-482-4388
Senegal....Owens, Susan Peace Corps 202-606-3185
Senegal....Palghat, Kathy Cnty Treasury 202-622-0332
Senegal....Seck, Mamadou Mansour Cnty Embassy 202-234-0540
Senegal....Woodruff, Neil Cnty AID 202-647-6321
Senile Dementia....Staff NIMH 301-443-4513
Senile Dementia....Staff NINDS 301-496-5751
Senile Dementia....Staff NIA 301-496-1752
Senile Macular Degeneration....Staff NEI 301-496-5248
Sensorimotor Research....Zoltick, Brad J. FAES 301-496-9375
Sensorineural Hearing Loss...Staff NIDCD 301-496-7243
Sentencing - Federal....Kaplan, Carol Justice Stat 202-307-0759
Sentencing....Baunach, Phyllis Jo Justice Stat 202-307-0361
Sentencing....Gaskins, Carla Justice Stat 202-508-8546
Sentencing....Kane, Patrick R. Justice Stat 202-307-3226
Septal Defects....Staff NHLBI 301-496-4236
Serbia....Jackson, Juhan Cnty Treasury 202-622-0766
Serbia....Staff Cnty State 202-647-2452
Serbia....Steblez, Walter Cnty Mines 202-501-9672
Serbia....Waxman-Lenz, Roberta Cnty Export-Import Bank 202-565-3742
Serbia-Montenegro....Corwin, Elizabeth Cnty USIA 202-619-5055
Service Industries, Census....Moody, Jack CENSUS 301-457-2689
Service Industries, Communication....Zabelsky, Thomas CENSUS 301-457-2766
Service Industries, Current Selected Service Report....Zabelsky, Thomas CENSUS 301-457-2766
Service Industries, Finance....Marcus, Sidney CENSUS 301-457-2790
Service Industries, Insurance....Marcus, Sidney CENSUS 301-457-2790
Service Industries, Real Estate....Marcus, Sidney CENSUS 301-457-2790
Service Industries, Transportation....Shoemaker, Dennis CENSUS 301-457-2786

Service Industries, Utilities....Shoemaker, Dennis CENSUS 301-457-2786
Service Industries....Parratt, Shelley SEC 202-942-1840
Service Industry Practices....Alcock, Jane FTC 404-347-7537
Service Industry Practices....Abdullah, Raouf M. FTC 202-326-3024
Service Industry Practices....Aliza, Ben FTC 202-326-2905
Services, Data Base....Cleveland, Douglas COMMERCE 202-482-3314
Services, Prices/Lv. Cond....Gerduk, Irwin LABOR 202-606-7748
Services, Telecom....Edwards, Daniel COMMERCE 202-482-4466
Services, Telecom....Elliot, Fred COMMERCE 202-482-1134
Services/trade matters....Broadman, Harry US Trade Rep 202-395-3606
Severe Accident Branch....Barrett, Richard J. NRC 301-415-3627
Sewage Sludge - Beneficial Use/Technology Transfer....Staff EPA 202-260-8488
Sewage Treatment - Industrial Pretreatment Program....Staff EPA 202-260-8488
Sewing and knitting needles....MacKnight, Peg USITC 202-205-3431
Sewing machine needles....Greene, William USITC 202-205-3405
Sewing machines....Greene, William USITC 202-205-3405
Sewing Notions....Rauch, Theodore CUSTOMS 212-466-5892
Sewing thread: cotton....Warlick, William USITC 202-205-3459
Sewing thread: manmade fibers....Warlick, William USITC 202-205-3459
Sewing thread: silk....Shelton, Linda USITC 202-205-3457
Sewing thread: wool....Shelton, Linda USITC 202-205-3457
Sex and Aging....Staff NIA 301-496-1752
Sex Change....Staff NICHD 301-496-5133
Sex Determination....Staff NICHD 301-496-5133
Sex Hormones....Staff NICHD 301-496-5133
Sexual Development....Staff NICHD 301-496-5133
Sexually Transmitted Diseases....Staff NIAID 301-496-5717
Sexually Transmitted Diseases and HIV Prevention....Morse, Stephen CDC 404-639-3222
Seychelles (Victoria)....Staff Cnty State 202-647-6473
Seychelles/Minerals....Antonides, Lloyd Cnty Mines 202-501-9686
Seychelles....Akpa, Emmanuel Cnty World Bank 202-473-4367
Seychelles....Imam, Fahmila Cnty Export-Import Bank 202-565-3738
Seychelles....Larsen, Mark Cnty USIA 202-619-4894
Seychelles....Marengo, Marc M. Cnty Embassy 212-687-9766
Seychelles....Schmitz, Virginia Peace Corps 202-606-3334
Seychelles....Shelton, Alison Cnty Treasury 202-622-0354
Seychelles....Watkins, Chandra Cnty Commerce 202-482-4564
Seychelles....Younge, Nathan Cnty TDA 703-875-4357
Sezary Syndrome....Staff NIAMS 301-496-8188
Shale oil....Foreso, Cynthia USITC 202-205-3348
Shared Energy Cooperatives....Gunn, Marvin Jr. NEIC 202-586-2826
Shared Instrumentation Grant....Staff NCRR 301-594-7947
Shawls....Jones, Jackie USITC 202-205-3466
Sheep....Steller, Rose USITC 202-205-3323
Sheet feeding....Olszewski, Robert PTO 703-308-2588
Sheet, plastics....Misurelli, Denby USITC 202-205-3362
Sheets, bed....Sweet, Mary Elizabeth USITC 202-205-3455
Shell, articles of....Spalding, Josphine USITC 202-205-3498
Shellac and other lacs....Reeder, John USITC 202-205-3319
Shellac, varnish....Johnson, Larry USITC 201-205-3351
Shellfish....Conte, Ralph CUSTOMS 212-466-5759
Shellfish....Newman, Douglas USITC 202-205-3328
Shells, crude....Steller, Rose USITC 202-205-3323
Shingles and older people....Staff NIA 301-496-1752
Shingles and shakes (wood)....Hoffmeier, Bill USITC 202-205-3321
Shingles, asphalt....Rhodes, Richard USITC 202-205-3322
Shingles (Herpes Zoster)....Staff NINDS 301-496-5751
Shingles, Wood....Wise, Barbara COMMERCE 202-482-0375
Ship Earth Stations....Staff FCC 202-632-7175
Ship Inspections....Staff FCC 202-632-7014
Ship Licensing....Staff FCC 717-337-1212
Ship Rules/Exemptions....Staff FCC 202-632-7175
Ships....Jordan, Charles PTO 703-308-0918
Shirts....Holoyda, Olha USITC 202-205-3467
Shock (Cardiogenic)....Staff NHLBI 301-496-4236
Shock (Hemorrhagic)....Staff NHLBI 301-496-4236
Shock Trauma Center....Staff UMD 301-528-6294
Shoe machinery....Fravel, Dennis USITC 202-205-3404
Shoe making....Sewell, Paul T PTO 703-308-2126
Shoe parts....Shildneck, Ann USITC 202-205-3499
Shoes....Sewell, Paul T PTO 703-308-2126
Shoes....Shildneck, Ann USITC 202-205-3499
Short Range Aids to Navigation....Kline, William USCG 202-267-0980

Short Stature....Staff NICHD 301-496-5133
Short-Term Forecasts of Energy Markets....Kilgore, Calvin NEIC 202-586-1617
Shorts....DeGaetano, Angela CUSTOMS 212-466-5540
Shorts: mens and boys....Sweet, Mary Elizabeth USITC 202-205-3455
Shorts: womens and girls....Sweet, Mary Elizabeth USITC 202-205-3455
Shotguns....Robinson, Hazel USITC 202-205-3496
Shrimp....Newman, Douglas USITC 202-205-3328
Shy-Drager Syndrome....Staff NINDS 301-496-5751
Shy-Drager Syndrome....Staff NIMH 301-443-4513
Shy-Drager Syndrome....Staff NHLBI 301-496-4236
Sickle Cell Disease....Staff Sickle Cell Disease Association of America, Inc. 800-421-8453
Sickle Cell Anemia....Staff NHLBI 301-496-4236
Sideroblastic Anemia....Staff NHLBI 301-496-4236
Siding (wood)....Hoffmeier, Bill USITC 202-205-3321
SIDS....Staff SIDS Alliance 800-221-7437
Sierra Leone (Freetown)....Staff Cnty State 202-647-4567
Sierra Leone/Minerals....Michalski, Bernadette Cnty Mines 202-501-9699
Sierra Leone....Waxman-Lenz, Roberta Cnty Export-Import Bank 202-565-3742
Sierra Leone....Palghat, Kathy Cnty Treasury 202-622-0332
Sierra Leone....Tallroth, Nils Borje Cnty World Bank 202-473-4876
Sierra Leone....O'Neal, Adrienne Cnty USIA 202-619-6904
Sierra Leone....Kargbo, Thomas Kahota Cnty Embassy 202-939-9261
Sierra Leone....Herring, Debra Peace Corps 202-606-3644
Sierra Leone....Michelini, Philip Cnty Commerce 202-482-4388
Sierra Leone....McCormick, Michael L. Peace Corps 202-606-3644
Sierre Leone....Williams, Gustavus Cnty Embassy 202-939-9261
Sight Substitution Systems....Staff NEI 301-496-5248
Signal Processing/Analysis....Staff DCRT 301-496-6561
Signal Processing/Analysis....Staff DCRT 301-496-2959
Silent Ischemia....Staff NHLBI 301-496-4236
Silica....White, Linda USITC 202-205-3427
Silicon Carbide Abrasive....Austin, Gordon MINES 202-501-9388
Silicon Characterization....Ehrstein, James R. NIST 301-975-2060
Silicon....Conant, Kenneth USITC 202-205-3346
Silicon....Cunningham, Larry D. MINES 202-501-9443
Silicone resins....Misurelli, Denby USITC 202-205-3362
Silicones....Michels, David USITC 202-205-3352
Silk....Freund, Kimberlie USITC 202-205-3456
Silk....Shelton, Linda USITC 202-205-3457
Silk....Warlick, William USITC 202-205-3459
Sillimanite....DeSapio, Vincent USITC 202-205-3435
Silver compounds....Greenblatt, Jack USITC 202-205-3353
Silver with options....Rosenfeld, David CFT 312-353-9026
Silver....McNay, Deborah USITC 202-205-3425
Silver....Reese, Jr., Robert G. MINES 202-501-9413
Silverware....Harris, John COMMERCE 202-482-1178
Singapore/Minerals....Tse, Pui-Kwan Cnty Mines 202-501-9696
Singapore (Singapore)....Staff Cnty State 202-647-3278
Singapore....Cung, Raphael Cnty Commerce 202-482-3877
Singapore....Gilroy, Meg Cnty USIA 202-619-5836
Singapore....Imam, Fahmila Cnty Export-Import Bank 202-565-3738
Singapore....Selverajah, A. Cnty Embassy 202-537-3100
Singapore....Shelton, Alison Cnty Treasury 202-622-0354
Single Family Housing....Staff HUD 202-708-3175
Sinusitis....Staff NIAID 301-496-5717
Sirups....Vacant USITC 202-205-3454
Sitters....Staff Safe Sitters 800-255-4089
Sjogren's Syndrome....Staff Sjogren's Syndrome Association 800-395-6772
Sjogren's Syndrome....Staff NEI 301-496-5248
Sjogren's Syndrome....Staff NINDS 301-496-5751
Sjogren's Syndrome....Staff NIDR 301-496-4261
Sjogren's Syndrome....Staff NIAMS 301-496-8188
Sjogren's Syndrome....Staff NIAID 301-496-5717
Ski equipment....Witherspoon, Richardo USITC 202-205-3489
Skin and Aging....Staff NIAMS 301-496-8188
Skin and Aging....Staff NIA 301-496-1752
Skin and Sunlight....Staff NIAMS 301-496-8188
Skin and Sunlight....Staff NCI 301-496-5583
Skin Cancer....Staff NCI 301-496-5583
Skin Diseases....Staff NIAMS 301-496-8188
Skins (animal)....Steller, Rose USITC 202-205-3323
Skirts, Knit and Woven....DeGaetano, Angela CUSTOMS 212-466-5540
Skirts....Sweet, Mary Elizabeth USITC 202-205-3455

Slack....Foreso, Cynthia USITC 202-205-3348
Slacks, mens and boys....Sweet, Mary Elizabeth USITC 202-205-3455
Slacks, womens and girls....Sweet, Mary Elizabeth USITC 202-205-3455
Slate....White, Linda USITC 202-205-3427
Slavic Republic....Schiel, Russell Peace Corps 202-606-3606
Slavic Republic....Lockwood, Jennifer Peace Corps 202-606-3607
Sleep and Aging....Staff NIA 301-496-1752
Sleep and Aging....Staff NIMH 301-443-4513
Sleep Apnea....Staff NHLBI 301-496-4236
Sleep Disorders....Staff NIMH 301-443-4513
Sleep Disorders....Staff NINDS 301-496-5751
Sleep Disturbances....Staff NIMH 301-443-4513
Sleepwear....Staff CPSC 301-504-0580
Slide fasteners....Shildneck, Ann USITC 202-205-3499
Slippers....Shildneck, Ann USITC 202-205-3499
Slovak Republic....Altheim, Stephen Cnty Treasury 202-622-0125
Slovak Republic....Hewer, Ulrich A. Cnty World Bank 202-473-2279
Slovak Republic....Ann Lien Cnty TDA 703-875-4357
Slovakia....Bazala, Razvigor Cnty USIA 202-619-5855
Slovakia....Burian, Peter Cnty Embassy 202-965-5161
Slovakia....Housh, Tony Cnty Treasury 202-622-7456
Slovakia....Lichardus, Branislav Cnty Embassy 202-965-5161
Slovakia....Staff Cnty State 202-647-3191
Slovakia....Steblez, Walter Cnty Mines 202-501-9672
Slovakia....Waxman-Lenz, Roberta Cnty Export-Import Bank 202-565-3742
Slovenia....Corwin, Elizabeth Cnty USIA 202-619-5055
Slovenia....Elwan, Ann E. Cnty World Bank 202-473-2435
Slovenia....Gallagher, Tricia Cnty Treasury 202-622-0117
Slovenia....Petric, Ernest Cnty Embassy 202-667-5363
Slovenia....Staff cnty State 202-736-7152
Slovenia....Steblez, Walter Cnty Mines 202-501-9672
Slovenia....Waxman-Lenz, Roberta Cnty Export-Import Bank 202-565-3742
Slovenia....Zore, Gregor S. Cnty Embassy 202-667-5363
Slow Viruses....Staff NINDS 301-496-5751
Small and Woman-Owned Business Opportunities....Staff HUD 202-708-1428
Small Business Innovation Research....Staff OD/OER 301-496-1968
Small Business Trade Policy....Lino Prosak, Sylvia COMMERCE 202-482-4792
Small Cell Carcinoma....Staff NCI 301-496-5583
Small Telcos....Staff FCC 202-418-1530
Smallpox....Staff NIAID 301-496-5717
Smell (Disorders)....Staff NINDS 301-496-5751
Smell (Disorders)....Staff NIDCD 301-496-7243
Smoke and Toxic Gas Prediction.....Mulholland, George W. NIST 301-975-6695
Smoke Detectors....Giles, Ken CPSC 301-504-0580
Smokeless powder....Johnson, Larry USITC 202-205-3351
Smokeless Tobacco (Oral Complications)....Staff NCI 301-496-5583
Smokeless Tobacco (Oral Complications)....Staff NIDR 301-496-4251
Smokers' Articles....Conte, Ralph CUSTOMS 212-466-5759
Smokers' articles....Burns, Gail USITC 202-205-3501
Smoking and Health....Eriksen, Michael P. CDC 404-488-5701
Smoking and Health....Hensley, Timothy CDC 404-488-5705
Smoking and Health....Staff NIDA 301-443-5583
Smoking and Health, Public Information....McKenna, Jeffrey P. CDC 404-488-5705
Smoking and Heart Disease....Staff NHLBI 301-496-4236
Smoking (Cancer related)....Staff NCI 301-496-5583
SMR-Business Opportunities....Staff FCC 202-418-0620
SMR-Enforcement: Channel....Staff FCC 800-322-1117
SMR-Interpretations....Staff FCC 202-418-0620
Smuggling Investigations....Cockrell, Robert Customs 202-927-1530
Snackfood....Manogue, Robert COMMERCE 202-482-2428
Snap fasteners....Shildneck, Anna USITC 202-205-3499
Soap, castile....Land, Eric USITC 202-205-3349
Soap, surface-active agents, synthetic detergent....Land, Eric USITC 202-205-3349
Soap, toilet....Land, Eric USITC 202-205-3349
Soaps, Detergents, Cleansers....Hurt, William COMMERCE 202-482-0128
Soaps....Joseph, Stephanie CUSTOMS 212-466-5768
Soapstone....White, Linda USITC 202-205-3427
Social and Behavioral Research on Aging....Staff NIA 301-496-1752
Social and Behavioral Sciences....Staff NICHD 301-496-6832
Social and Behavioral Sciences....Staff NIMH 301-443-4513
Social Security...Staff SSA 800-772-1213
Social Services Block Grant.... ACF 202-401-9215
Social Work Department....Staff CC 301-496-2381

Sociology of Journalism....Levy, Mark R. UMD 301-405-2389

Sociology....Caplow, Theodore UVA 703-924-6397

Soda ash....Conant, Kenneth USITC 202-205-3346

Sodium and potassium salts of oils, greases, fat....Land, Eric USITC 202-205-3349

Sodium Ash....Kostick, Dennis S. MINES 202-501-9410

Sodium benzoate....Matusik, Ed USITC 202-205-3356

Sodium bicarbonate....Conant, Kenneth USITC 202-205-3346

Sodium carbonate....Conant, Kenneth USITC 202-205-3346

Sodium compounds....Greenblatt, Jack USITC 202-205-3353

Sodium hydroxide....Conant, Kenneth USITC 202-205-3346

Sodium Sulfate....Kostick, Dennis S. MINES 202-501-9410

Sodium....Conant, Kenneth USITC 202-205-3346

Sodium....Lecos, Chris FDA 202-205-4144

Soft Drink....Manogue, Robert COMMERCE 202-482-2428

Software, Export Promo.....Fogg, Judy COMMERCE 202-482-4936

Software services....Warlick, William USITC 202-205-3459

Software....Hijikata, Heidi C. COMMERCE 202-482-0569

Software....Smolenskni, Mary COMMERCE 202-482-0551

Solar Burns (Eye Effects)....Staff NEI 301-496-5248

Solar Cells/Photovoltaic Devices/Small Hydro....Garden, Les COMMERCE 202-482-0556

Solar Energy Conversion....Kelly, Margurite NEIS 303-275-4099

Solar Energy Conversion....Annan, Robert H. NEIC 202-586-1720

Solar energy....Foreso, Cynthia USITC 202-205-3348

Solar Equipment, Geoth....Garden, Les COMMERCE 202-482-0556

Solar Equipment Ocean/Biomass....Garden, Les COMMERCE 202-482-0556

Solar Phenomena Research....Staff NASA 415-604-3937

Solar System Exploration....Farrar, Diane NASA 415-604-3934

Solar Thermal and Biomass Power....Burch, Gary NEIC 202-586-8121

Solid Waste Disposal (Radioactive)....Staff OD/ORS 301-496-2254

Solid Waste Disposal....Staff OD/ORS 301-496-3537

Solid Waste Information Clearinghouse Hotline....Staff EPA 800-677-9424

Solid Waste Management (Municipal)....Staff EPA 202-260-5856

Solid Waste Office of....Staff EPA 202-260-4627

Solomon Islands (Honiara)....Staff Cnty State 202-647-3546

Solomon Islands/Minerals....Lyday, Travis Cnty Mines 202-501-9695

Solomon Islands....Imam, Fahmila Cnty Export-Import Bank 202-565-3738

Solomon Islands....Davies, Irene Cnty World Bank 202-458-2481

Solomon Islands....Shelton, Alison Cnty Treasury 202-622-0354

Solomon Islands....Rahman, Talaat Cnty TDA 703-875-4357

Solomon Islands....Schell, Russell Peace Corps 202-606-3231

Solomon Islands....Morona, Catherine Peace Corps 202-606-0982

Solomon Islands....Lee, Allison Peace Corps 202-606-0983

Somalia/Minerals....Antonides, Lloyd Cnty Mines 202-501-9686

Somalia (Mogadishu)....Staff Cnty State 202-647-6453

Somalia....Ghani, Ejaz Syed Cnty World Bank 202-473-4819

Somalia....Gold, Ricki Cnty AID 202-647-7977

Somalia....Hutchings, Dayna Cnty Export-Import Bank 202-565-3737

Somalia....Larsen, Mark Cnty USIA 202-619-4894

Somalia....McKoy, Ethel Cnty Treasury 202-622-0336

Somalia....Watkins, Chandra Cnty Commerce 202-482-4564

Somatization Disorder...Staff NIMH 301-443-4513

Sorbitol....Randall, Rob USITC 202-205-3366

Sorting machines....Greene, William USITC 202-205-3405

Sound signaling apparatus....Baker, Scott USITC 202-205-3386

Sounding Rocket Program....Koehler, Keith NASA 804-824-1579

Sounding Rockets....Brown, Dwayne A. NASA 202-358-1726

South Africa/Minerals....van Oss, Henrik Cnty Mines 202-501-9687

South Africa, Republic of (Pretoria)....Staff Cnty State 202-647-8252

South Africa....Barrington, Belinda Cnty AID 202-647-4229

South Africa....Kilan, Andre Cnty Embassy 202-232-4400

South Africa....Mabury-Lewis, Anthony Cnty Export-Import Bank 202-565-3739

South Africa....Patel, Praful C. Cnty World Bank 202-473-4250

South Africa....Rauch, Margie Cnty Treasury 202-622-0251

South Africa....Schwartz, Larry Cnty USIA 202-619-6904

South Africa....Solomon, Emily Cnty Commerce 202-482-5148

South Africa....Sonn, Franklin Cnty Embassy 202-232-3400

South Asia/trade matters....Stillman, Betsy US Trade Rep 202-395-6813

South Asia/trade matters....Ruzicka, Rick US Trade Rep 202-395-6813

South Pacific Commission....Staff Cnty State 202-647-3546

Southeast Asia/trade matters....Damond, Joseph US Trade Rep 202-395-6813

Southeast MTC (Manufacturing Technology Center)....Bishop, Jim NIST 803-252-6976

Southern Cone Affairs....Murphy, Sean US Trade Rep 202-395-3324

Southern Cone Market....Chopra, Karen US Trade Rep 202-395-5190

Soy Products....Manogue, John COMMERCE 202-482-3428

Soybean Meal with options....Schambach, Duane CFT 312-353-9000

Soybean oil with options....Schambach, Duane CFT 312-353-9000

Soybeans and soybean oil....Reeder, John USITC 202-205-3319

Soybeans with options....Schambach, Duane CFT 312-353-9000

Space Communications....Brown, Dwayne C. NASA 202-358-1726

Space Derived Technology....Dunbar, Brian NASA 202-358-1547

Space Exploration....Keegan, Sarah NASA 202-358-1902

Space Flight Systems....Rachul, Lori NASA 216-433-8806

Space Flight....Campion, Edward S. NASA 202-358-1780

Space Flight....Cast, Jim NASA 202-358-1779

Space Industry Machinery, Nec....Farner, Kim COMMERCE 202-482-2232

Space Policy Development....Farner, Kim COMMERCE 202-482-2232

Space Propulsion....Rachel, Lori NASA 216-433-8806

Space Remote Sensing Commercialization....Sullivan, Nancy NASA 601-688-3341

Space Science and Applications....Braukus, Michael NASA 202-358-1979

Space Science and Applications....Cleggett-Haleim, Paula NASA 202-358-0883

Space Shuttle Engine Testing....Sullivan, Nancy NASA 601-688-3341

Space Shuttle Program....Staff NASA 713-483-5111

Space Shuttle Propulsion Testing....Sullivan, Nancy NASA 601-688-3341

Space Shuttle Research....Staff NASA 804-864-6122

Space Shuttle....Malone, June NASA 205-544-7061

Space Shuttle....James, Donald G. NASA 415-604-3935

Space Station Freedom....Rachul, Lori NASA 216-433-8806

Space Station Freedom....Simmons, Mike NASA 205-544-6537

Space technology....Norwood, Robert NASA 202-358-2320

Space Technology....Staff NASA 205-544-6538

Space Vehicle Testing....Buckingham, Bruce NASA 407-867-2468

Space Vehicle Testing....Buckingham, Bruce NASA 407-867-2468

Space Vehicle Testing....Buckingham, Bruce NASA 407-867-2468

Spacecraft....Anderson, Peder USITC 202-205-3388

Spacelab Missions Operations....Staff NASA 205-544-9492

Spacelab....Hess, Mark NASA 202-358-1778

Spain (Madrid)....Staff Cnty State 202-647-1412

Spain/Minerals....Newman, Harold R. Cnty Mines 202-501-9669

Spain....de Ojeda, Jaime Cnty Embassy 202-452-0100

Spain....Double, Mary Beth Cnty Commerce 202-482-4508

Spain....Gosnell, Peter Cnty Export-Import Bank 202-565-3733

Spain....Holloway, Barbara Cnty Treasury 202-622-0098

Spain....Rodriguez, Dario Polo Cnty Embassy 202-728-2340

Spain....Seifkin, David Cnty USIA 202-619-6582

Spanish, Italian and Portuguese languages....Opere, Fernando UVA 804-924-7159

Spasmodic Dysphonia....Staff NINDS 301-496-5924

Spasmodic Dysphonia....Staff NIDCD 301-496-7243

Spasmodic Torticollis....Staff NINDS 301-496-5751

Spasms (Arteries)....Staff NHLBI 301-496-4236

Spastic Hemiplegia....Staff NINDS 301-496-5751

Spastic Paraplegia....Staff NINDS 301-496-5751

Spastic Quadriplegia....Staff NINDS 301-496-5751

Spasticity....Staff NINDS 301-496-5751

Special classification provisions....Roth, Jordon USITC 202-205-3467

Special Collections Program....Pindell, Alvetta NAL 301-504-5204

Special Events...Staff CC 301-496-3475

Special Foreign Currency Program....Staff FIC 301-496-1653

Special Industry Machinery, Nec....Shaw, Eugene COMMERCE 202-482-3494

Special Investigations....Rosenbaum, Eli M. Justice 202-616-2492

Special Population Censuses....Csellar, Elaine CENSUS 301-457-1429

Special Topics - Agricultural History....Bowers, Douglas Agri 202-219-0787

Special Topics - Alternative Crops....Glaser, Lewrene Agri 202-219-0091

Special Topics - Biotechnology (Dairy)....Caswell, Margaret Agri 202-219-0417

Special Topics - Biotechnology....Reilly, John Agri 202-219-0450

Special Topics - Commodity Programs and Policies-Honey....Hoff, Fred Agri 202-219-0883

Special Topics - Commodity Programs and Policies-Sugar....Buzanelli, Peter Agri 202-219-0888

Special Topics - Commodity Programs and Policies-Tobacco....Grise, Verner Agri 202-219-0890

Special Topics - Commodity Programs and Policies....Harwood, Joy Agri 202-219-0840

Special Topics - Economic Linkages to Agriculture....Edmondson, William Agri 202-219-0785

Special Topics - Energy....Gill, Mohinder Agri 202-219-0464

Special Topics - Farm Labor Market....Whitener, Leslie Agri 202-219-0932

Special Topics - Farm Labor Laws....Runyan, Jack Agri 202-219-0932

Special Topics - Farm Machinery....Vesterby, Marlow Agri 202-219-0422

Special Topics - Farm Structure....Whitener, Leslie Agri 202-219-0932

Special Topics - Fertilizer....Rives, Sam Agri 202-720-2324

Special Topics - Fertilizer....Taylor, Harold Agri 202-219-0464

Special Topics - Geographic information Systems....Heimlich, Ralph Agri 202-219-0431

Special Topics - Macroeconomic Conditions (World)....Baxter, Tim Agri 202-219-0706

Special Topics - Macroeconomic Conditions....Denbaly, Mark Agri 202-219-0779

Special Topics - Natural Resource Policy (World)....Urban, Francis Agri 202-219-0717

Special Topics - Natural Resource Policy....Ribaudo, Marc Agri 202-219-0444

Special Topics - Natural Resource Policy....Osborn, Tim Agri 202-219-0401

Special Topics - Pesticides....Bull, Len Agri 202-501-8288

Special Topics - Pesticides....Love, John Agri 202-219-0388

Special Topics - Pesticides....Padgitt, Merritt Agri 202-219-0433

Special Topics - Pesticides....Rives, Sam Agri 202-720-2324

Special Topics - Pesticides....Vandeman, Ann Agri 202-219-0089

Special Topics - Population - World....Urban, Francis Agri 202-219-0705

Special Topics - Population....Beale, Calvin Agri 202-219-0482

Special Topics - Population....Swanson, Linda Agri 202-219-0557

Special Topics - Seeds....Gill, Mohinder Agri 202-219-0464

Special Topics - Soil Conservation....Magleby, Richard Agri 202-219-0436

Special Topics - Soil Conservation....Osborn, Tim Agri 202-219-1030

Special Topics - Sustainable Agriculture....Vandeman, Ann Agri 202-219-0433

Special Topics - Sustainable Agriculture....Baumes, Harry Agri 202-219-1019

Special Topics - Trade....Anderson, Margot Agri 202-219-0449

Special Topics - Trade....Krissoff, Barry Agri 202-219-0681

Special Topics - Transportation....Hutchinson, T.Q. Agri 202-219-0840

Special Topics - Water and Irrigation....Moore, Michael Agri 202-219-0411

Special Topics - Water and Irrigation....Gollehon, Noel Agri 202-219-0413

Special Topics - Water Quality....Rives, Sam Agri 202-720-2324

Special Topics - Water Quality....Ribaudo, Marc Agri 202-501-8387

Special Topics - Water Quality....Crutchfield, Steve Agri 202-219-0444

Special Topics - Weather....Preston, Greg Agri 202-219-7621

Special Topics - Weather....Ripley, Brad Agri 202-720-1444

Species Profiles, Fish and Wildlife....Staff FWS 703-358-1710

Specific Language Impairment (SLI)....Staff NIDCD 301-496-7243

Spectacles....Johnson, Christopher USITC 202-205-3488

Speech and Language Disorders....Staff NIDCD 301-496-7243

Speech and Language Disorders....Staff NICHD 301-496-5133

Speech and Language Disorders....Staff NINDS 301-496-5924

Speech....Staff American Speech-Language-Hearing Association Consumer Helpline 800-638-8255

Speech....Staff NIDCD 301-496-7243

Speech....Staff NIDR 301-496-4261

Speed changers....Fravel, Dennis USITC 202-205-3404

Speed Changers....Reise, Richard COMMERCE 202-482-3489

SPF (Specific Pathogen Free) Animal Breeding Research Program....Staff NCRR 301-594-7933

Sphingolipidoses Mucopolysaccaridoses and Stor. Dis.....Staff NINDS 301-496-5751

Sphingolipidoses....Staff NINDS 301-496-5751

Spices....Conte, Ralph CUSTOMS 212-466-5759

Spices....Schneider, Greg USITC 202-205-3326

Spielmeyer-Sjogren's Disease....Staff NINDS 301-496-5751

Spina Bifida....Staff Spina Bifida Association of America 800-621-3141

Spina Bifida....Staff NIDCD 301-496-7243

Spina Bifida....Staff NINDS 301-496-5751

Spina Bifida....Staff NICHD 301-496-5133

Spinal Arachnoiditis....Staff NINDS 301-496-5751

Spinal Cord Injuries....Staff Hotline 800-526-3456

Spinal Cord Injuries....Staff National Spinal Cord Injury Association 800-962-9629

Spinal Cord Injury....Staff NINDS 301-496-5751

Spinal Cord Lesions....Staff NINDS 301-496-5751

Spinal Cord Tumors....Staff NINDS 301-496-5751

Spinal Muscular Atrophy....Staff NINDS 301-496-5751

Spinning machines....Greene, William USITC 202-205-3405

Spinocerebellar Degeneration....Staff NINDS 301-496-5751

Split Channel Operations....Staff FCC 202-653-5560

Spondyloarthropathies....Staff NIAMS 301-496-8188

Spondylolisthesis....Staff NIAMS 301-496-8188

Sponge, articles of....Spalding, Josephine USITC 202-205-3498

Sponges, marine....Ludwick, David USITC 202-205-3329

Spongy Degeneration...Staff NINDS 301-496-5751

Sporting Goods and Athletic....Vanderwolf, John COMMERCE 202-482-0348

Sporting Goods, Export Promo.....Beckham, Reginald COMMERCE 202-482-5478

Sporting goods....Millin, Vincent PTO 703-308-1065

Sporting goods....Love, John PTO 703-308-0873

Sporting goods....Witherspoon, Ricardo USITC 202-205-3489

Sporting Goods....McKenna, Thomas CUSTOMS 212-466-5475

Sports Medicine....Staff NIAMS 301-496-8188

Spraying devices....Kashnikow, Andres PTO 703-308-1137

Spraying machinery: other....Lusi, Susan USITC 202-205-2334

Spraying machinery: agricultural/horticultural....Fravel, Dennis USITC 202-205-3404

Squamous Cell....Staff NCI 301-496-5583

Sri Lanka (Colombo)....Staff Cnty State 202-647-2351

Sri Lanka/Minerals....Kuo, Chin Cnty Mines 202-501-9693

Sri Lanka....Imam, Fahmila Cnty Export-Import Bank 202-565-3738

Sri Lanka....Benbrahim, Abderraouf Cnty World Bank 202-458-2637

Sri Lanka....McKoy, Ethel Cnty Treasury 202-622-0336

Sri Lanka....Gradisher, Thomas Cnty USIA 202-619-5529

Sri Lanka....Rahman, Talaat Cnty TDA 703-875-4357

Sri Lanka....Dhanapala, Janantha Cudah Cnty Embassy 202-338-8565

Sri Lanka....Dharmawardhane, Asoka G. Cnty Embassy 202-483-4026

Sri Lanka....Simmons, John Cnty Commerce 202-482-2954

Sri Lanka....Phillips, Scott Peace Corps 202-606-1053

St. Bartholomey....Brooks, Michelle Cnty Commerce 202-482-2527

St. Kitts and Nevis....Edwards, Erstein Mallet Cnty Embassy 202-686-2636

St. Kitts and Nevis....Rabchevsky, George Cnty Mines 202-501-9670

St. Kitts and Nevis....Marcus, Anthony Cnty Treasury 202-622-1218

St. Kitts-Nevis....Wilkins, Michele Cnty Export-Import Bank 202-565-3743

St. Kitts-Nevis....Brooks, Michelle Cnty Commerce 202-482-2527

St. Kitts/Nevis....Nallari, Raj R. Cnty World Bank 202-473-8697

St. Kitts....Irish, John P. Cnty Embassy 202-686-2636

St. Lucia....Brooks, Michelle Cnty Commerce 202-482-2527

St. Lucia....Edmunds, Joseph Edsel Cnty Embassy 202-364-6792

St. Lucia....John Herrman Cnty TDA 703-875-4357

St. Lucia....Mallet, Juliet Elaine Cnty Embassy 202-364-6793

St. Lucia....Marcus, Anthony Cnty Treasury 202-622-1218

St. Lucia....Nallari, Raj R. Cnty World Bank 202-473-8697

St. Lucia....Rabchevsky, George Cnty Mines 202-501-9670

St. Lucia....Wilkins, Michele Cnty Export-Import Bank 202-565-3743

St. Martin....Brooks, Michelle Cnty Commerce 202-482-2527

St. Vincent Grenadines....Brooks, Michelle Cnty Commerce 202-482-2527

St. Vincent Grenadines....Rabchevsky, George Cnty Mines 202-501-9670

St. Vincent....Layne, Kingsley Cnty Embassy 202-462-7806

St. Vincent....Marcus, Anthony Cnty Treasury 202-622-1218

St. Vincent....Nallari, Raj R. Cnty World Bank 202-473-8697

St. Vincent....Norris, Cecily A. Cnty Embassy 202-462-7846

St. Vincent....Wilkins, Michele Cnty Export-Import Bank 202-565-3743

St. Vitus Dance (Sydenham Chorea)....Staff NINDS 301-496-5751

Stained Teeth (Tetracycline)....Staff NIDR 301-496-4261

Stains....Johnson, Larry USITC 202-205-3351

Standard Industrial Classification, Empl/Unempl....Bennott, William LABOR 202-606-6474

Standard Occupational Classification, Empl/Unempl....McElroy, Michael LABOR 202-606-6516

Staphylococcal Infections....Staff NIAID 301-496-5717

Staple fibers, manmade....Sweet, Mary Elizabeth USITC 202-205-3455

Starches, chemically treated....Randall, Rob USITC 202-205-3366

Starches....Pierre-Benoist, John USITC 202-205-3320

Stargardt's Disease...Staff NEI 301-496-5248

State and Area Labor Force Data, Data Disk and Tapes....Marcus, Jessie LABOR 202-606-6392

State and Area Labor Force Data, Demog. Char. E/Un....Biederman, Edna LABOR 202-606-6392

State and Metropolitan Area Data Books....Cevis, Wanda CENSUS 301-457-1166

State and Outlying Area Estimates....Staff CENSUS 301-457-1099

State Data Center Program....Jones, Tim CENSUS 301-457-1305

State Drug Abuse Services (Standards and Requirements)....Staff NIDA 301-443-6245

State Energy Programs....Demetrops, James NEIC 202-586-9187

State Projections....Staff CENSUS 301-457-2422

State Rates/Infrastructure....Staff FCC 202-418-0940

States and Areas Establishment Survey, Data Disk.....Podgornik, Guy LABOR 202-606-6534

States and Areas Establishment Survey, Empl/Unempl....Shipp, Kenneth LABOR 202-606-6519

Static molds....Woo, Jay PTO 703-308-3793

Statistical Abstract....King, Glenn CENSUS 301-457-1171

Statistical Areas....Staff CENSUS 301-763-3827

Statistical Briefs...Bernstein, Robert CENSUS 301-457-1221

Statistical Consulting...Staff DCRT 301-496-6037

Statistical Engineering....Lundegard, Robert J. NIST 301-975-2840

Statistical Methods, Prices and Living Cond.....Hedges, Brian LABOR 202-606-6897

Statistical Research for Demographic Programs....Hoy, Easley CENSUS 301-457-4978

Statistical Research for Economic Programs....Hoy, Easley CENSUS 301-457-4978

Statistical Surveys, National Fish and Wildlife....Staff FWS 703-358-1730

Statistician, Chief....Young, Allan H. ECONOMIC 202-606-9607

Statistics (Blindness and Visual Disorders)....Staff NEI 301-496-5248

Statistics (Health)....Staff CDC 404-639-3286

Statistics (Health)....Staff NCHS 301-496-8500

Statistics....Dillingham, Steven Justice Stat 202-307-0765

Staurolite....Austin, Gordon MINES 202-501-9388

Stearic acid....Randall, Rob USITC 202-205-3366

Stearic acid esters....Randall, Rob USITC 202-205-3366

Steatite....White, Linda USITC 202-205-3427

Steel: angles, shapes, and sections....Kaplan, Stephanie USITC 202-205-3436

Steel: bars....Kaplan, Stephanie USITC 202-205-3436

Steel, Basic Shapes and Forms....Ilardi, Paula CUSTOMS 212-466-5476

Steel Industry Products....Bell, Charles COMMERCE 202-482-0608

Steel: Ingots, blooms, and billets....MacKnight, Peg USITC 202-205-3431

Steel: pipe and tube and fittings....Bello, Felix USITC 202-205-3120

Steel: Pipes....Bello, Felix USITC 202-205-3120

Steel: plate....MacKnight, Peg USITC 202-205-3431

Steel: rails....Yost, Charles USITC 202-205-3432

Steel: sheet....MacKnight, Peg USITC 202-205-3431

Steel: strip....MacKnight, Peg USITC 202-205-3431

Steel: tubes....Bello, Felix Karen USITC 202-205-3120

Steel: waste and scrap....Kaplan, Stephanie USITC 202-205-3436

Steel: wire rods....Yost, Charles USITC 202-205-3442

Steel: wire....Yost, Charles USITC 202-205-3442

Steele-Richardson Disease....Staff NINDS 301-496-5751

Stents...Staff NHLBI 301-496-4236

Stereo apparatus....Puffert, Douglas USITC 202-205-3402

Sterilization....Staff NICHD 301-496-5133

Sterilization....Warden, Robert PTO 703-308-2920

Steroid Contraceptives....Staff NICHD 301-496-5133

Steroid Hormones....Stoney, Simons S. FAES 301-496-6797

Steroid Hypertension....Staff NHLBI 301-496-4236

Steroids....Staff NIDA 301-443-6245

Stevens-Johnson Syndrome....Staff NIAID 301-496-5717

Stiff Man Syndrome....Staff NINDS 301-496-5751

Still's Disease....Staff NIAMS 301-496-8188

Stimulants....Staff NIDA 301-443-6245

Stomach Cancer....Staff NCI 301-496-5583

Stone and products....White, Linda USITC 202-205-3427

Stone, Crushed....Tepordei, Valentin V. MINES 202-501-9392

Stone, Dimension....Taylor, Harold A. MINES 202-501-9754

Stone House...Staff FIC 301-496-1213

Stone-processing machines....Greene, William USITC 202-205-3405

Stone....Bunin, Jacob CUSTOMS 212-566-5796

Stoneware articles....McNay, Deborah USITC 202-205-3425

Stoneworking machines....Fravel, Dennis USITC 202-205-3404

Storage Batteries...Larrabee, David COMMERCE 202-482-0607

Storm Water....Staff EPA 703-821-4823

Storm Water Hotline....Staff EPA 703-821-4823

Stoves/Woodburning....Staff EPA 919-541-2733

Strabismus....Staff NEI 301-496-5248

Stranger-to-Stranger Crime....Rand, Michael Justice Stat 202-616-3494

Streptococcal Infections....Staff NIAID 301-496-5717

Streptokinase....Staff NHLBI 301-496-4236

Stress and Aging....Staff NIA 301-496-1752

Stress (EKG)....Staff NHLBI 301-496-4236

Stress....Staff NIMH 301-496-4513

Striatonigral Degeneration....Staff NINDS 301-496-5751

Stroke (Hypertension)....Staff NHLBI 301-496-4236

Stroke....Staff American Heart Association Stroke Connection 800-553-6321

Stroke....Staff National Stroke Association 800-787-6537

Stroke....Staff NINDS 301-496-5751

Stroke....Staff NIDCD 301-496-7243

Strontium compounds....Greenblatt, Jack USITC 202-205-3353

Strontium pigments....Johnson, Larry USITC 202-205-3351

Strontium....Lundy, David USITC 202-205-3439

Strontium....Ober, Joyce A. MINES 202-501-9406

Structures of base metals....Kaplan, Stephanie USITC 202-205-3436

Structures....Lew, H.S. NIST 301-975-6061

Student Conservation Programs, Fish and Wildlife....Staff FWS 703-358-1786

Students, Youth, and Dropouts, Empl/Unempl. Stats.....Cohany, Sharon LABOR 202-606-6378

Studio Transmitter Links, Common Carrier....Staff FCC 202-418-1500

Studio Transmitter Links, Mass Media....Staff FCC 202-418-2600

Sturge Weber Syndrome....Staff Sturge Weber Foundation 800-627-5482

Sturge-Weber Syndrome....Staff NINDS 301-496-5751

Stuttering....Staff National Center for Stuttering 800-221-2483

Stuttering....Staff NIDCD 301-496-7243

Stuttering....Staff NINDS 301-496-5751

Sty....Staff NEI 301-496-5248

Styrene (monomer)....Matusik, Ed USITC 202-205-3356

Styrene resins....Misurelli, Denby USITC 202-205-3362

Subacute Necrotizing Encephalomyelopathy (Leighs')....Staff NINDS 301-496-5751

Subacute Sclerosing Panencephalitis....Staff NINDS 301-496-5751

Subarachnoid Cyst...Staff NINDS 301-496-5751

Subarachnoid Hemorrhage....Staff NINDS 301-496-5751

Subscriber line Charge....Staff FCC 202-418-1595

Subseabed Disposal Research....Warnick, Walter NEIC 301-903-3122

Substance Abuse....Staff Primary Care Management Systems 800-444-9999

Substance Abuse Prevention, Office of....Setal, Mel 301-443-9936

Sudan (Khartoum)....Staff Cnty State 202-647-6475

Sudan/Minerals....Antonides, Lloyd Cnty Mines 202-501-9686

Sudan....Abdalla, Elsadig Bakheit Cnty Embassy 202-338-8570

Sudan....Ghani, Ejaz Syed Cnty World Bank 202-473-4819

Sudan....Hill, Megan Cnty AID 202-647-8100

Sudan....Hutchings, Dayna Cnty Export Import Bank 202-565-3737

Sudan....Squire, Margo Cnty USIA 202-619-5529

Sudan....Suliman, Ahmed Cnty Embassy 202-338-8565

Sudan....VanRenterghem, Cynthia Cnty Treasury 202-622-0343

Sudan....Watkins, Chandra Cnty Commerce 202-482-4564

Sudanophilic Leukodystrophy....Staff NINDS 301-496-5751

Sudden Cardiac Death....Staff NHLBI 301-496-4236

Sudden Infant Death Syndrome....Staff NICHD 301-496-5133

Sugar and Sweeteners....Lord, Ronald Agri 202-219-0888

Sugar and Sweeteners....Buzzanell, Peter Agri 202-219-0886

Sugar and Sweeteners....Preston, Greg Agri 202-720-7621

Sugar....Maria, John CUSTOMS 212-466-5730

Sugar....Vacant USITC 202-205-3454

Suicide....Baldwin, Elaine NIDA 301-443-4536

Suicide....Staff NIMH 301-443-4513

Suit-Jackets....Crowley, Michael CUSTOMS 212-466-5852

Suits....Crowley, Michael CUSTOMS 212-466-5852

Suits: men's and boys'....Sweet, mary Elizabeth USITC 202-205-3455

Suits: women's and girls'....Sweet, Mary Elizabeth USITC 202-205-3455

Sulfides, nonmetallic....Conant, Kenneth USITC 202-205-3346

Sulfiting Agents....Lecos, Chris FDA 202-205-1144

Sulfur dioxide....Conant, Kenneth USITC 202-205-3346

Sulfur....Ober, Joyce MINES 202-501-9406

Sulfur....Trainor, Cynthia USITC 202-205-3354

Sulfuric acid....Trainor, Cynthia USITC 202-205-3354

Sulfuryl chloride....Conant, Kenneth USITC 202-205-3346

Summer Research Fellowship Program....Staff CC 301-496-2427

Sunlight and Skin Cancer....Staff NCI 301-496-5583

Sunshine....Staff FCC 202-418-1720

Supercomputers....Iverson, Sean COMMERCE 202-482-1987

Superconducting Super Collider Project....Hall, James NEIC 214-708-2521

Superconductivity....Eaton, Russell NEIC 202-586-0205

Superconductors....Lieberman, Paul PTO 703-308-2552

Superconductors....Chiarado, Roger COMMERCE 202-482-0402
Supercritical fluid extraction....Chesler, Stephen N. NIST 301-975-3102
Superfund Hazardous Waste....Staff EPA 800-231-3075
Superfund....Sims, Anne CDC 404-639-3286
Superfund....Staff EPA 202-260-7703
Superphosphates....Trainor, Cynthia USITC 202-205-3354
Supersonic (Mach 1-5) Engine Testing....Staff NASA 804-864-6125
Supervisory Training....Staff OD/DPM 301-496-6211
Supplemental Security Income (SSI)....Gambino, Phil SSA 410-965-8904
Supplies (Central Storeroom)....Staff OD/DAS 301-496-3273
Surety Guarantees....Kleeschulte, Dorothy D. SBA 202-205-6540
Surface Active Agents....Joseph, Stephanie CUSTOMS 212-466-5768
Surface-active agents....Land, Eric USITC 202-205-3349
Surgeon General....Manley, Audrey PHS 202-690-6467
Surgeons....Staff Association of American Physicians and Surgeons 800-635-1196
Surgery (Cancer)....Staff NCI 301-496-5583
Surgery, diagnostics....Howell, Kyle PTO 703-308-3256
Surgery, medicators....Rosenbaum, Fred PTO 703-308-2991
Surgery (Oral)....Staff NIDR 301-496-4261
Surgery, treatment....Howell, Kyle PTO 703-308-3256
Surgical apparatus....Johnson, Christopher USITC 202-205-3488
Surgical instruments (endoscopes)....Apley, Richard PTO 703-308-0305
Surgical instruments....Hafer, Robert PTO 703-308-2674
Surgical instruments....Mancene, Gene PTO 703-308-2696
Surgical instruments....Pellegrino, Stephen PTO 703-308-0871
Surgical Opinion, second....Staff National Second Surgical Opinion Program 800-638-6833
Surgical Treatment of Heart Disease....Staff NHLBI 301-496-4236
Suriname/Minerals....Gurmendi, Alfredo Cnty Mines 202-501-9681
Suriname (Paramaribo)....Staff Cnty State 202-647-2620
Suriname....Brooks, Michelle Cnty Commerce 202-482-2527
Suriname....Hume, Susan Cnty World Bank 202-473-2407
Suriname....John Herrman Cnty TDA 703-875-4357
Suriname....Korff, Michael Cnty USIA 202-619-6835
Suriname....Neil, Jeff Cnty Treasury 202-622-1268
Suriname....Udenhout, Willem E. Cnty Embassy 202-244-7489
Suriname....van Dillenburg, Georgine Cnty Embassy 202-244-7490
Suriname....Wilkins, Michele Cnty Export-Import Bank 202-565-3743
Survey Data and Tapes, Consumer Expend. Surv.....Passero, William LABOR 202-606-6900
Survey of Consumer Finances....Fries, Gerhard FRS 202-452-2578
Survey of Income and Program Participation (SIPP)....Eargle, Judy CENSUS 301-763-8375
Survey Operations, Consumer Expend. Survey. Pr/Lv....Dietz, Richard LABOR 202-606-6872
Surveys, Migratory Birds....Staff FWS 703-358-1714
Surveys, National Fish and Wildlife....Staff FWS 703-358-2156
Surveys, Waterfowl Harvest....Staff FWS 703-358-6300
Surveys, Waterfowls Population....Staff FWS 703-358-1838
Sutures, surgical....Randall, Rob USITC 202-205-3366
Swallowing Disorders...Staff NIDCD 301-496-7243
Swallowing Disorders....Staff NIDR 301-496-4261
Swaziland (Mbabane)....Staff Cnty State 202-647-8434
Swaziland/Minerals....van Oss, Hendrik Cnty Mines 202-501-9687
Swaziland....Barber, Ed Cnty Treasury 202-622-1730
Swaziland....Bezek, Jill Cnty TDA 703-875-4357
Swaziland....Burns, Paul Peace Corps 202-606-3634
Swaziland....Holm-Olsen, Finn Cnty Commerce 202-482-4228
Swaziland....Jewett, Woody Peace Corps 202-606-3635
Swaziland....Kanya, Mary M. Cnty Embassy 202-362-6683
Swaziland....Lane, Bernard Cnty AID 202-647-4228
Swaziland....Maybury-Lewis, Anthony Cnty Export-Import Bank 202-565-3739
Swaziland....Nhlabatsi, Lindiwe Audrey Cnty Embassy 202-362-6685
Swaziland....Patel, Praful C. Cnty World Bank 202-473-4250
Swaziland....Schwartz, Larry Cnty USIA 202-619-6904
Sweat Gland Disorders....Staff NIAMS 301-496-8188
Sweaters....Crowley, Michael CUSTOMS 212-466-5852
Sweaters....Sweet, Mary Elizabeth USITC 202-205-3455
Sweatshirts....Crowley, Michael CUSTOMS 212-466-5852
Sweatshirts....Sweet, Mary Elizabeth USITC 202-205-3455
Sweden/Minerals....Plachy, Josef Cnty Mines 202-501-9673
Sweden (Stockholm)....Staff Cnty State 202-647-5669
Sweden....Devlin, James Cnty Commerce 202-482-4414
Sweden....Ekman, Andreas Eric Cnty Embassy 202-462-2600

Sweden....Gosnell, Peter Cnty Export-Import Bank 202-565-3733
Sweden....Mackour, Oscar Cnty Treasury 202-622-0145
Sweden....Rankin-Galloway, Honore Cnty USIA 202-619-5283
Sweden....Sihver Liljegren, Carl Henrik Cnty Embassy 202-467-2600
Swimwear, Adult....Shea, Gerard CUSTOMS 212-466-5878
Swimwear, Childrens'....Kirschner, Bruce CUSTOMS 212-566-5865
Swimwear: womens and girls....Sweet, Mary Elizabeth USITC 202-205-3455
Swimwear....Hamey, Amy USITC 202-205-3465
Swimwear....Jones, Jackie USITC 202-205-3466
Swine Flu....Staff NIAID 301-496-5717
Switches, Electric....Malison, Andrew USITC 202-205-3391
Switches, telephone....Hylton, Lori USITC 202-205-3450
Switches....Recia, Henry PTO 703-308-1382
Switchgear and Switchboard Apparatus....Bodson, John COMMERCE 202-482-0681
Switzerland (Bern)....Staff Cnty State 202-647-1484
Switzerland/Minerals....Plachy, Josef Cnty Mines 202-501-9673
Switzerland....Combs, Philip/Wright, Corey Cnty Commerce 202-482-2920
Switzerland....Gosnell, Peter Cnty Export-Import Bank 202-565-3733
Switzerland....Jagmetti, Carlo Cnty Embassy 202-745-7900
Switzerland....Joseph, Jean-Claude Cnty Embassy 202-745-7900
Switzerland....Lemaistre, Alice Cnty USIA 202-619-6184
Switzerland....Mackour, Oscar Cnty Treasury 202-622-0145
Sydenham's Chorea....Staff NINDS 301-496-5751
Synchrotron Resources...Staff NCRR 301-594-7934
Syncope (Fainting)....Staff NHLBI 301-496-4236
Syndrome X....Staff NHLBI 301-496-4236
Synfuel Plants....Frye, Keith NEIC 301-903-2098
Synovitis....Staff NIAMS 301-496-8188
Synthesis Gas....Der, Victor NEIC 301-903-2700
Synthetic detergents....Land, Eric USITC 202-205-3349
Synthetic iron oxides and hydroxides....Johnson, Larry USITC 202-205-3351
Synthetic natural gas (SNG)....Land, Eric USITC 202-205-3349
Synthetic rubber....Misurelli, Denby USITC 202-205-3362
Syphilis....Staff NIAID 301-496-5717
Syria/Minerals....Michalski, Bernadette Cnty Mines 202-501-9699
Syria....Al-Moualem, Walid Cnty Embassy 202-232-6313
Syria....Austin, Ken Cnty Treasury 202-622-0174
Syria....Hutchings, Dayna Cnty Export-Import Bank 202-565-3737
Syria....Mukherjee, Mohua Cnty World Bank 202-473-3022
Syria....Sarra, Suleiman Cnty Embassy 202-232-6313
Syria....Winton, Donna Cnty USIA 202-619-6528
Syria....Wright, Corey/Sams, Thomas Cnty Commerce 202-482-5506
Syrian Arab Republic (Damascus)....Staff Cnty State 202-647-1131
Syringomyelia....Staff NINDS 301-496-5751
System Integration....Atkins, Robert COMMERCE 202-482-4781
Systemic Lupus Erythematosus....Staff NIAMS 301-496-8188
Systolic Hypertension in the Elderly (SHEP)....Staff NIA 301-496-1752
Systolic Hypertension in the Elderly (SHEP)....Staff NHLBI 301-496-4236

T

T-Bills, Technical Information....Decorleto, Donna FRS 202-452-3956
T-Bills with options....SIA Manasses CFT 312-353-9027
T-Bonds with options....Redheffer, Nancy L. CFT 312-353-9015
T-Cell Deficiency....Staff NIAID 301-496-5717
T-Notes (2,5, 6-10) with options....Redheffer, Nancy L. CFT 312-353-9015
T-Notes/Bonds (Zeros) with options....Redheffer, Nancy L. CFT 312-353-9015
T-Shirts, Knit....DeGaetano, Angela CUSTOMS 212-466-5540
T-Shirts....Sweet, Mary Elizabeth USITC 202-205-3455
Tablecloths....Sweet, Mary Elizabeth USITC 202-205-3455
Tachycardia....Staff NHLBI 301-496-4236
Tactile Devices....Staff NIDCD 301-496-7243
Taiwan Coordination....Staff Cnty State 202-647-7711
Taiwan/Minerals....Tse, Pui-Kwan Cnty Mines 202-501-9696
Taiwan....Aschneider, Todd Cnty Treasury 202-622-0335
Taiwan....Davis, Ian/Chu, Robert/Duvall, Dan Cnty Commerce 202-482-4390
Taiwan....Hutchings, Dayna Cnty Export-Import Bank 202-565-3737
Tajikistan....Ghasimi, Mohammad R. Cnty World Bank 202-473-6858
Tajikistan....Levine, Richard Cnty Mines 202-501-9682
Tajikistan....Resnick, Bonnie Cnty Treasury 202-622-0108
Tajikistan....Skipper, Thomas Cnty USIA 202-619-5057
Tajikistan....Staff Cnty State 202-647-6757

Tajikistan....Waxman-Lenz, Roberta Cnty Export-Import Bank 202-565-3742
Tajikistan....Eighmy, Thomas Cnty AID 202-647-6920
Takayasu's Arteritis....Staff NIAID 301-496-5717
Take Pride in America Program, Fish and Wildlife....Staff FWS 703-358-2156
Talc....Virta, Robert MINES 202-501-9384
Talc....White, Linda USITC 202-205-3427
Tall oil....Randall, Rob USITC 202-205-3366
Tangier Disease....Staff NINDS 301-496-5751
Tangier Disease....Staff NHLBI 301-496-4236
Tanning products and agents....Wanser, Stephen USITC 202-205-3363
Tantalum....Cunningham, Larry D. MINES 202-501-9443
Tantalum....Lundy, David USITC 202-205-3439
Tantalum....Presbury, Graylin COMMERCE 202-482-5158
Tanzania (Dar es Salaam)....Staff Cnty State 202-647-6473
Tanzania/Minerals....Izon, David Cnty Mines 202-501-9692
Tanzania....Burns, Paul Peace Corps 202-606-3634
Tanzania....Holm-Olsen, Finn Cnty Commerce 202-482-4228
Tanzania....Imam, Fahmila Cnty Export-Import Bank 202-565-3738
Tanzania....Jewett, Woody Peace Corps 202-606-3635
Tanzania....Kotze, Joan Cnty Treasury 202-622-0333
Tanzania....Larsen, Mark Cnty USIA 202-619-4894
Tanzania....Mwendwa, John Mathew Cnty Embassy 202-939-6125
Tanzania....Nyirabu, Charles Musama Cnty Embassy 202-939-6125
Tanzania....Pulaski, Stephan Cnty AID 202-647-5588
Tanzania....Shaw, William Cnty World Bank 202-473-0138
Tanzania....Younge, Nathan Cnty TDA 703-875-4357
Tape Players....Dicerbo, Mario CUSTOMS 212-466-5672
Tape players....Puffert, Douglas USITC 202-205-3402
Tape recorders and players, audio....Puffert, Douglas USITC 202-205-3402
Tape recordings....Puffert, Douglas USITC 202-205-3402
Tapestries....Hansen, John CUSTOMS 212-466-5854
Tapestries....Sweet, Mary Elizabeth USITC 202-205-3455
Taps....Mata, Ruben USITC 202-205-3403
Tar Sands....Der, Victor NEIC 301-903-2700
Tar sands oil....Foreso, Cynthia USITC 202-205-3348
Tardive Dyskinesia....Staff NINDS 301-496-5751
Tardive Dyskinesia....Staff NIMH 301-443-4513
Tarsal Tunnel Syndrome....Staff NINDS 301-496-5751
Tashkent....Eighmy, Thomas Cnty AID 202-647-6920
Taste and Smell Dysfunction....Staff NIDCD 301-496-7243
Taste and Smell Dysfunction....Staff NINDS 301-496-5751
Taste....Staff NIDCD 301-496-7243
Tax Policy....Stathis, Jennie S. GAO 202-512-5407
Tay-Sach's Disease....Staff NINDS 301-496-5751
Tea....Janis, William V. COMMERCE 202-482-2250
Tea....Maria, John CUSTOMS 212-466-5730
Tea....Schneider, Greg USITC 202-205-3326
Technical Assistance....Schulman, Lawrence FTA 202-366-4052
Technical Information Center....Rosicky, Henry PTO 703-308-0808
Technological Developments and Nursing Care....Staff NINR 301-496-0207
Technologists....Staff Association of Surgical Technologists 800-637-7433
Technology Assessment OD/OMAR 301-496-1143
Technology Centers, Fish....Staff FWS 703-358-1714
Technology Demonstration Center....Richardson, Deborah NAL 301-504-5779
Technology Services....Heydemann, P.L.M. NIST 301-975-4500
Technology Transfer Information Center....Hayes, Kathleen NAL 301-504-6875
Technology Transfer...Staff OD/OIA 301-496-7057
Technology Trends In Major Industries...Riche, Richard LABOR 202-606-5626
Technology....Shane, Richard SBA 202-205-6450
Teenage Pregnancy....Eddinger, Lucy ASH 202-690-8335
Teeth....Staff NIDR 301-496-4261
Telangiectasis (Rendu-Osler-Weber Dis., Syndrome)....Staff NHLBI 301-496-4236
Telecommunications, Cellular....Gossack, Linda COMMERCE 202-482-4466
Telecommunications, CPE....Pham, Phuangm COMMERCE 202-482-0399
Telecommunication Devices for the Deaf....Staff FCC 202-639-6999
Telecommunications, Fiber Optics....Mocenigo, Anthony COMMERCE 202-482-2953
Telecommunications for Deaf, Public and Spec. Studies....TDD LABOR 202-219-7090
Telecommunications, Major Projects....Paddock, Rick COMMERCE 202-482-5235
Telecommunications, Network Equipment....Henry, John COMMERCE 202-482-1193
Telecommunications, Network Equipment....Henry, John COMMERCE 202-482-1193

Telecommunications, Radio....Gossack, Linda COMMERCE 202-482-4466
Telecommunications, Satellites....Cooper, Patricia COMMERCE 202-482-4466
Telecommunications, Services....Elliot, Fred COMMERCE 202-482-1134
Telecommunications Services....Shefrin, Ivan COMMERCE 202-482-4661
Telecommunications, Trade Promo.....Vacant COMMERCE 202-482-2952
Telecommunications, TV Broadcast Equip.....Rettig, Thersa E. COMMERCE 202-482-4466
Telecommunications....Eisenzopf, Reinhard PTO 703-305-4711
Telecommunications....Edwards, Daniel COMMERCE 202-482-4466
Telegraph and telephone apparatus....Hylton, Lori USITC 202-205-3450
Telegraph Industry Group....Owings, Christopher SEC 202-942-1900
Telegraphy....Chin, Stephen PTO 703-305-4714
Telephone Equipment Interconnection....Staff FCC 202-418-0200
Telephone Lines....Staff FCC 202-418-0200
Telephone services....Hylton, Lori USITC 202-205-3450
Telephone Telegraph Rates....Staff FCC 202-418-0200
Telephones, Wireless....Dicerbo, Mario CUSTOMS 212-466-5672
Telephones....Vacant CUSTOMS 212-466-5673
Telephony....Dwyer, James L. PTO 703-305-4701
Telephony....Kuntz, Curt PTO 703-305-4708
Telescopes....Johnson, Christopher USITC 202-205-3488
Teletext Services....Elliot, Fred COMMERCE 202-482-1134
Television Advertising Intercity Relays....Staff FCC 202-418-1430
Television Advertising....Staff FCC 202-418-0200
Television camera....Razavi, Michael PTO 703-305-4713
Television equipment....Kitzmiller, John USITC 202-205-3387
Television Industry Group....Owings, Christopher SEC 202-942-1900
Television Political Broadcasting Fairness....Staff FCC 202-418-1440
Television Programming....Staff FCC 202-418-1430
Television Religious Petition....Staff FCC 202-418-0200
Television Translators....Staff FCC 202-418-1650
Television....Groody, James J. PTO 703-305-4702
Television...Chin, Tommy PTO 703-305-4715
Televisions....Dicerbo, Mario CUSTOMS 212-466-5672
TELEX, International and Domestic....Staff FCC 202-632-7265
Tellurium compounds....Greenblatt, Jack USITC 202-205-3353
Tellurium....Jasinski, Stephen MINES 202-501-9418
Temporal Arteritis....Staff NHLBI 301-496-4236
Temporal Arteritis (Eyes)....Staff NEI 301-496-5248
Temporal Arteritis (Neurological Aspects of)....Staff NINDS 301-496-5751
Temporomandibular Joint Disorders....Staff NIDR 301-496-4261
Tender Offers Proxy Contests....Staff FCC 202-418-1630
Tendonitis....Staff NIAMS 301-496-8188
Tennis equipment....Witherspoon, Richardo USITC 202-205-3489
Tents and tarpaulins....Cook, Lee USITC 202-205-3471
Territorial Exclusivity....Staff FCC 202-418-2120
Terrorism....Reynolds, James S. Justice 202-514-0849
Test Procedures-Equipment....Staff FCC 301-725-1585
Test Site Descriptions....Staff FCC 202-418-1430
Test Tube Babies....Staff NICHD 301-496-5133
Testicular Cancer....Staff NCI 301-496-5583
Tetanus....Staff NIAID 301-496-5717
Tethered Cord...NINDS 301-496-5751
Tetraethyl lead....Michels, David USITC 202-205-3352
Tetralogy of Fallot....Staff NHLBI 301-496-4236
Tetramer of proplyene....Raftery, Jim USITC 202-205-3365
Tetramethyl lead....Michels, David USITC 202-205-3352
Tetrapropylene....Raftery, Jim USITC 202-205-3365
Textile calendaring and rolling machines....Greene, William USITC 202-205-3405
Textile finishing agents....Land, Eric USITC 202-205-3349
Textile Machinery....Mangor, Jon COMMERCE 202-482-2732
Textile machines....Greene, William USITC 202-205-3405
Textile washing, bleaching, dyeing, machines....Greene, William USITC 202-205-3405
Textiles and Apparel Industry Group....Owings, Christopher SEC 202-942-1900
Textiles and Leather, Prices and Living Conditions....Paik, Soon LABOR 202-606-7714
Textiles, Trade Promo....Mangor, Jon COMMERCE 202-482-2732
Textiles....Dulka, William A. COMMERCE 202-482-4058
Textiles....Goldberg, Gerald PTO 703-308-5443
Textiles....Hubbard, Volenick Customs 202-482-7050
Thailand (Bangkok)....Staff Cnty State 202-647-7108
Thailand/Minerals....Lyday, Travis Cnty Mines 202-501-9695
Thailand....Camp, Bea Cnty USIA 202-619-5837

Thailand....Chompoopet, Wilaiwan Cnty Embassy 202-944-3600
Thailand....Dwor-Frecaut, Dominique Cnty World Bank 202-473-2970
Thailand....Frye, Lisa Peace Corps 202-606-0970
Thailand....Hower, Mark Peace Corps 202-606-5517
Thailand....Huston, Christine Peace Corps 202-606-0970
Thailand....Imam, Fahmila Cnty Export-Import Bank 202-565-3738
Thailand....Kelly, Jean Cnty Commerce 202-482-3877
Thailand....Respess, Rebecca Cnty TDA 703-875-4357
Thailand....VanRenterghem, Cynthia Cnty Treasury 202-622-0343
Thailand...Xuto, Manaspas Cnty Embassy 202-944-3600
Thalassemia....Staff NIDDK 301-496-3583
Thalassemia....Staff NHLBI 301-496-4236
Thallium compounds....Greenblatt, Jack USITC 202-205-3353
Thallium....Sehnke, Errol Mines 202-501-9421
Theater....McCord, Karyl NEA 202-682-5425
Theories of Aging....Staff NIA 301-496-1752
Therapeutic Compositions....Robinson, Douglas PTO 703-308-2897
Therapy devices....Apley, Richard PTO 703-308-0305
Thermal Switches....Picard, Leo PTO 703-308-0538
Thermodynamics....Lias, S. NIST 301-975-2562
Thermophysics....Kayser, R.F. NIST 301-975-2483
Thoracic-Outlet Syndrome....Staff NINDS 301-496-5751
Thoratic-Outlet Syndrome....Staff NHLBI 301-496-4236
Thorium compounds....Greenblatt, Jack USITC 202-205-3353
Thorium....DeSapio, Vincent USITC 202-205-3435
Thorium....Hedrick, James B. MINES 202-501-9412
Thread: cotton....Warlick, William USITC 202-205-3459
Thread: manmade fibers....Warlick, William USITC 202-205-3459
Thread: silk....Shelton, Linda USITC 202-205-3467
Threatened Species Permits, Fish and Wildlife....Staff FWS 703-358-2104
Thrift Acquisitions....Koonjy, Diane FRS 202-452-3274
Thrift Acquisitions....Wassom, Molly FRS 202-452-2305
Throat Disorders...Staff NIDCD 301-496-7243
Thrombasthenia....Staff NIDDK 301-496-3583
Thrombocythemia....Staff NHLBI 301-496-4236
Thrombocytopenia....Staff NHLBI 301-496-4236
Thrombocytopenia....Staff NIDDK 301-496-3583
Thromboembolism....Staff NHLBI 301-496-4236
Thrombolysis....Staff NHLBI 301-496-4236
Thrombophlebitis....Staff NHLBI 301-496-4236
Thrombosis....Staff NHLBI 301-496-4236
Thyroid (Adenoma of)....Staff NIDDK 301-496-3583
Thyroiditis....Staff NIDDK 301-496-3583
Thyroma....Staff NCI 301-496-5583
Thyrotoxic Myopathy...Staff NINDS 301-496-5751
Thyroxine-iodine....Staff NIDDK 301-496-3583
Tic Douloureux (Trigeminal Neuralgia)....Staff NINDS 301-496-5751
Ticks....Staff NIAID 301-496-5717
TIGER, Applications....Carbaugh, Larry CENSUS 301-457-1305
TIGER, Future Plans....Staff CENSUS 301-457-1100
Tiger, Products....Carbaugh, Larry CENSUS 301-457-1242
TIGER System Products....Staff CENSUS 301-457-4100
Tights....DeGaetano, Angela CUSTOMS 212-466-5540
Tiles, ceramic....McNay, Deborah USITC 202-205-3425
Timber Management...Hesse, David FS 202-205-0893
Timber Management, Fish and Wildlife....Staff FWS 703-358-2043
Time and Frequency....Sullivan, D.B. NIST 303-497-3772
Time Served in Prison - Federal....Kaplan, Carol Justice Stat 202-307-0759
Time Served in Prison....Greenfeld, Lawrence Justice Stat 202-616-3281
Time Served in Prison....Innes, Christopher Justice Stat 202-724-3121
Time Served in Prison....Beck, Allen Justice Stat 202-616-3277
Time switches....Luther, Dennis USITC 202-205-3497
Timing apparatus....Luther, Dennis USITC 202-205-3497
Tin compounds....Greenblatt, Jack USITC 202-205-3353
Tin Products....Presbury, Graylin COMMERCE 202-482-5158
Tin....Carlin, Jr., James F. MINES 202-501-9426
Tin....DeSapio, Vincent USITC 202-205-3435
Tinnitus....Staff NINDS 301-496-5751
Tinnitus....Staff NIDCD 301-496-7243
Tires and tubes, of rubber of plastics....Raftery, Jim USITC 202-205-3365
Tires....Prat, Raimundo COMMERCE 202-482-0128
Tires....Rauch, Theodore CUSTOMS 212-466-5892
Tissue Culture Cells (Freezing and Storage)....Staff OD/ORS 301-496-2960
Tissue Culture Media....Staff OD/ORS 301-496-6017

Tissue Plasminogen Activator (TPA)....Staff NHLBI 301-496-4236
Tissue Typing....Staff NHLBI 301-496-4236
Tissue Typing....Staff NIAID 301-496-5717
Titanium compounds....Greenblatt, Jack USITC 202-205-3353
Titanium dioxide....Johnson, Larry USITC 202-205-3351
Titanium pigments....Johnson, Larry USITC 202-205-3351
Titanium....DeSapio, Vincent USITC 202-205-3435
Titanium....Gambogi, Joseph MINES 202-501-9390
Tobacco and tobacco products....Harney, Amy USITC 202-205-3465
Tobacco machines....Jackson, Georgia USITC 202-205-3399
Tobacco pipes....Burns, Gail USITC 202-205-3501
Tobacco products....Love, John PTO 703-308-0873
Tobacco Products....Kenney, Cornelius COMMERCE 202-482-2428
Tobacco....Capehart, Tom Agri 202-219-0822
Tobacco....Conte, Ralph CUSTOMS 212-466-5759
Tobacco....Grise, Verner Agri 202-219-0890
Tobacco....Millin, Vincent PTO 703-308-1065
Tobacco....Preston, Greg Agri 202-720-7621
Tobago....Korff, Michael Cnty USIA 202-619-6835
Tobago....Lewin, Michael Cnty World Bank 202-473-8684
Tobago....Marcus, Anthony Cnty Treasury 202-622-1218
Tobago....Massiah, Joan Cnty Embassy 202-467-6490
Tobago....McKnight, Corinne Arvelle Cnty Embassy 202-467-6490
Togo (Lome)....Staff Cnty State 202-647-1540
Togo/Minerals....Izon, David Cnty Mines 202-501-9674
Togo....Baily, Jess Cnty USIA 202-619-5900
Togo....Barber, Ed Cnty Treasury 202-622-1730
Togo....Bezek, Jill Cnty TDA 703-875-4357
Togo....Dailly, Jean-Paul Cnty World Bank 202-473-4743
Togo....Henke, Debra Cnty Commerce 202-482-3317
Togo....Maybury-Lewis, Anthony Cnty Export-Import Bank 202-565-3739
Togo....Sanchez, Patricia Peace Corps 202-606-3237
Togo....Wickman, Cam Cnty AID 202-647-6335
Toilet preps, cosmetics, and perfumery....Land, Eric USITC 202-205-3349
Toilet soaps....Land, Eric USITC 202-205-3349
Toiletries....Mancene, Gene PTO 703-308-2696
Toll Fraud Complaints....Staff FCC 202-418-0960
Toluene....Raftery, Tim USITC 202-205-3365
Tomatoes....McCarty, Timothy USITC 202-205-3324
Toners....Wanser, Stephen USITC 202-205-3363
Tonga/Minerals....Lyday, Travis Cnty Mines 202-501-9695
Tonga (Nuku'alofa)....Staff Cnty State 202-647-3546
Tonga....Berghage, Jeff Peace Corps 202-606-1098
Tonga....Davies, Irene Cnty World Bank 202-458-2481
Tonga....Imam, Fahmila Cnty Export-Import Bank 202-565-3738
Tonga....Respess, Rebecca Cnty TDA 703-875-4357
Tongue....Staff NIDR 301-496-4261
Tongue....Staff NIDCD 301-496-7243
Tools/Dies/Jigs/Fixtures....Pilaroscia, Megan COMMERCE 202-482-0609
Tools, Machine....Losche, Robert CUSTOMS 212-466-5670
Topical drug products....Chkravarty, Alaka G. FAES 301-443-4595
Topographic Map (USGS) Indexes, Fish and Wildlife....Staff FWS 703-358-1713
Topped crude petroleum....Foreso, Cynthia USITC 202-205-3348
Torsion Dystonia (Dystonia Musculorum Deformans)....Staff NINDS 301-496-5751
Torticollis (Wryneck)....Staff NINDS 301-496-5751
Toto....Olson, Susan Peace Corps 202-606-3136
Tourette Syndrome....Staff TSA 800-237-0717
Tourette Syndrome....Staff NINDS 301-496-5751
Tourette Syndrome....Staff NIMH 301-443-4513
Tourette Syndrome....Staff NIDCD 301-496-7243
Tourism (Major Proj)....White, Barbara COMMERCE 202-482-4160
Tourism services....Ludolph, Josephine COMMERCE 202-482-3575
Tourism services....Sloane, Leonard USITC 202-205-3311
Tours (Campus)....Staff OD/VIC 301-496-1776
Tours....Staff CC 301-496-3475
Tours....Staff NLM 301-496-6308
Tow, manmade....Sweet, Mary Elizabeth USITC 202-205-3455
Towels....Hansen, John CUSTOMS 212-466-5854
Towels....Sweet, Mary Elizabeth USITC 202-205-3455
Towers--Painting and Lighting of....Staff FCC 202-632-7521
Toxic Shock Syndrome....Staff NICHD 301-496-5133
Toxic Shock Syndrome....Staff NIAID 301-496-5717
Toxic Shock Syndrome....Staff CDC 401-639-3286

Toxic Substances and Disease Registry, Agency for....Greenwell, Mike ATSDR 404-639-0727

Toxic Substances Library....Staff EPA 202-260-3944

Toxicology Branch....Staff EPA 703-305-6121

Toxicology/Pharmacology....Staff NIEHS 919-541-3345

Toxicology/Pharmacology....Staff NIGMS 301-496-7707

Toxicology Program, National....Stopinski, Helen NIEHS/NIH 919-541-3991

Toxicology Programs/Special. Information Services....Staff NLM 301-496-1131

Toxicology Programs/Specialized Information Services....Staff NLM 301-496-1131

Toxicology....Davis, Barbara D. FAES 703-603-8823

Toxicology....DeRosa, Christopher CDC 404-639-6300

Toxics Branch....Staff EPA 703-235-5320

TOXNET....Staff NLM 301-496-1131

Toxocariasis....Staff NEI 301-496-5248

Toxoplasmosis....Staff NEI 301-496-5248

Toxoplasmosis....Staff NIAID 301-496-5717

Toys and Games (Export Promo)....Beckham, Reginald COMMERCE 202-482-5478

Toys for pets, christmas deco, figurines, etc.....Raftery, Jim USITC 202-205-3365

Toys....Abrahamson, Dana USITC 202-205-3430

Toys....Hodgen, Donald COMMERCE 202-482-3346

Toys....Wong, Alice CUSTOMS 212-466-5538

Toys...Hafer, Robert PTO 703-308-2674

Trace Gas Measurement Techniques....Guenther, Franklin R. NIST 301-975-3939

Trace Metals (and CVD)....Staff NHLBI 301-496-4236

Trachoma....Staff NEI 301-496-5248

Track Suits....Crowley, Michael CUSTOMS 212-466-5852

Tractors (except truck tractors)....Fravel, Dennis USITC 202-205-3404

Tractors....Wholey, Patrick CUSTOMS 212-466-5668

Trade Related Employment....Teske, Gary R.A. COMMERCE 202-482-2056

Trademark Search Library....Staff PTO 703-308-9800

Traffic Safety Programs....Brownlee, Michael NHTSA 202-366-1755

Traffic Safety....Zawitz, Marianne Justice Stat 202-616-3499

Trailers and other vehicles not self-propelled....Polly, Laura USITC 202-205-3408

Training (Biological Safety and Control)....Staff OD/ORS 301-496-2960

Training Courses....Staff CENSUS 301-457-1210

Training....Rhile, Howard G. GAO 202-512-6418

Training....Staff OD/DPM 301-496-6211

Transceivers....Kitzmiller, John USITC 202-205-3387

Transformation (Cell)....Staff NCI 301-496-5583

Transformers....Bodson, John COMMERCE 202-482-0681

Transformers....Cutchin, John USITC 202-205-3396

Transformers....Josephs, Irwin CUSTOMS 212-466-5673

Transfusional Hemosiderosis....Staff NHLBI 301-496-4236

Transient Ischemic Attacks....Staff NHLBI 301-496-4236

Transient Ischemic Attacks....Staff NINDS 301-496-5751

Transplantation (Cornea)....Staff NEI 301-496-5248

Transplantation Immunology....Staff NIAID 301-496-5717

Transplants (He, Valv, Lung, Blo, Vess, Vei, Ar)....Staff NHLBI 301-496-4236

Transplants (Liver, Pancreas, Kidney)....Staff NIDDK 301-496-3583

Transplants (Organ Procurement)....Staff HRSA 301-443-7577

Transport....Staff FCC 202-418-1590

Transportation Equipment, Producer Price Index....Yatsko, Ralph LABOR 202-606-7747

Transportation Issues....Mead, Kenneth M. GAO 202-512-3766

Transportation Services....Johnson, William COMMERCE 202-482-5012

Transportation, Truck Inventory and Use....Bostic, William CENSUS 301-457-2797

Transportation....Staff OD/Motor Pool 301-496-3426

Transposition of the Great Vessels....Staff NHLBI 301-496-4236

Transsexuality....Staff NICHD 301-496-5133

Transverse Myelitis....Staff NINDS 301-496-5751

Trapping, Hatcheries....Staff FWS 703-358-1715

Trapping, Refuges....Staff FWS 703-358-2043

Trauma Research (Cent. Ner. Sys., Head, Spin. Cr.)....Staff NINDS 301-496-5751

Trauma Research....Staff NIDCD 301-496-7243

Trauma Research....Staff NIGMS 301-496-7301

Trauma....Staff American Trauma Society 800-556-7890

Travel and Tourism....Ludolp, Josephine COMMERCE 202-482-3575

Travel goods....Seastrum, Carl USITC 202-205-3493

Travel Surveys....Cannon, John CENSUS 301-457-3877

Treaties, Indian Fisheries....Staff FWS 703-358-1718

Treatment Improvement, Office for....Hurley, Joan NIDA 301-443-6549

Tremors....Staff NINDS 301-496-5751

Tremors....Staff NIDCD 301-496-7243

Trench Mouth....Staff NIDR 301-496-4261

Trichinosis....Staff NIAID 301-496-5717

Trichloroethylene....Michels, David USITC 202-205-3352

Trichomoniasis....Staff NIAID 301-496-5717

Trichotillomania....Staff NIMH 301-443-4513

Trichotillomania....Staff NINDS 301-496-5751

Tricks....Abrahamson, Dana USITC 202-205-3430

Tricuspid Atresia....Staff NHLBI 301-496-4236

Tricuspid Valve....Staff NHLBI 301-496-4236

Tricycles....Abrahamson, Dana USITC 202-205-3430

Trigeminal Neuralgia (Tic Douloureux)....Staff NINDS 301-496-5751

Triglycerides....Staff NHLBI 301-496-4236

Trimellitic acid esters...Johnson, Larry USITC 202-205-3351

Trinidad and Tobago/Minerals....Torres, Ivette Cnty Mines 202-501-9680

Trinidad and Tobago (Port-of-Spain)....Staff Cnty State 202-647-2621

Trinidad and Tobago....Brooks, Michelle Cnty Commerce 202-482-2527

Trinidad....Korff, Michael Cnty USIA 202-619-6835

Trinidad....Lewin, Michael Cnty World Bank 202-473-8684

Trinidad....Marcus, Anthony Cnty Treasury 202-622-1218

Trinidad....Massiah, Joan Cnty Embassy 202-467-6490

Trinidad....McKnight, Corinne Arvelle Cnty Embassy 202-467-6490

Trinidad....Wilkins, Michele Cnty Export-Import Bank 202-565-3743

Trinitrotoluene....Johnson, Larry USITC 202-205-3351

Tripoli....Austin, Gordon MINES 202-501-9388

Tropical Diseases....Staff NIAID 301-496-5717

Tropical Forestry....Martin, Michael R. FS 703-235-9461

Tropical Spastic Paraparesis....Staff NINDS 301-496-5751

Trousers....DeGaetano, Angela CUSTOMS 212-466-5540

Trousers: mens and boys....Sweet, Mary Elizabeth USITC 202-205-3455

Trousers: women's and girls'....Sweet, Mary Elizabeth USITC 202-205-3455

Truck tractors....Hagey, Michael USITC 202-205-3392

Trucking Services....Wolfe, Claudia COMMERCE 202-482-5086

Trucks....Hagey, Michael USITC 202-205-3392

Truncus Arteriosus....Staff NHLBI 301-496-4236

Truth in Leasing....Poindexter, Obrea FRS 202-452-2412

Truth in Lending....Williams, Manley FRS 202-452-3667

Trypanosomiasis....Staff NIAID 301-496-5717

Trypsinogen Deficiency....Staff NIDDK 301-496-3583

TSH, Excessive Secretion....Staff NIDDK 301-496-3583

TTY - Population Information....Staff CENSUS 301-763-5020

Tuberculosis....Jereb, John CDC 404-639-8123

Tuberculosis....Staff NIAID 301-496-5717

Tuberculosis....Staff CDC 404-639-1819

Tuberous Sclerosis....Staff National Tuberous Sclerosis Association 800-225-6872

Tuberous Sclerosis....Staff NINDS 301-496-5751

Tubes for pneumatic tires....Raftery, Jim USITC 202-205-3365

Tubes....Josephs, Irwin CUSTOMS 212-466-5673

Tubing, of rubber or plastics....Misurelli, Denby USITC 202-205-3362

Tularemia....Staff NIAID 301-496-5717

Tumor, Brain....Staff American Brain Tumor Association 800-886-2282

Tumor Immunology....Staff NCI 301-496-5583

Tumor....Staff NCI 301-496-5583

Tumors (Eye)....Staff NEI 301-496-5248

Tumors with Endocrine Function....Staff NIDDK 301-496-3583

Tuna....Corey, Roger USITC 202-205-3327

Tungsten compounds....Greenblatt, Jack USITC 202-205-3353

Tungsten....Amey, Earle B. MINES 202-501-9427

Tungsten....Lundy, David USITC 202-205-3439

Tunisia/Minerals....Dolley, Thomas Cnty Mines 202-501-9690

Tunisia (Tunis)....Staff Cnty State 202-647-3614

Tunisia....DiMeo, Pam Peace Corps 202-606-3196

Tunisia....Early, Evelyn Cnty USIA 202-619-6528

Tunisia....El Baroudy, Samia Cnty World Bank 202-4473-2370

Tunisia....Emmett, Anne Marie Peace Corps 202-606-3196

Tunisia....Ennifar, Azouz Cnty Embassy 202-862-1850

Tunisia....Imam, Fahmila Cnty Export-Import Bank 202-565-3738

Tunisia....Mandel, Pamela Cnty AID 202-663-2617

Tunisia....Romdhani, Oussama Cnty Embassy 202-862-1850

Tunisia....Schneider, Todd Cnty Treasury 202-622-0335

Tunisia....Stillwell, Carol Cnty TDA 703-875-4357

Tunisia....Wright, Corey/Sams, Thomas Cnty Commerce 202-482-1860

Turkey (Ankara)....Staff Cnty State 202-647-6114

Turkey/Minerals....van Oss, Hendrik Cnty Mines 202-501-9687
Turkey....Ayas, Esref Cnty Embassy 202-659-8200
Turkey....Corro, Ann Cnty Commerce 202-482-3945
Turkey....Hutchings, Dayna Cnty Export-Import Bank 202-565-3737
Turkey....Kandemir, Nuzhet Cnty Embassy 202-659-8200
Turkey....Lee, Nancy Cnty Treasury 202-622-2916
Turkey....Mehra, Suman Cnty World Bank 202-473-2247
Turkey....Santoro, Eugene Cnty USIA 202-619-6582
Turkmenistan....Annaberdiev, Tchamazar Cnty Embassy 202-737-4800
Turkmenistan....Eighmy, Thomas Cnty AID 202-647-6920
Turkmenistan....Leijonhufvud, Christina E. Cnty World Bank 202-473-8146
Turkmenistan....Resnick, Bonnie Cnty Treasury 202-622-0108
Turkmenistan....Rossate, Julie Peace Corps 202-606-3040
Turkmenistan....Shamson, Tanya Cnty TDA 703-875-4357
Turkmenistan....Staff Cnty State 202-647-6757
Turkmenistan....Ugur, Halil Cnty Embassy 202-737-4800
Turkmenistan....Waxman-Lenz, Roberta Cnty Export-Import Bank 202-565-3742
Turkmensistan....Skipper, Thomas Cnty USIA 202-619-5057
Turks/Caicos....Wilkins, Michele Cnty Export-Import Bank 202-565-3743
Turks and Caicos Islands....Siegelman, Mark Cnty Commerce 202-482-5680
Turner Syndrome....Staff NICHD 301-496-5133
Turntables....Puffert, Douglas USITC 202-205-3402
Turpentine....Randall, Rob USITC 202-205-3336
Turtles (Salmonellosis)....Staff CDC 404-639-3286
Tuvalu (Funafuti)....Staff Cnty State 202-647-3546
Tuvalu....Berghage, Jeff Peace Corps 202-606-1098
Tuvalu....Rahman, Talaat Cnty TDA 703-875-4357
Tuvalu....Shelton, Alison Cnty Treasury 202-622-0354
TV Answer....Staff FCC 202-418-0620
TV Broadcasting....Siegmund, John COMMERCE 202-482-4781
TV Channel Interference....Staff FCC 202-418-2190
TV Communications Eqmt....Gossack, Linda COMMERCE 202-482-4466
TV Receiver-Noise Figures....Staff FCC 301-725-1585
TV Satellite Stations-General Policy....Staff 202-418-2130
TV Satellite Stations-Specific TV Station....Staff FCC 202-418-1630
TV Technical Standards....Staff FCC 202-418-1630
TV Violence....Baldwin, Elaine 301-443-4536
Twine....Cook, Lee USITC 202-205-3471
Typewriters....Baker, Scott USITC 202-205-3386
Typewriting devices....Burr, Edgar PTO 703-308-0979
Typhoid Fever....Staff NIAID 301-496-5717

U

Uganda (Kampala)....Staff Cnty State 202-647-6479
Uganda/Minerals....Izon, David Cnty Mines 202-501-9692
Uganda....Downs, Peter Cnty AID 202-647-5583
Uganda....Goode, Sachiko Peace Corps 202-606-3695
Uganda....Katenta-Apuli, Stephen Cnty Embassy 202-726-7100
Uganda....Kotze, Joan Cnty treasury 202-622-0354
Uganda....Larsen, Mark Cnty USIA 202-619-4894
Uganda....Lucyk, Chris Cnty Commerce 202-482-1104
Uganda....Masutti, Maria L. Cnty World Bank 202-473-4751
Uganda....Maybury-Lewis, Anthony Cnty Export-Import Bank 202-565-3739
Uganda....Ssenyomo, Ahmed Cnty Embassy 202-726-7101
Uganda....Young, Nathan Cnty TDA 703-875-4357
Ukraine....Ann Lien Cnty TDA 703-875-4357
Ukraine....Balkind, Jeffrey Cnty World Bank 202-458-9116
Ukraine....Bloemenkamp, Sandra Cnty World Bank 202-458-9109
Ukraine....Carlen, James Cnty Treasury 202-622-0122
Ukraine....Marchuk, Vadym E. Cnty Embassy 202-333-0606
Ukraine....McCleod, Evelyn Cnty AID 202-736-7646
Ukraine....O'Keefe, Monica Cnty USIA 202-619-5057
Ukraine....Shcherbak, Yuriy Mikolayevych Cnty Embassy 202-333-0606
Ukraine....Staff Cnty State 202-647-8671
Ukraine....Viksnins, Helen Peace Corps 202-606-5517
Ukraine....Waxman-Lenz, Roberta Cnty 202-565-3742
Ukraine....Wooton, Nicholas Peace Corps 202-606-5519
Ulcerative Colitis....Staff NIDDK 301-496-3583
Ulcerative Lesions (Oral)....Staff NIDR 301-496-4261
Ulcers (Fingers, Toes, Arms, Legs)....Staff NHLBI 301-496-4236
Ulcers (Oral) NIDR 301-496-4261
Ulcers (Skin) NIAMS 301-496-8188

Ulcers (Stomach)....Staff NIDDK 301-654-3810
Ultrasonics Equipment....Staff FCC 202-653-8247
Umbrellas....Spalding, Josephine USITC 202-205-3498
Underground Nuclear Testing....Williams, Irvin NEIC 301-903-5341
Underwear....Burtnik, Brian CUSTOMS 212-466-5880
Underwear....Sweet, Mary Elizabeth USITC 202-205-3455
Unemployment and Labor Force, Foreign Countries....Sorrentino, Constance LABOR 202-606-5654
Unemployment Statistics....Palumbo, Thomas CENSUS 301-763-8574
Unfinished oils....Foreso, Cynthia USITC 202-205-3348
Uniform Crime Reports - Redesign Implementation....White, Paul Justice Stat 202-307-0771
Uniform Crime Reports - Redesign Implementation....Manson, Donald Justice Stat 202-616-3491
Unions, Employee Associations, Membership, Comp/Wk....Cimini, Michael LABOR 202-606-6275
Unit Labor Costs, Productivity....Neef, Arthur LABOR 202-606-5654
United Arab Emirates (Abu Dhabi)....Staff Cnty State 202-647-6558
United Arab Emirates/Minerals....Izon, David Cnty Mines 202-501-9674
United Arab Emirates....Al-Shaali, Mohammad bin Hussein Cnty Embassy 202-338-6500
United Arab Emirates....Al-Romaithi, Mohammed Cnty Embassy 202-338-6500
United Arab Emirates....Austin, Ken Cnty Treasury 202-622-0174
United Arab Emirates....Vacant Cnty USIA 202-619-6528
United Arab Emirates....Clement, Claude Cnty Commerce 202-482-5545
United Kingdom (London)....Staff Cnty State 202-647-6587
United Kingdom of Great Britain and Northern Ireland....Renwick, Sir Robin Cnty Embassy
United Kingdom/Minerals....Newman, Harold R. Cnty Mines 202-501-9669
United Kingdom....Gosnell, Peter Cnty Export-Import Bank 202-565-3733
United Kingdom....Kulla, Morgan Cnty USIA 202-619-6853
United Kingdom....Mackour, Oscar Cnty Treasury 202-622-0145
United Kingdom....McLaughlin, Robert Cnty Commerce 202-482-3748
United Kingdom....Phillips, Patricia Cnty Embassy 202-462-1340
Universal joints....Topolansky, Adam USITC 202-205-3394
Universal Service Fund....Staff FCC 202-418-0850
Universal Service....Staff FCC 202-418-1594
Unresectable Chrondosarcoma or Osteogenic Sarcoma....Staff NCI 301-496-5583
Upholstery fabrics....Sweet, Mary Elizabeth USITC 202-205-3455
Upper Atmosphere Research Satellite....Loughlin, John NASA 301-286-5565
Upper Atmosphere Research Satellite....Staff NASA 301-286-2806
Upper Midwest MTC (Manufacturing Technology Center)....Pounds, Jan NIST 612-338-7722
Uranium Enrichment....Haberman, Norton NEIC 301-903-4321
Uranium compounds....Greenblatt, Jack USITC 202-205-3353
Uranium oxide....Greenblatt, Jack USITC 202-205-3353
Uranium (statistics only) Hilliard, Henry Cnty MINES 202-501-9429
Uranium....DeSapio, Vincent USITC 202-205-3435
Uranium....Sugg, William COMMERCE 202-482-1466
Urban and Community Forestry Programs....Hatfield, Laura-Ziegler FS 202-205-0823
Urban Residence....Staff CENSUS 301-457-2381
Urban/Rural Residence....Staff CENSUS 301-457-2381
Urea resins....Misurelli, Denby USITC 202-205-3362
Urea....Trainor, Cynthia USITC 202-205-3354
Uremia....Staff NIDDK 301-654-4415
Uric Acid Kidney Stones....Staff NIDDK 301-654-4415
Urinary Incontinence....Staff NIA 301-496-1752
Urinary Tract Diseases....Staff NIDDK 301-654-4415
Urinary Tract Infections....Staff NIDDK 301-654-4415
Urinary Tract Tumors....Staff NIDDK 301-496-5583
Urine Volume....Staff NIDDK 301-654-4415
Urokinase....Staff NHLBI 301-496-4236
Urolithiasis....Staff NIDDK 301-654-4415
Urticaria....Staff NIAID 301-496-5717
Uruguay/Minerals....Gurmendi, Alfredo Cnty Mines 202-501-9681
Uruguay (Montevideo)....Staff Cnty State 202-647-2296
Uruguay....Hagerstrom, Mark V. Cnty World Bank 202-473-9208
Uruguay....John Herrman Cnty TDA 703-875-4357
Uruguay....Leeb, Howard Cnty USIA 202-619-5867
Uruguay....Macgillycuddy, Eduardo Cnty Embassy 202-331-1313
Uruguay....Moerzinger, Alvaro Cnty Embassy 202-331-1316
Uruguay....Neil, Jeff Cnty Treasury 202-622-1268
Uruguay....Prevot, Babette Cnty AID 202-647-4359

Uruguay....Ross, Rebecca Peace Corps 202-606-3575
Uruguay....Turner, Roger Cnty Commerce 202-482-1495
Uruguay....Vacant Peace Corps 202-606-3376
Uruguay....Wilkins, Michele Cnty Import Bank 202-565-3743
US Trade and Foreign Agriculture - Africa and Mideast....Kurtzig, Mike Agri 202-219-0636
US Trade and Foreign Agriculture - Asia - East....Dycke, John Agri 202-219-0610
US Trade and Foreign Agriculture - Asia - South....Vocke, Gary Agri 202-219-0610
US Trade and Foreign Agriculture - Canada....Stout, Jim Agric 202-219-0610
US Trade and Foreign Agriculture - China....Cooke, Frederick Agri 202-219-0610
US Trade and Foreign Agriculture - Developing Economies....Mathia, Gene Agri 202-219-0680
US Trade and Foreign Agriculture - Eastern Europe....Koopman, Robert Agri 202-219-0621
US Trade and Foreign Agriculture - Eastern Europe....Cochrane, Nancy Agri 202-219-0650
US Trade and Foreign Agriculture - Exports and Imports....Greene, Joel Agri 202-219-0816
US Trade and Foreign Agriculture - Exports....Ackerman, Karen Agri 202-219-0243
US Trade and Foreign Agriculture - Food Aid....Missiaen, Margaret Agri 202-219-0652
US Trade and Foreign Agriculture - Food Aid Programs....Suarez, Nydia Agri 202-219-0821
US Trade and Foreign Agriculture - Former Soviet Union....Foster, Christian Agri 202-219-0624
US Trade and Foreign Agriculture - Latin America....Link, John Agri 202-219-0689
US Trade and Foreign Agriculture - Pacific Rim....Coyle, William Agri 202-219-0610
US Trade and Foreign Agriculture - Programs....Ackerman, Karen Agri 202-219-0821
US Trade and Foreign Agriculture - Trade and Finance....Roningen, Vern Agri 202-219-0683
US Trade and Foreign Agriculture - Trade and Finance....Haley, Steve Agri 202-219-0666
US Trade and Foreign Agriculture - Western Europe....Normile, MaryAnn Agri 202-219-0774
US Trade and Foreign Agriculture....Baxter, Tim Agri 202-219-0708
US Trade and Foreign Agriculture....Stallings, David Agri 202-219-0688
Usher's Syndrome...Staff NIDCD 301-496-7243
Usher's Syndrome....Staff NEI 301-496-5248
USSR (Moscow)....Staff Cnty State 202-647-8671
Uterus....Staff NICHD 301-496-5133
Utility, Retail Prices....Adkins, Robert LABOR 202-606-6985
Uveitis....Staff NEI 301-496-5248
Uzbekistan....Butayarov, Turdiqui Cnty Embassy 202-638-4267
Uzbekistan....Eighmy, Thomas Cnty AID 202-647-6920
Uzbekistan....Koff, Allison S. Cnty TDA 703-875-4357
Uzbekistan....Rajagopalan, V.N. Cnty World Bank 202-473-2958
Uzbekistan....Resnick, Bonnie Cnty Treasury 202-622-0108
Uzbekistan....Rossate, Julie Peace Corps 202-606-3040
Uzbekistan....Skipper, Thomas Cnty USIA 202-619-5057
Uzbekistan....Staff Cnty State 202-647-6765
Uzbekistan....Teshabaev, Fatikah Cnty Embassy 202-638-4266

V

Vacancies, NIH Recording....Staff NIH 301-496-2403
Vaccine Licensing....Staff FDA 301-443-8995
Vaccines....Nesbitt, Elizabeth USITC 202-205-3355
Vaccines....Nucker, Christine M PTO 703-308-4028
Vaccines....Staff FDA/NCDB/OB 301-594-2090
Vaccines....Staff NIAID 301-496-5717
Vacuum cleaners....Jackson, Georgia USITC 202-205-3399
Vaginitis....Staff NIAID 301-496-5717
Valves and cocks....Mata, Ruben USITC 202-205-3403
Valves (Heart)....Staff NHLBI 301-496-4236
Valves, Pipefittings Ex Brass....Reise, Richard COMMERCE 202-482-3489
Valves....Riedl, Karl CUSTOMS 212-466-5493
Valvular Heart Disease....Staff NHLBI 301-496-4236
Valvuloplasty....Staff NHLBI 301-496-4236

Vanadium compounds....Greenblatt, Jack USITC 202-205-3353
Vanadium....Hilliard, Henry E. MINES 202-501-9429
Vanadium....Lundy, David USITC 202-205-3439
Vanatu (Port Vila)....Staff Cnty State 202-647-3546
Vanillin....Land, Eric USITC 202-205-3349
Vanuatu/Minerals....Lyday, Travis Cnty Mines 202-501-9695
Vanuatu....Davies, Irene Cnty World Bank 202-458-2481
Vanuatu....Imam, Fahmila Cnty Export-Import Bank 202-565-3738
Vanuatu....Lee, Allison Peace Corps 202-606-0983
Vanuatu....Marona, Catherine Peace Corps 202-606-0983
Vanuatu....Respess, Rebecca Cnty TDA 703-875-4357
Vanuatu....Schell, Russell Peace Corps 202-606-3231
Vanuatu....Shelton, Alison Cnty Treasury 202-622-0354
Varicella, Congenital....Staff NINDS 301-496-5751
Varicose Ulcers...Staff NHLBI 301-496-4236
Varicose Veins....Staff NHLBI 301-496-4236
Varnish....Brownchweig, Gilbert CUSTOMS 212-466-5744
Varnishes....Johnson, Larry USITC 202-205-3351
Vascular Collapse....Staff NHLBI 301-496-4236
Vasculitis....Staff NIAID 301-496-5717
Vasculitis....Staff NINDS 301-496-5751
Vasculitis....Staff NHLBI 301-496-4236
Vasectomy....Staff NICHD 301-496-5133
Vatican....Staff Cnty State 202-647-3746
VCRs....Dicerbo, Mario CUSTOMS 212-466-5672
VD (Control and Treatment)....Staff CDC 800-227-8922
VD....Staff NIAID 301-496-5717
Vector-Borne Infectious Diseases....Gubler, Duane J. CDC 303-221-6428
Vegetable fibers (except cotton)....Cook, Lee USITC 202-205-3471
Vegetable glue....Jonnard, Aimison USITC 202-205-3350
Vegetables - Fresh....Brewster, Jim Agri 202-720-7688
Vegetables - Proc.....Budge, Arvin Agri 202-720-4285
Vegetables....Hamm, Shannon Agri 202-219-0886
Vegetables....Hintzman, Kevin Agri 202-720-5412
Vegetables....Love, John Agri 202-219-0388
Vegetables....Lucier, Gary Agri 202-219-0884
Vegetables....Manogue, Robert COMMERCE 202-482-3428
Vegetables....McCarty, Timothy USITC 202-205-3324
Vehicle Crash Avoidance Research....Leasure, William NHTSA 202-366-5662
Vehicle performance....Clark, John NTSB 202-382-6634
Vehicle Propulsion Systems....Allsup, Jerry NEIC 202-586-9118
Vehicle Research....Monk, Michael NHTSA 513-666-4511
Vehicle Safety Compliance....Hellmuth, Robert NHTSA 202-366-2832
Vehicle Testing....Monk, Michael NHTSA 513-666-4511
Vehicles, Special Purpose....Desoucey, Robert CUSTOMS 212-466-5667
Veiling....Sweet, Mary Elizabeth USITC 202-205-3455
Vending machines....Jackson, Georgia USITC 202-205-3399
Venereal Disease (Control and Treatment)....Staff CDC 404-639-3286
Venereal Disease....Staff NIAID 301-496-5717
Venezuela (Caracas)....Staff Cnty State 202-647-3023
Venezuela/Minerals....Torres, Ivette Cnty Mines 202-501-9680
Venezuela....Bayly, Rachel Cnty Treasury 202-622-1266
Venezuela....Echeverria, Pedro Luis Cnty Embassy 202-342-2214
Venezuela....Hatfield, Ziegler Cnty Commerce 202-482-4303
Venezuela....Head, Alfred Cnty USIA 202-619-6835
Venezuela....Maybury-Lewis, Anthony Cnty Export-Import Bank 202-565-3739
Venezuela....Prevot, Babette Cnty AID 202-647-4359
Venezuela....Velez, Francisco Jose cnty Embassy 202-342-2214
Venezuela....Zermeno, Mayra R. Cnty World Bank 202-473-0141
Venous Insufficiency...Staff NHLBI 301-496-4236
Venous Thrombosis....Staff NHLBI 301-496-4236
Ventilation....Staff OD/ORS 301-496-2960
Ventricular Septal Defect...Staff NHLBI 301-496-4236
Vermiculite....Potter, Michael J. MINES 202-501-9387
Vertical Blanking Interval TV....Staff FCC 202-418-2190
Vertigo....Staff NIDCD 301-496-7243
Vertigo....Staff NINDS 301-496-5751
Vestibular Neuronitis....Staff NIDCD 301-496-7243
Vestibular System....Staff NIDCD 301-496-7243
Vests, mens'....Jones, Jackie USITC 202-205-3466
Veterans Affairs....Bechet, Leon J. SBA 202-205-6773
Veterans, Employment Statistics....Cohany, Sharon LABOR 202-606-6378
Veterans Status....Jones, Selwyn CENSUS 301-763-8574
Veterans Status....Palumbo, Thomas CENSUS 301-763-8574

Veterinary instruments....Johnson, Christopher USITC 202-205-3488
Veterinary Medicine....Snider, Sharon FDA 301-443-3285
Vibrotactile Aids....Staff NIDCD 301-496-7243
Victim and Witness Assistance Programs....Kaplan, Carol Justice Stat 202-307-0759
Victim and Witness Assistance Programs....Zawitz, Marianne Justice Stat 202-616-3499
Victims of Crime....Taylor, Bruce Justice Stat 202-616-3498
Victims of Crime....Klaus, Patsy Justice Stat 202-307-0776
Victims of Crime....Meister, Brenda G. Justice Stat 202-307-5983
Victims of Crime....Rand, Michael Justice Stat 202-616-3494
Video Data Service Interactive....Staff FCC 202-418-0680
Video Dialtone...Staff FCC 202-418-1580
Video games....Abrahamson, Dana USITC 202-205-3430
Video Marketplace....Staff FCC 202-418-1580
Video processing....Field, Bruce F. NIST 301-975-4230
Video Services....Elliot, Fred COMMERCE 202-482-1134
Video Transmission--Common Carrier....Staff FCC 202-418-1500
Videotape Productions....Staff NCRR 301-496-4700
Videotex Services....Elliot, Fred COMMERCE 202-482-1134
Vietnam/Minerals....Lyday, Travis Cnty Mines 202-501-9695
Vietnam....Camp, Bea Cnty USIA 202-619-5837
Vietnam....Ha, Huy Thong Cnty Embassy 202-861-0737
Vietnam....Haldane, Donna Cnty World Bank 202-458-0456
Vietnam....Imam, Fahmila Cnty Export-Import Bank 202-565-3738
Vietnam....Le, Bang Van Cnty Embassy 202-861-0737
Vietnam....Pho, Hong-Phong B. Cnty Commerce 202-482-3877
Vietnam....Rahman, Talaat Cnty TDA 703-875-4357
Vietnam....Schneider, Todd Cnty Treasury 202-622-0335
Vietnam....Staff Cnty State 202-647-3132
Vincent's Infection....Staff NIDR 301-496-4261
Vinyl chloride monomer....Michels, David USITC 202-205-3352
Vinyl resins or plastics....Misurelli, Denby USITC 202-205-3362
Violations, Fish and Wildlife Laws....Staff FWS 703-358-1949
Violent Crime....Reynolds, James S. Justice 202-514-0849
Viral products....Klinman, Dennis FAES 301-496-8492
Virgin Islands (US)....Soto, Rodrigo Cnty Commerce 202-482-5680
Virgin Islands (UK)....Brooks, Michelle Cnty Commerce 202-482-4464
Virology....Staff NIAID 301-496-5717
Virus (Cancer Related)....Staff NCI 301-496-5583
Virus Tumor Biology....Brady, John FAES 301-496-0988
Vision and aging....Staff The Lighthouse 800-334-5497
Vision and Aging....Staff NIA 301-496-1752
Vision and Aging....Staff NEI 301-496-5248
Vision Care (Statistics)....Staff NCHS 301-436-8500
Visitor Centers, Hatcheries....Staff FWS 703-358-1715
Visual Arts....Staff NEA 202-682-5448
Visual communications....Carter, H. UMD 301-405-2408
Visual displays....Oberley, Alvin E. PTO 703-305-4709
Visual signaling apparatus....Baker, Scott USITC 202-205-3386
Vital Statistics, Division of....Curtin, Lester CDC 301-436-8951
Vital Statistics, Family Growth Survey....Staff CDC 301-436-8500
Vitamin E (and Cardiovascular Disease)....Staff NHLBI 301-496-4236
Vitamin Supplements and Aging....Staff NIA 301-496-1752
Vitamins C,D,E, (and CVD)....Staff NHLBI 301-496-4236
Vitamins/Minerals....Corwin, Emil FDA 202-205-4144
Vitamins....Nesbitt, Elizabeth USITC 202-205-3355
Vitiligo....Staff NIAMS 301-496-8188
Vitrectomy....Staff NEI 301-496-5248
Vitreous Detachment....Staff NEi 301-496-5248
Vocal Cord Paralysis....Staff NINDS 301-496-5751
Vocal Cord Paralysis....Staff NIDCD 301-496-7243
Vocal Temor....Staff NIDCD 301-496-7243
Vocational Rehabilitation (Drug Related)....Staff NIDA 301-443-6245
Vogt-Koyanagi Disease....Staff NEI 301-496-5248
Voice Disorders....Staff NIDCD 301-496-5248
Volunteerism....Kharfen, Michael ACF 202-401-9215
Volunteers (Patients)....Staff CC 301-496-4763
Von Hipple-Lindau Disease....Staff NINDS 301-496-5751
Von Recklinghausen's Disease....Staff NINDS 301-496-5751
Von Willebrand's Disease....Staff NHLBI 301-496-4236
Voting and Registration....Jennings, Jerry CENSUS 301-457-2434
Voting Districts....McCully, Cathy CENSUS 301-457-1099
Voyager Flight Project....Doyle, Jim NASA 818-354-5011
Vulnerable Populations (Drug Abuse)....Staff NIDA 301-443-6245

W

Waardenburg Syndrome...Staff NIDCD 301-496-7243
Wage Developments, Current, Comp. and Working Cond....Cimini, Michael LABOR 202-606-6275
Wages/Industrial Relations, Collect Barg Settlements, Major....Devine, Janice M. LABOR 202-606-6276
Wages/Industrial Relations, Collect Barg Agreements Analysis....Cimini, Michael LABOR 202-606-6275
Wages/Industrial Relations, Current Wage Developments....Cimini, Michael LABOR 202-606-6275
Wages/Industrial Relations, Empl Benefit Surv, Other Benefits....Houff, James LABOR 202-606-6238
Wages/Industrial Relations, Empl Benefit Surv, Pension Plans....Houff, James LABOR 202-606-6238
Wages/Industrial Relations, Employment Cost Index....Shelly, Wayne LABOR 202-606-6206
Wages/Industrial Relations, Health Studies....Webber, William LABOR 202-606-6162
Wages/Industrial Relations, Special Projects....Webber, William LABOR 202-606-6162
Wages/Industrial Relations, Unions, Membership....Cimini, Michael LABOR 202-606-6275
Wages/Industrial Relations, Work Stoppages....Cimini, Michael LABOR 202-606-6275
Waldenstroms Macroglobulinemia....Staff NCI 301-496-5583
Walking sticks....Spalding, Josephine USITC 202-205-3498
Wall coverings, of rubber or plastics....Raftery, Jim USITC 202-205-3365
Wallets, Billfolds, Flatgoods....Byron, James E. COMMERCE 202-482-4034
Wallets....Seastrum, Carl USITC 202-205-3493
Walleye....Staff NEI 301-496-5248
Wallpaper....Twarok, Chris USITC 202-205-3314
Warm Air Heating Eqmt....Vacant COMMERCE 202-482-3509
Warts....Staff NIAID 301-496-5717
Washington issues....Callahan, Christopher UMD 301-405-2432
Waste and Chemical Policy Division....Staff EPA 202-260-5422
Waste and scrap (metals)....Lundy, David USITC 202-205-3439
Waste Detoxification....Lytle, Jill-Ellman NEIC 202-586-0370
Waste Heat Recovery....Lytle, Jill-Ellman NEIC 202-586-0370
Waste Management....Greeves, John T. NRC 301-425-7437
Waste Material Management....Sisson, Kurt NEIC 202-586-6750
Waste or scrap....Spalding, Josephine USITC 202-205-3498
Waste Products Utilization....Lytle, Jill-Ellman NEIC 202-586-0370
Waste Reduction Technologies....Lytle, Jill-Ellman NEIC 202-586-0370
Waste, textile: cotton....Sweet, Mary Elizabeth USITC 202-205-3455
Waste, textile: manmade fiber....Sweet, Mary Elizabeth USITC 202-205-3455
Waste, textile: silk....Shelton, Linda USITC 202-205-3457
Waste, textile: wool....Shelton, Linda USITC 202-205-3457
Waste Treatment and Disposal....Staff EPA 703-308-8434
Wastepaper....Stanley, Gary COMMERCE 202-482-0375
Watches....Harris, John COMMERCE 202-482-1178
Watches....Luther, Dennis USITC 202-205-3497
Watches....Scwartz, Stanley CUSTOMS 212-466-5895
Water and Sewage Treatment Plants....Vacant COMMERCE 202-482-3509
Water Division....Staff EPA 202-260-5700
Water Enforcement Division....Staff EPA 202-564-8304
Water Environmental Laws....Staff NEIC 202-586-4996
Water Hardness (and CVD)....Staff NHLBI 301-496-4236
Water Pollution....Staff EPA 202-260-2756
Water Projects, Federal....Staff FWS 703-358-1719
Water Quality Information Center....Makuch, Joseph NAL 301-504-6077
Water Resource Equipment....Vacant COMMERCE 202-482-3509
Water Resource Usage and Analysis....Staff FWS 703-358-1710
Water Rights Agreements, Fish and Wildlife....Staff FWS 703-358-1719
Water Supply....Staff OD/ORS 301-496-3537
Waterway rescues....McCormack, Michael USCG 202-267-1948
Waterway searches....McCormack, Michael USCG 202-267-1948
Waterway Services....Staff Coast Guard Hotline 800-368-5647
Wave communications systems....Tarcza, Thomas C. PTO 703-308-1689
Wave Energy....Loose, Ronald NEIC 202-586-5348
Wax, articles of....Spalding, Josephine USITC 202-205-3498
Waxes....Brownchweig, Gilbert CUSTOMS 212-466-5744
Waxes....Randall, Rob USITC 202-205-3366
Weapons and Crime....Taylor, Bruce Justice Stat 202-616-3498

Weapons and Crime....Rand, Michael Justice Stat 202-616-3494

Weapons Testing....Staff NEIC 301-903-3441

Weapons....Jordan, Charles PTO 703-308-0918

Wearing Apparel: Boys (sizes 2-7 only)....Kirschner, Bruce CUSTOMS 212-466-5865

Wearing Apparel: Girls (sizes 2-7 only)....Kirschner, Bruce CUSTOMS 212-466-5865

Wearing Apparel: Infants....Kirschner, Bruce CUSTOMS 212-466-5865

Weather....Whatley, David FAA 202-267-9090

Weatherization Assistance - Elderly....Staff NEIC 202-426-1698

Weatherization Assistance - Handicapped....Staff NEIC 202-426-1698

Weatherization Assistance - Low Income Individuals....Staff NEIC 202-426-1698

Weatherization Assistance....Staff NEIC 202-426-1698

Weaving machines....Greene, William USITC 202-205-3405

Weber-Christian Disease....Staff NIAID 301-496-5717

Weber-Christian Disease....Staff NIAMS 301-496-8188

Weekly and Annual Earnings--Current Pop. Survey....Mellor, Earl LABOR 202-606-6378

Weekly issue (new US patents)....Harris, Patricia PTO 703-305-7458

Wegener's Granulomatosis....Staff NIAMS 301-496-8188

Wegener's Granulomatosis....Staff NIAID 301-496-5717

Wegener's Granulomatosis....Staff NHLBI 301-496-4236

Weighing machinery....Lusi, Susan USITC 202-205-2334

Welding apparatus....Mata, Ruben USITC 202-205-3403

Welding/Cutting Apparatus....Abrahams, Edward COMMERCE 202-482-0312

Welfare and AFDC JOBS Programs....Checkan, Jane ACF 202-401-9215

Werdnig-Hoffmann Disease....Staff NINDS 301-496-5751

Werner's Syndrome....Staff NIDDK 301-496-3583

Wernicke's Disease....Staff NINDS 301-496-5751

West Bank....Roberts, Nigel Cnty World Bank 202-473-2241

West Bank....Young, Dorothy Cnty AID 202-663-2620

Western Europe/trade matters....Richards, Timothy US Trade Rep 202-395-3320

Western European Union (WEU)....Staff Cnty State 202-736-7299

Western Hemisphere Affairs....Huenemann, Jonathan US Trade Rep 202-395-5190

Western Hemisphere (policy planning)....Surobrodie, Carmen US Trade Rep 202-395-3900

Western Hemisphere Programs, Fish and Wildlife....Staff FWS 703-358-1754

Western Hemisphere/trade matters....Ives, Ralph US Trade Rep 202-395-5190

Western Hemisphere/trade matters....Allgeier, Peter US Trade Rep 202-395-6135

Western Sahara....Dolley, Thomas Cnty Mines 202-501-9690

Western Sahara....Staff Cnty State 202-647-3407

Western Samoa (Apia)....Staff Cnty State 202-647-3546

Western Samoa....Berghage, Jeff Peace Corps 202-606-1098

Western Samoa....Davies, Irene Cnty World Bank 202-458-2481

Western Samoa....Imam, Fahmila Cnty Export-Import Bank 202-565-3738

Western Samoa....Rahman, Talaat Cnty TDA 703-875-4357

Western Samoa....Shelton, Alison Cnty Treasury 202-622-0354

Western Samoa....Slade, Tuiloma Neroni Cnty Embassy 212-599-6196

Western Samoa....Stewart, Andrea W. Cnty Embassy 212-599-6196

Wetlands Division....Staff EPA 202-260-1799

Wetlands Inventory, National....Staff FWS 703-358-2201

Wetlands Protection Hotline....Staff EPA 800-832-7828

Whalebone, articles of....Spalding, Josephine USITC 202-205-3498

Wheat with options....Sepsey, Judy CFT 312-353-9025

Wheat....Reeder, John USITC 202-205-3319

Wheel goods: motorized....Hagey, Michael USITC 202-205-3392

Wheel goods: non-motorized....Seastrum, Carl USITC 202-205-3493

Whiplash....Staff NINDS 301-496-5751

Whipple's Disease....Staff NINDS 301-496-5751

Whipple's Disease....Staff NIAID 301-496-5717

Whips....Spalding, Josephine USITC 202-205-3498

Whiskey....Harney, Amy USITC 202-205-3465

Whistleblower Hotline....Staff EPA 800-424-4000

White Collar Crime....Kaplan, Carol Justice Stat 202-307-0759

Wholesale services....Luther, Dennis USITC 202-205-3497

Wholesale Trade, Census....Trimble, John CENSUS 301-457-2694

Wholesale Trade, Current Sales and Inventories....Piesto, Nancy CENSUS 301-457-2799

Wholesale Trade....Burroughs, Helen COMMERCE 202-482-1542

Whooping Cough....Staff NIAID 301-496-5717

Wilderness Planning, Fish and Wildlife....Staff FWS 703-358-1786

Wilderness Planning....Twiss, John FS 202-205-1422

Wildlife Assistance....Staff FWS 703-358-1713

Wildlife, Exotic....Staff FWS 703-358-1718

Wildlife Health Research....Staff FWS 202-208-5634

Wildlife, Injurious....Staff FWS 703-358-1718

Wildlife, Law Enforcement....Staff FWS 703-358-1949

Wildlife Management, Refuges....Staff FWS 703-358-2043

Wildlife Permits....Staff FWS 703-358-2104

Wildlife Protection....Staff FWS 703-358-1718

Wildlife, Range and Fish Habitat Research....Lennartz, Michael R. FS 202-205-1524

Wildlife, Refugees....Staff FWS 703-358-1744

Wildlife Research....Lennartz, Michael R. FS 202-205-1524

Wildlife....Kilbourne, James C. Justice 202-272-4421

William's Syndrome....Staff NHLBI 301-496-4236

Wilms' Tumor....Staff NCI 301-496-5583

Wilson Disease....Staff NIDDK 301-496-3583

Wilson Disease....Staff NINDS 301-496-5751

Wind Energy....Loose, Ronald NEIC 202-586-5348

Wind Engineering....Lew, H.S. NIST 301-975-6061

Windmill Components....Garden, Les COMMERCE 202-482-0556

Wines....Harney, Amy USITC 202-205-3465

Wire and Wire Products....Garden, Les COMMERCE 202-482-0556

Wire Cloth, Industrial....Reise, Richard COMMERCE 202-482-3489

Wire Cloth....McCauley, Patrick COMMERCE 202-482-0132

Wire Rods....Fitzgerald, John CUSTOMS 212-466-5492

Wire rods....Yost, Charles USITC 202-205-3442

Wire....Fitzgerald, John CUSTOMS 212-466-5492

Wire....Yost, Charles USITC 202-205-3442

Wireless Cable Applications....Staff FCC 202-418-1600

Wireless Microphones (licensed)....Staff FCC 717-337-1212

Wiring sets....Cutchin, John USITC 202-205-3396

Wiskott-Aldrich Syndrome....Staff NCI 301-496-5583

Wolff-Parkinson-White Syndrome (WPW)....Staff NHLBI 301-496-4236

Wollastonite....Potter, Michael J. MINES 202-501-9387

Women and Drugs....Staff NIDA 301-443-6245

Women, Employment/Unemployment Statistics....Hayghe, Howard LABOR 202-606-6378

Women in journalism....Beasley, Maurine UMD 301-405-2413

Women Owned Businesses....Emanuel, Elaine CENSUS 301-763-5726

Women, Population....Smith, Denise CENSUS 301-457-2378

Women's Businesses....Myers, Elizabeth SBA 202-205-6673

Women's Health and Fertility....Peterson, Herbert B. CDC 404-488-5250

Women's Health Initiative....Staff OD 301-402-3168

Women's Health Issues....Staff OD 301-402-1770

Women's Ownership Policy....Staff FCC 202-416-0934

Women's Sports....Staff Women's Sport Foundation 800-227-3988

Wood (densified)....Hoffmeier, Bill USITC 202-205-3321

Wood Containers....Wise, Barbara COMMERCE 202-482-0375

Wood Preserving....Wise, Barbara COMMERCE 202-482-0375

Wood Products, Misc.....Wise, Barbara COMMERCE 202-482-0375

Wood products, rough primary....Hoffmeier, Bill USITC 202-205-3321

Wood Products....Garretto, Paul CUSTOMS 212-466-5779

Wood Products....Wise, Barbara COMMERCE 202-482-0375

Wood pulp....Rhodes, Richard USITC 202-205-3322

Wood Technology....Howard, James FS 202-205-1558

Wood veneers....Hoffmeier, Bill USITC 202-205-3321

Wood Working Machinery....Cosslet, Patrick COMMERCE 202-482-0680

Wool and Mohair....Skinner, Robert Agri 202-219-0840

Wool and Mohair....Lawler, John Agri 202-219-0840

Wool and Mohair....Simpson, Linda Agri 202-720-3578

Wool grease, sulfonated or sulfated....Land, Eric USITC 202-205-3349

Wool....Shelton, Linda USITC 202-205-3457

Wool....Steller, Rose USITC 202-205-3323

Wool....Warlick, William USITC 202-205-3459

Word processors....Baker, Scott USITC 202-205-3386

Work Experience, Employment/Unemployment Stats....Mellor, Earl LABOR 202-606-6378

Work Injuries, Reports and Surveys of, Comp. and Work....Jackson, Ethel LABOR 202-606-6167

Work Injury, Report Surveys, Comp and Working Cond.....Jackson, Ethel LABOR 202-606-6167

Work-life Estimates, Employment Statistics....Horvath, Francis LABOR 202-606-6378

Work Stoppages, Compensation and Working Conditions....Cimini, Michael LABOR 202-606-6275

Workers, Older, Empl/Unempl. Stats.....Rones, Philip LABOR 202-606-6378

Working Conditions, Employment Cost Data....Shelly, Wayne LABOR 202-606-6206

Working Conditions, Safety and Health, Asst.Comm.....Eisenberg, William M. LABOR 202-606-6304

Working Conditions....Cimini, Michael LABOR 202-606-6275

Working Poor, Employment/Unemployment Statistics....Herz, Diane LABOR 202-606-6378

Workplace Drug Abuse....Staff NIDA 301-443-6245

Works of Art....Mushinske, Larry CUSTOMS 212-466-5739

Wound Healing (LDBA)....Staff NIDR 301-496-4261

Woven Outerwear: Boys'....Raftery, William CUSTOMS 212-466-5851

Woven Outerwear: Men's....Raftery, William CUSTOMS 212-466-5851

Woven Outerwear: Women's....Raftery, William CUSTOMS 212-466-5851

Wryneck (Torticollis)....Staff NINDS 301-496-5751

X

X-ray Crystallography....Staff NCRR 301-594-7934

X-ray, Radiation Effects on Fetus....Staff FDA 301-594-3533

X-ray Technician....Staff HRSA/BHPr 301-443-5794

X-ray apparatus....Johnson, Christopher USITC 202-205-3488

Xanthinuria....Staff NIDDK 301-654-4415

Xanthomatosis....Staff NHLBI 301-496-4236

Xeroderma Pigmentosum....Staff NIAMS 301-496-8188

Xeroderma Pigmentosum....Staff NCI 301-496-5583

Xerophthalmia....Staff NEI 301-496-5248

Xeroradiography....Staff NCI 301-496-5583

Xerostomia (Dry Mouth)....Staff NIDR 301-496-4261

Xylene....Raftery, Jim USITC 202-205-3365

Xylenol....Matusik, Ed USITC 202-205-3356

Y

YAG Laser....Staff NEI 301-496-5248

Yarns....Konzet, Jeffrey CUSTOMS 212-466-5885

Yarns....Shelton, Linda USITC 202-205-3457

Year 2000 Research and Development....Keeley, Catherine CENSUS 301-457-4036

Yeast Infections....Staff NIAID 301-496-5717

Yeast....Janis, William V. COMMERCE 202-482-2250

Yellow Fever....Staff NIAID 301-496-5717

Yellow Page Advertising....Staff FCC 202-632-7553

Yellowcake....Greenblatt, Jack USITC 202-205-3353

Yemen (Aden)/Minerals....Michalski, Bernadette Cnty Mines 202-501-9699

Yemen A.R.....Maybury-Lewis, Anthony Cnty Export-Import Bank 202-565-3739

Yemen Arab Republic (Sanaa)....Staff Cnty State 202-647-6572

Yemen, Republic of....Mukherjee, Mohua Cnty World Bank 202-473-3022

Yemen, Republic of....Thanos, Paul Cnty Commerce 202-482-1860

Yemen (Sana)/Minerals....Michalski, Bernadette Cnty Mines 202-501-9699

Yemen....Alaini, Mohsin Cnty Embassy 202-965-4760

Yemen....DiMeo, Pam Peace Corps 202-606-3196

Yemen....Mercer, Dorothy Cnty Treasury 202-622-0184

Yemen....Nasher, Ahmed Abdo Cnty Embassy 202-965-4761

Yemen....Schildwachter, Christy Peace Corps 202-606-3196

Yemen....Squire, Margo Cnty USIA 202-619-5529

Yemen...Vacant Cnty AID 202-663-2620

YMCA....Staff YMCA of the USA 800-872-9622

Youth Conservation Corps, Fish and Wildlife....Staff FWS 703-358-2029

Youth Development Information Center....Kane, John NAL 301-504-6400

Youth, Employment Statistics....Cohany, Sharon LABOR 202-606-6378

Youth, Students, and Dropouts, Empl./Unempl. Stats....Cohany, Sharon LABOR 202-606-6378

Youth with disabilities....Staff NCYD 800-333-6293

Yttrium....Hedrick, James B. MINES 202-501-9412

Yugoslavia (Belgrade)....Staff Cnty State 202-647-4138

Yugoslavia/Minerals....Steblez, Walter Cnty Mines 202-501-9671

Yugoslavia....Jackson, Juhka Cnty Treasury 202-622-0766

Yugoslavia....Keller, Jeremy Cnty Commerce 202-482-4915

Yugoslavia....Popovic, Zoran Cnty Embassy 202-462-6566

Yugoslavia....Vujovic, Nebojsa Cnty Embassy 202-462-6566

Z

Zaire/Minerals....Heydari, Michael Cnty Mines 202-501-9688

Zaire, Republic of (Kinshasa)....Staff Cnty State 202-647-2080

Zaire....Esposito, Dina Cnty AID 202-647-7887

Zaire....Henning, Herman Cnty USIA 202-619-5926

Zaire....Kotze, Joan Cnty Treasury 202-622-0333

Zaire....Maybury-Lewis, Anthony Cnty Export-Import Bank 202-565-3739

Zaire....Michelini, Philip Cnty Commerce 202-482-4388

Zaire....Tatanene, Manata Cnty Embassy 202-234-7690

Zaire...Grau, William J. Cnty World Bank 202-473-3309

Zambia (Lusaka)....Staff Cnty State 202-647-8432

Zambia/Minerals....Antonides, Lloyd Cnty Mines 202-501-9686

Zambia....Anderson, Sydney Cnty AID 202-647-2965

Zambia....Bezek, Jill Cnty TDA 703-875-4357

Zambia....Holm-Olsen, Finn Cnty Commerce 202-482-4228

Zambia....Jones, Donald Peace Corps 202-606-3256

Zambia....Kamana, Dunstan Weston Cnty Embassy 202-265-9717

Zambia....Kotze, Joan Cnty Treasury 202-622-0333

Zambia....Maybury-Lewis, Anthony Cnty Export-Import Bank 202-565-3739

Zambia....Nzala, George R. Cnty Embassy 202-265-9719

Zambia....Pomerantz, Phyllis Cnty World Bank 202-473-7170

Zambia....Schwartz, Larry Cnty USIA 202-619-6904

Zeolites....Virta, Robert MINES 202-501-9384

Zimbabwe (Harare)....Staff Cnty State 202-647-9429

Zimbabwe/Minerals....Izon, David Cnty Mines 202-501-9692

Zimbabwe....Burns, Paul Peace corps 202-606-3634

Zimbabwe....Holm-Olsen, Finn Cnty Commerce 202-482-4228

Zimbabwe....Jewett, Wood Peace Corps 202-606-3635

Zimbabwe....Keeys, Lynn Cnty AID 202-647-4289

Zimbabwe....Marongwe, Mark G. Cnty Embassy 202-332-7100

Zimbabwe....Maybury-Lewis, Anthony Cnty Export-Import Bank 202-565-3739

Zimbabwe....Midzi, Amos Bernard Muvengwa Cnty Embassy 202-332-7100

Zimbabwe....Patel, Praful C. Cnty World Bank 202-473-4250

Zimbabwe....Rauch, Margie Cnty Treasury 202-622-0251

Zimbabwe....Schwartz, Larry Cnty USIA 202-619-6904

Zimbabwe....Younge, Nathan Cnty TDA 703-875-4357

Zinc compounds....Greenblatt, Jack USITC 202-205-3353

Zinc....Jasinski, Stephen MINES 202-501-9418

Zinc....Larrabee, David Commerce 202-482-0607

Zinc....White, Linda USITC 202-205-3427

Zip Codes, Economic Data....Russell, Anne CENSUS 301-457-2687

Zip Codes, Demographic Data....Staff CENSUS 301-457-4100

Zip Codes, Geographic Relationships....Quarato, Rose CENSUS 301-457-1128

Zippers....Shildneck, Ann USITC 202-205-3499

Zirconium compounds....Greenblatt, Jack USITC 202-205-3353

Zirconium....DeSapio, Vincent USITC 202-205-3435

Zirconium....Gambogi, Joseph MINES 202-501-9390

Zollinger-Ellison Syndrome....Staff NIDDK 301-496-3583

Zoonoses....Staff NIAID 301-496-5717

Zoris....Sundar, Shetty USITC 202-205-3486

Index

Index

F

G

H

M

O